THE BARBECUE! BIBLE

THE BARBECUE! BIBLE

BY STEVEN RAICHLEN

PHOTOGRAPHY BY BEN FINK

WORKMAN PUBLISHING • NEW YORK

Library of Congress Cataloging-in-Publication Data is available.
ISBN: 978-0-7611-4943-9 (pb)
ISBN: 978-0-7611-4944-6 (hc)

Cover design by David Matt
Book design by Lisa Hollander
Photography by Ben Fink
Food stylist: Jamie Kimm
Prop stylist: Roy Finamore

Front Cover: author photo © Fernando Diez; center image © Willie Nash/Getty Images; fish © Lew Robertson/Jupiterimages; quesadillas, sauces, corn © Ben Fink; wood © Dorling Kindersley/Getty Images; ginger and spices © Feiler Fotodesign/Alamy Images; all other photographs © Greg Schneider. **Back Cover:** top © James Baigrie/Getty Images; middle © Ben Fink; lower © Greg Schneider

Workman books are available at special discounts when purchased in bulk for premiums and sales promotions as well as for fund-raising or educational use. Special editions or book excerpts can be created to specification. For details, contact the Special Sales Director at the address below.

Workman Publishing Company, Inc.
225 Varick Street
New York, NY 10014-4381

First printing April 2008
10 9 8 7 6 5 4

**Every family needs
a patriarch.
Ours was
my grandfather, Dear.**

. . . .

**This book is dedicated
in loving memory
to Samuel Israel
Raichlen.**

ACKNOWLEDGMENTS

MANY THANKS

The most gratifying part of writing any book is thanking the people who helped make it possible. *The Barbecue! Bible* involved a proverbial cast of thousands.

First and foremost, I thank my wife, Barbara, who brought me to an environment where I could grill all year round (Miami), accompanied me on much of the world's barbecue trail, and relived it in a three-year frenzy of recipe testing in our backyard. Barb, you're the best.

Next, I want to thank my indefatigable assistant, Nancy Loseke, and the whole crew at or directed by the people at Workman Publishing.

Peter Workman encouraged me to expand my original and rather modest proposal into a book of biblical proportions. Words simply aren't adequate, to thank my editor, Suzanne Rafer, who patiently wrestled a manuscript of more than two thousand pages into a book that actually fit between two covers, working with unwavering diligence, dedication, and verve to meet an impossible deadline. It's easy to see why authors would kill to work with her.

Then, too, there's the amazing Barbara Mateer (may I call you "Hawkeye"?), who spearheaded the revision with her customary thoroughness and good humor; the creative David Matt, who designed the lively cover of the revised edition; the prodigious Lisa Hollander, designer of the interior pages assisted by Carolyn Casey; crackerjack photo editor, Anne Kerman; the unerring photographer, Ben Fink, assisted by food stylist Jamie Kimm, and prop stylist Roy Finamore; and Cathy Dorsey, whose index made sense of it all.

It is always a pleasure to work with Workman publicists Ron Longe and Jen Pare Neugeboren, and the irrepressible Susan Schwartzman. As always, thanks go to Jenny Mandel, Pat Upton, Walter Weintz, David Schiller, and all my other colleagues at Workman.

Special thanks to Niman Ranch for their generous contribution of some of the best meats available. Their beautiful cuts helped make my recipes look delicious as well as taste great. To order directly from them, visit their website: www.nimanranch.com.

I was also assisted by a great staff of recipe testers, including Elida Proenza and Roger Thrailkill. Boris Djokic kept the computers humming and offered insight into the grilling of his native Yugoslavia, and my cousin David Raichlen helped with the anthropological research. While I was writing this book, my stepson Jake became a chef, and my stepdaughter Betsy became a dietitian. This is a very handy thing to have happen when you're developing recipes for a cookbook the size of this one. Jake traded his sushi knife for grill tongs and immersed himself in the world of smoke and fire. Betsy, and her husband, Gabriel Berthin, kept me nutritionally correct and up to speed on Andean grilling. I'd like to thank my colleagues and fellow cookbook authors—both in the United States and abroad—for sharing their enormous expertise (and their favorite barbecue joints): Burton Anderson, Najmieh Batmanglij, Giuliano Bugialli, Darra Goldstein, Jessica Harris, Madhur Jaffrey, Patsy Jamieson, Nancy Harmon Jenkins, Elizabeth Karmel, John Mariani, Joan Nathan, David Rosengarten, Nicole Routhier, Julie Sahni, Mimi Sheraton, Nina Simonds, Anya Von Bremsen, Patricia Wells, and Anne Willan.

I had a lot of great chefs in my court for this project, too. The short list would include Rick Bayless, Alain Ducasse, George Germon, Vinod Kapor, Johanne Killeen, Emeril Lagasse, Mark Miller, Mark Militello, Stephan Pyles, Charlie Trotter, and, of course, Chris Schlesinger (who brought grilling into the twenty-first century). Don Hysko, formerly of Peoples Woods, educated me on the fine points of grilling with natural wood and charwood.

I'd also like to thank my friends at Weber-Stephen Products Co., first for sharing their expertise with me (not to mention the opportunity to experience sub-zero grilling at their proving grounds in Palatine, Illinois, in the middle of winter): Jim Stephen, Mike Kempster Sr., Tom Wenke, Keith Wesol, Edna Schlosser, and the inimitable Sherry Bale.

A big thanks to three special friends: Kathleen Cornelia, Katherine Kenny, and the late Milton Eber.

In researching this book, I had the help of hundreds of tourism officials and barbecue buffs both in the United States and abroad. I could never thank all the people who helped me, but I'd like to acknowledge as many as I can.

ARGENTINA: Eduardo Piva, Enrique Capozzolo, and Gloria Pacheca of the Argentina National Tourist Office.

AUSTRALIA: Peter Hackworth of the Chili Queens and New York Latin restaurant in Brisbane.

AZERBAIJAN: Peter Richards of the Hyatt Regency Baku.

BRAZIL: Sara Widness of Kaufman Widness Communications; Marius Fontena of Churrascaria Marius; Yara Castro Roberts and Belita Castro.

CHINA/HONG KONG: Trina Dingler Ebert of Aman Resorts in Hong Kong; Angela Herndon of Lou Hammond & Associates; Margaret Sheriden, formerly of the South China Morning Post.

CURAÇAO: Traci La Rosa and Mark Walsh of Peter Martin Associates, Inc.; the Curaçao Tourist Development Bureau.

FRANCE: Marion Fourestier and Robin Massee of the French Government Tourist Office.

FRENCH WEST INDIES: Myron Clement and Joe Petrocik of Clement-Petrocik Co.; the French West Indies Tourist Board; my friend Eric Troncani of the Carl Gustaf Hotel.

INDIA: T. Balakrishnan, Y. K. Jain, Seema Schahi of the Indian Goverment Tourist Office; Chef Manjit S. Gill of the Welcomgroup; chefs Nakkul Anand, Geeta Kranhke, Shishir Baijal, Gev Desai, and J. P. Singh of the Maurya Sheraton Hotel & Towers in New Delhi; chefs Mohamed Farooq and Amitabh Devendra at the Mughal Sheraton in Agra; chefs Manu Mehta and Nisar Waris of the Rajputana Palace Sheraton in Jaipur.

INDONESIA: Fauzi Bowo, Madi Chusnun, and Yuni Syafril of the Indonesia Tourist Promotion Office; William W. Wongso of the William F & B Management Co. in Jakarta.

ISRAEL: Don Weitz of the Israeli Government Tourist Office; Ehud Yonay of Greater Galilee Gourmet, Inc.

ITALY: Juliet Cruz of the Italian Trade Commission; Maria and Angelo Leocastre of the Villa Roncalli in Foligno.

JAMAICA: Patricia Hannan and Jackie Murray of the Jamaica Tourist Board; Winston Stonar of Busha Browne's Company, Ltd.

JAPAN: Eriko Kawaguchi, M. B. Maslowski, Osamu Akiyama, and Nobuko Misawa of the Japan National Tourist Organization; Lucy Seligman, editor of the Gochiso-sama.

KOREA: Sang-hoon Rah, Sean Nelan, and Peter Jang of the Korea National Tourism Corporation; Mr. Park of Samwon Garden.

MACAO: Eric L. Chen of the Government Tourist Office in Macao.

MALAYSIA: Azizah Aziz of Tourism Malaysia.

MEXICO: Lori Jones and Patricia Echenique of the Mexican Tourism Board; Tom Fisher and Alina Gambor of Burson Marsteller; Jesus Arroyo Bergeyre of Arroy Restaurantes.

MONACO: Emmanuelle Perrier of the Monaco Tourism Bureau.

MOROCCO: Pamela Windo (friend and guide extraordinaire).

REPUBLIC OF GEORGIA: My e-mail pal Betsy Haskell of Betsy's Hotel in Tbilisi.

SINGAPORE: Mak Ying Kwan and Faizah Hanim Ahmad of the Singapore Tourist Promotion Board.

SOUTH AFRICA: Heather Kowadla and Laura Morrill of Lou Hammond & Associates; Christina Martin of the Christina Martin School of Food & Wine in KuaZulu Natal; Alicia Wilkinson of the Silwood Kitchen Cookery School in Capetown.

SPAIN: Alejandro Gomez Marco and Maria Luisa Albacar of the Oficina Española de Turismo; Ana Rodriguez of the Hotel Ritz in Madrid.

THAILAND: Kim Vacher-Ta of Tourism Authority of Thailand; Phenkhae Chattanont of the Oriental Bangkok Hotel; Ann Laschever of Lou Hammond and Associates.

TRINIDAD: Michael De Peaza, Nancy Pierre, and Tony Poyer of the Trinidad Tourism Development Bureau.

TURKEY: Murat Barlas and Ayfer Unsal; Mustafa Siyahhan of the Turkish Tourist Office in Washington, D.C.; Mehmet Dogan of the Tourism Office in Gaziantep.

UNITED STATES: Karen Adler of Pig Out Publications, Inc.; Judith Fertig, Danny Edwards of Little Jake's Eat It and Beat It, and Lindsey Shannon of BB's Lawnside in Kansas City; Mike Alexander and Mike DeMaster of Sonny Bryan's in Dallas; Roy and Jane Barber and Barry Maxwell of the Memphis in May International Festival, Inc.

URUGUAY: Alexis Parodi of the Ministerio de Turismo del Uruguay.

VIETNAM: Trai Thi Duong of the Truc Orient Express and Binh Van Duong of Le Truc.

Finally, a huge thanks to all the grill jockeys and pit bosses—both named in this book and unnamed—for sharing with me their skills, knowledge, time, food, and unbridled passion for grilling. Barbecue buffs have a reputation for secrecy, but everywhere I went, people welcomed me into their hearts and their kitchens. I thank them for three and a half extraordinary years on the barbecue trail.

CONTENTS

Preface to the New Edition:
More Great Grilling . . . xii

Introduction:
Three Years on the Barbecue Trail . . . xiii

CHAPTER 1

GRILLING BASICS: ANSWERS TO FREQUENTLY ASKED QUESTIONS

PAGE 1

Everything you need to know in order to grill and barbecue like a pro—in no time flat. How to master direct and indirect grilling; pit barbecuing; grilling on a rotisserie; and grilling without a grate. What to look for in equipment; how to buy the right fuel, how to light it, and how to keep it lit. Plus the scoop on accessories.

The Grilling Process . . . 1
The Grills . . . 5
The Fuels . . . 11
Setting Up the Grill . . . 15
  Grilling with Charcoal . . . 15
  Cooking with Gas . . . 20
  Cooking Satés . . . 23
  Smoking . . . 24
  Grilling Indoors . . . 26
  Grilling Over a Campfire . . . 26
Grill Maintenance and Cleaning . . . 28
Gearing Up . . . 29
The Food . . . 31
  Testing for Doneness . . . 31
  Beef . . . 32
  Pork . . . 37
  Game and "Exotic" Meats . . . 40
  Burgers and Sausages . . . 41
  Chicken . . . 42
  Seafood . . . 44
  Vegetarian Food on the Grill . . . 46
  Vegetables . . . 46
  Oddballs . . . 47
Seasoning and Sauces . . . 47
Now You're Smoking . . . 49

CHAPTER 2

THIRST QUENCHERS

PAGE 53

Cooking over a hot grill can work up a powerful thirst, and pit masters world-wide know that there are more ways to quench it than with beer. Here, then, is a mix of coolers—with and without alcohol—to accompany any barbecue.

Leaded . . . 54
Unleaded . . . 61
  The Afghan Grill . . . 64

CHAPTER 3

WARM-UPS

PAGE 67

Set your barbecue off to the happiest start with a selection of appetizing openers: Silver Paper Chicken, Honey-Glazed Hong Kong Wings, Shrimp Mousse on Sugarcane. Or how about a smoky Grilled Corn Chowder? They're all so good they taste like the main event themselves.

The Vietnamese Grill . . . 72
Stalking the Elusive Grilled Snail . . . 83

PAGE 86

CHAPTER 4

BLAZING SALADS

PAGE 95

Salads play two roles in the world of barbecue. Some, like Grilled Vegetable Caponata and Grilled Pork with a Sweet-Tart Dressing, are themselves grilled dishes. Others set off a grilled dish perfectly. You need go no farther than this chapter to enjoy both kinds.

On the Grill 96

A Tale of Three Barbecues: The Thai Grill 100

On the Side 110

CHAPTER 5

GRILLED BREAD

PAGE 125

From irresistible Grilled Garlic Bread Fingers to Catalan Tomato Bread to from-scratch Tandoori-Baked Flat Breads—whether ready-made or homemade, the grill gives bread unmatched flavor and crispness.

CHAPTER 6

WHATS YOUR BEEF?

PAGE 135

Texas-Style Barbecued Brisket and Brazilian Stuffed Rib Roast; Florentine-Style Steak and Bengali Shish Kebabs; Saigon Market Beef Sticks and Korean Grilled Short Ribs. Beef on the grill—savory, succulent, sensational—a perfect match of food and fire.

In Pursuit of the Best Tuscan Steak 148

Matambre: A Hunger-Killer from South America 152

Argentinean Roots 153

The Argentinean Grill 154

Hawkers' Centers 162

CHAPTER 7

HIGH ON HOG

PAGE 173

Time to go whole hog! Cook up the tenderest North Carolina Pulled Pork or fieriest Jamaican Jerk Pork Tenderloin. Feast on Pork with Moorish Seasonings, Sweet & Garlicky Pork Chops, or finger-licking Memphis-Style Ribs.

Jerk: The Jamaican Barbecue 184

PAGE 194

CHAPTER 8

A LITTLE LAMB

PAGE 199

So many of the world's barbecuers love to grill lamb that it's no wonder the selection of dishes is outstanding. Try Cape Town Lamb from South Africa, "Onion Water" Lamb Chops from Afghanistan, and The Real Turkish Shish Kebab from Turkey (of course!).

A Traditional Barbacoa 200

The Moroccan Grill 216

CHAPTER 9

GROUND MEAT, BURGERS & SAUSAGES

PAGE 223

The U.S. might have the best burgers, but wait till you taste the ground meat concoctions the rest of the world has to offer—Indonesian Flying Fox Satés, Oasis Kebabs from the Middle East, The Original Karim's Seekh Kebab from India—proving that the appeal of flavorful ground meat is universal.

From Hamburg to Hoboken: A Brief History of the Hamburger....225
Of Koftas, Lyulyas, and Seekh Kebabs....242
The Turkish Grill....244

CHAPTER 10

BIRD MEETS GRILL

PAGE 255

The world loves a great grilled chicken, and here are the recipes to help you achieve greatness: Chicken Satés Served in Lettuce Leaves, Sea Captain's Chicken Tikka, and Bahamian Grilled Chicken, to name a few. But don't overlook other birds that cook up deliciously on the grill, as well—check out the recipes for quail, duck, and turkey.

The Splendid Restaurant Karim....274
Uruguay's Mercado del Puerto....278
The Macanese Grill....296

CHAPTER 11

WATER MEETS FIRE: FISH ON THE GRILL

PAGE 303

Fresh fish, perfectly grilled, is spectacularly succulent. Don't miss Whole Grilled Snapper with South African Spices, Grilled Sea Bass with Fresh Artichoke Salad, Grilled Salmon Kiev, and Grilled Sole with Catalan Fruits & Nuts.

A New French Paradox....310
The Most Famous Fish House in Indonesia....315
On Trinidad's Shark and Bake....323

CHAPTER 12

HOT SHELLS: LOBSTER, SHRIMP, SCALLOPS, AND CLAMS

PAGE 353

Grilled Spiny Lobster with Basil Butter, Scallop Kebabs with Pancetta, Lemon, and Basil, Oysters with Horseradish Cream, and enough shrimp recipes to keep the barbie fired up for weeks. Here is shellfish at its best!

The Brazilian Grill....365

PAGE 367

CHAPTER 13

VEGETARIAN GRILL

PAGE 381

No longer only just for meat-eaters, now you can serve up a complete range of vegetarian dishes at a barbecue, including The Original Grilled Pizza, exotic Tabdoori Peppers, a lush Provençal Dagwood, and steak-like Grilled Portobello Mushroom Sandwiches with Basil Aioli.

The Indian Grill....383

CHAPTER 14

VEGETABLES: GREENS MEET GRILL

PAGE 395

There is probably no better way to heighten the natural flavor of a vegetable than by grilling. Proof is no farther away than Georgian Vegetable Kebabs, Catalan Grilled Artichokes, Argentinean Grilled Eggplant, Chorizo Grilled Mushrooms, and wonderfully warming Grilled Sweet Potatoes with Sesame Dipping Sauce.

The Japanese Grill....412

CHAPTER 15

RICE, BEANS, AND BEYOND

PAGE 423

Most of the world's great grilled dishes are accompanied by flavorfully prepared grains and beans. Dig into Persian-Style Steamed Rice and Quick and Smoky Baked Beans. And for something less expected, how about a Yorkshire Pudding on the Grill?

The Persian Grill: A Day with Najmieh Batmanglij 426

CHAPTER 16

SIDEKICKS:
PICKLES, RELISHES, SALSAS, AND SLAWS

PAGE 441

Bring on the condiments—those savory, fiery, sweet, and utterly satisfying go-withs that dress up any barbecue. Central Asian Pickles, Onion Relish with Pomegranate Molasses, Pineapple Chutney, "Dog's Snout" Salsa, and Tomato Peanut Sambal will add pizzazz to even the simplest grilled chicken, steak, or fish.

Stuck on Saté: The Indonesian Grill 450

CHAPTER 17

SAUCES

PAGE 463

All great pit masters are judged on their barbecue sauces and you'll match the best of them with this far-reaching collection. From a sweet-sour Basic Barbecue Sauce to a contemporary Ginger-Plum Barbecue Sauce to a mouth-scorching Portuguese *Piri-Piri,* there are plenty to match any grilled dish.

The Four Styles of an American Barbecue 468

CHAPTER 18

RUB IT IN

PAGE 489

Memphis Rub and Indian Roasted Spice Powder; Mexican Smoked Chile Marinade and Teriyaki Marinade; Roquefort Butter, Ketjap Butter, and Bourbon Butter Basting Sauce. A full selection of rubs, marinades, butters, and bastes add zip to even the simplest fare.

Barbecue Alley: The Mexican Grill. 500

CHAPTER 19

FIRE AND ICE:
DESSERTS

PAGE 511

No great barbecue is complete without a great dessert. Whether you end with a final flourish on the grill or with a luscious frozen dessert, you won't go wrong. Don't forget to leave room for Fire-Roasted Apples, Balinese Grilled Bananas in Coconut Milk Caramel, Persian Lemon and Rose Water "Sundae" with Sour Cherry Syrup, and Coconut Ice Cream.

Barbecue from the Land of Morning Calm: The Korean Grill. 520

PAGE 511

Metric Conversion Charts 526

Glossary of Special Ingredients. 527

Index. 531

GRILLED LAMB WITH HERBES DE PROVENCE | PAGE 213

MORE GREAT GRILLING

It's hard to believe ten years have passed since the initial publication of *The Barbecue! Bible*. Your enthusiasm for the first edition has been gratifying and amazing, and helped spark a veritable revolution in live-fire cooking. Americans are grilling more than ever before on an awe-inspiring array of new charcoal, gas, and wood-burning grills and smokers. Multiple grill–ownership is on the rise and what was once an activity for weekends in the summer has become for many people—even in the Frost Belt—the preferred method of cooking all year round.

What we grill has changed, too. Grilled dishes that once seemed exotic—*churrasco,* tandoori, saté—have become part of America's grilling repertory. Ingredients that once required a trip to a specialty market—tomatillos, coconut milk, lemongrass—now turn up at the supermarket—and, of course, on barbecue shopping lists. So do exotic fuels, like olive wood, grapevine trimmings, and Japanese *bincho tan* charcoal. Techniques that once seemed unfamiliar—rubbing and brining, for example, or indirect grilling and smoking—are now practiced comfortably by novices and experts alike. As the world grows smaller, our grilling repertory has grown and grown more global.

Which brings me with great pleasure to this edition of *The Barbecue! Bible*. I've completely updated the book from beginning to end. I've revised the techniques chapter based on the latest grills and accessories. I've recalibrated the recipes based on new ingredients. (In the last ten years, a baby back rib at your typical supermarket has nearly doubled in weight.) And because we eat with our eyes as well as our palates, I've added dozens of full-color photographs. Some are step-by-step technique sequences to show you how to prepare the food for the grill. Others are gorgeous full-page photographs to show you what the finished dishes should look like.

I look forward to many more decades of great grilling to come. As always, let me know your questions and comments, and especially what you're grilling, on my website:

www.barbecuebible.com

Steven Raichlen

THREE YEARS ON THE BARBECUE TRAIL

Half a million years ago, the world witnessed a revolution. An ape-like creature destined to become man became the first animal to cook its dinner. The mastery of fire by *Homo erectus* around 500,000 B.C. resulted in nothing less than the rise of civilization. Anthropologists have argued that the primitive act of roasting meat over fire ultimately led to language, art, religion, and complex social organization. In other words, you could say that grilling begat civilization.

How our forebears learned to grill remains a matter of speculation. Perhaps the first barbecue was the result of a forest fire, which roasted venison, bison, and other game on the hoof in a natural conflagration. Perhaps a haunch of meat fell into a campfire. Perhaps lightning struck a tree and transformed it into charcoal. In any case, archeological evidence suggests that by 125,000 B.C. man was using live fire to cook his meat and to help him extract from the bones a morsel particularly prized in prehistoric times: marrow.

The following millennia brought countless refinements to the art of cooking, from the invention of pottery and pots and pans to the bread machine and microwave oven. But when it comes to bringing out the primal flavor of food, nothing can rival grilling over a live fire.

This truth has not been lost to cultures as diverse as the Greek, Japanese, Australian, South African, and Argentinian. Grilling remains our most universal and universally beloved method of cooking. And in the past ten years, our own country has experienced a veritable grill mania.

It is this shared experience—and a desire to learn more about the cultures that produced its infinite regional variations—that led me to write this book.

WHY I WROTE THIS BOOK

The idea for the book came to me shortly after moving from Boston to Miami. South Florida is enough to sharpen anyone's appetite for grilling. First, there's the climate, which makes year-round grilling not only a possibility but almost a duty. (How different Miami is from Boston, where grilling in the winter requires donning arctic apparel!)

Then there's Miami's dizzying cultural diversity. Dade County, which includes Miami, is 50 percent Hispanic, and Miami itself is home to the nation's largest Cuban, Nicaraguan, Colombian, and Haitian communities. But "Hispanic" only begins to describe what's going on in Miami's markets and restaurants: Not only are the countries of the Caribbean and South America represented, but virtually every country in Europe, Africa, and Asia as well. Global cuisine isn't simply a curiosity or luxury here in South Florida. It's a way of life.

So an idea began to take hold of my imagination: to explore how the world's oldest and most universal cooking method varies from country to country, region to region, and culture to culture. To travel the world's barbecue trail—if such a trail existed—and learn how pit masters and grill jockeys solve that age-old problem: how to cook food over live fire without burning it.

I resolved to explore the *asados* of Argentina and the *churrascos* of Brazil; to taste Jamaica's jerk and Mexico's *barbacoa*. I'd visit Greece to discover the secret of souvlaki and Italy to learn how to make an authentic *bistecca alla fiorentina*. My research introduced me to eat *mechoui* in Morocco and *koftas* in the Middle East, donner kebab in Turkey, and tandoori in India. I would visit the birthplace of Japanese yakitori, Indonesian saté, and Korean *kui* and *bool kogi*.

Of course, there'd be lots of live-fire cooking to investigate in my own country: from the ribs of Kansas City and Memphis to the pulled pork of the Carolinas and the slow-smoked briskets of Texas. I'd check out the wood-burning grills of California and the hearthside cookery of New England. The more I delved into the world of barbecuing and grilling, the more I became convinced that it is more than just another technique in a cook's repertoire. It's even more than a cultural phenomenon. The world over, it's a way of life.

It wouldn't hurt, I reasoned, that grilling and barbecuing fit so nicely into the contemporary North American lifestyle. These ancient methods support the four dominant trends in modern American cooking: our passion for explosive flavors;

our fast-paced lifestyle, with its need for quick, easy cooking methods; our mushrooming health consciousness and desire to eat foods that are low in fat but high in flavor; our desire to turn our homes into our entertainment centers, to transform the daily necessity of food preparation into recreation—even fun.

If ever there was a cooking method to take us into the next millennium, it is grilling. We see its growing popularity in the skyrocketing sales of barbecue grills (currently, more than 70 percent of Americans own grills). We see it in the proliferation of barbecue festivals and restaurants with wood-burning grills.

The truth is that—in terms of ease, speed, and intensity of flavor—nothing can rival grilling. And as more Americans travel the barbecue trail and discover the regional subtleties of grilling, the movement will only grow.

I shared my idea with Peter Workman and Suzanne Rafer of Workman Publishing, who responded with an enthusiasm that matched my own. In fact, they encouraged me to broaden the scope of the original book from the twelve countries on which I had initially planned to focus to the entire world of grilling. (Easy for them to do! They wouldn't have to worry about jet lag, visas, complex travel arrangements, vaccinations that turned my arms into pincushions, and gastrointestinal perils that would challenge the limits of my culinary curiosity.)

A proposal was written. A contract was executed.

And only then did I panic.

How would I visit more than twenty-five countries in the space of three years? How would I overcome local language barriers and sometimes less than favorable attitudes to American journalists? And even if I could communicate with street cooks and chefs, how would I persuade them to share their grilling secrets? How would I ferret out the best barbecue in countries I knew only from guidebooks?

I realized I had taken on the biggest challenge of my life.

HOW I WROTE THIS BOOK

I began, as any journalist does, with research. I read exhaustively both cookbooks and travel books. I queried colleagues with expertise in the various countries I planned to visit. I consulted with tourism bureaus and cultural attachés. I spoke with food and cookware importers, travel agents, anthropologists, foreigners I met here and abroad—anyone who could shed insight into the grilling of a particular country.

My informants included fellow journalists, university professors, business travelers, diplomats, and flight attendants. Some of my best information came from taxi drivers. (Of all professions, cabbies seem to possess the most unerring knowledge of who serves the best barbecue.) I planned as much as I could, then I made sure I was in the right place to capitalize on chance.

I speak French and Spanish and a smattering of Italian, Portuguese, and German (the latter is useful in Turkey), so in countries where these languages are spoken, I was able to work on my own. In countries where I didn't speak the language, I found guides or interpreters. And of course I developed my own sign language:

"I" (point to me)

"write" (move my fingers to mime writing)

"about food" (raise an imaginary fork or chopsticks to my lips or rub my belly)

"I would like to" (again point to me)

"watch" (point to my eye)

"you cook." (mime the act of grilling, mixing, chopping, or stir-frying)

I took with me one of my previous cookbooks. I would show the recipes and point to the photograph of me on the back cover.

I feared my efforts would be met with suspicion, secrecy, and rejection, but almost everywhere I went I encountered openness, warmth, and welcome. Virtually all of the grill jockeys I interviewed were not only willing but happy to share their knowledge. On many occasions, I was invited into the kitchen. I tried my hand at molding *kofta* meat onto skewers, fanning the coals, or slapping *naan* on the inside walls of a blazing tandoor. My efforts generally evoked peals of good-natured laughter.

I found myself in many places not frequented by most travelers, having experiences that ranged from fascinating to hair-raising. In Mexico I nibbled cactus worms and crickets as a prelude to barbecue. (The latter tasted like potato chips with legs.) In Uruguay I sampled testicles, tripe, intestines, kidneys, and blood sausage. In Bali I paid a 6 A.M. visit to the local *babi guli* (roast pork) man, who rewarded my punctuality by letting me help him slaughter a suckling pig. In Bangkok I was the guest of honor at an Isarn (northeastern Thai) restaurant whose fly-filled kitchen overlooked a stagnant canal.

(I forced myself to eat with the enthusiasm appropriate to a guest of honor, and no one was more surprised than I when I *didn't* get sick.

Some of the world's best barbecue was off limits because of political turmoil. I would have liked to have visited Afganistan, Iraq, Iran, and some of the more turbulent former Soviet republics. Instead, I found experts and restaurants specializing in those cuisines in this country.

Barbecue buffs have a reputation for being a secretive bunch (at least in the United States), but virtually everywhere I traveled on the barbecue trail, cooks were happy to share their recipes and expertise. Some scrawled recipes for me, to be translated back at my hotel. Others drew pictures in my notebook to explain where a particular piece of meat came from or how to execute a particular cut. When possible, I credit the extraordinary grill hockeys I met by name (or at least by the name of their establishment).

Recipes are the heart of any cookbook, of course. In this one you'll find more than five hundred, covering everything from Brazilian *churrasco* to Balinese shrimp satés to Memphis-style ribs. The essays describing some of my experiences are intended for the traveler (both active and armchair), as well as the cook.

My three years on the barbecue trail passed in what seems like the blink of any eye.

As I sit here writing these words, I picture all the remarkable places I've been, the kind, generous people I've met, and the extraordinary food I've been lucky enough to sample. And yet I can't help but feel there's so much more I would have liked to have accomplished. The world of barbecue is so vast and complex, any survey is bound to have blind spots. I honestly believe I could spend the rest of my life writing about barbecuing and grilling and still find new things to discover.

ABOUT THE RECIPES

When writing the recipes, I've tried to be as authentic as possible. But I've also taken into account the fact that certain foods, seasonings, and cooking equipment simply aren't available in the United States (not to mention the fact that our tastes and aesthetics are different). Whenever I depart from a traditional recipe, I've tried to suggest the way it would be made in its country of origin.

In my three years on the barbecue trail, I sampled many dishes I know most Americans would never dream of preparing at home. (A couple that come to mind are Uruguay's *choto* (grilled coiled lamb's intestines) and Indonesia's *saté padang* (kebabs of beef entrails served in a fiery gravy). I've tried to describe these dishes in the essays and boxes in this book. I hope you'll give them a try when you travel.

As I quickly discovered on the barbecue trail, grilling is an art, not a science. Many cooks work in unbelievably primitive conditions. Indeed, one of the reasons I'm drawn to grilling is that it's so forgiving in terms of measurements and proportions. I hope you'll use the recipes in this book as I do, that is, as a broad guideline. If you don't feel like eating beef, make the recipe with chicken or seafood. Most of the marinades and rubs in this book—listed either as freestanding recipes or subrecipes in more elaborate preparations—can be used with any type of grilled fare. You'll also notice that there is often more than one way to cook a particular dish. As I always say in my cooking classes: There's no such thing as a mistake in the kitchen, just a new recipe waiting to be discovered.

Seasoning, marinating, and grilling are the cornerstones of live-fire cooking, which brings me to what I call the Barbecue Bible Method, and as you will see, it's very simple. First marinate the meat, or rub it with spices. Then let the meat absorb the seasonings for as long as recommended or as long as you have time for. Finally, grill it over whatever sort of fuel on whatever sort of equipment you feel most comfortable using. That's it.

Of course, I hope to expand your horizons—to inspire you to try new techniques and new flavors. But the bottom line is that I want you to make these recipes. Remember, cooking isn't brain surgery. This is especially true for what is surely the world's easiest cooking method, grilling.

BEATING A PATH TO THE WORLD'S BEST BARBECUE

Grilling is done, in some form or other, in virtually every country in the world. In some regions, it's a marginal technique—something you do outdoors, for example, when you lack access to a proper kitchen. Or something a street vendor does.

In other countries, grilling lies at the core of the culture's culinary identity. The grills may range from the shoebox–size braziers used in Southeast Asia to the behemoth fire pits found in South America and the American South. The preparations may be as simple as Argentina's *bife de lomo* (grilled tenderloin seasoned only with salt) or as complex as Vietnam's *bo bun* (thinly sliced, lemongrass-marinated beef eaten with noodles, chiles, crisp vegetables, aromatic herbs, and rice paper).

In researching my world tour of grilling and barbecue, I discovered that there is a barbecue belt that encircles the globe. Or more specifically, that there are six great barbecue zones. The United States and Mexico and the Caribbean comprise the first. Standing alone as the second is South America. On the other side of the Atlantic, the barbecue zone stretches from the Mediterranean Basin to the Middle East (number three) and from Arab North Africa to South Africa via the continent's western coast (number four).

The largest contiguous barbecue zone starts in Turkey and runs east through the Caucasus Mountains, Central Asia, Iraq, Iran, Afghanistan, Pakistan, and India (number five). In the thirteenth century, the Mongols, led by Genghis Khan, spread their love of grilled meats as far west as Turkey. The Arab world refined the idea, then shipped it back via the Mogul rulers to the Indian subcontinent and possibly beyond to Indonesia.

The last great barbecue zone (number six) follows the eastern rim of the Pacific, stretching from Australia and Indonesia to Korea. Along the way, some of the world's most interesting grilling can be found in Singapore, Malaysia, Thailand, Vietnam, Macao, and Japan.

Thus, most of the world's grilling takes place in the tropics, which you'd expect, given the proclivity of most humans in hot climates to cook outdoors. (Furthermore, most of the world's spices grow in the tropics, which adds interest to the marinades and condiments traditionally associated with grilling.) But a great deal of remarkable live-fire cooking lies squarely outside the tropics: Consider Japan, Argentina, and our own United States.

What's almost as interesting as where people do live-fire cooking is where they don't. Grilling has never played much of a role in two of the world's gastronomic superpowers: northern Europe and China. And although grilling is found in Central Africa, more often than not charcoal fires are used to heat stew pots and frying pans, not to cook the meats directly.

My first year on the barbecue trail, I focused my efforts in my own hemisphere. My first stop was the Jamaican town Boston Beach, birthplace of jerk. I island hopped my way across the Caribbean, stopping for French West Indian *boucanée* (chicken smoked over sugarcane), Trinidadian *choka* (spiced, grilled vegetables), *lechon asado* (Hispanic roast pig). The North American concept of barbecue (the intense spicing and slow smoky grilling) originated in the Caribbean, and the tradition remains alive and flourishing.

Next I headed for South America, home to some of the world's most heroic grilling. I dined in stylish *churrascarias* in Rio de Janeiro, at the homey grill stalls of Montevideo's Mercado del Puerto, and at landmark steak houses in Buenos Aires. I watched whole sides of beef being roasted in front of a campfire on an *estancia* (ranch) in the Pampas. South American grilling, I learned, represents one end of the barbecue spectrum, emphasizing simplicity and directness of flavor. Argentinians don't even bother with marinades for most meats: the seasonings are limited to sea salt and the perfume of wood smoke.

The second year, I turned my attention to Asia. I visited Indonesia, birthplace of the saté and home to what is probably the world's single largest repertoire of grilled dishes. I sampled dozens of different types of satés—a small fraction of what's actually eaten in Indonesia. I learned that small is beautiful: Indonesian satés are cooked on grills the size of a shoebox and served on skewers as slender as broom straws.

Indonesia and my next destinations, Singapore and Malaysia, possess some of the world's most complex marinades and spice mixtures. On the island of Penang in northern Malaysia, I watched grill jockeys pound ginger, chiles, galangal, lemongrass, kaffir lime leaves, shrimp paste, and coconut milk into fragrant pastes for seasoning grilled meats and seafood. I scorched my tongue on the fiery *achars* (pickles) and *sambals* (relishes) that accompany grilled fare in Southeast Asia. This complex seasoning of grilled meats stands at the opposite end of the spectrum from the simple grilled meats of South America.

One common complaint about barbecue in the West is that it's so, well, relentlessly carnivorous. In Thailand and Vietnam I found the perfect model for healthy barbecue: the pairing of small portions of grilled meats with large amounts of vegetables, rice, and noodles. The Thai often eat barbecued food wrapped in lettuce leaves (a practice echoed by Koreans), while in Vietnam the wrapping is done in crêpe-like sheets of rice paper. Fish sauce–based dipping sauces, toasted peanuts, sliced chiles, and fragrant basil and mint sprigs are often combined with grilled meats in a single, explosively flavorful bite.

As I moved north, the fish sauce and coconut milk marinades gave way to soy sauce and five-spice powder mixtures in Hong Kong and Macao and to sweet sesame marinades in Korea. In Japan (land of my birth, by the way), I sat elbow to elbow with Japanese businessmen in crowded Tokyo yakitori parlors, enjoying sweet-salty teriyaki and pungent barbecue sauces made from miso (cultured soybean paste) and *umeboshi* (pickled plums). I feasted on fabled Kobe beef and on ingredients I never knew you could grill, like okra and ginkgo nuts. Here, too, I learned that small is beautiful and that barbecue could be as subtle as haiku.

The third year, I focused my research on the Near East and the Mediterranean Basin. Turkish cooks introduced me to an astonishing array of kebabs and grilled vegetables. In Morocco I discovered *mechouie* (pit-roasted lamb), not to mention French-style brochettes flavored with pungent North African spices. In France I experienced the heady pleasures of grilling over grapevines. (One night, I drove four hundred miles to taste grilled escargots in a tiny village near Perpignon.) Italy, Spain, and Portugal impressed me with their wealth of simply grilled seafoods and vegetables.

Along the way, I filled in my travels: Mexico for its *barbacoas* and *carne asado;* India for its extraordinary tandoori and grilled breads; Israel for its *shwarma, kofta,* and grilled foie gras. I crisscrossed the United Stated, savoring pulled pork in the Carolinas, brisket in Texas, and ribs in Kansas City and Memphis.

All told, I traveled more than 150,000 miles to twenty-five countries on five continents.

Don't ask me what my favorite barbecue is. It would be a little like asking the parents of a large family to name their favorite child.

I loved the plate-burying abundance of an Argentinian steak as much as the delicacy of Japanese yakitori. I loved the straightforwardness of Italian *bistecca alla fiorentina* as much as the complex layering of flavor characteristic of Indian tandoori. I loved the eat-with-your-fingers informality of North American barbecue and the chic of a Brazilian *churrascaria.* I loved the Asian-style grilling, with its modest portions of grilled meats in relation to the generous serving of starches and vegetables. But I wouldn't snub my nose at a thick, juicy hamburger made from freshly ground sirloin charred over blazing hickory or mesquite.

Come to think of it, during three long years on the barbecue trail, there wasn't a single meal I didn't enjoy. So, as they say in Spanish, *buen provecho;* in Vietnamese, *chuc qui ban an ngon*; in Hindi, *aap kha lijiya;* in Japanese, *itadakimasu;* in Arabic, *bessahaa;* in Hebrew, *b'teavon;* in Korean, *jharr chop su se yo;* in French, *bon appétit;* in Chinese, *man man chi.* In other words, dig in!

—Steven Raichlen

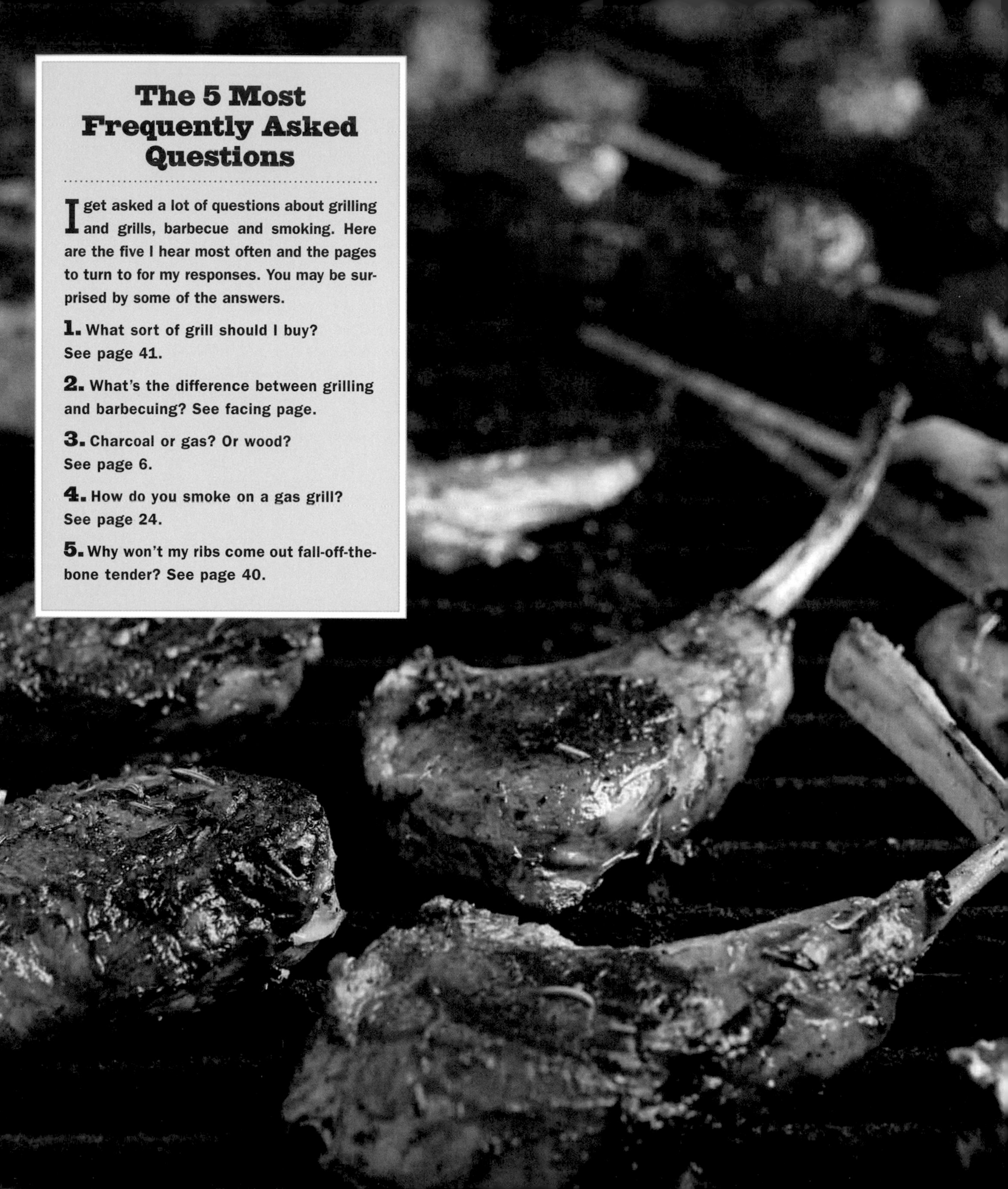

The 5 Most Frequently Asked Questions

I get asked a lot of questions about grilling and grills, barbecue and smoking. Here are the five I hear most often and the pages to turn to for my responses. You may be surprised by some of the answers.

1. What sort of grill should I buy? See page 41.

2. What's the difference between grilling and barbecuing? See facing page.

3. Charcoal or gas? Or wood? See page 6.

4. How do you smoke on a gas grill? See page 24.

5. Why won't my ribs come out fall-off-the-bone tender? See page 40.

CHAPTER 1

GRILLING BASICS ANSWERS TO FREQUENTLY ASKED QUESTIONS

Grilling is the oldest, most widespread and most forgiving method of cooking. Over the centuries, there have been countless refinements to the process of cooking food over fire, from grills and grates, to rotisseries and turnspits, to gas grills and infrared burners. These refinements have enabled us to cook an ever wider repertory of ingredients on the grill, but the basic principles remain the same, as does the primal pleasure of fire-cooked foods.

"Cooks are made, grillers are born."

—FRENCH PROVERB

THE GRILLING PROCESS

A lot of confusion surrounds just what the words grilling and barbecuing mean. This is compounded by the fact that we use the word barbecue to refer to many different aspects of live-fire cooking, everything from a piece of cooking equipment (the grill), to one or more cooking methods using that grill, to specific dishes, such as Texas- or North Carolina–style barbecue. We also use barbecuing more broadly—to refer to the act of cooking outdoors, to a meal cooked and served outdoors, and to a social gathering featuring barbecued food.

Much of the confusion lies in the fact that we often use the same piece of equipment (the barbecue grill) for the high-heat, direct cooking method known as grilling; for the low-heat, smoke-cook method that constitutes true barbecue; and for the moderate-heat method known as indirect grilling.

While related, all three methods are quite different. Understanding their differences will enable you to produce great fire-cooked fare every time.

What's the difference between grilling and barbecuing?

GRILLING is a quick, high-heat method of cooking directly over the flames or glowing coals. Grilling requires a high temperature—typically in excess of 600°F (some restaurant grills reach temperatures of 800° to 1,000°F)—and the cooking time is measured in minutes. Small or thin pieces of food that are tender and cook quickly are best suited to grilling—everything from steaks, chops, and burgers to fish fillets, vegetables, bread, pizza, and fruit. One of the greatest pleasures of grilled food is its immediacy: You can watch it being cooked. The high heat chars the surface, sealing in juices and creating the smoky, caramelized crust so prized in grilled fare.

Grilling is by far the world's most common live-fire cooking method, practiced on six continents in restaurants, street stalls, and backyards, by rich and poor alike. Whether done over a campfire-size pit in Argentina or on a shoebox-size saté grill in Bali, grilling is what 95 percent of the world's pit masters mean when they talk about barbecue.

BARBECUING in its truest form is a long, slow, low-heat, indirect cooking method that uses smoldering logs or charcoal and wood chunks to cook food, usually some sort of meat, in the presence of abundant wood smoke. The heat source is located away from the food, so it is cooked indirectly—next to, not directly over the fire. Born in the Caribbean, true barbecuing is practiced primarily in the United States—especially in Texas, Kansas City, Memphis, and the South. In traditional American pit barbecue, the heat source is a separate firebox, which is attached to but not part of the actual cooking chamber.

When I say slow cooking, I mean slow. Kansas City pit masters cook their baby back ribs for six hours and their pork shoulders for ten to twelve hours. When I say low, I mean *low*. The temperature of the pit at the original Sonny Bryan's in Dallas never rose above 225°F. Low heat generates smoke (the wood smolders, it doesn't burn), and this smoke gives barbecue its characteristic flavor. Smoke is a natural preservative, and in the days before refrigeration it was probably used first and foremost to keep meats and seafood from spoiling.

The slow, low, indirect heat of barbecue is ideally suited to large pieces of meat, like whole pigs and turkeys. It's also perfect for cuts with lots of tough connective tissue, like brisket and spareribs. Barbecue was traditionally associated with the poorer echelons of society, who created a cuisine based on inexpensive cuts, meats that are revered as barbecue today.

What is direct grilling?

Direct grilling involves using a high heat to cook relatively thin cuts of meat, like steaks, chops, kebabs; and vegetables, like peppers and portobello mushrooms. The food is cooked right over the fire and the high heat sears the surface and seals in the juices. When working over high heat, the total cooking time, depending on the size of the food, will be two to twenty minutes (two minutes for small shrimp and tiny satés, twenty minutes for a spatchcocked chicken). In many parts of the world, cooks boost the heat of the coals even further by oxygenating them with a fan or an electric blower.

For direct grilling, rake the lit coals out into an even layer covering the entire grill grate for a one-zone fire. For a two-zone fire, rake the coals out in an even layer but only cover two-thirds of the grill grate with them. Leave the remaining third coal-free. For a three-zone fire, bank the coals in a double layer on one side, a single layer in the center, and leave the far side coal free. (For more on zone cooking, see page 18.)

Direct grilling is generally done with the grill uncovered—especially when cooking smaller cuts of meat, like kebabs and satés, or highly flammable foods, like bread. You can cover the grill to speed up the cooking time for thicker steaks, like T-bones and porterhouses.

So what is indirect grilling?

Indirect grilling is a hybrid method, invented in this century, that bridges the gap between barbecuing and grilling. As in barbecuing, the food is cooked adjacent to, not directly over, the fire. But the cooking takes place in the same chamber as the fire and the temperature is usually higher—generally around 350°F—than it would be for barbecue. Wood chips or chunks are often placed on the coals or other heat source to generate smoke, as with barbecue. But just as often, indirect grilling is done without smoke.

When a charcoal grill is used for indirect grilling, the coals are placed on the sides or periphery of the firebox; the food goes in the center of the grate (see box, facing page). With a gas grill, the burners on one side (or the front and back of the grill) are lit and the food is placed over the nonlit area.

The beauty of indirect grilling is that it turns your barbecue grill into a sort of oven. This enables you to cook large cuts of meat, poultry, and fish or fatty cuts without burning them. Indirect grilling gives you the best of both grilling and barbecuing—grilling's charcoal and barbecue's tenderness and smokiness—without the drawbacks of either. Indirect grilling is a lot more forgiving than direct grilling in terms of timing and temperature control. And it's a lot faster than true barbecue, which can take six to twelve hours.

What foods should you indirect grill?

Foods that are too large, too tough, or too fatty to cook by direct grilling. The list includes whole chickens, ducks, and turkeys; rib roasts, pork shoulders, and loins; leg and shoulder of lamb; baby back ribs; whole fish; and whole vegetables and fruit, such as stuffed onions, cabbages, and apples.

What's the difference between indirect grilling and smoking?

All smoking is done using the indirect method, but not all indirect grilling is smoking. One difference lies in the temperature. Indirect grilling is generally done at a moderate heat (most typically at 350°F, although you can indirect grill at as low as 300°F and as high as 400°F). Smoking is typically done between 225° and 275°F.

The other difference lies, of course, in the smoke itself. When indirect grilling, you can add soaked wood chips or chunks to the fire to obtain a smoke flavor, but you can also indirect grill without smoke (for example, Asian recipes grilled using the indirect method are often cooked without smoke). When smoking, you always add wood chips or chunks to the fire.

INDIRECT GRILLING ON A CHARCOAL GRILL

Try cooking a whole chicken or a four-pound fish over a superhot fire, and you'll wind up with a carbonized exterior and a heart of uncooked flesh. Thicker foods should cook over a lower heat for a longer period of time, anywhere from thirty minutes to two hours. So how do you achieve this sort of heat on a charcoal grill?

Use the indirect method: In indirect grilling, the coals are pushed to the sides of the grill and the food cooks in the center—over a drip pan, not over the coals. The grill is always covered, and the vents in the lid and in the bottom of the grill are used to regulate the heat (open them to raise the temperature, close them to lower it). The temperature used in indirect grilling, about 350°F, is usually lower than that of direct grilling.

A grill set up for indirect grilling—charcoals on either side of the drip pan. This grill has baskets on either side of the grill to keep the coals in place.

To set up the grill for indirect grilling, light the charcoal and, when it is blazing red, dump it in two mounds at opposite sides of the grill. Some grills have special half-moon-shaped baskets to hold the coals at the sides; others have wire fences that hook onto the bottom grate to corral the coals. Let the coals burn until they are covered with a thin layer of gray ash. Set an aluminum foil drip pan in the center of the grill, between the mounds of coals. Place the food on the grate over the drip pan, and cover the grill. You'll need to add about ten to twelve fresh pieces of lump charcoal or briquettes to each side after an hour of cooking.

If you want a smoke flavor, you can add a half to three-quarters cup of presoaked wood chips, or one or two wood chunks, to the coals on each side just before you start to cook, and again whenever you replenish the coals (about once an hour).

Types of Grills

As grill fever continues to sweep North America, an ever-increasing selection of grills—from portable kettle grills to jumbo built-ins, from simple hibachis to high-tech gas grills—has become available. Here's a look at the basic styles, starting with the smallest.

HIBACHI: This small, portable charcoal grill, originally from Japan, is one of the world's best designed live-fire cooking devices. Making a virtue of simplicity, the hibachi consists of a rectangular or oval firebox (traditionally made of a heavy metal, like cast iron, for even heat conduction) surmounted by one or two metal grates. The hibachi is designed for the direct high-heat grilling of teriyaki, kebabs, satés, and small cuts of meat. The cooking temperature is controlled by air vents near the bottom of the grill and by raising and lowering the grate. The saté grills of Indonesia and the braziers of Turkey and North Africa are variations on the hibachi. The chief drawback of a hibachi is that it has no lid, so you can't use it for indirect grilling or smoking.

KETTLE GRILL: This uniquely American grill has a deep rounded bowl with a grate in the bottom for holding the charcoal (or wood chunks) and a grate above that for the food. The lid is also bowl-shaped and allows you to turn the grill into a smoker (when you use wood chips) or an outdoor oven. Kettle grills can be used for direct high-heat grilling, but what makes them unique is their ability to do indirect grilling and barbecuing. To this end, the best kettle grills have hinged food grates for easy access to the coals and slotted side baskets that hold the charcoal for indirect grilling. The cooking temperature is controlled by vents on the bottom and in the lid. Kettle-style grills come in both round and square designs.

The front-loading grill, which looks like a rectangular metal box with a door in the front, is a variation on the kettle grill. Front-loading grills are ideal for grilling with wood.

GAS GRILL: Another American invention, the gas grill consists of a metal box lined with tube-shaped liquid-propane burners. Surmounting these burners is a heating surface, sometimes a row of inverted V-shaped metal bars, sometimes lava stones or ceramic briquettes. Propane has no flavor of its own as it burns, but a smoke flavor is created when the meat juices and melting fat sizzle on the stones or metal bars. These days, most gas grills have two or three separate cooking zones, so you can set them up for indirect grilling.

KAMADO COOKERS: Shaped like a giant clay egg, the Kamado is a charcoal-burning grill with an ingenious venting system that allows you to cook at very low temperatures (225°F), very high temperatures (700°F), and everywhere in between (on the low vent setting, the Kamado is extremely fuel efficient). The thick ceramic walls hold in the heat and moisture, making the Kamado ideal for cooking inherently dry foods, like venison and turkey. The most popular Kamado cooker is the Big Green Egg, which enjoys a cultlike status among grillers. (See page 9 for more about Kamado cookers.)

TABLE GRILL: Also known as the Australian grill or Argentinean grill, this long, narrow grill (four to six feet long, one and a half to two feet wide) looks like a table surmounted by a grate. Legs or a trolley platform hold the grilling surface at waist height for comfortable cooking. Charcoal versions have a shallow firebox for the coals and an adjustable grate. Gas versions feature thermostatic heat control. Table grills are used for the direct high-heat cooking of large numbers of steaks, chops, shrimp, and lobster. You often find them at communal or charity barbecues. When Australians speak of barbecue grills, this is what they mean. Again, no lid means no indirect grilling.

55-GALLON STEEL DRUM GRILL: This variation on the kettle grill is especially popular on the professional barbecue circuit. A couple of hours of welding is all it takes to cut a 55-gallon industrial steel drum in half lengthwise and install legs, a chimney, a grate, and hinges and handles for raising and lowering the lid. The hefty size of these grills enables you to cook large cuts of meats (including whole pigs). It's also easy to build a fire on one side of the drum (or in a separate firebox) for the smoky, low-heat, indirect cooking needed to make fall-off-the-bone-tender barbecue. Variations on the 55-gallon steel drum grill include the smaller 10-gallon versions made from propane tanks, common in the Caribbean, and the jumbo 200- or 500-gallon versions made from furnace oil tanks, popular at barbecue festivals.

BUILT-IN GRILL: These brick or stone behemoths began to appear in the 1950s, the golden age of backyard barbecue. There are two types: the raised hearth style with a built-in chimney and the southern-style barbecue pit. The charcoal- or wood-burning raised hearth was designed for direct high-heat grilling of steaks, chicken, and burgers. The barbecue pit was built for the long, slow smoke cooking essential to making barbecue. With the increased mobility of the American family (the average American moves once every four years), built-ins have largely disappeared, and I must say I miss them. They gave me the sense of comfort and community I feel when I sit in front of a fireplace. However, a new generation of built-ins has started to appear—a veritable high-tech outdoor kitchen or cooking center that's as likely to be fueled by propane or natural gas as by wood or charcoal.

What's the difference between barbecuing and smoking?

Technically speaking, they are one and the same. Both are done at a low temperature (225° to 275°F). Both owe their distinctive flavor to the presence of abundant wood smoke. Practically speaking, barbecuing is generally done with large hunks of meat, like pork shoulders (or whole hogs) and brisket, while smoking is often done to fish, poultry, game, and, of course, red meat.

How did smoking come about?

Smoking is one of the oldest methods of preserving food—perhaps even older than salting. Smoke retards spoilage by slowing or impeding bacterial growth and by repelling flies and other insects. When combined with salting (the way you might brine and smoke salmon or turkey), it is an extremely effective method for preserving food without refrigeration.

What's the difference between hot smoking and cold smoking?

As the name implies, hot smoking is done at a temperature sufficient to both smoke and cook the food.

In cold smoking, the food is smoked far enough away from the heat source that it smokes without cooking. Typical cold-smoked foods include Scottish-style salmon and beef jerky. Cold smoking is beyond the scope of this book.

THE GRILLS

What sort of grill should I buy? How do I identify my "grilling personality"?

If I had a dollar (OK, a sawbuck) for every time I have been asked this question, I could retire. There's no such thing as a perfect single model or one-size-fits-all grill. The right grill for you depends on many factors: what you like to cook on the grill; how many people you typically cook for; how often you plan to use your grill (once a week or 24-7?); and of course how much space you have. (Would that stainless steel supergrill look fabulous in your backyard or would it be bigger than your whole deck?)

The Birth of the Kettle Grill

For a cooking method as ancient and universal as grilling, it seems unlikely that a single individual could be responsible for the invention of a new technique. Nonetheless, one person did revolutionize the art of outdoor cookery in North America by combining the techniques of grilling and barbecuing in a single device: the kettle grill. His name was George Stephen, and the method he pioneered is now known as indirect grilling.

The year was 1951. The place was Palatine, Illinois. Like many Americans in those halcyon days of the 1950s, Stephen was an avid barbecue buff. But the flat, brazier-style grills popular in those days didn't work well in rainy or windy weather. He was frustrated.

At the time, Stephen worked at the Weber Brothers Metal Works, a manufacturer of nautical buoys. In a stroke of genius, he had the idea to fit a metal grate into one of the spun metal bowls used for buoy making. He then fashioned a cover with vents out of the same metal. In July 1952, George Stephen began marketing his grill as George's Kettle, which was promptly nicknamed the "Sputnik" on account of its rotund shape.

The advantage of the deep, covered kettle grill wasn't simply that it deflected wind and rain. Rather, it was the way it enabled the user to transform the grill into a sort of oven where foods could be roasted—or for that matter barbecued—by the heat of glowing charcoal.

Today the Weber Kettle remains the world's best-selling charcoal grill.

There's even such a thing as your "grilling personality," and choosing the right grill to match your temperament will go a long way in making sure you buy a grill you'll actually use. For example, if you're a steak, chop, and burger sort of person (and I certainly hope this book will inspire you to expand your repertory), you can get away with a two- or three-burner gas grill or a simple charcoal kettle grill. If your tastes run to fork-tender briskets and crusty succulent pork shoulders, you'll need some sort of smoker. If you normally grill just for you and your spouse, a hibachi or 22 ½-inch kettle grill or a small gas grill will do the trick. If every weekend finds you cooking for twenty or thirty of your tailgating buddies, you'll most certainly want a jumbo charcoal grill, like a Weber Ranch, and a six-burner gas grill or table grill.

If you're the sort of person who enjoys the process of grilling—building a fire, waltzing the food from hot spots to cool spots, imbuing your food with the soulful flavor of wood smoke—you have a charcoal or wood-burning grill personality. If you're a more results- and destination-oriented person, if you care less about the process and sport of grilling than about getting the food on the table, you may be happier with a gas grill.

Eventually, you'll probably want to own several grills—a charcoal grill for simple smoking, for example, plus a gas grill for cooking a steak on a busy weeknight, plus maybe even a water smoker or offset barrel smoker for smoking salmon, ribs, or pork shoulders. Some people believe you can never be too thin or too rich; I believe you can never own too many grills (just ask my wife, Barbara—we own sixty).

Charcoal or gas? Or wood?

All three.

CHARCOAL has the advantage of burning hotter and drier than propane, so you can't beat it for searing meats, seafood, and vegetables. It's also easy to smoke on a charcoal grill and virtually impossible to really smoke on a gas grill. But charcoal—at least charcoal that's been properly lit—imparts no intrinsic flavor. (That's not to be confused with the half-lit charcoal soaked with lighter fluid we cooked over when I was growing up. For many people raised in the 1950s and '60s, that's the taste we associate with barbecue. Happily, times have changed.)

PROPANE and **NATURAL GAS** have the advantage of push button ignition and turn-of-the-knob heat control. And if you light and preheat a gas grill properly, you'll get virtually the same searing properties you get with charcoal coupled with a convenience that many grillers (about 68 percent of grilling families in the United States) prefer. Gas, too, imparts no intrinsic flavor, but many gas grills come with smoker boxes where you can put wood chips, which can add some smoke flavor.

WOOD for me is the ultimate fuel. Think logs or chunks of hardwoods, like hickory, oak, apple, or mesquite. You build a fire as you would in a fireplace or light wood chunks in a chimney starter, the same way you would charcoal. Grilling over wood gives you not only enough heat to sear but also a delicate, inimitable smoke flavor—not the heavy smoky flavor that comes from true barbecuing or smoking. Wood-grilled foods have a more subtle smoke flavor, which is why wood is the fuel preferred by pit masters from Tuscany to Buenos Aires.

For more about fuels for grilling, see page 11

What should I look for when buying a grill?

First, determine your "grilling personality" (see page 5). That will help you decide whether to buy a gas, charcoal, or wood burning grill; the size of the grill; and so on. Whatever grill you buy, you want to make sure it looks and feels sturdy and well made. And that the controls (vents on a charcoal grill, igniters and burner knobs on a gas one) move smoothly and easily.

A CHARCOAL GRILL should have a grate with hinged side panels, so you can add charcoal or wood without having to remove the whole grate with the food.

Pit Cooking

Pit cooking is probably the oldest method of live-fire cooking. But today the term can mean very different things depending on where you live. In Argentina, pit cooking is known as *asado*. Large cuts of meats (even whole lambs or pigs) are roasted on T-shaped spits placed upright in a circle around a blazing campfire. I've observed such campfires in ranch settings and in restaurants in downtown Buenos Aires. The heat is direct, but not directly under the meat, nor is it as hot as grilling over a grate. With a moderate flame, a side of beef or a whole goat cooks in four to six hours.

Barbecue buffs in the Carolinas, Texas, and the Midwest call their cookers "pits," although most are brick constructions that stand aboveground. Some are portable trailer-mounted cookers fashioned from fuel tanks. In these areas in the old days, barbecue was no doubt smoke cooked over shallow pits in the ground.

True pit cooking takes place in a hole in the ground. You've experienced it if you've ever been to a traditional New England clambake or to a Hawaiian luau. Pit cooking is popular in Mexico, where famous pit-cooked dishes include *barbacoa* (pit-cooked goat or lamb wrapped in cactus or avocado leaves) and *pebil* (pit-cooked pork wrapped in banana leaves).

In this type of pit cooking, a large hole is dug and then lined with stones and firewood. The fire is ignited and allowed to burn down to glowing coals. Then the food—usually a large cut of meat, like a whole pig or goat—is wrapped in a flame-retardant material, such as banana leaves or seaweed, and placed in the pit, which is covered with dirt, sand, more seaweed, or a tarpaulin. The food cooks underground for twelve to twenty-four hours. When dug out, it is incredibly flavorful and fall-off-the-bone tender.

But is it barbecue?

It's true, we're talking about an indirect cooking method, and the wood embers impart at least a trace of smoke flavor. But it's also true that the low, wet heat that does the cooking is actually more akin to steaming or roasting. Like so much in the realm of live-fire cooking, whether pit cooking is or isn't barbecue is a matter of debate.

It should also have a receptacle for collecting the ashes for easy removal.

A GAS GRILL should have a built-in thermometer (also a good feature for a charcoal grill), a gas gauge, and most important, a deep drip pan that's easy to remove and clean—I cannot overemphasize the importance of this. Try to buy a grill with side tables; you can never have enough workspace. Look for a multiyear guarantee; remember, grills spend most of their working lives outdoors at the mercy of the elements.

What are BTUs and how important are they?

A BTU (British thermal unit) is a measure of energy—specifically, the amount of energy required to raise one gram of water one degree Celsius. Practically

Checklist for Grill Shopping

With more choices than ever, buying a grill can be almost as daunting as purchasing a car or a computer. Here's what I look for when buying a grill.

Charcoal Grills

Essential features (applies to hibachis, kettle grills, table grills, and 55-gallon drums)

- Sturdy, nonwobbly legs
- A heavy-gauge metal bowl or firebox with a tight-fitting lid—except for hibachis, which have no lid
- A grate at the bottom of the grill for holding the charcoal
- Air vents in both the bottom and the lid for temperature control
- A solid-feeling cooking grate; for a hibachi or table grill, one that's easy to raise and lower
- Wooden or heatproof handles

Desirable optional features

- A built-in thermometer
- Slotted metal or wire side baskets to hold the coals for indirect cooking
- A hinged grate that offers easy access to the fire, so you can add coals as needed
- An ash catcher on the bottom for easy cleaning and disposal
- A side table for additional workspace
- Fittings for a rotisserie

Gas Grills

Essential features

- Sturdy construction
- A thick, heavy firebox and tight-fitting lid for even heat conduction
- Electric ignition
- At least two, and preferably three or more, separate heating zones
- Adjustable controls that enable you to set the grill on high, medium, and low. The high setting should give you a consistent grilling temperature of 600°F. This usually (but not always) means a grill with at least 10,000 to 12,000 BTUs per burner.
- A gas gauge
- A built-in thermometer

Desirable optional features

- Side tables for extra workspace
- A gas burner on one side for heating sauces and accompaniments
- Fittings for a rotisserie and smoker box
- A warming rack
- A spider guard for keeping insects out of the burners

speaking, it refers to the heat output of a gas grill. Most gas grills put out between 10,000 and 12,000 BTUs per burner, with some going as high as 15,000 BTUs. The monster Dragon Burners in the Kalamazoo grills put out 50,000 BTUs.

I wish I could tell you a minimum or magic number of BTUs to look for when buying a grill (12,000 isn't a bad starting point), but the fact is that a grill's heat output and performance have as much to do with the grill's overall design and type of heat diffuser (Flavorizer bars, ceramic bricks, lava stones, and so on), as with the number of BTUs. I often use the analogy of an engine in an automobile. A sports car with a four-cylinder motor may actually be faster and more agile than a six- or eight-cylinder engine in a large SUV. The best thing to do is patronize a store where you can actually see the grill you're thinking of buying in action. Shop at a grill store, like a Barbeques Galore (www.bbqgalore.com), or a grill-savvy hardware store. Here are some things to look for.

1. Grate placement: The grate should be three to four inches above the heat diffuser—any closer and the food tends to burn.

2. Grate level temperature: Whatever the number of BTUs, the grill should have no trouble getting up to at least 650°F after ten or fifteen minutes of preheating. You can check this by using the "Mississippi test" (hold your hand three inches above the grill grate and start counting "one Mississippi, two Mississippi," and so on). You'll be able to hold your hand over a 650°F grill for only about two seconds before the heat forces you to say "ouch" and withdraw your hand.

3. At least two separately controlled heat zones: This is the minimum you need for indirect grilling. You'll have even more control if the grill you own has three, four, or six burners.

What's the best material for grill grates?

For me, the best material for grill grates is cast iron, followed in order of preference by stainless steel rods (a quarter inch in diameter), stamped steel, porcelainized enamel, and finally the chrome-plated wire grates found on inexpensive charcoal grills.

So what's the big deal about cast iron? It holds and evenly conducts the heat and produces dark, well-defined grill marks. (After all, when cowboys brand cattle, they use cast iron, not porcelainized enamel.) The only downside to cast iron is that it rusts, so you need to season it. If you have a grill with a porcelainized enamel or chrome wire grate, you can buy a cast-iron Tuscan grill grate to place on top of it (see page 10).

What is meant by seasoning the grill grate?

Seasoning a grill grate means cooking a light film of oil into it. This both lubricates the grate and keeps it from rusting. Traditionally, seasoning is a process used for cast-iron grates, but you can also season grates made of other materials. Every time you heat, brush, and oil a grill grate, you season it.

So how do you season a cast-iron grate?

Start with a screaming hot grill grate. Brush it with a stiff wire brush. And oil it generously with a tightly folded paper towel dipped in vegetable oil (preferably grapeseed, safflower, or peanut oil, not corn oil). Hold the paper towel with tongs and draw it across the bars of the grate. (You can also oil a grill grate with a chunk of beef or pork fat.) Repeat this process before you start grilling and as soon as you're finished—the practice should become second nature. The more often you do this, the better seasoned your grill will be.

What's a Big Green Egg Kamado-style cooker?

The Big Green Egg, a large, ovoid, forest green, charcoal-burning ceramic cooker, has attracted a ton of press, not to mention a cultlike following. Its enthusiasts—and they are legion—flock to "Eggtober" fests around the country (indeed around the world), where they venerate the Big Green Egg's virtues: its remarkable fuel efficiency (with properly adjusted vents, a single load of charcoal will burn for as long as twenty-four hours) and its ability to cook at temperatures as low as 175°F, as high as 700°F, and at every stage in between. Thanks to its inch-thick ceramic walls and a unique felt seal, the Big Green Egg is unrivaled at retaining moisture. This makes it unsurpassed for smoke roasting a Thanksgiving turkey. The pizza stone accessory enables you to replicate the pizzas you'd get in a coal-burning oven.

The Big Green Egg belongs to a family of charcoal-burning pits called Kamado cookers. Other members include the squat Primo; the sleek, stainless steel–sheathed Viking C4; and the mosaic-crusted Kamado. All feature an efficient venting system to control the heat, thick ceramic walls to hold in the heat and moisture, and an endearing ovoid shape guaranteed to make the cookers a cult object. The only drawback? Should a Kamado cooker need refueling, you have to remove the grate and the food.

What is an infrared grill? Do I need an infrared burner?

You could think of an infrared grill as a gas grill on steroids. The technology—pioneered by the TEC Corporation—is typically based on a slab of ceramic honeycomb, which is heated literally red-hot by conventional propane. This singular configuration enables the grill to reach temperatures as high as 800° to 1,000°F, which approaches the heat used by commercial steak houses to sear steaks and chops. That's the good news. The bad news is that straight infrared grills work great for searing steaks but tend to burn everything else—even when used for indirect grilling.

For this reason, a growing number of manufacturers are including an infrared sear burner in conventional gas grills. This gives you the best of both worlds: blast-furnace heat for searing steaks and more moderate heat for grilling just about everything else.

I've been hearing a lot about pellet grills. What do you think of them?

The pellet grill, or more accurately, the pellet smoker, is a cooker that uses pellets of compressed sawdust—rather than conventional wood or charcoal—to generate heat and smoke. Some models, like the Traeger pellet grill, use a thermostatically controlled metal heating rod to ignite the pellets, giving you accurate, turn-of-a-knob heat control. Kansas City barbecue legend John Willingham used a custom designed pellet cooker to win multiple Grand Championships at the Memphis in May World Championship Barbecue Cooking Contest (one of his cookers resides at the Smithsonian Institution).

The advantage of a pellet cooker is its precise heat and smoke control (the pellets are fed to the burner by an electric auger). The disadvantage—at least for the purist—is that you plug it in, making it too darned easy to use.

What is a Tuscan grill?

A Tuscan grill is a heavy metal grate (usually cast iron) with legs; it's designed to allow you to grill in a fireplace. A simple model consists of a square or rectangular grate with four 4- to 6-inch-high legs. More elaborate models have a slotted vertical frame, so you can raise or lower the grate to control the intensity of the heat.

Why does charcoal-grilled food seem to taste better than food cooked on a gas grill?

A lot of people swear by the "charcoal" flavor of foods grilled over lump charcoal or briquettes. Actually, this is more the result of the way the high dry heat of lit charcoal sears the meat than about any flavor-producing compounds that rise from the lump charcoal or briquettes themselves. A high, dry heat does a better job of caramelizing the proteins in meat and fish and the plant sugars in vegetables and fruits than does the lower, moister heat traditionally associated with gas grills. Many of the newer gas grills burn virtually as hot and dry as charcoal. The one exception here is partially or improperly lit charcoal briquettes, especially when they're doused with petroleum-based lighter fluid. These briquettes impart an oily or unpleasantly acrid flavor to grilled food.

How would I go about building a brick barbecue pit in my backyard?

When I was growing up the 1950s, these brick beauties were the pride of suburban backyards. Brick barbecue pits fell out of fashion with the rise of freestanding charcoal and gas grills. To judge from the e-mails I receive, backyard pits are staging a comeback. The construction of a brick barbecue pit is beyond the scope of this book. There are, however, detailed instructions in *The Complete Book of Outdoor Cookery,* by James Beard and Helen Evans Brown, which was originally published in 1955 but was republished as recently as 1997. You may also find the following website helpful: www.backyardspaces.com/barbeque.html

THE FUELS

What's lump charcoal?

Sometimes called charwood or chunk charwood charcoal, lump charcoal is an all-natural product made by burning trees, logs, or chunks of pure wood in a kiln with little or no oxygen. This process eliminates most of the water in the wood and, interestingly, most of the aldehydes and other smoke and flavor-producing compounds. The result is a fuel that is easier to transport and light and that burns hotter, longer, and at a more consistent temperature than wood but that imparts little intrinsic flavor. Its reliability, consistency, purity, and neutral flavor make it the fuel of choice among many grill masters from around the world.

Lump charcoal can be made from a variety of hardwoods: for example, oak, hickory, or mesquite. Mesquite charcoal burns the hottest and is the most volatile—it often emits violent cracks and sparks as it burns. Whenever you can, use the lump charcoal that comes in jagged, irregular chunks (from real trees), rather than lump charcoal in rectilinear blocks, made from scrap lumber or flooring.

What is a charcoal briquette?

At the end of the nineteenthcentury, a chemist named Ellsworth Zwoyer devised a method for combining coal dust, wood scraps, borax, and petroleum binders into a composite fuel that could be stamped into a pillow-shaped briquette (he patented the pillow-shaped design in 1897). But it wasn't until a twentieth-century industrialist got involved that the charcoal briquette became a household fuel—and a household name. That industrialist was Henry Ford, and he saw in the briquette an opportunity to recycle the wood scraps left over from the manufacture of Model T Fords. He promptly launched the Ford Charcoal company (the factory was designed by Thomas Edison), which he eventually sold to a relative named Kingsford.

Black Gold—Charcoal

About 200,000 years ago, give or take a few millennia, our prehistoric forebears made a revolutionary discovery: Charred wood (charcoal) burns cleaner, hotter, and much more efficiently than fresh wood. Charcoal is made by burning wood without allowing complete combustion (it has nothing to do with coal, which is a carbon-based mineral). It was probably discovered by accident when someone shoveled dirt or sand on a campfire. Deprived of oxygen, the wood continued to smolder, just enough to evaporate the water and resins, but not enough to consume all the combustible components.

Cordwood contains 20 to 30 percent water; charred wood contains 2 to 3 percent. This gives charcoal many advantages: It burns faster and hotter (as much as 200°F hotter), and it's easier to transport and store. Charcoal is the preferred cooking fuel for more than half of the world's population; it is used throughout Africa, the Caribbean, and Asia. Coconut charcoal, made from coconut shells and used in Southeast Asia, produces particularly delicious results.

Most of the world uses lump charcoal, but in North America it's the composition briquette that reigns supreme. The good news about charcoal briquettes is that they're more uniform in shape, size, and consistency than charred wood. The bad news is that, like sausage, you never quite know what's in them. Some briquettes are made from charred hardwood with natural plant starches as a binder. Other briquettes contain wood scraps, tree bark, sawdust, coal dust, borax, limestone, and/or sodium nitrate held together with a petroleum-based binder. But before you say "yuk," consider that these commercial briquettes are what the pit masters at the big barbecue competitions use, and they produce some terrific barbecue. Charcoal briquettes can be OK if you make sure to ignite them completely.

Some charcoal briquettes contain bits of mesquite, oak, or other woods, which are designed to impart a smoke flavor. Others, like Kingsford's MatchLight charcoal briquettes, contain lighter fluid to help speed up the ignition. If you use charcoal briquettes, make sure the coals are completely lit and beginning to ash over before you start grilling—otherwise, you may get a petroleum taste to your food.

Is there such a thing as a "natural" briquette?

Yes. One example is made by Duraflame. It is borax free and, instead of petroleum, uses vegetable starch as a binder to hold the briquettes together.

So which is better, lump charcoal or briquettes?

Each has its partisans. I personally prefer lump charcoal on account of its purity and naturalness. The drawback to lump charcoal, however, is that it burns hot at the beginning, starts to lose its heat after thirty or forty minutes, and provides a less consistent heat than charcoal briquettes.

The charcoal briquette is designed to maintain a consistent temperature of about 600°F for a specific amount of time, usually one hour. The disadvantage of briquettes is that when not fully lit, they emit an unpleasant acrid flavor. However, as I've noted earlier, most of the contestants in the big barbecue contests use charcoal briquettes.

What Wood to Use

Does it really make a difference what sort of wood you grill on? Charlie Trotter thinks so. Chicago's preeminent chef varies the woods in his grill according to the season. "In the winter, we use heavier woods, like oak and hickory," explains Trotter, "moving to lighter woods, like alder and locust, in the springtime, and fruitwoods, like cherry, in the summer."

The fact is that woods are to grilling what spices are to rubs; they add flavor to whatever you cook over them. Bear in mind that grilling with wood as the fuel is different from smoking with wood—the flavor is lighter and more subtle.

ALDER: A good clean wood from the Pacific Northwest. Good for salmon, turkey, and chicken.

APPLE: Tangy and clean flavored. Goes with chicken, pork, and game.

CHERRY: Sweet and fruity, with distinct cherry overtones. Use it for salmon, and duck and other poultry.

GRAPEVINE TRIMMINGS: The preferred fuel in France. Grapevine trimmings burn at a high heat, imparting a clean, dare I say vinous, smoke flavor. Grape wood is well suited to steaks and other meats, seafood, and escargot.

HICKORY: Rich and smoky. The traditional wood for American barbecue in the South and Midwest. Good for pork.

MAPLE: Mellow, mild, and sweet. Use it with poultry, seafood, and pork.

MESQUITE: Robustly flavored and smoky. The ultimate wood for beef in the style of Texas and northern Mexico.

OAK: A European favorite, and the wood preferred by professional chefs. Its clean, well-rounded flavor is equally well suited to poultry, seafood, and meat.

PECAN: A southern American favorite. Similar to hickory, only milder.

Where to Buy Wood:

W W Wood, Inc.
P.O. Box 398
Pleasanton, Texas 78064
(830) 569-2501

What about using wood for grilling?

Wood is my personal favorite fuel for grilling, in particular, a hardwood like oak, hickory, beech, apple, or other fruitwood. Wood gives you both heat and flavor—a lighter smoke flavor than when you use wood chips or chunks for smoking, but a wood-grilled flavor, all the same. Grill masters from Tuscany to Montevideo back me up on this, and if you've ever had a simple sausage, steak, or s'more grilled over a campfire, you know how incredibly flavorful wood-grilled foods can be.

So why don't more people grill over wood?

Wood-grilled foods possess great flavor, but grilling over wood presents several challenges. First, wood is harder to transport and takes up more room than charcoal. It's also a bit trickier and more time-consuming to light and harder to control the heat. A wood fire starts out as hot or even hotter than a charcoal fire, but it quickly loses heat. And wood is easier to burn in a front-loading grill than a top-loading grill—and most people own top-loading grills.

Is there any easy way to achieve a wood-grilled flavor on a charcoal grill?

There are two excellent ways. The first is to build a wood fire using wood chunks instead of charcoal. You can buy these in bags in your local hardware store or grill shop. Place the chunks in a chimney starter and light them as you would charcoal. Once lit, rake out the chunks, let them burn to embers, and when most of the smoke subsides, start grilling. You'll be amazed by the flavor.

When grilling over wood, you need to keep two things in mind: First, wood embers burn out much more quickly than charcoal—one chimney starter's worth will give you twenty to thirty minutes of grilling time or even less. It's a good idea to light an extra chimney starter of wood chunks in another grill. Second, never cover a grill when you're burning wood, even when grilling using the indirect method. Your food will come out unbearably smoky.

The second way to achieve a wood-grilled flavor on a charcoal grill is to toss whole wood chunks or one or two small logs on a charcoal fire. The wood will burn, imparting a light wood flavor. The charcoal provides the actual heat. In this case the wood chunks should be dry, not soaked.

Tanked on Gas

Most gas grills run on liquid propane, which is available at grill shops, hardware stores, and gas stations. The standard tank holds about twenty pounds of propane, which will burn for twelve to eighteen hours, depending on the design, usage, and temperature of the grill. Most of the newer gas grills come with gas gauges. Some work by weight, others by pressure.

When filling a new propane tank, the air must be removed first. Advise the service person that you are filling a new tank, so he or she can bleed the tank properly. Transport the filled tank in an upright position. I keep a milk crate in the trunk of my car for this purpose.

How do you use wood for smoking and what's the best kind to use? Can you really match woods to foods?

To use wood for smoking, soak it for thirty minutes to one hour in water to cover. This slows the rate of combustion so the wood smolders and smokes. Toss the wood on lit charcoal, which will provide the actual heat (that's why it's so easy to smoke on a charcoal grill).

Almost any hardwood is a candidate for grilling (hardwood comes from deciduous trees—trees that lose their leaves in winter). The short list of commonly used woods for smoking includes oak, hickory, maple, alder, and fruitwoods, like apple, pear, and cherry. Never use a softwood like pine or spruce; the smoke will be unpleasant and oily tasting. Some softwood smoke is actually toxic. And never smoke with plywood or pressure-treated lumber, which contain toxic chemicals.

In terms of matching flavors, you can use particular woods like you would spices. Oak—and to a lesser extent, mesquite—work well with strong-tasting meats, like beef or lamb. The strong, sweet smoke of hickory is often associated with pork. Milder flavored meats, like poultry and fish, go well with the smoke of such fruitwoods as apple and cherry. But just as with using spices, there are no hard and fast rules. I always experiment, and you should feel free to, too. You'll find descriptions of the different wood "flavors" on page 12.

What's the difference between wood chips and chunks and when should you use each?

Both impart a similar flavor: Chips, on account of their size, do it faster than chunks. I use soaked wood chips on smaller grills, like a charcoal kettle grill, or for quicker cooking foods, like baby back ribs. I use larger chunks in larger cookers, like offset barrel smokers, and for foods that smoke all day, like briskets or pork shoulders.

I have a lot of pine trees on my property. Is it OK to grill and/or smoke over pine? Can I smoke on corncobs? Hickory nuts?

In barbecue, as in life, every rule has its exception. Grill masters in parts of Germany, for example, grill bratwurst over pinecones. But in general, pine, spruce, and other resiny softwoods should be avoided for grilling and smoking. Corncobs are not only fine for smoking, in some regions they're highly prized. Ditto for hickory nuts and shells and walnut shells.

I tried smoking with wood as my fuel in a kettle grill; the food was unbearably smoky. What did I do wrong?

When smoking on a kettle grill, add soaked wood chips or chunks to the mounds of lit charcoal. As I mentioned before, never smoke with straight wood in a covered grill. The fire will simply generate too much smoke.

What's the difference between propane and natural gas?

Both are hydrocarbon derivatives of petroleum. Natural gas, as the name suggests, comes from underground gas deposits and is ready to use as soon as it's captured. Propane is a refined distillate based on natural gases from underground. It passes through a refinery prior to being ready to use in your grill.

Practically speaking, both can be used to fuel grills, but they behave differently. Propane burns hotter and drier than natural gas: One unit of propane puts out 2.5 more BTUs when burned than an equal amount of natural gas. For this reason, natural gas–burning grills must be fitted with special manifolds with larger holes to achieve a heat comparable to what you'd get in a propane grill.

Natural gas also burns marginally cleaner than propane and is less expensive to buy. And, natural gas arrives at your home through convenient municipal piping, so you don't need to fuss with refilling tanks the way you do with propane (contact your local utility company for information about a hookup). We solved the dilemma at my house by having a thousand-gallon propane tank, which pipes directly to my grills.

My grill doesn't have a gas gauge. Is there any way to tell how much propane is in the tank?

There are several ways to measure the amount of gas: by gauge, by condensation, and by weight. Here are the options.

BY USING A GAUGE: Grill stores sell screw-on gas gauges you can install between the valve on the top of the propane cylinder and the hose that takes the gas to the grill. Gas gauges are available at grill shops or via the Web.

BY CONDENSATION: Pour a cup of boiling water over the outside of a propane tank. The water will form droplets of condensation over that part of the tank that's still full and will evaporate over that part of the tank that is empty, so you can see how much propane is left.

BY WEIGHT: A full propane tank weighs about thirty-eight pounds; an empty tank weighs about eighteen pounds. Many grills have built-in scales—or you can use an old bathroom scale to weigh the tank.

What's the best way to keep from running out of gas during a grill session?

That's easy: Always keep an extra propane tank (a full one) on hand.

SETTING UP THE GRILL

Now that you've got an overview of the various types of grills and fuels, the next thing to master is cooking over live fire. There are directions here for grilling with charcoal, followed by ones for gas grills. After that you can branch out—you'll find instructions and tips for smoking on the grill and for using a rotisserie and a smoker, plus some more unusual grilling techniques.

Grilling with Charcoal

What's the best way to light charcoal? My dad always used lighter fluid.

So did my dad, and we often ate steaks that reeked of petroleum by-products. It's not that I'm totally against lighter fluid, but many grillers today prefer to avoid the risk of petroleum by-products entirely and use a chimney starter to light the coals instead.

A chimney starter is a device of elegant simplicity—an upright metal tube or box that is roughly six inches wide and has a wire or slotted partition in the center and a heatproof handle. You place lump charcoal or briquettes in the top of the chimney starter and a crumpled sheet of newspaper or a paraffin fire starter (this looks like a waxy white ice cube; one brand of paraffin starter is manufactured by Weber) in the bottom. Place the chimney starter on the bottom grate of a charcoal grill and light the newspaper or fire starter. In about twenty minutes, you'll have a chimney full of uniformly lit coals. The chimney starter has three advantages over the traditional lighter fluid method.

1. It eliminates any risk of a petroleum residue flavor.

2. The confined vertical shape of the chimney funnels the heat upward so the coals ignite uniformly.

3. A chimney starter makes it easier to dump out the coals where you want them—at the sides of the grill for indirect grilling, for example.

Always wear heavy suede grill gloves when handling a lit chimney starter, and never light it on a wood or other flammable surface.

BUILDING A CHARCOAL FIRE

Grilling over charcoal has always been as much an art as it is a science because there's no perfectly precise way to control the heat. You need to start with enough coals to cover an area three inches larger on all sides than the size of the food you plan to cook. To cook a full meal on a standard 22½-inch kettle grill, this means about fifty briquettes.

For direct grilling, see page 2; for indirect grilling, see page 3. Use a grill hoe or garden hoe to rake out the coals). Let the coals burn until they are covered with a thin layer of gray ash, three to five minutes. You need about twenty-five minutes in all to light the coals and preheat a charcoal grill. Find more about controlling the heat on page 16.

1. *Light the coals, using one of the methods outlined above. Leave the coals in the chimney starter (or a pile) until they are all blazing red; this will take about twenty minutes.*

2. *Then pour out the coals and spread them over the bottom grate in the configuration you prefer. A two- or three-zone fire is good for direct grilling (see page 18).*

Heating Things Up

As you use the recipes in this book, you'll be instructed to preheat the grill to a particular temperature. Here are brief explanations of how to do this on both charcoal and gas grills.

If you are using a charcoal grill, light the charcoal, then rake the hot coals over the bottom of the grill. For better heat control when direct grilling, I suggest building a two- or three-zone fire, as described on page 18. Open the top and bottom vents wide. Use the "Mississippi" test (see the facing page) to determine when the coals are the proper temperature for cooking. When HOT, you should be able to hold your hand over the coals for only one to three seconds. If you have a grill thermometer, the surface temperature of the grilling area should be at least 600°F. Allow twenty to thirty minutes for the coals to come to the right temperature for cooking.

If you are using a gas grill, set all the burner dials on high. Preheat the grill until the internal temperature is at least 600°F. This will take ten to fifteen minutes.

PREHEAT THE GRILL TO MEDIUM-HOT: For a charcoal grill, light the coals as described above, but use fewer of them and rake them out into a thinner layer or let them burn for another five to ten minutes longer. On a three-zone fire, do the test where the hot zone and medium zone meet. Using the "Mississippi" test, you should be able to hold your hand over the coals for four to five seconds.

For a gas grill, preheat it to high, then turn the burner dials down to medium-high. The firebox temperature should be about 400°F.

PREHEAT THE GRILL TO MEDIUM: For a charcoal grill, light the coals as described previously but use fewer coals and rake them out into a yet thinner layer (or let them burn for another five to ten minutes). On a three-zone fire, test over the medium zone. You should be able to hold your hand over the fire for six to seven seconds.

For a gas grill, preheat it to high, then turn the burner dials down to medium. The firebox temperature should be about 350°F.

PREHEAT THE GRILL TO MEDIUM-LOW: For a charcoal grill, light the coals as described previously but use fewer coals and rake them out into a still thinner layer or let them burn for five to ten minutes longer than you did for medium. On a three-zone fire, test between the medium zone and the cool safety zone. You should be able to hold your hand over the fire for eight to ten seconds.

For a gas grill, preheat it to high, then turn the burner dials down to medium-low. The firebox temperature should be about 300°F.

PREHEAT THE GRILL TO LOW: For a charcoal grill, light the coals as described previously. Use fewer coals and rake them out in a very thin layer or let them burn for fifteen to twenty minutes longer. You should be able to hold your hand over the coals for twelve to fifteen seconds.

For a gas grill, preheat it to high, then turn the burner dials down to low. The firebox temperature should be about 250°F.

What's the slender silver bracket attached to the handle of many chimney starters?

You wouldn't believe how many people ask this question. It's called the bale—a second handle designed to help you lift and steer the chimney to where you want to dump the coals.

What if you want to use lighter fluid to light charcoal?

To start charcoal with lighter fluid, rake the charcoal into a round mound in the center of the bottom grate of the grill. Douse the charcoal with lighter fluid and ignite it with a match. Do not squirt additional lighter fluid onto

How *Not* to Light a Charcoal Grill

When I was eight years old, my mother gave me a lesson—and a heart-stopping fright—on the wrong way to light a charcoal grill. She threw a match on the briquettes, then poured gasoline on top. It was only the quick thinking of our neighbor that averted a tragedy: He knocked the exploding gas can out of Mom's hands and pushed her away from the fire. We all learned a valuable lesson: If you do use a petroleum-based starter, never, ever use gasoline. Pour the starter on the coals as directed in the instructions, seal the container, and move it away from the grill *before* you strike the match.

the fire once the coals are lit. Do make sure that the coals are completely lit (they should glow orange) and starting to ash over before you start grilling. This burns off any petroleum residue.

Is there any other way to light charcoal?

You can also use an electric starter, a loop-shaped metal heating element that glows bright orange when plugged in. You place the starter on the grate and arrange a mound of charcoal over the heating element, then plug in the starter. The charcoal will ignite in a matter of minutes. Electric starters are available at grill shops and are particularly handy for lighting deep grills like the Big Green Egg. They work equally well with wood chunks. The chief drawback to this device is that it requires an electric outlet next to the grill.

Can you light a charcoal grill in the garage when the weather gets cold? How about on a covered porch? How about using a hibachi?

No. No. And no. One of the by-products of burning charcoal is a toxic gas called carbon monoxide. Never light a charcoal grill in a closed area.

Is it safe to put a charcoal grill on a wood deck?

I have a wood deck under one of my "burn" areas, as active grill collections are known in the biz. I keep the deck safe by placing fireproof grill pads under each grill. Manufactured by DiversiTech, grill pads come in a variety of sizes, shapes, and colors and are available at grill shops, hardware and houseware stores, and via the Web at: www.grillpads.com.

A gas grill has knobs for controlling the heat. How do you control the heat on a charcoal grill?

There are three basic ways.

1. Adjust the heat by opening or closing the vents on the bottom and top of the grill. More air gives you a hotter fire; less air, a cooler fire.

The Mississippi Test

My grill doesn't have a thermometer. How do I check the heat?

Use the "Mississippi" test. Hold your hand about three inches over the grill grate and start counting "One Mississippi, two Mississippi, three Mississippi," and so on. After a certain number of Mississippis (seconds), the force of the heat will cause you to snatch away your hand. The number of seconds you can hold your hand above the coals roughly corresponds to the following temperatures:

TIME	LEVEL OF HEAT	TEMP
1 Mississippi	Very hot	650°F
2 to 3 Mississippi	Hot	600°F
4 to 5 Mississippi	Medium-hot	400°F
6 to 7 Mississippi	Medium	350°F
8 to 10 Mississippi	Medium-low	300°F
12 to 15 Mississippi	Low	250° to 275°F

2. Increase or decrease the number of coals in the grill. For example, to smoke at a low temperature on a kettle grill, I light only a half chimney starter of coals.

3. Build a two- or three-zone fire. That way you can move the food closer or farther away from the fire to control its exposure to the heat.

What's a two-zone fire? What's a three-zone fire?

In a **TWO-ZONE FIRE,** you spread the coals out in a single layer over about two thirds of the bottom grill grate, leaving one third of the grate coal free (use a grill hoe or garden hoe to rake the coals). The zone with the coals is your cooking area—use it for grilling simple foods for a small number of people. The coal-free zone is your cool or safety zone. To control the exposure to the heat, move the food closer to or farther away from the lit coals.

In a **THREE-ZONE FIRE,** you rake half of the coals into a double layer so they cover one third of the grill and spread the remaining coals out in a single layer in the center of the grill, leaving one third of the grill coal free. This arrangement gives you a high-heat zone (over the double-thick layer of coals) for searing; a moderate heat zone (over the single layer of coals) for cooking; and a cool, coal-free or "safety" zone. To control the exposure to the heat, start by searing the food over the hot zone, then move it to the moderate zone to cook it through. Should the food start to burn or if you get flare-ups, move the food to the cool zone.

Tips for Cold-Weather Grilling

When I was growing up, people living in the Frost Belt actually put their grills away from Labor Day to Memorial Day. Today, more and more grill masters are grilling all year long. As we in the business like to say, it's what separates the men from the boys. Ask yourself this simple question: When it snows, what do you shovel first—the path to your car or the path to your grill? Here are nine simple steps for successful cold-weather grilling.

1. Select foods that can be grilled quickly over direct heat, such as steaks, chops, chicken breasts, burgers, pork tenderloin, kebabs, fish fillets, and the like. Keep your menu simple.

2. Always position your outdoor grill in a well-ventilated area that is protected from the wind and open to the sky. Never grill in garages, outbuildings, or on covered porches.

3. Brush or knock any snow accumulation off the grill, if necessary, and salt any potentially icy patches around the grill.

4. If cooking with charcoal, line the inside of the grill with heavy duty aluminum foil, shiny side up, poking holes in the foil for the grill vents (This is very important.) The reflective foil will help build and maintain heat.

5. As always, preheat the grill to the desired temperature before adding the food.

6. Minimize heat loss by keeping the grill covered as much as possible after it is lit. Grills fitted with exterior thermometers are better suited to cold-weather grilling, as you don't have to uncover the grill to monitor its interior temperature.

7. If you are grilling with charcoal, you may have to add fresh coals more frequently—every half hour in cold temperatures versus every hour in warmer temperatures. I like to keep a second kettle grill or chimney starter going with hot coals so I can replenish the main fire as needed.

8. Odd, but because the outside air temperature is cold, it's easier to unthinkingly touch hot surfaces. Always wear heat-resistant grilling gloves (not ski gloves) to prevent burns.

9. Remember: Food takes longer (anywhere from 25 to 80 percent longer) to cook in cold weather.

A two-zone fire.

A three-zone fire.

How often should you add fresh charcoal? Can you add it as is, or does it need to be lit?

As charcoal burns, it gradually generates less and less heat. In general when you are using a prolonged cooking method, the coals need to be replenished once every hour. Charcoal briquettes may last a little longer; lump charcoal may burn out a little more quickly. When using lump charcoal, you can add fresh charcoal directly to the lit coals. Leave the grill uncovered for five to ten minutes while the lump charcoal lights.

If using briquettes, you can add them directly to the fire (leave the lid off until they light). However, I prefer to

When to Use a Drip Pan

When grilling food by the indirect method, including barbecuing, it's a good idea to use a drip pan. The drip pan serves three purposes: First, it helps you define the area for indirect grilling. Second, it collects the drippings from ribs, ducks, and other fatty foods. Finally, some grill jockeys use the drip pan to hold water, beer, wine, marinades, and other flavorful liquids to create a steamy environment that helps keep food moist during prolonged cooking.

The disposable aluminum foil roasting pans that you find in supermarkets make great drip pans. When you are indirect grilling on a charcoal grill, place the pan between the mounds of hot coals under the grate.

Many gas grills have built-in drip pans. If yours does, you don't have to add another one. Always be sure to empty the drip pan after each grill session. Otherwise, you run the risk of getting bad smells and raccoons.

Both side panels of this grate lift up to make adding fresh coals or wood chips easy.

light them in a chimney starter, in a second grill, or on the ground (never on a wood deck). Then, I add the lit coals to the fire. This avoids exposing the food to the acrid smoke generated when the briquettes are in the process of lighting.

Any suggestions for adding fresh coals to the fire without having to lift the grate with the food?

When you shop for a grill, look for one with a grate with hinged side panels. You lift the side panels to add fresh coals or wood chips (see photo, page 19).

What are the vents for on a charcoal grill?

The vents help you control the heat. When wide open, they let in more air, which makes the coals burn hotter. When partially closed, they restrict the airflow, which makes the coals burn cooler. If you close all the vents (bottom and top), you'll ultimately extinguish the fire.

Cooking with Gas

What's the safest way to light a gas grill? Do gas grills ever blow up?

Always have the grill lid open when lighting a gas grill. Gradually turn on one burner by rotating the burner knob counterclockwise. (On some grills, you may need to push the burner knob in first to rotate it. And on some grills, you must light one burner first—often an outside burner—which in turn lights the other burners.) One very important final step: Once you think the burner is lit, hold your hand a few inches over the grate for a minute or so to make sure the burner really is lit.

Never attempt to light a gas grill with the lid closed. The potential gas buildup and sudden ignition can cause a fatal explosion.

How do you test a gas grill for leaks?

Make a simple leak detection fluid by mixing equal parts liquid dish soap and water. Brush this over the hoses and couplings: Any leaks will show up as bubbles.

SETTING UP A GAS GRILL

You don't need a degree in engineering to light a gas grill, but there are a few watch points to get you started. (For more gas grilling safety tips, visit www.usepropane.com—the website of the Propane Education and Research Council.)

- **First, be sure you have enough gas (that's where the gas gauge comes in). There's nothing worse than cooking a whole brisket or ham and running out of gas halfway through.**

- **Uncover the grill, set the starting burner on high, and light it with the ignition switch. Make sure the burner is actually lit. Most gas grills have a peephole located under the burner control knob for viewing the burner. Or, hold your hand a few inches above the grate and make sure you can feel the heat.**

- **Should the gas fail to light after you've pushed the ignition switch for a few seconds, shut the grill down, wait a few minutes to let the grill air out, and then try again. Some people (myself included), lack a patience gene (not to mention a commonsense gene), so I mention this for anyone falling into that category: Do not keep the gas flowing while you keep pressing a balky ignition switch. The firebox will fill with gas, and when the spark finally comes, the gas will ignite with explosive force.**

- **Once the master burner is lit, light the others, setting all on high. Preheat the grill to the desired temperature. This will take about fifteen minutes—sometimes longer. Don't skimp on this preheating time—that's one of the most common mistakes people make when using a gas grill. (It is best to preheat the grill to high then lower to the desired temperature.)**

How to Grill Without a Grate

To most Americans, the grate (the metal grilling rack) is the most important part (or at least the defining part) of a barbecue grill. So you may be surprised to learn that in many parts of the world—from Turkey to Japan to India—grills do not have grates and the food is cooked in midair, as it were, directly over the fire.

Ground meat kebabs, like Indonesian satés and Persian *lula,* do particularly well grilled without a grate, because the meat tends to stick to the grate's metal bars. Many Indian tandoori dishes are covered with a chickpea batter that also tends to stick to the grate, as does the miso glaze so popular in Japanese grill joints.

The easiest way to do grilling off the grate on an American-style grill (charcoal or gas) is to place two flat one-inch-thick bricks or paving stones or pieces of metal pipe on the grill grate, far enough apart so that the ends of the skewers can rest comfortably on them. Place the skewer ends on the bricks; the food will be suspended above the grate and should be fully exposed to the heat.

If you've ever wrestled with ground meat kebabs sticking to the grate, you'll find this simple technique a revelation.

In order to grill these shrimp skewers without using the top grill grate at all, the charcoal was piled evenly in the center of the grill (on the bottom grate) and the bricks were placed on either side. The bricks rise up 2-inches higher than the layer of charcoal allowing the shrimp to grill above the fire.

What should you do if you smell gas from a gas grill?

If you smell gas, immediately turn off all the burners and close the valve on the propane tank. Disconnect the hose from the tank. Wait five minutes or so for any propane to dissipate. Reconnect the hose. Open the grill lid. Turn on the burners and click the ignition. If you still smell gas, *immediately* turn off the grill, disconnect the propane tank, and call the manufacturer.

How do you direct grill on a gas grill?

Set the burner dials on high and preheat the grill until the internal temperature is at least 600°F. (The temperature is usually measured at the lid level of the firebox, so it may be somewhat higher than the temperature at the grate.) You'll probably need to light all the burners to achieve this high heat. Once the desired temperature is reached, you can shut off one or more burners if you don't need to use the whole surface of the grate.

To direct grill at medium-high heat, set the burner dials on medium-high so that the internal temperature reaches at least 400°F.

How do you indirect grill on a gas grill?

To indirect grill on a two-burner gas grill, light one burner and place the food on the other side. On a three-burner gas grill, light the front and rear or left and right burners and place the food in the center. On a four- to six-burner grill, light the outside burners and place the food in the center of the grate. No matter how many burners there are, you need to cover the grill.

So what about a single-burner gas grill? To grill indirectly, you'll need some way to block the heat from the food. Place an inverted cake or pie pan in a larger metal pan or ovenproof skillet—the idea is to create an insulating pocket of air. Place the food on top of the inverted pan. Of course, having read this, if you own a one-burner gas grill, you may be inspired to graduate to a multiple-burner gas grill.

Rotisserie Cooking

You can spit roast foods on either a charcoal or a gas grill, and most grill manufacturers make rotisserie attachments. When buying a rotisserie attachment, look for a motor with an on-off switch (adjustable speeds are nice, too) and a cord that's long enough to reach the available electrical outlet. Be sure the device comes with a mounting bracket that will fit on your grill. The spit itself should have adjustable prongs for holding the food in place. Another nice feature is a counterweight, which helps reduce the strain on the motor.

To spit roast on a charcoal grill, set up the grill for indirect grilling and preheat it to medium-high or medium. When the coals are hot, rake them into two parallel rows, one about four inches in front of where the spit will turn and one about four inches behind where it will turn. Place a drip pan in the center, between the rows of coals. Skewer the food on the spit, attach the spit to the rotisserie mechanism, and turn on the motor. (Note: To spit roast on a kettle grill, you need a metal rotisserie collar, available from Weber, www.weber.com.) You'll need to add ten to twelve fresh coals per side after every hour of cooking.

Most of the newer high-end gas grills have an infrared rotisserie burner at the back of the firebox. When spit roasting, place a drip pan under where the food will be (you may need to remove the grill grates to get clearance). Preheat the rotisserie burner to high; to do this you may need to hold down the burner knob for fifteen seconds. Skewer the food on the spit, then insert it in the rotisserie mechanism and turn the motor on. That's all there is to it. If you're working on a four- to six-burner grill and you want to speed up the spit-roasting process, you can also light the outside burners; this combines spit roasting with indirect grilling.

To spit roast on a three-burner gas grill that has burners running from front to back, preheat the front and rear burners to medium-high or high. Leave the center burner off. Place a drip pan in the center of the grilling grate. Skewer the food on the spit, attach the spit to the rotisserie mechanism, and turn on the motor. If the food browns too quickly, turn off the front burner.

To spit roast on a three-burner gas grill with burners running left, center, and right or on a gas grill with four, five, or six burners, light the outside burners and leave the center burners off. Place a drip pan under the meat. This isn't true spit roasting because the meat is not exposed directly to the flame; it's more like indirect grilling on a rotisserie. But nonetheless, you'll get terrific results.

Approximate Times for Spit Roasting

1 chicken (3½ pounds)	40 minutes to 1 hour
1 game hen (2 pounds)	25 to 30 minutes
1 duck (4 to 5 pounds)	1¼ to 1½ hours
1 butterflied leg of lamb (2 to 3 pounds)	1 to 1½ hours
1 boneless pork loin (2 to 3 pounds)	1 to 1½ hours
1 boneless rib roast (about 3 pounds)	1 to 1½ hours

*Times given are for a covered grill. Add 15 to 20 minutes when using an uncovered grill.

When should you cook with the grill lid down and when should you leave the grill uncovered?

Always cover the grill when grilling using the indirect method. When grilling using the direct method, follow the "rule of palm." If what you're grilling is thinner than the palm of your hand (for example, skinless, boneless chicken breasts, thin pork chops, shrimp, many vegetables, garlic bread, and the like), grill them uncovered. These items cook quickly; you want to be able to watch them to make sure they don't overcook.

If what you're direct grilling is thicker than the palm of your hand (for example, a bible-thick swordfish or tuna steak or a thick porterhouse or T-bone steak), cover the grill. This holds in the heat and speeds up the cooking.

Cooking Satés

The saté is probably the most perfect morsel ever devised by a grill buff. This bite-size kebab on a small bamboo skewer is wildly popular all across Southeast Asia. Japan's yakitori and teriyaki are kissing cousins of saté. There's only one remotely challenging aspect to cooking a saté. Because bamboo is flammable, you must set up your grill so you can cook the meat without burning the ends of the skewers. There are three ways to accomplish this.

1. Do as they do in Southeast Asia—work on a slender grill, one just wide enough to expose the meat, but not the skewer ends, to the fire. Saté grills, long, narrow metal boxes that are quite tiny and portable, are specially designed for this purpose. Variations turn up from Jakarta to Kyoto and Kuala Lumpur. (I bought one in Jakarta that's twelve inches long and three inches wide and was fashioned from a large tin can.)

A Japanese-style hibachi is the closest thing to a saté grill available in North America, and it works quite well for cooking satés. You simply rake the coals right to the edge of the hibachi and place the satés on the grill with the exposed ends of the skewers hanging over the edge.

2. Protect the exposed part of bamboo skewers with a

Making an Aluminum Foil Grill Shield for Skewers

To make a grill shield for small bamboo skewers, fold a piece of aluminum foil in three like a business letter, shiny side out so it reflects the heat. Twelve by eighteen inches is a useful size piece of foil to start with to make a shield for small skewers. When you put the satés or kebabs on the grill grate, slide the foil under the ends of the skewers. Or, you can place the shield on the grate first and arrange the skewers on top. The aluminum foil will shield the flammable wood from the fire.

Rather than soaking bamboo skewers to prevent them from burning, use an aluminum foil shield. It's much more reliable.

skewer shield. This can be as simple as a folded piece of aluminum foil placed under the ends of the skewers, or you can buy a commercial skewer shield. Alternatively, you can wrap the exposed part of each skewer with aluminum foil.

3. It is often said you can prevent the ends of the skewers from burning by soaking the skewers in cold water for at least thirty minutes. This may slow the burning process slightly, but the first two methods are much more effective.

Smoking

What's the ideal temperature for smoking?

Tradition calls for the "big three" (brisket, pork shoulder, and spareribs) to be smoked "low and slow"—at a low temperature of 225° to 250°F for several hours. I find that whole chickens and quicker cooking ribs, like baby back ribs, have a crisper exterior (the skin in the case of chicken) and more pleasing texture (the actual meat in the case of baby back ribs) when smoke roasted at a higher temperature, 350°F, using the indirect grilling method.

I don't have a smoker. Can you smoke on a charcoal kettle grill?

You certainly can. Set it up for indirect grilling but use only half as much charcoal as you normally would. Less charcoal is the key to bringing the temperature down to a traditional low smoking temperature. You can also invest in a BBQ Baffle, a metal baffle that fits in a conventional charcoal grill and lowers the heat normally put out by charcoal by directing the flow of air through the grill (one source is www.bbqbaffle.com).

How do you smoke on a gas grill?

The short answer is, you don't. Gas grills can do many things well (they're terrific for direct and indirect grilling and for spit roasting). But because of the large vents in the back (required by the safety code), most gas grills do a poor job of smoking. Virtually all of the smoke goes pouring out the vents before it has a chance to flavor the food. Moreover, unless the grill is operating at full blast, it doesn't get hot enough to make the wood smolder (this is not a problem on a charcoal grill, where the wood comes in direct contact with the glowing coals). However, if you run a gas grill on high, the temperature will be too hot for indirect grilling or barbecuing.

Over the years, some grillers have come up with ingenious improvisations for smoking on gas grills. For example, you can place a pan of lit charcoal with soaked wood chips or chunks on the grate of a hot gas grill, turn off the burners, and plug up the vent holes in the back. Or you can invest in a device like Sam's Smoker Pro (a flat, metal box you fill with wood chips that goes under the grate over one of the burners—for information go to www.samssmoker.com).

If you insist on attempting to smoke on a gas grill, place all of the presoaked wood chips in the smoker box or in a smoker pouch and position them directly over one of the burners. Preheat the grill to high until the smoke billows, then lower the heat to the desired temperature for indirect grilling or barbecuing (or follow the manufacturer's instructions).

If your grill doesn't have a smoker box, you can buy one from a grill supply shop or you can improvise one, using a small loaf pan or metal pie tin. Or, make a couple of smoker pouches—wrap a cup or so of soaked, drained wood chips in heavy-duty aluminum foil to make a pillow-shaped pouch. Fold over the ends to seal it tightly, then to allow the smoke to escape, poke a half-dozen holes in the top with the end of an instant-read meat thermometer or a bamboo skewer.

The best solution? Even if you're a diehard gas griller or you just bought a stainless steel gas supergrill that costs as much as a car, if you really want to achieve the soulful smoke flavor of authentic barbecue, invest in an inexpensive charcoal kettle grill or an upright water smoker for smoking.

What do you do if your smoker doesn't have a thermometer?

If your smoker lacks a thermometer, insert the metal probe of an oven thermometer (not an instant-read meat thermometer) in one of the vent holes, or place it in the smoke chamber.

How often should you add fresh wood chips? Should you keep adding them until the food is done?

As a rule, I add fresh wood chips when I start smoking and then once an hour after that. With quicker-cooking food, like a whole chicken or a couple of racks of baby back ribs, one batch of wood chips (three quarters of a cup of soaked, drained wood chips or one to two chunks of hardwood per side) is sufficient. For pieces of meat that need to cook longer, like pork shoulder and briskets, I add wood every hour for the first half of the cooking time. I don't add wood during the second half of cooking—first because the meat seems to absorb less smoke flavor after a few hours, and second because I don't want the food to be unpleasantly smoky.

Is there such a thing as too much smoke?

Yes, and it brings us to one of the most commonly made mistakes in barbecue: the notion that if some is good, more is better. Oversmoked food tastes unpleasantly bitter and acrid.

The last few times I've cooked brisket, it's come out unpleasantly smoky. What am I doing wrong?

In a nutshell, you're using too much wood. Add 1 to 1½ cups of soaked chips or two to three soaked wood chunks to the charcoal embers every hour for the first half of the cooking time. There's no need to continue adding wood after five or six hours.

What should you use as the primary fuel in a smoker: charcoal or wood?

It depends on the pit master and smoker, but in general, I use lump charcoal for generating the heat and wood chunks for providing the wood smoke.

I have an offset barrel smoker and I have a hard time getting it up to temperature and keeping it hot. Any suggestions?

This is a common problem with these heavy iron or steel smokers. The quick fix is to build a larger fire. I use two, sometimes three, chimney starters' worth of coals in my offset barrel smoker. Make sure both the firebox vent and chimney vent are open. If you need a little more air in the firebox (remember, more air means more heat), you can leave the firebox side door open a quarter to a half inch.

If you do a lot of cold weather smoking, try to buy a smoker that has thick metal walls (at least a quarter inch thick). The thinner walled models just can't hold the heat in the winter.

Should you use a water pan and what should you put in it?

Your question refers to the so-called water smoker—an upright barrel smoker with the firebox on the bottom and a water-filled drip pan in the middle under the meat. (One of the common examples of this type of smoker is the Weber Smoky Mountain Cooker, aka the "Bullet"). The theory is that the liquid in the pan helps create a moist smoking environment and shields the meat from excessive heat.

I put water in the pan when smoking leaner meats, like turkey breast, but when I'm cooking fattier meats, like pork shoulders or briskets, I generally don't bother. I do line the water pan with aluminum foil to facilitate cleanup. Many people put wine, beer, cider, or another flavored liquid in the pan instead of water. I see no harm in this practice and it may even impart a subtle flavor (especially if you drink more of the wine or beer while the meat is smoking).

My smoker has two cooking grates. Can I smoke on both at the same time or just the top one? Wouldn't the food on the bottom grate cook faster because it's closer to the fire?

You probably have an upright barrel smoker or water smoker. Yes, you can smoke on two levels. I generally put the food that is fattier on the top grate and the leaner food on the bottom grate (brisket on the grate above a turkey, for example), so the dripping fat bastes the leaner meat. Yes, the food on the bottom will cook marginally quicker, so adjust the cooking time accordingly.

What do you think of electric smokers?

They work like a charm. The only drawback to electric smokers is they're too darned easy to use. (No pain, no glory.)

Grilling Indoors

How do you grill in the fireplace? And, how do you keep your indoor fireplace from getting all greasy?

The short answer is to invest in a Tuscan grill (see page 10 for a description). Build a roaring fire in your fireplace and let it burn down to embers. Rake the embers into a mound and place the Tuscan grill over them, then grill as you would outdoors.

To keep your fireplace from getting greasy, line it with aluminum foil (shiny side up to reflect the heat).

Indoor "Grills"

The advent of stovetop electric grills brought a traditionally outdoor cooking method into the kitchen. These grills feature an electric heating element positioned beneath a metal grate—a sort of inverted broiler. Indoor gas stovetop grills soon followed. But is this really grilling? In the case of an electric grill, a purist would say no. Indeed, the first qualification, live fire, is conspicuously absent. As for indoor gas grills, they function like outdoor models.

Both types of indoor grills offer the dry high-heat searing and charring so prized in outdoor grilling. I'm not sure that a blindfolded eater could tell the difference between outdoor and indoor grilled food that has been marinated well. And it certainly enables Frost Belters to enjoy grill-style food all year long.

Then there are skillet grills, frying pans with parallel raised ridges on the bottom that are designed to simulate grill marks. Here again, a purist might be tempted to dismiss these devices. Certainly there's no live fire. But the ridges create the smoky charring and inviting grill marks so typical of grilling. Skillet grilling is no substitute for outdoor grilling, but it can serve the apartment dweller who wants to approximate a grilled flavor.

I live in an apartment in Manhattan and can't put a grill on my fire escape. Which of your recipes can be grilled inside?

Almost anything you can grill outdoors can be grilled indoors, you just need to adapt the technique. As a matter of fact, there's a whole book on the subject—*Indoor Grilling*—written by yours truly. Just remember, outdoor grills should be used only outdoors.

Grilling Over a Campfire

What's the secret to grilling over a campfire? (My husband always burns the food.)

As a rule, it's better to grill over the embers than in the leaping flames of a roaring fire. Start your fire thirty to forty minutes before you plan to do the cooking. Shovel or rake the embers into a mound on one side of the fire and do your cooking over them. Burn fresh logs on the other side to continue generating embers.

How do you hold the food over the fire?

There are at least three ways.

1. S'MORE-STYLE: On the end of a stick or long skewer held over the fire. This is excellent for quick cooking foods, like sausages and s'mores.

2. *ASADO*-STYLE: Impaled on or tied to vertical stakes or skewers you stand in front of the fire. This is excellent for whole fish, split baby lambs and goats, beef ribs, and so on.

3. TUSCAN-STYLE: On a grate stretched between stones or bricks over the embers, or using a Tuscan grill, which has legs to hold it above the fire. Great for steaks and chops.

For every rule, there's an exception. When German grill masters make *speissbraten* (onion-stuffed, spit-roasted pork neck), they deliberately cook it in the flames of a beech wood fire to smoke it.

The Ten Commandments of Perfect Grilling

1. BE ORGANIZED. Have everything you need at grillside—the food, marinade, basting sauce, seasonings, and equipment—before you start grilling.

2. GAUGE YOUR FUEL. There's nothing worse than running out of charcoal or gas in the middle of grilling. When using charcoal, light enough to form a bed of glowing coals three inches larger on all sides than the surface area of the food you're planning to cook. (A 22½-inch grill needs one chimney starter's worth of coals.) When cooking on a gas grill, make sure the tank is at least one third full.

3. PREHEAT THE GRILL TO THE RIGHT TEMPERATURE. Remember: Grilling is a high-heat cooking method. In order to achieve the seared crust, distinctive flavor, and handsome grill marks associated with masterpiece grillmanship, you must cook over a high heat. How high? At least 600°F for high-heat direct grilling. Although I detail this elsewhere, it is worth repeating: When using charcoal, let it burn until it is covered with a thin coat of gray ash. Hold your hand about three inches above the grate. When the grill is hot enough to cook, after two to three seconds, the intensity of the heat should force you to snatch your hand away. If you are using a gas grill, preheat it to high (at least 600°F); this takes ten to fifteen minutes.

When indirect grilling, preheat the grill to 350°F.

4. KEEP IT CLEAN. There's nothing less appetizing than grilling on dirty old burnt bits of food stuck to the grate. Besides, the food will stick to a dirty grate. Clean the grate twice: once after you've preheated the grill and again when you've finished cooking. The first cleaning will remove any bits of food you may have missed after your last grilling session. Use the edge of a metal spatula to scrape off large bits of food and a stiff wire brush to finish scrubbing the grate.

5. KEEP IT LUBRICATED. Oil the grate just before placing the food on top. Use a tightly folded paper towel soaked in oil, or rub it with a piece of fatty bacon, beef fat, or chicken skin. Or, lift it off the hot grate, spray it with oil—away from the flames—then return it to the grill.

6. TURN, DON'T STAB. The proper way to turn meat on a grill is with tongs or a spatula. Never stab the meat with a carving fork—unless you want to drain the flavor-rich juices onto the coals.

7. KNOW WHEN TO BASTE. Bastes and marinades made with oil and vinegar, citrus, or yogurt can be brushed on the meat throughout the cooking time. If you want to use a marinade for basting, to avoid cross-contamination set some of it aside before you begin marinating the meat. Never use a marinade that has contained raw meat as a baste or a sauce.

When using a sugar-based barbecue sauce, apply it toward the end of the cooking time. The sugar in these sauces burns easily and should not be exposed to prolonged heat.

8. KEEP IT COVERED. When cooking larger cuts of meat and poultry, such as a whole chicken, leg of lamb, or prime rib, use the indirect method of grilling or barbecuing (see pages 2 and 3). Keep the grill tightly covered and resist the temptation to peek. Every time you lift the lid, you add to the cooking time.

9. GIVE IT A REST. Beef, steak, chicken—almost anything you grill—will taste better if you let it stand on a cutting board for a few minutes before serving. This allows the meat to "relax," making it juicier and tastier.

10. NEVER DESERT YOUR POST. Grilling is an easy cooking method, but it demands constant attention. Once you put something on the grill (especially when using the direct method), stay with it until it's cooked. This is not the time to answer the phone or mix up a batch of your famous mojitos.

Above all, have fun. Remember that grilling isn't brain surgery. And that's the gospel!

Can you indirect grill on a campfire?

Yes, there are two ways. The first is to stand the food on a stake (or on a brick in the case of onions and other round vegetables) in front of the fire (see *asado*-style grilling previously). The second is to cook the food in a Dutch oven, a large, deep cast-iron pot you set in the embers, shoveling more embers in the depressed section of the metal lid.

I once saw you cook sweet potatoes right on the embers. Why on earth would you do that and are they good?

Roasting food in the embers is probably the world's oldest method of grilling, and for some foods—especially for sweet potatoes and onions—it's one of the best. There are three compelling reasons to do this. First, it looks cool and is guaranteed to impress and amaze your guests. Second, the surface charring of the potato or onion skins imparts an incredible and inimitable smoke flavor. Third, you get to connect with your inner caveman—you're engaging in an act of cooking that's as old as mankind itself. One good example of this technique is the Onion an Potatoes Roasted in the Coals, page 418.

GRILL MAINTENANCE AND CLEANING

What do I do at the beginning of the season to get my grill ready?

This question assumes you put your grill away for the winter—something fewer and fewer of us do (see Cold-Weather Grilling on page 18). But if you mothball your grill during cold weather, here's what you need to do to get it ready for the start of the grilling season.

CHARCOAL GRILLS: Scrape out any ash you should have removed from the firebox at the end of the season. Make sure the metal vents at the top and bottom of the grill open and close easily; lubricate with WD-40 if necessary. Light the grill and preheat it screaming hot. Brush and oil the grill grate.

GAS GRILLS: If you forgot to clean the drip pan at the end of the season, do it now. Remove the grates and check to see that the burner tubes are free of obstructions, particularly spiders and spider webs, and that the holes in the tubes are open. If they are not, gently unclog them with a pin. Replace the grates.

Check the igniter buttons. When you press them, you should hear a click and spark. If you don't, you may need to replace the batteries. Finally, hook up the propane tank and open the valve, then light the grill. Brush and oil the grill grate.

In the unlikely event that you smell propane, turn off all the burners, disconnect and reconnect the hose to the gas tank, and try again. Use a leak detection liquid (see page 20) to check the couplings and hoses for leaks. If you find any leaks, immediately shut down the grill and call the manufacturer.

How often should I clean my grill? How clean does it *really* need to be?

My feeling is that the grill grates should be immaculate and the rest of the grill should be relatively clean at all times. Clean grates are essential for killer grill marks and they help keep food from sticking. Every time you fire up your grill, you should practice good grill hygiene—summed up by the simple phrase: "keep it hot, clean, and lubricated." In other words, preheat the grill to high, brush the grates with a stiff wire brush, and oil them with tightly folded paper towels dipped in oil and drawn across the bars of the grate with tongs. Do not attempt to clean a cold grill grate with soap, water, and steel wool. It will take you a long time and a lot of effort to achieve something that can be done in minutes.

"Guys, that fish skin or remnant of last week's pork chops burned onto the grill grate does not add flavor. If it looks disgusting, it probably is disgusting. When in doubt, ask your spouse."

If you are using a charcoal grill, you should scrape out the firebox and empty the ash catcher after every grill session. You may need to wait until the following morning to make sure the ash is completely cool.

With a gas grill, you should empty the drip pan after every grill session and hose off the exterior. Do not spray cold water on a hot grill thermometer or you may break the glass.

My grill grates are really rusty. What's the best way to clean them?

Preheat your grill to high (screaming hot) and brush the grates vigorously with a stiff wire brush. Then wipe the hot grate with a tightly folded paper towel dipped in oil and drawn across the grate at the end of tongs. Repeat as necessary. The more often you clean the grate in this fashion, the less likely it is to rust.

What's the best way to clean porcelainized enamel grill grates?

Porcelainized enamel grates are more prone to scratching and chipping than solid metal grates. To clean a porcelainized grate, preheat the grill to high, then brush the grate with a wire brush. (Many people like to use brass-bristled brushes, which are softer—and thus gentler on porcelainized enamel—than stainless steel bristles.) Oil the grate before grilling.

My grill grates corroded over the winter. Should I have stored them inside?

Ideally, if you use your grill on a regular basis throughout the winter, the grates will not corrode. But if you don't plan to use your grill during the winter, it's always a good idea to store it in a garage. If you have a gas grill, be sure to completely disconnect the propane canister. Of course, you should brush and oil the grill grates before shutting down the grill for the season. To restore corroded grates, follow the instructions above for cleaning a rusty grill.

What is an ash catcher and how often should I empty it?

The ash catcher is a pan, tray, or other receptacle under the firebox of a charcoal grill that is designed to hold the spent ashes. It should be emptied each time you use the grill. However, it takes several hours or even overnight for ashes to cool, so you may want to wait until the next morning. Never put spent ashes in a paper bag or plastic trash can. Often, there are a few live coals or sparks mixed in the ashes and these may set the receptacle on fire. I have seen this happen dozens of times.

GEARING UP

I want to get my dad a set of barbecue tools for Father's Day. What are the essential tools?

There are dozens, perhaps hundreds, of really cool grilling accessories, but you really need only three.

1. A long-handled stiff wire brush for cleaning the grill grate

2. Long-handled, spring-loaded tongs for oiling the grate and turning food

3. An instant-read meat thermometer for checking meat for doneness

That said, here are the near essentials and the not-so-essential-but-usefuls. A couple of good mail-order sources for grilling accessories:

www.barbecuebible.com/store/

www.barbecue-store.com (it also sells spare parts for gas grills)

Near Essentials

- Chimney starter (if you have a charcoal grill); see page 15
- One or more long-handled spatulas, preferably with crooked (offset) blades
- Two long-handled basting brushes (natural bristles, please; nylon will melt). You may also want to invest in a mop-style baster, which looks like a miniature mop.

Is It Done Yet?

The only remotely tricky part about barbecuing and grilling is knowing when the food is done. The pros use the poke test to check the doneness of steaks and chops (it's quite accurate when used by a seasoned griller). But for larger cuts of meat, nothing beats the "scientific" method for assessing doneness.

The "Artistic" Methods

There's an art to testing the doneness of steaks, chops, chicken breasts, and fish steaks or fillets. Here are three tried and true methods.

To test steaks and chops for doneness, the poke method is best. Press the thickest part of the steak or chop with your finger.

- When the meat is rare, it will feel soft, even squishy—a bit like the flesh at the base of your thumb when you touch the tip of your thumb lightly with the tip of your forefinger.

- When it is done to medium-rare, the meat will feel semisoft and yielding—like the flesh at the base of your thumb when you touch the tip of your thumb with the tip of your middle finger.

- When it is done to medium, the meat will yield just a little, like the flesh at the base of your thumb when you touch the tip of your thumb with the tip of your ring finger.

- When well-done, the meat will feel firm and springy—like the flesh at the base of your thumb when you touch the tip of your thumb with the tip of your pinky.

To test a whole chicken for doneness (less artistic, but still not scientific), insert a trussing needle or skewer into the thickest part of one thigh; the juices should come out clear. You can also try wiggling the drumstick; it should feel very loose. Or make a cut between the leg and the body. There should be no redness at the joint (unless you're smoking the chicken—smoke imparts a natural pink glow to meats).

To test fish for doneness, use the flake test: Press the thickest part with your finger. The flesh should break into large, firm flakes and should pull away from the bones easily.

The "Scientific" Method

Now on to larger cuts of meat like rib roasts and pork shoulders. The only really infallible test is to check the internal temperature with an instant-read meat thermometer. This handy device is available at any cookware shop. Insert it into the thickest part of the meat, but without touching any bones (bones, like metal, conduct heat). In the meat, poultry, and seafood chapters you'll find tables outlining degrees of doneness and their corresponding temperatures. Internal temperatures are also listed in the recipes when appropriate. Here's a broad guide to doneness.

BEEF AND LAMB

RARE	MEDIUM-RARE	MEDIUM	WELL-DONE
125°F	145°F	160°F	170° to 195°F

PORK

MEDIUM	WELL-DONE
160°F	170° to 190°F

CHICKEN, TURKEY, AND QUAIL

WELL-DONE
170° to 180°F

DUCK AND SQUAB

RARE	MEDIUM-RARE	MEDIUM	WELL-DONE
125°F	145°F	160°F	170°F

- One pair of heavy-duty grill gloves or mitts
- Three sharp knives: a chef's (8 to 12 inches), a paring, and a carving knife
- A carving fork
- Disposable aluminum foil drip pans (these are essential for indirect cooking and barbecuing and are also useful for soaking wood chips and holding marinades. They are available at just about any supermarket)
- Roll of heavy-duty aluminum foil
- Roll of paper towels
- Plastic or rubber gloves (wear them when you rub spices into pork and ribs or pull pork)
- An assortment of metal and bamboo skewers
- Stopwatch or timer
- An electric grill light for grilling at night (there's nothing harder than grilling when you can't see the food)
- Dry spray-type fire extinguisher

Luxuries

- A flat vegetable or fish grate (a wire grid or perforated metal plate that allows the smoke and flames to pass through but keeps small or fragile pieces of food from falling through or sticking to the grate)
- A hinged grill basket that allows you to grill and turn fish or other fragile foods without having to pry them off the grill grate
- Cedar or alder planks for grilling seafood
- A motorized rotisserie that mounts on the grill (great for whole chickens and legs of lamb)
- A grill hoe or garden hoe for raking out the coals
- A larding iron, a long slender tool with a V-shaped blade that enables you to insert strips of ham, cheese, or vegetables into a roast
- An electric spice mill (looks like a coffee grinder)—great for grinding whole spices to make rubs that taste like they mean it
- A meat grinder like grandma used to use (a grinder works much better than a food processor for grinding meat)
- A kitchen syringe—useful for injecting bastes into turkey breasts, pork roasts, and other dry meats to moisturize them from the inside
- A spray bottle or mister for basting grilled meats with vinegar or other flavorings (use the commonplace garden variety for vinegar or apple cider)

THE FOOD

You've got the tools, you understand the techniques. Now we get to the meat (and the vegetables and the seasonings) of the matter. After all, without food, what's the point of the grill?

Testing for Doneness

How can I tell when the food is done?

There are many ways to gauge doneness.

BY APPEARANCE: Does the food look done? Is it crusty and brown?

BY FEEL: When poked, squeezed, or pressed, does the food feel done?

BY INTERNAL TEMPERATURE: Does an instant-read meat thermometer show the meat to be rare, medium-rare, medium, and so on, in the center?

A true grill master uses several or all of these techniques to check for doneness. You'll find details about gauging doneness in the box on the facing page, plus a chart that lists the range of doneness temperatures for a number of foods.

What's the poke test? The flake test? The "Charmin" test?

The poke test is used for the doneness of steaks, chops, and other relatively thin cuts of meat. The flake test is used to check the doneness of grilled fish. For more on both these tests, see the box on page 30.

The "Charmin" test is used to check the doneness of round vegetables and fruits, like onions, cabbages, and apples, that have been grilled using the indirect method or have been smoked. Gently squeeze the sides between your thumb and forefinger. If the food feels "squeezably soft," it's done.

Do I really need an instant-read meat thermometer?

Unless you've been smoking meats for twenty years, the most accurate way to tell if a pork shoulder or rib roast is cooked is to use an instant-read meat thermometer. Insert it deep into the center of the roast, but not so that it touches a bone. (Bones conduct heat and will give you an inaccurate reading.) Leave the thermometer there for about fifteen seconds—it will tell you the internal temperature (see the doneness chart on page 30).

You can also use an instant-read meat thermometer to check the internal temperature of relatively thin foods, like porterhouse steaks: Insert the thermometer through the side of the steak. If there are any bones, make sure the thermometer does not touch them.

How do I know my instant-read meat thermometer is accurate?

To check the accuracy of an instant-read meat thermometer, insert the metal stem into a pot of boiling water. Water boils at 212°F at sea level—that's what should register on your thermometer. If the heat registers higher or lower, adjust the temperature using the lock nut on the back of the thermometer dial.

What do you think of those wireless thermometers with digital readouts and alarms?

They are very cool and they can certainly help you recognize when food is cooked. However, there's no substitute for your eyes, touch, and even sense of smell—and of course, for paying attention.

How do you cook a whole meal on the grill and have everything come off at once?

Excellent question! For starters, it helps to own multiple grills. This is not as extravagant as it sounds, for even if you're a dedicated gas griller, you'll probably want to own a charcoal grill for smoking. Especially after reading this book.

And now, here are some tips for menu planning.

1. Serve at least one dish that can be grilled ahead of time and served at room temperature. A platter of grilled vegetables, for example, like the Santa Margherita–style grilled vegetables on page 398, makes a spectacular centerpiece for a barbecue. Another great dish to grill ahead is an eggplant dip, like any of the ones on pages 82 through 85.

2. Serve at least one dish that is indirect grilled or smoked, for example the brisket on page 135, the *cochinita pibil*—pit-roasted pork Yucatán pork shoulder on page 186, or the prime rib on page 137. The cooking time for such dishes is much more forgiving than the split-second timing required when grilling a steak. Furthermore, once dishes like these come off the grill, they need to rest for fifteen to thirty minutes before serving, which gives you time to grill more quick-cooking items.

3. Make the grilling part of the evening's entertainment. For example, cook and serve the appetizer hot off the grill when guests arrive. This might be slices of Catalan Tomato Bread (page 128) or grilled garlic bread (page 126 or 127), or satés cooked on hibachis placed in the center of an outdoor table (on a heatproof pad, of course).

4. Grill the dessert to order at the end of the meal—for example, the grilled pineapple on page 513. Do this in front of your guests, or even better, get them involved in the grilling.

Beef

STEAK

What's the difference between prime and choice beef and which do you prefer?

The FDA grades meat according to marbling—those tiny flecks and streaks of fat found within the red meat. (In order to make such a determination, an inspector makes

Barbecue Countdown

In grilling, as in life, timing is everything. Here's a basic timetable that will help you get your grill lit, your food marinated and cooked, and your guests fed—without your having a nervous breakdown.

Preliminaries

- Twelve to two hours before you plan to serve, immerse the food in its marinade or rub it with its spice mix.
- Set the table.
- Prepare the drinks and side dishes.

Using a Charcoal Grill

- One hour before you plan to start cooking, soak wood chips or chunks, if you are using them, in cold water to cover.
- Light the charcoal twenty-five to thirty minutes before you plan to start cooking.
- When the coals blaze red (after fifteen to twenty minutes), dump them out of the chimney starter and spread them over the bottom of the grill. I like to build a three-zone fire (see page 18), so I have a high heat, a low heat, and a coal-free zone.

Let the coals burn until they glow orange and are covered with a thin layer of gray ash, three to five minutes longer for high heat. Now the fire is ready for grilling. If your recipe calls for a lesser heat, follow the timing instructions outlined on page 16.

- Clean the grate with a wire brush, and oil it as described in the seasoning question on page 9.
- If you are using wood chips, drain them well and toss them on the coals. Arrange the food on the grate and grill. If you will be indirect grilling for an extended period, light a second batch of coals in the chimney starter after forty-five minutes (about fifteen minutes before you will need them).
- After the food is cooked, don't forget to clean the grate again with the wire brush.

Using a Gas Grill

Follow the procedures described previously, preheating the grill for fifteen minutes. If you are using wood chips, place them in the smoker box when you preheat the grill. Keep the burners on high until the chips begin to smoke, then lower the heat as needed.

a cut between the twelfth and thirteenth ribs and visually inspects the meat for marbling.) Inspectors also look for fine muscle texture and bright red color.

PRIME is the highest grade, containing the most marbling, which in turn tends to give a steak the most tender consistency and richest mouthfeel and taste. Because it's the scarcest, prime beef is typically sold at steak houses, specialty butcher shops, and high-end markets. This is the grade of steak I personally prefer.

CHOICE beef contains somewhat less marbling and is slightly less tender, although it is still richly flavorful. Choice beef is the grade commonly sold at supermarkets, and I often cook with it.

There are several other grades, ranging in descending quality from Select to Canner. These are primarily for institutional and commercial use.

What's the difference between dry-aged and wet-aged beef and does either process make a difference?

Beef in its freshly slaughtered state is tough and stringy. All beef is aged for some period of time to make it tender and palatable. Dry aging takes the process to the

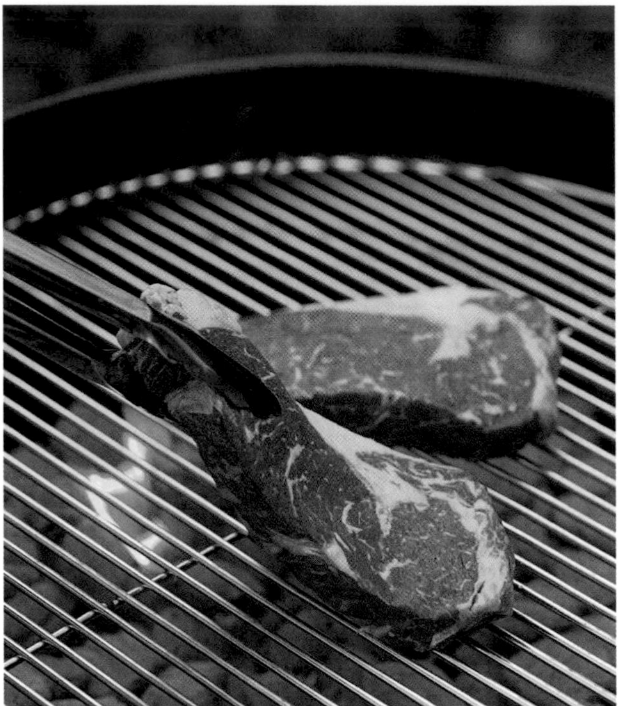

Always use tongs to move, turn, or remove meat from the grill. You don't want to poke the meat and lose valuable juices, as you would with these well-marbled, boneless New York strip steaks.

ultimate level. Dry-aged beef is hung, unwrapped, in a temperature-controlled meat locker for as long as four weeks. During that time, some of the water in the meat evaporates, concentrating the flavor of the meat and improving the texture. The aging also gives the beef a deeper, richer, more complex taste (much the way aging improves cheese or wine). The downside of the process is that the meat can lose up to 25 percent or more of its original weight through evaporation and trimming, which accounts for dry-aged beef's considerable expense. Still, for those occasions that you want beef at its best, this is the way to go.

Wet aging, as the name implies, involves aging beef in a vacuum-sealed plastic bag. You don't get the velvety texture and concentration of flavor achieved by dry aging, but you do get more flavor than you do in unaged beef.

What are some of the other factors that determine the quality and taste of a steak?

Well, first of all, there's the breed of cattle. Waygu (the breed used to make Kobe beef) heads the herd, as it were. Black Angus yields a rich, beefy tasting beef. It's also fast growing and fast fattening, which makes it one of the most popular and recognizable breeds—and brands—in the United States.

The steer's diet is also a factor. Grass is the natural diet for cattle, but most producers in the United States fatten their steers on corn. Grain-fed beef produces rich-tasting meat with a luscious, fatty (in a good sense) mouthfeel. In South America, grass is the feed of choice, producing beef with an interesting flavor but a somewhat less opulent mouthfeel. A growing number of boutique cattle growers in the United States are producing grass-fed beef. It's definitely worth trying.

Then there's the question of organic versus nonorganic, hormone-fed beef, and so on. When I grill at home, given the choice, I buy organic—even if the meat is tougher, I like the fact that it's chemical free.

Finally, there's the cut. Filet mignon is the leanest and most tender steak, but for me, it's the least interesting, possessing a flavor that might charitably be called "mild" and more accurately "bland." A rib steak or rib eye has the best marbling of all the so-called noble steaks, which gives it the most luxurious mouthfeel. My personal favorite is the New York strip, which is a little less tender than a rib eye but has a gutsy, robust flavor.

Ultimately, the best steak is a choice you'll have to make after trying different breeds fed different diets, different cuts, and prime versus choice. (You'll find a guide to some of the various cuts of steak on page 145.)

I've heard meat on the bone is better than boneless. Is this true for steaks and what is your favorite cut?

I agree and that's why, whenever possible, I order a bone-in New York strip, T-bone or porterhouse (the T-bone and porterhouse differ in the size of the attached filet mignon—larger in a porterhouse than in a T-bone), or rib steak. Some restaurants even serve a bone-in filet mignon. Bone-in steaks are more flavorful. And, besides, it's fun to gnaw the bone.

What is Kobe beef and is it worth the price?

Kobe, pronounced KO-bay and named for a city in southwest Japan, is one of many superpremium breeds available in Japan. The meat itself is supernaturally red and superabundantly well-marbled (a slice of raw Kobe beef looks like a lace doily laid upon a red tablecloth). It literally melts in your mouth. Part of what makes Kobe beef so special is the breed of steer (the waygu), its diet (which includes beer in the summer months), and the extraordinary care taken of each animal while it's raised. (Contrary to popular belief, Kobe steers are not massaged, but they are cared for almost like house pets.) Such care does not come cheaply, and in Japan, it's not uncommon to pay upward of $100 for a six-ounce Kobe steak.

So why don't you find me rushing to order Kobe beef in the U.S.? In the 1970s, waygu steers were brought to the States for breeding. Today, American raised "Kobe" beef or Kobe-style beef turns up on restaurant menus across the country. Some of it is excellent, with a buttery mouthfeel reminiscent of the Japanese product. (Reminiscent of, not identical to—even the best American Kobe beef pales in comparison to the Kobe served in Japan.) But much of it is quite ordinary and not worth the astronomical price. Unfortunately, at this writing, there is no rating system for American Kobe beef. Some specialty butchers carry Kobe beef if you're interested in trying it; one reliable source is Niman Ranch (www.nimanranch.com).

Should you season a steak before or after grilling? Let it warm to room temperature or grill it cold out of the refrigerator?

I recommend seasoning a steak right before it goes on the grill. I use coarse salt—kosher or sea—and freshly ground black pepper. I don't season the meat hours ahead because the salt would draw out some of the juices (this is not a problem when you season a few minutes ahead). I prefer to season before rather than after grilling because I find that grilling steak with the salt and pepper helps give it a crisp, savory crust.

As for letting the steaks warm to room temperature before grilling, I don't. It's dangerous to leave meat out at room temperature and you'll never observe this practice in a serious steak house. When you're grilling a steak over a 650° to 800°F fire, a steak cold out of the refrigerator cooks in virtually the same time as a steak at room temperature.

When I grill thick steaks the outside always gets charred before the inside is cooked. Any advice?

Many of the world's great steaks, from a Tuscan *bistecca alla fiorentina* to a Texas-style T-bone come two to three inches thick. There's an easy way to grill them. Build a three-zone fire with one hot zone, one medium zone, and one coal-free zone. After you've brushed and oiled the grate, arrange the steaks over the hot zone (running on a diagonal to the bars of the grate). Grill the steaks for two minutes to sear them. Then move the steaks to the medium zone, giving each a quarter turn if desired to create an attractive crosshatch of grill marks. Grill the steaks over medium heat for another four to six minutes, or as needed for the bottom to be crusty and brown.

Turn the steaks (always use tongs; never pierce the meat with a fork), returning them to the hot zone for two minutes to sear the other side. Then, move the steaks back to the medium zone, giving each a quarter turn. Finish grilling the steaks until they are cooked to taste; with a thick steak, you can use an instant-read meat thermometer to help you test for doneness. Insert it into the side of the steak (medium-rare is 140° to 145°F). If, while grilling, there are any flare-ups, move the steak to the coal-free zone.

The beauty of this method is that the high heat sears the steak and the medium heat cooks it through without burning the exterior.

My father likes his steak well-done. Is there anything I can do to keep the meat from drying out and toughening up?

Do as they do in Tuscany: Baste it with extra-virgin olive oil. Or as they do in New Orleans: Rub the top with a pat of butter when it comes off the grill.

How do you make a flank steak or skirt steak tender?

Well, marinating can help, but the main way is by slicing the cooked steak very thinly on a diagonal across the grain. (Shorter meat fibers mean less to chew and more tenderness.)

What is a flat iron steak? A hanger steak?

A flat iron steak is one of the so-called new steak cuts, in this case, a long, thin, flat, flavorful, tender steak, (with a slightly spongy consistency, cut from what is normally one of the toughest parts of a steer: the chuck (the shoulder).

Safety First

My boyfriend leaves the steaks, barbecue sauce, and mayonnaise out at room temperature for hours. He cuts meat, fish, and vegetables on the same cutting board. I say he's a health disaster waiting to happen. Am I right?

Yes. Your boyfriend violates two cardinal rules of grill safety. The first is to keep perishable foods refrigerated until just prior to grilling. If he likes to have the ingredients by the grill, tell him to keep them in an ice chest (filled with ice).

The second rule is to avoid cross-contamination. More than 75 percent (!) of the chickens sold in the United States are contaminated with salmonella. Outbreaks of E. coli contamination in ground beef are distressingly common. To work with these ingredients on a cutting board, then to cut vegetables or fish on the same board without washing it with soap (or better still, a sterilizing agent) is to court a massive outbreak of illness. Not fun at a barbecue.

A hanger steak is a long, full-flavored, fibrous steak cut from the belly of the steer. It's similar in taste to, but more tender than, skirt steak.

I've seen cuts of brisket that weigh as little as two pounds and others that weigh as much as eighteen pounds. What should I use?

This depends on many factors: What's readily available in your area; how many people you're planning to serve; what sort of grill or smoker you have; and so on. It also helps to know a little about brisket anatomy. The brisket is a large rectangular muscle from the chest of the steer. A whole brisket (also called a packer brisket) weighs about eighteen pounds and comprises three parts: the flat (a lean, flat, cigar box-shaped muscle located at the bottom of the brisket); the point (the lean triangular end of the flat); and the deckle (a fibrous fatty muscle that sits on the top of the flat and has a grain that runs at a 45 degree angle to the grain of the flat). Above and below the deckle are thick layers of hard, snowy white fat.

The flat is considered the choicest part of the brisket—it's the leanest and easiest to slice. A whole flat weighs around eight pounds; most supermarkets sell center cut sections of the flat, which commonly weigh two to five pounds. The good news about brisket flats is that they're all meat; the bad news is that, because they're so lean, they are the most prone to dry out.

My personal preference is to start with a whole packer brisket, which is about 40 percent fat. The fat melts during the cooking process, basting the leaner part of the meat, keeping it moist. However, you probably need to order a packer brisket ahead of time from your meat market; you need a fairly large smoker to cook it; and you need pretty much the whole day to cook it. For this reason, the recipe you'll find on page 135 of this book calls for a five- to six-pound piece of brisket flat.

BRISKET

I'm about to smoke a brisket and am wondering how much time it's going to take me.

Brisket is simultaneously the easiest and hardest meat in the world to cook. The easiest because all it requires is meat (and a less expensive cut of meat at that), spice (it can be as little as salt and pepper), and wood smoke. The hardest because unless you combine these ingredients in exactly the right proportions and, most important, take your time, you'll wind up with a mouthful of shoe leather.

So here's the secret in two words: *low* and *slow*. How low? Between 225° and 275°F (I try to keep the temperature around 250°F). How slow? A small piece of center cut brisket weighing three to four pounds needs to cook four to five hours. A full-size packer brisket (a whole untrimmed brisket with deckle and point (see above) takes ten to twelve hours. You want to cook the brisket to an internal temperature of 190° to 195°F, but you must do so slowly. To rush the process is to guarantee a mouthful of meat that will be unpalatably tough or dry—or both.

I just smoked my first brisket and was very disappointed in the results. It was tough and dry. Did I just get a bad piece of meat?

Probably not. Brisket, by its very nature, is a "bad" piece of meat. That is to say it's tough, ornery, and was once considered a "trash" cut. Chances are you started with a relatively lean section of the flat, and you may have cooked it at too high a temperature too quickly. I've developed four strategies for turning out moist brisket flats. Any or all of the following will help you.

1. Buy the fattiest piece you can find—ideally with a quarter inch layer of fat on top. If the brisket is fatty and you want to trim it somewhat, make sure you leave a quarter inch thick layer of fat.

2. Cook the brisket flat, fat side up (meat side down), in an aluminum foil pan. The pan shields the lean part of the meat from the heat and gathers the melting fat, which keeps the meat moist.

3. If your piece of flat looks really lean, drape strips of bacon over it. The melting bacon fat will keep it moist.

4. Wrap the brisket in aluminum foil (shiny side out) halfway through the cooking process (after two and a half hours for a five-hour brisket; after five hours for a ten-hour brisket; and so on). The foil seals in the steam, which breaks down the tough meat fibers. The process resembles braising. Wrap the brisket during the second half of the cooking process so it has plenty of time to absorb the smoke flavor at the beginning.

I am planning on making brisket for a party. Can I smoke it a couple days in advance and bring it back to room temperature on the day of the party?

Many people do this, and theoretically, a fatty, slow-cooked cut of meat like brisket is the perfect candidate for precooking and reheating. If I were to do so, I would let it cool to room temperature wrapped in aluminum foil, refrigerate it, and then warm it, wrapped, very slowly at a low temperature (no higher than 275°F). However, at my house, we always cook and eat our briskets the same day.

OTHER CUTS OF BEEF

Can you cook prime rib on the grill? At what temperature? For how long?

Prime rib is absolutely amazing when you make it on the grill—especially if you have a charcoal grill and you can smoke roast it. The basic procedure is to indirect grill it at a moderate heat (about 350°F). Stud the roast with garlic and thickly crust it with herbs. The cooking time will vary with the size of the roast. As a rough guide, figure twelve to fifteen minutes per pound. You'll find a great recipe for prime rib on page 137.

How do you cook beef ribs?

It depends on the rib. Beef long ribs taste great indirect grilled at a moderate temperature, like baby back ribs (be sure to toss soaked wood chips on the coals). Beef short ribs are better smoked low and slow in a smoker. Incidentally, the Koreans have a fabulous and singular way of cooking beef short ribs: They cut the meat into paper-thin slices, which they grill directly over charcoal—see the *kalbi kui* recipe on page 167.

What is a clod?

It's the best-kept barbecue secret in Texas—a whole beef shoulder (it's sometimes called a shoulder clod)—eighteen pounds of pure proteinacious pleasure. Cook it like a brisket.

Pork

I've been hearing a lot about *kurobuta* pork lately. What is it and is it worth the price?

What Kobe is to beef (or to use another metaphor, what Hermès is to handbags) *kurobuta* is to pork—a special breed of hog that's simply the richest-tasting on earth. *Kurobuta* (literally black pig) is the Japanese name for a Berkshire hog—a crossbreed of wild and domestic hogs developed in the English shire of Berk three-hundred years ago during the reign of Oliver Cromwell (whose troops were reported to be the first to discern its virtues). The English gave breeding stock to the United States and Japan in 1875: The rest, as they say, is history.

So what makes Berkshire pork special? *Kurobuta* are slower to mature than the average commercial pig, which gives them more time to fatten up and develop flavor. The muscle fibers are short and fine and the meat tastes like—well—it tastes like pork from a small farm in Europe. Look for *kurobuta* in fine butcher shops or via the Web; one good Internet source is Snake River Farms in Boise, Idaho (www.snakeriverfarms.com). Yes, it costs more than regular supermarket pork, but unlike Kobe beef, you won't need to take out a second mortgage to buy it. In other words, it's an affordable luxury.

What's the difference between a whole pork shoulder, a picnic shoulder, and a Boston butt?

A whole pork shoulder, cut from the front end of the hog, is a large rectangular hunk of meat, generously marbled and weighing twelve to fifteen pounds. It comprises two pieces: the picnic shoulder (sometimes called a picnic ham or shank end of the shoulder) and the Boston butt. The picnic shoulder is the foreleg end of the shoulder and it often contains the top of one of the forelegs. This gives it an interesting shape and flavor; some pit masters swear by it.

The Boston butt is the back part of the shoulder—it's more blocklike in shape and has a higher ratio of meat to skin or bone. It is the preferred cut for most enthusiasts of North Carolina–style pulled pork.

Should you pull or chop a pork shoulder? And which sauce—vinegar or mustard?

Whoa, you're getting into some serious polemics here. North Carolinians could come to fisticuffs debating the best way to serve their beloved pulled pork.

TO PULL OR TO CHOP? First thing you need to know if you're *not* familiar with Carolina-style pit-roasted pork shoulder is that it is always served pulled or chopped. Pulled refers to meat that's been torn into fine shreds by

HOW TO MAKE PROFESSIONAL GRILL MARKS

How do I get those "killer grill marks" you're always talking about?

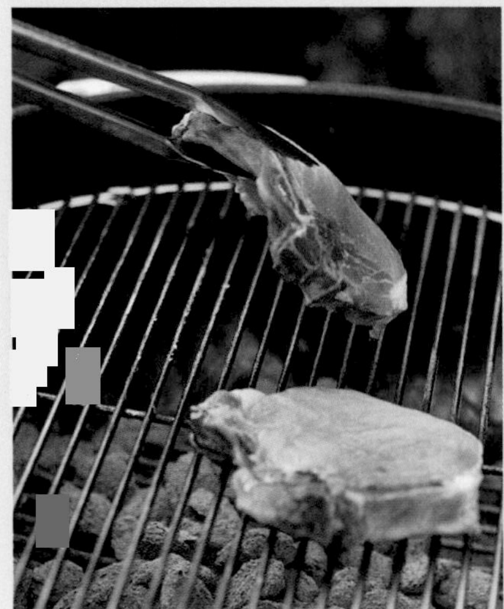

1. ***Start with a hot, clean grate. Arrange the food to be grilled on the grate so it is diagonal to the bars. Steaks and chops should all face in the same direction.***

2. ***After a few minutes, use tongs to give each piece a quarter turn; this creates a handsome crosshatch of grill marks.***

3. ***Once cooked on one side, turn the food and repeat on the other side.***

hand, while chopped indicates meat that has been reduced to a hashlike consistency with a cleaver. Pulled is how you get pork at barbecue competitions and at Carolina pig pickings, where a whole hog is pulled into meaty shreds to be doused with thin spicy vinegar sauce. Chopped is how the pork is generally served at restaurants. Pulling has the advantage of having been graced with a human touch, while chopped pork often contains "brownies"—crisp bits of chopped crust and skin. A few establishments, particularly in South Carolina, serve their pork shoulder thinly sliced.

VINEGAR OR MUSTARD SAUCE? The traditional sauce of North Carolina is vinegar sauce, a watery condiment made from distilled vinegar, salt, pepper, hot pepper flakes, and perhaps a little brown sugar to cut the edge. That's how they make it in the eastern part of the state. In the western part, they often add a little ketchup. The result is a tart, pugnacious sauce that has absolutely nothing in common with the sweet, thick, tomato-based barbecue sauce slathered on ribs in Kansas City (and in most of America). The fact is, you wouldn't really want to eat a vinegar sauce by itself. But mix it into pulled or chopped pork and it homogenizes with and counterbalances the fat, giving you one of the most perfect pork and sauce combinations in the world.

The preferred sauce in South Carolina is mustard sauce, made by combining mustard (usually ballpark style) with vinegar and sugar or honey. It, too, is wonderful and I'd have to taste several hundred more servings of both types of sauces in a comparative tasting to be able to pronounce one or the other my favorite.

What's better: spareribs or baby backs?

It's a matter of taste. Spareribs are bigger and tougher, but they're loaded with meaty flavor. Baby backs are more tender and better marbled, and they're also a lot quicker and easier to cook. Most people prefer baby backs. My suggestion is, if you're new to this game, start with baby backs. You can always graduate up to spares.

What are rib tips?

Rib tips are the cartilaginous ends of spareribs; they are often cut off and packaged with the spares. At least one pit master, Lindsay Shannon of BB's Lawnside BarB-Q in Kansas City, has made them a house specialty. Smoke rib tips low and slow, as you would spareribs.

What's the easiest way to remove the "skin" on the back of a rack of ribs?

The "skin" is a papery membrane (technically known as the pleura) found on the inside or concave side of a rack of ribs. The easiest way to remove it is to loosen it from a couple of the ribs by inserting a slender metal object, like the tip of an instant-read meat thermometer or a clean Phillips head screwdriver, under the membrane, then prying it away from the bones. Once you have the membrane loosened, grab it with a dry paper towel or dishrag (the membrane is slippery) and pull it away from the rack. The skin comes off of baby back ribs very easily; you need to work a little harder to remove it from spareribs and beef ribs.

Why bother? First, because the skin is a little tougher than the rest of the meat. And second, because if you leave the skin on, it impedes the absorption of spice and smoke flavors.

Following your recipe, I made ribs that had a dry rub applied first, then a mop sauce, then barbecue sauce. Did I wash off the rub with the mop sauce? Should I spray the mop sauce on next time?

The mop sauce (see page 48) goes on after the first forty-five minutes or so of cooking, which gives the meat ample time to absorb the rub first. The mop sauce combines with any rub that has not been absorbed to create a spicy paste that cooks into the meat, producing a savory crust. However, mop sauces should be applied with a light touch—not slopped on by the bucketful. You can certainly switch to a spray bottle. Incidentally, many pit masters spray ribs or pork shoulders with pineapple juice or apple cider.

No matter how closely I watch my ribs they always seem to burn after I put the barbecue sauce on. What am I doing wrong?

Most barbecue sauces contain a lot of sugar, and if you apply them too early, that sugar will burn before the meat is actually cooked. I almost always cook my ribs without sauce, serving the sauce on the side. If you do want to glaze the ribs with sauce, do so during the last three to five minutes of cooking.

Why won't my ribs come out fall-off-the-bone tender?

Because you have the wrong set of expectations. A properly cooked rib should be tender, of course, but it should also have a little chew to it—that's why God gave you teeth. You should be able to gnaw the meat off the bone. Fall-off-the-bone-tender ribs have been boiled or braised in the oven, and in my barbecue religion, that's heresy.

Should I boil, bake, or microwave ribs before grilling?

Absolutely not. You can achieve the requisite tenderness by smoke roasting the ribs on a grill or in a smoker.

I made ribs for the first time, and they turned out great. But I noticed there was a pinkish ring in the meat. Did I do something wrong?

On the contrary: You should pop open a bottle of Champagne (or microbrew) and celebrate. The pinkish ring is the smoke ring—a natural chemical reaction that takes place when meats are cooked low and slow in the presence of abundant wood smoke. Pit masters call it a "red badge of honor" (with apologies to Stephen Crane) and it lets you know you've smoked the ribs (or brisket or pork shoulder) to perfection.

My buddies and I want to grill a whole hog. What's the best way to proceed?

Entire books could be written on this subject. Perhaps they should. There are three basic methods: grilling, spit roasting, and smoking. Complete instructions are beyond the scope of this book, but here's a quick overview of each method.

GRILLING: If you have a small hog (up to fifty pounds) and a large grill (like a Weber Ranch), you can cook the hog using the indirect method. Most pit masters like to split the hog down the middle of the underside through the backbone (but not through the back skin) and open it up like a book. Start grilling the hog skin side up, then skin side down (you'll find instructions starting on page 154 in my book *How to Grill*). Figure on four to five hours for a fifty-pound hog.

For a larger hog, many people will dig a deep hole in the ground or make a raised pit with cinder blocks. They use metal rebar and chicken wire to make a grate that's big enough to fit over the pit and cook the pig as described above.

SPIT ROASTING: This is the method favored by Greeks and Greek-Americans and you also find it in the backyard of many a Southern bubba. The easiest way to do it is to rent a six-foot table grill with a rotisserie from a party supply house. Light the charcoal in a couple of chimney starters and make two mounds of coals—one where the shoulders will rotate and one where the hams will rotate. Spread out coals in a thinner layer in the center. Season the hog and sew it shut with a trussing needle and butcher's string. Place the pig on the spit, then on the rotisserie. Spit roast the hog until crackling crisp on the outside and cooked to about 190°F in the thickest part of the ham. For a fifty-pound pig, figure on four to five hours.

Note to do-it-yourselfers: You can also dig a pit in the ground (or build one with cinder blocks aboveground) and rig up a hand-cranked rotisserie over it. So, what turns the spit if you don't have a motor? Your friends plied with plenty of beer.

SMOKING: This is the method used by the pit masters on the competition circuit. Each team has its technical secrets, but all start with an industrial-size smoker. The cooking time is measured in half days—some pigs will go for twenty-four hours—and you can be sure the cooking temperature never exceeds 275°F. If you want to know more about smoking whole hogs, how to season and cook them, and where to buy large smokers, I recommend a subscription to *The National Barbecue News* (www.barbecuenews.com).

Game and "Exotic" Meats

My husband loves to hunt. Are there any special techniques for grilling venison?

Game is much leaner than commercial beef or pork, so however you cook it, you need to compensate for its inherent dryness. That generally means adding some sort of fat. For example, when grilling venison steaks or medallions, I always marinate them first in a mixture that contains at least 30 percent olive oil or vegetable oil. I also almost always wrap venison loins or steaks in bacon or pancetta, or if making shish kebabs, I place bacon pieces between the chunks of meat. When smoke roasting a leg or shoulder of venison, wrap it in aluminum foil after the first couple hours of cooking; this seals in the moistness. And why not add a couple of tablespoons of butter before wrapping up the meat?

I'm going to be grilling buffalo steaks (boneless rib eyes) for a family dinner. Do you have any suggestions for keeping them juicy?

Here, too, buffalo is leaner and drier than commercial beef. You can use a marinade (make sure it contains plenty of oil). If you do grill the steaks "dry," be sure to drizzle some olive oil or melted butter or beef fat over them just prior to serving. Or, when they come off the grill, you can top the steaks with a pat or two of a savory compound butter (see page 505).

I was wondering if you had any ideas for grilling "exotic" meats, like ostrich fillets and wild boar.

Once again, marinating is the way to go. A red wine–gin-olive oil marinade works great for the meats you're asking about.

Burgers and Sausages

I always have trouble with flare-ups when I'm cooking burgers. Any advice?

1. Build a three-zone fire (see page 18) with a hot zone for searing, a medium zone for cooking, and a cool safety zone where you can move the burgers to dodge any flare-ups.

2. Don't overcrowd the grill. Leave yourself plenty of room to maneuver so you can move the burgers away from the flames.

3. Never press a burger on the grill with the flat part of a spatula. This forces out the fat and juices, which can cause flare-ups and dry out your burgers.

My hamburgers always seem a little dry. How can I keep them juicy and moist?

Several possible solutions here.

- Don't use ground beef that's too lean. I like about 15 percent fat.
- If the meat is lean, when you form the patty, place a quarter-inch-thick slice of butter in the center. This is essential when cooking a burger medium or medium-well done, which, sadly, is what you should do to eliminate any risk of E. coli, if you're using supermarket ground beef.
- If you can, buy your ground beef from a trusted specialty butcher that grinds it fresh daily on the premises. That way, you can serve your burger rare or medium-rare in the center, which is another way to ensure moistness.
- Again, don't press the burger with the flat part of a spatula when grilling. This forces out the juices.

What do you put in your burgers? A lot of recipes seem to add everything but the kitchen sink.

I sprinkle the burgers with coarse salt and freshly ground black pepper just prior to grilling. That's it. I like the primal taste of the beef. The fireworks come from the garnishes: lettuce, tomato, onions, condiments—you name it.

I need help with bratwurst. Should you prick it first? Use the direct grilling or indirect grilling method?

The easiest way (and for me the best way) to grill a bratwurst or other fatty sausage is by using the indirect method. This gives you a crisp casing with unbelievably moist meat inside. Best of all, you never get flare-ups. And if you happen to be using a charcoal grill, you can toss handfuls of soaked wood chips on the coals. Once you've tasted smoke-roasted brats, you'll never want any other kind. And no, when using the indirect grilling method, you don't need to prick the brat.

Chicken

What's the big deal about free-range and organic chicken?

In a nutshell: purity and taste. Organic chickens are fed natural, organic feeds and are hormone and chemical free. Free-range chickens (and most of these are also organic) spend at least part of their lives outdoors, where they can run around—unlike commercial birds, which spend their whole lives crammed into tiny cages. This gives free-range and organic chicken a better flavor and texture, and it's better for you to eat.

What's the safe temperature to cook poultry to?

I always aim for 170°F (use an instant-read meat thermometer inserted into the deepest part of the thigh or breast, but not touching the bone, to check for doneness). This may be erring on the high side (many people cook their birds to medium—160°F). But I prefer to play it safe.

When I grill chicken breasts, they always come out dry.

That's the problem with skinless, boneless chicken breasts. They're almost pure protein, so there's nothing to keep them moist. There are at least seven solutions to your problem—feel free to use two or more at one time.

1. Once these chicken breasts have grilled for a few minutes, they are moved a quarter turn to get some expert grill marks.

2. Great grill marks turn chicken breasts from bland to boast-worthy.

1. Marinate the chicken breasts in a marinade that contains at least 25 percent olive oil or vegetable oil.

2. Marinate the chicken breasts in brine (a salt-sugar solution) before grilling. By the miracle of osmosis, brining actually adds moisture to the chicken. To make a basic brine, combine 1 tablespoon salt and 1 tablespoon sugar, for every 1 cup water in a bowl; whisk to mix.

3. Grill the chicken breasts under a brick, stone, or grill weight (wrap it in aluminum foil first). The weight compacts the meat and keeps it from drying out.

4. Wrap and grill the chicken breasts in a fatty food, such as bacon or prosciutto.

5. Baste the chicken breasts with melted butter or olive oil as they cook. Start applying the baste to the cooked side once you've turned the breast. Never brush a baste on raw chicken lest you contaminate the oil.

6. Like any grilled meat, chicken breasts should be allowed to rest for a couple minutes once off the grill before serving. This allows the meat to "relax," which makes the chicken more juicy.

7. Try grilling bone-in, skin-on breasts, which contain fat that will help keep the chicken moist during grilling. Better still, try grilling dark meat. It contains more fat than white, and dark meat is what the vast majority of grill masters around the world use when they want to grill chicken that's moist and flavorful.

I've noticed you marinate poultry for as little as one hour, while red meat might be marinated overnight. Why is this?

Chicken breasts are smaller and more delicate than large hunks of red meat, so they marinate more quickly. Also, when many people grill chicken breasts (as opposed to whole chickens or chicken pieces with the skin on), they're in a hurry, so I've tried to keep the marinating times brief.

A Rough Guide to Marinating Times

FOOD	MARINATING TIME
Very large pieces of meat, such as whole brisket and prime rib, pork shoulder, leg of lamb; turkeys, and capons	24 hours
Large pieces of meat, such as beef and pork tenderloins, pork loin, butterflied leg of lamb and rack of lamb; whole chickens; large whole fish	10 to 16 hours
Medium-size pieces of meat, such as porterhouse steaks, double cut pork chops; chicken halves or quarters; small whole fish	6 to 8 hours
Medium-small pieces of meat, such as steaks, pork and lamb chops; bone-in and large chicken breasts or legs; fish steaks; tofu; portobello mushrooms and other vegetables	2 to 4 hours
Small pieces of meat, such as satés; shrimp; chicken paillards (pounded chicken breasts) and the like	30 minutes to 1½ hours

When I was a girl, my uncle made the most fantastic barbecued chicken. I just can't seem to get it right. The skin burns (or catches fire!) before it's cooked through. Help!

Simple. Cook the bird using the indirect grilling method. Indirect grilling gives you moist meat and crisp skin and there's never any risk of flare-ups or setting the bird on fire. I don't know if your uncle's chicken recipe included barbecue sauce, but if it did, brush the sauce on during the last couple of minutes of grilling. The, move the sauced pieces directly over the fire so you can sizzle the sauce into the meat before serving.

My buddy made beer-can chicken on his gas grill for a neighborhood barbecue recently, but when I try, the lid on my charcoal grill won't close over the chicken. Any suggestions?

I'm not sure what sort of grill you do have, but a basic 22½-inch Weber kettle grill has a tall enough lid to accommodate a beer-can chicken cooked on a typical twelve-ounce beer can. I supposed you could try cooking the bird on a shorter eight-ounce can of beer. Or, the collar that comes with a Weber rotisserie will effectively raise the grill lid by several inches, giving you the clearance you need.

When cooking beer-can chicken, is there any danger that the paint will contaminate the chicken? How about the aluminum?

No. The paint (actually edible food dyes) is applied to the can at between 500° and 600°F. The can stays around 212°F when you cook a beer-can chicken on it—a much lower temperature than would be needed to melt the paint. Ditto with the aluminum. (And incidentally, aluminum occurs naturally in small quantities in most of the foods we eat.) We did a lot of laboratory testing to make sure the aluminum and paint stay on the can, not in the bird. The recipe for beer-can chicken on page 257 is perfectly safe.

How do you get a beer-can chicken off the can without burning yourself?

Excellent question. To take beer-can chicken off the grill, I use two sets of tongs. I grab the exposed part of the can and the bottom of the bird with one set and steady the top of the bird with the other. I transfer the bird to a platter and show it off, then take it into the kitchen (or away from the table). At that point, holding the can with one set of tongs, I lift the bird off of it with the other set, then carve the chicken into two leg pieces, two thigh pieces, two wing-breast pieces, and two breast pieces, and bring it back to the table.

I tried cooking beer-can chicken in my smoker. The skin was rubbery. How do I make it crisp?

You can't. That's why I prefer to make beer-can chicken in a charcoal grill rather than a smoker. You need a higher heat (350°F) to crisp the skin.

Can I make beer-can chicken in the oven?

You can, but you won't get a smoke flavor. Crackling-crisp skin and moist meat, yes. But no smoke flavor.

What do you do with the beer in the can?

Throw it out.

Can you really cook a Thanksgiving turkey on the grill?

Not only can you, you should. There's nothing like smoke roasting to maximize a turkey's flavor, while keeping the meat moist, especially when you flavor the bird with a marinade or brine beforehand. Note that I say smoke roasting (indirect grilling with wood smoke at a moderate temperature) rather than smoking. A smoker produces a succulent bird, but the skin will always be rubbery—and as everyone knows, the skin is the best part of the turkey. The Raichlens always cook their turkeys on the grill.

Seafood

My husband is an avid fisherman and we love to grill his catch. But the fillets usually stick to the grill or break when we turn them. Do you have any tips?

Do I ever! Basically, there are ten techniques you can use to prevent fish from sticking to the grill grate. I often use several at one time.

1. Pick the right kind of fish. Firm steak fish, such as swordfish and tuna, are the least likely to stick to the grate (they grill like beef). Soft fish fillets, like flounder or bluefish, are the most prone to sticking. Grill them on a fish grate or in a fish basket (see #7 and #8).

2. Follow the grill master's mantra: Keep it hot, clean, and lubricated. That is, start with a hot grill grate. Scrub it with a stiff-bristled wire brush. And oil it with a tightly folded paper towel dipped in oil and drawn across the bars of the grill grate. Brushing and oiling the grate is the best way I know to prevent sticking.

3. Oil and slide. Lightly brush the fish with oil just prior to placing it on the grate. And when you place it on the grate, gently slide it forward to brand it with grill marks.

4. Use a fish spatula. A wide-headed spatula slid under the fish can go a long way in helping you turn a fillet without breaking it.

5. Indirect grill the fish. This is especially useful with large whole fish, like the Bahamian grilled fish on page 304. Because with indirect grilling the top and bottom of the fish cook simultaneously, there's no need to turn the fish. Turning causes most fish that's stuck to the grill grate to break.

6. Grill fish without a grill grate. Grill masters in the Caribbean and Mexico eliminate the problem of fish sticking to the grill grate by grilling whole fish on a stick or skewer over the fire.

7. Grill on a fish grate. A fish grate is a wire grid or perforated sheet of metal, often nonstick. You oil it and preheat it on the regular grill grate, then place the fish on top. Fish is less likely to stick to a fish grate than to the wide-spaced bars of the grill grate.

8. Grill in a fish basket. Fish baskets come in a variety of shapes and sizes, but all are hinged so you can place a whole fish or fish fillets inside. The beauty of a fish basket is that you turn the basket to grill the fish on both sides. This works especially well for a delicate piece of fish. Remember to oil the fish basket with cooking spray oil or an oil-moistened paper towel before you add the fish.

9. Grill fish on a plank. Originating in the Pacific-Northwest, cedar-planked salmon (and other fish) is one of the most ingenious and tasty ways to grill fish. You'll need a cedar, alder, or other hardwood plank, available at grill shops and lumber yards—if you are buying a plank from a lumber yard, make sure you're buying natural, untreated wood.

Soak the plank in water to cover for one hour (this helps keep the plank from catching fire). Add your favorite seasonings to the fish and place it on top of the plank. Set up the grill for indirect grilling and preheat it to medium-high. Place the plank with the fish on top of it in the center of the grill away from the heat. The heat of the grill will not only cook the fish, but cause the plank to steam, releasing an incredible aromatic wood flavor. Best of all, because you're indirect grilling, there's no need to turn the fish.

10. Wrap and grill the fish in leaves. In the Yucatán, snapper is grilled in banana leaves (see *tikin xik* on page 334). There's a triple advantage to this process: The fish doesn't stick. It doesn't break. And the banana leaf imparts an intriguing flavor all its own.

My wife and I love planked salmon. Can you reuse the planks?

Yes, if they're not too burnt at the edges. After using a plank, soak it in water, then scrub it clean with a stiff brush. After three or four uses, the planks will get pretty ratty, but even then you can recycle them: Break the planks into pieces and toss them on the coals to generate wood smoke.

What's the best way to grill a whole fish?

Most pit masters around the world use a fish basket.

Whenever I grill shrimp, they come out dry. What's the best way to keep them moist?

Shrimp, like skinless, boneless chicken breasts, are almost pure protein, so they tend to dry out on the grill (the same is true for scallops and lobster). There are four strategies for keeping shrimp moist.

1. Marinate the shrimp in an oil-rich marinade—for example, as in the Honey Sesame Shrimp "on the Barbie" recipe on page 36. You can also brine the shrimp in a mixture of 1 tablespoon salt, 1 tablespoon sugar, and 1 cup water. Depending on their size, brine the shrimp for 15 to 30 minutes.

2. Wrap and grill the shrimp in bacon, pancetta, or another fatty meat. Not only does this keep the shrimp moist; it adds extra flavor.

3. Baste the shrimp with oil or butter while they're grilling. Always baste the cooked side, not the raw side, so you don't contaminate the oil.

4. Grill the shrimp in the shells. The shells shield the delicate meat from the fire. They also impart an interesting flavor all their own. You can even clean the shrimp in the shells before grilling them. Using kitchen shears, make a cut down the back of the shrimp through the shell, then scrape out the vein with a bamboo skewer or the tines of a fork.

How do you grill oysters?

There are two basic ways. Grill masters in the South Carolina Lowcountry place a mess of whole oysters in the shell on a grate or on a sheet of metal over a wood fire—often covering them with wet burlap. The oysters are grilled until the shells pop open, then eaten with melted butter or cocktail sauce.

Grill masters in Tomales Bay, California, shuck the oysters first to remove the top shell. Each oyster is seasoned with garlic butter or barbecue sauce (or both), then grilled in the bottom shell on the grate until bubbling. Grill shops sell special shellfish grilling grates to help you keep the shells steady so you don't lose the juices.

Mussels and clams can be grilled the same way.

What's the best way to grill lobster?

Here, too, there is more than one way to get the job done. The simplest is to grill the whole lobster right in the shell. To start place it back side down for a few minutes, then turn it back side up; as you do so, straighten out the tail so the lobster cooks evenly.

You can also cut the lobster in half lengthwise. I like to cut the lobster on a slotted cutting board or a cutting board set on a rimmed baking sheet. Then, once the lobster is cut in half, any juices can be collected and set aside in a bowl. Season and oil the lobster and grill it cut side down to brown the meat. Turn it over and pour the reserved juices over the meat, then continue grilling the lobster shell side down until the meat is cooked through.

When grilling Maine lobsters that have been cut in half, remove the claws and start grilling them about two minutes before the tail—the claws take longer to cook.

Vegetarian Food on the Grill

I just started dating a girl who's a vegetarian. I'm a carnivorous grill fanatic. Help!

First of all, I feel your pain. When I was writing the first edition of *The Barbecue! Bible,* my wife and daughter were vegetarians. (Happily, both have since become omnivores.) Take comfort in knowing that some of the best grilling in the world can be found in India and that country probably has more vegetarians than there are people in the United States (for some great Indian vegetarian recipes, see page 380). You may even learn to crave meatless grilling sometimes.

Can you really grill tofu?

Grilled tofu with miso barbecue sauce is one of Japan's national barbecue treasures (it tastes a lot better than it sounds). Two hundred and fifty million Japanese can't be wrong.

Is there such a thing as real grilled cheese?

Cheese is grilled and smoked along much of the world's barbecue trail, from Argentina, where thick slices of *provoletta* or aged provolone cheese are sizzled on the grill, to Switzerland, where chunks of raclette are melted in front of a wood-burning fireplace. You'll find recipes on pages 384 and 385.

Grilled pizza seems to be all the rage now. Is this something I can make at home?

Nothing could be easier. You drape the pizza dough on a well-oiled grill grate and use the heat of the fire to cook it. There are a few watch points.

■ Build a three-zone fire with a hot zone for searing the dough, a medium zone where you can move the crust while you add the toppings, and a coal-free zone where you can move it in case of flare-ups. (For more about three-zone fires, see page 18.)

■ Use lots of extra-virgin olive oil to stretch the dough and to keep it from sticking to the grill grate.

■ Add the toppings in the reverse order you would for an oven-baked pizza. The cheese goes on first because it takes the longest to melt. The sauce goes on last because it's already cooked and needs only warming. You'll find a recipe for grilled pizza on page 381.

Vegetables

My family loves kebabs, but all the vegetables never seem to be done at the same time. Should I microwave or parboil the vegetables first?

Not according to my *Barbecue! Bible.* The easiest way to grill mixed vegetables is to skewer and cook them by kind: onion wedges on one skewer; bell pepper slices or whole peppers on another; tomatoes on a third; and so on. Put the vegetable that takes longest to cook on the grill first (it's usually onions), and keep adding more skewered vegetables in decreasing order of cooking time. That way they'll all be done at once. If you do this, you'll be in good company. When Turks make shish kebab, they grill each type of vegetable on a separate skewer.

How do you grill small slender vegetables, like green beans and asparagus stalks?

Do as Japanese grill masters do: Arrange three or four of each individual vegetable side by side and pin them crosswise together with toothpicks to make rafts. It's much easier to turn and grill four asparagus rafts than sixteen individual stalks. For a great recipe, see page 396.

Can you really grill lettuce? Why would you bother?

Grilling imparts a smoky flavor to crunchy lettuces, like romaine. (Grilled Caesar salad was pioneered by a restaurant called Walt's Wharf in Seal Beach, California.) And as you know if you've been to the Veneto region in Italy, grilling helps heighten the sweetness and mitigate the bite of the bitter Italian radicchio and treviso.

Oddballs

Can you really cook dessert on the grill?

You sure can, and pit masters from Indonesia (see the Balinese Grilled Bananas on page 512) to Hawaii (see the Spice-Grilled Pineapple on page 513) back me up on this. The short list of things you can grill includes fruit (especially pineapple, peaches, apples, pears, and bananas); crisps and crumbles; pound cake; and of course, that childhood favorite, s'mores (see page 515).

My wife and I have an open bet on whether or not you could cook a cake on a grill. Please take us up on this challenge.

No problem, and I'll even give you two options.

1. Set up the grill for indirect grilling and preheat it to medium (about 350°F). You can "bake" the cake batter using the indirect method (with the grill covered). Ideally, you'll be using a charcoal grill, so you can toss a handful of soaked fruitwood chips on the coals to impart a delicate smoke flavor. If you've ever tried the "baked" apples on page 511 or one of the fruit crisps in my book *BBQ USA,* you know how much a whiff of wood smoke can enhance a dessert.

2. Start with a firm, dense, already-baked cake, like a pound cake. Cut it into slices and grill it as you would Catalan Tomato Bread (see page 126) or Tuscan Grilled Garlic Bread (see page 127). The grill was the original toaster and the taste of grill-toasted cake will come as nothing less than a revelation.

SEASONINGS AND SAUCES

What's the difference between a rub, a marinade, a brine, an injector sauce, a glaze, a basting sauce, a mop sauce, a finishing sauce, a compound butter, and a barbecue sauce, and when should I use each?

All are seasonings designed to enhance the flavor of grilled or smoked foods. What distinguishes them is their consistency (dry, wet, or somewhere in between), when they're applied, and how they react with the food. Here's a rundown.

BEFORE COOKING

A RUB is a dry seasoning, like a mixture of spices, applied to food before grilling or smoking. **A WET RUB** is a thick paste of spices and seasonings smeared on food prior to grilling or smoking.

A MARINADE is a flavorful wet seasoning in which the food is soaked before it's grilled or smoked.

A BRINE is a particular kind of marinade—a saline solution (often sweetened with sugar or honey) in which food is soaked prior to being smoked or grilled; the salt both flavors and cures the meat.

AN INJECTOR SAUCE is a flavorful liquid (like a marinade) that, prior to grilling or smoking, is injected deep into turkeys, pork shoulders, and other large roasts with a special injector that looks like a giant hypodermic needle.

DURING COOKING

A GLAZE is a thick, often sweet liquid brushed on food during grilling so that it "lacquers" and cooks into the meat.

A BASTING SAUCE, like a glaze, is also brushed on during cooking. It often contains melted butter and is designed both to add an extra layer of flavor and keep the food moist as it grills.

A MOP SAUCE is a thin, unsweetened or semisweet liquid swabbed on meats as they smoke or grill to keep them moist and add flavor. Mop sauces originated in the American South and Texas, where they were (and still are) traditionally applied with clean floor mop or barbecue mop.

AFTER COOKING

A FINISHING SAUCE is a thin sauce applied to cooked meats just after smoking to keep them shiny and moist and lock in the flavor. Finishing sauces are used almost exclusively on the competition barbecue circuit.

A COMPOUND BUTTER is a disk of flavored butter placed atop a grilled chop, steak, or piece of fish just prior to serving. The butter melts, subtly saucing the meat and keeping it moist and glossy. In general, compound butters are not sweet. (You'll find recipes for compound butters beginning on page 505.)

A BARBECUE SAUCE is a condiment served on or next to grilled or smoked meats when they're served. Many barbecue sauces, particularly American sauces—like the one on page 463—are sweet, but some, like the vinegar sauce on page 466, are not. My personal preference is to serve the barbecue sauce after the meat comes off the grill or smoker. If you apply a sweet sauce too early, the sugar will burn before the meat is completely cooked.

I also like to serve barbecue sauce on the side, not spooned directly over the meat. This allows you to appreciate the natural fire and smoke flavors before being bombarded by the sugar and spice in the sauce.

When do you use a dry rub and when do you use a wet rub?

There are no hard and fast rules. I'm tempted to say that dry rubs go on fatty foods, like ribs and briskets, while wet rubs go on lean foods, like fish and steak. But the world is full of counter examples, from Jamaican jerk (page 182) to Balinese *babi guling* (page 177).

I can tell you, however, that there are two ways to use wet and dry rubs. You can apply them right before smoking or grilling, in which case, they act like spices or seasoned salt. Or you can apply them several hours or even the day before smoking or grilling, in which case they both flavor and cure (chemically alter) the meat; in curing, the salt draws some of the water out of the meat, resulting in a more compact consistency.

What is the purpose of marinating? Is it to add flavor or tenderize the meat?

Actually, it's a bit of both. Many of the flavorings used in marinades (onion, garlic, soy sauce, beer, hot sauce, sesame or olive oil, and so on) add flavor to meats, and the oils help keep them moist.

Acids help break down meat fibers, tenderizing tough cuts of meat. Acidic marinade flavorings range from the lemon juice, vinegar, and wines used in the Mediterranean to the tamarind, yogurt, and buttermilk used in the Near East.

How long do you marinate a particular food?

This depends on three factors: the strength of the marinade and the size and tenderness of the meat. A strong vinegar- and chile-based marinade works more quickly, for example, than a delicate marinade of olive oil and herbs. Shrimp marinates much more quickly than a whole chicken or pork shoulder. And the tenderizing effects of a marinade work much faster on a tender cut, like filet mignon, than on a tough cut, like brisket.

Always keep marinating meats refrigerated.

What do you think of vacuum marinators, like the FoodSaver?

Some years ago, a clever grill master discovered that if you marinade meat in a vacuum (such as in a heavy plastic bag from which the air has been mechanically extracted), the marinade penetrates the meat more quickly. Enter the FoodSaver. Its manufacturer and many users claim you can achieve the same result of an overnight or even twenty-four hour marinade in thirty minutes.

Being an old-fashioned sort of guy, I don't often use them, but many grill masters swear by vacuum marinators and get great results using them. (Find out more at www.foodsaver.com.)

What about a kitchen injector?

A kitchen injector (sometimes called a Cajun injector) looks like an oversize hypodermic needle. You use it for injecting marinades deep into large cuts of meat, like turkeys and fresh hams. Note: If you are using spices in your marinade, be sure to strain it through a fine mesh sieve or several layers of cheesecloth so the spices don't clog the needle.

Is it OK to use a marinade for basting or sauce?

Not in its raw form; you run the risk of cross-contaminating the food. But yes, provided you either cook the used marinade at a rolling boil for at least three minutes or set some of the marinade aside for basting or sauce before you add the meat.

Do you have any sugar-free rubs or barbecue sauces?

There are several sugar-free rubs in the rub chapter of this book and several sugar-free barbecue sauces in the sauce chapter.

Do you have a favorite barbecue sauce?

Barbecue sauces vary as much as the meat grilled and the person grilling it. In general, my favorite barbecue sauce at any given time is the sauce traditionally served in that particular region. It can be sweet, as in Kansas City, or without a grain of sugar, as in the *chimichurri* of Argentina (see page 478). Time and tradition have established what sauce goes best with a particular cut and style of meat.

I'd like to make my own barbecue sauce but am not sure where to start. Any suggestions?

Most American barbecue sauces are based on either ketchup, tomato sauce, or mustard, so I'd start with one of those three (they taste pretty good already, so all you need to do is make them taste better). Add some sort of sweetener (sugar, honey, and/or molasses, for example) and some sort of acid (vinegar, lemon juice, wine) to offset the sweetness. Add aromatics, like onion or garlic, for depth of flavor, and something fiery, like hot sauce or ginger, for bite.

Many American barbecue sauces contain liquid smoke to reinforce the smoke flavor of the meats. (Contrary to the belief of some people, liquid smoke is a natural ingredient.) Add at least one unexpected ingredient (the short list of options might include coffee, cola, pureed fruit, bourbon, or another spirit) to give your sauce personality. Remember—the two most important ingredients in any barbecue sauce are originality and balance. And also remember: It's essential to write down what you add as you make the sauce, so you can duplicate it.

NOW YOU'RE SMOKING

How do I go about entering a barbecue contest?

The world of competition barbecue is one of the most fascinating subcultures in America. There are several ways to get involved. You could start by attending a national or regional competition. The three biggies are the Memphis in May World Championship Barbecue Cooking Contest, www.memphisinmay.org; the American Royal Barbecue in Kansas City, Missouri, www.americanroyal.com/; and the Jack Daniel's World Championship Invitational in Lynchburg, Tennessee, www.lynchburgtenn.com/jack_daniels_bar-b-q.html. But you'll have a better chance of actually talking to the individual pit masters at a local or regional competition: Contact the Kansas City Barbecue Society (KCBS, www.kcbs.us) for a list of regional contests.

The next step is to volunteer for a local team; you may soon find yourself becoming a team member. From there, the addiction can lead you to spending your nights developing sauces and your weekends perfecting ribs. Soon a mammoth smoker may appear in your driveway (and perhaps a Winnebago to haul it around). Before you know it, your vacations will be organized around entering barbecue competitions across the country. Note: It's a very good idea to involve your spouse or significant other in this hobby, as it quickly becomes all consuming.

If I attend the Memphis in May or the American Royal barbecue contest as a spectator, will I be able to taste the food made by the pit masters?

No. Regulations prevent the teams from serving the public. However, if you make friends with one of the team members, you may be invited to a private party at the team's prep site. Again, that's why the smaller local and regional competitions are so perfect for neophytes. You're much more likely to be invited to taste the food.

How do you pick what dish to enter in a barbecue contest?

There are several possible strategies here. Some teams play the odds. For example, there are far more contestants in the rib category at most competitions than there are for whole hogs, so statistically, at least, you have a better shot winning in whole hog than in any other category. Of course, it takes a lot of experience and know-how to nail the perfect hog.

Other teams go for shock value. Most barbecue contests have an "Anything But" category in which you can enter any dish save one of the big three (ribs, shoulders, or whole hog). Perhaps you have a killer smoke-roasted pecan pie, or nobody barbecues alligator like you do. Chances are there won't be a lot of direct competition in these categories. Thus, you improve your chances for winning.

My own advice is to go with the dish you're the most proud of (and the one you've had the most practice making). My grandmother always used to say that cream rises to the top. It's true.

People tell me I make really great barbecue. How do I go about opening a restaurant?

First, don't. Second, don't. Third, don't. And if I haven't dissuaded you yet, book a session with a psychotherapist. Few businesses have a poorer success rate than restaurants—the majority fail within the first three years. Running a successful restaurant requires a very different set of skills than smoking a prize-winning brisket and achieving the latter gives you no guarantee you'll succeed at running a restaurant.

If you still want to open a restaurant, I suggest first getting a job at an existing barbecue restaurant (or any restaurant) to see if you like it. You might even learn some skills should you decide to persist.

I have a killer sauce I'd like to manufacture. How do I bring it to market?

This is very difficult and, having a commercial line of rubs and sauces (and having failed at a previous line of spice mixes), I know whereof I speak. There are two routes: Partner with someone who's already in the business (what I did), or find a copacker—a company that will bottle, label, and warehouse the sauce for you. You'll need to develop a marketing plan, find distributors, and promote the product. But before you do, take a look at the sauce shelf of a barbecue store or even your local supermarket; there's plenty of competition. Not that I'm against entrepreneurship—on the contrary. I just want you to know what you're up against. Then again, a friend of mine started small in just such a way with a sauce he had spent several decades perfecting. It's called KC Masterpiece and my friend sold it to Clorox.

How do I locate the best places to eat barbecue when I travel?

Another good question. The minute you know you're going to be traveling somewhere, start asking. Check the Best BBQ Joint section of the Barbecue Board on www.barbecuebible.com. Check food and travel magazines. Write or call the local restaurant critic (I used to be a restaurant critic and I almost always answered such requests). When you get to your destination, start asking everyone for recommendations—especially taxi drivers. Taxi drivers almost everywhere in the world seem to have an unerring nose for great barbecue joints.

When you finally get to the place, make sure:

1. It's crowded.

2. There's a woodpile somewhere on the premises.

3. There's a real wood-burning grill or pit and you can actually smell smoke. (If there isn't, or if I can't, I walk out.)

4. And, that the food really tastes smoked.

The Six Most Common Mistakes in Grilling and How to Avoid Them

PREMATURE IGNITION: Don't light your grill too early—especially if using charcoal. Twenty to thirty minutes before you're ready to grill will do it. There's nothing worse than going to grill only to discover your coals have burned out. A related mistake: not preheating your gas grill properly before starting to grill. Proper direct grilling requires at least a 600°F fire.

THINKING MORE MEANS BETTER (a.k.a. "THE GUY SYNDROME"): A commonly but erroneously held belief (especially among males) is that if some is good, more is better. This applies to seasonings (if 1 tablespoon of rub is good, 4 tablespoons will be great), sauces (if ¼ cup Tabasco sauce is good, 1 cup must be better); smoke (if adding 1 cup of wood chips per hour for the first 4 hours is good, you can achieve even better results by adding all 4 cups the first hour); and so on. You know what I mean. The fact is that often in grilling, less is more. Try each of the recipes in this book with the recommended amount of an ingredient before increasing it.

GRILLING UNTIL BURNT: Cooking and burning are two different but related processes. The former transforms raw meats or vegetables into delectable—and digestible—pleasures. The latter takes the process one step further, turning good food into inedible cinders. Try to cook your food, not burn it. Golden brown is good; coal black is bad (except for some briskets). A crisp crust is good; a burnt carapace isn't. Enough said.

GRILLING OVER FLAMES, NOT OVER EMBERS: As a rule, charcoal and wood fires should be burned down to glowing embers before you put the food on. This gives you an even, powerful heat for searing. Grilling in the flames tends to produce uneven cooking (burnt exterior, raw center) and a sooty residue on the food. Note: As with every rule, this one has exceptions. Germans grill their *Spiessbraten* in the flames of a beech-wood fire. And there's nothing like a flaming campfire for toasting marshmallows for s'mores (see page 515).

OVERCROWDING THE GRILL: Filling the entire grill grate with food is a recipe for disaster. The reason is simple: You deprive yourself of maneuvering room in the event of hot spots on the grill or flare-ups. I work on what I call the "70 percent rule"—I never cook on more than 70 percent of the grate. In other words, I leave 30 percent of the grate empty (I call this the "safety zone") so I have someplace to move the food if the active part of the grill gets too hot or has too many flare-ups.

PRACTICING POOR GRILL HYGIENE: Some people (again mostly guys) confuse a dirty grill with a well-seasoned grill. A well-seasoned grill results from brushing and oiling the grate each time you use it (right before the food goes on and right after it comes off). A dirty grill results from failing to brush and oil the grate (and also from forgetting to empty the drip pan). Some people believe that burnt-on bits of salmon skin, beef scraps, pork ribs, and so on add flavor to what you're grilling. They well may—just not the flavor you really want.

FROM THE TOP CLOCKWISE:
SINGAPORE SLING | PAGE 59 • MINTED LIMEADE | PAGE 62 • MADRID-STYLE SANGRIA | PAGE 60 • PISCO SOUR | PAGE 58

CHAPTER 2

THIRST QUENCHERS

"Leaded or unleaded?" asked the bartender at a grill shack in Nassau, Bahamas. Leaded or unleaded, indeed! In local parlance, leaded refers to a gin-spiked coconut punch called sky juice, while unleaded describes the same drink made without gin. How better to begin a barbecue?

"Appetite comes with eating... but thirst departs with drinking."
—FRANÇOIS RABELAIS

You sure can work up an enormous thirst when grilling. First, because you're outdoors, standing next to a powerful heat source. Second, because the food that comes off the grill demands a full-flavored libation that matches the smoky taste of the fire.

It's hard to imagine a Brazilian barbecue without an icy pitcher of *caipirinhas* (Brazilian-style daiquiris) made with cane spirits and lime. Or Turkish kebabs without glasses of raki (an anise liquor) or a Caribbean cookout without Planter's Punch.

Here you'll find some of the world's best thirst quenchers, and not all of them are leaded.

Consider the Afghan Yogurt Drink, or *doh,* a refreshing Central Asian beverage made with yogurt, mint, and club soda and enjoyed in one form or another from Baghdad to Kabul. From Senegal's *gingere ananas* (Ginger Pineapple Punch) to the *bandung* (Rose Water Cooler) of Singapore and Malaysia, you'll find plenty of unleaded treasures to soothe the most stubborn thirst.

LEADED

BRAZIL

BRAZILIAN DAIQUIRI

CAIPIRINHA

ON THE SIDE
SERVES 8

Every rum-drinking nation has a version of the daiquiri, and Brazil's is the *caipirinha* (pronounced kai-pir-EEN-ya). Made with only three ingredients—fresh limes, sugar, and cane spirits—the *caipirinha* seems simple enough and it goes down with astonishing ease. But woe betide the person who drinks several in rapid succession, for the caipirinha is made with one of the strongest spirits in the western hemisphere: cachaça.

Cachaça (pronounced ka-SHAH-sa) is a spirit made from sugar cane and it's considerably stronger than rum. Cachaça can be found at well-stocked liquor stores, especially in cities with large Brazilian communities. If it's unavailable, you can use 151 rum or regular white rum. A similar drink, called *caipiroska,* is made with vodka.

What distinguishes the *caipirinha* from the commonplace daiquiri is the conscientious crushing of the limes in the pitcher, an act that extracts the flavorful oils from the rinds. It's hard to imagine a *churrasco* (Brazilian barbecue) that would not begin with a refreshing pitcher of *caipirinhas*.

8 large, juicy limes
1 cup turbinado sugar (Sugar in the Raw; see box, at right) or granulated sugar, or more to taste
2 cups cachaça, 151 rum, or regular white rum
4 cups ice cubes

1. Roll the limes on a cutting board, pressing them with the palms of your hands to loosen the juices from the pulp. Cut each lime into 8 pieces, then place the pieces in the bottom of a sturdy pitcher. Add the sugar and pound the lime pieces with a pestle, potato masher, or wooden spoon to extract as much juice as possible.

2. Stir in the cachaça and ice, then taste for sweetness, adding more sugar as necessary for just the right balance of sweet and sour. Serve, if desired, in daiquiri glasses, but regular tumblers will do.

Turbinado Sugar

A granulated light brown sugar, turbinado sugar is available at natural food stores. In supermarkets, look for the Sugar in the Raw brand.

PUERTO RICO

THE ORIGINAL PINA COLADA

ON THE SIDE
SERVES 2; CAN BE MULTIPLIED AS DESIRED

Ramon "Monchito" Marrero Perez knows a thing or two about piña coladas. The bar in San Juan where he works serves more than three hundred of these tropical refreshers a day. Perez claims to have invented the piña colada on a steamy summer day in 1954. Actually, according to Webster's, the term *piña colada* first appeared in print in 1923. Rum and pineapple juice had been a popular Puerto Rican cocktail for decades (if not centuries). Perez's innovation lay in adding coconut cream for richness and smoothness. Here is Perez's original recipe. For an even more luscious piña colada, substitute one cup of diced fresh pineapple for the pineapple juice.

¼ cup light rum (Perez uses Bacardi)
¾ cup unsweetened pineapple juice
3 tablespoons coconut cream, such as Coco López
2 tablespoons heavy cream
1 cup crushed ice
1 stick or thin wedge fresh pineapple
1 maraschino cherry with stem

Combine the rum, pineapple juice, coconut cream, and heavy cream in a blender with the ice and process until smooth. Pour into a large glass. Garnish with the pineapple stick and cherry and serve immediately.

CARIBBEAN

PLANTER'S PUNCH

ON THE SIDE
SERVES 4

Planter's punch is found throughout the Caribbean. Back in the days of the great plantations, it was the traditional beverage of welcome. The basic recipe calls for orange juice, pineapple juice, guava nectar, and rum, but there are as many variations as there are individual bartenders. Serve it with any of the West Indian–style barbecue dishes in this book.

ADVANCE PREPARATION

2 hours to 2 days for steeping the punch

FOR THE PUNCH

1 cup dark rum
1 cup fresh orange juice
1 cup unsweetened pineapple juice
1 cup guava nectar
2 tablespoons fresh lime juice
2 tablespoons sugar, or more to taste
½ teaspoon Angostura bitters
½ vanilla bean, split
2 cinnamon sticks (each 3 inches)
2 whole cloves
Ice cubes, for serving

FOR GARNISH

4 orange slices
4 maraschino cherries with stems
Freshly grated nutmeg

1. Combine the rum, orange juice, pineapple juice, guava nectar, lime juice, sugar, and bitters in a pitcher and stir until the sugar dissolves. Add the vanilla bean, cinnamon sticks, and cloves. Let the punch steep, covered, in the refrigerator for at least 2 hours or as long as 2 days.

2. Strain the punch into tumblers filled with ice. Garnish each glass with an orange slice and a maraschino cherry. Grate some nutmeg over each serving and serve immediately.

BAHAMAS

BAHAMIAN SKY JUICE

ON THE SIDE
SERVES 4

No Bahamian barbecue would be complete without sky juice, a potent brew of coconut water (the clearish liquid inside the coconut), evaporated milk, and gin. When I say potent, I mean potent—it goes down effortlessly and will turn your knees to rubber effortlessly, too.

Sky juice is generally made with gin in the Bahamas—odd for the rum-loving Caribbean, yet logical, given the islands' British heritage. But, I can report that it's equally delightful made with rum. I like to serve sky juice right in the coconut shells—a presentation that's especially festive at a cookout. Also, I like my sky juice on the sweeter side, but many people don't, so I've made the sugar optional.

4 ripe (hard) coconuts (see box, page 114)
1 cup evaporated milk
1 cup gin or rum
3 tablespoons sugar (optional)
1 teaspoon ground cinnamon
½ teaspoon freshly grated nutmeg

1. Using a screwdriver and hammer, poke through the "eyes" of the coconuts and drain the liquid from each through a strainer into a mixing bowl. You should have about 2 cups of coconut water. Set aside the emptied coconuts. Add the evaporated milk, gin, sugar (if using), cinnamon, and nutmeg to the coconut water and stir until the sugar dissolves. Refrigerate the sky juice until cold (at least 2 hours) or stir in a few ice cubes.

2. Using a funnel or squirt bottle, pour the sky juice into the reserved coconut shells. Insert straws and serve.

NOTE: When buying coconuts, shake them to hear if the water sloshes around inside. A dry coconut is sometimes rancid and is certainly past its prime.

BRAZIL

BRAZILIAN COCONUT SHAKE

BATIDO

ON THE SIDE
SERVES 4

Pronounced ba-CHEE-do, *batido* is the name Brazilians give to a variety of alcoholic milkshakes. The liquor of choice for this recipe would be cachaça (a potent Brazilian cane spirit). If it's unavailable, you can use regular white rum instead. I serve this exotic creamy milkshake with any barbecue that features Brazilian fare, for example the Brazilian Stuffed Rib Roast (page 139) and Brazilian Pork Rollatini (page 179).

1/3 cup coconut cream, such as Coco López
1/3 cup cachaça or regular white rum
1/4 cup sweetened condensed milk
4 cups crushed ice

Combine the coconut cream, cachaça, and condensed milk in a blender with the ice and process until smooth. Pour into tall glasses and serve immediately.

CARIBBEAN

PASSION FRUIT DAIQUIRI

ON THE SIDE
SERVES 4

The daiquiri originated at the turn of the century in the nickel-mining town of Daiquiri in southeast Cuba. You don't need a degree in mixology to know that its principle ingredients, then as now, are lime juice, sugar, and rum. Today daiquiris made with a multitude of fruits are enjoyed throughout the Americas. The passion fruit daiquiri here will give you a whole new perspective on, and appreciation for, a Caribbean classic.

3/4 cup frozen or bottled passion fruit juice, or 15 passion fruits
1/3 cup light rum
6 firmly packed tablespoons light brown sugar
3 cups crushed ice

1. If using frozen or bottled passion fruit juice, proceed to Step 2. If using fresh fruits, cut them in half and scrape out the pulp. Force the pulp through a strainer; you should have about 3/4 cup.

2. Combine the passion fruit, rum, and brown sugar in a blender with the ice and process until smooth. Pour into martini glasses and serve immediately.

U.S.A.

SMOKY MARTINI

ON THE SIDE
SERVES 1; CAN BE MULTIPLIED AS DESIRED

Steak is back. So are cigars and martinis. After a decade of rabid health consciousness, Americans seem to be relaxing a bit about food and eating wisely, without forsaking a sense of enjoyment. This martini is fortified with a drop of liquid smoke, which makes it perfect for a barbecue.

PASSION FRUIT DAIQUIRI | AT LEFT

¼ cup gin
½ teaspoon dry vermouth
1 drop liquid smoke
1 cup ice cubes
Strip of lemon zest

Combine the gin, vermouth, and liquid smoke in a shaker with the ice and stir (do not shake) to mix. Strain the drink into a martini glass. Twist the lemon zest, shiny side down, over the martini, then drop it into the drink. Serve immediately.

FRENCH WEST INDIES

FRENCH WEST INDIAN RUM PUNCH

'TI PUNCH

ON THE SIDE
SERVES 1; CAN BE MULTIPLIED AS DESIRED

'Ti punch (short for petit punch) is the most elemental of the French West Indian rum drinks—sipped with equal enthusiasm at casual cook shacks and tony restaurants. To partake of 'ti punch properly, the drinker squeezes the lime in the drink, then stirs it to dissolve the sugar. Some people add an ice cube or two, but most Guadeloupeans sip it straight.

Some versions call for the suavity of cane syrup, but most of the 'ti punch I had in Guadeloupe consisted simply of rum, lime, and sugar. Use either white rum or dark, depending on your taste.

3 tablespoons rum
2 teaspoons turbinado sugar (Sugar in the Raw; see box, page 54) or granulated sugar
1 lime wedge, for garnish

Place the rum and sugar in a glass (the locals prefer small brandy glasses) and stir lightly with a spoon. Rub the lime wedge around the rim of the glass, then press it onto the rim. Serve the 'ti punch with a small spoon or stirrer and a lime wedge for squeezing into the drink.

PERU

PISCO SOUR

ON THE SIDE
SERVES 4

The pisco sour isn't what you'd call a hot seller these days, but in the boom time following the California gold rush this lively cocktail was one of America's most popular drinks. Pisco is the name of a robust brandy made in Peru and Chile from muscat grapes. Serve pisco sours with any of the *anticuchos* (Peruvian kebabs) in this book or with any other South American barbecue.

½ cup sugar
1 lemon wedge
¼ cup fresh lemon juice
¾ cup pisco brandy
½ teaspoon Angostura bitters
White from one large egg (see Note)
3 cups crushed ice
4 fresh mint sprigs, for garnish

1. Spread ¼ cup of the sugar in a shallow dish. Rub the rims of 4 martini or whisky sour glasses with the cut side of the lemon wedge and dip each glass rim in the sugar, shaking off the excess.

2. Combine the remaining ¼ cup of sugar, the lemon juice, pisco brandy, Angostura bitters, and egg white in a blender with the ice and process until frothy.

3. Pour the mixture into the prepared glasses, garnish each with a mint sprig, and serve immediately.

NOTE: If you feel nervous about consuming a raw egg white, use 1 tablespoon egg substitute instead.

SINGAPORE

SINGAPORE SLING

ON THE SIDE
SERVES 4

It was a typical day on the barbecue trail, hours spent touring cook stalls, sampling satés under the blazing equatorial sun. Actually, tougher than it sounds. So I offered my wife and myself a treat at the end of the day: cocktails at the ultraluxurious Raffles Hotel, where legend has it, in 1915 the Singapore sling was invented by a Hainanese bartender named Ngiam Tong Boon. Today the hotel serves the drink in special monogrammed glasses in the vertiginously high-ceilinged Bar & Billiard Room. You can serve it with any of the Singapore- or Malaysian-style satés in this book.

- **½ cup gin**
- **¼ cup cherry brandy**
- **2 tablespoons fresh lime juice**
- **2 tablespoons unsweetened pineapple juice**
- **2 tablespoons fresh orange juice**
- **1 tablespoon Cointreau**
- **1 tablespoon Bénédictine**
- **4 dashes Angostura bitters**
- **Ice cubes, for serving**
- **3 cups club soda, or more as needed**
- **4 maraschino cherries, for garnish**
- **4 fresh pineapple slices, for garnish**

1. Combine the gin, cherry brandy, lime, pineapple and orange juices, Cointreau, Bénédictine, and Angostura bitters in a pitcher and stir to mix.

2. Place the ice cubes in tall glasses, then divide the gin mixture equally among them. Add club soda to fill each glass and garnish with a cherry and a slice of pineapple. Stir with a long-handled spoon and serve immediately.

MEXICO

FRONTERA MARGARITA

ON THE SIDE
SERVES 8

The potent tequila and lime thirst quencher known as a margarita is synonymous with good times and Mexican grilling. But, the best margarita I ever tasted was made not by a Mexican but by a gringo, Rick Bayless, owner of two popular Chicago restaurants, Frontera Grill and Topolobampo. Rick lets his tequila steep in the lime juice and lime zest for a good part of the day before mixing the drink, which creates a margarita with an uncommon depth of flavor.

ADVANCE PREPARATION

6 to 8 hours for steeping the tequila

INGREDIENTS

- **1¾ cups tequila (Rick uses Cuervo Especial gold)**
- **¼ cup orange liqueur (Rick uses the Spanish liqueur Gran Torres)**
- **½ cup fresh lime juice**
- **1 teaspoon finely grated lime zest**
- **⅓ cup sugar**
- **¼ cup coarse sea salt**
- **8 lime wedges, for garnish**
- **3 to 4 cups ice cubes, for serving**

1. The morning before you plan to serve the margaritas, combine the tequila, orange liqueur, lime juice and zest, sugar, and 1 cup of water in a pitcher. Stir until the sugar dissolves, then let the margarita mixture steep in the refrigerator, covered, for 6 to 8 hours.

2. Spread the salt out in a shallow dish. Rub the rims of 8 martini glasses with the cut side of a lime wedge and dip the rim of each glass in the salt, shaking off the excess. Add the ice to the margarita mixture and stir (or combine in a shaker and shake), then strain the margaritas into the prepared glasses. Drop a lime wedge in each glass and serve at once.

SPAIN

MADRID-STYLE SANGRIA

ON THE SIDE
SERVES 6

Sangria is one of the most popular beverages for a barbecue, but over the years there's been a tendency to turn it into a sort of wine-drenched fruit salad. Here's a sangria that's prepared in the style of the tapas bars of Madrid—minimal fruit, not too sweet, and very potent. My wife, Barbara, happens to like a fruity sangria, and when my back is turned, she's apt to add grapes and diced bananas to this recipe. If you like a fruity sangria, do the same.

1 bottle (750 milliliters) dry red wine, preferably Spanish
1 cup gin
1 cup Cognac
1 cup sugar, or more to taste
1 whole lemon
1 whole orange
½ cup fresh lemon juice
½ cup fresh orange juice
3 cinnamon sticks (each 3 inches)
Ice cubes, for serving

1. Combine the wine, gin, Cognac, and sugar in a pitcher and stir until the sugar dissolves. Cut the peel, including the white pith, off the lemon and orange, exposing the flesh. Cut the flesh into ¼-inch dice. Discard any seeds.

2. Stir the diced fruit, lemon and orange juice, and cinnamon sticks into the wine mixture. Taste for sweetness, adding more sugar to taste. You can serve the sangria right away, but it will be better if chilled for an hour or so to "ripen."

3. Serve the sangria in wine glasses over ice.

TURKEY

RAKI

ON THE SIDE
SERVES 4

It may be stretching it a bit to call this simple drink a recipe, but raki (and its Greek counterpart ouzo) is so essential to the enjoyment of barbecue in the eastern Mediterranean and Near East, I'd feel remiss if I didn't include it. Raki is a strong, clear, anise-flavored spirit. By some mysterious chemical reaction, it turns milky white the moment you add water.

1 cup raki or ouzo
1 to 2 cups water
Ice cubes, for serving

Pour two or three fingers (¼ cup) of raki into each of 4 tall glasses. Add water and ice to taste, then stir and serve.

UNLEADED

CARIBBEAN

MANGO NECTAR

ON THE SIDE
SERVES 4

Mango and other tropical fruit punches are found throughout the Caribbean, where they make a refreshing nonalcoholic alternative to the knee-weakening rum drinks associated with the region.

- **2 cups diced ripe mango (1 large or 2 medium-size fruits)**
- **2 tablespoons sugar, or more to taste**
- **2 tablespoons fresh lime juice, or more to taste**
- **Ice cubes, for serving**

Combine the mango, sugar, and lime juice with 2 cups of water in a blender and process until smooth. Add more water as needed to thin the punch to a pourable consistency. Taste for sweetness, adding more sugar and lime juice as necessary. Pour the Mango Nectar into tall glasses over ice and serve immediately.

SENEGAL

GINGER PINEAPPLE PUNCH

GINGERE ANANAS

ON THE SIDE
SERVES 4

Spicy, sweet, and refreshing—that's *gingere ananas,* a popular Senegalese drink that combines the fruitiness of fresh pineapple with the peppery bite of ginger. Serve it with Lamb with Onion-Mustard Sauce (page 209).

- **1 piece (4 inches) peeled fresh ginger**
- **3 cups diced fresh pineapple**
- **3 tablespoons sugar, or more to taste**
- **3 tablespoons fresh lime juice**
- **4 cups cold water**
- **Ice, for serving**

1. Cut the ginger into ¼-inch slices, then add it and the pineapple, sugar, lime juice, and cold water to a blender and process until smooth.

2. Strain the pineapple mixture into a pitcher, pressing the pulp against the strainer with the back of a spoon to extract all the juice. Taste for sweetness, adding more sugar, if necessary, then pour into tall glasses over ice and serve immediately.

TRINIDAD

PEANUT PUNCH

ON THE SIDE
SERVES 4

Peanuts turn up throughout the world of grilling—as a coating for kebabs in West Africa, for example, or as a sauce for satés in Southeast Asia. I discovered this unusual peanut punch at a rough-and-tumble eating pavilion called the Breakfast Shed in Port of Spain, the capital of Trinidad. I guarantee this will forever change the way you think about peanuts.

- **½ cup creamy peanut butter**
- **½ cup sweetened condensed milk**
- **1 teaspoon vanilla extract**
- **1 teaspoon Angostura bitters**
- **Ice cubes, for serving**

Combine the peanut butter, condensed milk, vanilla, Angostura bitters, and 4 cups of water in a pitcher and whisk until well combined. Pour the punch over ice in tall glasses and serve immediately.

SINGAPORE

ROSE WATER COOLER

BANDUNG

ON THE SIDE
SERVES 4

Visit the Indian section of any of Singapore's hawkers' centers and you'll find drink vendors purveying a rainbow-colored assortment of exotic drinks. *Bandung* may look like Pepto-Bismol, but its perfumy rose water flavor is as refreshing as it is unique. Serve it with Singapore- or Malaysian-style satés.

3 cups cold water
⅓ cup sweetened condensed milk
2 tablespoons rosewater (see Note)
2 tablespoons banana liqueur
2 tablespoons grenadine syrup
Ice cubes, for serving

Combine the water, condensed milk, rose water, banana liqueur, and grenadine syrup in a pitcher and stir to mix. Pour the cooler over ice in tall glasses and serve immediately.

NOTE: Rose water is available at Middle Eastern and Indian markets and many specialty food shops.

U.S.A.

MINTED LIMEADE

ON THE SIDE
SERVES 6 TO 8

This summery refresher takes advantage of the perfumed oils in the skin of the limes as well as the sour juice of their pulp. The mint adds a cooling touch that's most welcome next to a hot grill.

1 bunch fresh mint, rinsed and spun dry
8 limes (for about 1 cup juice)
1 cup sugar, or more to taste
Ice cubes, for serving

1. Set 6 to 8 sprigs of mint aside for garnish.

2. Using a vegetable peeler, remove the zest (the green oil-rich outer peel) from 4 of the limes, then set the limes aside. Combine the lime zest with the sugar, the remaining mint, and 1 cup of water in a small saucepan and bring to a boil over medium-high heat, stirring until the sugar dissolves. Reduce the heat to low and let simmer gently for 5 minutes. Remove the sugar mixture from the heat and let it cool to room temperature, then strain it into a pitcher.

3. Squeeze the juice from all of the limes; you should have about 1 cup. Add the lime juice and 4 cups of water to the sugar mixture. Taste for sweetness, adding more sugar if necessary. Pour the limeade over ice in tall glasses, garnishing each serving with a sprig of mint.

MOROCCO

MINT TEA

ON THE SIDE
SERVES 6 TO 8

Mint tea is more than the national drink of Morocco, it's the very lifeblood of this North African country, an elixir served to guests and family, in restaurants and private homes, at the beginning of a business negotiation or at the end of a meal. The tea contains only three ingredients, but its preparation has the solemnity of a religious rite. For best results, use a heavy teapot, preferably a metal one.

Traditionally, Moroccan mint tea is served in small, hand-painted glasses with gold rims. Serve it as a prelude or conclusion to Moroccan grilled fare.

4 cups boiling water, plus more for rinsing the teapot
1 bunch fresh mint, rinsed and spun dry
1 tablespoon loose black tea, such as Ceylon or English Breakfast
3 tablespoons sugar, or more to taste

Rinse out a 5-cup teapot with boiling water. Twist the bunch of mint a few times between your fingers to bruise the leaves, then place the mint, black tea, and sugar in the teapot. Add the 4 cups of boiling water and let the tea steep for 5 minutes. To serve, strain the tea into small heatproof glasses or small cups.

VIETNAM

VIETNAMESE ICED COFFEE

ON THE SIDE
SERVES 1; CAN BE MULTIPLIED AS DESIRED

This probably isn't like any iced coffee you've ever tasted—it combines strongly brewed espresso and sweetened condensed milk. For the Thai version, imagine you're sipping the coffee from an ice-filled plastic bag through a straw—which is how it's served by street vendors in Bangkok.

3 tablespoons sweetened condensed milk
¾ cup hot brewed espresso
Ice cubes, for serving

Place the condensed milk in the bottom of a tall heatproof glass. Pour in the espresso (in Vietnam it would be drip brewed right into the glass) and stir with a spoon to mix. Add enough ice cubes to fill the glass and serve immediately.

IRAN

PERSIAN YOGURT DRINK

DUGH

ON THE SIDE
SERVES 4 TO 6

Traditionally served with Iranian (Persian) kebabs, *dugh* is a close cousin of the Afghani beverage *doh,* which you'll find on page 65. *Dugh* is made with whole yogurt instead of whey and flavored with dried rose petals, available in Middle Eastern stores. Salted beverages may seem odd to most North Americans (not to mention ones with pepper), but they're uncannily refreshing.

2 cups plain whole-milk yogurt
1 tablespoon dried mint, plus a pinch or two for garnish
1 tablespoon dried rose petals, plus a pinch or two for garnish
1 teaspoon salt, or more to taste
1 teaspoon freshly ground black pepper, or more to taste
1 quart club soda
Ice cubes, for serving

Combine the yogurt, mint, rose petals, salt, and pepper in a pitcher and stir to mix. Add the club soda. Stir gently, then taste for seasoning, adding more salt and pepper, if necessary. Pour the *dugh* over ice in tall glasses and garnish each with a sprinkling of mint and rose petals.

AFGHANISTAN

AFGHAN YOGURT DRINK

DOH

ON THE SIDE
SERVES 1; CAN BE MULTIPLIED AS DESIRED

The national drink of Afghanistan, *doh* is one of a legion of sour, salted beverages popular throughout central and eastern Asia. I admit that the ingredient combination (yogurt whey, club soda, lemon juice, mint, and salt) may sound strange to a North American, but I promise that you will quickly grow to love it. The salt serves as a valuable rehydrating agent in warm climates.

To be strictly authentic, you'd need one special ingredient to prepare *doh*—yogurt whey, the clear sourish liquid left over when yogurt is drained, a procedure basic to many of the Afghan, Iranian, and Indian marinades found in this book. Fortunately, you'll have plenty of yogurt whey left over from making them, but because you shouldn't have to rely on whey to prepare *doh,* I call for an equal amount of undrained yogurt as a substitute.

The Afghan Grill

Of all the countries I wanted to visit, but couldn't because of political turmoil, Afghanistan was my biggest disappointment. This landlocked, mountainous nation of fifteen million lies at one of the great crossroads of the barbecue trail as well as at the confluence of four great civilizations: the Middle East, Central Asia, Eastern Asia, and the Indian subcontinent. Afghan grilling weaves culinary influences from all four regions into a cuisine that's uniquely its own.

This truth was brought home to me on my first meal at an Afghan restaurant, the Khyber Pass, in New York's East Village. The moment I stepped into the storefront dining room, with its soft lights, hand-hammered copperware, kilim carpets, and Afghan tapestries, I felt I was a million miles away from Manhattan. The house specialties—grilled lamb chops flavored with onion water; fire-charred game hens; and chicken marinated in yogurt and spices and cooked until fork-tender—were exotic but immediately accessible. I was won over by the way the side dishes of piquant *chatni* (chutneys—tangy table sauces that in Afghanistan are made from vinegar, herbs, most often cilantro, and ground nuts, not the fruits we are more familiar with) and bracingly tart *torshi* (vegetable pickles) counterpointed the richness of the grilled meats.

"Afghanistan lies at the crossroads of Asia," explained the restaurant's manager, Mohamed Noor. Noor reminded me that Alexander the Great conquered the region in the fourth century B.C. on his way from Greece to India. In the thirteenth century A.D., Genghis Khan subdued the area while on his march to Turkey and Eastern Europe. He was followed in the sixteenth century by King Babur, founder of India's Mogul Empire. (Indeed, King Babur is buried outside the capital city of Kabul.) Each of the conquerors and their armies left a mark on Afghan food.

Thus, olive oil, cinnamon, dill, fenugreek, and *kalonji* (nigella seeds, also known as black cumin or black onion seeds) are as popular in Afghanistan as they are in Middle and Near Eastern cooking. From India Afghans acquired a taste for garam masala (a spice blend with ingredients that Include cumin, cinnamon, cloves, and black cardamom seeds) and *chatnis*. As throughout northern India and Central Asia, meats are marinated before being grilled in tenderizing pastes of yogurt and spices. The Persian Empire provided the *torshis* and lavash (flat bread) that have become indispensable companions to Afghan barbecue.

The focal point of the Afghan kitchen is the grill. Afghanis use simple seasonings to make some of the best grilled food in the world. Marinades run to yogurt (or yogurt cheese) flavored with onion, garlic, chiles, hot red pepper flakes, cumin, and sometimes olive oil. It's not uncommon for meats to be marinated for forty-eight hours, which makes them extraordinarily juicy and tender. The accompaniments are simple: thin chewy Afghan bread, nutty rice pilaf, tangy pickles, and coriander sauce. There are recipes throughout the book for Afghan quail, chicken, and lamb dishes, plus such traditional accompaniments as *doh* (a yogurt drink) and *chatni*.

½ cup yogurt whey or plain whole-milk yogurt
½ cup club soda
1 tablespoon fresh lemon juice, or more to taste
1 teaspoon dried mint
½ teaspoon salt, or more to taste
Ice cubes, for serving

Combine the yogurt whey, club soda, lemon juice, mint, and salt in a small pitcher or glass and stir to mix. Taste for seasoning, adding more lemon juice and/or salt as necessary. To serve, pour the *doh* over ice in a tall glass.

INDIA

INDIAN YOGURT COOLER

LASSI

ON THE SIDE
SERVES 1; CAN BE MULTIPLIED AS DESIRED

Lassi is India's answer to the North American milkshake, and a splendid and refreshing response it is. It's also the perfect beverage to serve with hot and spicy food. (Contrary to popular belief, dairy products are much more effective than beer at extinguishing chile hellfire.) The rosewater and cardamom add a perfumed flavor you'll find exquisitely exotic.

1 cup plain whole-milk yogurt
1½ tablespoons sugar, or more to taste
1 teaspoon rose water
¼ teaspoon ground cardamom
5 ice cubes, cracked with a mallet
1 teaspoon chopped unsalted pistachios, for garnish

Combine the yogurt, sugar, rose water, cardamom, and ice in a blender and process until smooth. Taste for sweetness, adding more sugar as necessary. Pour the *lassi* into a tall glass, sprinkle the pistachios on top, and serve immediately.

STAR ANISE WINGS | PAGE 76 • PANCETTA GRILLED FIGS | PAGE 89

WARM-UPS

One of the things I like best about grilling is how it leaves you with so much free time. Sure, live-fire cooking can be quick and intense, but it also provides plenty of idle moments for standing around and chatting with friends.

"Even an old boot tastes good if it is cooked over char-coal."
—Italian Proverb

Just because you're standing around doesn't mean you have to go hungry—indeed, an empty plate is a sad thing at a barbecue. This chapter, a collection of dips, appetizers—even soups—will help your barbecue get off to a rousing start. From familiar dishes, like baba ghanoush (made the authentic way, by charring the eggplant on the grill) to the more exotic, such as *boka dushi* ("sweet mouth" chicken kebabs from the island of Curaçao), Vietnamese shrimp mousse grilled on sweet, crunchy sugarcane, and even Goat Cheese Grilled in Grape Leaves.

You'll find dishes you may never have realized could be grilled, like Indonesian quail egg kebabs or flame-cooked escargots. You'll also taste some of the world's greatest grilled (literally) cheese dishes, from Mexican quesadillas to Argentinean grilled provolone. And then there are those aforementioned grilled soups here (more precisely soups made with grilled vegetables) that will leave your guests raving long after the party is over.

INDONESIA

INDONESIAN BEEF AND COCONUT SATES

SATE LALAT

DIRECT GRILLING
SERVES 4-6 AS AN APPETIZER, 2 AS A MAIN COURSE

The smallest of Indonesian satés, *saté lalat* is not much bigger than a fly, which is what *lalat* literally means. Typically, the skewers for *saté lalat* are the size of broom straws; the meat portion is about one inch long; a serving would include three or four dozen satés. However, to suit American skewers and appetites, I make my *saté lalats* somewhat bigger.

A specialty of the island of Madura near Java, *saté lalat* owes its distinctive texture and flavor to the addition of shredded coconut. To be strictly authentic you should use freshly grated coconut, but I like the touch of sweetness (not to mention the convenience) offered by the shredded dried coconut sold at the supermarket. An Indonesian would use fresh turmeric; I approximate its flavor by combining the more readily available ground turmeric and fresh ginger.

These satés are so flavorful you really don't need a sauce.

SPECIAL EQUIPMENT

30 short bamboo skewers and an aluminum foil shield (see box, page 23)

INGREDIENTS

- 12 ounces lean ground beef chuck or sirloin
- ½ teaspoon ground turmeric
- 2 teaspoons minced or grated peeled fresh ginger
- ½ cup shredded coconut (dried or fresh, sweetened or unsweetened)
- 1 tablespoon sweet soy sauce (ketjap manis), or 1½ teaspoons each regular soy sauce and molasses
- 1 teaspoon fresh lime juice
- 2 tablespoons peanut or other vegetable oil
- ¼ teaspoon salt, or more to taste
- ½ teaspoon freshly ground black pepper, or more to taste

1. Combine the beef, turmeric, ginger, coconut, sweet soy sauce, lime juice, oil, salt, and pepper in a medium-size bowl and, using your hands, form a smooth paste. Cook a small amount of the beef mixture in a nonstick skillet until cooked through, then taste for seasoning, adding more salt and/or pepper to the remaining beef mixture as necessary.

2. Lightly wet your hands with cold water, then take a small amount (about 1 tablespoon) of the beef mixture and mold it around a skewer to form a thin strip about 5 inches long. Continue until all of the beef mixture is used up, placing the satés as they are finished on a platter or baking sheet lined with plastic wrap.

3. Set up the grill for direct grilling and preheat to high.

4. When ready to cook, brush and oil the grill grate. Arrange the satés on the hot grate with the aluminum foil shield under the ends of the skewers. Grill the satés, turning with tongs, until nicely browned on the outside and cooked through, 2 to 4 minutes in all. Serve at once.

VIETNAM

VIETNAMESE BEEF JERKY

THIT BO KHO

DIRECT GRILLING
SERVES 4 AS AN APPETIZER, 2-3 AS A MAIN COURSE

Grilled sugar-cured dried beef is a popular snack and street food throughout Southeast Asia. Vietnam's version (*thit bo kho*) owes its explosive flavor to a marinade made with lemongrass, chiles, and fish sauce. Traditionally, the cured beef is dried outdoors in the sun—a common sight in Vietnam but more difficult to execute in North America. The beef can also be dried on racks in the refrigerator, as I suggest here.

ADVANCE PREPARATION

1 to 2 days for marinating and drying the beef

INGREDIENTS

- 1 pound lean beef sirloin or bottom round, in a single piece
- 2 stalks fresh lemongrass, trimmed, or 2 strips lemon zest (each 2 by ½ inches), removed with a vegetable peeler
- 1 clove garlic, chopped
- 1 to 2 hot red chiles, stemmed and seeded (for a spicier jerky, leave the seeds in)
- 5 tablespoons sugar
- ½ teaspoon salt
- ½ teaspoon freshly ground black pepper
- 2 tablespoons Asian fish sauce
- 2 tablespoons soy sauce
- 2 tablespoons vegetable oil, for brushing

1. Cut the beef as thinly as possible into crosswise slices, place it in a baking dish, and set it aside while you prepare the marinade.

2. Combine the lemongrass, garlic, chiles, sugar, salt, and pepper in a mortar and pound to a smooth paste with a pestle, then work in the fish sauce and soy sauce. If you don't have a mortar and pestle, combine all these ingredients in a blender or food processor and process to a smooth puree. Pour the marinade over the meat in the baking dish and toss thoroughly to coat. Cover the beef and let marinate, in the refrigerator, for 2 hours.

3. Remove the beef from the marinade and spread out the slices on a wire rack in a shallow roasting pan. Refrigerate the beef, loosely covered with plastic wrap, until it is completely dry, 1 to 2 days.

4. Set up the grill for direct grilling and preheat to high.

5. When ready to cook, brush and oil the grill grate. Arrange the beef slices on the hot grate and grill, turning with tongs, until sizzling, brown, and crisp, 2 to 3 minutes per side, brushing the beef once or twice with the oil as it cooks. Serve at once.

TURKEY

PASTRAMI GRILLED IN GRAPE LEAVES

DIRECT GRILLING
MAKES 8 BUNDLES

Visit the Spice Market (also known as the Egyptian Market) in Istanbul and you'll see long, tongue-shaped strips of spice-crusted orange-brown meat hanging from the shop rafters. This is *basturma,* the cured beef of the Near East and precursor (both historically and linguistically) of North American pastrami. Usually the meat for *basturma* is beef, although it is sometimes made with camel, and the spices—salt, pepper, coriander, and paprika—will be familiar to anyone who likes pastrami. However, the flavor of *basturma* is more exotic.

That set me thinking about an appetizer I enjoyed at the Tuğra Restaurant at Istanbul's stately Çirağan Palace hotel: *basturma* grilled in grape leaves. If you live in an area with a large Middle or Near Eastern community (such as Fresno or Boston), you may be able to find real *basturma.* But a fine version of this dish can be made with pastrami. Cheese is not in the original recipe, but I very much like the way it rounds out the flavors.

ADVANCE PREPARATION

15 minutes for soaking the grape leaves

INGREDIENTS

16 bottled grape leaves packed in brine, drained
8 ounces thinly sliced pastrami or basturma
8 slices string cheese or mozzarella cut crosswise (each about ¼ inch thick, about 8 ounces; optional)
1 medium-size ripe tomato, cut into 8 thin slices
1 small onion, cut into 8 thin slices
8 paper-thin lemon slices, seeded, with rind removed

1. Place the grape leaves in a large bowl, add cold water to cover, and let soak for 15 minutes, changing the water two or three times.

2. Drain the grape leaves and blot dry with paper towels. Spread 8 of the leaves out on a work surface. Place a few slices of pastrami in the center of each. Top each portion of pastrami with a slice of cheese (if using), a slice of tomato, a slice of onion, and finally a slice of lemon. Bring the edges of a grape leaf up around the filling. Place a second grape leaf on top and turn the edges under so the filling is entirely covered. Repeat with the remaining grape leaves. Transfer the grape leaf bundles to a platter or baking sheet, cover them loosely with plastic wrap, and refrigerate.

3. Set up the grill for direct grilling and preheat to high.

4. When ready to cook, brush and oil the grill grate. Arrange the bundles on the hot grate, seam side up, and grill, turning with a spatula, until the grape leaves brown and the filling is heated through, 2 to 4 minutes per side. To eat, unwrap the grape leaves and eat the filling.

VIETNAM

GRILLED BEEF AND BASIL ROLLS

DIRECT GRILLING
MAKES 50 TO 60 ROLLS

A classic Vietnamese appetizer *bo goi la-lot,* beef grilled in *la-lot* leaves, inspired this recipe. *La-lot* leaves are the crinkly, round, aromatic leaves of a Southeast Asian vine. If you live in a city with a large Vietnamese community, you may be able to find fresh *la-lot* leaves, but if not, don't despair. The delicate rolls are equally delectable made with fresh basil, and that is what I prepare them with here. (For a Japanese touch, you could even use shiso leaves—also known as perilla or beefsteak leaves—which taste like a cross between mint and basil.) Sometimes these rolls are made with thin beef slices, sometimes with ground beef. I've followed the example of the Vietnam House restaurant in Saigon, using ground meat. Chopped peanuts add a nice crunchy finish.

SPECIAL EQUIPMENT

10 to 12 short bamboo skewers and an aluminum foil shield (see box, page 23)

INGREDIENTS

8 ounces very lean ground beef sirloin
2 cloves garlic, minced
5 teaspoons Asian fish sauce, or more to taste
1 tablespoon sugar, or more to taste
1 teaspoon freshly ground black pepper
1 or 2 large bunches basil, for about 60 large leaves
3 tablespoons coarsely chopped dry-roasted peanuts (optional)

1. Combine the beef, garlic, fish sauce, sugar, and pepper in a small bowl and, using your hands, form a smooth paste. Cook a small amount of the beef mixture in a nonstick skillet until cooked through, then taste for seasoning, adding more fish sauce and/or sugar to the remaining beef mixture as necessary; it should be both salty and sweet.

2. Select 50 to 60 of the largest basil leaves. Rinse them under cold running water, then drain and blot them gently dry with paper towels.

3. Place one leaf, underside up, on a work surface. Depending on the size of the leaf, mound up to 2 teaspoons of the beef mixture in the center. Starting with the stem end, roll the

WRAPPING BEEF

Grilled Beef and Basil Rolls are simple to make. Just be sure you buy the largest basil leaves—with no or few imperfections—that you can find.

1. ***Start with the pale, concave side of the basil leaves facing up. Place a nugget of the ground beef mixture in the center of each basil leaf.***

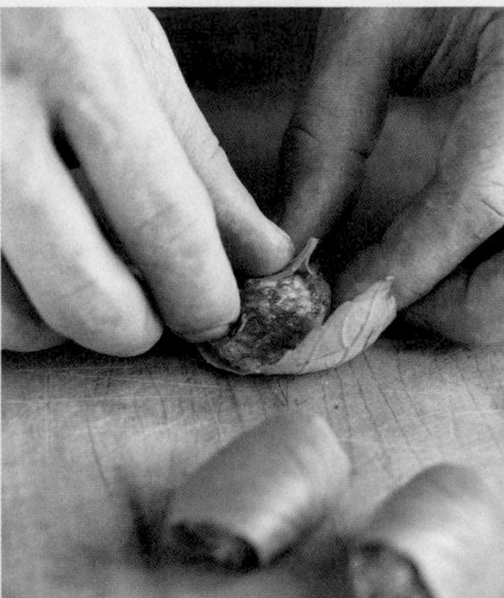

2. ***Beginning at the stem end, gently roll up the basil leaf around the meat.***

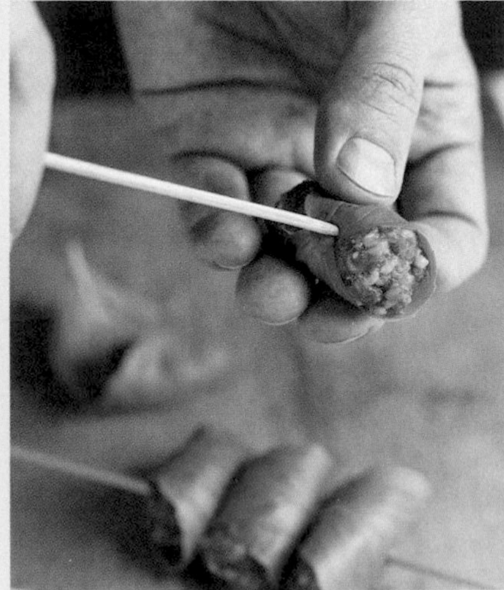

3. ***Skewer four or five basil and beef rolls on bamboo skewers; this will pin the rolls shut.***

GRILLED BEEF AND BASIL ROLLS | PAGE 69

The Vietnamese Grill

I have a theory about the best way to eat during the sweltering dog days of summer: Sun-belt lands that have scorching climates all year long inspire cooking styles suited to warm weather eating. And nowhere is this more true than Vietnam.

I visited Saigon hot on the barbecue trail and didn't have far to go to strike pay dirt. My hotel, the New World, was located across the street from Saigon's Ben Thanh central market. And like markets throughout Southeast Asia, Ben Thanh was teeming with grill jockeys.

A favorite stop was a stall where a woman grilled chicken wings that had been marinating in a fragrant paste of lemongrass, garlic, and fish sauce. Another vendor proffered an egg that had been "roasted" over a coconut shell charcoal fire. I wrapped it and a sprig of mint in a lettuce leaf and dipped it in *nuoc cham,* Vietnam's delicate table sauce—a piquant mixture of fish sauce, lime juice, and sugar. Amazing!

Grilling is ubiquitous in Vietnam, first because it produces such flavorful food, and second because it's so inexpensive. As in Thailand and Indonesia, coconut is a major crop here, and the tree's by-product, coconut husks, makes excellent charcoal.

But grilling isn't only for the poor. I stopped next at Vietnam House, a tiny restaurant located in a fashionable townhouse on Dong Khoi Street. It seemed to exist chiefly for the pleasure of deep-pocketed foreigners. This has both advantages and drawbacks: You get to dine surrounded by lacquered screens and gilded wood carvings, serenaded by live, twangy Vietnamese classical music, and served by waitresses in *ao dai* (slit dresses). But it feels a little like you're in Epcot.

Two items here rank as world-class barbecue. The first is *chao tom,* an ingenious combination of shrimp mousse that is grilled on a piece of sugarcane. You don't really eat the cane, so much as chew on it to release the sweet juices.

The other dish is *bo goi la-lot,* beef grilled in *la-lot* leaves and served on tiny skewers. *La-lot* is the piquant leaf of a Southeast Asian vine that reminds me a little of basil. The beef fairly sizzled, its fat counterbalanced by the herbal tang of the leaf.

Counterpointing grilled meats with vegetables, specifically with lettuce and aromatic herbs, and with noodles is one of the hallmarks of Vietnamese cuisine.

A Meal Outdoors

No dish represents the Vietnamese penchant for enriching small portions of grilled meats with a large proportion of noodles and vegetables than *banh hoi thit* (grilled pork with rice noodles) and its sister dish *bo bun* (grilled beef with rice paper). And no one makes these dishes better than the restaurant Thanh Nien.

I enjoyed my grilled pork in the restaurant's airy courtyard. To my left stood a grove of bamboo; to my right, a thatch-roofed portico. Oscillating fans stirred the torrid air. The tables around me were filled with fledgling capitalists chattering on cellular phones.

As I sipped an icy "33" Export beer, the waitress set before me three plates. The first contained neatly coiled, snowy rice noodles. The second held the actual pork, which had been thinly sliced, marinated in a fragrant mixture of lemongrass, shallots, and vodka, and smokily charred on the grill. The cooked slices were then dusted with an aromatic sprinkling of chopped scallions and toasted peanuts, the former for pungency, the latter for sweetness and crunch.

The final element was a salad platter that turns up on all Vietnamese tables. The refreshing assortment included lettuce and basil leaves, sliced cucumbers, mung bean sprouts, and crisp, pointed slices of star fruit. You wrap a coil of noodles and a slice of pork in a lettuce leaf and add basil for fragrance and slices of cucumber and star fruit for crispness. The result is a morsel perfect for summer, being simultaneously hot and cold; crisp, soft, and chewy; sweet, salty, lemony, and aromatic. I can't think of a dish in the West that comes close to achieving such a complex interplay of temperatures, textures, and tastes. And it's fun to eat.

leaf up into a compact cylinder. Place the rolled-up leaf on a baking sheet, with the leaf tip tucked under. Repeat with the remaining beef mixture and basil leaves.

4. Thread the beef rolls crosswise on the skewers, 5 rolls to a skewer, making sure to pierce the place where the leaf ends cross first (see Note).

5. Set up the grill for direct grilling and preheat to high.

6. When ready to cook, brush and oil the grill grate. Arrange the skewers on the hot grate with the aluminum foil shield under the ends of the skewers. Grill the rolls, turning with tongs, until the beef rolls are cooked through, 2 to 4 minutes in all. When done, the basil will be lightly browned and the rolls will be very hot to the touch. Serve the beef rolls on the skewers with the peanuts sprinkled on top (if using).

NOTE: You can make the beef rolls to this point up to several hours ahead of time. Cover the rolls loosely with plastic wrap and refrigerate them.

CURAÇAO

DUTCH WEST INDIAN CHICKEN KEBABS

BOKA DUSHI

DIRECT GRILLING
SERVES 4

This is a dish of three continents. I tasted it at a restaurant in Curaçao, but its roots lie in the East Indies, specifically Java. In Papiamento, the local dialect—a musical blend of Spanish, Portuguese, Dutch, and West African languages—*boka* means mouth and *dushi* means sweet. The seasonings and spices for the dish are sold at the Floating Market in Willemstad, a colorful flotilla of Venezuelan produce boats that make a thirty-five-mile journey to sell comestibles from South America. The assertive flavors of ginger and *sambal ulek* (chile paste) will light up your mouth like a Fourth of July sky.

As in Asia, dark meat is preferred to white, as it's thought to have a richer flavor. But you could certainly use skinless, boneless chicken breasts (you'll need one and a half pounds).

ADVANCE PREPARATION

30 minutes for marinating the chicken

SPECIAL EQUIPMENT

36 to 40 short bamboo skewers and an aluminum foil shield (see box, page 23)

INGREDIENTS

8 chicken thighs (2½ to 3 pounds)
¼ cup sweet soy sauce (ketjap manis), or 2 tablespoons each regular soy sauce and molasses
1 tablespoon fresh lime juice
2 teaspoons grated peeled fresh ginger
1 to 2 teaspoons sambal ulek or other chile paste or sauce
1 teaspoon ground cumin
½ teaspoon ground turmeric
1 cup Dutch West Indian Peanut Sauce (page 476)

1. Skin and bone the chicken thighs, then rinse them under cold running water. Drain and blot dry with paper towels. Cut the meat into strips the size of your little finger.

2. Combine the sweet soy sauce, lime juice, ginger, *sambal ulek*, cumin, and turmeric in a large bowl and stir well to blend. Add the chicken and toss to coat. Cover the chicken and let it marinate, in the refrigerator, for 30 minutes.

3. Set up the grill for direct grilling and preheat to high.

4. When ready to cook, drain the chicken strips, then thread them lengthwise on skewers. Brush and oil the grill grate, then arrange the skewers on the hot grate with the aluminum foil shield under the ends of the skewers. Grill the meat, turning with tongs, until it is cooked through, 2 to 4 minutes in all. Serve the *boka dushis* at once, with ramekins of the Dutch West Indian Peanut Sauce for dipping.

Sambal Ulek

***Sambal ulek* is a fiery paste made of hot red chiles. Look for it in specialty food shops or Asian markets, or substitute a Vietnamese or Thai chile paste or the hot sauce of your choice.**

CHINA

SILVER PAPER CHICKEN

DIRECT GRILLING
MAKES 16 PIECES

San Francisco's celebrated dim sum palace, Yank Sing, was the inspiration for this recipe. The original was deep-fried, but grilling produces equally tasty chicken with a fraction of the fat. An aluminum foil bundle helps seal in flavor and succulence—and also makes for an offbeat presentation. Five-spice powder is a Chinese seasoning composed of cinnamon, pepper, cloves, Sichuan peppercorns, and star anise. It imparts an exotically sweet, aromatic flavor to the chicken. Look for five-spice powder in Asian markets, specialty food shops, and in the ethnic foods sections of most supermarkets.

ADVANCE PREPARATION

2 to 4 hours for marinating the chicken

INGREDIENTS

8 chicken thighs (2½ to 3 pounds), or 4 skinless, boneless chicken breast halves (about 1½ pounds)
4 large scallions
½ cup soy sauce
¼ cup sugar
2 tablespoons Chinese rice wine or dry sherry
1 clove garlic, minced
½ teaspoon Chinese five-spice powder

1. If using chicken thighs, remove the skin. Using a sharp cleaver, cut each thigh, through the bone, crosswise in half. If using chicken breasts, cut each into 2-inch pieces for 16 pieces altogether. Rinse the chicken under cold running water, then drain and blot dry with paper towels. Trim the scallions and cut each into four 2-inch sections.

2. Combine the soy sauce, sugar, rice wine, garlic, and five-spice powder in a heavy saucepan and bring to a boil over medium heat. Let boil until thick and syrupy, about 5 minutes. Transfer the soy sauce mixture to a bowl and let cool to room temperature. Add the chicken pieces, toss to coat thoroughly, and let marinate, covered, in the refrigerator, for 2 to 4 hours.

3. Cut sixteen 6-inch squares of aluminum foil. Place a piece of foil, shiny side down, on a work surface. Drain the chicken, reserving the marinade, and place a piece of chicken, along with a piece of scallion, in the center of each square of foil. Spoon a little marinade on top of each piece of chicken, then wrap it by crinkling the foil together, rather than folding it neatly (see Note).

4. Set up the grill for direct grilling and preheat to high.

5. When ready to cook, arrange the foil bundles on the hot grate and grill, turning with tongs, until the chicken is cooked through, 2 to 4 minutes per side. To test for doneness, unwrap one of the bundles. The chicken should feel firm and hot to the touch. Much of the fun of eating this dish is the surprise that comes when unwrapping the foil, but do warn eaters to open their bundles carefully; the chicken will be very steamy and hot.

NOTE: The recipe can be prepared to this point up to 6 hours ahead. Refrigerate the foil bundles until ready to cook.

VIETNAM

SAIGON GARLIC LEMONGRASS WINGS

DIRECT GRILLING
MAKES 12 CHICKEN WINGS

I've always found the best window into a nation's cuisine to be its food markets. The moment I arrived in Saigon, I rushed to the colossal Ben Thanh market, located across the street from the hotel where I was staying. You can buy just about anything at Ben Thanh: eel, snake, all manner of innards, even grasshoppers. When you tire of shopping, an army of food vendors stands ready to ply you with Vietnamese soups, stews, and barbecue.

Here's how one vendor prepares chicken wings; her

recipe is as easy to make as it is flavorful. To increase the surface area of meat exposed to the flames, the wings are spread open as though poised for flight and threaded on skewers for grilling. Although I spoke no Vietnamese and the vendor spoke no English, the pleasure these delectable wings brought me was obvious.

To be strictly authentic, you'll need lemongrass and fish sauce for the marinade. In a pinch, you could substitute lemon zest and soy sauce.

ADVANCE PREPARATION

4 to 24 hours for marinating the chicken wings

SPECIAL EQUIPMENT

12 long bamboo skewers and an aluminum foil shield (see box, page 23)

INGREDIENTS

12 whole chicken wings (2½ to 3 pounds)
4 cloves garlic, peeled
¼ cup chopped shallots
1 piece (1 inch) fresh ginger, peeled and thinly sliced
2 stalks fresh lemongrass, trimmed and sliced, or 2 strips lemon zest (each 2 by ½ inches), removed with a vegetable peeler
2 tablespoons sugar
⅓ cup Asian fish sauce
3 tablespoons fresh lemon juice
3 tablespoons vegetable oil
¼ cup finely chopped dry-roasted peanuts, for garnish
¼ cup chopped fresh cilantro (optional), for garnish

1. Rinse the chicken wings under cold running water, then drain and blot dry with paper towels. Make two or three deep slashes, to the bone, in the meaty part of each wing. Set the wings aside while you prepare the marinade.

2. Combine the garlic, shallots, ginger, lemongrass, and sugar in a mortar and pound to a paste with a pestle, then work in the fish sauce, lemon juice, and 1 tablespoon of the oil. If you don't have a mortar and pestle, combine all these ingredients in a blender or food processor and process to a smooth puree. Scrape the marinade into a large bowl, add the chicken wings, and turn to coat thoroughly. Cover the wings and let marinate, in the refrigerator, for at least 4 hours, but preferably 24, turning the wings occasionally.

3. Set up the grill for direct grilling and preheat to medium-high.

4. When ready to cook, drain the chicken wings, reserving the marinade, then thread each wing on a skewer, running the skewer through all three sections of the wing to hold it open as widely as possible. Brush the wings on both sides with the remaining 2 tablespoons of oil.

5. Brush and oil the grill grate, then arrange the chicken wings on the hot grate with the aluminum foil shield under the ends of the skewers. Grill the wings, turning them several times with tongs, until the thicker wing sections are no longer pink near the bone, 12 to 16 minutes in all. Reduce the heat if the wings start to burn. Brush the wings once or twice with the reserved marinade, but do not brush them during the last 3 minutes of cooking.

6. Transfer the grilled wings to a serving platter, sprinkle the peanuts and cilantro (if using) over them, and serve.

AUSTRALIA

AUSTRALIAN BEER-BARBECUED WINGS

DIRECT GRILLING
MAKES 12 CHICKEN WINGS

The wing is the choicest morsel of the chicken for grilling, consisting chiefly of skin (rendered crackling crisp by the flames) and bones (which are fun to gnaw on, imparting a rich flavor in the process). The little meat there is, is well marbled, so it stays moist throughout the cooking. This truth is not lost on Australians, for whom the art of grilling chicken wings is something of a national pastime. You'll love the tangy, sweet-sour taste of these wings, which owe their uniqueness to a marinade flavored with Australian beer.

ADVANCE PREPARATION

4 hours for marinating the chicken wings

FOR THE CHICKEN AND MARINADE

12 whole chicken wings (2½ to 3 pounds)
¼ cup peanut oil
¼ cup fresh lemon juice
¼ cup Worcestershire sauce
¼ cup Australian beer, such as Foster's
1 teaspoon salt
1 teaspoon freshly ground black pepper

FOR THE BARBECUE SAUCE

2 tablespoons peanut oil
1 small onion, finely chopped
1 clove garlic, minced
2 teaspoons minced peeled fresh ginger
½ teaspoon hot red pepper flakes
1 cup ketchup
⅓ cup Australian beer, such as Foster's
2 tablespoons fresh lemon juice
2 tablespoons Worcestershire sauce
2 tablespoons red wine vinegar
1 tablespoon dark brown sugar
1 tablespoon honey
2 teaspoons soy sauce
1 teaspoon dry mustard
½ teaspoon freshly ground black pepper

1. Prepare the chicken: Rinse the wings under cold running water, then drain and blot dry with paper towels. Make two or three deep slashes, to the bone, in the meaty part of each wing. Place the wings in a large nonreactive bowl and stir in the ¼ cup of peanut oil, ¼ cup of lemon juice, ¼ cup of Worcestershire sauce, ¼ cup of beer, the salt, and the 1 teaspoon of pepper. Cover the wings and let marinate, in the refrigerator, for 4 hours, turning the wings occasionally.

2. Meanwhile, prepare the barbecue sauce: Heat the 2 tablespoons of peanut oil in a medium-size heavy saucepan over medium heat. Add the onion, garlic, ginger, and hot pepper flakes and cook, stirring with a wooden spoon, until the onion and garlic are lightly browned, about 5 minutes. Stir in the ketchup, ⅓ cup of beer, 2 tablespoons of lemon juice, 2 tablespoons of Worcestershire sauce, 2 tablespoons of vinegar, brown sugar, honey, soy sauce, mustard, and ½ teaspoon of pepper and bring to a boil. Reduce the heat to low and let the sauce simmer gently until thick and richly flavored, 10 to 15 minutes, stirring occasionally. Remove the barbecue sauce from the heat. Measure about 1 cup and set this aside for serving.

3. Set up the grill for direct grilling and preheat to medium-high.

4. When ready to cook, brush and oil the grill grate. Drain the wings and arrange them on the hot grate, pulling them open to expose as much skin as possible to the flames. Grill the wings, turning them several times with tongs, until the thicker wing sections are no longer pink near the bone, 12 to 16 minutes in all. Reduce the heat if the wings start to burn. Start brushing the wings with the barbecue sauce during the last 5 minutes of cooking.

5. Transfer the wings to a serving platter. Brush them again with the sauce, and serve with the reserved saucc.

MALAYSIA

STAR ANISE WINGS

DIRECT GRILLING OR ROTISSERIE
MAKES 12 CHICKEN WINGS

Lee Chun Hock is a jocular grill master who plies his trade in northern Malaysia. I met him on Gurney Road on Penang Island, where he runs a barbecue stall called Ipoh Famous Roasted Chicken Wings. (Ipoh is the name of his boss.) Hock's "pit" is a gleaming stainless rotisserie, where spring chickens are roasted snap crackle poppingly crisp over a charcoal fire. He offered me the following recipe on the condition that I give him a winning lottery number. I told him my age, birthday, and street address. I hope he won!

The powerfully flavorful marinade has everything you could wish for: soy sauce for saltiness, sugar and *ketjap manis* for sweetness, and star anise and cinnamon sticks for spice. The basting of sesame oil gives the wings a nutty crispness.

ADVANCE PREPARATION

8 to 24 hours for marinating the chicken wings

SPECIAL EQUIPMENT

Rotisserie (optional)

INGREDIENTS

- **12 whole chicken wings (2½ to 3 pounds)**
- **⅓ cup soy sauce**
- **⅓ cup sweet soy sauce (ketjap manis), or 7½ teaspoons each regular soy sauce and molasses**
- **⅓ cup Chinese rice wine or dry sherry**
- **⅓ cup sugar**
- **2 teaspoons freshly ground black pepper**
- **1 teaspoon Accent (MSG; optional)**
- **5 whole star anise**
- **2 cinnamon sticks (each 3 inches)**
- **2 tablespoons Asian (dark) sesame oil, for basting**

1. Rinse the chicken wings under cold running water, then drain and blot dry with paper towels. Make two or three deep slashes, to the bone, in the meaty part of each wing. Set the wings aside while you prepare the marinade.

2. Combine the soy sauces, rice wine, sugar, pepper, and Accent (if using) in a large nonreactive bowl and whisk until the sugar dissolves. Add the star anise and cinnamon, then add the wings and turn to coat thoroughly with the marinade. Cover the wings and let marinate, in the refrigerator, for at least 8 and as long as 24 hours, turning occasionally.

3. *If grilling directly on the grate,* set up the grill and preheat to medium-high.

If using a rotisserie, set up the grill for spit roasting following the manufacturer's instructions and preheat it to high. Place a large drip pan in the center of the grill directly under the spit.

4. When ready to cook, remove the wings from the marinade and discard the marinade.

If grilling directly on the grate, brush and oil the grill grate. Arrange the wings on the hot grate and grill, turning with tongs, until the thicker wing sections are no longer pink near the bone, 12 to 16 minutes in all. Reduce the heat if the wings start to burn.

If using a rotisserie, thread each wing onto the spit through the excess skin found at the joint. Attach the spit to the rotisserie mechanism and turn on the motor. Spit roast the wings until the thicker wing sections are no longer pink near the bone, 20 to 30 minutes.

5. Brush the wings once or twice with sesame oil as they cook. Transfer the grilled wings to a serving platter and serve at once.

CHINA

HONEY-GLAZED HONG KONG WINGS

DIRECT GRILLING
MAKES 12 CHICKEN WINGS

Here's a simple recipe for Hong Kong–style chicken wings. Brushing honey on as they cook creates an exceptionally crisp, sweet skin.

ADVANCE PREPARATION

2 to 4 hours for refrigerating the chicken wings

SPECIAL EQUIPMENT

12 long bamboo skewers and an aluminum foil shield (see box, page 23)

INGREDIENTS

- **12 whole chicken wings (2½ to 3 pounds)**
- **4 cloves garlic, minced**
- **1½ teaspoons salt**
- **1½ teaspoons freshly ground black pepper**
- **1 teaspoon Accent (MSG; optional)**
- **½ cup honey, for brushing**

1. Rinse the chicken wings under cold running water, then drain and blot dry with paper towels. Make two or three deep slashes, to the bone, in the meaty part of each wing. Place the wings in a large bowl and sprinkle the garlic, salt, pepper, and Accent (if using) over them. Turn the wings to coat with the seasonings, then cover and refrigerate them for 2 to 4 hours.

2. Set up the grill for direct grilling and preheat to medium-high.

3. When ready to cook, brush and oil the grill grate. Place the honey in a small saucepan and heat it until it's just warm on the grill's side burner, if it has one, or over low heat on the stovetop.

4. Thread each chicken wing on a skewer, running the skewer through all three sections to hold the wing open as wide as possible. Arrange the wings on the hot grate with the aluminum foil shield under the ends of the skewers. Grill, turning with tongs, until the thicker wing sections are no longer pink near the bone, 12 to 16 minutes in all, brushing the wings with the warm honey during the last 4 minutes of grilling. Reduce the heat if the wings start to burn. Transfer the grilled wings to a serving platter and serve at once.

SINGAPORE

SPICY CHILE WINGS

DIRECT GRILLING
MAKES 16 CHICKEN WINGS

These spicy wings reflect Singapore's incredible ethnic diversity. Five-spice powder is a Chinese flavoring, while the *ketjap manis* (sweet soy sauce) comes from Indonesia. The frying of the spice paste is characteristic of Malaysian and *nonya* ("grandmother") cooking, but the place where I actually sampled the wings was the Arab market. Frying the spice paste creates a complex flavor that will make these some of the best wings you've ever tasted.

The vendor who shared this recipe with me used parboiled wings, which he slathered with spice paste and finished on the grill. Given the hundreds of wings sold each morning, parboiling was a way for him to shorten the cooking time to a manageable duration. Since you and I are in less of a rush than the average market cook, I suggest you take the time to marinate the raw wings in the spice paste and cook them from start to finish on the grill. Although this recipe may look a little complicated, the actual preparation time is only about twenty minutes.

ADVANCE PREPARATION

6 to 24 hours for marinating the chicken wings

INGREDIENTS

16 whole chicken wings (about 3½ pounds)
3 large shallots, peeled
6 cloves garlic, peeled
1 piece (1 inch) fresh ginger, peeled
2 to 10 Thai chiles, serrano peppers, or small jalapeño peppers, stemmed, seeded, and coarsely chopped (for hotter wings, leave the seeds in; see Notes)
½ cup vegetable oil
2 tablespoons soy sauce
2 tablespoons sweet soy sauce (ketjap manis), or 1 tablespoon each regular soy sauce and molasses
1 teaspoon Chinese five-spice powder

1. Rinse the wings under cold running water, then drain and blot dry with paper towels. Make two or three deep slashes, to the bone, in the meaty part of each wing. Place the wings in a large bowl and refrigerate them while you prepare the spice paste.

2. Combine the shallots, garlic, ginger, and chiles in a food processor and process to a smooth paste. Add ¼ cup of the oil, the soy sauces, and the five-spice powder and process until smooth (see Notes).

3. Heat the remaining ¼ cup of oil in a wok or small, heavy skillet over medium heat. Add the spice paste and cook, stirring constantly, until thick, brown, and very flavorful, 8 to 12 minutes. Remove the spice paste from the heat and let cool completely.

4. Add the cooled spice paste to the chicken and turn the wings to coat thoroughly. Cover the wings and let them marinate, in the refrigerator, for at least 6 hours or as long as 24, turning them occasionally (the longer the wings marinate, the better).

5. Set up the grill for direct grilling and preheat to medium-high.

6. When ready to cook, brush and oil the grill grate. Arrange the wings on the hot grate and grill, turning with tongs, until the thicker wing sections are no longer pink near the bone, 12 to 16 minutes in all. Reduce the heat if the wings start to burn. Transfer the grilled wings to a serving platter and serve.

NOTES: As elsewhere in this book, I call for a range of chiles or peppers. Two seeded ones will give you piquant wings; 10 unseeded ones would make even a Malaysian firebrand feel at home.

The ingredients for the spice paste can also be pureed in a blender, in which case they can be processed all together.

CHINA

GRILLED CHICKEN WINGS WITH HONG KONG SPICES

SHEK O WINGS

DIRECT GRILLING
MAKES 12 CHICKEN WINGS

The seaside community of Shek O lies on the far side of Hong Kong Island, perhaps a half hour drive from the forest of skyscrapers. But the distance might be better measured in centuries than in kilometers. Here, on this island of relentless urban sprawl and frenzied economic development, you can find a bohemian seaside community with narrow streets, laid-back bars and open-air restaurants, and beaches that are crowded on Sundays with lots of families picnicking.

Grilling normally plays a minor role in Chinese cuisine, but the Sunday crowds transform Shek O beaches into barbecue central. Vendors do a lively business in charcoal and grilling utensils. The grills themselves are ingenious fabrications of chicken wire and rebar (the ribbed metal bars used for reinforcing concrete). The most popular food for grilling is chicken wings, which are marinated in soy sauce and honey. As elsewhere in Asia, the wings are spread open on the skewers in a zigzag to expose the maximum surface area to the fire.

ADVANCE PREPARATION

6 to 24 hours for marinating the chicken wings

SPECIAL EQUIPMENT

12 long bamboo skewers and an aluminum foil shield (see box, page 23)

INGREDIENTS

- **12 whole chicken wings (2½ to 3 pounds)**
- **½ cup soy sauce**
- **⅓ cup honey**
- **1 tablespoon minced peeled fresh ginger**
- **3 cloves garlic, minced**
- **3 scallions, both white and green parts, trimmed and very finely chopped**
- **2 teaspoons Chinese five-spice powder**

1. Rinse the chicken wings under cold running water, then drain and blot dry with paper towels. Make two or three deep slashes, to the bone, in the meaty part of each wing. Set the wings aside while you prepare the marinade.

2. Combine the soy sauce, honey, ginger, garlic, scallions, and five-spice powder in a large bowl and whisk until well combined. Set aside about half the marinade in a small bowl and cover and refrigerate it until you are ready to grill. Add the wings to the remaining marinade and turn to coat thoroughly. Cover the wings and let marinate, in the refrigerator, for at least 6 hours but preferably 24, turning the wings occasionally.

3. Set up the grill for direct grilling and preheat to medium-high.

4. When ready to cook, drain the chicken wings, then thread each wing on a skewer, running the skewer through all three sections to hold the wing open as wide as possible.

5. Brush and oil the grill grate. Arrange the wings on the hot grate with the aluminum foil shield under the ends of the skewers. Grill, turning with tongs, until the thicker wing sections are no longer pink near the bone, 12 to 16 minutes in all, brushing the wings with the reserved marinade as they cook. Reduce the heat if the wings start to burn. Don't baste the wings during the last 3 minutes of grilling. Transfer the grilled wings to a serving platter and serve at once.

U.S.A.

EAT IT & BEAT IT WINGS

INDIRECT GRILLING
MAKES 12 CHICKEN WINGS

A restaurant with a name like Kansas City's Lil' Jake's Eat It & Beat It (today known by the more dignified name of Danny Edwards) takes a pretty rapid-fire approach to customer turnover. When it comes to barbecue, however, proprietor Danny Edwards definitely takes his time. These wings absorb a spice rub overnight, then they're smoke-grilled until they are fall-off-the-bone tender. Quantities for the various seasonings are approximate: Add more or less to suit your taste.

ADVANCE PREPARATION

24 hours for curing the chicken wings

SPECIAL EQUIPMENT

1½ cups wood chips or chunks, preferably hickory, soaked for 1 hour in cold water to cover, then drained

INGREDIENTS

12 whole chicken wings (2½ to 3 pounds)
2 teaspoons garlic salt
2 teaspoons black pepper
2 teaspoons cayenne pepper
2 teaspoons crumbled dried oregano

1. Rinse the chicken wings under cold running water, then drain and blot dry with paper towels. Place the wings in a large bowl and sprinkle the garlic salt, black pepper, cayenne, and oregano over them. Turn the wings to coat them with the seasonings, then cover and refrigerate them, for 24 hours.

2. Set up the grill for indirect grilling and place a drip pan in the center.

If using a charcoal grill, preheat the grill to medium-low. When the coals are ready, toss half of the drained wood chips on them.

If using a gas grill, place all of the wood chips in the smoker box and preheat the grill to high; when smoke appears, lower the heat to medium-low.

3. When ready to cook, brush and oil the grill grate. Arrange the wings on the hot grate over the drip pan. Cover the grill and cook the wings until very tender, 1½ to 2 hours. If using a charcoal grill, you'll need to add 10 to 12 fresh coals and a handful of chips to each side after 1 hour.

4. Transfer the grilled wings to a serving platter and serve at once.

CHINA

GRILLED SHRIMP DIM SUM

DIRECT GRILLING
MAKES 12

Grilling is not one of the primary cooking techniques in Chinese cuisine. But many Chinese dishes lend themselves to live-fire cooking. Consider the following shrimp dish, which is traditionally served as dim sum. Grilling the shrimp instead of deep-frying them has the dual advantage of heightening the flavor and reducing the fat.

SPECIAL EQUIPMENT

12 short bamboo skewers and an aluminum foil shield (see box, page 23)

INGREDIENTS

12 large shrimp
12 scallions
6 lean slices of bacon

1. Peel and devein the shrimp (see the box on page 361). Trim the greens off the scallions, reserving them for another use, then trim off the roots; you should be left with approximately 2-inch sections of scallion white. Cut the slices of bacon in half crosswise.

2. Nestle each scallion white in the curved hollow of a shrimp, then wrap a piece of bacon around it and secure with a bamboo skewer or toothpick by running the skewer or toothpick through the wrapped shrimp.

3. Set up the grill for direct grilling and preheat to medium-high.

4. When ready to cook, brush and oil the grill grate. Arrange the dim sum on the hot grate with the aluminum foil shield under the ends of the skewers. Grill, turning once with tongs, until the shrimp are firm and pink and the bacon is crisp, 2 to 4 minutes per side. Serve at once.

VIETNAM

SHRIMP MOUSSE ON SUGARCANE

CHAO TOM

DIRECT GRILLING
MAKES 12 KEBABS

Chao tom, shrimp mousse grilled on sugarcane, is one of the most distinctive dishes in Vietnam. Talk about a dazzling contrast of flavors and textures, *chao tom* has it all: soft shrimp mousse and crispy, dulcet sugarcane. You don't really eat the cane so much as chew on it, releasing sweet juices that balance the saltiness of the shrimp. Fresh sugarcane is available in most major supermarkets.

ADVANCE PREPARATION

2 hours for chilling the mousse

INGREDIENTS

- **1 pound large shrimp, peeled and deveined (see box, page 361)**
- **2 ounces pork fat or salt pork (optional), diced**
- **1 clove garlic, minced**
- **1 scallion, both white and green parts, trimmed and minced**
- **1 tablespoon sugar, or more to taste**
- **1 tablespoon Asian fish sauce**
- **1 tablespoon peanut oil, plus additional oil for forming the kebabs**
- **1 teaspoon Vietnamese or Thai hot sauce**
- **½ teaspoon salt (see Notes), or more to taste**
- **½ teaspoon freshly ground black pepper, or more to taste**
- **3 pieces sugarcane (each 6 to 8 inches long)**

1. Combine the shrimp, pork fat (if using), garlic, scallion, and sugar in a food processor and process to a coarse puree. Running the food processor in spurts, add the fish sauce, peanut oil, hot sauce, salt, and pepper. Cook a small amount of the shrimp mousse in a nonstick skillet until cooked through, then taste for seasoning, adding more sugar, salt, and/or pepper to the remaining shrimp mixture as necessary; it should be highly seasoned. Transfer the shrimp mousse to a bowl, cover, and refrigerate until well chilled, about 2 hours.

2. Using a sharp, heavy knife, peel the sugarcane and cut each piece lengthwise into 4 quarters. Lightly oil the fingers of one hand. Take about 3 tablespoons of the shrimp mousse and mold it around the top half of a piece of sugarcane. This will feel awkward at first, but soon you'll be doing it like a pro. Continue in this fashion until all the sugarcane pieces are prepared. Arrange the kebabs on a lightly oiled plate, cover with plastic wrap, and refrigerate until ready to grill.

3. Set up the grill for direct grilling and preheat to high.

4. When ready to cook, brush and oil the grill grate. Arrange the kebabs on the hot grate and grill, turning once with tongs, until the shrimp mousse is lightly browned, firm, and cooked through, 2 to 3 minutes per side. Serve the kebabs at once, eating them by nibbling the shrimp mousse off the cane. Be sure to chew on the cane to extract the sweet juice.

NOTES: If you are using salt pork, add only ¼ teaspoon of salt to the shrimp.

You can substitute 12 sugarcane swizzle sticks for the pieces of sugarcane. Swizzle sticks are available at specialty food shops at many supermarkets.

FRANCE

GRILLED SNAILS

ESCARGOTS GRILLES

DIRECT GRILLING
MAKES 2 DOZEN SNAILS

No one can accuse me of not going the distance for a recipe. Consider this one, from the restaurant L'Hostal in Castellnou, France (read about it on page 83). L'Hostal's chef uses lard for basting the snails. That's right, lard. I know that lard is not the most fashionable ingredient in the United States, but, for starters, it has a unique meaty flavor you just can't duplicate with butter. It's also healthier than butter, believe it or not, containing half the cholesterol and one third of the saturated fat. But you can certainly use butter in this dish if lard turns you off. By the way, the shallots, garlic, and celery should be chopped so fine they would blow away if you breathed too hard.

Under the best circumstances, you'd build your fire with grapevine trimmings. The second best alternative is charcoal, with a few soaked grapevine trimmings or wine barrel chips tossed on the coals. But rest assured that eminently respectable grilled snails can be cooked on a gas grill.

SPECIAL EQUIPMENT

Vegetable grate or wire cake rack

INGREDIENTS

2 dozen canned escargots with shells (if possible, try to buy petits gris)
12 tablespoons lard or unsalted butter, or a mixture of both, at room temperature
2 large shallots, very finely minced
3 cloves garlic, very finely minced
1 medium-size rib celery, very finely minced
3 tablespoons minced fresh flat-leaf parsley
1 teaspoon fresh thyme leaves, or ½ teaspoon dried thyme
½ teaspoon curry powder
Salt and freshly ground black pepper

1. Drain the escargots in a colander and rinse well under cold running water. Drain again and blot dry with paper towels. Melt 3 tablespoons of the lard in a medium-size saucepan over medium heat. Add the shallots, garlic, celery, parsley, thyme, and curry powder, then season with salt and pepper to taste. Cook the vegetables until they are soft and translucent but not brown, about 3 minutes. Remove the pan from the heat and let the vegetable mixture cool to room temperature.

2. Whisk the remaining 9 tablespoons of lard into the cooled vegetable mixture. Using the tip of a butter knife, place a portion of the vegetable mixture about the size of a hazelnut in each escargot shell. Insert an escargot in each shell, then fill it with some of the remaining vegetable mixture. After each snail shell has been filled, place it on a baking sheet or platter (see Note).

3. Set up the grill for direct grilling and preheat to high.

4. When ready to cook, place a vegetable grate or wire cake rack on top of the grill grate. Arrange the snails, open side up, on the rack and grill until the filling is bubbling and fragrant, 3 to 5 minutes. Use tongs to transfer the snails to plates and serve at once.

NOTE: The recipe can be prepared to this point up to several hours in advance. Refrigerate the snails, loosely covered with plastic wrap, until you are ready to grill.

TRINIDAD

GRILLED EGGPLANT DIP

CHOKA DIP

DIRECT GRILLING
MAKES ABOUT 2½ CUPS

There is no shortage of grilled eggplant dishes in the world, but this one—a dip that is a specialty of Trinidad's Indian community—is one of the few I know of in which the eggplant is studded with garlic cloves before grilling. What results is an incredible depth of flavor. I often use this Trinidadian technique when I grill eggplant for another use.

Serve this as a dip with Grilled Pita Chips.

2 long, slender eggplants (about 2 pounds in all)
8 cloves garlic, peeled and cut lengthwise in half
½ cup plain whole-milk yogurt
¼ cup chopped fresh cilantro
3 scallions, both white and green parts, trimmed and finely chopped
2 teaspoons ground coriander
2 teaspoons grated peeled fresh ginger
2 tablespoons fresh lemon juice
2 tablespoons vegetable oil
Salt and freshly ground black pepper
Grilled Pita Chips (page 125)

1. Using the tip of a paring knife, make 8 small slits in each eggplant. Insert a half clove of garlic in each slit.

2. Set up the grill for direct grilling and preheat to high.

3. When ready to cook, place the eggplants on the hot grate and grill, turning with tongs, until the skin is charred all over and the flesh is very soft, 20 to 30 minutes; the eggplants will have lost their firm shape. Transfer the eggplants to a plate to cool.

Stalking the Elusive Grilled Snail

Barbecue lends itself to obsession. If you're afflicted with an obsessive personality like me and you start to delve into the world of barbecue, you may soon find all your spare time literally going up in smoke. The truth is well known to the legions of barbecue "widows" who have lost their husbands to barbecue contests and smoke fests. This truth became apparent during a ten-day swing through the south of France to study the elusive art of French grilling.

Barbara (my wife) and I had been on the road for about a week, and this being Sunday, it was to be our first night "off" (without any special dining plans). Then I made the fatal mistake of calling French culinary authority Patricia Wells, who told me about grilled snails.

Grilled snails are the specialty of a restaurant called L'Hostal in the hamlet of Castellnou near Perpignan in southwestern France. The problem was that we were in Arles (the Provençal town immortalized by Van Gogh), some four hundred miles away.

A call to the restaurant confirmed that yes, they had grilled snails. Yes, I could order them for this evening. No, the restaurant would not be open Monday or Tuesday. Yes, it was too bad we were leaving France on Wednesday. Yes, if we wanted grilled snails, we'd have to eat them that night.

I did some quick calculations. If we left our hotel in ten minutes and drove a hundred miles an hour, we could be in Castellnou by sundown. I turned to Barbara and said, "I've just found a place that serves grilled snails."

"Great," she said. "Let's go."

"There's only one problem," I said. "The restaurant is near the Spanish border."

Luckily, when it comes to barbecue, my wife is nearly as obsessive as I am.

True to my calculations, we arrived in Castellnou four hours later, having averaged a hundred miles an hour on the autoroute. The last six miles took us up a steep, winding road to a perfectly restored medieval citadel. We found L'Hostal without much trouble (it being the only restaurant in town). Still vibrating from the drive, we took our seats on a cliffside terrace that had a dazzling view of the Roussillon valley.

In the summer, L'Hostal does its grilling in a huge outdoor fireplace. In the winter, the operations are moved to the manorial hearth in the low-ceilinged dining room. The favored fuel here is vine trimmings—branches for delicate fare, like snails; vine stalks and roots for large cuts of meat. When we arrived, sure enough, four dozen tiny snails were sizzling away on a circular wire grill over blazing vine trimmings.

With tolls, gas, and a place to stay for the evening, the trip to Castellnou cost $400. Which makes this one of the most expensive dishes of escargots I've ever eaten. It was worth the drive—and the money—for I've never seen grilled escargots anywhere else.

In one sense, neither you nor I will ever be able to reproduce this recipe at home. We probably can't get the tiny, succulent escargots known locally as *petits gris* (little grays). We certainly can't buy them live or feed them fresh thyme in special cages in our basements. We can't buy snail grills, although a vegetable grate or round cake rack perched on a couple of bricks will work in a pinch.

Ultimately, we will never be able to duplicate the texture and flavor of L'Hostal's grilled snails: the texture being soft, moist, even a little "drooly" (*baveuse* in French); the taste being pungent, salty, and aromatic, with overtones of thyme and even curry.

But I love a challenge. So, although we may not be able to duplicate the dish, I've come up with a recipe for highly delicious grilled snails inspired by L'Hostal's preparation (see page 81). As for the grill, well, Barbara is still wondering what happened to our cake rack.

4. Cut the stem end off the eggplants. Then, using a paring knife, scrape off the charred skin. Transfer the eggplant flesh, with its garlic, to a medium-size bowl and mash to a coarse puree with a fork or puree it in a food processor. Stir in the yogurt, cilantro, scallions, coriander, ginger, lemon juice, and oil. Season the dip with salt and pepper to taste. Serve at once with the pita chips.

IRAN

PERSIAN EGGPLANT DIP WITH WALNUTS

DIRECT GRILLING
MAKES ABOUT 1½ CUPS

I first sampled this tangy dip at a Persian (Iranian) restaurant in New York called Persepolis. If you think baba ghanoush is good (see the next recipe), wait until you taste this. What makes this dip so distinctive is the addition of walnuts and a tangy farmer cheese called *kashk-bibi*. Before you despair of finding the latter (it's available in Middle Eastern markets), know that its sharp flavor is easily approximated by using feta cheese and a spoonful of feta brine (the liquid in which most fetas come packed).

Serve this as a dip with Grilled Pita Chips.

1 large or 2 small eggplants (about 1 pound in all)
¼ cup walnut pieces, lightly toasted (see box, page 113)
1 ounce feta cheese packed in brine, drained, 1 tablespoon brine reserved
1 clove garlic, minced
3 tablespoons plain yogurt, preferably whole milk
3 tablespoons extra-virgin olive oil
1 teaspoon fresh lemon juice, or more to taste
Salt and freshly ground black pepper
1 tablespoon dried mint
Grilled Pita Chips (page 125)

1. Set up the grill for direct grilling and preheat to high.

2. When ready to cook, place the eggplant on the hot grate and grill, turning with tongs, until the skin is charred all over and the flesh is very soft, 20 to 30 minutes; the eggplant will have lost its firm shape. Transfer the eggplant to a plate to cool.

3. Grind the walnuts to a coarse powder in a food processor, running the machine in bursts. Cut the stem end off the eggplant. Then, using a paring knife, scrape off the charred skin. Add the eggplant flesh to the ground nuts in the food processor.

4. Crumble the feta and add it to the processor along with the garlic, then process to a smooth puree. Add the reserved feta brine, yogurt, 2 tablespoons of the olive oil, and the lemon juice. Season with salt and pepper to taste, then process until smooth. Taste for seasoning, adding more lemon juice and/or salt as necessary; the dip should be highly seasoned. Transfer the dip to a serving bowl. Make a slight hollow in the center of the dip with the back of a spoon and set it aside.

5. Heat the remaining 1 tablespoon of olive oil in a small skillet over medium heat. Add the mint and cook, stirring, until fragrant, about 1 minute. Pour the mint oil into the hollow in the dip and serve at once with the pita chips.

MIDDLE EAST

MIDDLE EASTERN EGGPLANT PUREE WITH TAHINI

BABA GHANOUSH

DIRECT GRILLING
MAKES ABOUT 2¼ CUPS

Baba ghanoush is one of those ethnic dishes that has crossed over to the North American mainstream. To prepare it correctly, you must char the eggplant on a grill. The charring imparts an intense characteristic smoke flavor that makes this one of the most popular items on a Middle Eastern meze (appetizer) platter. There's one nontraditional element here—the studding of the eggplant with garlic cloves before grilling—a technique I picked up in Trinidad.

Serve this as a dip with Grilled Pita Chips.

2 long, slender eggplants (about 2 pounds in all)
7 cloves garlic, 6 peeled and cut lengthwise in half, 1 minced
2 scallions, both white and green parts, trimmed and finely chopped
3 tablespoons tahini
4 tablespoons extra-virgin olive oil, or more to taste
3 tablespoons fresh lemon juice, or more to taste
Salt and freshly ground black pepper
Grilled Pita Chips (page 125)

1. Using the tip of a paring knife, make 6 small slits in each eggplant. Insert a half clove of garlic in each slit.

2. Set up the grill for direct grillling and preheat to high.

3. When ready to cook, place the eggplants on the hot grate and grill, turning with tongs, until the skin is charred all over and the flesh is very soft, 20 to 30 minutes; the eggplants will have lost their firm shape. Transfer the eggplants to a plate to cool.

4. Cut the stem end off the eggplants. Then, using a paring knife, scrape off the charred skin. Transfer the eggplant flesh to a food processor. Add the minced garlic, scallions, tahini, 3 tablespoons of the olive oil, and the lemon juice. Season with salt and pepper to taste, then process until smooth. Taste for seasoning, adding more lemon juice and/or salt as necessary; the mixture should be very tangy.

5. Spoon the baba ghanoush into a serving bowl and drizzle the remaining 1 tablespoon of olive oil over it. Serve at once with the pita chips.

TURKEY

YOGURT-CUCUMBER SALAD WITH MINT

CACIK

ON THE SIDE
MAKES ABOUT 2 CUPS

Part dip and part salad, *cacik* (pronounced ja-jik) turns up on meze (hors d'oeuvre) platters throughout Turkey—not to mention in Greece, where it goes by the name of *tzatziki*. (I think of it as eastern Mediterranean guacamole.) There isn't a more refreshing dish for warm weather than this cooling combination of yogurt, mint, and cucumber—a perfect dip for a summer cookout. For an exceptionally rich *cacik,* drain the yogurt for four hours, as described in Step 1. But don't worry if you don't have time to drain the yogurt; the *cacik* will still be extremely tasty.

Serve this as a dip with wedges of fresh pita bread.

ADVANCE PREPARATION

4 hours for draining the yogurt (optional), plus 20 minutes for draining the cucumber

INGREDIENTS

2 cups plain whole-milk yogurt (see Notes)
1 European (seedless) cucumber, or 1 large regular cucumber
1 teaspoon salt, or more to taste
1 to 2 cloves garlic, minced
3 tablespoons finely chopped fresh mint or dill (see Notes)
2 tablespoons extra-virgin olive oil
Freshly ground black pepper
Pita bread, for serving

1. If draining the yogurt, set a yogurt strainer, or regular strainer lined with a double layer of dampened cheesecloth, over a medium-size bowl. Add the yogurt and let drain, in the refrigerator, for 4 hours. You should wind up with about 1¼ cups.

2. Peel the cucumber and seed it, if necessary (see the box on page 85), then coarsely grate or finely chop it. Place the grated cucumber in a colander and toss it with ½ teaspoon of salt. Place the colander over a bowl or in the sink and let the cucumber stand for 20 minutes to drain off some of the excess water. Rinse the cucumber and blot it dry with paper towels.

3. Transfer the drained yogurt to a serving bowl. Stir the cucumber, garlic, 2 tablespoons of the mint, 1 tablespoon of the olive oil, and the remaining ½ teaspoon of salt into the yogurt. Taste for seasoning, adding pepper to taste and more salt as necessary.

4. To serve, make a slight hollow in the center of the *cacik* with the back of a spoon and pour the remaining 1 tablespoon of olive oil into the depression (for a less formal presentation, simply drizzle the remaining olive oil on top). Decorate the top of the *cacik* with the remaining 1 tablespoon of mint. (One traditional presentation is to sprinkle the mint in two intersecting lines to make a cross. If you decide to serve the *cacik* this way, don't make a hollow in the yogurt; simply drizzle the olive oil over the top.) Serve the *cacik* at once with pita bread.

NOTES: You'll need only 1¼ cups of yogurt if you don't plan to drain it.

If fresh mint or dill is not available, you can substitute 1 tablespoon dried mint or dill. Add 2 teaspoons to the yogurt in Step 3 and sprinkle the remaining teaspoon over the *cacik* before serving.

ARGENTINA

GRILLED PROVOLONE

PROVOLONE ASADO

DIRECT GRILLING
SERVES 6 TO 8

This popular Argentinean appetizer defies the laws of culinary physics. Doesn't cheese melt when heated? Wouldn't it become unmanageably gooey on the grill? The fact is that provolone holds its shape beautifully during grilling, acquiring a silky texture and a charred, smoky flavor that balances the cheese's peppery, pungent bite. One thing is for sure, this dish is certainly popular: Visit any steak house in Buenos Aires and you'll see huge platters of provolone slices, stacked up like chips at a casino, ready for grilling.

SPECIAL EQUIPMENT

Two-pronged barbecue fork

INGREDIENTS

2 slices (each about 8 ounces and 1½ inch thick) aged provolone (the older and firmer the better)
1 to 2 tablespoons extra-virgin olive oil
2 teaspoons dried oregano
Freshly ground black pepper
Crusty Italian bread, for serving (see Note)

1. Set up the grill for direct grilling and preheat to high.

2. When ready to cook, brush and oil the grill grate. Brush the cheese slices on both sides with olive oil and sprinkle ½ teaspoon of the oregano and some pepper on top of each. Place the cheese slices on the hot grate. Cook until the bottom side is browned and beginning to bubble, but not completely melted. This will take 2 to 4 minutes.

3. Using the prongs of a barbecue fork, pry the cheese off the grill. Turn the cheese slices over and sprinkle the remaining teaspoon of oregano on top, dividing it evenly between them. Sprinkle some pepper over the cheese, then grill the second side the same way, 2 to 4 minutes longer.

4. Transfer the grilled cheese to a plate. To eat, spread the melted cheese on chunks or slices of bread.

NOTE: Although it's not traditional, for an even richer charcoal flavor you could slice the bread and toast it on the grill.

MEXICO

GRILLED QUESADILLAS

DIRECT GRILLING
MAKES 48 WEDGES

Ten years ago, few of us had heard of quesadillas. Now we can't seem to live without them. These Mexican grilled cheese "sandwiches," made from chiles and cheese sandwiched between tortillas, have taken the United States by storm. Most are panfried, but this recipe features a quesadilla that's actually cooked on the grill. Feel free to vary the ingredients for the filling, but don't wander away when cooking them. Tortillas burn like paper.

1¼ cups coarsely grated Jack or sharp white Cheddar cheese
½ cup sour cream
2 scallions, both white and green parts, trimmed and thinly sliced
1 Flame-Roasted Tomato (recipe follows), seeded (see box, page 454) and diced
¼ cup fresh cilantro leaves
2 to 3 pickled jalapeño peppers, thinly sliced (see Note)
½ teaspoon ground cumin
Salt and freshly ground black pepper
8 flour tortillas (8 inches each)

1. Combine the cheese, sour cream, scallions, tomato, cilantro, jalapeños, and cumin in a small bowl and stir to mix. Season with salt and black pepper to taste.

2. Set up the grill for direct grilling and preheat to medium-high.

3. When ready to cook, place 4 tortillas on a work surface and spread the cheese mixture evenly over them. Press the remaining tortillas on top to make sandwiches.

4. Brush and oil the grill grate. Place the quesadillas on the hot grill grate and grill until lightly browned on both sides, 2 to 4 minutes per side, turning them carefully with a large spatula. Cut each quesadilla into 8 wedges before serving.

NOTE: For spicier quesadillas, use thinly sliced fresh jalapeños, with or without the seeds.

FLAME-ROASTED TOMATOES

DIRECT GRILLING

Some of the recipes in this book call for peeled and seeded tomato. Why bother doing either? Tomato skin, especially when cooked, can turn into red filaments that get caught in your teeth. Tomato seeds come in a watery pulp that can dilute the flavor of the dish.

Mexicans have devised an ingenious method for peeling tomatoes. They char the tomatoes on the grill (or on a *comal,* or griddle). The charred skins impart a great smoky flavor and slip off easily.

Ripe tomatoes

1. Set up the grill for direct grilling and preheat to high.

2. When ready to cook, arrange the tomatoes on the hot grill grate and grill, turning with tongs, until the skin blackens and blisters, 8 to 12 minutes. Transfer the tomatoes to a plate or platter to cool.

3. Scrape the burnt skin off the tomatoes with a paring knife. Don't worry if you can't remove every last bit; a little burnt skin adds a nice smoky flavor.

GRILLED QUESADILLAS | AT LEFT

U.S.A.

GOAT CHEESE GRILLED IN GRAPE LEAVES

DIRECT GRILLING
MAKES 8 BUNDLES

A rustic French cheese called *banon* (BAN-awh) inspired this dish. It's a specialty of the Alps Maritime region. The cheese is made from cow's or goat's milk, then wrapped in chestnut leaves and cured with marc (a brandy made from the residue of grapes after the juice has been extracted), which gives it a nutty, slightly winey flavor. I've taken the idea one step further, grilling the cheese in grape leaves. The grilled grape leaves impart a piquant, woodsy flavor to the cheese while keeping it exquisitely moist and creamy. You want to use a soft goat cheese for this recipe; good choices would include Montrachet, bûcheron, or a young crottin de Chavignol.

ADVANCE PREPARATION

15 minutes for soaking the grape leaves, plus 15 minutes to 8 hours for refrigerating the grape leaf bundles

INGREDIENTS

16 bottled grape leaves packed in brine, drained
8 sun-dried tomatoes, plain or packed in oil
8 ounces goat cheese, cut into 8 slices
3 tablespoons pine nuts (optional), toasted (see box, page 113)
1 teaspoon fresh thyme leaves, or ½ teaspoon dried thyme
Freshly ground black pepper
1 tablespoon extra-virgin olive oil
16 small, thin slices of French bread or pumpernickel

1. Place the grape leaves in a large bowl, add cold water to cover, and let soak for 15 minutes, changing the water two or three times.

2. If using dry sun-dried tomatoes, soak them in hot water to cover for 15 minutes. If using oil-packed dried tomatoes, there is no need to soak them.

3. Drain the grape leaves and blot them dry with paper towels. Spread out 8 of the leaves on a work surface. Drain the tomatoes, blot them dry, and cut into thin slivers. Place a slice of cheese in the center of each grape leaf. Sprinkle the slivered tomatoes, pine nuts (if using), thyme, and some pepper over the cheese and drizzle the olive oil on top. Bring the edges of a grape leaf up around the cheese. Place a second grape leaf on top and turn the edges under so the cheese is entirely covered. Repeat with the remaining grape leaves. Transfer the grape leaf bundles to a baking sheet or platter, cover them loosely with plastic wrap, and refrigerate them for at least 15 minutes or up to 8 hours.

4. Set up the grill for direct grilling and preheat to high.

5. When ready to cook, brush and oil the grill grate. Arrange the grape leaf bundles on the hot grate seam side up and grill, turning once with a spatula, until the grape leaves brown and the cheese begins to melt, about 2 minutes per side.

6. Place the bread slices on the grate and grill until golden brown, 1 to 2 minutes per side. Serve at once, unwrapping the grape leaves (they are not eaten) and eating the melted cheese with a fork or spread on the toasted bread.

U.S.A.

BACON GRILLED PRUNES

DIRECT GRILLING
MAKES 16

Here's proof that some of the world's tastiest dishes are also the most simple. This recipe consists of only two ingredients—bacon and prunes—but the contrast of sweet and salty, meaty and fruity, crisp and chewy makes this an irresistible appetizer. I like to use an artisanal cob-smoked bacon, but a lean supermarket brand would do perfectly well.

SPECIAL EQUIPMENT

16 short, thin bamboo skewers and an aluminum foil shield (see box, page 23)

INGREDIENTS

4 lean slices of bacon, or more as needed
16 pitted prunes

1. Cut each slice of bacon crosswise into 4 pieces; each piece should be just large enough to wrap up a prune. Wrap each prune in bacon and secure it with a bamboo skewer or toothpick by running the skewer or toothpick through the center of the prune and out the other side.

2. Set up the grill for direct grilling and preheat to medium-high.

3. When ready to cook, brush and oil the grill grate. Arrange the bacon-wrapped prunes on the hot grate with the aluminum foil shield under the ends of the skewers. Grill, turning once with tongs, until the prunes are heated through and the bacon is crisp, 2 to 3 minutes per side. Transfer the grilled prunes to a platter and serve at once.

ITALY

PANCETTA GRILLED FIGS

DIRECT GRILLING
MAKES 12

Using fresh figs and pancetta adds an Italian twist to the preceding recipe. Fresh figs were once deemed fairly exotic, but you can now find them in most supermarkets (and certainly in Italian markets), especially in late spring and summer. Pancetta is often described as cured Italian bacon. Unlike our bacon, though, it's never smoked. Pancetta can be found in Italian markets, specialty food shops, and an increasing number of supermarkets.

SPECIAL EQUIPMENT

12 small bamboo skewers and an aluminum foil shield (see box, page 23)

INGREDIENTS

6 thin slices pancetta
12 ripe figs (see Note)
12 fresh sage leaves

1. Cut each strip of pancetta in half; each piece should be just large enough to wrap up a fig. Top each fig with a sage leaf, then wrap it in pancetta, and secure it with a small bamboo skewer by running the skewer through the center of the fig and out the other side.

2. Set up the grill for direct grilling and preheat to medium-high.

3. When ready to cook, brush and oil the grill grate. Arrange the figs on the hot grate with the aluminum foil shield under the ends of the skewers. Grill, turning once with tongs, until the figs are heated through and the pancetta is crisp, 2 to 4 minutes per side. Transfer the grilled figs to a platter and remove the skewers before serving.

NOTE: You could also use dried figs for this recipe. Soak them in a bowl of boiled water (or, better yet, hot Marsala wine or port) for about 30 minutes, or until soft, then drain them and proceed with the recipe.

INDONESIA

QUAIL EGG SATES

SATE TELOR

DIRECT GRILLING
MAKES 24

One of the most unusual satés in Indonesia, *saté telor* is a tiny kebab of immature chicken eggs—a specialty of the city of Kudus in central Java. *Saté telor* is the traditional accompaniment to *ayam soto* (Javanese chicken soup). I make it with quail eggs, but quartered hard-cooked chicken eggs are acceptable substitutes. The sweet, peppery glaze and crisply fried shallots make this a must try for the adventurous griller. Serve these satés as a pass-around or at-table hors d'oeuvre.

ADVANCE PREPARATION

1 hour for cooling and marinating the eggs

SPECIAL EQUIPMENT

8 short bamboo skewers and an aluminum foil shield (see box, page 23)

INGREDIENTS

24 quail eggs, or 6 chicken eggs
1 cup sweet soy sauce (ketjap manis), or ½ cup each regular soy sauce and molasses
2 cloves garlic, minced
2 tablespoons firmly packed light brown sugar
1 teaspoon freshly ground black pepper
½ teaspoon Accent (MSG; optional)
1 cup vegetable oil, for frying
4 shallots, cut into thin wedges

1. Place the quail or chicken eggs in a large saucepan with cold water to cover and bring gradually to a gentle boil over medium-low heat. Cook the quail eggs for 5 minutes or the chicken eggs for 11 minutes, then remove them from the heat. Immediately set the pan with the eggs in the sink and run cold water into it until the eggshells are cool. Shell the eggs under cold running water and blot them dry with paper towels. If using chicken eggs, cut them into quarters lengthwise. Set the eggs aside while you prepare the glaze.

2. Combine the sweet soy sauce, garlic, brown sugar, pepper, and Accent (if using) in a small deep saucepan (see Note) and bring to a boil over medium-high heat, stirring until the sugar dissolves. Remove the glaze from the heat and set aside to cool to room temperature, about 30 minutes.

3. Add the eggs to the room temperature glaze and stir them gently to coat. Let the eggs marinate for 30 minutes.

4. Heat the oil to 350°F in a small skillet (test the heat by adding a piece of shallot; the oil bubbles should dance). Add the shallots and fry until they are golden brown and crisp, about 2 minutes. Using a slotted spoon, transfer the shallots to paper towels to drain.

5. Set up the grill for direct grilling and preheat to high.

6. When ready to grill the eggs, remove them from the marinade and thread them lengthwise on the skewers, 3 to a skewer. If you are working with egg quarters, gently insert the skewers lengthwise through both the white and the yolk. Brush and oil the grill grate, then arrange the satés on the hot grate with the aluminum foil shield under the ends of the skewers. Grill the eggs, basting them with the glaze and turning once with tongs, until the eggs are heated through, 2 to 4 minutes per side. Sprinkle the satés with the fried shallots and serve at once.

NOTE: The saucepan must be large enough to hold the eggs but narrow enough so the eggs will be covered by the glaze.

VIETNAM

GRILLED EGGS WITH VIETNAMESE SEASONINGS

DIRECT GRILLING
SERVES 4

Here's a Southeast Asian twist on Western hard-cooked eggs. If you're familiar only with the mayonnaise and mustard treatment that hard-boiled eggs receive in the West, the vibrant dipping sauce of chile, lime juice, and fish sauce will come as a revelation. The eggs are roasted over a low flame on the grill instead of being boiled. This particular recipe was inspired by a street vendor in Saigon, but I've seen similar preparations in Thailand and Singapore.

3 tablespoons Asian fish sauce
2 tablespoons fresh lime juice
1 tablespoon sugar
1 clove garlic, minced
1 Thai or bird chile or serrano pepper, stemmed, seeded, and thinly sliced (for a hotter sauce, leave the seeds in)
1 head Boston lettuce, separated into leaves, rinsed, and spun dry
1 small bunch fresh mint, trimmed of large stems
4 large eggs, at room temperature

1. Combine the fish sauce, lime juice, sugar, garlic, and chile in a small bowl and stir until the sugar dissolves. Divide the sauce among 4 tiny bowls. Arrange the lettuce leaves and mint on a platter.

2. Set up the grill for direct grilling and preheat to medium.

3. When ready to cook, pierce a tiny hole in the end of each egg with an egg pricker or needle. Place the eggs on the grill and cook until the shells are browned and the eggs are completely cooked, 10 to 15 minutes, turning often with tongs to ensure even cooking.

4. Serve the eggs in the shell. To eat, shell an egg and cut it in quarters lengthwise. Wrap the quarter eggs in lettuce leaves with a sprig of mint, then dip them in the sauce.

U.S.A.

FIRE-CHARRED TOMATO SOUP

DIRECT GRILLING
SERVES 8 AS A FIRST COURSE

This smoky tomato soup is a long way from the canned version we're all so familiar with. The charred flavor of the vegetables is reinforced by the fire-toasted ancho chile (the dried version of a poblano pepper), and the soup is delectable both hot and cold.

Note that I've made wood chips—not soaked this time—optional. You'll get a richer, smokier flavor if you use them, but the soup will be perfectly delicious even if you don't. Do use gorgeous fresh, ripe tomatoes.

4 large ripe tomatoes (about 3 pounds)
2 medium-size onions, peeled and quartered (leave the root ends on)
2 medium-size red bell peppers
4 tablespoons extra-virgin olive oil
Salt and freshly ground black pepper
1 ancho chile (or 2 if you like spicy food) or another large dried chile, such as pasilla
7 cups homemade vegetable or chicken stock or canned low-sodium broth, or more as needed
3 cloves garlic, minced
1 tablespoon balsamic vinegar, or more to taste
1 tablespoon honey, or more to taste
3 tablespoons mixed chopped fresh herbs, such as basil, thyme, chives, and/or flat-leaf parsley
½ cup plain yogurt, preferably whole milk, or sour cream

1. Cut the tomatoes crosswise into 1-inch-thick slices, removing the stem ends. Brush the tomato slices, onion wedges, and bell peppers generously with olive oil, using 2 tablespoons of it, and season the vegetables with salt and black pepper to taste.

2. Set up the grill for direct grilling and preheat to high. If using a gas grill, place the wood chips (if using) in the smoker box.

3. When ready to cook, if using a charcoal grill, toss the wood chips (if using) on the coals. Brush and oil the grill grate. Arrange the tomatoes, onions, and bell peppers on the hot grate and grill, turning the onions and bell peppers with tongs and the tomato slices with a spatula, until the vegetables are nicely charred all over. The bell peppers will take the longest, 15 to 20 minutes, the tomatoes the shortest, about 8 minutes in all. As they are done, transfer vegetables to a platter to cool.

4. Place the ancho chile on the grill grate and toast quickly, about 20 seconds per side, just until it becomes smoky and brittle. Take care not to let it burn.

5. Using a paring knife, scrape the charred skin and burned bits off the bell peppers and onions (don't worry about removing every last bit). Cut the onion quarters into thin crosswise slices, discarding the roots. Core, seed, and chop the bell peppers.

6. Place 1 cup of the stock in a small saucepan and crumble the toasted ancho chile over it. Heat over medium heat until warm, then remove from the heat and let the chile soak until soft, about 5 minutes.

7. Heat the remaining 2 tablespoons of olive oil in a large saucepan over medium heat. Add the garlic and sliced onions and cook until lightly browned, about 5 minutes. Stir in the grilled tomatoes and bell peppers, the remaining 6 cups of stock, the vinegar and honey, and the ancho chile and its soaking liquid. Season with salt and black pepper to taste. Let the soup simmer for 5 minutes. If it seems too thick, add a little more stock.

8. Transfer the soup to a blender and process to a smooth puree, then return it to the saucepan, pressing it through a strainer if necessary to remove any remaining pieces of charred skin. Stir in 2 tablespoons of the mixed herbs and season with salt and black pepper to taste. If a sharper tasting soup is desired, add a little more vinegar; for a sweeter soup, add a little more honey.

9. To serve, ladle the soup into bowls. Top each serving with a dollop of yogurt and sprinkle the remaining 1 tablespoon of chopped herbs on top.

U.S.A.

GRILLED CORN CHOWDER

DIRECT GRILLING
SERVES 4 TO 6 AS A FIRST COURSE

If you like a smoky flavor and you like chowder, then you'll love this grilled corn chowder—especially if you grill the corn with wood chips. The open flame seems to intensify the sweetness of all the vegetables.

SPECIAL EQUIPMENT

1 cup wood chips, soaked for 1 hour in cold water to cover, then drained

INGREDIENTS

3 ears of corn, shucked
1 medium-size onion, peeled and quartered (leave the root end on)
1 medium-size green bell pepper or poblano pepper
1 medium-size red bell pepper
2 tablespoons olive oil or melted butter, or more as needed
Salt and freshly ground black pepper
2 medium-size all-purpose potatoes, peeled and cut into ¼-inch dice
2 tablespoons all-purpose flour
½ teaspoon fresh thyme leaves, or ¼ teaspoon dried thyme
4 cups homemade chicken or vegetable stock or canned low-sodium broth
1 bay leaf
¾ cup heavy cream or half-and-half
2 tablespoons chopped fresh flat-leaf parsley (optional), for garnish

1. Set up the grill for direct grilling and preheat to high. If using a gas grill, place the wood chips in the smoker box.

2. When ready to cook, if using charcoal, toss the wood chips on the coals. Brush the corn, onion, and bell peppers with a little olive oil and season with salt and black pepper to taste. Arrange the vegetables on the hot grate and grill, turning with tongs, until nicely charred on all sides, 16 to 20 minutes for the bell peppers, 10 to 12 minutes for the onion quarters, and 8 to 12 minutes for the corn. As they cook, baste the vegetables with additional olive oil and season them with more salt and black pepper. As they are done, transfer the vegetables to a platter to cool.

3. Cut the corn kernels off the cobs and place them in a large saucepan. Using a paring knife, scrape the charred skin and burned bits off the bell peppers and onion (don't worry about removing every last bit). Core and seed the bell peppers and cut them into ¼-inch dice. Cut the onion quarters into thin crosswise slices, discarding the roots. Add the bell peppers and onion to the corn in the saucepan.

4. Stir the potatoes, flour, and thyme into the vegetables and cook over medium-high heat for 2 minutes, stirring frequently to prevent burning. Add the stock and bay leaf and bring to a boil, then reduce the heat to low and cook, uncovered, at a gentle simmer until the potatoes are cooked, 8 to 10 minutes. Stir in the cream and cook for 2 minutes longer. Season the soup with salt and black pepper to taste and remove it from the heat. Remove and discard the bay leaf.

5. Spoon the chowder into bowls, sprinkle the parsley (if using) on top, and serve at once.

SPAIN

GRILLED GAZPACHO

DIRECT GRILLING
SERVES 8 AS A FIRST COURSE

Gazpacho is Spain's culinary lifeblood, a refreshing puree of vegetables that blurs the distinction between soup and salad. Grilling adds a smoky dimension that transforms this warm-weather soup from the realm of refreshing to unforgettable. If you are using a food processor, puree the vegetables first, then add the liquids.

SPECIAL EQUIPMENT

2 long bamboo skewers and an aluminum foil shield (see box, page 23)

INGREDIENTS

4 scallions, both white and green parts, trimmed
2 cloves garlic, peeled
1 medium-size red onion, peeled and quartered (leave the root end on)
1/3 cup extra-virgin olive oil
2 slices (each 3/4 inch) country-style white bread or French bread
5 medium-size ripe tomatoes (about 2½ pounds)
1 medium-size red bell pepper
1 medium-size green bell pepper
1 medium-size cucumber, peeled
1/4 cup mixed chopped fresh herbs, such as basil, oregano, tarragon, and/or flat-leaf parsley
2 tablespoons red wine vinegar, or more to taste
½ to 1 cup cold water
Salt and freshly ground black pepper

1. Finely chop the scallion greens and set aside for garnish. Thread the scallion whites crosswise on a skewer and add the garlic cloves. Thread the onion quarters on a second skewer. Lightly brush the scallion whites, garlic, and onion quarters with about 1 tablespoon of the olive oil.

2. Set up the grill for direct grilling and preheat to high.

3. When ready to cook, brush and oil the grill grate. Place the skewered vegetables on the hot grate with the aluminum foil shield under the ends of the skewers. Grill, turning with tongs, until nicely browned, 4 to 8 minutes in all. Transfer the vegetables to a plate to cool. Add the bread slices to the grill grate and grill until darkly toasted, 1 to 2 minutes per side. Set the bread aside. Grill the tomatoes and bell peppers until the skins are nicely charred, about 8 to 12 minutes in all for the tomatoes, 16 to 20 minutes for the peppers. Transfer the tomatoes and bell peppers to a platter to cool. Using a paring knife, scrape the charred skins and burned bits off the tomatoes, onion, and bell peppers (don't worry about removing every last bit). Core and seed the peppers.

4. Cut the scallion whites, garlic, onion, toast, tomatoes, bell peppers, and cucumber into 1-inch pieces. Place the pieces in a blender or food processor, adding the tomatoes first, along with the mixed herbs, wine vinegar, and the remaining olive oil. Process to a smooth puree. Thin the gazpacho to pourable consistency with cold water as needed, and season with salt and black pepper to taste.

5. The gazpacho can be served now, but it will taste even better if you chill it for an hour or so to allow the flavors to blend. Just before serving, taste for seasoning, adding more vinegar and/or salt as necessary. To serve, ladle the gazpacho into bowls and sprinkle the chopped scallion greens on top.

SPICY THAI BEEF SALAD | PAGE 102

CHAPTER 4

BLAZING SALADS

As you travel the world's barbecue trail, you come to recognize certain constants. Consider the pairing of salads with grilled meats. Every culture has a selection of salads that are traditionally served with barbecue, from the *kimchis* (pickled salads) that accompany Korean grilled meats to the lavish salad bars (sometimes offering four dozen different items) found at Brazilian *churrascarias* (barbecue restaurants). Most of these salads are served cold as side dishes (their cool crunch counterpoints the sizzle of the grilled fare), but many are cooked and served hot.

"What is more refreshing than salads when your appetite seems to have deserted you. . . ."

—Alexis Soyer

No ingredient is beyond a diehard grill jockey. In this chapter, you'll find recipes for Grilled Eggplant, Tomato, and Pepper Salad, for a Thai grilled pork salad flavored with roasted rice and chiles, and for grilled chicken salads from both India and Iran. And you'll learn how to prepare a classic *salade niçoise* on the grill—well, not so classic, as it calls for fresh tuna, rather than canned.

You'll also encounter some of the traditional salad platters that accompany Turkish, Mexican, Indonesian, and Lebanese barbecue. They may not be grilled, but are a must alongside dishes that are flame cooked. If all this sounds too exotic, there's also a potato salad that would do a good old North American barbecue proud.

ON THE GRILL

ARMENIA

GRILLED EGGPLANT, TOMATO, AND PEPPER SALAD

FASOULI

DIRECT GRILLING
SERVES 4 TO 6

Love of barbecue cuts across race, nationality, and economic class. Some of my best informants have been taxi drivers, most of whom seem to come from other countries. This salad was inspired by a conversation with an Armenian cabbie in Philadelphia. He called it *fasouli,* which he said means crazy or all mixed up. He preferred to remain anonymous, so wherever he is, thanks for the tip.

The salad can be prepared up to a day ahead of time, but taste it just before serving and adjust the seasoning as needed.

1 medium-size eggplant (about 1 pound)
1 large green bell pepper
1 large red bell pepper
1 pound ripe plum tomatoes
½ cup finely chopped onion
2 cloves garlic, minced
3 tablespoons extra-virgin olive oil
2 tablespoons red wine vinegar, or more to taste
½ cup coarsely chopped fresh flat-leaf parsley
Salt and freshly ground black pepper

1. Set up the grill for direct grilling and preheat to high.

2. When ready to cook, brush and oil the grill grate. Place the eggplant on the hot grate, and grill, turning with tongs, until the skin is charred all over and the flesh is very soft, 20 to 30 minutes; the eggplant will have lost its firm shape. Char the bell peppers and tomatoes the same way, 16 to 20 minutes for the bell peppers, about 8 minutes for the tomatoes. Cook the tomatoes enough to blister the skins but not so much that they become soft. The centers should remain firm. Transfer the charred vegetables to a cutting board to cool.

3. Cut the stem end off the eggplant. Then, using a paring knife, scrape the charred skin off the eggplant, bell peppers, and tomatoes. Core and seed the peppers and core the tomatoes. Cut the vegetables into 1-inch cubes and transfer them to a serving bowl. Stir in the onion, garlic, olive oil, wine vinegar, and parsley. Season the salad with salt and black pepper to taste and more vinegar, as necessary; the salad should be highly seasoned. Serve the salad at once or cover and refrigerate it for up to 24 hours before serving.

SPAIN

SPANISH GRILLED VEGETABLE SALAD

ESCALIVADA

DIRECT GRILLING
SERVES 4 TO 6

Sometimes spelled *escalibada, escalivada* is a Catalan grilled vegetable salad. (*Escalivar* means, in Catalan, to cook in hot ashes.) At a minimum, the vegetables would include onions, red bell peppers, and eggplant, with a generous drizzle of fruity Spanish olive oil. A more elaborate version might include leeks, scallions, celery, and tomatoes, topped with a proper vinaigrette. Traditionally, the vegetables are grilled whole and sliced into thin strips for serving, but you get a richer smoke flavor by preslicing the onions and eggplant. Some grill masters display the vegetables separately on a plate, but you can also toss them together—making a great topping for grilled bread.

FOR THE VEGETABLES

1 large onion
1 large or 2 small long, slender eggplants (about 1 pound)
1 bunch leeks (the smallest, tenderest ones you can find)
1 bunch scallions
2 medium-size red bell peppers
4 medium-size ribs celery
About 2 tablespoons extra-virgin olive oil, preferably Spanish
Salt and freshly ground black pepper

FOR THE VINAIGRETTE

2 tablespoons sherry vinegar or red wine vinegar, or more to taste
½ teaspoon salt, or more to taste
⅓ cup extra-virgin olive oil, preferably Spanish
3 tablespoons finely chopped fresh flat-leaf parsley
Freshly ground black pepper
Lemon wedges, for serving

1. Prepare the vegetables: Peel the onion, leaving the root end intact, then cut through the root into 6 or 8 wedges. Cut the eggplant on the diagonal into ¼-inch slices. Trim the roots and dark green parts off the leeks, leaving only the white portion, then cut the leeks lengthwise in half and rinse well. Blot the leeks dry with paper towels. Trim the roots off the scallions. Brush the onion, eggplant slices, leeks, scallions, bell peppers, and celery generously with olive oil and season with salt and pepper to taste.

2. Set up the grill for direct grilling and preheat to high.

3. When ready to cook, brush and oil the grill grate. Arrange all of the vegetables on the hot grate and grill, turning with tongs, until nicely browned, about 12 minutes in all. Transfer the vegetables as they are done to a cutting board to cool.

4. When cool enough to handle, cut the roots off the onion wedges and thinly slice the onions crosswise. Cut the eggplant slices into ¼-inch slivers. Scrape any burnt skin off the bell peppers, then core, seed, and thinly slice them. Cut the leeks, scallions, and celery into thin crosswise slices. Arrange the vegetable slices in separate piles on plates or a platter or toss to mix.

5. Prepare the vinaigrette: Whisk together the vinegar and ½ teaspoon of salt in a small bowl until the salt dissolves. Whisk in the ⅓ cup of olive oil and the parsley. Season the vinaigrette with black pepper to taste and more salt, if necessary. Spoon the vinaigrette over the vegetables and serve with lemon wedges.

NORTH AFRICA

MOROCCAN EGGPLANT SALAD

SALADE D'AUBERGINES

DIRECT GRILLING
SERVES 4

Like many Moroccan salads, this one is traditionally made by frying the eggplant in oil. I've lightened the recipe by charring the eggplant on the grill. In Morocco you'd use small eggplants, but larger, American-style eggplants work well, too. (Increase the cooking time for the latter.) If you're used to Middle Eastern–style eggplant salads, you'll find that the addition of cumin, paprika, and white pepper lends a soulful North African accent to this one.

4 to 6 small (Italian-style) eggplants, or 2 regular eggplants (1½ pounds in all)
3 tablespoons extra-virgin olive oil
3 tablespoons chopped fresh flat-leaf parsley
2 tablespoons fresh lemon juice, or more to taste
1 clove garlic, minced
½ teaspoon ground cumin
½ teaspoon paprika
½ teaspoon freshly ground white pepper
½ teaspoon salt, or more to taste

1. Set up the grill for direct grilling and preheat to high.

2. When ready to cook, brush and oil the grill grate. Brush the eggplants with about 1½ teaspoons of the olive oil, then place them on the hot grate and grill, turning with tongs, until the skin is charred all over and the flesh is very soft, 15 to 20 minutes for small eggplants; up to 30 minutes for large. Transfer the eggplants to a cutting board to cool.

3. Cut the stem ends off the eggplants and, using a paring knife, scrape off the charred skin. Finely chop the eggplant flesh and transfer it to a serving bowl. Stir in the remaining 1½ teaspoons of olive oil, and the parsley, lemon juice, garlic, cumin, paprika, white pepper, and salt. Taste for seasoning, adding more lemon juice and/or salt as necessary; the salad should be highly seasoned. Serve at room temperature.

LEBANON

LEBANESE EGGPLANT SALAD

SALAFAT EL AHAB

DIRECT GRILLING
SERVES 4

Eggplant has a wonderful ability to absorb the smoky flavors of the grill—a truth appreciated by cooks throughout the Middle East. The contrast of charred eggplant and fresh tomato produces an amazingly flavorful salad. I like to use small Italian-style eggplants, which cook through more quickly than the large American eggplants. If the only thing available is the latter, try to find a long, relatively thin eggplant.

3 to 4 small (Italian-style) eggplants, or 1 regular eggplant (about 1 pound in all)
2 medium-size ripe tomatoes, seeded (see box, page 454) and cut into ¼-inch dice
1 bunch fresh flat-leaf parsley, stemmed and thinly sliced (about ¾ cup)
2 scallions, both white and green parts, trimmed and finely chopped
1 clove garlic (optional), minced
2 tablespoons extra-virgin olive oil, or more to taste
2 tablespoons fresh lemon juice, or more to taste
Salt and freshly ground black pepper

1. Set up the grill for direct grilling and preheat to high.

2. When ready to cook, brush and oil the grill grate. Place the eggplants on the hot grate and grill, turning with tongs, until the skin is charred all over and the flesh is very soft, 15 to 20 minutes for small eggplants; up to 30 minutes for large. Transfer the eggplants to a cutting board to cool.

3. Cut the stem ends off the eggplants. Then, using a paring knife, scrape off the charred skin. Cut the flesh into ¼-inch dice and transfer to a serving bowl. Stir in the tomatoes, parsley, scallions, garlic (if using), olive oil, and lemon juice. Season with salt and pepper to taste. Taste for seasoning, adding more olive oil if the salad seems too dry and/or more lemon juice as necessary; the salad should be highly seasoned.

MOROCCO

GRILLED ZUCCHINI SALAD

DIRECT GRILLING
SERVES 4

Here's a North American twist on a traditional Moroccan salad. Moroccans would fry the zucchini, but I like the robust flavor imparted by grilling. In Morocco it's customary to serve sixteen to twenty different salads at one time. Try matching this with the Moroccan Eggplant Salad (page 97) and the Armenian Grilled Eggplant, Tomato, and Pepper Salad (page 96).

4 small or 3 medium-size zucchini (about 1 pound in all), scrubbed and trimmed
3 tablespoons extra-virgin olive oil
Salt and freshly ground black pepper
12 large fresh mint leaves, slivered, or 1 teaspoon dried mint
2 tablespoons finely chopped fresh flat-leaf parsley
1 tablespoon fresh lemon juice, or more to taste
1 clove garlic, minced
½ teaspoon paprika
¼ teaspoon ground cumin
¼ teaspoon freshly ground white pepper, or more to taste

1. Cut the zucchini into ¼-inch lengthwise slices. Brush each slice with olive oil (you'll need about 1 tablespoon in all) and season with salt and pepper to taste.

2. Set up the grill for direct grilling and preheat to high.

Grilling Vegetables

When scraping the blackened skins from grilled vegetables, don't worry about removing every last bit of charred skin. A little bit left on adds flavor.

3. When ready to cook, brush and oil the grill grate. Arrange the zucchini slices on the hot grate and grill, turning with tongs, until tender and well browned, 10 minutes in all. Transfer the zucchini to a cutting board to cool.

4. Cut each zucchini slice crosswise on the diagonal into ¼-inch strips. Transfer the strips to a serving bowl and stir in the remaining 2 tablespoons of olive oil, and the mint, parsley, lemon juice, garlic, paprika, cumin, and white pepper. Taste for seasoning, adding salt and more white pepper and/or lemon juice as necessary; the salad should be highly seasoned. Serve at room temperature.

ITALY

GRILLED VEGETABLE CAPONATA

DIRECT GRILLING
SERVES 6 AS AN APPETIZER, 4 AS A SALAD

Caponata is Sicily's answer to Russia's eggplant caviar—a cross between a dip and a salad made with sautéed eggplants, bell peppers, and other vegetables, invigorated with olives, capers, and pine nuts. It's just the sort of dish that can be electrified by grilling. Caponata can be served by itself as an antipasto, salad, or side dish, and it would be delicious as a topping for bruschetta. The one unexpected ingredient in this recipe—cocoa powder—adds a pleasant, bittersweet flavor.

The caponata will keep for a week; just be sure to reseason it before serving.

2 long, slender eggplants (about 1½ pounds in all)
8 cloves garlic, peeled and cut lengthwise in half
2 medium-size ripe tomatoes
2 medium-size onions, peeled and cut in quarters (leave on the root ends)
2 medium-size ribs celery, trimmed
1 medium-size red bell pepper
1 medium-size green bell pepper
5 tablespoons extra-virgin olive oil, or as needed
Salt and freshly ground black pepper
3 tablespoons chopped fresh flat-leaf parsley
2 tablespoons pine nuts, toasted (see box, page 113)
2 tablespoons drained capers
2 tablespoons chopped pitted green or black olives
2 tablespoons balsamic vinegar, or more to taste
1½ teaspoons unsweetened cocoa powder

1. Using the tip of a paring knife, make 8 small slits in each eggplant. Insert a half clove of garlic in each slit. Lightly brush the eggplants, tomatoes, onions, celery, and bell peppers with olive oil, using about 2 tablespoons, and season with salt and black pepper to taste.

2. Set up the grill for direct grilling and preheat to high.

3. When ready to cook, brush and oil the grill grate. Arrange the vegetables on the hot grate. Grill the eggplants, turning with tongs, until the skin is charred all over and the flesh is very soft, 20 to 30 minutes. Grill the tomatoes, turning with tongs, until the skin is black and blistered, 8 to 12 minutes. Grill the onions, celery, and bell peppers the same way; these will take 10 to 20 minutes in all. Transfer the vegetables as they are done to a cutting board to cool.

4. Using a paring knife, scrape the charred skin off the vegetables. Cut the stem ends off the eggplants and coarsely chop the flesh. Core the tomatoes, then cut them crosswise in half, wring out the seeds, and coarsely chop the flesh. Cut the root ends off the onions, then thinly slice them and the celery. Core, seed, and thinly slice the bell peppers. Transfer the vegetables to a serving bowl.

5. Stir in the remaining 3 tablespoons of olive oil and the parsley, pine nuts, capers, olives, balsamic vinegar, and cocoa powder. Toss well to mix. Taste for seasoning, adding salt and pepper to taste and more vinegar as necessary; the caponata should be highly seasoned. Serve at room temperature.

A Tale of Three Barbecues: The Thai Grill

This is a tale of one city—and three barbecues. The first embodies the privileged world of Somerset Maugham, the world of the jet-setting gentry that frequents one of Asia's grandest hotels. The second and third reflect a more realistic style of Third World dining. All three take place in Thailand's political and cultural capital: Bangkok. And all reflect the Thais' love of explosive flavors and their profound reverence for food.

Curiously, I did not think of Thailand as one of the world's great barbecue centers. There isn't a single great barbecued dish in Thailand's pantheon of culinary masterpieces. There's no Thai equivalent to Brazilian *churrasco,* to Italian *bistecca alla fiorentina,* to Persian *chelow kebab,* or American ribs.

Yet everywhere I went in Thailand, I experienced grilling—on the beaches of Koh Samui, in the highlands of Chiang Mai, on the crowded streets and back alleys of Bangkok. So strong is the Thai love of *yaang* (live-fire cooking), they reserve it not just for special occasions, but for everyday fare.

Everyday fare? Well that's a mundane way to describe my first experience with Thai grilling: the riverside barbecue at the Oriental hotel. The Oriental is one of those pleasure palaces built in the last century, on the banks of the Chao Phraya river. Joseph Conrad resided there; so did Herman Melville and Somerset Maugham. My room in the Authors' Wing was a veritable two-story town house, with every architectural amenity and electronic convenience known to modern man.

But what had my jaw dropping was a torchlit barbecue on the riverside terrace. Seated at a pink granite table with teak chairs, I was surrounded by globe lights entwined with bougainvillea. Here a whiff of frangipani, there the perfume of jasmine. The long-tail boats skimming the river seemed close enough to touch.

As with everything at the Oriental, barbecue is done in a grandiose way, with banks of grills and a buffet line stretching a good fifty feet. There's a seafood station that fairly sparkles with spiny lobsters, slipper lobsters, fresh and salt water prawns, and a fishmonger's assortment of fish, neatly bedded in ice. There are poultry and meat stations, where chicken, duck, squab, beef, and pork emerge sizzling from the grills.

But despite the fancy surroundings, the basic preparations are really quite simple. The marinades are variations on a mixture of fish sauce (*nam pla*), lime juice, sugar, and garlic. The accompanying table sauces range from a mild, sweet lemon-honey-garlic sauce to an incendiary tincture of chiles, shallots, and fish sauce. I could spend a couple of paragraphs describing the side dishes—the salad spreads, elaborate carved fruit displays, dessert stations where young women in sarongs cook coconut cakes called *kenoms.* But what really impressed me was the straightforwardness of the grilled fare, the elegant simplicity of the fish.

The Hawkers' Center

A few days later, I experienced a similar barbecue in a considerably different setting: a hawkers' center on a tiny side street off traffic-clogged Silom Road. Hawkers' centers are where ordinary Thais eat—a motley assortment of food stalls and pushcarts selling every imaginable Thai street food, from stir-fries and soups to noodle dishes, like pad thai. The air was thick with smoke from charcoal braziers.

I stopped at the cart of a tiny woman for a popular local snack, squid on a stick. She fished the tiny sea creature from a jar where it was marinating in an aromatic mixture of fish sauce, lime juice, palm sugar, garlic, chiles, and lemongrass. The squid went onto a tiny skewer for a two-minute sizzle over the coals. It was sweet, salty, tender, smoky, and absolutely delicious. These, of course, are the same flavors I experienced at the Oriental. But this feast cost all of 10 baht (about 45 cents).

It's no accident that fish sauce is a recurring theme in Thai barbecue. This malodorous condiment—made from salted, fermented anchovies—is as essential to Thai cooking as soy sauce is to Japanese and

Chinese. Fish sauce has a wonderful way of reinforcing the briny flavor of seafood. I suppose this is the reason it's so popular in Thailand as a marinade and dip for grilled fish.

Barbecue in Esarn

Talk to Thais long enough about barbecue and you'll hear the name Esarn. The term refers to both a region and a people: the province in northeastern Thailand adjacent to the Laotian and Cambodian borders, whose inhabitants are of Lao descent.

According to my guide, Nilcharoen Prasertsak, the Esarn became masters of grilling by simple economic necessity. They couldn't afford the oil necessary for stir-frying. So they turned to cooking food over the one commodity even the poor in Thailand have plenty of—coconut shell charcoal. Esarn street vendors are famous throughout Thailand for their *gai yaang* (grilled chicken) and *pla yaang* (grilled fish).

And that is why my next destination was an Esarn neighborhood in the Dusit district of Bangkok. There, houses open directly onto the sidewalks, and women sit crosslegged, washing dishes, clothes, and children in plastic tubs on the ground. Sun filters through the leaves of scraggly trees, and mangy dogs lie in the middle of the streets. The scene is more reminiscent of a village in a jungle than of an Asian metropolis with seven million inhabitants.

To judge from the smoke in the air, I was certainly in barbecue central. Every square foot of sidewalk seemed to be devoted to some sort of culinary activity. On one street corner a man fanned a charcoal fire that was blazing in a hub cap. Elsewhere, women were pounding garlic and spices in mortars with pestles and shredding green papayas to make a fiery Esarn salad called *som tum*.

My destination was a restaurant on Sukhantharam Road. It was clearly a classy joint—you could tell by the flashing jukebox. There were also a framed picture of the King of Thailand, plastic chairs, and pink-clothed tables, and scrawny kittens foraging for scraps on the floor. There was even air-conditioning—a rare luxury in these parts—although there was a 5 baht charge per person for the management to turn it on.

Mr. Noi specializes in the sort of simple but pungent fare for which the Esarn are famous: a *som tum* so laced with chiles, it all but melts your molars; an oxtail soup that soothes your soul while it scorches your gullet; a spatchcocked grilled chicken, all smoky and crisp, redolent of cilantro and garlic. As with most Esarn grilled meats, the chicken was accompanied by a platter of cabbage and celery leaves, basil sprigs, and green beans. The sticky rice came Laotian style, steamed in bamboo. I devoured it Esarn style—with my fingers.

Despite dubious hygienic conditions, there was such goodwill and warm hospitality on the part of the staff, I decided to eat whatever was put in front of me. I survived without so much as a hiccough.

Thai Satés

Incidentally, there's one grilled dish you don't have to risk your gastrointestinal track to enjoy, a dish you'll find wherever you go in Thailand—high-style restaurant or down-home street stall—which is all the more curious, because the dish was invented in a country a thousand miles away: Indonesia. I'm talking, of course, about saté.

Named for the Javanese word meaning to stick or skewer, saté consists of tiny pieces of chicken, pork, or other meats grilled on tiny bamboo skewers. Saté has become quite popular in North America, but nothing here can rival the tiny size and delicate flavor of Thai satés. The sweet soy sauce marinade of Java has given way to a fish sauce–coconut milk mixture. (The oil-rich coconut milk keeps the meat from drying out.) Thai saté is traditionally accompanied by a creamy peanut sauce and a tangy cucumber salad.

Thai barbecue makes the perfect alternative to the meat-laden cookouts of the West. Seafood and vegetables play a major role in Thai grilling. When meats are eaten, it's in small quantities, with a high proportion of vegetables and rice. But even if health is not a concern, you can't beat the dynamic flavor of the Thai grill.

THAILAND

SPICY THAI BEEF SALAD

YAM NUA YANG

DIRECT GRILLING
SERVES 4

This recipe is modeled on Thailand's famous *yam nua yang,* grilled beef salad. I can't think of a better starter or light main course on a warm summer day. The combination of flavors—fiery chiles, fragrant mint, ginger, and garlic—is explosive . . . and addictive. As in other recipes, I offer a range of chiles: one for the tender of tongue and six (or more) for the pyromaniac. Sometimes the salad is topped with roasted rice powder (see the box on page 104) instead of peanuts.

ADVANCE PREPARATION

2 to 8 hours for marinating the meat

FOR THE BEEF AND MARINADE

1 flank steak (1¼ to 1½ pounds)
3 tablespoons soy sauce
2 tablespoons Asian fish sauce
2 tablespoons sugar
3 cloves garlic, minced
1 tablespoon minced peeled fresh ginger

FOR THE DRESSING

3 cloves garlic, peeled
1 to 6 Thai or bird chiles or seranno or jalapeño peppers, stemmed, seeded, and thinly sliced (for a hotter dressing, leave the seeds in)
4½ teaspoons sugar
3 tablespoons Asian fish sauce
3 tablespoons fresh lemon juice

FOR THE SALAD

1 head Boston or Bibb lettuce, separated into leaves, rinsed, and spun dry
1 cucumber, peeled and thinly sliced
12 cherry tomatoes, cut in half
12 fresh mint leaves (optional)
1 small red onion, very thinly sliced
¼ cup fresh cilantro leaves
¼ cup coarsely chopped dry-roasted peanuts

1. Prepare the beef: Lightly score the flank steak in a crosshatch pattern, making the cuts ¼ inch deep. Place the meat in a glass baking dish. Combine the soy sauce, 2 tablespoons of fish sauce, 2 tablespoons of sugar, minced garlic, and ginger in a mixing bowl and whisk until the sugar dissolves. Pour this mixture over the flank steak and let marinate, covered, in the refrigerator for at least 2 hours or as long as 8, turning several times.

2. Prepare the dressing: Combine the garlic cloves, chiles, and 4½ teaspoons of sugar in a mortar and pound to a paste with a pestle. Work in the 3 tablespoons of fish sauce and the lemon juice. If you don't have a mortar and pestle, the ingredients for the dressing can be pureed in a blender or food processor.

3. Prepare the salad: Line a platter with the lettuce leaves and arrange the cucumber, cherry tomatoes, and mint leaves (if using) on top.

4. Set up the grill for direct grilling and preheat to high.

5. When ready to cook, drain the steak. Brush and oil the grill grate, then place the steak on the hot grate and grill until cooked to taste (3 to 5 minutes per side for medium-rare), turning with tongs.

6. Transfer the grilled steak to a cutting board and let cool slightly or completely (the salad can be served warm or at room temperature). Thinly slice the steak across the grain on the diagonal. Spoon the dressing over the salad and arrange the beef slices on top. Sprinkle the onion, cilantro, and roasted peanuts over the salad and serve.

THAILAND

GRILLED PORK WITH A SWEET-TART DRESSING

PORK LAAB

DIRECT GRILLING
SERVES 4 TO 6

Sometimes written *larb, laab* refers to a family of Thai salads made with grilled meats, crisp vegetables, and explosively flavored seasonings. This one features

HOW TO PREPARE FLANK STEAK

A quick-cooking, flavorful cut of meat, flank steak is a favorite for the grill. When sliced correctly on the diagonal, the resulting pieces are tender and attractive.

1. *Using a chef's knife, score the top and bottom of the flank steak in a crosshatch pattern. The cuts should be shallow—about ¼-inch deep.*

2. *Grill the flank steak until nicely browned on the bottom, 3 to 5 minutes. If you like, rotate the steak 90 degrees after 1½ minutes to create an attractive crosshatch of grill marks.*

3. *Turn the flank steak over and grill the second side the same way.*

4. *To serve, thinly slice the flank steak sharply on the diagonal across the grain.*

pork, which is marinated in a pungent mixture of fish sauce and garlic and grilled just prior to serving.

Roasted rice powder gives the salad a nutty flavor and gritty-crunchy consistency much prized by Southeast Asians. If it seems like too much trouble to make, the salad is still amazingly tasty without it. (Or you could use coarsely chopped peanuts in its place.) As elsewhere in this book, I've called for a range of chiles. A Thai would use the full six—or even more.

ADVANCE PREPARATION

1 to 2 hours for marinating the meat

FOR THE PORK AND MARINADE

1 pork tenderloin, or 2 pork chops (each about ½-inch thick; about 8 ounces total)
¼ cup Asian fish sauce
¼ cup fresh lime juice
2 tablespoons firmly packed light brown sugar, or 2 tablespoons honey
3 cloves garlic, minced
½ teaspoon freshly ground black pepper

FOR THE SALAD

1 cucumber, peeled, seeded (see box, page 454), and thinly sliced
2 cups thinly sliced napa cabbage or iceberg lettuce
1 cup mung bean sprouts
2 shallots, sliced paper-thin
1 to 6 Thai chiles or serrano or jalapeño peppers, stemmed, seeded, and thinly sliced (for a hotter salad, leave the seeds in)
2 scallions, both white and green parts, trimmed and thinly sliced
¼ cup fresh mint leaves, plus a few whole sprigs for garnish
¼ cup fresh basil leaves
¼ cup fresh cilantro leaves (or more mint or basil)
2 tablespoons rice powder, for garnish (optional; see box, page 104)

1. Prepare the pork and marinade: Trim any sinew or large pieces of fat off the pork. Combine the fish sauce, lime juice, brown sugar, garlic, and pepper in a medium-size bowl and stir until the sugar dissolves. Transfer half

How to Make Rice Powder

Set a dry skillet over medium heat (do not use a nonstick skillet for this). Add a quarter cup of rice and heat until the grains are lightly toasted and just beginning to brown, two to three minutes, shaking the pan to ensure even cooking (the rice will crackle as it toasts). Transfer the rice to a bowl to cool, then grind it to a fine powder in a spice mill or blender. You should end up with one third cup of rice powder.

of the marinade to a second bowl and set aside for the dressing. Add the pork to the remaining marinade and let marinate, covered, in the refrigerator for 1 to 2 hours, turning the meat several times.

2. Set up the grill for direct grilling and preheat to medium-high if you are cooking pork tenderloin, high if you are cooking pork chops.

3. When ready to cook, drain the pork and blot dry. Set aside the marinade. Brush and oil the grill grate, then place the pork on the hot grate. Grill the pork until cooked through, 6 to 8 minutes per side for a tenderloin, 3 to 5 minutes per side for chops, turning with tongs and basting only the first side with the reserved marinade. When done, the internal temperature of the pork should register 160°F on an instant-read meat thermometer. Transfer the pork to a cutting board and let rest for 5 minutes.

4. Meanwhile, make the salad: Add the cucumber, napa cabbage, bean sprouts, shallots, chiles, scallions, mint, basil, and cilantro to the dressing in the bowl and toss gently but thoroughly to mix. Mound the salad on plates or a platter. Thinly slice the pork on the diagonal and fan out the slices on top of the salads. Sprinkle the salads with the rice powder (if using), garnish with mint sprigs, and serve at once.

INDIA

GRILLED CHICKEN SALAD WITH INDIAN SPICES

MURGH CHAAT

DIRECT GRILLING
SERVES 4

Here's the perfect way to use up leftover chicken or any grilled chicken. The tangy flavors of tomato, cilantro, and lemon juice make this salad particularly refreshing in the summer.

To be strictly authentic, prepare the salad with a spice mix called *chaat masala*. The mix owes its tartness to the addition of *amchur* powder (ground green mango) and its sulphury flavor to a mineral called black salt. *Chaat masala* can be bought ready-made at an Indian grocery store. Or use the Quick Chaat Mix on page 105. The flavor won't be quite the same, but the salad will be delectable nonetheless.

ADVANCE PREPARATION

The chicken must be grilled ahead of time

INGREDIENTS

1 medium-size ripe tomato
½ medium-size green bell pepper, cored and seeded
¼ medium-size red onion
3 cups finely diced (¼ inch) cold grilled chicken
¾ cup chopped fresh cilantro
3 tablespoons vegetable oil
3 tablespoons fresh lemon juice, or more to taste
½ teaspoon ground cumin
½ teaspoon ground coriander
½ teaspoon freshly ground black pepper
2 teaspoons chaat masala or Quick Chaat Mix (recipe follows)
Salt (optional)
Curly leaf lettuce, rinsed and spun dry, for serving

1. Cut the tomato, bell pepper, and onion into ¼-inch dice and place in a large bowl with the chicken.

2. Combine the cilantro, oil, lemon juice, cumin, coriander, pepper, and half of the *chaat masala* in a small bowl and whisk to blend; then pour the mixture over the salad. Toss well to mix and taste for seasoning, adding salt (if using) and/or more lemon juice as necessary; the chicken salad should be highly seasoned.

3. Spoon the salad onto plates lined with lettuce leaves, sprinkle the remaining *chaat masala* over each serving, and serve immediately.

QUICK CHAAT MIX

MAKES ABOUT 1 TABLESPOON

Use the Quick Chaat Mix as a toasted seasoning mix for grilled chicken or sprinkle it over the *raitas* (yogurt sauces) in this book (see page 459).

¼ teaspoon cumin seeds
¼ teaspoon coriander seeds
¼ teaspoon black peppercorns
¼ teaspoon ground ginger
1 teaspoon dried mint leaves
1 teaspoon salt

1. Set a dry skillet over medium heat (do not use a nonstick skillet for this). Add the cumin seeds, coriander seeds, and peppercorns and heat, shaking the pan occasionally, until the spices are fragrant and toasted, about 2 minutes.

2. Allow the spices to cool, then grind them to a powder in a spice mill. Add the ginger, mint leaves, and salt and continue to grind until finely ground. The Quick Chaat Mix can be stored in a tightly capped small jar in a cool, dry place for up to 2 months.

How to Rinse and Dry Cilantro

When it comes to flavoring grilled fare, it's hard to beat cilantro. The leaves of the coriander plant have an unusually pungent flavor that has endeared cilantro to grill jockeys all over the world.

Once the province of ethnic markets, fresh cilantro is now available in virtually any major supermarket. If you're lucky enough to live in an area with a large Hispanic or Asian community, you may be able to find fresh bunches of cilantro with the roots attached. (The roots are used as a flavoring for marinades and spice pastes throughout Southeast Asia.) Fresh cilantro is often very sandy, so before using it, it's best to give the leaves a good rinsing.

To rinse cilantro, hold the bunch by the stems and agitate the leaves in a large bowl of cold water. Change the water once or twice—until it is free of grit.

To dry cilantro, still holding it by the stems, shake it firmly in a wide arc. (This is best done outdoors, of course, so as not to spatter your walls with water.) Alternatively, shake it (somewhat less enthusiastically) in the sink or blot it dry with paper towels. Or, you can use a salad spinner, once you've cut off the roots.

To stem cilantro, pluck small sprigs off the large stems. (It's OK to keep and chop the small stems.)

To keep leftover cleaned cilantro fresh for later use, loosely wrap it in a moist paper towel and store it in an unsealed plastic bag in the refrigerator. It's important that the bag be left unsealed, so that the cilantro leaves can "breathe."

IRAN

PERSIAN CHICKEN SALAD WITH PICKLES AND OLIVES

DIRECT GRILLING
SERVES 4

I first tasted this dish at a fine Persian restaurant in New York called Persepolis. The combination of chicken and potatoes in a salad is as delectable as it's unexpected. It's another great way to use up leftover grilled chicken.

ADVANCE PREPARATION

The chicken must be grilled ahead of time

How to Rinse Salad Greens

Salad greens, such as spinach, are often gritty—especially if you buy them by the bunch at farm stands. To get rid of the grit, separate the leaves from any heavy stems. Place the leaves in a large bowl of cold water and agitate them gently with your fingers, allowing the grit to fall to the bottom of the bowl. Lift the leaves out of the water with your hands and place them in a colander. Pour out the water and refill the bowl with fresh water. Continue rinsing the greens in this fashion—as many as six times—until they are grit free. Always transfer the greens to a colander before discarding the water. If you pour the greens with the water into the colander, you'll just wash the grit back on.

INGREDIENTS

1 pound large red-skinned potatoes, scrubbed
2 large eggs
Salt
2 cups finely diced (1/4 inch) cold grilled chicken
3 tablespoons finely chopped cornichons or dill pickles
2 medium-size ribs celery, very finely diced
1 tablespoon chopped pitted green olives
6 tablespoons mayonnaise
2 tablespoons chopped fresh dill, plus a few sprigs for garnish
Freshly ground black pepper
8 lettuce leaves, rinsed and spun dry, for serving
2 medium-size ripe tomatoes, thinly sliced, for serving
12 black olives, preferably oil-cured, for garnish

1. Place the potatoes and eggs in a pot of cold salted water and bring to a boil over medium heat. Reduce the heat to low and let simmer until the potatoes are tender (they will be easy to pierce with a skewer) and the eggs are hard cooked; 11 minutes should do it (see Note). Drain the potatoes and eggs in a colander and rinse under cold water until cool. Drain well.

2. Cut the potatoes into ¼-inch dice and place them in a large bowl. Add the chicken, cornichons, celery, green olives, mayonnaise, and chopped dill and toss gently but thoroughly to mix. Season with salt and pepper to taste. Shell the hard-cooked eggs, cut them into ¼-inch dice, and add them to the bowl.

3. To serve, line plates or a platter with lettuce leaves. Arrange the tomato slices in a ring around the edge of the plate, overlapping them slightly. Mound the chicken salad in the center and garnish it with the black olives and dill sprigs.

NOTE: The eggs will be done after 11 minutes. The potatoes may take longer.

FRANCE

GRILLED SALADE NIÇOISE

DIRECT GRILLING
SERVES 4 AS A LIGHT MAIN COURSE

The classic salad from Nice is the epitome of Provençal cooking—bright colors and bold flavors in a dish that's refreshing, nourishing, and sustaining. Traditional *salade niçoise* is made with boiled vegetables and canned tuna. To make a more interesting salad, I took to grilling fresh tuna instead. It wasn't long before I was grilling the potatoes, onions, and green beans, too.

Grilling transforms *salade niçoise* into an unforgettable main course. It's practical, too, as all the ingredients can be grilled ahead. Haricots verts are skinny French green beans. Look for them in the produce section of specialty food shops and at some greengrocers, or use the skinniest regular green beans you can find.

ADVANCE PREPARATION

30 minutes for marinating the tuna

SPECIAL EQUIPMENT

Vegetable grate (optional)

FOR THE DRESSING

1 tablespoon fresh lemon juice
1 tablespoon red wine vinegar, or more to taste
2 teaspoons Dijon mustard
1 clove garlic, minced
Salt and freshly ground black pepper
¼ cup extra-virgin olive oil
1 to 2 anchovy fillets (optional), rinsed, blotted dry, and finely chopped
1 tablespoon capers, drained
12 fresh basil leaves, thinly slivered, plus 4 to 6 small sprigs for garnish

FOR THE SALAD

4 tuna steaks (each about 1 inch thick and 6 ounces)
4 tablespoons extra-virgin olive oil
2 tablespoons fresh lemon juice
Coarse sea salt
Cracked black peppercorns
1 pound small red potatoes, scrubbed and cut in half
12 ounces haricots verts or regular green beans, ends trimmed
1 large red onion, peeled and cut into 12 wedges (leave the root ends on)
Freshly ground black pepper
6 cups mesclun (mixed baby salad greens)
2 large ripe tomatoes, cut into wedges
2 hard-cooked eggs, cut into wedges
⅓ cup niçoise or other black olives, rinsed and drained

1. Make the dressing: Place the 1 tablespoon of lemon juice and the wine vinegar, mustard, and garlic in a mixing bowl. Season with salt and pepper to taste and whisk until the salt dissolves. Whisk in the ¼ cup of olive oil in a thin stream, then whisk in the anchovies (if using), capers, and basil. Taste for seasoning, adding more vinegar and/or salt as necessary; the dressing should be highly seasoned. Set the dressing aside.

2. Make the salad: Place the tuna in a shallow dish with 2 tablespoons of the olive oil and the 2 tablespoons of lemon juice. Season with sea salt and cracked black peppercorns to taste. Turn the fish a couple of times to coat thoroughly and let marinate; in the refrigerator, covered, for 30 minutes.

Mesclun Mix

Mesclun is a mix of baby lettuces and greens. It can include arugula, oak leaf lettuce, tatsoi, mizuna, mustard greens, and other greens. Mesclun is available as a mix at specialty food shops and most supermarkets. But, certainly, you can make your own using a combination of any of the greens listed here (make sure each has been picked young—the leaves should be very small): arugula, mizuna, bok choy, mustard greens, chicory, spinach, lettuces, tatsoi.

GRILLED SALADE NIÇOISE | PAGE 107

3. Place the potatoes in a medium-size saucepan and add lightly salted water to cover. Bring the potatoes to a boil, reduce the heat, and let simmer until just tender, 8 to 10 minutes. Using a slotted spoon, transfer the potatoes to a colander, run cold water over them, and let them drain. Let the water in the saucepan return to a boil. Add the haricots verts and let cook in the rapidly boiling water until they are crisp-tender, about 1 minute. Drain the beans, run cold water over them, then drain them again.

4. Set up the grill for direct grilling and preheat to high.

5. When ready to cook, if using a vegetable grate, preheat it for 5 minutes (see Notes). Toss the potatoes, green beans, and onion wedges with the remaining 2 tablespoons of olive oil and season with salt and pepper to taste. Arrange the vegetables on the hot vegetable grate or grill grate and grill, turning with tongs, until nicely charred on the outside, 3 to 5 minutes per side. Transfer to a platter and let cool.

6. Brush and oil the grill grate. Drain the tuna steaks and place them in the basket or on the hot grate. Grill the tuna until cooked to taste, 3 to 5 minutes per side for medium-rare. Transfer the tuna to a cutting board, let it rest for 3 minutes, then cut it into thin crosswise slices (see Notes).

7. Just before serving, mound the mesclun in the center of a large platter and arrange the tomato wedges, haricots verts, potatoes, onion wedges (cut off the root end), hard-cooked eggs, and olives in an attractive pattern around the greens. Fan the tuna slices out over the greens. Whisk the dressing again, then spoon it over the salad. Garnish the salad with the basil sprigs and serve.

NOTES: If you aren't using a vegetable grate, the easiest way to grill the haricots verts is to skewer them side by side together; that way they won't fall through the grill grate.

The salad can be prepared ahead up to this point, unless you wish to serve the tuna hot. In that case, grill it at the last minute.

ON THE SIDE

GREECE

A DIFFERENT GREEK SALAD

MARLO SALATA

ON THE SIDE
SERVES 4 TO 6

This is a little different from the Greek salads most of us are used to, made as it is with crisp romaine lettuce and aromatic fresh dill. The lemon juice is squeezed directly over the salad; I like to squeeze each half between my fingers to catch the seeds before they fall into the salad. Serve this salad with the Rotisseried Leg of Lamb with Lemon and Butter (page 206), Swordfish Souvlaki (page 345), or any other Greek grilled fare.

1 head romaine lettuce, separated into leaves, rinsed, and spun dry
1 clove garlic, cut in half
1 bunch dill, chopped
½ to 1 bunch scallions, both white and green parts, trimmed and finely chopped
1 to 2 lemons, cut in half
3 to 4 tablespoons extra-virgin olive oil
Salt and freshly ground black pepper
½ cup kalamata or other Greek olives
4 to 6 ounces feta cheese, drained and thinly sliced

1. Cut the romaine leaves crosswise into ½-inch strips. Rub a salad bowl with the cut garlic. Add the romaine, dill, and scallions (see Note).

2. Just before serving, squeeze the lemon juice to taste over the salad and pour the olive oil on top. Season the salad generously with salt and pepper and toss well to mix. Garnish the salad with the olives and feta and serve.

NOTE: The salad can be prepared ahead to this point. Cover it with a damp paper towel, then loosely with plastic wrap and refrigerate it until you are ready to serve.

KOREA

KOREAN LETTUCE AND ONION SALAD

ON THE SIDE
SERVES 4

Steak and onions are a marriage made in steak house heaven. Koreans display an equal enthusiasm for the combination—witness this tangy onion and lettuce salad, another one that is served with grilled meats at the sprawling Samwon Garden steak house in Seoul. Elsewhere in Korea, I found spring onion and scallion salads prepared in a similar fashion. The sesame seeds and vinegar tend to neutralize the pungency of the onion, especially if you use a sweet onion. Serve the salad with Korean Sesame-Grilled Beef (page 150) or Korean Grilled Short Ribs (page 167).

2 tablespoons soy sauce, or more to taste
2 tablespoons rice vinegar, or more to taste
½ teaspoon sugar, or more to taste
½ teaspoon hot paprika or cayenne pepper
2 teaspoons Asian (dark) sesame oil
1½ tablespoons sesame seeds, toasted (see box, page 113)
½ teaspoon freshly ground black pepper
6 to 8 romaine lettuce leaves, rinsed, spun dry, and cut crosswise into ¼-inch strips (about 3 cups)
1 medium-size sweet onion, such as Vidalia, Maui, or Walla Walla, thinly sliced (see Note)

1. Combine the soy sauce, rice vinegar, sugar, and paprika in a serving bowl and whisk until the sugar dissolves. Whisk in the sesame oil, sesame seeds, and pepper.

2. Add the lettuce and onion to the dressing and toss gently but thoroughly. Taste for seasoning, adding more soy sauce, rice vinegar, and/or sugar as necessary; the salad should be highly seasoned. Serve at once.

NOTE: If the stronger-tasting yellow onions are the only ones available, to blunt the bite you may wish to blanch the slices in boiling water for 10 seconds, then rinse them under cold water.

ARGENTINA

LA CABANA'S HOUSE SALAD

ON THE SIDE
SERVES 6

La Cabaña opened in 1935 and quickly became the premier chophouse in Buenos Aires. Named for the huts gaucho cowboys slept in during their cattle drives, La Cabaña served as a magnet for big-spending beef buffs, and its magnificent high-ceilinged dining rooms, done in dark wood, wrought iron, and gilded wallpaper, were a favorite haunt of presidents and kings (including the king of Spain, who would hold court in a private dining room in the back when visiting Argentina). So imagine the shock when the landmark restaurant closed its doors after nearly three quarters of a century of service. Happily, La Cabaña is back—in smart new digs in a fashionable new neighborhood, serving the same plate-burying cuts of grass-fed beef that made it a Buenos Aires legend. Here's the house salad from the old restaurant, a welcome respite from the carnivorian onslaught that characterizes a typical Argentinean meal.

FOR THE SALAD

- **1 small or ½ large head iceberg lettuce**
- **1 bunch arugula, stemmed, rinsed, and dried**
- **2 medium-size ripe tomatoes**
- **2 hard-cooked eggs, shelled**
- **1 medium-size red bell pepper, cored and seeded**
- **1 cup diced cooked beets**
- **2 medium-size ribs celery, thinly sliced**
- **1 can (14 ounces) hearts of palm, drained and thinly sliced**

FOR THE DRESSING

- **2 teaspoons Dijon mustard**
- **1 tablespoon red wine vinegar, or more to taste**
- **1 tablespoon fresh lemon juice**
- **½ teaspoon salt, or more to taste**
- **½ cup extra-virgin olive oil**
- **½ teaspoon freshly ground black pepper**

1. Make the salad: Core the lettuce and cut it crosswise into ¼-inch slices. Gently toss the lettuce with the arugula in a bowl. Arrange the lettuce mixture in the bottom of 6 shallow salad bowls, mounding it toward the center.

2. Cut each tomato into 12 wedges. Cut each hard-cooked egg into 6 wedges. Cut the bell pepper into 18 thin strips. Arrange the tomato and hard-cooked egg wedges and the bell pepper strips on top of the lettuce in a sunburst pattern (radiating away from the center like the spokes of a wagon wheel), alternating colors.

3. Drain off any liquid that may still remain on the beets and blot them dry with paper towels. Mound the beets, celery, and hearts of palm in the center of each portion of salad.

4. Make the dressing: Combine the mustard, wine vinegar, lemon juice, and salt in a small bowl and whisk until the salt dissolves. Whisk in the olive oil and black pepper. Taste for seasoning, adding more wine vinegar and/or salt as necessary; the dressing should be highly seasoned. Pour the dressing over the salads and serve at once.

JAPAN

SESAME SPINACH SALAD

ON THE SIDE
SERVES 4 TO 6

Simplicity and color are the hallmarks of Japanese salads: the bright greens of spinach, the oranges of carrots, the whites of daikon radish and bean sprouts. This spinach salad, commonly served at yakitori parlors, owes its wonderful nutty flavor to sesame oil and toasted sesame seeds. For the best results, use the young, tender, flat-leaf spinach leaves sold in bunches at specialty greengrocers, not those in cellophane bags. Serve the salad with any of the Japanese grilled dishes in this book.

1 pound fresh spinach, stemmed and rinsed thoroughly (see box, page 106)
Salt
2 tablespoons sesame seeds, toasted (see box, page 113)
1 clove garlic, minced
2 tablespoons mirin (sweet rice wine) or cream sherry, or more to taste
1 tablespoon soy sauce, or more to taste
1 tablespoon Asian (dark) sesame oil

1. Cook the spinach in a large saucepan of boiling salted water until just tender, about 30 seconds. Drain the spinach in a colander and rinse with ice water. Blot the spinach leaves dry with paper towels.

2. Combine 1 tablespoon of the sesame seeds, the garlic, mirin, soy sauce, and sesame oil in a serving bowl and whisk to mix. Stir in the spinach. Taste for seasoning, adding more mirin and/or soy sauce as necessary; the salad should be a little sweet and a little salty. Sprinkle the remaining 1 tablespoon of sesame seeds over the spinach and serve at room temperature or chilled.

KOREA

"THREE HOTS" SALAD

ON THE SIDE
SERVES 4 TO 6

This spicy salad is one of the half dozen or so condiments that traditionally accompany Korean grilled meat dishes. I first sampled it at Samwon Garden, a mammoth restaurant in Seoul that takes an almost Disneyesque approach to Korean barbecue. The salad acquires its peppery bite from three sources: watercress, mustard greens, and wasabi (Japanese "horseradish"). Wasabi is available at Asian markets, natural foods stores, and specialty food shops. If unavailable, use prepared horseradish. Serve the salad with the Korean Sesame-Grilled Beef (page 150) or the Korean Grilled Short Ribs (page 167).

2 teaspoons wasabi
3 tablespoons rice vinegar
1½ tablespoons sugar
2 teaspoons soy sauce
½ teaspoon salt
½ teaspoon freshly ground black pepper
1 bunch watercress, rinsed, spun dry, and torn into small sprigs
1 bunch mustard greens, stemmed, rinsed, spun dry, and torn into bite-size pieces (2 to 3 cups), or the equivalent in additional watercress

1. Combine the wasabi and 2 teaspoons of water in the bottom of a serving bowl and whisk to make a paste. Let stand 5 minutes.

2. Add the rice vinegar, sugar, soy sauce, salt, and pepper to the wasabi mixture and whisk until the sugar and salt dissolve.

3. Just before serving, add the watercress and mustard greens and toss to mix.

KOREA

SPICY DAIKON SALAD

ON THE SIDE
SERVES 4 TO 6

It's hard to imagine a Korean meal without this refreshing salad of crunchy chunks of daikon radish emblazoned with chile powder, vinegar, and garlic. Daikon is a succulent Asian radish that looks like our white (icicle) radish but is much longer and thicker; it has a moist, crisp flesh. Look for it at Asian markets, natural foods stores, and many supermarkets. In a pinch, you could use regular red radishes.

ADVANCE PREPARATION

30 minutes to 8 hours for marinating the salad

INGREDIENTS

- **1 daikon radish (12 to 14 ounces)**
- **3 cloves garlic, minced**
- **1 tablespoon minced peeled fresh ginger**
- **2 teaspoons sugar, or more to taste**
- **1 teaspoon salt, or more to taste**
- **1 to 3 teaspoons hot paprika, or ½ teaspoon cayenne pepper**
- **2 tablespoons rice vinegar, or more to taste**
- **2 teaspoons soy sauce**
- **1 teaspoon Asian (dark) sesame oil**
- **3 scallions, both white and green parts, trimmed and finely chopped**
- **1½ teaspoons sesame seeds, toasted (see box, below)**

1. Using a vegetable peeler, peel the radish. Cut the ends off the radish, then cut it in quarters lengthwise and crosswise into ½-inch slices.

2. Combine the garlic, ginger, sugar, salt, and paprika in a serving bowl and mash them together with the back of a wooden spoon. Stir in the rice vinegar, soy sauce, sesame oil, scallions, sesame seeds, and daikon. Let stand for 30 minutes, or as long as 8 hours (if letting the salad stand for 8 hours, cover and refrigerate it).

3. Just before serving, taste for seasoning, adding more sugar, salt, and/or rice vinegar, as necessary; the salad should be highly seasoned.

How to Toast Seeds, Nuts, and Breadcrumbs

Set a dry skillet over medium heat (do not use a nonstick skillet for this). Add the seeds, nuts, or breadcrumbs and heat until lightly toasted, three to five minutes, shaking the skillet occasionally. Transfer the seeds, nuts, or breadcrumbs to a plate to cool.

You can also toast in a preheated 350°F oven. Spread out the seeds, nuts, or crumbs on a rimmed baking sheet and bake them until lightly browned, five to ten minutes. Watch carefully to avoid burning.

JAPAN

SPICY JAPANESE BEAN SPROUT SALAD

ON THE SIDE
SERVES 4 TO 6

A meal at a yakitori parlor would include several small dishes of salads as well as grilled fare on a skewer. This salad comes from Ton Ton, a bare-bones yakitori joint under the elevated railroad near the Ginza district in Tokyo. The dressing contains only six ingredients, but the flavors—sweet, salty, sour, nutty, and fiery—will play pinball with your taste buds.

- **1 clove garlic, peeled**
- **½ teaspoon salt, or more to taste**
- **1 tablespoon sugar, or more to taste**
- **3 tablespoons rice vinegar, or more to taste**
- **2 teaspoons Asian (dark) sesame oil**
- **½ to 1 teaspoon hot red pepper flakes**
- **4 cups mung bean sprouts (about 8 ounces)**

Place the garlic and salt in a small bowl and mash it with the back of a spoon. Add the sugar, rice vinegar, sesame oil, and hot pepper flakes and whisk until the sugar and salt dissolve. Stir in the bean sprouts and let stand for 5 minutes. Just before serving, taste for seasoning, adding more salt, sugar, or rice vinegar as necessary; the salad should be highly seasoned.

INDONESIA

JAVANESE LONG BEAN SALAD PLATE WITH CABBAGE WEDGES

LALAPAN

ON THE SIDE
SERVES 4 TO 6

This colorful herb and vegetable platter is the traditional Javanese accompaniment to grilled fish. You won't be able to duplicate it exactly, as they use strange aromatic herbs, like *daun mangi* and *daun rispong,* that simply don't exist in the West. (To hint at their flavor, I've called for epazote—a Mexican herb—with a clean, woodsy, pleasantly bitter flavor.) Long beans are Asian green beans that can measure up to eighteen inches in length. Look for them at Asian markets or substitute skinny green beans. Serve *lalapan* with any of the Indonesian grilled fish dishes included in this book. Traditionally, the Fiery Chile and Shallot Relish (*sambal chobek,* page 444) would be served as well.

12 ounces long beans or thin green beans, ends trimmed
Salt
½ medium-size white cabbage, cored and cut into ½-inch-thick wedges
1 medium-size cucumber, peeled and cut into ¼-inch slices
2 medium-size ripe tomatoes, cored and cut into wedges
1 bunch lemon balm or basil, rinsed and patted dry
1 bunch epazote or flat-leaf parsley, rinsed and patted dry

1. Cook the long beans in a saucepan of rapidly boiling salted water until crisp-tender, about 3 minutes. Drain well, rinse under cold water, and drain again.

2. Arrange the long beans, cabbage, cucumber, tomatoes, lemon balm or basil, and epazote or parsley attractively on a platter and serve.

How to Prepare Fresh Coconut

How can you tell if a coconut is fresh? When buying one, shake it to hear if the coconut water sloshes around inside. A dry coconut is sometimes rancid and is certainy past its prime.

To open a fresh coconut, hold it in your hand over a bowl in the sink. Tap all the way around the middle of the coconut repeatedly with the back of a cleaver. Rotate the coconut as you tap: Soon a crack will appear, then the coconut will break in half. Save the coconut water that pours into the bowl; it's great for drinking or cooking rice. Now, wrap the coconut halves in a kitchen towel and, using a hammer, break them into pieces. Using a paring knife, pry the coconut meat off the shell. (If it's hard to get out, bake the pieces in a 400°F oven for ten minutes.) Trim the brown skin off the meat. Grate the coconut on a hand grater or in a food processor, using the grating blade.

If you're not going to use all the coconut, place it (either in chunks or grated) in a plastic bag; it can be refrigerated for up to two days. To keep the prepared coconut fresh longer, wrap it in plastic and then in aluminum foil; it can be frozen for up to two months. When grated, the average coconut yields about five cups.

BALI

LONG BEANS WITH FRESH COCONUT

URAP SAYUR

ON THE SIDE
SERVES 4 TO 6

As complex and delightful as traditional Balinese music, this salad has an intricate interplay of flavors and textures—the crunch of long beans, the crispness of coconut, the succulent sweetness of bean sprouts and bell peppers. Long beans are Asian green beans that grow up to eighteen inches in length. Look for them at Asian markets or use regular green beans (the skinniest you can find) or haricots verts. Don't be disconcerted by the seemingly large amount of oil. Most of it is discarded. Serve the salad with any of the Balinese satés or grilled dishes in this book.

FOR THE GARNISH AND DRESSING

½ cup vegetable oil, preferably canola
9 cloves garlic, thinly sliced (about 3 tablespoons), plus 2 cloves minced
4 to 5 shallots (about 4 ounces), thinly sliced (about ⅔ cup), plus 1 shallot, minced
1 stalk lemongrass, trimmed and minced, or 1 strip lemon zest (2 by ½ inches) removed with a vegetable peeler)
1 tablespoon minced galangal or peeled fresh ginger
¼ cup canned coconut milk
¼ cup fresh lime juice
2 tablespoons palm sugar or firmly packed light brown sugar
2 tablespoons Asian fish sauce or soy sauce

FOR THE SALAD

Salt
8 ounces long beans or thin green beans, ends trimmed off
2 cups mung bean sprouts
¼ to ½ cup grated fresh coconut (see box, at left) or unsweetened dried coconut
1 medium-size red bell pepper, cored, seeded, and cut into ¼-inch dice
1 to 4 jalapeños or other hot peppers, minced
Freshly ground black pepper

1. Prepare the garnish: Heat the oil in a small skillet over medium-high heat. Add the sliced garlic and cook until crisp and golden brown, about 1 minute. Using a wire skimmer or slotted spoon, transfer the garlic to paper towels to drain. Cook the sliced shallots the same way, working in several batches if necessary to avoid crowding the skillet. Take care not to let the garlic and shallots burn, or they'll become bitter. Blot the garlic and shallots with a paper towel and set aside. Pour off and discard all but 3 tablespoons of the oil from the skillet.

2. Prepare the dressing: Reheat the oil in the skillet over medium heat. Add the minced garlic and shallot, lemongrass, and galangal and cook until lightly browned, about 1 minute. Stir in the coconut milk and bring to a boil. Cook until reduced by about half, about 3 minutes. Stir in the lime juice, palm sugar, and fish sauce and bring to a boil. Remove the pan from the heat and let the dressing cool.

3. Prepare the salad: Bring a saucepan with 2 quarts of salted water to a boil.

4. Cut the long beans into ½-inch pieces. Place the mung bean sprouts in a colander in the sink. Cook the long beans in the boiling water until crisp-tender, about 2 minutes. Drain the beans in the colander (the boiling water will blanch the sprouts). Rinse the vegetables under cold running water until the beans are cool, then drain the beans and mung beans well and blot both dry with paper towels.

5. Transfer the long beans and bean sprouts to a large bowl. Stir in the grated coconut, bell pepper, jalapeños, fried garlic, fried shallots, and dressing (see Note). Toss well to mix. Taste for seasoning, adding salt and black pepper to taste. Transfer the salad to an attractive platter and serve.

NOTE: The salad can be assembled ahead of time but add the fried garlic and shallots and the dressing at the last minute.

LEFT TO RIGHT: VIETNAMESE SALAD PLATE | AT RIGHT • JAVANESE LONG BEAN SALAD PLATE | PAGE 114 • TURKISH RADISH SALAD PLATE | AT RIGHT

Salad Plates

Salad and vegetable plates are one of the constants in the world of grilling—the indispensable accompaniment to grilled meats, be they Indonesian satés, Turkish kebabs, Mexican *carne asada,* or anything in between.

I've included five traditional salad plates here that I encountered on the barbecue trail. Use them as a starting point to customize your own accompaniments.

VIETNAM

VIETNAMESE SALAD PLATE

ON THE SIDE
SERVES 4 TO 6

This fragrant assortment of herbs and vegetables is served alongside Vietnamese grilled fare and noodles. The lettuce leaves are used as wrappers for bite-size portions of meat and its various accompaniments. The Vietnamese are adept at using chopsticks to do the wrapping—a skill that definitely improves with practice. Basil provides explosive blasts of flavor (often mint and/or cilantro are served as well), while the bean sprouts and cucumber provide a delicious moist crunch. If you live in an area with a large Asian community, you may be able to find Thai basil, which has overtones of mint.

1 head Boston or Bibb lettuce
1 bunch fresh basil, mint, and/or cilantro
2 cups fresh bean sprouts
2 to 4 serrano or jalapeño peppers, to taste, seeded, if desired
1 medium-size cucumber, peeled (see box, page 454)
1 star fruit (optional)

Separate the lettuce into leaves, trying to keep the leaves as whole as possible. Rinse and spin dry the lettuce and basil separately, leaving the basil on the stem. Rinse and drain the bean sprouts. Thinly slice the jalapeños, cucumber, and star fruit (if using). Arrange the various ingredients in attractive piles on a platter and serve.

TURKEY

TURKISH RADISH SALAD PLATE

ON THE SIDE
SERVES 4 TO 6

Here's the Turkish version of the fresh vegetable platter that, in one form or another, seems to accompany grilled meats all over the world. If you go to Turkey to experience this, you may be intrigued by a vegetable that looks like a bright red tennis ball. It's actually a jumbo radish. The parsley is for eating, not just to look pretty, so make sure it is very fresh. Serve the salad with any of the Turkish grilled meat dishes you'll find in this book, squeezing the lemon over all.

1 bunch fresh flat-leaf parsley
1 bunch radishes, trimmed and cut in half
2 lemons, cut into wedges and seeded

Rinse the parsley and spin dry, leaving the stems attached. Arrange the parsley, radishes, and lemon wedges on plates or a platter and serve.

LEBANON

LEBANESE CRUDITES PLATE

ON THE SIDE
SERVES 4 TO 6

Whenever a Lebanese meal is served, this vegetable platter (or a variation on it) appears on the table. The vegetables are eaten by themselves as an hors d'oeuvre or as an accompaniment to grilled meats or seafood (often rolled up in a piece of pita). As you move east, you find a similar vegetable platter accompanying grilled meats in Iran, Iraq, India, and even Indonesia. Serve this with Grilled Shrimp with Taratoor or Spiced Lamb and Beef Kebab (pages 368 and 238).

1 bunch scallions, both white and green parts, trimmed
1 bunch radishes, trimmed of roots and leaves
1 cucumber, cut lengthwise in half, then cut into wedges
2 dill pickles, cut lengthwise in half, then cut into wedges
2 hearts of romaine lettuce, separated into leaves, rinsed, and spun dry

Arrange the scallions, radishes, cucumber, pickles, and lettuce in an attractive pattern on a platter and serve.

IRAN

SHIRAZI CUCUMBER, TOMATO, AND ONION SALAD

ON THE SIDE
SERVES 4 TO 6

Cucumber, tomato, and onion salads seem to turn up whenever meats are run through by skewers and seared smokily over fire. Here's the Iranian version, named for its birthplace, the city of Shiraz, and robustly flavored with parsley, fresh mint, and lime juice. Serve this salad with any of the Persian kebabs in this book, accompanied by pieces of lavash or pita bread for dipping.

1 large cucumber, peeled, seeded (see box, page 454), and cut into ½-inch dice
2 medium-size ripe tomatoes, cored and cut into ½-inch dice
1 small or medium-size onion, cut into ½-inch dice
½ cup chopped fresh flat-leaf parsley
½ cup chopped fresh mint
1 to 2 cloves garlic, minced
3 scallions, both white and green parts, trimmed and finely chopped
¼ cup fresh lime juice, or more to taste
¼ cup extra-virgin olive oil
Salt and freshly ground black pepper

Combine the cucumber, tomatoes, and onion in a serving bowl with the parsley, mint, garlic, scallions, lime juice, and olive oil. Toss gently but thoroughly to mix. Taste for seasoning, adding salt and pepper to taste and more lime juice as necessary; the salad should be highly seasoned. Serve at once.

TURKEY

SHEPHERD'S SALAD

ÇOBAN SALATASI

ON THE SIDE
SERVES 4

There are probably as many versions of this colorful salad as there are Turkish cooks to make it. The basic ingredients are tomatoes, bell peppers, and onions. Here's a more elaborate version of *çoban salatasi* that's bursting with Anatolian freshness. Serve it as a prelude to any of the Turkish kebabs in this book.

1 large or 2 small ripe tomatoes
1 medium-size cucumber
1 medium-size green bell pepper
½ small red onion
3 tablespoons chopped fresh flat-leaf parsley (optional)
½ cup brine-cured black olives
3 tablespoons extra-virgin olive oil
1 tablespoon red wine vinegar, or more to taste
Salt and freshly ground black pepper
3 ounces feta cheese, drained and crumbled

1. Core and seed the tomatoes (see the box on page 454) and cut them into ¼-inch dice. Peel and seed the cucumber (see the box on page 454) and cut it into ¼-inch dice. Core and seed the bell pepper and cut it into ¼-inch dice. Cut the onion into ¼-inch dice.

2. Combine the tomatoes, cucumber, bell pepper, onion, parsley (if using), and most of the olives in a serving bowl (see Note). Add the olive oil and wine vinegar and toss gently but thoroughly to mix. Taste for seasoning, adding salt and pepper and more wine vinegar as necessary; the salad should be highly seasoned.

3. Sprinkle the crumbled feta cheese over the salad, garnish it with the remaining olives, and serve at once.

NOTE: The vegetables can be cut and tossed ahead of time, but for best results don't mix in the dressing more than 20 minutes before serving.

SRI LANKA

TOMATO AND SHALLOT SALAD

ON THE SIDE
SERVES 4

Part relish and part salad, this tangy dish is one of the innumerable variations on the theme of tomato and onion salad found wherever meat or fish are cooked on a grill. As elsewhere in this book, I offer a range of peppers.

The salad can be served immediately, but it will taste better if you let it stand for fifteen or twenty minutes, so the flavors have a chance to blend. Be sure to reseason the salad just before serving. Serve it with the Sri Lankan satés or any of the Indian tandoori in this book.

3 tablespoons distilled white vinegar, or more to taste
1 teaspoon salt, or more to taste
½ teaspoon freshly ground black pepper
3 tablespoons vegetable oil
2 large ripe tomatoes, cut into ¼-inch dice
½ cup diced (¼-inch) shallots
1 to 4 serrano or jalapeño peppers, thinly sliced crosswise
¼ cup finely chopped fresh cilantro or mint

Combine the vinegar, salt, and black pepper in a serving bowl and whisk until the salt dissolves. Whisk in the oil. Add the tomatoes, shallots, peppers, and cilantro. Taste for seasoning, adding more vinegar and/or salt as necessary; the salad should be highly seasoned. Serve at once.

BULGARIA

TOMATO SALAD WITH FETA CHEESE
SHOPSKA SALATA

ON THE SIDE
SERVES 4

Late one evening in Washington, D.C., after a grueling day on a book tour, I sat back in my room at the Jefferson Hotel and ordered room service. I was obligingly served by Kiril Mitov, a young Bulgarian putting himself through school by working the swing shift at the hotel. We got to talking about books and barbecue, and soon he was telling me about cookouts in Sofia. No Bulgarian barbecue would be complete without this salad, he said, which takes its name from a rural region outside Sofia, and it owes its distinctive tang to snow-white Bulgarian feta cheese. *Shopska salata* is the traditional accompaniment to Bulgarian Burgers (page 226) and Bosnian Three-Meat Patties (page 228).

2 large ripe tomatoes
1 medium-size green bell pepper, cored and seeded
1 to 2 spring onions, both white and green parts (see Note)
¼ cup coarsely chopped fresh flat-leaf parsley
¼ cup extra-virgin olive oil
1 tablespoon red wine vinegar, or more to taste
Salt and freshly ground black pepper
3 ounces feta cheese, preferably Bulgarian, drained

1. Core the tomatoes and cut them into 1-inch cubes. Cut the bell pepper and onion into ¼-inch dice. Combine the tomatoes, bell pepper, and onion in a serving bowl with the parsley, olive oil, and wine vinegar and toss gently but thoroughly to mix. Taste for seasoning, adding salt and black pepper and more vinegar as necessary; the salad should be highly seasoned.

2. Coarsely grate or crumble the feta cheese on top of the salad and serve at once.

NOTE: If spring onions are not available, you can substitute 4 scallions (both white and green parts) or ½ small red onion.

INDONESIA

BALINESE CUCUMBER SALAD

ON THE SIDE
SERVES 4

This curious salad looks a little like green spaghetti. Actually, it's made with long, thin, noodlelike slivers of cucumber. (The easiest way to cut these is on a mandoline or with the julienne disk of a food processor.) Cucumber salads are just about universally served with barbecue. But what better way to relieve the heat of the fire and the day than with a salad that's as cool as the proverbial cucumber?

3 tablespoons dry-roasted peanuts, coarsely chopped
1 hothouse (seedless English) cucumber (see Note), or 1 large regular cucumber
¼ large sweet onion, such as Vidalia
3 tablespoons rice vinegar
4½ teaspoons sugar, or more to taste
½ teaspoon salt, or more to taste

1. Set a dry skillet over medium heat (do not use a nonstick skillet for this). Add the peanuts and heat until lightly browned, about 2 minutes, shaking the skillet occasionally. Transfer the peanuts to a plate to cool.

2. Peel the cucumber and seed it if necessary (see the box on page 454). Cut the cucumber crosswise into 3-inch sections, then lengthwise into spaghetti-thin strips. Cut the onion into as thin crosswise slices as possible.

3. Combine the rice vinegar, sugar, and salt in a serving bowl and whisk until the sugar and salt dissolve. Taste for seasoning, adding more sugar and/or salt as necessary; the dressing should be both tart and sweet. Stir in the cucumber and onion. Sprinkle the peanuts over the salad and serve.

NOTE: An English cucumber is the long, thin variety that has few seeds. It is often sold sealed in plastic.

SRI LANKA

POTATO SALAD WITH CARAMELIZED ONIONS

ON THE SIDE
SERVES 4

Potato salad is an immutable fixture for an American barbecue. Here's the Sri Lankan version—spiked with spicy-fried onions—just right for accompanying the Sri Lankan chicken satés or any of the Indian, Pakistani, or Bangladeshi kebabs in this book. I've taken a few liberties with the recipe, such as leaving the potato skins on. As elsewhere, I give a range of heat: Use one teaspoon of hot paprika if you like a milder potato salad and four teaspoons if you like to eat fire.

1½ pounds red-skinned potatoes, preferably very small, scrubbed
Salt
¼ cup vegetable oil, or more as needed
1 to 4 teaspoons hot paprika (or for a much milder salad, use sweet paprika)
1½ teaspoons ground coriander
½ teaspoon freshly ground black pepper
⅛ teaspoon ground cardamom
1 large onion, very thinly sliced
2 tablespoons fresh lemon juice
3 tablespoons chopped fresh cilantro

1. If using very small new potatoes, cut them in half; cut larger potatoes into ½-inch chunks. Place the potatoes in a medium-size saucepan, add lightly salted water to cover, and bring to a boil. Reduce the heat to medium and let the potatoes simmer until just tender, 8 to 10 minutes.

2. Meanwhile, prepare the onion mixture. Heat the oil in a large skillet over high heat. Add the paprika (start with a small amount), coriander, pepper, and cardamom and cook, stirring, for 15 seconds. Add the onion and cook for 1 minute. Reduce the heat to medium, then medium-low, and cook the onion until it is caramelized—that is, very soft and a deep golden brown—which will take about 20 minutes in all.

3. When the potatoes are done, drain them in a colander, rinse them under cold running water until they are cool, and drain them again. Set aside while finishing the onion mixture.

4. Stir the cooled potatoes and lemon juice into the onion mixture and cook over medium heat stirring until thoroughly coated, 1 to 2 minutes. Taste for seasoning, adding salt and/or more paprika as necessary; the salad should be highly seasoned. If it looks too dry, add a little more oil. Transfer the salad to a bowl and let cool, then sprinkle cilantro on top before serving.

U.S.A.

TWO-TONE POTATO SALAD

ON THE SIDE
SERVES 6

No barbecue would be complete without potato salad. One day, short on regular potatoes, my wife, Barbara, made this two-tone salad using sweet and baking potatoes. The result was so colorful and tasty we've made it a family standby. You'll be amazed by how much flavor the olives and capers add. If you wish to make a conventional potato salad, use all baking potatoes.

2 large baking potatoes (each 10 ounces)
2 large sweet potatoes (each 10 ounces)
Salt
⅓ cup mayonnaise
2 tablespoons Dijon mustard
2 tablespoons extra-virgin olive oil
2 tablespoons red wine vinegar, or more to taste
2 tablespoons drained capers
2 tablespoons chopped pitted green olives (with or without pimientos)
Freshly ground black pepper
2 medium-size ribs celery (with leaves, if possible), finely chopped
2 hard-cooked eggs (optional), coarsely chopped
3 scallions, both white and green parts, trimmed and finely chopped
½ cup finely chopped red onion
¼ cup chopped fresh flat-leaf parsley, plus a few sprigs for garnish
8 pitted black olives, for garnish

1. Peel all of the potatoes and cut them into ¾-inch cubes. Place the baking potatoes in a large saucepan with 2 quarts of lightly salted water. Bring to a boil and cook for 4 minutes. Add the sweet potatoes and let simmer until all the potatoes are just tender, 4 to 6 minutes more.

2. Meanwhile, make the dressing: Combine the mayonnaise and mustard in a large serving bowl and whisk until blended and smooth. Whisk in the olive oil, wine vinegar, capers, and green olives. Season with pepper to taste.

3. Drain the potatoes, then stir them into the dressing while still hot. Set the potatoes aside to cool and absorb the dressing.

4. Stir the celery, eggs (if using), scallions, onion, and chopped parsley gently but thoroughly into the cooled potato mixture. Taste for seasoning, adding salt and/or more wine vinegar as necessary; the salad should be highly seasoned. Garnish the salad with the parsley sprigs and black olives and serve.

INDONESIA

SPICY FRUIT
IN A TAMARIND DRESSING
RUJAK

ON THE SIDE
SERVES 4

An offbeat salad, *rujak,* pronounced RUE-jack, is one of the national dishes of Indonesia. (Indeed, it turns up throughout Southeast Asia, especially in Singapore and Malaysia.) The pairing of crunchy vegetables and acidic fruits makes an uncommonly refreshing combination for a barbecue. As for the dressing—a sweet, hot, piquant mixture of peanuts, tamarind, and peppers—few salad dressings are more distinctively flavorful or refreshing. There's nothing else quite like it. If tamarind pulp or puree is unavailable, use balsamic vinegar instead.

FOR THE DRESSING

- **3 tablespoons dry-roasted peanuts**
- **3 tablespoons tamarind pulp or puree or balsamic vinegar (see Note)**
- **¾ cup hot water**
- **1 piece (2 inches) ripe banana**
- **2 cloves garlic, chopped**
- **1 shallot, chopped**
- **1 to 3 jalapeño or other hot peppers, seeded and chopped (for a hotter rujak, leave the seeds in)**
- **2 tablespoons Asian fish sauce, sweet soy sauce (ketjap manis), or regular soy sauce**
- **2 tablespoons molasses**
- **1 tablespoon firmly packed brown sugar**
- **1 tablespoon fresh lime juice, or more to taste**
- **Salt**

FOR THE SALAD

- **1 star fruit or Asian pear**
- **1 small jicama or large Granny Smith apple (about 8 ounces)**
- **½ fresh pineapple**
- **1 cucumber**
- **1 cup mung bean sprouts, rinsed and drained**
- **¼ cup chopped fresh cilantro or scallion greens, for garnish**

1. Make the dressing: Grind the peanuts to a coarse powder in a food processor, running the machine in spurts. Transfer the peanuts to a small bowl.

2. If using tamarind pulp, combine it and the hot water in a food processor and let stand until softened, about 5 minutes. Pulse the machine in short bursts until the flesh comes away from the seeds, about 1 minute. Don't process the tamarind pulp so much that you crush the seeds. Strain the resulting mixture into the bowl with the peanuts. Discard the tamarind seeds and pulp. If using tamarind puree or balsamic vinegar, add it and the hot water to the peanuts.

3. Return the peanut mixture to the processor and add the banana, garlic, shallot, jalapeños, fish sauce, molasses, brown sugar, and lime juice, then season with salt to taste. Run the processor until a smooth paste forms. Taste for seasoning, adding more lime juice and/or salt as necessary; the dressing should be highly seasoned.

4. Make the salad: If using the star fruit, cut it crosswise into ¼-inch slices and set aside; if using the Asian pear, cut it in half lengthwise, core it, and then cut each half crosswise into ¼-inch slices. If using the jicama, peel it, cut it in half lengthwise, and cut the halves crosswise into ¼-inch slices; if using the apple, prepare it in the same way as the Asian pear. Peel and core the pineapple; cut it into 1-inch chunks. Peel the cucumber and cut it crosswise into ¼-inch slices.

5. To serve, pool the dressing on a platter or 4 large salad plates. Arrange the star fruit or pear, jicama or apple, pineapple, cucumber, and bean sprouts on top. Garnish the salad with the cilantro and serve.

NOTE: Tamarind is a tan seedpod filled with a tart, reddish-brown pulp. If you buy whole pods, you'll need to peel them and soak the pulp in warm water for 30 minutes to soften it, before proceeding with Step 2. You can also buy peeled tamarind pulp (look for it at Indian and Asian markets) and frozen tamarind puree (found in Hispanic markets). The puree is already strained; it's the easiest to use. Tamarind extract is not recommended for this recipe.

Rujak

Malaysian *rujak* vendors sometimes serve this salad on skewers as ungrilled kebabs. I, too, like to serve it on skewers, but when I do, I lightly grill the kebabs first.

If you want to give this a try, thread the fruit attractively onto short bamboo skewers and grill it over high heat for two to four minutes per side (four to eight minutes in all). Serve each skewer in a pool of tamarind dressing.

SPICY FRUIT IN A TAMARIND DRESSING | AT LEFT

TANDOORI BAKED FLAT BREADS | PAGE 131

CHAPTER 5

GRILLED BREAD

It was bound to happen. After decades of firing up such predictable fare as meat, seafood, and vegetables, grill jockeys finally discovered bread. Of course, grilling may have been the original method used to make bread. The first breads made by our Neolithic ancestors were likely grain pastes cooked crisp on heated stones next to a campfire. Today, villagers in Lebanon still use this technique for cooking pita bread. And in India, the flat breads called naan are baked on the sides of charcoal-fired clay barbecue pits called tandoors, while in Mexico commercially prepared tortillas are cooked on a metal conveyer belt that passes over open flames.

"It is better to have loafed and lost than never to have loafed at all."

—JAMES THURBER

The easiest way to grill bread is to use the glowing coals as a toaster. But you can also use the flames to cook raw dough. In the following pages you'll find recipes for grilled focaccia and flat bread cooked directly over the embers, as well as a direct-grilled version of Indian naan. Grilling also makes wonderfully crisp *papadoms* (Indian lentil crisps) that are completely free of the oil normally associated with them.

Whether you start with ready-made bread or homemade dough, you'll find it tastes better cooked on the grill.

MIDDLE EAST

GRILLED PITA CHIPS

DIRECT GRILLING
MAKES 24 PITA WEDGES

Grilling is a great way to crisp wedges of pita bread for dipping. (It's also a great way to add fresh life to stale pita bread.) For extra color and flavor, sprinkle the chips with white or black sesame seeds before putting them on the grill.

- **3 large or 4 small pita breads**
- **3 tablespoons extra-virgin olive oil**
- **1 tablespoon regular or black sesame seeds (optional)**

1. Cut larger pitas into 8 wedges, smaller pitas into 6 wedges (see Note). Generously brush both sides of each wedge with olive oil. Sprinkle one side of each wedge with sesame seeds (if using).

2. Set up the grill for direct griling and preheat to medium-high.

3. When ready to cook, arrange the pita wedges on the hot grate and grill, turning with tongs, until they are nicely browned, 1 to 2 minutes per side. Don't take your eyes off the grill for a second; grilled pita burns very easily.

4. Place the grilled pita wedges in a single layer on a tray, platter, or cake rack and let cool. The wedges will crisp as they cool.

NOTE: For extra crisp chips, separate each pita into two rounds by cutting it in half horizontally. Cut each round into wedges, brush these on both sides with olive oil (you'll need more oil), and grill them. This gives you a thinner and therefore crisper pita chip.

U.S.A.

GRILLED BREAD WITH GARLIC CILANTRO BUTTER

DIRECT GRILLING
MAKES 20 TO 24 SLICES

Grilling produces a garlic bread that is crunchy on the outside and softly chewy on the inside, with a smoky charcoaled flavor. The cilantro lends a Latin touch.

1 loaf bakery-style French bread (about 20 inches long)
8 tablespoons (1 stick) unsalted butter, at room temperature
4 cloves garlic, minced
½ cup minced fresh cilantro
Salt and freshly ground black pepper

1. Slice the bread sharply on the diagonal ¾ inch thick.

2. Using a whisk, cream the butter in a mixing bowl. Add the garlic and cilantro and season with salt and pepper to taste.

3. Set up the grill for direct griling and preheat to medium-high.

4. When ready to cook, generously brush or spread the bread slices on both sides with the cilantro butter. Arrange the bread slices on the hot grate and grill, turning with tongs as needed, until nicely browned, 2 to 4 minutes per side. Don't take your eyes off the grill for a second; grilled bread burns very easily. Transfer the grilled bread to a bread basket and serve at once.

U.S.A.

GRILLED GARLIC BREAD FINGERS

DIRECT GRILLING
MAKES 16 PIECES

Barbecue, by its very nature, requires a lot of standing around the grill waiting for foods to cook. But idle time shouldn't be hungry time. These slender bread strips—nice and garlicky—make a perfect munchie while you're waiting for more substantial fare to cook. Cutting the bread into fingers maximizes the surface area, ensuring even crusting and browning on all sides. The lemon zest adds a dimension you won't find in most garlic breads. And because you maximize the surface area, this recipe works well even on supermarket French bread. In the interest of health, I like to brush the bread with olive oil, but you could certainly use melted butter.

1 loaf French bread (about 20 to 24 inches long; see Note)
½ cup extra-virgin olive oil or melted unsalted butter
4 cloves garlic, minced
1 teaspoon grated lemon zest
¼ cup minced fresh flat-leaf parsley
Salt and freshly ground black pepper

1. Cut the loaf crosswise into 4 equal pieces. Then cut each piece lengthwise into 4 equal pieces to make 16 "fingers," each 5 to 6 inches long.

2. Heat the olive oil in a small saucepan over medium-low heat. Add the garlic, lemon zest, and parsley and simmer until the garlic just begins to brown, 3 to 5 minutes. Remove the garlic oil from the heat and season with salt and pepper to taste.

3. Set up the grill for direct griling and preheat to medium-high.

4. When ready to cook, generously brush the bread fingers all over with the garlic oil. Starting crust side down, arrange the fingers on the hot grate and grill, turning with tongs, until nicely browned, 2 to 4 minutes per side. Don't take your eyes off the grill for a second; grilled bread burns very easily.

5. Transfer the grilled bread to a bread basket and serve at once.

NOTE: My favorite bread for this recipe is the soft, puffy "French" or "Italian" loaves sold in the supermarket bread aisle. You can also use a long, crusty bakery-style baguette, but the result will be very crusty.

ITALY

TUSCAN GRILLED GARLIC BREAD

BRUSCHETTA

DIRECT GRILLING
MAKES 8 SLICES

A slice of grilled bread rubbed with garlic and drizzled with olive oil—bruschetta (pronounced broo-SKEH-ta)—is the ancestor of American garlic bread. Most of us have grown up with baked or toasted versions, but real bruschetta, cooked over coals, comes as a revelation. To be strictly authentic, you'd use Tuscan bread, which is remarkable for its dense, slightly crumbly texture and its curious lack of salt. This makes the bread taste rather insipid—until you pair it with fruity Tuscan olive oil and a generous sprinkling of sea salt.

Bruschetta offers a remarkable contrast of flavors: the intense, granular saltiness of the topping, the fruitiness of the olive oil, the fragrance of the garlic (which is mellowed by warming), and the scent of smoke. Oh, sure, there are fancier versions of bruschetta, but none can rival the elemental flavor of this one. Note that there is no need to soak the wood chips. Unsoaked, the chips will give the bruschetta more of a wood flavor than a smoky flavor. Use them with a charcoal grill only.

SPECIAL EQUIPMENT

1 cup unsoaked wood chips, preferably oak (charcoal grill only; optional)

INGREDIENTS

8 slices of Italian bread (preferably unsalted Tuscan bread), cut ½ inch thick
1 to 2 cloves garlic, cut in half
2 to 3 tablespoons of the best cold-pressed extra-virgin olive oil you can find, preferably Tuscan
Coarse salt (kosher or sea) and freshly ground black pepper

1. Set up the grill for direct griling and preheat to medium-high.

2. When ready to cook, throw a cupful of unsoaked wood chips on the coals (if using). Arrange the bread slices on the hot grate and grill until nicely browned on both sides, 2 to 4 minutes per side, rotating the slices 60 degrees after 30 seconds or so to create an attractive crosshatch of grill marks. Don't take your eyes off the grill for a second; grilled bread burns very easily.

3. Transfer the bread slices to the cool edge of the grill or to a platter. Rub the top of each bread slice generously with cut garlic. Drizzle olive oil over the bread and generously sprinkle salt and pepper on top. Serve at once.

SPAIN

CATALAN TOMATO BREAD

PA AMB TOMAQUET

DIRECT GRILLING
MAKES 8 SLICES

My first meal in Barcelona—at the venerable Los Caracoles restaurant in the medieval quarter—began with this simple bread appetizer, and scarcely a day went by when I wasn't served some variation of it. Catalan Tomato Bread belongs to an ancient family of grilled breads that includes Italian bruschetta and Indian naan. It offers irrefutable proof that the best dishes are often the easiest.

At its most rudimentary, *pa amb tomàquet* consists simply of a slice of grilled bread rubbed with ripe tomatoes and drizzled with olive oil. Like all simple dishes, it requires the best raw materials: crusty country-style bread; squishily ripe tomatoes; fragrant, cold-pressed olive oil. When prepared properly, the bread will be crisp from grilling, but the surface will be just beginning to soften thanks to the juices from the tomatoes. Not everyone in Catalonia uses garlic, so I've made it optional.

There are two ways to serve tomato bread. The first is for the cook to do the rubbing and drizzling. The second is to set out a cruet of olive oil and a bowl of salt, provide each person with a clove of garlic and half a tomato, and let him or her do the work. The second way is more fun.

4 very ripe tomatoes, cut in half
4 cloves garlic (optional), cut in half
8 slices country-style bread, cut ½ inch thick
Cruet of extra-virgin olive oil
Small bowl of coarse (kosher or sea) salt
Freshly ground black pepper (optional)

1. Place a half tomato and half garlic clove (if using) on each serving plate.

2. Set up the grill for direct griling and preheat to medium-high.

3. When ready to cook, arrange the bread slices on the hot grate and grill until nicely browned, 2 to 4 minutes per side. Don't take your eyes off the grill for a second; grilled bread burns very easily.

4. Place a piece of grilled bread on each plate. Serve immediately. To eat, rub a bread slice with the cut side of the garlic (if using), then with the cut side of the tomato. Drizzle olive oil over each slice and sprinkle salt and pepper, if desired, on top.

ITALY

GRILLED FOCACCIA

DIRECT GRILLING
MAKES 8 *FOCACCE*

It's hard to imagine a time when we didn't eat focaccia. In the last decade this puffy Italian flat bread has jumped from the ethnic fringe to the culinary mainstream. Focaccia is a very ancient bread; its name comes from the Latin word *focus,* meaning hearth. There is archeological evidence that the first *focacce* were baked right in or on the embers on hearthstones heated by coals. That set me thinking about cooking the dough directly on the grill. This will make a thinner focaccia than the deep-dish pizza thickness you may be accustomed to—it's almost like a cracker.

ADVANCE PREPARATION

1 to 2 hours for the dough to rise

FOR THE DOUGH

1 envelope active dry yeast
1 cup warm water
1½ teaspoons sugar
3 tablespoons extra-virgin olive oil
1½ teaspoons table salt
3¼ cups unbleached all-purpose flour, plus more for dusting
¼ cup fine cornmeal, for dusting

TO FINISH THE FOCACCIA

3 tablespoons sesame seeds
1 tablespoon coarse salt (kosher or sea)
3 to 4 tablespoons extra-virgin olive oil, for brushing

CATALAN TOMATO BREAD | AT LEFT

1. Combine the yeast with the warm water and sugar in a large bowl and let stand until foamy, about 10 minutes. Stir in 2 tablespoons of olive oil, the table salt, and 3 cups of flour. You want a dough that comes away from the side of the bowl; add more flour if necessary.

2. Knead the dough until smooth and elastic either by hand on a floured work surface, in a food processor, or in a mixer fitted with the dough hook. The dough should be soft and pliable, but not sticky; add more flour, if necessary. It should take 6 to 8 minutes to knead.

3. Use some of the remaining tablespoon of olive oil to oil a large bowl. Place the dough in the bowl, brush the top with the remaining olive oil, cover it loosely with plastic wrap, and let rise in a warm, draft-free spot until doubled in bulk, 1 to 2 hours.

4. Punch down the dough and roll it into a cylinder about 2 inches in diameter. Cut the cylinder into 8 equal pieces. Roll each piece of dough into a ball and keep covered with a damp kitchen towel.

5. When you are ready to roll out the *focacce,* set up the grill for direct grilling and preheat to high.

6. Lightly dust the work surface and rolling pin with flour. Roll out the balls one at a time (keeping the others covered) to form circles 6 inches in diameter and ¼ inch thick. Lightly dust the circles with cornmeal and stack them on a plate with a piece of plastic wrap or waxed paper in between. For the best results, finish rolling out the breads not more than 15 minutes before you plan to cook them.

7. When ready to cook, combine the sesame seeds and coarse salt in a small bowl. Lightly brush the top of each focaccia with some olive oil and sprinkle some of the sesame mixture on top.

8. Place the *focacce* a few at a time, oiled side down, on the hot grate. Brush the tops with more olive oil and sprinkle more of the sesame mixture over them. Cook the *focacce* until nicely browned and blistered, 2 to 4 minutes per side, turning with tongs. Don't take your eyes off the grill for a second; grilled bread burns very easily. Repeat with the remaining *focacce* and serve.

U.S.A.

BRUCE FRANKEL'S GRILLED BREAD

DIRECT GRILLING
MAKES 6 BREADS

This recipe takes me down memory lane, specifically to a restaurant that helped launch the dining revolution in Boston, a romantic, innovative restaurant run by a visionary chef named Bruce Frankel. Although Panache in Central Square, Cambridge, Massachusetts, closed its doors more than a decade ago, and although Frankel has turned his talents to the Internet, my generation of Boston foodies will forever remember Panache with fondness. Bruce used to serve this wonderful grilled bread with goat cheese as an appetizer.

ADVANCE PREPARATION

1½ to 2½ hours for the dough to rise

INGREDIENTS

½ envelope active dry yeast (1¼ teaspoons)
1 tablespoon molasses
⅔ cup warm water
1½ cups unbleached all-purpose flour, plus more for dusting
¾ cup whole-wheat flour
3 tablespoons cornmeal, plus more for dusting
½ teaspoon coarse salt (kosher or sea), plus more for sprinkling
3 tablespoons extra-virgin olive oil
1 tablespoon fresh thyme leaves
Coarsely ground black pepper

1. Combine the yeast with the molasses and 2 tablespoons of the warm water in a large bowl and let stand until foamy, 5 to 10 minutes. Stir in the remaining warm water, 1½ cups of all-purpose flour, the whole-wheat flour, 3 tablespoons of cornmeal, and ½ teaspoon of salt to form a dough that is soft and pliable, but not sticky. Knead the dough until smooth and elastic either by hand on a floured work surface, in a food processor, or a mixer fitted with a dough hook; add more all-purpose flour, if the dough is too sticky to work with. It should take 6 to 8 minutes.

2. Use about 1½ teaspoons of the olive oil to lightly oil a large bowl. Place the dough in the bowl, brush the top with another 1½ teaspoons of olive oil, cover it with a dampened kitchen towel, and let rise in a warm, draft-free spot until doubled in bulk, 1 to 2 hours. Punch the dough down, cover it again, and let rise until doubled in bulk again, about 30 minutes.

3. Punch the dough down and divide it into 6 equal pieces. Roll each piece into a ball and keep covered with a damp kitchen towel.

4. When you are ready to roll out the bread, set up the grill for direct grilling and preheat to high.

5. Lightly dust the work surface and rolling pin with flour. Roll out the balls one at a time (keeping the others covered) to form circles 5 inches in diameter and ⅛ inch thick. Lightly dust the circles with cornmeal and stack them on a plate with a piece of plastic wrap or waxed paper in between.

6. When ready to cook, brush the breads with the remaining 2 tablespoons of olive oil and place them, a few at a time, on the hot grate. Grill, turning once with tongs, until puffed and golden brown, 2 to 4 minutes per side. Don't take your eyes off the grill. Sprinkle the breads with the thyme leaves and pepper to taste. Serve at once.

INDIA

TANDOORI-BAKED FLAT BREADS

NAAN

DIRECT GRILLING
MAKES 14 TO 16 NAANS

Flat breads were the first food cooked in a tandoor (Indian oven) and for me they remain the best—especially, the light, buttery, yeasted bread known as naan. The traditional way to cook naan is on the walls of the tandoor. Virtually every residential neighborhood in northern India has a bakery (more like an open-air stall), where barefoot bakers roll and bake naan to order.

The procedure is simple enough. When you order naan, the baker takes a soft white ball of dough and rolls it into a flat bread. A few slaps from hand to hand stretch the bread into its traditional teardrop shape. The baker presses the bread onto the wall of a hot tandoor using a pillowlike holder called a *gaddi* (literally throne). The *gaddi* protects the baker's hand—a must when you consider that the temperature of the tandoor can reach 700°F. The bread emerges from the oven puffed and blistered on top and crisp and brown on the bottom. It's sweet and smoky, pliable and moist, and about as delicious as bread gets.

Most of us don't have tandoors, but good results can be obtained with an American-style barbecue grill. Over the years I've experimented with various techniques, including placing a baking stone in the grill. The best results come with cooking the naan directly on the grate over the flames.

ADVANCE PREPARATION

1½ to 2 hours for the dough to rise

INGREDIENTS

1 envelope active dry yeast
5 tablespoons sugar
1 cup warm water
1 large egg, beaten
3 tablespoons milk
2 teaspoons salt
4½ to 5 cups unbleached all-purpose flour, plus additional for dusting and rolling
1 tablespoon vegetable oil
4 tablespoons (½ stick) unsalted butter, melted

1. Combine the yeast, 1 tablespoon of the sugar, and ¼ cup of the warm water in a large bowl and let stand until foamy, 5 to 10 minutes. Stir in the remaining 4 tablespoons of sugar, ¾ cup of warm water, and the egg, milk, and salt. Add 4 cups of the flour and stir to form a dough that is soft and pliable, but not sticky. Knead the dough until smooth and elastic either by hand on a floured work surface, in a food processor, or in a mixer fitted with a dough hook; add more flour, if the dough is too sticky to work with. It should take 6 to 8 minutes.

2. Use 1½ teaspoons of the oil to lightly oil a large bowl. Place the dough in the bowl, brush the top with the remaining 1½ teaspoons of oil, cover it with a clean kitchen towel, and let rise in a warm, draft-free spot until doubled in bulk, 1 to 1½ hours. Punch down the dough and pinch off 2-inch pieces. Roll them between your palms into smooth balls. You should have 14 to 16 balls. Place the balls on a lightly floured baking sheet and cover with a lightly dampened clean kitchen towel. Let rise again until puffy, about 30 minutes.

3. Set up the grill for direct grilling and preheat to high.

4. When ready to cook, place a rolling pin, cutting board, bowl of flour, and the melted butter near the grill. (This is incredibly theatrical; your guests will be amazed.) Lightly flour the cutting board, then roll out a dough ball on it to form a disk about 5 inches in diameter. Gently slap the disk from one hand to the other to stretch it into an elongated 7- to 8-inch circle. (The motion is rather like the "patty cake, patty cake" motion in the nursery rhyme.) Stretch the circle into a traditional teardrop shape and immediately place it on the hot grate.

5. Cook the naan until the bottom is crusty and browned and the top is puffed and blistered, 2 to 4 minutes. Brush the naan with butter, turn it over, and grill the other side until lightly browned, 2 to 4 minutes. Don't take your eyes off the grill; naan burns quickly. Prepare the remaining naan the same way. Brush each naan with more butter as it comes off the grill and serve while piping hot. Serve whole, or cut each naan into 3 wedges to serve the traditional way.

INDIA

PAPADOMS
COOKED OVER THE COALS

METHOD: DIRECT GRILLING
MAKES 8 *PAPADOMS*

Crisp, spicy, and wafer-thin, *papadoms* are Indian flat breads made from lentil flour and spices. You've probably had them if you've eaten at an Indian restaurant, for *papadoms* are served as both an hors d'oeuvre and with the main course. They usually come deep-fried at Indian restaurants in North America, an admittedly tasty but greasy preparation, but in India *papadoms* are often cooked on the lid of a tandoor oven or over direct flames to produce audibly crisp wafers without a drop of added fat.

Papadoms are commonly sold in boxes, canned, or frozen at Indian markets and specialty food shops. (They're one of the few commercially prepared foods consumed widely in India.) Here's how *papadoms* are served on Bombay's Khau Galli, a kaleidoscopically colorful street of food stalls near the Zaveri market.

8 papadoms

1. Set up the grill for direct grilling and preheat to high.

2. When ready to cook, place a few *papadoms* on the hot grill grate. Cook until the bottoms begin to brown and blister, 20 to 40 seconds. Turn the *papadoms* with tongs and cook the other side the same way. Don't take your eyes off the grill; *papadoms* burn quickly. Repeat with the remaining *papadoms*. Serve at once.

JAMAICA

JAMAICAN FRY BREAD
FESTIVALS

ON THE SIDE
MAKES ABOUT 24 FESTIVALS

Festivals—deep-fried breads—are the traditional accompaniment to Jamaican jerk chicken or pork. The following were inspired by a jerk joint in Boston Beach called Sufferer's. (The name is certainly appropriate when you stop to consider how many Scotch bonnet chiles go into a single batch of jerk!) For a more dramatic presentation, I like to braid the dough into twists, but you can roll it out and fry it in the traditional cigar shapes.

2 cups unbleached all-purpose flour
¼ cup cornmeal
3 tablespoons sugar

2 tablespoons baking powder
1 teaspoon salt
5 tablespoons unsalted butter, chilled
¾ cup evaporated milk, or more as needed
2 cups peanut oil for frying, or more as needed

1. Combine the flour, cornmeal, sugar, baking powder, and salt in a large mixing bowl. Using two knives, cut in the butter. Alternatively, mix the ingredients in a food processor fitted with a chopping blade. The mixture should feel crumbly, like sand. Add enough evaporated milk to obtain a stiff but pliable dough. Stir just to mix.

2. Pinch off walnut-size pieces of dough and roll them between your palms to make long thin ropes. You should have about 24, each one about 10 inches long and ¼ inch thick. Fold the ropes in half and twist them together.

3. Place the peanut oil in a deep-fat fryer or large, deep skillet. Heat over medium-high heat until it reaches 350°F on a deep-frying thermometer.

4. Gently and carefully lower the festivals into the hot oil and fry, turning with a slotted spoon, until golden brown, 2 to 4 minutes in all. Transfer the festivals to paper towels to drain and serve while still hot.

GRILLED PRIME RIBS OF BEEF | PAGE 137

CHAPTER 6

WHAT'S YOUR BEEF?

To judge from the quantity of bison bones found near the fire pits of prehistoric cave dwellers, beef was man's first barbecue. To this day, the popularity of beef remains universal—not to mention at an all-time high. After all, nothing matches the primeval pleasure of sanguine, smokily charred, perfectly cooked beef.

"Carve the bone completely out of the steak with a sharp knife and hide it for yourself."
—*James Beard*

Beef is some of the best food the barbecue trail has to offer, whether you're a Korean enjoying *bool kogi* (sesame-grilled beef), a Russian savoring shashlik (kebabs), or a Texan cutting into an oversize steak. What you may not realize is just how widespread and passionate the world's beef eaters are or how astonishingly diverse are the ways to cook beef with live fire.

In this chapter you'll find grilled beef dishes of all sizes, shapes, and cooking methods. Indonesia's tiny satés, mammoth prime ribs from Great Britain, T-bones from Tuscany, teriyaki from Tokyo, short ribs from Seoul, quickly seared Vietnamese beef, and slow-cooked, smoky briskets from Texas.

You'll also learn how to properly grill a steak and how to stuff and roll a *matambre* (South American flank steak). In fact, no matter what your beef is, you'll find it in this chapter.

U.S.A.

TEXAS-STYLE BARBECUED BRISKET

INDIRECT GRILLING
SERVES 10 TO 12

Pork may be the preferred barbecue east of the Mississippi (think of the pork shoulder of the Carolinas and the ribs of Kansas City and Memphis), but in Texas beef is king—especially beef brisket, which comes moist and smoky and tender enough to cut with a fork. (Not that any self-respecting Texas barbecue buff would use a fork.) Barbecued brisket is simultaneously one of the easiest and most challenging recipes in the world of barbecue. Easy because it requires only one main ingredient: brisket (even the rub is optional). Challenging because pit masters spend years learning the right combination of smoke (lots), heat (low), and time (measured in half days rather than hours) to transform one of the toughest, most ornery parts of the steer into tender, meaty perfection.

Over the years, I've found that two things help above all: choosing the right cut of brisket—

namely, untrimmed, with a thick sheath of fat—and then cooking the brisket in a shallow pan. The pan keeps the juices from dripping onto the fire and the meat from drying out, while allowing for the maximum smoke penetration from the top. A whole brisket (the sort cooked by a restaurant) weighs eighteen to twenty pounds. Here I call for a partially trimmed brisket—a cut weighing five to six pounds. Do not attempt to make this with a two-pound trimmed, fatless brisket; it will turn out much too dry.

To achieve the requisite smoke flavor, you need to smoke the brisket in a charcoal grill—or in a smoker. A gas grill will not produce enough smoke.

ADVANCE PREPARATION

4 to 8 hours for curing the meat (optional); also, allow yourself about 6 hours cooking time

SPECIAL EQUIPMENT

6 cups hickory or mesquite chips or chunks, soaked for 1 hour in cold water to cover and drained

INGREDIENTS

- **1 beef brisket (5 to 6 pounds), with a layer of fat at least ¼ inch thick, preferably ½ inch thick**
- **1 tablespoon coarse salt (kosher or sea)**
- **1 tablespoon chili powder**
- **2 teaspoons sugar**
- **1 teaspoon freshly ground black pepper**
- **1 teaspoon ground cumin**

1. Rinse the brisket under cold running water and blot it dry with paper towels.

2. Combine the salt, chili powder, sugar, pepper, and cumin in a bowl and toss with your fingers to mix. Rub the spice mixture on the brisket on all sides. If you have time, wrap the brisket in plastic and let it cure, in the refrigerator, for 4 to 8 hours (or even overnight), but don't worry if you don't have time for this—it will be plenty flavorful, even if you cook it right away.

3. Set up a charcoal grill for indirect grilling and preheat it to low. No drip pan is necessary for this recipe.

Barbecue Sauce, the Texas Way

The best Texas-style barbecue sauce combines the sweetness of Kansas City–style tomato sauces with the mouth-puckering tartness of a North Carolina vinegar sauce. I've come up with my own version—mix together equal parts of the Basic Barbecue Sauce (page 463) and the North Carolina Vinegar Sauce (page 466). Serve this with barbecued brisket. For a really good sauce, add some meat drippings or a little chopped brisket.

4. When ready to cook, toss 1½ cups of the wood chips on the coals (¾ cup per side). Place the brisket, fat side up, in an aluminum foil pan (or make a pan with a double sheet of heavy duty aluminum foil). Place the pan in the center of the hot grate, away from the heat. Cover the grill.

5. Smoke cook the brisket until tender enough to shred with your fingers; 6 hours will likely do it, but it may take as long as 8 (the cooking time will depend on the size of the brisket and heat of the grill). Baste the brisket from time to time with the fat and juices that accumulate in the pan. You'll need to add 10 to 12 fresh coals to each side every hour and toss more wood chips on the fresh coals; add about ¾ cup chips per side every time you replenish the coals during the first 3 hours.

6. Remove the brisket pan from the grill and let rest for 15 minutes. Transfer the brisket to a cutting board and thinly slice it across the grain, using a sharp knife, electric knife, or cleaver. Transfer the sliced meat to a platter, pour the pan juices on top, and serve at once.

U.S.A.

GRILLED PRIME RIBS OF BEEF WITH GARLIC AND ROSEMARY

INDIRECT GRILLING
SERVES 12 TO 16

If you're like most people (including me), you're probably intimidated by the prospect of cooking a standing rib roast. Who wouldn't be? A prime rib represents a formidable piece of meat for even the most seasoned chef: an eighteen-pound mass of beef and bones that literally takes both hands to lift. It's also expensive—a seven-rib roast can cost upward of $150. Well, be intimidated no more, because here's an easy, virtually foolproof method for cooking perfect, crusty on the outside, meltingly tender inside prime ribs every time: Cook the rib roast on your barbecue grill using the indirect method.

The only remotely challenging aspect to cooking prime ribs is the timing, and if you figure on twelve to fourteen minutes per pound (for a bone-in roast), you'll make a perfect roast every time. Besides, you can let a cooked prime-rib roast stand for up to thirty minutes before carving. Indeed, at least ten to fifteen minutes of standing time is recommended to allow the juices to flow from the center of the roast back to the exterior.

The following recipe calls for a seven-rib roast, which will weigh sixteen to eighteen pounds and will serve eight Paul Bunyans and twelve to sixteen normal people. A two-, four-, or six-rib roast would be prepared the same way. For that matter, a boneless rib roast could also be prepared this way (just shorten the cooking time). When buying prime ribs, be sure to choose a roast with a thick jacket of fat. The fat melts as the roast cooks, basting and tenderizing the meat.

And don't fret if you can't find fresh rosemary. The beef will have plenty of flavor grilled with dried rosemary.

Yorkshire Pudding (page 439) makes the perfect accompaniment to the roast.

ADVANCE PREPARATION

None, but allow yourself about 4 hours cooking time

FOR THE BEEF

- **1 prime rib beef roast (7 ribs; 16 to 18 pounds), tied at 2-inch intervals**
- **6 cloves garlic, each clove peeled and cut lengthwise into 4 pieces**
- **4 to 6 sprigs fresh rosemary, or 1 tablespoon dried rosemary**

FOR THE RUB

- **2 tablespoons black peppercorns**
- **2 tablespoons dried rosemary**
- **2 tablespoons coarse salt (kosher or sea)**
- **2 tablespoons sweet paprika**

1. Prepare the beef: Using the tip of a slender paring knife, make a series of ½-inch-deep holes in the roast, mostly in the sheath of fat on top, but also in the sides and bottom. The holes should be about 2 inches apart. Insert slivers of garlic in half of the holes. Strip the leaves off one or two of the rosemary sprigs and insert them in the remaining holes (or insert the dried rosemary). Slide

the remaining sprigs of rosemary under the string used to tie up the roast.

2. Make the rub: Grind the peppercorns and dried rosemary to a fine powder in a spice mill or blender. Add the salt and paprika and grind to mix. Rub this mixture all over the roast, especially over the sheath of fat on top.

3. Set up the grill for indirect grilling, place a large drip pan in the center, and preheat the grill to medium.

4. When ready to cook, brush and oil the grill grate. Place the roast, fat side up, on the hot grate over the drip pan and cover the grill.

5. Grill the roast until cooked to taste, 3½ to 4 hours for a medium-rare roast of this size, figuring on 12 to 14 minutes per pound. (If using a charcoal grill, you'll need to add 10 to 12 fresh coals to each side every hour. If using a gas grill, keep the cover closed at all times.) Use an instant-read meat thermometer to test for doneness;

Beef Grilling Chart

CUT	METHOD	HEAT	DONENESS		
			Rare (125°F)	Medium (160°F)	Well-Done (170°F)
STEAKS					
½ inch thick	direct	high	1 to 2 minutes per side	2 to 3 minutes per side	3 to 4 minutes per side
1 inch thick	direct	high	3 to 4 minutes per side	4 to 6 minutes per side	6 to 7 minutes per side
1½ inches thick	direct	high	4 to 6 minutes per side	6 to 8 minutes per side	8 to 9 minutes per side
Flank Steak	direct	high	2 to 3 minutes per side	4 to 5 minutes per side	6 to 7 minutes per side
ROASTS AND RIBS					
Tenderloin: 2 to 3 pounds	indirect	high	40 to 50 minutes	1 hour	Don't do it
Tenderloin: 4 to 5 pounds	indirect	high	1 hour	1¼ hours	Don't do it
Boneless Rib: 4 to 6 pounds	indirect	medium	1 to 1½ hours	1½ to 2 hours	Don't do it
Standing Rib: 16 to 18 pounds, bone-in	indirect	medium	3 hours	4 hours	Don't do it
Brisket: 5 to 6 pounds	indirect	low			5 to 7 hours; 190°F
Ribs	indirect	medium		1½ to 2 hours	1½ to 2 hours; done when tender

This chart is offered as a broad guideline to cooking times for the various cuts of meat. Remember, grilling is an art, not a science. When in doubt, refer to times in the individual recipes.

you'll want to cook the roast to 145°F for medium-rare, 160°F for medium.

6. Transfer the roast to a platter or carving board and cover it loosely with aluminum foil. Let the roast rest for 10 to 15 minutes before carving and serving. The easiest way to carve the roast is to cut it into rib sections using a long, slender knife, then slice it into thin slices to serve.

LARDING THE BEEF

Don't despair if you don't have a larding iron. A sharpening steel works just as well. Wash and wipe the steel to remove any metal fillings.

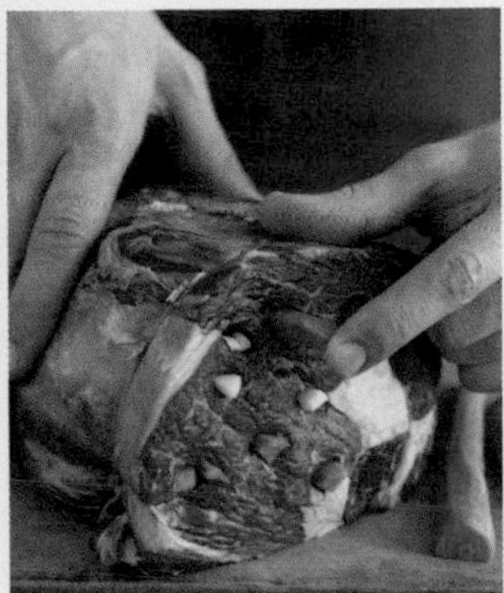

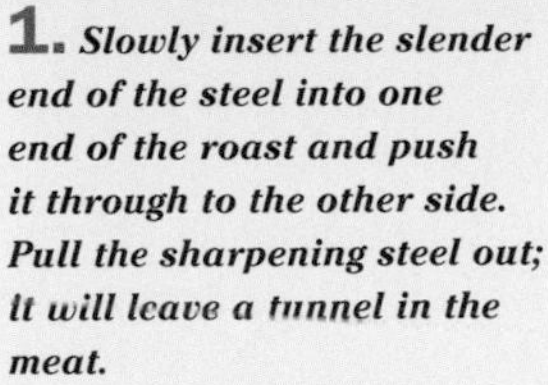

1. *Slowly insert the slender end of the steel into one end of the roast and push it through to the other side. Pull the sharpening steel out; it will leave a tunnel in the meat.*

2. *Gently worm the vegetable slivers, cheese, and ham into the tunnel. With shorter vegetables, like bell pepper strips, you'll have to insert them from both ends. Freezing the ham and cheese first makes them easier to insert.*

BRAZIL

BRAZILIAN STUFFED RIB ROAST

INDIRECT GRILLING OR ROTISSERIE
SERVES 8

This grilled stuffed roast is one of the most colorful *churrascaria* offerings ever to grace a plate in Rio. Imagine a boneless beef rib roast generously larded with ham, cheese, carrots, bell peppers, and other vegetables, then roasted to fork-tenderness on a rotisserie (or using the indirect-grilling method). The stuffing serves a dual purpose, both flavoring the meat and forming a colorful mosaic when the roast is sliced. This recipe was inspired by the restaurant Porcão in Ipanema in Rio de Janeiro.

The easiest way to insert the various ingredients for the stuffing that goes into the meat is to use a larding iron, a sharp implement with a V-shaped metal blade, which you may be able to find at a cookware shop. Alternatively, follow the instructions for larding in the box at right.

SPECIAL EQUIPMENT

Rotisserie (optional)

INGREDIENTS

1 boneless beef rib roast (3½ to 4 pounds), rolled and tied
2 long slender carrots, peeled and cut lengthwise in half
½ green bell pepper, cored, seeded, and cut lengthwise into ½-inch strips
½ red bell pepper, cored, seeded, and cut lengthwise into ½-inch strips
1 medium-size onion, cut into 10 wedges
1 slice (¼ inch thick) smoked ham (about 2 ounces), cut into ¼-inch strips and frozen
1 slice (¼ inch thick) aged provolone or other firm white cheese (about 2 ounces), cut into ¼-inch strips and frozen
2 cloves garlic, cut into matchstick slivers
Salt and freshly ground black pepper

1. Using a larding iron or sharpening steel, pierce the roast from end to end in 16 to 20 places. The idea is to riddle the meat with slender tunnels that run along the grain.

2. Insert the carrot halves, bell pepper strips, thin onion wedges, and ham and cheese strips into these tunnels, gently inching them into the holes. The carrot strips will be long enough to go all the way through the meat, but you'll need to double or triple up on the remaining ingredients; insert shorter pieces from both ends.

3. Using the tip of a paring knife, make tiny slits, 1 inch apart, in the surface of the roast. Insert a sliver of garlic in each. Generously season the roast with salt and pepper (see Note).

4. *If grilling using the indirect grilling method,* set up the grill for indirect grilling, place a large drip pan in the center, and preheat the grill to medium. When ready to cook, brush and oil the grill grate. Place the roast on the hot grate over the drip pan. Cover the grill and cook the roast to taste: 1 to 1½ hours for medium-rare (145°F on an instant-read meat thermometer), 1½ to 2 hours for medium (160°F). If using a charcoal grill, you'll need to add 10 to 12 fresh coals to each side every hour.

If using a rotisserie, set up the grill for spit roasting following the manufacturer's instructions. If using a gas grill, preheat the front and rear burners to high. If using a charcoal grill, light the coals and rake into rows in front and back, leaving a gap in the center. Skewer the roast on the spit. Cover the grill and cook the roast to taste: 1¼ to 1½ hours for medium-rare (145°F on an instant-read meat thermometer), 1½ to 2 hours for medium (160°F). If using a charcoal grill, you'll need to replenish the coals after an hour.

5. Transfer the roast to a cutting board and let it rest for 10 minutes. Using an electric knife or sharp carving knife, cut the roast into thin crosswise slices and serve.

NOTE: The roast can be prepared up to 8 hours ahead to this point. Refrigerate it, covered.

CUBA

STEAKS IN GARLIC LIME MARINADE

PALOMILLA

DIRECT GRILLING
SERVES 4

Mention *palomilla* to Cubans and their eyes will light with pleasure. Like so much grilled fare, *palomilla* (pronounced pal-o-ME-ya) is a poor man's dish that has been elevated to a gastronomic indulgence. The term refers to a thin, flavorful steak cut from the bottom round (*la bola* in Spanish). Because bottom round can be rather tough, the steak is cut thin (about the width of your baby finger) to make it seem more tender.

Where I live in Miami, *palomilla* turns up at Cuban restaurants throughout the city. For the ultimate *palomilla,* use prime top butt and grill the meat over oak, instead of the traditional pan-frying method. Like most Cuban meats, *palomilla* would traditionally be marinated in *adobo* (a cumin, lime, garlic marinade) before cooking. You can also baste the steak with *adobo* as it cooks.

If you can't find steaks cut from the top butt, you could use shell steaks, or sirloin. The important thing is to cut the steaks thin (no more than a half inch thick).

Serve the steaks with Grilled Polenta (page 433) or Bahamian Peas and Rice (page 431).

ADVANCE PREPARATION

30 minutes for marinating the steaks

INGREDIENTS

4 cloves garlic, peeled
Salt and freshly ground pepper
½ teaspoon ground cumin
½ cup fresh lime juice or sour orange juice
4 tablespoons extra-virgin olive oil
4 beef steaks (each 6 to 8 ounces), cut ½ inch thick
2 large onions, cut crosswise into ½-inch slices

1. Combine the garlic, 1 teaspoon of salt, ½ teaspoon of pepper, and the cumin in a mortar and pound to a paste with a pestle. Work in the lime juice and 2 tablespoons of the olive oil to form a smooth paste. If you don't have a mortar and pestle, combine all these ingredients in a blender or food processor and process to a smooth puree. Taste for seasoning, adding more salt and/or pepper as necessary; the *adobo* should be highly seasoned. Spread half of the *adobo* over the steaks and let marinate, in the refrigerator, for 30 minutes. Set the remaining *adobo* aside.

2. Set up the grill for direct grilling and preheat to high.

3. When ready to cook, brush and oil the grill grate. Brush the onion slices with the remaining 2 tablespoons of olive oil and arrange them on the hot grate. Place the steaks and onion slices on the hot grate. Grill the steaks until cooked to taste, 2 to 3 minutes per side for medium-rare, basting them with some of the remaining *adobo* and rotating them 90 degrees

How to Grill the Perfect Steak

When Americans are polled about their favorite foods for grilling, steak always heads the list. A slab of beef is the perfect food for the grill: Its broad surface area soaks up charcoal and smoke flavors, and its relative thinness allows for quick cooking. The most common mistake made in grilling steak is overcooking it; the second most common is undercooking. Here's how to do it just right.

1. Pick the right kind of steak. Tender cuts like sirloin, tenderloin, porterhouse, strip steak, and shell steak are the best. Fibrous steaks, like skirt and flank, also taste great grilled, provided that they are thinly sliced on the diagonal. Save tough cuts like chuck and blade steak for long, slow, moist cooking methods like braising. (You'll find a gallery of some of the different cuts of steak on page 145.)

2. Some people let the steak come to room temperature before grilling. Most professionals, myself included, don't bother. The difference in cooking time is negligible and certainly not worth the risk of meat spoiling at room temperature.

3. Preheat the grill to high. If you are cooking a very thick steak (say a T-bone that's two inches thick), build a two-zone fire (see page 18). On a gas grill, preheat one side to high, one side to medium-high.

4. Season the steaks generously with salt and pepper. Use a coarse-grained salt, like kosher or sea salt. Coarse grain salt crystals dissolve more slowly than fine table salt, so they hold up better during cooking, and steak pros all over the world use this. I always use freshly ground or freshly cracked black pepper, and I apply it generously both before and after grilling.

Some people don't add the salt until after cooking. The salt, they argue, draws out the juices. Believe me, you won't get much juice loss in the short time it takes to cook a medium-rare steak. And besides, you can't beat the flavor of salt mixed with caramelized meat juices.

5. Oil the grill grate. The easiest way to do this when grilling steak is to use a piece of steak fat held by tongs or on the end of a carving fork. Rub the fat over the bars of the grate. An oiled rag or folded up paper towel works fine, too.

6. Arrange the steaks on the oiled grate so they are all lined up in the same direction. After two minutes, rotate each steak. Normally I rotate them 45 degrees. This creates an attractive diamond crosshatch of grill marks on the steaks. Sometimes I rotate them 90 degrees; this produces a square crosshatch. Cook the steaks until beads of blood appear on the surface, one to two minutes for a steak a half inch thick, three to five minutes for one that's an inch thick, six to nine minutes for a thickness of one and a half to two inches. Turn the steak with tongs or a spatula; never use a fork. The holes made by a fork allow the juices to escape.

7. Continue cooking the steaks on the second side, rotating them after two minutes. The steaks will need slightly less time on the second side. The best test for doneness is feel: Press the top with your index finger. A rare steak will be softly yielding; a medium steak will be firmly yielding; a well-done steak will be firm (see Is It Done Yet? on page 30). Avoid cutting into a steak to test for doneness. This, too, drains the juices.

8. Transfer the steaks to plates or a platter and season them again with salt and pepper. At this stage, I like to drizzle my steaks with extra-virgin olive oil (à la Tuscany) or with melted butter (à la Ruth's Chris). This is optional, but it sure rounds out the flavor.

9. The last step is usually overlooked, but it's the most important. Let the steaks rest for two to five minutes before you serve them. This allows the meat to relax, giving you a moister, juicier steak.

STEAKS FROM HELL | AT RIGHT

after 1 minute on each side to create an attractive crosshatch of grill marks. Always use tongs when moving or turning the steaks. Grill the onions until nicely charred, 3 to 4 minutes per side, seasoning them with salt and pepper.

4. Transfer the steaks to plates or a platter and brush them one final time with the *adobo*. Let stand for 3 minutes, then serve with the grilled onions on the side.

MEXICO

STEAKS FROM HELL

DIRECT GRILLING
SERVES 4

This recipe literally *is* steaks from hell. It comes from an unassuming steak house in Juarez, Mexico, called Mitla, and *mitla* is the Nahuatl Indian word for hell. Mitla's steaks owe their extraordinary flavor to the fact that they're cooked over blazing mesquite logs. You can approximate the flavor by tossing mesquite chips on the grill.

I grill the tomatoes used to make the salsa on a stovetop burner. You can do this while the barbecue grill is heating up, letting you prepare the salsa in advance. You'll have about a cup and a half and any left over is great with chips.

SPECIAL EQUIPMENT

2 cups mesquite wood chips or chunks (optional), soaked for 1 hour in cold water to cover and drained

INGREDIENTS

2 to 4 chiles de arbol or other dried hot red chiles (4 give you a nice heat)
2 large ripe tomatoes
⅓ medium-size onion, sliced
1 clove garlic, sliced
3 tablespoons coarsely chopped fresh cilantro
1 to 2 tablespoons fresh lime juice
Salt and freshly ground black pepper
4 T-bone or sirloin beefsteaks (each about ¾ inch thick)
4 large or 8 small flour tortillas, for serving

1. Soak the chiles in a bowl of warm water until pliable, about 20 minutes.

2. Meanwhile, set each tomato directly on a gas stove burner and roast it over high heat until the skin is charred and blistered on all sides, 6 to 8 minutes in all. Transfer the tomatoes to a plate and let them cool.

3. Drain the chiles and remove the seeds if you prefer a milder salsa. Place the chiles in a blender with the cooled tomatoes and the onion, garlic, and cilantro and process to a coarse paste. Add the lime juice and season with salt and pepper to taste. Transfer the salsa to a serving bowl.

4. Set up the grill for direct grilling and preheat to high. If using a gas grill, add the wood chips (if using) to the smoker box before preheating.

5. When ready to cook, if using a charcoal grill, toss the wood chips on the coals. Brush and oil the grill grate. Salt the steaks generously on one side. Arrange the steaks on the oiled grate, salt side down, and grill, turning once with tongs, until cooked to taste, 2 to 4 minutes per side for medium-rare. Transfer the steaks to a platter and let rest for 3 minutes.

6. Meanwhile, arrange the tortillas on the grate and grill until soft, pliable, but not browned, about 20 seconds per side. Serve the steaks with the tortillas and the salsa on the side.

U.S.A.

MUSTARD LIME STEAKS

DIRECT GRILLING
SERVES 4

A few ingredients thoughtfully combined can utterly transform a commonplace dish—and this recipe is the perfect example. There are lots of steaks you could use here: sirloin, T-bone, rib eyes, New York strips, even skirt steaks.

4 sirloin beefsteaks (10 to 12 ounces each), cut 1 inch thick
¼ cup dry mustard, such as Colman's
¼ cup Worcestershire sauce
1 large, juicy lime
Coarse salt (kosher or sea) and freshly ground white pepper

1. Place the steaks on a platter and sprinkle 2 tablespoons of the dry mustard over them. Pat the steaks with the flat part of a fork to spread the mustard evenly. Sprinkle the steaks with 2 tablespoons of the Worcestershire sauce, then squeeze half of the lime juice over them. Pat the steaks with the fork. Season the steaks generously with salt and pepper. Turn the steaks over and spread them with the remaining 2 tablespoons each of mustard and Worcestershire and the remaining lime juice. Season the steaks with salt and pepper, patting them with the fork. Let the steaks marinate for 15 to 20 minutes while you preheat the grill.

2. Set up the grill for direct grilling and preheat to high.

3. When ready to cook, brush and oil the grill grate. Place the steaks on the hot grate and grill, turning with tongs, until cooked to taste, 4 to 6 minutes per side for medium-rare. Do not rotate steaks here; if you do, you'll knock off the mustard mixture. (This is a good steak to serve "Pittsburgh rare"—black on the outside, bloody inside.) Transfer the steaks to a platter and let rest for 3 minutes.

4. Thinly slice the steaks on the diagonal, as you would London broil. Let the slices marinate in the meat juices for a minute or two, then serve.

FRANCE

RIB STEAKS WITH RED WINE SAUCE AND MARROW

ENTRECOTES A LA BORDELAISE

DIRECT GRILLING
SERVES 4

Here's a dish from my cooking school days in Paris. An *entrecôte* is a French rib steak, often cooked and served on the bone in plate-burying proportions. In the U.S. I use rib eyes, which are generously marbled and delicious on the grill. As for the term *bordelaise* (Bordeaux style), it refers, logically enough, to a sauce made with reduced red wine and shallots and a garnish of poached marrow. I like to enrich the sauce further by adding sautéed mushrooms.

You needn't open a *grand cru* for this recipe, but try to use a wine you wouldn't mind drinking straight. (This is a great way to use up leftover Bordeaux.) Marrow bones can be found at butcher shops and ethnic markets: Ask your butcher to cut the bones on his saw and extract the marrow for you. But even if you can't find marrow, the steaks will still be fabulous without it.

3 tablespoons unsalted butter
½ cup minced shallots
8 ounces white mushrooms, wiped clean, and thinly sliced
2 cups dry red wine
1 cup homemade beef stock or low-sodium canned beef broth
1 teaspoon cornstarch dissolved in 1 tablespoon dry red wine (optional)
Coarse salt (kosher or sea) and freshly ground black pepper
¼ cup marrow, from 4 marrow bones
4 beef rib eye steaks (8 to 10 ounces each), cut 1 inch thick
2 tablespoons olive oil
2 tablespoons chopped fresh flat-leaf parsley

1. Melt the butter in a heavy medium-size saucepan over medium heat. Add the shallots and cook, stirring, until softened and translucent but not brown, about 3 minutes. Add the mushrooms and cook until lightly browned and most of the liquid has evaporated, 3 to 5 minutes. Add the 2 cups of wine and bring to a boil over medium-high heat, then reduce the heat slightly and let simmer briskly until the wine is reduced by half, about 5 minutes. Add the beef stock and let simmer briskly until the mixture is reduced by half again, 5 minutes longer. If you start with very good stock, the mixture may be thick enough to serve as a sauce without the cornstarch. If not, stir the cornstarch and wine mixture into the sauce and bring to a boil; the sauce should thicken slightly. Whisk in salt and pepper to taste; the sauce should be highly seasoned. Remove the sauce from the heat and set it aside while you poach the marrow.

2. Pour water to a depth of 1 inch in a shallow pan and heat to a simmer. Add the marrow and poach until waxy and white, with no remaining red color, turning with a skimmer, 15 to 30 seconds. Do not overcook or the marrow will melt. Transfer the marrow to paper towels to drain; then cut it into thin crosswise slices (see Note).

CUTS OF BEEF

The first step in mastering the art of grilling a steak is to pick the right one—and to understand its cooking properties. Rib steak (or rib eye) and filet mignon, for example, are the most tender, requiring little more than a hot fire and a reasonable sense of cooking time to produce meat that's tender enough to cut with the proverbial side of a fork. Flank steaks and skirt steaks are tough fibrous cuts, but when thinly sliced across the grain, they reward you with a rich flavor and as much tenderness as anyone could wish for. Here's a field guide to the players.

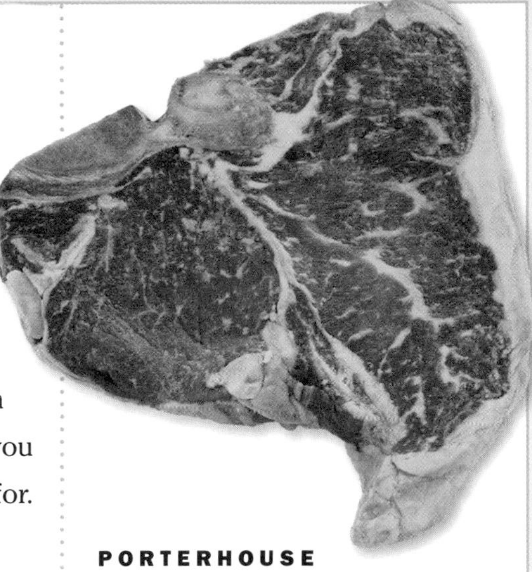

PORTERHOUSE

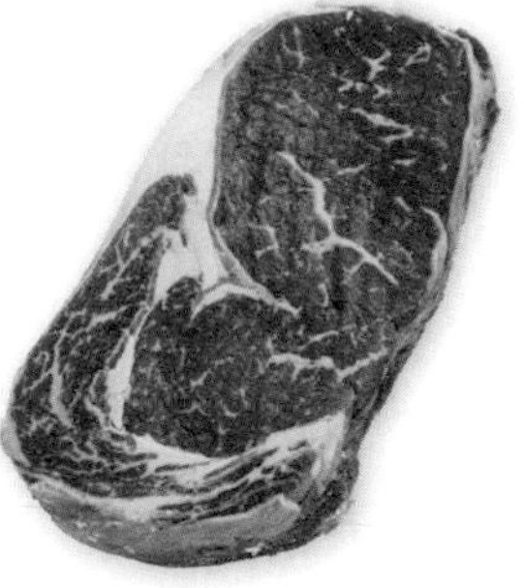

RIB EYE

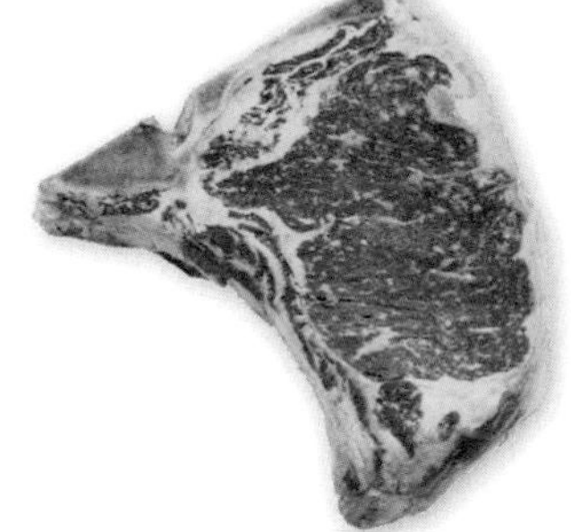

T-BONE

TOP SIRLOIN STEAK

FILET MIGNON

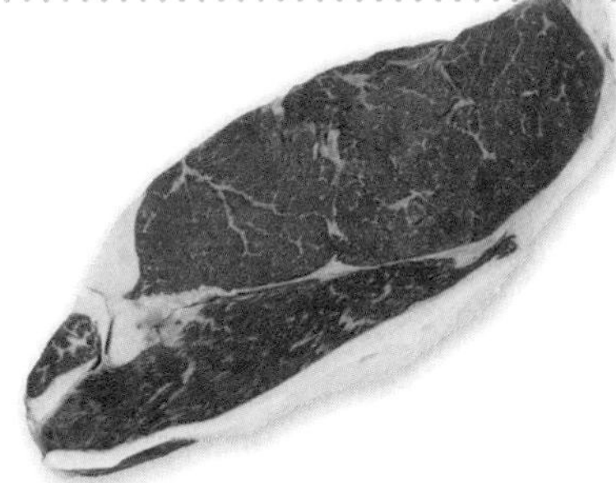

SIRLOIN

TENDERLOIN

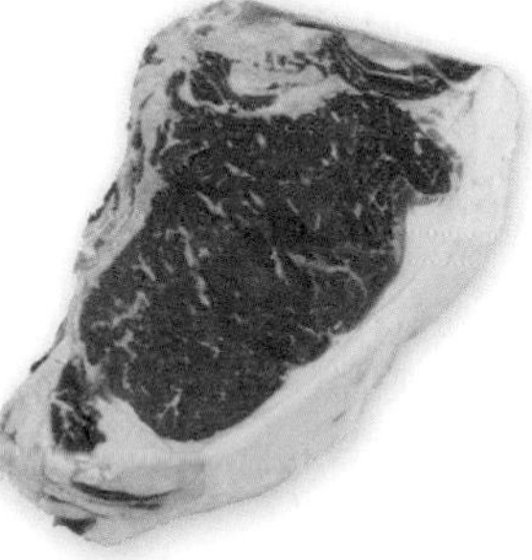

NY STRIP STEAK

FLANK STEAK

SKIRT STEAK

3. Set up the grill for direct grilling and preheat to high.

4. When ready to cook, rub the steaks on both sides with the olive oil and season them with salt and pepper to taste. Brush and oil the grill grate. Place the steaks on the hot grate and grill until cooked to taste, 3 to 5 minutes per side for medium-rare, rotating the steaks 45 degrees after 2 minutes on each side to create an attractive crosshatch of grill marks; use tongs when moving or turning the steaks.

5. While the steaks grill, reheat the sauce, tasting it for seasoning and adding more salt and/or pepper as necessary. Warm the marrow in a small saucepan or skillet.

6. Transfer the steaks to a platter and let rest for 2 to 3 minutes. Spoon the sauce over the steaks and top them with slices of marrow and a sprinkling of parsley. Serve at once.

NOTE: The recipe can be prepared several hours ahead to this point.

ITALY

FLORENTINE-STYLE STEAK

BISTECCA ALLA FIORENTINA

DIRECT GRILLING
SERVES 2 TO 3;
CAN BE MULTIPLIED AS DESIRED

Although I know that it doesn't sound like much when you describe it—an olive oil–basted, grilled porterhouse steak—*bistecca alla fiorentina* is one of the high holies of Tuscan cuisine. But here, as in so much of art, perfection lies in the details. The details in this instance include a lengthily aged steak from a rare breed of cattle cooked over an uncommonly high heat and basted with the best olive oil money can buy. *Bistecca* is commonly translated as T-bone steak, although it's actually closer to a porterhouse: Because *bistecca* is cut closer to the center of the steer, it has a larger piece of tenderloin attached than a T-bone.

On page 148, you can read about a true master in the art of making *bistecca alla fiorentina.* It would be impossible to duplicate his recipe outside of Italy, but his techniques can be adapted to make a highly respectable version with North American beef. The main secret is to find a butcher who will sell you an aged T-bone steak. Oh, you'll also need one unexpected piece of equipment—a hair dryer for fanning the coals!

SPECIAL EQUIPMENT

Handheld hair dryer (optional; for use with a charcoal grill)

INGREDIENTS

1 porterhouse or T-bone beefsteak (about 2 pounds), cut at least 1½ inches thick
Coarse salt (kosher or sea) and freshly ground white pepper
½ cup of the best cold-pressed extra-virgin olive oil you can find (preferably Tuscan)

1. Set up the grill for direct grilling and preheat to high. (Ideally, you'll be using wood or charcoal; the coals should just be beginning to ash over.) If using wood or charcoal, blow the ash off with a hair dryer.

2. When ready to cook, brush and oil the grill grate. Place the steak on the hot grate and, if using charcoal, point the hair dryer at the coals to fan them to a glowing red. Grill the steak until cooked to taste (about 6 to 8 minutes per side for medium-rare) turning with tongs. Generously salt and pepper the steak when you turn it.

3. When done, transfer the steak to a deep serving platter and generously salt and pepper it again. Drizzle the olive oil over the hot steak and let stand for 3 minutes before serving. Then cut servings of the beef off the bone for each eater. Mix the olive oil that collects in the bottom of the platter with the meat juices and spoon these over the steak as a sauce. Uncork an old bottle of Barolo and get ready to enjoy one of the world's best steaks.

CENTRAL AMERICA

NICARAGUAN-STYLE STEAK

CHURRASCO

DIRECT GRILLING
SERVES 4

The word *churrasco* is used throughout Latin America to describe beef cooked on the grill, although the precise meaning varies from country to country. In Brazil, for example, *churrasco* is the generic term for barbecue. In Nicaragua it refers to a broad, thin steak cut from a beef tenderloin. Most steaks are cut across the muscle grain, but Nicaragua's *churrasco* is cut along the grain. What results is a flat, thin piece of meat with a remarkable texture, a steak that's tender enough to cut with a fork. (And the steak's broad surface area readily picks up the smoke flavor from the coals.)

Nicaraguan *churrasco* is always served with a trio of sauces: *chimichurri* (here used as a marinade as well), *salsa marinara* (Nicaraguan Tomato Sauce, page 472), and a spicy pickled onion sauce called *cebollita.* Other accompaniments might include fried plantains (Grilled Plantains, a tasty substitute, appear in this book; see page 416).

ADVANCE PREPARATION

30 minutes for marinating the meat

INGREDIENTS

- **1 piece (1½ pounds) beef tenderloin, preferably center cut**
- **1 large or 2 medium-size bunches fresh flat-leaf parsley, stemmed (about 2 cups leaves)**
- **4 cloves garlic, peeled**
- **1 cup extra-virgin olive oil**
- **¼ cup red wine vinegar, or more to taste**
- **1½ teaspoons salt, or more to taste**
- **1 teaspoon finely ground black pepper, or more to taste**

1. Place the piece of tenderloin on a cutting board. Holding the knife parallel to the cutting board, cut the meat into four flat, even horizontal strips. Place each strip between two sheets of plastic wrap and, using the side of a cleaver or a rolling pin, pound them to a thickness of ¼ inch. Arrange the steaks in a nonreactive baking dish.

2. Place the parsley and garlic in a food processor and process until finely chopped. Add the olive oil, wine vinegar, salt, pepper, and 3 tablespoons of water and process to make a thick sauce. Taste for seasoning, adding more vinegar, salt, and/or pepper as necessary; the *chimichurri* marinade should be highly seasoned. Place half of the *chimichurri* in a bowl or crock for serving; pour the remainder over the meat. Let marinate in the refrigerator, covered, for 30 minutes, turning several times.

3. Set up the grill for direct grilling and preheat to high.

4. When ready to cook, brush and oil the grill grate. Drain the beef and place it on the hot grate. Grill, turning with tongs, until cooked to taste, 1 to 2 minutes per side for medium-rare. Serve with the remaining *chimichurri.*

CHURRASCO OF TENDERLOIN TIPS

PUNTAS DE CHURRASCO

Butchers sometimes sell tenderloin "tips" or "tails"—the narrow ends that are too slender to cut into filets mignons. These tips make a wonderful *churrasco* (they're better marbled than the center cuts) and they're a lot less expensive to boot. You may need to butterfly them to obtain thin, broad strips (see the box How to Butterfly Pork or Beef on page 181 for instructions).

Substitute 1¾ pounds of tenderloin tips for the center cut tenderloin in the Nicaraguan-Style Steak at left (you'll need a little more meat because the tips are a fattier cut). Trim off any excess fat and proceed with the recipe.

In Pursuit of the Best Tuscan Steak

It was one of those days when life on the barbecue trail didn't seem very glamorous. When my destination seemed to recede with each passing kilometer. When the "just another twenty minutes" turned into one hour after another.

My wife, Barbara, and I had come to Tuscany to sample *bistecca alla fiorentina* (Florentine steak). But here we were driving away from Florence, indeed, leaving Tuscany for Umbria. The winding roads and scenic hilltop towns I associate with Tuscany gave way to a roadway clogged with diesel belching trucks and a city crowded with traffic. It seemed an inauspicious start to a quest for a disappearing regional dish.

Yet our destination had come recommended by a highly reliable source. Italian food and wine expert Burton Anderson had mentioned the Villa Roncalli in the sort of conspiratorial whisper that foodies reserve for their personal favorite haunts. "You'll find one of the last people in Italy who serves real Chianina beef," explained Anderson. "I think you'll find his grilling techniques of interest."

We pulled off a crowded road into a long tree-shaded driveway. At the end rose a tall, yellow building with green shutters and brick-colored trim—the Villa Roncalli, formerly a seventeenth century hunting lodge. We stowed our skepticism long enough to check into a simple room with the gorgeous linens and bathroom fixtures we'd come to associate with even the most modest lodgings in Italy.

The dining room opened at 8 P.M., and there we were. The setting certainly looked promising: a large square chamber with a half dozen elegantly set tables. A huge bronze chandelier hung from a dizzyingly high-domed ceiling. An equally monumental mahogany breakfront filled with wine bottles lined the back wall. A waist-high fireplace stood in one corner, but much to my dismay, there was nary a fire in sight.

Because of antipollution measures, many restaurants in Florence have given up cooking over the traditional oak fire. But here in the countryside? Well, I couldn't imagine why the Villa Roncalli's fireplace was still cold and bare.

A handsome young woman in a starched, immaculately white, floor-length apron made a majestic entrance. Maria Luisa Leocastre is the owner's daughter, dining room manager, and chef. "If you wouldn't mind," she explained, "the kitchen would like to prepare a menu *degustazione*." (They give out menus, but everyone has the *degustazione*.) Of course we wouldn't mind, I said, but I noted that I would like to try a *bistecca alla fiorentina*.

In gradual succession we were served a delicate salad of *ortie* (wild greens) and shaved Parmesan cheese; a squash blossom filled with velvety ricotta and herbs; and a tiny square of fish cooked in a crust of paper-thin sliced potatoes. There was an exquisite soup made from beans and tiny clams. There was an exquisitely creamy barley risotto. The only thing missing was the beef.

ON WITH THE SHOW

Then at 10:30 P.M., just when I'd completely despaired of ever having my *bistecca*, Maria's father, Angelo Leocastre, made his appearance. Pressed denim shirt. Pleated wool pants. Alligator belt and leather shoes. He looked less like a grill master than an executive on vacation. Angelo dumped a few handfuls of oak on the stone slab floor of the fireplace and with a flourish ignited it with a blowtorch. He switched on a device that looked like a giant hair blower and within minutes the coals blazed red.

A true *bistecca* turns out to be a cross between a T-bone steak and a porterhouse. (It's cut closer to the center of the steer than a North American T-bone, so it includes a full circle of the tenderloin.) The steak Angelo showed me was three fingers thick and as dark red as the local sagrantino wine that filled my glass. He tossed it on a square grill that had legs to hold it over the fire.

"Veloce, veloce," (fast, fast) Angelo said, passionately explaining the secret to great *bistecca alla fiorentina.* The key is high heat. Using local oak and a blower to stoke the coals, Angelo claimed he could achieve a temperature of 900°F. Within minutes, the outside of the meat had seared to a golden-brown crust. The inside remained moist and sanguine. I noted with interest that Angelo seasoned the meat—a huge sprinkling of salt and white pepper from separate stone bowls—only after he had turned it.

I timed the cooking with a stop watch: exactly six minutes per side. Angelo transferred the steak to a platter and basted it generously with olive oil. Generous? I'd say he poured half a cup of green-gold oil over the steak. The aroma generated when the fragrant oil hit the hot meat made my mouth water.

There are people who maintain that a steak is a steak is a steak. They haven't tasted Angelo's *bistecca.* To say it cut like butter wouldn't do justice to its extraordinary tenderness. As for the flavor, I've simply never had beef like it. Somehow, Angelo has achieved the sort of complexity and depth of flavor you would get by aging a Parmesan cheese for three years or a red wine for a couple of decades. It's rich, sonorous, complex, and full flavored, without being heavy or gamy. It's beef the way it was meant to be eaten before the industrialization of cattle raising.

Angelo waved away a plate of vegetables the waitress had brought. "When you eat *fiorentina, fiorentina* is all you eat. The only suitable vegetable is wine." We drank fishbowl-size glasses of a dark red, cedary Santoroso wine. Amazingly enough, considering all the food we'd eaten, with Angelo's help we managed to finish the *bistecca.* The T-bone went to Angelo's waist-high mastiff, "Tiny."

Angelo's eyes lit with passion as he described the animal that supplies his *bistecca.* The Chianina is a huge, snow-white, one-and-a-half-ton steer that owes its extraordinary flavor to a diet of corn, beans, and barley. It's not an animal that lends itself to industrial production, explained Angelo. It takes too long to reach maturity and the "yield" is not efficient.

Angelo knows, perhaps, ten farmers who still raise it. "A labor of love," he said. The future for Chianina does not look particularly promising. "Some day, all our meat will come from Argentina or France," he said, wincing noticeably. "Then there will be no more *fiorentina.*"

LET IT AGE

After dinner, we followed Angelo into an outbuilding that serves as his studio, where we learned the final secrets of his extraordinary *bistecca.* It's here he ages the beef for thirty days at around 33°F. It will lose about 15 percent of its weight in the process. We admired the *prosciutti* and sausages hanging from the rafters—all homemade and aged for three years. "We make everything from scratch here," Angelo said with pride.

As the nights turn cool and darkness comes earlier, many of us will forsake our barbecue grills. But this is precisely the sort of weather a Tuscan cherishes for grilling. In Tuscany, grilling is generally done indoors in a fireplace. There's even a special grate with legs at each corner for holding the meat over a pile of coals.

On page 146 you'll find a recipe for *bistecca alla fiorentina* that comes as close as possible to the Italian classic. I can't think of a more compelling reason to keep the fire in your grill burning all autumn or winter long.

KOREA

KOREAN SESAME GRILLED BEEF

BOOL KOGI

DIRECT GRILLING
SERVES 6

Korean barbecue comes in two main varieties: *kalbi kui* (Korean Grilled Short Ribs, page 167) and *bool kogi,* thin shavings of beef steeped in a sweet-salty sesame marinade. The dish takes its name from the Korean words for *fire* and *meat* and is cooked on a grill that looks like a perforated inverted wok. *Bool kogi* is eaten like moo shu or fajitas, using lettuce instead of a pancake or tortilla. You roll the meat in a romaine lettuce leaf, dip it in sauce, then pop it into your mouth. The contrast of sweet and salty, of pungent and fruity, of crisp vegetable and chewy but tender meat is unique in the world of barbecue.

ADVANCE PREPARATION

1 to 2 hours for marinating the meat

INGREDIENTS

- 2 pounds beef tenderloin tips, or boneless sirloin
- ½ cup soy sauce
- ⅓ cup sugar
- 3 tablespoons sake, rice wine, or sherry
- 2 tablespoons Asian (dark) sesame oil
- 8 cloves garlic, thinly sliced
- 4 scallions, both white and green parts, trimmed and minced
- 2 tablespoons sesame seeds, toasted (see box, page 113)
- ½ teaspoon freshly ground black pepper
- Garlic Kebabs, prepared through Step 2 (optional, page 408)
- Asian Pear Dipping Sauce (page 486)
- 1 head romaine lettuce, separated into leaves, rinsed, and spun dry

BUTTERFLYING A FLANK STEAK

The flank steak you buy should be ten to twelve inches long and about six inches wide. Arrange the flank steak at the edge of the cutting board so that the short side is closest to you and the narrower edge of the long side is to your right, if you are right-handed, or to your left, if you are left-handed. You can apply the same technique to tenderloin tips.

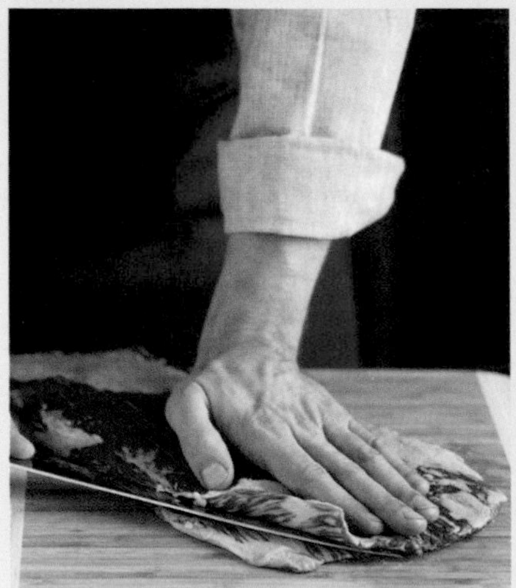

1. *Holding the flank steak flat with one hand, carefully start cutting it in half. Work with the knife parallel to the cutting board.*

2. *Continue cutting the steak to but not through the opposite side; stop cutting about ¼ inch from the edge.*

3. *Open up the butterflied steak, cover it with plastic wrap, and pound it flat and even with the side of a heavy cleaver (you can also use a rolling pin for this).*

1. If using tenderloin tips, butterfly them (see the box at left as reference) to obtain broad flat pieces of meat; each should be about 4 inches long and wide and ¼ inch thick. If using sirloin, cut it across the grain into ¼-inch slices. Whichever cut you use, using the side of a cleaver or a rolling pin, pound the slices between two sheets of plastic wrap to flatten them to a thickness of ⅛ inch. Place the meat in a large nonreactive baking dish and set aside while you prepare the marinade.

2. Combine the soy sauce, sugar, sake, sesame oil, garlic, scallions, sesame seeds, and pepper in a small bowl and whisk until the sugar dissolves. Pour the marinade over the meat in the baking dish and toss thoroughly to coat. Let marinate in the refrigerator, covered, for 1 to 2 hours.

3. Set up the grill for direct grilling and preheat to high.

4. When ready to cook, brush and oil the grill grate. Add the garlic kebabs (if using) to the hot grate and grill for 4 to 5 minutes. Then arrange the pieces of meat on the grate and grill, turning with tongs, until nicely browned on both sides, 1 to 2 minutes per side. Turn the garlic kebabs as the meat cooks. Transfer the meat to a platter when it is done and unwrap the garlic.

5. Pour the Asian Pear Dipping Sauce into 6 small bowls, one for each diner. To eat, take a piece of meat and a grilled garlic clove (if using) and wrap them in a lettuce leaf. Dip the leaf in the dipping sauce and eat at once.

MEXICO

GRILLED BEEF OAXACA STYLE

DIRECT GRILLING
SERVES 8

Carne asado (grilled meat) and *carnitas* (little pieces of grilled meat) are snack/street/party foods so popular in Mexico, they could qualify as official state dishes. You find these smoky beef bits wherever crowds gather and an enterprising cook has space to set up a grill.

The best *carne asado* I've ever tasted was at the Mercado 20 de Noviembre (November 20 Market) in Oaxaca. The contrast of textures and flavors—chewy meat, crisp scallions, juicy salsa, cooling guacamole, and fiery chiles—was as dazzling as the baroque architecture in the local churches.

Serving Oaxacan *carne asado* makes a wonderful way to entertain, offering your guests a taste experience they're not likely to forget. The recipe here may seem involved, but it's really a series of simple steps. To be strictly authentic, you'd cook the ingredients over wood or charcoal, not gas. But gas will do the trick, too.

2 bunches scallions, both white and green parts, trimmed
8 chiles de agua, cubanelle peppers, bull's horn peppers, jalapeño peppers, or poblano peppers
Coarse salt (kosher or sea)
2 pounds boneless sirloin steak, cut into broad sheets ¼ inch thick (see Note)
16 corn or flour tortillas, or more as needed
4 limes, cut into wedges
Oaxacan-Style Guacamole (page 455)
Salsa Mexicana (page 192)

1. Set up the grill for direct grilling and preheat to high.

2. When ready to cook, if using charcoal, toss the scallions and peppers right on the coals. If using gas (or you don't have easy access to the coals), arrange the scallions and peppers on the hot grate. Cook, turning with tongs, until nicely charred and tender, about 5 minutes per side. Leave the fire burning.

3. Transfer the grilled scallions to a serving plate, cover with plastic wrap, and set aside until ready to serve. Scrape the charred skin off the peppers with a sharp knife (don't worry about removing every last bit). Cut the peppers in half and scrape out the seeds. Transfer the peppers to a bowl, cover with plastic wrap, and set aside.

4. When ready to grill the beef, brush and oil the grill grate. Generously salt the beef and place it on the hot grate. Grill, turning with tongs, 1 to 4 minutes per side for well-done (the way Oaxacans like their beef cooked). While you're at it, arrange the tortillas, a few at a time, on the grill for a few seconds to heat them, then keep them warm in a cloth-lined basket. Transfer the grilled beef to a cutting board and cut it into thin strips or ½-inch dice.

5. To serve, set out bowls of lime wedges, guacamole, and salsa along wth the scallions and peppers. To eat, place a

Matambre: A Hunger-Killer from South America

El Palenque may not be the fanciest restaurant in Montevideo, Uruguay, but when it comes to eating beef, there's no place I'd rather be. Located in the Mercado del Puerto (port market), a nineteenth-century covered market that today serves as Montevideo's barbecue headquarters, El Palenque offers a staunchly carnivorous bill of fare that includes *mollejas* (grilled sweetbreads), *choto* (crisp rolled small intestines), and an *asado de tira* (long, thin cross-section of the rib roast) that literally spills off your plate.

But my favorite dish here bears the curious name of *matambre.* Actually, the name says it all. *Hambre* is the Spanish word for hunger. *Matar* means to kill. Put them together and you get one of the most distinctive dishes in South America.

Matambres are usually described as rolled, stuffed, baked, or grilled flank steaks. But travel around South America and you'll find that they can come flat and plain, as well, and be made with a variety of cuts of meat, not just flank steak. Traditionally served as an appetizer, *matambres* also come in portions large enough to dwarf the average North American main course.

For me, the *matambre* reaches its apotheosis at El Palenque. The Montevidean version features a belt-loosening array of sausages, carrots, bell peppers, and cheese rolled in an oregano and sage–scented sheet of flank steak. When sliced crosswise, the *matambre* forms a handsome spiral of beef studded with a colorful mosaic of vegetables, cheese, and sausage. Knowing about the restaurant's mighty portions, I ordered a half serving of Palenque's hunger-killer. The slice was as thick as a phone book. I'd hate to see a full portion.

few pieces of beef on a tortilla. Place a grilled scallion and pepper half on top. Top with spoonfuls of guacamole and salsa, and a squeeze of lime juice. Roll the whole thing up and eat it.

NOTE: Ask your butcher to cut the beef for you on a meat slicer. Cutting the steaks this thin makes them tender and maximizes the surface area exposed to the heat and smoke.

ARGENTINA

A SIMPLE MATAMBRE

MATAMBRE

DIRECT GRILLING
SERVES 6 AS AN APPETIZER, 4 AS A MAIN COURSE

Literally hunger killer, *matambre* refers both to a cut of meat and to the series of dishes that are made from it. The cut, which doesn't exist in North America, is a large, half-inch-thick rectangular muscle from the chest of the cow. Tough but flavorful, *matambre* is always served well done: The prolonged cooking helps break down the tough meat fibers.

The simplest version of *matambre*—the one served as an appetizer at *estancias* (ranches) and steak houses in Argentina—consists of the flat piece of the meat sprinkled with spices, grilled, and cut into one-inch squares to be served on toothpicks. To re-create it in North America, I like to use skirt steak. Skirt steak is a smaller cut than *matambre,* but the thinness and muscle structure are similar. Skirt steak is more tender, however, so you don't need to cook it as long.

To make a more elaborate *matambre,* the meat is stuffed and rolled into a compact cylinder and grilled over low heat for several hours. You'll find instructions for making a stuffed *matambre* on page 156.

ADVANCE PREPARATION

4 to 8 hours for marinating the meat

SPECIAL EQUIPMENT

Toothpicks, for serving

Argentinean Roots

The first *matambres* appeared in Argentina as steaks seasoned with salt and herbs and cooked flat over glowing coals. Such was the *matambre* I received by way of a welcome at the Estancia La Cinacina, a ranch west of Buenos Aires that stages barbecues and equestrian shows for sightseers. Cut into one-inch squares and served on toothpicks, this sort of *matambre* makes for a tasty hors d'oeuvre.

Matambre embellishments vary from restaurant to restaurant and chef to chef. The Estancia restaurant in Buenos Aires (not to be confused with the aforementioned ranch) rolls its *matambre* with only a sprinkling of olive oil, salt, pepper, garlic, oregano, and bay leaves.

In Brazil, I feasted on a splendid *matambre* at the Barra Grill in Rio de Janeiro. True to Brazilian tradition, the meat had been marinated in a spicy garlic-and-lime-based mixture, prior to being rolled with bacon and cheese and roasted on a spit.

Because of the innate toughness of the cut of meat used in the dish, *matambre* requires lengthy cooking to attain the proper tenderness. You might think that lengthy cooking would be difficult, if not impossible, over a live fire. But South American grill jockeys resort to an ingenious method. They swaddle the *matambre* in aluminum foil and cook it for several hours over a low fire. The foil prevents the outside of the meat from burning, while holding the *matambre* neatly in shape.

Below and on page 156 you'll find recipes for two different *matambres* you can prepare on your grill. Whether you serve them as colorful appetizers or main courses, one thing's for sure: They certainly will kill your hunger!

FOR THE STEAK AND MARINADE

1½ pounds beef skirt steaks
1 medium-size green bell pepper, cored, seeded, and finely chopped
2 cloves garlic, minced
¼ cup extra-virgin olive oil
2 tablespoons red wine vinegar
1 teaspoon dried oregano
½ teaspoon hot red pepper flakes
½ teaspoon salt
½ teaspoon finely ground black pepper
2 bay leaves

FOR THE SPICE MIXTURE

1 teaspoon dried oregano
½ teaspoon hot red pepper flakes
½ teaspoon salt
½ teaspoon finely ground black pepper

1. Prepare the steaks and marinade: Arrange the steaks in a nonreactive baking dish and set aside while you prepare the marinade.

2. Combine the bell pepper, garlic, olive oil, wine vinegar, 1 teaspoon of oregano, ½ teaspoon of red pepper flakes, ½ teaspoon of salt, and ½ teaspoon of black pepper in a small bowl and stir to mix well. Pour the marinade over the steaks in the baking dish and toss well to coat. Add the bay leaves, cover, and let marinate in the refrigerator for at least 4 hours, preferably overnight.

3. Make the spice mixture: Combine the 1 teaspoon of oregano, ½ teaspoon of red pepper flakes, ½ teaspoon of salt, and ½ teaspoon of black pepper in a small bowl.

4. Set up the grill for direct grilling and preheat to high.

5. When ready to cook, brush and oil the grill grate. Drain the steaks and place them on the hot grate, sprinkling half of the spice mixture on top. Grill the steaks, turning with tongs, until medium to medium-well done, about 4 minutes per side. After turning the steaks, sprinkle the remaining spice mixture on top.

6. Transfer the steaks to a cutting board and let rest about 3 minutes, then cut them into 1-inch squares and serve on toothpicks.

The Argentinean Grill

To say that Argentineans love meat is the understatement of the year. This nation of more than forty million consumes beef on a scale our own country hasn't seen since the 1950s. Buenos Aires fairly bulges with *parrillas* (grills), *asado* restaurants, and chop houses. Statistics are hard to come by (misplaced, I was told, during the last change of government), but my casual poll suggests that the average Argentinean eats meat ten to twelve times a week.

Actually, Argentina offers two very different grilled meat experiences: *asado* and *parrilla* (pronounced par-EE-yha). *Asado* is traditional ranch-style barbecue: whole baby goats, suckling pigs, sides of beef ribs, and briskets roasted upright on stakes in front of a fire. The *parrilla* corresponds to a North American steak house. Sausages, innards, and belly-bludgeoning steaks are the specialty, and meats are cooked to order. If you like fall-off-the-bone tender kid, pork, or beef ribs, your best bet is an *asado*. If you fancy succulent steaks, sizzling and rare, head for a *parrilla*. Can't make up your mind? Don't worry—many restaurants serve both.

Gauchos and Grilled Meat

Argentina's love affair with grilled meats began with the gauchos, rugged cowboys who herded cattle on the grassy plains of the Pampas. The arrival in Buenos Aires of the first refrigerated ship from Europe in 1876 ushered in a golden age for cattlemen. The *estancieros* (ranchers) became millionaires selling Europeans Argentinean beef. By 1910, Buenos Aires was South America's largest city and, in the Western Hemisphere, second in size and affluence only to New York. Beef money built the wide avenues, plazas, and extravagant buildings that make Buenos Aires the "Paris of South America."

There's a tendency to romanticize the gauchos. The real gauchos, often *mestizos* (of mixed Spanish and Indian heritage), lived a less than glamorous life. Yes, they wore *boinas* (berets) and *rastras* (coin-studded leather belts; the coins were a way of showing off their wages) festooned with *faccas* (South American bowie knives). Yes, they danced the *malambo,* a solitary male dance that imitates the motions of a horse. Still, they lived a lonely existence, on the margins of society, with little or no female contact.

The gauchos developed *asado*. To experience the phenomenon firsthand, I signed up for a bus tour of a ranch called Estancia La Cinacina. An hour outside of Buenos Aires, the land becomes flat and spacious, with clumps of trees punctuating the grasslands. Cinacina is owned by the Ramirez family, three generations of ruggedly handsome gauchos decked out in berets, bandanas, and riding boots. For three hours, they entertained us with carriage rides, gaucho music, handkerchief dancing, and demonstrations of equestrian prowess. Then, we piled into a mess hall for a communal cowboy lunch.

In an adjacent courtyard was a circular fire pit where one of the Ramirezes worked as an *asador* (pit master) tending a bonfire that had been started early that morning. By the time we arrived, whole rib sections of beef and *vacios* (a cut that corresponds to the breast and brisket) had been tied to cruciform metal stakes and stood before the fire. The stakes were angled slightly away from the flames, so that the juices dripped on the ground, not the coals. The meat roasted for two to three hours and, when removed from the stakes, it was tender enough to eat with a spoon. The only seasoning was salt and fresh air. It was the only seasoning needed.

Cinacina's *asado* came with the traditional accompaniments: salad, *salsa criollo* (onion and tomato relish), and a vinaigrette-like condiment called *chimichurri*. *Chimichurri* is Argentina's national steak sauce, and there are probably as many different versions as there are individual pit masters. At its simplest, *chimichurri* consists of olive oil flavored with a little dried oregano, hot pepper flakes, salt, and pepper. This is the sort of *chimichurri* served at Cinacina.

In cities, one finds a more elaborate *chimichurri:* fresh parsley, garlic, olive oil, and wine vinegar. I make a sort of pesto, sometimes with hot peppers. There's even a red *chimichurri* made from tomatoes and bell peppers.

La Cabaña

Once back in Buenos Aires, I set out to investigate *parrilla*. My destination was the granddaddy of Argentinean steak houses: the venerable La Cabaña. Founded in 1935, La Cabaña has since upscaled, downsized, and relocated under new ownership, but at the time it was to the kingdom of barbecue what Windsor Castle is to the royal family of England. As you entered, you passed an ancient wooden meat locker and a wood-burning grill with a gleaming copper hood. The dining room had the grandeur of a Tudor hunting lodge.

You warmed up with crusty *mollejas* (grilled sweetbreads). Meltingly tender *riñones* (kidneys). Creamy *chinchulin* (intestines). Handsome coils of *longaniza* (spicy Calabrian-style sausage). Crisp-skinned *morcillas* (raisin-studded sweet blood sausages). These and other equally delicious items were served as a *parrillada* (mixed grill) on a tabletop hibachi stoked with blazing coals. But the specialty was clearly the beef. A ranch in the Junín district west of Buenos Aires supplied La Cabaña with specially raised steers, each weighing half a ton. A *bife de lomo* (filet mignon) at La Cabaña probably dwarfed a grapefruit. A single *costilla* (bone-in rib steak) tipped the scale at more than three and a half pounds.

A most unusual *chimichurri* accompanied the beef—a tangy red paste of garlic, peppers, anchovies, canned tuna, and tomato sauce. The anchovies suggest parentage with two other of the world's great steak sauces: A.1. and Worcestershire. The presence of tuna recalls Italy's great *tonnato* sauce, traditionally served with cold roast veal.

As at most Argentinean steak houses, dessert is a simple affair. A wood-fired oven-baked apple. Or perhaps a flan with *dulce de leche*—dark, thick milk caramel—the burnt-sugar flavor of which echoes the smokiness of charcoal-seared meat. Dinner is an event—late, long, and a lot.

A Visit to Costanera Norte

Today the epicenter of *parrilla*-style grilling is an area called the Costanera Norte, about fifteen minutes from downtown Buenos Aires. Thirty years ago, there was nothing there, save a seawall along the Plata river. The Costanera lies on the road city dwellers would take driving back to Buenos Aires from weekend trips to the country and seaside. Then, a few enterprising cooks began setting up makeshift grills and serving steak dinners out of the backs of their cars.

Today, the Costanera is lined with dozens of stylish restaurants, with names like Happening and Los Años Locos. The decors vary from retro to modern, but the bill of fare is pretty much the same—which is to say every imaginable type of steak and organ meat expertly grilled and served without artifice. Well-dressed customers flock here from Buenos Aires for lunch on the weekends.

I was able to find an establishment that maintained a sense of what the Costanera must have been like in the old days. In a nearby port area, a couple of young men set up a grill shack. Here, under the shadow of a huge derrick, amid thick clouds of smoke, men in sweaty red jackets grilled an astonishing assortment of meats.

The grill consisted of a metal table piled with glowing coals surmounted by a chain-link grate. The grate sloped gently upward from front to back, offering a range of cooking temperatures. Meats are seared on the hotter front part of the grill, then moved back to finish cooking at a lower temperature. I could make a meal on the aroma alone. At El Potro, salads are dished up without ceremony from plastic tubs. Guests get to eat on a rickety terrace overlooking a power plant. The entertainment takes the form of a soccer game on a small black-and-white TV.

Argentina can be a forbidding place for a vegetarian. In recent years many generally health-conscious North Americans have come to regard meat with suspicion if not downright contempt, but while I consider myself as nutritionally correct as the next guy, nonetheless I feel obliged to note that after a week of restaurant hopping in Buenos Aires, I was one happy fella.

URUGUAY

MONTEVIDEAN STUFFED BEEF ROLL

MATAMBRE

INDIRECT GRILLING
SERVES 8 AS AN APPETIZER, 4 AS A MAIN COURSE

While it may sound complicated, this recipe can be assembled in fifteen minutes. When people see the results, they'll think you've been working for hours. The cut called for here is flank steak, but I've also made it with brisket. If you're not comfortable with your knifesmanship, ask your butcher to butterfly the meat. You'll find more about *matambre* on page 152.

MONTEVIDEAN STUFFED BEEF ROLL

SPECIAL EQUIPMENT

Heavy-duty aluminum foil; metal skewers or butcher's string for securing the matambre

INGREDIENTS

- ½ large red bell pepper, cored and seeded
- ½ large green bell pepper, cored and seeded
- 1 piece (6 ounces) Romano cheese
- 1 piece (6 ounces) kielbasa sausage
- 2 large eggs (optional), hard-cooked, peeled, and cooled
- 1 long carrot, peeled
- 6 thin slices of bacon
- 1 beef flank steak (1½ to 1¾ pounds), butterflied (see box, page 150)
- Salt and freshly ground black pepper
- 1 teaspoon dried oregano
- ½ teaspoon dried sage

1. Cut the bell peppers into ½-inch lengthwise strips. Cut the cheese and kielbasa lengthwise into ½-inch-thick strips. Cut the eggs (if using) lengthwise into quarters. Cut the carrot lengthwise in quarters.

2. Arrange the bacon strips on a large (24 by 24 inch) square of heavy-duty aluminum foil, leaving a space of about 1 inch between each slice (if necessary, use 2 pieces of foil); the strips should run parallel to the edge of the work surface. Place the butterflied flank steak on top of the bacon so that the grain of the meat (and the seam between the halves of meat) runs parallel to the bacon.

3. Season the flank steak generously with salt and black pepper and sprinkle the oregano and sage over it. Arrange strips of sausage in a neat row, end to end, along the edge of the meat closest to you. Place a row of red bell pepper strips next to it, then a row of cheese strips, then carrot strips, then green bell pepper strips, then hard-cooked eggs. Repeat the process until all of the ingredients are used up. Leave the last 3 inches of meat uncovered.

4. Starting at the edge closest to you and using the foil to help you, roll up the meat with the filling to make a compact roll; it's a lot like rolling a jelly roll. Pin the top edge shut with metal skewers or tie the *matambre* closed with a few lengths of butcher's string. Encase the roll in the foil, twisting the ends to make what will look like a large sausage. Poke a few holes in the foil at each end to allow for the release of steam.

5. Set up the grill for indirect grilling and preheat to medium. No drip pan is necessary for this recipe.

6. When ready to cook, place the *matambre* in the center of the grill, away from the fire. Cover the grill. Cook the *matambre* until very tender, 1½ to 2 hours. To test for doneness, insert a metal skewer right through the foil covering; it should pierce the meat easily and be piping hot to the touch when withdrawn. If using a charcoal grill, you'll need to add 10 to 12 fresh coals to each side after 1 hour.

7. Transfer the *matambre* to a cutting board and let rest for 10 minutes. Remove the foil and skewers or string, then cut the *matambre* crosswise into 1-inch slices to serve.

WEST AFRICA

GRILLED BEEF WITH PEANUT FLOUR

KYINKYINGA

DIRECT GRILLING
SERVES 4

I first learned of *kyinkyinga* (pronounced chin-CHIN-ga) from an anthropologist who spent several years studying tribes in West Africa. When cooking beef, they hang long strips of it on vertical skewers and cook it upright in front of a campfire. The peanut flour used to coat the meat adds an unexpected crunch and sweet nutty flavor that counterpoints the fiery chile marinade on the beef.

The only remotely difficult aspect to this dish is finding peanut flour. If you live in a city that has a West African community, you may be able to find it at a West African grocery store or sometimes at an Asian market. In a pinch, you can easily grind dry-roasted peanuts with a little flour in a food processor.

For the sake of convenience, I cook the meat kebab style. As always, I offer a range of chiles. Four will give you a really hot *kyinkyinga*.

ADVANCE PREPARATION

2 to 3 hours for marinating the meat

SPECIAL EQUIPMENT

4 long metal skewers, or 8 short bamboo skewers and an aluminum foil shield (see box, page 23)

FOR THE BEEF AND MARINADE

1½ to 2 pounds boneless beef sirloin
1 large onion, cut into chunks
1 green bell pepper, cored, seeded, and cut into chunks
6 cloves garlic, peeled
1 to 4 Scotch bonnet chiles, or 2 to 8 jalapeño peppers, seeded and coarsely chopped (for a hotter kyinkyinga, leave the seeds in)
2 tablespoons chopped peeled fresh ginger
1½ teaspoons salt
1 teaspoon freshly ground black pepper
¼ cup peanut oil

FOR THE KEBABS

2 large green bell peppers, cored, seeded, and cut into 1-inch pieces
1 large onion, cut into 1-inch pieces
1½ cups peanut flour (see Note)

1. Prepare the beef and marinade: Trim any sinews and excess fat off the beef, then cut the meat into 1-inch cubes. Place the beef in a large baking dish.

2. Combine the onion and bell pepper chunks and the garlic, Scotch bonnets, ginger, salt, and pepper in a food processor and finely chop. Add the peanut oil and process to a smooth puree. Add the marinade to the beef and toss to coat. Let marinate in the refrigerator, covered, for 2 to 3 hours.

3. Assemble the kebabs: Remove the beef from the marinade and thread it onto the skewers, alternating it with the pieces of bell pepper and onion. Place the flour on a large plate and roll the kebabs in it so that all sides are generously covered.

4. Set up the grill for direct grilling and preheat to high.

5. When ready to cook, brush and oil the grill grate. Arrange the skewers on the hot grate with the aluminum foil shield under the ends of the skewers. Grill the kebabs, turning with tongs, until the beef is cooked to taste, 2 to 3 minutes per side (8 to 12 minutes in all) for medium-rare. Serve at once.

NOTE: If you don't have peanut flour, grind 1¼ cups dry-roasted peanuts with ¼ cup all-purpose flour as fine as possible in a food processor, running the machine in short bursts. Take care not to overgrind; peanut flour quickly becomes peanut butter.

PERU

PERUVIAN BEEF KEBABS

ANTICUCHOS

DIRECT GRILLING
SERVES 4

Peru's national snack, *anticuchos* are spicy kebabs of beef heart grilled to order by street vendors. Because beef hearts aren't part of most North American diets, I've redesigned the dish for sirloin. The traditional recipe calls for *aji amarillo* and achiote. *Aji amarillo* is a fiery yellow chile powder made from a potent Peruvian chile. Achiote are the orange seeds of the Caribbean annatto plant. (Annatto seeds, available in Latin American markets, are very hard; grind them in a spice mill.) But if you can't find these ingredients, rest assured that you can make perfectly delectable *anticuchos* using the substitutions suggested below.

Peruvian Potato Mixed Grill (page 418) would make a good accompaniment to the *anticuchos.*

ADVANCE PREPARATION

2 hours for marinating the meat

SPECIAL EQUIPMENT

4 long metal skewers

FOR THE BEEF AND MARINADE

1½ pounds boneless beef sirloin or tenderloin
2 cloves garlic, minced
2 to 4 teaspoons aji amarillo (chile powder or paste) or hot paprika
½ teaspoon ground annatto seeds, or ½ teaspoon ground turmeric
1 teaspoon ground cumin
1 teaspoon salt
1 teaspoon freshly ground black pepper
½ cup extra-virgin olive oil
⅓ cup red wine vinegar

FOR THE GLAZE

3 tablespoons vegetable oil
1 to 3 teaspoons aji amarillo (chile powder or paste) or hot paprika
1 teaspoon salt
½ teaspoon freshly ground black pepper
3 tablespoons finely chopped fresh flat-leaf parsley

FOR THE KEBABS

1 medium-size green bell pepper, cored, seeded, and cut into ½-inch pieces
1 medium-size red or yellow bell pepper, cored, seeded, and cut into ½-inch pieces

1. Prepare the beef and marinade: Trim any sinews and excess fat off the beef, then cut the meat into ½-inch cubes. Toss the beef with the garlic, 2 to 4 teaspoons of *aji amarillo,*

On Trimming Fat from Meat

Throughout this book I ask you to trim various cuts of meat. What you want to remove is any sinew, gristle, and silverskin. And excess fat—not *all* fat.

By excess fat, I mean large pieces (an inch or more) of fat or a layer of fat that's more than a half inch thick. Fat may be bad in nutritional circles (I should know; my stepdaughter is a dietitian), but when it comes to barbecue, fat is good. Well-marbled steaks or briskets covered with a sheath of fat always taste better than absolutely lean cuts of meat.

The reason is simple: Grilling is a dry-cooking method. The blast of dry heat tends to dry meats out. As a well-marbled piece of meat cooks, the fat melts, basting the meat fibers, keeping them moist and succulent. Besides, there's nothing more delicious than the flame-charred fat at the edge of a steak or rib. Just don't make a steady diet of it!

So the next time you go to trim meat, resist the temptation to remove all the fat. Your barbecue will be the better for it.

annatto, cumin, 1 teaspoon of salt, and 1 teaspoon of black pepper in a large nonreactive baking dish. Cover and refrigerate the beef for 30 minutes.

2. Stir in the olive oil and wine vinegar, re-cover the beef, and let it marinate in the refrigerator for 1½ hours.

3. Make the glaze: Heat the vegetable oil in a small skillet or saucepan. Add the 1 to 3 teaspoons of *aji amarillo,* 1 teaspoon of salt, and ½ teaspoon of black pepper. Cook the glaze, stirring, over low heat until orange and fragrant, about 5 minutes. Stir in the parsley and cook for 1 minute. Remove the glaze from the heat and set aside to cool.

4. Assemble the kebabs: Thread the pieces of beef onto the skewers, alternating with pieces of bell pepper. Brush the kebabs with half of the glaze.

5. Set up the grill for direct grilling and preheat to high.

6. When ready to cook, brush and oil the grill grate. Arrange the skewers on the hot grate. Grill the kebabs, turning once with tongs, until the meat is cooked to taste, 3 to 4 minutes per side (6 to 8 minutes in all) for medium-rare. Brush the kebabs as they cook with the remaining glaze. Do not brush the kebabs during the last 2 minutes of grilling. Serve at once.

BANGLADESH

BENGALI SHISH KEBABS

DIRECT GRILLING
SERVES 8 AS AN APPETIZER, 4 AS A MAIN COURSE

Shish kebab is the world's most popular barbecue dish. The meat and the kind of skewers may vary but the principle—meat grilled on a stick—remains constant. Here's a Bengali version that's as popular an after-school snack in Bangladesh as burgers are in the U.S. The spicing is more restrained than Indian tandoori kebabs, and the spice mix is rubbed onto the meat before the oil is added for marinating; it gets into the meat better this way. I call for beef tenderloin here, but you can also use tenderloin tips or sirloin.

ADVANCE PREPARATION

2 hours for marinating the meat

SPECIAL EQUIPMENT

4 long metal skewers, or 8 short bamboo skewers and an aluminum foil shield (see box, page 23)

FOR THE BEEF AND MARINADE

1½ pounds beef tenderloin
3 cloves garlic, minced
1 tablespoon minced peeled fresh ginger
1½ teaspoons salt
1 tablespoon ground coriander (see Note)
1 teaspoon ground cumin (see Note)
1 teaspoon freshly ground black pepper
½ to 1 teaspoon cayenne pepper
3 tablespoons vegetable oil

FOR SERVING

Tandoori-Baked Flat Breads (page 131) or pita bread
1 cucumber, seeded (see box, page 454) and cut into ½-inch dice
1 tomato, seeded (see box, page 454) and cut into ½-inch dice
1 small onion, cut into ½-inch dice
1 lemon, cut into wedges
Bengali Mango-Tamarind Barbecue Sauce (optional; page 470)

1. Prepare the beef: Trim any sinews and excess fat off the beef, then cut the meat into 1-inch cubes.

2. Combine the beef, garlic, ginger, salt, coriander, cumin, black pepper, and cayenne in a bowl and toss thoroughly to mix. Add the oil and toss again. Let the beef marinate in the refrigerator, covered, for 2 hours. Then, thread the beef cubes onto the skewers.

3. Set up the grill for direct grilling and preheat to high.

4. When ready to cook, brush and oil the grill grate. Arrange the kebabs on the hot grate (place the aluminum foil shield under the ends of the bamboo skewers). Grill, turning the kebabs with tongs, until the beef is cooked to taste, 2 to 3 minutes per side (8 to 12 minutes in all) for medium-rare. Transfer the kebabs to a platter.

5. To serve: Arrange the breads of your choice in one layer on the grate and grill until pliable, about 20 seconds per side. Divide the breads among serving plates (if serving the kebabs as an appetizer, cut each bread in half). Unskewer the beef onto the breads (or fold a bread around the meat on each skewer and remove the skewer). Sprinkle the diced cucumber, tomato, and onion over the meat and squeeze a little lemon juice on top. Spoon the Bengali Mango-Tamarind Barbecue Sauce (if using) on top, or use it as a dipping sauce. Serve the kebabs at once.

NOTE: For extra flavor, start with whole cumin and coriander seeds. Lightly toast them in a dry skillet over medium heat until lightly colored and fragrant, 3 to 5 minutes, shaking the pan frequently (don't use a nonstick skillet for this). Then let the seeds cool and grind them in a food processor.

RUSSIA

RUSSIAN SHASHLIK

DIRECT GRILLING
SERVES 4 TO 6

Muscovites love to take to the country on the weekends, and when they do, chances are they'll cook these robust beef kebabs. Grating the onion is a traditional Slavic technique that produces a fuller, richer onion flavor than dicing.

ADVANCE PREPARATION

4 to 8 hours for marinating the meat

SPECIAL EQUIPMENT

4 to 6 long metal skewers

FOR THE BEEF AND MARINADE

- **1½ to 2 pounds boneless beef sirloin or tenderloin tips**
- **1 large onion, coarsely grated**
- **6 cloves garlic, minced**
- **½ cup dry red wine**
- **¼ cup red wine vinegar**
- **3 tablespoons extra-virgin olive olive oil**
- **2 bay leaves**
- **1½ teaspoons salt**
- **1 teaspoon freshly ground pepper**

FOR THE KEBABS

- **1 large onion, cut into 1-inch pieces**
- **1 large green bell pepper, cored, seeded, and cut into 1-inch pieces**

1. Prepare the beef and marinade: Trim any sinew and excess fat off the beef, then cut the meat into 1½-inch cubes.

2. Combine the grated onion, garlic, wine, wine vinegar, olive oil, bay leaves, salt, and black pepper in a large nonreactive baking dish. Add the beef and toss thoroughly to coat. Let the beef marinate in the refrigerator, covered, for at least 4 hours, preferably 8, stirring once or twice.

3. Assemble the kebabs: Remove the beef from the marinade, setting aside the marinade. Thread the beef onto the skewers, alternating it with pieces of onion and bell pepper.

4. Set up the grill for direct grilling and preheat to high.

5. When ready to cook, brush and oil the grill grate. Arrange the kebabs on the hot grate and grill, turning with tongs, until the meat is cooked to taste, 2 to 3 minutes per side (8 to 12 minutes in all) for medium-rare. Baste the beef with the marinade as it cooks but do not baste during the last 3 minutes of grilling. Serve the kebabs at once.

NIGERIA

FIERY STICK MEAT

SUYAS

DIRECT GRILLING
SERVES 8 AS AN APPETIZER,
4 AS A MAIN COURSE

I first encountered "stick meat" (fiery beef kebabs) at a Nigerian restaurant in Washington, D.C. But it was Dozie Nnamah, a cab driver in Chicago, who set the scene for properly enjoying this West African snack: Imagine you're in your twenties and it's Saturday night in Lagos. You and a bunch of friends crowd into a car for a spin. You crank up the radio until it rattles the windshield, listening to Ebenezer Obey, King Sunny Ade, or whoever else is rocking the Nigerian airwaves. And, you pick up a couple of six-packs of Gulder or Premier beer. (None for the driver, of course!)

The last stop is the nearest stick meat vendor, where you buy a few dozen *suyas,* fiery beef kebabs. You eat the stick meat with raw onion and as much cayenne pepper as you can stand, and that's how it goes—for an evening, at least, it's hard to imagine that life gets better than this.

Note that the meat shouldn't be too lean for stick meat; you need a few pieces of fat to baste and tenderize the beef as it cooks. As usual, I offer a range of heat from the cayenne. At my house, I would use a tablespoon of cayenne for the marinade.

Serve the beef kebabs with plenty of ice-cold beer.

ADVANCE PREPARATION

1 to 2 hours for marinating the meat

SPECIAL EQUIPMENT

20 short bamboo skewers and an aluminum foil shield (see box, page 23)

INGREDIENTS

- **1½ pounds boneless beef sirloin (try to choose a piece with some fat on it, or ask your butcher to give you a piece of beef fat)**
- **3 beef bouillon cubes**
- **1 to 3 teaspoons cayenne pepper, plus 1 tablespoon for serving**
- **1 teaspoon freshly ground black pepper**
- **½ teaspoon salt**
- **2 tablespoons vegetable oil**
- **1 medium-size onion, cut into ½-inch pieces, for serving**

1. Trim any sinews and excess fat off the beef, then cut the beef into ½-inch cubes. Crumble the bouillon cubes in a large bowl and mix with 1 tablespoon of water to make a thick paste. Stir in the 1 to 3 teaspoons of cayenne and the black pepper and salt. Add in the meat and toss thoroughly to coat. Let the beef marinate in the refrigerator, covered, for 1 to 2 hours.

2. Remove the beef from the marinade and thread it onto skewers, 6 to 8 cubes to a skewer, leaving the point (the last ¼ inch of the skewer) exposed. Pour the oil on a plate and roll the skewers around in it to coat the meat.

3. Set up the grill for direct grilling and preheat to high.

4. When ready to cook, brush and oil the grill grate. Arrange the skewers on the hot grill grate with the aluminum foil shield under the ends of the skewers. Grill, turning with tongs, until the meat is cooked to taste, 2 to 3 minutes per side (8 to 12 minutes in all; see Note).

5. Place the onion in a small bowl and the remaining 1 tablespoon of cayenne pepper in another. To eat, spear a piece of onion on the end of the skewer, then sprinkle the meat with as much additional cayenne as you can bear.

NOTE: These times will give you meat that is well-done. All the stick meat I've had has been served that way—it was made with cheap cuts of meat, so prolonged cooking was required to tenderize it. To serve medium-rare stick meat, use a more tender cut and cook the kebabs 1½ to 2 minutes per side.

IRAN

QUICK PERSIAN BEEF KEBABS

DIRECT GRILLING
SERVES 4

As a rule, Iranian kebabs are easy to make, but they do require a day or two of marinating. Here, however, is a beef kebab from that country that you can make and serve in the time it takes you to preheat the grill. The secret is to use thinly sliced beef tenderloin, which is so tender it needs no advance marinating.

SPECIAL EQUIPMENT

4 flat metal skewers

INGREDIENTS

- **1½ pounds beef tenderloin, all fat and sinew trimmed off**
- **1 large onion, cut into 1-inch chunks**
- **3 tablespoons fresh lime juice**
- **3 tablespoons extra-virgin olive oil**
- **1 tablespoon cracked black peppercorns**
- **Salt**
- **2 tablespoons (¼ stick) unsalted butter, in one piece**
- **Lavash (flat bread), for serving**

1. Cut the tenderloin crosswise into 1-inch-thick slices. Place the slices flat on the cutting board and cut them into 1-inch-wide strips. Cut each strip crosswise into ½-inch-thick pieces. Thread the beef onto the skewers and place them on a large nonreactive platter.

2. Puree the onion in a food processor. Strain the onion puree over the kebabs, turning to coat all sides.

3. Place the lime juice, olive oil, and peppercorns in a small bowl and beat them with a fork. Season with salt to taste, then pour the marinade over the kebabs, turning to coat all sides. Let the kebabs marinate for 15 minutes.

4. Set up the grill for direct grilling and preheat to high.

5. When ready to cook, brush and oil the grill grate. Drain the kebabs, arrange them on the hot grate, and grill until cooked to taste. I recommend 1½ to 2 minutes per side (6 to 8 minutes in all); Iranians like their beef on the medium side of medium-rare.

6. Transfer the kebabs to a platter. Skewer the butter on the end of a fork for easy handling and rub some of it over each kebab. Serve the kebabs immediately, with the lavash, using a piece of the bread to protect your hand as you slide the beef off the skewer.

Hawkers' Centers

I am an enthusiastic eater of street food. I love everything about it—its immediacy, its directness, its in-your-face flavors, the fact that you can watch it being made to order and eat it the second it's ready. I love street food for the same reason that I love homey ethnic restaurants: because the owner is putting his energy and money into the food, not the decor.

This is especially true for the satés, kebabs, *anticuchos, tacos al pastor,* and other grilled fare that constitutes some of the world's greatest curbside eating. Many of my happiest moments on the barbecue trail were spent at outdoor markets and street stalls, where you sit so close to the grill, you feel like you're at a barbecue in your own backyard.

The one drawback to street food is hygiene (or its lack). Running water (never mind hot water) is a luxury at many Third World street stalls, as is refrigeration. Food is usually prepared and served with the vendor's bare hands. Eating street food can be like playing culinary roulette. You never know which bite will lead to gastrointestinal distress.

Some years ago, in an effort to make street food more sanitary, the government of Singapore organized the vendors into hawkers' centers, where the cooks—and their customers—could enjoy the health benefits of electricity, refrigeration, running water, and a roof over their heads. The hawkers' centers are rigorously regulated by the government, which makes Singapore one of the safest places in the world to enjoy street food. There are dozens of hawkers' centers around Singapore—three of the best are located at Newton Circus, Bugis Square, and the newly restored Clarke Quay.

Hawkers' centers represent democracy and ecumenism at their best. Visit a hawkers' center in Singapore, for example, and you'll find Indonesian saté stands, Muslim bakeries, Chinese noodle stalls, and Indian drink shops. Cell phone–toting Chinese businessmen dine elbow to elbow with turbaned Sikhs.

Following Singapore's example, other nations have begun to organize their street vendors into regulated hawkers' centers. The Sarinah food court in the basement of the Sarinah shopping center in Jakarta groups street vendors specializing in dishes from all over Indonesia into a clean, modern Western-style setting. Similar hawkers' centers exist in the basement of department stores throughout Korea, Japan, and Malaysia. One of the world's best hawkers' centers—Gurney Drive in Penang, Malaysia—enjoys a spectacular seaside setting. Where else can you feast on saté and *rujak* with a view of the Andaman Sea?

MOROCCO

BANI MARINE STREET BEEF KEBABS

DIRECT GRILLING
SERVES 4

Bani Marine Street is one of the barbecue lanes in Marrakech, a crowded street off the Jema al-Fna marketplace lined with simple storefront grill restaurants. You don't really need a menu, since the bill of fare is displayed in the windows: lamb chops, liver, *merguez* sausages reddened with paprika and cayenne, and decoratively sculpted mounds of *kefta* (ground spiced lamb).

A meal at one of these restaurants is a simple but soul-satisfying experience: a dish of olives and a plate of kebabs, served with fiery *harissa,* fire-toasted bread, and shallot relish (a rather ingenious condiment since the parsley neutralizes the pungency of the shallots).

As in Indonesia, the meat for the kebabs is diced very small to keep it tender. And it doesn't hurt to put a little fatty beef or beef fat on the kebabs as well as the lean sirloin to keep the meat moist.

ADVANCE PREPARATION

2 to 8 hours for marinating the meat

SPECIAL EQUIPMENT

20 short bamboo skewers and an aluminum foil shield (see box, page 23)

INGREDIENTS

1½ pounds boneless beef sirloin
1 medium-size onion, finely chopped or grated
¼ cup finely chopped fresh flat-leaf parsley
1 teaspoon sweet paprika
1 teaspoon of salt, plus 1 tablespoon, for serving
½ teaspoon ground cumin, plus 1 tablespoon, for serving
½ teaspoon freshly ground white pepper
2 tablespoons vegetable oil
Moroccan Shallot Relish (page 445)
A Simple Harissa (page 481)
Moroccan bread, French bread, or pita bread

1. Trim any sinews and excess fat off the beef, then cut the beef into ½-inch cubes. Combine the onion, parsley, paprika, 1 teaspoon of salt, ½ teaspoon of cumin, and the white pepper and oil in a large baking dish. Add the beef and toss thoroughly to coat. Let marinate in the refrigerator, covered, for at least 2 hours, preferably 8. Then, thread the beef onto the skewers.

2. Set up the grill for direct grilling and preheat to high.

3. When ready to cook, brush and oil the grill grate. Arrange the kebabs on the hot grate with the aluminum shield under the ends of the skewers. Grill, turning once with tongs, until the meat is cooked to taste, 3 to 4 minutes per side for medium (6 to 8 minutes in all; Moroccans tend to eat their beef well-done).

4. To serve, place 1 tablespoon each of salt and cumin in separate tiny bowls and place them on the table side by side, along with bowls of the shallot relish and *harissa.* Slide the meat off the skewers onto plates. Let each person season his or her portion to taste with the salt and cumin, then spoon the relish and *harissa* on top. Serve the bread, in chunks, to soak up the juices.

PORTUGAL

MADEIRA BEEF AND BAY LEAF KEBABS

ESPETADAS

DIRECT GRILLING
SERVES 4 TO 6

Grilled beef is beloved throughout Portugal, but nowhere as much as on the island of Madeira. Restaurants on this hilly island have a unique accoutrement: an inverted L-shaped metal pole attached to one end of each table. The beef is grilled on special metal skewers with eyelets at the end, which are then brought to the table and hung with great ceremony from the L-shaped pole, over a bowl piled with Portuguese bread. As the kebabs hang, the meat juices drip onto the bread, which becomes as much a delicacy as the beef.

You can approximate the effect by serving the kebabs on a platter lined with sliced Portuguese bread. It's interesting to note that in the old days (and now, deep in the countryside), the beef was skewered and grilled on branches of a bay leaf tree.

ADVANCE PREPARATION

4 to 6 hours for marinating the meat

SPECIAL EQUIPMENT

4 to 6 long metal skewers

INGREDIENTS

1½ pounds beef tenderloin or boneless sirloin
¼ cup extra-virgin olive oil
¼ cup red wine vinegar
1 onion, finely chopped
½ cup chopped fresh flat-leaf parsley
4 cloves garlic, finely chopped
1 teaspoon salt
1 teaspoon freshly ground black pepper
14 bay leaves
Portuguese or other crusty country-style bread, for serving

1. Trim any sinews and excess fat off the beef, then cut the meat into 1½-inch cubes. Combine the olive oil, wine vinegar, onion, parsley, garlic, salt, pepper, and 2 of the bay leaves in a large nonreactive baking dish. Add the beef and toss thoroughly to coat. Let marinate in the refrigerator, covered, for 4 to 6 hours.

2. Remove the beef and bay leaves from the marinade, discarding the bay leaves. Set the marinade aside. Thread the meat and the remaining 12 bay leaves onto the skewers, dividing the bay leaves among the kebabs.

3. Set up the grill for direct grilling and preheat to high.

4. When ready to cook, brush and oil the grill grate. Arrange the kebabs on the hot grate and grill, turning with tongs, until the meat is cooked to taste, 2 to 3 minutes per side (8 to 12 minutes in all) for medium-rare. Baste the *espetadas* with the marinade but not during the last 3 minutes of grilling.

5. Serve the *espetadas* on or off the skewers on slices or chunks of Portuguese bread to soak up the juices.

VIETNAM

LETTUCE BUNDLES WITH GRILLED BEEF

DIRECT GRILLING
SERVES 4 AS AN APPETIZER, 2-3 AS A MAIN COURSE

This dish could be thought of as a Vietnamese taco. Although it doesn't really exist there, I was inspired to create it by a classic Vietnamese dish called *bo bun* (beef with rice paper). It's a fun combination of salad, pasta, and meat courses mixed into a single, satisfying mouthful. It's also a versatile dish that you can prepare with any type of meat (or seafood) and a variety of noodles—I've used Thai rice vermicelli, Japanese soba, and Western-style spaghetti. The recipe calls for sirloin, but you could also use shell steak or New York strip steak.

Rice vermicelli are hair-thin rice noodles. Look for them in Asian markets, natural foods stores, and an increasing number of supermarkets.

ADVANCE PREPARATION

30 minutes for marinating the meat and soaking the noodles

SPECIAL EQUIPMENT

24 short bamboo skewers and an aluminum foil shield (see box, page 23)

INGREDIENTS

1 boneless sirloin beefsteak (about 1 pound), cut about 1 inch thick
Aromatic Lemongrass Marinade (recipe follows)
4 ounces rice vermicelli, soba noodles, angel hair pasta, or spaghetti
1 bunch fresh basil, preferably Thai basil, stemmed
1 bunch fresh mint (optional), stemmed
2 jalapeño peppers, seeded and thinly sliced (optional—for hotter lettuce bundles leave the seeds in)
1 head Boston or Bibb lettuce, separated into leaves, rinsed, and spun dry
Thai Peanut Sauce (page 476)

1. Place the steak flat on a cutting board. Using a sharp knife, cut it lengthwise into ⅛-inch-wide strips, then transfer these to a nonreactive baking dish. Add the

LETTUCE BUNDLES WITH GRILLED BEEF | AT LEFT

Aromatic Lemongrass Marinade and toss the beef to coat thoroughly. Let marinate in the refrigerator, covered, for 30 minutes.

2. If using rice vermicelli, place it in a bowl, add cold water to cover, and let soak until soft and pliable, about 30 minutes. (If using soba, angel hair, or spaghetti, no soaking is necessary.) Drain the rice noodles and cook in 3 quarts rapidly boiling water until tender, 1 to 3 minutes (6 to 8 minutes if using the other noodles). Drain the noodles in a colander and rinse them with cold water. Drain again and transfer the noodles to a bowl. Arrange the basil, mint (if using), jalapeños (if using), and lettuce leaves on plates or in bowls. Divide the peanut sauce among 4 small bowls. Weave the beef strips lengthwise onto the skewers.

3. Set up the grill for direct grilling and preheat to high.

4. When ready to cook, brush and oil the grill grate. Arrange the skewers on the hot grate with the aluminum foil shield under the ends of the skewers. Grill, turning with tongs, until the meat is cooked to taste, 1 to 2 minutes per side (2 to 4 minutes in all) for well-done. Transfer to a platter.

5. To eat, wrap a strip of beef on its skewer, a forkful of noodles, some basil, and some mint leaves and jalapeño slices (if using) in a lettuce leaf. Slide the skewer out (you can use the lettuce leaves as pot holders for sliding the beef off the skewers). Dip the resulting bundle in the Thai Peanut Sauce, and then pop it into your mouth—the contrast of textures, temperatures, and flavors is dazzling.

AROMATIC LEMONGRASS MARINADE

MAKES ABOUT 1 CUP; ENOUGH FOR 1½ POUNDS BEEF, CHICKEN, OR FISH

This marinade demonstrates the universal appeal of one of the oddest and most ancient food pairings: anchovies with beef. The Romans did it when they seasoned their meats with *liquamen* (pickled anchovy sauce). Italians carry on the tradition with their steak *pizzaiola* (garnished with anchovies and tomatoes). The Vietnamese version features a highly aromatic marinade based on *nuoc mam* (fish sauce), a malodorous but highly tasty condiment made with pickled anchovies.

- **3 stalks fresh lemongrass, trimmed and coarsely chopped, or 3 strips lemon zest (each 2 by ½ inches), removed with a vegetable peeler**
- **2 large shallots, coarsely chopped**
- **5 cloves garlic, coarsely chopped**
- **3 tablespoons sugar**
- **5 tablespoons Asian fish sauce**
- **3 tablespoons fresh lime juice**
- **1 teaspoon freshly ground black pepper**

Combine the lemongrass, shallots, garlic, and sugar in a mortar and pound to a coarse paste with a pestle, then work in the fish sauce, lime juice, and pepper. If you don't have a mortar and pestle, combine all these ingredients in a blender and process to a smooth puree.

THAILAND

LEMONGRASS BEEF WITH PEANUTS

DIRECT GRILLING
SERVES 4

Variations on these delicate kebabs are to be found throughout Southeast Asia. Coriander and sugar may seem like odd flavorings for beef, but the combination is brilliant. (After all, we North Americans slather sugar-based barbecue sauces on brisket and ribs!)

SPECIAL EQUIPMENT

About 30 short bamboo skewers and an aluminum foil shield (see box, page 23)

INGREDIENTS

- **1½ pounds boneless beef sirloin or top round**
- **2 stalks lemongrass, trimmed and cut into ¼-inch slices, or 2 strips lemon zest (each 2 by ½ inches), removed with a vegetable peeler**

2 cloves garlic, peeled
1 tablespoon coriander seeds
2 tablespoons light brown sugar
¼ cup Asian fish sauce
¼ cup coarsely chopped dry-roasted peanuts, for garnish

1. Place the steaks flat on a cutting board and cut them crosswise into long, thin strips; each should be about ⅛ inch thick, 1 inch wide, and 4 to 5 inches long. Weave the beef strips lengthwise onto the skewers and set aside in a large baking dish while you prepare the marinade.

2. Combine the lemongrass, garlic, coriander seeds, and brown sugar in a mortar and pound to a coarse paste with a pestle. If you don't have a mortar and pestle, combine all these ingredients in a blender or food processor and process to a puree. Stir in the fish sauce. Drizzle the marinade over the beef skewers and rub it on the meat to coat it as thoroughly as possible. Let marinate in the refrigerator, covered, for 30 minutes, or until the grill is ready.

3. Set up the grill for direct grilling and preheat to high.

4. When ready to cook, brush and oil the grill grate. Arrange the skewers on the hot grate with the aluminum foil shield under the ends of the skewers. Grill, turning with tongs, until the meat is cooked to taste, 1 to 2 minutes per side (2 to 4 minutes in all) for medium. Sprinkle the kebabs with the chopped peanuts and serve at once.

VIETNAM

SAIGON MARKET BEEF STICKS

DIRECT GRILLING
SERVES 6 AS AN APPETIZER, 4 AS A MAIN COURSE

These tiny kebabs are the Vietnamese version of satés. You'll find them at the hawkers' stands clustered in and around Saigon's markets. The Vietnamese use a modest cut of meat, but I like to take the dish uptown by using tenderloin tips (which cost considerably less than filet mignon). You could also use thinly sliced sirloin or New York strip steak.

ADVANCE PREPARATION

30 minutes to 1 hour for marinating the meat

SPECIAL EQUIPMENT

24 small bamboo skewers and an aluminum foil shield (see box, page 23)

INGREDIENTS

1 pound beef tenderloin tips
Aromatic Lemongrass Marinade (page 166)
1 to 2 tablespoons vegetable oil, for basting
¼ cup finely chopped dry-roasted peanuts (optional), for garnish

1. Cut the beef into strips 4 inches long, 1 inch wide, and ¼ inch thick. Weave the beef lengthwise onto the skewers and place in a nonreactive baking dish. Add the Aromatic Lemongrass Marinade and toss the beef to coat thoroughly. Let marinate in the refrigerator, covered, for 30 minutes to 1 hour.

2. Set up the grill for direct grilling and preheat to high.

3. When ready to cook, brush and oil the grill grate. Arrange the skewers on the hot grate with the aluminum foil shield under the ends of the skewers. Baste the beef with some of the oil and grill, turning once with tongs, until the meat is cooked to taste, 1 to 2 minutes per side (2 to 4 minutes in all) for medium (the Vietnamese-preferred doneness for this dish). Baste the meat again with the oil after turning. Serve the kebabs at once, sprinkled with peanuts, if desired.

KOREA

KOREAN GRILLED SHORT RIBS

KALBI KUI

DIRECT GRILLING
SERVES 4

Mention *kalbi* to a Korean and watch his mouth water. Beef short ribs are something of a national obsession here, served braised to fall-off-the-bone tenderness or savored in the delicate soups and soulful stews for which the Land of Morning Calm is famous. But the most popular way to eat *kalbi* is grilled (*kui*). Korean chefs have developed an ingenious method for handling this flavorful but hard-to-eat cut of beef: The meat is sliced and butterflied to create a long, paper-thin strip, which is grilled right on the bone.

Dine at a restaurant in Korea and the waitress will set a charcoal-filled brazier in the center of the table. Each person cooks his *kalbi* to taste, then wraps the meat in lettuce leaves and dips it in a sweet-salty pear sauce.

ADVANCE PREPARATION

3 hours for marinating the meat

FOR THE RIBS AND MARINADE

2 pounds beef short ribs, cut into 2-inch lengths and butterflied (see box, below)
½ Asian pear or regular pear, peeled and cored
2 cloves garlic, peeled
2 scallions, both white and green parts, trimmed
¼ cup soy sauce
2 tablespoons Asian (dark) sesame oil
2 tablespoons honey
2 tablespoons sake or dry sherry
1 tablespoon sugar
½ teaspoon freshly ground black pepper

FOR SERVING

1 head romaine lettuce, separated into leaves, rinsed, and spun dry
Asian Pear Dipping Sauce (page 486)

1. Prepare the ribs and marinade: Place the butterflied ribs in a large nonreactive baking dish.

2. Coarsely chop the pear, garlic, and scallions and place them in a blender with the soy sauce, sesame oil, honey, sake, sugar, and pepper. Process to a smooth puree. Pour the marinade over the ribs in the baking dish, cover it, and let marinate, in the refrigerator, for 3 hours.

How to Butterfly Short Ribs for Korean-Style Grilling

Have your butcher cut the short ribs into two-inch lengths. (You can butterfly the longer ribs sold at the supermarket, but it will be a little more difficult.)

1. Position one piece of short rib at the lower right corner of a cutting board with the cut side (the sawed bone end) facing you and the thick meaty part of the rib on top. (If you're left-handed, position the rib on the lower left corner of the cutting board and reverse the directions.)

2. Using a small, sharp knife, holding the blade parallel to the cutting board, and working from right to left, slide the knife through the meat along the top of the bone, almost to the left edge to free it. Don't cut all the way through; you want to leave the meat attached to the bone. Fold the meat flap over to the left to make a flat rectangle of meat attached to the bone.

3. Now, holding your knife parallel to the cutting board, make another cut through the meat two thirds of the way down, again almost to the left edge, and open this flap up, too. You'll have a strip of meat with a left half that is twice as thick as the right.

4. Make a final cut through that thicker section on the left, this time through the center, to but not through the left edge. Again, the knife should be parallel to the cutting board. Open up this last flap of meat. You should wind up with a very thin strip of meat 4 to 5 inches long and about 2 inches wide, with the bone attached at the right side.

5. The last step is to tenderize the meat. Place the strip of meat flat on the cutting board and score it slightly by tapping it with the back of a heavy knife on the diagonal—first in one direction, then in the other—to make a crosshatch pattern.

This sounds a good deal more complicated than it really is. Cutting and unfolding the beef is quite similar to unrolling a flattened roll of paper towels.

3. Set up the grill for direct grilling and preheat to high.

4. When ready to cook, brush and oil the grill grate. Arrange the butterflied short ribs on the hot grate and grill, turning with tongs, until done to taste, 2 to 3 minutes per side (4 to 6 minutes in all) for well done (as Koreans tend to like their short ribs).

5. To eat: Cut the meat off the bone of a short rib and wrap it in a lettuce leaf. Dip the beef and lettuce in the dipping sauce and pop it into your mouth. Don't forget to gnaw on the bone, which may well be the best part of *kalbi kui*!

U.S.A.

DINOSAUR RIBS

INDIRECT GRILLING
SERVES 4

Beef ribs play second fiddle to pork ribs—at least in North America. A very different mind-set exists in Asia, where grilled short ribs—*kalbi kui*—are the national dish of Korea (see page 167) and where braised beef ribs are popular in China. The following recipe merges East and West, featuring a rub based on traditional Chinese five-spice powder and a sweet, sticky glaze made with hoisin sauce. The cooking method—long, slow, smoke-grilling—is a hundred percent American. The mammoth size of these ribs led a young friend of mine to call them "dinosaur ribs." So dinosaur ribs they remain at our house.

ADVANCE PREPARATION

1 to 6 hours for marinating the meat

SPECIAL EQUIPMENT

2 cups wood chips or chunks, soaked for 1 hour in cold water to cover and drained

FOR THE RIBS

2 racks beef ribs skinned (2½ to 3 pounds each; see Note)
4 teaspoons Chinese five-spice powder
1 tablespoon coarse salt (kosher or sea)
1 tablespoon freshly ground black pepper
2 teaspoons garlic powder

FOR THE BASTING MIXTURE AND SAUCE

⅔ cup hoisin sauce
¼ cup rice wine, sake, or dry sherry, or more if needed
2 tablespoons honey
2 cloves garlic, minced
2 teaspoons grated peeled fresh ginger

1. Prepare the ribs: Rinse the ribs under cold running water and blot them dry with paper towels. Combine the five-spice powder, salt, pepper, and garlic powder in a small bowl. Place the ribs in a large baking dish and rub them all over with the spice mixture. Let the ribs cure in the refrigerator, covered, for at least 1 hour, ideally for 4 to 6 hours.

2. Make the basting mixture and sauce: Combine the hoisin sauce, rice wine, honey, garlic, and ginger in a bowl and whisk to mix. Add more rice wine as needed to thin the sauce to a basting consistency. Set aside about ½ cup of the hoisin mixture to use for serving.

3. Set up the grill for indirect grilling and place a drip pan in the center.

If using a gas grill, place all of the wood chips in the smoker box and preheat the grill to high; when smoke appears, lower the heat to medium.

If using a charcoal grill, preheat it to medium.

4. When ready to cook, if using a charcoal grill, toss half of the wood chips on the coals. Brush and oil the grill grate. Place the ribs on the oiled grate over the drip pan and cover the grill. Cook the ribs until the meat is very tender and has shrunk back from the ends of the bones, 1½ to 2 hours. If using a charcoal grill, you'll need to add 10 to 12 fresh coals to each side and toss the remaining wood chips on the fire after 1 hour.

5. Start basting the ribs with the hoisin mixture during the last 30 minutes of grilling; baste the ribs several times, giving them one final basting just before serving. Serve the ribs accompanied by the reserved hoisin sauce.

NOTE: I use racks of long beef ribs 6 to 8 inches long and 10 to 12 inches wide, with each rack containing 7 ribs—what remain after the butcher cuts a rib roast off the bones. They may not look meaty, but they're incredibly succulent, with quite a bit of meat between the bones.

ARGENTINA

ARGENTINEAN VEAL & CHICKEN KEBABS

DIRECT GRILLING
SERVES 4

I first sampled these belt-loosening kebabs at La Estancia (literally the ranch), a boisterous steak house on an equally boisterous street, the Lavalle pedestrian mall, in downtown Buenos Aires. The combination of sweet (the prunes) and salty (the meat and bacon) is a savory one that weaves a common thread through Latin American cooking. Serve the kebabs accompanied by Tomato Salsa (page 457) or a *chimichurri,* one of the classic Argentinean garlic and parsley sauces (see page 478).

SPECIAL EQUIPMENT

4 long metal skewers

INGREDIENTS

1 pound boneless veal loin cut into 1½-inch chunks
1 pound skinless, boneless chicken breasts or thighs, cut into 1½-inch chunks
6 ounces thick-sliced pancetta or slab bacon (rind removed), cut into 1½-inch pieces
1 medium-size red bell pepper, cored, seeded, and cut into 1-inch pieces
1 medium-size onion, cut into 1-inch pieces
16 large pitted prunes
¼ cup extra-virgin olive oil
2 lemon wedges
Coarse salt (kosher or sea) and freshly ground black pepper

1. Thread the veal, chicken, pancetta, bell pepper, onion, and prunes onto the skewers, alternating the ingredients. Try to place the pancetta next to the pieces of veal and chicken; the melting fat will help keep the meats from drying out as they cook.

2. Place the olive oil in a small bowl and squeeze the juice from the lemon wedges into it. Drop in the lemon rinds and set the bowl aside.

3. Set up the grill for direct grilling and preheat to high.

4. When ready to cook, brush and oil the grill grate. Arrange the kebabs on the hot grate and grill, turning with tongs, until the veal and chicken are cooked through, 3 minutes per side (12 minutes in all). Brush the kebabs with the lemon oil as they cook. Season the grilled kebabs with salt and black pepper and serve at once.

PHILIPPINES

GRILLED OXTAILS

KARE KARE

DIRECT GRILLING
SERVES 4

Every nation has its comfort foods—hearty, uncomplicated dishes that are enjoyed without fuss or culinary pretense. A Filipino favorite is *kare kare,* oxtails. Traditionally, the oxtails would be stewed, but chef Romy Dorotan likes the smoky flavor achieved by finishing the meat on the grill. Dorotan is the Luzon-born owner-chef of the restaurant Cendrillon in New York's Soho, where he presents innovative remakes of Filipino dishes.

Cooks seem divided into two camps when it comes to oxtails. There are those, like me, who love their soulful, meaty flavor—and there are those who are afraid to try them. If you belong to the latter group, please know that oxtails are amazingly flavorful, inexpensive, and probably available at your local supermarket. Try them—I bet you'll like them.

Finally, to be strictly authentic, you should garnish the oxtails with *bagoong* (Filipino fermented shrimp). If you're feeling adventurous, you can find this tangy, salty ingredient at Filipino and Asian markets, but you should be warned that *bagoong* can be pretty robust tasting. I find that a splash of fish sauce or a diced anchovy or two works just as well, with a much milder odor.

ADVANCE PREPARATION

1½ hours for boiling the oxtails

FOR THE OXTAILS

2 pounds oxtails, cut into 1½-inch slices
1 medium-size onion, cut in quarters
3 cloves garlic, peeled
1 bay leaf
Salt and freshly ground black pepper

FOR THE TOMATO-PEANUT SAUCE

1 tablespoon extra-virgin olive oil
1 small onion, finely chopped
1 clove garlic, chopped
¾ cup tomato puree, fresh or canned
¾ cup broth from cooking the oxtails
3 tablespoons chunky peanut butter
3 tablespoons minced fresh flat-leaf parsley
Salt and freshly ground black pepper

FOR FINISHING THE OXTAILS

1 tablespoon olive oil, for basting
Salt and freshly ground black pepper
2 to 3 teaspoons bagoong, chopped anchovies, or Asian fish sauce, for garnish (optional)

1. Prepare the oxtails: Place the oxtails in a large, heavy pot with cold water to cover by 4 inches. Add the onion quarters, garlic cloves, and bay leaf and season with salt and pepper to taste. Bring to a boil over medium-high heat, skimming off any foam that rises to the surface. Reduce the heat to low and let the oxtails simmer gently, uncovered, until very tender, 1 to 1½ hours, skimming the broth from time to time to remove any fat. Let the oxtails cool in the broth, then transfer them to a plate. Reserve ¾ cup of the broth for the tomato-peanut sauce; save the remainder for soups or stews (see Note).

2. Make the sauce: Heat the olive oil in a nonstick skillet. Add the chopped onion and garlic and cook over medium heat until softened but not brown, about 3 minutes. Add the tomato puree and bring to a boil. Stir in the oxtail broth and peanut butter and let simmer until the sauce is thick (the consistency of heavy cream) and richly flavored, about 5 minutes. Add the parsley and cook for 1 minute longer. Remove the sauce from the heat and season with salt and pepper to taste, then keep warm over low heat.

3. Set up the grill for direct grilling and preheat to high.

4. When ready to cook, brush and oil the grill grate. Lightly brush the oxtails with olive oil and season them with salt and pepper. Arrange the oxtails on the hot grate and grill, turning with tongs, until heated thoroughly, 2 to 4 minutes per side (4 to 8 minutes in all). Rotate the oxtails 90 degrees after 1 to 2 minutes on each side to create an attractive cross-hatch of grill marks.

5. Spoon the sauce on plates or a platter and arrange the grilled oxtails on top. If desired, place a spoonful of *bagoong* or chopped anchovies or a splash of fish sauce on each serving and serve at once.

NOTE: The recipe can be prepared a day, or even several days, ahead to this point. Refrigerate the boiled oxtails, covered.

MEMPHIS-STYLE RIBS | PAGE 194

CHAPTER 7

HIGH ON HOG

Every May, tens of thousands of barbecue buffs from around the world flock to Memphis, Tennessee, for a three-day orgy of barbecuing and feasting known as the Memphis in May World Championship Barbecue Cooking Contest. The colorful names of the teams at this self-proclaimed Barbecue Super Bowl—Patio Porkers, Sultans of Swine, Jurassic Pork—indicate loud and clear the preferred meat of these grill maestros: pork.

"Oldfield with more than Harpy throat endu'd, Cries 'send me, Gods! a whole Hog barbecu'd!'"

—ALEXANDER POPE

Pork is just about the perfect meat for barbecuing and grilling. Blessed with a generous marbling, the meat stays moist during prolonged cooking and has a robust flavor that stands up to fiery chiles, lively Chinese five-spice powder, and dulcet barbecue sauces.

Americans aren't the only ones who like to live high off the hog. A survey of the world's great barbecue dishes would surely include Jamaican Jerk Pork Tenderloin, Bali's *babi guling* (Balinese Roast Pork), and Mexico's *cecina adobada* (Chile-Marinated Pork in the Style of Oaxaca). I even found pork satés in a primarily Muslim country—Indonesia—the legacy of Chinese merchants who settled in the Old Port district of Jakarta.

So stir up the barbecue sauce and get ready to make a perfect hog of yourself.

CUBA

CHRISTMAS EVE "PIG"

LECHON ASADO

INDIRECT GRILLING
SERVES 16 TO 20

Pit-roasted pig is the traditional centerpiece of a Cuban *Nochebuena,* or Christmas Eve supper, a holiday that stirs the same sort of emotions—and digestive juices—in a Cuban heart that Thanksgiving does in ours. Come Christmas Eve day in Miami, the sky fills with fragrant smoke, as thousands of backyard barbecue buffs—everyone from bricklayers to bankers—cook whole young pigs that have been marinating overnight in tangy *adobo,* a garlic–sour orange marinade flavored with cumin and oregano. This recipe calls for a cut of meat of a more manageable size, a fresh (uncured) ham, which has the advantage of being both more widely available than a whole pig and able to fit in your refrigerator.

Cubans don't generally go in for smoke flavor, but you could certainly add a couple of cups of soaked wood chips to the coals or the smoker box while the pork cooks. If you are using a gas grill, be sure that you start with a full tank of gas.

ADVANCE PREPARATION

8 to 24 hours for marinating the meat; also, allow yourself 6 to 8 hours cooking time

INGREDIENTS

- **1 whole fresh ham (18 to 20 pounds; see Note)**
- **2 heads garlic, broken into cloves and peeled**
- **2 tablespoons coarse salt (kosher or sea)**
- **1 tablespoon dried oregano**
- **1 tablespoon ground cumin**
- **1 tablespoon freshly ground black pepper**
- **2 cups fresh sour orange juice (see box, page 186), or 1½ cups fresh lime juice plus ½ cup fresh regular orange juice**
- **¼ cup extra-virgin olive oil**
- **1 cup dry sherry**
- **2 large onions, thinly sliced**
- **4 bay leaves**
- **3 cups (2 batches) Cuban Mojo (recipe follows)**

1. Using the tip of a sharp paring knife, make ½-inch deep slits in both the skin and meat sides of the ham, spacing them about 1½ inches apart. Set the ham aside while you prepare the marinade.

2. Combine the garlic, salt, oregano, cumin, and pepper in a mortar and pound to a smooth paste with a pestle, then work in 1 cup of the sour orange juice and the olive oil. If you don't have a mortar and pestle, puree all of these ingredients in a food processor or blender. Rub the marinade all over the ham, forcing it into the slits. Place the ham in a large container and add the remaining 1 cup of sour orange juice and the sherry, onions, and bay leaves. Let the ham marinate overnight or even up to 24 hours, turning it several times.

3. Set up the grill for indirect grilling, place a drip pan in the center, and preheat the grill to medium.

4. When ready to cook, place the ham, meat side down, on the hot grate over the drip pan and cover the grill (discard the marinade). Cook the ham until the skin is well browned and very crisp and the meat is fork-tender. When tested with

Pork Grilling Chart

CUT	METHOD	HEAT	DONENESS	
			Medium (160°F)	Well-Done (170°F)
CHOPS AND STEAKS	direct	high	4 to 6 minutes per side	DON'T DO IT
ROASTS				
Loin: 2½ to 3 pounds	indirect	medium	1 to 1½ hours	Don't do it
Shoulder: 5 to 6 pounds	indirect	medium to medium-low		4 to 6 hours
Fresh ham: 18 to 20 pounds	indirect	medium to medium-low		6 to 10 hours
RIBS				
Baby backs: 2 to 2½ pounds	indirect	medium to medium-low		1¼ to 1½ hours
Spare ribs: 3 to 4 pounds	indirect	medium to medium-low		1½ to 2 hours

This chart is offered as a broad guideline to cooking times for the various cuts of meat. Remember, grilling is an art, not a science. When in doubt, refer to times in the individual recipes.

an instant-read meat thermometer, the internal temperature should register about 190°F (Cubans like their pork more well done than we do). The whole process will take 6 to 7 hours. If the skin begins to brown too much, drape a piece of aluminum foil loosely over it or lower the heat. If using charcoal, you'll need to add 10 to 12 fresh coals to each side every hour.

5. Transfer the ham to a cutting board and let it rest for 15 minutes. Cut the meat off the bone and chop it with a cleaver or thinly slice it (be sure to include a little skin). Splash the meat with the Cuban Mojo and serve at once.

NOTE: You can also prepare a pork shoulder (4 to 6 pounds) or loin (2½ to 3 pounds) the same way. You'd need only half as much marinade, and the cooking time would be 4 to 6 hours for the pork shoulder, 1 to 1½ hours for the loin.

CUBAN MOJO

MAKES ABOUT 1½ CUPS

No, it's not pronounced mo-jo. *Mojo* (mo-ho) is Cuba's barbecue sauce, a sort of cumin and fried garlic vinaigrette that's splashed over every imaginable dish, from *palomilla* (Cuban steak) on page 140 to the Christmas Eve "Pig" (*lechon asado*) on page 173. Cubans make their *mojo* with sour orange juice. Sour oranges can be found at Hispanic grocery stores, but excellent *mojo* can be made with fresh lime juice mixed with a little regular orange juice for sweetness. Serve the *mojo* in a jar or bottle with a tight-fitting lid, so you can shake it up before pouring. This recipe is easily doubled; if you are making the *lechon asado,* you will need to do so. Just make sure you use a saucepan deep enough to safely accommodate a cup of boiling olive oil.

½ cup extra-virgin olive oil
8 large cloves garlic, cut into paper-thin slices or finely chopped
⅔ cup fresh sour orange juice, or ½ cup fresh lime juice plus 3 tablespoons fresh regular orange juice
1 teaspoon ground cumin
1 teaspoon dried oregano
1 teaspoon salt, or more to taste
1 teaspoon freshly ground black pepper, or more to taste
3 tablespoons chopped fresh cilantro or flat-leaf parsley

1. Heat the olive oil in a deep saucepan over medium heat. Add the garlic and cook until fragrant and pale golden brown, 1 to 2 minutes. Do not let the garlic brown too much or it will become bitter. Remove the pan from the heat and let cool for 5 minutes.

2. Stir the sour orange juice, cumin, oregano, salt, pepper, and ½ cup of water into the saucepan off the heat. Return the pan to the heat, let the sauce come to a rolling boil, and cook for 2 minutes. Taste for seasoning, adding more salt and/or pepper as necessary. Let the *mojo* cool to room temperature, then stir in the cilantro. Transfer the *mojo* to a jar or bottle with a tight-fitting lid. Serve the *mojo* in the jar, shaking it well first.

U.S.A.

NORTH CAROLINA PULLED PORK

INDIRECT GRILLING
SERVES 10 TO 12

Barbecue means different things to different people in different parts of the country. In North Carolina it means pork, or more precisely smoked pork shoulder, that has been grilled using the indirect method until it's fall-off-the-bone tender, then pulled into meaty shreds with fingers or a fork. Doused with vinegar sauce and eaten with coleslaw on a hamburger bun, it's one of the most delicious things on the planet, and it requires only one special ingredient: patience.

My friend and barbecue buddy Elizabeth Karmel makes some of the best pork shoulder I've ever tasted. Elizabeth comes from Greensboro, North Carolina, where she grew up on pulled pork. Her secret is to cook the pork to an internal temperature of 195°F—higher than is recommended by most books. But this is the temperature needed for the pork to separate easily into the fine, moist, tender shreds characteristic of true Carolina barbecue. Elizabeth doesn't use a rub, although many of her compatriots do. (I personally like a rub, but I've made it optional in the recipe.)

A true pork shoulder includes both the Boston butt (the upper part of the leg with the shoulder blade) and the picnic ham (the actual foreleg), a cut of meat that weighs fourteen to eighteen pounds in its entirety and is used chiefly at professional barbecue competitions. The recipe here calls for Boston butt alone (five to six pounds), which, thanks to its generous marbling, gives you superb barbecue. The appropriate beverage for all this? Cold beer or Cheerwine (a sweet red soda pop).

ADVANCE PREPARATION

3 to 8 hours for marinating the meat (optional); also, allow yourself 4 to 6 hours cooking time

SPECIAL EQUIPMENT

6 cups hickory chips or chunks, soaked for 1 hour in cold water to cover and drained

FOR THE RUB (OPTIONAL)

1 tablespoon mild paprika
2 teaspoons light brown sugar
1½ teaspoons hot paprika
½ teaspoon celery salt
½ teaspoon garlic salt
½ teaspoon dry mustard
½ teaspoon freshly ground black pepper
½ teaspoon onion powder
¼ teaspoon salt

FOR THE BARBECUE

1 Boston butt (bone-in pork shoulder roast; 5 to 6 pounds), covered with a thick (½ inch) layer of fat
Vinegar Sauce (recipe follows)
10 to 12 hamburger buns
North Carolina–Style Coleslaw (opposite)

1. If using the rub, combine the mild paprika, brown sugar, hot paprika, celery salt, garlic salt, dry mustard, pepper, onion powder, and salt in a bowl and toss with your fingers to mix. Wearing rubber or plastic gloves if desired, rub the spice mixture onto the pork shoulder on all sides, then cover it with plastic wrap and refrigerate it for at least 3 hours, preferably 8.

If not using the rub, generously season the pork all over with coarse (kosher or sea) salt and freshly ground black pepper; you can start cooking immediately.

2. Set up the grill for indirect grilling and place a drip pan in the center.

If using a gas grill, place all of the wood chips in the smoker box and preheat the grill to high; when smoke appears, reduce the heat to medium.

If using a charcoal grill, preheat the grill to medium-low and adjust the vents to obtain a temperature of 300°F.

3. When ready to cook, if using charcoal, toss 1 cup of the wood chips on the coals. Place the pork shoulder, fat side up, on the hot grate over the drip pan. Cover the grill and smoke cook the pork shoulder until fall-off-the-bone tender and the internal temperature on an instant-read meat thermometer reaches 195°F, 4 to 6 hours (the cooking time will depend on the size of the pork roast and the heat of the grill). If using charcoal, you'll need to add 10 to 12 fresh coals to each side every hour and toss more wood chips on the fresh coals; add about ½ cup per side every time you replenish the coals. With gas, all you need to do is be sure that you start with a full tank of gas. If the pork begins to brown too much, drape a piece of aluminum foil loosely over it or lower the heat.

4. Transfer the pork roast to a cutting board, loosely tent it with aluminum foil, and let rest for 15 minutes.

5. Wearing heavy-duty rubber gloves if desired, pull off and discard any skin from the meat, then pull the pork into pieces, discarding any bones or fat. Using your fingertips or a fork, pull each piece of pork into shreds 1 to 2 inches long and ⅛ to ¼ inch wide. This requires time and patience, but a human touch is needed to achieve the perfect texture. If patience isn't one of your virtues, you can finely chop the pork with a cleaver (many respected North Carolina barbecue joints serve chopped 'cue). Transfer the shredded pork to a nonreactive roasting pan. Stir in 1 to 1½ cups of the vinegar sauce, enough to keep the pork moist, then cover the pan with aluminum foil and place it on the grill for up to 30 minutes to keep warm.

6. To serve, mound the pulled pork on the hamburger buns and top with coleslaw. Let each person add more vinegar sauce to taste.

VINEGAR SAUCE

MAKES ABOUT 4 CUPS

Peppery and piquant, this vinegar sauce is the preferred condiment of eastern North Carolina. In the western part of the state, the sauce becomes more tomatoey, while in southern parts of the Carolinas, mustard sauce reigns supreme.

2 cups cider vinegar
½ cup plus 2 tablespoons ketchup
¼ cup firmly packed brown sugar, or more to taste
5 teaspoons salt, or more to taste
4 teaspoons hot red pepper flakes
1 teaspoon freshly ground black pepper
1 teaspoon freshly ground white pepper

Combine the vinegar, ketchup, brown sugar, salt, red pepper flakes, black pepper, and white pepper with 1⅓ cups of water in a nonreactive medium-size bowl and whisk until the sugar and salt dissolve. Taste for seasoning, adding more brown sugar and/or salt as necessary; the sauce should be piquant but not quite sour.

NORTH CAROLINA–STYLE COLESLAW

MAKES ABOUT 6 CUPS

This is coleslaw at its simplest and best. No onions. No carrots. No peppers. No mayonnaise. Just cabbage and peppery barbecue sauce.

1 small or ½ large head green cabbage
(about 2 pounds), cored
1 cup Vinegar Sauce (above), or more to taste
Salt (optional)

Finely chop the cabbage by hand or shred it on a mandoline or using the shredding disk of a food processor. Place the cabbage in a large bowl and stir in the Vinegar Sauce. Let stand for 10 minutes, then taste for seasoning, adding salt and/or more sauce as needed.

INDONESIA

BALINESE ROAST PORK

BABI GULING

INDIRECT GRILLING OR ROTISSERIE
SERVES 6 TO 8

Spiced roasted pig—*babi guling*—is the most famous dish in Bali. Traditionally, *babi guling* is made with a whole suckling pig that has been stuffed with a fragrant *bumbu* (spice paste) and spit roasted over a charcoal fire. Turmeric, galangal, lemongrass, and coriander give it an explosive, unforgettable flavor.

The following recipe comes from Iingah Kepidana, a Balinese pit master extraordinaire, who showed me how to pound the ingredients for the spice paste in a tub-size mortar with a pestle the size of a baseball bat. Kepidana cooks his *babi guling* over fire in half of a fifty-five-gallon drum, turning the rickety spit by hand.

I've retooled the recipe to be made with boneless pork shoulder. Long Beans with Fresh Coconut (page 115) and Balinese Yellow Rice (page 430) both make great accompaniments.

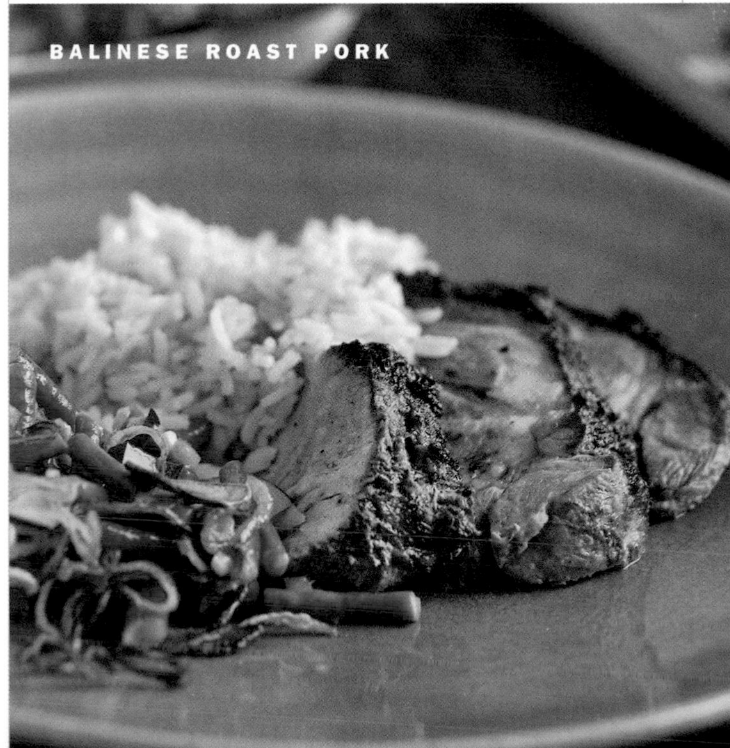
BALINESE ROAST PORK

SPECIAL EQUIPMENT

Butcher's string or metal skewers; rotisserie (optional)

INGREDIENTS

1 boneless pork shoulder roast (3 to 4 pounds)
4 large shallots, peeled
4 to 8 Thai chiles, or 2 to 4 jalapeño peppers
4 cloves garlic, peeled
1 tablespoon chopped peeled fresh ginger
1 tablespoon chopped fresh turmeric, or ½ teaspoon ground turmeric
1 tablespoon chopped fresh galangal or additional fresh ginger
3 stalks fresh lemongrass, trimmed and finely chopped (about ¼ cup), or 3 strips lemon zest (each 2 by ½ inches), removed with a vegetable peeler
1½ teaspoons ground coriander
1 teaspoon freshly and finely ground black pepper
2 tablespoons fresh lime juice
1 tablespoon light brown sugar
2 teaspoons salt
5 tablespoons vegetable oil, or more as needed

1. Using a sharp, heavy knife, cut a deep pocket in one side of the pork roast, starting and ending about ¾ inch from each end and cutting almost all the way through to the other side. Set the roast aside while you prepare the spice paste.

2. Combine the shallots, Thai chiles, garlic, ginger, turmeric, galangal, lemongrass, coriander, black pepper, lime juice, brown sugar, and salt in a mortar and pound to a smooth paste with a pestle. If you don't have a mortar and pestle, combine all these ingredients in a food processor or blender and process to a smooth paste.

3. Heat 3 tablespoons of the oil in a wok or small nonstick skillet over medium heat. Add the spice paste and cook until fragrant and shiny, about 5 minutes, stirring occasionally (see Frying Chiles, at right). Remove the spice paste from the heat and let cool to room temperature, about 15 minutes.

4. Spread half of the cooled spice paste in the pocket you cut in the side of the pork roast. Using butcher's string, tie the roast at 1-inch intervals or pin the opening shut with metal skewers. Using a rubber spatula, spread the remaining spice paste over the entire surface of the roast and set it aside while you prepare the grill.

Frying Chiles

The fumes from frying the spice paste for the Balinese Roast Pork can be irritating to people who are sensitive to chiles. Be sure your exhaust fan is running on high or fry the chiles outdoors using the grill side burner.

5. *If grilling using the indirect grilling method,* set up the grill for indirect grilling, place a large drip pan in the center, and preheat the grill to medium. When ready to cook, brush and oil the grill grate. Place the roast on the hot grate over the drip pan. Cover the grill and cook the roast until nicely browned on all sides and cooked through, 1 to 1½ hours, basting the roast with the remaining oil occasionally. When tested with an instant-read meat thermometer, the internal temperature should read 190°F for very well-done. (This is the way Indonesians prefer their pork.) If using a charcoal grill, you'll need to add 10 to 12 fresh coals to each side after 1 hour.

If using a rotisserie, set up the grill for spit roasting following the manufacturer's instructions and preheat the grill to high. When ready to cook, skewer the roast lengthwise on the rotisserie spit, attach the spit to the grill, and let the roast rotate until nicely browned on all sides and cooked through, 1 to 1½ hours, basting the roast with the remaining oil occasionally. When tested with an instant-read meat thermometer, the internal temperature should read 190°F for very well-done. If using a charcoal grill, you'll need to add 10 to 12 fresh coals to each side after 1 hour.

6. Transfer the pork roast to a cutting board or platter, removing it from the spit, if necessary. Let the roast rest for 10 minutes, then remove the string or skewers and cut the roast into crosswise slices to serve.

BRAZIL

RIO PORK ROLLATINI

DIRECT GRILLING
MAKES 12 ROLLS; SERVES 4

These tangy pork rolls come from Rio's legendary Porcão restaurant chain, where they're cooked on a spit. I like to think of them as Brazilian rollatini. For the sake of authenticity, I should note that the Dijon mustard and cornichons are my contributions to the recipe. Their flavors contrast perfectly with the richness of the Gruyère. Because you want these rollatini lean, it's best to start with trimmed pork.

SPECIAL EQUIPMENT

Butcher's string or toothpicks

INGREDIENTS

1½ pounds boneless pork loin, trimmed
Salt and freshly ground black pepper
½ cup finely grated Gruyère or Parmesan cheese
3 tablespoons Dijon mustard
1 slice smoked or cooked ham (about 2 ounces and ¼ inch thick), cut into pencil-thin strips
1 small onion, cut into 12 wedges
12 cornichon pickles (optional)
2 tablespoons extra-virgin olive oil, for brushing

1. Cut the pork loin crosswise into 12 thin slices, or have your butcher do it. (It helps to partially freeze the pork before slicing.) Each slice should be about 4 inches long, 3 inches wide, and ¼ inch thick; if the slices are too thick, you can pound them between sheets of plastic wrap, using the side of a heavy cleaver or a rolling pin. Season the slices of pork with salt and pepper.

2. Spread the grated cheese in a shallow bowl. Dip each slice of pork in the grated cheese, turning it to lightly coat both sides and shaking off the excess. Arrange the pork slices flat on a work surface and spread the top of each lightly with mustard. Place a strip of ham, an onion wedge, and a cornichon (if using) at a narrow end of each slice, then roll the pork tightly around the filling to form a compact roll. Tie each roll in the center with butcher's string or pin it shut with toothpicks. Brush the rolls with the olive oil, place them on a plate, and sprinkle any remaining cheese on top (see Note).

3. Set up the grill for direct grilling and preheat to medium-high.

4. When ready to grill, brush and oil the grate. Arrange the pork rolls on the hot grate and grill, turning with tongs, until nicely browned on all sides and just cooked through (firm to the touch), 8 to 10 minutes in all. Remember to remove the strings or toothpicks before serving.

NOTE: The rollatini can be prepared several hours ahead of time. Refrigerate the pork rolls, loosely covered with plastic wrap, until you are ready to grill. Brush them with the olive oil and sprinkle any remaining cheese on top just before grilling.

ITALY

ROSEMARY-GRILLED PORK LOIN

INDIRECT GRILLING OR ROTISSERIE
SERVES 4

For sixteen years Aiello Rosario and his wife, Luccia D'Ambrosio, of Florence, Italy, have turned their spotless white truck into a rotisserie. Their specialty is a whole pig that has been artfully boned, stuffed with a pungent paste of garlic and rosemary, and roasted over smoldering oak. I met the couple at the weekly market in the medieval town of San Gimignano near Siena. There, lines quickly formed for their herb-scented, meltingly tender pork sandwiches.

I've prepared this recipe using both the rotisserie and the indirect grilling method. It's the next best thing to spending an afternoon in the Tuscan countryside.

ADVANCE PREPARATION

2 to 4 hours for marinating the meat (optional)

SPECIAL EQUIPMENT

Butcher's string; rotisserie (optional)

INGREDIENTS

6 cloves garlic, peeled
1 bunch fresh rosemary, stemmed (about ¼ cup leaves)
1 tablespoon coarse salt (kosher or sea)
1 tablespoon freshly ground black pepper
2 tablespoons extra-virgin olive oil
1 boneless pork loin roast (2½ to 3 pounds)

1. Combine the garlic, rosemary, salt, and pepper in a mortar and pound to a smooth paste with a pestle, then work in the oil. If you don't have a mortar and pestle, combine all these ingredients in a food processor or blender and process to a smooth paste.

2. Using a long, sharp knife, cut the pork loin roast almost in half lengthwise, starting at one side, as directed in the box on butterflying on page 181 (do not pound the roast). Open out the meat as you would a book, then cut a lengthwise pocket down the center of each side, starting and ending about ½ inch from each end and cutting almost all the way through to the other side. Spread half of the herb paste over the surface and in the pockets of the opened-out roast, then bring the sides back together so the roast resumes its original shape. Using butcher's string, tie the roast at 1-inch intervals, then spread the remaining herb paste over the entire surface of the roast. If desired, loosely cover the roast with plastic wrap and let marinate, in the refrigerator, for 2 to 4 hours, letting it come to room temperature while you preheat the grill.

3. *If grilling using the indirect grilling method,* set up the grill for indirect grilling, place a large drip pan in the center, and preheat the grill to medium. When ready to cook, brush and oil the grill grate. Place the roast on the hot grate over the drip pan. Cover the grill and cook the roast until well browned on all sides and cooked through, 1 to 1½ hours. When tested with an instant-read meat thermometer the internal temperature should register 160°F. If using a charcoal grill, you'll need to add 10 to 12 fresh coals to each side after 1 hour.

If using a rotisserie, set up the grill for spit roasting following the manufacturer's instructions and preheat the grill to high. When ready to cook, skewer the roast lengthwise on the rotisserie spit, attach the spit to the grill, and let the roast rotate until well browned on all sides and cooked through, 1 to 1½ hours. When tested with an instant-read meat thermometer the internal temperature should register at least 160°F.

4. Transfer the pork roast to a cutting board or platter. Let the roast rest for 5 minutes, then remove and discard the string. Cut the roast into thin crosswise slices and serve it hot, warm, or (as they do in Italy) at room temperature.

SPAIN

PORK WITH MOORISH SEASONINGS

PINCHOS MORUNOS

DIRECT GRILLING
SERVES 8 AS AN APPETIZER, 4 AS A MAIN COURSE

I've always been fascinated by the dishes that result from the clash of two cultures—like these kebabs, a popular tapa in Spain. The Spanish name for the dish means Moorish kebabs, and the seasonings—hot pepper flakes cumin, and coriander—are characteristic of North Africa. But no self-respecting Muslim would prepare the kebabs with what is probably Spain's most popular meat: pork. So, here's a dish born of two cultures and continents.

ADVANCE PREPARATION

4 to 8 hours for marinating the meat

SPECIAL EQUIPMENT

8 long metal skewers

INGREDIENTS

2 pounds boneless pork loin or tenderloin
1 medium-size onion, finely diced
3 cloves garlic, minced
3 tablespoons minced fresh flat-leaf parsley
1 tablespoon paprika, preferably Spanish
½ teaspoon hot red pepper flakes
½ teaspoon ground cumin
½ teaspoon ground coriander
½ teaspoon dried oregano
¼ teaspoon saffron threads, crumbled
4 tablespoons extra-virgin olive oil
2 tablespoons red wine vinegar
2 tablespoons dry sherry or white wine
1 teaspoon salt
½ teaspoon freshly ground black pepper

HOW TO BUTTERFLY PORK OR BEEF

Various recipes in this book call for cuts of pork or beef that have been butterflied. In some cases the meat needs to be pounded to an even thickness. Here's how to do it.

For broad thick (1 inch) pieces of pork or beef loin

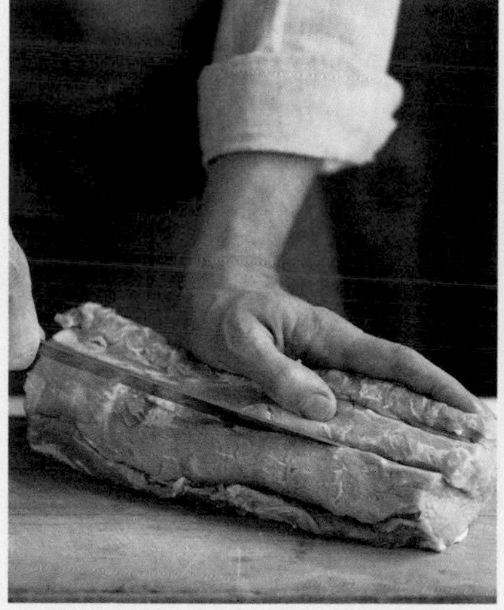

1. *First butterfly the loin: Place the meat on a cutting board so an end is facing you. Holding a long, slender, sharp knife parallel to the cutting board and starting on a long side, slice through the middle of the loin horizontally,*

2. *cutting almost all the way through to the opposite side, stopping about 1 inch from the edge.*

3. *Then, open up the piece of meat as you would a book, place it between two sheets of plastic wrap, and pound it gently with the side of a heavy cleaver or with a rolling pin to make a rectangle that is uniformly about 1 inch thick.*

For thin pieces of pork or beef follow the procedure outlined in Steps 1, 2, and 3, but you may want to cut the tenderloin in half crosswise first. Pound the butterflied tenderloin to a thickness of ¼ inch, or as desired.

For thin pieces of chops or steaks

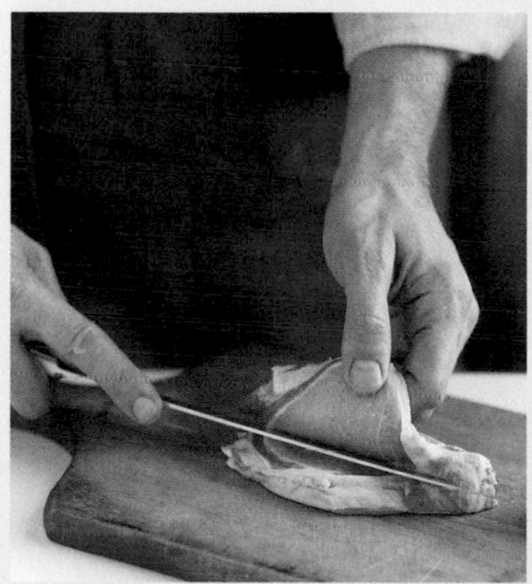

Place the meat on a cutting board, hold it flat with one hand, and keeping the knife parallel to the cutting board, slice through it horizontally, stopping about ½ inch from the edge. After opening the meat up like a book and placing it between plastic wrap, you can pound it to a uniform thickness.

1. Cut the pork into ¾-inch cubes. Combine the onion, garlic, parsley, paprika, red pepper flakes, cumin, coriander, oregano, and saffron in a large nonreactive baking dish. Stir in 2 tablespoons of the olive oil and the wine vinegar, sherry, salt, and black pepper. Add the meat and toss thoroughly to coat. Let marinate in the refrigerator, covered, for 4 hours, or as long as overnight, then thread the pork cubes onto the skewers.

2. Set up the grill for direct grilling and preheat to high.

3. When ready to cook, brush and oil the grill grate, then arrange the kebabs on the hot grate. Grill the pork until it is browned on all sides and cooked through, 2 to 3 minutes per side, 8 to 12 minutes in all, brushing it occasionally with the remaining 2 tablespoons of olive oil. Serve at once.

JAMAICA

JERK PORK TENDERLOIN

DIRECT GRILLING
SERVES 4 TO 6

Traditional Jamaican jerk would be made with a whole pig, boned and spread open like a book, marinated with fiery jerk seasoning, and smoke grilled over smoldering allspice wood (see page 184 for a complete description of jerk). Here's a home version that can be made with pork tenderloin. To achieve the right flavor, you must use Scotch bonnet chiles or their Mexican cousins, habañero peppers. If you can't find either, use fresh jalapeño peppers and a few tablespoons of a Scotch bonnet–based hot sauce, like Busha Browne's Pukka Sauce, Matouk's Hot Pepper Sauce, or Coyote Cocina Howlin' Hot Sauce. If you have sensitive skin, wear rubber gloves when handling Scotch bonnets. I've suggested a range of chiles: tender tongues should start with two to four; fiery food buffs can use the full amount.

The traditional accompaniments to jerk pork are Jamaican Fry Bread (page 132) and Fire-Roasted Breadfruit (page 403).

ADVANCE PREPARATION

At least 4 hours for marinating the meat

SPECIAL EQUIPMENT

2 cups hickory or oak chips or chunks, soaked for 1 hour in cold water to cover and drained

INGREDIENTS

- 2 pounds pork tenderloin (3 to 4 tenderloins)
- 2 to 16 Scotch bonnet chiles, seeded (for a hotter jerk, leave the seeds in)
- 2 bunches scallions, both white and green parts, trimmed and cut into 1-inch pieces
- ½ medium-size onion, cut into 1-inch pieces
- 1 piece (1 inch) peeled fresh ginger, thinly sliced
- 3 cloves garlic, peeled
- 1 tablespoon fresh thyme, or 2 teaspoons dried thyme
- 2½ teaspoons ground allspice
- ½ teaspoon freshly ground black pepper
- ½ teaspoon freshly grated nutmeg
- ¼ teaspoon ground cinnamon
- ¼ cup distilled white vinegar
- 3 tablespoons soy sauce
- 3 tablespoons coarse salt (kosher or sea)
- 1 tablespoon light brown sugar
- 2 tablespoons vegetable oil, plus 1 to 2 tablespoons vegetable oil, for basting

1. Using the tip of a paring knife, make holes ¼ inch deep all over each pork tenderloin. Place the tenderloins in a large nonreactive baking dish and set aside while you prepare the seasoning.

2. Combine the Scotch bonnets, scallions, onion, ginger, and garlic in a food processor and process until finely chopped. Add the thyme, allspice, pepper, nutmeg, cinnamon, vinegar, soy sauce, salt, brown sugar, and the 2 tablespoons of oil and process to a smooth puree. Or puree all of these ingredients in a blender.

3. Using a rubber spatula, spread the seasoning mixture over the tenderloins, stuffing it into the holes. Let the tenderloins marinate in the refrigerator, covered, for at least 4 hours, or as long as overnight, turning the meat several times.

4. Set up the grill for direct grilling.

If using a gas grill, place the wood chips in the smoker box and preheat the grill to high; when smoke appears, lower the heat to medium.

If using a charcoal grill, preheat it to medium.

5. When ready to cook, if using a charcoal grill, toss the wood chips on the coals. Brush and oil the grill grate. Arrange the pork tenderloins on the hot grate and grill, turning with tongs and brushing occasionally with oil, until nicely browned on both sides and cooked through, 8 to 10 minutes per side. When not turning the meat, keep the grill covered to hold in the smoke.

6. Transfer the pork to a cutting board and let rest for 5 minutes, then cut it into thin diagonal slices and serve.

MEXICO

CHILE-MARINATED PORK IN THE STYLE OF OAXACA

CECINA ADOBADA

DIRECT GRILLING
SERVES 4

Variations of this dish turn up all over Mexico. The Oaxacan version (*cecina adobada*) uses broad, thin slices of pork that have been marinated in an aromatic (but not particularly fiery) paste of dried chiles, vinegar, garlic, and spices. *Cecina* is a popular item in the restaurants of Oaxaca, but the best place to eat it is at one of the grill stalls in the Mercado 20 de Noviembre (the November 20 Market). In fact, this recipe was inspired by market stall #189, manned by a shy woman (and eighteen-year barbecue veteran) who would give only her first name: Laura. The only remotely tricky part is butterflying the pork to make the thin sheets that are traditionally used for grilling. The idea is to obtain what looks like pork scaloppine.

Cecina adobada is traditionally served with guacamole and a spicy salsa, and warm corn tortillas for wrapping everything up.

ADVANCE PREPARATION

4 to 6 hours for marinating the meat

FOR THE PORK AND ADOBO

6 guajillo chiles, or ¼ cup pure chile powder
½ cup distilled white vinegar
4 cloves garlic
1 teaspoon salt
1 teaspoon freshly ground black pepper
1 teaspoon dried oregano
½ teaspoon ground cinnamon
¼ teaspoon ground cloves
2 pork tenderloins (about 1½ pounds total)

FOR SERVING

8 corn tortillas (6 inches)
Oaxacan-Style Guacamole (page 455)
Salsa Mexicana (page 192)

1. Prepare the pork and *adobo:* If using the guajillo chiles, tear them open and remove the veins and seeds. Soak the chiles in the vinegar until soft, about 30 minutes.

2. Place the guajillo chiles or chile powder, vinegar, garlic, salt, pepper, oregano, cinnamon, and cloves in a food processor or blender and process to form a smooth, wet paste.

3. Cut each pork tenderloin into 4 broad, thin (¼ inch thick) pieces, using the butterflying technique that's described on page 181. Spread each piece of pork with the *adobo* mixture and stack them in a nonreactive baking dish. Let the pork marinate in the refrigerator, covered, for 4 to 6 hours.

4. Set up the grill for direct grilling and preheat to high.

5. When ready to grill, brush and oil the grill grate. Arrange the slices of pork on the hot grate and grill, turning with tongs, until nicely browned and cooked through, 2 to 3 minutes per side.

6. Serve the pork at once, accompanied by the tortillas, guacamole, and salsa. To eat, wrap the pork in the tortillas with some guacamole and salsa.

Jerk: The Jamaican Barbecue

I have eaten Jamaica's national dish and I can tell you this much: It hurts. Smoke stings your eyes and Scotch bonnet chiles scorch the gullet. I experienced my first real fiery jerk pork in Boston Beach on the northeastern coast of Jamaica. After making it through one order, I wiped my brow . . . and promptly ordered seconds!

Jerk is Jamaican barbecue. Like its North American counterpart, jerk is simultaneously a dish, a cooking method, and a way of life. It turns up at rugged roadside eateries and respectable restaurants from one end of Jamaica to the other. To make jerk, the meat (usually pork or chicken) is washed with lime juice or vinegar, marinated in a fiery paste of Scotch bonnet chiles and other spices, and smoke cooked over smoldering hardwood.

Some people cook jerk on a barbecue grill, others in a steel drum or over a pit. As for the seasoning, as the jerk marinade is called, there are probably as many different formulas as there are individual cooks in Jamaica. And, in recent years, the traditional jerk pork and jerk chicken have given way to such newfangled creations as jerk snapper, jerk lobster, even jerk pasta.

Historically, jerk is associated with the Maroons, runaway slaves who settled in the St. Thomas highlands in eastern Jamaica in the late seventeenth century. To preserve meats while on the run from British soldiers, the Maroons rubbed wild boar with a fiery paste of salt, spices, and Scotch bonnet chiles, then smoked it over smoldering wood.

Actually, the preparation probably dates back to the region's first inhabitants, the Arawak Indians. After all, the raw materials for jerk—the incendiary Scotch bonnet chile, the pimento berry (allspice), thyme, wild cinnamon, and scallions—have existed in Jamaica for centuries. The very term *barbecue* seems to have come from an Arawak word, a grill made of green branches called *barbacoa*.

According to Winston Stoner, the charismatic director of the Busha Browne's Company (which manufactures a popular line of Jamaican seasonings), the term *jerk* is derived from a Jamaican patois word *juk*, meaning to stab or stick with a sharp implement. "The first thing to be jukked was the wild boar," Stoner explained to me at his office in a Kingston warehouse. "Today it's a tame pig." Once dressed, the meat would be jukked a second time to speed the absorption of the spice mix. "But to really understand Jamaican jerk," insisted Stoner, "you've got to go to Boston Beach."

Twist my arm. This tiny seaside community, a twenty-minute drive from the city of Port Antonio in northeastern Jamaica, has the sort of serene horseshoe-shaped beach you dream about on a cold winter night. Brightly painted canoes dot the golden sands, which are lapped by the turquoise Caribbean. Named for the Boston Fruit Company, which had a Jamaican outpost, Boston Beach was once a center of the banana trade. Today, it's renowned for another gastronomic specialty: jerk. Although jerk is served all over Jamaica, Boston Beach is the best place to find traditional jerk pits.

For, like the barbecue of the American South and the bean hole beans of New England, jerk is born quite literally from a hole in the ground. Even the fanciest steel drum rig (and there are some fancy ones in Jamaica) can't compete with the elemental flavor of meat cooked over an open pit.

A jerk pit consists of a shallow trough, framed on either side by a row of cinderblocks. Arranged across these blocks is a sort of grate made of inch-thick sticks cut from green pimento (allspice tree). Spaced an inch apart, the sticks literally burn up during the cooking process and must be replaced every few hours. As the sticks burn, they impart a smoky flavor that is unique to Jamaican jerk.

What's in a Name?

There are many jerk shacks in Boston Beach. My first experience there is inextricably associated with a restaurant that was popular in the 1990s—Sufferer's

Jerk Pork Front Line No. 1. To call it a restaurant might be stretching things a bit. The dining room was a rickety pavilion made of bamboo slats with four mismatched tables. An American health inspector would have winced at the sight of the open-air kitchen, with its dirt floor, corrugated tin roof, concrete work table, and cutting board made from an old tree stump. There were only three basic items on the menu: jerk chicken, jerk pork, and jerk sausage. But to come to Jamaica without visiting one of the jerk purveyors in Boston Beach would be to miss one of the most intense gastronomic experiences in the world.

Prince Duncan Sufferer didn't know the origins of his restaurant. The serious, soft-spoken man took over from his parents in 1975. The day I was there he was assisted by a half dozen young men at an operation that began at 6 A.M. and didn't finish until seven or eight at night.

When I arrived, the crew had been working for hours. A wiry young man named Darrick Minot had the painful task of pureeing twenty-four pounds of Scotch bonnet chiles in a hand-cranked meat grinder. When you stop to consider that the Scotch bonnet is the world's hottest chile—up to fifty times hotter than a jalapeño—painful is the operative word here. "Don't touch your eyes when doing this," Minot warned, as the stinging pepper fumes swirled all around us. I guess it's not for nothing that he works at a place called Sufferer's.

The tongue-torturing chile paste that emerged from the meat grinder formed the backbone of the seasoning. But it wasn't until twenty-one different spices and condiments were added that the marinade was complete. The spices included wild cinnamon sticks, whole nutmegs, and fistfuls of pungent allspice berries. The bittersweet flavor of those berries is one of the defining flavors of jerk.

Other essential seasonings included bushy branches of thyme, antler-shaped clusters of ginger, and escallions (Caribbean chives), which taste like a cross between a North American scallion and a shallot. Garlic powder, soy sauce, brown sugar, vinegar, and a generous measure of sea salt were all added to the marinade, which was mixed in a plastic bucket. The resulting mixture was so hot it would probably qualify for regulation by the Atomic Energy Commission.

Pit master William Gallimore, a tall black man dressed in a battered blue shirt and shoes that literally fell off his feet, tended the four pits where the jerk was cooked. The first was a ground-level barbecue grill, where thick coils of homemade sausage sizzled over blazing embers. The second held split chickens on a wire grill, with a sheet of metal over them to keep in the fragrant smoke. The third was a round hole in the ground where whole breadfruits roasted among blazing pimento wood. The fourth pit was the rallying point for all this activity, for it was there that a whole pig was transformed into meltingly tender jerk pork.

According to Gallimore, the secret to great jerk is the slow cooking over low heat. Every half hour, he shoveled fresh coals under the pork. It took about an hour to cook a chicken and five hours to cook a pig. The pork was turned every thirty minutes, an operation that plunged the pit master into dense clouds of eye-stinging smoke. The lengthy cooking produced pork of astonishing succulence, pork that was meltingly tender, richly flavored, subtly smoky, and spicy but not unbearably hot. The slow cooking seemed to attenuate the bite of the chiles.

The service of jerk is as simple as the cooking process is complex. You order it by the pound. The pit master hacks off pieces with a cleaver and serves them to you in a sheet of waxed paper. That's it.

Festival and breadfruit are the traditional accompaniments to jerk pork. Festival is a cigar-shaped fritter made from flour, cornmeal, and sugar. Breadfruit, a tropical fruit brought to the West Indies by Captain Bligh himself, tastes a little like a baked potato. If you ever tasted breadfruit and thought it bland, you haven't tasted the likes of Sufferer's. To wash down this princely repast, choose from icy bottles of Red Stripe Beer, dark sweet Dragon Stout, or for the teetotaler, a refreshing grapefruit soda called Ting.

Jerk has now spread far beyond the shores of Jamaica. I've eaten jerk at a strip mall in Fort Lauderdale and a trendy restaurant in SoHo, New York. My neighborhood eatery in Miami serves jerk scrambled eggs for breakfast. But to taste the real McCoy, you must make a pilgrimage to Boston Beach in northern Jamaica. Which isn't the worst assignment—especially as winter approaches!

Smoky Grilled Pork

You can prepare a smoky version of the Oaxacan-style pork by substituting chipotle peppers (smoked jalapeños) for the guajillo chiles.

MEXICO

GRILLED PORK WITH FIERY SALSA

POC CHUC

DIRECT GRILLING
SERVES 4

There are many reasons people visit the Yucatán: To explore the Mayan ruins at Uxmal and Chichén Itzá. To lounge on the beaches of Cozumel and Cancún. For me, I came to this peninsula on the southeastern coast of Mexico for the purpose of eating *poc chuc.*

Poc chuc is one of the world's great pork dishes—and best-kept secrets. Unless you've been to the Yucatán, you've probably never heard of it. The name suggests that *poc chuc* is an ancient dish: *poc* is the Mayan word for to grill; *chuc* means burning embers. Fire charring is an important element, not only for the meat, but for the salsa and pickled onions.

Poc chuc originated in the villages of central Yucatán, where *campesinos* (farmers) would cure pork in salt water to prevent it from spoiling in the hot sun. The seasoning was equally simple and flavorful: fire-charred onions marinated in sour orange juice and a salsa—called *salsa de chiltomate*—made of charred tomatoes at their reddest and ripest and local habañero peppers.

Poc chuc is easy to make, dramatic to serve, and astonishingly tasty. But you need all three components—the cured pork, the grilled pickled onions, and the charred tomato sauce—to achieve the full effect. Serve this grilled pork with plenty of warm corn tortillas for wrapping up the meat.

ADVANCE PREPARATION

10 minutes for brining the meat

FOR THE PORK

2 pork tenderloins (about 1½ pounds total)
3 tablespoons coarse salt (kosher or sea)

FOR THE PICKLED ONION

1 large red onion, peeled, root end left intact
1 cup fresh sour orange juice (see box, page 186), or ¾ cup fresh lime juice plus ¼ cup fresh regular orange juice
2 teaspoons table salt

FOR THE SALSA DE CHILTOMATE

2 ripe medium-size tomatoes
1 to 3 habañero peppers or Scotch bonnet chiles
1 clove garlic, minced
¼ cup chopped fresh cilantro
3 tablespoons fresh sour orange juice (see box, page 186), or 2 tablespoons fresh lime juice plus 1 tablespoon fresh regular orange juice
½ teaspoon coarse salt (kosher or sea), or more to taste
8 tortillas (6 inches or larger), for serving

1. Prepare the pork: Butterfly each pork tenderloin following the directions in the box on page 181 to obtain a total of 8 broad sheets of meat about ¼ inch thick.

2. Combine the 3 tablespoons of coarse salt and 1 cup of water in a shallow bowl and whisk until the salt dissolves. Add the pork pieces to the brine, cover, and let marinate for 10 minutes, turning the pieces once or twice to make sure all are equally exposed to the brine. Drain and refrigerate the pork until ready to cook.

3. Make the pickled onion: Cut the onion into 8 wedges. Do not trim away the root end of the wedges; they will help hold the onion together as it grills.

4. Set up the grill for direct grilling and preheat to high.

5. When ready to cook, brush and oil the grill grate.

Arrange the onion wedges on the hot grate and grill, turning with tongs, until nicely charred on both sides, about 4 minutes per side. Leave the fire burning.

6. Trim the root ends off the onions and transfer the onions to a small serving bowl; stir in the 1 cup of sour orange juice and 2 teaspoons of table salt. Let the onions marinate for at least 10 minutes.

7. Meanwhile, make the *salsa de chiltomate:* Arrange the tomatoes and habañero peppers on the grate and grill, turning with tongs, until nicely charred on all sides, 8 to 12 minutes in all. The idea is to char the skins without cooking the vegetables through. Transfer the tomatoes and peppers to a plate to cool for 5 minutes. Leave the fire burning.

8. Place the cooled tomatoes and peppers and the garlic in a food processor or blender and process to a coarse puree. Add the cilantro, 3 tablespoons of sour orange juice, and ½ teaspoon of coarse salt and process just to mix. Taste for seasoning, adding more salt as necessary. Transfer the salsa to a serving bowl.

9. Just before serving, brush and oil the grill grate and add 20 fresh coals, if using charcoal, to bump up the heat. Arrange the pork on the hot grate and grill, turning with tongs, until cooked through, 2 to 3 minutes per side. Press the pieces of meat against the grate with the back of a metal spatula to make well-defined grill marks.

10. Transfer the pork to a platter. Arrange the tortillas on the grate just long enough to warm them, about 20 seconds per side. Serve the pork, accompanied by the pickled onions, *salsa de chiltomate,* and a basket of the warmed tortillas.

Sour Orange

Sour orange is one of the defining flavors in Yucatán and Caribbean grilling, essential for marinades and for squeezing over dishes at the table.

The juice of the bumpy, roundish, greenish-orange, irregularly sized fruit is sharply acidic, like lime juice, with just a hint of orange flavor. If you live in an area with a large Hispanic or West Indian community, you may be able to find sour oranges. If not, the flavor can be approximated by combining three or four parts fresh lime juice with one part fresh regular orange juice.

CHINA

SUSUR LEE'S BARBECUED PORK

DIRECT GRILLING
SERVES 4 TO 6

Susur Lee, Hong Kong–born owner of the restaurant Lotus in Toronto, is one of Canada's most celebrated chefs. This recipe takes an East-meets-West approach to classic Chinese barbecue. Actually, "barbecue" is something of a misnomer, seeing as the Chinese roast and/or fry their barbecued pork, but almost never resort to grilling. In this exception, pork's natural affinity for sweet flavorings shines through. The dish is as simple and easy to make as the results are delectable.

ADVANCE PREPARATION

12 to 24 hours for marinating the meat

INGREDIENTS

1½ pounds pork tenderloin (2 to 3 tenderloins)
1 medium-size rib celery, finely chopped
1 medium-size carrot, finely chopped
1 medium-size onion, finely chopped
1 tablespoon minced peeled fresh ginger
5 strips fresh tangerine or orange zest (each 2 by ½ inches), removed with a vegetable peeler
⅔ cup rice wine or dry sherry
⅓ cup soy sauce
⅓ cup pure maple syrup
2 tablespoons Asian (dark) sesame oil

1. Trim any excess fat or sinew off the pork tenderloins. Combine the celery, carrot, onion, ginger, tangerine zest, rice wine, soy sauce, maple syrup, and 1 tablespoon of the sesame oil in a nonreactive baking dish and stir to mix. Add the tenderloins, turning to coat. Let marinate in the refrigerator, covered, for 12 to 24 hours, the longer the better, turning occasionally.

2. Remove the tenderloins from the marinade and blot dry with paper towels. Strain the marinade into a small nonreactive saucepan and bring to a boil over medium-high heat. Let the marinade boil until thick and syrupy, 5 to 8 minutes.

3. Set up the grill for direct grilling and preheat to medium-high.

4. When ready to cook, brush the tenderloins with the remaining 1 tablespoon of sesame oil. Arrange the tenderloins on the hot grate and grill, turning with tongs, until the pork is browned on all sides and cooked through, 16 to 20 minutes in all. When tested with an instant-read meat thermometer, the temperature should register at least 160°F. Start brushing the tenderloins with the boiled marinade after 8 minutes.

5. Transfer the grilled tenderloins to a cutting board and let rest for 5 minutes. Cut each tenderloin on the diagonal into ½-inch slices. Fan the slices out on plates or a platter and serve with any remaining marinade.

URUGUAY

URUGUAYAN ROLLED PORK

PAMPLONA DE PUERCO

DIRECT GRILLING
SERVES 6 AS AN APPETIZER, 4 AS A MAIN COURSE

A *pamplona* is a stuffed rolled roast that is grilled over a gentle fire. This specialty of the grill stalls and restaurants at Montevideo's Mercado del Puerto is made with few ingredients, but the peppers and provolone fill the pork with flavor, and the resulting mosaic of color makes the dish a visual knockout, too. Uruguayans would serve a whole *pamplona* per person—as an appetizer! (Then again, South Americans eat a lot more meat than do their North American neighbors.) Don't be intimidated: This recipe is really quite easy—even if you've never butterflied a roast before.

If desired, serve one of the *chimichurris* (see pages 477 and 478) as an accompaniment.

SPECIAL EQUIPMENT

Butcher's string or small metal skewers

INGREDIENTS

2 pork tenderloins (about 1½ pounds in all)
Salt and freshly ground black pepper
1 large red bell pepper
2 slices (¼ inch thick; 2 ounces each) provolone cheese
1 to 2 tablespoons extra-virgin olive oil, for basting

1. Trim any excess fat and sinew off the pork tenderloins, then cut each crosswise in half. Butterfly and pound each piece following the directions in the box on page 181 to obtain four 7-inch squares that are ¼ inch thick (a total of 8 squares). Season the pork with salt and pepper.

2. Core and seed the bell pepper, then cut it lengthwise into ¼-inch strips. Cut each slice of provolone into ¼-inch strips.

3. Place the pieces of pork on a work surface. Arrange 4 to 5 strips each of bell pepper and provolone lengthwise on top of each piece of pork, alternating strips of bell pepper and cheese and leaving a ½-inch border on each side. Roll up a piece of the pork to enclose the filling and form a compact cylinder. Tie the roll in several places with butcher's string or pin it shut with small metal skewers. Assemble the remaining *pamplonas* the same way (see Note).

4. Set up the grill for direct grilling and preheat to medium-high.

5. When ready to cook, brush the *pamplonas* lightly with olive oil and season them with salt and pepper.

Arrange the *pamplonas* on the hot grate and grill, turning with tongs, until the pork is browned on all sides and is cooked through, 16 to 20 minutes in all. When done, a metal skewer inserted in a *pamplona* will come out hot to the touch.

6. Transfer the *pamplonas* to a platter and remove the string or skewers. Let rest for 5 minutes before slicing. Traditionally, the roll would be served whole on a plate, but I like to cut it crosswise into ½-inch slices and fan the slices out on the plate to create a spiral effect.

NOTE: The *pamplonas* may be prepared to this point up to 6 hours ahead of time. Cover them loosely with plastic wrap and refrigerate them if you are planning to wait more than 15 minutes before grilling.

INDONESIA

SWEET PORK SATES

SATE BABI MANIS

DIRECT GRILLING
SERVES 4 AS AN APPETIZER, 2-3 AS MAIN COURSE

This may seem like a straightforward saté recipe, but it's also a profound comment on religious tolerance in modern Indonesia. Like most of the Indonesian archipelago, Java is a Muslim island, yet here's a pork kebab from a bustling hawkers' center in the heart of Batavia (the port section of Jakarta). The explanation is simple: Batavia was Jakarta's Chinatown (although the current Chinese community is a fraction of what it once was), and the Chinese love pork.

This recipe comes from the Saté Babi Sop Bakut Shop in the Pecenongan district, near the Radisson Hotel. If you have the time and you're feeling adventurous, dinner here makes a fun outing. (Come late to avoid Jakarta's hellish traffic.) You'll sit at an oilcloth-covered table under an awning with fluorescent lights and be served satés—sizzling hot from the grill—on red plastic plates.

ADVANCE PREPARATION

1 hour for marinating the meat

SPECIAL EQUIPMENT

16 short bamboo skewers and an aluminum foil shield (see box, page 23)

INGREDIENTS

1 pound boneless pork loin or shoulder, with some fat, cut into ½-inch dice
⅔ cup sweet soy sauce (ketjap manis), or ⅓ cup each regular soy sauce and molasses
2 cloves garlic, minced
2 shallots, thinly sliced
1 cucumber, peeled and seeded (see box, page 454), then cut into ½-inch dice
1 tablespoon ground dried galangal
4 kaffir limes or key limes, or 2 Persian limes, cut into wedges
Mixed Vegetable Achar (optional; page 449)

1. Thread the pork onto the skewers, 5 to 6 pieces per skewer. Combine ⅓ cup of the sweet soy sauce and the garlic and shallots on a plate and roll the satés around in the mixture. Let marinate in the refrigerator, covered, for 1 hour, turning the skewers occasionally.

2. Set out plates. On one side of each plate place a mound of diced cucumber, a small pool of the remaining sweet soy sauce, a small pile of the galangal powder, and a few lime wedges.

Galangal

Galangal is a root in the ginger family with a pungent, peppery flavor. You can find it fresh in Asian markets and dried in Asian markets and specialty food stores. The dried version often goes by the name *laos*. If fresh or dried galangal is not available, fresh or dried ginger makes an acceptable substitute. The flavor is somewhat different—a little sweeter—but the resulting dish will still taste great and reasonably authentic.

SWEET & GARLICKY PORK CHOPS | AT RIGHT

3. Set up the grill for direct grilling and preheat to high.

4. When ready to cook, brush and oil the grill grate. Arrange the satés on the hot grate with the aluminum foil shield under the ends of the skewers. Grill, turning with tongs, until the meat is nicely browned and cooked through, 6 to 8 minutes in all.

5. To eat, place a piece of cucumber on the end of a skewer. Dip the saté first into the sweet soy sauce, then into the galangal powder. Squeeze a little lime juice over all, then pop the saté into your mouth. The Mixed Vegetable Achar (if using) will serve as a palate cleanser between satés.

THAILAND

SWEET & GARLICKY PORK CHOPS

DIRECT GRILLING
SERVES 4

One of the constants in the world of barbecue is the pairing of grilled meats with garlic. Another is the use of a sugar- or honey-based marinade to counterpoint the richness of a meat like pork. Put them together and you get this Thai-style barbecue, which is made here with pork chops but could also be used for pork tenderloin or loin. I like to use one-inch-thick loin chops for this recipe, but you can also use twice as many of the more widely available thin chops. Jasmine Rice (page 428) would make a good accompaniment.

ADVANCE PREPARATION

1 to 2 hours for marinating the meat

INGREDIENTS

4 thick (1 inch) or 8 thin (½ inch) pork chops (about 2 pounds in all)
1 head garlic, broken into cloves and peeled
3 tablespoons sugar
⅓ cup Asian fish sauce or soy sauce
3 tablespoons honey
3 tablespoons rice wine
2 tablespoons Asian (dark) sesame oil
1 tablespoon grated peeled fresh ginger
2 teaspoons salt
1 teaspoon freshly ground black pepper

1. Make 1 or 2 cuts in the fat side of each pork chop to keep it from curling during grilling. Arrange the chops in a baking dish and set aside.

2. Combine the garlic and sugar in a mini-chopper or food processor and process to a paste or pound to a paste in a mortar using a pestle. Work in the fish sauce, honey, rice wine, sesame oil, ginger, salt, and pepper. Using a rubber spatula, spread the mixture over both sides of the chops. Let marinate in the refrigerator, covered, for 1 to 2 hours.

3. Set up the grill for direct grilling and preheat to high.

4. When ready to cook, brush and oil the grill grate. Arrange the chops on the hot grate and grill until nicely browned on both sides and cooked through, 4 to 6 minutes per side for thick chops, 2 to 4 minutes per side for thin chops. Transfer the chops to a platter and serve at once.

MEXICO

OAXACAN-STYLE PORK RIBS

DIRECT GRILLING
SERVES 4

La Capilla (The Chapel) plays to the sort of nostalgia city dwellers everywhere have for the countryside. Located about a half hour outside Oaxaca, the restaurant offers its patrons the opportunity to spend an afternoon in the country, dining at communal tables under open-air thatch-roofed huts, serenaded by a mariachi band, and surrounded by wooden ox carts and caged farm animals. You sip locally brewed mescal and feast on simply grilled meats, cooked the old-fashioned way—in an open kitchen over a blazing charcoal fire. And after you've eaten—an activity that seems to take a couple of hours—there are hammocks for a siesta. It is, in short, the perfect way to spend an afternoon in the country.

At the time I visited La Capilla, its chef was a short, serious woman named Manuela Martinez Torres, and her pork ribs would do a Kansas Citian proud. The first thing I noticed about them was that the bones of each rack were neatly cracked in the center. This allowed the *adobo* (spice paste) to penetrate the meat on all sides, explained Torres, and it also released the marrow and juices from the bones, adding flavor and succulence to the meat. If you have a cooperative butcher, ask him to do this for you.

The second curious thing about Manuela's ribs was the *adobo* itself, a dark green paste of dried herbs and vinegar made without chiles (unusual for these parts). The preparation had the rare virtue of seeming to intensify the flavor of the meat without masking or altering it.

The third surprise was the cooking method: direct grilling over charcoal, not the slow, smoky, indirect cooking method used by most barbecue joints in the United States. If you like a rib that has some chew to it (not everyone likes them almost fall-off-the-bone tender), these are the ribs for you. And they're great served with tortillas, Oaxacan-Style Guacamole (page 455), and the Salsa Mexicana that follows this recipe.

Note that Manuela used spareribs. You could certainly use baby back ribs.

ADVANCE PREPARATION

8 to 24 hours for marinating the ribs

INGREDIENTS

2 racks pork spareribs (6 to 8 pounds total)
6 cloves garlic, peeled
1 tablespoon dried thyme
1 tablespoon dried oregano
1 tablespoon dried marjoram
2 teaspoons salt
1 piece (½ inch) cinnamon stick, or ½ teaspoon ground cinnamon
2 allspice berries, or ⅛ teaspoon ground allspice
2 whole cloves, or ⅛ teaspoon ground cloves
¼ cup distilled white vinegar
Salsa Mexicana (recipe follows)

1. Remove the thin, papery skin from the back of each rack of ribs by pulling it off in a sheet with your fingers, using one corner of a kitchen towel to gain a secure grip, or with pliers. Place the ribs in a roasting pan.

2. Combine the garlic, thyme, oregano, marjoram, salt, cinnamon stick, allspice berries, cloves, vinegar, and 3 tablespoons of water in a food processor or blender and process to a smooth paste, adding more water, if necessary. Rub the spice paste over the ribs on both sides. Let the ribs marinate in the refrigerator, covered, at least 8 hours, or for up to 24 hours.

3. Set up the grill for direct grilling and preheat to medium.

4. When ready to cook, season the ribs with salt. Brush and oil the grill grate, then arrange the ribs on the hot grate, meaty side down. Grill the ribs until nicely browned and cooked through, 30 to 40 minutes in all, turning once or twice with tongs (see Note).

5. Cut the racks into sections of 2 or 4 ribs for serving. Pass the Salsa Mexicana alongside.

NOTE: You'll probably get flare-ups—especially as the fat melts in the beginning. Control them by moving the ribs around on the grate or by squirting the fire a few times with a water pistol. Lower the heat as needed.

SALSA MEXICANA

MAKES ABOUT 2 CUPS

This simple salsa is a constant on Mexico's culinary landscape. The name changes from region to region (*pico de gallo* in the north; *salsa mexicana* in the south), but the basic elements—tomatoes, crisp white onions, and fiery green and red peppers so luscious that eating them is almost carnal—remain the same.

2 ripe medium-size tomatoes
1 medium-size or ½ large white onion
2 to 8 serrano or jalapeño peppers
¼ cup chopped fresh cilantro
3 tablespoons fresh lime juice, or more if needed
½ teaspoon salt, or more if needed

Cut the tomatoes, onion, and peppers into ¼-inch dice. (You can soften the bite of the peppers by scraping out the veins and seeds.) Place the tomatoes, onion, and peppers in a serving bowl. Add the cilantro, lime juice, and salt and toss to mix. Taste for seasoning, adding more lime juice and/or salt as necessary.

PHILIPPINES

ROMY'S RIBS WITH FILIPINO SEASONINGS

INDIRECT GRILLING
SERVES 4

Romy Dorotan is a man with a mission: to introduce New Yorkers to the soulful flavors of his native Philippines. His Mercer Street restaurant, Cendrillon, has the industrial look of the Soho gallery scene (bare brick walls, exposed heating ducts), but his food hums with complex flavors. Romy's ribs are a cross-cultural triumph, fragrant with citrus and Szechuan peppercorns. He cooks the ribs in what he calls a Chinese smoker (actually, it's more like a steamer). I adapted them to cook on the grill using the indirect grilling method.

The ribs can be served as is, but for a truly amazing experience, try painting them with Ginger-Plum Barbecue Sauce during the last five minutes of cooking.

ADVANCE PREPARATION

6 to 8 hours for marinating the ribs

SPECIAL EQUIPMENT

1½ cups wood chips or chunks, soaked for 1 hour in cold water to cover and drained

INGREDIENTS

2 racks baby back pork ribs (4 to 5 pounds)
⅔ cup soy sauce
Juice and grated zest of 1 orange
Juice and grated zest of 1 lemon
Juice and grated zest of 1 lime
2 stalks fresh lemongrass (optional), trimmed and thinly sliced
1 tablespoon minced peeled fresh ginger
2 cloves garlic, minced
1 tablespoon sweet paprika
2 teaspoons Szechuan peppercorns
2 teaspoons coriander seeds
2 teaspoons cumin seeds
2 teaspoons mustard seeds
1 teaspoon fennel seeds
1 dried hot red chile, or ½ teaspoon cayenne pepper
2 teaspoons light brown sugar
2 teaspoons salt
Ginger-Plum Barbecue Sauce (optional; page 470)
Thinly sliced scallions (optional), for serving
Toasted sesame seeds (optional; see box, page 113)

1. Remove the thin, papery skin from the back of each rack of ribs by pulling it off in a sheet with your fingers, using one corner of a kitchen towel to gain a secure grip, or with pliers. Place the ribs in a nonreactive roasting pan.

2. Combine the soy sauce, orange juice and zest, lemon juice and zest, lime juice and zest, lemongrass, ginger, and garlic in a blender and process to a smooth puree. Pour the marinade over the ribs, turning to coat both sides. Let marinate in the refrigerator, covered, for 6 to 8 hours, turning once or twice.

3. Combine the paprika, Szechuan peppercorns, coriander seeds, cumin seeds, mustard seeds, fennel seeds, dried chile, brown sugar, and salt in a spice mill or blender and grind to a fine powder (see Note).

4. Remove the ribs from the marinade and blot dry with paper towels (discard the marinade). Rub the spice mix over the ribs on both sides.

5. Set up the grill for indirect grilling and place a large drip pan in the center.

If using a gas grill, place all of the wood chips in the smoker box and preheat the grill to high; when smoke appears, reduce the heat to medium.

If using a charcoal grill, preheat it to medium.

6. When ready to cook, if using a charcoal grill, toss the wood chips on the coals. Arrange the ribs on the hot grate, bone side down, over the drip pan. Cover the grill and smoke cook the ribs until the meat is very tender and has shrunk back from the ends of the bones, 1¼ to 1½ hours. If using a charcoal grill, you'll need to add 10 to 12 fresh coals to each side after 1 hour.

7. To serve, transfer the racks of ribs to a cutting board and cut them into 2- or 3-rib sections. The ribs explode with flavor as is, but for a truly over-the-top experience, drizzle Ginger-Plum Barbecue Sauce over them and sprinkle sliced scallions and sesame seeds on top. Bet you can't eat just one.

NOTE: For extra flavor, before grinding you can toast the spices in a dry skillet over medium heat until fragrant, about 3 minutes (don't use a nonstick skillet for this).

U.S.A.

MEMPHIS-STYLE RIBS

INDIRECT GRILLING
SERVES 6

It never fails to amaze me how one simple idea can give birth to so many great regional variations. Consider ribs. The pork rib is one of the most perfect morsels ever to occupy a grill. The meat is generously marbled, which keeps it moist during prolonged cooking. As the fat melts, it crisps the meat fibers and bastes the meat naturally. The bones impart a rich meaty flavor (meat next to the bone always tastes best), while literally providing a physical support—a gnawable rack on which to cook the meat. Yet depending on whether you eat ribs in Birmingham or Kansas City, or Bangkok or Paris for that matter, you'll get a completely different preparation.

I've always been partial to Memphis-style ribs. Memphians don't mess around with a lot of sugary sauces. Instead, they favor dry rubs—full-flavored mixtures of paprika, black pepper, and cayenne, with just a touch of brown sugar for sweetness. The rub is massaged into the meat the night before grilling, and additional rub is sprinkled on the ribs at the end of cooking. This double application of spices creates incredible character and depth of flavor, while at the same time preserving the natural taste of the pork. Sometimes a vinegar and mustard based sauce—aptly called a mop sauce—is swabbed over the ribs (with said mop) during cooking; I've included one here, for you to use if you like.

You can choose any type of rib for this recipe: baby back ribs, long ends, short ends, rib tips—you name it (for more on these cuts see The Four Styles of American Barbecue on page 468). Cooking times are approximate. The ribs are done when the ends of the bones protrude and the meat is tender enough to pull apart with your fingers. I like my ribs served dry, in the style of Memphis's legendary barbecue haunt, the Rendezvous. If you want to serve them with a sauce, you'll find a number to choose from in this chapter.

ADVANCE PREPARATION

4 to 8 hours for marinating the ribs

SPECIAL EQUIPMENT

1½ cups wood chips or chunks (preferably hickory), soaked for 1 hour in cold water to cover and drained

FOR THE RIBS AND RUB

3 racks baby back pork ribs (about 7 pounds), or 2 racks pork spareribs (6 to 8 pounds total)
¼ cup sweet paprika
4½ teaspoons freshly ground black pepper
4½ teaspoons dark brown sugar
1 tablespoon salt
1½ teaspoons celery salt
1½ teaspoons cayenne pepper
1½ teaspoons garlic powder
1½ teaspoons dry mustard
1½ teaspoons ground cumin

FOR THE MOP SAUCE (OPTIONAL)

2 cups cider vinegar
½ cup yellow (ballpark) mustard
2 teaspoons salt

1. Prepare the ribs and rub: Remove the thin, papery skin from the back of each rack of ribs by pulling it off in a sheet with your fingers, using the corner of a kitchen towel to gain a secure grip, or with pliers.

2. Combine the paprika, black pepper, brown sugar, salt, celery salt, cayenne, garlic powder, dry mustard, and cumin in a small bowl and whisk to mix. Rub two thirds of this mixture over the ribs on both sides, then transfer the ribs to a roasting pan. Cover and let cure, in the refrigerator, for 4 to 8 hours.

CUTS OF RIBS

Ribs are a constant on the world's barbecue trail—dished up by grill masters from Kansas City to Kuala Lumpur. The meat next to the bone always seems to taste the most flavorful and this is especially true of ribs. But not all ribs are the same. You can't play the game of smoke and fire without a scorecard: The photos here will help you identify the players. Note: The lamb ribs pictured are delicious prepared following the Dinosaur Rib recipe on page 169 (shorten the cooking time by 30 percent).

TRUE BABY BACKS (1 POUND)

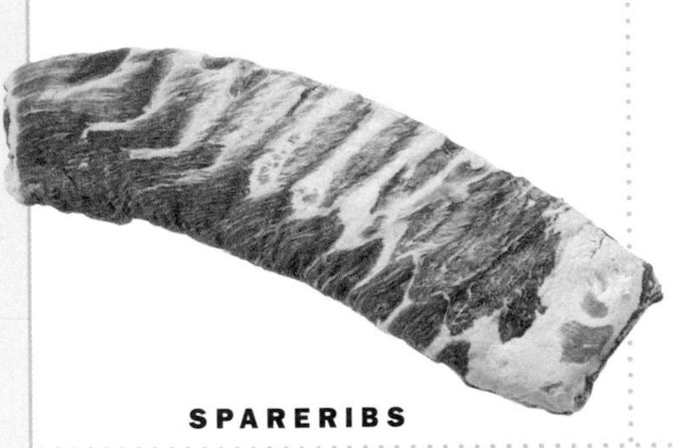

SPARERIBS

BEEF SHORT RIBS

RIB TIP

FULL-SIZE BABY BACKS (2 TO 2½ POUNDS)

ARGENTINEAN CROSSCUT BEEF SHORT RIBS

DENVER LAMB RIBS

LAMB RIBLETS

3. Prepare the mop sauce (if using): Mix together the cider vinegar, mustard, and salt in a bowl and set aside.

4. Set up the grill for indirect grilling and place a large drip pan in the center.

If using a gas grill, place all of the wood chips in the smoker box and preheat the grill to high; when smoke appears, reduce the heat to medium.

If using a charcoal grill, preheat it to medium.

5. When ready to cook, if using a charcoal grill, toss the wood chips on the coals. Brush and oil the grill grate. Arrange the ribs on the hot grate over the drip pan. Cover the grill and smoke cook the ribs for 1 hour.

6. When the ribs have cooked for an hour, uncover the grill and brush the ribs with the mop sauce (if using). Re-cover the grill and continue cooking the ribs until tender and almost done, ¼ to ½ hour longer for baby back ribs, ½ to 1 hour longer for spareribs. The ribs are done when the meat is very tender and has shrunk back from the ends of the bones. If using a charcoal grill, you'll need to add 10 to 12 fresh coals to each side after 1 hour. Fifteen minutes before the ribs are done, season them with the remaining rub, sprinkling it on.

7. To serve, cut the racks in half or, for a plate-burying effect, just leave them whole.

JAMAICA

RASTA RIBS

INDIRECT GRILLING
SERVES 4

Memphis meets Montego Bay in this rib recipe, a takeoff on Jamaican jerk. To make it, I replace the traditional wet jerk seasoning with a dry rub made with Jamaican spices. The method—applying the rub in two stages, once before cooking, once before serving—is Memphis barbecue at its best. The Scotch bonnet chile and its cousin, the habañero pepper, are two of the world's hottest chiles, so don't use more of the powder than you mean to. Neophytes should make the rub with two teaspoons of the powder. Masochists can use the whole two tablespoons. Good accompaniments would be Two-Tone Potato Salad, Jamaican Fry Bread, and Haitian Slaw (pages 121, 132, and 461).

ADVANCE PREPARATION

5 hours for marinating the ribs

SPECIAL EQUIPMENT

1½ cups wood chips or chunks (preferably oak or hickory), soaked for 1 hour in cold water to cover and drained

FOR THE RIBS

2 racks baby back pork ribs (4 to 5 pounds total)
2 cups dark rum

FOR THE DRY JERK SEASONING

2 teaspoons to 2 tablespoons Scotch bonnet or habañero chile powder (see Note)
2 tablespoons freeze-dried chives
1 tablespoon dried onion flakes
1 tablespoon dried garlic flakes
1 tablespoon coarse salt (kosher or sea)
2 teaspoons ground coriander
2 teaspoons ground ginger
1 teaspoon freshly ground black pepper
1 teaspoon ground allspice
½ teaspoon ground cinnamon
¼ teaspoon ground cloves
¼ teaspoon freshly grated nutmeg

1. Prepare the ribs: Remove the thin, papery skin from the back of each rack of ribs by pulling it off in a sheet with your fingers, using one corner of a kitchen towel to gain a secure grip, or with pliers. Place the ribs in a nonreactive roasting pan and pour the rum over them, turning the ribs to coat completely. Let marinate in the refrigerator, covered, for 4 hours, turning occasionally.

2. Meanwhile, make the dry jerk seasoning: Combine the chile powder, chives, onion flakes, garlic flakes, salt, coriander, ginger, pepper, allspice, cinnamon, cloves, and nutmeg in a spice mill or blender and grind to a fine powder.

3. Drain the ribs and blot dry with paper towels. Rub half of the jerk mixture over the ribs on both sides. Let marinate in the refrigerator, covered, for 1 hour.

4. Set up the grill for indirect grilling and place a large drip pan in the center.

If using a gas grill, place all of the wood chips in the smoker box and preheat the grill to high; when smoke appears, reduce the heat to medium.

If using a charcoal grill, preheat it to medium.

5. When ready to cook, if using a charcoal grill, toss the wood chips on the coals. Arrange the ribs on the hot grate over the drip pan. Cover the grill and smoke cook the ribs until the meat is very tender and has shrunk back from the ends of the bones, 1¼ to 1½ hours. If using a charcoal grill, you'll need to add 10 to 12 fresh coals to each side after 1 hour.

6. Transfer the ribs to a platter and season them with the remaining dry jerk seasoning, sprinkling it on. Serve at once.

NOTE: If Scotch bonnet or habañero chile powder sounds too incendiary, you can use your favorite hot chili powder. The flavor won't be quite as authentic, but the ribs will still taste killer.

Naming Baby Backs

The "baby back" ribs I've called for here are top loin ribs, which weigh in at two to two-and-a-half pounds per rack (one rack is enough to feed two people). "True" baby backs are smaller—one rack weighs about one pound. They come from younger, smaller hogs and are frequently imported from Denmark. If you want to substitute them in these recipes, you'll need four racks.

THE REAL TURKISH SHISH KEBAB | PAGE 214

CHAPTER 8

A LITTLE LAMB

Lamb is the preferred meat for grilling on a huge stretch of the world's barbecue trail. You could start enjoying it in Morocco and eat your way east through North Africa, the Middle East, Turkey, and Central Asia, continuing on to the Indian subcontinent to Indonesia, Australia, and New Zealand.

Throughout the Arab world, birthdays, weddings, and other happy occasions are celebrated with a pit-roasted lamb called *mechoui,* and no Greek holiday feast would be complete without a whole spit-roasted lamb. As for Australians, you'd expect great grilled lamb in a country where sheep are said to outnumber humans by twenty to one.

In this chapter you'll find familiar favorites, such as shish kebab and lamb Provençal, as well as many exotic ways to grill lamb, including Afghan lamb chops marinated in onion water and Mexican *barbacoa* (chile-slathered leg of lamb wrapped in avocado leaves). Did I mention Senegalese lamb with mustard sauce, Indian tandoori lamb with chickpea flour, and Cape Town leg of lamb with a brown-sugar mustard crust?

When you travel the world's barbecue trail, a little lamb quickly becomes a lot of lamb. And that's good news for so many of us who love this flavorful meat.

MEXICO

MEXICAN BARBECUED LAMB

BARBACOA

INDIRECT GRILLING
SERVES 8

Mexico's answer to barbecue, *barbacoa* is intriguingly delicious and easy to adapt for the backyard barbecue grill. I've chosen a recipe for Oaxacan-style *barbacoa,* featuring a guajillo chile marinade and a wrapping of avocado leaves. The avocado leaves can be found dried at Mexican markets and specialty food shops and impart a pleasant aniselike flavor. But don't worry if you can't find avocado leaves because the lamb will still be quite delectable barbecued without a wrapping.

Barbacoa is traditionally served in two courses: first a soup (flavored with lamb drippings), then the lamb, which is eaten with tortillas. You can read more about *barbacoa* on page 200.

"*Don't think—cook!*"
—LUDWIG WITTGENSTEIN

ADVANCE PREPARATION

4 to 8 hours for marinating the lamb, plus about 4 hours cooking time

A Traditional Barbacoa

Barbacoa helped build at least one Mexican mom-and-pop eatery into a multimillion-dollar restaurant that serves up to five thousand guests a day. Arroyo, founded in 1940 in the Mexico City suburb of Coyoacán (located about forty minutes south of downtown), has become a gustatory amusement park. Occupying a city block, it is complete with roving orchestras and a private bullfighting ring.

Jesus Arroyo Bergeyre is the third-generation owner of the restaurant and a passionate spokesman for the cultural traditions it strives to preserve. I began my tour of the restaurant in a garden of maguey cactus. Its leaves are an essential part of *barbacoa,* not to mention that they are home to the *gusano,* a cactus worm that is a beloved delicacy in Mexico (it's enjoyed crisply fried).

Next, Bergeyre led me to the focal point and pride of the restaurant, a row of *barbacoa* pits, six kettle-shaped holes built into a raised brick dais. Each pit was so deep, I could have stood in one and still barely seen over the edge. The evening before, the pits had been loaded with wood and ignited. It's only when the wood burns down to glowing coals that the cooking of the *barbacoa* begins.

A cook appeared with a huge steel kettle filled with water, beans, vegetables, garlic, and bunches of cilantro and epazote. This became the *consommé de cordeiro* (lamb soup, flavored with the drippings), which is also an essential part of *barbacoa.* The pot was lowered into the pit on top of the coals. Meanwhile, whole hindquarters or shoulders of lamb were wrapped and tied in flame-scorched maguey cactus leaves. The cook positioned the lamb on a metal rack over the kettle. The pit was then closed with a metal lid, the edges of which were sealed the old-fashioned way: with dirt.

The *barbacoa* would roast "underground," as it were, for eight to ten hours. When it emerges from the pit, it will be tender enough to pull apart with your fingers. The herbal-tequila taste of the cactus leaves, the herb-scented steam from the soup kettle, and the smoke from the wood combine to produce a lamb with an extraordinary flavor—a lamb unique in the world of barbecue.

SPECIAL EQUIPMENT

8 to 10 fresh or dried avocado leaves (optional; soak dried leaves for 20 minutes in cold water to cover)

FOR THE CHILE PASTE AND LAMB

6 guajillo chiles (see Chile Notes, page 201)
5 cloves garlic, coarsely chopped
¼ medium-size onion, coarsely chopped
½ teaspoon dried oregano
2 whole cloves
2 whole allspice berries
1 small piece (½ inch) cinnamon stick, or ½ teaspoon ground cinnamon
1 teaspoon salt
¼ cup distilled white vinegar
½ leg of lamb bone-in (about 4 pounds), trimmed of any papery skin

FOR THE CONSOMME

1 medium-size onion, cut into ½-inch dice
2 carrots, peeled and cut into ½-inch dice
1 zucchini, scrubbed and cut into ½-inch dice
1 piece (12 ounces) calabaza (West Indian pumpkin) or butternut squash, peeled and cut into ½-inch dice
½ small green cabbage, cored and cut into ½-inch dice
1 large ripe tomato, cut into ½-inch dice
1 medium-size potato, peeled and cut into ½-inch dice
1 ear corn (optional), shucked and cut into ½-inch rounds
2 bay leaves, 2 sprigs cilantro, and 2 sprigs epazote (optional), tied in a piece of cheesecloth
¼ cup finely chopped fresh cilantro leaves
1 chipotle pepper, minced (see Chile Notes, page 201)
Salt and freshly ground black pepper

FOR SERVING

Warm tortillas
Salsa Mexicana (page 192)

1. Prepare the chile paste and lamb: Stem the guajillo chiles, tear them open, and remove the veins and seeds. Soak the chiles in water to cover until they are soft and pliable, about 20 minutes. Drain the chiles and place them in a blender with the garlic, coarsely chopped onion, oregano, cloves, allspice berries, cinnamon, salt, vinegar, and ¼ cup of water. Process to a smooth paste.

2. Using the tip of a paring knife, make a series of slits in the lamb, ¼ inch deep and 1 inch apart. Smear the chile paste all over the lamb, working it into the slits. Cover the lamb loosely with plastic wrap and let marinate, in the refrigerator, for 4 to 8 hours (the longer the better).

3. Prepare the consommé: Combine the diced onion, carrots, zucchini, calabaza, cabbage, tomato, potato, corn (if using), herb bundle, and 10 to 12 cups of water in a large fire-proof pot.

4. Set up the grill for indirect grilling and preheat to medium-low.

5. You're now ready to assemble the *barbacoa*. Place the consommé pot in the center of the grate that holds the charcoal, or if using gas, in the center of the grill grate (away from the heat). Place a metal rack, like a sturdy cake rack, on top and layer half of the avocado leaves (if using) on top; if not using avocado leaves, oil the rack. Place the lamb, fat side up, on top of the rack and avocado leaves and carpet it with the remaining leaves (if using). Cover the grill tightly.

6. Cook the *barbacoa* until the lamb is fall-off-the-bone tender, 3 to 4 hours. When the lamb is done, an instant-read meat thermometer inserted in the thickest part of the leg (but not touching the bone) will register between 180° and 190°F. If using a charcoal grill, you'll need to add 10 to 12 fresh coals to each side every hour.

7. To serve the *barbacoa,* discard the top layer of avocado leaves and transfer the lamb and bottom layer of leaves to a platter. Let rest for 5 minutes, then thinly slice the meat or cut it into chunks. Remove and discard the herb bundle from the consommé. Using a ladle, skim off any fat floating on the surface of the soup. Stir in the chopped cilantro and chipotle and season the consommé with salt and pepper to taste; the soup should be highly seasoned. Serve the consommé first, then the meat, accompanying both with tortillas and salsa.

INDIA

LEG OF "MUTTON" WITH SAFFRON AND ROSE WATER

INDIRECT GRILLING
SERVES 4

This is one of the most remarkable tandoori dishes I had anywhere in India. "Mutton" is what Indians call baby goat. Here its haunting flavor comes from a marinade perfumed with rose water, mace, and saffron, seasonings that suggest the Persian roots of this dish. (Don't forget, the Mogul rulers of northern India were descended from Persians.) Muhammad Farooq, master chef of the Mughal Sheraton in Agra, uses goat so young that a whole leg is about the size of a turkey leg! Baby goat tastes like a cross between lamb and veal. You may be able to order it from a specialty butcher, but leg of lamb makes a perfectly delicious substitute.

This recipe may sound a little involved, but actually it's a series of simple steps. The only challenging part is remembering to drain the yogurt ahead of time. By the way, the liquid you drain from the yogurt can be made into the refreshing Afghan Yogurt Drink (page 65). Chickpea flour, or *besan*—which imparts a nutty taste—is available at Indian markets and natural foods stores. Indian-style basmati rice and Pineapple Chutney (page 454) would make good accompaniments.

Chile Notes

Guajillo chiles are smooth-skinned, mild, sweet, dried chiles with a taste similar to sweet paprika. If they are unavailable, you can use a quarter cup of pure chile powder.

Chipotles are smoked jalapeño peppers. They come both in cans and dried. If you are using canned chipotles for the soup, simply chop them. If the chipotles are dried, soak them in hot water for twenty minutes, then chop them.

ADVANCE PREPARATION

4 hours for draining the yogurt, plus 6 hours for marinating the meat

INGREDIENTS

- 1½ cups plain whole-milk yogurt
- ¼ teaspoon saffron threads
- 1 teaspoon rose water
- ½ cup chickpea flour (besan; optional)
- 1 green cardamom pod
- 1 black cardamom pod (optional)
- ½ teaspoon black peppercorns
- 2 blades mace, or ¼ teaspoon freshly grated nutmeg
- ½ teaspoon salt
- ½ teaspoon cayenne pepper
- 1 teaspoon grated peeled fresh ginger
- 1 clove garlic, minced
- 1 tablespoon unsalted butter, melted
- ½ leg of lamb bone-in (about 4 pounds; see Note), preferably shank end, trimmed of any papery skin

1. Set a yogurt strainer, or a regular strainer lined with a double layer of dampened cheesecloth, over a small bowl. Add the yogurt to the strainer and let drain, in the refrigerator, until a firm "cheese" forms, about 4 hours; you should have about 1 cup.

2. When ready to marinate the lamb, place the saffron in a small bowl and grind it to a fine powder with a pestle or the end of a wooden spoon. Add the rose water, stir, and let stand for 10 minutes.

3. Meanwhile, cook the chickpea flour (if using) in a dry skillet over medium heat until lightly toasted and aromatic, about 3 minutes, shaking the pan occasionally (don't use a nonstick skillet for this). Remove the toasted flour from the heat and transfer it to a medium-size bowl. Add the green and black cardamom pods, peppercorns, and mace (if using) to the skillet and toast over medium heat until aromatic, about 2 minutes, shaking the pan once or twice. Remove the spices from the heat and let cool, then grind them in a spice mill or clean coffee grinder. Add the ground spices to the chickpea flour (if using).

4. Using a wooden spoon, mash the yogurt cheese into the spice mixture to blend thoroughly, then add the saffron rose water mixture and the grated nutmeg (if using), and the salt, cayenne, ginger, garlic, and butter. Stir the yogurt mixture with the spoon or knead it with your fingers until blended and smooth; it will be a thick paste.

5. Using a sharp paring knife, make slits about ¾ inch deep all over the lamb and rub in the yogurt paste. Place the meat in a deep bowl, cover, and let marinate, in the refrigerator, for 6 hours.

6. Set up the grill for indirect grilling, place a large drip pan in the center, and preheat the grill to medium.

7. When ready to cook, place the lamb on the hot grate over the drip pan and cover the grill. Cook the lamb until done to taste, 1¼ to 1¾ hours for fall off-the-bone tender (Indians like their lamb—and kid—well-done); when the lamb is very well-done an instant-read thermometer inserted in the thickest part of the leg (but not touching the bone) will register between 180° and 190°F. If using a charcoal grill, you'll need to add 10 to 12 fresh coals to each side after 1 hour.

8. Transfer the lamb to a cutting board and let it rest for 10 minutes before carving and serving.

NOTE: If you can get kid, use two 1½-pound legs, trimmed of fat and sinews, instead of the lamb. Cook it as described but reduce the time to about 1 hour.

SOUTH AFRICA

CAPE TOWN LAMB

INDIRECT GRILLING
SERVES 12

This recipe is simplicity itself, and it makes a pleasant switch from the usual lamb with mint sauce. The preparation reflects the ecumenism of the South African kitchen. Asia is represented by the use of ginger, soy sauce, and Chinese mustard. A British influence can be seen in the Worcestershire sauce and brown sugar. Put them together and you get an energizing jolt of flavor—sweet, sour, and spicy—that will give you a whole new perspective on lamb. I like to serve this lamb with equally ecumenical accompaniments: naan (Tandoori-Baked Flat Breads, page 131), Persian-Style Steamed Rice (page 425), and Pineapple Achar (page 449).

CAPE TOWN LAMB | AT LEFT

Lamb Grilling Chart

CUT	METHOD	HEAT	DONENESS		
			Rare (140°F)	Medium (160°F)	Well-Done (170°F)*
CHOPS					
½ inch thick	direct	high	1 to 2 minutes per side	2 to 3 minutes per side	3 to 4 minutes per side
1 inch thick	direct	high	2 to 4 minutes per side	4 to 6 minutes per side	6 to 8 minutes per side
1½ inches thick	direct	high	4 to 6 minutes per side	6 to 8 minutes per side	8 to 10 minutes per side
RACKS	indirect	medium	30 to 40 minutes	40 to 50 minutes	50 minutes to 1 hour
LEG, boneless 4 to 6 pounds	indirect	medium	1 hour	1 to 1½ hours	1½ to 2 hours
LEG, bone-in 6 to 8 pounds	indirect	medium	1½ to 2 hours	2 to ½ hours	2½ to 3 hours

This chart is offered as a broad guideline to cooking times for the various cuts of meat. Remember, grilling is an art, not a science. When in doubt, refer to times in the individual recipes.

*Really well-done lamb will be 180° to 190°F.

ADVANCE PREPARATION

3 to 8 hours for marinating the meat

FOR THE LAMB

1 bone-in leg of lamb (6 to 8 pounds), trimmed of any papery skin
6 cloves garlic, cut into thin slivers
6 thin slices peeled fresh ginger, cut into thin slivers

FOR THE GLAZE

¼ cup Worcestershire sauce
¼ cup soy sauce
¼ cup firmly packed brown sugar
3 tablespoons Dijon mustard
2 tablespoons hot Chinese-style mustard, or 1 tablespoon dry mustard
3 tablespoons fresh lemon juice
3 tablespoons vegetable oil
3 cloves garlic, minced
1 tablespoon minced peeled fresh ginger
Salt and freshly ground black pepper

1. Prepare the lamb: Using the tip of a sharp paring knife, make slits about an inch deep all over the surface of the lamb. Insert a sliver each of garlic and ginger into each slit. Place the lamb in a nonreactive roasting pan and set aside while you prepare the glaze.

2. Make the glaze: Combine the Worcestershire sauce, soy sauce, brown sugar, Dijon and Chinese-style mustards, lemon juice, oil, and minced garlic and ginger in a small, heavy saucepan and bring to a boil over medium heat, stirring to dissolve the sugar. Cook the glaze until thick and syrupy, about 3 minutes, stirring frequently to prevent sticking. Remove the glaze from the heat and taste for seasoning, adding salt and pepper as necessary. Let cool to room temperature.

3. Pour half of the cooled glaze over the lamb in the roasting pan, brushing to coat it on all sides. Cover and let marinate, in the refrigerator, for 3 to 8 hours (the longer the better). Refrigerate the remaining glaze, covered.

4. Set up the grill for indirect grilling, place a large drip pan in the center, and preheat the grill to medium.

5. When ready to cook, place the lamb on the hot grate over the drip pan and cover the grill. Cook the lamb until done to taste, 2 to 2½ hours; when done to medium, an instant-read meat thermometer inserted in the thickest part of the leg (but not touching the bone) will register 160°F. Start brushing the lamb with the remaining glaze during the last 45 minutes of grilling; brushing it two or three times. If using a charcoal grill, you'll need to add 10 to 12 fresh coals to each side every hour.

6. Transfer the lamb to a cutting board and brush it one last time with glaze, then let rest for 10 minutes before carving. While the lamb rests, heat any remaining glaze to serve as a sauce with the lamb.

NORTH AFRICA

MOROCCAN BARBECUED LAMB

MECHOUI

DIRECT GRILLING
SERVES 8

Mechoui is North African barbecued lamb. Traditionally, a whole lamb is gutted, spitted, rubbed with butter and spices, and cooked over an open pit fire. The quality of the local lamb, the intensity of Moroccan spices, and the heady scent of wood smoke make this one of the most memorable dishes you'll find on the planet. Here's an easy, satisfying version made with a more manageable leg of lamb; it captures the open-air drama of the original. Serve the *mechoui* with A Simple Harissa, Moroccan Shallot Relish, Moroccan Eggplant Salad (pages 481, 445, and 97), and pita.

There are three options for how you grill the lamb. The closest to the original would be on a rotisserie over the fire. Alternatively, you could use the indirect grilling method in a covered grill. In the third method (the least traditional, but the most unabashedly delicious, which is why I have chosen it here), you grill a butterflied leg of lamb directly over the fire. Your butcher can bone and butterfly the lamb for you.

FOR THE LAMB AND SPICED BUTTER

1 leg of lamb, boned and butterflied (3½ to 4 pounds after boning), trimmed of any papery skin
Salt and freshly ground black pepper
8 tablespoons (1 stick) salted butter, at room temperature
4 cloves garlic, minced
16 fresh mint leaves, minced, or 1 tablespoon dried mint
1 teaspoon ground coriander
1 teaspoon sweet paprika
½ teaspoon ground cumin, plus more for serving

FOR THE SAUCE

3 tablespoons salted butter
1 onion, finely chopped
2 cloves garlic, minced
3 tablespoons distilled white vinegar or fresh lemon juice, or more to taste
16 fresh mint leaves, thinly slivered, or 3 tablespoons mint jelly
2 cups homemade chicken stock, or canned low-sodium chicken broth, or water
Salt

1. Prepare the lamb and spiced butter: Open out the butterflied leg of lamb on a work surface so the inside is up and season it with salt and pepper. Set the lamb aside while you make the spiced butter.

2. Combine the 8 tablespoons of butter, 4 cloves of garlic, minced mint, and the coriander, paprika, and cumin in a food processor and process to a smooth paste.

3. Set up the grill for two-zone grilling (see page 18) and preheat one zone to medium-high and one zone to medium.

4. When ready to cook, spread about one third of the spiced butter over the inside of the lamb. Spread about 1 tablespoon more over the outside of the lamb. Arrange the lamb, outer side down, over the hotter section of the grill and cook, turning with tongs, until done to taste, 15 to 20 minutes per side. If the lamb starts to burn, move it to the cooler section of the grill. Every 5 minutes, spread the top of the lamb with some of the remaining spiced butter.

5. Meanwhile, make the sauce: Melt the 3 tablespoons of butter in a small, heavy saucepan over medium-high heat. Add the onion and the 2 cloves of garlic and cook until lightly browned, about 5 minutes. Add the vinegar and the slivered mint and bring to a boil, then stir in the chicken stock. Let come to a boil, then reduce the heat to medium and let the sauce simmer until it is richly flavored and slightly reduced, about 5 minutes. Remove the sauce from the heat and taste for seasoning, adding salt and/or more vinegar as necessary.

6. Transfer the lamb to a cutting board and let it rest for 5 minutes before slicing. Serve the lamb with the sauce and tiny bowls of salt and cumin on the side for seasoning.

GREECE

ROTISSERIED LEG OF LAMB WITH LEMON AND BUTTER

ROTISSERIE GRILLING
SERVES 8

Lamb is the preferred meat of the Greeks—especially at Easter. It's hard to imagine an Easter celebration in Athens (not to mention in Chicago, Boston, or Astoria, New York), without a fire pit where whole lambs are spit roasted to the color of mahogany and the crispness of cellophane. This recipe calls for a butterflied leg of lamb, which can easily be cooked on a backyard barbecue grill. The turning motion of a rotisserie will give you the best results, but you can also cook the lamb over medium heat using the indirect grilling method; this will take an hour and a half to two hours. Have your butcher bone and butterfly the lamb for you.

ADVANCE PREPARATION

4 to 6 hours for marinating the meat

SPECIAL EQUIPMENT

Butcher's string; rotisserie

FOR THE LAMB AND MARINADE

1 tablespoon coarse salt (kosher or sea)
1 tablespoon freshly ground white pepper
1 tablespoon dried oregano, preferably Greek
1 leg of lamb, boned and butterflied (3½ to 4 pounds after boning), trimmed of any papery skin
1 lemon, cut in half and seeded
6 tablespoons (¾ stick) unsalted butter, at room temperature

FOR THE BASTING MIXTURE

½ cup extra-virgin olive oil
¼ cup fresh lemon juice
¼ cup dry white wine
2 cloves garlic, minced
2 teaspoons dried oregano, preferably Greek
1 teaspoon freshly ground black pepper

1. Prepare the lamb and marinade: Combine the salt, white pepper, and 1 tablespoon of oregano in a small bowl.

2. Open out the butterflied leg of lamb on a work surface so the inside is up and sprinkle one third of the spice mixture over it. Squeeze the juice from one lemon half over the meat, then cut the used lemon half into quarters. Set the remaining lemon half aside. Rub the inside of the lamb with 3 tablespoons of the butter, then scatter the lemon quarters on top. Fold the lamb back into its original cylindrical shape and tie it at 1-inch intervals with butcher's string. Place the lamb on a baking sheet, cover it loosely with plastic wrap, and let marinate, in the refrigerator, for 4 to 6 hours.

3. Meanwhile, prepare the basting mixture: Combine the olive oil, lemon juice, wine, garlic, 2 teaspoons of oregano, and black pepper in a medium-size nonreactive bowl and whisk to mix.

4. Set up the grill for spit roasting following the manufacturer's instructions and preheat it to high.

5. When ready to cook, skewer the lamb roast lengthwise on the spit and rub it all over with the cut side of the second lemon half and the remaining 3 tablespoons of butter. Add another generous sprinkling of the spice mixture. Attach the spit to the rotisserie mechanism, cover the grill, and turn on the motor.

6. After the meat has been rotating for 30 minutes, whisk the basting mixture again and, using a long-handled basting brush, brush some of it all over the lamb. Cook the lamb until crusty and brown on the outside and done to taste, 1 to 1½ hours; when done to medium-well, an instant-read meat thermometer inserted in the thickest part of the roast will register

170°F. Uncover the grill to brush the lamb every 15 minutes with the basting mixture and season it with more spice mixture from time to time. If using a charcoal grill, you'll need to add 10 to 12 fresh coals to each side after 1 hour.

7. Transfer the lamb roast, on the spit, to a cutting board. Remove the spit and let the roast rest for 5 minutes. Remove the strings before slicing.

AUSTRALIA

LAMB STEAKS WITH SZECHUAN PEPPER RUB

DIRECT GRILLING
SERVES 4

For centuries, lamb was Australia's preferred meat—in many places its only meat—a legacy of the vast sheep farms that represented the continent's first industry. Even today, no Down Under cookout would be complete without lamb. My choice for this dish would be steaks cut from the leg of lamb. If you have a butcher who will do this, you will be richly rewarded with an uncommonly flavorful piece of meat. Otherwise, use chops from the shoulder, loin, or rib.

Coriander and Szechuan peppercorns may not seem like traditional seasonings, but the proximity of this former British colony to Southeast Asia has made Australia one of the epicenters of Pacific Rim cuisine. The Szechuan peppercorns lend the lamb a clean, woodsy flavor that is unexpected but right on the money.

1 tablespoon Szechuan peppercorns
1 tablespoon black peppercorns
1 tablespoon coriander seeds
1 tablespoon coarse salt (kosher or sea)
4 lamb steaks, cut from the leg or shoulder (each about 8 ounces and ¾ inch thick; see Note)

1. Combine the Szechuan and black peppercorns, coriander seeds, and salt in a dry skillet (don't use a nonstick skillet for this). Toast the spices over medium heat until the peppercorns are very fragrant, about 3 minutes, stirring or shaking the pan occasionally. Transfer the spice mixture to a spice mill and grind to a powder (you can also grind the spices in a mortar with a pestle).

2. Rub as much of the spice mixture as you wish over both sides of the lamb steaks. Place the steaks on a platter and let sit while you preheat the grill.

3. Set up the grill for direct grilling and preheat to high.

4. When ready to cook, brush and oil the grill grate. Arrange the lamb steaks on the hot grate and grill, turning with tongs, until cooked to taste, 3 to 4 minutes per side for medium-rare. Use the poke test (page 31) to check for doneness. When medium-rare the meat will be gently yielding and an instant-read meat thermometer inserted through the side of the steak will register about 145°F.

5. Transfer the steaks to serving plates or a platter. Season them with a little more of the spice mixture, if any remains, and serve at once.

NOTE: If desired, you can substitute 8 loin or 12 rib lamb chops for the steaks. Each loin chop should weigh 4 to 5 ounces and be 1½ inches thick (grill loin chops about 6 minutes per side for medium-rare); each rib chop should be about 3 ounces and 1 inch thick (grill rib chops about 4 minutes per side for medium-rare).

TURKEY

RACKS OF LAMB ÇIRAGAN PALACE

DIRECT GRILLING
SERVES 4

The Çirağan Palace (pronounced Chee-raan) is one of the world's most celebrated hotels, an eleven-acre pleasure palace (former summer home of Sultan Abdül Aziz) located on the banks of the Bosporus on the outskirts of Istanbul. There you can get an exquisite Ottoman meal at the hotel's Turkish restaurant, Tuğra.

I'd spent the week sampling grilled lamb at kebab parlors and street stalls. What a refreshing change of pace to enjoy it in a formal dining room surrounded by chandeliers and sweeping views of the Bosporus. The chef starts with the most expensive of all cuts of lamb—tenderloin—which he marinates overnight in a mixture of olive oil, milk, and onion juice. A sauce made of charred eggplant and yogurt reinforces the smoky flavor of the lamb. Since lamb tenderloin costs a sultan's fortune, I've retooled the recipe for the more affordable and readily available rack of lamb.

ADVANCE PREPARATION

24 hours for marinating the meat

FOR THE LAMB AND MARINADE

2 racks of lamb (3 to 4 pounds in all)
1 large white onion, finely chopped (enough to make ½ cup juice)
1 cup whole milk or half-and-half
1 cup extra-virgin olive oil
1 teaspoon freshly ground black pepper

FOR THE EGGPLANT SAUCE

1 cup plain whole-milk yogurt
2 long, slender eggplants (about 1 pound in all)
1 small green bell pepper
1 clove garlic, minced
2 tablespoons (¼ stick) unsalted butter, at room temperature
1 teaspoon fresh lemon juice, or more to taste
Salt and freshly ground black pepper

1. Prepare the lamb and marinade: Trim most of the fat off the lamb, then scrape the rib bones clean with a sharp paring knife (or have your butcher do this). Place each rack in a large, heavy-duty resealable plastic bag and set them aside while you prepare the marinade.

2. Process the onion in a blender or food processor to a smooth puree, then strain the puree through a strainer lined with a double layer of dampened cheesecloth into a medium-size bowl; you should have about ½ cup juice. Whisk in the milk, olive oil, and black pepper. Pour half of the onion mixture over each rack of lamb in its plastic bag, then seal the bags and turn them over several times so the racks are coated with the marinade. Let the racks of lamb marinate in the refrigerator for 24 hours, turning the bags several times.

3. Make the eggplant sauce: About 4 hours before you plan to grill, set a yogurt strainer, or a regular strainer lined with a double layer of dampened cheesecloth, over a small bowl. Add the yogurt to the strainer and let drain, in the refrigerator, until a firm "cheese" forms.

4. When you are ready to continue with the sauce, set up the grill for direct grilling and preheat to high.

5. Arrange the eggplants on the hot rack and grill, turning with tongs, until charred all over and the flesh is very soft, 20 to 30 minutes. About 10 minutes before the eggplant is done, add the bell pepper to the grate and grill, turning with tongs as necessary, until charred all over and soft. Transfer the charred vegetables to a plate and let cool. Leave the fire burning.

6. Using a paring knife, scrape the skin off the cooled eggplant and bell pepper and core and seed the pepper. Combine the vegetables in a food processor with the garlic, drained yogurt, butter, and lemon juice and season with salt and black pepper to taste. Process to a smooth puree, then transfer the sauce to a small, heavy saucepan and let come to a simmer over low heat. Cook the sauce until thick and creamy, about 2 minutes, stirring occasionally. Remove the sauce from the heat and taste for seasoning, adding more lemon juice and/or salt as necessary; the sauce should be highly seasoned. If you are planning on grilling the lamb right away, cover the sauce and keep it warm (see Note).

7. If using a gas grill, reduce the heat to medium-high; if using charcoal, the grill should now be at medium-high. If not, bump up the heat with 20 to 24 fresh coals.

8. When ready to cook, drain the lamb, setting aside the marinade. Season the racks generously with salt, then brush and oil the grill grate. Arrange the lamb on the hot grate, bone side up, and grill until nicely browned and cooked to taste, 8 to 12 minutes per side, turning with tongs. When done, an instant-read thermometer inserted in the center of the rack (but not touching a bone) will register 145°F for medium-rare, 160°F for medium. Baste the racks with the reserved marinade during the first 15 minutes of cooking only. At the end, stand each rack upright to grill the ends.

9. Transfer the lamb racks to a cutting board and let rest for 5 minutes before carving. Spread the warm eggplant sauce over serving plates or a platter. Carve each rack into chops and arrange them on top of the sauce. Serve at once.

NOTE: The sauce may be made up to 24 hours ahead and refrigerated, covered. Reheat it over low heat.

SENEGAL

LAMB WITH ONION-MUSTARD SAUCE

DIBI

DIRECT GRILLING
SERVES 4

As a rule, West Africans favor stews and boiled dishes over grilled fare. But *dibi* (grilled lamb) is so popular in Senegal, it could qualify as an official state dish. You'll find it being served at sidewalk stalls and roadside eateries throughout Dakar almost any time of day or night. All manner of cuts of lamb hang in sanguine glory from the walls of the stalls—chops, shoulders, legs, and organ meats. Customers simply point to the cut they want and the vendor cooks it on a simple grill, then slathers it with an oniony mustard sauce. This princely repast is served up in foil or newspaper, and it's so good, you want to lick your fingers when you're finished. The popularity of grilled lamb here can be explained by religion: Senegal is 95 percent Muslim. Arab traders brought the art of grilling, not to mention the love of lamb, to this West African nation.

8 loin lamb chops (each 4 to 5 ounces and 1½ inches thick), or 12 rib lamb chops (each about 3 ounces and 1 inch thick)
1 tablespoon plus ¼ cup vegetable oil
Salt and freshly ground black pepper
1 medium-size onion, finely chopped
¼ cup grainy French mustard
½ teaspoon sugar (optional)

1. Brush the lamb chops lightly on both sides with 1 tablespoon of the oil and season them with salt and pepper. Place the chops on a platter and let marinate while you prepare the onion mustard sauce.

2. Combine the onion, the remaining ¼ cup of oil, and the mustard in a small, heavy saucepan and bring to a boil, stirring. Reduce the heat to low and let simmer gently until the onion is soft and lightly browned, about 10 minutes, stirring frequently. Use 3 tablespoons of water to thin the mixture to the consistency of a sauce, adding up to 1 tablespoon more, if needed. Remove the sauce from the heat and taste for seasoning, adding salt and/or pepper to taste, or the sugar if the sauce tastes too tart. Cover the sauce to keep warm.

3. Set up the grill for direct grilling and preheat to high.

4. When ready to cook, brush and oil the grill grate. Arrange the chops on the hot grate and grill, turning with tongs, until cooked to taste, about 6 minutes per side for medium.

5. Transfer the chops to serving plates or a platter and spoon the onion mustard sauce on top. Serve at once.

AFGHANISTAN

"ONION WATER" LAMB CHOPS

O BE PEYAZ

DIRECT GRILLING
SERVES 4

The Afghan name of this dish—*o be peyaz*—means, literally, onion water. The lamb chops are marinated in an intensely flavored mixture of saffron, onion juice, chiles, and turmeric. Most Afghan meats are marinated for several days prior to cooking, but these chops can be grilled after a couple of hours. The recipe was inspired by the Khyber Pass restaurant in New York City. The onion juice has a tenderizing and aromatizing effect on the lamb, and it's used throughout the Islamic world. Serve the chops with pita bread, Quick-Cook Basmati Rice (page 424), and Persian Yogurt Drink (page 63).

ADVANCE PREPARATION

2 hours for marinating the meat

INGREDIENTS

8 loin lamb chops (each 4 to 5 ounces and 1½ inches thick)
¼ teaspoon saffron threads
1½ pounds onions, peeled and quartered
1 to 3 serrano peppers or other hot chiles, minced
2 teaspoons salt
1 teaspoon ground turmeric
1 teaspoon freshly ground black pepper

1. Trim most of the excess fat off of the lamb chops.

2. Place the saffron in a small bowl and grind it to a fine powder with a pestle or the end of a wooden spoon. Add 1 tablespoon of warm water, stir, and let stand for 5 minutes.

3. Place the onions in a food processor and process, in batches if necessary, until they are pureed and quite watery. Transfer the pureed onions to a fine-meshed strainer and set it over a large, deep nonreactive bowl. Let the onions drain, pressing the solids with the back of a rubber spatula or wooden spoon to extract the juice; you should have about 2 cups. Discard the contents of the strainer.

4. Add the serranos, salt, turmeric, black pepper, and the soaked saffron to the onion juice. Whisk until the salt dissolves. Add the lamb chops and turn to coat thoroughly. Let the chops marinate in the refrigerator, covered, for 2 hours, turning several times.

5. Preheat the grill to high.

6. When ready to cook, remove the chops from the marinade, drain them well, and discard the marinade. Brush and oil the grill grate, then arrange the chops on the hot grate and grill, turning with tongs, until cooked to taste, about 6 minutes per side for medium.

7. Transfer the chops to serving plates or a platter and serve at once.

IRAN

LAMB CHOPS
WITH YOGURT AND SAFFRON
SHISHLIK

DIRECT GRILLING
SERVES 4

One of the most sumptuous dishes in the Iranian repertoire, *shishlik* consists of double-thick lamb chops cut from the rack, marinated in a saffron-scented mixture of yogurt, lemon juice, and garlic. Don't trim away too much fat—you need it to melt and baste the lamb as the chops cook. This recipe comes from Iranian cooking authority Najmieh Batmanglij, who adds homemade candied orange peel for a touch of sweetness. I've had good results with both commercial candied peel and strips of orange zest.

For equally delicious results, try the marinade with chicken and use the basting sauce while grilling chicken, veal, and other cuts of lamb. Serve the lamb with Persian-Style Steamed Rice (page 425).

ADVANCE PREPARATION

24 to 48 hours for marinating the meat

FOR THE LAMB AND MARINADE

- ½ teaspoon saffron threads
- 2 cups plain whole-milk yogurt
- ½ cup fresh lemon juice
- 1 medium-size onion, finely chopped
- 8 cloves garlic, finely chopped
- 2 tablespoons cracked black peppercorns
- 2 tablespoons chopped candied orange peel, or 4 strips orange zest (each 2 by ½ inches), removed with a vegetable peeler
- 8 double rib lamb chops (each 5 to 6 ounces and 2 inches thick)

FOR THE SAFFRON BASTING SAUCE

- ¼ teaspoon saffron threads
- 3 tablespoons salted butter
- 3 tablespoons fresh lemon juice
- Salt and freshly ground black pepper

1. Prepare the marinade: Place the ½ teaspoon of saffron in a large, deep nonreactive bowl and grind to a fine powder with a pestle or the end of a wooden spoon. Add 1 tablespoon of warm water to the saffron, stir, and let stand for 10 minutes.

2. Add the yogurt, ½ cup of lemon juice, and the onion, garlic, peppercorns, and orange peel to the soaked saffron and stir to mix. Add the lamb chops, making sure they are completely submerged in the marinade. Cover the bowl with plastic wrap and let the chops marinate, in the refrigerator, for 24 to 48 hours (the longer the better).

3. Meanwhile, prepare the saffron basting sauce: Place the ¼ teaspoon of saffron in a small, heavy nonreactive saucepan and grind it to a fine powder with a pestle or the end of a wooden spoon. Add 1 tablespoon of warm water, stir, and let stand for 10 minutes.

4. Add the butter and 3 tablespoons of lemon juice to the soaked saffron and stir over low heat until the butter melts and the basting sauce is blended and heated through. Remove the sauce from the heat and set aside.

5. Set up the grill for direct grilling and preheat to high.

6. When ready to cook, remove the chops from the marinade, and discard the marinade. Season the chops with salt and pepper. Brush and oil the grill grate, then arrange the chops on the hot grate. Grill the chops, turning with tongs, until cooked to taste, 6 to 8 minutes per side for medium-well, which is how Iranians like their lamb ("It's more tender that way," explains Najmieh). After they have cooked for several minutes brush the chops several times with the saffron basting sauce.

7. Transfer the chops to serving plates or a platter and serve at once.

MOROCCO

LAMB CHOPS STALL #26

DIRECT GRILLING
SERVES 4

The lamb chops served at the stall of Muhammad Moutawakel in the Jema al-Fna probably aren't any better than those served at a hundred other eateries in Marrakech. They just taste that way, served as they are under the open sky, amid the carnivalesque surroundings of the liveliest public square in North Africa. This recipe is extremely simple to prepare, but to get the full effect you need all three simple components: the grilled lamb, the tomato sauce, and the shallot relish.

SPECIAL EQUIPMENT

- 4 long metal skewers

INGREDIENTS

- 12 rib lamb chops (each 3 to 4 ounces and 1 inch thick)
- 1 tablespoon coarse salt (kosher or sea)
- 1 teaspoon ground cumin
- 1 teaspoon garlic powder
- 1 teaspoon freshly ground black pepper
- 4 pita breads
- Moroccan Tomato Sauce (recipe follows)
- Moroccan Shallot Relish (page 445)

GRILLED LAMB WITH HERBES DE PROVENCE | AT RIGHT

1. Arrange three lamb chops flat in a row on a cutting board, ribs on the diagonal all pointing in the same direction. Run a metal skewer through the meat of all three chops at a 60 degree angle to the bones. Skewer the remaining chops the same way.

2. Combine the salt, cumin, garlic powder, and pepper in a small bowl. Using some of the spice mixture, season the lamb chops on both sides. Place the remaining spice mixture in tiny bowls for serving and set aside.

3. Set up the grill for direct grilling and preheat to high.

4. When ready to cook, brush and oil the grill grate. Arrange the skewered lamb chops on the hot grate and grill, turning with tongs, until the lamb is cooked to taste, 4 to 6 minutes per side for medium.

5. Using a pita to protect your hand, unskewer the chops onto serving plates. Serve the chops and pitas with a hefty dollop of tomato sauce, a spoonful of shallot relish, and a generous pinch of spice mixture.

MOROCCAN TOMATO SAUCE

MAKES ABOUT 1½ CUPS

There are probably as many versions of this tomato sauce as there are individual grill jockeys in Morocco. This one offers the refreshing taste of fresh mint.

2 large ripe tomatoes (about 1 pound)
1 large shallot, or ½ small onion, peeled
3 tablespoons chopped fresh mint or flat-leaf parsley
1 tablespoon fresh lemon juice
Salt and freshly ground black pepper

Cut the tomatoes in half crosswise. Grate the tomatoes through the large holes of a four-sided grater into a shallow bowl. Grate in the shallot the same way. Stir in the mint and lemon juice, season with salt and pepper to taste, and serve immediately.

FRANCE

GRILLED LAMB WITH HERBES DE PROVENCE

DIRECT GRILLING
SERVES 4

This is about the easiest and best way I know to cook lamb chops. You find them everywhere in Provence, from backyard cookouts to country inns and roadside restaurants. The basic seasoning is Herbes de Provence, a fragrant mixture of rosemary, thyme, marjoram, savory, basil, bay leaf, and—for a touch of sweetness—fennel and lavender. Herbes de Provence is sold in most gourmet shops, often in decorative jars at inflated prices. But it's easy to make your own for a lot less money so I've provided a recipe.

12 rib lamb chops (each 3 to 4 ounces and 1 inch thick)
¼ cup extra-virgin olive oil
2 lemons
Salt and freshly ground black pepper
3 tablespoons Herbes de Provence (page 491)

1. Arrange the chops in a nonreactive baking dish just large enough to hold them in a single layer. Place the olive oil in a small bowl, then cut one lemon in half and squeeze the juice from both halves into the oil and whisk to blend. Set half aside for basting.

2. Brush the lamb chops on both sides with the remaining olive oil mixture and season the chops with salt and pepper to taste. Sprinkle the chops with 2 tablespoons of the Herbes de Provence and let them marinate, at room temperature, for 10 minutes.

3. Set up the grill for direct grilling and preheat to high.

4. When ready to cook, brush and oil the grill grate. Arrange the lamb chops on the hot grate and grill, turning with tongs, until cooked to taste, about 4 minutes per side for medium-rare. As the lamb chops cook, baste them from time to time with the remaining olive oil mixture.

5. Transfer the grilled chops to a platter and season them with the remaining Herbes de Provence. Serve at once, accompanied by the remaining lemon, cut into wedges.

FRANCE

LATIN QUARTER LAMB KEBABS

DIRECT GRILLING
SERVES 4

Arresting in their simple beauty, these kebabs caught my eye in a shop window on the rue de la Huchette in Paris. This area, a warren of medieval lanes on the Left Bank has become the Plaka of Paris, lined with dozens of Greek restaurants and grill joints. I love the idea of putting whole lamb chops on kebabs—you get to gnaw on the bones after you eat the meat. Serve the chops with Grilled Polenta (page 433).

SPECIAL EQUIPMENT

4 long metal skewers

INGREDIENTS

1 large onion, peeled
1 large green bell pepper
12 rib lamb chops (each 3 to 4 ounces and 1 inch thick)
8 ripe plum tomatoes
1 tablespoon coarse salt (kosher or sea)
1 teaspoon freshly ground black pepper
1 teaspoon dried mint
1 teaspoon dried oregano
1 teaspoon dried rosemary
3 tablespoons extra-virgin olive oil, or more as needed, for brushing
4 pita breads

1. Cut the onion into eight wedges and break each wedge into segments. Core and seed the bell pepper, then cut it into strips 1½ inches long and ½ inch wide.

2. Thread the ingredients for the kebabs onto the skewers in the following sequence: first a lamb chop, then a piece of onion, a piece of bell pepper, a tomato (skewered crosswise), another piece of onion, piece of bell pepper, and lamb chop, more onion and bell pepper, a tomato, more onion and bell pepper, and another lamb chop. Run the metal skewer through the meat of each chop at a 60 degree angle to the bone. Arrange the kebabs on a platter or baking sheet, cover them loosely with plastic wrap, and set aside, in the refrigerator, until ready to grill.

3. Combine the salt, black pepper, mint, oregano, and rosemary in a small bowl, crumbling the rosemary between your fingers. Brush the skewered chops and vegetables all over with some olive oil and season them generously with some of the spice mixture.

4. Set up the grill for direct grilling and preheat to high.

5. When ready to cook, brush and oil the grill grate, then arrange the kebabs on the hot grate and grill, turning with tongs, until the lamb is cooked to taste, 4 to 6 minutes per side for medium. As the kebabs cook, brush them with more olive oil and season them with more of the spice mix.

6. Using a pita to protect your hand, unskewer the chops onto serving plates. Serve the chops at once with the pitas.

TURKEY

THE REAL TURKISH SHISH KEBAB

DIRECT GRILLING
SERVES 4

Shish kebab is Turkey's most celebrated kebab (although the average Turk eats it far less often than ground lamb kebabs). There are probably as many versions in Turkey as there are individual cooks. This one—from the restaurant Develi in Istanbul—owes its tangy flavor to a twenty-four-hour soak in olive oil and yogurt. Contrary to American versions of the dish, Turkish shish kebab rarely comes with vegetables on the same skewer as the meat. Rather, the vegetables are grilled on separate skewers, so each can be cooked the proper length of time.

For the tenderest possible kebabs, use lamb tenderloin or loin. You can also use leg or shoulder meat, but the kebabs will be a little tougher. It doesn't hurt to intersperse lean pieces of lamb with a few fatty pieces; the fat will tenderize the lean meat as it melts.

ADVANCE PREPARATION

24 hours for marinating the meat

SPECIAL EQUIPMENT

6 long metal skewers, including 2 flat ones for the vegetables

INGREDIENTS

- 1 cup plain whole-milk yogurt
- ¼ cup extra-virgin olive oil
- 2 cloves garlic, minced
- 2 teaspoons Aleppo pepper flakes, or 1 teaspoon hot red pepper flakes
- 1 teaspoon salt
- 1 teaspoon freshly ground black pepper
- 1½ pounds boneless loin or shoulder of lamb, cut into 1-inch cubes (include some fatty pieces)
- 8 ripe plum tomatoes or small round tomatoes
- 12 bull's horn peppers (see page 502), stemmed
- 4 pita breads
- 2 tablespoons ground sumac (optional), for serving

1. Combine the yogurt, olive oil, garlic, pepper flakes, salt, and black pepper in a nonreactive bowl. Add the lamb cubes and toss to coat thoroughly. Let the lamb marinate in the refrigerator, covered, for 24 hours, stirring once or twice.

2. Remove the lamb from the marinade and discard the marinade. Thread the cubes of meat onto the thin skewers, alternating lean and fatty pieces. Thread the tomatoes onto a separate, flat skewer; thread the bull's horn peppers onto another flat skewer.

3. Set up the grill for direct grilling and preheat to high.

4. When ready to cook, brush and oil the grill grate, then arrange all of the kebabs on the hot grate, and grill, turning with tongs, until the skins on the vegetables are blistered and browned and the lamb is browned and done to taste, 8 to 12 minutes in all for well-done.

5. Using a pita to protect your hand, unskewer the lamb and vegetables onto serving plates, dividing the vegetables evenly. Serve at once, accompanied by the pitas and sumac (if using) for sprinkling on top.

HOW TO UNSKEWER SHISH KEBABS

Shish kebab is one of the most world's most beloved methods for cooking meats, especially lamb. But unskewering the meat can be challenging—as anyone knows who's tried to unskewer a kebab too vigorously and then sent cubes of meat sailing across the dining room.

Cooks in the Near East and Central Asia have developed an ingenious method for unskewering kebabs. They hold the end of the skewer in one hand and grab the meat with the other, using a piece of pita bread or a sheet of lavash as a pot holder. They pull the meat toward them a tiny bit to loosen it from the skewer, then slide it off the skewer onto the plate.

The Moroccan Grill

Marrakech: Everything you've heard about this legendary red city at the foot of the Atlas Mountains lives up to its reputation—the splendor, the squalor, the stately mosques, the labyrinthine souks, the kaleidoscopically colorful markets bursting with everything from robes to rugs to rose water.

As for the food, it's easy to see why chefs from all over the world take inspiration from Morocco. The cuisine combines the refinement of France (its former colonial ruler) with the exoticism of Africa and the Middle East. Moroccan cooking challenges your taste buds but is familiar enough to be comfort food. It's a cuisine of intense flavors, built on a lavish use of spices.

This is certainly the case of the kebabs, sausages, chops, roasts, organ meats, and seafood that constitute the Moroccan grill. Grilling occupies a central position in Morocco's culinary life, practiced in public squares and crowded markets, at sidewalk cafés and waterfront restaurants. Almost anywhere you turn, you will smell the sweet scent of lamb roasting over charcoal. Look skyward at dusk and the sky will be filled with plumes of smoke rising from a thousand open air cook shacks.

Interestingly, Moroccan haute cuisine relies mainly on such wet cooking methods as stewing, steaming, and deep-frying. Think of Morocco's most famous dishes: couscous, *tagine, bisteeya.* None are cooked on a grill. Grilled fare is the popular food of Morocco, what people eat when they're in a hurry, on a budget, or in the mood for casual dining. And they eat it with gusto.

Jema al-Fna

This quickly became apparent my first day in Marrakech, when I stopped at Jema al-Fna. This fabled piazza, the entryway to the old city, immerses you in everything that is exotic and wondrous about Morocco: the shrill trumpets of the snake charmers (those are real cobras coiled on the blankets), the singsong shouts of the storytellers, the cries of the hustlers and beggars. The din continues from morning to midnight.

Come nightfall, the Jema al-Fna fills with open-air cook stalls, like the one run by Muhammad Moutawakel, a ruggedly handsome man in a crisp white paper cap. Each evening, around five o'clock, he sets out white enamel trays piled high with couscous, hand-cut french fries, and shiny salads of peppers, carrots, and other vegetables. But the star attraction here is the lamb chops and kebabs sizzling away on his grill.

The secret to a great kebab, explains Muhammad, is to intersperse the cubes of meat with pieces of lamb tail fat. The fat melts during the grilling, basting the lamb, keeping it moist and tender. Unlike many American backyard grillers, Muhammad is not afraid of the flare-ups that explode when drops of melting fat hit the fire. "Flare-ups are the best way to give the meat a charred, smoky flavor," he says.

Muhammad seasons his lamb with a mixture of cumin, salt, and garlic powder. The accompaniments, variations of which I experienced throughout Morocco, include a spicy fresh tomato sauce, a tangy shallot and parsley relish, and a wedge of a crusty flat Moroccan bread called *chobs*. You dine under the stars, surrounded by the circuslike swirl of activity in the Jema al-Fna. Barbecue just doesn't get any better.

Bani Marine Street

Well, actually, it's not half bad on Bani Marine Street, a few blocks away from the Jema, either. Bani Marine Street is one of the many "barbecue lanes" in the newer quarters of Marrakech. The crowded street is lined with simple storefront grill restaurants. You don't need a menu, because the bill of fare is displayed in the windows: stacks of lamb chops, trays of liver, coils of *merguez* sausage (reddened with paprika and cayenne), and decoratively sculpted mounds of *kefta* (ground spiced lamb).

There are plenty of items Americans would relish, like the lamb steaks, chops, and shish kebabs. To combat the toughness of Moroccan beef, cooks cut the meat for kebabs into cubes as small as your thumbnail. There are also plenty of items most Americans wouldn't eat, like lamb's brains, testicles, and spleen. The spleen comes stuffed with chopped onions and parsley and tastes like tough, spongy, strong-flavored liver. In the interest of science, I tried it, but it seems to be one of those foods you have to have been brought up on to enjoy.

A meal at one of the Bani Marine Street restaurants is a simple but soul-satisfying experience: a dish of olives and a plate of kebabs, served with fire-toasted bread, shallot relish, and fiery *harissa,* the North African hot sauce made with cayenne pepper and pureed tomatoes. Shallot relish is a rather ingenious concoction: The parsley in it is a natural mouthwash that neutralizes the pungency of the shallots. You also get a tiny dish of salt and ground cumin.

The Mechoui Mystique

At least one Moroccan grilled meat dish has made the leap from street food to the stratosphere of haute cuisine: *mechoui.* Like American barbecue or Brazilian *churrasco, mechoui* refers simultaneously to a single dish, a style of cooking, and a kind of meal. The original *mechoui* was a whole lamb, stuffed with herbs, rubbed with butter and spices, and roasted on a spit over an open pit fire. You can still find this style of *mechoui* in villages in the countryside.

As *mechoui* moved from the country to the city, cooks abandoned the open fire for a wood-fired underground oven. My next stop took me to the heart of the souk, that Ali Baba–esque labyrinth of shops and alleyways that constitutes the main market of Marrakech. My destination was the *mechoui* shop of Housseine Admov. A wiry man with a salt and pepper mustache, wearing a black djellaba, Housseine has owned this tiny shop, in the center of the souk, for forty years. He proudly showed me his trade license—#E67830—qualifying him as a "master *rôtisseur.*"

Actually, when I arrived, there wasn't much to look at: Four white tile walls. A bare earthenware floor from which rose a rickety cast-iron stovepipe. It turned out that the action at a *mechoui* parlor takes place not aboveground, but beneath it. Under the floor is an urn-shaped clay oven, nine feet deep, five feet across, and tapering to an opening perhaps fourteen inches wide in the center of the floor. The *mechoui* pit resembles a giant underground tandoor (Indian barbecue oven).

Twice a day Housseine builds a roaring fire in the underground oven, letting the logs burn down to embers. Twice a day he spits whole, freshly slaughtered lambs on thick wooden poles and lowers them into the oven. The lambs are seasoned with salt, pepper, and cumin, then smoke roasted in the underground oven for two to three hours. The meat that emerges is fall-off-the-bone tender, with buttery-crisp skin and a subtle smoky flavor that made me think of American barbecue. It is nothing short of sublime.

Over the next two days I spent a fair amount of time at Housseine's shop. I watched him build the fires: one at 5:00 A.M. (for the noon lambs), one at 2:30 P.M. (for the night lambs), using discarded cardboard boxes for kindling. I watched him lower the lambs into the oven, haul them out, and line them up, like soldiers, against the white-tile wall, to be packaged in plastic garbage bags and sent home with their owners.

Housseine doesn't sell the lambs; he levies a fee for roasting them. The pit can accommodate up to ten lambs, so when it's full for both the noon and night shifts, he turns a tidy profit. The pit requires regular maintenance. Once a month, Housseine hires a dwarf to climb down into the oven and clean it. Once every twenty years, he digs the oven up and replaces it with a new one.

Owning a *mechoui* pit is an upbeat occupation. Because *mechoui* is a rich man's dish or a ceremonial treat served on happy occasions, such as birthdays and weddings, people who order *mechoui* from Housseine generally have something to celebrate. But, you don't need an underground pit to make great *mechoui*—restaurants in Marrakech roast it on rotisseries or in the oven. A North American–style kettle grill produces a great *mechoui*. Leg of lamb gives you the spirit of the dish in proportions that don't require a whole community to enjoy (see page 205 for a recipe).

MOROCCO

MOROCCAN LAMB KEBABS

DIRECT GRILLING
SERVES 4

There is nothing exotic about the flavorings here; they just happen to produce exceptionally tasty lamb. Kebabs are a culinary common denominator in Morocco, found at palatial restaurants, open-air cook shops, and just about everywhere in between. The secret to good kebabs is to intersperse the lean meat with cubes of fatty meat or lamb fat—preferably from the tail. I've given a range of marinating times: Thirty minutes of marinating will give you tasty lamb for a week-night supper; eight hours will give you incredibly rich flavored lamb for a special occasion. Serve the kebabs with Grilled Zucchini Salad (page 98).

ADVANCE PREPARATION

30 minutes to 8 hours for marinating the meat

SPECIAL EQUIPMENT

4 to 6 long metal skewers

INGREDIENTS

1 medium-size onion, grated
3 tablespoons chopped fresh flat-leaf parsley
3 tablespoons chopped fresh cilantro
½ teaspoon ground cumin
½ teaspoon sweet paprika
½ teaspoon freshly ground white or black pepper
½ teaspoon salt
1 tablespoon extra-virgin olive oil
1½ to 2 pounds boneless leg or shoulder of lamb, cut into 1-inch cubes (include some fatty pieces)
4 pita breads

1. Combine the onion, parsley, cilantro, cumin, paprika, pepper, salt, and olive oil in a large bowl and stir to mix. Add the lamb cubes and toss to coat thoroughly. Let the lamb marinate in the refrigerator, covered, for at least 30 minutes, or up to 8 hours (the longer the better).

2. Remove the lamb from the marinade and discard the marinade. Thread the cubes of meat onto the skewers, dividing them evenly and alternating lean and fatty pieces.

3. Set up the grill for direct grilling and preheat to high.

4. When ready to cook, brush and oil the grill grate, then arrange the kebabs on the hot grate and grill, turning with tongs, until nicely browned and cooked to taste, 8 to 12 minutes in all, for well-done (as the Moroccans tend to like their lamb).

5. Using a pita to protect your hand, unskewer the lamb onto serving plates. Serve at once.

GREECE

SOUVLAKI FLAMBEED WITH METAXA

DIRECT GRILLING
SERVES 4

Souvlaki is the Greek version of shish kebab, a popular street food consisting of lamb bathed in a tangy marinade of olive oil, lemon juice, garlic, and bay leaves and grilled over blazing coals. The retsina (a Greek wine flavored with resin) in this recipe isn't strictly traditional, nor is flambéing the souvlakis with Metaxa (Greek brandy). But both beverages would be served at a Greek barbecue, and both add flavor and drama to the meat, and so I decided to add them. The purist could omit them. Serve the souvlaki with pita bread, Yogurt-Cucumber Salad with Mint (page 85), and A Different Greek Salad (page 110).

ADVANCE PREPARATION

6 to 24 hours for marinating the meat

SPECIAL EQUIPMENT

4 long metal skewers

INGREDIENTS

- ¼ cup extra-virgin olive oil, preferably Greek
- ¼ cup retsina wine or dry red wine
- ¼ cup fresh lemon juice
- 4 bay leaves
- 3 cloves garlic, minced
- 1 teaspoon dried oregano, preferably Greek
- Salt and freshly ground black pepper
- 1½ pounds boneless leg or shoulder of lamb, cut into 1-inch cubes (include some fatty pieces)
- 1 medium-size onion, cut into 1-inch pieces
- ⅓ cup Metaxa (Greek brandy) or other brandy
- Lemon wedges, for serving
- 4 pita breads, for serving

1. Combine the olive oil, wine, and lemon juice in a large nonreactive bowl and whisk to blend. Stir in the bay leaves, garlic, oregano, 1 teaspoon of salt, and 1 teaspoon of pepper. Add the cubes of lamb and toss to coat thoroughly, then let marinate in the refrigerator, covered, for at least 6 hours, or up to 24 hours.

2. Remove the lamb from the marinade, reserving the marinade, and thread the cubes of meat onto the skewers, alternating them with pieces of onion.

3. Set up the grill for direct grilling and preheat to high.

4. When ready to cook, brush and oil the grill grate, then arrange the kebabs on the hot grate and grill, turning with tongs, until nicely browned and cooked to taste, 8 to 12 minutes in all, for well-done (as Greeks tend to like their lamb). Brush the kebabs as they cook with the reserved marinade (but not during the last 3 minutes) and season them with salt and pepper.

5. Transfer the souvlakis to a heatproof platter. Warm the Metaxa in a small saucepan over very low heat; do not allow it to boil or even become hot. Remove the pan from the heat and then, making sure your sleeves are rolled up, light a long match and use it to ignite the brandy, averting your face as you do so. Very carefully pour the flaming brandy over the souvlakis and serve at once, accompanied by lemon wedges and pitas.

REPUBLIC OF ARMENIA

ARMENIAN SHISH KEBAB

DIRECT GRILLING
SERVES 4

Shish kebab is common currency in the cuisines of the Middle and Near East and Central Asia. The Armenian version owes its richness to the addition of tomato paste to the marinade—a tangy mixture of red wine, olive oil, and wine vinegar. This recipe is equally delicious prepared with beef. Either way the shish kebabs go well with lavash and bulgur, and with Grilled Eggplant, Tomato, and Pepper Salad (page 96), and Onion Relish with Pomegranate Molasses (page 446).

ADVANCE PREPARATION

8 to 24 hours for marinating the meat

SPECIAL EQUIPMENT

4 long metal skewers

INGREDIENTS

- ½ cup dry red wine
- ¼ cup tomato paste
- ¼ cup extra-virgin olive oil
- 2 tablespoons red wine vinegar
- 1 medium-size onion, finely chopped
- 1 clove garlic, finely chopped
- 1 teaspoon dried marjoram or summer savory
- 1 teaspoon salt
- ½ teaspoon freshly ground black pepper
- ½ teaspoon hot red pepper flakes
- ¼ teaspoon ground allspice
- 1½ pounds boneless leg or shoulder of lamb, cut into 1-inch cubes (include some fatty pieces)
- 24 pearl onions, peeled and cut in half, or 2 medium-size onions, cut into 1-inch pieces
- 2 green bell peppers, cored, seeded, and cut into 1-inch pieces
- Lavash (flat bread), for serving

1. Combine the red wine, tomato paste, olive oil, and wine vinegar in a large nonreactive bowl and whisk to blend. Stir in the chopped onion, garlic, marjoram, salt, black pepper, hot pepper flakes, and allspice. Add the cubes of lamb and toss to coat thoroughly, then cover and let marinate, in the refrigerator, for at least 8 hours, or up to 24 hours.

2. Remove the lamb from the marinade and discard the marinade. Thread the cubes of meat onto the skewers, alternating them with pearl onion halves and bell pepper pieces.

3. Set up the grill for direct grilling and preheat to high.

4. When ready to cook, brush and oil the grill grate, then arrange the kebabs on the hot grate and grill, turning with tongs, until nicely browned and cooked to taste, 8 to 12 minutes in all, for well-done.

5. Using a piece of lavash to protect your hand, unskewer the lamb and vegetables onto serving plates and serve at once.

REPUBLIC OF GEORGIA

ALEXANDRE DUMAS' GEORGIAN-STYLE LAMB KEBABS

DIRECT GRILLING
SERVES 4

Alexandre Dumas was one of the most prolific and beloved novelists of the nineteenth century, writing such classics as *The Count of Monte Cristo* and *The Man in the Iron Mask.* What you may or may not know is that he was also a passionate trencherman, and in addition to penning a volume entitled *Le grand dictionnaire de cuisine,* he wrote extensively about the food he encountered during his travels.

The following recipe was inspired by Dumas' travels through the Caucasus Mountains in 1859. Concerning the cooking equipment, he imparts some curious advice, quoted in Darra Goldstein's fine book *The Georgian Feast:* "Even if you don't have a skewer or happen to be traveling in a place where skewers are unknown, you can always substitute something else. Throughout my travels the cleaning-rod of my rifle served as a skewer, and I didn't notice any harm to the worthiness of my weapon from using it in this humble role."

Amen!

I've embellished Dumas' original recipe, adding a distinctive traditional Georgian mixture of spices called *khmeli-suneli.* I think you'll find the results incredibly aromatic. You probably haven't tasted ground marigold before; it's available at markets specializing in Russian products. On page 248 you'll find a description of sumac. Serve these kebabs with grilled tomatoes, Georgian Pickled Plum Sauce (page 467), and Georgian Pickles (page 442).

ADVANCE PREPARATION

1 to 8 hours for marinating the meat

SPECIAL EQUIPMENT

4 long metal skewers

INGREDIENTS

- **½ teaspoon ground coriander**
- **½ teaspoon dried dill**
- **½ teaspoon dried basil**
- **½ teaspoon dried mint**
- **½ teaspoon ground marigold (optional)**
- **Salt and freshly ground black pepper**
- **1½ pounds boneless leg of lamb, cut into 1-inch cubes (Dumas calls them "walnut size")**
- **1 medium-size onion, finely chopped**
- **1 cup red wine vinegar**
- **2 tablespoons olive oil, for basting**
- **2 tablespoons ground sumac (optional), for serving**

1. Combine the coriander, dill, basil, mint, ground marigold (if using), and 1 teaspoon of salt, and ½ teaspoon of pepper in a large bowl. Add the lamb and toss to coat thoroughly. Let marinate in the refrigerator, covered, for 30 minutes.

2. Add the onion and wine vinegar to the lamb, tossing

again to mix well. Re-cover the lamb and let marinate, in the refrigerator, for at least another 30 minutes, up to 8 hours total (the longer it marinates, the tangier the lamb).

3. Set up the grill for direct grilling and preheat to high.

4. When ready to cook, thread the lamb onto the skewers. Brush and oil the grill grate, then arrange the kebabs on the hot grate and grill, turning with tongs, until nicely browned and cooked to taste, 8 to 12 minutes in all, for well-done. Brush the kebabs several times as they cook with olive oil and season them with salt and pepper.

5. Unskewer the lamb onto serving plates and serve at once, accompanied by ground sumac (if using) for sprinkling.

THE GREAT AMERICAN HAMBURGER | AT RIGHT

CHAPTER 9

GROUND MEAT, BURGERS & SAUSAGES

The hamburger is the U.S.'s most famous contribution to the world of barbecue. And while we may think that nothing can beat the succulence of a thick, hand-patted burger expertly charred over fire, grill jockeys around the world offer some stiff competition, elevating lowly ground meat to the level of art.

"There's a lot more future in hamburgers than in baseball."
—Ray Kroc

Bulgarians have earned bragging rights for their *kufteh* (cumin-scented veal and pork burgers). Romanians deserve raves for their *mititei* (spicy pork and lamb sausages). And Croatians should be proud of their *ćevapčići* (three-meat burgers flavored with coriander). Moving east, the burger gives way to a sort of skinless sausage, that's molded and cooked on a flat metal skewer. It's called *kofta kebab* in the Middle East, *lyulya kebab* in Azerbaijan, and *seekh kebab* in India.

As for actual sausages, there is no shortage on the barbecue trail, from the chorizo of Spain and Latin America to the *kupati* (beef sausage studded with pomegranate seeds) of the Republic of Georgia. These recipes may seem a long way from hamburgers and hot dogs. Yet the appeal of grilled ground meats is universal.

U.S.A.

THE GREAT AMERICAN HAMBURGER

DIRECT GRILLING
SERVES 6

What makes a great hamburger? First there's the meat. You want to use a flavorful cut, like sirloin (for uptown burgers), or chuck or round (if you're feeling more democratic). And it shouldn't be too lean: 15 to 20 percent fat is ideal.

I adhere to the "less is more" school when it comes to making hamburgers. Namely, the fewer ingredients you add to the meat, the better. Oh, I know how tempting it is for cooks to want to season the meat with onion, garlic, spices, and condiments. But to taste a burger at its best, keep it utterly simple. The garnishes will add all the flavor you need.

One final bit of advice: Handle the meat as little as possible: a few pats to form it into patties. Anything more will rob the burger of its juiciness and primal flavor.

FOR THE BURGERS

2¼ pounds ground round, chuck, or sirloin
6 slices (½ inch thick) Vidalia or other sweet onion (optional)
2 tablespoons unsalted butter, melted, or 2 tablespoons extra-virgin olive oil
Salt and freshly ground black pepper
6 hamburger buns

FOR THE TOPPINGS—ANY OR ALL

Iceberg lettuce leaves
Sliced ripe tomatoes
Sliced dill pickles or sweet pickles
Cooked bacon (2 slices per burger)
Ketchup, Mustard, and Mayonnaise

1. Divide the meat into six equal portions. Lightly wet your hands with cold water, then form each portion of meat into a round patty, 4 inches across and of an even thickness (see Note).

2. Set up the grill for direct cooking and preheat to high.

3. When ready to cook, brush and oil the grill grate.

4. If using onion slices, brush them on both sides with melted butter and season with salt and pepper. Place the onion on the hot grate and grill until nicely browned, about 4 minutes per side, then transfer to a plate.

5. Brush one side of the meat patties lightly with melted butter and season with salt and pepper. Arrange the burgers, buttered side down, on the hot grate and grill until the bottoms are nicely browned, 4 to 5 minutes. Brush the tops lightly with some of the melted butter and season them with salt and pepper. Using a spatula, turn the burgers and grill until they are browned and cooked to taste, 4 to 5 minutes longer for medium. Meanwhile, brush the cut sides of the buns with the remaining melted butter and toast them, cut sides down, on the grill during the last 2 minutes the burgers cook.

6. Set out the toppings. Put the burgers and onion slices on buns and serve.

NOTE: If you are not planning on cooking the burgers immediately, place them on a large plate, cover them loosely with plastic wrap, and refrigerate them.

Cooking Hamburgers

When I was growing up, an E. coli outbreak was a freak occurrence. Today you can hardly pick up the newspapers without reading about some sort of mass food contamination.

Ground meats seem to be particularly susceptible to contamination. In order to kill E. coli (or other bacteria), you need to cook hamburgers (and other meats) to an internal temperature of 160°F. That's the temperature of medium-done meat.

Some other ways to make hamburgers safer:

- Buy your meat at a top-notch butcher shop where the meat is ground daily. If possible, choose your meat before it's ground and have the butcher grind it while you wait.
- Store the meat in the refrigerator until you're ready to cook it.
- Wash any cutting board you've cut meat on with very hot water and plenty of soap immediately after each use.

CHEESEBURGERS

SERVES 6

To make this popular classic, in addition to the ingredients in the main recipe for hamburgers, above, you'll need:

6 slices (¼ inch thick) sharp Cheddar cheese or Swiss cheese, or 6 pieces of Roquefort

Follow the instructions through cooking the first side of the burgers in Step 4. After you turn the burgers, place a piece of cheese on top. Cover the grill and cook the burgers until the cheese is melted and the meat is done to taste; check after 3 minutes. When done, assemble the burgers.

From Hamburg to Hoboken: A Brief History of the Hamburger

The hamburger ranks as one of the most popular dishes in the world—at least, if you figure by numbers. According to Jeffrey Tennyson, author of *Hamburger Heaven: The Illustrated History of the Hamburger,* Americans consume more than 38 billion burgers a year—three a week for each man, woman, and child. Add foreign consumption and you've got a food phenomenon unique in human history.

The hamburger's history begins, logically enough, in Hamburg, Germany, which in the eighteenth century was the largest port in Europe. According to Tennyson, German seafarers acquired a taste for chopped beef in Russia, where steak tartare had been a staple for centuries. Tartare takes its name from the Tartary (or Tatary) plains in Central Asia, home to the nomadic warriors known as the Mongols. Mongol horsemen, so the legend goes, enjoyed their beef raw, tenderizing it by placing it under their saddles (the riding action reduced it to a tender pulp).

History neglects to tell us whether it was a Mongol, Russian, or German who first had the idea to cook the chopped beef. We do know that by the time the hamburger reached North America, with German immigrants, it was cooked—and beloved and respected. The first North American restaurant to propose hamburger on its menu was the legendary Delmonico's in New York, which in 1834 offered "hamburger steaks" for the princely sum of 10 cents—twice the price of roast beef or veal cutlet.

As the hamburger became more familiar, the price dropped. By the turn of the century, hamburgers had become the food of the masses; they were sold everywhere from horse-drawn lunch wagons to soda fountains to the newly invented luncheonettes. Somewhere along the line tomatoes and pickles were added as a topping. And, the patty was placed on a bun, making the hamburger the ultimate convenience food—something you could eat on the run.

BACON AND SMOKED CHEESE BURGERS

SERVES 6

Think of these as "barbecue" burgers, redolent with the wood smoke scent of bacon and smoked cheese. In addition to the ingredients for the hamburgers on the opposite page, you'll need:

12 thin slices of bacon
6 slices (1/4 inch thick) smoked mozzarella or other smoked cheese

In Step 2, wrap each meat patty with 2 slices of bacon. Cook the burgers as described in the main recipe at left. Put the burgers on buns and top with the cheese. The heat of the burgers will melt the cheese.

AVOCADO, SPROUT, AND SALSA BURGERS

SERVES 6

Tired of the same old, same old? For a refreshing new take on hamburgers, replace the toppings suggested in the main recipe on the opposite page with these:

1 large ripe avocado, peeled, pitted, and cut into 1/4-inch slices
1½ cups alfalfa sprouts
1½ cups Salsa Mexicana (page 192)

Cook the burgers as described in the main recipe at left. Put them on buns and top with avocado slices, sprouts, and salsa.

BULGARIA

BULGARIAN BURGERS

KUFTEH

DIRECT GRILLING
SERVES 4

Kufteh, aka *kafta, kofta,* and *kefta,* generally refers to the grilled ground lamb kebabs or meatballs popular throughout the Arab world. But in Bulgaria, the term describes a meat patty similar to a hamburger. The lamb used in Muslim countries gives way to ground pork and veal in Bulgaria—an exceptionally flavorful combination of meats. *Kufteh* and *kebabche* (the same mixture formed into a sausage shape) are popular enough to qualify as the national snack in Bulgaria, where they're served with crusty rolls or country-style bread and tomato salad (Tomato Salad with Feta Cheese, see page 119).

8 ounces ground veal
8 ounces ground pork
1 small onion, minced
3 tablespoons minced fresh parsley
1 teaspoon salt, or more to taste
Generous ½ teaspoon ground cumin, or more to taste
½ teaspoon freshly ground black pepper, or more to taste

1. Combine the veal, pork, onion, parsley, salt, cumin, and pepper in a mixing bowl and stir to mix with a wooden spoon. To test the mixture for seasoning, cook a teaspoon of it in a nonstick skillet until cooked through, then taste, adding more salt, cumin, and/or pepper to the remaining mixture as necessary; the mixture should be highly seasoned.

2. Divide the meat mixture into four equal portions. Lightly wet your hands with cold water, then form each portion into a patty 3 inches across and about ¾ inch thick (see Note).

3. Set up the grill for direct grilling and preheat to high.

4. When ready to cook, brush and oil the grill grate. Arrange the burgers on the hot grate and grill, turning with a spatula, until browned on both sides and cooked through, 3 to 4 minutes per side. Serve at once.

NOTE: If you are not planning on cooking the burgers immediately, place them on a large plate, cover them loosely with plastic wrap, and refrigerate them.

PAKISTAN

"SLIPPER" BURGERS

CHAPLI KEBAB

DIRECT GRILLING
SERVES 4

His name was Mohammed Bashir and he wore a powder blue *shilwar* (pantaloon) and *kamiz* (tunic). I met him not in his hometown of Faisalabad, Pakistan, but in a taxi in Philadelphia. As is my wont with cabbies wherever I travel, I asked him about the barbecue of his homeland. He told me about a dish with the curious name of *chapli kebab,* literally slipper or sandal patties. (The word *kebab* is used here in the original sense of meat, not food on a skewer.)

To make *chapli kebab,* ground meat is shaped in a large, flat patty that looks like the sole of a slipper or sandal. *Chapli kebab* is a specialty of the town of Peshawar on the India-Pakistan border—Muslim country, so you can use either beef or lamb. Pakistani restaurants in the U.S. tend to serve *chapli kebab* pan-fried. But I like them grilled—the way I imagine they're made in Peshawar—with naan (Tandoori-Baked Flat Breads, see page 131) alongside.

ADVANCE PREPARATION

1 to 2 hours for chilling the patties

INGREDIENTS

1 pound ground lamb or beef
½ medium-size onion, minced
2 cloves garlic, minced
1 to 2 serrano or other hot peppers, seeded and minced (for hotter patties, leave the seeds in)
¼ cup finely chopped fresh cilantro
1 tablespoon grated peeled fresh ginger
2 teaspoons ground or crushed coriander seeds
1 teaspoon salt, or more to taste
½ teaspoon freshly ground black pepper, or more to taste

½ teaspoon cayenne pepper
½ teaspoon ground cumin

1. Combine the lamb, onion, garlic, peppers, cilantro, ginger, coriander seeds, salt, black pepper, cayenne, and cumin in a large bowl. Knead and squeeze until thoroughly blended, 3 to 4 minutes. To test the mixture for seasoning, cook a small amount in a nonstick skillet until cooked through, then taste, adding more salt and/or black pepper to the remaining mixture as necessary; the mixture should be highly seasoned.

2. Line a large plate with plastic wrap. Divide the meat mix-

A Word About the Recipes in This Chapter

The recipes in this chapter are easy, but they do involve some special care.

■ First, a word about grinding. The kebabi and saté men I met on the barbecue trail grind their own meat from scratch, and time permitting, I like to do the same. But I know that perfectly delicious results can be obtained with a lot less fuss and time by using preground meat, so that is what I call for in the recipes.

■ If you do grind your own meat (see page 232 for instructions), unless otherwise instructed, use a fairly fatty cut like shoulder (for lamb and pork) or chuck (for beef). Put it through the fine plate of the meat grinder (the plate with one-eighth-inch holes).

■ Sometimes I call for kneading the kebab mixture by hand, either over a low heat or at room temperature. Kneading (especially over heat) creates a smooth, tightly knit, almost spongy texture much prized by Central Asians. There is no need to knead the meat unless instructed to do so in a recipe.

■ Some of the recipes call for molding the ground meat onto skewers. In general, chilling the meat before molding it will make the task easier. If it is necessary to chill the meat, it's noted in the recipe. I also like to chill molded kebabs for one to two hours before grilling. This makes the meat less likely to fall off the skewers. Chilling is a luxury not available to many kebab and saté chefs in the Third World, who have no refrigeration. If you're pressed for time, most of the *koftas,* kebabs, and satés in this chapter can be assembled and grilled without chilling. If you're preparing the meat ahead of time, always refrigerate it until you're ready to grill.

■ The ground meat should be molded on flat skewers (these are available at Middle Eastern and Iranian markets and at http://store.grilling4all.com). Ideally, the skewers will be a half inch wide, but you can get away with using a quarter-inch-wide skewer. Use slender metal or bamboo skewers only as a last resort; the meat is more likely to fall off them.

■ Because ground meat satés are fairly fragile, I suggest arranging them on a baking sheet lined with plastic wrap as you prepare them. When I prepare larger kebabs, I rest both ends of the skewers on the sides of a roasting pan so that the meat is suspended. This prevents the kebabs from flattening out.

■ I also recommend grilling ground meat kebabs without a grate, a procedure in which the ends of the skewers are positioned on bricks or metal pipes so they are raised above the grill grate. This makes the kebabs less likely to stick and fall apart. (For instructions on grateless grilling, see page 21).

If you're in a hurry or you don't have bricks or pieces of pipe, you can cook ground meat kebabs directly on the grill grate. Just remember to oil it well before adding the kebabs.

■ Use tongs for turning the kebabs. Try to hold the ends of the skewers, rather than the meat part, when turning them.

■ To unskewer a ground meat kebab, do as an Iranian kebabi man does: Use a piece of pita bread or lavash as a pot holder. Gently pull the portion of meat toward you to loosen it, then push it away from you to unskewer it.

Ground Meats Grilling Chart

CUT	METHOD	HEAT	COOKING TIME
BURGERS	direct	high	8 to 10 minutes in all
SAUSAGES	direct	medium	16 to 20 minutes in all
KOFTAS AND *LULAS*	direct	high	6 to 8 minutes in all
SATES	direct	high	4 to 8 minutes in all depending on size

*To eliminate the risk of bacterial contamination, cook all ground meats to at least 160°F.

ture into four equal portions. Lightly wet your hands with cold water, then form each portion of meat into an oval patty about 5 inches long and ¾ inch thick. As it is made, place each patty on the prepared plate. Cover loosely with plastic wrap and refrigerate for 1 to 2 hours.

3. Set up the grill for direct grilling and preheat to high.

4. When ready to cook, brush and oil the grill grate. Arrange the patties on the hot grate and grill, turning with a spatula, until nicely browned on both sides and cooked to taste, 4 to 5 minutes per side for medium. Serve at once.

BOSNIA

THREE-MEAT PATTIES

CEVAPCICI

DIRECT GRILLING
MAKES 8 PATTIES; SERVES 4

Pronounced che-VAP-chee-chee, *ćevapčići* are one of the many grilled ground meat patties popular in the Balkans; compare them with the *mititei* (Romanian Pork and Lamb Sausages, opposite) and *kufteh* (Bulgarian Burgers, page 226) in this chapter. This version calls for an equal amount of beef, veal, and pork, but *ćevapčići* are also made with just lamb or any combination of these meats. The resulting flavor is so richly complex it tastes like a hamburger that's gone to finishing school. The addition of baking soda helps to make the mixture light. Note that the meat shouldn't be too lean.

ADVANCE PREPARATION

1 to 2 hours for chilling the patties

FOR THE PATTIES

8 ounces ground beef chuck
8 ounces ground pork butt
8 ounces ground veal or lamb
½ medium-size onion, grated
3 tablespoons chopped fresh flat-leaf parsley
1½ teaspoons salt, or more to taste
½ teaspoon ground coriander
½ teaspoon freshly ground black pepper, or more to taste
½ teaspoon baking soda
⅓ cup homemade beef stock, canned low-sodium beef broth, or water

FOR SERVING

1 medium-size onion, finely chopped
1 ripe tomato, finely chopped
1 red bell pepper, cored, seeded, and finely chopped, or 3 tablespoons chopped pickled peppers
4 crusty rolls

1. Make the patties: Combine the beef, pork, veal, onion, parsley, salt, coriander, black pepper, and baking soda in a large bowl. Knead and squeeze the mixture with your hands until thoroughly blended, 3 to 4 minutes. Knead in the broth. To test the mixture for seasoning, cook a small amount in a nonstick skillet until cooked through, then taste, adding more salt and/or black pepper to the remaining mixture as necessary; it should be highly seasoned.

2. Lightly oil a large plate. Divide the meat mixture into eight equal portions. Lightly wet your hands with cold water, then roll each portion between your palms to form a sausage shape about 1 inch in diameter and 2 inches long. As they are made, place the *ćevapčići* on the prepared plate. Cover them loosely with plastic wrap and refrigerate for 1 to 2 hours.

3. Prepare the toppings: Place the onion, tomato, and bell pepper in separate serving bowls. Cover and set aside until ready to serve.

4. Set up the grill for direct grilling and preheat to high.

5. When ready to cook, brush and oil the grill grate. Arrange the *ćevapčići* on the hot grate and grill, turning with a spatula, until they are nicely browned and cooked through, 6 to 8 minutes in all.

6. Serve the *ćevapčići* on crusty rolls (2 per roll), topped with spoonfuls of onion, tomato, and bell pepper.

ROMANIA

ROMANIAN PORK AND LAMB SAUSAGES

MITITEI

DIRECT GRILLING
MAKES 8 SAUSAGES; SERVES 4

Legend credits La Iordachi restaurant in Bucharest as the birthplace of *mititei,* the skinless sausages so popular in Romania. One particularly busy night, the story goes, the kitchen ran out of regular sausages and ground pork and lamb were mixed together, patted into short, stubby sausage shapes (*mititei* means little in Romanian), and grilled without casings. The blend of spices used, including caraway, allspice, and cloves, makes this one of the most interesting ground meat dishes around. Some people like to use beef instead of pork; in either case, the meat shouldn't be too lean.

ADVANCE PREPARATION

1 to 2 hours for chilling the patties

INGREDIENTS

12 ounces ground pork or beef
12 ounces ground lamb shoulder
1 small onion, minced as fine as possible
2 cloves garlic, minced as fine as possible
1 tablespoon extra-virgin olive oil
1½ teaspoons salt, or more to taste
1 teaspoon baking soda
1 teaspoon hot or sweet paprika, preferably imported
½ teaspoon dried marjoram
½ teaspoon caraway seeds
½ teaspoon freshly ground black pepper, or more to taste
¼ teaspoon ground allspice
Tiny pinch of ground cloves

1. Combine the pork, lamb, onion, garlic, olive oil, salt, baking soda, paprika, marjoram, caraway seeds, pepper, allspice, and cloves in a large bowl. Knead and squeeze the mixture with your hands until thoroughly blended, 3 to 4 minutes. To test the mixture for seasoning, cook a small amount in a nonstick skillet until cooked through, then taste, adding more salt and/or pepper to the remaining mixture as necessary; it should be highly seasoned.

2. Lightly oil a large plate. Divide the meat mixture into eight equal portions. Lightly wet your hands with cold water, then roll each portion between your palms to form sausage shapes about 1 inch in diameter and 3½ inches long. As they are made, place the *mititei* on the prepared plate. Cover them loosely with plastic wrap and refrigerate for 1 to 2 hours.

3. Set up the grill for direct grilling and preheat to high.

4. When ready to cook, brush and oil the grill grate. Arrange the *mititei* on the hot grate and grill, turning with a spatula, until nicely browned and cooked through, 6 to 8 minutes in all. Serve at once.

SAMBA DOGS | AT RIGHT

BRAZIL

SAMBA DOGS

DIRECT GRILLING
SERVES 8

I tasted these unusual hot dogs at a samba school in Rio. From midnight to 4 A.M. the cavernous concrete hall reverberated with the thunderous rhythm of samba. An army of street vendors stood by to assuage the hunger of the dancers, and I was particularly intrigued by the hot dog stand: The vendor crowned her hot dogs with a luscious relish of corn, tomatoes, peas, black and green olives, and hard-cooked eggs.

- 1 large egg, hard-cooked and cut into ¼ inch dice
- 1 ripe medium-size tomato, seeded (see box, page 454) and finely chopped
- ¼ cup corn kernels, freshly cooked, or drained canned corn
- ¼ cup cooked fresh or frozen green peas, or drained canned petits pois
- ¼ cup pimiento-stuffed green olives, cut into ¼-inch dice
- ¼ cup pitted black olives, cut into ¼-inch dice
- ¼ cup diced red onion
- 3 tablespoons extra-virgin olive oil
- 4½ teaspoons red wine vinegar, or more to taste
- Salt and freshly ground black pepper
- 8 best-quality hot dogs
- 8 best-quality hot dog buns, split

1. Combine the egg in a medium-size bowl with the tomato, corn, peas, olives, onion, olive oil, and vinegar and toss gently but thoroughly to mix. Taste for seasoning, adding more vinegar and salt and pepper to taste; the relish should be highly seasoned.

2. Set up the grill for direct grilling and preheat to high.

3. When ready to cook, brush and oil the grill grate. Arrange the hot dogs on the hot grate and grill, turning with tongs, until crusty and nicely browned all over, 6 to 8 minutes in all. While the hot dogs cook on the second side, place the buns, cut side down, on the grate and toast lightly.

4. Serve the hot dogs on the buns, topped with the relish.

SPAIN

SPICY CHORIZOS

DIRECT GRILLING
MAKES TWELVE 5-INCH LINKS; SERVES 6

To judge by geographic distribution, chorizo is the world's most popular sausage. Born in Spain, this spicy reddish-orange link is found throughout Spain's former colonies, from the Caribbean to South America to the Philippines and beyond. Vinegar, paprika, and garlic give chorizo loads of flavor; hot and black pepper impart a deliciously fiery bite.

ADVANCE PREPARATION

1 hour for soaking the sausage casing (optional)

SPECIAL EQUIPMENT

Sausage stuffer (optional); small skewers or toothpicks (optional)

INGREDIENTS

- 7 feet of sausage casing (optional; see Note)
- 2½ pounds ground pork (about 20 percent fat)
- ⅓ cup red wine vinegar
- ¼ cup ice water
- 3 tablespoons sweet paprika
- 1 tablespoon hot paprika or ancho chile powder
- 1 tablespoon hot red pepper flakes, or more to taste
- 1 tablespoon coarse (kosher or sea) salt, or more to taste
- 2 teaspoons dried oregano
- 2 teaspoons ground cumin
- 2 teaspoons ground coriander
- 5 cloves garlic, minced
- 1 tablespoon sugar
- 1 teaspoon freshly ground black pepper, or more to taste
- 1 to 2 tablespoons vegetable oil, for brushing the sausages
- Crusty rolls (optional)

1. If using the sausage casing, soak it in a large bowl of cold water for 1 hour, changing the water several times.

2. Combine the pork, wine vinegar, ice water, sweet and hot paprikas, hot pepper flakes, salt, oregano, cumin, coriander, garlic, sugar, and black pepper in a large mixer bowl and mix with a mixer fitted with a paddle or dough hook or stir to mix with a wooden spoon. To test the mixture for seasoning, cook a small amount in a nonstick skillet until cooked through, then taste, adding more hot pepper flakes, salt, or black pepper to the remaining mixture as necessary; it should be highly seasoned.

3. Stuff the sausage into the casing (if using), by first soaking the casing and rinsing out the insides as directed in the box below, then stuffing the sausage into it following the instructions shown on page 233. If you're not planning to cook the sausage immediately, cover it loosely with plastic wrap and refrigerate it.

4. Set up the grill for direct grilling and preheat to medium if cooking sausage links, high if cooking kebabs.

5. When ready to cook, brush and oil the grill grate. If the sausage is in casings, brush it lightly with oil. Arrange the sausage on the hot grate and grill, turning with tongs, until nicely browned all over and cooked through; when done a metal skewer inserted in a sausage with a casing will come out very hot to the touch, 16 to 20 minutes in all.

6. Serve the chorizos, hot dog style, on crusty rolls or cut them into pieces and serve on small skewers or toothpicks.

NOTE: If you don't want to make sausages in casings, you can mold the sausage mixture onto flat skewers as described in Step 2 of Oasis Kebabs (page 238), then proceed to cook the kebabs as directed in that recipe.

Grinding It Out

Somewhere in the recesses of my grandmother's cellar is an ancient hand-crank meat grinder. It's a piece of equipment I saw often on the barbecue trail, and when it comes to grinding meat for burgers and *koftas,* nothing can beat it—or its motorized cousins. The reason is simple: Inside the meat grinder is a cross-shaped blade that rotates against a perforated metal plate. Together, they function like a knife on a cutting board. The grinder cleanly chops the meat into tiny pieces, just as a well-wielded knife or cleaver would do.

Hard-core grill buffs may wish to invest in a motorized or hand-crank meat grinder or a meat grinder attachment for an appliance like a KitchenAid mixer. How different is the food processor, today's high-tech answer to the meat grinder? A food processor tears and mashes the meat instead of chopping it. The result tends to be mushy and stringy, with an uneven texture.

Grinding in a Food Processor

If you wish to grind your own meat and must use a food processor, be sure it's fitted with a metal chopping blade. First cut the meat into half-inch dice. Do not fill the processor bowl more than one quarter full. Run the machine in short bursts.

The Fat Factor

Two other factors determine the flavor and succulence of your grilled ground meat: the cut of meat and the fat content. In general, you want to use a flavorful cut of meat: when it comes to pork or lamb pick shoulder; for beef use chuck, round, or sirloin.

You need fat to keep ground meat succulent. For the recipes in this chapter, I recommend a fat content of 15 to 20 percent to keep ground meat dishes moist and tender.

The fat content of ground beef is frequently marked on the package at the supermarket (remember, ground sirloin is leaner than ground round or chuck). When in doubt about the fat content, ask the butcher.

Sausage Casings

Sausage casings are available at butcher shops, ethnic markets, and some supermarkets. To prepare them for use, soak them for one hour in several changes of cold water. Drain the casing, then pull one end over the end of the faucet of your kitchen sink. Gently turn the cold water tap on and let the running water rinse out the inside of the casing for five minutes.

HOW TO STUFF SAUSAGES LIKE A PRO

When using the meat grinder attachment of a mixer

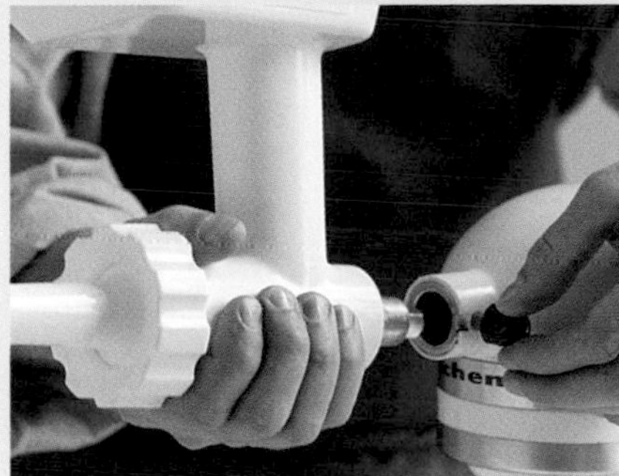

1. *Attach the meat grinder/sausage stuffer attachment to the mixer and screw it in place.*

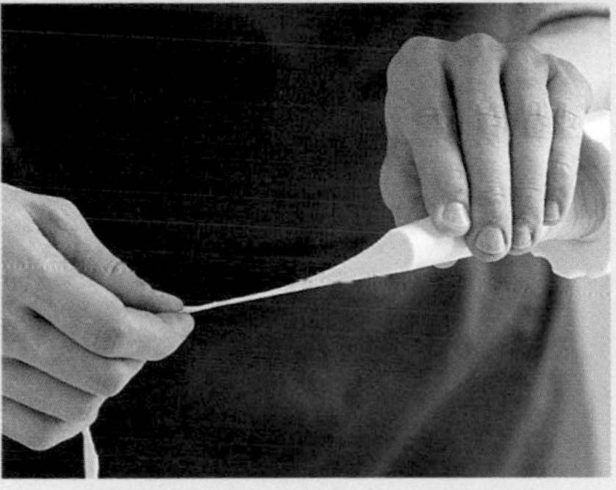

2. *Pull one end of the sausage casing over the plastic sausage stuffer tube, bunching it up on the tube the way an old-time Hollywood starlet would put on a stocking.*

3. *Tie a knot at the end of the sausage casing.*

4. *Place the sausage filling in the feed tray of the meat grinder.*

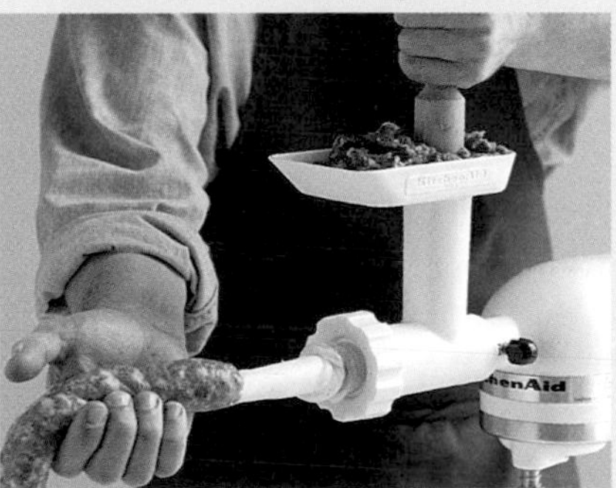

5. *Using a wooden plunger, force the sausage filling into the feed chute. The meat will come out the end of the tube into the casing. Grab the emerging sausage to support it.*

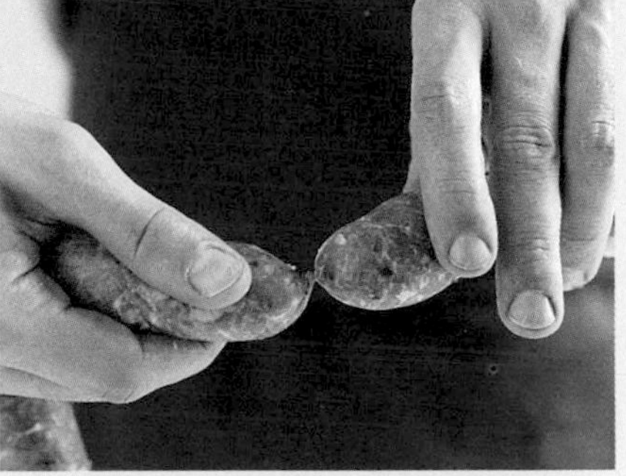

6. *Twist the sausage a couple of times every 3 or 4 inches to form links. Then, tie each link off with a short piece of butcher's string; this helps hold the sausage together as it cooks.*

When using a pastry bag with a round tip

1. *Fold the top of the pastry bag down to form a 2-inch cuff. Fill the pastry bag with sausage filling, scraping the spatula against the top of the cuff.*

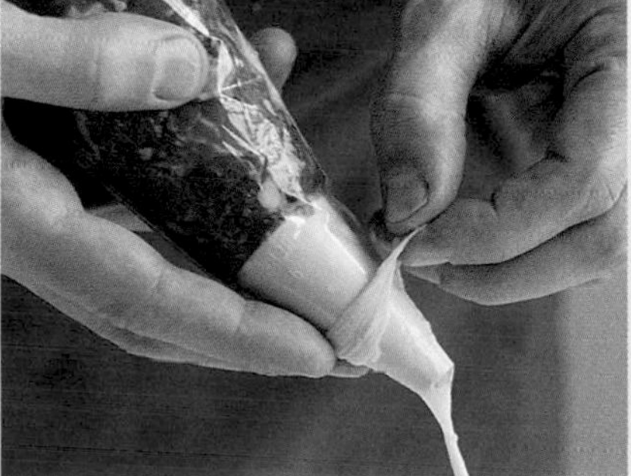

2. *Pull the sausage casing over the round piping tip and bunch it up. You'll need to use one hand to hold the casing in place on the piping tip.*

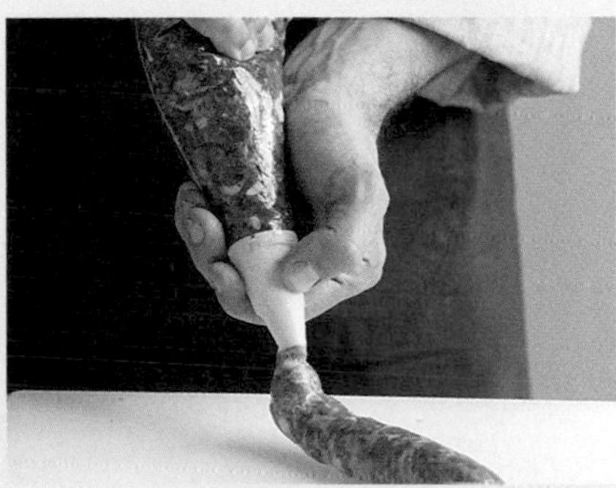

3. *Use your other hand to gently squeeze the pastry bag, starting at the top, to force the sausage filling into the casing. Release a little of the casing at a time to form sausage links.*

TYPES OF SAUSAGES

The world of sausages is nearly as diverse as the world of barbecue. Sausages come both raw and cooked. Grill raw sausages for eight to ten minutes per side (sixteen to twenty minutes in all) over a medium fire. They should be cooked through. To test for doneness, insert the probe of an instant-read meat thermometer lengthwise through one of the narrow ends; the internal temperature should be 160°F. Already cooked sausages need only to be warmed on the grill.

SPANISH CHORIZO

KNOCKWURST

ANDOUILLE

MEXICAN CHORIZO

KNACKWURST

MERGUEZ

BRATWURST

KIELBASA

HOT DOGS

SWEET

HOT

ITALIAN SAUSAGE

BRAZIL

SAMBA SAUSAGES

CHORIÇOU

DIRECT GRILLING
SERVES 4

This simple recipe is the perfect symbol of Brazil's sensuality and scintillating spirit. Grilled sausages are, of course, common currency among the world's street foods, but it's only in Brazil that street vendors take the time to make tiny slits in those sausages, fill them with minutely diced onions and bell peppers, and lovingly baste them with olive oil as they cook. The "grill" of the vendor who passed his version on to me was the charcoal-filled hubcap of an old car. Virtually any type of cooked sausage could be prepared this way. I've called for chorizos, but kielbasa, knockwurst, or even hot dogs would work well, too.

SPECIAL EQUIPMENT

4 long bamboo skewers and an aluminum foil shield (see box, page 23)

INGREDIENTS

4 cooked chorizos, homemade (page 233) or store-bought, or other cooked sausages (each 1 inch thick and 4 to 5 inches long)
½ small onion, very finely minced
½ medium-size red or green bell pepper, cored, seeded, and very finely minced
2 cloves garlic, minced
2 tablespoons extra-virgin olive oil

1. Push a skewer lengthwise through each sausage. Make a series of diagonal parallel slits, ¼ inch deep and ½ inch apart in one side of each sausage. Turn the sausage over and make a similar set of slits going the opposite direction.

2. Combine the onion, bell pepper, and garlic in a small bowl, then stuff some of this mixture into each of the slits in the sausages.

3. Set up the grill for direct grilling and preheat to medium-high.

4. When ready to cook, brush and oil the grill grate. Arrange the sausages on the hot grate with the aluminum foil shield under the ends of the skewers. Grill, turning with tongs, until lightly browned on all sides and heated through, turning as necessary, 6 to 8 minutes in all. As the sausages cook, drizzle the olive oil over the slits.

5. Serve the sausages right on the skewers and eat them like Popsicles with any remaining onion mixture.

REPUBLIC OF GEORGIA

PORK AND POMEGRANATE SAUSAGES

KUPATI

DIRECT GRILLING
MAKES TWELVE 4-INCH STUFFED SAUSAGES OR 3-INCH PATTIES; SERVES 4

The pairing of meats with fruit is one of the hallmarks of the cuisines of the Caucasus Mountains. A case in point: these sausages, a popular breakfast dish in the Republic of Georgia, especially in the fall, when fresh pomegranates are in season. The meat mixture is traditionally stuffed into sausage casings, but excellent *kupati* can be cooked in free-form patties or molded on flat skewers in the form of *kofta* (see page 238).

There are several ways these sausages can be enjoyed. You can cut them into inch-long pieces and skewer them on toothpicks for hors d'oeuvres, or you can serve them with rolls or Georgian bread for a different kind of sandwich. I think you'll find the combination of pomegranate, dill, cilantro, and cinnamon a delectable addition to pork.

ADVANCE PREPARATION

1 hour for soaking the sausage casing (optional)

SPECIAL EQUIPMENT

Sausage stuffer (optional)

INGREDIENTS

- **7 feet of sausage casing (optional)**
- **1 large pomegranate**
- **1½ pounds ground pork (not too lean)**
- **2 cloves garlic, chopped**
- **2 tablespoons chopped fresh dill, or 1 tablespoon dried dill**
- **2 tablespoons chopped fresh cilantro**
- **1½ teaspoons salt, or more to taste**
- **1 teaspoon freshly ground pepper**
- **¼ teaspoon ground cinnamon, or more to taste**
- **1 to 2 tablespoons vegetable oil, for brushing the sausages**

1. If using the sausage casing, soak it in a large bowl of cold water for 1 hour, changing the water several times.

2. Break the pomegranate into quarters and seed it.

3. Place the pork in a large bowl and stir in the pomegranate seeds, garlic, dill, cilantro, salt, pepper, and cinnamon. Knead and squeeze the mixture with your hands until blended, 3 to 4 minutes. To test the mixture for seasoning, cook a small amount in a nonstick skillet until cooked through, then taste, adding more salt and/or cinnamon to the remaining mixture as necessary; it should be highly seasoned.

4. *If making sausages in casings,* first soak the casing and rinse out the insides as directed in the box on page 232, then stuff the sausage into it following the instructions shown on page 233.

If making sausage patties, line a baking sheet with plastic wrap. Divide the mixture into eight equal portions, then lightly wet your hands with cold water and form each portion into a patty about 3 inches across and about ½ inch thick. As they are made, place the sausages on the prepared baking sheet.

If you are not planning to cook the sausages immediately, cover them loosely with plastic wrap and refrigerate them.

5. Set up the grill for direct grilling and preheat to medium if cooking sausage links, high if cooking patties.

6. When ready to cook, brush and oil the grill grate. If the sausages are in casings, brush them lightly with oil. Arrange the sausages on the hot grate and grill, turning with tongs, until nicely browned all over and cooked through; when done a metal skewer inserted in a sausage with a casing will come out very hot to the touch, 16 to 20 minutes in all; sausage patties will be done after about 4 minutes on each side. Serve the sausages at once.

INDONESIA

BEEF SATES WITH CORIANDER

SATE AGE

DIRECT GRILLING
SERVES 4 AS AN APPETIZER, 2 AS A MAIN COURSE

This lovely coriander-scented beef saté, *saté age,* which comes from Solo in central Java, is traditionally served on a flat bamboo skewer that looks like an ice cream stick. The closest thing to a *saté age* skewer here is a Popsicle stick—an item easy enough to find at most supermarkets. Otherwise, try using tongue depressors or flat bamboo skewers for the satés. The aromatic satés are also good made with lamb or a mixture of beef and lamb.

SPECIAL EQUIPMENT

16 wide, short bamboo skewers, or Popsicle sticks, and an aluminum foil shield (see box, page 23)

INGREDIENTS

- **1 pound lean ground beef chuck or sirloin**
- **3 tablespoons chopped fresh cilantro**
- **2 shallots, minced**
- **1 clove garlic, minced**
- **4 teaspoons ground coriander**
- **1 teaspoon salt, or more to taste**
- **1 teaspoon freshly ground black pepper, or more to taste**
- **⅔ cup sweet soy sauce (ketjap manis), or ⅓ cup each regular soy sauce and molasses**

1. Combine the beef, cilantro, shallots, garlic, 2 teaspoons of the coriander, and the salt and pepper in a food processor and process until well blended. To test for seasoning, cook a small amount of the mixture in a nonstick skillet until cooked through, then taste, adding more salt and/or pepper to the remaining mixture as necessary.

2. Line a baking sheet with plastic wrap. Lightly wet your hands with cold water. Take a handful (3 to 4 tablespoons) of the meat mixture and mold it onto a skewer or Popsicle stick to form a flat sausage about 3 inches long, ¾ inch wide, and ½ inch thick. Continue until all of the meat mixture is used up, placing the satés on the prepared baking sheet as they are made (see Note).

3. Prepare a glaze by stirring the sweet soy sauce and remaining 2 teaspoons of coriander in a shallow dish. Set the glaze aside.

4. Set up the grill for direct grilling and preheat to high.

5. When ready to cook, brush and oil the grill grate. Arrange the satés on the hot grate with the aluminum foil shield under the ends of the skewers. Grill, turning with tongs, for 2 minutes per side. Remove the satés from the grill, roll them in the sweet soy glaze until lightly coated, then grill until nicely browned on the outside and cooked through, 1 to 2 minutes per side. Serve the satés at once.

NOTE: If you are not planning to cook the satés immediately, cover them loosely with plastic wrap and refrigerate.

INDONESIA

FLYING FOX SATES

SATE KALONG

DIRECT GRILLING
MAKES 16 SATES; SERVES 4 AS AN APPETIZER, 2 AS A LIGHT MAIN COURSE

These beef and garlic satés take their curious name from the nocturnal mammal called the flying fox. The squirrel-like creature comes out at dusk, sailing from tree to tree on folds of skin that extend, parachute-like, from the sides of its body. That's precisely the time of day that saté vendors traditionally set up shop in the town of Cirebon in northwestern Java.

Saté kalong is one of Indonesia's most delicate kebabs, traditionally measuring three inches long and a mere quarter inch wide. (Lacking the patience of an Indonesian saté maker, I tend to make them a bit larger.) The pairing of sugar and garlic with beef may seem odd—until you stop to think about the sweet sauces that accompany American barbecue.

ADVANCE PREPARATION

1 to 2 hours for chilling the satés

SPECIAL EQUIPMENT

16 long bamboo skewers and an aluminum foil shield (see box, page 23)

INGREDIENTS

12 ounces ground beef chuck or sirloin
5 cloves garlic, minced
3 tablespoons palm sugar or light brown sugar, or more to taste
½ teaspoon salt, or more to taste
½ teaspoon freshly ground black pepper

1. Combine the beef, garlic, palm sugar, salt, and pepper in a large bowl, then knead and squeeze the mixture with your hands until thoroughly blended, 3 to 4 minutes. To test the mixture for seasoning, cook a small amount in a nonstick skillet until cooked through, then taste, adding more palm sugar and/or salt to the remaining mixture as necessary; the mixture should be both savory and a little sweet.

2. Line a baking sheet with plastic wrap. Divide the meat mixture into sixteen portions. Lightly wet your hands with cold water, then mold each portion around a skewer, preferably in the traditional shape, a strip about 5 inches long, ½ inch wide, and ⅛ inch thick. To achieve the requisite flatness, pinch the meat between your thumb and forefinger. As they are made, place the satés on the prepared baking sheet, then cover them loosely with plastic wrap and refrigerate for 1 to 2 hours.

3. Set up the grill for direct grilling and preheat to high.

4. When ready to cook, brush and oil the grill grate. Arrange the satés on the hot grate with the aluminum foil shield under the ends of the skewers. Grill, turning with tongs, until nicely browned on both sides and cooked through, 1 to 2 minutes per side. Serve at once.

MIDDLE EAST

OASIS KEBABS

KOFTA

DIRECT GRILLING
MAKES 8 *KOFTAS*;
SERVES 4 AS A MAIN COURSE

Kofta (also called *kefta, kafta,* and *kufte*) describes a sort of skinless sausage enjoyed throughout North Africa, the Balkans, and the Middle East. Depending on where you eat it, the meat will be lamb or beef (in the Arab world), pork or veal (in the Balkans), or a mixture of meats. The seasonings reflect local taste preferences, too, ranging from the onion-garlic-parsley triumvirate of the Balkans to the mint and cinnamon of the Middle East. Here's a Middle Eastern–style *kofta*. The mint and cinnamon add an unexpected sweet touch.

These *kofta* are easy to make, but there are a few things to watch for. First, because there's no casing to seal in the juices, it's best to use a fairly fatty meat—look for 15 to 20 percent—to keep them moist. Also, it's essential to use wide, flat skewers; the meat will fall off the slender metal skewers used for traditional shish kebab. Serve the *kofta* with Moroccan Eggplant Salad (see page 97).

ADVANCE PREPARATION

1 to 2 hours for chilling the meat

SPECIAL EQUIPMENT

8 flat, wide, long metal skewers

FOR THE MEAT

1½ pounds ground beef, lamb, or a mixture of the two
½ large onion, very finely chopped
1 cup finely chopped fresh flat-leaf parsley
½ cup chopped fresh mint, or 1 tablespoon dried mint
1 teaspoon ground cinnamon
1½ teaspoons salt, or more to taste
1 teaspoon freshly ground black pepper, or more to taste

FOR SERVING

Pita bread or lavash
Finely chopped onion
Ground sumac (optional; see box, page 248)

1. Combine the beef, onion, parsley, mint, cinnamon, salt, and pepper in a large bowl, then knead and squeeze the mixture with your hands until thoroughly blended, 3 to 4 minutes. To test the mixture for seasoning, cook a small amount in a nonstick skillet until cooked through, then taste, adding more salt and/or pepper to the remaining mixture as necessary.

2. Divide the meat mixture into eight equal portions. Lightly wet your hands with cold water. Then, starting about 1 inch from the tip, mold each portion around a skewer to form a flattish sausage 8 to 10 inches long and 1 to 1½ inches wide. To keep from flattening the meat, place each *kofta* on a baking pan so the ends of the skewers rest on the sides of the pan. Cover the *koftas* loosely with plastic wrap and refrigerate them for 1 to 2 hours.

3. Set up the grill for direct grilling and preheat to high. If desired, use a grateless grill setup (see box, page 21).

4. When ready to cook, arrange the *koftas* on the grill as described for grateless grilling or brush and generously oil the grill grate and place the *koftas* directly on it. Grill the *koftas,* turning with tongs, until nicely browned and cooked through, 6 to 8 minutes in all.

5. Using a pita to protect your hand, slide each *kofta* off its skewer onto a plate. Serve the *koftas* sprinkled with chopped onion and ground sumac (if using) and accompanied by pitas.

AFGHANISTAN

SPICED LAMB AND BEEF KEBABS

LULA KEBAB

DIRECT GRILLING
MAKES 8 KEBABS; SERVES 8 AS AN APPETIZER, 4 AS A MAIN COURSE

Here's the Afghan version of a ground meat kebab that is known elsewhere in the Muslim world as *kofta, kubideh,* and *lyulya.* The spicing reflects Afghanistan's unique location at Asia's crossroads: The dill and cilantro are characteristic of Central Asian cooking; the chiles and turmeric of the Indian subcontinent. Made with both lamb and beef, *lulas* are some of the most flavorful ground meat kebabs ever to grace a skewer. Serve them with pita bread, accompanied by Coriander Sauce (page 482) and Central Asian Pickles (page 441).

ADVANCE PREPARATION

1 to 8 hours for chilling the kebabs

SPECIAL EQUIPMENT

8 flat, wide, long metal skewers

INGREDIENTS

1 pound lean ground lamb
1 pound lean ground beef, such as round or sirloin
1 small onion, grated
1 to 2 bird chiles or serrano peppers, seeded and minced (for hotter kebabs, leave the seeds in)
1 large egg
3 tablespoons minced fresh dill
3 tablespoons minced fresh cilantro
2 teaspoons salt, or more to taste
1 teaspoon freshly ground black pepper
1 teaspoon ground cumin, or more to taste
½ teaspoon ground turmeric

1. Combine the lamb, beef, onion, chiles, egg, dill, cilantro, salt, pepper, cumin, and turmeric in a large bowl. Knead and squeeze the mixture with your hands until thoroughly blended, 3 to 4 minutes. Transfer the mixture to a large heavy skillet and set over very low heat. Cook the meat mixture just until it is warmed through, stirring constantly with a wooden spoon. Remove meat mixture from the heat and let stand until completely cooled.

2. To test the meat mixture for seasoning, cook a small amount in a nonstick skillet until cooked through, then taste, adding more salt and/or cumin to the remaining mixture as necessary; it should be highly seasoned.

3. Line a baking sheet with plastic wrap. Divide the meat mixture into eight equal portions. Lightly wet your hands with cold water. Then, starting about 1 inch from the tip, mold each portion around a skewer to form a flattish sausage that is 8 to 10 inches long and 1 to 1½ inches wide. Using the first two fingers of one hand in a scissors fashion, make a series of shallow ridges across the length of the sausage. As it is made, place each kebab on the prepared baking sheet, then cover loosely with plastic wrap and refrigerate for at least 1 hour, or as long as overnight.

4. Set up the grill for direct grilling and preheat to high. If desired, use a grateless grill setup (see box, page 21).

5. When ready to cook, arrange the kebabs on the grill as described for grateless grilling or brush and generously oil the grill grate and place the kebabs directly on it. Grill the kebabs, turning with tongs, until nicely browned and cooked through, 6 to 8 minutes in all. Serve at once.

IRAN

PERSIAN LAMB AND BEEF KEBABS

KUBIDEH

DIRECT GRILLING
MAKES 8 *KUBIDEH*; SERVES 8 AS AN APPETIZER, 4 AS A MAIN COURSE

Ground lamb and beef kebabs (*kubideh*) are the truest test of the competency of an Iranian kebabi man. *Kubideh* is the Persian word for chopped or mashed and, when properly prepared, these kebabs are moist, succulent, and feather light—no small feat considering that the principal ingredients are beef and lamb, and rather fatty (at least 25 percent) beef and lamb at that. The following recipe requires a little work, but the results are astonishing. Serve *kubideh,* unskewered, on a mound of Persian Rice with a Golden Crust (page 425).

Be sure you grate or puree the onion just prior to adding it to the meat; this will keep the flavor from becoming too overpowering (the longer onion remains in contact with air, the stronger it becomes).

ADVANCE PREPARATION

1 to 2 hours for chilling the kebabs

SPECIAL EQUIPMENT

8 wide, flat, long metal skewers

INGREDIENTS

1 pound ground lamb
1 pound ground beef round or sirloin
2 teaspoons salt, or more to taste
1 teaspoon freshly ground black pepper, or more to taste
½ teaspoon baking soda
1 large onion, peeled
Lavash or pita bread

1. Place the lamb, beef, salt, pepper, and baking soda in a large bowl and stir to blend. Transfer the mixture to a large heavy saucepan. Set the saucepan over very low heat and knead the mixture with your hands until it's warmed through and very smooth, about 5 minutes. Remove the meat mixture from the heat.

2. Cut the onion into chunks, then grate it through the next-to-smallest holes of a four-sided hand grater or process it in a food processor; you should have about 1 cup of grated onion. Add the onion to the meat mixture in the saucepan and knead it again, this time off the heat, until the onion is thoroughly mixed in, another 5 minutes.

3. To test the mixture for seasoning, cook a small amount in a nonstick skillet until cooked through, then taste, adding more salt and/or pepper to the remaining mixture as necessary.

4. Line a baking sheet with plastic wrap. Divide the meat mixture into eight equal portions. Lightly wet your hands with cold water. Then, starting about 1 to 1½ inches from the tip, mold each portion around a skewer to form a flattish sausage 8 to 10 inches long and 1 to 1½ inches wide. Using the first two fingers of one hand in a scissors fashion, make a series of shallow ridges across the length of the sausage. As it is made, place each kebab on the prepared baking sheet, then cover loosely with plastic wrap and refrigerate for 1 to 2 hours.

5. Set up the grill for direct grilling and preheat to high. If desired, use a grateless grill setup (see box, page 21).

6. When ready to cook, arrange the kebabs on the grill as described for grateless grilling or brush and generously oil the grill grate and place the kebabs directly on it. Grill the kebabs, turning with tongs, until nicely browned and cooked through, 6 to 8 minutes in all.

7. Using a piece of lavash to protect your hand, slide the kebabs off their skewers onto plates. Serve at once accompanied by lavash.

INDONESIA

LAMB SATES WITH TAMARIND SAUCE

SATE BUNTEL

DIRECT GRILLING
SERVES 4 AS AN APPETIZER, 2 AS A MAIN COURSE

The largest of all Indonesian satés (at least of the ones I sampled) is a sausage-size kebab of ground lamb that takes four skewers to hold it. I first tasted it in Jakarta at a simple but spotless eatery called Asli. The saté originated in the city of Solo in Java, explains Asli's owner, Mr. Budiyanto, whose grandparents came from Solo and founded the restaurant in 1949. The Solo influence is apparent in the sweet-sour tamarind sauce used for basting and serving the satés.

To be strictly authentic, you'll need caul fat (a lacy membrane from the belly of a pig used in sausage making). You can ask for it at a specialty butcher. But don't worry if you can't find caul fat, for free-form *saté buntel* is easy to make and equally delicious.

ADVANCE PREPARATION

1 to 2 hours for chilling the satés

SPECIAL EQUIPMENT

4 short bamboo skewers (if using caul fat) or 4 Popsicle sticks, or wide, short bamboo skewers, and an aluminum foil shield (see box, page 23)

FOR THE LAMB

1 pound ground lamb
1 teaspoon ground coriander
1 teaspoon salt
1 teaspoon freshly ground black pepper
4 squares (each 6 inches) caul fat (optional)

FOR THE TAMARIND SAUCE

1 cup Tamarind Water (recipe follows) or frozen tamarind puree, thawed
⅓ cup firmly packed light brown sugar
1 tablespoon sweet soy sauce (ketjap manis), or 1½ teaspoons each regular soy sauce and molasses

FOR THE GARNISH

1 cucumber, peeled and thinly sliced
1 large or 2 medium-size shallots, thinly sliced

1. Prepare the lamb: Combine the lamb, coriander, salt, and pepper in a medium-size bowl and stir to blend. Divide the lamb mixture into four equal portions.

2. *If using caul fat,* arrange the 4 pieces on a work surface. Place one portion of the lamb mixture on each piece of caul fat and roll the caul fat around the meat to form a sausage about 4 inches long and about 1 inch in diameter. Push a skewer into one end of each sausage. Carefully transfer the sausages to a plate, cover them, and refrigerate for 1 to 2 hours.

If making free-form satés, lightly oil a plate and lightly wet your hands with cold water. Take a portion of lamb mixture and mold it onto a Popsicle stick to form a sausagelike kebab that is 4 inches long and 1 to 1½ inches thick. Place the satés on the oiled plate, cover them loosely with plastic wrap, and refrigerate for 1 to 2 hours.

3. Make the tamarind sauce: Combine the Tamarind Water, brown sugar, and sweet soy sauce in a small nonreactive saucepan and boil, stirring to dissolve the brown sugar, until thick and syrupy, about 3 minutes. Let cool completely. Pour half of the tamarind sauce into one or more small bowls and set aside for serving.

4. Set up the grill for direct grilling and preheat to medium-high.

5. When ready to cook, brush and oil the grill grate. Arrange the satés on the hot grate with the aluminum foil shield under the ends of the skewers. Grill, turning with tongs, until the lamb is nicely browned and cooked through, 6 to 8 minutes in all. Halfway through the cooking process, begin brushing the satés with the remaining tamarind sauce.

6. Transfer the satés to a platter and brush them one final time with tamarind sauce. Garnish the satés with the sliced cucumber and shallots. Serve the reserved tamarind sauce on the side for dipping.

TAMARIND WATER

MAKES ABOUT ½ CUP

Tamarind is the fruit of a tall tropical tree, a fava bean–shaped pod filled with a fruity, orange-brown, sweet-sour pulp. The fruit takes its name from the Arabic words *tamr hindi,* literally Indian date. Actually, tamarind tastes more like a prune than a date—prune mixed with lime juice and a drop of liquid smoke. This distinctive sweet-sour flavor has endeared tamarind to cooks all along the world's barbecue trail, from Asia to the Caribbean. You've probably tasted it, for tamarind is a key flavoring in Worcestershire sauce and A.1. steak sauce.

You can buy fresh tamarind pods in Caribbean and Asian markets Look for fleshy, heavy pods with cracked skins that reveal the sticky brown pulp inside; tamarind with an unbroken skin is underripe. Peeling fresh tamarind is time-consuming, so most ethnic markets and many supermarkets sell peeled tamarind pulp, which is quicker and easier to use.

Stringy and full of seeds, tamarind is rarely used in its natural state. The first step is to transform the sticky flesh into tamarind water, also known as tamarind puree. This is done by pureeing the pulp from peeled tamarind pods with boiling water.

If you live in an area with a large Hispanic community, you may be able to find frozen tamarind puree, which eliminates the need to make this recipe.

8 ounces tamarind pods (8 to 10 pods), or ½ cup peeled tamarind pulp (see Note)
1¾ cups boiling water

1. If using tamarind pods, first peel the skin off with a paring knife to expose the pulp. Break the pulp into 1-inch pieces and place it in a food processor or blender with 1 cup of the boiling water. Let the tamarind soften for 5 minutes.

2. Run the blender or food processor in short bursts at low speed for 15 to 30 seconds to obtain a thick brown liquid. Don't overblend, or you'll break up the seeds. Pour the resulting liquid through a strainer, pressing hard with a wooden spoon to extract the juices, scraping the underneath side of the strainer with a spatula.

3. Return the tamarind pulp in the strainer to the food processor or blender and add the remaining ¾ cup of hot water. Blend again and pour the mixture through the strainer, pressing hard to extract the juices. The Tamarind Water can be stored in a tightly covered container in the refrigerator for up to 5 days or frozen for several months (I like to freeze it in plastic ice-cube trays, so I have convenient premeasured portions).

NOTE: Indian markets sell plastic jars of smooth, dark, syrupy tamarind extract. This product has an interesting flavor, but you can't use it to make tamarind water.

TURKEY

SHALLOT KEBABS WITH POMEGRANATE MOLASSES

SOGAR KEBAB

DIRECT GRILLING
MAKES 8 KEBABS, SERVES 8 AS AN APPETIZER, 4 AS A MAIN COURSE

A specialty of the Imam Cagdas restaurant in Gaziantep, Turkey, this simple kebab is made with a small, red-skinned onion that looks like the familiar shallot. I've used both shallots and pearl onions to make them with equal success. One unexpected touch: After grilling, the lamb and onions and a few drops of pomegranate molasses are placed in a covered dish for a few minutes. This steams the onions, imparting an incredible sweet-sour flavor to the meat.

SPECIAL EQUIPMENT

8 flat, wide, long metal skewers

Of Koftas, Lyulyas, and Seekh Kebabs

Arabs call them *koftas*. Iranians call them *kubideh*. Afghanis and Azerbaijanis know them as *lula* (or *lyulya kebabs*), while Indians and Pakistanis call them *seekh kebabs*. Whatever you call them, ground meat molded on a skewer and grilled is one of the world's most popular treats.

Kofta country begins in Morocco and stretches as far east as Bangladesh. Perhaps even farther—you could certainly argue that Indonesia's ground beef and lamb satés are actually a sort of *kofta*. The name, main ingredients, and flavorings change along the way, but the result remains the same. That result is a sort of skinless sausage. The secret to making these is to mold a sausage-shaped portion of meat on a flat metal skewer and cook it over a grateless grill.

At its simplest, *kofta* consists merely of ground lamb or beef flavored with onion, garlic, and parsley. Sometimes egg or cracked wheat is added to give the kebab a firmer consistency. Sometimes the meat is kneaded by hand in a pan over a low flame to create the close-knit texture of fine fabric. Cooks in the Balkans and Iran add baking soda or seltzer water to make their *mititeis* and *ćevapčićis* (the Balkan version of *kofta*) light.

The spicing, too, reflects the country of origin. As you move east, the cumin and paprika popular in Morocco give way to cinnamon and mint in the Middle East. Kebabi men in Central Asia flavor their *lula kebabs* with hot peppers, dill, and cilantro. Indians turn to the evocative flavors of ginger, cumin, and turmeric to give their *seekh* (ground lamb) kebabs pizzazz.

In this chapter, you'll find many variations on the theme of ground meat grilled on a stick. To be strictly authentic, you'd cook these kebabs using the grateless grilling technique shown on page 21. If you're careful and you oil the grate well, you can also cook the kebabs directly on the grate.

INGREDIENTS

1 pound ground lamb
1 clove garlic, minced
1 teaspoon salt, or more to taste
½ teaspoon ground cumin, or more to taste
½ teaspoon freshly ground black pepper, or more to taste
20 large shallots or pearl onions
Pita breads, for serving
2 to 3 teaspoons Pomegranate Molasses (recipe follows)

1. Combine the lamb, garlic, salt, cumin, and pepper in a large bowl. Knead and squeeze the mixture with your hands until thoroughly blended, 3 to 4 minutes. To test the mixture for seasoning, cook a small amount in a nonstick skillet until cooked through, then taste, adding more salt, cumin, and/or pepper to the remaining mixture as necessary.

2. Peel the shallots and cut each lengthwise in half. Starting on the round sides, thread 5 shallot halves onto each skewer, leaving about 1 inch between each.

3. Line a baking sheet with plastic wrap. Divide the meat mixture into thirty-two equal portions. Lightly wet your hands with cold water, then take one portion of the meat and mold it around a skewer, between two shallot halves, trying to make it as close to the size of the shallots as possible. Repeat with the remaining portions of meat so each skewer contains 5 shallot halves alternating with 4 portions of meat. As it is made, place each kebab on the prepared baking sheet. If you are not planning to cook the kebabs immediately, cover them loosely with plastic wrap and refrigerate them.

4. Set up the grill for direct grilling and preheat to high. If desired, use a grateless grill setup (see box, page 21).

5. When ready to cook, arrange the kebabs on the grill as described for grateless grilling or brush and generously oil the grill grate and place the kebabs directly on it. Grill the kebabs, turning with tongs, until the shallots are nicely browned and soft and the meat is browned as well and cooked through, 8 to 10 minutes in all.

6. Using a pita to protect your hand, slide the meat and shallots off their skewers into a serving bowl. Toss them with the Pomegranate Molasses, cover the bowl, and let stand for 3 minutes. Divide the meat and shallots among serving plates and serve at once, accompanied by the pitas.

POMEGRANATE MOLASSES

NARSHRAB

MAKES ABOUT 1½ CUPS

Order grilled meats or seafood in eastern Turkey, the Republics of Georgia or Armenia, or pretty much anywhere in Central Asia, and you'll be served an explosively flavorful, sweet-sour condiment that looks like liquid tar. Often it's drizzled on the food before it is served, as well. Known locally as *narshrab,* and as pomegranate molasses in the West, it consists of fresh pomegranate juice boiled down to a thick, perfumed syrup. A few drops drizzled over chops or kebabs has an amazing way of bringing out the flavor of grilled meats. Bottled *narshrab* can be found at Middle Eastern and Armenian markets. Here's how to make it from scratch.

8 to 10 pomegranates (for 4 cups juice)
¼ cup sugar

1. Cut the pomegranates in half and juice them on a citrus reamer. You should have about 4 cups of juice. Strain the juice into a large, wide, heavy saucepan and add the sugar.

2. Bring the pomegranate juice to a boil, reduce the heat, and cook at a brisk simmer until dark, thick, syrupy, and reduced by two thirds, 15 to 20 minutes. Transfer the pomegranate syrup to a sterile bottle or jar. It will keep for 2 months in the refrigerator.

TURKEY

LAMB AND PISTACHIO KEBABS

DIRECT GRILLING
MAKES 4 KEBABS; SERVES 4 AS A MAIN COURSE

These lovely ground lamb kebabs—flecked with crunchy green bits of pistachio nuts—are a specialty of the popular Develi restaurant in Istanbul. The restaurant's

The Turkish Grill

You probably won't find the name Imam Cagdas—or Gaziantep—in your typical Turkish guide book. But mention either place to a Turk and you'll get the sly, conspiratorial look reserved not for tourists but insiders. Imam Cagdas (pronounced ee-mam cha-dahsh), which is also the name of the owner, is arguably the most famous kebab house in Turkey, a boisterous, two-story storefront founded by Imam's great-grandfather in 1887. The day of my visit, guests included the city mayor and the commander of the local army base, not to mention seven hundred other hungry customers. And it was slow season!

Turkish gastronomes have the sort of reverential regard for Gaziantep that Americans have for New Orleans. Gaziantep is the sixth largest city in Turkey, a booming, dusty metropolis located thirty miles west of the Euphrates river near the Syrian border in south central Turkey. Foodies know it as the pistachio capital of Turkey, not to mention a city with a collective fondness for chile peppers that would rival those from Santa Fe.

But the stars of the show are the kebabs, which are stacked in towering piles on metal trays in Imam Cagdas's open kitchen. The variety bears testimony to the Turkish culinary imagination. There is *sogar kebab*—skewers of ground lamb and whole shallots that are seasoned with a few drops of pomegranate molasses before serving. There is *semit kebab,* springy sausages of ground lamb and bulgur wheat spiced up with fresh mint and allspice. For sheer visual appeal you can't beat *sedzeli kebab:* shiny purple chunks of eggplant spit roasted with ground lamb. And that's just in winter. Imam Cagdas varies the half dozen kebabs it serves according to the seasons.

Gaziantep might seem like an odd place to begin a story on Turkish grilling. It's not particularly easy to get to and it's certainly not on the tourist circuit, but the love of barbecue there is evident even before you land at the airport. A few years ago, an airline pilot passing over Gaziantep radioed the fire department to report a forest fire. Closer investigation revealed the thick cloud of smoke to be the output of thousands of portable grills brought to the woods by families for their holiday picnics.

Almost every restaurateur worth his salt in Turkey claims to have a chef from Gaziantep—as I was to discover on my next stop: the restaurant Develi in Istanbul.

When in Istanbul

Develi is the sort of restaurant I came to love so much in Turkey: fancy enough to have tablecloths, but relaxed enough for men to pass the evening drinking *raki* (anise liquor) and eating *meze* (appetizers) with their buddies after work. According to its fifth-generation owner, Ali Develier, Develi was opened in 1912 by a camel trader from Gaziantep. Today the four-story restaurant seats 450.

I started with *pilaki,* a variety of dips and salads seasoned with fruity Turkish olive oil. *Lamejun,* Turkish ground lamb pizza, came next, followed by freshly baked *pida,* a Turkish bread that tastes like a cross between focaccia and pita. In short order, I was served the house specialty, ground lamb and pistachio nut kebabs, followed by lemony shish kebab and Ali Nasik kebab, a sausage of ground lamb served on a bed of pureed grilled eggplant and yogurt.

Street Kebabs

I don't mean to give the impression that grilled fare is solely restaurant food. Indeed, Turkey's most popular "barbecue" is a street food known as *donner kebab. Donner* means twirling or turning in Turkish; the kebab in question consists of thin flat strips of spiced lamb (or sometimes chicken), layered and stacked to make a giant roast that turns on a vertical spitrotisserie.

The genius of *donner kebab* is that each portion comes off the rotisserie freshly grilled and delicately crusty. (Good *donner kebab* is like a prime rib with nothing but end cuts.) *Donner* is always carved from the bottom up to allow the dripping fat from the top to baste the meat. Actually, there are two types of *donner: yaprak,* made with whole lamb, and *kyma,* made with ground.

The sliced *donner* is rolled in a piece of pita bread or a sheet of lavash along with sliced lettuce and tomatoes and yogurt sauce. It's fresh, hot, and succulent, and a serving cost me less than a dollar.

Short-Order Kebabs

My last night in Turkey, I wandered the streets of the Beyolu (a lively neighborhood in Istanbul that reminds me of the Latin Quarter in Paris). I came upon a smoky grill restaurant tucked away amid the area's taverns and cafés. No one spoke English, but it really didn't matter, for the menu was self-explanatory. In the center of the restaurant stood a troughlike brazier perhaps twelve feet long and two feet wide, crowned by a hand-hammered copper hood decorated with scenes of Turkish country life. Around the brazier ran a marble counter with seats for a dozen guests. It reminded me of a sushi bar that specialized in grilled lamb instead of raw fish.

Kiyi's (the name of the restaurant) pit master is Murat Dademir, a big, gracious man in his thirties, from Adana in southern Turkey, who tilts his head in a kindly way when you ask him a question. When I met him, he was making *adana kebab,* molding ground lamb spiced with fiery Aleppo peppers onto flat metal skewers by hand. In rapid succession he turned out some of Turkey's most popular grilled dishes: First *iskander kebab,* thinly sliced ground lamb served over diced pida with yogurt, hot tomato sauce, and melted butter. Next came *durum*—thinly sliced grilled lamb wrapped with lettuce, tomato, onion, and yogurt in a sheet of lavash.

When Murat learned of my interest in Turkish grilling, he offered to make me a special salad called *ezmeli.* He laid a skewer of bull's horn peppers directly on the coals until the skins were charred and blistered. Murat charred tomatoes and slender Turkish eggplants the same way. He scraped off most of the burnt skin, leaving a little on for flavor, then cut the vegetables into bite-size pieces. He tossed them with chopped parsley, fruity Turkish olive oil, and lemon juice—proof that even a vegetarian can eat well in Turkey.

founder came from Gaziantep, Turkey's culinary capital near the Syrian border. In addition to its spicy cooking, Gaziantep is famed for its pistachios, which have an intense flavor and supernaturally bright green color. The nuts lend the meat a wonderful texture and flavor. For the best results, use Turkish pistachios, which are available at Middle or Near Eastern markets. Turkish Radish Salad (page 117), Onion Relish with Pomegranate Molasses (page 446), and pita bread would make great accompaniments.

ADVANCE PREPARATION

1 to 2 hours for chilling the meat

SPECIAL EQUIPMENT

4 flat, wide, long metal skewers

INGREDIENTS

1 pound ground lamb
½ cup shelled pistachio nuts, preferably Turkish, coarsely chopped by hand or in a food processor
¼ cup minced red onion
1 clove garlic, minced
1 teaspoon salt, or more to taste
1 teaspoon ground or flaked Aleppo pepper (see box, page 250) or pure chile powder
½ teaspoon ground cumin
½ teaspoon freshly ground black pepper, or more to taste
Pita bread

1. Combine the lamb, pistachios, onion, garlic, salt, Aleppo pepper, cumin, and black pepper in a large bowl. Knead and squeeze the mixture with your hands until thoroughly blended, 3 to 4 minutes. To test the mixture for seasoning, cook a small amount in a nonstick skillet until cooked through, then taste, adding more salt and/or black pepper to the remaining mixture as necessary. Cover and refrigerate the meat mixture for 1 to 2 hours.

2. Line a baking sheet with plastic wrap. Divide the meat mixture into four equal portions. Lightly wet your hands with cold water. Then, starting about 1 inch from the tip, mold each portion of the meat mixture around a skewer to form a flattish sausage 8 to 10 inches long and about 1 inch wide. As it is made, place each kebab on the prepared baking sheet.

3. Set up the grill for direct grilling and preheat to high. If desired, use a grateless grill setup (see box, page 21).

4. When ready to cook, arrange the kebabs on the grill as described for grateless grilling or brush and generously oil the grill grate and place the kebabs directly on it. Grill the kebabs, turning with tongs, until nicely browned and cooked through, 6 to 8 minutes in all.

5. Using a pita to protect your hand, slide each kebab off its skewer onto a serving plate. Serve at once with pitas.

INDIA

THE ORIGINAL KARIM'S SEEKH KEBAB

DIRECT GRILLING
MAKES 4 KEBABS;
SERVES 4 AS A MAIN COURSE

The Indian version of sausage, *seekh kebab* is ground spiced meat (or vegetables) molded onto square or flat skewers and grilled over charcoal. Sometimes the kebabs are cooked in the extremely high heat of a tandoor oven (especially at fancy restaurants), but traditionally they're grilled on a brazier. Flat skewers (at least a half inch wide) work well, but don't use slender metal skewers or the meat will fall off.

There are probably as many versions of *seekh kebab* as there are grill jockeys in India. This one comes from the venerable Karim restaurant in New Delhi. Note the addition of dal (cooked split peas), which gives these kebabs a unique earthy flavor and texture. Don't be bashful about the fat in this recipe: The meat should have at least 20 percent—you need it to keep the kebabs moist. Besides, much of the fat melts out during the cooking. Accompany these succulent kebabs with an Indian bread; naan—Tandoori-Baked Flat Bread (page 131)—is my first choice, and Coriander Sauce (page 482), which is similar to Indian chutney.

ADVANCE PREPARATION

1 to 2 hours for chilling the meat

SPECIAL EQUIPMENT

4 flat, wide, long metal skewers

INGREDIENTS

½ cup dried yellow split peas
¼ teaspoon ground turmeric
1 pound ground lamb
1 clove garlic, minced
2 scallions, both white and green parts, trimmed and minced
2 tablespoons chopped fresh cilantro
2 teaspoons grated peeled fresh ginger
1 teaspoon salt, or more to taste
½ teaspoon cumin seeds, toasted (see box, page 113)
½ teaspoon freshly ground black pepper, or more to taste
¼ teaspoon cayenne pepper, or more to taste
Naan (Tandoori-Baked Flat Breads, page 131; optional), for serving
1 small red onion or large shallot, very thinly sliced, for serving
Lemon wedges, for serving

1. Place the split peas and turmeric in a medium-size saucepan and add water to cover. Bring to a boil over high heat, then reduce the heat to medium and let the peas simmer, uncovered, until just tender but not mushy, 12 to 15 minutes; you should be able to crush a properly cooked pea between your thumb and forefinger. Drain the peas in a colander and let cool.

2. Grind the cooled peas to a coarse meal in a food processor. Place the lamb in a large bowl and stir in the cooled peas along with the garlic, scallions, cilantro, ginger, salt, cumin seeds, black pepper, and cayenne, then knead and squeeze the mixture with your hands until thoroughly blended, 3 to 4 minutes. To test the mixture for seasoning, cook a small amount in a nonstick skillet until cooked through, then taste, adding more salt, black pepper, and/or cayenne to the remaining mixture as necessary; it should be highly seasoned. Cover and refrigerate the meat mixture for 1 to 2 hours.

3. Line a baking sheet with plastic wrap. Divide the meat mixture into four equal portions. Lightly wet your hands with cold water. Then, starting about 1 inch from the tip, mold each portion of the meat mixture around a skewer to form a sausage about 10 inches long and 1 inch in diameter. As it is made, place each kebab on the prepared baking sheet (see Note).

4. Set up the grill for direct grilling and preheat to high. If desired, use a grateless grill setup (see box, page 21).

5. When ready to cook, arrange the kebabs on the grill as described for grateless grilling or brush and generously oil the grill grate and place the kebabs directly on it. Grill the kebabs, turning with tongs, until nicely browned and cooked through, 6 to 8 minutes in all.

6. Slide each kebab off its skewer onto a serving plate; if you are serving the kebabs with naan, you can use it to protect your hand as you remove the kebabs from the skewers. Serve the kebabs accompanied by the sliced onion and lemon wedges.

NOTE: If you are not planning to cook the kebabs immediately, cover them loosely with plastic wrap and refrigerate them.

AZERBAIJAN

LAMB IN LAVASH

LYULYA KEBAB

DIRECT GRILLING
MAKES 24 PIECES; SERVES 8 TO 12 AS AN APPETIZER, 4 TO 6 AS A MAIN COURSE

Ground lamb kebabs are enjoyed throughout the Muslim world, from Sumatra to Marrakech, but they reach their apotheosis in Turkey, Iran, and the former Soviet republics of Central Asia. *Lyulya* is the Azerbaijani version, and the use of fragrant fresh basil and sweet-sour pomegranate seeds make it unique among the ground meat kebabs. This particular rendition, which comes from the restaurant in the Hyatt Regency in Baku, is served wrapped with fresh herbs in thin sheets of the paperlike Middle and Near Eastern flat bread called lavash. (Lavash is widely available in Middle Eastern markets and even many supermarkets.) The lavash—a sort of edible napkin—makes these kebabs perfect finger fare for a cookout.

SPECIAL EQUIPMENT

8 flat, wide, long metal skewers

FOR THE KEBABS

- 1½ pounds ground lamb
- 1 small onion, finely chopped
- 2 tablespoons whole-wheat flour
- ¼ cup coarsely chopped fresh flat-leaf parsley
- ¼ cup thinly slivered fresh basil leaves
- 1½ teaspoons salt, or more to taste
- ½ teaspoon freshly ground black pepper, or more to taste

FOR SERVING

- 2 large lavash, or 4 pita breads
- 24 fresh basil leaves
- 24 flat-leaf parsley sprigs
- 4 scallions, both white and green parts, trimmed and thinly sliced
- 1 large pomegranate, broken into seeds
- 3 tablespoons ground sumac (optional; see page 248)

1. Place the lamb and onion in a food processor and process until the onion is ground very fine. Add the flour, chopped parsley, slivered basil, salt, and pepper and process briefly to combine. To test the mixture for seasoning, cook a small amount in a nonstick skillet until cooked through, then taste, adding more salt and/or pepper to the remaining mixture as necessary; it should be highly seasoned. Transfer the meat mixture to a large bowl and refrigerate it, covered, for 20 minutes.

2. Line a baking sheet with plastic wrap. Divide the meat mixture into eight equal portions. Lightly wet your hands with cold water. Then mold each portion around a skewer to form a sausage 8 to 10 inches long and about 1 inch in diameter. As it is made, place each kebab on the prepared baking sheet (see Note).

3. Set up the grill for direct grilling and preheat to high. If desired, use a grateless grill setup (see box, page 21).

4. When ready to cook, arrange the kebabs on the grill as described for grateless grilling or brush and generously oil the grill grate and place the kebabs directly on it. Grill the kebabs, turning with tongs, until nicely browned on both sides and cooked through, 6 to 8 minutes in all.

5. Transfer the kebabs to a platter and arrange the lavash in one layer on the grill grate. Grill until just warm and pliable, about 20 seconds per side. Remove the lavash from the grill and cut it into 5 by 4 inch strips.

6. Using a strip of lavash to protect your hand, slide each kebab off its skewer onto a platter. Cut each kebab into three 4-inch pieces. Wrap each piece, along with a whole basil leaf and a sprig of parsley, in a strip of lavash. Arrange the bundles on a serving platter and sprinkle the scallions and pomegranate seeds over them. Serve accompanied by ground sumac (if using).

NOTE: If you are not planning to cook the kebabs immediately, cover them loosely with plastic wrap and refrigerate them.

TURKEY

LAMB AND EGGPLANT KEBABS

SEDZELI KEBAB

DIRECT GRILLING
SERVES 4

This colorful skewer is one of the most popular kebabs in Turkey, and given the mild, sweet flavor of Turkish eggplants, it's easy to see why. As the kebabs cook, the eggplant absorbs the lamb juices, creating one luscious combination. Another plus for health-conscious eaters is the high proportion of vegetables to meat. Choose eggplants that are rather long and narrow: Asian eggplants work well. Serve these kebabs with Onion Relish with Pomegranate Molasses (page 446) and Turkish Radish Salad (page 117).

SPECIAL EQUIPMENT

8 long metal skewers, or 8 bamboo skewers and an aluminum foil shield (see box, page 23)

INGREDIENTS

1 pound ground lamb
¼ cup minced red onion
1 clove garlic, minced
3 tablespoons finely chopped fresh flat-leaf parsley
1 teaspoon salt, or more to taste
½ teaspoon ground cumin
½ teaspoon freshly ground black pepper, or more to taste
8 Asian or other long slender eggplants (each 6 to 7 inches long and 1½ inches wide)
Lavash or pita bread

1. Place the lamb in a large bowl and mix in the onion, garlic, parsley, salt, cumin, and pepper. Knead and squeeze the mixture with your hands until thoroughly blended, 3 to 4 minutes. To test the mixture for seasoning, cook a small amount in a nonstick skillet until cooked through, then taste, adding more salt and/or pepper to the remaining mixture as necessary; it should be highly seasoned.

2. Trim the ends off the eggplants and discard them; cut each eggplant crosswise into 1½-inch rounds. Thread each round, through the cut side, on a skewer, 4 to a skewer, spacing them about 1½ inches apart.

3. Line a baking sheet with plastic wrap. Divide the meat mixture into twenty-four equal portions. Lightly wet your hands with cold water, then take one of the portions of meat and mold it around a skewer, between two eggplant rounds, making it as much as possible the same size and shape as the eggplant. Repeat with the remaining portions of meat so each skewer contains 4 eggplant rounds

Sumac

Whenever you sit down to a meal of kebabs or *kofta* in the Middle East and Central Asia, you will be offered a dish of purplish red powder with a tart, lemony, almost sour plum flavor. This is sumac. Made from a Middle Eastern berry and available at Middle and Near Eastern and Armenian markets, sumac is used throughout the region as a seasoning for grilled meats and seafood. If unavailable, you can use a squeeze of lemon juice instead.

LAMB AND EGGPLANT KEBABS | AT LEFT

alternating with 3 portions of meat. As it is made, place each kebab on the prepared baking sheet (see Note).

4. Set up the grill for direct grilling and preheat to high. If desired, use a grateless grill setup (see box, page 21).

5. When ready to cook, arrange the kebabs on the grill as described for grateless grilling or brush and generously oil the grill grate and place the kebabs directly on it. (If using bamboo skewers, place an aluminum foil shield under the ends of the skewers.) Grill, turning with tongs, until nicely browned and cooked through, 8 to 12 minutes in all.

6. Using a piece of lavash to protect your hand, slide the meat and eggplant off the skewers onto serving plates. If desired, trim away the charred eggplant skin before eating. Serve accompanied by lavash.

NOTE: If you are not planning to cook the kebabs immediately, cover them loosely with plastic wrap and refrigerate them.

TURKEY

CRACKED WHEAT AND LAMB KEBABS

SEMIT KEBAB

DIRECT GRILLING
SERVES 4

The combination of lamb and bulgur (cracked wheat) is popular in the Near and Middle East. My favorite variation on this theme of grain and meat is Turkish *cig kofte,* a fiery pâté of chile-spiced bulgur and uncooked lean ground lamb. From this pâté, it's not much of a leap to *semit kebab* (bulgur kebab), a highly unusual and amazingly tasty kebab that's a specialty at the restaurant Cagdas in Gaziantep, Turkey. Bulgur gives the ground lamb kebabs a firm, chewy texture; the mint and allspice reinforce the sweet flavor of the wheat; while the Aleppo pepper and hot paprika turn up the heat.

ADVANCE PREPARATION

2 hours for soaking the bulgur, plus 1 to 2 hours for chilling the kebabs

SPECIAL EQUIPMENT

4 flat, wide, long metal skewers

INGREDIENTS

- **½ cup fine bulgur**
- **1 pound ground lamb**
- **1 small onion, minced**
- **1 clove garlic, minced**
- **2 teaspoons dried mint**
- **1 teaspoon Aleppo pepper (see box, this page) or hot paprika, or more to taste**
- **1 teaspoon salt, or more to taste**
- **½ teaspoon freshly ground black pepper, or more to taste**
- **½ teaspoon hot red pepper flakes**
- **¼ teaspoon ground allspice**
- **Lavash or pita bread**

1. Place the bulgur in a bowl, add cold water to cover by 1 inch, and let soak for 2 hours.

2. Place the lamb in a large bowl. Drain the bulgur in a strainer, then squeeze it between your fingers to wring out all the water. Add the bulgur to the lamb along with the onion, garlic, mint, Aleppo pepper, salt, black pepper, hot pepper flakes, and allspice. Knead and squeeze the mixture with your hands until thoroughly blended, 3 to 4 minutes. To test the mixture for seasoning, cook a small amount in a nonstick skillet until cooked through, then taste, adding more Aleppo pepper, salt, and/or black

Aleppo Pepper

The Aleppo pepper is a small, round, reddish brown chile hailing from Syria and eastern Turkey. Usually sold powdered or in flakes, it has a clean, tart, almost metallic, ancho-like flavor with considerable heat. Look for it in Middle Eastern grocery stores.

pepper to the remaining mixture as necessary; it should be highly seasoned.

3. Line a baking sheet with plastic wrap. Divide the meat mixture into four equal portions. Lightly wet your hands with cold water, then mold each portion of the meat mixture around a skewer to form a sausage 10 to 12 inches long and about 1 inch in diameter. As it is made, place each kebab on the prepared baking sheet (see Note). Loosely cover the kebabs with plastic wrap and refrigerate them for 1 to 2 hours.

4. Set up the grill for direct grilling and preheat to high. If desired, use a grateless grill setup (see box, page 21).

5. When ready to cook, arrange the kebabs on the grill as described for grateless grilling or brush and generously oil the grill grate and place the kebabs directly on it. Grill the kebabs, turning with tongs, until nicely browned and cooked through, 6 to 8 minutes in all.

6. Using a piece of lavash to protect your hand, slide each kebab off its skewer onto a serving plate. Serve at once, accompanied by lavash.

NOTE: If not planning to cook immediately, cover loosely with plastic wrap and refrigerate.

TURKEY

"GENTLE AL" KEBABS WITH FIRE-CHARRED EGGPLANT AND YOGURT

DIRECT GRILLING
MAKES 4 KEBABS; SERVES 4

This is one of the most popular kebabs in Turkey—a glory of smoke and fire featuring two of the best ingredients ever to hit a barbecue grill: lamb and eggplant. Legend credits its invention to a kebab maker named Ali Nasik ("Gentle Al") from the city of Bursa. Gentle Al's brainstorm was to serve grilled, spiced ground lamb kebabs over a tangy puree made from fire-charred eggplant and yogurt. Today, you find these kebabs all over Turkey. For the sake of convenience, the eggplant puree can be prepared ahead (I like to grill the eggplant the day before). For a really great-tasting puree, use whole-milk yogurt from a Middle Eastern market. The dill in the lamb isn't strictly traditional, but I like the way it rounds out the flavor.

ADVANCE PREPARATION

1 to 2 hours for chilling the kebabs

SPECIAL EQUIPMENT

4 flat, wide, long metal skewers

FOR THE KEBABS

- 1 pound ground lamb
- 3 tablespoons minced onion
- 1 clove garlic, minced
- 1 tablespoon chopped fresh dill, or 1½ teaspoons dried dill (optional)
- 1 teaspoon salt, or more to taste
- ½ teaspoon ground cumin
- ½ teaspoon freshly ground black pepper, or more to taste

FOR THE EGGPLANT PUREE

- 2 Asian or other long slender eggplants (about 10 ounces each)
- 2 cloves garlic, minced
- 1 to 1¼ cups whole-milk yogurt
- 1 tablespoon fresh lemon juice, or more to taste
- ½ teaspoon salt, or more to taste
- ½ teaspoon freshly ground black pepper, or more to taste

FOR SERVING

- Pita bread
- 1 cup whole-milk yogurt
- 2 tablespoons chopped fresh flat-leaf parsley

1. Make the kebabs: Combine the lamb, onion, 1 clove of garlic, dill (if using), 1 teaspoon of salt, cumin, and ½ teaspoon of pepper in a large bowl. Knead and squeeze the mixture with your hands until thoroughly blended, 3 to 4 minutes. To test the mixture for seasoning, cook a small amount in a nonstick skillet until cooked through, then taste, adding more salt and/or pepper to the remaining mixture as necessary.

2. Line a baking sheet with plastic wrap. Divide the meat mixture into four equal portions. Lightly wet your hands with cold water, then mold each portion around a skewer to form a sausage 10 to 12 inches long and about 1 inch in diameter. As it is made, place each kebab on the prepared baking sheet. Cover and refrigerate the kebabs for 1 to 2 hours.

3. Set up the grill for direct grilling and preheat to high.

4. When ready to cook, brush and oil the grill grate. Make the eggplant puree: Place the eggplants on the hot grate and grill, turning with tongs, until the skin is charred on all sides and the flesh is soft, 20 to 30 minutes. Transfer the eggplants to a plate and let cool.

5. Scrape as much of the charred skin as possible off the eggplant (it's not necessary to remove every bit). Then, cut the eggplant into chunks and process in a food processor until pureed. Transfer the eggplant puree to a bowl and stir in the garlic, 1 cup of the yogurt, the lemon juice, ½ teaspoon of salt, and ½ teaspoon of pepper. The puree should be quite loose; add the remaining ¼ cup yogurt as needed. Taste for seasoning, adding more lemon juice, salt, and/or pepper as necessary; the eggplant puree should be highly seasoned. Cover the puree and set it aside.

6. If necessary, add 20 to 24 fresh coals to increase the heat of the grill to high. If desired, use a grateless grill setup (see box, page 21).

7. When ready to cook, arrange the kebabs on the grill as described for grateless grilling or brush and generously oil the grill grate and place the kebabs directly on it. Grill the kebabs, turning with tongs, until nicely browned and cooked through, 6 to 8 minutes in all.

8. Meanwhile, warm the eggplant puree on one side of the grill in an uncovered medium-size saucepan.

9. Using a pita to protect your hand, slide each kebab off its skewer onto a platter, then cut the kebabs into 2-inch pieces. Spoon the warmed eggplant puree into the center of 4 serving plates. Top each portion with ¼ cup of yogurt and arrange pieces of sausage on top. Sprinkle parsley over the sausage and serve at once with the pitas.

IRAQ

FOUR PEPPER CHICKEN KEBABS

KAFTA

DIRECT GRILLING
MAKES 4 KEBABS; SERVES 4

Kafta (with its myriad other spellings) refers to a huge family of ground meat kebabs found as far east as India and as far west as Morocco. The traditional meat for *kafta* is lamb, often fatty lamb at that. How refreshing to find a *kafta* made with America's favorite low-fat meat—boneless chicken breast. This recipe was inspired by a dish from Detroit's Fendi restaurant, which is owned by Chaldeans, Iraqi Christians. These kebabs may be low in fat, but they're long on flavor, thanks to the colorful addition of paprika and the bell peppers. For a milder *kafta,* use sweet paprika; for a spicier one, use hot. Serve the kebabs with Central Asian Pickles (page 441), Persian-Style Steamed Rice (page 425), or Persian Rice with a Golden Crust (page 425).

SPECIAL EQUIPMENT

4 flat, wide, long metal skewers

INGREDIENTS

1¼ pounds skinless, boneless chicken breasts, trimmed of fat and sinews and cut into 1-inch cubes
1 clove garlic, minced
1 teaspoon salt, or more to taste
½ teaspoon freshly ground white pepper, or more to taste
½ teaspoon hot or sweet paprika, or more to taste
½ teaspoon ground cumin, or more to taste
3 tablespoons finely chopped flat-leaf parsley
3 tablespoons minced green bell pepper
3 tablespoons minced red bell pepper
1 tablespoon olive oil, for brushing

1. Combine the chicken, garlic, salt, white pepper, paprika, and cumin in a food processor and process just to a coarse paste. Mix in the parsley and bell peppers, running the machine in short bursts; don't overgrind, or the parsley and peppers will make the mixture a drab color. To test the mixture for seasoning, cook a small amount in a nonstick skillet until cooked through, then taste, adding more salt, white pepper, paprika, and/or cumin to the remaining mixture as necessary; the mixture should be highly seasoned.

2. Line a baking sheet with plastic wrap. Divide the chicken mixture into four equal portions. Lightly wet your hands with cold water, then mold each portion around a skewer to form a flattish sausage 10 to 12 inches long and about ¾ inch thick. As it is made, place each kebab on the prepared baking sheet (see Note).

3. Set up the grill for direct grilling and preheat to high.

4. When ready to cook, brush and generously oil the grill grate. Brush one side of the kebabs lightly with some of the olive oil and arrange them on the hot grate, oiled side down. Grill until nicely browned on the first side, 2 to 4 minutes. Brush the tops of the kebabs with the remaining oil, turn with tongs, and continue cooking until cooked through, 2 to 4 minutes longer. Serve at once.

NOTE: If you are not planning to cook the kebabs immediately, cover them loosely with plastic wrap and refrigerate them.

PIRI-PIRI CHICKEN | PAGE 258

BIRD MEETS GRILL

I'm standing at a rotisserie at a market in Provence, where rows of chickens slowly rotate on spits in front of a wall of fire. I could just as easily be in Turkey or Bali or Tuscany or the West Indies. Grilled chicken ranks among the world's most popular barbecue. The diversity of its preparation is limited only by the imagination of the world's grill jockeys.

"Poultry is for the cook what canvas is for the painter."
—ANTHELME BRILLAT-SAVARIN

In this chapter you'll learn how to grill all forms of chicken and other poultry, from quick cooking cuts like wings and breasts to whole chickens, ducks, and turkeys, which take advantage of the indirect grilling method to achieve smoky, fall-off-the-bone tenderness. I'll tell you how to avoid the dual perils of serving undercooked chicken and burning the highly flammable skin.

The sheer variety of grilled chicken dishes from around the world is mind-boggling. During my travels I discovered fiery Portuguese Piri-Piri Chicken, fragrant game hens grilled with Moroccan spices, Pakistani Sea Captain's Chicken Tikka (marinated with yogurt and cardamom), and—a favorite on the American barbecue circuit—Beer-Can Chicken (a bird that has been smoke grilled on top of an open can of beer).

So pop the tops of your favorite six-pack and get ready to cook the perfect bird on the grill.

JAMAICA

DIMPLES' BARBECUED CHICKEN

INDIRECT GRILLING
SERVES 2 TO 4

Jerk, especially jerk pork, is so famous in Jamaica, it's easy to forget that the island has other barbecued dishes. Among them is this incredibly flavorful, fall-off-the-bone-tender chicken, which I enjoyed by flickering torchlight at a riverside eatery called Boar Hill outside Kingston. The chef, although she would blush to be identified as such, was a pretty, short, shy woman named Fastina Sherman. Compliment her on her cooking, or simply ask her a question, and she would break into an embarrassed, deep-dimpled smile. No wonder everyone called her Dimples!

The marinade for this chicken is a lot milder than Jamaica's infamous jerk, but being Jamaican, it still calls for a fiery Scotch bonnet chile. Seeding the chile blunts the heat, or you can use a milder chile, like a Caribbean rocotillo. Shaped like a patty pan squash, this chile has the smoky flavor of the Scotch bonnet, but without the heat.

ADVANCE PREPARATION

12 to 24 hours for marinating the chicken

SPECIAL EQUIPMENT

1 cup oak or fruit wood chips or chunks, soaked for 1 hour in cold water to cover and drained

FOR THE CHICKEN

1 whole chicken (3½ to 4 pounds)
1 bunch scallions, both white and green parts, trimmed and finely chopped
2 cloves garlic, minced
½ to 1 Scotch bonnet chile, seeded and finely chopped, or ½ to 1 teaspoon Scotch bonnet–based hot sauce
1 tablespoon sweet paprika
1 teaspoon fresh thyme, or ½ teaspoon dried thyme
½ teaspoon salt
½ teaspoon freshly ground black pepper
4½ teaspoons soy sauce
1 tablespoon vegetable oil

FOR THE BARBECUE SAUCE

1 cup ketchup
⅓ cup soy sauce
4 scallions, both white and green parts, trimmed and minced
2 cloves garlic, minced
2 tablespoons minced peeled fresh ginger
¼ to ⅓ cup firmly packed dark brown sugar
¼ cup distilled white vinegar
2 tablespoons dark rum, or more to taste

1. Prepare the chicken: Remove and discard the fat just inside the body cavities of the chicken. Remove the package of giblets and set aside for another use. Rinse the chicken, inside and out, under cold running water, then drain and blot dry, inside and out, with paper towels. Set the chicken aside while you prepare the seasoning.

Poultry Grilling Chart

CUT	METHOD	HEAT	DONENESS well (170°F)
CHICKEN			
whole	indirect	medium	1¼ to 1½ hours
whole	rotisserie	high	1 to 1¼ hours
whole, spatchcocked	direct	medium	40 minutes to 1 hour
boneless breast	direct	high	3 to 6 minutes per side
bone-in breast	direct	medium	8 to 10 minutes per side
legs	direct	medium	8 to 10 minutes per side
wings	direct	medium	6 to 8 minutes per side
GAME HEN			
whole, spatchcocked	direct	medium	8 to 10 minutes per side
DUCK			
whole	rotisserie	medium-high	1½ to 2 hours
whole	indirect	medium	2 to 2½ hours
TURKEY			
whole	indirect	medium	15 to 20 minutes per pound

*This chart is offered as a guideline to cooking times for the various types of poultry. Remember, grilling is an art, not a science. When in doubt, refer to times in the individual recipes.

2. Combine the chopped scallions, 2 cloves of minced garlic, Scotch bonnet, paprika, thyme, salt, pepper, 4½ teaspoons of soy sauce, and the oil in a small bowl and stir to mix or, for a richer flavor, place these ingredients in a food processor or blender and process to a smooth puree. Spoon half of the scallion mixture into the neck and body cavities of the chicken, then rub the rest over the skin (or under it; see box, page 261) covering it completely. Place the chicken in a large, heavy-duty resealable plastic bag. Seal the bag and let the chicken marinate, in the refrigerator, for 12 to 24 hours, turning the bag over several times.

3. Make the barbecue sauce: Combine the ketchup, ⅓ cup of soy sauce, minced scallions, 2 cloves of minced garlic, ginger, brown sugar, and vinegar in a medium-size nonreactive saucepan and bring to a boil over medium heat, stirring until the sugar dissolves. Reduce the heat to low and let simmer, uncovered, until thick and richly flavored, 10 to 15 minutes. Stir in the rum during the last 2 minutes of cooking, taste for seasoning, adding more rum as necessary, then remove the barbecue sauce from the heat. You should have about 2 cups.

4. Set up the grill for indirect grilling and place a drip pan in the center.

If using a gas grill, place all of the wood chips in the smoker box and preheat the grill to high; when smoke appears, reduce the heat to medium.

If using a charcoal grill, preheat it to medium.

5. When ready to cook, if using a charcoal grill, toss half of the wood chips on the coals. Brush and oil the grill grate. Remove the chicken from the plastic bag and place it, breast side up, on the hot grate over the drip pan. Cover the grill and cook the chicken for 45 minutes.

6. Uncover the grill and brush the chicken liberally with the barbecue sauce. Re-cover the grill and continue cooking the chicken until the skin is mahogany brown and the juices run clear when the tip of a skewer or sharp knife is inserted in the thickest part of a thigh, 30 to 45 minutes more. When done, an instant-read meat thermometer inserted in the thickest part of a thigh, but not touching the bone, should register about 170°F. Continue to brush the chicken with the barbecue sauce as it cooks. If using charcoal, you'll need to add 10 to 12 fresh coals to each side and toss the remaining wood chips on the fire after 1 hour.

7. Transfer the chicken to a cutting board or platter and let rest for 5 minutes before carving. Serve accompanied by the remaining barbecue sauce. Any leftover sauce can be refrigerated, covered, for up to 2 weeks.

U.S.A.

BEER-CAN CHICKEN

INDIRECT GRILLING
SERVES 2 TO 4

This iconic recipe makes some of the most moist, succulent, flavorful barbecued chicken I've ever tasted. The secret? Inserting an open can of beer into the cavity of the bird and cooking it upright on the grill. The bird makes a great conversation piece. The recipe was inspired by the Bryce Boar Blazers, a barbecue team from Texas I met at the Memphis in May World Championship Barbecue Cooking Contest and it went on to become an American classic.

SPECIAL EQUIPMENT

1½ cups mesquite chips or chunks, soaked in cold water to cover for 1 hour and drained

INGREDIENTS

1 large whole chicken (4 to 5 pounds)
3 tablespoons Memphis Rub (page 489), or your favorite dry barbecue rub
1 can (12 ounces) beer

1. Remove and discard the fat just inside the body cavities of the chicken. Remove the package of giblets and set aside for another use. Rinse the chicken, inside and out, under cold running water, then drain and blot dry, inside and out, with paper towels. Sprinkle 1 tablespoon of the rub inside the body and neck cavities, then rub another 1 tablespoon of rub all over the skin of the bird. If you wish, rub another ½ tablespoon of the mixture between the flesh and skin (see box, page 261). Cover and refrigerate the chicken while you preheat the grill.

2. Set up the grill for indirect grilling and place a drip pan in the center.

If using a gas grill, place all of the wood chips in the smoker box and preheat the grill to high; when smoke appears, reduce the heat to medium.

If using a charcoal grill, preheat it to medium.

3. Pop the tab on the beer can. Using a "church key"–style can opener, make 2 or 3 holes in the top of the can. Pour out half of the beer, then spoon the remaining dry rub through the holes into the beer. Holding the chicken upright, with the opening of the body cavity facing down, insert the beer can into the cavity.

4. When ready to cook, if using charcoal, toss half the wood chips on the coals. Brush and oil the grill grate. Stand the chicken up in the center of the hot grate, over the drip pan. Spread out the legs to form a sort of tripod to support the bird (the beer can will be the third "leg").

5. Cover the grill and cook the chicken until fall-off-the-bone tender, 1¼ to 1½ hours. If using a charcoal grill, you'll need to add 10 to 12 fresh coals to each side and toss the remaining wood chips on the fire after 1 hour.

6. Using tongs, transfer the bird to a cutting board or platter, holding a large metal spatula underneath the beer can for support. (Place the board or platter right next to the bird to make the move shorter and be careful not to spill the hot beer.) Let the chicken rest for 5 minutes before removing it from the beer can and carving it. (Toss the beer can out along with the carcass.)

SOUTH AFRICA

PIRI-PIRI CHICKEN

INDIRECT GRILLING
SERVES 4 TO 8

Piri-piri is the Portuguese name for a hot sauce made with tiny fiery chiles and vinegar. The chile was a New World food, of course, and the Portuguese seafarers of the fifteenth and sixteenth centuries deserve credit for introducing it to the rest of the world. You still find the sauce in Portugal and in the former Portuguese colonies of Brazil, Macao, Goa, Angola, and Mozambique. The South African love of *piri-piri* no doubt comes from the two last, its northern neighbors.

At Brazilian markets, *piri-piri* goes by the name of *molho malagueta* (malagueta pepper sauce). In a pinch you could use Tabasco sauce or even a Caribbean Scotch bonnet chile–based hot sauce, but if you do, add a tablespoon or two of vinegar to the marinade as well.

ADVANCE PREPARATION

4 to 12 hours for marinating the chicken

INGREDIENTS

2 whole chickens (3½ to 4 pounds each)
½ cup extra-virgin olive oil
8 tablespoons (1 stick) salted butter, melted
⅓ cup fresh lemon juice
3 to 4 tablespoons Portuguese Hot Sauce (page 480), malagueta pepper sauce, or other hot sauce (as much as you and your guests can bear)
1 tablespoon sweet paprika
1 teaspoon ground coriander
3 cloves garlic, peeled
3 scallions, both white and green parts, trimmed and sliced
3 tablespoons coarsely chopped fresh flat-leaf parsley
1 piece (1 inch) peeled fresh ginger, thinly sliced
2 bay leaves, crumbled
1 teaspoon salt
½ teaspoon freshly ground black pepper

1. Remove and discard the fat just inside the body cavities of the chickens. Remove the packages of giblets and set aside for another use. Rinse the chickens, inside and out, under cold running water, then drain and blot dry, inside and out, with paper towels. Spatchcock the chickens (see page 289) and place them in a large, nonreactive bowl or baking dish and set aside while you prepare the marinade and sauce.

2. Combine the olive oil, butter, lemon juice, Portuguese Hot Sauce, paprika, coriander, garlic, scallions, parsley, ginger, bay leaves, salt, and pepper in a food processor or blender and process to a smooth puree. Pour half of this sauce over the chickens and, using your hands, coat them with it. Let the chickens marinate in the refrigerator, covered, for 4 to 12 hours (the longer the better). Refrigerate the remaining hot sauce mixture, covered; you will use it as a sauce for the chickens. Let the hot sauce come to room temperature before serving.

How to Grill the Perfect Whole Chicken

In my estimation, if you want to cook a whole chicken, you need a grill with a rotisserie. Why is spit roasting such a perfect way to cook chicken? I have a few theories. First, the slow rotation in front of a live fire provides a gentle, even heat that cooks the legs through without drying out the breast meat. Second, as the bird cooks, the fat under the skin melts, basting the meat continuously. Third, the steady, even exposure to the flame crisps the skin without burning it. Here are some tips on grilling chicken on—and off—a spit.

Grilling on a Rotisserie

1. Start with a good chicken, preferably grain fed, free range, and organic. Remove and discard the fat just inside the body cavities of the chicken. Remove the package of giblets and set it aside for another use. Rinse the chicken, inside and out, under cold running water, then drain and blot it dry, inside and out, with paper towels.

2. Generously salt and pepper the bird, inside and out. For extra flavor you can put a peeled garlic clove, bay leaf, strip of lemon zest, and/or sprig of rosemary inside the body and neck cavities. (My editor, Suzanne Rafer, inserts slices of garlic under the skin.)

3. Tightly truss the bird, using butcher's string and a trussing needle or skewers. Trussing helps the chicken cook evenly and gives it an attractive shape.

4. Set up the grill for rotisserie cooking following the manufacturer's instructions. If you are grilling with charcoal, fill a chimney starter, light the charcoal, and let it burn until glowing red, about two minutes. Rake one row of coals just in front of where the chicken will be turning on the spit and one row just behind it. Place a drip pan directly under where the chicken will be.

   If you are using a gas grill, place the drip pan in the center of the grill. Then, if there is a rotisserie burner at the back of the grill, preheat the burner. If you have a three-burner gas grill without a rotisserie burner, turn the front and rear burners on high and leave the middle burner turned off.

5. Skewer the chicken to the spit, then attach the spit to the grill and turn the rotisserie on. Cook the chicken, covered if possible, until the skin is gorgeously browned and the flesh is cooked through; this will take one to one and a quarter hours. Every fifteen minutes or so, baste the rotating bird with the juices that accumulate in the drip pan. When done, the bird's internal temperature will read 170°F on an instant-read meat thermometer inserted in the thickest part of a thigh, but not touching the bone. Another test is to pierce the thickest part of the thigh with the tip of a skewer or sharp knife; the juices should run clear.

6. Remove the chicken from the spit and transfer the bird to a cutting board or platter. Let it rest for five minutes before carving. Remove the trussing strings (or skewers) and get ready for the ultimate chicken.

Grilling Without a Rotisserie

You can also make a delicious chicken using the indirect grilling method. As with the rotisserie, you must start with a good chicken and season and truss it.

1. Set up the grill for indirect grilling, place a drip pan in the center of the grill, under the grate, and preheat the grill to medium. Place the chicken, breast side up, on the hot grate over the drip pan.

2. Cover the grill and cook the chicken until the skin is nicely browned and the meat is cooked through (as described in Step 5 above), one and a quarter to one and a half hours. Baste the bird with the drippings from the drip pan every twenty minutes or so as it cooks. If you are using a charcoal grill, you'll need to add ten to twelve fresh coals to each side after one hour. Let the chicken rest for five minutes before carving and serving.

3. Set up the grill for indirect grilling, place a large drip pan in the center, and preheat the grill to medium (see Note).

4. When ready to cook, brush and oil the grill grate. Place the chickens, skin side up, on the hot grate over the drip pan, reserving any marinade in the bowl. Brush the chickens with the marinade, then cover the grill and cook for 30 minutes. Uncover the grill and brush the chickens with any remaining marinade. Re-cover the grill and continue cooking the chickens until the juices run clear when the tip of a skewer or sharp knife is inserted in the thickest part of a thigh, 20 to 30 minutes longer. When done, an instant-read meat thermometer inserted in the thickest part of a thigh, but not touching the bone, should register about 170°F. If you want the chicken skin to be browned and crisp, place the chickens, skin side down, on the grill grate directly over the fire for the last 5 to 10 minutes of grilling.

5. Using long spatulas, carefully transfer the chickens to a cutting board or platter and let rest for 5 minutes before carving. Serve accompanied by the reserved hot sauce.

NOTE: For a crustier bird, you can cook the chickens using the direct method. Preheat the grill to medium, brush and oil the grill grate, and arrange the chickens on the hot grate skin side down. Grill, uncovered, for 15 to 20 minutes per side, turning the birds very carefully with long spatulas so they stay in one piece.

BAHAMAS

BAHAMIAN GRILLED CHICKEN

DIRECT GRILLING
SERVES 4

On most of the islands of the Caribbean, it's common to rinse chicken and meats in lime juice before cooking. The practice probably originated in the days before refrigeration, when the citrus juice served as both a flavoring and disinfectant. Today we prize the lime juice for the tart, tangy flavor it imparts to the chicken. Serve the chicken with Bahamian Peas and Rice (page 431).

ADVANCED PREPARATION

30 minutes to 2 hours for marinating the chicken

INGREDIENTS

- 1 chicken (3½ to 4 pounds), quartered, or 4 bone-in chicken breast halves with skin
- 1 cup fresh lime juice
- 1 small onion, thinly sliced
- 2 cloves garlic, minced
- ½ to 2 Scotch bonnet or other hot chiles, thinly sliced
- 2 teaspoons chopped fresh thyme, or 1 teaspoon dried thyme
- 2 tablespoons vegetable oil
- 1 tablespoon sweet paprika
- 1 teaspoon salt
- ½ teaspoon freshly ground white pepper

1. Rinse the chicken pieces under cold running water, then drain and blot dry with paper towels. Place the pieces in a nonreactive bowl or baking dish and pour the lime juice over them; turn the pieces to coat. Let the chicken marinate, at room temperature, for 15 minutes, turning the pieces once or twice.

2. Pour off and discard the lime juice, then add the onion, garlic, Scotch bonnet(s), thyme, oil, paprika, salt, and pepper and turn the chicken pieces to coat thoroughly. Let the chicken marinate in this mixture for at least 15 minutes or as long as 1 to 2 hours (the longer the better), covering and refrigerating it if marinating for the longer time.

3. Set up the grill for two-zone direct grilling (see page 18), preheating two thirds of the grill to medium and leaving one third heat free as a safety zone.

4. When ready to cook, brush and oil the grill grate. Using a rubber spatula, scrape any bits of onion or garlic off the chicken pieces. Arrange the chicken, skin side down, on the grate over the hot zone of the grill and cook until the skin is golden brown and the meat is cooked through without any trace of red at the bone, 8 to 12 minutes per side. If you get flare-ups, move the chicken to the safety zone until the flames die down.

5. Transfer the chicken pieces to serving plates or a platter and serve.

SENEGAL

CHICKEN WITH LEMON-MUSTARD SAUCE

YASSA

DIRECT GRILLING
SERVES 4

I first encountered this dish at a Senegalese restaurant in Washington, D.C. It was a fairly mild version of a dish that can be quite fiery, flavored as it traditionally is with the African equivalent of a Scotch bonnet chile. The recipe is unusual by Western barbecue standards, but quite typical of Africa, in that the meat is grilled first, then simmered in the lemon-mustard sauce.

ADVANCE PREPARATION

2 to 12 hours for marinating the chicken

FOR THE CHICKEN AND SPICE PASTE

1 chicken (3½ to 4 pounds), quartered
8 cloves garlic, peeled
1 to 2 Scotch bonnet chiles, seeded (for a hotter spice paste, leave the seeds in)
1 teaspoon salt
1 teaspoon freshly ground black pepper
3 tablespoons vegetable oil

FOR THE LEMON-MUSTARD SAUCE

1 large onion, finely chopped (about 2 cups)
1 cup grainy French mustard
½ cup vegetable oil
¼ cup fresh lemon juice
12 green olives, pitted and thinly sliced
1 bay leaf
½ to 1 Scotch bonnet chile, seeded (for a hotter sauce, leave the seeds in)
Salt and freshly ground black pepper

SEASONING UNDER THE SKIN

When it comes to giving chicken or other birds the maximum flavor, nothing beats putting the seasoning under the skin before grilling. So, from time to time pit masters are required to perform feats of surgery. Chicken skin is not the highly permeable membrane you'd expect it to be; spices find it difficult to get through. But spread the rub or marinade under the skin and the meat will soak up the flavorings like a sponge, while the skin seals in the juices. It may feel awkward at first, but soon you'll be doing it like a pro. Here's how.

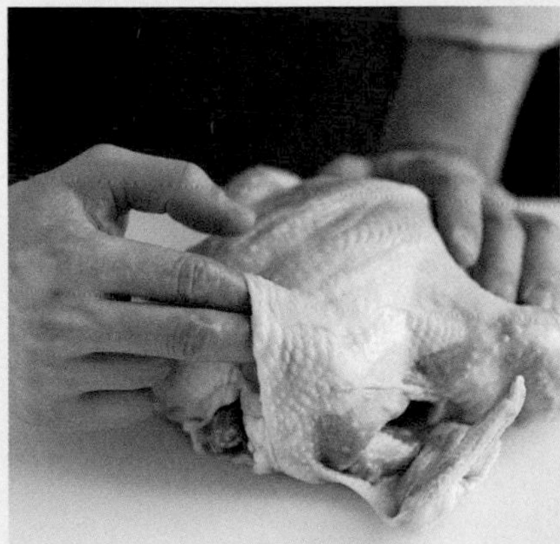

1. *Starting at the neck, tunnel your forefinger and middle finger under the skin to loosen it from the meat. Hold the bird steady with the other hand.*

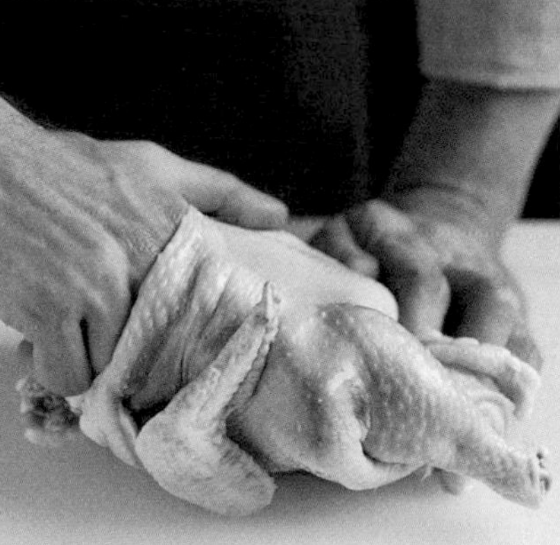

2. *Slide your hand in deeper to loosen the chicken skin from the breasts, thighs, and drumsticks. Work carefully so as not to tear the skin.*

3. *Then, sprinkle the rub or spoon the marinade over the chicken meat under the skin. You can use the same technique to flavor halved or quartered birds as well as whole chicken breasts.*

1. Prepare the chicken and spice paste: Rinse the chicken pieces under cold running water, then drain and blot dry with paper towels. Make 1 or 2 deep slashes, to the bone, in each piece, then place the chicken in a nonreactive baking dish large enough to hold all the pieces in a single layer. Set the chicken aside while you prepare the spice paste.

2. Combine the garlic, Scotch bonnets, 1 teaspoon of salt, and 1 teaspoon of pepper in a mortar and pound to a paste with a pestle, then work in the 3 tablespoons of oil. If you don't have a mortar and pestle, combine all of these ingredients in a food processor or blender and process until smooth.

3. Using your fingers, stuff half the spice paste into the slashes in each piece of chicken, then spread the remainder over the skin. Let the chicken marinate in the refrigerator, covered, for 2 to 12 hours (the longer the better).

4. Make the lemon-mustard sauce: Combine the onion, mustard, ½ cup of oil, and the lemon juice, olives, bay leaf, and Scotch bonnet. Season with salt and pepper to taste. Stir to mix well and bring to a boil over medium heat, then reduce the heat to low. Let simmer, uncovered, stirring frequently, until the onion is soft, the sauce is thick and creamy, and the oil has started to separate out, about 15 minutes. Remove the sauce from the heat and taste for seasoning, adding more salt and/or pepper as necessary. Discard the bay leaf and Scotch bonnet. Set the sauce aside, covered.

5. Set up the grill for two-zone direct grilling (see page 18), preheating two thirds of the grill to medium and leaving one third heat free as a safety zone.

6. When ready to cook, brush and oil the grill grate. Arrange the chicken pieces, skin side down, on the grate over the hot zone of the grill and cook until the skin is golden brown and the meat is cooked through without any trace of red at the bone, 8 to 12 minutes per side. If you get flare-ups, move the chicken to the safety zone until the flames die down.

7. Transfer the chicken to the saucepan with the sauce and bring to a simmer over low heat, spooning the sauce over the chicken to coat. Cover and cook until the chicken is well flavored by the sauce, 4 to 5 minutes.

8. Transfer the chicken pieces to serving plates or a platter, spoon the sauce over them, and serve.

BRAZIL

BRAZILIAN BEER CHICKEN

DIRECT GRILLING
SERVES 4

The United States isn't the only place where beer and barbecue are inextricably interwoven. In Rio de Janeiro I came across this savory grilled chicken, which owes its exceptional succulence to a two-day bath in beer. Try, if possible, to find a Brazilian beer: Antarctica (a pilsner-style brew) will produce a mild-flavored chicken; Xingu Black Beer (a dark bitter stout) will produce a bird with a rich, malty flavor. Serve the chicken with Crazy Rice (page 432) or Brazilian Black Beans with Bacon (page 438).

ADVANCE PREPARATION

6 hours to 2 days for marinating the chicken

INGREDIENTS

2 cups beer
½ cup vegetable oil
½ cup Dijon mustard
1 tablespoon sweet paprika
1 teaspoon freshly ground black pepper
1 medium-size onion, thinly sliced
12 cloves garlic, thinly sliced
2 bay leaves
1 chicken (3½ to 4 pounds), quartered
Coarse salt (kosher or sea)

1. Combine the beer, oil, mustard, paprika, and pepper in a nonreactive bowl large enough to hold the chicken pieces and whisk thoroughly to blend. Stir in the onion, garlic, and bay leaves.

2. Rinse the chicken pieces under cold running water, then drain and blot dry with paper towels. Add the chicken to the marinade and turn to coat. Let the chicken marinate in the refrigerator, covered, for 6 hours, or up to 2 days (the longer the better), turning the chicken pieces occasionally.

3. Set up the grill for two-zone direct grilling (see page 18), preheating two thirds of the grill to medium and leaving one third heat free as a safety zone.

How to Grill Perfect Chicken Halves and Quarters

Chicken is one of the most popular foods to grill, yet it causes more trouble than just about any other grilled fare. Way too often, people serve birds that are burnt on the outside and raw in the center. It's understandable: A halved or quartered chicken with the skin on presents a twofold challenge.

The first problem is that the fat in the skin melts and causes flare-ups. The second problem is that, because it contains bones, chicken pieces take longer to cook than, say, steaks or burgers. And because of food safety issues, you don't want to eat chicken anything less than well-done.

To cook chicken halves or quarters to perfection, use a two-zone grilling method, which will enable you to control the heat by moving the birds back and forth over hotter and cooler sections of the grill. Here's how.

1. First, season the chicken pieces with salt, pepper, and any other seasonings you plan to use.

2. **If you are using a charcoal grill,** spread the coals out in a single layer over two thirds of the grill, leaving one third of the grill bare to use as a safety zone.

If you are using a gas grill, preheat most of the grill to medium, leaving one burner off to create a heat-free safety zone.

In either case, you are giving yourself plenty of room so you can move the birds around to avoid flare-ups.

3. After brushing and oiling the grill grate, arrange the pieces of chicken, skin side down, on the grate over the hot zone of the grill. Cook the chicken until the skin is crisp and golden brown and the meat is cooked through without any trace of red at the bone, eight to twelve minutes per side, turning with tongs (the total cooking time will be sixteen to twenty-four minutes). When the chicken is done, the juices will run clear when the meat is pierced. If there are flare-ups, move the chicken pieces to the heat-free safety zone until the flames die down.

4. If the recipe calls for basting and you are using an oil- or wine-based marinade, you can brush the chicken continuously. If you are using a sugar-based marinade, start brushing it on the chicken during the last five minutes of grilling.

For the Chickenhearted: Bird Without Flames

You can avoid the risk of flare-ups entirely by grilling halved or quartered chickens using the indirect method. Set up the grill for indirect grilling, place a drip pan in the center, under the grate, and preheat the grill to medium. When you are ready to cook, brush and oil the grill grate. Place the chicken pieces, skin side down, on the hot grate, over the drip pan. Cover the grill and cook the chicken until the juices run clear, about forty minutes for half birds, thirty to forty minutes for chicken quarters. In general, breast pieces require less cooking time than leg pieces. The advantage of this method is that it's absolutely foolproof; the disadvantage is that the bird will lack the charred flavor you get from cooking over direct flames.

4. When ready to cook, remove the chicken pieces from the marinade, setting aside the marinade. Blot the chicken dry with paper towels and season it generously with salt.

5. Brush and oil the grill grate. Arrange the chicken pieces, skin side down, on the grate over the hot zone of the grill and cook until the skin is golden brown and the meat is cooked through without any trace of red at the bone, 8 to 12 minutes per side. If you get flare-ups, move the chicken to the safety zone until the flames die down. During the first 10 minutes of grilling only, brush the chicken several times with the reserved marinade.

6. Transfer the chicken pieces to serving plates and serve.

INDONESIA

BALINESE GRILLED CHICKEN WITH APPLE-MACADAMIA SAUCE

DIRECT GRILLING
SERVES 4

I first tasted this sweet-spicy grilled chicken at the Amandari resort in Ubud, Bali. It was so good I all but ate the bones. Amandari is a luxurious hotel perched on the top tier of a rice paddy. You can stroll out onto your terrace and observe a method of agriculture that's as ageless as Bali itself.

The original recipe calls for wonderful-sounding exotic ingredients, including candlenuts and kencur (lesser galangal). To make the recipe more user-friendly, I've substituted macadamia nuts and ginger, but if you can find candlenuts and kencur, by all means use them. To make the recipe more health conscious, I've substituted vegetable oil for the original coconut oil. Tamarind Water is exotic, but it's easy to prepare. Balsamic vinegar makes a readily available substitute. Serve the chicken with Balinese Yellow Rice (page 430).

ADVANCE PREPARATION

4 to 12 hours for marinating the chicken

FOR THE CHICKEN AND MARINADE

- ½ cup Tamarind Water (page 241), or ¼ cup balsamic vinegar
- 2 tablespoons vegetable oil
- 2 cloves garlic, minced
- 1 teaspoon salt
- ½ teaspoon freshly ground black pepper
- 1 chicken (3½ to 4 pounds), quartered, or 4 bone-in chicken breast halves with skin

FOR THE APPLE-MACADAMIA SAUCE

- 2 tablespoons vegetable oil
- 2 shallots, minced
- 2 cloves garlic, minced
- 1 to 2 fresh hot red chiles, seeded and minced (for a hotter sauce, leave the seeds in)
- 1 tablespoon minced peeled fresh ginger
- ½ teaspoon ground turmeric
- 5 macadamia nuts, coarsely chopped
- 1 large Granny Smith apple, peeled, cored, and finely chopped
- 1 cup homemade chicken stock or canned low-sodium chicken broth
- 2 teaspoons Asian fish sauce or soy sauce, or more to taste
- 1 teaspoon fresh lime juice, or more to taste
- Salt and freshly ground black pepper

1. Prepare the chicken and marinade: Combine the Tamarind Water, 2 tablespoons of oil, 2 cloves of garlic, 1 teaspoon of salt, and ½ teaspoon of pepper in a nonreactive bowl large enough to hold the chicken and whisk to mix.

2. Rinse the chicken pieces under cold running water, then drain and blot dry with paper towels. Add the chicken to the marinade and turn to coat. Let the chicken marinate in the refrigerator, covered, for 4 to 12 hours.

3. Make the apple-macadamia sauce: Heat the 2 tablespoons of oil in a medium-size nonreactive saucepan over medium heat. Add the shallots, 2 cloves of garlic, and the chile(s) and ginger and cook until lightly browned, about 4 minutes. Stir in the turmeric, macadamia nuts, and apple and cook until the apple is soft, 3 to 5 minutes. Add the chicken stock, fish sauce, and lime juice and bring to a boil. Let boil, uncovered, for 3 minutes, stirring occasionally.

4. Transfer the sauce to a food processor or blender and process to a smooth puree. Return the sauce to the pan and let simmer, uncovered, over low heat until thick and richly flavored, 3 to 5 minutes. Remove the sauce from the heat and taste for seasoning, adding salt and pepper and more fish sauce and/or lime juice as necessary; the sauce should be highly seasoned. Keep the sauce warm, covered. It can be prepared up to 48 hours ahead of time and refrigerated, covered. Reheat before serving.

5. Set up the grill for two-zone direct grilling (see page 18), preheating two thirds of the grill to medium and leaving one third heat free as a safety zone.

6. When ready to cook, brush and oil the grill grate. Remove the chicken pieces from the marinade and discard the marinade. Arrange the chicken pieces, skin side down, on the grate over the hot zone of the grill and cook until the skin is golden brown and the meat is cooked through without any trace of red at the bone, 8 to 12 minutes per side. If you get flare-ups, move the pieces of chicken to the safety zone until the flames have died down.

7. Transfer the chicken pieces to serving plates or a platter, spoon the sauce over them, and serve.

BARBADOS

BAXTER ROAD GRILLED CHICKEN

DIRECT GRILLING
SERVES 4

Foodies of a certain age may remember Baxter Road of the old days—back when it was a rough-and-tumble row of cook stalls that sprung up nightly along an equally rough-and-tumble street on the outskirts of Bridgetown, Barbados. This chicken owes its exceptional succulence and flavor to Barbados's national marinade, which is called, simply, seasonin'. A tangy paste based on garlic, chives, peppers, and thyme, seasonin' is considerably—and mercifully—milder than Jamaican jerk, which makes it ideal for people who can't stand chile hellfire.

ADVANCE PREPARATION

4 to 12 hours for marinating the chicken

INGREDIENTS

1 chicken (3½ to 4 pounds), quartered
4 cloves garlic, peeled
3 shallots, coarsely chopped
1 bunch of chives or scallions, both white and green parts, trimmed
1 medium-size green bell pepper, cored, seeded, and coarsely chopped
1 medium-size rib celery, coarsely chopped
1 Scotch bonnet chile, or 2 jalapeño peppers, seeded and minced (for a hotter marinade, leave the seeds in)
3 tablespoons chopped fresh flat-leaf parsley
2 teaspoons chopped fresh thyme, or 1 teaspoon dried thyme
2 tablespoons fresh lime juice, or more to taste
2 tablespoons soy sauce
2 tablespoons extra-virgin olive oil
Salt and freshly ground black pepper

1. Rinse the chicken pieces under cold running water, then drain and blot dry with paper towels. Place the chicken in a large nonreactive bowl or baking dish and set aside while you prepare the marinade.

2. Combine the garlic, shallots, chives, bell pepper, celery, Scotch bonnet, parsley, and thyme in a food processor and process to a smooth paste. Add the lime juice, soy sauce, and olive oil and process until blended and smooth. Taste for seasoning, adding salt, black pepper, and/or more lime juice as necessary; the mixture should be highly seasoned. Pour the marinade over the chicken and turn the pieces to coat. Let the chicken marinate in the refrigerator, covered, for 4 to 12 hours (the longer the better).

3. Set up the grill for two-zone direct grilling (see page 000), preheating two thirds of the grill to medium and leaving one third heat free as a safety zone.

4. When ready to cook, brush and oil the grill grate. Remove the chicken pieces from the bowl, setting aside the marinade. Arrange the chicken, skin side down, on the grate over the hot zone of the grill and cook until the skin is golden brown and the meat is cooked through without any trace of red at the bone, 8 to 12 minutes per side. If you get flare-ups, move the chicken to the safety zone until the flames die down. During the first 10 minutes of grilling only, brush the chicken once or twice with the reserved marinade.

5. Transfer the chicken pieces to serving plates or a platter and serve.

GUADELOUPE

BUCCANEER CHICKEN

POULET BOUCANEE

INDIRECT GRILLING
SERVES 8

When the Europeans first came to the wilds of Hispaniola, they observed a singular style of cooking. The Carib Indians would cure wild boar and other game with salt and spices, then dry it over a smoky fire. The Carib word for this technique sounded to European ears like *boucan.* As for the first Europeans to practice this style of cooking, they were shipwrecked sailors and religious iconoclasts who hid out in the wilds of what is now northwestern Haiti. They became known as the buccaneers. *Poulet boucanée* (buccaneer-style chicken) remains popular in the French West Indies.

The recipe may seem a little involved, but actually it's a series of simple steps. The only tricky part will be finding sugarcane, and thanks to exotic produce companies, like Frieda's, fresh cane can be found at many supermarkets and specialty produce shops. Other good outlets include Hispanic and Asian markets.

The recipe is designed for a charcoal or gas barbecue grill. If you have a smoker, you can smoke the chicken in it, using sugarcane instead of wood chips. For any type of cooker, if you can't find sugarcane, use the chips.

ADVANCE PREPARATION

24 hours for marinating the chicken

SPECIAL EQUIPMENT

1 pound fresh sugarcane, split lengthwise, or 1½ cups hardwood chips or chunks, soaked for 1 hour in cold water to cover and drained

INGREDIENTS

- **2 chickens (each 3½ to 4 pounds), quartered**
- **3 limes**
- **8 cloves garlic, peeled and crushed**
- **1 bunch scallions, both white and green parts, trimmed and coarsely chopped**
- **1 small onion, finely chopped**
- **½ cup chopped fresh flat-leaf parsley**
- **1 to 3 Scotch bonnet chiles or other hot peppers, seeded and thinly sliced (for a hotter marinade, leave the seeds in)**
- **1 tablespoon chopped fresh thyme, or 1½ teaspoons dried thyme**
- **1 tablespoon whole cloves**
- **2 teaspoons black peppercorns**
- **2 teaspoons allspice berries**
- **1 cinnamon stick (3 inches long)**
- **1 whole nutmeg**
- **1 cup dark rum**
- **1 tablespoon red wine vinegar**
- **3 tablespoons salt**
- **2 tablespoons brown sugar**

1. Rinse the chicken pieces under cold running water, then drain and blot dry with paper towels. Set aside while you prepare the marinade.

2. Cut the limes in half and squeeze the juice into a large nonreactive bowl. Toss in the lime rinds, then add the garlic, scallions, onion, parsley, Scotch bonnets, thyme, cloves, peppercorns, allspice berries, cinnamon stick, nutmeg, rum, wine vinegar, salt, brown sugar, and 6 cups of water and stir until the salt and sugar dissolve. Add the chicken pieces and turn to coat with the marinade. Let the chicken marinate in the refrigerator, covered, for 24 hours.

3. Set up the grill for indirect grilling and place a drip pan in the center.

If using a gas grill, place the sugarcane in the smoker box and preheat the grill to high; when smoke appears, reduce the heat to medium.

If using a charcoal grill, preheat it to medium.

4. When ready to cook, if using charcoal, toss all of the sugarcane on the coals. Remove the chicken pieces from the marinade, discarding the marinade, and blot the chicken dry.

5. Brush and oil the grill grate. Arrange the chicken pieces, skin side down, on the hot grate over the drip pan and cover the grill. Cook the chicken until the juices run clear when the tip of a skewer or sharp knife is inserted in the thickest part of a thigh and the breast meat near the bone shows no trace of pink, 1 to 1½ hours (see Note). If using a charcoal grill, you'll need to add 10 to 12 fresh coals to each side after 1 hour.

6. Transfer the chicken to serving plates or a platter and serve or refrigerate it, covered, to serve cold later.

NOTE: Because the chicken is smoked rather than grilled, the meat near the joints may remain a little pink, even when the chicken is fully cooked.

INDIA

TANDOORI CHICKEN

TANDOORI MURGH

DIRECT GRILLING
SERVES 4

Tandoori chicken is the most popular of all Indian barbecue dishes—exquisite to eat by itself and a starting point for many more sophisticated dishes, including Grilled Chicken Salad with Indian Spices (page 104). The bird owes its extraordinary moistness, tenderness, and flavor to a double marinade—first a tenderizing bath of lemon juice and cayenne pepper, then a flavorful paste made with yogurt, saffron, garlic, and ginger.

If you have the time to drain the yogurt, as called for in Step 1, you'll get a richer tandoori. If you're in a hurry, use one cup undrained yogurt. I've given a range for the cayenne: one teaspoon will give you gently spicy tandoori; three teaspoons will produce a bird that bites back. I've made the orange food coloring optional, but most Indian chefs would use it. This recipe calls for a cut up whole chicken, but you could certainly make chicken tandoori with boneless breasts. For those, cut the marinating times in half and cook as directed on page 277.

Serve the chicken with naan (Tandoori-Baked Flat Breads, page 131), Quick-Cook Basmati Rice (page 424), and Coriander Sauce (page 482).

ADVANCE PREPARATION

4 hours for making the yogurt cheese (optional), plus 4 hours for marinating the chicken

SPECIAL EQUIPMENT

2 or 3 long metal skewers

FOR THE YOGURT MARINADE

1½ cups plain whole-milk yogurt
¼ teaspoon saffron threads
5 cloves garlic, sliced
1 piece peeled fresh ginger (2 inches), sliced
1 teaspoon salt
½ teaspoon freshly ground black pepper
½ cup heavy (whipping) cream or sour cream
1 teaspoon Quick Garam Masala (page 496)
1 to 2 drops orange food coloring (optional)

FOR THE CHICKEN

1 chicken (3½ to 4 pounds), cut into 8 pieces (see The American Cut, page 268)
1 to 3 teaspoons cayenne pepper
1½ teaspoons salt
½ teaspoon freshly ground black pepper
½ cup fresh lemon juice
3 tablespoons unsalted butter, melted

1. Make the yogurt marinade: Set a yogurt strainer, or regular strainer lined with a double layer of dampened cheesecloth, over a bowl. Add the yogurt to the strainer and let drain, in the refrigerator, until a firm "cheese" forms, about 4 hours.

2. When ready to finish making the marinade, place the saffron in a small bowl and grind it to a fine powder with a pestle or the end of a wooden spoon. Stir in 3 tablespoons warm water and let stand for 2 minutes. Combine the saffron mixture with the garlic and ginger in a food processor or blender and process to a smooth paste, adding more water if necessary.

3. Discard the liquid from the drained yogurt. Transfer the yogurt to a large bowl and stir in the saffron mixture, the 1 teaspoon of salt, ½ teaspoon of black pepper, and the cream and garam masala until thoroughly blended and smooth. If desired, stir in enough food coloring to create the desired tint. Refrigerate the marinade.

4. Prepare the chicken: Rinse the chicken pieces under cold running water and remove and discard the skin. Then drain and blot dry the chicken with paper towels. Make 2 deep slashes, to the bone, in the fleshy side of each piece of chicken. Place the chicken in a nonreactive baking dish large enough to hold the pieces in a single layer. Combine the cayenne, 1½ teaspoons of salt, and ½ teaspoon of black pepper in a small bowl, then sprinkle the mixture over the chicken, rubbing it in thoroughly with your fingers, making sure it gets into the slashes. Add the lemon juice and turn the chicken pieces to coat. Let the chicken marinate, at room temperature, for 15 minutes.

5. Drain the chicken and add it to the yogurt marinade, stirring to coat the pieces completely. Let the chicken marinate in the refrigerator, covered, for 4 hours, stirring occasionally.

HOW TO CUT UP A CHICKEN

Many recipes in this book call for cut-up chickens. Sure, you can buy chicken pieces, but it's handy to know how to cut up a whole chicken yourself. Here are instructions for my version of the American cut, which leaves a piece of breast meat attached to each wing, for a more equitable division of the chicken, and the French cut, which isn't available commercially. The American cut gives you eight pieces of chicken in addition to the backbone (save that for making stock). The French cut produces four pieces, including two *suprêmes*—boneless half breasts with the first joint of the wing attached. For best results, use good-quality knives with sharp edges.

The American Cut

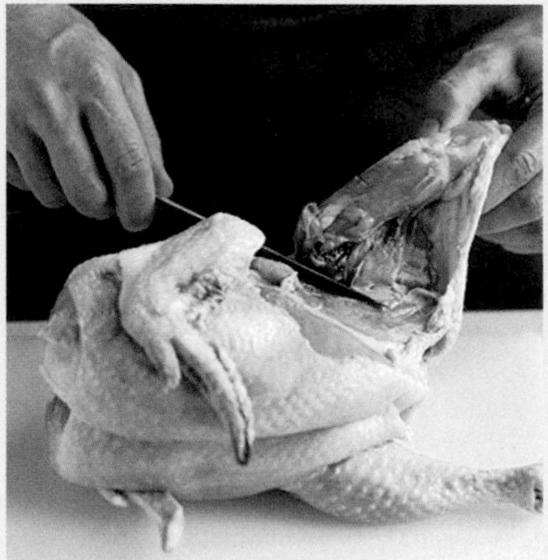

1. *Place the chicken on its side and pull the top leg away from the body. Slicing between that leg and the carcass, make a cut to the joint connecting the thigh to the bird's body.*

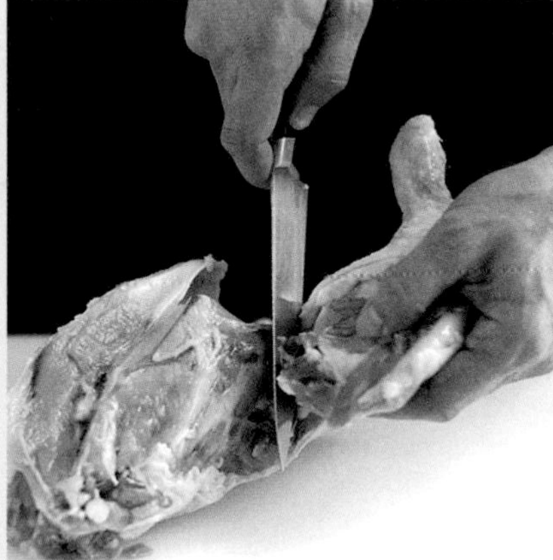

2. *When you get to the joint, pop the thigh bone out of the hip socket and continue cutting to remove the leg. Repeat with the second leg.*

3. *Cut each leg in half through the "knee" joint, following the yellow line of fat to separate the leg into thigh and drumstick.*

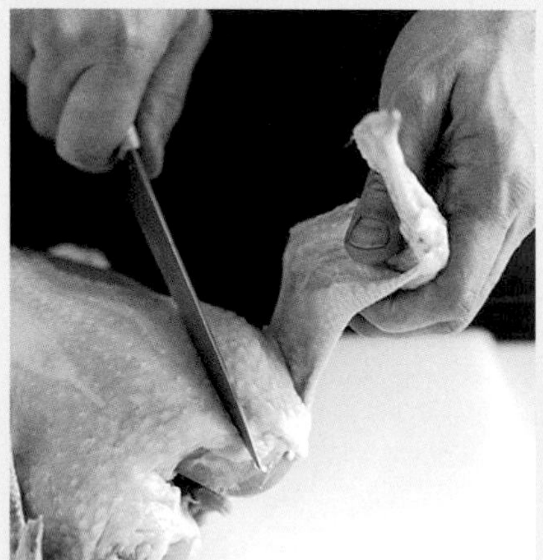

4. *Place the chicken breast side up. Make a downward diagonal cut to remove the wing on each side; include a two-inch piece of breast meat with each wing.*

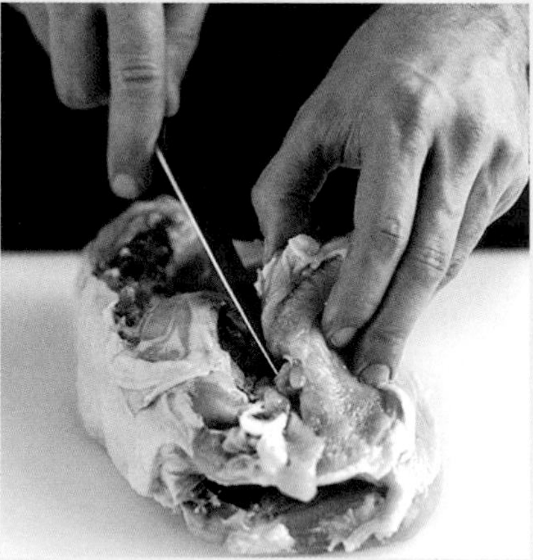

5. *Cut the breast section off the backbone, following the yellow line of fat that runs between the wing joint and the bottom of the rib cage.*

6. *Cut the breast section in half through the breastbone. You will have eight pieces of chicken (plus the backbone), each about the same size.*

The French Cut

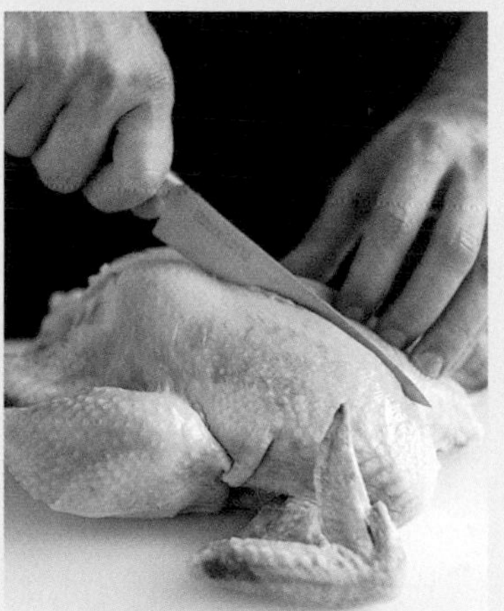

1. ***Place the chicken breast side up. Starting at the neck end, make a lengthwise cut through the meat along one side of the breastbone, keeping the knife pressed against the rib cage as you cut down through the carcass.***

2. ***When the knife reaches the wing, cut through the joint, leaving the wing attached to the breast meat so you remove a breast half and wing in a single piece. Repeat on the other side.***

3. ***Cut the two end sections off each wing, leaving only the mini "drumstick" attached to the breast. Then cut the legs off the carcass as depicted in photos 1 and 2 of the American cut; leave the drumsticks attached to the thighs. You will have four pieces of chicken, plus the carcass.***

6. Remove the chicken from the marinade and discard the marinade. Thread the chicken onto skewers, leaving 1 inch between each piece to allow for better heat circulation.

7. Set up the grill for direct grilling and preheat to high.

8. When ready to cook, brush and oil the grill grate, then arrange the skewers on the hot grate. Grill the chicken, turning with tongs, until browned but not fully cooked, about 4 minutes per side (8 minutes in all). Transfer the skewers to a large platter (see Note). Brush the chicken pieces generously on all sides with the melted butter and return the skewers to the grate. Grill the chicken until it is nicely charred on the outside and the juices run clear when the tip of a skewer or sharp knife is inserted in the thickest part of a thigh and the breast meat near the bone shows no trace of pink, 2 to 4 more minutes per side (4 to 8 more minutes in all).

9. Unskewer the chicken pieces onto serving plates or a platter and serve.

NOTE: Many Indian chefs cook the chicken ahead of time to this point, finishing it at the last minute to order. If you decide to do this, refrigerate the chicken, covered, if you are going to wait longer than 30 minutes.

BRITISH WEST INDIES

ANGUILLAN ROAST CHICKEN

DIRECT GRILLING
SERVES 4

A tiny island in the British West Indies, Anguilla is located a five-minute plane ride from St. Martin. Its long, low-lying profile inspired Columbus to call it Anguilla, which is the Spanish word for eel. In keeping with the island's small scale, barbecue grills here are made not from fifty-gallon drums, but from empty propane tanks that are cut in half and propped up on spidery welded legs. The following recipe was inspired by a fine Anguillan cook, octogenarian Allyne Hazel Guichard, mother of the catering director of the stunning Cap Juluca resort.

Allyne cooks her chicken Anguillan style, over sea grape wood. To achieve a similar smoke flavor, I like to toss a cup of soaked and drained apple, cherry, or maple wood chips on the coals. Smoke flavor, combined with a rum and Scotch bonnet chile based marinade and hot sauce, conspire to make this one of the tastiest chicken preparations in the Caribbean. Serve the chicken with Bahamian Peas and Rice (page 431).

ADVANCE PREPARATION

12 hours for marinating the chicken

SPECIAL EQUIPMENT

1½ cups wood chips or chunks of choice, soaked for 1 hour in cold water to cover and drained

INGREDIENTS

- **1 chicken (3½ to 4 pounds), cut into 8 pieces (see The American Cut, page 268)**
- **1 bunch scallions, both white and green parts, trimmed and coarsely chopped**
- **1 shallot, coarsely chopped**
- **4 cloves garlic, coarsely chopped**
- **1 small onion, coarsely chopped**
- **½ to 2 Scotch bonnet chiles, seeded and chopped (for a hotter seasoning, leave the seeds in)**
- **2 teaspoons salt, or more to taste**
- **2 teaspoons chopped fresh thyme, or 1 teaspoon dried thyme**
- **½ teaspoon freshly ground black pepper**
- **2 bay leaves, crumbled**
- **½ cup extra-virgin olive oil**
- **¼ cup rum, preferably 151 proof**
- **Anguillan Barbecue Sauce (recipe follows)**

1. Rinse the chicken pieces under cold running water, then drain and blot dry with paper towels. Place the chicken in a large nonreactive bowl. Combine the scallions, shallot, garlic, onion, Scotch bonnets, salt, thyme, pepper, and bay leaves in a food processor and process to a coarse paste. Add the olive oil and rum and process until blended and smooth. Taste for seasoning, adding more salt as necessary; the mixture should be highly seasoned. Pour the marinade over the chicken and turn the pieces to coat thoroughly. Let the chicken marinate in the refrigerator, covered, for 12 hours.

2. Set up the grill for two-zone direct grilling (see page 18).

If using a gas grill, place all of the wood chips in the smoker box and preheat two thirds of the grill to high; when smoke appears, reduce the heat to medium. Leave one third of the grill heat free as a safety zone.

If using a charcoal grill, preheat two thirds of the grill to medium and leave one third heat free as a safety zone.

3. When ready to cook, if using a charcoal grill, toss all of the wood chips on the coals. Brush and oil the grill grate. Remove the chicken pieces from the marinade and discard the marinade. Arrange the chicken, skin side down, on the grate over the hot zone of the grill and cook until the skin is golden brown and the meat is cooked through without any trace of red at the bone, 8 to 12 minutes per side. If you get flare-ups, move the chicken to the safety zone until the flames die down. During the last 5 minutes of cooking, brush the chicken with a small amount of the Anguillan Barbecue Sauce.

4. Transfer the chicken to a serving platter and serve with the remaining Anguillan Barbecue Sauce on the side.

ANGUILLAN BARBECUE SAUCE

MAKES 3 TO 4 CUPS

Here's a barbecue sauce bursting with island flavor. Half of a Scotch bonnet chile will give you a gentle heat; culinary pyromaniacs can certainly leave the seeds in or add more chiles. This makes much more barbecue sauce than you need for a single chicken. It keeps well in the refrigerator.

- **3 tablespoons extra-virgin olive oil**
- **1 medium-size onion, finely chopped**
- **2 cloves garlic, minced**
- **½ to 2 Scotch bonnet chiles, seeded and minced**
- **3 pounds ripe tomatoes, peeled and seeded (see box, page 454), then chopped**
- **¼ cup tomato paste**
- **¼ cup commercial barbecue sauce**
- **2 tablespoons Anguillan or other Caribbean hot sauce**
- **¼ cup cider vinegar, or more as needed**
- **¼ cup firmly packed dark brown sugar, or more as needed**
- **¼ cup dark rum**
- **1 teaspoon dried oregano**
- **1 teaspoon chopped fresh thyme, or ½ teaspoon dried thyme**
- **Salt and freshly ground black pepper**

ANGUILLAN ROAST CHICKEN | PAGE 269

1. Heat the olive oil in a large saucepan over medium heat. Add the onion, garlic, and Scotch bonnets and cook until just beginning to brown, about 5 minutes. Stir in the tomatoes and cook until most of the liquid has evaporated, 5 to 7 minutes.

2. Stir in the tomato paste, barbecue sauce, hot sauce, vinegar, brown sugar, rum, oregano, thyme, and ¼ cup of water. Season with salt and pepper to taste, then bring to a boil, stirring to dissolve the sugar. Reduce the heat to low and let the sauce simmer, uncovered, until thick and richly flavored, 20 to 30 minutes, stirring occasionally.

3. Remove the sauce from the heat and taste for seasoning, adding more vinegar, brown sugar, or salt as necessary; the sauce should be highly seasoned. Add more water if the sauce seems too thick. The sauce can be refrigerated, covered, for 2 to 3 weeks.

Bombay Tikka "Taco"

The Bademyia food stall also serves a version of chicken tikka that uses the seasoning paste from the recipe for Chile-Coriander Chicken on page 275. To make it, use 1½ pounds of skinless, boneless chicken breasts cut into two-inch squares. Prepare the seasoning paste as directed in Step 2 of the Chile-Coriander Chicken recipe. Place the chicken pieces in a baking dish, then spread the seasoning paste over them. Let the chicken marinate in the refrigerator, covered, for one to two hours.

Preheat the grill to high, and when ready to cook, thread the chicken pieces on four long metal skewers, dividing them evenly. Brush and oil the grill grate. Grill the chicken until nicely browned and cooked through, three to five minutes per side. To serve, heat four flour tortillas or lavash on the grill until they are soft and pliable, about thirty seconds per side. Unskewer the chicken onto the tortillas or lavash and top each serving with sliced red onion and drizzles of Coriander Sauce (page 482) and Tamarind Dipping Sauce (page 487). Roll the tortillas up tightly to eat. Serves four.

PAKISTAN

SEA CAPTAIN'S CHICKEN TIKKA

DIRECT GRILLING
SERVES 4

This recipe demonstrates the ambassadorial powers of barbecue. I got it from a Pakistani sea captain, one Mushtaque Ahmad, whom I met on a Singapore Airlines flight from Singapore to Bangkok. (The captain was on his way home to Karachi after seven months at sea.) Our conversation began about the O. J. Simpson trial—the first one—and eventually led to cooking. Here's how the captain prepares a spicy, yogurt-marinated Pakistani favorite: chicken tikka.

ADVANCE PREPARATION

6 to 12 hours for marinating the chicken

INGREDIENTS

1 chicken (3½ to 4 pounds), cut into 8 pieces (see The American Cut, page 268)
Salt
3 whole cardamom pods
3 cloves garlic, coarsely chopped
3 tablespoons finely chopped peeled fresh ginger
1 cup plain whole-milk yogurt
3 tablespoons fresh lemon juice
1 teaspoon freshly ground black pepper
½ to 1 teaspoon cayenne pepper
1 to 2 drops orange food coloring (optional)
1 onion, thinly sliced lengthwise, for serving

1. Rinse the chicken pieces under cold running water and remove and discard the skin. Then drain and blot dry the chicken with paper towels. Place the chicken pieces in a large nonreactive bowl. Sprinkle 1 teaspoon salt over the chicken and toss to mix. Let stand for 5 minutes.

2. Meanwhile, crush the cardamom pods in a mortar with a pestle, then add the garlic and ginger and pound to a coarse paste. If you don't have a mortar and pestle, combine all these ingredients in a mini chopper or spice mill and process to a coarse paste. Transfer the cardamom mixture to a small bowl and stir in the yogurt, lemon juice, black pepper, and cayenne. Season the marinade with salt to taste. If desired, stir in enough food coloring to create the desired tint. Pour the marinade over the chicken and turn the pieces to coat. Let the chicken marinate in the refrigerator, covered, for 6 to 12 hours (the longer the better).

3. Set up the grill for direct grilling and preheat to medium-high.

4. When ready to cook, brush and oil the grill grate. Remove the chicken pieces from the marinade and discard the marinade. Arrange the chicken pieces on the hot grate. Grill, turning with tongs, until nicely browned and the juices run clear when the tip of a skewer or sharp knife is inserted in the thickest part of a thigh and the breast meat near the bone shows no trace of pink, 6 to 8 minutes per side.

5. Transfer the chicken to serving plates or a platter and serve topped with the sliced onion.

IRAN

GRILLED CHICKEN WITH SAFFRON

JOOJEH KEBAB

DIRECT GRILLING
SERVES 8

This will be one of the easiest and tastiest recipes you will ever prepare. The yogurt and lemon juice tenderize the chicken, while the saffron perfumes the flavor. In an Iranian restaurant, the chicken would be cooked kebab style on skewers, breast pieces on one skewer, thighs on another, drumsticks on a third, and so on. This allows the chef to cook each part for the exact amount of time it needs. There is no reason why you couldn't do that with this recipe if it makes things easier for you. Serve the chicken with lavash and Central Asian Pickles (page 441).

ADVANCE PREPARATION

24 hours for marinating the chicken

FOR THE CHICKEN AND MARINADE

½ teaspoon saffron threads
1½ cups plain whole-milk yogurt
1 large onion, finely chopped (about 2 cups)
½ cup fresh lemon juice
2 teaspoons salt
1 teaspoon freshly ground black pepper
2 chickens (3½ to 4 pounds each), each cut into 8 pieces (see The American Cut, page 268)

FOR THE BASTING MIXTURE

¼ teaspoon saffron threads
1 tablespoon fresh lemon juice
3 tablespoons unsalted butter
Salt and freshly ground black pepper

1. Prepare the chicken and marinade: Place the ½ teaspoon of saffron in a medium-size bowl and grind to a fine powder with a pestle or the end of a wooden spoon. Add 1 tablespoon of warm water, stir, and let stand for 5 minutes, then stir in the yogurt, onion, ½ cup of lemon juice, and the salt and pepper.

2. Rinse the chicken pieces under cold running water, then drain and blot dry with paper towels. Place the chicken in a very large nonreactive bowl or baking dish and pour the marinade over them, turning the pieces to coat thoroughly. Let the chicken marinate in the refrigerator, covered, for 24 hours, turning the pieces occasionally.

3. Make the basting mixture: Place the ¼ teaspoon of saffron in a small bowl and grind to a fine powder with a pestle or the end of a wooden spoon. Stir in the 1 tablespoon of lemon juice and let stand for 5 minutes. Melt the butter in a small saucepan over low heat, then remove from the heat and stir in the saffron and lemon juice mixture.

4. Set up the grill for two-zone direct grilling (see page 18), preheating two thirds of the grill to medium and leaving one third heat free as a safety zone.

5. When ready to cook, brush and oil the grill grate. Remove the chicken pieces from the marinade and discard the marinade. Arrange the chicken, skin side down, on the grate over the hot zone of the grill and cook until the skin is golden brown and the meat is cooked through without any trace of red at the bone, 8 to 12 minutes per side. Brush the chicken with the basting mixture once or

The Splendid Restaurant Karim

A trip to the famous restaurant Karim in New Delhi, India, will take you through a National Geographic–esque warren of narrow lanes teeming with veiled women and white-robed men, noisy street merchants and swarming beggars, wandering cows and nose-tweaking aromas. The lanes are too narrow for a taxi to take you directly to the restaurant, but a squadron of turbaned *sieks* in red livery, positioned every thirty yards, will guide you. After a short walk, you arrive at the last place you'd expect to find in this colorful neighborhood: a proper restaurant with air conditioning, wood paneling, coffered ceilings, and nattily set, tableclothed tables.

Karim's founder was Hazi Karimuddin ("Karim" was his nickname), scion of a long line of royal chefs and chef himself to one of the region's last kings, Bahadur Shah Zafar. Like the chefs of the Ancienne Régime in France, Karim found himself unemployed when changing socioeconomic conditions forced the closure of the palace kitchen. So in 1913 he opened a restaurant in the shadow of the Jamma Masjid, a mosque outside the walls of the Red Fort.

The original Karim's still stands in the courtyard of a small building. Over the years half a dozen dining rooms have been added, including one where men can dine with their families (the bulk of the clientele is male). We're in Muslim territory now, and I was reminded of this by the sight of Karim's great-grandson (also a chef), who wore a white skull cap and sat cross-legged before a bank of pots simmering over charcoal, like a potentate surveying his fiefdom. As in most Muslim neighborhoods, the restaurant doesn't get busy until after sundown.

The original Karim's specializes in the butter- and cream-enriched stews of the Moguls. Indeed, there's only one grilled meat on the menu: *seekh kebab.* You can watch these ground lamb kebabs being cooked on rectangular metal braziers over charcoal that an electric fan blows to bright red. What comes off these heavy skewers is a sort of tube-shaped sausage that's perfumed with spices, extraordinarily succulent, and in its own way fully as splendid as the famous mosque.

In 1970, the family opened a second restaurant in another colorful Muslim neighborhood, Nizamuddin. Endowed with a larger kitchen and fancier dining room, the Nizamuddin Karim offers a wider selection of grilled dishes, including *tandoori bakra,* a whole goat stuffed with dried fruits, hard-cooked eggs, and a basmati rice preparation called *biryanl.* I succumbed to *tandoori barra* (lamb ribs), *seekh kebab,* and an astonishing variety of grilled breads. But the one dish I still dream about is Karim's Afghani *murgh,* Afghan-style chicken, and to try to get the recipe, I asked for a tour of the kitchen.

The good news is that the food prep area here was as immaculate as the dining room (not always the case in this part of the world). The cooks wore gray jumpsuits, which made them look a little like convicts. Two sat barefoot and cross-legged before a pair of giant tandoors, where the meats and breads were cooked. Marinades were mixed in flat metal pans on a floor clean enough to eat off of.

The bad news is that the family keeps tight wraps on its recipes—to the point where the spice mixes used to flavor the lamb marinades are blended at a separate location. So not even the chef knows the full recipe. In the *murgh,* I was able to detect the tangy presence of yogurt cheese and lemon juice, with a generous dose of pureed garlic and ginger. A taste of the marinade also revealed the heat of cayenne and the pungency of cumin. Curiously, the overall effect reminded me of Hungarian liptauer cheese. You'll find my way of duplicating the results on page 276.

twice as it cooks, watching to see that it doesn't burn. Season the chicken with salt and pepper to taste. If you get flare-ups, move the chicken to the safety zone until the flames die down.

6. Transfer the chicken pieces to serving plates or a platter and serve.

INDIA

BADEMIYA'S JUSTLY FAMOUS CHILE-CORIANDER CHICKEN

DIRECT GRILLING
SERVES 4

The Taj Mahal hotel is the most famous hotel in Bombay. But for me the real attraction of the neighborhood is a food stall called Bademiya, located on tiny Tulloch Road behind the venerable Taj. Founded by Muhammad Yaseen in the 1940s and now run by his jean- and Nike-clad son Jamal, this sidewalk eatery attracts Bombay barbecue buffs of all castes and classes for its fiery grilled chicken, meltingly succulent *seekh* (minced lamb) kebabs, and grilled lamb's udder. (The last tastes like chewy liver and is for adventurous eaters only.)

The original version of the chicken dish is hot, hot, hot. For the full effect, use an entire tablespoon of cayenne. For a milder but highly flavorful rendition, use one to two teaspoons of cayenne, or substitute hot paprika, which isn't quite as fiery. To round out your meal at Bademiya, two fulltime bakers work nonstop tossing paper-thin disks of dough onto charcoal-fired metal domes to make freshly cooked *ruoomali* ("handkerchief" bread). Because these are difficult to make, I suggest serving this chicken with either of two thoroughly non-Indian but definitely satisfactory alternatives, flour tortillas or lavash. Afghan Coriander Sauce (page 482) and Tamarind Dipping Sauce (page 487) make great accompaniments.

ADVANCE PREPARATION

4 to 6 hours for marinating the chicken

INGREDIENTS

4 whole chicken legs (thigh and drumstick), or 1 chicken (3½ to 4 pounds), quartered
1½ tablespoons coriander seeds
2 teaspoons whole black peppercorns
1 teaspoon cumin seeds
6 cloves garlic, peeled
1 piece (2 inches) peeled fresh ginger, thinly sliced
3 tablespoons vegetable oil
2 tablespoons fresh lemon juice
1 teaspoon to 1 tablespoon cayenne pepper
1½ teaspoons salt
½ cup chopped fresh cilantro
Thinly sliced red onion, for garnish
Wedges of limes or lemons, for garnish

1. Remove and discard the skin from the chicken. Rinse the chicken under cold running water and drain and blot dry with paper towels. Place the chicken in a baking dish large enough to hold it in a single layer and set aside while you prepare the seasoning paste.

2. Heat a dry skillet over medium heat (do not use a nonstick skillet for this) and add the coriander seeds, peppercorns, and cumin seeds. Toast the spices until fragrant, 2 to 3 minutes, shaking the skillet occasionally. Let the spices cool, then transfer them to a spice mill and grind to a fine powder. Combine the ground spices in a food processor or blender with the garlic, ginger, oil, lemon juice, cayenne, salt, and ¼ cup of water. Process to a smooth paste, adding more water if necessary to obtain a pourable consistency. Add the cilantro and process just to mix.

3. Using your fingers, spread the seasoning paste over the chicken, coating it all over. Let the chicken marinate in the refrigerator, covered, for 4 to 6 hours.

4. Set up the grill for direct grilling and preheat to medium.

5. When ready to cook, brush and oil the grill grate. Arrange the chicken on the hot grate. Grill, turning with tongs, until the juices run clear when the tip of the skewer or sharp knife is inserted in the thickest part of a thigh, 8 to 10 minutes per side (16 to 20 minutes in all).

6. Transfer the chicken to serving plates or a platter and serve at once, garnished with sliced red onion and lime or lemon wedges.

INDIA

AFGHAN-STYLE CHICKEN

DIRECT GRILLING
SERVES 6

Despite its name, this recipe comes from India, not Afghanistan (although it may have originated in the latter country). It's the specialty of New Delhi's famous Karim restaurant. In the eighteenth and nineteenth centuries, the borders of the countries we now know as Afghanistan, Pakistan, and India were considerably more fluid. Recipes and culinary philosophies traveled with merchandise and politics along a trade route known as the Silk Road. So it's not surprising to find Karim's chefs serving a yogurt and chile marinade characteristic of Afghanistan—it is an electrifying paste of flavors. Hopefully you'll experience the restaurant's slogan when you taste it: Secret of good mood [sic] Taste Karim's food!

ADVANCE PREPARATION

4 to 6 hours for making the yogurt cheese, plus 4 to 6 hours for marinating the chicken

FOR THE CHICKEN AND MARINADE

3 cups plain whole-milk yogurt
6 cloves garlic, minced
2 tablespoons grated peeled fresh ginger
1 small onion, minced
3 tablespoons fresh lemon juice
½ to 1 tablespoon cayenne pepper
1½ teaspoons salt
1 teaspoon freshly ground black pepper
1 teaspoon cumin seeds, toasted (see box, page 113)
6 chicken legs (2 to 2½ pounds total), cut into drumsticks and thigh sections

FOR SERVING

Sliced red onion
Sliced tomato
Sliced cucumber
Sliced radishes
Lemon wedges

1. Prepare the chicken and marinade: Set a yogurt strainer, or regular strainer lined with a double layer of dampened cheesecloth, over a bowl. Add the yogurt to the strainer and let drain, in the refrigerator, until a firm "cheese" forms, 4 to 6 hours.

2. Discard the liquid from the drained yogurt (it will be quite thick). Transfer the yogurt to a large nonreactive bowl. Add the garlic, ginger, onion, lemon juice, cayenne, salt, black pepper, and cumin seeds and whisk to blend.

3. Remove and discard the skin from the chicken. Rinse the chicken under cold running water and drain and blot it dry with paper towels. Make 2 or 3 deep slashes, to the bone, in each piece. Add the chicken to the marinade and turn the pieces to coat. Let the chicken marinate in the refrigerator, covered, for 4 to 6 hours.

4. Set up the grill for direct grilling and preheat to medium (for the best results, use charcoal).

5. When ready to grill, brush and oil the grill grate. Remove the chicken from the marinade and discard the marinade. Arrange the chicken on the hot grate. Grill the chicken, turning with tongs, until nicely browned on the outside and the juices run clear when the tip of a skewer or sharp knife is inserted in the thickest part of a drumstick or thigh, 8 to 10 minutes per side (16 to 20 minutes in all).

6. To serve: Transfer the chicken to serving plates or a platter and serve at once, garnished with onion, tomato, cucumber, and radish slices and lemon wedges.

MIDDLE EAST

PALESTINIAN CHICKEN

DIRECT GRILLING
SERVES 4

Yogurt, lemon, and garlic are common seasonings in the Middle East. But the sweet touch of ground cinnamon and cardamom add indicate the Palestinian/Jordanian origin of this dish. The recipe came from a lady grill master from the West Bank. The traditional way to prepare it would be with boneless breast meat on kebabs, but I like to use whole, bone-in chicken breasts (I like the extra flavor the bones add).

Serve the chicken breasts with grilled or fresh pita, rice, and Charred Tomato Sauce with Pomegranate Molasses (page 473).

ADVANCE PREPARATION

4 to 12 hours for marinating the chicken

INGREDIENTS

2 whole, bone-in chicken breasts with skin (12 to 16 ounces each), split in half
1 cup plain whole-milk yogurt
3 tablespoons fresh lemon juice
6 cloves garlic, minced
1 teaspoon salt
½ teaspoon ground cinnamon
½ teaspoon freshly ground black pepper
¼ teaspoon ground cardamom
⅛ teaspoon ground cloves

1. Rinse the chicken breasts under cold running water, then drain and blot dry with paper towels. Place the breasts in a nonreactive baking dish large enough to hold them in a single layer and set aside.

2. Combine the yogurt, lemon juice, garlic, salt, cinnamon, pepper, cardamom, and cloves in a small nonreactive bowl and whisk to blend. Pour the yogurt mixture over the chicken and, using your fingers, spread it over the breasts to cover them completely. Let the chicken marinate, covered, in the refrigerator, for 4 to 12 hours (the longer the better).

3. Set up the grill for two-zone direct grilling (see page 18), preheating two thirds of the grill to medium and leaving one third heat free as a safety zone.

4. When ready to cook, brush and oil the grill grate. Remove the chicken breasts from the marinade and discard the marinade. Arrange the chicken, skin side down, on the grate over the hot zone of the grill and cook until the skin is golden brown and the meat is cooked through without any trace of red at the bone, 8 to 12 minutes per side. If you get flare-ups, move the chicken to the safety zone until the flames die down.

5. Transfer the chicken breasts to serving plates or a platter and serve.

How to Grill Perfect Chicken Breasts

Skinless, boneless breasts are the easiest part of the chicken to grill. Because they're so lean, you don't get the flare-ups associated with whole chicken or chicken legs, and you can grill skinless, boneless breasts directly over high flames. But the lack of fat can also be a drawback: Chicken breasts must be generously basted with oil or melted butter during grilling to keep them from drying out. Here's how to grill chicken breasts so they come out just right.

1. Rinse and drain the chicken breasts under cold running water, then drain and blot them dry.

2. Preheat the grill to high.

3. When ready to cook, brush and oil the grill grate. For extra smoke flavor, toss a few soaked wood chips on the coals, inverted V bars, or lava stones before grilling. Arrange the breasts so that they all go in the same direction on the hot grate. Grill them for two minutes, then using tongs, rotate the breasts 45 degrees and grill them for two to four minutes more; this creates an attractive crosshatch of grill marks.

4. Turn the breasts with tongs and grill the other side, again rotating each breast 45 degrees after two minutes. The total cooking time for a skinless, boneless chicken breast will be four to six minutes per side.

5. Generously baste the breasts with oil, melted butter, or a marinade as they cook. Baste the cooked side only, so you don't cross-contaminate the basting liquid with uncooked chicken juices. If you are using a sugar-based barbecue sauce, apply it only during the last two minutes of grilling on each side.

Uruguay's Mercado del Puerto

"Where's the beef?" asked a popular TV commercial a few years back. Where, indeed! Many people in North America are cutting back on meat consumption or eliminating it entirely. How different life is south of the equator, where meat remains the bedrock of the Latin American diet. This truth became apparent to me the moment I landed in Montevideo, Uruguay.

"Beef is cheaper here than chicken," explained my taxi driver, pointing out the profusion of butcher shops (one every couple blocks) on the way to my hotel. During my stay, the Montevideans I met proudly admitted to eating meat between ten and twelve times a week. If this seems like a cultural flashback, just a stroll through the old quarter of Montevideo proves it. Studebakers, panel trucks, even Model T Fords ply the tree-lined avenues and cobblestone streets. Laundry hangs on the wrought-iron balconies of moldering eighteenth-century town houses. Here, in the old quarter of the capital of the smallest nation in South America, time seems to have stood still.

Time has surely stood still at the Mercado del Puerto. Montevideans flock to this once-stately covered market for a carnivorian orgy of grilled steaks, sausages, roasts, roulades, and organ meats. Built in 1868, the Mercado del Puerto is a soaring temple of girders and glass. Access to the block-long market is gained through grandiose iron gates, and a three-story-high skylight, blackened with smoke and age, towers over an ornate clock tower. The dilapidated stone floor gives the Mercado a slightly seedy feel—which is what a proper market should have. And one thing's for sure: The beef is definitely here.

Follow Your Nose

As you walk through the old town, you can smell the market before you actually see it. It's a common aroma in South America—a comforting blend of fire-seared meat and wood smoke. Formerly Montevideo's main food market, the Mercado of today is its barbecue headquarters, home to more than a dozen bare-bones restaurants specializing in grilled meats. Take a seat at one of the counters and you'll taste some of the best barbecue in South America—as well as parts of animals you never knew you could eat.

Consider the Estancia del Puerto (Port Ranch), a lively grill founded more than a quarter century ago by Antonio and Marono Fraga. The latter is a short, bald, bespectacled man who remembers when the Mercado was a working food market with only one or two simple eateries. The boom came in the 1980s, when gentrification turned most of the food stalls into restaurants. The Estancia alone will serve five hundred people a day, going through more than a ton of beef a week.

Patrons, many of them regulars since the restaurant opened, take their seats at black marble counters surrounding the kitchen. (There's also a separate seating area with proper tables and chairs.) Some are office workers, while others are city employees or dock hands, although the crowd is dressier than you'd expect for the portside location. There's no doubt that the focal point of the restaurant is the massive grill, where pork, lamb, chicken, and especially beef are charred to smoky perfection.

The Uruguayan grill has two working parts. The first is a U-shaped metal basket that holds blazing hardwood logs. As the logs disintegrate, the glowing coals are raked under the *parilla,* a large, rectangular metal grate that serves as the actual grill. The grate slopes gently upward in the back: The front (the part closest to the coals) is used for searing the meat; the rear is used for roasting and warming.

The *asador* (grill man) is recognizable by his white coat and *gorra* (short-brimmed cap). He remains in constant motion, now adding a log to the fire box, now raking a fresh load of coals under the grate, now moving meats from hot spots to cool spots or back again. When not actually grilling meats, he may be boning a chicken to make a *pamplona* (a stuffed roast—you'll find a recipe on page 280), or rolling carrots, peppers, hard-cooked eggs, and flank steak into a belt-loosening roast called a *matambre,* literally hunger-killer (see pages 152 and 156).

The first thing that strikes you at a Montevidean grill is how limited the North American notion is of what makes suitable barbecue. No part of the animal is overlooked by a Montevidean grill master. A typical meal might start with *mollejas* (grilled sweetbreads), *choto* (a crisp coiled roll of sheep's small intestines that tastes better than it sounds), *chinchulin* (buttery, crescent-shaped spirals of lamb's small intestine), or *riñones* (veal kidneys).

Uruguayans are also great fans of sausage—a love they may have acquired from the German immigrants who settled here in the early part of this century. Chorizo is the most famous Latin American sausage. To most North Americans, chorizo means the spicy Mexican variety. Uruguayan chorizo, on the other hand, is salty and garlicky, but not in the least bit spicy. It's rather like kielbasa.

Another tasty sausage is *salchicha,* which comes in a slender, tightly coiled casing. *Morcilla* is blood sausage, recognizable by its shiny black, crackling-crisp casing. It, too, tastes a lot better than it sounds. There are, in fact, two different types of *morcilla* in Uruguay, savory and sweet. The latter is flavored with sugar and raisins and is absolutely delicious. I wish I could find it at home.

Uruguayan beef cuts will be equally unfamiliar to most North Americans. The most popular is *asado de tira*—a long, thin cross-section of beef ribs that literally buries the plate. The noises of the market are punctuated by the high-pitched whine of the meat saw, cutting sides of beef into *asados.* The generous marbling makes the meat incredibly succulent, while the rib bones provide extra flavor. Another popular cut is the *pulpa,* smokily charred "breast," which is similar to brisket.

No-Frills Dining

Whatever you order, know that it will be served with the utmost simplicity. The plate is cheap stamped metal. The accompaniments are limited to a parsley and garlic sauce called *chimichurri* (think of it as South American pesto) and a tomato, onion, and pepper relish known as *salsa criolla.* Some restaurants follow the example of Uruguay's northern neighbor, Brazil, serving *farofa* (toasted manioc flour) to sprinkle over the meat to absorb the juices. To round out your meal, you might have a baked potato or simple salad of lettuce, tomato, and onions. Desserts are usually packaged confections that are as intensely sugary as the espresso served after the meal.

Another popular lunch spot is Don García, named for its jovial proprietor, who runs the restaurant with his dark-eyed wife, Alicia. This tiny eatery has no tables, and you'll probably have to wait awhile for a seat at the red granite counter. However long it takes, don't miss it, for Don Garcia serves some of the best, most reasonably priced food at the Mercado. Two could eat themselves silly by ordering the *parillada* (mixed grill). You'll be presented with a sizzling-hot plate heaped with chorizo, *morcilla, salchicha,* several types of innards, and even a steak. Another of the Don's specialties is grilled bread, which Garcia slathers with oil and garlic. To wash it down there's a sort of Uruguayan sangria made with ginger ale and red wine.

The Mercado del Puerto is mainly a lunch spot, but at least one restaurant reopens for dinner: El Palenque. Founded in 1964, this popular eatery straddles the east wall of the market. At lunchtime, patrons line up at its marketside counter. At night, there's a streetside dining room with country hams hanging from the rafters and a terrace with plastic café chairs.

El Palenque serves the sort of staunchly carnivorous fare found throughout the Mercado del Puerto, but there are two house specialties that will delight nonmeat eaters. The first is *provolone asado,* grilled slabs of provolone cheese sprinkled with olive oil, oregano, and paprika. The second are grilled sardines—among the rare seafood I saw at the market.

El Palenque's owner, Emilio Gonzales Portela, came to work here in the 1960s as a humble grill man. Today he owns the restaurant, which serves four hundred customers a day. I guess you could call it the American dream—Montevidean style.

URUGUAY

MONTEVIDEAN CHICKEN BREASTS

PAMPLONA DE POLLO

DIRECT GRILLING
SERVES 6 AS AN APPETIZER, 2-4 AS A MAIN COURSE

The term *pamplona* refers to the stuffed, rolled, grilled meats popular at Uruguayan steak houses and barbecues. Almost any meat is a candidate for stuffing, especially chicken, pork, and veal. (Beef is considered so noble, it's generally cooked by itself.) This recipe was inspired by a chicken *pamplona* served at a Mercado del Puerto restaurant. The bell pepper, ham, egg, and prunes, make this a particularly colorful stuffing. The juxtaposition of sweet prunes and salty ham gives an orchestral range of flavor.

In Montevideo, these rolls would be wrapped and cooked in caul fat, a lacy membrane of fat from the belly of a pig. Caul fat is often used in charcuterie for wrapping sausages and pâtés. If you want to try using caul fat here, ask for it at butcher shops. Caul fat doesn't have much of a flavor, but as it cooks the fat bastes the meat. The olive oil in the recipe here supplies a similar moistness.

Don't be intimidated by the prospect of making stuffed roll-ups; this one can literally be assembled in five minutes—even if you've never stuffed a chicken breast before. It's a foolproof recipe, and the results will look like a million bucks. Serve the stuffed chicken with any one of the *chimichurris* in the sauce chapter (pages 477 through 478).

SPECIAL EQUIPMENT

Short metal skewers or butcher's string

INGREDIENTS

2 whole skinless, boneless chicken breasts (12 to 16 ounces each; see Note)
Salt and freshly ground black pepper
1 teaspoon dried oregano
½ medium-size red bell pepper, cored and seeded
1 slice (¼ inch thick) cooked or smoked ham (about 1½ ounces)
1 hard-cooked egg, peeled
12 pitted prunes
2 to 3 tablespoons extra-virgin olive oil, for brushing

1. Rinse the chicken breasts under cold running water, then drain and blot dry with paper towels. Spread the breasts open, smooth side down and with one long side facing you, on a work surface. Cut off the fillets (the long, slender strip of meat on each half breast) and set aside for another use. Season the breasts with salt and black pepper to taste and ½ teaspoon of the oregano.

2. Cut the bell pepper lengthwise into ¼-inch strips. Cut the ham into ¼-inch strips. Cut the hard-cooked egg into 6 lengthwise wedges. Arrange the bell pepper and ham strips flat on the opened chicken breasts. Place the egg wedges and prunes lengthwise on top, leaving a ½-inch border on each side.

3. Starting at the side facing you, roll each chicken breast up to form a compact cylinder. Pin the rolls closed with short metal skewers or tie them with butcher's string as follows: Tie a piece of string around one end of each roll and then wrap it around the roll until you reach the other end; tie the ends to secure them.

4. Rub the outsides of the rolls with olive oil and season them with salt and black pepper to taste and the remaining ½ teaspoon of oregano. Place the *pamplonas* on a platter, loosely cover them with plastic wrap, and refrigerate until ready to grill, up to 6 hours.

5. Set up the grill for direct grilling and preheat to medium-high.

6. When ready to cook, brush and oil the grill grate. Arrange the *pamplonas* on the hot grate and grill, turning with tongs and basting with a small amount of olive oil, until nicely browned, firm to the touch, and a skewer inserted in the center of each comes out very hot to the touch, 15 to 25 minutes in all.

7. Transfer the *pamplonas* to a cutting board. Traditionally, *pamplonas* are served whole on plates, but I like to cut them crosswise into ½-inch slices, fanning the slices out on serving plates or a platter to create a mosaic effect. Let the *pamplonas* rest for 5 minutes before removing the skewers or string.

NOTE: Each whole skinless, boneless chicken breast called for here must be in one piece—breast halves just won't do.

THAILAND

CHICKEN SATES SERVED IN LETTUCE LEAVES

DIRECT GRILLING
SERVES 4 AS AN APPETIZER, 2-3 AS A MAIN COURSE

Satés originated in Indonesia, but Thais and Malaysians adopted these tiny kebabs with passion. Along the way, the seasoning changed from Indonesia's sweet soy-based marinade to the fish sauce so prized in Thai cooking. I like to serve satés the way they are commonly eaten in Southeast Asia—wrapped in lettuce leaves.

ADVANCE PREPARATION

20 minutes to 2 hours for marinating the chicken

SPECIAL EQUIPMENT

16 long bamboo skewers and an aluminum foil shield (see box, page 23)

INGREDIENTS

1 pound skinless, boneless chicken breasts
¼ cup coconut milk, canned or homemade (page 114)
2 tablespoons Asian fish sauce
2 tablespoons fresh lime juice
2 teaspoons honey or sugar
2 cloves garlic, minced
½ teaspoon ground turmeric
Thai Peanut Sauce (page 476)
1 head Boston lettuce, separated into leaves, rinsed, and trimmed

1. Rinse the chicken breasts under cold running water, then drain and blot them dry with paper towels. Cut the chicken breasts lengthwise (with the grain) into a total of 16 strips, each 4 inches long, ½ inch wide, and ¼ inch thick.

2. Combine the coconut milk, fish sauce, lime juice, honey, garlic, and turmeric in a medium-size nonreactive bowl and whisk to blend. Add the chicken to the marinade and toss to coat thoroughly. Let the chicken marinate in the refrigerator, covered, for 20 minutes to 2 hours (the longer the better).

3. Remove the chicken strips from the marinade and discard the marinade. Weave the strips of chicken lengthwise onto the skewers.

4. Set up the grill for direct grilling and preheat to high.

5. When ready to cook, brush and oil the grill grate. Arrange the satés on the hot grate with the aluminum foil shield under the ends of the skewers. Grill, turning with tongs, until lightly browned and cooked through, 1 to 3 minutes per side (2 to 6 minutes in all).

6. Transfer the satés to serving plates. Serve, accompanied by bowls of the peanut sauce. To eat, place a saté on a lettuce leaf and top the chicken with a spoonful of peanut sauce; wrap it up in the lettuce and pull out the skewer.

MALAYSIA

MALAYSIAN CHICKEN SATES

DIRECT GRILLING
SERVES 8 AS AN APPETIZER, 4 AS A MAIN COURSE

Satés are enjoyed throughout Southeast Asia, where each country boasts that it makes the best. The Malaysian version is particularly aromatic, thanks to the fragrant paste of shallots, lemongrass, peanuts, turmeric, and coriander in which the meat is marinated. A Malaysian would use fresh turmeric. As this is difficult to find in North America, I've substituted a mix of fresh ginger and turmeric powder.

Asians prefer the rich flavor of dark-meat chicken (chicken thighs or drumsticks). For ease in preparation, I've called for boneless breasts, but you could certainly use dark meat.

ADVANCE PREPARATION

1 hour for marinating the chicken

SPECIAL EQUIPMENT

About 40 short bamboo skewers and an aluminum foil shield (see box, page 23); 1 stalk fresh lemongrass, untrimmed

INGREDIENTS

- 1½ pounds skinless, boneless chicken breasts
- 4 large or 6 medium-size shallots, quartered
- 2 stalks fresh lemongrass, trimmed and cut into ½-inch pieces, or 2 strips lemon zest (each 2 by ½ inches; removed with a vegetable peeler)
- 1 tablespoon chopped peeled fresh ginger
- 3 tablespoons dry-roasted peanuts
- 6 tablespoons vegetable oil
- 2 tablespoons fresh lemon or lime juice, or more to taste
- 1 tablespoon soy sauce
- 1 teaspoon salt, or more to taste
- 1 teaspoon ground turmeric
- 1 teaspoon ground cumin
- 1 teaspoon ground coriander
- ¼ teaspoon ground cinnamon
- ½ teaspoon freshly ground black pepper
- Dutch West Indian Peanut Sauce (see page 476)

1. Rinse the chicken breasts under cold running water, then drain and blot them dry with paper towels. Cut the chicken breasts lengthwise (with the grain) into 2½-inch-long strips about the size of your little finger. Place the chicken in a large bowl.

2. Combine the shallots, lemongrass pieces, ginger, peanuts, 3 tablespoons of the oil, and the lemon juice, soy sauce, salt, turmeric, cumin, coriander, cinnamon, and pepper in a food processor and process to a smooth paste. Taste for seasoning, adding more salt and/or lemon juice as necessary; the marinade should be highly seasoned. Add the marinade to the chicken, stirring to coat completely. Let the chicken marinate in the refrigerator, covered, for 1 hour, stirring once or twice.

3. Remove the chicken from the marinade; discard the marinade. Weave the strips of chicken lengthwise onto skewers.

4. Set up the grill for direct grilling and preheat to high.

5. When ready to cook, brush and oil the grill grate. Arrange the satés on the hot grate with the aluminum foil shield under the ends of the skewers. Grill, turning with tongs, until lightly browned and cooked through, 1 to 3 minutes per side (2 to 6 minutes in all). Using the whole lemongrass stalk as a brush, baste the satés with the remaining 3 tablespoons of oil once or twice as they cook.

6. Transfer the satés to serving plates or a platter and serve with the Dutch West Indian Peanut Sauce.

SRI LANKA

SRI LANKAN SATES

DIRECT GRILLING
SERVES 8 AS AN APPETIZER, 4 AS A MAIN COURSE

Most people associate satés (aka satays) with Southeast Asia, particularly with Indonesia, Malaysia, or Singapore. But you also find them in Sri Lanka—a notion that isn't as far-fetched as it might seem. The principle of kebabs seems to have arrived in Indonesia with Arab traders in the twelfth century A.D. Sri Lanka certainly could have been a stopping point on the way. Or maybe, and even more likely, meat on a stick was an obviously good idea that sprang up in many parts of the world at once.

This Sri Lankan version of saté features a lively marinade of paprika and coriander. It comes with an equally lively sauce, gilded with turmeric and enriched with coconut milk. I like the bite provided by hot paprika, but sweet paprika may be easier on the taste buds.

ADVANCE PREPARATION

30 minutes to 6 hours for marinating the chicken

SPECIAL EQUIPMENT

About 40 short bamboo skewers and an aluminum foil shield (see box, page 23)

FOR THE CHICKEN

- 1½ pounds skinless, boneless chicken breasts
- 1 tablespoon sweet or hot paprika
- 2 teaspoons ground coriander
- 1 teaspoon salt
- 1 teaspoon freshly ground black pepper
- 2 cloves garlic, minced
- 3 tablespoons vegetable oil

FOR THE SAUCE

- 3 tablespoons vegetable oil
- 1 large onion, thinly sliced

1 tablespoon minced peeled fresh ginger
2 cloves garlic, minced
1 teaspoon ground cumin
1 teaspoon ground coriander
½ teaspoon hot paprika or cayenne pepper
½ teaspoon ground turmeric
Salt and freshly ground black pepper
1 cup coconut milk, canned or homemade (page 114)
2 teaspoons distilled white vinegar, or more to taste

1. Prepare the chicken: Rinse the chicken breasts under cold running water, then drain and blot them dry with paper towels. Cut the chicken breasts lengthwise (with the grain) into 2½-inch-long strips about the size of your little finger. Place the chicken in a large bowl. Add the 1 tablespoon of paprika, 2 teaspoons of coriander, 1 teaspoon of salt, 1 teaspoon of black pepper, and 2 cloves of minced garlic, rubbing them onto the meat with your fingers. Stir in the 3 tablespoons of oil to coat thoroughly. Let the chicken marinate in the refrigerator, covered, for 30 minutes, or up to 6 hours (the longer the better).

2. Meanwhile, make the sauce: Heat the 3 tablespoons of oil in a medium-size saucepan over high heat. Add the onion, ginger, 2 cloves of minced garlic, cumin, 1 teaspoon of coriander, ½ teaspoon of hot paprika, and the turmeric. Season with salt and black pepper to taste and cook for 1 minute, stirring to coat the onion with the seasonings. Reduce the heat to medium and cook, stirring occasionally, until the onion is very soft and a deep golden brown, 5 to 10 minutes. Stir in the coconut milk and vinegar and let simmer until you have a thick, spoonable sauce, about 5 minutes. Taste for seasoning, adding more salt and/or vinegar as necessary; the sauce should be highly seasoned. Remove the sauce from the heat and set aside.

3. Weave the strips of chicken lengthwise onto skewers.

4. Set up the grill for direct grilling and preheat to high.

5. When ready to cook, brush and oil the grill grate. Arrange the satés on the hot grate with the aluminum foil shield under the skewers. Grill, turning with tongs, until lightly browned and cooked through, 1 to 3 minutes per side (2 to 6 minutes in all).

6. Transfer the satés to serving plates or a platter and spoon a little of the sauce over each. Serve at once.

THAILAND

SCHOOLYARD CHICKEN SATES

DIRECT GRILLING
SERVES 4 AS AN APPETIZER, 2-3 AS A MAIN COURSE

The same impulse that sends American schoolchildren rushing out to Pizza Hut and McDonald's when the lunch bell rings has the uniformed youngsters of Nat Monekugrasae High School in Bangkok heading to the saté stand of Suay and Pong Pochana. The Pochana sisters are just two among the twenty or so vendors who fill the stalls in the parking lot across the street from the school, but it's their satés that the children seem to prefer above everything else.

Pong sits cross-legged on a raised dais, threading the meat of chicken legs on skewers, while Suay fans a narrow brazier to heat the coconut shell charcoal used for grilling. Saté originated in Indonesia, of course (see page 450), but the coconut milk in the marinade and tangy Tamarind Dipping Sauce the satés are served with are distinctly Thai. The latter, thanks to the smoky tartness of the tamarind, is one of the tastiest sweet-and-sour sauces ever to grace grilled chicken. You can also serve the satés with Jasmine Rice (page 428).

ADVANCE PREPARATION

1 to 2 hours for marinating the chicken

SPECIAL EQUIPMENT

About 40 short bamboo skewers and an aluminum foil shield (see box, page 23)

INGREDIENTS

1 pound skinless, boneless chicken breasts or leg meat
3 cloves garlic, minced
1 piece (1 inch) peeled fresh ginger, thinly sliced
1 tablespoon sugar
1 teaspoon salt
2 tablespoons Asian fish sauce
½ cup coconut milk, canned or homemade (see page 114)
Tamarind Dipping Sauce (page 487)

1. Rinse the chicken under cold running water, then drain and blot it dry with paper towels. Cut the chicken lengthwise (with the grain) into 2½-inch-long strips about the size of your little finger. Place the chicken in a large bowl.

2. Combine the garlic, ginger, sugar, and salt in a mortar and pound to a coarse paste with a pestle, then work in the fish sauce and coconut milk. If you don't have a mortar and pestle, combine all these ingredients in a food processor or blender and process to a coarse paste. Add the marinade to the chicken, turning the strips to coat. Let the chicken marinate in the refrigerator, covered, for 1 to 2 hours (the longer the better), stirring occasionally.

3. Remove the chicken strips from the marinade, reserving the marinade, and weave the chicken lengthwise onto the skewers.

4. Set up the grill for direct grilling and preheat to high.

5. When ready to cook, brush and oil the grill grate. Arrange the satés on the hot grate with the aluminum foil shield under the ends of the skewers. Grill, turning with tongs, until lightly browned and cooked through, 1 to 3 minutes per side (2 to 6 minutes in all). Brush the satés once or twice with the reserved marinade before turning.

6. Transfer the satés to serving plates or a platter and serve at once, accompanied by small bowls of the Tamarind Dipping Sauce.

INDONESIA

JAKARTA CHICKEN SATES

SATE AYAM

DIRECT GRILLING
SERVES 4 AS AN APPETIZER, 2-3 AS A MAIN COURSE

This is probably the most popular saté in Jakarta—the street food equivalent of, say, a hot dog in New York City. This particular recipe comes from Nurul Phamid, a willowy young man with a faint mustache, who sells his satés from a pushcart on Jabang Street. Phamid loads his satés with chicken livers and chicken skin, as well as dark chicken meat. For the sake of simplicity, I make the liver and skin optional; you certainly could add either or both, if you wish. What really makes Phamid's satés so succulent is what he uses for basting: chicken fat!

SPECIAL EQUIPMENT

About 28 short bamboo skewers and an aluminum foil shield (see box, page 23)

INGREDIENTS

1 pound boneless chicken breasts or leg meat, with skin if desired
4 ounces chicken livers (optional), trimmed
6 tablespoons sweet soy sauce (ketjap manis), or ⅓ cup each regular soy sauce and molasses
¾ cup Thai Peanut Sauce (page 476)
3 tablespoons finely chopped onion
1 tablespoon fresh lime juice
2 tablespoons rendered chicken fat (see box, page 285) or unsalted butter, melted
1 tablespoon chile paste (sambal ulek) or your favorite hot sauce, for serving

1. If the chicken has skin and you plan to use it in the satés, remove it from the chicken and set it aside; otherwise, discard it. Rinse the chicken, chicken skin (if using), and chicken livers (if using) under cold water, then drain and blot them dry with paper towels. Cut the chicken and livers into ½-inch dice and the skin into ½-inch squares. Thread the chicken pieces alternately on the skewers; each saté should be about 3 inches long. Place the satés on a platter, cover them loosely with plastic wrap, and refrigerate them while you prepare the marinade.

2. Combine 4 tablespoons of the sweet soy sauce, ¼ cup of the peanut sauce, and the onion and lime juice in a shallow dish and stir to mix. Roll the satés in the marinade to coat thoroughly.

3. Set up the grill for direct grilling and preheat to high.

4. When ready to cook, brush and oil the grill grate. Arrange the satés on the hot grate with the aluminum foil shield under the ends of the skewers. Grill, turning with tongs, until lightly browned and cooked through, 1 to 3 minutes per side (2 to 6 minutes in all). Brush the satés once or twice with the chicken fat as they cook.

5. To serve, place the remaining ½ cup of peanut sauce in a small bowl and spoon the remaining 2 tablespoons of sweet soy sauce and the chile paste into the center (the motion of dipping the satés into this sauce will mix the ingredients together). Transfer the satés to serving plates or a platter and serve accompanied by the sauce.

JAPAN

YAKITORI

DIRECT GRILLING
SERVES 4 TO 6

Yakitori (literally grilled chicken) is Japan's most popular snack—enjoyed daily at innumerable yakitori parlors, where office workers gather after work for drinks, eats, and camaraderie. (To read about a quintessential yakitori parlor in Tokyo, see page 412.) Traditionally, the chicken is skewered with *negi,* a member of the green onion family that's thicker than a scallion but thinner than a leek. If you can find slender young leeks, use them in this recipe; otherwise, use scallions. Also, to be strictly authentic use chicken thighs, which the Japanese believe to be more flavorful than breast meat. For speed and convenience, use boneless breasts, my first choice here. Serve the yakitori with Grilled Rice Cakes (page 431), Spicy Japanese Bean Sprout Salad (page 113), or Sesame Spinach Salad (page 111).

SPECIAL EQUIPMENT

16 short bamboo skewers, or more as needed, and an aluminum foil shield (see box, page 23)

INGREDIENTS

- **2 pounds skinless, boneless chicken breasts or thighs**
- **2 pounds slender young leeks (8 or 9 in all, see Notes)**
- **½ cup soy sauce**
- **½ cup sake**
- **½ cup mirin (sweet rice wine) or cream sherry**
- **3 tablespoons sugar**
- **3 slices peeled fresh ginger (each ¼ inch thick)**
- **3 cloves garlic, peeled and crushed**
- **3 scallions, both white and green parts, trimmed and coarsely chopped**

1. Rinse the chicken under cold running water, then drain and blot dry with paper towels. Cut it crosswise into pieces that are 2 inches long and both ½ inch wide and thick. Set the chicken aside while you prepare the leeks.

2. Cut off and discard the green parts of the leeks. Cut the white parts in half lengthwise as far as the roots. Rinse the leeks carefully under cold running water, then drain them and cut off the roots. Cut each half leek crosswise into 2-inch pieces.

3. Thread the chicken pieces crosswise on the skewers, alternating them with pieces of leek; you should be able to get 4 pieces of chicken on each skewer. Arrange the skewers on a platter and cover them loosely with plastic wrap. Refrigerate the chicken until you are ready to grill, up to 6 hours.

4. Combine the soy sauce, sake, mirin, sugar, ginger, garlic, and scallions in a small, heavy saucepan and bring to a boil over medium heat, stirring until blended and the sugar dissolves. Reduce the heat to low and let simmer, uncovered, until the sauce is glossy and syrupy and reduced to about ¾ cup, about 5 minutes. Remove the yakitori sauce from the heat and strain into a bowl (see Notes).

5. Set up the grill for direct grilling and preheat to high.

To Render Chicken Fat

Remove the large pieces of fat from just inside the main body cavity of the bird. Place them in a small skillet over medium heat and cook until the fat renders out, five to ten minutes. Strain the fat into a jar and cover. The main cavity of an average chicken will contain one to two ounces of fat. This will yield one to two tablespoons rendered fat. You can render this amount or, alternatively, save lumps of fat in the freezer and render a cup or two at a time. (The lumps of fat will keep, frozen, for about two months.) Rendered chicken fat will keep in the refrigerator for several weeks.

6. When ready to cook, brush and oil the grill grate. Arrange the skewers on the hot grate with the aluminum foil shield under the ends of the skewers. Grill, turning with tongs, until the chicken is nicely browned and cooked through, 3 to 5 minutes per side (6 to 10 minutes in all). Halfway through cooking start brushing the yakitori with the sauce. Brush only the cooked part of the chicken.

7. Transfer the yakitori to serving plates or a platter and serve at once with any remaining sauce spooned on top.

NOTES: If young leeks are not available, substitute 2 bunches of thick scallions. Trim off the roots and cut the white parts into 2-inch pieces; cut the scallion greens into 4-inch pieces and fold them in half.

The yakitori sauce can be made up to 6 hours ahead. Refrigerate it, covered, until ready to use.

U.S.A.

TURKEY PASTRAMI

INDIRECT GRILLING
SERVES 4 TO 6

Pastrami is truly a dish of three continents. Most Americans associate this cured meat with delicatessens. The first delicatessens were opened by Jews from Eastern Europe to provide immigrants with the beloved foods they left behind in Germany, Russia, and Poland. Actually, pastrami seems to have originated in Central Asia (particularly in eastern Turkey and Armenia), where it goes by the name of *basturma*. *Basturma* can be made with a variety of different meats, including beef, horse, and even camel. The meat is cut into two-foot-long strips, which are cured in salt, garlic, paprika, and other spices.

As for turkey pastrami, well, that's a uniquely North American invention—designed to be high in flavor, low in fat, and requiring only one day curing time, instead of the traditional two weeks needed to make beef pastrami.

ADVANCE PREPARATION

24 hours for curing the turkey

SPECIAL EQUIPMENT

1 cup wood chips or chunks, soaked for 1 hour in cold water to cover and drained

INGREDIENTS

2 pounds skinless, boneless turkey breast
1 tablespoon coriander seeds
2 teaspoons cracked black peppercorns
4½ teaspoons coarse salt (kosher or sea)
2 teaspoons dark brown sugar
2 teaspoons sweet paprika
1½ teaspoons mustard seeds
1 teaspoon ground ginger
3 cloves garlic, minced

1. Rinse the turkey breast under cold running water, then drain and blot it dry with paper towels.

2. Coarsely crush the coriander seeds and peppercorns in a spice mill or under the edge of a cast-iron skillet. Place the crushed spices in a bowl and whisk in the salt, brown sugar, paprika, mustard seeds, ginger, and garlic. Using your fingers, pat the spice mixture over the entire surface of the turkey breast and rub it in thoroughly. Wrap the breast in plastic wrap or place it in a large resealable plastic bag and let the turkey cure in the refrigerator for 24 hours.

3. Set up the grill for indirect grilling and place a drip pan in the center.

If using a gas grill, place all of the wood chips in the smoker box and preheat the grill to high; when smoke appears, reduce the heat to medium.

If using a charcoal grill, preheat it to medium.

4. When ready to cook, if using a charcoal grill, toss all of the wood chips on the coals. Brush and oil the grill grate. Unwrap the turkey and place it on the hot grate over the drip pan. Cover the grill and cook the turkey until an instant-read thermometer inserted in the thickest part of the breast registers 170°F, 1 to 1½ hours. If using a charcoal grill, you'll need to add 10 to 12 fresh coals to each side after 1 hour.

5. Transfer the turkey pastrami to a rack to cool, then refrigerate it, covered, until cold. To serve, cut the pastrami into thin slices across the grain.

U.S.A.

ANNATTO-SPICED GRILLED TURKEY

INDIRECT GRILLING
SERVES 10 TO 12

This certainly isn't like the turkey grandmother used to make! Unless grandmother wore cowboy boots and hailed from Santa Fe, New Mexico. Southwestern cooking mogul Mark Miller marinates his turkey in a tangy tincture of annatto seeds, marjoram, and citrus juice. Annatto seeds (also known as achiote) are a rust-colored spice native to Central America, with an earthy, iodine-like flavor. Annatto comes to Southwest cooking via the Yucatán and can be found in Hispanic markets and many supermarkets. Cascabel chiles are fiery round dried chiles that rattle like sleigh bells when you shake them. If unavailable, use two small dried hot red peppers.

For extra flavor and moistness, I like to loosen the skin from the bird and place some of the marinade underneath it; on page 261 you'll find instructions for doing this. If it seems too tricky, omit Step 3. If you want, you can prepare the marinade the day before. This will deepen the flavor.

ADVANCE PREPARATION

4 hours for marinating the turkey

SPECIAL EQUIPMENT

About 3 cups wood chips, soaked for 1 hour in cold water to cover and drained

INGREDIENTS

- **1 turkey (10 to 12 pounds)**
- **Salt and freshly ground black pepper**
- **3 cascabel chiles, or 2 small dried hot red peppers**
- **1 tablespoon annatto seeds**
- **1 bunch fresh marjoram, or 1 tablespoon dried marjoram**
- **2 cups fresh orange juice**
- **3 tablespoons fresh lime juice**
- **4 cloves garlic, minced**
- **½ teaspoon ground cumin**
- **1 tablespoon extra-virgin olive oil, for brushing**

1. Remove and discard the fat from just inside the body cavities of the turkey. Remove the package of giblets and set aside for another use. Rinse the turkey, inside and out, under cold running water, then drain and blot it dry, inside and out, with paper towels. Season the turkey inside and out with salt and pepper; then cover and refrigerate it while you prepare the marinade.

2. Combine the cascabel chiles, annatto seeds, and 1 cup of water in a small saucepan and bring to a boil over medium-high heat. Let cook, uncovered, until the chiles have softened and all liquid has been absorbed, 5 to 10 minutes. Transfer the chiles and annatto seeds to a food processor or blender and add the marjoram, orange juice, lime juice, garlic, cumin, 1 teaspoon of salt, and ¼ of teaspoon pepper. Process until smooth. Pour the marinade into a strainer set over a medium-size bowl and press it through using a wooden spoon. Taste for seasoning, adding more salt and/or pepper as necessary; the marinade should be highly seasoned.

3. If you wish to put some of the marinade between the skin and flesh of the turkey, follow the directions in the box on page 261 for loosening the skin. Spoon a few tablespoons of the marinade into the body cavity of the turkey and a tablespoon into the neck cavity. Brush the outside of the bird with additional marinade—liberally if you didn't put marinade under the skin—and a little olive oil. Place the turkey in a roasting pan and cover it loosely with plastic wrap. Let the turkey marinate in the refrigerator for 4 hours.

4. Set up the grill for indirect grilling and place a large drip pan in the center.

If using a gas grill, place as many of the wood chips as you can in the smoker box and preheat the grill to high; when smoke appears, reduce the heat to medium.

If using a charcoal grill, preheat it to medium.

5. When ready to cook, if using a charcoal grill, toss 1½ cups of the wood chips on the coals. Brush and oil the grill grate. Place the turkey on the hot grate over the drip pan. Cover the grill and cook the turkey until the juices run clear when the tip of a skewer or sharp knife is inserted in the thickest part of a thigh and the legs wiggle freely in the joint, 2½ to 3 hours (figuring on 15 to 20 minutes per pound). When done, an instant-read meat thermometer inserted in the thickest part of a thigh, but not touching the bone, should register about 170°F. If using charcoal, you'll need to add 10 to 12 fresh coals to each side every hour and toss about ¾ cup of wood chips on the fresh coals.

6. Transfer the turkey to a platter and let rest, loosely covered with aluminum foil, for 15 minutes before carving.

MOROCCO

GRILLED GAME HENS WITH MOROCCAN SPICES

DIRECT GRILLING
SERVES 4

For the most part in Morocco, grilled fare means lamb, but here's a dish for poultry lovers that's fairly bursting with Moroccan spice flavors. Cilantro, cumin, paprika, and ginger combine to transform a commonplace bird into a flame-cooked triumph.

ADVANCE PREPARATION

2 to 8 hours for marinating the chicken

INGREDIENTS

4 game hens (each about 1 pound)
1 medium-size onion, grated
2 tablespoons chopped fresh flat-leaf parsley
2 tablespoons chopped fresh cilantro
3 tablespoons fresh lemon juice
2 tablespoons extra-virgin olive oil
1 teaspoon salt
½ teaspoon ground cumin
½ teaspoon hot or sweet paprika
½ teaspoon ground ginger
½ teaspoon freshly ground white pepper
Lemon wedges, for garnish

1. Remove and discard the fat just inside the body cavities of the game hens. Remove the packages of giblets (if any) and set aside for another use. Rinse the hens, inside and out, under cold running water, then drain and blot dry, inside and out, with paper towels. Spatchcook the game hens as shown at right or cut each lengthwise in half with poultry shears. Place the birds in a large, deep nonreactive bowl or baking dish and set aside while you prepare the marinade.

2. Combine the onion, parsley, cilantro, lemon juice, olive oil, salt, cumin, paprika, ginger, and white pepper in a small bowl and whisk to mix. Pour the marinade over the game hens and turn the birds to coat thoroughly. Let the game hens marinate in the refrigerator, covered, for 2 to 8 hours (the longer the better), turning the birds occasionally.

3. Set up the grill for two-zone direct grilling (see page 18), preheating two thirds of the grill to medium and leaving one third heat free as a safety zone.

4. When ready to cook, brush and oil the grill grate. Remove the game hens from the marinade and discard the marinade. Arrange the game hens, skin side down, on the grate over the hot zone of the grill and cook until the skin is golden brown and the meat is cooked through without any trace of red at the bone, 15 to 20 minutes per side. If you get flare-ups, move the game hens to the safety zone until the flames die down.

5. Transfer the game hens to serving plates or a platter and let rest for 5 minutes. Serve garnished with lemon wedges.

AFGHANISTAN

AFGHAN-STYLE GAME HENS

ROTISSERIE OR DIRECT GRILLING
SERVES 4

Afghans are some of the world's best grill masters, as this dish aptly demonstrates. The marinade uses familiar ingredients, many of which you probably have on hand, but the birds come out so exotic tasting, succulent, and flavorful that your guests will think they're dining in a great ethnic restaurant. You can get away with marinating the game hens for only eight hours, but after the full twenty-four hours, the hens will taste their best.

ADVANCE PREPARATION

8 to 24 hours for marinating the hens

SPECIAL EQUIPMENT

Rotisserie (optional; see Note)

HOW TO SPATCHCOCK A CHICKEN OR GAME HEN

A spatchcocked chicken or game hen is one that has been partially boned and then butterflied—spread open. Spatchcocking speeds up the cooking process and enables you to cook a whole bird using the direct grilling method; a lot more of the surface area of the meat is exposed to the flames, so it cooks evenly. While spatchcocking may seem intimidating the first time you do it, you'll get the hang of it quickly.

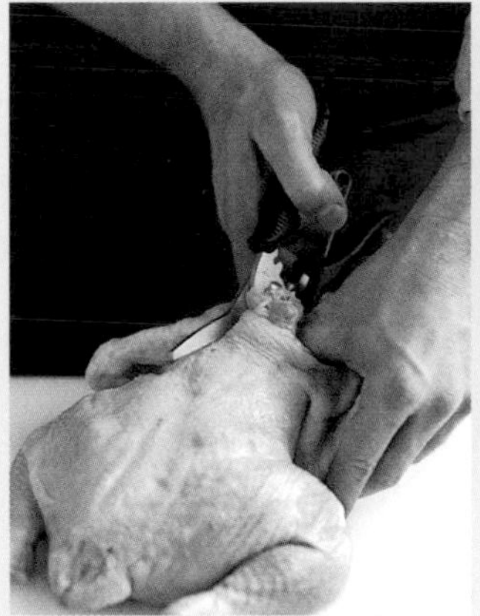

1. *Place the bird, breast side down, on a cutting board. Using poultry shears, cut through the flesh and bone along one side of the backbone, starting at the neck.*

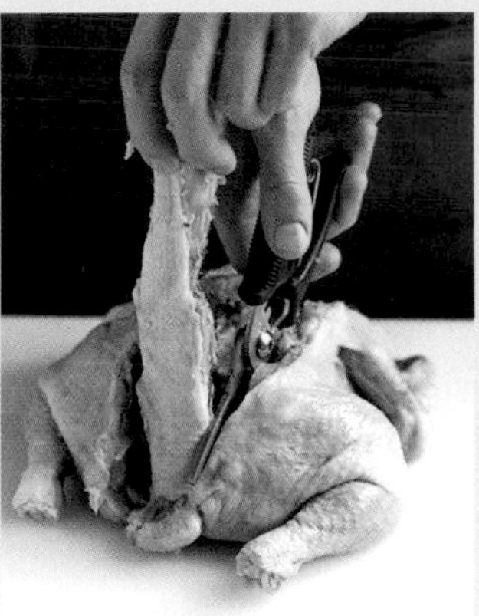

2. *Completely remove the backbone by cutting along the other side until you reach the tail.*

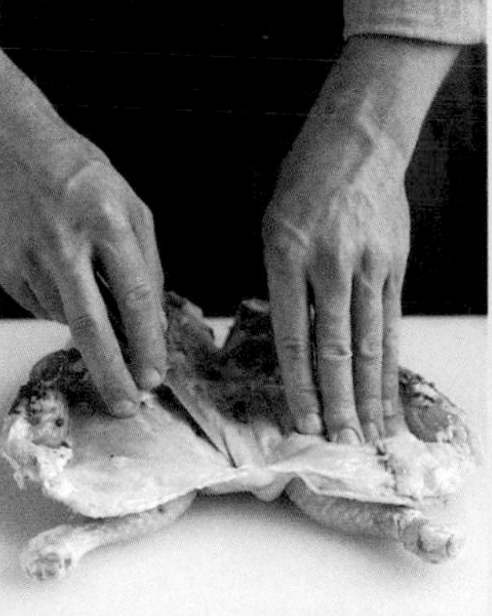

3. *Spread out the bird, like opening a book, by gently pulling the halves apart. Using a sharp paring knife, lightly score the top of the breastbone.*

4. *Run your fingers along and under the sides of the breastbone and attached cartilage and pop them out.*

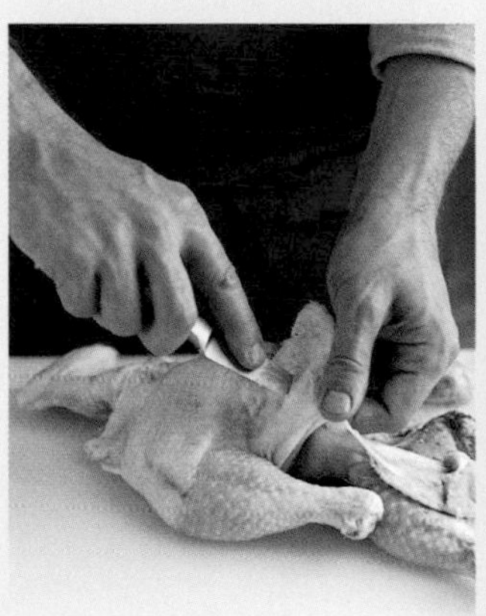

5. *The next two steps are optional but they produce a more attractive bird: Turn the bird over and, using a sharp knife, make a slit on each side, in the skin near the bottom of each breast, 1-inch long for a chicken, ½-inch long for a game hen.*

6. *Insert the end of each drumstick through the slit you have made on that side of the bird.*

7. *When you have tucked the drumsticks through the slits, the spatchcocked bird will look like this.*

8. *Finally, cut the tips of the wings off and fold the wings under so that they are flat. The backbone and wing tips can be saved to use for stock.*

INGREDIENTS

4 game hens (each about 1 pound)
¾ cup extra-virgin olive oil
¾ cup plain whole-milk yogurt
⅓ cup fresh lemon juice
1 tablespoon sweet paprika
1 teaspoon ground cumin
2 teaspoons salt
1 teaspoon freshly ground black pepper
3 medium-size onions, thinly sliced
8 cloves garlic, thinly sliced
1 lemon, thinly sliced
1 to 4 bird peppers or jalapeño peppers, thinly sliced

1. Remove and discard the fat just inside the body cavities of the game hens. Remove the packages of giblets (if any) and set aside for another use. Rinse the hens, inside and out, under cold running water, then drain and blot dry, inside and out, with paper towels. Place the game hens in a large, deep nonreactive bowl or baking dish and set aside while you prepare the marinade.

2. Combine the olive oil, yogurt, lemon juice, paprika, cumin, salt, and black pepper in a medium-size bowl and whisk to blend. Stir in the onions, garlic, sliced lemon, and bird peppers, then pour the marinade over the game hens and turn the birds to coat thoroughly. Let the game hens marinate in the refrigerator, covered, for 8 to 24 hours (the longer the better), turning the hens occasionally.

3. Set up the grill for spit roasting following the manufacturer's instructions and preheat to medium-high.

4. When ready to cook, skewer the game hens on the spit. Attach the spit to the rotisserie mechanism and turn on the motor. Cook the game hens until they are nicely browned and the juices run clear when the tip of a skewer or sharp knife is inserted in the thickest part of a thigh, 30 to 40 minutes if the grill is covered, somewhat longer if the grill is uncovered.

5. Remove the game hens from the spit, transfer them to a cutting board or platter, and let rest for 5 minutes before serving.

NOTE: If you prefer, you can cook the game hens directly on the grill. Spatchcook the birds (see page 289) or cut them lengthwise in half with poultry shears, then marinate them as directed in Step 2. Grill the birds using the two-zone method following the directions for Grilled Game Hens with Moroccan Spices on page 288.

U.S.A.

GRILLED DUCK
WITH GARLIC AND GINGER

INDIRECT GRILLING
SERVES 2

I'm about to make an extravagant claim: There is no better way to cook duck than on a grill. This may sound iconoclastic coming from a cook who was trained in France, where duck is almost always roasted in the oven and where it is served fashionably rare, like steak. The truth is that the ducks we get in North America taste best cooked long and slow to tenderize the meat and melt out the fat. And indirect grilling is about the best way I know to produce crackling crisp skin and well-done meat that is virtually fat free and fall-off-the-bone tender. Besides, it takes the mess of cooking a fatty bird, like duck, out of your kitchen.

Here's a basic recipe for grilled duck, flavored by slivers of garlic and ginger inserted in slits in the flesh. The slits perform a second function—the same as making pricks all over the skin with a fork: They allow the fat to drain off, crisping the skin in the process. If you like a smoke flavor with duck, throw a cupful of soaked wood chips on the coals (or into the smoker box of a gas grill). Fruit woods, like apple and cherry, go particularly well with duck. The duck is wonderful served with the cinnamon cherry and orange sauces that follow. Then again, it's pretty outrageous eaten just by itself.

1 duck (4½ to 5 pounds), thawed if frozen
2 cloves garlic, quartered lengthwise
2 slices (each ¼ inch thick) peeled fresh ginger, cut into ¼-inch slivers
Salt and freshly ground black pepper
Cinnamon Cherry (recipe follows), or Orange, Sauce for Duck (pages 291 and 292)

1. Remove and discard the fat just inside the body cavities of the duck. Remove the package of giblets and set aside for another use. Rinse the duck inside and out, under cold running water, then drain and blot dry, inside and out, with paper towels.

2. Place the duck on its breast so that the back side is up. Using the tip of a sharp, slender knife, make a slit in the fatty part of the duck under each wing and a slit in the underside of each thigh. Insert a sliver of garlic and a sliver of ginger into each slit, then place the remaining garlic and ginger in the body cavity. Prick the duck skin all over with a sharp carving fork, being careful not to pierce the meat; then season the duck, inside and out, very generously with salt and pepper.

3. Set the grill up for indirect grilling, place a large drip pan in the center, and preheat the grill to medium-low.

4. When ready to cook, place the duck, breast side up, on the hot grate over the drip pan. Cover the grill and cook the duck for 1½ hours. If using a charcoal grill, you'll need to add 10 to 12 fresh coals to each side after each hour of cooking.

5. After it has cooked for 1½ hours, turn the duck on its end over a bowl to drain off any juices that have accumulated in the cavity and discard the juices. Continue cooking the duck until the skin is mahogany brown and crackling crisp and the meat is well-done and tender, 30 to 45 minutes longer. When done, an instant-read meat thermometer inserted in the thickest part of a thigh, but not touching the bone, should register about 170°F.

6. Transfer the duck to a platter and let rest for 5 minutes before carving. Serve with either of the suggested sauces on the side.

CINNAMON CHERRY SAUCE FOR DUCK

MAKES ABOUT 2 CUPS, ENOUGH FOR 2 DUCKS

Duckling à la Montmorency represents classical French cuisine at its best. I've made the sauce with both sweet and tart cherry varieties and both fresh and canned fruit. Fresh cherries are obviously better, but canned pitted cherries are certainly convenient and still quite tasty. (Be sure to use canned fruit, not the thick pie filling that also comes in cans.) Adjust the sugar accordingly. To reinforce the cinnamon flavor, place a cinnamon stick in the cavity of the duck before you grill it.

12 ounces fresh cherries, or 1 can (15 ounces) cherries packed in light syrup
¼ cup sugar, or more to taste
¼ cup red wine vinegar
½ cup port wine
1 tablespoon fresh lemon juice
¼ teaspoon grated fresh lemon zest
1 cup rich duck or chicken stock, or canned low-sodium chicken broth
1 stick (3 inches) cinnamon
1½ teaspoons cornstarch or arrowroot
1 tablespoon kirsch
Salt and freshly ground black pepper
1 teaspoon honey (optional)

1. If using fresh cherries, stem them and rinse under cold running water, then drain. Pit the cherries using a cherry pitter; you should have about 1½ cups. If using canned cherries, drain, rinse, and drain them again. Set the cherries aside.

2. Combine the sugar and 3 tablespoons of water in a small, deep, heavy saucepan over high heat and cook, covered, for 2 minutes. Uncover the pan, reduce the heat to medium-high, and cook until the sugar caramelizes (turns a deep golden brown), gently swirling the pan to ensure even cooking. This should take 6 to 8 minutes, but watch carefully—the sugar can burn quickly. Remove the pan from the heat and add the wine vinegar. (Stand back: The mixture will emit a Vesuvian hiss, releasing eye-stinging vinegar vapors.) Place the caramel mixture over low heat and let simmer, whisking until the caramel is completely dissolved, 2 to 3 minutes.

3. Stir the port, lemon juice, and lemon zest into the caramel mixture and bring to a boil over medium heat, then cook, uncovered, for 2 minutes. Add the stock and cinnamon stick and cook until reduced slightly, about 5 minutes. Reduce the heat to low, add the cherries, and let the sauce simmer gently until the cherries are soft but not mushy, about 5 minutes for fresh cherries, 2 minutes for canned. Remove and discard the cinnamon stick.

4. Dissolve the cornstarch in the kirsch and whisk this mixture into the sauce. Let boil until the sauce thickens slightly, about 1 minute. Remove the sauce from the heat and taste for seasoning, adding salt and pepper to taste; if additional sweetness is desired, whisk in the honey or more sugar. The sauce can be refrigerated, covered, for up to 5 days. Reheat it before serving.

ORANGE SAUCE FOR DUCK

MAKES ABOUT 2 CUPS, ENOUGH FOR 2 DUCKS

Duckling à l'orange is another French classic, not to mention one of the first dishes I learned to make at the La Varenne cooking school in Paris. The sauce owes its unique sweet-sour-caramel flavor to a mixture of burnt sugar and vinegar called a *bigarade*. The traditional preparation calls for oranges, but I also like the exotic flavor you get with tangerines. To reinforce the orange flavor, place a few strips of the orange zest in the cavity of the duck before grilling.

2 large oranges, preferable navel oranges
¼ cup sugar
¼ cup red wine vinegar
1½ cups rich duck or chicken stock, or canned low-sodium chicken broth
1 tablespoon orange marmalade
1½ teaspoons cornstarch
2 tablespoons Grand Marnier or other orange liqueur
Salt and freshly ground black pepper

1. Finely grate enough zest off one of the oranges to make 1 teaspoon. Cut the remaining rind and all the white pith off this orange to expose the flesh. Working over a bowl to catch any juices and using a sharp paring knife, make V-shaped cuts between the membranes to release neat segments of orange. Set the orange segments aside, first removing any seeds with a fork. Juice the second orange: You should have about ⅔ cup of juice.

2. Combine the sugar and 3 tablespoons of water in a small, deep, heavy saucepan over high heat and cook, covered, for 2 minutes. Uncover the pan, reduce the heat to medium-high, and cook until the sugar caramelizes (turns a deep golden brown), gently swirling the pan to ensure even cooking. This should take 6 to 8 minutes, but watch carefully—the sugar can burn quickly. Remove the pan from the heat and add the wine vinegar. (Stand back: The mixture will emit a Vesuvian hiss, releasing eye-stinging vinegar vapors.) Place the caramel mixture over low heat and let simmer, whisking until the caramel is completely dissolved, 2 to 3 minutes.

3. Stir the orange juice and stock into the caramel mixture and bring to a boil over medium heat. Cook, uncovered, until reduced by half, 10 to 15 minutes. Reduce the heat to low and whisk in the orange marmalade. Let simmer until the marmalade melts, about 1 minute.

4. Dissolve the cornstarch in the Grand Marnier, whisk this mixture into the sauce, and cook until the sauce thickens slightly, about 1 minute. Add the orange segments and remove the sauce from the heat. Season with salt and pepper to taste. The sauce can be refrigerated, covered, for up to 5 days. Reheat it before serving.

Grating Citrus Peel

You can grate orange zest, or that of any other citrus fruit, on a box grater—use the side with the smallest holes. But, there's an easier to use tool called a Microplane. If you don't own one, run don't walk to the nearest cookware shop to buy it. A few strokes of this ingenious device gives you the finest imaginable grated zest. Whichever grater you use, grate only the oil-rich outer rind, not the bitter white pith beneath it.

MACAO

PEKING DUCK

INDIRECT GRILLING
SERVES 4

Peking duck is one of the glories of Chinese gastronomy. I never thought of it as barbecue until I visited Macao. This tiny Portuguese enclave, located an hour south of Hong Kong by hydrofoil, boasts some of the best food in Asia. (That's what happens when you marry two cultures who love to eat: the Portuguese and the Chinese.)

You may not find Lam Yam Wing in any of the guidebooks, but coming to Macao and visiting the restaurant afforded me a major gastronomic experience. The real pride and joy of the house is Peking duck, which has been brushed with honey and roasted to the color of mahogany. The waiter carves the skin into crackling crisp shards and serves it with silver dollar-size scallion pancakes. (No papery Peking pancakes here, but velvety, delicate, thin crêpes.) The actual meat of the duck is returned to the kitchen to be stir-fried with shallots and garlic. The recipe here is inspired by Lam Yam Wing.

Cooking duck in a covered grill using the indirect method produces a succulent and crisp duck without a lot of mess and work. Leaving the duck to dry uncovered in the refrigerator overnight crisps the skin even more.

Here, then, is a not strictly traditional, but eminently tasty Peking duck cooked on the grill. Don't be intimidated by the length of the recipe—the actual preparation time is minimal. I've included a recipe for scallion crêpes, which you can make while the duck cooks. If you're in a hurry, you could use packaged Peking pancakes or even flour tortillas, but neither is as delicate as the crêpes.

ADVANCE PREPARATION

24 hours for drying the duck skin

FOR THE DUCK

1 duck (4½ to 5 pounds), thawed if frozen
Salt and freshly ground black pepper
1 teaspoon Chinese five-spice powder
1 clove garlic, peeled
1 scallion, both white and green parts, trimmed
3 thin slices peeled fresh ginger
1 tablespoon Asian (dark) sesame oil

FOR THE SAUCE

1 cup hoisin sauce
¼ cup honey
¼ cup soy sauce
¼ cup rice wine or sake
3 cloves garlic, minced
1 tablespoon minced peeled fresh ginger

FOR SERVING

16 Scallion Crêpes (recipe follows), or Peking pancakes or flour tortillas
16 scallion brushes (page 295; see Note)

1. Prepare the duck: The day before you plan to serve the duck, remove and discard the fat just inside the body cavities. Remove the package of giblets and set aside for another use. Rinse the duck, inside and out, under cold running water, then drain and blot dry, inside and out, with paper towels. Place the duck in a roasting pan and let stand, uncovered, in the refrigerator overnight to dry out the skin.

2. Season the body cavity of the duck with salt, pepper, and ½ teaspoon of the five-spice powder. Place the garlic clove, scallion, and ginger slices in the body cavity, then turn the duck over on its breast so that the back side is up. Using the tip of a sharp, slender knife, make a small slit in the fatty part of the duck under each wing and a slit on the underside of each thigh. Prick the duck skin all over with a sharp carving fork, being careful not to pierce the meat. Brush the outside of the duck all over with the sesame oil and rub the skin all over with the remaining ½ teaspoon of five-spice powder and some salt and pepper.

3. Set the grill up for indirect grilling, place a large drip pan in the center, and preheat the grill to medium-low.

4. When ready to cook, place the duck, breast side up, on the hot grill grate over the drip pan. Cover the grill and cook the duck for 1½ hours. If using a charcoal grill, you'll need to add 10 to 12 fresh coals to each side after each hour of cooking.

5. Meanwhile, make the sauce: Combine the hoisin sauce, honey, soy sauce, rice wine, and minced garlic and ginger in a small, heavy saucepan and bring to a simmer over low heat. Let the sauce simmer gently, uncovered, until well flavored and syrupy, about 5 minutes.

6. After it has cooked for 1½ hours, turn the duck on its end over a bowl to drain off any juices that have accumulated in the cavity and discard the juices. Prick the skin again with a fork and make fresh slits under the wings and thighs to encourage draining. Continue cooking the duck until the skin is mahogany brown and crackling crisp and the meat is well-done and tender, 30 to 45 minutes longer. When done, an instant-read meat thermometer inserted in the thickest part of a thigh, but not touching the bone, should register about 170°F.

7. To serve: Transfer the duck to a platter. Present it to your guests, then using a sharp knife, carve the skin and meat off

PEKING DUCK WITH SCALLION CREPES | PAGE 292

the bones (you may want to do this in the kitchen). Spoon the sauce into small bowls or ramekins, one per guest. Arrange the duck meat and skin on one platter, the Scallion Crêpes and scallion brushes on another. Have each guest brush a crêpe with sauce, using a scallion brush. Place a slice of duck skin and meat on the crêpe (and a scallion brush, if desired) and roll it into a cone for eating.

NOTE: You'll need to allow a couple of hours for soaking the scallion brushes.

How to Make Scallion Brushes

Cut the roots and dark green tops off scallions, reserving the green parts for crêpes or another use. You want to wind up with three-inch pieces of scallion white. To form the individual "bristles" of the brushes, make a series of one-inch lengthwise cuts in each end of the scallion whites, gradually rotating the scallions. Soak the scallions in a bowl of ice water for a couple of hours to curl the ends of the brushes.

SCALLION CREPES

MAKES ABOUT SIXTEEN 4-INCH CREPES

These crêpes are much more delicate than Peking pancakes or tortillas. You can make them up to twenty-four hours ahead and store them wrapped in plastic in the refrigerator.

2 large eggs
½ teaspoon sugar
½ teaspoon salt
¾ cup milk
1 cup unbleached all-purpose flour
3 tablespoons very finely chopped trimmed scallion greens
1 tablespoon Asian (dark) sesame oil
Nonstick cooking oil spray, melted butter, or more sesame oil for oiling the crêpe pan

1. Place the eggs, sugar, and salt in a bowl and whisk until the sugar and salt dissolve. Whisk in the milk and ½ cup of water to blend well, then add the flour and whisk just to mix. If the batter looks lumpy, strain it into another bowl. Whisk in the scallions and sesame oil. The batter should be the consistency of heavy cream. If it is too thick, thin it with a little more water.

2. Lightly spray a 5-inch crêpe pan with oil (or brush it with a little butter or more sesame oil) and heat over medium heat (when the pan is hot enough, a drop of water placed in it will evaporate in 2 to 3 seconds). Off the heat, add 2 tablespoons of the crêpe batter to the pan all at once. Gently tilt and rotate the pan to form a thin 4-inch round crêpe.

3. Return the pan to the heat and cook the crêpe until lightly browned on both sides, 1 to 2 minutes per side, turning with a spatula. As the crêpes are done, stack them on top of one another on a plate. For best results, spray the pan lightly with oil between crêpes.

ITALY

TUSCAN GRILLED PHEASANT

INDIRECT GRILLING OR ROTISSERIE
SERVES 2

Da Delfina, in the village of Artimino near Florence, is just the sort of restaurant you want to wind up at after a long day on the barbecue trail. You drive up progressively narrower roads to a village perched atop a precipitously steep Tuscan hilltop. You come to a dining establishment that feels less like a restaurant than a private home. You're in Chianti country now, and Da Delfina has a terrace where, weather permitting, you can dine with an almost extraterrestrial view of the manicured vineyards below you.

The Macanese Grill

As a frequent and fervent traveler, I am fascinated by crossroads cuisines. The meeting—and sometimes clash—of two cultures along a narrow geographic interface has produced some of the world's most interesting food, as in Macao. This tiny Portuguese enclave on the southeastern coast of China is the very embodiment of what contemporary American chefs have come to call "fusion cuisine." Except that in this case the fusion has been going on for more than four hundred years, merging two cultures from opposite ends of the earth.

Macao is a tiny snippet of land located in the mouth of China's Pearl River estuary. Tiny? Its population of 450,000 lives on two small islands and a peninsula only two and a half square miles in size. Macao was founded as a Portuguese colony in 1557, when Iberian traders established an outpost there to serve as mercantile go-betweens to the Chinese and Japanese. Portugal is one of the smallest countries in Europe, but in the seventeenth century it projected its sphere of influence around the world. Macao was the easternmost outpost of an empire that stretched from Brazil to Angola and Mozambique to Goa in India and Timor.

Today Macao is a Special Administrative Region of China, and 5 percent of the mostly Chinese population speaks Portuguese, but you still find baroque churches, markets selling salt cod and olive oil, and pastry shops specializing in Portuguese pastries. This is also one of the few places in China where grilling is widespread, for the Portuguese brought grilling to China, a country whose complex cuisine is remarkable, and surprising, for its lack of live-fire cooking. In other words, you have a fusion of Chinese and Portuguese culinary cultures—known locally as Macanese cuisine.

Like most of the million-plus tourists who come here each year, I arrived on a jetfoil from Hong Kong. The ride took less than an hour, but it took me decades back in time. At first glance, Macao looks like any emerging Asian city—relentless construction, hellish traffic, high-rise apartments, and casinos crowding the waterfront. But step onto a side street, like the Rua de la Felicidade (the appropriately named "street of happiness" that once served the colony's red light district), and you could be in prewar China.

Merchandise spills from storefronts onto rickety tables lining the sidewalks. Vendors cook sheets of *au jok kohn,* a sort of sweet, salty, and deliciously fatty pork jerky, over braziers filled with blazing charcoal. Restaurants specialize in foods you didn't know you could eat: Snakes slither in the window of one establishment; another boasts cages of a small tapirlike mammal that are empty at the end of the evening. Come nightfall, the street fills with the heady aroma of cooking, as locals converge here for doorsill dining and outdoor socializing.

You'd expect to find grilling at Macao's Portuguese restaurants and you will. Consider Fernando's, opened by an Azores Islander and located on the most tranquil of Macao's islands, Coloane. In the center of Fernando's open-air kitchen stands a barbecue pit, where sardines, salt cod, even cuttlefish are grilled over burning charcoal. In true Portuguese fashion, grilled seafoods and meats are served with a tomato, bell pepper, and olive oil "salsa" and fiery *piri-piri* sauce.

Many of Macao's Chinese have adopted live-fire cooking. My next stop was a roadside barbecue joint called Lam Yam Wing on the island of Taipa. Run by four brothers, Lam Yam Wing is the farthest thing from a tourist trap. Instead the place is hopping with locals who come here for Chinese barbecue. The focal point of the restaurant is the grill, a twenty-foot-long metal trough with half a dozen different cooking zones. There's a rotisserie area, where whole chickens (with heads still intact) spin on mechanized turnspits. There's a gridiron on which chicken wings, sea crabs, and fat, buttery local eels sizzle. The cooking technique may be Portuguese, but the flavorings are pure Chinese: soy sauce, sesame oil, rice wine, ginger, and scallions. The food is cut into bite-size pieces so you can eat it with chopsticks. But many customers have adopted the Western practice of eating the 'cue with their hands.

The first thing you see when you enter the restaurant is an open kitchen with a massive hearth equipped with a multispit rotisserie and wood-burning grill. Cords of Tuscan oak lie stacked on the floor and in the courtyard below. The white-haired woman shelling cannellini beans at a table by the door is none other than Delfina Cioni herself, who founded the restaurant, after a stint as a private chef for a nearby countess, in 1961. Today the restaurant is run by her son, Carlo.

According to Carlo, it makes sense to cook game on the grill. After all, it wasn't so long ago that our hunter-gatherer forebears caught their own food and cooked it over communal campfires. Nonetheless, when grilling game, you have to keep its inherent dryness in mind. Game is much leaner than domesticated animals; as a result, it tends to dry out during cooking. The best way to avoid this is to wrap the game in pancetta, bacon, or caul fat.

I was the only person at my table eating pheasant the day I dined at Da Delfina, so they served me a boned, stuffed pheasant leg. The recipe here calls for a whole pheasant, which you can bone if you're feeling ambitious (I've provided instructions). But the pheasant will be perfectly delicious even if you don't bone it. Note that if you can't find pheasant, chicken and game hen are delicious prepared in this fashion.

ADVANCE PREPARATION

30 minutes for soaking the bread

SPECIAL EQUIPMENT

Butcher's string; skewers (optional); rotisserie (optional)

INGREDIENTS

1 pheasant (about 2¼ pounds)
1 cup milk
4 thick slices stale country-style white bread, crusts removed
8 ounces Swiss chard leaves, trimmed
Salt
1 clove garlic, minced
⅓ cup freshly grated Parmesan cheese
Freshly ground black pepper
8 thin slices pancetta (about 6 ounces)
4 sprigs fresh rosemary

1. Rinse the pheasant, inside and out, under cold running water, then drain and blot dry, inside and out, with paper towels. If you're feeling ambitious, partially bone the pheasant: Start at the neck opening. Using the tip of a sharp paring knife, cut the flesh away from the rib cage. When you get to the wing joints, cut right through them. As you bone the bird, pull the flesh back over the rib cage, the way you would peel off a glove. Continue boning until you get to the leg joints. Cut through them as well. Cut out the thigh bones. Pull out the rib cage and turn the pheasant back inside in (like turning an inside-out sock back to right side out). This sounds a good deal more complicated and messy than it really is. You can certainly stuff and cook the pheasant without removing the bones. Refrigerate the bird, covered, while you prepare the stuffing.

2. Pour the milk over the bread in a shallow bowl and let soak for 30 minutes.

3. Meanwhile, cook the Swiss chard in a large pot of rapidly boiling salted water until tender, about 5 minutes. Rinse the chard under cold water, drain it well, and blot dry with paper towels. Chop the Swiss chard as finely as possible and squeeze it in your hands to wring out any water. Place the chard in a medium-size bowl.

4. Squeeze the bread to wring out the milk. Add the bread to the Swiss chard along with the garlic and Parmesan and mix well. Season the stuffing mixture with salt and pepper to taste, then spoon the stuffing into the pheasant and sew or skewer the bird shut.

5. Season the outside of the pheasant with salt and pepper. Wrap the bird in strips of the pancetta, tucking the sprigs of rosemary underneath them. Use butcher's string to tie the pancetta in place.

6. There are two ways to cook the pheasant: using the indirect grilling method or spit roasting it.

If grilling using the indirect grilling method, set up the grill for indirect grilling, place a drip pan in the center, and preheat the grill to medium. When ready to cook, brush and oil the grill grate. Place the pheasant on the hot grate over the drip pan and cover the grill. Cook the pheasant until nicely browned and the tip of a metal skewer or sharp knife inserted into the thickest part of the thigh comes out very hot to the touch, about 1 hour.

If using a rotisserie, set up the grill for spit roasting following the manufacturer's instructions and preheat to medium-high.

When ready to cook, skewer the pheasant on the spit. Attach the spit to the rotisserie mechanism, turn on the motor, and cover the grill. Cook the pheasant until nicely browned and the tip of a metal skewer or sharp knife inserted into the thickest part of the thigh comes out very hot to the touch, 40 minutes to 1 hour.

7. To serve, remove the trussing string and skewers (if using). Let the pheasant rest for 10 minutes, then cut it in half and serve.

GRILLED PHEASANT LEGS

DIRECT GRILLING
SERVES 4

The Italian preparation for a whole pheasant also works well when used to stuff pheasant or chicken legs. You can use wooden toothpicks to pin the stuffed legs closed or tie them with butcher's string.

4 pheasant or chicken legs (about 2 pounds in all)
Stuffing from Tuscan Grilled Pheasant (Steps 2 through 4, page 295)
8 thin slices pancetta (about 6 ounces; see Note)
4 sprigs fresh rosemary

1. Rinse the pheasant legs under cold running water, then drain and blot them dry with paper towels. Partially bone the pheasant legs by cutting out each thigh bone, working from the inside of the top of the leg.

2. Prepare the stuffing as described, then stuff the pheasant legs with the stuffing and tie or sew the openings shut, or pin them shut with wooden toothpicks. Wrap each pheasant leg in 2 slices of pancetta, tucking a sprig of rosemary underneath. Tie the pancetta in place with butcher's string.

3. Set up the grill for two-zone direct grilling (see page 18), preheating two thirds of the grill to medium-high and leaving one third heat free as a safety zone.

4. When ready to cook, brush and oil the grill grate. Arrange the pheasant legs on the grate over the hot zone of the grill and cook, turning with tongs, until the skin is nicely browned and the tip of a skewer or sharp knife inserted into a thigh comes out very hot, 8 to 12 minutes per side. If you get flare-ups, move the legs to the safety zone until the flames die down. Remove the string from the legs before serving.

NOTE: You'll need butcher's string to tie the pancetta around the pheasant legs.

GREECE

GRILLED QUAIL SANTORINI

DIRECT GRILLING
SERVES 4

Santorini is one of the most heartachingly beautiful of the Greek islands, a collapsed shell of volcano on the steep sides of which whitewashed villas and churches cling. The island has given its name to an equally picturesque restaurant in Chicago's Greektown, a softly lit, split-level dining room where guests dine amid copper cookware, rustic wicker chairs, baskets hanging from the rafters, and a blazing fireplace. Quail is a house specialty here, and despite the simplicity of the preparation, this is one of the best ways I know to grill the tiny bird.

ADVANCE PREPARATION

1 to 2 hours for marinating the quail

INGREDIENTS

8 quail (about 2 pounds in all)
½ cup red wine vinegar, or more to taste
½ cup fresh lemon juice
1½ tablespoons crumbled dried oregano (see Greek Oregano, opposite page)
2 teaspoons salt, or more to taste
2 teaspoons freshly ground black pepper, or more to taste
¾ cup extra-virgin olive oil, preferably Greek

1. Remove and discard any fat just inside the body cavities and rinse the quail, inside and out, under cold running water, then drain and blot dry with paper towels. Spatchcock the quail following the directions on page 289 or cut them in half. Arrange the quail, skin side down, in a nonreactive baking dish and set aside while you prepare the vinaigrette marinade.

2. Combine the wine vinegar, lemon juice, oregano, salt, and pepper in a large bowl and whisk until the salt dissolves. Whisk in the olive oil to blend. Taste for seasoning, adding more wine vinegar, salt, and/or pepper as necessary; the mixture should be highly seasoned. Pour half of the vinaigrette over the quail, turning the birds to coat thoroughly. Let the quail marinate in the refrigerator, covered, for 1 to 2 hours, turning once or twice. Set aside the remaining vinaigrette until serving time.

3. Set up the grill for two-zone direct grilling (see page 18), preheating two thirds of the grill to medium-high and leaving one third heat free as a safety zone.

4. When ready to cook, brush and oil the grill grate. Remove the quail from the marinade and discard the marinade. Arrange the quail, skin side down, on the grate over the hot zone of the grill. Cook the quail until they are nicely browned and the juices run clear when the tip of a skewer or sharp knife is inserted in the thickest part of a thigh, 5 to 8 minutes per side. If you get flare-ups, move the quail to the safety zone until the flames die down.

5. Transfer the quail to serving plates or a platter and let rest for 2 minutes before serving. Whisk the reserved vinaigrette to recombine and serve it spooned over the quail.

Greek Oregano

Greek oregano has a richer, mintier flavor than the oregano most North Americans are accustomed to. Ferret out Greek oregano at Greek or Middle Eastern markets.

AFGHANISTAN

AFGHAN GRILLED QUAIL

DIRECT GRILLING
SERVES 4

If you've always found quail to be a little on the dry side, this recipe is for you. The spiced yogurt marinade makes the birds exceptionally moist and succulent. The only "difficult" thing is remembering to drain the yogurt ahead of time. By the way, even if you don't like quail, you can enjoy this dish. The marinade makes a wonderful dip for crudités. This recipe was inspired by a New York restaurant called Khyber Pass.

ADVANCE PREPARATION

2 to 3 hours for draining the yogurt, plus 3 to 12 hours for marinating the quail

INGREDIENTS

- **4 cups plain whole-milk yogurt**
- **2 teaspoons hot or sweet paprika**
- **1 teaspoon salt, or more to taste**
- **1 teaspoon ground coriander**
- **½ teaspoon cayenne pepper, or more to taste**
- **½ teaspoon curry powder**
- **½ teaspoon ground cumin**
- **½ teaspoon ground turmeric**
- **½ teaspoon freshly ground black pepper**
- **8 quail (about 2 pounds in all)**

1. Set a yogurt strainer, or regular strainer lined with a double layer of dampened cheesecloth, over a bowl. Add the yogurt to the strainer and let drain, in the refrigerator, for 2 to 3 hours.

2. Discard the liquid from the drained yogurt. Transfer the yogurt (it will be semifirm but not dry), to a large nonreactive bowl or baking dish. Add the paprika, salt, coriander, cayenne, curry powder, cumin, turmeric, and black pepper and whisk to blend. Taste for seasoning, adding more salt and/or cayenne as necessary; the mixture should be highly seasoned. Set the marinade aside while you prepare the quail.

3. Remove and discard any fat just inside the body cavities, rinse the quail inside and out, under cold running water, then drain and blot dry with paper towels. Spatchcock the quail following the directions on page 289 or cut them in half.

4. Add the quail to the bowl with the marinade, turning to coat thoroughly. Let the quail marinate in the refrigerator, covered, for 3 to 12 hours, turning the birds occasionally.

5. Set up the grill for two-zone direct grilling (see page 18), preheating two thirds of the grill to medium-high and leaving one third heat free as a safety zone.

6. When ready to cook, brush and oil the grill grate. Remove the quail from the marinade and discard the marinade. Arrange the quail, skin side down, on the grate over the hot zone of the grill. Cook the quail until they are nicely browned and the juices run clear when the tip of a skewer or sharp knife is inserted in the thickest part of a thigh, 5 to 8 minutes per side. If you get flare-ups, move the quail to the safety zone until the flames die down.

7. Transfer the quail to serving plates or a platter and let rest for 2 minutes before serving.

UZBEKISTAN

SPICED GRILLED QUAIL

DIRECT GRILLING
SERVES 4

This recipe comes from what I call the barbecue belt of the former Soviet Union. Grilling plays a central role in the cuisines of the Central Asian republics of Turkmenistan, Tajikistan, and Uzbekistan. The quail here are popular in Uzbekistan, where according to the Russian scholar Darra Goldstein, the birds would be wrapped in pumpkin leaves and roasted in hot ashes. The garlic, cumin, and coriander marinade creates complex layers of flavor.

Goldstein, author of many books, including *The Georgian Feast: The Vibrant Culture and Savory Food of the Republic of Georgia,* has adopted a more streamlined method for cooking the quail than the traditional leaf-wrapped one. She splits the quail, marinates them, and grills them over direct flames. Instructions for the traditional method follow. Either way you'll be amazed how such a tiny bird can have such a big taste.

ADVANCE PREPARATION

4 hours for marinating the quail

INGREDIENTS

8 quail (about 2 pounds in all)
2 teaspoons coarse salt (kosher or sea)
2 teaspoons cumin seeds
2 teaspoons coriander seeds
2 teaspoons whole black peppercorns
2 cloves garlic, chopped
2 tablespoons extra-virgin olive oil

1. Remove and discard any fat just inside the body cavities and rinse the quail, inside and out, under cold running water, then drain and blot dry with paper towels. Spatchcock the quail following the directions on page 289 or cut them in half. Place the quail in a large bowl or baking dish and set aside while you prepare the spice paste.

2. Combine the salt, cumin and coriander seeds, and peppercorns in a mortar and crush to a powder with a pestle, then work in the garlic and olive oil; or grind the salt and spices to a powder in a spice mill and combine them with the garlic and olive oil in a small bowl. Using your fingers, rub the spice paste all over the quail. Let the quail marinate in the refrigerator, covered, for 4 hours.

3. Set up the grill for two-zone direct grilling (see page 000), preheating two thirds of the grill to medium-high and leaving one third heat free as a safety zone.

4. When ready to cook, brush and oil the grill grate. Arrange the quail, skin side down, on the grate over the hot zone of the grill. Cook the quail until they are nicely browned and their juices run clear when the tip of a skewer or sharp knife is inserted in the thickest part of a thigh, 5 to 8 minutes per side. If you get flare-ups, move the quail to the safety zone until the flames die down.

5. Transfer the quail to serving plates or a platter and let rest for 2 minutes before serving.

UZBEKISTAN

QUAIL GRILLED IN GRAPE LEAVES

DIRECT GRILLING USING CHARCOAL
SERVES 4

Intrigued by the traditional recipe for Uzbekistani spiced quail, I tried wrapping the birds in grape leaves (different from pumpkin leaves, of course, but more widely available in this country) and roasting them in the embers. The results were amazing. In order to cook the quail using this method, you need to have a charcoal grill.

ADVANCE PREPARATION

1 hour for soaking the grape leaves plus 4 hours for marinating the quail

SPECIAL EQUIPMENT

Butcher's string to tie the grape leaves around the quail

INGREDIENTS

40 grape leaves packed in brine (see Note)
8 quail (about 2 pounds in all)
Spice paste as prepared in Spiced Grilled Quail (Step 2, at left)

1. Rinse the grape leaves under cold running water, then let them soak in a bowl of cold water to cover for 1 hour, changing the water several times.

2. Remove and discard the fat just inside the body cavities and rinse the quail inside and out, under cold running water, then drain and blot dry with paper towels. Leave the quail whole. Place a little spice paste in the cavity of each bird; rub the remaining spice paste on the skin.

3. Drain the grape leaves and blot dry. Wrap each quail in five grape leaves and tie securely with butcher's string. Let the quail marinate in the refrigerator, covered, for 4 hours.

4. Set up a charcoal grill for direct grilling and preheat to medium-high.

5. When ready to cook, nestle the wrapped quail in the ashes. Roast the birds until they are cooked through, 15 to 20 minutes, turning the quail from time to time with tongs. To test for doneness, insert the tip of a metal skewer or sharp knife into the thickest part of a thigh. It should come out very hot to the touch.

6. Serve the quail in the grape leaves, brushing off any excess ash. Since the quail have been grilled in the ashes, the grape leaves will be inedible and should be removed before the quail are eaten.

FENNEL-GRILLED BASS FLAMBEED WITH PERNOD | PAGE 307

CHAPTER 11

WATER MEETS FIRE: FISH ON THE GRILL

Fish live in water. But they acquire their maximum flavor from fire. This truth is not lost on grill jockeys around the world, who grill everything imaginable, from tiny sardines to spectacular whole flamed sea bass, from Turkish and Brazilian swordfish kebabs to chile-laced Bahamian-style snapper. Grilling was probably the first way man cooked fish and, as my travels suggest, it remains the best.

"Food is meant to tempt as well as nourish, and everything that lives in water is seductive."

—Jean-Paul Aron

This chapter covers the fine points of grilling fish, from steaks and fillets to dramatically presented whole sea creatures. Have you ever had a problem with fish that fell apart or stuck to the grill? Here's where I explain how to avoid these pitfalls. I also explore some of the ingenious techniques that grilling experts have evolved for keeping fish moist and flavorful, including wrapping and grilling it in grape leaves, as they do in the Republic of Georgia, or cooking it on lemongrass skewers like they do in Bali.

For many people the subject of grilling fish begins and ends simply with salmon or tuna steaks. Journey with me on the barbecue trail and you'll discover a whole new, thrilling world of grilled seafood.

SOUTH AFRICA

WHOLE GRILLED SNAPPER WITH SOUTH AFRICAN SPICES

FISH BRAI

INDIRECT GRILLING
SERVES 4

B*rai* is the South African word used to describe a barbecue. You may be surprised by the Indian and Malaysian flavorings (curry, ginger, and coconut milk) in this recipe, but not once you take into account that South Africa has large Indian and Malaysian communities. I find that the curry and coconut milk have a wonderful way of bringing out the sweetness of fish.

Cooking a whole fish on the grill always presents a challenge. If you cook it directly over live fire, you run the risk of burning the skin before the center of the fish is cooked. You also face the tricky task of inverting the fish without having it fall apart. South Africans solve the problem by using the indirect grilling method, so you don't need to turn the fish.

ADVANCE PREPARATION

3 to 8 hours for marinating the fish

INGREDIENTS

1 whole snapper, bluefish, sea bass, or other large fish (3½ to 4 pounds), cleaned and trimmed of fins, head and tail left on
Salt and freshly ground black pepper
1 tablespoon curry powder
1 tablespoon hot paprika, or 1 to 2 teaspoons cayenne pepper
1½ teaspoons ground cumin
3 tablespoons vegetable oil
3 tablespoons unsweetened canned coconut milk
2 tablespoons fresh lemon juice
1 bunch scallions, both white and green parts, trimmed and finely chopped
5 cloves garlic, peeled and crushed
1 piece (½ inch) fresh ginger, peeled and thinly sliced
¾ cup coarsely chopped fresh cilantro leaves

1. Rinse the fish, inside and out, under cold running water, then drain it and blot dry with paper towels. Make 4 diagonal slashes, to the bone, in each side of the fish. Season the fish, inside and out (including the side slashes), with salt and black pepper. Place the fish in a nonreactive roasting pan and set aside while you prepare the spice paste.

2. Combine the curry powder, paprika, cumin, oil, coconut milk, lemon juice, scallions, garlic, ginger, and cilantro with 1 teaspoon of salt and ½ teaspoon of black pepper in a food processor or blender and process to a smooth paste. Taste for seasoning, adding more salt and/or black pepper as necessary; the spice paste should be highly seasoned.

3. Spoon half of the spice paste into the cavity and under the gills of the fish. Spread the remaining spice paste over the outside of the fish, working it into the slashes in the sides. Let the fish marinate in the refrigerator, covered, for at least 3 hours, or up to 8 hours for a richer flavor.

4. Set up the grill for indirect grilling, place a drip pan in the center, and preheat the grill to high.

5. When ready to cook, brush and oil the grill grate. Place the fish on the hot grate and cover the grill. Grill the fish until it breaks into firm flakes when pressed with a finger, 45 minutes to 1 hour. If the fish starts to brown too much, lower the heat by closing the vents or turning down the gas.

6. Using two long spatulas, carefully transfer the fish to a serving platter. At the table, fillet the fish as described on page 309 and serve at once.

BAHAMAS

BAHAMIAN-STYLE WHOLE GRILLED SNAPPER

INDIRECT GRILLING
SERVES 4

This recipe comes from a cook shack in Nassau in the Bahamas, but it typifies the way fish is cooked throughout the Caribbean. There they start with a whole fish so fresh it was still swimming a few hours earlier. They rub it with fiery goat peppers and marinate it in a piquant mixture of fresh lime juice, garlic, ginger, and black pepper. Then it's grilled using the indirect method or directly over a low flame. The lucky diner can't help but marvel at how something so simple can taste so good.

I can't think of a more dramatic showpiece for a summery Caribbean-style cookout. No sweat on the advance preparation, which takes a couple of minutes and can be done several hours ahead. No sweat on the cooking—fish grilled using the indirect method eliminates the worry of burning. For maximum drama, I like to use one large fish—a four- to five-pound snapper or mahimahi, for example, which will serve four people. Good northern fish to prepare this way include striped bass, sea bass, and bluefish.

Goat peppers are the Bahamian version of a Scotch bonnet. The tender of tongue could use a milder chile, but the flavor won't be strictly authentic. (Don't worry—goat peppers and Scotch bonnets lose a lot of their heat during cooking.) I like to cook the fish on a banana leaf or piece of aluminum foil. Grilling this way retains some of the juices and keeps the fish from sticking to the grate.

How to Grill the Perfect Whole Fish

A beach. A campfire. A glistening fish—minutes out of the water—cooked on a stick or grate over blazing coals. It's a scene that's almost as old as mankind itself and as enjoyable as perfect beach weather. And it serves to remind us that fish never tastes better than when cooked over open fire.

That's the good news. The bad news is that most of us either burn fish to a crisp, serve it raw in the center, or leave half the fish sticking to the grate of the grill. Fortunately, there are three methods for grilling a perfect whole fish every time. And, you may want to invest in a fish-grilling basket. These hinged, fish-shaped devices keep the fish off the grate (where it can stick), enabling you to turn the fish without having it slide off a spatula. Essential? Of course not. But fish baskets can make the grilling process a whole lot easier.

But before you even start your fire, choose the right fish for grilling whole. Flat fish, like snappers, pompano, black bass, sole, and trout are ideal. You can also grill large fish, like salmon and bluefish, using the indirect method. The fish you grill should be impeccably fresh. The eyes should be shiny and clear; the gills should be red; and the fish should be utterly free of a fish smell. When you are ready to grill, make three or four deep diagonal slashes to the bone in each side of the fish. This allows any marinade or basting mixture to penetrate the flesh and speeds up the cooking time.

And, you need to know how to tell when the fish is done. To do this, press the fish with your finger. When properly cooked the flesh will break into firm flakes. It should easily pull away from the bones. Use a long spatula to gently slide the fish off the grate, or if you are using a fish-grilling basket, simply remove it from the grate. Then transfer the fish to a platter.

The Direct Flame Method

Preheat the grill to medium-high. Generously oil the grill grate or hinged fish-grilling basket. Brush both sides of the fish with oil or melted butter. Place the fish on the hot grate directly over the heat and grill until the skin is dark and crisp and the flesh is cooked through to the bone, four to fifteen minutes per side, depending on the size of the fish. Turn the fish using a long spatula or by inverting the fish-grilling basket.

The Indirect Method

This method is particularly well suited to large fish, like whole salmon: Set up the grill for indirect cooking and preheat it to high or medium-high. (You don't really need a drip pan because fish is so lean, but if you wish, set one in place.) Generously oil the grate or hinged fish-grilling basket and brush the fish on both sides with oil or melted butter. Place the fish in the center of the grate, away from the heat; cover the grill; and cook the fish until done, thirty minutes to one hour (sometimes more), depending on the size of the fish.

The Banana Leaf Method

This method from Southeast Asia is the easiest way to grill a one- or two-pound whole fish. A fresh or frozen banana leaf will keep the fish from drying out. You can find these at an Asian or Hispanic market. Cut the banana leaf into a rectangle that is a little larger than the size of the fish you will be grilling. In a pinch, you can make a "high-tech" banana leaf by cutting four to six pieces of aluminum foil slightly larger than the fish and stacking them in layers.

Then, preheat the grill to high. Generously oil the grate. Brush both sides of the fish with oil or melted butter. Place the fish on the hot grate directly over the heat and grill it on one side until the skin is dark and crisp, six to twelve minutes, depending on its size.

Place the banana leaf on the grate next to the fish and invert the fish onto it. Cook the fish until it is cooked through, six to twelve minutes, depending on its size. Discard the banana leaf before serving.

Fish Grilling Chart

CUT	METHOD	HEAT	DONENESS (cooked through)
WHOLE FISH			
1 to 1½ pounds	direct	medium-high	6 to 10 minutes per pound
2 to 5 pounds	indirect	medium	12 to 15 minutes per pound
FILLETS			
½ inch thick	direct	high	2 to 4 minutes per side
1 inch thick	direct	high	3 to 6 minutes per side
STEAKS			
½ inch thick	direct	high	2 to 4 minutes per side
1 inch thick	direct	high	3 to 6 minutes per side

This chart is offered as a broad guideline to cooking times for the various cuts of fish. Remember, grilling is an art, not a science. When in doubt, refer to times in the individual recipes.

ADVANCE PREPARATION

30 minutes for marinating the fish

SPECIAL EQUIPMENT

1 banana leaf (see Note), cut in a rectangle the size of the fish, or 4 to 6 layers of aluminum foil, folded to the size of the fish

INGREDIENTS

- 1 whole snapper, pompano, or other large fish (4 to 5 pounds), cleaned and trimmed of fins, head and tail left on
- 3 goat peppers, Scotch bonnet chiles, or habañero peppers
- 4 large, juicy limes
- Salt and freshly ground black pepper
- 1 piece (2 inches) fresh ginger, peeled and thinly sliced
- 2 cloves garlic, thinly sliced
- 1 to 2 tablespoons extra-virgin olive oil (optional; not traditional, but I like it)

1. Rinse the fish, inside and out, under cold running water, then drain it and blot dry with paper towels. Make 4 or 5 diagonal slashes, to the bone, in each side of the fish.

2. Thinly slice 2 goat peppers; cut the remaining goat pepper lengthwise in half. Cut one of the limes in half lengthwise, then cut it into thin crosswise slices. Cut a second lime in half crosswise. Juice the remaining 2 limes and set the juice aside in a small cup.

3. Rub the fish all over with the cut sides of the goat pepper and lime halves. Sprinkle salt and black pepper in the fish cavity and the slashes in the sides of the fish. Place a slice each of goat pepper, lime, ginger, and garlic in each slit and under each gill, then place the remaining slices in the fish cavity.

4. Place the banana leaf or aluminum foil on a large platter and place the fish on top. Pour the lime juice over the fish and season it again with salt and black pepper, then drizzle the olive oil (if using) over it. Let the fish marinate in the refrigerator, covered, for 30 minutes while you preheat the grill.

5. Set up the grill for indirect cooking and preheat to high.

6. When ready to cook, place the fish, on the banana leaf, in the center of the grill away from the heat. Cover the grill and cook the fish until the flesh breaks into firm flakes when pressed with a finger, 1 to 1½ hours. If using a charcoal grill, you'll need to add 10 to 12 fresh coals to each side after 1 hour. If the fish starts to brown too much, lower the heat.

7. Using two long spatulas, carefully transfer the fish to a serving platter. At the table, fillet the fish as described on page 309 and serve at once.

NOTE: If you're lucky enough to live in a city with a large Asian or Hispanic community, you may be able to find fresh or frozen banana leaves for this. Otherwise use aluminum foil.

FRANCE

FENNEL-GRILLED BASS FLAMBEED WITH PERNOD

LOUP DE MER AU FENOUIL FLAMBE

DIRECT GRILLING
SERVES 4

Here's a dish for cooks with a penchant for theatrics. Freshly caught *loup de mer* (literally, wolf of the sea, corresponding to our sea bass) grilled over burning fennel stalks and dramatically flambéed at the tableside is the ultimate culinary showpiece of the French Riviera. It's easy to make and impressive to serve. There are only two remotely challenging aspects to the recipe: finding whole fennel stalks and remembering to dry them ahead of time.

Fennel, a bulbous green-white vegetable with the flavor of licorice and the crunch of celery, grows wild in Provence, in the south of France. My wife, Barbara, and I often found it on roadside picnics. Once considered exotic in the United States, it can now be found at most supermarkets, but to get fennel with the stalks attached, you may need to go to a farm stand, an Italian market, or a specialty greengrocer (although there are supermarket produce departments that do carry untrimmed fennel). Once you find the fennel, cut off the stalks and dry them as described in the box at right (the dried stalks will keep for months).

Here's the authentic recipe for *loup de mer au fenouil flambé* from the Auberge des Glycines on the tiny island of Porquerolles. You can grill the fennel bulbs (see page 408 for instructions). An alternative recipe, for people who can't find fennel stalks, follows the main recipe.

ADVANCE PREPARATION

24 hours to dry the fennel stalks, if using

INGREDIENTS

2 whole sea bass (each about 2 pounds), cleaned and trimmed of fins, heads and tails left on (see Note)
Salt and freshly ground black pepper
10 to 12 dried fennel stalks (see box, below)
3 tablespoons extra-virgin olive oil
¼ cup Pernod or other anise-flavored liqueur
Lemon wedges, for serving

1. Rinse the fish, inside and out, under cold running water, then drain them and blot dry with paper towels. Make 3 diagonal slashes, to the bone, in each side of each fish. Season the fish, inside and out (including the side slashes), with salt and pepper. Place 2 dried fennel stalks in the cavity of each fish. Brush the fish on both sides with the olive oil and season again with salt and pepper.

2. Set up the grill for direct grilling and preheat to medium-high.

3. When ready to cook, arrange 6 fennel stalks on a serving platter. Place the remaining fennel stalks directly on the hot coals or, if using a gas grill, on the grill grate. Brush and oil

How to Dry Fennel Stalks

Preheat the oven to 200°F. Take two to three bulbs of fennel with their stalks and leaves attached and cut the stalks off flush with the bulbs; reserve the fennel bulbs for another use. Cut away the leaves and arrange the stalks in one layer on a baking sheet. Bake the stalks for three hours. Turn off the heat and leave the fennel stalks in the oven overnight to finish drying. (Alternatively, you can tie the fennel stalks together and hang them upside down in a cool, dry place until brittle and dry, one to two weeks.) If not using the stalks immediately, they can be stored in a resealable plastic bag for up to three months.

the grill grate. If you're worried about the fish sticking, use hinged fish-grilling baskets (see page 305); otherwise, place both fish directly on the hot grate or on top of the fennel stalks and grill until the skin on the first side is dark and crisp and the flesh is cooked through to the bone on that side, 8 to 12 minutes. Turn each fish carefully with a long spatula and cook on the second side until the flesh breaks into firm flakes when pressed with a finger, 8 to 12 minutes longer.

4. During the last 2 or so minutes the fish cooks, warm the Pernod in a heavy saucepan at the side of the grill; don't let it boil or even get too warm to touch.

5. Using a spatula, carefully transfer each fish to the fennel stalk–lined platter. Pour the warmed Pernod over the fish and then carefully ignite the liqueur with a long match. Carefully bring the flaming fish to the table. When the flame dies out, fillet the fish as described on page 309 and serve at once, with lemon wedges.

NOTE: *Loup de mer* is a long, slender, dark gray fish with a fine-flavored, tender white flesh. While it corresponds most closely to North American sea bass, snapper, striped bass, or sea trout could be substituted here.

FENNEL-GRILLED BASS FLAMBEED WITH PERNOD II

Prepare the sea bass as described in the Fennel-Grilled Bass Flambéed with Pernod recipe on page 307, substituting a trimmed bulb of fresh fennel for the dried fennel stalks. Cut the fresh fennel lengthwise into thin slices. Place a few slices of fennel in the cavity of each fish and toss a few strips on the coals or place them on the grate before grilling. Brush the remaining fennel slices with olive oil and season them with salt and pepper, then grill the fennel slices, along with the fish, until tender and nicely browned, 3 to 4 minutes per side, turning with tongs. Arrange the grilled fennel slices on a serving platter and place the grilled fish on top. Flambé the fish as described in Step 5 and serve. (The advantage of this method is that you can eat the grilled fennel.)

FRANCE

GRILLED SEA BASS
WITH FRESH ARTICHOKE SALAD
LOUP DE MER GRILLE AUX ARTICHAUTS

DIRECT GRILLING
SERVES 4

My wife and I arrived in Nice in June, just in time for the first of the season's *artichauts violets.* These purple-tinged baby artichokes are so mild flavored and tender, you needn't even bother to cook them. Rather, the tough outside leaves are pulled off and discarded (there's no hairy choke to remove), then the artichokes are sliced paper-thin on a mandoline to be enjoyed raw. Their softly crunchy texture and delicate licorice flavor are a revelation.

Baby artichokes are usually served in salads, but at least one restaurant in Nice serves them atop grilled sea bass—a combination that is as unforgettable as it is unexpected. The traditional fish for this recipe is *loup de mer* (sea bass), but you can also use whole snappers, porgies, striped bass, or even one and a half to two pounds of a steak fish, like swordfish or tuna.

ADVANCE PREPARATION

20 minutes for marinating the fish

FOR THE FISH

2 whole sea bass (each about 2 pounds), cleaned and trimmed of fins, heads and tails left on
Coarse salt (kosher or sea) and freshly ground black pepper
2 tablespoons extra-virgin olive oil, plus additional olive oil for brushing

FOR THE ARTICHOKE SALAD

16 baby artichokes (see Note)
2 tablespoons fresh lemon juice
1 large or 2 small ripe tomatoes, peeled and seeded (see box, page 454), then cut into ¼-inch dice
8 fresh basil leaves, thinly slivered
2 tablespoons finely chopped fresh chives or scallion greens
1 small clove garlic, minced
1 anchovy fillet, drained and finely chopped, or 1 teaspoon anchovy paste (optional)
¼ cup extra-virgin olive oil
Salt and freshly ground black pepper

HOW TO FILLET A WHOLE GRILLED FISH

Maître d's do it at the tony restaurants on the Côte d'Azur. You, too, can fillet a whole grilled fish at tableside, and with a little practice, you'll display the panache of a pro. First, you'll need a large serving fork and spoon and a platter.

1. *Carefully peel the skin off the top side of the fish (if you want to serve it skinless) and set the skin on a refuse platter.*

2. *Using the side of the spoon, make a lengthwise cut down the back of the fish, just above the backbone. Gently ease the spoon into the cut, loosening the fish from the bones along the entire top side of the fish frame.*

3. *Using the spoon and fork, remove the top half of the fish and transfer it to a platter.*

4. *Now, using the side of the spoon, make a lengthwise cut down the back of the fish, just below the backbone. Slide the spoon under the backbone.*

5. *Using the spoon and fork, lift off the backbone, frame, and fish head and transfer them to the refuse platter.*

6. *Carefully turn the bottom half of the fish over; peel off and discard the skin, if desired. If the fish breaks into large pieces strategically place lemon slices on top. Cut the fish into individual portions and transfer these to plates.*

A New French Paradox

This is a story about a French paradox. Not the one that explains how the French can consume endless quantities of butter and foie gras without gaining excess weight or keeling over from heart disease. (The solution to that paradox, seemingly, lies in drinking lots of red wine.) No, the paradox puzzling me has to do with how a nation that reputedly has the world's greatest cuisine can do without what is arguably the world's most basic, primal, and universal cooking method: grilling.

That's right, grilling. Thumb through any of the great reference books on French cuisine—from Escoffier to Bocuse—and you'll find few if any recipes for grilling. Dine at a Michelin-starred restaurant in Paris and you'd be hard-pressed to find a single dish that is grilled. Sautéed? Yes. Roasted? Yes. Baked. Broiled. Fried. Even steamed. But grilling simply isn't a part of the classic French culinary repertory.

So does this mean that the French don't like barbecue? Not on your life. It turns out that the French are ardent grillers. Just not at their high-profile restaurants. So where do you find French grilling? Well, first of all, in the countryside. Especially in Provence. This most Mediterranean of French provinces is the epicenter of grilling, featuring casual grill eateries and country inns where embers blaze away in fireplaces. Traditionally, live-fire cooking was done indoors over the hearth, and it remains as much a winter as summer activity.

One of these establishments bears the evocative name of La Grillade au Feu de Bois (The Wood Fire Grill). Located in an eighteenth-century Provençal farmhouse in the hamlet of Flassans-Sur-Issole, the restaurant–country inn features simple lamb chops and massive rib steaks grilled over blazing vine trimmings in an ancient stone fireplace. As in most French grilling, the seasonings are simple: olive oil, salt, pepper, and a sprinkling of herbes de Provence.

Seafood restaurants are another source of live-fire cooked French fare, especially on the coast. One of the most famous dishes of the Côte d'Azur is sea bass flamed with fennel. The fish is grilled over dried fennel stalks and flambéed—theatrically at tableside—with an anise-flavored liqueur, like Pernod. Less well known but no less delectable is *raïto,* a dish of grilled tuna served with a red wine, olive, and caper sauce that I first tasted at an inn on a remote Mediterranean island called Porquerolles.

The French also do a lot of grilling at home. One of a Frenchman's favorite social gatherings bears the curious name of *mechoui.* The term comes from North Africa, where it refers to a whole spit-roasted lamb. It's interesting to note that the French had to borrow a term from another language to describe a backyard barbecue.

Some years ago, I attended a *mechoui* with friends at a farmhouse in the Champagne region. A huge fire had been built using vine stalks. The fare ranged from grilled lamb to sanguine sirloin steaks to pork chops. The only remotely North African element in this *mechoui* was a spicy Algerian sausage called *merguez.* This lurid red sausage has become a fixture on the French culinary landscape.

But with a little persistence, you don't even need to leave Paris to find great live-fire cooking. In fact, in most cases you don't have to go much farther than a neighborhood charcuterie. The French do all things culinary well, but no one can beat them at spit-roasted chicken. The French rotisserie is an awesome contraption, a tall vertical hearth with horizontal rows of mechanical turnspits that spin in front of what looks like a wall of flame created by rows of horizontal gas burners. Fresh chickens are placed on the top turnspit, and as they turn, the dripping fat bastes the more cooked birds below. Sure, the quality of the poultry helps. But equally important is the cooking method: the high, even heat of the wall of flames.

So, barbecue buffs, when you visit France, don't despair of finding great grilling—you just have to know where to look for it. Which just goes to show that even a Frenchman knows a good paradox when he sees one.

1. Prepare the fish: Rinse the fish, inside and out, under cold running water, then drain them and blot dry with paper towels. Make 3 diagonal slashes, to the bone, in each side of each fish. Season the fish, inside and out (including the side slashes), with salt and pepper and brush the fish on both sides with the 2 tablespoons of olive oil. Let the fish marinate for 20 minutes.

2. Make the artichoke salad: Tear the green outer leaves off the artichokes and, using a sharp knife, cut off the ends of the stems. Cut the artichokes into paper-thin slices, preferably by using a mandoline. Place the artichoke slices in a nonreactive bowl and toss with the lemon juice.

3. Add the tomato, basil, chives, garlic, anchovy (if using), and ¼ cup of olive oil to the artichokes and toss gently but thoroughly to mix. Season with salt and pepper to taste; the mixture should be highly seasoned. Set the artichoke salad aside.

4. Set up the grill for direct grilling and preheat to medium-high.

5. When ready to cook, brush each fish lightly on both sides with more olive oil and season with more salt and pepper. If you're worried about the fish sticking, use hinged fish-grilling baskets (see page 350); otherwise, brush and oil the grill grate and place both fish directly on it. Grill the fish until the skin on the first side is dark and crisp and the flesh is cooked through to the bone on that side, 8 to 12 minutes. Turn each fish carefully with a long spatula and cook on the second side until the flesh breaks into firm flakes when pressed with a finger, 8 to 12 minutes longer.

6. Using a spatula, carefully transfer the fish to a serving platter. Fillet the fish as described on page 309, then spoon the artichoke salad on top to serve.

NOTE: Baby artichokes are most often available in the spring at Italian markets, specialty greengrocers, and many supermarkets. If you can't find them, use one 10-ounce package of frozen artichoke hearts prepared according to package directions, then thinly slice and toss them with lemon juice. In a real pinch, you can use canned artichoke hearts; just make sure you rinse and drain them well before slicing.

FRANCE

JOHN DORY WITH SAUCE VIERGE

DIRECT GRILLING
SERVES 4

One of the best seafood restaurants on the Côte d'Azur bears the unlikely name of Bacon. This has less to do with a smoked meat that, on occasion, is used to enhance grilled fish than with the location of the restaurant, Bacon Point, on the Cap d'Antibes, overlooking the medieval city. Simplicity is the name of the game at Bacon (as it is at all great fish houses), and to this day I can still remember the taste of the perfectly grilled John Dory fish I had there served with a simple but equally perfect *sauce vierge*.

The sauce takes its name (literally, virgin sauce), it is said, from the fact that none of its ingredients are cooked—which is about the closest the French get to salsa. John Dory (or St. Pierre, as it is called, in French) is a delicate, white-fleshed fish found throughout the Mediterranean. You rarely find it in the United States (unless you know someone in the airfreight business). But almost any mild white fish (whole, steak, or fillet) will be enhanced by this preparation. Good candidates include striped bass, sea bass, halibut, cod, snapper, or mahimahi. This recipe calls for small whole fish; for fish steak and fillet how-to's, see pages 324 and 309.

FOR THE FISH

4 John Dory or other small whole fish (each about 1 pound), cleaned and trimmed of fins, heads and tails left on
2 tablespoons extra-virgin olive oil
Salt and freshly ground black pepper

FOR THE SAUCE VIERGE

2 large ripe tomatoes, peeled and seeded (see box, page 454), then diced
2 cloves garlic, minced
20 fresh basil leaves, thinly slivered
½ cup extra-virgin olive oil
2 tablespoons fresh lemon juice, or more to taste
2 teaspoons red wine vinegar
Salt and freshly ground black pepper

1. Prepare the fish: Place the fish in a nonreactive baking dish. Brush the fish on all sides with some of the 2 tablespoons of olive oil and season them with salt and pepper.

2. Make the *sauce vierge:* Combine the tomatoes, garlic, basil, ½ cup of olive oil, lemon juice, and wine vinegar in a nonreactive bowl and toss gently to mix. Taste for seasoning, adding salt and pepper to taste and more lemon juice as necessary; the sauce should be highly seasoned.

3. Set up the grill for direct grilling and preheat to medium-high.

4. When ready to cook, brush the fish lightly on both sides with more olive oil and sprinkle more salt and pepper on them. If you're worried about the fish sticking, use hinged fish-grilling baskets (see page 350); otherwise, brush and oil the grill grate and place the fish directly on it. Grill the fish until the skin on the first side is dark and crisp and the flesh is cooked through to the bone on that side, 6 to 10 minutes. Turn each fish carefully with a long spatula and cook on the second side until the flesh breaks into firm flakes when pressed with a finger, 6 to 10 minutes longer.

5. Using a spatula, carefully transfer the fish to a serving platter. If desired, fillet the fish as described on page 309 and serve at once, topped with a generous spoonful of the sauce.

MALAYSIA

GRILLED MACKEREL GURNEY DRIVE

DIRECT GRILLING
SERVES 4

Charcoal Grill Seafood is one of the many open-air cook stalls lining scenic bay-front Gurney Drive in Penang, Malaysia. One of many, but certainly not average. There, nothing is served that isn't at its freshest. A bank of aquariums keeps eels and prawns alive until the moment of cooking. Other fish that swam in the Andaman Sea just hours earlier are displayed under a thatched roof on a bed of banana leaves in a miniature wooden dingy.

I ordered something called *ikan tumone,* a small fish that looks like a tiny mackerel. My waitress cleaned it on the spot and handed it to a grill man, who stuffed it with a fragrant paste of lemongrass, shallots, and chiles. He fanned the coconut-shell charcoal fire until it glowed red and basted the fish with coconut milk. What came off the grill had to be one of the tastiest fish I've had anywhere, East or West.

There are lots of possibilities for fish to use here. The spice paste is designed to counterpoint the oiliness of a fatty fish like mackerel. You could also use whole porgies, grunts, or pompanos; steak fish, like salmon or swordfish; or even a fillet fish, like bluefish. And because it keeps well, you might think about doubling the spice paste to have some on hand whenever you get that urge to grill; I've used it to coat just about everything—chicken, beef, pork, and even tofu.

FOR THE SPICE PASTE

2 large shallots, coarsely chopped
6 cloves garlic, coarsely chopped
2 large or 6 small stalks fresh lemongrass, trimmed and coarsely chopped
4½ teaspoons chopped peeled fresh ginger
2 serrano peppers, seeded and coarsely chopped (for a hotter dish, leave the seeds in)
2 tablespoons peanut oil
2 tablespoons soy sauce
2 tablespoons fresh lime juice
Salt

FOR THE FISH AND BASTING MIXTURE

4 mackerel or other small whole fish (each about 1 pound), cleaned and trimmed of fins, heads and tails left on
2 tablespoons canned unsweetened coconut milk
2 tablespoons (¼ stick) unsalted butter, melted

1. Make the spice paste: Combine the shallots, garlic, lemongrass, ginger, and serrano peppers in a mortar and pound to a smooth paste with a pestle, then work in the peanut oil, soy sauce, and lime juice. Season the spice paste with salt to taste. If you don't have a mortar and pestle, combine all these ingredients in a blender and process to a smooth paste. Transfer the spice paste to a small nonstick skillet and cook over medium heat until richly flavored and shiny with oil, 5 to 10 minutes, stirring frequently to prevent sticking. Remove from the heat and let cool (see Note).

2. Prepare the fish and basting mixture: Rinse the fish, inside and out, under cold running water, then drain them and blot dry with paper towels. Using a thin, sharp knife, cut a pocket in each side of each fish from head to tail. Setting half the spice paste aside, spoon the rest first into the cavities of the fish, then into the pockets on the sides, dividing the paste evenly.

3. Combine the coconut milk and melted butter in a small bowl and whisk to blend; brush this basting mixture on both sides of each fish.

4. Set up the grill for direct grilling and preheat to medium-high.

5. When ready to cook, brush and oil the grill grate. If you're worried about the fish sticking, use hinged fish-grilling baskets (see page 350); otherwise, place the fish directly on the hot grate and grill until the skin on the first side is dark and crisp and the flesh is cooked through to the bone on that side, 6 to 10 minutes. Turn each fish carefully with a long spatula and brush them with any remaining coconut milk mixture; spoon the remaining spice paste on top. Cook the fish on the second side until the flesh breaks into firm flakes when pressed with a finger, 6 to 10 minutes longer.

6. Using a spatula, carefully transfer the fish to a serving platter. Fillet the fish as described on page 309 (if desired) and serve at once.

NOTE: The spice paste can be prepared ahead of time; refrigerate it in a tightly covered container for up to 1 week.

THAILAND

SWEET AND SOUR GRILLED SNAPPER

PLA POW

DIRECT GRILLING
SERVES 4

I encountered this dish not in Thailand, but at the stunning Amanusa resort at Nusa Dua beach in Bali (it turned out that the chef worked for many years in Thailand). We don't usually serve sweet sauces with seafood in the West, but this sweet-sour tamarind sauce is great paired with the charcoaled flavor of grilled fish. Try it with small whole fish such as porgies or small snappers. You could also use fish steaks, such as swordfish or tuna (see page 324 for grilling instructions). Serve the fish with Balinese Cucumber Salad (page 120) and Jasmine Rice (see page 428).

ADVANCE PREPARATION

30 minutes for marinating the fish

FOR THE FISH

4 small snappers or other small whole fish (each about 1 pound), cleaned and trimmed of fins, heads and tails left on
5 tablespoons Asian fish sauce
5 tablespoons fresh lemon juice
1 lemon, thinly sliced
1 teaspoon freshly ground black pepper

FOR THE SWEET-SOUR TAMARIND SAUCE

¾ cup palm sugar or firmly packed light brown sugar
⅔ cup Tamarind Water (page 241)
⅓ cup Asian fish sauce
1 cup peanut oil, for frying
3 shallots, very thinly sliced
6 cloves garlic, very thinly sliced
4 jalapeño or serrano peppers, thinly sliced
2 tablespoons fresh lemon juice

1. Prepare the fish: Rinse the fish, inside and out, under cold running water, then drain them and blot dry with paper towels. Make 3 or 4 diagonal slashes, to the bone, on each side of each fish. Place the fish in a nonreactive baking dish or roasting pan just large enough to hold them in a single layer.

2. Combine the 5 tablespoons of fish sauce and 5 tablespoons of lemon juice in a small nonreactive bowl and whisk to blend, then pour the mixture over the fish. Turn the fish once or twice to coat, then sprinkle the lemon slices and black pepper on top. Let the fish marinate, covered, in the refrigerator for 30 minutes.

3. Make the sauce: Combine the palm sugar, Tamarind Water, and ⅓ cup of fish sauce in a small, heavy saucepan and bring to a boil over medium heat, stirring until the sugar dissolves. Reduce the heat to low and let simmer gently, uncovered, until thick and well flavored, 5 to 10 minutes, stirring occasionally.

4. Meanwhile, heat the peanut oil to 350°F in a small, heavy skillet over medium-high heat. Add the shallots and fry until crisp, 1 to 2 minutes. Using a wire skimmer, transfer the shallots from the oil to paper towels to drain. Add the garlic to the hot oil and fry until crisp, 1 to 2 minutes, then using the skimmer, transfer the garlic to paper towels. Add the jalapeños to the hot oil and fry until crisp, 1 to 2 minutes, then using the skimmer transfer the jalapeños to paper towels. Set the oil aside to cool.

5. Remove the palm sugar mixture from the heat and stir in the 2 tablespoons of lemon juice and half each of the fried shallots, garlic, and jalapeños, setting the remainder aside for garnish. Cover the sauce and set aside to keep warm.

6. Set up the grill for direct grilling and preheat to medium-high.

7. When ready to cook, remove the fish from the marinade and discard the marinade. Blot the fish dry with paper towels. Brush each fish on both sides with the reserved frying oil. If you're worried about the fish sticking, use hinged fish-grilling baskets (see page 350); otherwise, brush and oil the grill grate and place the fish directly on it. Grill the fish until the skin on the first side is dark and crisp and the flesh is cooked through to the bone on that side, 6 to 10 minutes. Turn each fish carefully with a long spatula and cook on the second side until the flesh breaks into firm flakes when pressed with a finger, 6 to 10 minutes longer.

8. Using a spatula, carefully transfer the fish to a serving platter. Fillet the fish as described on page 309, then spoon half of the sauce over the fillets and sprinkle the remaining fried shallots, garlic, and peppers on top. Serve the fish at once, accompanied by the remaining sauce.

INDONESIA

GRILLED FISH SUNDA KELAPA

DIRECT GRILLING
SERVES 4

One of my favorite ways to cook seafood comes from a fish house in Jakarta called Sunda Kelapa (see opposite page). Sometimes it's tricky to adapt a cooking technique from halfway around the world to the North American kitchen, but Sunda Kelapa's grilling techniques are perfectly suited to cooking fish on an American grill.

This recipe is ideal for grilling whole fish. Good candidates in this country, depending on where you live, include porgies, small snappers, mackerel, pompano, redfish, or small bluefish. You can also cook your favorite steak fish this way (find instructions on page 324); fresh tuna prepared in this manner is absolutely delicious.

ADVANCE PREPARATION

20 minutes for marinating the fish

SPECIAL EQUIPMENT

2 to 4 banana leaves (see Note), cut into 4 pieces the size of the fish, or 4 to 6 layers of aluminum foil, folded into 4 rectangles the size of the fish

FOR THE FISH

4 small whole fish, such as pompano or small snappers (each about 1 pound), cleaned and trimmed of fins, heads and tails left on
1 cup fresh lime juice
½ cup coarse salt (kosher or sea)

FOR THE SPICED BUTTER

6 tablespoons (¾ stick) unsalted butter
4½ teaspoons fresh lime juice
1 tablespoon soy sauce
3 cloves garlic, minced
1 large shallot, minced
2 teaspoons minced peeled fresh ginger
½ teaspoon ground turmeric

1. Prepare the fish: Rinse the fish, inside and out, under cold running water, then drain them and blot dry with paper towels. Make 3 or 4 diagonal slashes, to the bone, in each side of each fish. Place the fish in a nonreactive baking dish or roasting pan just large enough to hold them in a single layer.

2. Combine the 1 cup of lime juice, the salt, and 1 cup of water in a medium-size nonreactive bowl and whisk until the salt dissolves. Pour the lime juice mixture over the fish and turn them once or twice to coat. Let the fish marinate in the refrigerator, covered, for 20 minutes.

3. Make the spiced butter: Melt the butter in a small, heavy saucepan over low heat, then stir in the 4½ teaspoons of lime juice and the soy sauce, garlic, shallot, ginger, and turmeric.

The Most Famous Fish House in Indonesia

I'd heard that Sunda Kelapa was one of the best restaurants in Jakarta, but I never would have guessed it by the neighborhood. The ride there took me through a dilapidated stretch of the port section of Batavia, past derelict warehouses, down trash-strewn streets lined with shanties. Then I turned into a walled compound guarded by attendants in paramilitary garb and began to see why this fish house had fetched rave reviews in dozens of languages in publications all over the world: The sheer variety of seafood offered made my jaw drop.

I had come to Indonesia as a globe-trotting student of barbecue. I wasn't disappointed. This sprawling country spanning thousands of islands—and boasting the world's fourth largest population—is home to some of the most interesting grilling in the world. When most people think of Indonesian grilling, what comes to mind is a tiny kebab called saté. It's true that the saté is Indonesia's national snack, and there are dozens if not hundreds of different types to choose from. But saté is only part of Indonesia's barbecue story, as I quickly learned at Sunda Kelapa.

Sunda Kelapa was the brainchild of Sri Rosilowati, a short, stylishly dressed woman from western Java. In 1972 Mrs. Rosilowati opened a fish shack adjacent to the harbor to feed the crews of the wooden freighters from the island of Sulawesi. Mrs. Rosilowati's concept was simple: Serve impeccably fresh fish, grilled simply over charcoal, in clean, unpretentious surroundings. It was a winning formula, to say the least! At the time of my visit Mrs. Rosilowati and her daughter Suripah presided over 120 employees and two cavernous dining rooms that must have seated five hundred.

The warehouse-size kitchen was an immaculate jumble of blazing grills, stainless-steel work tables, and plastic barrels filled with Indonesian seafood with unfamiliar names—*baronangs* (rabbit fish), *ikan grapu* (a sort of grouper), and *gourame* (a large flat fish that reminds me of pompano), to list a few. The grills were stoked with Indonesia's favorite fuel, coconut shell charcoal, and young boys fanned the grills with rattan flags to make the embers glow. Sunlight filtered through the slat walls and ceiling, illuminating the smoke rising from the grills. The overall effect was less that of a restaurant kitchen than of cooking over a campfire in the woods.

What fascinated me most about Sunda Kelapa was the techniques used by the grill cooks. If you've ever tried to grill a whole fish, you know how it has a tendency to burn on the outside, remain raw on the inside, and generally dry out. At Sunda Kelapa they used three popular Indonesian techniques to obtain perfectly cooked fish every time: brine marinating, double basting, and grill roasting on banana leaves.

The marinade—called a *bumboo*—was a tangy mixture of lime juice, water, and brine-strength quantities of salt. The fish was slashed to the bone to allow the mixture (and heat) to penetrate the flesh. The brine both moisturized and slightly cured the fish. The marinating time was brief and most of the *bumboo* dripped into the coals.

To further moisturize the fish, it was basted as it grilled with the *bumboo* and also with a mixture of melted butter flavored generously with garlic, shallots, and turmeric.

To cook the fish through without burning it, the cook seared it on one side directly over the fire, then inverted it onto a rectangle of banana leaf to finish cooking. The banana leaf shielded the fish from the flames, preventing it from drying out and overcooking.

Sunda Kelapa served its grilled fish with a *lalapan,* a plate of herbs and raw vegetables that included lemon balm, parsley, basil, sliced cucumber, tomato and cabbage wedges, and boiled long beans. You also got bowls of *achar* (a sort of mango and shallot pickle) and *chobal,* a painfully hot relish made from chiles, shallots, and shrimp paste, named for the small black stone mortar in which these ingredients are traditionally pounded and served. I've included recipes for all these in this book; now fire up the grill and enjoy. Oh, and to be like the locals, eat the fish with your fingers!

Let simmer until fragrant but not brown, about 5 minutes, then remove the spiced butter from the heat.

4. Set up the grill for direct grilling and preheat to medium-high.

5. When ready to cook, drain the fish, reserving the marinade. Brush each fish on both sides with some of the spiced butter. Brush and generously oil the grill grate and arrange the fish on it. Brush the fish lavishly with some of the reserved marinade. Grill the fish until the first side is nicely browned, 6 to 10 minutes, brushing the fish with additional spiced butter and marinade as they cook.

6. Using a long spatula, carefully turn each fish, inverting each onto a banana leaf or aluminum foil rectangle. Brush the fish again with spiced butter and continue grilling until nicely browned on the second side and the flesh breaks into firm flakes when pressed with a finger, 6 to 10 minutes longer. Brush the fish once more with the spiced butter as they finish cooking.

7. Using a spatula, carefully transfer the fish to a serving platter. Fillet the fish as described on page 309 or serve them whole, to be eaten with fingers.

NOTE: If you're lucky enough to live in a city with a large Asian or Hispanic community, you may be able to find fresh or frozen banana leaves for this. Otherwise use aluminum foil.

GUADELOUPE

GRILLED SNAPPER WITH CUCUMBER SAUCE

DIRECT GRILLING
SERVES 4

The night I stopped at Agoupa, a popular eatery in the resort community of Gosier in Guadeloupe, its first-year anniversary party was in full swing. Souk music blared from the sound system, bodies swayed in the heat, and the rum flowed like water. This open-air eatery (located just outside Pointe-à-Pitre) draws tourists and locals alike for its exuberant ambience and reasonable prices. (*Agoupa* means something extra in Creole, a little like *lagniappe* in Cajun French.) From a distance, the steel-drum barbecue grills blazed like blast furnaces in the night.

The sauce for this fish dish is a sort of gazpacho made with cucumbers and green tomatoes. It's very original and very tasty. Don't be put off by the seemingly large number of ingredients. Most you'll have on hand already, and the actual preparation time is only fifteen or twenty minutes. Serve the snappers with Bahamian Peas and Rice (page 431).

ADVANCE PREPARATION

1 to 2 hours for marinating the fish

FOR THE FISH AND MARINADE

- **4 small whole snappers (each about 1 pound), cleaned and trimmed of fins, heads and tails left on**
- **2 bunches fresh chives, or 1 bunch scallions, both white and green parts, trimmed and finely chopped**
- **1 head garlic, cut in half crosswise**
- **1 medium-size onion, thinly sliced**
- **2 bay leaves**
- **1 Scotch bonnet or other hot chile, seeded and cut in half (for a hotter dish, leave the seeds in)**
- **2⁄3 cup fresh lime juice**
- **1⁄4 cup dark rum**
- **3 tablespoons salt**

FOR THE CUCUMBER SAUCE

- **1 cucumber, peeled and seeded (see box, page 454)**
- **1 green (unripe) tomato, cored and peeled, or 4 tomatillos, husked, cored, and peeled**
- **1⁄4 cup diced onion**
- **3 scallions, both white and green parts, trimmed and finely chopped**
- **1⁄4 cup chopped fresh flat-leaf parsley**
- **3 tablespoons white wine vinegar or distilled white vinegar, or more to taste**
- **3 tablespoons extra-virgin olive oil, plus additional oil for brushing**
- **Salt and freshly ground black pepper**

1. Prepare the fish and marinade: Rinse the fish, inside and out, under cold running water, then drain them and blot dry with paper towels. Make 3 or 4 diagonal slashes, to the bone, on each side of each fish. Place the fish in a nonreactive baking dish or roasting pan just large enough to hold them in a single layer. Scatter the chives, garlic, onion slices, bay leaves, and Scotch bonnet over the fish.

2. Combine the lime juice, rum, 3 tablespoons of salt, and 4 cups of water in a medium-size nonreactive bowl, stirring until the salt dissolves. Pour the marinade over the fish and let marinate in the refrigerator, covered, for 1 to 2 hours.

3. Make the cucumber sauce: Combine the cucumber, green tomato, diced onion, scallions, parsley, vinegar, and olive oil in a food processor or blender and process to a smooth puree. Taste for seasoning, adding salt and pepper to taste and more vinegar as necessary; the sauce should be highly seasoned.

4. Set up the grill for direct grilling and preheat to medium-high.

5. When ready to cook, remove the fish from the marinade and discard the marinade. Blot the fish dry with paper towels and brush each lightly on both sides with olive oil. If you're worried about the fish sticking, use hinged fish-grilling baskets (see page 350); otherwise, brush and oil the grill grate and place the fish directly on it. Grill the fish, basting them once or twice with olive oil, until the skin on the first side is dark and crisp and the flesh is cooked through to the bone on that side, 6 to 10 minutes. Turn each fish carefully with a long spatula and cook on the second side until the flesh breaks into firm flakes when pressed with a finger, 6 to 10 minutes longer; continue to baste the fish with the marinade.

6. Using a spatula, carefully transfer the fish to a serving platter. Fillet the fish as described on page 309 (if desired) and serve at once, accompanied by the cucumber sauce.

THAILAND

GRILLED FISH WITH ESARN SEASONING

DIRECT GRILLING
SERVES 4

Simple but amazingly flavorful, this way to prepare fish comes from the Esarn region in northeast Thailand. To be strictly authentic, you'll need cilantro roots, which taste like a cross between cilantro and celery root. Asian, Indian, and Hispanic markets sell cilantro with the roots intact, but if you can't find the whole plant, cilantro leaves produce a highly tasty spice mix, too. I like to use small whole fish, like sea bass or snappers, for this recipe. Serve the grilled fish with Jasmine Rice (page 428) and Lemon Honey Sauce with Garlic (see page 483).

ADVANCE PREPARATION

1 to 2 hours for marinating the fish

FOR THE FISH AND SPICE PASTE

4 small whole fish, such as black bass or small snappers (each about 1 pound), cleaned and trimmed of fins, heads and tails left on
12 cloves garlic, peeled and crushed
½ cup chopped cilantro roots or leaves, roots rinsed well and drained before chopping
1 tablespoon salt
2 teaspoons ground coriander
2 teaspoons freshly ground white pepper

FOR THE BASTING SAUCE

3 tablespoons Asian fish sauce
3 tablespoons vegetable oil
3 tablespoons fresh lime juice
4½ teaspoons sugar

1. Prepare the fish and spice paste: Rinse the fish, inside and out, under cold running water, then drain them and blot dry with paper towels. Make 3 or 4 diagonal slashes, to the bone, on each side of each fish.

2. Combine the garlic, cilantro, salt, coriander, and white pepper in a mortar and pound to a paste with a pestle. If you don't have a mortar and pestle combine these ingredients in a food processor and process to a paste. Stuff half of the spice paste into the slashes in the sides of the fish, dividing it evenly, then spread the remainder in the cavities and over the surface of the fish. Arrange the fish in a baking dish. Let the fish marinate in the refrigerator, covered, for 1 to 2 hours.

3. Make the basting sauce: Combine the fish sauce, oil, lime juice, and sugar in a small bowl and stir until the sugar dissolves.

4. Set up the grill for direct grilling and preheat to medium-high.

5. When ready to cook, if you're worried about the fish sticking, use hinged fish-grilling baskets (see page 350); otherwise, brush and oil the grill grate and place the fish directly on it. Grill the fish, brushing them with the basting sauce, until the skin on the first side is dark and crisp and the flesh is cooked through to the bone on that side, 6 to 10 minutes. Turn each fish carefully with a long spatula and cook on the second side, brushing again with the basting sauce, until the flesh breaks into firm flakes when pressed with a finger, 6 to 10 minutes longer.

6. Using a spatula, carefully transfer the fish to a serving platter. Fillet the fish as described on page 309 (if desired) and serve at once.

GUADELOUPE

GRILLED SNAPPER WITH FRENCH WEST INDIAN CAPER SAUCE

DIRECT GRILLING
SERVES 4

Here's how fish is served at the open-air cook stalls lining the beaches of Guadeloupe. The marinade features the four essential flavors of the French Antilles: lime juice, Scotch bonnet chiles, garlic, and fresh thyme. Pair them with a caper sauce invigorated with more Scotch bonnet and you get an electrifying dish your taste buds won't soon forget. This recipe calls for snappers, but any whole fish would work. (For that matter, you could use fish steaks; see page 324 for grilling instructions.) The larger the fish, the lower the heat you'll need to work over, so as to cook the fish through without burning.

ADVANCE PREPARATION

1 hour for marinating the fish

FOR THE FISH AND MARINADE

4 whole small snappers (each about 1 pound), cleaned and trimmed of fins, heads and tails left on
3 cloves garlic, peeled
1 to 2 Scotch bonnet chiles, seeded and chopped (for a hotter fish, leave the seeds in)
2 teaspoons salt
1 teaspoon freshly ground black pepper
1 teaspoon chopped fresh thyme, or ½ teaspoon dried thyme
½ cup fresh lime juice

FOR THE CAPER SAUCE

1 clove garlic, minced
1 shallot, minced
2 tablespoons minced fresh flat-leaf parsley
2 tablespoons drained capers
½ Scotch bonnet chile, seeded and minced
2 tablespoons fresh lime juice
1 tablespoon red wine vinegar
½ cup extra-virgin olive oil, plus 2 tablespoons for brushing
Salt and freshly ground black pepper

1. Prepare the fish and marinade: Rinse the fish, inside and out, under cold running water, then drain them and blot dry with paper towels. Make 3 to 4 diagonal slashes, to the bone, on each side of each fish. Place the fish in a nonreactive baking dish just large enough to hold them in a single layer.

2. Combine the cloves of garlic, chopped Scotch bonnets, 2 teaspoons of salt, 1 teaspoon of pepper, and the thyme in a mortar and pound to a paste with a pestle, then work in the ½ cup of lime juice. If you don't have a mortar and pestle, combine all these ingredients in a food processor and process to a paste. Pour the marinade over the fish, turning it to coat and working the marinade into the slashes in the sides. Let the fish marinate in the refrigerator, covered, for 1 hour, turning once or twice.

3. Make the caper sauce: Combine the minced garlic, shallot, parsley, capers, minced Scotch bonnet, 2 tablespoons of lime juice, and the wine vinegar in a small bowl and whisk to mix. Whisk in the ½ cup of olive oil and season with salt and pepper to taste; the sauce should be highly seasoned (see Note).

4. Set up the grill for direct grilling and preheat to medium-high.

5. When ready to cook, remove the fish from the marinade and discard the marinade. Blot the fish dry with paper towels and brush it on both sides with the 2 tablespoons of olive oil. If you're worried about the fish sticking, use hinged fish-grilling baskets (see page 350); otherwise, brush and oil the grill grate and place the fish directly on it. Grill the fish until the skin on the first side is dark and crisp and the flesh is cooked through to the bone on that side, 6 to 10 minutes. Turn each fish carefully with a long spatula and cook on the second side until the flesh breaks into firm flakes when pressed with a finger, 6 to 10 minutes longer.

6. Using a spatula, carefully transfer the fish to a serving platter. Fillet the fish as described on page 309 (if desired). Spoon some of the caper sauce on top of the fish and serve at once, accompanied by the remaining sauce.

NOTE: For a smoother sauce, you can process the ingredients in a food processor or blender.

PORTUGAL

PORTUGUESE GRILLED SARDINES

DIRECT GRILLING
SERVES 6 AS AN APPETIZER, 3 TO 4 AS A MAIN COURSE

Grilled fresh sardines are as popular in Portugal as hot dogs and hamburgers are in North America. People devour them by the dozen from street vendors, in informal seaside fish houses and proper restaurants, and at backyard cookouts. So beloved are sardines in Portugal that they turn up in Portuguese outposts and former colonies all over the world. I've enjoyed this popular Portuguese dish in Macao, Brazil, and my former home of Cambridge, Massachusetts, where there is a large Portuguese American community.

If your experience with sardines is limited to the canned variety, you're in for a revelation. The only challenge is where to find fresh sardines. If you live in an area with a large Iberian or Italian population, you may be able to find fresh sardines at an ethnic fishmonger—especially in the warmer months. (The best time of year to eat sardines is between May and October, when the fish fatten for spawning.) Alternatively, you may have to settle for frozen sardines.

The salting that's done here gives the sardines extra flavor—almost like a cured fish. In Macao, grilled sardines are served with tomato salsa and crusty Portuguese bread or corn bread.

ADVANCE PREPARATION

30 minutes to 1 hour for salting the sardines

INGREDIENTS

24 fresh sardines, cleaned, heads and tails left on
1 cup coarse salt (kosher or sea)
2 tablespoons extra-virgin olive oil
Freshly ground black pepper (optional)
Lemon wedges, for serving

1. Rinse the sardines under cold running water, then drain and blot dry with paper towels. Sprinkle ⅓ cup of the salt in the bottom of a baking dish. Arrange 12 of the sardines on top and sprinkle them with ⅓ cup of the remaining salt. Arrange the remaining sardines on top and sprinkle the remaining ⅓ cup of salt over all. Cover the sardines and let cure in the salt, in the refrigerator, for 30 minutes to 1 hour.

2. Set up the grill for direct grilling and preheat to high.

3. When ready to cook, rinse the salt off the sardines and blot them dry with paper towels. Brush the sardines with the olive oil and season them with pepper, if desired. If you're worried about the fish sticking, use hinged fish-grilling baskets (see page 350); otherwise, brush and oil the grill grate and arrange the sardines directly on it. Grill the sardines until their skins are lightly charred and the flesh breaks into firm flakes when pressed with a finger, 3 to 6 minutes per side.

4. Using a long spatula, transfer the sardines to a serving platter and serve at once with lemon wedges for squeezing. Let your diners remove the head, tail, and bones.

MOROCCO

SEAFOOD MIXED GRILL IN THE STYLE OF ESSAOUIRA

DIRECT GRILLING
SERVES 8

Essaouira is a port town on the northwest coast of Morocco. Here, on the concrete wharf where the fishing boats tie up, fish lovers will find a most remarkable seafood barbecue. To get to this spot, you must navigate a tangled web of fishing nets, a gauntlet of touts (each one attempting to drag you to the stall of his employer), and a disconcerting cloud of flies. Take courage, because once you are seated, you will enjoy impeccably fresh seafood the way it is meant to be served: in sight of the bobbing fishing boats and the blue, blue ocean from which it was taken only a few hours earlier. Talk about fresh—the vendors clean the fish the moment you order it. Seasoned by the sea breeze and served under the whirling gulls in the wide blue sky, there's nothing that can beat it.

This feast is elemental in its simplicity: grilled fish, tangy tomato salad, crusty bread. I've written the recipe as a mixed grill, based on the most commonly served seafoods in Essaouira. Feel free to vary the selection based on whatever looks freshest in your area. In Essaouira, the shrimp would be served with the heads on and grilled in the shells.

FOR THE SEAFOOD

2 pounds shrimp, ideally in the shell
16 fresh sardines, cleaned and trimmed of fins, heads and tails left on
8 whole whiting or sea bream, cleaned and trimmed of fins, heads and tails left on
2 pounds squid, cleaned (see Note)
¾ cup extra-virgin olive oil, or more as needed
Coarse salt (kosher or sea) and freshly ground black pepper

FOR THE TOMATO SALAD

8 ripe tomatoes, seeded (see box, page 454) and finely chopped
2 large red onions, finely chopped
½ cup chopped fresh flat-leaf parsley
½ cup extra-virgin olive oil
¼ cup fresh lemon juice, or more to taste
2 teaspoons red wine vinegar
Salt and freshly ground black pepper

FOR SERVING

Moroccan bread or pita bread
Lemon wedges

1. Prepare the seafood: Leaving the shrimp shells on, if desired, devein the shrimp according to the instructions on page 361. Rinse the shrimp, sardines, whiting, and squid under cold running water, then drain them and blot dry with paper towels. Brush the shrimp, fish, and squid on both sides with some of the ¾ cup of olive oil and season them with salt and pepper to taste.

2. Make the tomato salad: Combine the tomatoes, onions, parsley, ½ cup of olive oil, lemon juice, and wine vinegar in a large nonreactive bowl and toss gently but thoroughly to mix. Taste for seasoning, adding salt and pepper to taste and more lemon juice as necessary. Set the tomato salad aside.

3. Set up the grill for direct grilling and preheat to high.

4. When ready to cook, brush and oil the grill grate. Arrange the seafood on the hot grate and grill, turning the whole fish with a long spatula and the shrimp and squid with tongs, until nicely browned and cooked through. The sardines will take 3 to 6 minutes per side and the whiting will take 4 to 8 minutes per side (when done the flesh will break into firm flakes when pressed with a finger). The shrimp and squid will be done after 1 to 2 minutes per side. When the shrimp are cooked, they will be pinkish white and firm; the squid will be white and firm. After turning, brush the seafood again with olive oil and reseason it with salt and pepper.

5. To serve: Divide the seafood among 8 serving plates. Serve at once, accompanied by the tomato salad, Moroccan or pita breads, and lemon wedges.

NOTE: The squid pieces for this recipe should be large—whole bodies and whole tentacles. If you can only get squid that's been cut into rings or chunks, thread them on a skewer to grill.

SEAFOOD MIXED GRILL IN THE STYLE OF ESSAOUIRA | AT LEFT

BRAZIL

GRILLED FISH WITH BRAZILIAN GARLIC MARINADE

DIRECT GRILLING
SERVES 4

Marius Fontana is one of the most celebrated restaurateurs in Rio de Janeiro, a charismatic guy with shoulder-length brown hair and a stratospheric energy level. Marius created the garlic marinade here for fish kebabs, but I've discovered that it also works great on fish steaks or small whole fish. Swordfish, tuna, or salmon steaks, or small whole snappers or black bass all shine prepared this way. Serve up Brazilian Daiquiris (page 54) beforehand and Crazy Rice (page 432) alongside.

ADVANCE PREPARATION

1 hour for marinating the fish

INGREDIENTS

4 swordfish, tuna, or salmon steaks (each 6 to 8 ounces and 1 inch thick)
6 cloves garlic, peeled
½ medium-size onion, quartered
½ medium-size red bell pepper, cored, quartered, and seeded
¼ cup extra-virgin olive oil
¼ cup dry white wine
2 tablespoons ketchup
2 tablespoons sweet paprika
1 teaspoon salt
½ teaspoon freshly ground black pepper
¼ cup finely chopped fresh cilantro

1. Rinse the fish steaks under cold running water, then drain them and blot dry with paper towels. Place the fish in a nonreactive baking dish just large enough to hold them flat in a single layer.

2. Combine the garlic, onion, bell pepper, olive oil, white wine, ketchup, paprika, salt, and black pepper in a food processor or blender and process to a smooth puree. Add the cilantro and pulse just to mix. Pour the marinade over the fish steaks, turning them to coat. Let the fish marinate in the refrigerator, covered, for 1 hour.

3. Set up the grill for direct grilling and preheat to high.

4. When ready to cook, brush and oil the grill grate. Remove the fish steaks from the marinade and discard the marinade. Arrange the fish steaks, facing in the same direction, on the hot grill grate. Cook the fish steaks until done to taste, turning them carefully with a long spatula. If you are grilling tuna, the steaks will be done to medium-rare after 3 to 4 minutes per side. If you are grilling swordfish or salmon, cook the steaks until opaque in the center when pierced with a knife, 4 to 6 minutes per side. For an attractive crosshatch of grill marks, rotate the fish steaks 90 degrees after the first 2 minutes of grilling on each side.

5. Transfer the fish steaks to serving plates or a platter and serve at once.

TRINIDAD AND TOBAGO

GRILLED SHARK AND BAKE

DIRECT GRILLING
SERVES 4

One of the most popular dishes in Trinidad is shark and bake, a shark steak marinated in "seasoning" (a tangy tincture of chiles and West Indian herbs), then deep-fried and served on a puffy pillow of fried bread, called a bake. The combination is so flavorful Trinidadians eat it for breakfast, lunch, dinner, and between-meal snacks.

Much as I enjoyed the traditional dish, I couldn't help thinking it would also be tasty—and healthier—if the ingredients were grilled. After all, the firm texture of shark makes it ideal for grilling. And grilled bread is a part of Indian cooking, which certainly inspired many Trinidadian dishes.

ADVANCE PREPARATION

2 to 4 hours for marinating the fish

On Trinidad's Shark and Bake

Several varieties of shark are marketed in the United States, including mako, blue shark, and black tip. All three have a firm, white, mild-flavored flesh that belies the predatory fierceness of their source. Mako tastes quite similar to swordfish; blue shark has a whiter flesh and more delicate flavor; and black shark shares these qualities, but tends to be a little dry.

Although shark may seem exotic, even weird, to many Americans, it's more commonplace than you think. A fair amount of what passes for swordfish in this country is actually shark. Anxious to avoid unpleasant connotations, though, many fishmongers market shark by the benign name of dogfish; a rather strange choice considering the idea was to make the fish sound more attractive. There's another reason to love shark, besides its fine-flavored flesh: It's virtually boneless. Endowed with a cartilaginous backbone, shark lacks the tiny bones found in ordinary fish.

As for the seasoning, it's based on traditional Trinidadian fresh herbs, including chives, parsley, thyme, mint leaves, and *culantro* (*culantro* is a saw-tooth-leafed herb that tastes like strong cilantro). These herbs grow in profusion in Paramin, a hilltop community a half hour north of Port of Spain.

To round out the seasoning, you'd ideally add the Trinidadian chile called a seasoning pepper, which tastes like a Scotch bonnet without the heat. Possible substitutes in this country include green bell pepper, cachucha pepper (a small, pattypan squash–shaped pepper sometimes called *chile rocotillo* or *aji dulce*), or even a seeded, deveined Scotch bonnet.

The recipe here is a North American's take on a Trinidadian classic—inspired by a beautiful restaurant I visited called Natalie's Shark and Bake Shop at Maracas Bay on Trinidad's north coast. If you're in a hurry, you could omit the bakes, substituting grilled slices of your favorite store-bought bread, instead. This recipe also works well made with swordfish.

FOR THE FISH AND MARINADE

4 shark steaks, such as mako (each 6 to 8 ounces and about ¾ inch thick)
1 bunch chives, or ½ bunch scallions, trimmed
2 shallots, or ½ small onion, coarsely chopped
2 cloves garlic, coarsely chopped
1 medium-size rib celery, coarsely chopped
¼ cup fresh cilantro leaves
¼ cup fresh flat-leaf parsley leaves
2 tablespoons fresh mint leaves
2 teaspoons fresh thyme leaves, or 1 teaspoon dried thyme
½ Scotch bonnet chile, seeded and deveined, or ¼ cup chopped green bell pepper
¼ cup fresh lime juice, or more to taste
2 teaspoons salt, or more to taste
½ teaspoon freshly ground black pepper

FOR THE BAKES

1 tablespoon active dry yeast
1 tablespoon sugar
2½ cups unbleached all-purpose flour, plus more as needed
2 teaspoons baking powder
1¼ teaspoons salt

FOR GRILLING AND SERVING

2 to 3 tablespoons vegetable oil, for brushing
Salt and freshly ground black pepper
Garlic Sauce (page 482)
Matouk's, Busha Browne's, or other Caribbean hot sauce, for serving

1. Prepare the fish and marinade: Rinse the shark steaks under cold running water, then drain them and blot dry with paper towels. Place the shark steaks in a nonreactive baking dish just large enough to hold them flat in a single layer.

2. Combine the chives, shallots, garlic, celery, cilantro, parsley, mint, thyme, Scotch bonnet, lime juice, 2 teaspoons of salt, ½ teaspoon of pepper, and ¾ cup of water in a blender or food processor and puree. Taste for seasoning, adding more lime juice and/or salt as necessary; the mixture should be

How to Grill the Perfect Fish Steak

Steaks cut from firm, meaty fish like salmon, swordfish, and tuna are fantastic when grilled. You cook them pretty much as you would beef steaks. Actually, this isn't completely true: I cover the grill when cooking thick fish steaks. Restaurant chefs invert a metal pie pan over each one. Both methods help speed up the cooking process.

1. Start with the freshest possible fish. Tuna, for example, should be sushi quality. If you like it rare in the center, look for fish steaks that are 1 to 2 inches thick. If you like it cooked through, you want fish steaks that are ½ to ¾ inch thick. Swordfish can be cut ¾ to 1 inch thick. When grilling salmon steaks, leave the bones in. They help hold the fish together.

2. Then, set up the grill for direct grilling and preheat it to high.

3. When ready to cook, brush the fish steaks on both sides with oil or melted butter and season them with salt and pepper. If you've marinated the fish in a mixture rich with oil, butter, or coconut milk, it is unnecessary to blot the fish dry, brush it with more oil, or season it. The grill grate should be oiled, and the fish can go on the grate right after you've done that.

4. Arrange the fish steaks on the hot grill grate, all facing the same direction. Grill the fish steaks on one side for about two minutes if they are ½ inch thick; three to six minutes for steaks 1 to 2 inches thick. If desired, after two minutes of grilling, using a long spatula, rotate the steaks 90 degrees to create an attractive crosshatch of grill marks.

5. Carefully turn the fish steaks over, using the spatula, and cook the second side the same way, rotating the fish steaks 90 degrees after two minutes of grilling, if desired. Tuna tastes best served rare or pink in the center, so the cooking time will be a bit shorter. Swordfish and salmon should be cooked through.

6. To test fish steaks for doneness, gently pierce the steak in the center with a knife; it should look done to taste. When properly cooked through, if you press the fish with your finger the area around where you press will break into firm flakes. If there is a center bone, the fish should pull away easily.

highly seasoned. Pour the marinade over the shark steaks, turning them to coat. Let the shark marinate in the refrigerator, covered, for 2 to 4 hours.

3. At least 2 hours before you plan to grill, make the dough for the bakes: Combine the yeast, sugar, and ½ cup of warm water in a large bowl and stir until the yeast and sugar dissolve. Let the yeast mixture stand until foamy, 5 to 10 minutes, then stir in ¾ cup of warm water. Sift in the flour, baking powder, and 1¼ teaspoons of salt. Stir the mixture with a wooden spoon to form a stiff but moist dough, adding more flour as necessary (you can also make the dough in a mixer using a dough hook). The dough should be moister than conventional bread dough but not so wet that you can't roll it. Knead the dough in the bowl until smooth and elastic, about 5 minutes.

4. Cover the bowl with plastic wrap, place it in a warm, draft-free spot, and let the dough rise until doubled in bulk, 1 to 2 hours.

5. Set up the grill for direct grilling and preheat to high.

6. Punch the dough down by stirring it with a wooden spoon. Divide the dough into 4 equal pieces and roll each piece into a ball. Dust the balls with flour. Working on a liberally floured work surface with an equally liberally floured rolling pin, roll each dough ball out to a circle 6 to 7 inches in diameter and ¼ inch thick.

7. When ready to grill the bakes, brush and oil the grill grate. Lightly brush the bakes with oil and arrange them on the hot grill grate. Grill the bakes until blistered and lightly browned,

2 to 4 minutes per side, turning them with a long spatula. Keep the bakes warm in a bread basket lined with a towel.

8. When ready to cook the shark steaks, remove them from the marinade and discard the marinade. Blot the shark steaks dry with paper towels, brush them lightly on both sides with oil, and season them with salt and pepper to taste. Arrange the shark steaks, facing in the same direction, on the hot grill grate. Grill the shark steaks until cooked through in the center when pierced with a knife, 3 to 6 minutes per side, turning them carefully with a long spatula. For an attractive crosshatch of grill marks, rotate the shark steaks 90 degrees after the first 2 minutes of grilling on each side.

9. To serve: Using a spatula, carefully transfer the shark steaks to serving plates or a platter. Fold a shark steak in a bake and pour Garlic Sauce and hot sauce to taste on top before eating.

MEXICO

GRILLED SWORDFISH EN PIPIAN

DIRECT GRILLING
SERVES 6

Pipián refers to a family of Mexican sauces made with *pepitas,* hulled green pumpkin seeds. The toasted, ground seeds serve as both a flavoring and thickener. *Pipián* is found all over Mexico, but especially in the southwestern state of Guerrero, where it goes by the name of *mole verde* (green sauce). The sauce's relative mildness makes it heaven-sent for seafood. This recipe pairs the sauce with swordfish, but you can also serve it with salmon, snapper, shrimp, or one of my favorite fishes, pompano. For that matter, grilled pork or chicken would be delicious with pumpkin seed sauce.

The recipe includes two unusual ingredients: tomatillos and epazote. Tomatillos are a small, green tomato-like fruit, recognizable by their papery husks. Fresh tomatillos can be found in the produce section of most supermarkets, but you can also use canned ones. Epazote is a jagged-leafed herb with a pungent smell and flavor. Also known as pigweed, it's available at Mexican markets and is often found growing in vacant lots. I've made the epazote optional; the sauce will be quite delicious, if not strictly authentic, without it.

As I do throughout the book, I've given a range of peppers. The larger amount is the more authentic. (Remember, the peppers lose some of their heat when blanched.) Don't be intimidated by the number of ingredients—the sauce is quite quick and easy to make—but if you want to simplify things, you can omit the marinade and just brush the swordfish steaks with olive oil, seasoning them with a little salt and pepper before grilling. The sauce itself can be made up to three days in advance and can even be frozen.

ADVANCE PREPARATION

1 hour for marinating the fish

FOR THE FISH AND MARINADE

6 swordfish steaks (each 6 to 8 ounces and about 1 inch thick)
2 to 6 jalapeño or serrano peppers, seeded and thinly sliced (for a hotter marinade, leave the seeds in)
¼ cup coarsely chopped fresh cilantro
3 tablespoons fresh lime juice
3 tablespoons extra-virgin olive oil
Salt and freshly ground black pepper

FOR THE SAUCE

1 cup hulled pumpkin seeds
2½ cups fish stock, bottled clam broth, chicken broth, or water
8 fresh tomatillos (see Note)
4 to 6 fresh jalapeño peppers, 6 to 10 serrano peppers, or 1 poblano pepper, cut in half lengthwise and seeded (for a hotter sauce, leave the seeds in)
½ small onion
4 cloves garlic, peeled
2 scallions, both white and green parts, trimmed and cut into 1-inch pieces
½ cup coarsely chopped fresh cilantro, plus a few tablespoons for garnish
2 tablespoons coarsely chopped fresh flat-leaf parsley
2 romaine lettuce leaves, cut crosswise into 1-inch slices
1 tablespoon fresh lime juice, or more to taste
¼ teaspoon ground cumin
2 tablespoons lard or extra-virgin olive oil
2 sprigs epazote (optional), finely chopped
Salt

1. Prepare the fish and marinade: Rinse the swordfish steaks under cold running water, then drain and blot them dry with paper towels. Place the swordfish steaks in a nonreactive baking dish just large enough to hold them flat in a single layer.

2. Combine the sliced jalapeño peppers, ¼ cup of cilantro, 3 tablespoons of lime juice, and olive oil in a small nonreactive bowl and whisk briefly to blend the liquids. Season the marinade with salt and pepper to taste and pour it over the swordfish steaks. Let the swordfish steaks marinate in the refrigerator, covered, for 1 hour, turning once or twice.

3. Make the sauce: Toast the pumpkin seeds in a dry skillet (do not use a nonstick skillet for this) over medium heat until they begin to brown and pop, 3 to 5 minutes. Shake the pan as the seeds cook; do not let them burn. Transfer the pumpkin seeds to a shallow bowl to cool. Set 3 tablespoons of seeds aside for garnish, then grind the remaining seeds to a fine powder in a food processor, running the machine in bursts. Stir in 1 cup of the fish stock and set aside.

4. Discard the papery husks from the tomatillos and place the tomatillos in a small saucepan with water to cover. Add the jalapeño pepper halves and bring to a boil over medium heat. Reduce the heat to low and let simmer gently until the tomatillos are soft, about 5 minutes. Drain the tomatillos and jalapeños and place them in a food processor or blender with the remaining 1½ cups of fish stock and the onion, garlic, scallions, ½ cup of cilantro, the parsley, lettuce, lime juice, and cumin and process to a smooth puree.

5. Heat the lard or olive oil in a large, deep saucepan over medium heat. Add the pumpkin seed mixture and cook until dark, thick, and fragrant, about 5 minutes, stirring frequently to prevent splattering. Stir in the tomatillo mixture and continue cooking the sauce until thick and richly flavored, 15 to 20 minutes, stirring often. During the last 5 minutes of cooking, stir in the epazote (if using). Remove the sauce from the heat and taste for seasoning, adding salt to taste and/or more lime juice as necessary; the sauce should be highly seasoned. Set the sauce aside and keep it warm.

6. Set up the grill for direct grilling and preheat to high.

7. When ready to cook, brush and oil the grill grate. Remove the swordfish steaks from the marinade and discard the marinade. Arrange the swordfish steaks, facing in the same direction, on the hot grill grate. Grill the swordfish steaks until cooked through the center when pierced by a knife, 3 to 6 minutes per side, turning them carefully with a long spatula. For an attractive crosshatch of grill marks, rotate the swordfish steaks 90 degrees after the first 2 minutes of grilling on each side.

8. Using a spatula, carefully transfer the steaks to a serving platter and spoon the sauce over them. Sprinkle the reserved toasted pumpkin seeds and chopped cilantro on top and serve at once.

NOTE: If fresh tomatillos are not available, 28 ounces of canned tomatillos, drained, rinsed, and drained again, can be substituted; it is not necessary to cook canned tomatillos before adding them to the blender.

AZERBAIJAN

STURGEON SHASHLYK

DIRECT GRILLING
SERVES 4

Azerbaijan is an oil-rich former Soviet republic located to the east of the world's sturgeon capital, the Caspian Sea. *Shashlyk* is the Russian (and former Soviet Republic's) term for a shish kebab. You could certainly grill the fish on spits in this recipe, but here I've called for it to be marinated and cooked as steaks. The sour cream has both a tenderizing and enriching effect. Sweet-tart pomegranate molasses can be bought commercially at Middle Eastern markets or made fresh following the recipe I've included in this book. Sumac is a sour red spice served as a seasoning for grilled meats throughout the Near East; it, too, can be found in Middle Eastern markets and specialty food stores.

ADVANCE PREPARATION

1 to 2 hours for marinating the fish

FOR THE FISH AND MARINADE

4 fresh sturgeon (see box, page 324), monkfish, or swordfish steaks (each 6 to 8 ounces and about 1 inch thick)

2 tablespoons vegetable oil
Salt and freshly ground black pepper
1 cup sour cream
3 tablespoons fresh lemon juice
2 tablespoons chopped fresh dill, or 1 tablespoon dried dill
1 clove garlic, minced

FOR SERVING

4 scallions, both white and green parts, trimmed and thinly sliced
1 ripe tomato, cut into wedges
Lemon wedges
1 cucumber, thinly sliced
2 to 3 tablespoons Pomegranate Molasses (page 243)
3 tablespoons ground sumac (see page 248)

1. Prepare the fish and marinade: Rinse the fish steaks under cold running water, then drain them and blot dry with paper towels. Brush the fish steaks on both sides with the oil and season with salt and pepper to taste, then place the fish in a nonreactive baking dish just large enough to hold them flat in a single layer.

2. Combine the sour cream, lemon juice, dill, and garlic in a small nonreactive bowl. Pour the marinade over the fish steaks, turning them to coat completely. Let the fish steaks marinate in the refrigerator, covered, for 1 to 2 hours, turning the fish steaks occasionally.

3. Set up the grill for direct grilling and preheat to high.

4. When ready to cook, brush and oil the grill grate. Remove the fish steaks from the marinade and discard the marinade. Arrange the fish steaks, facing in the same direction, on the hot grill grate. Grill the fish steaks until cooked through in the center when pierced with a knife, 3 to 6 minutes per side, turning them carefully with a long spatula. For an attractive crosshatch of grill marks, rotate the fish steaks 90 degrees after the first 2 minutes of grilling on each side.

5. To serve: Using a spatula, carefully transfer the fish steaks to a serving platter. Sprinkle the sliced scallions on top and garnish the fish steaks with the tomato and lemon wedges and cucumber slices. Serve at once, accompanied by the Pomegranate Molasses and ground sumac.

SENEGAL

FISH YASSA

DIRECT GRILLING
SERVES 4

The term *yassa* refers to a family of dishes popular in West Africa, especially in Senegal. The basic preparation centers on a tangy sauce of onions, mustard, and lemon juice. Traditionally, the onions are fried in palm oil, a richly flavored, reddish oil sold at African and Brazilian markets. Palm oil is high in saturated fat, so here I approximate its color and flavor by cooking canola oil with a spoonful of paprika. There are lots of possibilities for fish here: The traditional choice would be a dark, rich fish, like kingfish or bluefish, but salmon is also excellent prepared in this fashion. Serve the fish accompanied by a pitcher of Ginger Pineapple Punch (page 61) and steamed white rice.

ADVANCE PREPARATION

1 to 2 hours for marinating the fish

FOR THE FISH

4 fish steaks, such as salmon, (each 6 to 8 ounces and about 1 inch thick)
Salt and freshly ground black pepper
¼ cup fresh lemon juice
2 tablespoons canola oil

FOR THE SAUCE

¼ cup canola oil
1 teaspoon sweet paprika
4 medium-size onions, cut into ¼-inch wedges (about 3 cups)
1 medium-size carrot, peeled and thinly sliced
½ to 2 Scotch bonnet chiles, seeded and thinly sliced (for a hotter sauce, leave the seeds in)
¼ cup fresh lemon juice, or more to taste
¼ cup grainy French mustard, or more to taste
2 tablespoons distilled white vinegar
Salt and freshly ground black pepper

1. Prepare the fish: Rinse the fish steaks under cold running water, then drain them and blot dry with paper towels. Season the fish steaks with salt and pepper and place them in a nonreactive baking dish just large enough to hold them flat in a single layer.

GRILLED TUNA WITH RED WINE, CAPER, AND OLIVE SAUCE | AT RIGHT

2. Whisk the ¼ cup of lemon juice and the canola oil in a small nonreactive bowl to blend and pour it over the fish. Turn the fish steaks once or twice to coat, then cover them and let marinate, in the refrigerator, for 1 to 2 hours.

3. Make the sauce: Heat the canola oil in a nonstick skillet over medium heat. Stir in the paprika, then add the onions, carrot, and chiles and cook until the onion is translucent, 3 to 4 minutes. Add ⅓ cup of water, ¼ cup each lemon juice, mustard, and the vinegar and bring to a boil. Reduce the heat to low and simmer the sauce until reduced, thick, and richly flavored, 10 to 15 minutes, stirring often; the onions should remain a little crisp. Remove from the heat and taste for seasoning, adding salt, pepper, and more lemon juice or mustard as necessary; the sauce should be highly seasoned. Cover and keep warm.

4. Set up the grill for direct grilling and preheat to high.

5. When ready to cook the fish steaks, brush and oil the grill grate. Remove the steaks from the marinade and discard the marinade. Arrange the fish steaks, facing in the same direction, on the hot grill grate. Grill the fish steaks until cooked through in the center when pierced with a knife, 3 to 6 minutes per side, turning them carefully with a long spatula. For an attractive crosshatch of grill marks, rotate the fish steaks 90 degrees after the first 2 minutes of grilling on each side.

6. Using a spatula, carefully transfer the fish steaks to serving plates or a platter and spoon the sauce on top. Serve at once.

FRANCE

GRILLED TUNA WITH RED WINE, CAPER, AND OLIVE SAUCE

THON GRILLE AU JUS DE RAITO

DIRECT GRILLING
SERVES 4

I first tasted this dish (or one very nearly like it) on the end of a barely inhabited island located a few miles off the Côte d'Azur. The Ile de Porquerolles is where to go to escape the crowds and traffic of the Riviera. Immortalized by the mystery writer Georges Simenon, the island has a single town you can cross on foot in about ten minutes, set amid acres of national parkland. The residents had the good sense to ban cars from the mainland.

But in France nowhere is so remote that you can't find a good meal—in this case at a gracious, Michelin one-star restaurant in the hotel Mas de Langoustier. Chef Joël Guillet takes a contemporary approach to Provençal cooking, but one dish on his menu may date back to the Phoenicians. According to local lore, the red wine, olive, and caper sauce known as *raïto* originated in Greece and was brought to Massilia (as Marseilles was known in ancient times) by Phoenician sailors. Provence is the only place in France where you find it, and it's rooted deeply enough to have several names, including *rayte* and *raïte.* Whatever its origins, it's a sauce richly rooted in the Mediterranean, with a deep flavor that goes well with grilled tuna.

ADVANCE PREPARATION

30 minutes for marinating the fish

FOR THE FISH

- 4 tuna steaks (each 6 to 8 ounces and about 1 inch thick)
- 2 tablespoons extra-virgin olive oil
- Salt and freshly ground black pepper

FOR THE RAITO

- About ⅓ cup extra-virgin olive oil
- 1 medium-size onion, finely chopped
- 3 cloves garlic, minced
- 1 small ripe tomato, peeled and seeded (see box, page 454), then finely chopped
- 2 cups dry red wine
- 1 tablespoon tomato paste
- 1 sprig fresh thyme, or ¼ teaspoon dried thyme
- 1 bay leaf
- ¼ cup black olives, preferably tiny niçoise olives, pitted
- 2 tablespoons drained capers
- Salt and freshly ground black pepper

1. Prepare the fish: Brush the tuna steaks on both sides with the 2 tablespoons of olive oil and season them with salt and pepper to taste. Place the tuna in a baking dish, cover it, and let marinate, in the refrigerator, for 30 minutes.

2. Make the *raïto:* Heat 3 tablespoons of olive oil in a large saucepan over medium-high heat. Add the onion and garlic and cook until golden brown, about 5 minutes. Add the tomato and cook for 2 minutes. Stir in the red wine, tomato paste, thyme, bay leaf, olives, and capers and bring to a boil. Reduce the heat to medium and let simmer briskly until the *raïto* is reduced by half, about 10 minutes.

3. Remove the *raïto* from the heat and discard the thyme sprig and bay leaf. Whisk in the remaining 2½ tablespoons of olive oil and season the *raïto* with salt and pepper to taste; the *raïto* should be highly seasoned (see Note). Cover the *raïto* and keep it warm.

4. Set up the grill for direct grilling and preheat to high.

5. When ready to cook, brush and oil the grill grate. Arrange the tuna steaks, facing in the same direction, on the hot grill grate. Grill the tuna steaks until cooked to taste, 1 to 2 minutes per side for rare, 2 to 3 minutes per side for medium-rare, turning them carefully with a long spatula. For an attractive crosshatch of grill marks, rotate the tuna steaks 45 degrees after the first minute of grilling on each side.

6. Transfer the steaks to serving plates or a platter and serve at once, with the *raïto* spooned on top.

NOTE: Chef Guillet likes the refinement of pureeing the *raïto* in a blender, adding the olives and capers at the end instead of before the sauce is reduced; he returns the *raïto* to the pan just to heat it through. Being a robust sort of guy, I like the gutsiness of an unpureed *raïto*. Take your choice.

PORTUGAL

TUNA STEAKS, MADEIRA STYLE

DIRECT GRILLING
SERVES 4

Readers of my books will know of my love for Portugal and Portuguese cooking. I would venture to say that Portugal is the best-kept culinary secret in Europe—and this includes its outdoor cooking. The following dish comes from Portuguese-owned Madeira, a volcanic island off the coast of Africa, which is famed for its fortified wine, tropical flowers, and vertiginously steep terraced hillsides. I suppose it's no accident that grilling should be popular in Madeira. The island was once covered with trees that were used for making charcoal.

ADVANCE PREPARATION

3 to 4 hours for marinating the fish

INGREDIENTS

4 cloves garlic, peeled
1 tablespoon coarse salt (kosher or sea)
1 tablespoon dried oregano leaves
1 tablespoon dried basil leaves
1 teaspoon freshly ground black pepper
½ cup extra-virgin olive oil, preferably Portuguese, or more as needed
4 tuna steaks (each 6 to 8 ounces and about 1 inch thick)
8 bay leaves

1. Combine the garlic, salt, oregano, basil, and pepper in a mortar and pound to a paste with a pestle, then work in enough olive oil to achieve a spreadable consistency, 1 to 2 tablespoons. If you don't have a mortar and pestle, mash these ingredients together in a bowl using the back of a wooden spoon or process them in a mini chopper or blender, adding the olive oil gradually.

2. Rinse the tuna steaks under cold running water, then drain them and blot dry with paper towels. Using your fingers or a spatula, spread the spice paste on both sides of each of the tuna steaks, then place them in a baking dish just large enough to hold them flat in a single layer. Pour ¼ cup of the remaining olive oil over the tuna and turn the steaks once or twice to coat. Place a bay leaf under each tuna steak and one on top, then cover the tuna and let marinate, in the refrigerator, for 3 to 4 hours, spooning the olive oil over the tuna steaks occasionally.

3. Set up the grill for direct grilling and preheat to high.

4. When ready to cook, brush and oil the grill grate. Remove the tuna steaks from the marinade and discard the marinade. Rinse the tuna and blot it dry with paper towels, then brush the remaining 1 to 2 tablespoons of olive oil on both sides of each tuna steak. Arrange the tuna steaks, facing in the same direction, on the hot grill grate. Grill the tuna steaks until done to taste, 4 to 6 minutes per side for medium-well (the Portuguese like their tuna on the medium side of medium-well), turning them carefully with a long spatula. For an attractive crosshatch of grill marks, rotate the tuna steaks 90 degrees after the first 2 minutes of grilling on each side.

5. Using a spatula, transfer the tuna steaks to serving plates or a platter and serve at once.

EQUATORIAL GUINEA

SPANISH GUINEAN FISH GRILL WITH THREE SAUCES

DIRECT GRILLING
SERVES 8

The Claris is one of the smartest hotels in Barcelona, an ultramodern hideaway with quiet, luxurious rooms nestled behind the ornate facade of a nineteenth-century mansion. It's an odd place, to be sure, to begin an account of a fish barbecue from Equatorial Guinea. But it was here that I met Arsenio Pancho Sobe, doorman extraordinaire and passionate barbecue buff. Sobe is one of the 100,000 or so Guineans living in Spain, the former colonial ruler of Guinea.

Sobe comes from Malabo, the capital of Equatorial Guinea, located on the tiny island of Bioko, off the coast, where seafood is grilled over coconut logs and served with a triumvirate of spicy sauces. The first is an irresistible peanut sauce flavored with dried shrimp; the second, an intriguing green sauce made with a spinachlike edible leaf called *machea;* the third, a tangy avocado sauce.

All three sauces owe their firepower to the large, bright red Guinea pepper, a cousin of the habañero. If you live near a West African market, you may be able to find Guinea peppers; if not, use habañeros or Scotch bonnets. As for fish, a Guinean would use a full-flavored, dark-fleshed fish like kingfish or mackerel. I've had equal success with bluefish, tuna steaks (which I suggest here), and whole snappers.

Although this may seem like an imposing recipe, it's actually just a series of simple steps. A couple of things can make it even easier. First, you could cook a smaller amount of fish and just prepare one of the sauces. In this case, I'd go with the Peanut Sauce, which is the most unusual. Second, the peanut and spinach sauces keep well, so you could prepare them ahead and use them later or as needed—the sauces are what make the dish Guinean.

ADVANCE PREPARATION

1 hour for marinating the fish

INGREDIENTS

8 fish steaks, such as tuna or kingfish (each 6 to 8 ounces and about 1 inch thick)
Salt and freshly ground black pepper
3 cloves garlic, peeled and crushed
½ to 2 Guinea peppers or Scotch bonnet chiles (optional), seeded and minced
1 cup fresh lime juice
2 to 3 tablespoons coconut oil or other vegetable oil, for brushing
Peanut Sauce (recipe follows)
Spinach Sauce (see page 332)
Avocado Sauce (see page 332)

1. Rinse the fish steaks under cold running water, then drain them and blot dry with paper towels. Season the fish steaks generously on both sides with salt and black pepper and place them in a nonreactive baking dish just large enough to hold them flat in a single layer. Add the garlic and Guinea peppers. Pour the lime juice over the fish steaks and turn them once or twice to coat. Let the fish steaks marinate in the refrigerator, covered, for 1 hour, turning once or twice.

2. Set up the grill for direct grilling and preheat to high (see Note).

3. When ready to cook, remove the fish steaks from the marinade and discard the marinade. Drain the fish steaks well, then brush them on both sides with coconut oil and season them with salt and black pepper to taste.

4. Brush and oil the grill grate, then arrange the fish steaks, facing in the same direction, on the hot grill grate. Grill the fish steaks until cooked to taste, 2 to 3 minutes per side for medium-rare, turning them carefully with a long spatula. (If you are grilling steaks other than tuna, cook them 4 to 6 minutes per side.) For an attractive crosshatch of grill marks, rotate the fish steaks 90 degrees after the first minute of grilling on each side.

5. Transfer the fish steaks to serving plates and serve at once, with the peanut, spinach, and avocado sauces.

NOTE: If you're using a charcoal grill and you have coconut-shell charcoal or husks left over from a fresh coconut that you can add to the coals, so much the better. Make sure the husks are really dry before throwing them on the grill.

PEANUT SAUCE

MAKES ABOUT 2 CUPS

Dried shrimp aren't particularly popular in North America—which is a shame, because their sweet, briny flavor is delectable—but they turn up widely in Africa, Asia, the Caribbean, and Brazil. Brazilians, in fact, boast a dish very similar to this one, a stew based on dried shrimp and peanuts called *vatapá,* from the state of Bahia in northern Brazil. If you can't find dried shrimp, use fresh ones.

½ cup finely chopped onion
2 cloves garlic, minced
1 large ripe tomato, finely chopped, with its juices
½ to 2 Guinea peppers or Scotch bonnet chiles, seeded and minced (for a hotter sauce, leave the seeds in)
2 teaspoons minced peeled fresh ginger
1 bay leaf
1 ounce (3 to 4 tablespoons) dried shrimp, coarsely chopped, or 4 ounces fresh shrimp, shelled and deveined (see page 361), then coarsely chopped
½ cup chunky peanut butter
3 to 4 tablespoons minced fresh cilantro (optional)
Salt and freshly ground black pepper

1. Combine the onion, garlic, tomato, Guinea peppers, ginger, bay leaf, shrimp, and 1½ cups of water in a saucepan and bring to a boil over medium heat. Reduce the heat to low and let simmer gently until dried shrimp are soft, fresh shrimp are firm, about 5 minutes.

2. Remove the pan from the heat and discard the bay leaf, then whisk in the peanut butter and cilantro (if using). Season the sauce with salt and black pepper to taste. Place the pan back over low heat and continue simmering the sauce until it is thick and richly flavored, about 5 minutes. Transfer the sauce to a small bowl, and cover and refrigerate it until ready to use. Let come to room temperature to serve.

SPINACH SAUCE

MAKES ABOUT 2 CUPS

This sauce is traditionally made with an edible green leaf called *machea.* In this country spinach gives a pretty close approximation. Palm oil has a distinctive orange color and sourish flavor. Look for it in African or Brazilian markets, but if you can't find it, or have health concerns (palm oil is high in saturated fat), use olive oil instead. Add some paprika to give the olive oil a touch of reddish color.

½ medium-size onion, finely chopped
1 clove garlic, minced
1 bay leaf
½ to 1 Guinea pepper or Scotch bonnet chile, seeded and minced
½ teaspoon salt, or more to taste
½ package frozen chopped spinach (about 5 ounces), thawed, or 4 cups stemmed fresh leaf spinach, rinsed well, drained, and chopped
1 tablespoon palm oil or extra-virgin olive oil
Freshly ground black pepper
1 to 2 teaspoons fresh lime juice (optional)

1. Combine the onion, garlic, bay leaf, Guinea pepper, and salt with 1½ cups of water in a large, heavy saucepan and bring to a boil over medium heat. Cook, uncovered, until the onion is tender, about 5 minutes.

2. Remove and discard the bay leaf, then add the spinach and let boil until tender, about 2 minutes. Stir in the palm oil. Transfer the spinach mixture to a food processor or blender and process to a coarse puree. Put the puree in a small bowl and taste for seasoning, adding black pepper, more salt, and lime juice (if using) as necessary. Cover and refrigerate until ready to use. Let come to room temperature to serve.

AVOCADO SAUCE

MAKES ABOUT 2 CUPS

This sauce finds an analog on the other side of the Atlantic: the avocado sauces of Mexico, which are also served with grilled fish.

1 ripe Hass avocado, peeled, pitted, and cut into ¼-inch dice
1 tablespoon fresh lime juice, or more to taste
½ cup finely chopped onion
2 cloves garlic, minced
1 bay leaf
½ to 1 Guinea pepper or Scotch bonnet chile, seeded and minced
¼ cup finely chopped fresh flat-leaf parsley
¼ cup finely chopped fresh cilantro
1 large ripe tomato, seeded (see box, page 454) and finely diced
Salt and freshly ground black pepper

1. Combine the avocado and lime juice in a nonreactive small, heavy saucepan and toss to mix. Stir in the onion, garlic, bay leaf, Guinea pepper, parsley, and ½ cup of water. Bring to a simmer over low heat and cook until the avocado and onion are soft, about 5 minutes. Stir in the cilantro and tomato, season with salt and black pepper to taste, and let simmer for 1 minute longer.

2. Remove the sauce from the heat and taste for seasoning, adding more lime juice and/or salt as necessary; add a little water if it is too thick. Put the sauce in a small bowl, cover, and refrigerate until ready to use. Remove the bay leaf before serving at room temperature.

HOW TO SKIN AND BONE FISH FILLETS

Fish fillets can be grilled with or without the skin. Some skin (I'm thinking salmon) is exquisitely tasty when brushed with oil, sprinkled with salt, and grilled over a medium-high flame until crisp. But if a recipe calls for the skin of the fish fillet to be removed, here's how to do it.

1. *Place the fillet, skin side down, at the edge of the cutting board closest to you, tail (or narrow end) to the left (or right, if you're left-handed). Holding the tail in one hand and using a long, slender knife, make a cut through the flesh but not through the skin. The cut should be made about ½ inch in from the end so you have a small piece to hold on to.*

2. *Holding the knife blade roughly parallel to the cutting board, gradually cut toward the wider end of the fillet. Use a sawing motion and pinch the skin between the knife blade and the cutting board. The fillet will come cleanly away from the skin.*

3. *It's always a good idea to check a fillet for any remaining bones. Run your fingers over the top of the fillet, feeling for bones. Pull out any you find with needle-nose pliers, tweezers, or a strawberry huller.*

MEXICO

YUCATAN-STYLE GRILLED FISH

TIKIN XIK

DIRECT GRILLING
SERVES 4

Le Saint Bonnet is just the sort of restaurant you want to wind up at after a long, hot morning driving the monotonously straight roads of the Yucatán. Its open-air dining area, shaded by a thatch roof and cooled by sea breezes, overlooks the blue-green waters of the Gulf of Mexico. It's the kind of place where ordering a beer brings you half a dozen tiny plates of *botanas* (cocktail snacks) and where you can easily spend three hours over lunch.

The restaurant's founder was French, which accounts for the restaurant's name. The French heritage notwithstanding, it was here that I learned to make the most famous fish dish in the Yucatán: *tikin xik* (pronounced tee-ken-SHEEK). As the Mayan-sounding name suggests, *tikin xik* is one of the oldest dishes in the Yucatán, predating the arrival of the Spanish. *Xik* is the Mayan word for marinated fish; *tikin* means something that is turned or rotated. And though *tikin xik* is not actually on Le Saint Bonnet's menu, regulars know to ask for it, and the chef is always happy to oblige.

At the restaurant, as is traditional, a whole fish is cleaned and boned through the back (a fairly complicated process), spread open like a book, and marinated in a special *recado,* a bright orange spice paste made with annatto seeds, garlic, and sour orange juice. The day I tried it, the fish was a freshly caught grouper that underwent the process, but other good fish for *tikin xik* include mahimahi and snapper. Because the boning of the whole fish is so complicated, I suggest using fish fillets; if you wish to try a whole fish, see the box on page 309.

ADVANCE PREPARATION

30 minutes for marinating the fish

SPECIAL EQUIPMENT

1 banana leaf (see Note), cut into 4 rectangles a little larger than the pieces of fish, or 4 rectangles of aluminum foil, each 4 to 6 layers thick; a fish grate (optional)

FOR THE FISH AND RECADO

- **4 mahimahi fillets (each 6 to 8 ounces and ¾ to 1 inch thick)**
- **1 teaspoon annatto seeds**
- **½ teaspoon black peppercorns**
- **2 allspice berries**
- **2 whole cloves**
- **½ teaspoon ground cinnamon**
- **2 tablespoons fresh sour orange juice (see box, page 186), or 1 tablespoon each fresh regular orange juice and lime juice**
- **2 tablespoons fresh regular orange juice**
- **2 tablespoons distilled white vinegar**
- **2 cloves garlic, minced**
- **1 bay leaf**
- **Salt**
- **2 to 4 tablespoons vegetable oil or unsalted butter, melted, for brushing**
- **Freshly ground black pepper**

FOR COOKING THE FISH (OPTIONAL)

- **1 small white onion, cut into ¼-inch wedges**
- **1 large ripe tomato, cut into ¼-inch wedges**
- **4 sprigs fresh epazote**

FOR SERVING

- **Shredded lettuce**
- **Cucumber slices**
- **Tomato slices**
- **Lime slices**
- **Fresh flat-leaf parsley sprigs**
- **"Dog's Snout" Salsa (page 459)**

1. Rinse the mahimahi fillets under cold running water, then drain them and blot dry with paper towels. Place the fillets in a nonreactive baking dish just large enough to hold them flat in a single layer.

2. Combine the annatto seeds, peppercorns, allspice berries, cloves, and cinnamon in a spice mill or clean coffee mill and grind to a fine powder. Transfer the spice powder to a small nonreactive bowl and add the sour orange juice, regular orange juice, vinegar, garlic, bay leaf, and 1 teaspoon of salt. Stir until the salt dissolves and the *recado* is well blended, then taste it and add enough water to take out the sharpness, about ¼ cup. Pour the *recado* over the mahimahi, turning the fillets to coat. Let the fish marinate in the refrigerator, covered, for 30 minutes.

3. Set up the grill for direct grilling and preheat to high.

4. When ready to cook, preheat a fish grate (if using) for 5 minutes. Drain the mahimahi fillets and discard the *recado*. Brush both sides of the fillets with some oil and season them with salt and pepper.

5. Generously oil the hot fish grate (if using) or the grill grate, then arrange the fillets on it. Grill the mahimahi for 3 to 4 minutes. Using a long spatula, carefully turn the fillets, inverting each one onto a banana leaf. Arrange the onion and tomato wedges and the epazote (if using) on top of the fillets and grill until the fish breaks into firm flakes when pressed with a finger, 3 to 4 minutes longer.

6. Using a spatula, carefully transfer the mahimahi fillets to a serving platter. Surround the fish with the lettuce and the cucumber, tomato, and lime slices and top it with parsley sprigs. Serve the fish at once, accompanied by the "Dog's Snout" Salsa.

NOTE: If you're lucky enough to live in a city with a large Asian or Hispanic community, you may be able to find fresh or frozen banana leaves. Otherwise you can use aluminum foil. Or, you can omit the banana leaf, if you like, and just turn the fish fillets over on the fish grate, but the fish won't be quite as moist.

WHOLE FISH, *TIKIN XIK* STYLE

INDIRECT GRILLING
SERVES 4

Here's how to prepare *tikin xik* with a whole fish. In place of the mahimahi fillets called for in Yucatán-Style Grilled Fish on the opposite page, substitute one large whole fish, such as snapper, grouper, or pompano, trimmed of fins and cleaned, with its head and tail left on.

1. Rinse the fish, inside and out, under cold running water. Drain and blot it dry with paper towels. Make 5 or 6 deep diagonal slashes, to the bone, in each side of the fish. Place the fish in a nonreactive roasting pan while you prepare the *recado* marinade as directed in Step 2. Pour the *recado* over the fish, using your fingers to spread it over both sides and working it into the slashes as well. Let the fish marinate in the refrigerator, covered, for 1 to 3 hours.

2. Set up the grill for indirect grilling and preheat to high. No drip pan is necessary for this recipe.

3. When ready to cook, set the fish on a piece of banana leaf or 4 to 6 layers of aluminum foil cut just larger than the fish and place it in the center of the grill grate, away from the flame. Cover the grill and cook the fish until it flakes easily when pressed with a finger, 40 minutes to 1 hour. Arrange the onion, tomato wedges, and epazote (if using) on top of the fish 10 minutes before the end of the cooking time.

4. Using two long spatulas, carefully transfer the fish to a serving platter. Garnish the fish as directed in Step 6 and serve it with the "Dog's Snout" Salsa (page 459), filleting the fish as directed on page 309.

AUSTRALIA

BARRAMUNDI IN ASIAN-SPICED COCONUT MILK

DIRECT GRILLING
SERVES 4

Barramundi is one of the most beloved fish in Australia, a gold-flecked beauty with a firm, sweet, white flesh that forms large meaty flakes when cooked. You may not be able to find barramundi easily (do try it when you go to Australia), but sea bass, grouper, and especially mahimahi make good substitutes.

The Southeast Asian roots of this recipe are obvious. You'll love the haunting flavors of the lemongrass and kaffir lime leaves, not to mention the wonderful way the coconut milk moisturizes and enriches the fish. This recipe was inspired by The Bathers Pavillion restaurant on Balmoral Beach in Sydney.

ADVANCE PREPARATION

2 hours for marinating the fish

SPECIAL EQUIPMENT

Fish grate (optional)

INGREDIENTS

4 barramundi, sea bass, grouper, or mahimahi fillets (each 6 to 8 ounces and ¾ to 1 inch thick), checked over for bones (see box, page 333)
1 large shallot, finely chopped
3 cloves garlic, minced
2 stalks fresh lemongrass, trimmed and minced, or 2 strips lemon zest (each 2 by ½ inches), removed with a vegetable peeler
1 piece (1 inch) peeled fresh ginger, minced
1 piece (1 inch) fresh galangal (see Note), minced, or an additional tablespoon of peeled minced fresh ginger
2 Thai chiles or serrano peppers, seeded and minced (for a hotter sauce, leave the seeds in)
2 tablespoons vegetable oil, preferably peanut oil
½ teaspoon shrimp paste (see Note), or 1 chopped anchovy fillet
2 cups coconut milk, canned or homemade (see page 114)
3 tablespoons Asian fish sauce
1 tablespoon fresh lime juice
1 teaspoon palm sugar or light brown sugar
2 kaffir lime leaves (see Note), cut crosswise into hair-thin slivers, or 2 strips lime zest (each 2 by ½ inches), removed with a vegetable peeler

1. Rinse the fish fillets under cold running water, then drain them and blot dry with paper towels. Place the fillets in a nonreactive baking dish just large enough to hold them flat in a single layer. Set the fillets aside while you prepare the marinade and sauce.

How to Grill Perfect Fish Fillets

Fillets are the hardest cut of fish to grill, yet people like them because they're free of bones and the broad surface area readily absorbs charcoaled flavors. The problem is that fish fillets tend to stick to the grill grate and crumble when turned.

One secret to preventing this is to use a grill basket—you'll find information about those on page 350. Another trick is to use a fish grate, a flat metal sheet or plate (sometimes nonstick or enameled) that rests on top of the grill grate and has rows of small holes or slits to let in the fire and smoke. Because it's smooth and flat, fish fillets are less apt to stick to a fish grate and are easier to slide off it than from the grill grate itself—provided, of course, you oil the hot fish grate well. Here's how to use one.

Skinless Fillet Method

1. Preheat the grill to high.

2. When ready to cook, place the fish grate on the grill and preheat it for five minutes. Brush the fish fillets with oil or melted butter and season them with salt and pepper. Generously oil the fish grate. Arrange the fillets on the grate and cook them until they are browned on the bottom and starting to turn opaque on the top, three to six minutes.

3. Brush the tops of the fish fillets again with oil or melted butter and, using a long spatula, turn them carefully and cook them until browned on the second side, three to six minutes longer. When done, the fish should break into firm flakes when pressed with a finger.

Skin-On Method

This method works well for fillets of fish with a thick skin, like salmon or bluefish.

1. Preheat the grill to medium-high.

2. When ready to cook, brush the skin of the fish with oil or melted butter. Place the fillets, skin side down, on the hot grate. Cover the grill. Cook the fish without turning until the skin is darkly browned and crackling crisp and the meat flakes easily when pressed with a finger, six to twelve minutes. (The trapped-in heat will cook the top side of the fillets.) If the skin starts to burn, using a spatula, slide the fillets onto a piece of aluminum foil.

2. Combine the shallot, garlic, lemongrass, ginger, galangal, and Thai chiles in a mortar and pound to a thick paste with a pestle. If you don't have a mortar and pestle, combine these ingredients in a food processor and process until a thick paste forms. Set the shallot paste aside.

3. Heat the oil in a wok or large, heavy skillet over medium heat. Add the shrimp paste and cook until fragrant, about 1 minute. Add the shallot paste and cook, stirring constantly, until brown and fragrant, about 10 minutes.

4. Stir in the coconut milk, fish sauce, lime juice, palm sugar, and half of the kaffir lime leaves into the skillet. Increase the heat to medium-high and bring to a boil, then reduce the heat to medium and let the sauce mixture simmer until thick and richly flavored, about 5 minutes. Remove the sauce from the heat and let cool to room temperature.

5. Pour half of the cooled sauce over the fish fillets in the baking dish, refrigerating the remaining sauce, covered, until just before serving. Turn the fish once or twice to coat, then let it marinate in the refrigerator, covered, for 2 hours, turning the fillets occasionally so that they marinate evenly.

6. Set up the grill for direct grilling and preheat to high.

7. When ready to cook, preheat a fish grate (if using) for 5 minutes, then oil it or the grill grate. Remove the fish fillets from the marinade and discard the marinade. Arrange the fish fillets on the hot grate and grill them for 3 to 6 minutes. Using a long spatula, turn the fillets carefully and grill until the fish breaks into firm flakes when pressed with a finger, 3 to 6 minutes longer. While the fish cooks, heat the reserved sauce in a saucepan on the side burner of the grill, if it has one, or over low heat on the stovetop.

8. Using the spatula, transfer the fillets to serving plates or a platter and spoon the warmed sauce over them. Garnish each piece of fish with a tuft of shredded kaffir lime leaves and serve at once.

NOTE: The unusual ingredients in this recipe—galangal, shrimp paste, and kaffir lime leaves—are available at Asian markets. But don't be discouraged if you can't find these ingredients; I've given substitutions. Even with these stand-ins you'll have a voluptuously flavorful dish.

UKRAINE

SALMON KIEV ON THE GRILL

DIRECT GRILLING
SERVES 4

OK, OK, I know this dish is traditionally made with chicken, not salmon, and it's supposed to be deep-fried, not grilled. But I can think of few experiences more pleasurable than cutting into a smokily grilled piece of fish to release the fragrant squirt of melted herb butter inside.

ADVANCE PREPARATION

2 hours to 2 days for chilling the butter

SPECIAL EQUIPMENT

4 long wooden toothpicks or small metal skewers; fish grate or grill basket (optional)

INGREDIENTS

- **4 tablespoons (½ stick) unsalted butter, at room temperature**
- **2 tablespoons minced fresh flat-leaf parsley**
- **1 clove garlic (optional), minced**
- **½ teaspoon grated lemon zest**
- **2 teaspoons fresh lemon juice, or more to taste**
- **Salt and freshly ground black pepper**
- **4 salmon fillets (each 6 to 8 ounces and ¾ to 1 inch thick), skinned and checked over for bones (see box, page 333)**
- **1 tablespoon extra-virgin olive oil or unsalted butter, melted**

1. Combine the butter, parsley, garlic (if using), lemon zest, and lemon juice in a small bowl and whisk until smooth and creamy. Taste for seasoning, adding salt and pepper to taste and more lemon juice as necessary. Place the "Kiev" butter on a large piece of plastic wrap and shape it into a cylinder. Refrigerate the butter until hard, at least 2 hours, or up to 2 days.

2. Rinse the salmon fillets under cold running water, then drain them and blot dry with paper towels. Place the fillets on a cutting board. Holding a thin, sharp knife parallel to the cutting board, cut a pocket about 2 inches long in the center of one side of each piece of fish, stopping about ½ inch from the opposite side.

3. Cut the hardened Kiev butter lengthwise into 4 equal pieces and stuff one piece into the pocket in each piece of fish. Pin each pocket shut with a long toothpick or small metal skewer, then transfer the salmon fillets to a plate and brush them on both sides with olive oil or melted butter. Season both sides of the fish with salt and pepper and refrigerate until ready to grill.

4. Set up the grill for direct grilling and preheat to high.

5. When ready to cook, preheat a fish grate (if using) for 5 minutes, then oil it or the grill grate. Arrange the salmon fillets on the hot grate and grill for 3 to 6 minutes. Using a long spatula, carefully turn the fillets and grill until a skewer inserted into a salmon piece comes out very hot to the touch, 3 to 6 minutes longer. If desired, after 2 minutes of grilling on each side, rotate the fillets 45 degrees with the spatula to create an attractive crosshatch of grill marks.

6. Using the spatula, carefully transfer the salmon pieces to serving plates or a platter. Remove the toothpicks or skewers and serve the salmon at once.

REPUBLIC OF GEORGIA

SALMON GRILLED IN GRAPE LEAVES

KOLHEEDA

DIRECT GRILLING
SERVES 4

One of the most intriguing grilled fish dishes I've ever enjoyed is a Georgian specialty called *kolheeda*. Named for a mythical gold mine in the Caucasus Mountains, *kolheeda* features a boned whole salmon trout stuffed with walnuts and dill, wrapped in grape leaves, and grilled. The grape leaves impart a delectable tartness to the fish, while offsetting the richness of the walnuts. They also keep the fish from drying out.

This recipe was inspired by Nancy and Gogetidze Gelody of the Pearl Café in Brighton Beach, Brooklyn, New York. I've called for salmon fillets, which are easier to get than salmon trout in most parts of the country, but do use salmon trout, if you can find it. Grape leaves preserved in brine are available in jars at Middle Eastern markets and most supermarkets

Kolheeda makes an excellent introduction to Georgian cuisine, not to mention a dramatic dish for entertaining.

ADVANCE PREPARATION

30 minutes for soaking the grape leaves

INGREDIENTS

16 to 24 grape leaves packed in brine
4 salmon fillets (each 6 to 8 ounces and ¾ to 1 inch thick), skinned and checked over for bones (see box, page 333)
Salt and freshly ground black pepper
1 cup shelled walnuts
2 cloves garlic, chopped
2 tablespoons chopped fresh dill, or 1 tablespoon dried dill
2 tablespoons chopped fresh cilantro or flat-leaf parsley
1 tablespoon fresh lemon juice, or more to taste
4 paper-thin lemon slices

1. Rinse the grape leaves thoroughly under cold running water, then place them in a bowl with cold water to cover and let soak for 30 minutes, changing the water once or twice. Drain the grape leaves and blot dry with paper towels.

2. Meanwhile, rinse the salmon fillets under cold running water, then drain them and blot dry with paper towels. Place the fillets on a cutting board. Holding the knife parallel to the cutting board, cut a deep pocket in one long side of each fillet, starting and ending about 1 inch from each end and cutting almost but not quite through to the other side. Season the fillets, inside and out, with salt and pepper, then set them aside.

3. Combine the walnuts, garlic, dill, cilantro, and lemon juice in a food processor and process to a very coarse paste. Taste for seasoning adding salt and pepper to taste and more lemon juice as necessary; the mixture should be highly seasoned. Spoon the stuffing into the pockets in the salmon, dividing it evenly among them.

SALMON GRILLED IN GRAPE LEAVES | AT LEFT

4. Working with one piece of fish at a time, arrange 2 or 3 grape leaves on a work surface to form a rectangle 2 inches larger than the piece of salmon; the grape leaves should overlap slightly. Place a piece of salmon on top of the grape leaves, then repeat with the remaining pieces of salmon. Place a lemon slice on top of each piece of salmon. Cover the salmon with the remaining grape leaves, tucking the ends under each piece (see Note).

5. Set up the grill for direct grilling and preheat to high.

6. When ready to cook, brush and oil the grill grate. Place the wrapped fish on the hot grate. Grill the fish until the grape leaves are nicely browned and the fish is cooked through, 3 to 6 minutes per side, testing for doneness by inserting a thin metal skewer into the thickest part of the fish; if it comes out very hot to the touch, the fish is cooked.

7. Using a spatula, transfer the fish to serving plates or a platter and serve at once. Unwrap the salmon and discard the grape leaves before eating.

NOTE: The salmon can be prepared to this point several hours ahead of time and refrigerated covered. If you like, secure the bundles by tying them with butcher's string.

ITALY

PINO'S GRILLED SALMON WITH BASIL CREAM

DIRECT GRILLING
SERVES 4

Salmon has a natural affinity for basil, especially when paired with the basil cream sauce here. This is an invention of my friend Pino Savarino, a fine chef from the Ligurian coast in Italy.

SPECIAL EQUIPMENT

Fish grate (optional)

FOR THE FISH

4 salmon fillets (each 6 to 8 ounces and ¾ to 1 inch thick), skinned and checked over for bones (see box, page 333)
2 tablespoons extra-virgin olive oil
2 tablespoons fresh lemon juice
Salt and freshly ground black pepper

FOR THE BASIL SAUCE

20 fresh basil leaves, plus 4 basil sprigs for garnish
⅓ cup dry white wine
2 cloves garlic
1 cup heavy (whipping) cream
1 tablespoon fresh lemon juice
2 tablespoons (¼ stick) unsalted butter
Salt and freshly ground black pepper

1. Prepare the fish: Rinse the salmon fillets under cold running water, then drain them and blot dry with paper towels. Place the fillets on a platter and brush them on both sides with the olive oil. Drizzle the 2 tablespoons of lemon juice over both sides and season the fillets with salt and pepper to taste. Set the salmon aside while you prepare the sauce.

2. Make the basil sauce: Combine the basil, white wine, and garlic in a food processor or blender and process to a smooth puree. Transfer the puree to a small, heavy saucepan and stir in the cream. Bring to a simmer over medium heat and cook until reduced by half, about 15 minutes, stirring frequently. Whisk in the 1 tablespoon of lemon juice and the butter. When the butter is incorporated, remove the sauce from the heat and season it with salt and pepper to taste. Keep the basil sauce warm, covered.

3. Set up the grill for direct grilling and preheat to high.

4. When ready to cook, preheat a fish grate (if using) for 5 minutes, then oil it or the grill grate. Arrange the salmon fillets on the hot grate and grill for 3 to 6 minutes. Using a long spatula, carefully turn the fillets and grill until the fish breaks into firm flakes when pressed with a finger, 3 to 6 minutes longer.

5. Using the spatula, carefully transfer the fillets to serving plates or a platter. Spoon the basil sauce on top. Garnish each fillet with a sprig of basil and serve at once.

SPAIN

GRILLED SOLE WITH CATALAN FRUITS & NUTS

DIRECT GRILLING
SERVES 4

Grilling isn't particularly prevalent in Spain, but live-fire cooking lends itself to a number of Spanish preparations. Consider the following specialty from La Cuineta, a restaurant in Barcelona's Barri Gòtic (medieval district) that positively oozes charm. The chef uses sole (Dover sole, that is), which is much firmer and meatier than what passes for sole in the United States. If you live in a large city, you may be able to find fresh Dover sole or halibut, but any grillable fish will work—I often make this dish with mahimahi. The contrast of sweet with savory (currants and sugar, in this case, with pine nuts and seafood) is quite typical of Catalan cooking.

ADVANCE PREPARATION

30 minutes for marinating the fish

SPECIAL EQUIPMENT

Fish grate (optional)

FOR THE FISH

4 pieces (each 6 to 8 ounces) Dover sole or mahimahi fillet, checked over for bones (see box, page 333)
Salt and freshly ground black pepper
2 tablespoons extra-virgin olive oil
¼ cup fresh orange juice
1 clove garlic, minced

FOR THE SAUCE

2 tablespoons (¼ stick) unsalted butter
½ cup minced shallots
1 tablespoon all-purpose flour
2 tablespoons brandy
¾ cup fresh orange juice, or more to taste
1 tablespoon sugar, or more to taste
½ cup heavy (whipping) cream
3 tablespoons currants
3 tablespoons pine nuts, toasted (see box, page 113)
Salt and freshly ground black pepper
Fresh lemon juice (optional)

1. Prepare the fish: Rinse the fish fillets under cold running water, then drain them and blot dry with paper towels. Season the fish on both sides with salt and pepper and place in a nonreactive baking dish just large enough to hold the pieces in a single layer. Drizzle the olive oil and ¼ cup of orange juice over the fish and sprinkle the garlic on top, turning the fillets a few times to coat. Let the fish fillets marinate in the refrigerator, covered, for 30 minutes.

2. While the fish marinates, make the sauce: Melt the butter in a small, heavy saucepan over medium heat. Add the shallots and cook until soft and translucent but not browned, about 2 minutes. Stir in the flour and cook, stirring, for 1 minute. Remove the pan from the heat and whisk in the brandy and the ¾ cup of orange juice, then return the pan to medium heat and bring the orange juice mixture to a boil. Add the sugar and cream and stir until the sugar dissolves. Let the sauce simmer until thick and richly flavored, 5 to 10 minutes. Remove the sauce from the heat and stir in the currants and pine nuts (see Note). Taste for seasoning, adding salt and pepper to taste and more sugar as necessary; the sauce should be a little sweet. If you want the sauce to be more acidic, add a little more orange juice or even a drop of lemon juice. Keep the sauce warm, covered.

3. Set up the grill for direct grilling and preheat to high.

4. When ready to cook, preheat a fish grate (if using) for 5 minutes, then oil it or the grill grate. Remove the fish from the marinade and set aside any remaining marinade. Arrange the fillets on the hot grate and grill for 3 to 6 minutes, basting them with the leftover marinade, but do not baste during the last 4 minutes of grilling. Using a long spatula, carefully turn the fillets and grill until the fish breaks into firm flakes when pressed with a finger, 3 to 6 minutes longer.

5. Spoon the sauce onto 4 serving plates, dividing it evenly. Using the spatula, carefully transfer the fish fillets to the plates, arranging them on top of the sauce. Or serve the sauce separately. In any case, serve the fish at once.

NOTE: If you're feeling fancy, you can strain the sauce through a fine-meshed strainer before adding the currants and pine nuts. I'm a rustic kind of guy, and I like a rustic kind of sauce with the shallot pieces still in it.

MALAYSIA

GRILLED SKATE WINGS WITH NONYA SWEET-AND-SOUR SAUCE

DIRECT GRILLING
SERVES 4

Meltingly tender, buttery, and crisp, these skate wings are the specialty of Mrs. Goh Choi Eng, owner of a cook stall on Gurney Drive in Penang. The fish receives a double barrage of flavor—first from a tangy basting sauce made from aromatic, locally grown cloves, then from a Malaysian sweet-and-sour sauce redolent of lemongrass, shallots, and chiles. If skate is impossible to find in your neighborhood, this is also delicious made with bluefish, swordfish, or halibut.

Nonya is the Malay word for grandmother. It refers to a hybrid style of cooking developed in the nineteenth century in Singapore and Malaysia. The Nonyas were local women (usually Muslims) who married immigrant Chinese laborers who had immigrated to the Malaysian peninsula to work—often for the British. The Nonyas adopted Chinese seasonings, like soy sauce and five-spice powder, and Chinese cooking techniques, like stir-frying, while retaining their passion for such Malay ingredients as lemongrass and fiery chiles. The frying of the spice paste is another Nonya technique.

SPECIAL EQUIPMENT

Fish grate (optional)

INGREDIENTS

2 pounds skate wings, cleaned
1 tablespoon ground coriander
2 teaspoons curry powder
¼ teaspoon ground cloves
1 to 2 serrano or other hot peppers, seeded and minced (for a hotter mixture, leave the seeds in)
2 tablespoons Worcestershire sauce
Salt and freshly ground black pepper
1 to 2 tablespoons vegetable oil, for brushing
½ cup Nonya Sweet-and-Sour Sauce (recipe follows), or more as needed

1. Cut the skate wings crosswise (in the same direction as the bones) into 1-inch strips. Butterfly each strip by cutting it in half lengthwise as far as, but not through, the bottom piece of skin. Spread the halves open, then set the strips of skate aside while you prepare the basting mixture.

2. Combine the coriander, curry powder, cloves, peppers, Worcestershire sauce, and 6 tablespoons of water in a bowl and whisk until smooth. Season with salt and black pepper to taste (see Note).

3. Set up the grill for direct grilling and preheat to high.

4. When ready to cook, preheat a fish grate (if using) for 5 minutes, then oil it or the grill grate. Arrange the skate pieces on the hot grate and grill until nicely browned on the bottom, 2 to 4 minutes. As the skate grills, brush it alternately with the basting liquid and the oil.

5. Using a long spatula, carefully turn the skate pieces and brush each with 1 to 2 tablespoons of the Nonya Sweet-and-Sour Sauce. Grill the skate until browned on the second side and the meat flakes easily when pressed with a finger, 2 to 4 minutes longer.

6. Using the spatula, transfer the skate to serving plates or a platter and serve at once.

NOTE: This makes a wonderful basting liquid for any type of seafood; it will keep for weeks in the refrigerator.

NONYA SWEET-AND-SOUR SAUCE

MAKES 1½ TO 2 CUPS

This sauce bears the name sweet-and-sour, but I promise you it's unlike any sweet-and-sour sauce you've ever tasted. Garlic and shallots give it pungency and lemongrass provides fragrance, while jalapeños instill a gentle heat. To be strictly authentic, you'd thin the spice paste to a spreadable consistency with oil, but I like to use another popular Nonya ingredient, coconut milk. Also, a Nonya would probably add a teaspoon of MSG (which of course you can do, too).

8 ounces shallots (about 1½ cups), coarsely chopped
6 to 8 jalapeños or other hot peppers, seeded and coarsely chopped (for a hotter sauce, leave the seeds in)
3 to 4 large stalks fresh lemongrass, trimmed and coarsely chopped, or 3 strips lemon zest (each 2 by ½ inches) removed with a vegetable peeler
2 heads garlic, peeled
½ cup vegetable oil
⅓ cup fresh lime juice, or more to taste
2 tablespoons fresh orange juice or additional lime juice
2 tablespoons sugar, or more to taste
4½ teaspoons soy sauce, or more to taste
1 teaspoon salt, or more to taste
½ teaspoon ground turmeric
½ cup coconut milk, canned or homemade (see page 114)

1. Combine the shallots, jalapeños, lemongrass, garlic, oil, lime juice, orange juice, sugar, soy sauce, salt, and turmeric in a food processor or blender and process to a coarse paste.

2. Transfer the sauce mixture to a small, heavy saucepan and cook over medium heat until slightly reduced and richly flavored, 15 to 20 minutes, stirring frequently. Stir in the coconut milk and let the sauce simmer until thick and creamy, about 5 minutes longer. Remove the sauce from the heat and taste for seasoning, adding more lime juice, sugar, soy sauce, and/or salt as necessary; the sauce should be a little sweet, a little tart, and very aromatic.

3. If not using the sauce immediately, let it cool to room temperature, then transfer it to a clean jar and store it, tightly covered, in the refrigerator. It will keep for several weeks.

PORTUGAL

GRILLED SALT COD

BACALHAO GRELHADO

DIRECT GRILLING
SERVES 4

There's an old saying in Portugal, the gist of which is that a woman isn't ready to get married until she knows 365 ways to prepare *bacalhao* (salt cod). Hyperbole (and a touch sexist), perhaps, but the dictum serves to remind us of the important role salt cod plays in Portuguese cuisine and culture.

One of the most original salt cod preparations I've ever experienced is grilled salt cod, or *bacalhao grelhado*. The fish is soaked for a day to soften and desalinate it, then it's grilled and topped with sizzling fried garlic and olive oil. You can make a meal on the aroma alone! When buying salt cod, choose a one-inch-thick center cut of the whitest fish you can find (yellowish salt cod and thin, stringy tail pieces are inferior). The best place to buy salt cod is at a Portuguese, Spanish, or Italian market.

ADVANCE PREPARATION

24 hours for soaking the fish

SPECIAL EQUIPMENT

Fish grate (optional)

INGREDIENTS

2 pounds salt cod
⅔ cup extra-virgin olive oil
8 cloves garlic, thinly sliced
½ teaspoon cracked or coarsely ground black pepper
Lemon wedges, for serving

1. Place the salt cod in a large bowl and add enough cold water to cover by 1 inch. Cover the cod with plastic wrap and place it in the refrigerator to soak for 24 hours. (If the cod has skin on it, soak it skin side up.) Change the water 3 or 4 times to make the cod less salty.

2. Drain the salt cod, then rinse it under cold running water. Drain the salt cod again and pat it dry with paper towels. Cut the salt cod into 4 equal portions and remove any skin.

3. Set up the grill for direct grilling and preheat to high.

4. When ready to cook, preheat a fish grate (if using) for 5 minutes. Meanwhile, lightly brush each piece of cod with some of the olive oil, using 1½ to 2 tablespoons in all. Oil the fish or grill grate as well, then arrange the pieces of cod on the hot grate and grill until nicely browned on the bottom, 3 to 6 minutes. Using a long spatula, carefully turn the pieces of cod and grill until browned on the second side and flaky and piping hot in the center, 3 to 6 minutes longer.

5. While the fish finishes grilling, place the remaining olive oil in a small saucepan and heat it almost to smoking on the side burner of the grill, if you have one, or over medium heat on the stovetop.

6. Using the spatula, transfer the fish to a heatproof platter. Divide the garlic slices among the pieces of cod, concentrating them in the center. Sprinkle the cod with the coarse pepper. Pour the hot olive oil over the cod, especially where the garlic is (the garlic should sizzle and brown). Serve at once, accompanied by lemon wedges.

PERU

PERUVIAN FISH KEBABS

ANTICUCHOS DE PESCADO

DIRECT GRILLING
SERVES 4

The idea for this recipe comes from a Peruvian-Italian restaurant in Coral Gables, Florida. It's a refined version of Peru's most popular street food (traditional *anticuchos* are made with beef hearts). Here in Miami we use mahimahi for the kebabs, but swordfish, halibut, or even shark are all good choices.

To be strictly authentic, you would use a chile powder or paste called *aji amarillo* (literally, yellow pepper) in the glaze. If you live in a city with a large Peruvian community, you may be able to find it at a Hispanic grocery store, but if not, the flavor can be approximated by combining hot paprika with a pinch of turmeric. Don't be put off by the seemingly large quantity of salt; most of it drains onto the coals. Serve the kebabs with Peruvian Potato Mixed Grill (page 418).

ADVANCE PREPARATION

30 minutes to 1 hour for marinating the fish

SPECIAL EQUIPMENT

4 long metal skewers

INGREDIENTS

1½ pounds firm white fish, such as swordfish, halibut, or mahimahi (about 1 inch thick)
Salt
2 red bell peppers, cored and seeded
6 cloves garlic, peeled
1 teaspoon ground cumin
⅓ cup distilled white vinegar
⅓ cup fresh lemon juice
Freshly ground black pepper
3 tablespoons vegetable oil
1 tablespoon aji amarillo powder or paste, ancho chile powder, or hot paprika
¼ teaspoon ground turmeric (optional)
Lemon wedges, for serving

1. Rinse the fish under cold running water, then drain it and blot dry with paper towels. Cut the fish into 1-inch cubes, place it in a medium-size nonreactive bowl, and toss it with 1½ teaspoons of salt. Let the fish stand for 5 minutes. Meanwhile, cut the bell peppers into 1-inch squares and set aside.

2. Combine the garlic, cumin, vinegar, lemon juice, and ½ teaspoon of black pepper in a food processor or blender and process until blended and smooth. Pour this marinade over the fish and toss to coat. Let the fish marinate in the refrigerator, covered, for 30 minutes to 1 hour.

3. While the fish marinates, prepare the glaze. Heat the oil in a small skillet or saucepan over medium-low heat. Add the *aji amarillo,* turmeric (if using), and 1 teaspoon of salt and 1 teaspoon of black pepper. Gently cook the glaze, stirring with a wooden spoon, until red and fragrant, about 5 minutes. Set the glaze aside to cool (see Note).

4. Remove the fish cubes from the marinade and discard the marinade. Thread the fish cubes onto the skewers, alternating them with squares of bell pepper.

5. Set up the grill for direct grilling and preheat to high.

6. When ready to cook, brush and oil the grill grate. Arrange the kebabs on the hot grate and brush them with half of the glaze. Grill the kebabs, turning with tongs, until the fish cubes are nicely browned on the outside and cooked through, 2 to 3 minutes per side (8 to 12 minutes in all). Brush the kebabs with the remaining glaze after turning.

7. Transfer the kebabs to serving plates or a platter and serve them at once with lemon wedges.

NOTE: You can also simply mix the ingredients for the glaze in a bowl without cooking them. The result will still be very flavorful, but not quite as rich as it would be if you cooked them first.

GREECE

SWORDFISH SOUVLAKI

DIRECT GRILLING
SERVES 4

My friend Patsy Jamieson, food stylist for the magazine *EatingWell,* prepares fish kebabs the way the Greeks make souvlaki (shish kebab), using the traditional Greek flavorings of olive oil, lemon, garlic, oregano, and bay leaves. There are lots of options when it comes to the fish: swordfish, tuna—any firm fish will do, or for that matter even shrimp or scallops. Couscous, rice, or warmed pita bread would make a good accompaniment.

ADVANCE PREPARATION

30 minutes for marinating the fish

SPECIAL EQUIPMENT

4 long metal skewers

INGREDIENTS

1½ pounds swordfish or tuna steaks (about 1 inch thick)
3 tablespoons extra-virgin olive oil
3 tablespoons fresh lemon juice
3 tablespoons dry white wine
2 cloves garlic, minced
1 tablespoon chopped fresh oregano, or 1½ teaspoons dried oregano
1 teaspoon grated lemon zest
1 teaspoon salt, or more to taste
½ teaspoon freshly ground black pepper
24 bay leaves
1 medium-size onion
Lemon wedges, for serving

1. Trim the skin, if any, off the fish steaks. Rinse the fish under cold running water, then drain and blot dry with paper towels. Cut the fish into 1-inch cubes.

2. Combine the olive oil, lemon juice, white wine, garlic, oregano, lemon zest, salt, and pepper in a large nonreactive bowl and whisk until blended and the salt dissolves. Taste for seasoning, adding more salt as necessary; the mixture should be highly seasoned. Add the fish to the marinade and turn to coat. Let the fish marinate in the refrigerator, covered, for 30 minutes, turning occasionally.

3. Place the bay leaves in a bowl of cold water to cover and let soak for 20 minutes.

4. Cut the onion in half crosswise, then cut each half in quarters and break these into layers. Drain the bay leaves. Remove the fish cubes from the bowl, reserving whatever marinade is left, and thread the fish cubes onto the skewers, placing a piece of onion and a bay leaf between each cube and dividing them evenly.

5. Set up the grill for direct grilling and preheat to high.

6. When ready to cook, brush and oil the grill grate. Arrange the kebabs on the hot grate and grill, turning with tongs, until the fish cubes are nicely browned on the outside and cooked through, 2 to 3 minutes per side (8 to 12 minutes in all). As the kebabs cook, baste them with any remaining marinade, but do not baste during the last 2 minutes of grilling.

7. Transfer the kebabs to serving plates or a platter and serve at once, accompanied by lemon wedges.

BRAZIL

SWORDFISH KEBABS WITH COCONUT MILK

DIRECT GRILLING
SERVES 4

This recipe comes from the most unlikely of sources, a Rio de Janeiro meat emporium called Porcão (Big Pig). Like most *churrascarias* (barbecue restaurants), Porcão specializes in an astonishing assortment of grilled meats presented on swordlike spits and carved directly onto your plate at the table. Conspicuous consumption is the name of the game: The waiters keep bringing food until you expressly ask them to stop.

These kebabs caught my eye (and taste buds) precisely because they weren't meat. Porcão makes them with *surubinho,* a giant mild, sweet freshwater fish from the Amazon. The closest equivalent in North America would be halibut—which you could use—as well as tuna, sea bass, or any firm, meaty fish. I usually make the recipe with swordfish.

Coconut milk is a traditional ingredient in northern Brazilian cooking. Its high fat content keeps the fish moist and flavorful. Be sure to use unsweetened coconut milk: reliable brands include A Taste of Thai, which is available at most supermarkets. For additional flavor, Porcão's chef bastes the kebabs with garlic butter as they cook. The fish will have plenty of flavor without this step, but it does offer added richness. Crazy Rice (page 432) makes a good accompaniment.

ADVANCE PREPARATION

1 to 4 hours for marinating the fish

SPECIAL EQUIPMENT

4 long metal skewers

FOR THE FISH AND MARINADE

1½ pounds swordfish steaks (about 1 inch thick)
1 cup coconut milk, canned or homemade (see page 114)
2 tablespoons extra-virgin olive oil
6 cloves garlic, coarsely chopped
1 medium-size onion, quartered
½ medium-size green bell pepper, cored, seeded, and quartered
1 teaspoon salt, or more to taste
1 teaspoon freshly ground black pepper
¼ cup chopped fresh flat-leaf parsley

FOR THE BASTING MIXTURE (OPTIONAL)

2 tablespoons (¼ stick) salted butter
1 clove garlic, minced

FOR THE KEBABS

1 medium-size onion
1 red bell pepper, cored, seeded, and cut into 1-inch squares
1 green bell pepper, cored, seeded, and cut into 1-inch squares

1. Prepare the fish and marinade: Trim the skin off the swordfish steaks. Rinse the fish under cold running water, then drain it and blot dry with paper towels. Cut the fish into 1-inch cubes and place it in a medium-size nonreactive bowl. Set the fish aside while you prepare the marinade.

2. Combine the coconut milk, olive oil, coarsely chopped garlic, the quartered onion, ½ green bell pepper, and the salt and black pepper in a food processor or blender and process to a smooth puree. Add the parsley and blend for 30 seconds. Taste for seasoning, adding more salt as necessary; the mixture should be highly seasoned. Pour the marinade over the fish cubes and toss to coat. Let the fish marinate in the refrigerator, covered, for at least 1 hour, or up to 4 hours (the longer the better), stirring occasionally.

3. If using the basting mixture: Place the butter in a saucepan and melt it over low heat, either on the burner attachment of the grill, if it has one, or on the stovetop. Stir in the minced garlic and remove the basting mixture from the heat.

4. Assemble the kebabs: Cut the whole onion in half crosswise; cut each half in quarters and break these into layers.

Remove the fish cubes from the marinade and discard the marinade. Thread the fish cubes onto the skewers, placing a piece of onion and a bell pepper square between each cube and dividing them evenly.

5. Set up the grill for direct grilling and preheat to high.

6. When ready to cook, brush and oil the grill grate, then arrange the kebabs on the hot grate and grill, turning with tongs, until the fish cubes are nicely browned on the outside and cooked through 2 to 3 minutes per side (8 to 12 minutes in all). Brush the kebabs with the basting mixture (if using) during the last minute of cooking.

7. Transfer the kebabs to serving plates or a platter and serve at once.

TURKEY

PANDELI SWORDFISH KEBABS

DIRECT GRILLING
SERVES 4

Pandeli is a landmark restaurant located on the second floor of the entryway into Istanbul's Spice Bazaar. It has the most famous staircase in Istanbul, with shimmering blue and white tiles that line an ancient passageway. But to come to Pandeli solely for the visual virtuosity of its stairway would be to overlook a bill of fare so appealing and tasty that modern Turkey's founder, Kemal Atatürk, made the restaurant his regular lunch spot. If you arrive early enough, you may be able to get a seat at a table overlooking the spice market or the Bosporus. But wherever you sit, be sure to order the seafood meze (a sampler of cured Black and Caspian Sea seafoods) and these swordfish kebabs.

Turkish cooks paint with a simple but powerful palette, so although there may not seem to be anything extraordinary about this recipe, I think you'll find, as I do, that the results are exceedingly tasty. See A Griller's Guide to the World's Chiles on page 502 for a description of bull's horn peppers.

ADVANCE PREPARATION

30 minutes for marinating the kebabs

SPECIAL EQUIPMENT

4 long metal skewers

INGREDIENTS

- 1½ pounds swordfish steaks (about 1 inch thick)
- 12 bull's horn peppers, or 2 large green bell peppers (see Note)
- 12 bay leaves
- 2 large ripe tomatoes, each cut into 6 wedges
- 1 large lemon, cut into ¼-inch slices (12 slices in all)
- Salt and freshly ground black pepper
- ¼ cup extra-virgin olive oil
- 3 tablespoons fresh lemon juice
- 1 bunch fresh flat-leaf parsley, stemmed, ½ bunch coarsely chopped, ½ bunch broken into large sprigs
- Lemon wedges, for serving

1. Trim the skin off the swordfish steaks. Rinse the fish under cold running water, then drain it and blot dry with paper towels. Cut the fish into 2-inch squares about 1 inch thick. Thread the fish onto the skewers through the short side alternately with the bull's horn peppers, bay leaves, tomato wedges, and lemon slices, dividing all of the ingredients evenly among the skewers. Season the kebabs with salt and black pepper to taste.

2. Place the kebabs in a large nonreactive baking dish. Combine the olive oil and lemon juice in a small bowl and whisk to blend, then pour the olive oil mixture over the kebabs. Sprinkle the chopped parsley on the kebabs. Let the kebabs marinate in the refrigerator for 30 minutes, turning them once or twice.

3. Set up the grill for direct grilling and preheat to high.

4. When ready to cook, remove the kebabs from the baking dish, reserving whatever marinade is left. Brush and oil the grill grate, then arrange the kebabs on the hot grate. Grill the kebabs, turning with tongs, until the vegetables and swordfish are nicely browned and the fish is cooked through, 4 to 6 minutes per side (8 to 12 minutes total). As the kebabs cook, baste them with any remaining marinade, but do not baste during the last 3 minutes of grilling.

5. Transfer the kebabs to serving plates or a platter and serve at once, accompanied by lemon wedges and garnished with parsley sprigs.

NOTE: If you are using bull's horn peppers, leave them whole and core but do not seed them. If you are using green peppers, core and seed them, then cut them into 2 by 1–inch strips.

RUSSIA

STURGEON KEBABS

DIRECT GRILLING
SERVES 4

Russians often grate onions for marinades rather than chop them. This exposes more of the onion to air, producing a stronger flavor. The sweet-sour trickle of pomegranate molasses is a hallmark of the soulful cooking of the former Soviet Republics of the Caucasus Mountains.

ADVANCE PREPARATION

2 to 4 hours for marinating the fish

SPECIAL EQUIPMENT

4 long metal skewers

INGREDIENTS

1½ pounds fresh sturgeon (see box, at right), monkfish, or swordfish steaks (about 1 inch thick)
1 onion, coarsely grated
½ cup dry white wine
¼ cup vegetable oil, plus 1 to 2 tablespoons vegetable oil, for brushing the kebabs
3 tablespoons fresh lemon juice
1 tablespoon sweet paprika
1½ teaspoons salt
1 bay leaf, crushed
½ teaspoon freshly ground black pepper
2 to 3 tablespoons Pomegranate Molasses (page 243), for serving
Lemon wedges, for serving

1. Trim the skin off the fish steaks and cut the meat off the bones, if necessary. Rinse the fish under cold running water, then drain it and blot dry with paper towels. Cut the fish into 1-inch cubes and set aside while you prepare the marinade.

2. Combine the onion, white wine, ¼ cup of oil, and the lemon juice, paprika, salt, bay leaf, and pepper in a large nonreactive bowl and stir to mix. Add the fish cubes and toss to coat. Let the fish marinate in the refrigerator, covered, for at least 2 hours, or up to 4 hours, stirring occasionally.

3. Set up the grill for direct grilling and preheat to high.

4. When ready to cook, remove the fish cubes from the marinade and discard the marinade. Thread the fish cubes

Sturgeon

Most people think of sturgeon as the source of fine caviar or as smoked fish for bagels. But in the former Soviet Union, this whiskered, prehistoric-looking fish is a popular item for grilling, as I quickly discovered during a day of restaurant hopping in the Brighton Beach area of Brooklyn, New York's "Little Odessa." Sturgeon has a mild, sweet flavor and firm, almost gelatinous consistency, and its dense texture makes it ideal for grilling on skewers or as steaks, as on page 324. If you live in an area with a large Russian community (such as in the Pacific Northwest), you may be able to find it fresh. Monkfish has a similar texture. Another possibility is swordfish, which has a much softer consistency but tastes equally delicious prepared in this fashion.

onto the skewers, dividing them evenly. Brush and oil the grill grate, then arrange the kebabs on the hot grate and brush them generously with oil. Grill the kebabs, turning with tongs, until nicely browned on the outside and cooked through, 2 to 3 minutes per side (8 to 12 minutes in all), brushing them again with oil after turning.

5. Transfer the kebabs to serving plates or a platter and serve them at once with Pomegranate Molasses drizzled on top and accompanied by lemon wedges.

INDONESIA

BALINESE FISH MOUSSE SATES

SATE LILIT

DIRECT GRILLING
SERVES 4 TO 6 AS AN APPETIZER, 2 AS A MAIN COURSE

Saté lilit rank among the most exquisite of Indonesia's satés. Their birthplace is Bali, where they are used in and served at religious festivals. To make them, a delicate mousse is flavored with explosively aromatic spices, then enriched with coconut milk and grilled on fragrant lemongrass stalks. The mousse can be made of fish, shrimp, chicken, duck, and even turtle.

Even if you can't locate a few of the special ingredients here, you can still prepare *saté lilit.* Kaffir lime leaves, electrifying with their perfumed lime flavor, can be found fresh or frozen at Asian markets, but if none is available, a little grated lime zest will work instead. Shrimp paste (*trassi*) is a strong-smelling seasoning made from fermented shrimp. Substitutes include Asian fish sauce or anchovy paste.

Don't be frightened by the long list of ingredients. These satés are easy to make and aren't as time consuming as they may appear. The results will light up your mouth like a Fourth of July sky.

ADVANCE PREPARATION

2 hours for chilling the mousse

SPECIAL EQUIPMENT

24 stalks fresh lemongrass, each trimmed to 6 inches long (see Notes), or 24 small flat bamboo skewers or Popsicle sticks

FOR THE SPICE PASTE

- 4 large shallots, sliced
- 4 macadamia nuts
- 3 cloves garlic, sliced
- 1 to 3 Thai chiles or serrano peppers, sliced
- 1 piece (1 inch) galangal or fresh ginger, peeled and sliced
- 2 teaspoons ground coriander
- ½ teaspoon freshly ground black pepper
- ½ teaspoon ground turmeric
- 1 teaspoon shrimp paste or anchovy paste, or 1 tablespoon Asian fish sauce
- ½ teaspoon salt
- 4½ teaspoons vegetable oil

FOR THE FISH MOUSSE

- 12 ounces firm white fish fillets, such as snapper, mahimahi, bass, or catfish
- 8 ounces shrimp, peeled and deveined
- ¼ cup canned unsweetened coconut milk
- 1 large egg white
- 1 tablespoon fresh lime juice, or more to taste
- 2 kaffir lime leaves, cut into hair-thin slivers, or ½ teaspoon grated lime zest
- 4 teaspoons palm sugar or light brown sugar
- Salt (optional)

1. Make the spice paste: Combine the shallots, macadamia nuts, garlic, Thai chiles, galangal, coriander, pepper, turmeric, shrimp paste (see Notes), and ½ teaspoon of salt in a food processor and process to a smooth paste. Heat the oil in a small, heavy skillet over medium heat. Add the spice paste and cook until dark and fragrant, 5 to 10 minutes, stirring constantly. Remove the spice paste from the heat and transfer it to a small bowl to cool.

2. Make the fish mousse: Combine the fish fillets and shrimp in the food processor and process to a smooth puree. Add the cooled spice paste, coconut milk, egg white, lime juice, kaffir lime leaves, and palm sugar and process until thoroughly blended. To test the mixture for seasoning, cook a small amount of it in a nonstick skillet until cooked through, then taste, adding salt and more lime juice to the remaining mixture as necessary; the mousse mixture should be highly seasoned. Refrigerate the mousse mixture, covered, for 2 hours.

3. Divide the mousse mixture into 24 equal portions. Lightly wet your hands with cold water, then take each portion of mousse mixture and mold it around the bulbous part of a lemongrass stalk to make a sausage shape about 3 inches long. As they are finished, place the satés on a baking sheet lined with plastic wrap. Loosely cover the satés with more plastic wrap and refrigerate them until ready to cook, for up to 6 hours.

4. Set up the grill for direct grilling and preheat to high.

5. When ready to cook, brush and oil the grill grate. Arrange the satés on the hot grate and grill until nicely browned on the outside and cooked through, 3 to 4 minutes per side (6 to 8 minutes in all). If the fish mixture sticks to the grate, use a spatula to help turn the satés.

6. Using the spatula, carefully transfer the satés to serving plates or a platter. Serve at once.

NOTES: If you can buy large lemongrass stalks (ones about 12 inches long with bases ½ inch in diameter), the tops may be thick enough to use as skewers; then, because you'll be cutting the stalks crosswise in half, you'll need only 12 stalks.

If you are using fish sauce, add it to the mousse mixture along with the spice paste in Step 2.

Grill Baskets

One easy way to keep fish from sticking to the grill grate—whether you are cooking fillets or whole fish—is to use a grill basket. A grill basket is a hinged metal basket with two flat or slightly rounded wire sides. You place the basket on top of the grill grate; the beauty of this technique is that it's a lot easier to turn the whole basket than individual fish fillets or whole fish.

When you are ready to grill, oil the grill basket well to prevent sticking. Place the fish in the basket and fasten the two sides together; usually there's a ring or clip on the basket for this purpose. Place the fish in the basket on the grill grate and cook until browned on both sides and cooked through, turning the basket when the first side is done.

Transfer the grill basket to a heatproof platter or cutting board. Release the clip, taking care not to burn your fingers. Open the basket and slide the fish out with a spatula and you're ready to serve.

U.S.A.

FLORIDA SNAPPER BURGERS

DIRECT GRILLING
SERVES 4

Here's a "meatless" burger from one of the pioneers of the new Floridian style of cooking, Allen Susser of Chef Allen's in North Miami Beach. Susser uses red snapper; in areas of the country where snapper isn't available, you could use monkfish or halibut (you need a fish that contains a lot of gelatin). The texture of these burgers is rather like that of fish mousse, and the fish sauce and fresh dill make them exceptionally flavorful. In keeping with the tropical theme, Chef Allen's serves this burger with a mango ketchup Susser bottles and distributes nationally. If you can't find it, Mark Militello's Mango Barbecue Sauce makes a good substitute. Susser suggests serving the burgers on crusty French bread topped with spinach.

ADVANCE PREPARATION

1 to 6 hours for chilling the fish

INGREDIENTS

1¼ pounds skinless fresh red snapper fillets, cut into 1-inch pieces
3 large egg whites, lightly beaten
1 tablespoon Thai fish sauce
1 teaspoon coarse salt (kosher or sea), or more to taste
¼ teaspoon freshly ground black pepper, or more to taste
¼ teaspoon cayenne pepper, or more to taste
2 tablespoons chopped scallions, both white and green parts
2 tablespoons chopped fresh dill
3 to 4 tablespoons fresh bread crumbs
2 tablespoons extra-virgin olive oil
1 loaf French bread (about 16 inches long), cut in half lengthwise, then each half cut crosswise into 4 equal pieces
12 fresh spinach leaves, rinsed and patted dry
½ cup Mark Militello's Mango Barbecue Sauce (optional; page 465)

1. Run your fingers over the snapper fillets, feeling for bones, then use needle-nose pliers or tweezers to remove any you may find. Transfer the snapper to a food processor and process it, in short bursts, just until finely chopped. Do not overprocess; you don't want a puree (see Note). Still processing in short bursts, add the egg whites, fish sauce, salt, black pepper, and cayenne. Add the scallions, dill, and enough bread crumbs to bind the mixture together (start with 3 tablespoons). To test the mixture for seasoning, cook a small amount of it in a nonstick skillet until cooked through, then taste, adding more salt and/or black pepper to the remaining fish mixture as necessary; it should be highly seasoned.

2. Divide the fish mixture into 4 equal portions. Lightly wet your hands with cold water and form each portion into a patty 3½ inches across and about ½ inch thick. Place the patties on a generously oiled plate, cover them, and refrigerate for at least 1 hour, or up to 6 hours.

3. Set up the grill for direct grilling and preheat to high.

4. When ready to cook, brush the tops of the fish patties generously with olive oil. Brush and oil the grill grate, then arrange the patties, oiled side down, on the hot grate. Grill, turning with tongs, until nicely browned on both sides and cooked through, 3 to 4 minutes per side, adding the French bread pieces, cut sides down, to the grill to toast when you turn the patties. Do not overcook the burgers.

5. Serve the burgers on the toasted French bread, topped with spinach leaves and barbecue sauce, if desired.

NOTE: As an alternative, you can chop the fish by hand with a cleaver or sharp, heavy knife; transfer it to a bowl and work in the remaining ingredients by hand.

MORTON BAY "BUGS" WITH GINGER-MINT BUTTER | AT RIGHT

CHAPTER 12

HOT SHELLS: LOBSTERS, SHRIMP, SCALLOPS, AND CLAMS

I've often pondered how early man figured out how to eat oysters. Certainly not with an oyster knife! I like to think he placed them on the coals of a campfire and let the smoky heat open the shells. And while you may not think of the grill when it comes to cooking shellfish, grilling remains one of the best methods I know for cooking clams, mussels, shrimp, and even lobster.

"Many shrimps, many flavors; many men, many whims."
—MALAYSIAN PROVERB

This chapter will introduce you to the world of grilled shellfish, from Greek grilled octopus to Caribbean shrimp grilled on skewers made of sugar cane. You'll find out how Australians cook their famous shrimp "on the barbie," not to mention their beloved Morton Bay "bugs" (rock lobsters).

Grilling is a great way to cook lobster. It keeps shrimp moist and soft-shell crabs crackling crisp. Broaden your repertoire with the likes of Flaming Prawns, Penganese Grilled Shrimp with Painfully Hot Salsa, and Bahamian Grilled Conch.

Shellfish never tasted so good!

AUSTRALIA

MORTON BAY "BUGS" WITH GINGER-MINT BUTTER

DIRECT GRILLING
SERVES 4

I love the affectionate disrespect that fishermen everywhere seem to have for Neptune's noblest creature. That is, whether you buy lobsters from a fisherman on the coast of Maine or in Morton Bay, Australia, you're likely to hear them called "bugs." The Morton Bay "bug" is one of Australia's most prized shellfish, a clawless crustacean similar to a Florida (or rock or spiny) lobster. I call for lobster tails in the recipe here, but you could also use Maine lobster or spot prawns—even jumbo shrimp would take to this preparation, as well. Ginger, lime, and mint create an explosively flavorful butter that is brushed on the lobster as it grills. The preparation is simple, but powerfully good.

4 lobster tails (8 to 9 ounces each), thawed if frozen, or 4 live Maine lobsters (1¼ to 1½ pounds each)
8 tablespoons (1 stick) unsalted butter
2 tablespoons chopped fresh mint, or 2 teaspoons dried mint
1 tablespoon minced peeled fresh ginger
1 clove garlic, minced
1 teaspoon grated lime zest
3 tablespoons Asian fish sauce or soy sauce
2 tablespoons fresh lime juice
Salt and freshly ground black pepper
Lemon wedges, for serving

1. *If using lobster tails,* cut them in half lengthwise with kitchen shears or a sharp, heavy knife; use a fork to remove the intestinal vein that runs the length of the tail.

If using live lobsters, kill each by inserting a sharp knife in the back of the head between the eyes; this will dispatch them instantly (or see the box below). Cut the lobsters in half lengthwise and remove the vein and the papery gray sac from the head. Break off the claws and crack them with a chef's knife.

2. Melt the butter in a small, heavy saucepan over low heat. Add the mint, ginger, garlic, and lime zest and increase the heat to medium. Cook the butter mixture until it is fragrant but not brown, about 3 minutes. Stir in the fish sauce and lime juice and bring to a boil, then remove the ginger-mint butter from the heat.

3. Brush the cut sides of the lobster tails or lobsters with some of the ginger-mint butter and season them with salt and pepper to taste.

4. Set up the grill for direct grilling and preheat to high.

5. When ready to cook, brush and oil the grill grate. Arrange the lobster tails or lobster halves and claws, cut side down, on the hot grate and grill for 4 to 8 minutes. Using tongs, turn the lobster and grill on the shell side until the flesh is firm and white, 4 to 8 minutes longer, brushing it generously several times with the ginger-mint butter.

6. Transfer the lobster to serving plates or a platter and pour any remaining ginger-mint butter over them. Serve at once with lemon wedges.

When You're Feeling Less Than Brave

The parboiling technique described here is for those of you who don't take too well to the idea of dispatching a lobster with a knife.

If you are cooking as many as four lobsters, bring eight quarts of water to a boil in a large pot with a lid. Add the lobsters, cover the pot tightly, and let boil for two minutes. Using tongs, transfer the lobsters to a platter and let them cool. Then cut the lobsters in half and grill them according to the recipe.

FRENCH WEST INDIES

GRILLED SPINY LOBSTER WITH BASIL BUTTER

DIRECT GRILLING
SERVES 4

This imposing dish is the speciality of a New Age inn called Hostellerie des Trois Forces in St. Barthélemy. Astrologer-chef Hubert Delamotte makes it with spiny lobster, which has a broad tail and fiercely barbed carapace, but no claws. If you live in Florida or Texas, the equivalent would be a "Florida" lobster. Maine lobster can be prepared the same way. Whichever lobster you use, you'll surely enjoy the way the fragrance of the basil brings out the sweetness of the lobster meat. Serve the lobster with Grilled Polenta (page 433).

4 lobster tails (8 to 9 ounces each), thawed if frozen, or 4 live Maine lobsters (1¼ to 1½ pounds each)
8 tablespoons (1 stick) salted butter, melted

Salt and freshly ground black pepper
½ cup coarsely chopped fresh basil
1 to 2 limes, cut in half

1. *If using lobster tails,* cut them in half lengthwise with kitchen shears or a sharp, heavy knife; use a fork to remove the intestinal vein that runs the length of the tail.

If using live lobsters, kill each by inserting a sharp knife in the back of the head between the eyes; this will dispatch them instantly (or see the box at left). Cut the lobsters in half lengthwise and remove the vein and the papery gray sac from the head. Break off the claws and crack with a chef's knife.

2. Brush the cut sides of the lobster tails or lobsters with some of the melted butter and season them with salt and pepper to taste. Place the remaining melted butter in a small saucepan over medium heat, add the chopped basil, and let simmer for 2 minutes.

3. Set up the grill for direct grilling and preheat to high.

4. When ready to cook, brush and oil the grill grate. Arrange the lobster tails or lobster halves and claws, cut side down, on the hot grate and grill for 4 to 8 minutes. Using tongs, turn the lobster and grill on the shell side until the flesh is firm and white, 4 to 8 minutes longer, squeezing lime juice over the lobster as it cooks and brushing generously several times with the basil butter.

5. Transfer the lobster to serving plates or a platter and serve at once, accompanied by the remaining basil butter in ramekins on the side.

FRENCH WEST INDIES

SPINY LOBSTER WITH CREOLE SAUCE

DIRECT GRILLING
SERVES 4

My wife and I first tasted this dish on our honeymoon in Saint Barthélemy in 1990. The place was a tiny beach restaurant called the Marigot Bay Club, run by a fisherman friend named Michel Ledée. The lobster had emerged from the water about an hour before we ate it. To enjoy it any fresher, we'd have had to have dined in bathing suits!

Michel's Creole sauce has complex layers of flavor: the bass tones of garlic and scallions, the brassy notes of thyme and lime juice, and the shrill accent of Scotch bonnet–based hot sauce. I note with sadness that Michel died tragically while rescuing his daughter from a swimming accident. This recipe is dedicated to his memory.

4 lobster tails (8 to 9 ounces each), thawed if frozen, or 4 live Maine lobsters (1¼ to 1½ pounds each)
4 tablespoons lard (see Note)
½ cup finely chopped shallots
4 scallions, both white and green parts, trimmed and finely chopped
3 cloves garlic, minced
3 tablespoons chopped fresh flat-leaf parsley
2 teaspoons chopped fresh thyme, or 1 teaspoon dried thyme
1 cup ketchup
2 tablespoons fresh lime juice, or more to taste
1 teaspoon hot pepper sauce, preferably a Scotch bonnet–based sauce such as Matouk's, or more to taste
Salt and freshly ground black pepper

1. *If using lobster tails,* cut them in half lengthwise with kitchen shears or a sharp, heavy knife; use a fork to remove the intestinal vein that runs the length of the tail.

If using live lobsters, kill each by inserting a sharp knife in the back of the head between the eyes; this will dispatch them instantly (or see the box at left). Cut the lobsters in half lengthwise and remove the vein and the papery gray sac from the head. Break off the claws and crack them with a chef's knife. Refrigerate the lobster, covered, while you prepare the Creole sauce.

2. Melt 2 tablespoons of the lard in a medium-size saucepan over medium heat. Add the shallots, scallions, garlic, parsley, and thyme and cook until the shallots and scallions are lightly browned, 3 to 5 minutes. Stir in the ketchup, lime juice, hot pepper sauce, and ⅔ cup of water and bring to a boil. Reduce the heat to low and let simmer gently, uncovered, until the sauce is thickened and nicely flavored, 5 to 10 minutes.

Shellfish Grilling Chart

TYPE	METHOD	HEAT	COOKING TIME
CLAMS, IN SHELL	direct	high	until shells open, 6 to 8 minutes
LOBSTER			
half lobster	direct	high	until cooked through, 4 to 8 minutes per side
lobster tail	direct	high	until cooked through, 4 to 8 minutes per side
OYSTERS, IN SHELL	direct	high	until shells open, 6 to 8 minutes
SCALLOPS	direct	high	until cooked through, about 2 minutes per side
SHRIMP	direct	high	until cooked through, about 2 minutes per side

This chart is offered as a broad guideline to cooking times for the various types of shellfish. Remember, grilling is an art, not a science. When in doubt, refer to times in the individual recipes.

Remove the sauce from the heat and taste for seasoning, adding salt and pepper to taste and more lime juice and/or hot pepper sauce as necessary; the Creole sauce should be highly seasoned.

3. Melt the remaining 2 tablespoons of lard in a small saucepan over low heat, then brush it over the cut side of the lobster tails or lobsters. Season the lobster with salt and pepper to taste.

4. Set up the grill for direct grilling and preheat to high.

5. When ready to cook, brush and oil the grill grate. Arrange the lobster tails or lobster halves and claws, cut side down, on the hot grill grate and grill for 4 to 8 minutes. Turn the lobster, using tongs, and spoon the Creole sauce over it, dividing the sauce evenly. Grill the lobster on the shell side until the flesh is firm and white, 4 to 8 minutes longer.

6. Transfer the lobster to serving plates or a platter and serve at once.

NOTE: Lard may seem like a strange, even off-putting ingredient, but it's often used for basting at French barbecues. Here it is used as a base for the Caribbean lobster seasoning. You can certainly substitute melted butter or oil.

SOUTH AFRICA

GRILLED ROCK LOBSTER

INDIRECT GRILLING
SERVES 4

South Africans have an ingenious way of preparing rock lobster for grilling. They snip open the thin shell covering the bottom of the tail. Then they cook the lobster in the shell, belly side up, using the indirect method. This keeps the lobster moist and tender—ideal for rock or spiny lobsters. There is nothing flashy about the basting sauce used with the lobsters, but the butter, wine, and Worcestershire add a world of flavor without masking the pristine taste of the lobster.

4 live spiny or rock lobsters (1¼ to 1½ pounds each), or 4 lobster tails (8 to 9 ounces each), thawed if frozen
4 tablespoons (½ stick) unsalted butter
3 tablespoons extra-virgin olive oil
2 tablespoons Worcestershire sauce
2 tablespoons fresh lemon juice
2 tablespoons dry white wine
2 cloves garlic, minced
3 tablespoons minced fresh flat-leaf parsley

½ teaspoon cayenne pepper, or more to taste
Salt and freshly ground black pepper

1. *If using live lobsters,* kill each by inserting a sharp knife in the back of the head between the eyes; this will dispatch them instantly (or see the box on page 354). Then, using kitchen shears, make 4 cuts, 2 lengthwise and 2 crosswise, in the "belly" side of the tail; remove the thin shell.

If using lobster tails, using kitchen shears or a sharp, heavy knife, cut them in half lengthwise through the top shell but not all the way through the underside. Open out the tails like a butterfly. Using a fork, remove the intestinal vein that runs the length of the tail.

Set the lobsters or lobster tails aside while you prepare the basting and serving sauce.

2. Melt the butter in a small, heavy saucepan over medium-low heat. Add the olive oil, Worcestershire sauce, lemon juice, white wine, garlic, parsley, and cayenne and let simmer gently until the garlic is fragrant and has lost its raw edge, 3 to 5 minutes. Remove the sauce from the heat, taste for seasoning, and add salt and black pepper to taste and more cayenne as necessary. Set half of the sauce aside for serving.

3. Set up the grill for indirect grilling. No drip pan is necessary for this recipe. Preheat the grill to medium (see Note).

4. When ready to cook, place the lobsters or lobster tails in the center of the grate, belly side up, and brush them generously with the basting sauce. Cover the grill and cook the lobster until the flesh is firm and white, 30 to 40 minutes for lobsters and 20 to 30 minutes for tails. Brush the exposed lobster meat once or twice with the basting sauce as it grills.

5. Transfer the lobsters to serving plates or a platter and serve at once, accompanied by the reserved sauce in ramekins for dipping.

NOTE: The lobster tails may also be grilled over direct heat: Preheat the grill to high and cook the tails cut side down for 4 to 8 minutes to sear the meat. Using tongs, turn the tails over and cook, cut side up, until the flesh is firm and white, 4 to 8 minutes longer. Brush the lobsters with the basting sauce as they cook and again just before serving.

U.S.A.

GRILLED SOFT-SHELL CRABS WITH SPICY TARTAR SAUCE

DIRECT GRILLING
SERVES 4 TO 6

Like all crustaceans, crabs periodically shed their shells to make room for future growth. Soft-shell crabs are freshly molted blue crabs. You eat the molted crab carapace and all; the crabs are in season from May through August. Most recipes call for soft-shells to be panfried or deep-fried. Grilling produces great-tasting crabs with a fraction of the fat. You still get the wonderful soft-shell crab flavor and texture: briny as the ocean and potato-chip crisp.

The crabs should be live when you buy them. Ask the fishmonger to clean them, and always cook them the same day you buy them. Serve the crabs with Grilled Garlic Bread Fingers (page 126) and Your Basic Slaw (page 460).

FOR THE TARTAR SAUCE

1 cup good-quality mayonnaise
1 to 2 fresh or pickled jalapeño peppers, seeded and finely chopped
1 tablespoon Dijon mustard
1 tablespoon fresh lime juice, or more to taste
1 tablespoon capers, drained and chopped
1 tablespoon chopped fresh chives or trimmed scallion greens
1 tablespoon chopped sour pickles, preferably cornichons
1 tablespoon chopped fresh tarragon or basil
Salt (optional)

FOR THE CRABS

8 tablespoons (1 stick) unsalted butter, melted, or ½ cup extra-virgin olive oil
1 tablespoon fresh lemon juice
12 soft-shell crabs, cleaned
Salt and freshly ground black pepper

1. Make the tartar sauce: Combine the mayonnaise, jalapeños, mustard, lime juice, capers, chives, pickles, and tarragon in a small bowl and whisk thoroughly to mix. Taste for seasoning, adding salt and/or more lime juice as necessary; the tartar sauce should be highly seasoned. Set the tartar sauce aside until serving time (see Note).

2. Prepare the crabs: Combine the melted butter and lemon juice in a small bowl and whisk to blend. Brush the crabs on both sides with some of the lemon butter and season them generously with salt and pepper.

3. Set up the grill for direct grilling and preheat to high.

4. When ready to cook, brush and oil the grill grate. Arrange the crabs on the hot grate and grill, turning with tongs, until the shells are bright red, 3 to 6 minutes per side. Brush the crabs with the remaining lemon butter once or twice as they cook.

5. Transfer the crabs to serving plates or a platter and serve at once, accompanied by the tartar sauce.

NOTE: The tartar sauce can be made up to 2 days ahead of time. Refrigerate it, covered.

INDONESIA

PRAWNS WITH KETJAP BUTTER

DIRECT GRILLING
SERVES 4

Prawns the size of lobsters, grilled crackling crisp in the shells, basted with a succulent, sweet-salty mixture of butter and sweet soy sauce—this is one of the specialties of Jakarta's famous fish house, Sunda Kelapa, and those prawns are delicious enough to eat with your hands, which is what most of the customers do. We can't get those huge prawns here, but if you live in the Pacific Northwest or Hawaii, try making this recipe with spot prawns; otherwise, use jumbo shrimp in the shells. Serve this with the Javanese Long Bean Salad Plate with Cabbage Wedges (page 114), Penang Shallot Relish (page 444), and steamed rice.

3 tablespoons unsalted butter
3 tablespoons sweet soy sauce (ketjap manis), or 1½ tablespoons each regular soy sauce and molasses
1 tablespoon fresh lime juice
1½ pounds spot prawns or jumbo shrimp, deveined and butterflied (see box, page 361), shells left on

1. Melt the butter in a small saucepan, then remove it from the heat and stir in the sweet soy sauce and lime juice. Rinse the prawns under cold running water, then drain them and blot dry with paper towels. Brush the cut sides of the prawns with some of the butter mixture.

2. Set up the grill for direct grilling and preheat to high.

3. When ready to cook, brush and oil the grill grate. Arrange the prawns, cut side down, on the hot grate and grill until lightly browned on that side, about 2 minutes. Brush the shell sides with the butter mixture and, using tongs, turn the prawns over. Grill the prawns until lightly browned on the second side and firm and pink inside, about 2 minutes longer, brushing them once or twice more with the butter mixture.

4. Transfer the prawns to serving plates or a platter, pour any remaining butter mixture over them, and serve at once.

GUADELOUPE

GRILLED "CRAYFISH" WITH CURRY BEURRE BLANC

DIRECT GRILLING
SERVES 4

Guadeloupe is famous throughout the Caribbean for a large, sweet-fleshed shellfish known as *oassou* (pronounced wa-sou). Although commonly translated as crayfish, the *oassou* is actually a type of prawn. The preferred cooking method is grilling: The shellfish are skewered, heads and all, and roasted over glowing coals. *Oassous* are not available in the U.S. (at least not yet), but the spot prawns found in Hawaii and the Pacific Northwest have a similar flavor. Jumbo shrimp can be prepared the same way.

In Guadeloupe (this is part of France, after all), the *oassou* would be accompanied by a beurre blanc (butter sauce) flavored with a French West Indian curry powder called *colombo,* available in West Indian markets. My version of the sauce offers you the option of using *colombo* or a standard (though good-quality) curry powder.

ADVANCE PREPARATION

30 minutes to 1 hour for marinating the shellfish

SPECIAL EQUIPMENT

4 long metal skewers

FOR THE PRAWN BROCHETTES AND MARINADE

20 spot prawns or jumbo shrimp in the shell
1 onion, halved crosswise, each half cut into 6 to 8 wedges
1 red bell pepper, cored, seeded, and cut into 1-inch squares
3 tablespoons fresh lime juice
3 tablespoons extra-virgin olive oil
2 cloves garlic, minced
Salt and freshly ground black pepper

FOR THE BEURRE BLANC

1 cup dry white wine
¼ cup white wine vinegar
⅓ cup minced shallots
1½ teaspoons colombo powder, homemade (page 497) or store-bought, or good-quality regular curry powder, or more to taste
¼ cup heavy (whipping) cream
8 tablespoons (1 stick) cold unsalted butter, cut into ½-inch pieces
Salt and freshly ground black pepper

1. Prepare the prawn brochettes and marinade: Rinse the prawns under cold running water, then drain them and blot dry with paper towels. Thread the prawns lengthwise onto the skewers, dividing them evenly and threading a chunk of onion and a piece of bell pepper between each. Place the prawn brochettes on a platter and set aside while you prepare the marinade.

2. Combine the lime juice, olive oil, and garlic in a small bowl and whisk to mix. Season with salt and pepper to taste. Brush some of the marinade over the brochettes and set aside the rest for brushing on the brochettes later. Cover the brochettes loosely with plastic wrap and let them marinate in the refrigerator for 30 minutes to 1 hour.

3. Make the beurre blanc: Place the white wine, wine vinegar, shallots, and *colombo* powder in a small, heavy saucepan over medium-high heat and stir to mix. Let the wine mixture boil, uncovered, until reduced to about ¼ cup, 6 to 8 minutes. Add the cream and let boil, uncovered, until the mixture is reduced to about ¼ cup, 2 to 4 minutes longer. Reduce the heat to medium. Add the butter, one piece at a time, whisking continuously to obtain an emulsified sauce. Wait until each piece of butter is thoroughly incorporated before adding the next. Once all the butter has been added remove the pan from the heat; do not allow the beurre blanc to boil or it may curdle. Taste for seasoning, adding salt and pepper to taste and more *colombo* powder as necessary; the beurre blanc should be highly seasoned. Set the beurre blanc aside until serving time, keeping it warm on a shelf over the stove or in a pan of hot (not boiling) water. Do not place it over direct heat or it may curdle.

4. Set up the grill for direct grilling and preheat to high.

5. When ready to cook, brush and oil the grill grate. Arrange the brochettes on the hot grate and grill, turning with tongs, until the prawn shells turn bright red and the flesh is opaque, 3 to 5 minutes per side. Brush the brochettes with the reserved marinade once or twice as they grill.

6. Using a fork, slide the prawns and vegetables off the skewers onto serving plates and serve at once, accompanied by the beurre blanc.

GREECE • FRANCE

LATIN QUARTER SHRIMP KEBABS

DIRECT GRILLING
SERVES 4

The prettiest kebabs I've ever seen were prepared on the rue de la Huchette in the Latin Quarter of Paris. This warren of narrow streets—one of the oldest neighborhoods in Paris—is home to dozens of Greek restaurants, each one vying to outdo the next with the drama of its shish kebabs. Everything is fair game for a skewer—lamb, beef, tightly coiled *merguez* (Moroccan sausage), seafoods ranging from oval, bright orange salmon steaks to jumbo prawns with their heads still attached. The kebabs are composed with the precision of a Swiss watchmaker and a painterly eye to form and color. Subtle variations distinguish the kebabs of one establishment from another. The kebabs here feature an aromatic rub of oregano, thyme, and rosemary. You're not actually meant to eat the grilled lemon but it sure imparts a great flavor.

SPECIAL EQUIPMENT

4 long metal skewers

FOR THE HERB RUB

1 tablespoon coarse salt (kosher or sea)
1 teaspoon freshly ground white pepper
1 teaspoon dried oregano
1 teaspoon dried rosemary
1 teaspoon dried thyme

FOR THE KEBABS

1½ pounds jumbo shrimp or spot prawns (2 pounds if using ones with the heads on, which is preferable), deveined, shells left on (see box, page 361)
2 medium-size onions, peeled
1 large green bell pepper, cored, seeded, and quartered lengthwise
1 lemon, cut into 8 wedges
12 large cherry tomatoes
3 tablespoons extra-virgin olive oil, or as needed for brushing
Pita bread, for serving

1. Make the herb rub: Combine the salt, white pepper, oregano, rosemary, and thyme in a bowl, crumbling the rosemary between your fingers. Set aside.

2. Prepare the kebabs: Rinse the shrimp under cold running water, then drain them and blot dry with paper towels. Cut each onion lengthwise into 4 wedges and cut each wedge crosswise in half. Cut each bell pepper quarter crosswise into 4 equal pieces.

3. Arrange the ingredients for the kebabs on a cutting board, then assemble the kebabs. Here's a sequence I like (but feel free to follow any you desire): a lemon wedge (cut edge toward you), a piece of bell pepper, a wedge of onion, a shrimp (underside facing you) with a cherry tomato placed in the hollow space formed by the curve in the shrimp, another piece of bell pepper and onion, another shrimp with a tomato, and more bell pepper and onion. Follow these with another shrimp with a tomato, more bell pepper and onion, and, finally, another lemon wedge (cut edge away from you). Run a skewer through these ingredients to make an attractive kebab, then thread the remaining kebabs the same way (see Note).

4. Set up the grill for direct grilling and preheat to high.

5. When ready to cook, brush the kebabs on both sides with olive oil and sprinkle some of the herb rub over them. Brush and oil the grill grate. Arrange the kebabs on the hot grate and grill until the shrimp flesh is firm and pink and the tomatoes and onions are lightly charred, about 2 minutes per side. Brush the kebabs once or twice with additional olive oil and season them liberally with the herb rub as they grill.

6. Using a pita to protect your hand, unskewer the kebabs onto plates and serve with pitas.

NOTE: The kebabs may be prepared up to 6 hours ahead of time. Refrigerate them, loosely covered with plastic wrap.

VIETNAM

SALT AND PEPPER GRILLED SHRIMP

DIRECT GRILLING
SERVES 4

Like much grilled fare, this recipe is simplicity itself, but the addition of three commonplace seasonings to shrimp grilled in the shells makes an irresistible combination. I first heard about the preparation from my friend, travel correspondent Jane Wooldridge. Sure enough, when I tasted it in Saigon, I understood Jane's enthusiasm. In Vietnam the shrimp would be grilled with the heads and shells intact and this, indeed, enhances the flavor. If you live in a coastal region, you may be lucky enough to find shrimp with heads on. At the very least, try to use shrimp in the shells.

1½ pounds jumbo shrimp (2 pounds if using shrimp with the heads on), deveined, shells left on (see box at right)
3 tablespoons fresh lime juice, plus 1 large, juicy lime
3 teaspoons coarse salt, preferably sea salt
3 teaspoons freshly ground white pepper

1. Rinse the shrimp under cold running water, then drain them and blot dry with paper towels. Place the shrimp in a large nonreactive baking dish, sprinkle the lime juice and 1 teaspoon each salt and white pepper over them, and toss to coat. Let the shrimp marinate at room temperature for 10 minutes.

2. Meanwhile, cut the lime lengthwise into 4 wedges. Put a lime wedge in each of 4 tiny shallow bowls or dishes. Place a small mound of salt (½ teaspoon) on one side of the lime wedge and a mound of white pepper (½ teaspoon) on the other. Set aside.

3. Set up the grill for direct grilling and preheat to high.

4. When ready to cook, brush and oil the grill grate. Arrange the shrimp, in their shells, on the hot grate and grill, turning with tongs, until the meat is firm and pink, about 2 minutes per side.

5. Transfer the shrimp to serving plates. To eat, squeeze the lime wedge over the salt and pepper and stir two or three times with chopsticks; peel the shrimp and dip it in the lime mixture.

AUSTRALIA

HONEY SESAME SHRIMP "ON THE BARBIE"

DIRECT GRILLING
SERVES 4

Shrimp "on the barbie," aka grill, is Australia's most famous culinary export. Even if you know nothing else about Down Under cooking, you're surely aware of how much Australians love grilling—especially seafood. If the truth be told, shrimp is something of a misnomer, as most Australians would say "prawns." The Chinese roots

HOW TO PEEL AND DEVEIN SHRIMP

Shrimp is delectable grilled both in and out of the shell—leaving the shell on keeps the shrimp moist and flavorful—but sooner or later that shell has got to come off.

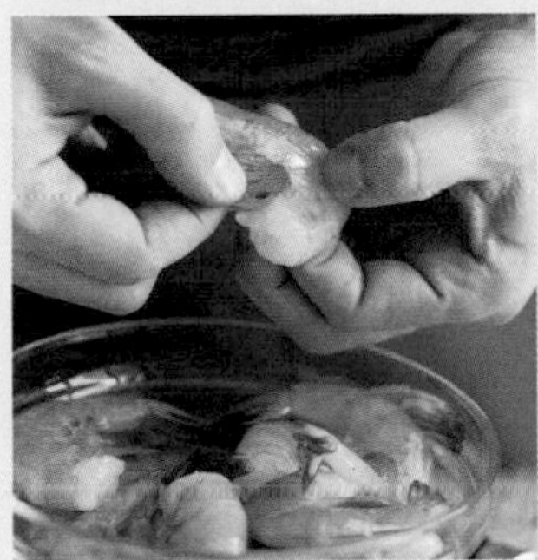

TO PEEL A RAW SHRIMP BY HAND: ***Pull off the legs; this will open up the shell on the underside. Loosen the shrimp from the shell with your fingers, then pull it free. Make sure you get all of the shell; the only part you might want to leave on, for aesthetic reasons, is the feathery tail.***

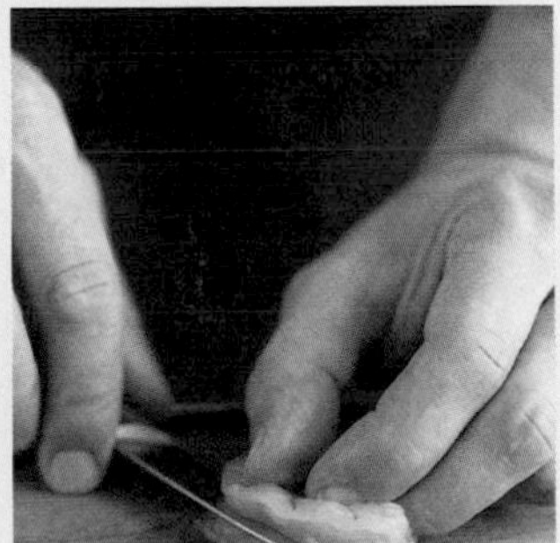

TO DEVEIN A PEELED SHRIMP: ***The classic way is to cut a V-shaped groove down the back of the shrimp; the groove should be just deep enough to include the vein. Remove the wedge of flesh and the vein will come with it.***

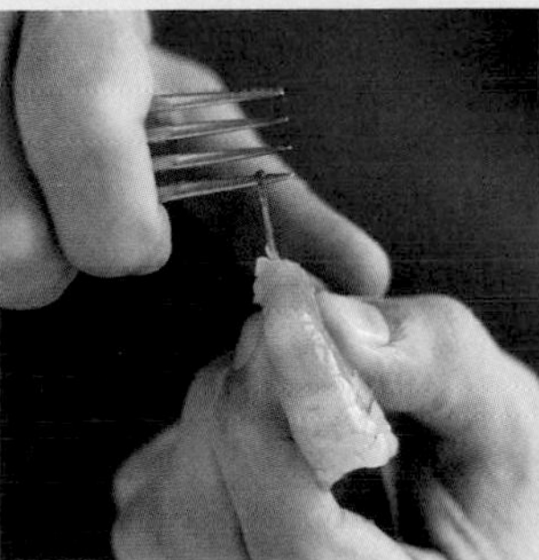

There's a lightning-quick method for deveining a peeled shrimp, one taught to me by a Louisianan. Insert the tine of a fork in the back of the shrimp, midway between the head and tail. Pull the fork gently away from the shrimp and the vein will come with it.

HONEY SESAME SHRIMP "ON THE BARBIE" | PAGE 361

of this dish are obvious—a legacy of the huge influx of Asian immigrants to Australia in the 1970s and 80s. I love the way the sweetness of the honey and five-spice powder play off the nuttiness of the sesame seeds and sesame oil and the brininess of the shrimp and soy sauce.

ADVANCE PREPARATION

30 minutes to 1 hour for marinating the shrimp

INGREDIENTS

1½ pounds jumbo shrimp, peeled and deveined (see box, page 361)
5 tablespoons Asian (dark) sesame oil
3 tablespoons rice wine, sake, or dry sherry
3 tablespoons soy sauce
4½ teaspoons honey
4½ teaspoons sesame seeds
1 tablespoon Thai sweet chile sauce (optional; see Note)
½ teaspoon Chinese five-spice powder
2 cloves garlic, peeled and crushed with the side of a cleaver
2 slices (¼ inch thick) peeled fresh ginger
2 scallions, trimmed, white part flattened with the side of a cleaver, green part finely chopped and set aside for garnish
Lime wedges, for serving

1. Rinse the shrimp under cold running water, then drain them and blot dry with paper towels.

2. Combine 3 tablespoons of the sesame oil, the rice wine, soy sauce, honey, sesame seeds, chile sauce (if using), and five-spice powder in a large bowl and whisk to blend. Stir in the garlic, ginger, scallion whites, and shrimp and toss to coat, then cover and let marinate, in the refrigerator, for 30 minutes to 1 hour.

3. Using a slotted spoon, transfer the shrimp from the marinade to a bowl and toss it with the remaining 2 tablespoons of sesame oil. Pour the marinade into a saucepan. Using the slotted spoon, remove and discard the garlic, ginger, and scallion whites. Bring the marinade to a boil over medium-high heat and cook, uncovered, until it is a thick, syrupy glaze, about 3 minutes. Remove the glaze from the heat and set aside.

4. Set up the grill for direct grilling and preheat to high.

5. When ready to cook, brush and oil the grill grate. Arrange the shrimp on the hot grate and grill, turning with tongs, until nicely browned on the outside and firm and pink inside, about 2 minutes per side. Brush the shrimp with the glaze as they cook.

6. Transfer the shrimp to serving plates or a platter, sprinkle the scallion greens on top, and serve with lime wedges.

NOTE: Thais use sweet chile sauce like Americans use ketchup. Many supermarkets carry it (one good brand is A Taste of Thai), but if it's not available, simply omit it.

Butterflying Shrimp

Once you have deveined the shrimp, following the instructions on page 361, you can butterfly them by making a deeper lengthwise cut in the flesh. Slice almost, but not quite entirely, through a shrimp and you will be able to open it up like a book.

BRAZIL

SHRIMP WITH BAHIAN PEANUT SAUCE

DIRECT GRILLING
SERVES 6 TO 8 AS AN APPETIZER, 4 AS A MAIN COURSE

This recipe takes its inspiration from Bahia in northern Brazil. Bahia has been called the New Orleans of Brazil. Nowhere are African influences on Brazilian cooking more evident or more delicious. Coconut milk, cilantro, fiery chiles, and peanuts are the cornerstones of Bahian cooking. They come together here to provide a rich, hauntingly flavorful sauce for grilled shrimp.

ADVANCE PREPARATION

30 minutes for marinating the shrimp

SPECIAL EQUIPMENT

8 long bamboo skewers and an aluminum foil shield (see box, page 23)

FOR THE SHRIMP AND MARINADE

- 1½ pounds jumbo shrimp, peeled and deveined (see box, page 361)
- ¾ cup coconut milk, canned or homemade (page 114)
- ¼ cup fresh lime juice
- 2 cloves garlic, minced
- 1 teaspoon salt
- ½ teaspoon freshly ground black pepper

FOR THE SAUCE

- 2 tablespoons extra-virgin olive oil
- 4 cloves garlic, minced
- 1 bunch scallions, both white and green parts, trimmed and minced
- 1 tablespoon minced peeled fresh ginger
- ½ medium-size green bell pepper, cored, seeded, and finely chopped
- ½ medium-size red bell pepper, cored, seeded, and finely chopped
- 2 ripe tomatoes, peeled and seeded (see box, page 454), then finely chopped
- 1¼ cups coconut milk, canned or homemade (page 114)
- ½ cup creamy peanut butter
- 3 tablespoons fresh lime juice
- ½ cup chopped fresh cilantro
- ¼ teaspoon cayenne pepper, or more to taste
- Salt and freshly ground black pepper
- ¼ cup chopped peanuts, toasted (see box, page 113), for garnish

1. Prepare the shrimp and marinade: Rinse the shrimp under cold running water, then drain and blot dry with paper towels.

2. Combine the ¾ cup of coconut milk, ¼ cup of lime juice, 2 cloves of garlic, 1 teaspoon of salt, and ½ teaspoon of pepper in a large nonreactive bowl and stir to blend. Add the shrimp and toss to coat. Let the shrimp marinate at room temperature, covered, for 30 minutes.

3. Make the sauce: Heat the olive oil in a medium-size saucepan over medium heat. Add the 4 cloves of garlic, scallions, ginger, and green and red bell peppers and cook until lightly browned, about 5 minutes. Add the tomatoes, increase the heat to high, and cook until some of the tomato liquid evaporates, about 1 minute.

4. Stir in the 1¼ cups of coconut milk, peanut butter, 3 tablespoons of lime juice, and half of the cilantro. Reduce the heat to low and let simmer gently, uncovered, until the sauce is well flavored and slightly thickened, 5 to 10 minutes. Stir in the cayenne, then taste for seasoning, adding salt and black pepper to taste and more cayenne as necessary; the sauce should be highly seasoned. Keep the peanut sauce warm, covered.

5. Remove the shrimp from the marinade and discard the marinade. Thread the shrimp onto the skewers.

6. Set up the grill for direct grilling and preheat to high.

7. When ready to cook, brush and oil the grill grate. Arrange the shrimp kebabs on the hot grate with the aluminum foil shield under the ends of the skewers. Grill the shrimp, turning with tongs, until they are nicely browned on the outside and firm and pink inside, about 2 minutes per side. Brush the shrimp with some of the peanut sauce after turning.

8. Spoon the peanut sauce onto serving plates, dividing it evenly. Using a fork, slide the shrimp off the skewers onto the peanut sauce. Sprinkle chopped peanuts and the remaining cilantro over the shrimp and serve at once.

INDIA

TANDOORI PRAWNS

DIRECT GRILLING
SERVES 4

I landed in New Delhi after an eighteen-hour flight from New York. My reason for coming was simple: I wanted to sample tandoori (Indian barbecue) in its land of birth. Fortunately, I didn't have to travel much farther: India's most famous barbecue restaurant, Bukhara, was located in my hotel. One look at the exhibition kitchen, with its blazing tandoors and hammered copper walls hung with barbecue skewers, and I knew that I'd struck pay dirt.

A tandoor is a cross between a barbecue pit and an oven. The waist-high, urn-shaped clay vessel holds a charcoal fire in the bottom. Seafood, meats, even vegetables are roasted on vertical spits over the coals, while breads are baked directly on the tandoor's walls.

At Bukhara, this dish would be made with huge, juicy prawns from the Bay of Bengal. In this country I've used both shrimp and lobster tails. Whichever shellfish you use, the

The Brazilian Grill

Let the Turks have their shish kebab, Indonesians their saté. I raise my fork for *churrasco,* Brazil's version of barbecue. *Churrasco* makes a prodigious meal and an evening's entertainment. *Churrasco* (pronounced shoe-HRA-skoo) is served with belt-loosening largesse by a ceremonious procession of waiters bearing sword-like spits to carve at your table. And no one does it better than Marius Fontana.

Marius is the owner of three upscale *churrascarias* (grills) in Rio de Janeiro. You'd never guess it to meet him. Tasseled loafers. Designer jeans. Meticulously combed shoulder-length hair. He looks more like a movie star than a pit jockey. But ask a *carioca* (a Rio resident) where to go for *churrasco* and you're almost sure to be told Marius. The night I arrived at his Ipanema district restaurant, the four hundred seats were packed.

Churrasco is a method of cooking, but it's also a way of life. This rustic style of eating originated in Brazil's cattle country, Rio Grande do Sul. The traditional cooking equipment for *churrasco* was simple enough: an open fire, a sword for skewering meats, and a razor-sharp knife for carving them. The seasonings were even simpler: coarse sea salt and fresh air. For the better part of four centuries the cowboys of southern Brazil enjoyed *churrasco* in this fashion.

More recently, *churrasco* spread from the Rio Grande to the rest of Brazil. As it moved north, it evolved from rustic cookout to a culinary extravaganza. Baptisms, birthdays, sporting events, even political rallies are celebrated over *churrasco.* Today, some of the fanciest restaurants in Rio are *churrascarias.*

Consider Marius (the restaurant). The sleekly contemporary dining room boasts polished wood paneling, frosted glass partitions, brass rails, and coffered ceilings with recessed pin spots. It's a long way from a cowboy campfire! So is the clientele, which includes an air-kissing crowd of moguls, movie stars, and upscale tourists.

The large portions of a traditional *churrasco* have evolved into a curious display of conspicuous consumption. You're not simply handed a cocktail menu. The waiter rolls a portable bar right to your table. The hors d'oeuvre course is nothing less than a personal buffet that includes *pão de queijo* (tiny steaming cheese buns), crisply fried manioc, hard-cooked quail eggs, and a dozen other Brazilian appetizers. Come time for the main course, well, all I can say is that it's a good thing they supply you with the "sign."

The "sign" is a fixture at most *churrascarias.* It enables you to control the pace of what is otherwise a relentless assault on your waistline. The miniature sign-post at Marius comes with three panels: normal, *lento* (slow), and *suspenso* (stop). (Elsewhere, you may get a wheel with an arrow that points to the particular cut of meat you want more of or a placard that reads "stop.")

A squadron of waiters circulates through the dining room, each one bearing a different cut of meat. One staggers under the weight of whole spit-roasted prime rib. Others bear coils of *linguiça* (Portuguese sausage), *picanha* (spit-roasted sirloin), *cupim* (steer hump), chicken hearts, mint-glazed lamb kebabs—perhaps twenty different items in all. And as long as the "normal" sign is in place, each and every waiter will make a trip to your table. The only way to ward them off is to flip the sign to *suspenso.*

Each item arrives at the table sizzling hot off the grill. To learn how this amazing feat is achieved, I asked if I might visit the kitchen. Built into one wall is a giant stainless-steel rotisserie with motorized spits. The fatty cuts of meat are placed on the highest level, so that the melting fat bastes the leaner cuts roasting below. Ingenious. The waiters carry the spits to the dining room, carve off the cooked portion, then return the spits to the kitchen for more cooking.

A meal at a Brazilian *churrascaria* may sound like a relentlessly carnivorian experience. It is a relentlessly carnivorian experience, but Brazil's *churrascarias* serve some pretty amazing seafood dishes as well—see the Grilled Fish with Brazilian Garlic Marinade (page 322) and the Shrimp with Bahian Peanut Sauce (page 363). Whatever you order, I promise you won't go hungry!

exotic ginger, cream, and spice marinade makes this some of the most succulent and explosively flavorful fare you'll taste on the world's barbecue trail. You'll need to know about two special ingredients: Chickpea flour (*besan*) is available at Indian and some Italian markets and natural foods stores; in a pinch you could substitute whole-wheat flour in place of the besan or simply omit it. Garam masala is an Indian spice mix. I have included a recipe for it in this book, but you can also use a commercial blend. And, to simulate the type of grilling done in an Indian tandoor, use the grateless grilling method outlined on page 21 to cook these shrimp.

ADVANCE PREPARATION

2 hours for marinating the shrimp

SPECIAL EQUIPMENT

4 long metal skewers

INGREDIENTS

1½ pounds jumbo shrimp, peeled and deveined (see box, page 361)
3 tablespoons coarsely chopped peeled fresh ginger
6 cloves garlic, sliced
1 teaspoon salt, or more to taste
2 tablespoons fresh lemon juice, or more to taste
⅔ cup heavy (whipping) cream or plain whole-milk yogurt
1 large egg
3 tablespoons chickpea flour (optional)
½ teaspoon cayenne pepper
½ teaspoon ground turmeric
½ teaspoon ground cumin
½ teaspoon Quick Garam Masala (page 496) or a commercial blend
½ teaspoon freshly ground white pepper
2 to 3 tablespoons melted salted butter, for brushing
Lemon wedges, for serving

1. Rinse the shrimp under cold running water, then drain them and blot dry with paper towels.

2. Combine the ginger, garlic, and salt in a mortar and pound to a paste with a pestle, then work in the lemon juice and 2 tablespoons of the cream. If you don't have a mortar and pestle, combine all of these ingredients in a food processor or blender and process to a smooth paste.

3. Transfer the ginger-garlic paste to a large nonreactive bowl and whisk in the remaining cream, egg, chickpea flour (if using), cayenne, turmeric, cumin, garam masala, and white pepper. Taste for seasoning, adding more salt and/or lemon juice as necessary; the ginger-garlic paste should be highly seasoned. Add the shrimp and toss to coat. Let the shrimp marinate in the refrigerator, covered, for 2 hours.

4. Remove the shrimp from the bowl and discard the marinade. Thread the shrimp onto the skewers.

5. Set up the grill for direct grilling and preheat to high.

6. When ready to cook, brush and oil the grill grate. Arrange the kebabs on the hot grate and grill, turning with tongs, until the shrimp are nicely browned on the outside and firm and pink inside, about 2 minutes per side. Brush the shrimp with the melted butter once or twice as they cook.

7. Using a fork, slide the shrimp off the skewers onto serving plates or a platter and serve at once with lemon wedges.

INDIA

FLAMING PRAWNS

DAHAKTE JHINGA

DIRECT GRILLING
SERVES 4

Muhammed Ishtiyaque Qureshi comes from a long line of Indian master chefs. To look at him, you'd think he was straight out of California. A ponytail peeps out from under his toque. A gold earring gleams in one ear. Ishtiyaque is the chef of the Indian Harvest restaurant at the Leela hotel in Bombay, and his penchant for theatrics certainly extends to his cooking. Every few minutes, the dining room erupts with a volcanic roar and tower of flames from a sizzling platter of *dahakte jhinga*, "flaming prawns." The show is designed to delight Japanese and Western businessmen (and their Indian hosts), but according to Ishtiyaque, there is a tradition of serving flambéed food in India. After all, Indian barbecue originated with the Mogul rulers from Persia, and Ishtiyaque claims that they seasoned their grilled fare with flaming wine.

Ishtiyaque's prawns come from the Bay of Bengal and are the size of small lobsters. Their flavor is reinforced by a two-stage marinating process: first in vinegar, then in yogurt. In North America, either jumbo shrimp or lobster tails work well. To be strictly authentic, you'd marinate the prawns in a fruity black vinegar made from an Indian berry called *jamun*. I approximate its flavor by combining cider vinegar with apricot nectar. Ishtiyaque uses yogurt cheese for his marinade, but plain yogurt will produce tasty results, too.

ADVANCE PREPARATION

1 hour for marinating the shrimp

FOR THE SHRIMP AND VINEGAR MARINADE

1½ pounds jumbo shrimp, in their shells (see Note)
3 tablespoons cider vinegar
2 tablespoons apricot nectar
2 tablespoons fresh lemon juice

FOR THE YOGURT MARINADE

1 cup plain whole-milk yogurt
3 cloves garlic, minced
1 tablespoon grated peeled fresh ginger
1 to 3 teaspoons cayenne pepper or hot paprika
¼ teaspoon ground cloves
1 teaspoon salt
2 to 3 tablespoons melted butter, for brushing
¼ cup rum, preferably 151 proof, for flambéing

1. Prepare the shrimp and vinegar marinade: Cut each shrimp lengthwise through the belly almost all the way through to the back shell and devein them. Spread the shrimp halves open but leave them attached and in their shells. Rinse the shrimp under cold running water, then drain them and blot dry with paper towels.

2. Combine the vinegar, apricot nectar, and lemon juice in a nonreactive baking dish large enough to hold the shrimp in a single layer. Add the shrimp, cut side down, and let marinate, at room temperature, for 15 minutes.

3. Make the yogurt marinade: Combine the yogurt, garlic, ginger, cayenne, cloves, and salt in a large nonreactive bowl and whisk to blend. Add the shrimp, turning to coat, then cover and let marinate, in the refrigerator, for 45 minutes.

4. Set up the grill for direct grilling and preheat to high.

5. When ready to cook, brush and oil the grill grate. Remove the shrimp from the marinade and discard the marinade. Arrange the shrimp, cut side down, on the hot grate. Grill the shrimp for 2 minutes, then turn them, using tongs, and grill until nicely browned on the outside and firm and pink inside, about 2 minutes longer. Brush the shrimp once or twice with the melted butter as they cook.

6. Transfer the grilled shrimp to a platter. Make sure the area is clear of flammable material and that no one is standing too close. Gently warm the rum, over very low heat, in a small saucepan; do not let it boil or even get hot. Remove the pan from the heat and, using a long match, carefully ignite the rum. Very carefully pour it over the shrimp and serve at once.

NOTE: Lobster tails are also good fixed this way. You can prepare 4 lobster tails following the directions for the shrimp in Step 1 and marinating them as directed, first in the vinegar mixture and then in the yogurt. Grill as directed in Step 5, for 4 to 8 minutes per side.

INDONESIA

BALINESE PRAWN SATES

SATE UDANG

DIRECT GRILLING
SERVES 6 TO 8 AS AN APPETIZER, 4 AS A MAIN COURSE

Balinese shrimp satés owe their extraordinary fragrance to the skewers on which they're cooked: fresh lemongrass stalks. When buying lemongrass, try to choose slender stalks. But don't worry too much if you can't find lemongrass—satés cooked on bamboo skewers will still have plenty of flavor.

ADVANCE PREPARATION

1 hour for marinating the shrimp

SPECIAL EQUIPMENT

12 thin stalks fresh lemongrass, trimmed of roots, tips, and outer leaves, or 12 long bamboo skewers, and an aluminum foil shield (see box, page 23)

INGREDIENTS

1½ pounds extra large shrimp (about 24), peeled and deveined (see box, page 361)
¼ cup sweet soy sauce (ketjap manis), or 2 tablespoons each regular soy sauce and molasses
3 cloves garlic, minced
1½ teaspoons ground coriander
2 tablespoons fresh lime juice
2 tablespoons palm sugar or light brown sugar
3 tablespoons vegetable oil

1. Rinse the shrimp under cold running water, then drain them and blot dry with paper towels.

2. Combine the sweet soy sauce, garlic, coriander, lime juice, palm sugar, and 1 tablespoon of the oil in a large bowl and whisk until blended and the sugar dissolves. Add the shrimp and toss to coat. Let the shrimp marinate in the refrigerator, covered, for 1 hour.

3. Drain the shrimp. If using the lemongrass stalks as skewers, using a metal skewer, make a "starter" hole in each shrimp. Thread the shrimp on the lemongrass stalks, or on the bamboo skewers, 2 shrimp to each.

4. Set up the grill for direct grilling and preheat to high.

5. When ready to cook, brush and oil the grill grate. Arrange the satés on the hot grate with the aluminum foil shield under the ends of the skewers. Grill the shrimp, turning with tongs, until they are nicely browned on the outside and firm and pink inside, about 2 minutes per side. Brush the shrimp once or twice with the remaining oil as they cook.

6. Transfer the satés to serving plates or a platter and serve.

LEBANON

GRILLED SHRIMP WITH TARATOOR

DIRECT GRILLING
SERVES 4

This is another favorite grilled shrimp dish around my house. It's quick, easy, and wonderfully exotic. What sets the recipe apart is the dipping sauce that accompanies the lightly marinated shrimp. *Taratoor* is a creamy, nutty, lemony white sauce made from sesame paste and lemon. Tahini (sesame paste) is widely available at Middle Eastern markets, natural food stores, and in many supermarkets. For a cool presentation, arrange the shrimp on a platter, cut side up, and spoon the sauce on top. In this case, I'd sprinkle the shrimp with a little chopped parsley.

ADVANCE PREPARATION

30 minutes for marinating the shrimp

SPECIAL EQUIPMENT

About 40 short bamboo skewers and an aluminum foil shield (see box, page 23)

FOR THE SHRIMP

1½ pounds jumbo shrimp, in their shells
2 tablespoons extra-virgin olive oil
2 tablespoons fresh lemon juice
1 clove garlic, minced
Salt and freshly ground black pepper

FOR SERVING

½ cup tahini
2 cloves garlic, minced
½ cup fresh lemon juice, or more to taste
3 tablespoons minced fresh flat-leaf parsley
Salt and freshly ground white pepper
Pita bread, for serving

1. Cut each shrimp in half lengthwise, starting at the underside and cutting to but not through the top shell. Fold the shrimp open and devein them, then rinse them under cold running water. Drain and blot dry with paper towels. Place the shrimp in a nonreactive baking dish and sprinkle the olive oil, 2 tablespoons of lemon juice, and 1 clove of garlic over them. Season the shrimp with salt and black pepper to taste. Let the shrimp marinate in the refrigerator, covered, for 30 minutes, turning occasionally.

2. Make the *taratoor:* Combine the tahini, 2 cloves of garlic, ½ cup of lemon juice, and the parsley in a small bowl and whisk to mix. Whisk in enough warm water to obtain a pourable sauce (start with 3 tablespoons). Taste the *taratoor* for seasoning, adding salt and white pepper to taste and more lemon juice as necessary; the *taratoor* should be highly seasoned. Transfer the *taratoor* to 4 ramekins or small bowls, dividing it evenly, and set aside until serving time.

3. Remove the shrimp from the baking dish, setting aside any marinade. Arrange the shrimp flat on a work surface and pin them open crosswise with 2 skewers, one at each end.

4. Set up the grill for direct grilling and preheat to high.

5. When ready to cook, brush and oil the grill grate. Arrange the shrimp, cut side down, on the hot grate with the aluminum foil shield under the ends of the skewers. Grill the shrimp, turning with tongs, until nicely browned on the outside and firm and pink inside, about 2 minutes per side. Brush the shrimp once or twice with any reserved marinade while cooking.

6. Using a pita bread to protect your hand, unskewer the shrimp onto serving plates or a platter and serve accompanied by pitas and the *taratoor* for dipping.

WEST INDIES

PLANTATION SHRIMP

DIRECT GRILLING
SERVES 6 TO 8 AS AN APPETIZER, 4 AS A MAIN COURSE

You won't actually find this dish in the Caribbean, although it's made with some of the most typical ingredients of the West Indies: sugarcane (hence the *plantation* in the name), rum, allspice, and nutmeg. I created the recipe for a Caribbean restaurant in Hong Kong that bore the name of my book *Miami Spice*.

You're not really meant to eat the sugarcane. The idea is to chew on the cane skewers as you eat the shrimp to release the sweet juices. If you're in a hurry, simply marinate the shrimp in the honey-soy mixture and grill them. They'll be amazing—even without the sugarcane and glaze. Serve the shrimp with Bahamian Peas and Rice (page 431).

ADVANCE PREPARATION

1 hour for marinating the shrimp

SPECIAL EQUIPMENT

1 package fresh sugarcane swizzle sticks (see Note)

FOR THE SHRIMP AND MARINADE

1½ pounds extra-large shrimp (about 24), peeled and deveined (see box, page 361)
2 cloves garlic, minced
2 scallions, both white and green parts, trimmed and minced
1 tablespoon minced peeled fresh ginger
½ Scotch bonnet chile, or 1 jalapeño pepper, seeded and minced
2 tablespoons soy sauce
2 tablespoons honey
2 tablespoons peanut oil

FOR THE RUM GLAZE

⅓ cup plus 1 tablespoon dark rum
2 tablespoons tomato paste
2 tablespoons dark brown sugar
1 tablespoon honey
1 tablespoon distilled white vinegar
1 tablespoon Worcestershire sauce
1½ teaspoons Tabasco or other hot sauce
⅛ teaspoon ground allspice
⅛ teaspoon ground cloves
Salt and freshly ground black pepper

1. Prepare the shrimp and marinade: Rinse the shrimp under cold running water, then drain them and blot dry with paper towels.

2. Combine the garlic, scallions, ginger, Scotch bonnet, soy sauce, 2 tablespoons of honey, and the peanut oil in a large bowl and whisk to mix. Add the shrimp, tossing to coat. Let the shrimp marinate in the refrigerator, covered, for 1 hour.

3. While the shrimp marinates, prepare the sugarcane skewers: Using a sharp knife, cut the sugarcane swizzle sticks into 3-inch lengths, slicing them sharply on the diagonal to make a sharp point. You will need one sugarcane skewer for each shrimp.

4. Make the rum glaze: Combine the ⅓ cup rum, the tomato paste, brown sugar, 1 tablespoon of honey, vinegar, Worcestershire sauce, Tabasco sauce, allspice, and cloves in a small, heavy saucepan and bring to a boil over medium-high heat, stirring until blended and the sugar melts. Reduce the heat to medium and let simmer until a syrupy glaze forms, 3 to 5 minutes. Remove the rum glaze from the heat, stir in the remaining 1 tablespoon of rum, and season with salt and pepper to taste.

5. Remove the shrimp from the marinade and discard the marinade. Using a metal skewer, make a "starter" hole in each shrimp. Thread one shrimp on each sugarcane skewer, starting with the pointed end.

6. Set up the grill for direct grilling and preheat to high.

7. When ready to cook, brush and oil the grill grate. Arrange the shrimp on the hot grate and grill, turning with tongs, until nicely browned on the outside and firm and pink inside, about 2 minutes per side. Brush the shrimp with the rum glaze as they cook.

8. Transfer the shrimp to serving plates or a platter. Spoon any remaining rum glaze over the shrimp and serve at once.

NOTE: Sugarcane swizzle sticks are available at specialty food stores and many supermarkets. One good, widely distributed brand is Frieda's.

U.S.A.

EMERIL LAGASSE'S NEW ORLEANS–STYLE BARBECUED SHRIMP

DIRECT GRILLING
SERVES 4

You may be surprised to find a New Orleans–style recipe in this book: After all, grilling isn't traditionally associated with Louisianan cooking. Indeed, the first time I tasted this dish, the shrimp were sautéed, not grilled. But grilling works great here—I love the way the smoky, charcoaled flavor of the shrimp counterpoints the lemony richness of the cream-based barbecue sauce.

ADVANCE PREPARATION

1 hour for marinating the shrimp

INGREDIENTS

1½ pounds jumbo shrimp
3 tablespoons extra-virgin olive oil
3 tablespoons Cajun Rub, (page 490) or a commercial brand of Cajun seasoning
1 small onion, finely chopped
2 tablespoons minced garlic
3 bay leaves
2 lemons, peeled, cut into thin crosswise slices, and seeded
2 cups bottled clam broth or water
½ cup Worcestershire sauce
¼ cup dry white wine
2 cups heavy (whipping) cream
2 tablespoons (¼ stick) unsalted butter
Salt and freshly ground black pepper

1. Peel and devein the shrimp (see box, page 361), leaving the feathery tail shells intact and setting aside the shells. Rinse the shrimp under cold running water, then drain them and blot dry with paper towels.

2. Place the shrimp in a large bowl and sprinkle 2 tablespoons of the olive oil and 4½ teaspoons of the Creole seasoning over them. Rub the oil and seasonings into the shrimp with your hands to coat well, then cover them and let marinate, in the refrigerator, for 1 hour.

3. While the shrimp marinates, make the barbecue sauce. Heat the remaining 1 tablespoon of olive oil in a large saucepan over medium heat. Add the onion and garlic and cook until just beginning to brown, about 3 minutes. Increase the heat to high and add the reserved shrimp shells, the remaining 4½ teaspoons of Creole seasoning, and the bay leaves, lemon slices, clam broth, Worcestershire sauce, and white wine. Bring to a boil, stirring, then reduce the heat to medium and let simmer, uncovered, until only about 1½ cups of liquid remain, 20 to 30 minutes.

4. Strain the barbecue sauce mixture into a second saucepan and place it over high heat. Let the sauce boil, uncovered, until thick, syrupy, and dark brown, about 15 minutes, stirring it often to prevent scorching; you should have about ½ cup. Whisk in the cream and bring to a boil. Reduce the heat slightly and cook the barbecue sauce mixture until only about 2 cups of liquid remain, 5 to 10 minutes. Remove the sauce from the heat and whisk in the butter until melted. Season the sauce with salt and pepper to taste; the sauce should be highly seasoned. Set ½ cup of the sauce aside for basting. Keep the remaining sauce warm, covered, for serving.

5. Set up the grill for direct grilling and preheat to high.

6. When ready to cook, brush and oil the grill grate. Arrange the shrimp on the hot grate and brush some of the ½ cup barbecue sauce on it. Grill the shrimp until nicely browned on the outside and firm and pink inside, about 2 minutes per side. Brush the shrimp liberally with the barbecue sauce once or twice as they cook.

7. Transfer the shrimp to a serving platter and serve at once, topped with the remaining barbecue sauce.

MALAYSIA

PENANGESE GRILLED SHRIMP WITH PAINFULLY HOT SALSA

DIRECT GRILLING
SERVES 4

The mere mention of Penang is enough to make most Malaysians' mouths water. This tropical island off the northeastern coast is reputed to have some of the best food in Asia—a reputation easily verified by visiting the food stalls on Gurney Drive. You'd expect the fiendishly hot *nam choh* (shallot "salsa") in this recipe to overpower the delicate butter and coconut milk–basted shrimp, but in fact it does just the opposite: The heat seems to sensitize your taste buds to the mild, sweet flavor of the shrimp.

You'll need to know about one special ingredient to prepare this recipe: shrimp paste (called *belacan* in Malaysian and *trassi* in Indonesian), a pungent paste made from fermented shrimp and salt. Despite its off-putting aroma, shrimp paste adds a complex and pleasing flavor that has endeared it to chefs from one end of Southeast Asia to the other. Toasting helps mellow the nose-jarring smell of the paste. It can be found at Asian markets and in some specialty food shops. In a pinch you can use a dab of anchovy paste or a teaspoon or two of fish sauce (omitting the toasting, of course). Malaysians use shrimp with the heads still on, which are not that easy to find in this country. If you can get them, by all means use them.

SPECIAL EQUIPMENT

8 long bamboo skewers and an aluminum foil shield (see box, page 23)

INGREDIENTS

1½ pounds jumbo shrimp (2 pounds if using shrimp with the heads on), shells left on
2 tablespoons (¼ stick) salted butter, at room temperature
¼ teaspoon shrimp paste
3 tablespoons fresh lime juice, or more to taste
1 teaspoon sugar, or more to taste
¾ teaspoon salt, or more to taste
¾ cup thinly sliced shallots
6 to 8 Thai chiles or serrano peppers, seeded and thinly sliced (for a hotter salsa, leave the seeds in)
1 cup coconut milk, canned or homemade (page 114), for brushing

1. Devein the shrimp (see box, page 361), then run a knife along the top of each to make the slit deeper, because you will be stuffing the shrimp with butter. Rinse the shrimp under cold running water, then drain them and blot dry with paper towels. Spread the butter inside the slits in the shrimp, then thread the shrimp lengthwise on the skewers so both ends are secured. Place the shrimp on a platter and set aside.

2. Place the shrimp paste on the end of one tine of a grill fork. Hold it over the grill until lightly toasted and aromatic, about 2 minutes. Transfer the shrimp paste to a small bowl and add the lime juice, sugar, and salt. Stir until blended and the sugar and salt dissolve, then stir in the shallots and Thai chiles. Taste for seasoning, adding more lime juice, sugar, and/or salt as necessary; the *nam choh* should be highly seasoned. Set aside until serving time.

3. Set up the grill for direct grilling and preheat to high.

4. When ready to cook, brush and oil the grill grate. Brush the shrimp with some of the coconut milk and arrange the skewers on the hot grate with the aluminum foil shield under the ends of the skewers. Grill the shrimp, turning with tongs, until they are nicely browned on the outside and firm and pink inside, about 2 minutes per side. Brush the shrimp with the coconut milk once or twice as they grill.

5. Transfer the skewered shrimp to serving plates or a platter and serve at once with tiny bowls of the *nam choh.*

U.S.A.

GULF COAST SHRIMP

DIRECT GRILLING
SERVES 6 TO 8 AS AN APPETIZER, 4 AS A MAIN COURSE

These Gulf Coast Shrimp have jumped from the proverbial frying pan to the fire, since traditionally the shrimp would be sautéed, not grilled. Hot, sweet, and smoky, the shrimp are definitely worth putting tradition aside for.

ADVANCE PREPARATION

2 to 4 hours for marinating the shrimp

INGREDIENTS

- **1½ pounds jumbo shrimp, peeled and deveined (see box, page 361), shells reserved**
- **1 cup bottled clam broth, chicken broth, or water**
- **8 tablespoons (1 stick) unsalted butter**
- **6 cloves garlic, minced**
- **4 scallions, both white and green parts, trimmed and finely chopped**
- **1 to 2 tablespoons Tabasco or other Louisiana-style hot sauce**
- **1 tablespoon Worcestershire sauce**
- **2 bay leaves**
- **2 teaspoons cayenne pepper**
- **2 teaspoons sweet paprika**
- **2 teaspoons dried thyme**
- **2 teaspoons dried oregano**
- **1½ teaspoons salt**
- **1 teaspoon freshly ground black pepper**
- **¾ cup dark cane syrup (see Note)**

1. Combine the shrimp shells and the clam broth in a medium-size saucepan and bring to a boil. Reduce the heat to low and let simmer, uncovered, until slightly reduced and well flavored (the shrimp shells will turn orange), 10 to 15 minutes. Strain the broth into another medium-size saucepan; you should have about ¾ cup.

2. Add the butter, garlic, scallions, Tabasco, Worcestershire sauce, bay leaves, cayenne, paprika, thyme, oregano, salt, black pepper, and cane syrup to the shrimp broth. Bring to a boil over medium heat and cook, uncovered, whisking often until thick, syrupy, and richly flavored, about 10 minutes. Remove the marinade from the heat and let cool to room temperature.

3. Meanwhile, rinse the shrimp under cold running water, then drain them and blot dry with paper towels.

4. Add the shrimp to the cooled marinade in the saucepan and toss to coat. Let the shrimp marinate in the refrigerator, covered, for 2 to 4 hours.

5. Set up the grill for direct grilling and preheat to high.

6. When ready to cook, brush and oil the grill grate. Remove the shrimp from the marinade, setting aside the marinade. Arrange the shrimp on the hot grate and grill, turning with tongs, until nicely browned on the outside and firm and pink inside, about 2 minutes per side. Brush the shrimp with 2 to 3 tablespoons of the reserved marinade while they grill.

7. Transfer the shrimp to a serving platter. Bring the remaining marinade to a boil over medium heat whisking it well. Remove and discard the bay leaves, then pour the marinade over the shrimp and serve at once.

NOTE: Cane syrup can be found in stores specializing in Southern products or can be bought by mail order; one popular brand is Steen's. If you can't find cane syrup, you can always substitute a dark corn syrup, such as Karo.

U.S.A.

SCALLOP KEBABS WITH PANCETTA, LEMON, AND BASIL

DIRECT GRILLING
SERVES 4

These kebabs are as easy to make as they are full of flavor. The salty pancetta (Italian bacon) and the piquant lemon combine to deliver a tangy two punch. If you live on the East Coast, in the winter you may be able to find true bay scallops—small, meaty nuggets of incredible sweetness. But larger sea scallops will work, too, provided you cut them down to size. Most scallops come with a crescent-shaped muscle on one side, which should be removed before cooking. (It is noticeably tougher than the rest of the shellfish.)

ADVANCE PREPARATION

30 minutes for marinating the scallops

SPECIAL EQUIPMENT

8 long bamboo skewers and an aluminum foil shield (see box, page 23)

INGREDIENTS

- **1½ pounds bay or sea scallops**
- **3 tablespoons extra-virgin olive oil**
- **3 tablespoons fresh lemon juice**
- **4 strips lemon zest (each 2 by ½ inches), removed with a vegetable peeler**
- **Plenty of freshly ground black pepper**
- **1 bunch fresh basil, stemmed**
- **8 thin slices (6 to 8 ounces) pancetta (Italian bacon) or regular bacon, cut into 1-inch pieces**

1. Using your fingers, pull off and discard the small, half moon–shaped muscle from the side of any scallop that has one. If using sea scallops, cut any large ones in quarters and cut medium-size ones in half, so that all of the pieces are the same size. Rinse the scallops under cold running water, then drain them and blot dry with paper towels.

2. Combine the olive oil, lemon juice, lemon zest, and pepper in a medium-size bowl and whisk to mix. Add the scallops and toss to coat. Let the scallops marinate at room temperature, covered, for 30 minutes.

3. Remove the scallops from the marinade, setting aside the marinade. Thread the scallops onto the skewers, inserting a basil leaf and a piece of pancetta between each.

4. Set up the grill for direct grilling and preheat to high.

5. When ready to cook, brush and oil the grill grate. Arrange the kebabs on the hot grate with the aluminum foil shield under the ends of the skewers. Grill the scallops until they are just firm and white, 1 to 2 minutes per side (2 to 4 minutes in all). Brush the scallops once or twice with the reserved marinade as they cook.

6. Using a fork, slide the scallops off the skewers onto serving plates or a platter and serve at once.

FRENCH WEST INDIES

GRILLED CLAMS WITH COLOMBO BUTTER

DIRECT GRILLING
SERVES 4 TO 6 AS AN APPETIZER, 2 TO 3 AS A MAIN COURSE

Clams are probably the last thing to come to mind when most of us think of grilled seafood. But grilling over or in the coals of a fire was most likely the first way man cooked bivalves, and the tradition survives in many regions, including the French West Indies, one of the birthplaces of barbecue. *Colombo* is a French West Indian curry powder made with rice as well as spices. Its nutty, spicy, aromatic flavor has an uncanny way of bringing out the sweetness of the clams. I've included a recipe, but commercially made *colombo* can be found in West Indian markets or you can substitute a good curry powder.

SPECIAL EQUIPMENT

Shellfish grate (optional)

INGREDIENTS

8 tablespoons (1 stick) salted butter
3 cloves garlic, minced
2 teaspoons colombo powder, homemade (see page 497) or store-bought, or good-quality regular curry powder, or more to taste
Freshly ground black pepper
2 dozen littleneck or cherrystone clams (see Note), scrubbed

1. Melt the butter in a small, heavy saucepan over medium heat. Add the garlic and *colombo* powder and cook until very fragrant and the garlic is softened but not browned, about 2 minutes. Remove the *colombo* butter from the heat and taste for seasoning, adding pepper to taste and more *colombo* powder as necessary; the mixture should be highly seasoned.

2. Set up the grill for direct grilling and preheat to high.

3. When ready to cook, preheat a shellfish grate (if using) for 5 minutes, then arrange the clams on it. Otherwise, arrange the clams directly on the grill grate. Grill the clams until the shells open, 6 to 8 minutes.

4. Transfer the clams to serving plates or a platter, discarding any clams that did not open. Spoon a little of the *colombo* butter into each clam shell and serve at once.

NOTE: Clams are graded by size, littlenecks being the smallest. For best results, do not use clams that are any wider than 2 inches across for this recipe, or they will be too tough.

FRANCE

GRILLED MUSSELS

ECLADE

DIRECT GRILLING
SERVES 4

One of the world's most distinctive styles of barbecuing, *éclade* consists of cooking mussels using a blazing pile of dry pine needles. (The name may come from the French verb *éclore,* to open.) This not only sounds like the way our prehistoric ancestors cooked shellfish, it probably *is* the way. To this day, *éclade* remains popular picnic fare in the Cognac region of France.

Unless you live in the country, your access to dry pine needles may be limited. Fortunately, mussels grilled over charcoal have very nearly as fine a flavor—with a lot less fuss. The mussels taste best eaten hot off the grill, which means the shells may burn your fingers a little. That's why another name for this dish is *moules brûles-doigts* (finger burners).

SPECIAL EQUIPMENT

Shellfish grate (optional)

INGREDIENTS

4 pounds mussels
¾ cup (1½ sticks) unsalted butter
3 cloves garlic, minced
⅓ cup minced fresh flat-leaf parsley
Salt and freshly ground black pepper

1. Scrub the mussels under cold running water, discarding any with cracked shells or shells that fail to close when tapped. Using a needle-nose pliers, pull out and discard any clumps of threads gathered at the hinges of the mussels.

2. Melt the butter in a small, heavy saucepan over medium heat. Add the garlic and parsley and season with salt and pepper to taste. Cook the garlic until it is softened but not browned, about 2 minutes. Remove the garlic-parsley butter from the heat and transfer it to 4 small bowls, one for each person for dipping, covering the bowls to keep warm.

3. Set up the grill for direct grilling and preheat to high.

4. When ready to cook, preheat a shellfish grate (if using) for 5 minutes, then arrange the mussels on it, rounded side down (see Note). Otherwise, arrange the mussels directly on the grill grate. Grill the mussels until the shells open, 2 to 6 minutes if you cover the grill, somewhat longer if you don't.

5. Transfer the mussels to serving bowls, discarding any that didn't open. To eat, remove the mussels from the shells with your fingers or a small seafood fork and dip them in the garlic-parsley butter. Provide a platter or plates for the discarded shells.

NOTE: If you look at a mussel closely, you will see it has a rounded and a flat side.

U.S.A.

OYSTERS WITH HORSERADISH CREAM

DIRECT GRILLING
SERVES 4 TO 6 AS AN APPETIZER, 2 TO 3 AS A MAIN COURSE

Oysters possess a natural affinity for horseradish—a fact appreciated by anyone who has passed an hour or two at a raw bar. In this recipe the horseradish is folded into unsweetened whipped cream, which melts as it hits the hot oysters. Nothing can beat the pungency of freshly grated horseradish, but the bottled product will produce highly delicious results, too.

SPECIAL EQUIPMENT

Shellfish grate (optional)

INGREDIENTS

1 cup heavy (whipping) cream
1 tablespoon grated plain horseradish, drained if bottled, or more to taste
1 tablespoon chopped fresh chives or scallion greens
1 teaspoon grated lemon zest
2 teaspoons fresh lemon juice, or more to taste
Salt and freshly ground black pepper
2 dozen oysters in the shell, scrubbed

1. Beat the cream in a chilled medium-size bowl until soft peaks form, then fold in the horseradish, chives, lemon zest, and lemon juice and season with salt and pepper to taste. Taste for seasoning, adding more horseradish and/or lemon juice as necessary.

2. Set up the grill for direct grilling and preheat to high.

3. When ready to cook, preheat a shellfish grate (if using) for 5 minutes, then arrange the oysters on it, rounded side down (see Note). Otherwise, arrange the oysters directly on the grill grate. Grill the oysters until the shells open, 6 to 8 minutes.

4. Transfer the oysters to serving plates or a platter, discarding any top shells or oysters that did not open. Place a spoonful of horseradish cream on each oyster and serve at once.

NOTE: If you look at an oyster closely, you will see that one side is more rounded than the other.

BAHAMAS

BAHAMIAN GRILLED CONCH

DIRECT GRILLING
SERVES 4

Conch (pronounced konk) is the whitest, sweetest, most delicately flavored of all shellfish. Although it's not well known in North America, it's virtually the national dish of the Bahamas. Stroll along the Potter's Cay market beneath the bridge to Paradise Island or along the Arawak Cay recreation area (a popular local hangout) and you'll find dozens of stalls specializing in the preparation of this giant sea snail. After you've had fiery conch salad (the most popular way to eat conch) and "cracked" (fried) conch, you'll be ready for the most delicious preparation of all: grilled conch.

The basic procedure is to grill the conch wrapped in aluminum foil with onions, garlic, chiles, and butter. To enhance the smoke flavor, Nassau chef Basil Dean chars the conch directly over the coals before wrapping it. Any white fish fillets can be prepared in this fashion (omitting the tenderizing), with delectable results.

SPECIAL EQUIPMENT

Heavy-duty aluminum foil

Conch

If you live in Florida or Louisiana, you may be able to find fresh or at least thawed frozen conch at your local fishmonger. Elsewhere in the country, you'll have to settle for frozen conch. Fortunately, conch freezes well. Thaw the conch in the refrigerator.

INGREDIENTS

- 1½ pounds trimmed, cleaned conch (4 large or 8 small steaks; see Conch, page 375)
- Salt and freshly ground black pepper
- ⅔ cup very finely chopped onion
- 2 cloves garlic, minced
- ½ to 1 bird pepper, or other hot chile, seeded and minced (for a hotter dish, leave the seeds in)
- 2 tablespoons fresh lime juice
- 4 tablespoons (½ stick) salted butter
- 4 lime wedges, for serving

1. Tenderize the conch steaks by pounding them to a ¼-inch thickness using a meat mallet or a rolling pin. Season the conch steaks on both sides with salt and pepper.

2. Set up the grill for direct grilling and preheat to high.

3. When ready to cook, brush and oil the grill grate. Arrange the conch steaks on the hot grate and grill them quickly, turning with tongs, about 1 minute per side. (The idea is to leave grill marks on the conch and impart a charcoaled flavor.) Transfer the steaks to a platter to cool. Leave the fire burning.

4. Cut four 12 by 8–inch pieces of heavy-duty aluminum foil. Place 1 large or 2 small conch steaks in the center of each piece of foil.

5. Place the onion, garlic, and bird pepper in a bowl, stir to mix, and spoon 3 to 4 tablespoons of the onion mixture on top of each conch steak. Drizzle 1½ teaspoons of lime juice over each conch steak and top with 1 tablespoon of butter. Pull the sides of the aluminum foil up over the top of a conch steak and pleat them together to make an airtight package. Wrap the remaining conch steaks the same way.

6. When ready to cook, arrange the foil packages on the hot grate and grill until the conch is cooked through and tender, about 5 minutes (when done, a metal skewer inserted into the conch through the foil will be very hot when withdrawn).

7. Open the foil packages and slide the conch steaks, with their toppings, onto plates. (Or let each person unwrap his or her own bundle. But warn everyone to avoid the escaping steam.) Serve the conch steaks with wedges of lime for squeezing.

Ouzo and Octopus

The traditional beverage to drink with grilled octopus is ouzo, Greece's national anise-flavored spirit. Pour a few fingers of ouzo in a glass and fill the glass with water. The ouzo will turn the color of milk. Ouzo goes down with astonishing ease. Make sure you have a designated driver!

GREECE

GRILLED OCTOPUS

KHTAPOTHI STI SKHARA

DIRECT GRILLING
SERVES 4 TO 6

If I were to pick the quintessential taste of the Greek islands, it would be this popular meze (appetizer). Octopus is one of those foods that seems to have been put on earth expressly for grilling: The fire brings out the sweetness of the delicate white meat, which in turn absorbs the flavors of olive oil, oregano, and charcoal without surrendering its own. Cleaning and tenderizing an octopus can be an intimidating process: Fortunately, virtually all the octopus sold in North America is cleaned and tenderized already. This leaves you the easy task of grilling the octopus (preferably over charcoal) until it's nicely charred on all sides, without quite being burnt. Octopus is available frozen at Greek markets, Japanese markets, and specialty seafood shops. Squid or shrimp can be prepared in a similar fashion. This recipe is unusual in that the octopus is grilled dry, then marinated. Serve it with A Different Greek Salad (page 110).

- 2 pounds cleaned, trimmed octopus
- 2 tablespoons red wine vinegar, or more to taste
- 2 tablespoons fresh lemon juice
- 2 teaspoons dried oregano, preferably Greek
- 1 teaspoon coarse salt (kosher or sea), or more to taste
- ½ teaspoon freshly ground black pepper
- 6 to 8 tablespoons extra-virgin olive oil
- ¼ cup finely chopped fresh flat-leaf parsley
- Lemon wedges, for serving

GRILLED OCTOPUS | AT LEFT

1. Using a paring knife, peel or scrape any reddish skin off the octopus (you probably won't need to do this, as most octopus comes already cleaned). Leave the legs whole, but cut the body in quarters. Rinse the octopus under cold running water, then drain it and blot dry with paper towels.

2. Set up the grill for direct grilling and preheat to high.

3. When ready to cook, brush and oil the grill grate. Arrange the octopus pieces on the hot grate and grill, turning with tongs, until nicely charred (but not quite burnt) on all sides, 3 to 6 minutes per side (6 to 12 minutes in all).

4. Transfer the octopus to a cutting board and cut it into bite-size pieces. Place the pieces in a serving bowl.

5. Combine the wine vinegar, lemon juice, oregano, salt, pepper, olive oil, and parsley in a small bowl and whisk to mix, then pour the marinade over the octopus and toss to coat. Let the octopus marinate for at least 5 minutes, or up to 30 (the octopus can be served warm or at room temperature). Taste for seasoning, adding more salt or wine vinegar as necessary; the octopus should be highly seasoned. Serve the octopus accompanied by lemon wedges.

SOUTH AFRICA

GRILLED SQUID DURBAN

DIRECT GRILLING
SERVES 4

You probably know that South Africa's culinary roots go back to England, Holland, and, of course, Africa. What you may not realize is that many cities, like the east coast port of Durban, boast large Indian and Malaysian communities—a throwback to the days when Asian laborers were brought there to work in the gold and diamond mines. These grilled squid have the gustatory fireworks you'd associate with India or Southeast Asia. The scoring of the surface of the squid prior to marinating is optional, but it will give you a dramatic presentation.

ADVANCE PREPARATION

1 to 2 hours for marinating the squid

SPECIAL EQUIPMENT

Fish grate (optional)

INGREDIENTS

2 pounds cleaned squid, including tentacles
2 teaspoons coriander seeds
1 teaspoon cumin seeds
3 cloves garlic, peeled
½ small onion, peeled
1 piece (1 inch) peeled fresh ginger
3 stalks fresh lemongrass, trimmed and thinly sliced, or 3 strips lemon zest (each 2 by ½ inches), removed with a vegetable peeler
1 to 3 serrano or jalapeño peppers, seeded (for hotter squid, leave the seeds in)
¾ cup coconut milk, canned or homemade (page 114)
½ teaspoon salt, or more to taste
½ teaspoon freshly ground black pepper, or more to taste
½ cup fresh cilantro leaves
Lime wedges, for serving

1. Rinse the squid under cold running water, then drain it and blot dry with paper towels. Make a lengthwise cut in one side of the bodies to open them up into broad, thin sheets. If desired, lightly score the outside of each piece of squid in a crosshatch pattern, using a sharp knife and cutting about halfway through the squid. Leave the tentacle sections whole. Place the squid in a large bowl and set it aside in the refrigerator, covered, while you prepare the marinade.

2. Heat a dry, small skillet over medium heat (do not use a nonstick skillet for this). Add the coriander and cumin seeds and cook until toasted and fragrant, about 3 minutes, shaking the pan occasionally. Remove the spices from the heat and let cool, then place them in a food processor or blender and grind them to a coarse powder (see Note). Add the garlic, onion, ginger, lemongrass, serrano peppers, coconut milk, salt, and black pepper and process to a smooth paste. Taste for seasoning, adding more salt and/or pepper as necessary; the marinade should be highly seasoned. Stir in ¼ cup of the cilantro, then pour the marinade over the squid and toss to coat. Let the squid marinate in the refrigerator, covered, for 1 to 2 hours, turning the pieces occasionally.

3. Set up the grill for direct grilling and preheat to high.

4. When ready to cook, preheat a fish grate (if using) for 5 minutes, then brush and oil it or the grill grate. Arrange the squid pieces on the hot grate and grill, turning with tongs, until just firm and white, 1 to 2 minutes per side.

5. Transfer the squid to serving plates or a platter and sprinkle the remaining ¼ cup of cilantro on top. Serve the squid at once, accompanied by lime wedges.

NOTE: If you're in a hurry, you can omit the whole seeds and toasting procedure and use ground spices instead.

MACAO

FERNANDO'S GRILLED CUTTLEFISH WITH MACANESE "SALSA"

DIRECT GRILLING
SERVES 4

Fernando Gomes knows a good thing when he sees it. When the Azores Islander landed in the early 1980s, in what was the Portuguese colony of Macao (soon to be part of China), it was love at first sight—and bite. So he did what many Portuguese do in Macao: He opened a restaurant. Behind a funky brick storefront is a spacious courtyard where guests dine under whirling paddle fans in an open-air pavilion. Fernando's is located on the quietest of Macao's islands, Coloane, and it backs up to Hac Sa Beach. The grilled cuttlefish alone is worth the trip.

Cuttlefish is a larger, wider, fleshier, somewhat sweeter cousin of squid. If you live in an area with a large Asian, Iberian, or Italian community, you may be able to find cuttlefish at an ethnic fish market. Squid also works well for this recipe and is much more widely available. If possible, use charcoal for grilling here.

ADVANCE PREPARATION

30 minutes for marinating the cuttlefish

SPECIAL EQUIPMENT

Fish grate (optional)

INGREDIENTS

1½ to 2 pounds cleaned cuttlefish or squid, with tentacles
⅔ cup extra-virgin olive oil
3 tablespoons red wine vinegar, or more to taste
1 small onion, finely chopped
¼ cup finely chopped fresh flat-leaf parsley
½ teaspoon salt, or more to taste
½ teaspoon freshly ground black pepper
1 ripe medium-size tomato, seeded (see box, page 454) and diced

1. Rinse the cuttlefish under cold running water, then drain it and blot dry with paper towels. Place the cuttlefish in a nonreactive baking dish.

2. Combine the olive oil, wine vinegar, onion, parsley, salt, and pepper in a nonreactive bowl and whisk to mix. Taste for seasoning, adding more vinegar and/or salt as necessary; the olive oil mixture should be highly seasoned. Pour half of the olive oil mixture over the cuttlefish. Let the cuttlefish marinate in the refrigerator, covered, for 30 minutes. Transfer the remaining olive oil mixture to an attractive bowl and stir in the tomato. Set the tomato mixture aside.

3. Set up the grill for direct grilling and preheat to high.

4. When ready to cook, preheat a fish grate (if using) for 5 minutes, then brush and oil it or the grill grate. Remove the cuttlefish from the marinade, setting aside the marinade. Arrange the cuttlefish on the hot grate and grill, turning with tongs, until nicely charred and just firm, 2 to 3 minutes per side (4 to 6 minutes in all). Brush the cuttlefish once or twice with the remaining marinade as it cooks.

5. Transfer the cuttlefish to serving plates or a platter. Serve at once, accompanied by the tomato mixture.

PROVENÇAL DAGWOOD | PAGE 392

CHAPTER 13

VEGETARIAN GRILL

Traditionally, the American barbecue was a relentless procession of meat dishes. If you didn't like hamburgers, hot dogs, shish kebab, or steak, you were pretty much out of luck. No wonder many vegetarians found it easier to stay at home rather than to deal with making a meal from coleslaw and potato salad.

"The one who constantly eats vegetable roots can do anything."

—CHINESE PROVERB

Fortunately, times have changed. As more and more Americans switch to at least a partially vegetarian diet, chefs and pit masters have turned their talents to meatless grilling. Vegetarian barbecue has gone full force from the fringe into the culinary mainstream.

This chapter focuses on a number of the world's great grilled vegetarian main dishes, from Swiss raclette to Indian vegetable kebabs to Japanese *dengaku* (a whimsical dish with a name that means tofu on stilts). Who says you need meat?

That's not just boosterism on my part. When I was writing *The Barbecue! Bible,* both my wife and daughter had given up eating meat (both have since come to take a more accepting view of animal protein). Vegetarian grilling was one way we could continue to have family meals. But, don't take my word for it. Try the recipes in this chapter and you, too, will see: You don't need meat to have a great time at a barbecue.

U.S.A.

THE ORIGINAL GRILLED PIZZA

I'll never forget the first time I tasted grilled pizza. The year was 1985, and the place was Al Forno restaurant in Providence, Rhode Island. The waitress set before me a rectangle of dough, cracker crisp at the edges, smokily singed on the bottom, moistly chewy in the center, and simply topped with puddles of fresh tomato sauce, a dusting of grated cheese, and a handful of chopped fresh basil. It was everything pizza should be—and more—boasting the primeval smoke flavor of Indian tandoori breads combined with the puffy moistness of freshly baked pita. It was love at first bite.

Al Forno owners Johanne Killeen and George Germon created their grilled pizza somewhat by accident. "A vendor told us about a grilled pizza he'd had in Italy," recalls Johanne. "We realized he had probably mistaken a wood-fired oven for a grill, but we were intrigued enough to try to cook the dough on the grill."

Grilled pizza is easy to make, impressive to serve, and about one of the best tasting things you'll ever put in your mouth. Just remember a few simple points to watch. First, set up the grill for two-zone grilling, so that you have a hotter section (over which to sear the dough) and a cooler section (over which to keep the pizza warm without burning the bottom while you put on the toppings).

Second, make the pizzas by stretching out the dough in olive oil instead of rolling it in flour (the oil helps the dough crisp). The first stretch you make will shrink most of the way back. Keep stretching; eventually, you'll achieve the proper shape and thinness.

Finally, keep in mind that the topping goes on a grilled pizza in the opposite sequence of a conventional pizza: first the olive oil, then the cheese, and finally the tomato sauce or tomatoes. This allows the cheese to melt even though it isn't exposed to direct heat. Here's the basic dough, plus two grilled pizzas that will change the way you think about pizza forever.

BASIC PIZZA DOUGH

MAKES ENOUGH DOUGH FOR TWO 13 BY 9-INCH RECTANGULAR PIZZAS

Al Forno's dough owes its earthy flavor to the use of three different types of flour: white flour, whole wheat flour, and stone-ground cornmeal.

ADVANCE PREPARATION

2 to 3 hours for making and raising the dough

INGREDIENTS

1 envelope active dry yeast
1 teaspoon sugar
2 teaspoons coarse salt (kosher or sea)
3 tablespoons fine white cornmeal
3 tablespoons whole-wheat flour
1 tablespoon extra-virgin olive oil, plus oil for the bowl
3 to 3½ cups unbleached all-purpose flour, or more as needed

1. Place 1 cup of warm water in a large bowl and add the yeast and sugar. Stir until the sugar dissolves, then let the yeast mixture sit for 5 minutes. Stir in the salt, cornmeal, whole-wheat flour, and olive oil. Gradually stir in enough all-purpose flour to form a dough that comes away from the side of the bowl. Knead the dough on a floured work surface, or in a food processor or mixer fitted with a dough hook, until it is smooth and elastic. The dough should be soft and pliable, but not sticky. Kneading should take 6 to 8 minutes.

2. Lightly oil a clean large bowl. Place the dough in the bowl, brush the top with olive oil, and cover it loosely with plastic wrap. Let the dough rise in a warm, draft-free spot until doubled in bulk, 1 to 2 hours. Punch down the dough.

3. Let the dough rise until doubled in bulk again, 40 to 50 minutes. Punch the dough down and divide it into 2 equal pieces. Shape each piece of dough into a ball, then flatten them slightly so they resemble thick disks. You're now ready to make the pizzas.

GRILLED PIZZA
WITH TOMATO, BASIL & CHEESE

DIRECT GRILLING
MAKES TWO 13 BY 9-INCH PIZZAS

Here's a grilled version of the simplest of all pizzas, the Margherita. To heighten the grilled flavor, I like to char the tomatoes. Once the slices are charred, you can dice the tomatoes before using them to top the crust.

2 large ripe tomatoes, cored and sliced crosswise ½ inch thick
6 tablespoons extra-virgin olive oil, or more as needed
Coarse salt (kosher or sea) and freshly ground black pepper
1 recipe Basic Pizza Dough (at left)
2 cloves garlic, minced
⅔ cup shredded or diced Italian Fontina cheese
⅓ cup freshly grated Pecorino Romano cheese
16 fresh basil leaves

1. Set up the grill for two-zone grilling (see page 18), preheating two thirds of the grill to medium and leaving one third heat free as a safety zone.

2. When ready to cook, brush each tomato slice with a small amount of olive oil and season it with salt and pepper to taste. Char the tomato slices on the hot side of the grill, turning them with a spatula, about 2 minutes per side. Transfer the tomato slices to a plate and let cool. Leave the fire burning.

3. Generously oil a large baking sheet and place one disk of pizza dough on it. Using your fingers and the palms of your hands, stretch out the dough into a 13 by 9–inch

The Indian Grill

India? Barbecue? Mention Indian cooking and what most comes to mind are curries, chutneys, and rice dishes. What you may not realize is that India is one of the world's great barbecuing centers, home to a unique style of live-fire cooking called tandoori. Named for a giant clay cooking vessel, tandoori combines the charcoal flavor of Western-style grilling with the fall-off-the-bone tenderness of food cooked in a barbecue pit or oven.

When I first visited Bukhara, a restaurant located in New Delhi's Maurya Sheraton hotel, the executive chef was Manjit Gill. The secret to tandoori cooking, he explained, is the ovens. He pointed to the tandoors, the waist-high, urn-shaped clay ovens that are the focal point of the restaurant's exhibition kitchen. These sort of ovens have been in use in India and Central Asia for at least five thousand years, and they turn up in Iran, where they're called *tanoors,* and in the Caucasus Mountains, where they're called *tones.* They're an indispensable element of northern Indian cooking.

According to Gill, the term *tandoor* may come from the Sanskrit word *kandu* (a bowl-shaped vessel) or perhaps from the Persian words *tata andar,* literally hot inside. That's putting it mildly. It takes Gill three hours to preheat the tandoors at Bukhara; by the time the food goes in for cooking, the internal temperature exceeds 800°F. This blast furnace–level heat handsomely chars bull's horn peppers and cauliflower (popular Indian grilled vegetables) in a matter of minutes and produces *raan gosht* (baby leg of goat marinated in yogurt and chickpea flour) so tender you can pull it apart with your fingers. (Which is how Indians eat it.) Kebabs emerge dappled with Rembrandtesque browns, while breads baked directly on the walls of the tandoor come out as smoky and light as wood-oven-baked pizzas.

Lest the lightning-quick activity of the chefs give you the impression that tandoori is fast food, know that each spice-scented mouthful is the result of a lot of advance preparation. Meats and vegetables are patiently marinated—sometimes twice—in tangy pastes of yogurt or yogurt cheese and mouth-puckering mixtures of vinegar, tamarind, or lemon juice. Pungent purees of ginger and garlic build the background flavor, while spice mixes, called *masalas,* weave intricate tapestries of taste. The marinating period can last anywhere from thirty minutes to overnight, and it tenderizes meats so that they can quickly cook to perfection in the blast furnace heat.

Once marinated, the foods are threaded onto long metal skewers and lowered into the tandoor. The vertical position of the skewers is another reason tandoori fare is so succulent: The juices drip on the food below, not on the coals. Additionally, most kebabs are generously basted with ghee (clarified butter) before serving.

Vegetarians get short shrift at most North American barbecue joints. Not so in India, where a sizable percentage of the population of one billion doesn't eat meat. Vegetarian kebabs include *paneer tikka* (fresh cheese kebabs coated with chickpea flour) and *tandoori aloo* (spit-roasted potatoes stuffed with a fragrant mixture of cashew nuts, raisins, and coriander). The traditional accompaniments for tandoori include mint chutney, cooling *raita* (a yogurt-based condiment), and an astonishing assortment of breads.

Bread was the first food cooked in a tandoor, and it remains a staple. Every village in northern India has an open-air bakery, where *roti* (whole-wheat flat breads), *paratha* (buttered, layered flat breads), and naan (sweet, yeasted white breads) emerge piping hot from the tandoor. If you're lucky enough to dine at Bukhara with a large party, order the "family" naan, a huge, bowl-shaped bread that measures a full two feet across.

While it's impossible to make authentic tandoori fare at home without a tandoor, you can produce a reasonable approximation using a backyard charcoal or gas grill. The trick is to set up the grill for grateless grilling (see the box on page 21), so the meat doesn't touch the grate. After all, the tandoor is only part of what makes Indian barbecue so distinctive. The marinades, spices, and basting play a significant role, too. Bottom line: You can't lose, no matter which way you grill the dish.

rectangle (it doesn't need to be too even). This stretching technique takes a little practice, so don't be discouraged if your first rectangle isn't picture-perfect. Stretch out the remaining disk of pizza dough to the same size on a second oiled baking sheet.

4. Working with one rectangle of dough at a time and using both hands, gently lift the dough from the baking sheet. Drape it on the grill grate over the hot zone of the grill. Within a minute or so, the underside of the dough will crisp, darken, and harden and the top will puff slightly. Using tongs or two spatulas, turn the dough over and move it to the cool zone of the grill.

5. Quickly brush the top of the pizza with 1 tablespoon of the olive oil. Scatter half of the garlic on top, then sprinkle half of the Fontina and Pecorino Romano cheese over it and arrange half of the tomato slices and 8 basil leaves on top. Drizzle another tablespoon of olive oil over the top of the pizza and season it with salt and pepper to taste.

6. Slide the pizza back over the hot zone of the grill, rotating it to ensure even cooking. Cook the pizza until the underside is slightly charred and the cheese is melted on top, 2 to 4 minutes.

7. Remove the pizza from the grill, cut it into serving pieces, and serve it, then repeat the procedure with the second rectangle of dough and the remaining ingredients.

GRILLED PIZZA WITH ARUGULA & ITALIAN CHEESES

DIRECT GRILLING
MAKES TWO 13 BY 9-INCH PIZZAS

When making grilled pizza, Al Forno owners Johanne and George urge that you keep the toppings simple. You don't want to mask the flavor of the grilled dough.

1 recipe Basic Pizza Dough (page 382)
6 tablespoons extra-virgin olive oil, or more as needed
2 cloves garlic, minced
1 cup shredded Bel Paese cheese
6 tablespoons freshly grated Parmesan cheese
2 large ripe tomatoes, peeled and seeded (see page 454), then coarsely chopped
24 arugula leaves (from 1 bunch, rinsed and stemmed)

1. Prepare the pizza as described in the recipe for Grilled Pizza with Tomato, Basil, and Cheese, working with one rectangle of dough at a time. After you turn over the dough for each pizza, sprinkle the top of each with half of the Bel Paese and Parmesan cheese, followed by half of the chopped tomatoes. Arrange 12 arugula leaves on top of each pizza.

2. Slide the pizza back over the hot zone of the grill, rotating it to ensure even cooking. Cook the pizza until the underside is slightly charred and the cheese is melted on top, 2 to 4 minutes.

3. Remove each pizza from the grill when it is done and cut it into serving pieces.

SWITZERLAND

RACLETTE

DIRECT GRILLING
SERVES 6

Raclette is the original grilling cheese. For centuries, this Franco-Swiss favorite has been melted in front of a fire and served over boiled potatoes or bread. The term *raclette* describes both the dish and the cheese used to make it. The latter is a large, disk-shaped semifirm cow's milk cheese, about three inches thick and weighing thirteen to seventeen pounds. It has a 45 percent butterfat content. The nonedible, dark beige rind encases a robustly flavored cheese.

2 pounds small red potatoes, scrubbed and cut in half
Salt
30 tiny pickled (cocktail) onions, drained
30 small sour pickles, such as cornichons, drained

6 thick slices rye bread or country-style bread
1 wedge (2½ to 3 pounds) raclette cheese (see Note)

1. Place the potatoes in a pot with salted water to cover. Bring to a boil over high heat, then reduce the heat to medium and let the potatoes simmer until tender, about 10 minutes. Drain the potatoes in a colander, rinse them with cold water, and drain again. Divide the potatoes, onions, and pickles among 6 serving plates and set aside.

2. If cooking the raclette next to a fireplace or wood stove, build a brisk fire. If using a grill, set it up for direct grilling and preheat to high.

3. When ready to cook, spear the bread on a long-handled fork (or hold it with tongs) and toast it in front of the fire. Alternatively, you can toast the bread on the hot grill grate, turning it with tongs, 1 to 3 minutes per side. Divide the toasted bread among the serving plates with the potatoes, onions, and pickles.

4. To make the raclette:

If cooking in a fireplace, using long-handled, spring-loaded tongs, hold the cheese next to the fire until the surface begins to melt, 2 to 4 minutes. Scrape a small amount of the melted cheese onto each plate over the bread, potatoes, onions, and pickles. Return the cheese to the fire and continue until you have melted as much as you need.

If cooking on a grill, brush and oil the grill grate and place the cheese directly on it. Cook the cheese until the bottom is melted, about 2 minutes. Scrape a small amount of the melted cheese onto each plate over the bread, potatoes, onions, and pickles. Return the cheese to the grate and continue until you have melted as much as you need.

NOTE: You'll need about 2½ pounds of cheese to serve 6 people. But when working in front of a fire, it's easier to work with a larger piece—say 4 to 6 pounds. It will hold up better in front of the flames. Use the leftover cheese at another grill session.

Raclette

Ski lodges in the Alps in the winter are the last places you'd expect to find live-fire cooking—especially for an ingredient most people don't associate with grilling: cheese. But the French and Swiss Alps are home to one of the world's great live-fire dishes, the après-ski favorite raclette. The word comes from the French verb *racler,* to scrape.

Raclette (the dish) is traditionally made by placing a half or quarter wheel of cheese on a stone in front of the fireplace. (Today, most restaurants use electric raclette burners instead of a fireplace to do the melting.) As the part of the cheese next to the fire melts, it is scraped onto plates to be enjoyed with such sturdy Alpine fare as crusty bread and boiled potatoes, tangy pickled onion, and cornichons (small sour pickles). *Heidi* fans may remember reading about Grandfather melting the cheese in front of the fireplace in Johanna Spyri's beloved novel.

Raclette (the cheese) has an aroma that might charitably be described as "pungent"—off-putting to all but the most ardent devotees of Limburger. But melt the cheese next to an open flame and the infamous odor disappears. The cheese becomes as creamy as butter and as mild and sweet as mozzarella. It is widely available at cheese markets and specialty food shops. You won't have trouble locating it: Just use your nose. Raclette is made in both France and Switzerland, and the best ones are made with unpasteurized milk. Steven Jenkins, author of the *Cheese Primer,* recommends raclette from the towns of Bagnes, Conches, Gosmer, and Orsières in Switzerland and the Brunnerois and Perrin brands from France.

Who says you can't enjoy live-fire cooking in the winter? Never did something that smells so bad taste so good!

INDIA

TANDOORI PEPPERS

INDIRECT GRILLING
SERVES 4

Stuffed peppers turn up at tandoori parlors throughout northern India. The pepper in question looks like a miniature green bell pepper but is hotter. The overall effect is a cross between an American green bell pepper and a Mexican *chile poblano.* I compensate for the lack of heat in our peppers by adding a good dose of cayenne to the filling. Incidentally, the filling is a meal in itself—a soulful stew of onion, potato, cabbage, and cashew nuts assertively seasoned with spices and cheese. Indians would roast the stuffed peppers on vertical spits in a tandoor. The upright position keeps the filling from falling out. Lacking a tandoor, the best way to cook the peppers is to stand them upright on the grate, and grill them using the indirect method. Although not traditional, yellow or red bell peppers are delicious for stuffing too.

FOR THE BELL PEPPERS AND MARINADE

4 large yellow, red, or green bell peppers
2 tablespoons fresh lemon juice
1 tablespoon vegetable oil
1 clove garlic, coarsely chopped
1 piece (½ inch) peeled fresh ginger
¼ teaspoon salt

FOR THE FILLING

2 tablespoons vegetable oil
½ teaspoon cumin seeds
½ teaspoon ground turmeric
¼ teaspoon cayenne pepper, or more to taste
1 medium-size onion, finely chopped
1 clove garlic, minced
1 potato (about 10 ounces), peeled and cut into ¼-inch dice
⅓ small head green cabbage, cored and thinly sliced
1 large ripe tomato, finely chopped
2 tablespoons cashew nuts, coarsely chopped
2 tablespoons golden raisins (optional)
¼ cup finely chopped fresh cilantro
½ cup grated Gouda or mild Cheddar cheese
Salt

1. Prepare the bell peppers and marinade: Carefully cut the caps (the stem ends) off the bell peppers and set them aside. (Each cap section should be about ½ inch deep.) Using a spoon or melon baller, scrape the veins and seeds out of the bell peppers. Set the bell peppers aside, with their caps.

2. Combine the lemon juice, 1 tablespoon of oil, chopped garlic, ginger, and ¼ teaspoon of salt in a food processor or blender and process until smooth. Using a pastry brush, paint the insides of the bell peppers and their caps with the marinade, then set the peppers aside to marinate.

3. Make the filling: Heat the 2 tablespoons of oil in a large skillet or saucepan over medium heat. Add the cumin seeds, turmeric, cayenne, onion, and minced garlic and cook until the onion is just beginning to brown, about 5 minutes. Stir in the potato, cabbage, tomato, cashews, and raisins (if using) and cook for 2 minutes. Reduce the heat to low, cover the pan, and cook the vegetables until soft, stirring occasionally, 10 to 15 minutes. Check after 10 minutes, and if the vegetables look wet, uncover the pan for the last 5 minutes of cooking to evaporate any excess liquid. Stir in the cilantro and cook for 1 minute. Stir in the cheese. Remove pan from heat and taste for seasoning, adding salt to taste and more cayenne as necessary; the filling should be highly seasoned.

4. Spoon the filling into the bell peppers. If they don't stand up on their own, position them on rings made from crumpled aluminum foil. Place the caps on top. The peppers can be stuffed up to 6 hours ahead and refrigerated, covered loosely with plastic wrap.

5. Set up the grill for indirect grilling, place a drip pan in the center, and preheat to high.

6. When ready to cook, place the stuffed peppers in the center of the hot grate away from the heat. Cover the grill and cook the peppers until they are nicely browned and tender, 20 to 30 minutes. I like to move the peppers directly over the flames for a few minutes at the end to lightly char the skins. Serve the peppers at once.

TANDOORI PEPPERS | AT LEFT

INDIA

WHITE RABBIT

DIRECT GRILLING
SERVES 4

This ingenious recipe was inspired by Manu Mehta, executive chef at the Sheraton Rajputana hotel in Jaipur. Mehta caters to a large vegetarian clientele, so he created a meatless version of the local barbecue, *sula*—literally rabbit. He makes the dish with *paneer* (a white Indian cheese) instead of the traditional game—hence the nickname "white rabbit." *Paneer* is a soft but solid cheese, not unlike farmer's cheese or Hispanic *queso blanco*.

The chef and I agreed you could also make this dish with a thoroughly non-Indian ingredient with a consistency very similar to *paneer:* tofu. If you've ever complained that tofu is bland, this is the recipe for you. The bean curd receives a double blast of flavor: first from the cilantro and mint stuffing, then from the garlic, ginger, and jalapeño marinade. Add the charcoal flavor imparted by grilling and you have a dish guaranteed to turn skeptics into believers.

ADVANCE PREPARATION

30 minutes for draining the tofu, plus 4 hours for marinating the tofu

FOR THE TOFU AND FILLING

2 pieces (each 1 pound) extra-firm tofu
3 tablespoons chopped fresh cilantro
3 tablespoons chopped fresh mint or additional cilantro
1 scallion, both white and green parts, trimmed and coarsely sliced
1 to 2 jalapeño peppers or other hot peppers, seeded
1 tablespoon fresh lemon juice
1 tablespoon vegetable oil
¼ teaspoon salt

FOR THE MARINADE

3 cloves garlic, sliced
1 piece (1 inch) peeled fresh ginger, sliced
1 jalapeño pepper, seeded
2 tablespoons vegetable oil
1 tablespoon sweet paprika
1 teaspoon ground coriander
½ teaspoon cayenne pepper, or more to taste
½ teaspoon salt, or more to taste
¾ cup plain whole-milk yogurt
¼ cup heavy (whipping) cream or sour cream
3 tablespoons chopped fresh cilantro
1 tablespoon fresh lemon juice, or more to taste
3 tablespoons unsalted butter, melted

1. Prepare the tofu and filling: Rinse the tofu under cold running water and drain it. Place a cutting board on a slight incline in the sink. Place the tofu on the cutting board and put a heavy plate or pot lid on top of the tofu to press out the excess liquid; this will take about 30 minutes.

2. Cut each piece of drained tofu horizontally in half, then cut each of these pieces in half crosswise. Arrange the pieces of tofu flat at the edge of a cutting board. Holding the blade of a paring knife parallel to the cutting board, cut a deep pocket in one side of each piece of tofu.

3. Combine the 3 tablespoons of cilantro, the mint and scallion, 1 to 2 jalapeños, lemon juice, 1 tablespoon of oil, and ¼ teaspoon of salt in a food processor and process to a coarse paste. Spoon equal amounts of filling into the pocket in each piece of tofu.

4. Prepare the marinade: Combine the garlic, ginger, jalapeño, 2 tablespoons of oil, and 2 tablespoons of water in a food processor or blender and process to a smooth paste. Transfer the marinade to a small bowl and stir in the paprika, coriander, cayenne, ½ teaspoon salt, yogurt, cream, 3 tablespoons of cilantro, and 1 tablespoon lemon juice. Taste for seasoning adding more cayenne, salt, and/or lemon juice as necessary; the marinade should be highly seasoned. Pour one third of the marinade over the bottom of a nonreactive baking dish and arrange the stuffed tofu on top. Pour the remaining marinade over the tofu. Let the tofu marinate in the refrigerator, covered, for 4 hours.

5. Set up the grill for direct grilling and preheat to high.

6. When ready to cook, brush and oil the grill grate. Remove the tofu from the marinade and discard the marinade. Arrange the tofu on the hot grate. Grill the tofu, turning it carefully with a spatula, until nicely browned and thoroughly heated through, about 4 minutes per side. Brush the tofu once or twice with some of the melted butter as it grills.

7. Transfer the tofu to serving plates or a platter and brush it once more with melted butter before serving.

JAPAN

TOFU ON STILTS
DENGAKU

DIRECT GRILLING
SERVES 4

Dengaku is a popular dish at the teahouses that line the lovely Philosopher's Walk in Kyoto. The dish takes its curious name from the Japanese word for stilt. The stilts in question are two bamboo skewers that are used to hold the piece of tofu over the coals as it grills. The traditional grill for cooking *dengaku* does not have a grate. Instead, the skewers are propped up over the flames and the tofu is grilled in midair—what I call grateless grilling. Acceptable results can be obtained on a regular grill or hibachi, but you will lose some glaze.

ADVANCE PREPARATION

30 minutes for draining the tofu

SPECIAL EQUIPMENT

16 long bamboo skewers and an aluminum foil shield (see box, page 23)

INGREDIENTS

2 pieces (each 1 pound) extra-firm tofu
½ cup white miso
2 tablespoons mirin (sweet rice wine) or cream sherry
2 tablespoons sake
2 tablespoons sugar
1 tablespoon mayonnaise
1 tablespoon sesame seeds, toasted (see box, page 113)

1. Rinse the tofu under cold running water and drain it. Place a cutting board on a slight incline in the sink. Place the tofu on the cutting board and put a heavy plate or pot lid on top of the tofu to press out the excess liquid; this will take about 30 minutes.

2. Combine the miso, mirin, sake, sugar, and mayonnaise in the top of a double boiler and whisk until smooth. Cook the miso glaze over gently simmering water until thick and creamy, about 3 minutes.

3. Cut each piece of drained tofu horizontally in half, then cut each of these pieces in half crosswise. Push 2 skewers through each piece of tofu, starting at a narrow end.

4. Set up the grill for direct grilling and preheat to high. If desired, use a grateless grill setup (see box, page 211).

5. When ready to cook, arrange the tofu on the grill as described for grateless grilling or brush and oil the grill grate and place the tofu directly on it with the aluminum foil shield under the ends of the skewers. Grill the tofu, turning with a spatula, until it is lightly browned on each side, 3 to 4 minutes per side. Brush the tofu with the miso glaze as it cooks.

6. Transfer the tofu to serving plates or a platter, sprinkle the sesame seeds on top, and serve at once.

U.S.A.

MUSHROOM-RICE BURGERS
WITH CHEDDAR CHEESE

DIRECT GRILLING
SERVES 6

When I was growing up, no one knew from vegetarian burgers. Today, they've become big business, as more and more health-conscious Americans adopt at least partial vegetarian diets. The following recipe combines mushrooms, oats, and brown rice in a patty that looks somewhat like a hamburger and has a rich, earthy flavor that could almost be described as meaty. It's also a great way to use up leftover brown rice. Note that vegetarian burgers are more fragile than beef or lamb burgers. Cook them on a well-oiled vegetable grate and turn them as gently as possible with a spatula.

ADVANCE PREPARATION

4 to 5 hours total for chilling the burger mixture and patties

SPECIAL EQUIPMENT

Vegetable grate

FOR THE BURGERS

2 tablespoons extra-virgin olive oil
1 medium-size onion, finely chopped
2 cloves garlic, minced
8 ounces white mushrooms, wiped clean with dampened paper towels and finely chopped
1 cup cooked brown rice
½ cup quick oats
4 ounces coarsely grated sharp Cheddar cheese (about ¾ cup)
1 egg, lightly beaten
Salt and freshly ground black pepper
2 to 3 tablespoons fine dry bread crumbs, as needed

FOR SERVING

½ head iceberg lettuce, thinly sliced
1 large ripe tomato, thinly sliced
1 large onion (optional), thinly sliced
Pickle slices
4 whole-wheat hamburger buns
Ketchup and/or mayonnaise and/or mustard

1. Prepare the burger mixture: Heat the olive oil in a nonstick skillet over medium heat. Add the onion and garlic and cook until soft but not brown, about 4 minutes. Increase the heat to medium-high, add the mushrooms, and cook, stirring occasionally, until tender and most of the mushroom liquid has evaporated, about 4 minutes.

2. Stir in the brown rice and cook for 1 minute. Transfer the mushroom mixture to a large bowl. Stir in the oats, Cheddar cheese, and egg. Season with salt and pepper to taste. If the burger mixture seems too moist, add the bread crumbs. Cover the burger mixture and refrigerate it until firm, 3 to 4 hours.

3. Line a baking sheet or large plate with plastic wrap. Divide the burger mixture into equal portions. Lightly wet your hands with cold water, then form each portion of the burger mixture into a patty. Place the patties on the prepared baking sheet, cover them loosely with plastic wrap, and refrigerate for 1 hour. Arrange the lettuce, tomato slices, onion slices (if using), and pickles on a platter and set aside.

4. Set up the grill for direct grilling and preheat to high.

5. When ready to cook, place a vegetable grate on the hot grill and preheat it for 5 minutes. Oil the vegetable grate and arrange the patties on it. Grill the patties, turning them carefully with a spatula, until nicely browned on both sides, 4 to 6 minutes per side. As the patties cook, toast the hamburger buns on the grate as well.

7. Serve the patties as you would any burger, piling the buns high with tomato, onion (if desired), lettuce, pickles, and smearing on ketchup, mayonnaise, or mustard—or all three.

INDIA

YAM AND NUT KEBABS

DIRECT GRILLING
SERVES 4

How do you cater to a large, affluent vegetarian community in a land of avid meat eaters? Nisar Waris faces this challenge daily. Waris is the chef of Peshawar, the signature restaurant in the Sheraton Rajputana hotel in Jaipur. His staff has created a huge repertoire of vegetarian barbecue items, including these singular kebabs. Talk about an amazing set of flavors! Chef Waris skillfully combines the sweetness of yams and raisins, the nuttiness of cashews and pistachios, and the spicy zing of cardamom and cilantro. It's enough to make you want to give up meat! Waris molds and grills the yam mixture on skewers, but you can also form it into burger-like patties. To start with, the yams can be either grilled, using the indirect method, or baked.

ADVANCE PREPARATION

3 hours for chilling the yam mixture (optional)

SPECIAL EQUIPMENT

4 long, flat, metal skewers

FOR THE KEBABS

1 pound yams or sweet potatoes (enough to make 1 cup puree; see Notes)
¼ cup chickpea flour (besan; see Notes) or whole-wheat flour

2 cups coarsely chopped nut mixture, including cashews, pistachios, and almonds, and/or sunflower seeds
1 tablespoon heavy (whipping) cream or sour cream
1 teaspoon fresh lemon juice, or more to taste
½ cup golden raisins, finely chopped
⅓ cup chopped fresh cilantro
1 teaspoon freshly ground white pepper
½ teaspoon Quick Garam Masala (page 496) or ground coriander
¼ teaspoon ground cardamom
½ teaspoon salt, or more to taste
3 tablespoons unsalted butter, melted

FOR SERVING

Naan, pita bread, or lavash
Lemon wedges
Sliced onions
Sliced cucumbers
Sliced tomatoes
Sliced chile peppers

1. If you are using the grill to cook the yams, set it up for indirect grilling, place a drip pan in the center, and preheat the grill to medium-high. If you are using the oven to cook the yams, preheat it to 400°F.

2. To grill the yams, place them in the center of the hot grill, over the drip pan and away from the heat, and cover the grill. Or bake the yams in the oven. Either way the yams will be done when soft, 40 minutes to 1 hour.

3. Transfer the yams to a plate and let cool. Peel the yams, then mash them in a large bowl with a potato masher, fork, or pestle. (Don't puree the yams in a food processor or the mixture will become gummy.)

4. Cook the chickpea flour in a dry skillet over medium heat until lightly toasted and fragrant, about 2 minutes (do not use a nonstick skillet for this). Stir the chickpea flour into the yams. Add the mixed nuts to the skillet and cook, stirring, over medium heat until lightly toasted and fragrant, 3 to 5 minutes. Stir the nuts into the yams.

5. Stir the cream, lemon juice, raisins, cilantro, white pepper, garam marsala, cardamom, and salt into the yam mixture. Taste for seasoning, adding more lemon juice and/or salt as necessary; the yam mixture should be highly seasoned. You can form the kebabs now, but the mixture will be easier to work with if you refrigerate it, covered, for 3 hours. You can also make the kebab mixture the day before and chill it overnight if desired.

6. Oil the skewers. Divide the yam mixture into four equal portions. Lightly wet your hands with cold water, then mold each portion onto a skewer to make a sausage shape 9 to 10 inches long and 1 inch in diameter. If you are making the kebabs ahead of time, place them on oiled baking sheets and cover them loosely with plastic wrap. Refrigerate the kebabs until ready to cook.

7. Set up the grill for direct grilling and preheat to high. If desired, use a grateless grill setup (see box, page 21).

8. When ready to cook, lightly brush the kebabs with melted butter and arrange them on the grill as described for grateless grilling or brush and oil the grill grate and place the kebabs directly on it. Grill the kebabs, turning once or twice, until lightly browned on all sides, about 8 minutes in all. Brush the kebabs with butter again as they grill.

9. To serve: Using a piece of naan, pita bread, or lavash to protect your hand, unskewer the kebabs onto serving plates or a platter. Serve the kebabs with the bread, lemon wedges, and a platter of sliced onions, cucumbers, tomatoes, and chile peppers.

NOTES: The best yam to use here is a true yam, a starchy tuber with minimal sweetness. Look for true yams at Hispanic or Caribbean markets. I've also made the dish with boniatos (white-fleshed Caribbean sweet potatoes, which taste like roasted chestnuts) and, of course, American sweet potatoes.

Chickpea flour (*besan*) is made from roasted chickpeas. It has a tart, nutty, earthy flavor and is available at Indian and some Italian markets and natural foods stores. You can substitute whole-wheat flour.

FRANCE

PROVENÇAL DAGWOOD

DIRECT GRILLING
SERVES 4

If you like grilled vegetables and goat cheese, you'll love this sandwich, which fairly explodes with the evocative flavors of Provence. Rosemary and garlic lend a Mediterranean fragrance to vegetables that are traditionally associated with ratatouille, the classic vegetable stew from this region of France. The tangy cheese provides a counterpoint in texture to the vegetables. Use a soft, spreadable fresh goat cheese like Montrachet for best results. These sandwiches can be made a few hours ahead of time and are great to take on picnics, with the vegetable juices soaking into the bread.

FOR THE VEGETABLES

1 medium-size eggplant (12 to 14 ounces), stem end trimmed off
2 medium-size zucchini, stem ends trimmed off
2 medium-size yellow squash, stem ends trimmed off
2 medium-size red bell peppers
1 medium-size red onion, peeled but root end left attached

FOR THE BASTING MIXTURE

3 tablespoons extra-virgin olive oil
2 tablespoons fresh lemon juice
2 cloves garlic, minced
1 sprig fresh rosemary, or 1 teaspoon dried rosemary
Salt and freshly ground black pepper

FOR SERVING

1 long baguette
8 ounces fresh goat cheese, at room temperature

1. Prepare the vegetables: Cut the eggplant, zucchini, and yellow squash lengthwise into ¼-inch-thick slices. Core, seed, and quarter the bell peppers. Quarter the onion, leaving the root end attached to each piece (the root will help the onion hold together as it grills).

2. Make the basting mixture: Combine the olive oil, lemon juice, and garlic in a small bowl. If using dried rosemary, add it directly to the olive oil mixture.

3. Set up the grill for direct grilling and preheat to high.

4. When ready to cook, brush the eggplant, zucchini, squash, bell pepper, and onion slices with some of the olive oil mixture, using the rosemary sprig as a basting brush. (If you are not using fresh rosemary, use a pastry brush.) Arrange the vegetables on the hot grate and grill, turning with tongs, until nicely browned, 3 to 6 minutes per side. Brush the vegetables once or twice more with the olive oil mixture and season them with salt and black pepper as they cook. Transfer the vegetables to a platter to cool. Cut the root end off the onion wedges and break the layers apart.

5. To serve: Cut the bread crosswise into four equal pieces. Split each piece lengthwise in half for the sandwiches. Brush the insides of each piece of bread with any remaining olive oil mixture and spread the goat cheese over them. Sandwich the eggplant, zucchini, squash, bell pepper, and onion slices inside the bread. Cut the sandwiches in half and serve warm or at room temperature.

U.S.A.

GRILLED PORTOBELLO MUSHROOM SANDWICHES WITH BASIL AIOLI

DIRECT GRILLING
SERVES 4

The portobello mushroom has become the fin de siècle "steak," a grilled vegetable alternative to beef. The broad fleshy mushroom cap has a rich meaty flavor, and luckily, portobellos are available at most supermarkets and specialty food shops. To this, add a fresh basil-flavored aioli (French garlic mayonnaise) and you've got a sandwich that tap dances on your taste buds!

SPECIAL EQUIPMENT

Vegetable grate

INGREDIENTS

4 large portobello mushrooms, wiped clean with dampened paper towels
3 cloves garlic, cut into thin slivers
Leaves from 1 sprig fresh rosemary (optional)
3 tablespoons extra-virgin olive oil
3 tablespoons balsamic vinegar
1 large ripe tomato, cut crosswise into ½-inch slices
Salt and freshly ground black pepper
4 onion rolls, hamburger buns, or 5-inch sections of baguette, split
Basil Aioli (recipe follows) or mayonnaise
1 bunch arugula, rinsed and spun dry

1. Cut the stems off the portobello mushrooms flush with the mushroom caps. Using the tip of a paring knife, make tiny holes in the caps and insert the garlic slivers and rosemary leaves (if using).

2. Combine the olive oil and balsamic vinegar in a small bowl and whisk to mix. Generously brush the portobello caps and tomato slices with some of the oil and vinegar mixture and season them with salt and pepper.

3. Set up the grill for direct grilling and preheat to high.

4. When ready to cook, place a vegetable grate on the hot grill and preheat it for 5 minutes. Arrange the portobello caps, rounded side down, and the tomato slices on the hot grate and grill, turning with a spatula, until nicely browned and soft, 3 to 6 minutes per side. Brush the vegetables once or twice as they cook with the oil and vinegar mixture.

5. Spread the insides of the rolls or bread with Basil Aioli or mayonnaise. Add the grilled mushrooms and tomato slices and the arugula and serve at once.

BASIL AIOLI

MAKES ABOUT 1 CUP

Aioli is a garlic mayonnaise from the south of France. This version uses commercial mayonnaise as a base to avoid the small but worrisome health risks associated with eating raw egg yolks.

1 cup mayonnaise
3 cloves garlic, put through a garlic press
24 fresh basil leaves, thinly slivered
1 tablespoon fresh lemon juice
Salt and freshly ground black pepper

Combine the mayonnaise, garlic, basil, and lemon juice in a small bowl and whisk to mix. Season with salt and pepper to taste.

GRILLED VEGETABLES IN THE STYLE OF SANTA MARGHERITA | PAGE 398

VEGETABLES: GREENS MEET GRILL

When I was growing up, barbecue meant meat. Especially steak. The idea of grilling a bell pepper or a portobello mushroom would have seemed as strange as landing a man on the moon.

"What was paradise but a garden full of vegetables."
—WILLIAM LAWSON

Well, we did land a man on the moon and we have discovered grilled vegetables. In fact, North Americans may be newcomers to a wide range of grilled vegetables, but we've embraced the cause with religious fervor. And why not? Because no other cooking method produces a better taste. Grilling evaporates some of the water in a vegetable, concentrating the flavor. High, dry heat caramelizes natural plant sugars, heightening a vegetable's sweetness. Unlike boiling, which removes flavor from vegetables, grilling seems to intensify their natural taste. Add a whiff of smoke (from wood chips or wood chunks) and you'll have vegetables with an astonishing depth of flavor.

This chapter offers a mouthwatering tour of the world of grilled vegetables, from Korean grilled oyster mushrooms to tandoori cauliflower fragrant with Indian spices. Along the way, you'll learn how to grill corn, fennel, long beans, and even breadfruit. If you had trouble eating your vegetables when you were a kid, it's probably because they weren't grilled.

REPUBLIC OF GEORGIA

GEORGIAN VEGETABLE KEBABS

DIRECT GRILLING
SERVES 4

These colorful vegetable kebabs turn up at any barbecue in the Republic of Georgia. Their simplicity makes a nice counterpoint to the complex flavors of Georgian marinated meats. Georgian Pickled Plum Sauce (page 467) would be a good accompaniment, but the vegetable kebabs are also delicious plain. Choose tomatoes that are ripe but still a little firm, so they won't fall off the skewers. A Georgian would use a flat, wide steel skewer.

How to Grill Perfect Vegetables Every Time

In general, vegetables benefit from a direct, high-heat grilling method. The exceptions are dense root vegetables, like potatoes and turnips, that are best grilled by the indirect method or parboiled and finished over the fire. To see some of the grilling techniques described here, take a look at the vegetables on the grill on page 399.

ASPARAGUS, OKRA, GREEN BEANS, AND OTHER LONG, SKINNY, FIBROUS VEGETABLES: Snap or cut the ends off of the vegetables and arrange four to six vegetables side by side on a work surface. Skewer the vegetables crosswise with slender bamboo skewers, then brush them with olive oil or sesame oil and sprinkle them with salt and pepper. Grill the vegetables over high heat until nicely browned on both sides. Asparagus will take 6 to 8 minutes in all. Okra and green beans will be done in 8 to 10 minutes. Scallions need a total grilling time of 4 to 8 minutes.

CORN: There are two schools of thought on this one. The easiest way to grill corn is simply to toss unshucked ears on the grate and cook them over high heat until the husks are completely charred. Then, you scrape off the charred husks with paper towels (the silk will come off with the husks). It will take 15 to 20 minutes in all for the corn to grill and the result will be sweet and mildly smoky.

My favorite way to grill corn is to start with ears that have the husks pulled back to use as a handle and the silk removed. I generously brush them with melted butter or olive oil and equally generously season with salt and pepper and maybe a little chopped parsley. I grill the corn over high heat, directly over the flames, until the kernels are darkly browned and starting to pop. This takes 8 to 12 minutes in all.

EGGPLANTS: Choose eggplants that are long and slender. Grill the eggplant over high heat until the skin is black and charred on all sides and the flesh is soft; test it by gently poking the top. You're supposed to burn the skin; that's what gives the eggplant its smoky flavor. Turn the eggplant with tongs as it cooks: The whole process will take 20 to 30 minutes. Transfer the grilled eggplant to a plate and let cool, then scrape off the charred skin (you don't have to remove all the burnt pieces; they add a terrific flavor). The eggplant is now ready for chopping to make salads or pureeing to make dips.

Some of the recipes in this book call for Asian eggplants, which are 1 to 2 inches in diameter and about 6 inches long. They cook in 9 to 12 minutes.

MUSHROOMS: Mushrooms tend to get somewhat dry if you grill them plain, so it's best to marinate them for a few hours in an oil-based marinade or slather them with an herb or flavored butter as they grill. For easy grilling and turning, thread small, flat mushrooms on skewers so that they will lie flat on the grill grate (across the cap, not through the stem). Larger mushrooms can be sliced or quartered and skewered. Grill mushrooms over high heat, cooking them 3 to 6 minutes per side (6 to 12 minutes in all).

When grilling portobellos, cook them gill side down first, then turn them. Portobellos will be done after 4 to 6 minutes per side (8 to 12 minutes in all). Stuffed mushroom caps should be grilled rounded side down, using the indirect method (with the grill covered), for 15 to 20 minutes. Generously baste all mushrooms as they cook.

ONIONS: Cut onions in quarters, but leave the root intact on each piece. Peel the skin back to the root end (the root holds the onion together as it grills) and brush the onion quarters with oil or melted butter. Grill onions over a high flame until they are nicely charred on the outside and cooked through, turning them to ensure even cooking. You'll need 10 to 12 minutes in all. Cut the root off the onions and scrape away the burnt skin before serving. You can also grill onion slices.

PEPPERS: This method works for both bell peppers and chile peppers—choose peppers that are rotund and smooth, with relatively few depressions or crevasses. Preheat the grill to high. Place the whole peppers on the grill and cook until darkly charred on all sides, 4 to 5 minutes per side (16 to 20 minutes in all) for larger peppers; smaller chiles will take less time. Don't forget to grill the tops and bottoms of the peppers; if necessary, hold the peppers with tongs if they won't balance properly on either end. This is another vegetable you're supposed to burn. Transfer the grilled peppers to a large bowl and cover it with plastic wrap or place the grilled peppers in a paper or plastic bag and close it. This creates steam, which makes it easy to remove the skin. When the pepper is cool enough to handle, scrape off the skin with a paring knife. Cut out the stem and remove the seeds.

Another way to grill peppers is to brush them lightly with olive oil and grill them until they are nicely browned but not burnt. In this case, you won't have to bother peeling the peppers.

LEAFY VEGETABLES: Cut radicchio in quarters, wedges, or thick slices. Grill kale leaves whole. Grill other leafy vegetables over high heat until the leaves start to brown, 2 to 4 minutes per side. Watch them carefully—do not allow the leaves to burn to a crisp.

TOMATOES: Thread small tomatoes or plum tomatoes on wide, flat skewers and grill them over high heat, turning, until the skins are browned and blistered all over. Grill individual tomatoes the same way, turning them with tongs. To grill really large tomatoes (such as beefsteaks), cut them crosswise into 1-inch-thick slices. Brush the tomato slices with olive oil, season them with salt and pepper, and grill over high heat. Small tomatoes and plum tomatoes will be done in 8 to 12 minutes in all. Larger, whole tomatoes take twice as long, and tomato slices take 2 to 4 minutes per side.

ZUCCHINI AND SUMMER SQUASH: Cut the squash lengthwise into ¼- or ½-inch-thick slices. Brush each side with olive oil or walnut oil. Season the squash with salt and pepper and grill over high heat. It will be done after 4 to 6 minutes per side.

SPECIAL EQUIPMENT

4 long, flat metal skewers

INGREDIENTS

- 8 small green bell peppers, cored and seeded
- 6 ripe plum tomatoes
- 16 large white mushrooms, stemmed, caps wiped clean with dampened paper towels
- 3 tablespoons extra-virgin olive oil
- Coarse salt (kosher or sea) and freshly ground black pepper
- 1 lemon, cut in half

1. Thread the vegetables on the skewers, alternating bell peppers and tomatoes and placing mushrooms between each. Brush the kebabs with olive oil and season them with salt and pepper.

2. Set up the grill for direct grilling and preheat to high.

3. When ready to cook, brush and oil the grill grate. Arrange the kebabs on the hot grate and grill, turning with tongs, until nicely browned, 4 to 6 minutes per side (8 to 12 minutes in all), brushing with olive oil. Remove the skewers, squeeze lemon juice on the vegetables, and serve at once.

JAPAN

JAPANESE VEGETABLE MIXED GRILL

ROBATAYAKI

DIRECT GRILLING
SERVES 4 TO 6

Robatayaki refers to a theatrical, upscale style of Japanese grilling (you can read about it on page 412). Traditionally, the foods were grilled over a prized Japanese charcoal called *bincho,* and in certain sections of Tokyo—among the eateries near the Yurakucho train station, for example—you still find restaurants with charcoal grills. Others take a more contemporary approach, cooking food over high-tech gas grills. This mixed vegetable grill has many virtues, not the least of which is that it's the very best way I know of to cook okra.

SPECIAL EQUIPMENT

50 to 60 bamboo skewers (assorted lengths) and an aluminum foil shield (see box, page 23)

INGREDIENTS

1 pound okra
1 pound sugar snap peas, stems and strings removed
1 pound thick asparagus, fibrous ends removed, stalks trimmed to matching lengths
12 ounces fresh shiitake or large white mushrooms, stemmed, caps wiped clean with dampened paper towels
1 bunch scallions, both white and green parts, trimmed and cut into 2-inch pieces
1 tablespoon coarse salt (kosher or sea)
2 teaspoons freshly ground white pepper (optional)
2 to 4 tablespoons Asian (dark) sesame oil

1. Trim the tips off the stems of the okra, but do not cut into the pods; this would expose the insides to air, making the okra slimy. Arrange 4 or 5 okra side by side in a neat row on a cutting board. Stick a bamboo skewer through each end of each piece. The idea is to create a sort of raft that will hold the okra flat for grilling. Transfer the skewered okra to a large platter. Skewer the sugar snap peas the same way and transfer them to the okra platter.

2. Cut the asparagus stalks in half crosswise. Thread these halves crosswise on skewers (so the asparagus stalks are at a 90 degree angle to the skewers), 4 to 5 pieces to a skewer, alternating tip halves and stalk pieces. Transfer the skewered asparagus to the platter with the okra and sugar snap peas.

3. Cut any large shiitakes in half or quarters; leave small ones whole. Thread the shiitake caps onto skewers, 4 caps to a skewer, alternating them with pieces of scallion. The caps should be threaded on so they will lie flat on the grill (skewer them across the cap, not through the stem). Transfer the shiitake skewers to the platter.

4. Mix the salt and white pepper (if using) in a small bowl. Brush the vegetables with the sesame oil and sprinkle the salt and pepper on top.

5. Set up the grill for direct grilling and preheat to high.

6. When ready to cook, brush and oil the grill grate. Arrange the okra, sugar snap peas, asparagus, and shiitakes on the hot grate with the aluminum foil shield under the ends of the skewers and grill, turning with tongs, until browned and tender, 3 to 6 minutes per side, depending on the vegetable. Serve the various skewers of vegetables as soon as they're ready. Don't worry about serving everything at once; it's more fun if the vegetables arrive sequentially.

ITALY

GRILLED VEGETABLES IN THE STYLE OF SANTA MARGHERITA

DIRECT GRILLING
SERVES 8

After two grueling weeks on the barbecue trail, the town of Santa Margherita on the Italian Riviera appeared like an oasis in the desert. Imagine a spectacularly craggy cove surrounding a harbor filled with bobbing yachts and fishing boats. Trompe l'oeil painted houses. Cafés crowded with chic young Italians. Come lunchtime, it was impossible to ignore a buffet served on a bluff overlooking the bay—especially the centerpiece of that buffet, an enormous platter of grilled vegetables.

In keeping with the Italian understatement when it comes to grilling, the vegetables were cooked without the benefit of a marinade and with only a drizzle of olive oil and squirt of lemon juice by way of a sauce. But I guarantee you'll never taste better grilled vegetables, nor feast your eyes on a prettier platter. Use the following ingredient list as a starting point, substituting whatever vegetables look freshest.

SPECIAL EQUIPMENT

Vegetable grate (optional)

HOW TO GRILL PERFECT VEGETABLES EVERY TIME | PAGE 396

INGREDIENTS

- 2 medium-size red bell peppers
- 2 medium-size yellow bell peppers
- 2 Belgian endives
- 1 pound fresh cremini or regular white mushrooms, stemmed, caps wiped clean with dampened paper towels
- 4 small eggplants or zucchini
- ½ cup extra-virgin olive oil
- Coarse salt (kosher or sea) and freshly ground black pepper
- 1 pound thick asparagus, fibrous ends removed
- 8 small ripe tomatoes
- 2 tablespoons balsamic vinegar (optional)
- 8 lemon wedges, for serving

1. Core, halve, and seed the red and yellow bell peppers, then cut each pepper in half lengthwise into 3 strips. Cut the endives lengthwise in quarters, leaving the stem ends attached. Cut the mushrooms in half and the eggplants in half lengthwise.

2. Set up the grill for direct grilling and preheat to high.

3. When ready to cook, preheat a vegetable grate (if using) for 5 minutes, then brush and oil it or the grill grate. Lightly brush the bell pepper pieces with some of the olive oil, season them with salt and black pepper to taste, and arrange them on the hot grate. Grill the bell peppers until lightly charred on both sides, leaving the skins intact, 4 to 6 minutes per side. Brush the bell peppers lightly with

Vegetable Grilling Chart

VEGETABLE	METHOD	HEAT	COOKING TIME
ARTICHOKES	direct	medium-low	1 to 1¼ hours
ASPARAGUS	direct	high	6 to 8 minutes in all
CORN	direct	high	8 to 12 minutes in all
EGGPLANT, whole			
Asian	direct	high	9 to 12 minutes, until cooked through
regular, long slender	direct	high	20 to 30 minutes, until cooked through
GREEN BEANS	direct	high	6 to 8 minutes in all
MUSHROOM CAPS			
portobello	direct	high	4 to 6 minutes per side
regular	direct	high	3 to 5 minutes per side
ONIONS			
quartered	direct	high	10 to 12 minutes per side
sliced	direct	high	4 to 8 minutes per side
PEPPERS, whole	direct	high	16 to 20 minutes (let the skin burn)
SUMMER SQUASH, sliced (yellow and zucchini)	direct	high	4 to 6 minutes per side
TOMATOES			
sliced	direct	high	2 to 4 minutes per side
whole	direct	high	8 to 24 minutes in all

This chart is offered as a broad guideline to cooking times for various vegetables. Remember, grilling is an art, not a science. When in doubt, refer to times in the individual recipes. See page 396 for tips on grilling vegetables.

olive oil and season them with salt and black pepper once or twice as they grill. Transfer the bell peppers to a platter. Leave the fire burning.

4. Oil, season, and grill the endives, mushrooms, eggplants, asparagus, and tomatoes the same way as the bell peppers. Each vegetable should be nicely charred on the outside and soft and tender inside; depending on the vegetable, this will take 3 to 6 minutes per side. Brush all of the vegetables lightly with olive oil and season them with salt and black pepper once or twice as they grill.

5. Arrange the grilled vegetables in rows on a platter, varying the colors and shapes. Drizzle the remaining olive oil on top of the hot vegetables and let cool.

6. Just before serving, season the vegetables again with salt and pepper. If you like, drizzle a little balsamic vinegar on top. Serve lemon wedges on the side for squeezing over the vegetables.

TRINIDAD

WEST INDIAN GRILLED VEGETABLES

CHOKA

DIRECT GRILLING
SERVES 8

In general, Trinidadians aren't big grillers, preferring the deep-fat frying of their British heritage or the stewing of their African forebears. That's not to say that you don't see a lot of charcoal fires at roadside stalls in Port of Spain. But by and large, they are used to heat bubbling stockpots and fryers, not for direct grilling. One exception are the *chokas* enjoyed by the Indian community. A *choka* is a fire-roasted vegetable that is chopped and seasoned with oil.

The traditional vegetable for *choka* is eggplant, but you can also use tomatoes, potatoes, even pumpkin. *Choka* is customarily served with *sada roti* (flat bread)—often for breakfast. In this country, you can use pita bread or any of the grilled breads featured in this book. Here's a *choka* inspired by a stylish Port of Spain restaurant called Monsoon.

FOR THE CHOKA

- 2 smallish eggplants (10 to 12 ounces each)
- 6 cloves garlic, peeled and cut in half lengthwise
- 2 ripe medium-size tomatoes
- 1 medium-size green bell pepper
- 1 large onion, peeled and cut into quarters (leave the root ends intact)
- 1 tablespoon vegetable oil
- Salt and freshly ground black pepper

FOR THE SPICE MIXTURE

- 2 tablespoons vegetable oil
- 2 teaspoons mustard seeds, preferably black
- 1 medium-size onion, finely chopped
- 2 cloves garlic, minced
- 1 tablespoon finely chopped peeled fresh ginger
- ½ to 1 Scotch bonnet chile, seeded and minced
- 2 tablespoons fresh lime juice
- ¼ cup chopped fresh cilantro, for garnish

1. Prepare the *choka:* Using the tip of a paring knife, make 6 randomly placed slits around each eggplant. Insert a half clove of garlic in each slit. Lightly brush the eggplants, tomatoes, bell pepper, and onion quarters with the 1 tablespoon of oil and season with salt and black pepper to taste.

2. Set up the grill for direct grilling and preheat to high.

3. When ready to cook, brush and oil the grill grate. Arrange the eggplants, tomatoes, bell pepper, and onion quarters on the hot grate and grill, turning with tongs, until the skins are charred, about 20 minutes for the eggplant (the flesh should be very soft as well) and bell pepper and about 12 minutes for the tomatoes and onion quarters. Transfer the vegetables to a plate and let cool.

4. Scrape most of the charred skin off the vegetables. Cut the eggplant and tomatoes into 1-inch dice. Core, seed, and finely dice the bell pepper. Cut the root end off the onion quarters and thinly slice the onion crosswise. Transfer the vegetables to a shallow heatproof serving bowl and stir to mix, then season them with salt and black pepper to taste (see Note).

5. Just before serving, prepare the spice mixture: Heat the 2 tablespoons of oil in a small, heavy skillet over medium-high heat. Add the mustard seeds, chopped onion, minced garlic, ginger, and Scotch bonnet and cook until fragrant and golden brown, about 5 minutes. Add the lime juice, let come to a boil, then pour the hot spice mixture over the vegetables. Toss gently to mix, sprinkle the cilantro on top, and serve the vegetables warm or at room temperature.

NOTE: The recipe can be prepared to this point up to 2 days ahead of time. Keep, covered, in the refrigerator.

SPAIN

CATALAN GRILLED ARTICHOKES

DIRECT GRILLING
SERVES 8

La Tomaquera is a one-room chop house in a working-class neighborhood in Barcelona. It's the sort of place that takes pride in not serving Coca-Cola; the sort of place that closes early when there's a soccer game on TV. For about $30, you could eat yourself into oblivion in this lively restaurant. For me that meant feasting on snails in a rich gravy, followed by an assortment of grilled beef, lamb, and other meats.

What most captivated me was an unusual vegetable dish, grilled artichokes—one of the best things I have eaten in my life. The long, low-heat grilling process renders the leaves so crisp, you can almost eat them whole. I know of only one other dish with artichokes so delectably crisp—Rome's *carciofi alla giudia,* artichokes in the Jewish style.

For best results, choose medium-size artichokes, ones with leaves that are fairly spread open. You could also use baby artichokes, but if you do, cook them for a shorter amount of time. Avoid the dense jumbo globe artichokes, which are delicious boiled, but difficult to grill.

8 medium-size artichokes
½ lemon
1 cup (2 sticks) unsalted butter
6 cloves garlic, minced
¼ cup minced fresh flat-leaf parsley
Coarse salt (kosher or sea)
Lots of cracked or coarsely ground black pepper

1. Cut the stems off the artichokes so the artichokes stand upright. Rub the artichoke bottoms with the cut side of the lemon to prevent discoloring. Using kitchen shears, trim off the spiny tips of the leaves. Using your fingers, gently push the leaves apart to open the artichoke like a flower.

2. Melt the butter in a small, heavy saucepan over low heat, then add the garlic and parsley. Increase the heat to medium and let the butter mixture come to a simmer. Let simmer until the garlic loses its rawness, about 3 minutes. Brush the artichokes all over with a generous amount of the garlic butter and sprinkle them with salt and pepper. Pour a spoonful of the garlic butter over the top of each artichoke, letting it drip into the leaves.

3. Set up the grill for direct grilling and preheat to medium-low.

4. When ready to cook, brush and oil the grill grate. Arrange the artichokes on the hot grate, stem side down, and grill until the bottoms are a deep golden brown, about 30 minutes, rotating the artichokes frequently with tongs to ensure even cooking. Baste the artichokes often with the garlic butter and season them generously with salt and pepper.

5. Starting in the center and working with tongs, again spread the artichoke leaves out to open each artichoke like a flower. Baste the artichokes with more garlic butter and season them with more salt and pepper. Invert the artichokes and cook them until they are a deep golden brown, 30 to 40 minutes longer. The leaves should be crisp and should pull out easily; the heart should be tender (test it for doneness by inserting a skewer). If using a charcoal grill, you'll need to add 25 fresh coals after 1 hour.

6. Invert the artichokes (the artichoke bottoms will now be on the grate) and baste and season them again. Let the artichokes cook a few minutes longer to rewarm the bottoms. Drizzle any remaining garlic butter over the artichokes and serve at once.

JAMAICA

FIRE-ROASTED BREADFRUIT

DIRECT GRILLING (SEE NOTE)
SERVES 4 TO 6

Breadfruit was brought to the Caribbean from the South Pacific by the infamous Captain Bligh and has become one of the classic accompaniments to Jamaica's jerk pork. Some restaurants in Jamaica even have a special charcoal pit for roasting breadfruits, which are buried in the embers. Char roasting is one of the best ways to cook this large, round (think bowling ball), pebbly, and green-skinned fruit, the chief characteristic of which is its mild flavor (some people might say utter blandness)—perfect for taming the blast furnace heat of jerk pork.

Breadfruit may be fruit, botanically speaking, but it's usually served as a vegetable or starch. Charring imparts a smoky flavor that is readily absorbed by the starchy, white flesh. The most authentic way to cook it is on a charcoal grill, but you can also char it on a gas grill using either the direct or indirect method. Breadfruit can be found at West Indian markets and specialty greengrocers. Choose a firm, unblemished specimen and let it ripen at room temperature until it just begins to yield when pressed with your thumb. It should still be rather firm.

1 breadfruit (3 to 4 pounds)
4 tablespoons (½ stick) salted butter, for serving
Salt and freshly ground black pepper

1. *If using a charcoal grill,* build a nice bed of glowing embers. When ready to cook, nestle the breadfruit in the coals, raking them around the breadfruit to cover as much of it as possible.

If using a gas grill, preheat it to medium. When ready to cook, place the breadfruit on the hot grate.

2. Cook the breadfruit until the skin is charred and the flesh is very soft, 40 minutes to 1 hour, depending on the size and ripeness of the breadfruit. If using a gas grill, turn the breadfruit often with tongs. To test for doneness, insert a metal skewer; the breadfruit should be soft in the center.

3. To serve, cut or break the breadfruit into wedges and trim away the burnt part. Spread the butter over the breadfruit, season it with salt and pepper, and mash it with a fork.

NOTE: You can also grill the breadfruit on a gas grill using the indirect method; preheat the grill to medium-high. When ready to cook, place the breadfruit in the center of the grill, away from the heat, cover the grill, and cook the breadfruit until well browned on the outside and soft in the center, 1 to 1½ hours. (I prefer the direct method, because you actually char the skin of the breadfruit, but the indirect method requires less intervention.)

INDIA

TANDOORI CAULIFLOWER

INDIRECT GRILLING
SERVES 6 TO 8

When it comes to barbecue, few Westerners would think of cauliflower. Not so in India. There, *gobi* is appreciated for its ability to absorb smoke and spice flavors and maintain its firm texture. You'll need to know about two special ingredients for this recipe: *besan* (chickpea flour) and *ajwain* (carum seeds). Both are available at Indian markets, and chickpea flour can also be found at natural foods stores and many specialty food shops. If it's unavailable, whole-wheat flour makes an acceptable substitute. I've made the *ajwain* optional, as it's somewhat more difficult to find. The cauliflower will still be plenty flavorful without it.

ADVANCE PREPARATION

2 hours for marinating the cauliflower

SPECIAL EQUIPMENT

8 long metal skewers

INGREDIENTS

- 2 cups plain whole-milk yogurt (see Note)
- 1 whole cauliflower (about 1½ pounds)
- 3 cloves garlic, minced
- 1½ tablespoons grated peeled fresh ginger
- ¼ cup vegetable oil
- 1 tablespoon sweet paprika
- 1 teaspoon cayenne pepper
- 1 teaspoon salt
- ½ teaspoon freshly ground black pepper
- ½ teaspoon ajwain (optional)
- ½ teaspoon ground cumin
- 2 teaspoons fresh lemon juice
- ¾ cup chickpea flour (besan), or ¼ cup whole-wheat flour, or more as needed
- 3 tablespoons unsalted butter, melted, for brushing

1. Set a yogurt strainer, or a regular strainer lined with a double layer of dampened cheesecloth, over a medium-size bowl. Add the yogurt and let drain, in the refrigerator, for 4 hours. You should wind up with about 1¼ cups.

2. Cut the cauliflower into florets, leaving about 1 inch of stem on each floret. Prick each floret 8 to 10 times with a trussing needle or carving fork to allow the marinade to penetrate to the center.

3. Combine the garlic, ginger, and oil in a food processor or mini chopper and process to a smooth paste. Alternatively, you can pound the garlic and ginger to a paste in a mortar with a pestle, then work in the oil. Transfer the garlic paste to a large nonreactive bowl. Whisk in the paprika, cayenne, salt, black pepper, *ajwain* (if using), cumin, lemon juice, drained yogurt, and enough chickpea flour to make a smooth mixture. Stir in the cauliflower. Let the cauliflower marinate in the refrigerator, covered, for 2 hours.

4. Remove the cauliflower florets from the marinade, setting aside the marinade, and thread the florets through the stems onto the skewers. (The flower ends of the cauliflower should all be pointing up.)

5. Set up the grill for indirect grilling, place a drip pan in the center, and preheat the grill to high.

6. When ready to cook, spoon any remaining marinade over the cauliflower, arrange the skewers on the hot grate over the drip pan, and cover the grill. Grill the cauliflower for 10 minutes, then brush the florets with a little melted butter. Continue grilling the cauliflower until nicely browned and tender, 10 to 20 minutes longer. Move the skewers directly over the flames for the last 2 to 3 minutes to lightly brown the cauliflower.

7. Brush the cauliflower with the remaining butter and slide it off the skewers onto plates or a platter. Serve at once.

NOTE: If you prefer not to drain the yogurt, you will need only 1½ cups.

TRINIDAD

GRILLED CORN WITH SHADON BENI BUTTER

DIRECT GRILLING
SERVES 8

Despite the wide use of charcoal as a cooking fuel, Trinidadians aren't particularly keen on grilling. One exception is corn. Stroll through Queen's Park Savannah in Port of Spain at dusk and you'll find large crowds at the corn vendors lining up for crackling crisp ears of a mature variety of corn most Americans would consider too large, old, and dried out to eat. But it's these very defects that make the corn so munchable and delicious.

Traditionally, the cooked ears are brushed with melted butter and sprinkled with salt and pepper. Inspired by a popular Trinidadian herb, I've come up with a more interesting topping: *shadon beni* butter. *Shadon beni* (literally false cilantro) is a dark green, thumb-shaped, sawtooth-edged herb with a taste similar to cilantro. It's generally sold in North America by its Hispanic name, *culantro* (look for it in Hispanic and West Indian markets). But don't despair if you can't find *shadon beni:* cilantro makes an equally delicious butter. By the way, you can use *shadon beni* butter as a great topping for other simply grilled vegetables and seafood.

Grate Expectations: Some Tips on Grilling Vegetables

You know the scenario: You love grilled vegetables, but when you go to turn those mushrooms, scallions, and onion wedges sizzling away on the grill, they fall between the bars of the grate into the fire. There are a couple of ways to avoid this problem. Some savvy grill buffs use a vegetable grate—an auxiliary grate that goes on top of the main grill grate. Often made of porcelain- or nonstick-coated metal, the vegetable grate has numerous small holes that allow the flames and smoke flavor to reach the vegetables but keep those veggies from falling into the fire.

A variation on the vegetable grate is the vegetable basket, a hinged wire basket into which you can put loose mushrooms, cherry tomatoes, slices of summer squash and zucchini, and other small pieces of vegetables. Instead of trying to turn each piece on the grill grate, you simply invert the basket.

Vegetable grates and baskets are sold at cookware shops and by mail order. If you use one, you should preheat it on the regular grill grate for about five minutes before adding the vegetables.

Barbecue buffs are divided on whether or not to oil the grate—regular or vegetable—before grilling vegetables. Vegetables don't tend to stick to the bars of the grate as much as meats and seafood do (it's the proteins in the meats and seafood that do the sticking). But if you want the better grill marks that oiling the grate gives you, and if you feel it's better to be safe than sorry, go ahead and oil your grate right before grilling—after it has been preheated.

And please don't feel that you can't grill vegetables if you don't have a vegetable grate. I traveled the barbecue trail on five continents and only on one—North America—did I find cooks using vegetable grates.

8 ears of corn (the larger and older, the better)
8 tablespoons (1 stick) salted butter, at room temperature
3 tablespoons finely chopped fresh culantro or cilantro
2 scallions, both white and green parts, trimmed and minced
1 clove garlic, minced
Freshly ground black pepper

1. Shuck the corn and set it aside while you prepare the *shadon beni* butter.

2. Place the butter, *culantro,* scallions, and garlic in a food processor and process until smooth. Season the butter with pepper to taste and transfer it to a bowl. Alternatively, if the herbs and garlic are very finely minced, you can stir them right into the butter in a bowl.

3. Set up the grill for direct grilling and preheat to high.

4. When ready to cook, brush and oil the grill grate. Arrange the corn on the hot grate and grill, turning with tongs, until nicely browned all over, 8 to 12 minutes. As the corn cooks, brush it occasionally with the *shadon beni* butter.

5. Remove the corn from the grill and brush it once more with the *shadon beni* butter. Serve at once.

JAPAN

GRILLED EGGPLANTS WITH MISO "BARBECUE" SAUCE

DIRECT GRILLING
SERVES 6

Grilled eggplant might seem like an odd bar snack to Westerners, but it's a best seller in the teriyaki bars near the train stations in Tokyo. I like to think of it as a vegetarian hot dog. The "barbecue sauce" used to glaze the eggplants is a sweet-salty mix made from miso (cultured soy bean paste). White miso, the most common variety, can be found in the refrigerator case of natural foods stores and in many large supermarkets. For this recipe, the eggplant of choice would be a slim Asian variety. The advantage to a small eggplant is that it cooks quickly and can be eaten in a couple of bites. You can also serve the eggplants as a main course; they'll feed two to three people.

6 Asian eggplants (about 4 ounces each)
⅓ cup white miso
1 tablespoon sake
1 tablespoon mirin (sweet rice wine) or cream sherry
1 tablespoon sugar
1 tablespoon mayonnaise
1 tablespoon Asian (dark) sesame oil, for brushing
1 teaspoon black sesame seeds or toasted regular sesame seeds (see box, page 113)

1. Cut the eggplants in half lengthwise. Using a sharp knife, make shallow crisscrosses on the skin and cut sides of each half eggplant. The cuts should be about ⅛ inch deep and ⅛ inch apart.

2. Combine the miso, sake, mirin, sugar, and mayonnaise in a bowl and whisk until smooth.

3. Set up the grill for direct grilling and preheat to high.

4. When ready to cook, brush and oil the grill grate. Brush the eggplants on both sides with the sesame oil. Arrange the eggplants, cut side down, on the hot grate and grill until nicely browned, 3 to 4 minutes. Turn the eggplants with tongs and spread a generous spoonful of miso sauce over the cut side of each. Continue grilling the eggplants until the undersides are nicely browned and the flesh is soft, 6 to 8 minutes longer. To test for doneness, gently squeeze the sides of the eggplants; they should be softly yielding.

5. Transfer the eggplants to a serving platter, sprinkle the sesame seeds on top, and serve at once.

ARGENTINA

ARGENTINEAN GRILLED EGGPLANT

DIRECT GRILLING
SERVES 6

Argentineans don't generally dilute their staunchly carnivornian meals with superfluous side dishes or vegetables. However, grilled eggplant has become part of the steak house repertoire. The eggplant of choice is a small (four inch long) Italian variety—the sort you'd find in an Italian market or specialty food shop. Larger eggplants can be cooked this way, too.

3 small (4 to 6 ounces each) Italian eggplants
2 cloves garlic, minced
3 tablespoons extra-virgin olive oil
1 teaspoon dried oregano
1 teaspoon dried basil
1 teaspoon fresh thyme leaves, or ½ teaspoon dried thyme
1 teaspoon sweet or hot paprika
½ teaspoon hot red pepper flakes (optional)
Salt and freshly ground black pepper

1. Cut the eggplants crosswise into ½-inch slices. Mix the garlic and olive oil in a small bowl, then brush some of the garlic oil over the cut sides of the eggplants.

2. Combine the oregano, basil, thyme, paprika, and hot pepper flakes (if using) in a small bowl and set aside.

3. Set up the grill for direct grilling and preheat to high.

4. When ready to cook, brush and oil the grill grate. Arrange the eggplant slices on the hot grate and grill until nicely browned on the bottom, 3 to 5 minutes. Lightly brush the top of the eggplant slices with some of the garlic oil. Turn the eggplants with tongs and brush the other side with the remaining garlic oil.

5. Sprinkle the herb mixture over the eggplants and season them with salt and black pepper to taste. Continue cooking the eggplants on the second side until they are nicely browned and the flesh is soft, 3 to 5 minutes longer. Serve the eggplants at once.

ARGENTINEAN GRILLED EGGPLANT | AT LEFT

ITALY

GRILLED FENNEL

DIRECT GRILLING
SERVES 4

You've probably seen it in the produce section of the supermarket: the weird vegetable with the fern-like, feathery leaves, crisp green stalks, and bulbous, green-white bottom. The taste of fresh fennel might well be described as licorice-flavored celery. Grilling seems to bring out its sweetness. Add a sweet-sour balsamic vinegar marinade and you have a vegetable you're not likely to soon forget. It can be served at room temperature as an antipasto or hot as a vegetable side dish. The balsamic vinegar marinade doubles as the dressing.

ADVANCE PREPARATION

2 hours for marinating the fennel

INGREDIENTS

4 small or 2 large fennel bulbs (1½ to 2 pounds)
⅓ cup extra-virgin olive oil
⅓ cup balsamic vinegar
2 tablespoons honey
2 cloves garlic, minced
2 small shallots, minced
3 tablespoons chopped fresh tarragon or basil
Salt and freshly ground black pepper

1. Cut the stalks and outside leaves off the fennel. (Reserve the stalks for another use, such as the Fennel-Grilled Bass on page 307.) Cut each fennel bulb lengthwise into ½-inch-wide slices through the narrow side.

2. Place the olive oil, balsamic vinegar, honey, garlic, shallots, and tarragon in a large nonreactive bowl and whisk to mix. Add the sliced fennel and toss to coat thoroughly. Let the fennel marinate, covered, for 2 hours; it does not have to be refrigerated.

3. Set up the grill for direct grilling and preheat to high.

4. When ready to cook, brush and oil the grill grate. Remove the fennel slices from the marinade, setting aside the marinade. Place the fennel on the hot grate, and grill, turning with tongs, until just tender, 8 to 12 minutes in all, seasoning it with salt and pepper to taste.

5. Toss the grilled fennel with any remaining marinade and serve warm or at room temperature.

KOREA

GARLIC KEBABS

DIRECT GRILLING
SERVES 4 TO 8

These tiny kebabs traditionally accompany Korean grilled meats, like Korean Sesame-Grilled Beef (bool kogi; page 150). The grilling imparts a delicate charcoal flavor, while the foil covering prevents the garlic cloves from burning.

SPECIAL EQUIPMENT

8 large wooden toothpicks

INGREDIENTS

2 to 3 heads garlic (for 24 large cloves)
1 tablespoon Asian (dark) sesame oil
Salt and freshly ground black pepper

1. Break the heads of garlic into cloves. Peel each clove (see Note). Skewer the garlic cloves crosswise on toothpicks, 3 cloves to a toothpick. Brush the garlic cloves with the sesame oil and season them with salt and pepper to taste. Loosely wrap each kebab in aluminum foil.

2. Set up the grill for direct grilling and preheat to high.

3. When ready to cook, arrange the toothpicks of garlic on the hot grate and grill until the garlic is tender, about 5 minutes per side, turning with tongs to ensure even cooking. Remove the foil from the garlic a few minutes before the garlic is done grilling to allow it to brown lightly.

NOTE: To loosen the skin, gently flatten the cloves of garlic using the side of a cleaver or chef's knife. Or use a flexible tube-shaped garlic peeler.

CARIBBEAN

GRILLED LONG BEANS

DIRECT GRILLING
SERVES 4

Long beans (aka yard-long beans) are a traditional Chinese vegetable. Shaped like green beans but up to eighteen inches long, they found their way to the Caribbean via the Chinese indentured laborers who came to Trinidad in the mid-1800s. Long beans taste similar to green beans but are a little earthier. Perhaps the niftiest thing about them is that they are so long, you can tie them into decorative knots.

SPECIAL EQUIPMENT

Vegetable grate (optional)

INGREDIENTS

1 pound long beans or green beans
2 tablespoons Asian (dark) sesame oil
Salt and freshly ground black pepper
1 tablespoon sesame seeds, toasted (see box, page 113)

1. Bring a large pot of salted water to a boil and cook the long beans until crisp-tender, about 3 minutes. Rinse the beans under cold running water and drain well. Cut each long bean into an 8 to 9-inch length and tie each into a loose knot (see Note). Let the beans dry on paper towels.

2. Set up the grill for direct grilling and preheat to high.

3. When ready to cook, preheat a vegetable grate (if using) for 5 minutes, then brush and oil it or the grill grate. Brush the knotted beans with the sesame oil and season them with salt and pepper to taste. Arrange the beans on the hot grate and grill, turning with tongs, until nicely browned, 8 to 10 minutes in all.

4. Transfer the long beans to serving plates or a platter, sprinkle the sesame seeds on top, and serve at once.

NOTE: If using regular green beans, thread 4 or 5 crosswise on short bamboo skewers and use an aluminum foil shield when you grill them (see box, page 23). Young, slender green beans don't need to be parboiled.

KOREA

GRILLED MUSHROOM AND SCALLION KEBABS

DIRECT GRILLING
SERVES 4 TO 6

Mushrooms are the perfect vegetable for grilling. The high heat caramelizes the outside of the mushrooms, intensifying their flavor. The mushrooms' high water content keeps them moist. These virtues aren't lost on Koreans, who enjoy a wide variety of grilled mushroom dishes. These kebabs are vegetarian, but Koreans will often grill mushrooms with strips of chicken or beef.

ADVANCE PREPARATION

1 to 2 hours for marinating the kebabs

SPECIAL EQUIPMENT

12 long bamboo skewers (or as needed) and an aluminum foil shield (see box, page 23)

INGREDIENTS

12 ounces fresh shiitake or cremini mushrooms, stemmed, caps wiped clean with dampened paper towels
2 bunches large scallions, both white and green parts, trimmed
1 medium-size yellow bell pepper, cored, seeded, and cut into 1½ by ½-inch strips
¼ cup soy sauce
3 tablespoons sugar
1 tablespoon Asian (dark) sesame oil
4 cloves garlic, minced
2 tablespoons sesame seeds, toasted (see box, page 113)
½ teaspoon freshly ground black pepper

1. Cut each mushroom into ½-inch-thick slices. Cut the white part of the scallions into pieces the length of the mushroom strips (about 1½ inches long). Finely chop the scallion greens. Thread the mushroom strips onto skewers so they will lie flat on the grill, alternating them with scallion whites and bell pepper strips threaded onto the skewers the short way. Place the kebabs in a baking dish.

2. Whisk together the soy sauce, sugar, sesame oil, garlic, 1 tablespoon of sesame seeds, and the black pepper in a large bowl. Pour the soy sauce mixture over the kebabs and let marinate at room temperature for 1 to 2 hours, turning once.

3. Set up the grill for direct grilling and preheat to high.

4. When ready to cook, brush and oil the grill grate. Remove the kebabs from the marinade, setting aside the marinade. Arrange the kebabs on the hot grate with the aluminum foil shield under the ends of the skewers and grill, turning with tongs and brushing often with the marinade, until the mushrooms are tender and the scallions and bell pepper are nicely browned, 3 to 5 minutes per side (6 to 10 minutes in all).

5. Sprinkle the chopped scallion greens and remaining tablespoon of sesame seeds over the kebabs and serve them hot or at room temperature.

KOREA

SESAME-GRILLED OYSTER MUSHROOMS

DIRECT GRILLING
SERVES 4

Oyster mushrooms are elongated gray mushrooms that have something oysterlike about their slippery, softly chewy consistency. If you can't find them, you can substitute other exotic mushrooms or even quartered white mushrooms. This recipe was inspired by the Korea House in Seoul, where it was part of a *hanjongshik,* a dazzling array of more than two dozen different miniature dishes that comprise a traditional Korean table d'hôte.

SPECIAL EQUIPMENT

Vegetable grate, or 12 short bamboo skewers, and an aluminum foil shield (see box, page 23)

INGREDIENTS

1 pound oyster or medium-size white mushrooms
½ medium-size green bell pepper, cored and seeded
½ medium-size red bell pepper, cored and seeded
2 cloves garlic, minced
3 scallions, both white and green parts, trimmed and minced
3 tablespoons soy sauce
1½ tablespoons Asian (dark) sesame oil
1 tablespoon sugar
1 tablespoon sesame seeds, toasted (see box, page 113)
Salt and freshly ground black pepper

1. Trim the ends off the oyster mushrooms. Cut the bell pepper halves on the diagonal into thin slices.

2. Combine the garlic, scallions, soy sauce, sesame oil, sugar, and sesame seeds in a small bowl. Season the sesame oil mixture with salt to taste and plenty of black pepper and stir until the sugar dissolves. Add the mushrooms and bell peppers and toss to mix, then let marinate for 15 minutes. Then, if not using a vegetable grate, thread the mushrooms and bell peppers onto skewers.

3. Set up the grill for direct grilling and preheat to high.

4. When ready to cook, preheat a vegetable grate (if using) for 5 minutes, then brush and oil it or the grill grate. Arrange the mushrooms and bell peppers on the hot grate with the aluminum foil shield under the ends of the skewers. Grill, turning with tongs, until the vegetables are nicely browned and tender, 3 to 5 minutes per side (6 to 10 minutes in all).

5. Transfer the mushrooms and bell peppers to a serving platter, plates, or bowls. This dish can be served hot, cold, or at room temperature.

JAPAN

SHIITAKE AND SCALLION KEBABS

DIRECT GRILLING
SERVES 4 AS AN APPETIZER OR SIDE DISH

These colorful kebabs turn up at yakitori joints around Tokyo and make a terrific side dish or vegetarian appetizer. I love the way the flavor of the grilled scallions permeates the shiitakes. Fresh shiitakes are widely available, but you could also use dried Chinese black mushrooms (soaked in hot water for twenty minutes) or another type of mushroom.

SPECIAL EQUIPMENT

8 long bamboo skewers and an aluminum foil shield (see box, page 23)

INGREDIENTS

1 bunch large scallions, both white and green parts, trimmed
24 small fresh shiitakes, stemmed, caps wiped clean with dampened paper towels
3 tablespoons soy sauce
3 tablespoons mirin (sweet rice wine) or cream sherry
1 tablespoon sugar
1 clove garlic, minced

1. Cut the scallions crosswise into pieces the size of the mushroom caps, about 1½ inches long. Thread the shiitake caps onto the skewers so they will lie flat on the grill, alternating them with pieces of scallion, threaded on crosswise. Place 3 mushroom caps and 4 scallion pieces on each skewer. Reserve any leftover scallion pieces for another use.

2. Combine the soy sauce, mirin, sugar, and garlic in a small bowl and whisk until the sugar dissolves.

3. Set up the grill for direct grilling and preheat to high.

4. When ready to cook, brush and oil the grill grate. Arrange the kebabs on the hot grate with the aluminum foil shield under the ends of the skewers and grill, turning with tongs and brushing with the soy mixture, until the shiitakes are tender and the scallions are nicely browned, 3 to 5 minutes per side (6 to 10 in all). Serve at once.

SPAIN

CHORIZO GRILLED MUSHROOMS

INDIRECT GRILLING
SERVES 4 AS AN APPETIZER, 8 AS A SIDE DISH

Mushroom caps grilled with chorizo, garlic, and olive oil are a popular Spanish tapa—so popular, in fact, that there's a tapas bar in Madrid, the Mesón del Champiñón, that serves this and only this dish. The Mesón stands in a row of tapas bars—each with its own specialty—built directly into the retaining wall of the Plaza Mayor. It should be noted that the Mesón cooks its mushroom caps on a *plancha* (griddle), but grilling produces a more interesting flavor. It's also a lot more fun because you get to do it outdoors. This recipe can be served either as an appetizer or as a vegetable side dish.

SPECIAL EQUIPMENT

Vegetable grate (optional); toothpicks, for serving

INGREDIENTS

16 large white mushrooms, stemmed, caps wiped clean with dampened paper towels
⅓ cup extra-virgin olive oil, or more as needed
4 slices (each ¼ inch thick, 1 to 2 ounces total) cooked chorizo sausage (see Note)
4 cloves garlic, minced
¼ cup chopped flat-leaf parsley
½ lemon
Salt and freshly ground black pepper

1. Generously brush the mushrooms on both sides with some of the olive oil and place the mushrooms in a baking dish, rounded side down.

2. Cut each chorizo slice in quarters and place one quarter in each mushroom cap. Divide the garlic and parsley among the mushroom caps. Squeeze a little lemon juice into each mushroom cap and drizzle any remaining olive oil over them. Generously season the mushrooms with salt and pepper.

3. Set up the grill for indirect cooking, place a drip pan in the center, and preheat the grill to high.

4. When ready to cook, preheat a vegetable grate (if using) for 5 minutes. Arrange the chorizo-stuffed mushrooms in the center of the hot grate, away from the heat, and cover the grill. Cook the mushrooms until tender and nicely browned and the sausage and garlic are sizzling, about 20 minutes. For a smokier flavor, move the mushroom caps directly over the flames for the last 5 minutes of grilling.

5. Transfer the grilled mushrooms to a platter and stick a toothpick in each for serving.

NOTE: Chorizo is a spicy Spanish sausage. I've also prepared these mushroom caps with country ham instead of chorizo. You'd need about 2 ounces of ham cut into tiny slivers.

The Japanese Grill

To most people, Japanese food means sushi, sashimi, sukiyaki, or soba noodles. But Japan has a venerable tradition of grilling. Actually, two traditions of grilling exist there: an haute cuisine style called *robatayaki* and a more populist style called yakitori. This became clear on a trip to a country that happens to be especially dear to me: I was born in Nagoya, Japan.

In the course of my grill hopping in Japan, I savored delicate *dengaku* (tofu grilled on "stilts") at a tranquil tea house on the Philosopher's Walk in Kyoto. I munched crisp barbecued rice cakes brushed with mouth-puckeringly tart plum paste from street vendors outside Tokyo's venerated Sensoji Temple. I ate chicken teriyaki and miso-glazed eggplants in the rough and tumble yakitori joints under the train station near the neon-lit Ginza. But my ultimate experience in Japanese grilling was dinner at Tokyo's Inakaya.

Unassuming from the outside, the restaurant occupies a post-war high-rise in the fashionable Rapongi district. You pass by a bowl of salt (a symbol of hospitality) and a bamboo vase filled with peach blossoms on your way to a dining experience quite unlike anything in North America.

Very Welcomed Guests

The moment my wife, Barbara, and I entered, a waiter in a blue and white robe shouted out our arrival. His coworkers repeated the announcement in voices that could have roused the dead. We took our seats amid more shouting ("the customer is sitting down," "the customer is ordering") at a U-shaped bar surrounding a dazzling marketlike array of ingredients. There were wicker baskets filled with vegetables (okra, shiitakes, leeks, yams, and baby taro roots to name a few); glistening blocks of ice piled with whole fish, giant prawns, and monstrously large king crab claws; trays of pork, chicken, and marbled Kobe beef. I tried to enumerate the individual items displayed here, but lost count after forty.

Kneeling on a platform overlooking all this bounty was a chef wearing a blue and white bandana around his head. We ordered sake. There was another round of shouting and then the chef thrust a ten-foot-long wooden paddle at us with a bowl in a small wooden box at the end. A waiter appeared with a flask and proceeded to fill the bowl with sake, spilling the wine into the shallow box underneath. Generosity is the name of the game at Inakaya, and for the next two hours we were treated to a largesse that bordered on conspicuous consumption.

Appetizers arrived without our ordering them: a plate of sashimi, a small carrot and *kampyo* (gourd) salad, a cold kebab of Kobe beef, the world's most expensive meat (the cows are raised on beer and grain and their meat is rich and tender). We don't speak Japanese, so we pointed to the various ingredients displayed on the U-shaped counter in front of the chef and the real meal—the *robatayaki*—began.

Robatayaki takes its name from the Japanese words *ro* and *yaki*. *Ro* refers to a square hearth around which peasants would gather for warmth and cooking. *Yaki* means grilled, and in the old days the grilling would have been done over charcoal. Many yakitori parlors still grill this way, but Inakaya takes a more high-tech approach, cooking the food over infrared gas grills that are tiny by American standards. Our entire dinner was cooked on a grill not much longer than my forearm and not much wider than the palm of my hand.

In rapid succession we were served tiny kebabs of grilled asparagus, shiitake mushroom caps, even okra (the okra was downright amazing grilled). Nothing is too weird for a *robatayaki* chef: baby yams, quail eggs, even ginko nuts, which taste like waxy potatoes. The shouting went unabated, the paddle delivered an endless succession of treats. We wanted to continue like this for the rest of the evening, which is exactly what we did.

The most remarkable aspect of *robatayaki*—even beyond the noisy theatrics and belt-loosening generosity—is perhaps the utter simplicity of the preparation. Sure, there's a brushing of teriyaki sauce here, a dollop of miso sauce there, and a drizzle of melted butter. But most of the fare is seasoned solely with salt. The flavors are direct and natural, but from these simple seasonings the chef creates a symphonic range of flavors. The tallest soufflé, the richest French pastry, couldn't rival the simple, unadorned slice of exquisitely ripe melon Inakaya serves for dessert.

Given the meticulousness of Japanese cooking, the precise, almost painterly plate presentations, it's easy to lose sight of the joyful aspect of Japanese cuisine. Yet *joyful* and *festive* are the operative words at Inakaya, not to mention at virtually every place we dined in Japan. You might expect such refined food to be eaten in sacerdotal silence. But Japanese epicures drink hard and party heartily—especially when partaking of their favorite foods.

Happy Hour, Japanese-Style

This is especially true at the yakitori joints one finds in or under virtually all of the train stations in Tokyo. The yakitori parlor is a uniquely Japanese institution: part pub, part barbecue joint, to which Japanese office workers (aka "salary men") flock after work for a snack, a cigarette, a couple of beers, and some earsplitting conversation before embarking on the long commute home by train.

Yakitori parlors aren't big (some have only a half dozen seats) and certainly aren't fancy. For example, one of the most infamous yakitori parlors in Tokyo, Tonton, doesn't even have four walls. But to come to Japan without visiting a yakitori parlor would be missing an important cultural experience.

Yakitori takes its name from the Japanese words for grilled (*yaki*) and chicken (*tori*). Unlike upscale grill restaurants, like Inakaya, yakitori parlors still use charcoal grills—often a troughlike brazier mounted on legs in the front of the restaurant. The traditional charcoal is *bincho,* made from the slow-burning holm oak in the Wakayama Prefecture near Kyoto.

According to some authorities, yakitori (or at least the practice of grilling) originated with the Dutch traders who settled in Nagasaki. Indeed, one popular Tokyo yakitori chain goes by the name Nanbantei, which translates as Restaurant of the Southern Barbarians, what the Japanese called the early European traders.

As for the *tori* (chicken), most yakitori parlors offer an impressive selection of different cuts. There are *momo yaki* (chicken legs—preferred to breast meat because they have more fat and flavor), shiitake *toriyaki* (chicken and mushroom kebabs), *negi toriyaki* (chicken and leek kebabs), and *tsukune yaki* (chicken meatballs). Adventurous eaters can move on to *kawa yaki* (grilled chicken skin), *hatsu yaki* (chicken hearts), *bonchiri yaki* ("pope's noses"), and *uzura yaki* (grilled embryonic chicken eggs). Nor are vegetarians neglected: Just order some *nasu yaki* (grilled eggplant brushed with miso glaze), *piiman yaki* (tiny grilled peppers), or *ginnan yaki* (grilled ginkgo nuts).

Not bad for a restaurant that in most incarnations occupies less space than your bedroom! You pay by the skewer, which makes yakitori relatively inexpensive. (This is one of the few dining experiences you will have in Tokyo that leaves you change from a 2,000 yen note—about $19.) The traditional beverage at a yakitori parlor is beer.

In the West (particularly in North and South America), the quality of a barbecue is measured in part by how many notches it forces you to loosen your belt. You'd certainly never call it health food. How different Japanese grilling is. Whether at a *robatayaki* restaurant or at a humble yakitori joint, meats are used almost as a condiment. Sauces tend to be based on broths, not oils, eggs, or other fats. The portions are moderate, even modest, with most items being served in bite-size pieces. Small is beautiful in Japan. The food, at least, speaks to you in whispers, not shouts.

For me this sense of moderation is the most important lesson Western grill buffs can learn from Japan. That, and to keep shouting and have fun.

U.S.A.

MUSHROOM CAPS WITH ARUGULA BUTTER

INDIRECT GRILLING
SERVES 8 AS AN APPETIZER, 4 AS A MAIN COURSE

Stuffed mushrooms was one of the first dishes I ever learned to make and I'm still fascinated by the fungus's ability to absorb the flavors of a filling while retaining its own. I like to make this dish with jumbo mushroom caps, behemoths measuring three inches across that seem custom grown for stuffing. I fill them with arugula butter and cook them on the grill using the indirect method. Amazing.

SPECIAL EQUIPMENT

Vegetable grate (optional)

INGREDIENTS

1 bunch arugula, stemmed, rinsed, spun dry, and coarsely chopped
1 clove garlic, minced
8 tablespoons (1 stick) unsalted butter, at room temperature
A few drops of fresh lemon juice
Salt and freshly ground black pepper
8 jumbo or 16 large white mushrooms, stemmed, caps wiped clean with dampened paper towels
¼ cup freshly grated Parmesan cheese

1. Finely chop the arugula and garlic in a food processor. Add the butter and lemon juice, season with salt and pepper to taste, and process until smooth. Spread the arugula butter in the mushroom caps and sprinkle the Parmesan cheese on top.

2. Set up the grill for indirect cooking, place a drip pan in the center, and preheat the grill to high.

3. When ready to cook, preheat a vegetable grate (if using) for 5 minutes, then brush and oil it or the grill grate. Arrange the mushrooms in the center of the hot grate, away from the heat, and cover the grill. Cook the mushrooms until browned and tender and the butter is melted and sizzling, about 20 minutes. For a smokier flavor, move the mushroom caps directly over the flames for the last 5 minutes of grilling. Serve the mushrooms at once.

Black Gold

Back in the nineteenth century, when you could buy a black truffle without having to take out a second mortgage, the French would cook truffles in the coals the same way as described in the recipe for onions and potatoes on page 418. Should you win the lottery, this is a wonderfully extravagant way to enjoy the odoriferous black fungus. You'd need fifteen to twenty minutes' cooking time for a two-inch truffle.

JAPAN

SESAME-GRILLED OKRA

DIRECT GRILLING
SERVES 4

Okra is the vegetable people love to hate. What they dislike is its tendency to get slimy, especially when boiled or stewed. Others, like me, are drawn to its crunch—when not overcooked—and sweet, earthy flavor. I discovered grilled okra in Tokyo, where it's part of the stunning array of grilled vegetables, meats, and seafood served at *robatayaki* restaurants (which specialize in Japanese grilling). For a Mediterranean touch, use olive oil instead of sesame oil.

SPECIAL EQUIPMENT

8 short bamboo skewers and an aluminum foil shield (see box, page 23)

INGREDIENTS

1 pound fresh okra (see Note)
1 tablespoon Asian (dark) sesame oil or extra-virgin olive oil
Salt and freshly ground black pepper

1. Trim the tips off the stems of the okra, but do not cut into the pods; this would expose the insides to air, making the okra slimy. Arrange 4 or 5 okra side by side in a neat row at the edge of a cutting board. Stick a bamboo skewer through each end of each okra, skewering group of 4 or 5 okra with 2 skewers. The idea is to make a sort of raft that holds the okra flat for grilling. Transfer the skewered okra to a platter. Lightly brush both sides of the okra with sesame oil and season them with salt and pepper to taste.

2. Set up the grill for direct grilling and preheat to high.

3. When ready to cook, brush and oil the grill grate. Arrange the skewered okra on the hot grate with the aluminum foil shield under the ends of the skewers and grill, turning with a flat spatula, until tender and lightly browned, about 4 to 5 minutes per side (8 to 10 minutes in all). Serve the okra at once, letting everyone remove the skewers themselves.

NOTE: When buying okra, choose smallish pods of uniform size. They should be about the length and width of your forefinger. Look for crisp, springy, bright green pods, avoiding okra that look brown or shriveled.

SPAIN

GREEN ONIONS ROMESCO

CALÇOTS

DIRECT GRILLING
SERVES 4

Succulent, tender *calçots* (pronounced CAL-sots) are Catalan green onions—and what onions. The sweet, fleshy shoots are buried with earth as they grow (much like Belgian endives) to keep them pale and delicately flavored. The *calçots* are charred over burning vine trimmings, then wrapped in newspaper to steam and finish cooking. Every January, when *calçots* are harvested, huge *calçadas* (onion feasts) take place throughout Catalonia. Traditionally, the onions are dipped in an almond and roasted tomato sauce called *romesco* and messily devoured by hand. But, you can also enjoy them with olive oil, salt, and pepper.

This recipe can be prepared with green onions or large scallions. I particularly like using green Vidalia onions, which are available from December to April from Bland Farms.

INGREDIENTS

- **2 bunches green onions, or 4 bunches large scallions, both white and green parts, trimmed**
- **Coarse salt (kosher or sea)**
- **Romesco Sauce, for serving (optional; page 472)**
- **Spanish extra-virgin olive oil (optional), for serving**
- **Freshly ground black pepper (optional), for serving**

1. Set up the grill for direct grilling and preheat to high.

2. When ready to cook, brush and oil the grill grate. Arrange the onions on the hot grate and grill, turning with tongs, until charred all over, 8 to 12 minutes (scallions will take less time than green onions). Season the onions with plenty of salt as they cook. When done, wrap the charred onions in a thick layer of paper towels (or use newspaper as they do in Spain) and let them rest for 15 minutes.

3. Unwrap the onions and pick away the charred skin with your fingers. Serve the onions warm with Romesco Sauce for dipping or drizzle olive oil on top, season them with pepper, and pop them into your mouth.

ITALY

MARINATED GRILLED PEPPERS

WITH OLIVES AND ANCHOVIES

DIRECT GRILLING
SERVES 4

Like most Italian grilled dishes, this one is simple. Good results depend on the quality of the raw ingredients, rather than on complex marinades or lots of ingredients. You can use any type of bell pepper or even a kaleidoscopic mixture of red, green, yellow, and purple peppers. I first tasted the dish made solely with red bell peppers and that's how I prefer it. For a more rustic dish, leave the pepper skins on as I do here. For a more refined dish, grill the peppers whole and peel them as described in the box about grilling vegetables on page 396.

SPECIAL EQUIPMENT

Vegetable grate (optional)

INGREDIENTS

4 red bell peppers
¼ cup extra-virgin olive oil
Coarse salt (kosher or sea) and freshly ground black pepper
2 to 4 oil-packed anchovy fillets, drained and cut into ¼-inch pieces
2 tablespoons drained capers
4 fresh basil leaves, thinly slivered
¼ cup niçoise or other oil-cured black olives
1 tablespoon balsamic vinegar, or more to taste

1. Cut the bell peppers in half, then stem and seed them. Cut each half lengthwise into 2 pieces. Toss the bell pepper pieces with 1 tablespoon of the olive oil and season them with salt and pepper to taste.

2. Set up the grill for direct grilling and preheat to high.

3. When ready to cook, preheat a vegetable grate (if using) for 5 minutes, then brush and oil it or the grill grate. Arrange the peppers on the hot grate and grill, turning with tongs, until blistered and nicely browned all over, 3 to 5 minutes per side (6 to 10 minutes in all). Transfer the grilled bell peppers to a cutting board and let cool. Cut each bell pepper piece into ½-inch-wide strips and place the strips in a shallow serving bowl.

4. Add the anchovies, capers, basil leaves, olives, balsamic vinegar, and remaining 3 tablespoons of olive oil to the bowl with the peppers and stir to combine. Let the bell peppers marinate for at least 15 minutes or as long as 2 hours before serving.

CARIBBEAN

GRILLED PLANTAINS

DIRECT GRILLING
SERVES 4

The plantain is a jumbo cousin of the banana. It's always served cooked, usually as a starch or vegetable. A green plantain tastes bland like a potato. When ripe (the skin will be black), plantains become as sweet as a ripe banana. Both green and ripe plantains can be grilled, but I prefer the ripe ones: The fire caramelizes the sugars in the plantains and makes them candy sweet. Grilling the plantain pieces in their skins keeps them moist and tender.

4 very ripe (black) plantains (see Note), unpeeled

1. Cut 1 inch off each end of the plantains, then cut each plantain crosswise sharply on the diagonal into 2-inch pieces.

2. Set up the grill for direct grilling and preheat to high.

3. When ready to cook, place the plantains on the hot grate and grill, turning often with tongs, until the skins are charred, the exposed ends are nicely caramelized, and the flesh in the center is soft. This will take 12 to 15 minutes. To test for softness, press the plantains with your finger.

4. Serve the grilled plantains in the skins. Cut off the skin before eating.

NOTE: If you live in an area with a large Hispanic community, you may be able to buy ripe plantains. Otherwise, let green ones ripen at room temperature until their skins are black (this can take up to a week).

TWO FOIL-GRILLED POTATOES

INDIRECT GRILLING

The inspirations for the following similarly prepared potatoes—both great—couldn't hail from two more disparate sources. When my wife, Barbara, was a young girl, she and her bunkmates at summer camp would prepare a campfire dish called potatoes à la ketchup. Sliced potatoes were tossed with ketchup and butter and grilled in a foil bundle on the fire. Eaten steamy hot, they were camp comfort food at its best. Years later, in quite a different setting, we had another foil-grilled potato dish—this one flavored with sesame seeds and soy sauce—at a Japanese steak house at the Sahid Jaya hotel in Jakarta.

U.S.A.

POTATOES A LA KETCHUP

SERVES 4

Yukon Gold potatoes were not available when Barbara was a kid, but we love their buttery flavor when we make this dish today.

SPECIAL EQUIPMENT

Heavy-duty aluminum foil

INGREDIENTS

2 tablespoons ketchup
1 tablespoon Worcestershire sauce
1 tablespoon fresh lemon juice
4 tablespoons (½ stick) unsalted butter, at room temperature
4 medium-size potatoes (each about 6 ounces), cut into ¼-inch slices
1 small onion, thinly sliced
Salt and freshly ground black pepper

1. Mix the ketchup, Worcestershire sauce, and lemon juice in a small nonreactive bowl and set aside.

2. Cut 4 pieces of heavy-duty aluminum foil, each 14 by 8 inches. Place a piece of foil, shiny side down and narrow edge toward you, on a work surface. Smear a tablespoon of the butter in the center of the bottom half of the foil rectangle (the half closest to you). Arrange one quarter of the potatoes in a mound on top of the butter. Place one quarter of the onion on top of the potatoes. Spoon 1 tablespoon of the ketchup mixture over the potatoes and season them with salt and pepper to taste. Fold the top half of the foil over the potatoes and bring the top and bottom edges together. Fold the edges over several times to make a tight seal. Prepare packages of the remaining potatoes the same way.

3. Set up the grill for indirect grilling and preheat to medium-high. No drip pan is necessary for this recipe.

4. When ready to cook, place the foil packages in the center of the hot grate, away from the heat, and cover the grill. Cook the packages until dramatically puffed, 20 to 30 minutes. Carefully open a package to check the potato for doneness.

5. Serve the potatoes in the foil packages, warning everyone to open the packages at arm's length, using knives and forks, as the escaping steam will be very hot.

INDONESIA

FOIL-GRILLED POTATOES WITH ASIAN SEASONINGS

SERVES 4

Most Westerners don't associate potatoes with such Asian seasonings as ginger and soy sauce, but the combination is really quite pleasing.

SPECIAL EQUIPMENT

Heavy-duty aluminum foil

INGREDIENTS

2 tablespoons soy sauce
2 tablespoons sesame seeds, toasted (see box, page 113)
1 clove garlic, thinly sliced
2 scallions, both white and green parts, trimmed and finely chopped
4 tablespoons (½ stick) unsalted butter, at room temperature
4 medium-size potatoes (each about 6 ounces), cut into ¼-inch slices
Salt and freshly ground black pepper

1. Place the soy sauce, sesame seeds, garlic, and scallions in a small bowl and stir to mix.

2. Cut 4 pieces of heavy-duty aluminum foil, each 14 by 8 inches. Place a piece of foil, shiny side down and narrow edge toward you, on a work surface. Smear a tablespoon of the butter in the center of the bottom half of the foil rectangle (the half closest to you). Arrange one quarter of the potatoes in a mound on top of the butter. Spoon one quarter of the soy sauce mixture over the potatoes and season them with salt and pepper to taste. Fold the top half of the foil over the potatoes and bring the top and bottom edges together. Fold the edges over several times to make a tight seal. Prepare packages of the remaining potatoes the same way.

3. Set up the grill for indirect grilling and preheat it to medium-high. No drip pan is necessary for this recipe.

4. When ready to cook, place the foil packages in the center of the hot grate, away from the heat, and cover the grill. Cook the packages until they are dramatically puffed, 20 to 30 minutes. Carefully open a package to check the potato for doneness.

5. Serve the potatoes in the foil packages, warning everyone to open the packages at arm's length, using knives and forks, as the escaping steam will be very hot.

EUROPE

ONIONS AND POTATOES ROASTED IN THE COALS

GRILLING IN THE EMBERS
SERVES 4

This is the most basic, primal way to cook root vegetables—a method as old as mankind itself. The process is simple enough: You bury the vegetables in a mound of glowing coals. The exterior burns, imparting a wonderful smoke flavor, leaving the flesh inside sweet and tender. Sweet onions like Vidalias or Walla Wallas are particularly good cooked this way, as are rich-fleshed potatoes, like Yukon Golds.

FOR ROASTING

4 large baking potatoes, unpeeled
4 large sweet onions, in their skins

FOR SERVING

Balsamic vinegar
Extra-virgin olive oil
Coarse salt (kosher or sea) and freshly ground black pepper
Unsalted butter
Sour cream

1. Set up a charcoal grill for direct grilling and preheat to high.

2. When ready to cook, rake half of the coals to one side of the grill. Arrange the potatoes and onions on top of the remaining coals, with the potatoes together in one spot and the onions in another (they cook at different rates and this allows you to remove each when done). Using tongs, place the reserved coals on top of the potatoes and onions.

3. Grill the potatoes and onions until very soft, 40 minutes to 1 hour for the potatoes, 20 to 30 minutes for the onions. To test for doneness, poke a skewer into the center of each. It should slip in very easily. Remove the potatoes and onions from the coals with tongs. Brush away the ashes with a pastry brush and place the potatoes and onions on a serving platter.

4. To eat, cut open the potatoes and onions and eat the flesh out of the skins (the skins of the potatoes will be too ashy to eat). Sprinkle the onions with a few drops of balsamic vinegar and olive oil and some salt and pepper (if desired; the onions are pretty darn good by themselves). Eat the potatoes with butter and/or sour cream and salt and pepper.

PERU

ANDEAN POTATO MIXED GRILL

DIRECT GRILLING
SERVES 4 TO 6

Where did the universally popular potato originate? There are numerous theories, but the evidence seems to point to Peru. This mountainous country in northern South America is the home of such distinctive potatoes as the purple potato and the *camote* (a type of sweet potato, but not as sweet as those in the U.S.). In fact, more different types of potatoes probably grow in Peru than in any other country in the world. The following recipe uses a variety of Peruvian potatoes, which are available at specialty food shops and greengrocers. The purple potato tastes similar to the North American boiling potato. The *camote* has a mild, nutty, semisweet flavor reminiscent of roasted chestnuts. (The Yukon Gold variety isn't strictly traditional, but it sure tastes good.)

SPECIAL EQUIPMENT

Vegetable grate (optional)

INGREDIENTS

2 pounds mixed potatoes, including purple potatoes, camotes or sweet potatoes, boniatos (Caribbean sweet potatoes), and/or Yukon Gold potatoes, scrubbed but unpeeled
4 tablespoons (½ stick) unsalted butter, or ¼ cup extra-virgin olive oil
2 cloves garlic, minced
2 tablespoons chopped fresh flat-leaf parsley
Salt and freshly ground black pepper

1. Place the potatoes in a large pot and add cold water to cover. Bring to a boil over medium heat and cook, uncovered, until tender, about 10 minutes for small potatoes, 20 to 30 minutes for large. Drain the potatoes, then rinse them under cold running water to stop the cooking. Peel the potatoes with a paring knife and cut them lengthwise into ½-inch-thick slices.

2. Melt the butter, with the garlic and parsley, in a saucepan over high heat. Bring the butter to a sizzle but do not let the garlic brown. Remove the pan from the heat.

3. Set up the grill for direct grilling and preheat to high.

4. When ready to cook, preheat a vegetable grate (if using) for 5 minutes, then brush and oil it or the grill grate. Brush the potato slices with the butter mixture and arrange them on the hot grate. Grill the potatoes, turning with tongs, until golden brown on both sides, 2 to 3 minutes per side. Season the potatoes with salt and pepper as they cook. Serve at once.

GREECE

GREEK GARLIC AND LEMON ROASTED POTATOES

INDIRECT GRILLING
SERVES 6 TO 8

These potatoes are a traditional accompaniment to Greek spit-roasted lamb (page 206). Lemon is one of the dominating flavors, and although North Americans don't usually associate it with potatoes, I must say it adds a whole new dimension. For extra richness, stir a few tablespoons of butter into the potatoes at the end.

SPECIAL EQUIPMENT

1 cup wood chips, soaked for 1 hour in cold water to cover and drained

INGREDIENTS

3 pounds small red potatoes, scrubbed and cut in half
¼ cup extra-virgin olive oil
4 cloves garlic, coarsely chopped
2 bay leaves
1 teaspoon dried oregano
Coarse salt (kosher or sea) and freshly ground black pepper
1 lemon, cut in half
2 tablespoons unsalted butter (optional)
2 tablespoons chopped fresh dill

1. Place the potatoes in a roasting pan, toss them with the olive oil, garlic, bay leaves, and oregano, and season them with salt and pepper to taste. Squeeze lemon juice over the potatoes, then place the lemon rind halves on top, with the cut side up.

2. Set up the grill for indirect cooking. No drip pan is necessary for this recipe.

If using a gas grill, place the wood chips in the smoker box and preheat the grill to high; when smoke appears, reduce the heat to medium.

If using a charcoal grill, preheat it to medium.

3. When ready to cook, if using a charcoal grill, toss the wood chips on the coals. Set the roasting pan in the center of the grill and cover the grill. Cook the potatoes until browned and tender, 1 to 1¼ hours, stirring them from time to time to ensure even cooking. Stir in the butter (if using) and dill during the last 15 minutes of cooking.

4. To serve, remove and discard the lemon rinds and bay leaves from the potatoes. Taste for seasoning, adding more salt and/or pepper as necessary, and serve.

CARIBBEAN

WEST INDIAN PUMPKIN GRATIN

INDIRECT GRILLING
SERVES 6 TO 8

This recipe is one of my favorite ways to prepare pumpkin. It is especially good served with Jerk Pork Tenderloin (page 182), Buccaneer Chicken (page 265), or Bahamian Grilled Chicken (page 260). It does require using your grill twice, however: first to cook the pumpkin, then to grill the gratin. For this reason, you may wish to prepare the pumpkin on the weekend (when you have plenty of time) and grill the gratin just before serving. This has an added benefit. If bad weather should prevent you from grilling the following day, you can always finish the gratin in the oven. I guarantee the extra grilling is worth the effort—this is one of the tastiest gratins ever.

The traditional pumpkin for this recipe is calabaza, a dense, heavy, dark orange squash with an intense pumpkin flavor. Calabaza is sold in halves or pieces. The closest North American squash would be a butternut.

1 piece (about 2 pounds) calabaza, or 2 medium-size butternut squash
2 cloves garlic
3 tablespoons unsalted butter, chilled, cut into ¼-inch pieces, plus additional butter for greasing the gratin dish
1 cup heavy (whipping) cream
Salt and freshly ground black pepper
Freshly grated nutmeg
1 cup freshly grated Parmesan cheese
3 tablespoons fresh bread crumbs, toasted (see box, page 113)

1. Scoop the seeds out of the calabaza or cut the butternut squash in half and remove the seeds. Wrap the squash loosely in aluminum foil.

2. Set up the grill for indirect grilling and preheat it to medium. No drip pan is necessary for this recipe.

3. When ready to cook, place the squash in the center of the hot grate, away from the heat, and cover the grill. Cook the squash until it is very tender, about 1 hour. Remove the squash, open the foil (being careful to avoid the escaping steam), and let the squash cool to room temperature. Leave the grill burning. (If you are cooking the gratin the next day, you'll have to set up the grill for indirect grilling again and preheat to high.)

4. Trim the skin off the squash and then cut the flesh into ¼-inch-thick slices. Mince one of the garlic cloves and set it aside. Cut the remaining garlic clove in half and rub a 10-inch flame proof gratin dish with it; lightly butter the dish. Arrange one fourth of the squash in a layer in the bottom of the dish. Pour ⅓ cup of the cream on top and sprinkle it with salt, pepper, nutmeg, one third of the minced garlic, ⅓ cup of the Parmesan cheese, and some of the pieces of butter. Arrange another layer of squash on top and pour ⅓ cup of cream over it. Top this with salt, pepper, nutmeg, half the garlic, ⅓ cup of the Parmesan cheese, and some butter. Repeat in this fashion to make another complete layer of squash (save a little butter for the top). Arrange the remaining squash on top, sprinkle the bread crumbs over it, and dot it with the remaining butter. The recipe can be prepared ahead to this stage. If making ahead, cover it loosely with plastic wrap and refrigerate until ready to grill, up to 48 hours.

5. If you are making and serving the gratin on the same day, you'll need to increase the heat to high. If you are using a charcoal grill, you'll need to add 10 to 12 fresh coals to each side.

6. When ready to cook, place the gratin in the center of the hot grate, away from the heat, and cover the grill. Cook the gratin until it is bubbling, crusty, and brown, 20 to 30 minutes. Serve at once.

KOREA

GRILLED SWEET POTATOES WITH SESAME DIPPING SAUCE

DIRECT GRILLING
SERVES 4

Grilled sweet potatoes are a popular Korean street food. I first tasted this snack at the Tongdaemun Market in Seoul, where it offered a double dose of pleasure. The first was gustatory—the unexpected contrast between the sweetness of the potato and the sesame saltiness of the dipping sauce. The second pleasure was purely tactile: The potato has a wonderful way of warming your hands in Korea's frigid winter air. Sweet potatoes were brought to Korea from Japan in the eighteenth century as a famine-prevention food, and there's nothing quite as satisfying to eat when you're strolling through the market. If you're used to the butter/brown sugar approach to sweet potatoes, this preparation will come as a revelation.

4 medium-size sweet potatoes (each 4 to 5 inches long and about 1½ inches wide)
5 tablespoons soy sauce
5 tablespoons sake or dry sherry
2 tablespoons sugar
2 scallions, both white and green parts, trimmed and minced
2 cloves garlic, minced
2 tablespoons sesame seeds, toasted (see box, page 113)

1. Scrub the sweet potatoes and blot them dry with paper towels.

2. Set up the grill for direct grilling and preheat to medium-high.

3. When ready to cook, brush and oil the grill grate. Place the sweet potatoes on the hot grate and grill, turning often with tongs, until very well browned and squeezably soft, 30 to 40 minutes.

4. Meanwhile, make the sauce. Combine the soy sauce, sake, sugar, scallions, garlic, and sesame seeds in a small bowl and whisk until blended and the sugar dissolves. Spoon the sauce into 4 small bowls or ramekins.

5. Serve the sweet potatoes with the bowls of sauce. To eat out of hand, simply dip the potatoes in the sauce. To serve the sweet potatoes as a side dish, cut them open and spoon the sauce over them.

CENTRAL ASIA

GRILLED DILLED TOMATOES

DIRECT GRILLING
SERVES 4

Grilled tomatoes accompany kebabs throughout Central Asia, from Iraq to the Republic of Georgia. Use smallish tomatoes (two and a half to three inches across) that are firm but ripe. Flat metal skewers work the best for holding the tomatoes, which would slip off a skinny metal skewer.

SPECIAL EQUIPMENT

2 long, flat metal skewers

INGREDIENTS

8 ripe small round or plum tomatoes
2 tablespoons extra-virgin olive oil
2 tablespoons chopped fresh dill
Salt and freshly ground black pepper

1. Thread the tomatoes crosswise on the skewers, brush them with the olive oil, and season with the dill and salt and pepper to taste.

2. Set up the grill for direct grilling and preheat to high.

3. When ready to cook, brush and oil the grill grate. Place the skewered tomatoes on the hot grate and grill, turning as necessary with tongs, until the skins are charred and blistered and the flesh inside is hot and soft, 8 to 12 minutes in all.

4. Ease the tomatoes off the skewers with a fork onto a serving platter or plates and serve at once.

CHAPTER 15

RICE, BEANS, AND BEYOND

Rice and beans may not be the glamour dishes of a barbecue, but no self-respecting cookout is complete without them. This chapter focuses on those stalwart dishes that add heft to your plate and help to round out what could otherwise be a relentlessly carnivorian meal.

"Who could ever weary of moonlit nights and well-cooked rice?"
—*Japanese Proverb*

Rice is the traditional accompaniment to much of the world's grilled fare, from the sticky short-grain rices popular in Asia to the fluffy long-grain rices featured in the West.

Beans are also universal. North American–style baked beans are familiar, but did you know that Indians serve *dal* (gingery stewed beans) with their tandoori or that Brazilians enjoy *tutu mineira* (cowboy-style black beans) with their *churrasco* (grilled meats)? In this chapter, you'll find recipes for these delectable dishes and more.

This brings me to the less expected accompaniments to barbecue, such as polenta and grits, which are delicious grilled, and Yorkshire pudding, which can be cooked on the grill while the rib roast is resting. You'll even find a recipe for toasted manioc flour, which Brazilians like to sprinkle over grilled meats.

Armed with these recipes, no one will go hungry. Which is the ultimate goal of any barbecue.

INDIA

INDIAN-STYLE BASMATI RICE

ON THE SIDE
SERVES 4

The traditional Indian method for cooking basmati rice involves an elaborate but easy sequence of rinsing, soaking, and steaming the rice. This produces the most delicate basmati rice I know.

SPECIAL EQUIPMENT

Wok ring or flame tamer

INGREDIENTS

2 cups basmati rice
1 teaspoon salt

Basmati Rice Five Ways

Basmati is the Rolls-Royce of rices, a long, slender grain with an intensely aromatic taste that is buttery, nutty, milky, and sweet. And that's before you add any flavorings. Grown in the foothills of the Himalayas, basmati owes its extraordinary flavor to several years' aging in silos. Unlike most rices, it doubles in length, not width, when cooked.

Basmati rice is traditionally associated with India, but it's eaten almost on a daily basis as far west as the Caucasus Mountains and as far east as Bangladesh. The traditional method for cooking basmati rice involves multiple washings, soakings, and steaming. This is the Indian-style recipe you'll find on page 423. But because basmati rice plays such an important role in the world of barbecue, I offer several recipes, ranging from Quick-Cook Basmati Rice, ideal for the weeknight cook, to an elaborate Persian Rice with Cranberries.

Note that basmati rice is sold at most specialty food shops and many supermarkets. If you like it as much as I do, you'll probably want to buy it in bulk at an Indian, Pakistani, or Near or Middle Eastern market.

1. Place the rice in a large bowl and add cold water to cover by 3 inches. Swirl the rice around with your fingers until the water becomes cloudy, then put the rice in a strainer to drain. Repeat the process until the water remains clear. This will take 4 to 6 rinsings. Drain the rice, return it to the bowl, and add 2 cups of water. Let the rice soak for 30 minutes.

2. Drain the rice through a strainer set over a large, heavy pot. Bring the soaking water to a boil over high heat. Add the salt, stir in the rice, and let the water return to a boil. Reduce the heat to medium-low and let simmer gently, partially covered, until the surface of the rice is riddled with steamy holes, 10 to 12 minutes.

3. Reduce the heat to low and use a wok ring or a flame tamer to raise the pot 1 inch above the burner. Wrap a clean kitchen towel around the pot lid, piling any excess cloth on top of the lid. (You want to keep the cloth away from the heat.) Place the cloth-covered lid over the rice and let steam, over very low heat, for 10 minutes.

4. Gently fluff the rice with a fork and serve at once.

U.S.A.

QUICK-COOK BASMATI RICE

ON THE SIDE
SERVES 4

Here's a quick-cook method that produces quite tasty basmati rice for a hurried weeknight. You can also use an American-grown basmati-style rice like Texmati.

2 tablespoons unsalted butter
1 teaspoon salt
½ teaspoon freshly ground white pepper (optional)
2 cups basmati rice

1. Place the butter, salt, white pepper (if using), and 6 cups of water in a large, heavy pot and bring to a boil. Stir in the rice and let the water return to a boil over high heat.

For Saffron Rose Water Basmati

Soak a half teaspoon of saffron threads in two tablespoons of rose water in a small jar with a lid. Sprinkle a few drops over the rice and toss before serving. Store any extra saffron rose water in the refrigerator.

2. Reduce the heat to low, cover the pot tightly, and cook the rice until the grains are tender and all the water is absorbed, about 18 minutes. Remove the pot from the heat and let stand, covered, for 5 minutes.

3. Gently fluff the rice with a fork and serve at once.

IRAN

PERSIAN-STYLE STEAMED RICE

ON THE SIDE
SERVES 6

No Persian meal would be complete without rice. Here's a simple steamed rice recipe that's great with any of the Persian or Afghan kebabs in this book. Use this rice or the one at right to prepare Iran's most famous grilled meal: *chelow kebab* (see box, page 426).

3 cups basmati rice
1½ teaspoons salt
4 tablespoons (½ stick) unsalted butter, cut into small pieces

1. Place the rice in a large bowl and add cold water to cover by 3 inches. Swirl the rice around with your fingers until the water becomes cloudy, then put the rice in a strainer to drain. Repeat the process until the water remains clear. This will take 4 to 6 rinsings.

2. Place the rice, salt, and 6 cups of water in a deep, nonstick saucepan. Bring to a boil over high heat. Reduce the heat to medium and let the rice simmer gently, uncovered, for about 18 minutes. When the rice has absorbed all the water, reduce the heat to the lowest possible setting and sprinkle the pieces of butter over the top.

3. Wrap a clean kitchen towel around the pot lid, piling any excess cloth on top of the lid. (You want to keep the cloth away from the heat.) Place the cloth-covered lid over the rice and steam for 20 minutes. Remove the pot from the heat and let stand, covered, for 5 minutes.

4. Gently fluff the rice with a fork and serve at once.

IRAN

PERSIAN RICE WITH A GOLDEN CRUST

CHELOW

ON THE SIDE
SERVES 6

One of the glories of Persian (Iranian) gastronomy, *chelow* is tender, sweet, saffroned rice served with an audibly crisp, yogurt-flavored crust. The theory is simple enough (you brown the rice in a single layer on the bottom), but it takes years of practice to achieve a perfect dark-golden crust that comes away from the bottom of the pan in one piece. Here's how my Persian cooking guru, Najmieh Batmanglij, prepares this classic accompaniment to an Iranian barbecue.

3 cups basmati rice
1½ teaspoons salt
¼ teaspoon saffron threads
⅔ cup clarified melted unsalted butter (see Note), or olive oil
3 tablespoons plain whole-milk yogurt

1. Place the rice in a large bowl and add cold water to cover by 3 inches. Swirl the rice around with your fingers until the water becomes cloudy, then put the rice in a strainer to drain. Repeat the process until the water remains clear. This will take 4 to 6 rinsings.

2. Place 8 cups of water and the salt in a large shallow pot (preferably nonstick; the pot should be 10 to 12 inches across and about 6 inches deep) and bring to a boil over high heat. Reduce the heat to medium-high, add the rice, and cook, uncovered, at a brisk simmer for 6 minutes. Pour the rice into a strainer, rinse it under cool running water, and drain well. Wipe out and dry the rice pot with paper towels.

3. Place the saffron threads in a small bowl and grind to a fine powder with a pestle or the end of a wooden spoon. Add 1 tablespoon of warm water, stir, and let stand for 5 minutes.

4. In a separate bowl, combine the clarified butter, yogurt, and ½ cup of water and whisk to mix. Pour the butter mixture evenly over the bottom of the rice pot. Spoon a ½-inch layer of rice evenly over the butter mixture. Without disturbing this

The Persian Grill: A Day with Najmieh Batmanglij

Najmieh Batmanglij is my guru of Persian grilling. I met her on what was probably the least likely day of the year for a barbecue. The charcoal lay neatly piled in her custom-made grill on the terrace of her Georgetown townhouse in Washington, D.C. But by the time I arrived, a freak snowstorm had blanketed the grill, terrace, and gardens with a thick layer of snow.

Never mind—Najmieh Batmanglij is not the sort of cook to let a snowstorm ruin a cookout. A short woman with dark eyes and a cascade of black hair, Najmieh is an author and cooking instructor who comes by her passion for Persian barbecue naturally. One of eleven children, she was born and raised in Tehran in the country now called Iran, but with the ancient and more exotic name Persia. Her books include *Food of Life: A Book of Ancient Persian.* So essential is grilling to Iranian cuisine that she has equipped her kitchen with an indoor grill that would be the envy of many a restaurant. I shook the snow off my overcoat and boots and we set about the task of marinating and skewering meats for Iranian-style grilling.

On the day I visited, she demonstrated ten dishes in three hours with a dexterity that bordered on legerdemain. A whole beef tenderloin was speedily reduced to neat bite-size strips and doused with onion juice, lime juice, and cracked peppercorns. Lamb and beef shoulder were fed through a noisy meat grinder, then kneaded together by hand over low heat to make Iran's famous *kubideh,* ground meat kebab. Earthenware crocks held chunks of chicken and lamb that had been marinating for two days in a colorful mixture of yogurt and saffron. Impressive any time of the year, the display was made more remarkable by the inclement weather outside.

It's unlikely that a cooking technique as universal as roasting meats on a stick over a fire originated at a single time in a single country. But if it had, Iran would make a likely birthplace. Grilling has been inextricably interwoven with Persian culture for thousands of years.

Linguistic evidence suggests Iran as the wellspring of Near Eastern–style grilling. After all, *kebab* is the Persian word for meat. Early Persian literature and art abound with images of grilling. A fourth-century coming-of-age manual, for example, describes a spit-roasted capon that had been raised on a diet of hemp seeds and olive butter. The tenth-century poet Ferdowsi gives a detailed description of a veal marinade made with saffron, rose water, musk, and old wine.

Persian-style kebabs, with their emphasis on lamb and yogurt-based marinades, turn up as far west as the Balkans and as far east as Bangladesh. They probably inspired Greek souvlaki and Indian tandoori. Souvlaki may have arrived via the Turks during the Ottoman Empire (if not before, during the Persian Wars in the sixth century B.C.). Tandoori was imported by the Moguls, Persian rulers who brought Islam to northern India in the sixteenth century A.D. (The spicing is more extravagant in the Indian version, but the yogurt and garlic–based marinade is the same).

What accounts for the long-standing popularity of grilled fare in the region we now call Iran? "Ours is an outdoor culture," explains Najmieh. "For eight months a year, most Persians cook, dine, and even sleep outdoors." This love of the outdoors has given rise to a singular style of grilling.

Chelow Kebab

If Iran had a single national dish, it would surely be *chelow kebab,* skewers of lamb, veal, or beef served on a snowy mountain of rice with fire-charred tomatoes, raw egg, raw onions, and a tart purplish powder made from sumac berries. But, almost anything is fair game for the *kebabi* man: lamb, veal, beef, organ meats, tomatoes, onions, even sumac-dusted fish. Of course, the most popular meat is lamb. "In Iran sheep graze on herbs, which gives them an exceptional flavor," explains Najmieh. Loin and tenderloin are her preferred cuts, but leg and shoulder will do if marinated for at least forty-eight hours. Tradition calls for interspersing the lamb chunks with moisturizing lumps of tail fat.

Lengthy marinating is one of the cornerstones of Persian grilling. The basic marinade consists of yogurt, lemon or lime juice, onion, garlic, saffron, pepper, and salt. Sometimes olive oil is substituted for the yogurt—especially for beef and veal. Marinating for two to three days is not uncommon. A soak that long in an acidic yogurt and lemon juice marinade can work wonders for breaking down tough meat fibers. It also produces an uncommon depth of flavor. "Iranians always have some sort of meat marinating in the refrigerator," explains Najmieh. "That way, we can make kebabs at a moment's notice."

Another hallmark of Persian grilling is the basting mixture, brushed on the meat while it cooks. The basic formula includes lime juice, saffron, and melted butter. The saffron imparts a golden glow to the meat. And the mixture as a whole keeps the meat moist, essential when you grill over very high heat.

Given the importance of kebabs in Persian cuisine, it's not surprising that Iranians have developed highly distinctive skewers: long, flat ribbons of steel of varying widths with pointed tips for easy penetration. Narrow skewers are used for skewering chunks of meat; medium-width skewers for holding thin strips of chicken and beef. The widest skewers measure a half to one inch across and are designed for holding ground meats.

But grilled fare is only part of what makes a Persian barbecue so remarkable—the side dishes are also stars of the show. Guests would be welcomed with tiny, gold-rimmed glasses of dulcet tea. The table would be sagging under the weight of a *mokhalafat,* a stunning assortment of dips, salads, chutneys, *torshis* (pickles), and paper-thin lavash bread for wrapping around the meats.

Najmieh accompanied her barbecue with a platter of basil, mint, watercress, and other fresh herbs, not to mention tomatoes, cucumbers, and scallions. She also included chopped onion and tart sumac powder to sprinkle over the meat. To wash it down, she served cool, frothy glasses of *dugh,* a refreshing beverage made from yogurt, mint, and rose petals. By the end of the day I felt like I was at a cookout in Tehran, not in a snowstorm in Washington, D.C.

layer, add the remaining rice, mounding it toward the center. Sprinkle the top of the mound with the saffron mixture. Cover the pan and place it over medium heat for 8 minutes.

5. Remove the lid and sprinkle the rice with an additional ½ cup of water. Reduce the heat to low. Wrap a clean kitchen towel around the pot lid, piling any excess cloth on top of the lid. (You want to keep the cloth away from the heat.) Place the cloth-covered lid over the rice and cook until the rice on top is tender and the rice on the bottom of the pot has formed a dark golden crust, about 40 minutes. Check the rice after 30 minutes; if you don't see a crust, increase the heat slightly.

6. To serve, spoon the loose rice from the top into a serving bowl, leaving the crusty rice at the bottom. Place a round platter over the pot. Invert the pot and give it a little shake. The crusty rice should slide out in a golden brown disk. Cut the crust into wedges and serve these next to the loose rice.

NOTE: To clarify butter, melt 1 cup (2 sticks) butter in a small saucepan over medium heat. Remove it from the heat and skim off any white foam on top. Pour off the golden liquid (the clarified butter) into a glass measure or heatproof jar, discarding the white liquid and milk solids that have settled in the bottom of the pan. Any unused clarified butter can be refrigerated, covered, for up to a month.

IRAN

PERSIAN RICE WITH CRANBERRIES

ON THE SIDE
SERVES 6

Rice with sour cherries or bilberries is a popular accompaniment to Persian kebabs. One evening, lacking both, I made the rice with dried cranberries: Their sweet-sour flavor was right on the money. Dried cranberries and cherries are sold at specialty food shops, natural foods stores, many supermarkets, and by mail from American Spoon Foods.

3 cups basmati rice
1½ teaspoons salt
1½ cups dried cranberries or dried sour cherries
¼ cup sugar
2 tablespoons unsalted butter, plus 2 tablespoons butter, melted
2 tablespoons plain whole-milk yogurt

1. Place the rice in a large bowl and add cold water to cover by 3 inches. Swirl the rice around with your fingers until the water becomes cloudy, then put the rice in a strainer to drain. Repeat the process until the water remains clear. This will take 4 to 6 rinsings.

2. Place 8 cups of water and the salt in a large shallow pot (preferably nonstick; the pot should be 10 to 12 inches across and about 6 inches deep) and bring to a boil over high heat. Reduce the heat to medium-high, add the rice, and cook, uncovered, at a brisk simmer for 6 minutes. Pour the rice into a strainer, rinse it under cool running water, and drain well. Wipe out and dry the rice pot with paper towels.

3. Meanwhile, place the cranberries, sugar, and 1½ cups of water in a medium-size saucepan. Bring to a simmer over medium heat and cook until the cranberries are soft and most of the cooking liquid has evaporated, 5 to 8 minutes; the juice of the cranberries should be thick and syrupy. Using a slotted spoon, transfer the cranberries to a bowl. Add the 2 tablespoons of butter to the cranberry juice and bring to a boil, stirring until the butter melts. Remove the cranberry juice from the heat and set it aside, covered, at room temperature.

4. Combine the yogurt, melted butter, and 2 tablespoons of water in a bowl and whisk to mix. Pour the yogurt mixture evenly over the bottom of the rice pot. Spoon a ½-inch layer of rice evenly over the yogurt mixture. Stir the cranberries into the remaining rice, and without disturbing the rice layer in the pot, add the cranberry rice, mounding it toward the center. Place the pot, uncovered, over medium heat and cook until the rice begins to brown on the bottom, 6 to 8 minutes.

5. Reduce the heat to low. Wrap a clean kitchen towel around the pot lid, piling any excess cloth on top of the lid. (You want to keep the cloth away from the heat.) Place the cloth-covered lid over the rice and cook until the rice on top is tender and the rice on the bottom of the pot has formed a dark golden crust, about 40 minutes. Check after 30 minutes; if you don't see a crust, increase the heat slightly.

6. Remove the pot from the heat and pour the reserved cranberry juice over the rice. Let the rice stand, covered, for 5 minutes.

7. To serve, spoon the loose rice from the top into a bowl, leaving the crusty rice at the bottom. Place a round platter over the pot. Invert the pot and give it a little shake. The crusty rice should slide out in a golden brown disk. Cut the crust into wedges and serve these with the loose rice.

THAILAND

JASMINE RICE

ON THE SIDE
SERVES 4

Jasmine rice is a relative newcomer to the North American table, but it's taken the country by storm. With its sweet, delicate, almost floral flavor, it's easy to see why. Jasmine rice can be found at Asian markets and specialty food shops. Serve this rice with any of the Thai grilled dishes in this book.

2 cups jasmine rice

1. Place the rice in a large bowl and add cold water to cover by 3 inches. Swirl the rice around with your fingers until the water becomes cloudy, then put the rice in a strainer to drain. Repeat this process until the water remains clear. This will take 4 to 6 rinsings.

2. Place 3½ cups of water in a large, heavy saucepan and bring to a boil over high heat. Stir in the rice and let the water return to a boil. Reduce the heat to low and cover the pot tightly. Cook the rice until just tender, 15 to 18 minutes.

3. Remove the pan from the heat. Remove the lid and wrap a clean kitchen towel around the pot lid, piling any excess cloth on top of the lid. Place the cloth-covered lid over the rice and let the rice stand for 5 minutes.

4. Gently fluff the rice with a fork and serve at once.

PERSIAN RICE WITH CRANBERRIES | PAGE 427

INDONESIA

BALINESE YELLOW RICE

NASI KUNING

ON THE SIDE
SERVES 6

This towering cone of rice—gilded with turmeric and perfumed with lemongrass and galangal or ginger—symbolizes Bali's sacred Mount Agung. As such, it's a fitting centerpiece for a *megibung,* the Balinese rice table. A *megibung* is a sort of smorgasbord of Balinese delicacies, which would invariably include *babi guling* (Balinese Roast Pork, page 177) and a variety of satés.

The traditional rice for this dish is Balinese long-grain rice. The closest approximation available in this country is Thai jasmine rice. Coconut water is the liquid inside the coconut.

3 cups jasmine rice
1½ cups coconut water (see box, page 114) or plain water
1½ cups homemade chicken stock or canned low-sodium chicken broth
¾ cup coconut milk, canned or homemade (page 522)
1 stalk fresh lemongrass, trimmed and flattened with the side of a cleaver, or 1 teaspoon grated lemon zest
4 slices (each ¼ inch thick) peeled fresh galangal or peeled fresh ginger, lightly crushed with the side of a cleaver
½ teaspoon ground turmeric
1 tablespoon salt

1. Place the rice in a large bowl and add cold water to cover by 3 inches. Swirl the rice around with your fingers until the water becomes cloudy, then put the rice in a strainer to drain. Repeat the process until the water remains clear. This will take 4 to 6 rinsings.

2. Place the coconut water, chicken stock, coconut milk, lemongrass, galangal, turmeric, and salt in a large, heavy pot and bring to a boil over high heat. Add the rice and let the water return to a boil. Reduce the heat to low and cover the pot tightly. Cook the rice until just tender, 15 to 18 minutes. Remove the pot from the heat and let the rice stand, covered, for 5 minutes.

3. Gently fluff the rice with a fork. Remove and discard the lemongrass and galangal slices. To serve *nasi kuning* in the traditional Balinese manner, pack it into a lightly oiled large funnel or other cone-shaped mold. Place the mold, with the wide opening facing up, in a deep bowl or pot covered with aluminum foil and let stand for 3 minutes. Place a platter over the base of the mold and invert and unmold the rice onto the platter.

JAPAN

JAPANESE STEAMED RICE

ON THE SIDE
SERVES 6

Rice is more than just a food in Japan. It's the very soul of Japanese culture. Japanese culinary authority Shizuo Tsuji devoted eight pages to the preparation of simple boiled rice in his seminal book *Japanese Cooking: A Simple Art.* It's the inspiration for the recipe here.

You'll need to use a short-grain (aka oval) Asian-style rice for this recipe. Most of the short-grain rice sold in North America is grown in California. Good brands include Calrose and Kokuho Rose. The choicest rice in Japan is *shinmai,* freshly harvested "new rice," which comes to market in the fall. You may be able to find *shinmai* at a Japanese market.

3 cups short-grain rice
2 teaspoons black sesame seeds (optional)

1. Place the rice in a large bowl and add cold water to cover by 3 inches. Swirl the rice around with your fingers until the water becomes cloudy, then put the rice in a strainer to drain. Repeat the process until the water remains clear. This will take 4 to 6 rinsings. Once well rinsed, let the rice remain in the strainer for 30 minutes, so it is well drained.

2. Combine the rice and enough water to cover the rice by

1 inch (about 4 cups) in a large heavy pot with a tight-fitting lid. Cook the rice, covered, over medium-high heat until you can hear the water begin to boil. Increase the heat to high and bring the rice to a vigorous boil (the lid might move from the pressure of the steam). Boil the rice for 2 minutes. Reduce the heat to low and cook the rice until all the water is absorbed, 15 to 20 minutes. Do not uncover the rice until it has cooked for a minimum of 15 minutes.

3. Remove the pot from the heat. Remove the lid and wrap a clean kitchen towel around the pot lid, piling any excess cloth on top of the lid. Place the cloth-covered lid over the rice and let the rice stand for 15 minutes.

4. Gently fluff the rice with a fork before serving. Sprinkle black sesame seeds (if using) on top and serve at once.

JAPAN

GRILLED RICE CAKES

DIRECT GRILLING
MAKES 16 TO 18 CAKES; SERVES 6 TO 8

Grilled rice cakes are a popular dish in Japan, turning up at street vendors' stalls, at yakitori parlors, and even at highfalutin restaurants. The following recipe was inspired by the vendors outside the Sensoji Temple in Tokyo. You could probably use brown rice, although the Japanese barbecue buffs I met in Japan have an almost universal preference for white. Japanese grill jockeys don't oil the rice cakes. Their grills don't have grates, so the cakes are grilled on chopsticklike skewers held over the fire. The oil enables you to grill the cakes on a Western-style grill.

ADVANCE PREPARATION

2 to 8 hours for chilling the rice cakes

INGREDIENTS

Japanese Steamed Rice (page 430), cooled
1 tablespoon canola oil, plus more for oiling the plate
Classic Teriyaki Sauce (page 473), White Miso Barbecue Sauce (page 475), or both

1. Place the rice in a bowl and have a bowl of cold water handy. Lightly oil a large plate. Lightly wet your hands and pinch off 2-inch balls of rice. Mold them into circles, ovals, or heart shapes, rewetting your hands as necessary. Each shape should be about 1 inch thick. As they are made, place the rice cakes on the prepared plate. When all of the rice has been used up, refrigerate the rice cakes, loosely covered with plastic wrap, for at least 2 and as long as 8 hours.

2. Set up the grill for direct grilling and preheat to high.

3. When ready to cook, brush and oil the grill grate. Lightly brush the rice cakes on both sides with the canola oil. Brush one side with one or both of the sauces, then arrange the rice cakes, sauce side down, on the hot grate. Cook the rice cakes until nicely browned on both sides, 4 to 5 minutes per side, brushing the cakes with the sauces again before turning. Serve at once.

BAHAMAS

BAHAMIAN PEAS AND RICE

ON THE SIDE
SERVES 8

Peas and rice are a staple on every island in the Caribbean. The "peas" in this case are pigeon peas, a greenish-brown, earthy-flavored bean native to Africa. The African origins are evident in some of the bean's local names. Jamaicans call it Gunga pea (Congo pea). In the French West Indies, it's known as *pois d'angole* (pea from Angola), a name echoed in the Spanish term *gandule*. If you live in the American South, you probably know it as "crowder."

Whatever you call it, pigeon peas come in ridged pods and are widely available canned and frozen at Hispanic markets and most supermarkets. If you can't find them, you can certainly substitute black-eyed peas or small red kidney beans.

1 tablespoon vegetable oil
4 slices of bacon, cut into ¼-inch slivers
1 medium-size onion, finely chopped
1 medium-size red bell pepper, cored, seeded, and finely chopped
3 cloves garlic, minced
6 fresh basil leaves, thinly slivered, or 1 teaspoon dried basil
1 teaspoon fresh thyme, or ½ teaspoon dried thyme
2 teaspoons salt, or more to taste
½ teaspoon freshly ground black pepper, or more to taste
2 tablespoons tomato paste
½ teaspoon sugar
3 cups long-grain white rice
1 tablespoon fresh lime juice
2 cups cooked pigeon peas, black-eyed peas, or kidney beans

1. Heat the oil in a large, heavy pot over medium heat. Add the bacon and cook until lightly browned, about 4 minutes. Pour off all but 2 tablespoons of the fat. Add the onion, bell pepper, garlic, basil, thyme, salt, and black pepper and cook until the onion is golden brown, about 5 minutes. Stir in the tomato paste and sugar and cook about 2 minutes longer.

2. Add 5½ cups of water and bring to a boil. Stir in the rice and lime juice and let return to a boil. Reduce the heat to low and cover the pot tightly. Cook the rice until it is tender, about 18 minutes, but check it after 15 minutes: If the rice is too wet, set the pot lid ajar to allow some of the liquid to evaporate; if the rice is too dry, add 2 to 3 more tablespoons of water. Stir in the pigeon peas during the last 3 minutes of cooking.

3. Remove the pot from the heat and let the peas and rice stand for 5 minutes. Just before serving, fluff the peas and rice with a fork and taste for seasoning, adding more salt and/or black pepper as necessary.

A Fancy Presentation

You can mold Bahamian Peas and Rice in lightly oiled one-cup ramekins or custard cups (you will need eight). Spoon the peas and rice into the cups and pack them tightly, pressing down with the back of a spoon. Wait two minutes, then invert each mold onto a serving plate. Give the mold a gentle shake; an attractive dome or cylinder of rice should slide out easily.

BRAZIL

CRAZY RICE
ARROZ LOCO

ON THE SIDE
SERVES 4

This colorful side dish is the Brazilian version of fried rice. It turns up at *churrascarias* and restaurants in Rio de Janeiro and São Paolo, with each chef trying to outdo his peers with the elaborateness of the flavorings. The version here comes from a wonderful restaurant called Candidos, located in the port town of Pedra de Guaratiba, an hour south of Rio.

FOR THE RICE

1½ cups long-grain rice
½ teaspoon salt
1 tablespoon unsalted butter

FOR THE FLAVORINGS

1 tablespoon extra-virgin olive oil
3 slices of bacon, cut into ¼-inch slivers (see Note)
½ medium-size red onion, diced
1 clove garlic, minced
½ medium-size green bell pepper, cored, seeded, and cut into ¼-inch dice
½ medium-size red bell pepper, cored, seeded, and cut into ¼-inch dice
½ cup cooked corn kernels
¼ cup dark raisins
¼ cup golden raisins
3 tablespoons chopped fresh flat-leaf parsley
Salt and freshly ground black pepper

1. Prepare the rice: Place the rice in a large bowl and add cold water to cover by 3 inches. Swirl the rice around with your fingers until the water becomes cloudy, then put the rice in a strainer to drain. Repeat the process until the water remains clear. This will take 4 to 6 rinsings.

2. Place the rice in a large, heavy pot. Add enough water to cover by ¾ inch (about 2½ cups). Stir in the salt and butter and bring to a boil over high heat. Tightly cover the pan, reduce the heat to low, and cook the rice until it is tender, about 18 minutes, but check after 15 minutes: If the rice is too wet, set the lid ajar to allow some of the liquid to evaporate; if the rice is too dry, add 2 to 3 more tablespoons of water. Remove the pot from the heat and let the rice stand, covered, for 5 minutes. Fluff it with a fork and set aside.

3. Prepare the flavorings: Heat the olive oil in a large skillet over medium heat. Add the bacon and cook until lightly browned, about 4 minutes. Pour off all but 2 tablespoons of the fat. Add the onion, garlic, green and red bell peppers, corn, dark and golden raisins, and the parsley. Cook until the onion is golden, about 5 minutes. Stir the rice into the flavorings and cook until thoroughly heated through, about 2 minutes. Taste for seasoning, adding salt and black pepper to taste, then serve.

NOTE: To make a vegetarian version of Crazy Rice, simply leave out the bacon and increase the olive oil to 2 tablespoons.

ITALY

GRILLED POLENTA

DIRECT GRILLING
SERVES 4

Polenta is Italian cornmeal mush—but, oh, what mush: cornmeal simmered to a savory paste and, here, enriched with butter and cream, then smokily browned on the grill. You can serve grilled polenta by itself as a side dish or you can top it with your favorite tomato sauce. For an artistic touch, use a cookie cutter to cut out the polenta in stars, triangles, circles, or other fanciful shapes.

If you're in a hurry, you can buy precooked polenta, sold in bologna-shaped tubes. Cut it crosswise a half inch thick, brush it with melted butter, and grill as described in Step 6.

ADVANCE PREPARATION

4 hours to 2 days for chilling the polenta

INGREDIENTS

2 cups coarse yellow cornmeal
1 teaspoon salt, or more to taste
½ teaspoon freshly ground black pepper, or more to taste
½ cup heavy (whipping) cream
2 to 4 tablespoons unsalted butter, melted, or extra-virgin olive oil

1. Combine the cornmeal, salt, pepper, and 6 cups of water in a large, heavy saucepan and whisk until smooth. Bring the mixture to a boil over high heat and let boil for 2 minutes, whisking steadily.

2. Reduce the heat to a gentle simmer and stir in the cream and, if desired, 2 tablespoons of melted butter or olive oil. Let the polenta simmer gently, uncovered, until it thickens enough to pull away from the side of the pan, 30 to 40 minutes. The polenta should be the consistency of soft ice cream. You don't need to whisk the polenta continuously, but you should keep a careful eye on it, giving it a stir every 5 minutes. As it thickens, you'll need to switch from a whisk to a wooden spoon. Taste for seasoning, adding more salt and/or pepper as necessary; the polenta should be highly seasoned.

3. Pour the polenta into a nonstick jelly-roll pan or cake pan and even out the top with a spatula. The polenta should be about ½ inch thick. Let cool to room temperature, then cover the polenta loosely with plastic wrap and refrigerate until firm, at least 4 hours or as long as 2 days.

4. Cut the cold polenta with a knife or cookie cutter into squares, rectangles, or other shapes; the pieces should be no more than 3 to 4 inches across. Use a spatula to transfer the pieces of polenta from the pan to a large plate.

5. Set up the grill for direct grilling and preheat to high.

6. When ready to cook, brush and oil the grill grate. Brush both sides of the polenta pieces with 2 tablespoons of melted butter or with olive oil. Arrange the polenta on the hot grate and cook, turning with a spatula, until sizzling hot and nicely browned on both sides, 3 to 4 minutes per side. Serve the grilled polenta at once.

U.S.A.

GRILLED GRITS

DIRECT GRILLING
SERVES 6

Grilling polenta is a long-standing Italian tradition. This gave me the idea to grill the American equivalent, grits. Grilled grits go really well with southern or Texas-style barbecue.

ADVANCE PREPARATION

4 hours to 2 days for chilling the grits

INGREDIENTS

- **3 cups homemade chicken stock, canned low-sodium chicken broth, or water**
- **1 clove garlic, minced**
- **1 teaspoon of your favorite hot sauce**
- **1 teaspoon salt, or more to taste**
- **½ teaspoon freshly ground black pepper, or more to taste**
- **3 cups quick-cook grits**
- **4 tablespoons (½ stick) unsalted butter, melted, or olive oil**

1. Combine the chicken stock, garlic, hot sauce, salt, and pepper in a large, deep pot and bring to a boil over high heat. Stir in the grits and 2 tablespoons of melted butter and let return to a boil. Reduce the heat to a gentle simmer and cook the grits, uncovered, until thick, 5 to 8 minutes, or for the time given on the package, stirring often. The heat should be high enough to cause bubbles to break the surface but low enough so that the grits don't spatter. Taste for seasoning, adding more salt and/or pepper as necessary.

2. Pour the cooked grits onto a nonstick baking sheet or pie pan and even out the top with a spatula. The grits should be about ½ inch thick. Let cool to room temperature, then cover the grits loosely with plastic wrap and refrigerate until firm, for at least 4 hours or as long as 2 days.

3. Cut the grits into rectangles or wedges. Use a spatula to transfer these from the baking sheet to a large plate.

4. Set up the grill for direct grilling and preheat to high.

5. When ready to cook, brush and oil the grill grate. Brush both sides of the pieces of grits with some of the remaining melted butter. Arrange the grits on the hot grate and cook, turning with a spatula, until sizzling hot and nicely browned on both sides, 3 to 4 minutes per side. Brush the grits with any remaining butter as they grill. Serve the grits at once.

Grilled Grits Plus

Add any of the following ingredients in Step 1 when you stir in the grits.

For cheese grits: Add a half cup finely grated sharp Cheddar, Gouda, or Manchego cheese.

For corn grits: Add one cup grilled corn kernels (see the box on page 396 for grilling instructions).

For jalapeño grits: Add two to six chopped pickled jalapeño peppers and a half cup grated Jack or Cheddar cheese.

BRAZIL

RAINBOW MANIOC

FAROFA

ON THE SIDE
SERVES 6 TO 8

Although it is little known outside its native Brazil, *farofa* is one of the world's most unusual accompaniments to barbecue. In its simplest form, it looks somewhat like sautéed bread crumbs, but the flavor is nutty, earthy, and buttery—much more complex. The texture is delectably gritty.

Farofa (accent on the second syllable) is made from ground dried manioc (also known as cassava), the starchy tuber that gives us tapioca. There's a basic version (see the box at right), but a more elaborate *farofa,* like this one,

Toasted Manioc

A simpler *farofa* is served as a condiment at Brazilian grill joints, where it is sprinkled over steaks and chops to soak up the meat juices. It may strike you as odd but it quickly becomes addictive. To make it, sauté manioc flour in butter or oil with a little onion or garlic.

is garnished with a rainbow-colored array of dried fruits, vegetables, and scrambled eggs.

2 tablespoons unsalted butter
4 tablespoons extra-virgin olive oil
1 large onion, finely chopped
2 cloves garlic, minced
1 medium-size red bell pepper, cored, seeded, and cut into ½-inch diamonds
1 medium-size green bell pepper, cored, seeded, and cut into ½-inch diamonds
1 medium-size yellow bell pepper, cored, seeded, and cut into ½-inch diamonds
⅓ cup raisins or dried currants
⅓ cup diced pitted prunes
2 cups manioc flour (see Note)
2 large eggs, beaten
Salt and freshly ground black pepper

1. Heat the butter and 2 tablespoons of the olive oil in a large nonstick skillet over medium heat. Add the onion and garlic and cook until soft but not brown, about 4 minutes. Add the bell peppers, raisins, and prunes and cook until the onion is golden brown, about 4 minutes longer.

2. Add the manioc flour and cook, stirring frequently, until golden brown, about 6 minutes. Push the manioc mixture to the edge of the pan.

3. Add the remaining 2 tablespoons of olive oil to the center of the skillet and heat well. Pour the eggs into the skillet and cook, stirring vigorously with a wooden spoon, until scrambled. Stir the scrambled eggs into the manioc mixture and cook until thoroughly heated, 2 to 4 minutes more. Season the *farofa* with salt and black pepper to taste, transfer it to a serving platter, and serve at once.

NOTE: Manioc flour can be found at Brazilian and Portuguese grocery stores and at specialty food shops. Matzo meal could be used as a substitute, although the flavor won't be quite the same.

INDIA

INDIAN "BAKED BEANS"

DAL BUKHARA

ON THE SIDE
SERVES 8

It's hard to conceive of a North American barbecue without baked beans. Halfway around the world, New Delhi's famous tandoori palace, Bukhara, attracts a cultlike following for an exquisitely rich, creamy bean dish called *dal bukhara*. In other words, baked beans. Like traditional Yankee beans, *dal bukhara* is cooked overnight in a giant pot over charcoal.

The bean of choice for *dal bukhara* is the *urad dal* (also called *kali dal*), a small black bean that looks like a mung bean. (The English name is "whole black gram bean.") The cream and butter give the beans a silky consistency and concentrated richness unequaled by other Indian bean dishes. *Urad dal* is available at Indian markets and natural foods stores. In a pinch, you can use mung beans.

Traditional *dal bukara* takes twelve hours to make. I've streamlined the recipe by making it in a pressure cooker.

1 cup (8 ounces) dried whole black gram beans, or mung beans
1 large ripe tomato
1 tablespoon grated peeled fresh ginger
3 cloves garlic, minced
½ medium-size onion, minced
1 tablespoon tomato paste
2 teaspoons ground coriander
1 teaspoon salt, or more to taste
½ teaspoon ground black pepper, or more to taste
¼ teaspoon cayenne pepper, or more to taste
6 tablespoons unsalted butter
½ cup heavy (whipping) cream

QUICK AND SMOKY BAKED BEANS | AT RIGHT

1. Spread out the beans on a baking sheet and pick out and discard any twigs or stones. Place the beans in a large bowl and add cold water to cover by 3 inches. Swirl the beans with your fingers, then place them in a strainer to drain. Repeat the process another 3 or so times.

2. Place the beans in a pressure cooker and add 4 cups of water. Pressure cook the beans over medium heat until you hear an even hiss and the valve in the lid dances in a lively fashion, about 10 minutes.

3. Meanwhile, core the tomato and cut it into chunks. Place the tomato in a food processor and process until pureed.

4. Run cold water over the pressure cooker for 5 minutes to cool it completely (both top and sides), then remove the lid.

5. Stir the ginger, garlic, onion, pureed tomato, tomato paste, coriander, salt, black pepper, cayenne, and 4 tablespoons of the butter into the beans. Pressure cook the beans again until they are reduced to a thick, creamy puree, about 5 minutes (see Note). Once again, cool the cooker completely under cold running water before removing the lid.

6. Shortly before serving, stir the cream into the beans and let them simmer gently in the pressure cooker (with its lid off) or in a saucepan until rich and creamy, 2 minutes. Taste for seasoning, adding more salt, black pepper, and/or cayenne as necessary. Transfer the beans to a serving bowl and dot the top with the remaining 2 tablespoons of butter. Serve the beans at once.

NOTE: The beans can be prepared several hours or even a day ahead to this point and stored, covered, in the refrigerator. Reheat them over medium heat, stirring well.

U.S.A.

QUICK AND SMOKY BAKED BEANS

INDIRECT GRILLING
SERVES 6 TO 8

Not everyone has the time to make baked beans from scratch. This recipe starts with canned beans, but a quick smoke on the grill produces such rich flavor, you'd swear the beans had been cooked for hours. For the best results, add a couple of cups of diced barbecued pork, ham, or brisket and/or meat drippings left over from a previous cookout.

SPECIAL EQUIPMENT

2 cups wood chips or chunks, soaked for 1 hour in cold water to cover and drained

INGREDIENTS

4 thick-cut slices of bacon (about 4 ounces), cut into ¼-inch slivers
1 large onion, finely chopped
3 cloves garlic, minced
1 tablespoon grated peeled fresh ginger
2 cans (each 15 ounces) Great Northern or kidney beans, rinsed and drained
¼ cup firmly packed dark brown sugar
¼ cup molasses
¼ cup barbecue sauce
¼ cup ketchup
2 tablespoons Worcestershire sauce
1 tablespoon dry mustard
1 tablespoon prepared mustard
1 tablespoon cider vinegar
1 to 2 cups diced smoked or barbecued pork, ham, or brisket (optional)
1 tablespoon barbecued meat drippings (optional)
Salt and freshly ground black pepper

1. Place the bacon in a large, heavy pot and cook over medium heat until lightly browned, about 5 minutes. Discard all but 2 tablespoons of the bacon fat.

2. Add the onion, garlic, and ginger and cook until the onion is golden brown, about 5 minutes. Remove the pot from the heat and stir in the beans, brown sugar, molasses, barbecue sauce, ketchup, Worcestershire sauce, dry mustard, prepared mustard, cider vinegar, pork (if using), and drippings (if using). Transfer the beans to a baking dish (an aluminum-foil turkey pan works well).

3. Set up the grill for indirect grilling. No drip pan is necessary for this recipe.

If using a gas grill, place all of the wood chips in the smoker box and preheat to high; when smoke appears, reduce the heat to medium.

If using a charcoal grill, preheat it to medium.

4. When ready to cook, if using a charcoal grill, toss all of the wood chips on the coals. Place the baking pan with the beans in the center of the hot grate, away from the heat, and cover the grill. Smoke roast the beans until thick and richly flavored, about 30 minutes. Season with salt and pepper to taste and serve at once.

NOTE: These beans can also be prepared in the oven; bake them for 30 minutes at 350°F.

BRAZIL

BRAZILIAN BLACK BEANS WITH BACON
TUTU MINEIRA

ON THE SIDE
SERVES 8

Here's the Brazilian version of baked beans. Actually, it's only one of the versions. Brazilians love beans so much they have dozens of dishes to choose from. *Tutu* comes from Minas Gerais (a mining state in northwest Brazil), where it's made with black beans and bacon. I've lightened up the recipe a little—the original is the sort of fare you want to eat before engaging in strenuous physical labor. Serve *tutu mineira* with any of the Brazilian barbecue main dishes in this book.

4 slices of bacon (about 4 ounces)
1 medium-size onion, finely chopped
4 cloves garlic, minced
¼ cup chopped fresh flat-leaf parsley
1 bay leaf
4 cups cooked black beans (if using canned beans, you'll need two 15-ounce cans)
½ to 1 cup homemade chicken stock, canned low-sodium chicken broth, or liquid reserved from cooking the beans
¼ teaspoon Portuguese Hot Sauce (page 480) or your favorite hot sauce, or more to taste
3 to 4 tablespoons manioc flour (see Note)
Salt and freshly ground black pepper
2 hard-cooked eggs, coarsely chopped

1. Place the bacon in a large skillet and cook over medium heat until lightly browned, about 5 minutes. Pour off all but 2 tablespoons of the bacon fat. Add the onion, garlic, 2 tablespoons of the parsley, and the bay leaf to the skillet and cook until the onion is golden brown, about 4 minutes.

2. Add the beans, ½ cup of the chicken stock, and the hot sauce to the skillet and let simmer for 5 minutes. Discard the bay leaf. Using a pestle, potato masher, or the back of a wooden spoon, mash half the beans in the skillet. Stir in 3 tablespoons of manioc flour. Let the beans simmer, uncovered, until nice and thick, about 3 minutes. If the beans are too thick, add a little more bean cooking liquid; if they are too thin, add the remaining 1 tablespoon of manioc flour.

3. Taste for seasoning, adding salt and pepper to taste and more hot sauce as necessary. Sprinkle the *tutu* with the chopped eggs and the remaining 2 tablespoons of parsley and serve at once.

NOTE: If manioc flour is not available (see the Note on page 435), you can substitute toasted bread crumbs (see box, page 113).

ENGLAND

YORKSHIRE PUDDING ON THE GRILL

INDIRECT GRILLING
SERVES 8

Grilled Prime Ribs of Beef with Garlic and Rosemary (page 137) just isn't complete without Yorkshire pudding. And you can cook the pudding on the grill while the meat rests before you carve it. The trick to achieving a dramatic puff is to start with ice-cold batter and add it to a smoking hot pan. For the most authentic flavor, use melted meat drippings—however nutritionally incorrect they may be. You can collect drippings from a roast while it cooks, using a turkey baster to extract them from the drip pan, or save drippings from a previous grill session.

ADVANCE PREPARATION

30 minutes for chilling the batter

INGREDIENTS

6 large eggs
2¼ cups milk
1 teaspoon salt
½ teaspoon freshly ground black pepper
2 cups all-purpose unbleached flour
¼ cup prime rib drippings, melted unsalted butter, or extra-virgin olive oil

1. Place the eggs, milk, salt, and pepper in a large bowl and whisk to mix. Whisk in the flour and 2 tablespoons of the drippings. Cover and chill the batter in the freezer for 30 minutes.

2. Set up the grill for indirect grilling and preheat it to high (see Note). No drip pan is necessary for this recipe.

3. When ready to cook, add the remaining 2 tablespoons of drippings to a clean 13 by 9–inch roasting pan, place it in the center of the hot grill grate, and heat to smoking, about 3 minutes. Pour the chilled batter into the roasting pan and cover the grill tightly. Cook the Yorkshire pudding until it is puffed and nicely browned, 20 to 30 minutes (don't peek). Cut the pudding into squares and serve at once.

NOTE: If you have just prepared a roast, your grill will already be set up for the indirect method. If you are using a charcoal grill, just add 10 to 12 fresh coals to each side.

CENTRAL ASIAN PICKLES | AT RIGHT

SIDEKICKS: PICKLES, RELISHES, SALSAS, AND SLAWS

"Hunger is the best pickle."
—BENJAMIN FRANKLIN

Every great performance has its divas and chorus lines. So it is with barbecue. The meats or seafood may fetch the lion's share of the bravos, but it's the condiments—the pickles, relishes, salsas, and slaws—that expand what would be a simple solo into a performance of operatic virtuosity.

Pickles and relishes play an important role in the world of barbecue, where their texture and bite offer an exquisite contrast to grilled meats. In this chapter you'll find recipes for the *encurtidos* (pickled onion mixtures) of Central America, the *torshis* (pickled vegetables) of Central Asia, the fiery *sambals* of Indonesia and Malaysia, and the chutneys of the Indian subcontinent.

A large and distinguished family of salsas comes from closer to home, ranging from Argentina's mild *salsa criolla* (Tomato Salsa) to the excruciatingly fiery *xni pec* ("Dog's Snout" Salsa) of the Yucatán to the Smoky Apple-Banana Salsa, Grilled Pineapple Salsa, and Mango Mint Salsa found in the U.S.

Finally, no barbecue is complete without slaw. In this chapter you'll find several, including a scorcher with fiery Scotch bonnet chiles. I can hear the bravos already.

AFGHANISTAN

CENTRAL ASIAN PICKLES

TORSHI

ON THE SIDE
MAKES ABOUT 3 QUARTS; SERVES 12

Torshi refers to a family of pickled vegetables found throughout Central Asia, especially in Afghanistan, Iraq, and Iran. Obviously, the formula varies from country to country, but the basic recipe includes carrots, celery, cauliflower, and turnips or cucumbers cured in vinegar, salt, and *sev gundig* (black onion seeds found in Middle and Near Eastern groceries). No Central Asian barbecue would be complete without one or more bowls of *torshi*. This recipe makes a mild pickle. If you'd prefer yours hot, add two to twelve dried red chile peppers.

ADVANCE PREPARATION

3 days for pickling the vegetables

SPECIAL EQUIPMENT

1 large jar (3 quarts or larger), well washed

FOR THE PICKLING SOLUTION

4½ cups distilled white vinegar
⅓ cup salt
¼ cup sugar, or more to taste
1 teaspoon black onion seeds (sev gundig; optional)
1 teaspoon dried oregano
1 teaspoon black peppercorns
½ teaspoon ground turmeric

FOR THE VEGETABLES

1 head cauliflower, cut into bite-size florets
4 medium-size carrots (about 8 ounces), peeled and cut into 1-inch pieces
4 medium-size celery ribs, cut into 1-inch pieces
1 turnip, peeled and cut lengthwise in half, then crosswise into ¼-inch slices
1 medium-size onion, cut into ¼-inch slices
3 cloves garlic, peeled

1. Make the pickling solution: Combine the vinegar, salt, sugar, black onion seeds (if using), oregano, peppercorns, turmeric, and 3 cups of water in a large jar. Cover the jar tightly and shake until the salt and sugar dissolve.

2. Prepare the vegetables: Add the cauliflower, carrots, celery, turnip, onion, and garlic to the jar and stir. Taste for seasoning, adding more sugar as necessary. Press a piece of plastic wrap directly on top of the vegetable mixture to keep the vegetables submerged. Cover the jar, placing another piece of plastic wrap between the mouth of the jar and the lid (to prevent the vinegar from corroding the metal lid). Let the vegetables pickle, at room temperature or in the refrigerator, for at least 3 days; the *torshi* can be refrigerated, tightly covered, for several weeks.

REPUBLIC OF GEORGIA

GEORGIAN PICKLES

ON THE SIDE
MAKES ABOUT 3 QUARTS; SERVES 10 TO 12

Whenever Georgians eat barbecue (indeed, whenever they feast in general), you'll find a lavish assortment of pickles—vegetables you expect to find pickled, like cucumbers and cabbage, and vegetables you wouldn't think of pickling, like lettuce and watermelon (the whole fruit, not just the rind). Georgian pickles can be made in a matter of minutes, but leave yourself three days for the vegetables to cure.

ADVANCE PREPARATION

3 days for pickling the vegetables and watermelon

SPECIAL EQUIPMENT

Three 1-quart jars, well washed

FOR THE PICKLING SOLUTION

5 cups distilled white vinegar
5 tablespoons salt
5 tablespoons sugar, or more to taste
8 cloves garlic, peeled
8 sprigs fresh cilantro
8 sprigs fresh dill
8 dried hot peppers

FOR THE VEGETABLES AND MELON

1 head iceberg lettuce
1 pound ripe plum tomatoes
1 pound pickling cucumbers, such as Kirby
1 piece (1 pound) watermelon with rind

1. Make the pickling solution: Combine the vinegar, salt, sugar, and 3 cups of water in a nonreactive saucepan and bring to a boil over high heat. Remove from the heat and stir in the garlic, cilantro, dill, and dried hot peppers. Let the pickling solution cool to room temperature, about 1 hour. Taste for seasoning, adding more sugar as necessary.

2. Prepare the vegetables and melon: Trim the lettuce and cut it into 1-inch wedges. Rinse the tomatoes and cucumbers under cold running water, blot them dry with paper towels, and prick each 5 to 6 times with a fork. Cut the watermelon, both rind and flesh, into 1-inch wedges. Divide the vegetables and melon among three clean 1-quart jars. Add enough cooled pickling mixture to cover. Press a piece of plastic wrap directly on top of the vegetable and melon mixture in each jar to keep the vegetables and melon submerged.

3. Cover the jars, placing another piece of plastic wrap between the mouth of the jar and the lid (to prevent the vinegar from corroding the metal lid). Let the vegetables and melon pickle in the refrigerator for at least 3 days. The pickles can be refrigerated, tightly covered, for several weeks.

MEXICO

CARROT AND PINEAPPLE ESCABECHE

ON THE SIDE
MAKES ABOUT 2 QUARTS; SERVES 8 TO 10

Escabeche is the Spanish term for a food preserved in vinegar. Part relish, part pickle, part salsa, this one, made with carrots and pineapple, is 100 percent delicious. Serve it as an accompaniment to turkey, for example, the way you would cranberry sauce. One chile will give you a warm *escabeche,* six chiles an infernally hot one.

ADVANCE PREPARATION

At least 2 hours for chilling the *escabeche*

INGREDIENTS

2 cups rice vinegar
⅔ cup sugar
5 cups julienned carrots (6 to 8 medium-size carrots; about 10 ounces)
1 to 6 serrano or jalapeño peppers, sliced crosswise as thinly as possible
3 cups diced fresh pineapple
Salt and freshly ground black pepper
3 tablespoons chopped fresh cilantro

1. Bring the rice vinegar and sugar to a boil in a large, shallow nonreactive saucepan over high heat. Add the carrots, reduce the heat to medium, and let simmer until just tender, 1 to 2 minutes. Add the serrano peppers and let simmer for 20 seconds. Using a slotted spoon, transfer the carrots and peppers to a heatproof serving bowl.

2. Add the pineapple to the simmering rice vinegar mixture and cook until just tender, 2 to 4 minutes. Using a slotted spoon, transfer the pineapple to the serving bowl. Add enough of the poaching liquid to nicely coat the vegetables and pineapple. Season the *escabeche* with salt and black pepper to taste.

3. Let the *escabeche* cool to room temperature, then refrigerate it, covered, until serving time, at least 2 hours (see Note).

4. Just before serving, taste the *escabeche* for seasoning, adding more salt and/or black pepper as necessary, and stir in the cilantro.

NOTE: The *escabeche* can be prepared to this point up to 2 days ahead.

CENTRAL AMERICA

PICKLED VEGETABLES

ENCURTIDO

ON THE SIDE
MAKES ABOUT 2 PINTS; SERVES 8 TO 10

The tangy condiment *encurtido* turns up throughout Central America, where it's used as an all-purpose accompaniment for grilled steaks and sausages, rice and bean dishes—and just about everything else. The chile of choice is the habañero pepper, a Mexican and Central American cousin of the Caribbean Scotch bonnet chile. The two are interchangeable.

ADVANCE PREPARATION

At least 1 day for pickling the vegetables

SPECIAL EQUIPMENT

Two 1-pint jars, well washed

INGREDIENTS

2 cups distilled white vinegar
1 tablespoon salt, or more to taste
2 large white onions, finely diced
1 cup finely diced carrots
½ medium-size green bell pepper, cored, seeded, and finely diced
½ medium-size red bell pepper, cored, seeded, and finely diced
1 to 3 fresh habañero peppers, thinly sliced
3 tablespoons chopped fresh cilantro
1 tablespoon chopped fresh oregano, or 2 teaspoons dried oregano
8 black peppercorns
2 allspice berries

1. Combine the vinegar and salt in a nonreactive bowl and whisk until the salt dissolves. Stir in the onions, carrots, green and red bell peppers, habañeros, cilantro, oregano, peppercorns, and allspice berries. Taste for seasoning, adding more salt as necessary. Transfer the *encurtido* to two 1-pint jars.

2. Cover the jars, placing a piece of plastic wrap between the mouth of each jar and the lid (to prevent the vinegar from corroding the metal lid). Let the vegetables pickle, at room temperature, for at least 1 day (see Note).

NOTE: *Encurtido* will keep for several weeks in the refrigerator (the flavor improves as the mixture sits).

MALAYSIA

PENANG SHALLOT RELISH

CHUNG GAO JAI

ON THE SIDE
MAKES ABOUT 1¼ CUPS; SERVES 4 TO 6

Shallot relishes turn up widely on the world's barbecue trail. I've enjoyed them in countries as diverse as Morocco, Malaysia, and Turkey. One reason for their popularity is that shallots have a milder, more refined flavor than onions. This relish comes from the island of Penang in northwestern Malaysia, where it is served with Grilled Skate Wings (page 342). In fact, it's delicious with just about any type of fish and even over steak. Warning, though: This baby is hot!

Sambal ulek is a fiery red chile paste from Indonesia and Malaysia, widely available at Asian markets and in some specialty food shops. Substitutes include unsweetened Thai and Vietnamese red chile sauces and Chinese chile pastes.

1 cup thinly sliced shallots
½ cup fresh lime juice, or more to taste
1½ teaspoons salt, or more to taste
1½ teaspoons sugar
1 tablespoon sambal ulek or other hot chile paste, or more to taste

Place the shallots in a large nonreactive bowl, add the lime juice, salt, sugar, *sambal ulek,* and ¼ cup of water, and stir until the salt and sugar dissolve. Taste for seasoning, adding more lime juice, salt, and/or or *sambal ulek* as necessary. The relish will taste good right away and even better after 30 minutes, as the flavors blend and merge.

INDONESIA

FIERY CHILE AND SHALLOT RELISH

SAMBAL CHOBEK

ON THE SIDE
MAKES ABOUT 1 CUP; SERVES 4 TO 6

This relish (or *sambal,* as it is called in Indonesia) features an incendiary blend of shallots and red chiles. *Chobek* is a black lava-stone mortar and pestle traditionally used to grind the ingredients for *sambals* in Java. There are lots of options for chiles: red jalapeño or serrano peppers, bird peppers or tabasco peppers. I've given a range to suit every degree of heat tolerance (an Indonesian would use the full fifteen). You'll need to know about one offbeat ingredient, shrimp paste. Called *trassi* in Indonesia and *belacan* in Malaysia, it's a malodorous purple-brown paste of ground, salted, fermented shrimp.

It tastes a lot better than it smells. If shrimp paste is not available, you could use a few drops of Asian fish sauce or omit it entirely.

½ teaspoon shrimp paste (optional)
5 to 15 fresh red chiles, stemmed and thinly sliced
4 shallots, coarsely chopped
⅔ cup fresh lime juice, or more to taste
2 teaspoons salt, or more to taste

1. Roll the shrimp paste (if using) into a ball and place it on the end of a fork or skewer. Hold it over a live flame (either a barbecue grill or gas burner) until lightly toasted and very aromatic, 2 to 4 minutes. Alternatively, you can place the shrimp paste on a piece of aluminum foil and roast it under the broiler.

2. Combine the shrimp paste, chiles, shallots, lime juice, and salt in a blender or food processor and blend to a coarse paste. Taste for seasoning, adding more lime juice and/or salt as necessary; the *sambal* should be very spicy. *Sambal chobek* can be refrigerated, tightly covered, for at least 3 days.

MOROCCO

MOROCCAN SHALLOT RELISH

ON THE SIDE
MAKES ABOUT 1 CUP; SERVES 4

This simple relish is a traditional accompaniment to Moroccan barbecue. Serve it with any of the Moroccan lamb dishes in the lamb chapter or the Bani Marine Street Beef Kebabs (page 163).

½ cup finely chopped shallots
½ cup finely chopped flat-leaf parsley
2 tablespoons extra-virgin olive oil
2 tablespoons fresh lemon juice, or more to taste
½ teaspoon salt, or more to taste
½ teaspoon freshly ground black pepper, or more to taste

Combine the shallots, parsley, olive oil, and lemon juice in a mixing bowl and toss to mix. Add the salt and pepper and toss again. Taste for seasoning, adding more lemon juice, salt, and/or pepper as necessary. The relish tastes best served within 2 hours.

NICARAGUA

PICKLED ONIONS

CEBOLLITA

ON THE SIDE
MAKES ABOUT 2 CUPS; SERVES 6

In Nicaragua, grilled beef is always served with pickled onions. This is one of the quickest and easiest pickle recipes there is—perfect for any grilled meat.

ADVANCE PREPARATION

6 to 8 hours for pickling the onions

SPECIAL EQUIPMENT

One 1-pint jar, well washed

INGREDIENTS

1 cup distilled white vinegar
1½ teaspoons salt
½ teaspoon sugar
1 large white onion, cut into thin wedges
1 to 2 fresh jalapeño peppers, thinly sliced

1. Place the vinegar, salt, and sugar in a nonreactive bowl and whisk until the salt and sugar dissolve. Stir in the onion and jalapeños. Press a piece of plastic wrap directly on top of the mixture to keep the onions submerged.

2. Let the onions and jalapeños pickle at room temperature for 6 to 8 hours, then transfer them to a clean 1-pint jar. Cover the jar, placing a piece of plastic wrap between the mouth of the jar and the lid (to prevent the vinegar from corroding the metal lid). The *cebollita* can be refrigerated, tightly covered, for several weeks.

MEXICO

ONION-CILANTRO RELISH

ON THE SIDE
SERVES 6 TO 8

This simple relish turns up in Mexico wherever you find *barbacoa* (see page 200 for a description), grilled fish, or grilled meats. I love the way the relish launches a triple assault on your tongue: the pungency of the onion, the peppery bite of the radishes, and the aromatic punch of fresh cilantro. By the way, the cilantro has a neutralizing effect on the onion; you're less likely to get "onion breath" when you eat the two ingredients together.

1 bunch fresh cilantro
1 bunch radishes
1 sweet white onion, peeled

Rinse the cilantro under cold running water, blot it dry with paper towels, and pluck the leaves from the stems. Trim and rinse the radishes, then cut them into ¼-inch dice. Cut the onion into ¼-inch dice. Combine the cilantro, radishes, and onion in a serving bowl and toss to mix. The relish tastes best served within 2 hours of being made.

TURKEY

ONION RELISH WITH POMEGRANATE MOLASSES

ON THE SIDE
MAKES ABOUT 2 CUPS; SERVES 4 TO 6

This tangy relish turns up in one form or another at kebab houses and private homes throughout Turkey. A simple version might consist solely of parsley and sliced onions. Here's a more elaborate relish—flavored with sumac, Aleppo pepper, and pomegranate molasses. I first sampled it at the home of Turkish cooking authority Ayfer Unsal.

1 medium-size white onion, thinly sliced lengthwise
1 medium-size red bell pepper, cored, seeded, and thinly sliced
¼ cup coarsely chopped flat-leaf parsley
1 tablespoon Aleppo pepper flakes or sweet or hot paprika
1 tablespoon ground sumac (see box, page 248), or 2 teaspoons fresh lemon juice
1 tablespoon Pomegranate Molasses (page 243)
Salt

Place the onion, bell pepper, parsley, pepper flakes, sumac powder, and Pomegranate Molasses in an attractive bowl and mix them together well with your hands or a wooden spoon (mixing with your hands helps soften the onions). Let the relish stand 5 to 10 minutes, then season with salt to taste. Serve at once.

GUYANA

MANGO FIRE RELISH

ON THE SIDE
MAKES ABOUT 2 CUPS; SERVES 8

This popular condiment from Guyana is alarmingly hot and delectably fruity. Tradition calls for the relish to be made with green mangoes, but I like the peach and apricot tones that come from ripe ones. Use the relish sparingly—it's *really* hot. To make a slightly less fiery version, seed the Scotch bonnets before pureeing. Serve this relish with any simply grilled seafood, poultry, or meat dish.

1 pound ripe mangoes, peeled, pitted, and cut into ½-inch dice (about 2 cups)
1 to 4 Scotch bonnet chiles, or more if you can bear it, stemmed
4 cloves garlic, crushed
2 teaspoons salt, or more to taste
2 teaspoons sugar
⅓ cup fresh lime juice, or more to taste

ONION-CILANTRO RELISH | AT LEFT

MIXED VEGETABLE ACHAR | AT RIGHT

Combine the mangoes, Scotch bonnets, garlic, salt, and sugar in a food processor and process to a coarse puree. Add the lime juice and 2 tablespoons of water and process just to mix. Add more water as needed to obtain a thick but pourable relish. Taste for seasoning, adding more salt and/or lime juice as necessary. The relish can be refrigerated, tightly covered, for at least 1 week.

SINGAPORE

PINEAPPLE ACHAR

ON THE SIDE
MAKES ABOUT 3 CUPS; SERVES 6

Achar is an Indian and Southeast Asian relishlike dish often made with fruit. This one contrasts the cooling succulence of fresh pineapple with the fiery bite of chiles. There is one ingredient that may take you by surprise here: fish sauce. Yet, throughout Southeast Asia this briny condiment is paired with fruit. You'll be amazed how the salt in the fish sauce brings out the sweetness of the pineapple. And how the acidity in the fruit eliminates the fishy flavor of the fish sauce. So try it even if you have misgivings. I promise you'll be delighted. This recipe was inspired by an *achar* I tasted at a food stall in the Arab market in Singapore.

1 tablespoon Asian fish sauce, or more to taste
1 tablespoon fresh lime juice, or more to taste
1 tablespoon sugar, or more to taste
3 cups diced fresh pineapple
1 to 3 hot Asian red or green chiles or jalapeño peppers, seeded and thinly sliced (for a hotter achar, leave the seeds in)

Combine the fish sauce, lime juice, and sugar in an attractive bowl and whisk until the sugar dissolves. Stir in the pineapple and Asian chiles. Taste for seasoning, adding more fish sauce, lime juice, and/or sugar as necessary; the *achar* should be sweet, fruity, tart, and a little salty. Serve at once.

INDONESIA

MIXED VEGETABLE ACHAR

ON THE SIDE
SERVES 6

Here's another *achar*—this one from the Amandari resort in Bali. It's one of the most refreshing relishes ever to grace a table. I love the way the sweetness of the cinnamon and star anise balance the bite of the shallots and vinegar.

ADVANCE PREPARATION

8 to 10 hours for marinating the relish

FOR THE VEGETABLES

1 cucumber, peeled and seeded (see box, page 454)
3 carrots, peeled
1 medium-size red bell pepper, cored and seeded
1 medium-size green bell pepper, cored and seeded
4 shallots, peeled

FOR THE MARINADE

1⅓ cups distilled white vinegar
½ cup sugar
5 whole cloves
4 cinnamon sticks (3 inches each)
2 star anise
2 slices (each ¼ inch thick) peeled fresh ginger, smashed with the side of a cleaver
Salt (optional)

1. Prepare the vegetables: Cut the cucumber, carrots, and red and green bell peppers into 4 by ¼ inch strips. Thinly slice the shallots. Place the vegetables in a large nonreactive bowl, toss to mix, and set aside.

2. Make the marinade: Combine the vinegar, sugar, cloves, cinnamon sticks, star anise, and ginger in a small nonreactive saucepan. Bring to a boil over high heat. Reduce the heat to medium and let the marinade simmer until richly flavored, about 10 minutes. Taste for seasoning, adding salt if desired. Let the marinade cool slightly, then strain it over the vegetables. Let the vegetables marinate in the refrigerator, covered, for 8 to 10 hours, stirring from time to time. The *achar* can be refrigerated, covered, for 1 week.

Stuck on Saté: The Indonesian Grill

Indonesia is a country of mind-boggling ethnic diversity, with three hundred different races and religions. I visited two of the best known of the 12,000 islands in the Indonesian archipelago—Java and Bali—and no matter where I went I found saté (pronounced sah-TAY). Indonesia's culinary common denominator, these tiny kebabs are served everywhere, from roadside pushcarts to swank hotel restaurants, as a snack or full meal, at religious festivals, sporting events, and at the beach, pretty much any time of the day or night.

Simple to make, easy to eat, economical, nutritious, infinitely varied in shape and flavor, satés are one of the most perfect foods devised by man. Not surprisingly, their popularity extends far beyond Indonesia's borders. Satés have become an integral part of the Thai, Malaysian, and Singaporean diet (*satay* is the Malaysian spelling). In the last decade, they've been embraced with equal enthusiasm by American chefs.

A great many misconceptions surround saté, not the least of which is its main ingredient. To most Americans, saté means a small (although rather large by Indonesian standards) chicken or beef kebab served with peanut sauce. In Indonesia, however, there are hundreds of different types of satés to choose from, ranging from the tiny *saté lalat* (a beef and coconut saté made in such diminutive proportions, its name literally means fly saté) to the *saté buntel* (a ground lamb saté so large it takes four skewers to hold it).

The saté—or at least the idea of grilling meat on a stick—seems to have originated with Arab spice traders, who arrived on the island of Sumatra in the eleventh century A.D. The Arabs introduced the Islamic religion to the region, and it's possible they also introduced the Middle Eastern-style kebab. To support this theory, scholars point to Padang, which was one of the first cities in Sumatra to adopt Islam. *Saté padang* became one of Indonesia's most beloved satés and remains so to this day. (Of course, the idea of meat on a stick is so universal, it may have originated long before the arrival of the Arabs.)

If saté was inspired by the Arab kebab, it quickly acquired its own personality. First, it shrank. The average *saté ayam* (chicken saté) or *saté kambing* (lamb or goat saté) is about the size of your baby finger. This makes for great snacking: It's not uncommon for an Indonesian to down twenty or thirty satés at a single sitting. And still not leave the table stuffed.

According to Jakarta tourism representative Yuni Syafril, the saté takes its name from a Sumatran word meaning to stick, stab, or skewer. When you're really angry with someone, explained Syafril, you threaten to "saté" them. This sort of etymology is certainly not without precedent in the world of barbecue: Jamaican jerk, for example, is named for *juk*, the local dialect word for to stab.

Searching Out the Best

Syafril was my host in Jakarta, the capital of Indonesia, and the largest city on Java, and he acquitted his duties with the hospitality for which Indonesians are famous. My first night there, he took me on the Indonesian equivalent of a bar crawl. Our first stop was the Jalan Sabang, a noisy street lined with restaurants (including the famous Padang restaurant Natrabu, not to mention a Kentucky Fried Chicken and a Sizzler steak house). Our destination wasn't a dining establishment, however, but a tiny pushcart on bicycle wheels run by Nurul Phamid, a willowy young man with a faint moustache.

Like his father, who set up shop here in 1960, Phamid begins work at 5 P.M. and continues until

3 A.M. His stock in trade is *saté ayam,* which he prepares and grills by the light of a kerosene lamp. Phamid spends his afternoons threading tiny pieces of chicken thigh, liver, skin, and embryonic chicken eggs onto bamboo skewers not much bigger than broom straws.

When you place your order, Phamid prepares the marinade on the spot, mixing *ketjap manis* (sweet soy sauce), peanut sauce, a squeeze of lime juice, and chopped onion on a dinner plate. He dabs a handful of satés into the mixture, as you would a paint brush, then places them on a tiny charcoal brazier. A few waves of a bamboo fan—the most important piece of equipment in a saté man's kitchen after the grill—and the coconut husk charcoal blazes to life. Phamid bastes the sizzling satés with his secret ingredient, rendered chicken fat. A moment later, they're ready to eat.

The accompaniments to this splendid saté include a dollop of peanut sauce, a splash of *ketjap manis,* and a spoonful of *sambal* (fiery chile sauce), which are mixed together in a bowl. We were also served a steamed cake of sticky rice, called *lontong,* which is cooked in a banana leaf. We sprinkled everything with fried shallots. The cost for this princely feast—and it is princely—was 3,000 rupiahs, about 35 cents.

Now for Saté Pedang

Our next stop was a brightly lit sidewalk eatery called Gunung Sari, near Jakarta's lively Kota district. Jakarta operates on a diurnal economy: daytime businesses close their shutters at nightfall and a veritable city of portable restaurants spring up on the sidewalks in front of them. Some, like Gunung Sari, are quite elaborate, complete with generators, fluorescent lighting systems, and white Formica tables. I peered into an enormous cauldron bubbling away over a charcoal fire to see the next dish I was to sample: *saté pedang.*

To make it, beef hearts, tongue, and tripe are simmered for several hours in a fiery broth flavored with ginger, galangal, turmeric, garlic, and palate-blasting doses of black pepper. Then, the cooked meats are cut into tiny dice, threaded on skewers, and grilled over coconut husk charcoal. Meanwhile, the broth has been heavily thickened with rice flour into a starchy gravy. The kebabs and gravy are served on a banana leaf. To wash them down there's iced tea chilled with chips off a huge block of ice that sits on the sidewalk.

I must confess, I'm not a big fan of heart or tongue, and years of restaurant reviewing have conditioned me to disdain starchy gravies. But Gunung Sari's *saté padang* was one of the most delicious things I've ever tasted. I understood why this rough-and-tumble eatery does such a lively business.

During the weeks I spent on the islands of Bali and Java, I sampled an astonishing array of satés: Sausage-size *saté buntel* (ground lamb and coriander satés) served with sweet-sour tamarind sauce. Tiny *saté kalong* ("flying fox" satés), a sweet, garlicky ground beef saté named for a nocturnal squirrel that comes out about the same time of day the saté vendors do in the city of Cirebon on the north coast of Java. One night, I feasted on what was the last kind of saté I expected to find in this staunchly Muslim country: *saté babi manis* (sweet pork saté). I ate it, logically enough, in Jakarta's Chinatown. In Bali I enjoyed one of my all-time favorites, *saté lilit,* a spicy fish mousse flavored with exquisitely aromatic Kaffir lime leaves and grilled on fresh lemongrass stalks.

Recipes for these satés and others appear throughout this book—some are better as appetizers, some are better as main dishes, and most work well as either. Satés are the perfect grilled food for today's lifestyle: high in flavor, low in fat, great for casual eating and entertaining, and quick and easy to make. And traditionally you eat a relatively small amount of meat in proportion to the vegetable-based accompaniments.

MALAYSIA

MANGO ACHAR

ON THE SIDE
MAKES ABOUT 4 CUPS; SERVES 6 TO 8

Here's the third of our trio of *achars,* this one from Malaysia. I like to think of it as Southeast Asian coleslaw. The sweetness of the mango and coconut milk makes a particularly welcome addition to a barbecue, as does the contrast of sweet and savory, of hot and cold. As elsewhere in the book, I've given a range of chiles. One will make a mild *achar;* six will be Malaysian in its firepower.

FOR THE DRESSING

½ cup coconut milk, canned or homemade (page 522)
¼ cup distilled white vinegar
1 tablespoon sugar, or more to taste
1 tablespoon Asian fish sauce or soy sauce (see Note)
2 teaspoons minced peeled fresh ginger
1 clove garlic, minced
½ teaspoon salt, or more to taste
½ teaspoon freshly ground black pepper, or more to taste

FOR THE RELISH

1 pound ripe mangoes, peeled, pitted, and cut into ½-inch dice (about 2 cups)
¼ head green cabbage (8 ounces), cut into ½-inch dice (about 2 cups)
2 shallots, thinly sliced
1 to 6 hot chiles, such as Thai chiles or serrano peppers, seeded and thinly sliced (for a hotter achar, leave the seeds in)

1. Make the dressing: Combine the coconut milk, vinegar, sugar, fish sauce, ginger, garlic, salt, and pepper in a small nonreactive saucepan and bring to a boil over medium heat, whisking until the sugar and salt dissolve. Transfer the dressing to a serving bowl and let cool to room temperature.

2. Prepare the relish: Stir the mango, cabbage, shallots, and chiles into the dressing. Taste for seasoning, adding more sugar, salt, and/or pepper as necessary; the *achar* should be a little sweet, a little salty, and electrifyingly spicy. You can serve the *achar* right away, but it will taste even richer if you let it stand for an hour (no longer) before serving.

NOTE: Traditionally, the *achar* would be flavored with a malodorous condiment called shrimp paste. I call for fish sauce, which has a similar flavor and is easier to find and use.

INDONESIA

LEMONGRASS SAMBAL

ON THE SIDE
MAKES ABOUT 1¼ CUPS; SERVES 4 TO 6

Spicy pastes made of hot chiles and aromatic vegetables (sometimes with seafood added), *sambals* are served as condiments in Indonesia and Malaysia. A tiny bowl or spoonful of *sambal* (or several different *sambals*) is placed on the plate and served as an accompaniment to saté or grilled chicken or fish. This one features the perfumed flavor of fresh lemongrass. To be strictly authentic, you'd use fresh turmeric, palm sugar, and tamarind water—all available at Asian markets. But a highly tasty *sambal* can be made using ginger and ground turmeric instead of the fresh; brown sugar in place of the palm sugar; and lemon juice in place of the tamarind.

6 stalks fresh lemongrass, trimmed and thinly sliced
2 to 3 large shallots, coarsely chopped
6 cloves garlic, peeled
1 to 3 Thai chiles or serrano peppers, seeded and coarsely chopped (for a hotter sambal, leave the seeds in)
1 ripe plum tomato, cut into ½-inch dice (with its juices)
1 tablespoon chopped peeled fresh ginger
1 tablespoon chopped fresh turmeric, or an additional 1 tablespoon chopped peeled fresh ginger mixed with ½ teaspoon ground turmeric
1 tablespoon palm sugar or light brown sugar
2 tablespoons Tamarind Water (page 241) or fresh lemon juice
1 tablespoon sweet soy sauce (ketjap manis), or 1½ teaspoons each regular soy sauce and molasses
½ teaspoon salt, or more to taste
½ teaspoon freshly ground black pepper, or more to taste
½ cup peanut oil

1. Place the lemongrass, shallots, garlic, Thai chiles, tomato with its juices, ginger, turmeric, and palm sugar in a food processor. Process to a coarse paste. Add the Tamarind Water, sweet soy sauce, salt, and pepper. Process to blend.

2. Heat the peanut oil in a wok or frying pan over medium heat. Add the lemongrass mixture. Cook, stirring with a wooden spoon, until lightly browned and very fragrant, about 10 minutes. Taste for seasoning, adding more salt and/or pepper as necessary. Let the *sambal* cool to room temperature before serving. This delicious *sambal* can be refrigerated, tightly covered, for at least 1 week.

INDONESIA

TOMATO PEANUT SAMBAL

SAMBAL ACHAN

ON THE SIDE
MAKES ABOUT 1¼ CUPS; SERVES 4 TO 6

This is one of the milder *sambals* in the Indonesian repertory—a creamy condiment made nutty with peanut butter, aromatic with cilantro and coriander, and piquant with lime juice. Serve this *sambal* with any of the Indonesian satés in this book or with Vietnamese, Thai, or Malaysian style grilled meats.

¼ cup chunky peanut butter
¼ cup fresh lime juice or distilled white vinegar, or more to taste
¼ cup sweet soy sauce (ketjap manis), or 2 tablespoons each regular soy sauce and molasses, or more to taste
2 to 3 teaspoons sambal ulek or other hot chile paste, or more to taste
1 large ripe tomato, peeled and seeded (see box, page 454), then diced
2 scallions, both white and green parts, trimmed and minced
1 clove garlic, minced
3 tablespoons minced fresh cilantro leaves
1 teaspoon ground coriander
½ teaspoon salt
½ teaspoon freshly ground black pepper

1. Combine the peanut butter, lime juice, sweet soy sauce, and *sambal ulek* in a small bowl and whisk to mix.

2. Stir in the tomato, scallions, garlic, cilantro, coriander, salt, and pepper. Taste for seasoning, adding more lime juice, sweet soy sauce, and/or *sambal ulek* as necessary. The *sambal* can be refrigerated, tightly covered, for at least 1 week.

MOROCCO

TOMATO JAM

ON THE SIDE
MAKES ABOUT 1 CUP; SERVES 4 TO 6

This thick, spicy "jam" is unlike any tomato dish you've ever tasted. Sweet, fruity, and perfumed, it is traditionally part of the lavish assortment of salads served at the beginning of a Moroccan meal. I like to serve it in a more unconventional fashion—as a relish for grilled meats.

8 ripe tomatoes (3 to 3½ pounds)
½ cup sugar, or more to taste
3 tablespoons vegetable oil
2 tablespoons red wine vinegar, or more to taste
2 teaspoons ground cinnamon, or more to taste

1. Cut the tomatoes in half crosswise and gently squeeze the halves, cut side down, over a bowl to wring out the seeds (you can save the seeds and liquid for stock or soups). Grate the tomatoes, on the coarse side of a grater, into a large nonstick skillet.

2. Stir in the sugar, oil, wine vinegar, and cinnamon and bring the mixture to a boil over high heat. Reduce the heat to medium and let the mixture gently cook, stirring occasionally with a wooden spoon, until thick and jamlike, 5 to 10 minutes. Taste for seasoning, adding more sugar, wine vinegar, and/or cinnamon as necessary. The tomato jam should be sweet and spicy. Transfer the jam to a dish or bowl and let cool to room temperature. The jam can be refrigerated, covered, for at least 1 week.

SRI LANKA

PINEAPPLE CHUTNEY

ON THE SIDE
MAKES ABOUT 2 CUPS; SERVES 4 TO 6

Here's a quick, easy pineapple chutney that is often served with chicken satés in Sri Lanka. Tamarind gives the chutney a complex, smoky, sweet-sour flavor. For best results, use one of the golden pineapples, which are richer and sweeter than the conventional hard, green variety.

2 cups diced fresh, ripe pineapple (with its juices)
½ medium-size red bell pepper, cored, seeded, and cut into ¼-inch dice
¼ cup dark or golden raisins
1 to 4 serrano peppers or another hot chile, seeded and finely chopped
3 tablespoons chopped fresh cilantro
½ cup Tamarind Water (page 241), or ¼ cup balsamic vinegar mixed with 1 tablespoon light brown sugar
½ cup pineapple juice
¼ cup cider vinegar
2 tablespoons firmly packed light brown sugar, or more to taste
1 cinnamon stick (3 inches)
3 white cardamom pods, or 1 teaspoon ground cardamom
½ teaspoon sambal ulek or other hot chile paste

1. Combine the pineapple with its juices, bell pepper, raisins, serrano pepper, cilantro, Tamarind Water, pineapple juice, cider vinegar, brown sugar, cinnamon stick, cardamom, and *sambal ulek* in a heavy nonreactive saucepan and bring to a boil over high heat. Cook the chutney, uncovered, until the pineapple is soft and the chutney is thick and richly flavored, about 5 minutes. Remove the chutney from

HOW TO SEED TOMATOES AND CUCUMBERS

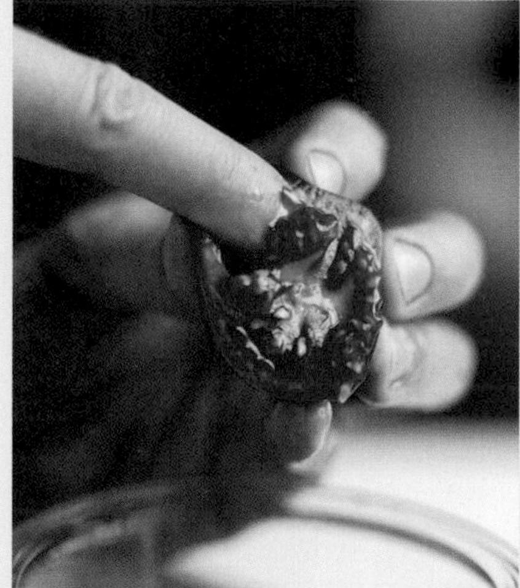

TO SEED A TOMATO: *Cut the tomato (fresh or grilled) in half crosswise. Holding a half in one hand, gently squeeze it to pop out the seeds and drain the liquid. You can help ease the seeds out with your fingertip.*

You may wish to work over a strainer placed on top of a bowl. Using the back of a spoon, press on the pulp and seeds to extract the liquid. Cover and refrigerate the tomato liquid to use for sauces, soups, or drinking.

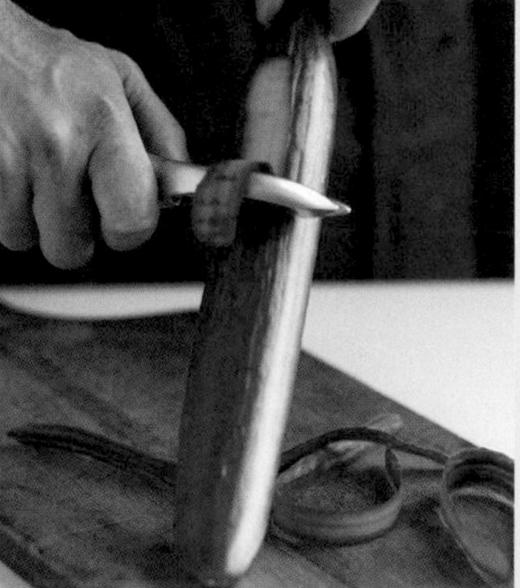

TO PEEL A CUCUMBER: *Remove the cucumber peel in lengthwise strips with a vegetable peeler, leaving about an eighth of an inch between each peeled-off strip. That way, when you slice the cucumbers crosswise, you'll get attractive green stripes on each slice.*

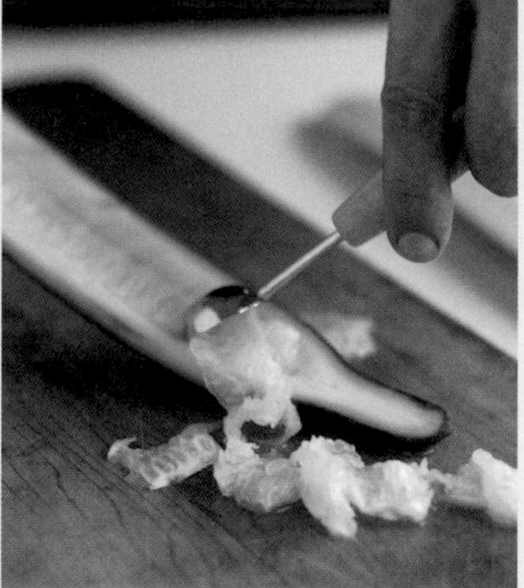

TO SEED A CUCUMBER: *Cut the cucumber in half lengthwise. Then, using a melon baller or a teaspoon, it's easy to scrape out the cucumber seeds.*

the heat and taste for seasoning, adding more brown sugar as necessary.

2. Transfer the chutney to a bowl and let cool to room temperature. Discard the cinnamon stick before serving. The chutney can be refrigerated, tightly covered, for several weeks.

MEXICO

OAXACAN-STYLE GUACAMOLE

ON THE SIDE
SERVES 4 TO 6

Just about everybody is familiar with the pureed avocado preparation known as guacamole. What you may not realize is that it serves more as a sauce than a dip in Mexico and that it changes from region to region. Guacamole is easy to prepare, but if you don't use ripe avocados (the sort that go splat when you drop them), it will never taste right. Here's the Oaxacan version—perfect for spooning over grilled meats.

2 ripe avocados
¼ cup chopped onion
1 clove garlic, minced
1 to 3 serrano or jalapeño peppers, coarsely chopped
¼ cup fresh lime juice, or more to taste
¼ cup chopped fresh cilantro
½ teaspoon salt, or more to taste

1. Peel, pit, and coarsely chop the avocados.

2. Combine the onion, garlic, and serrano peppers in a food processor and process until finely chopped. Add the avocados and process to a puree. Add the lime juice, cilantro, and salt and process just to blend. Taste for seasoning, adding more lime juice and/or salt as necessary.

3. Transfer the guacamole to an attractive bowl and serve at once.

MEXICO

GRILLED HABANERO SALSA

DIRECT GRILLING
MAKES ABOUT 1 CUP; SERVES 8

The habañero is one of the world's two or three hottest chiles. Grilling blunts its fiery bite and enhances its smoky, fruity flavor. Still, this is one of the most scorching salsas you'll ever taste. If you like them hellish, also try the "Dog's Snout" Salsa on page 459.

SPECIAL EQUIPMENT

Vegetable grate (optional)

INGREDIENTS

12 to 15 habañero peppers or Scotch bonnet chiles
1 small onion, cut lengthwise in half
1 clove garlic, minced
¼ cup fresh sour orange juice (see box, page 186), or fresh lime juice
¼ cup fresh regular orange juice
½ teaspoon salt
¼ teaspoon sugar (optional)

1. Set up the grill for direct grilling and preheat to high.

2. When ready to cook, preheat a vegetable grate (if using) for 5 minutes, then brush and oil it or the grill grate.

3. Arrange the habañero peppers and onion halves, cut side down, on the hot grate and grill, turning often, until browned all over, 3 to 6 minutes (the skins should be charred but the peppers and onion should not be cooked through). Transfer the peppers and onions to a cutting board and let cool.

4. Scrape off any particularly burnt pieces of skin, finely chop the peppers and onion halves, and place them in a serving bowl. Stir in the garlic, sour orange juice, regular orange juice, salt, and sugar (if using). Use this salsa sparingly; it's vicious! It is best served within 3 hours of being made.

GRILLED PINEAPPLE SALSA | AT RIGHT

ARGENTINA

TOMATO SALSA

SALSA CRIOLLA

ON THE SIDE
MAKES 3 TO 4 CUPS; SERVES 6 TO 8

This colorful salsa turns up wherever grilled meats are served in Argentina. The recipe varies from restaurant to restaurant and from family to family. Sometimes it's nothing more than chopped tomatoes and onions. The *salsa criolla* here is a slightly more elaborate version that tastes great with just about any type of grilled fare.

2 large ripe tomatoes (about 1 pound), cored and seeded (see box, page 454), then cut into ¼-inch dice
1 sweet onion, such as Vidalia or Walla Walla, cut into ¼-inch dice
1 medium-size green bell pepper, cored, seeded, and cut into ¼-inch dice
2 tablespoons extra-virgin olive oil
2 tablespoons red wine vinegar, or more to taste
3 tablespoons fresh flat-leaf parsley
1 teaspoon dried oregano
Salt and freshly ground black pepper

Combine the tomatoes, onion, bell pepper, olive oil, wine vinegar, parsley, and oregano in a nonreactive medium-size bowl and toss to mix. Taste for seasoning, adding salt and black pepper to taste and more wine vinegar as necessary; the salsa should be highly seasoned. The salsa can be prepared up to 4 hours ahead of time. Taste for seasoning and add salt and/or pepper as necessary just before serving.

U.S.A.

THREE FRUIT SALSAS

ON THE SIDE

Fruit salsas are a uniquely North American invention and are of relatively recent date. They've become an indispensable part of the American table and are a perfect companion for grilled meats, poultry, and seafood. They're also healthy, containing little if any fat. Here are three of my favorites. Once you have the basic idea, you can make salsa with just about any type of fruit.

GRILLED PINEAPPLE SALSA

DIRECT GRILLING
MAKES 4 TO 6 CUPS; SERVES 6 TO 8

Grilling imparts a distinctive smoky flavor to the pineapple and peppers in this salsa, but if you're in a hurry, a perfectly delectable salsa can be made without grilling. Serve the pineapple salsa over grilled pork.

1 ripe pineapple
1 medium-size red bell pepper
1 medium-size yellow bell pepper
1 poblano pepper or medium-size green bell pepper
½ to 1 Scotch bonnet chile or other hot chile, seeded and minced (for a hotter salsa, leave the seeds in)
1 tablespoon minced candied ginger
½ medium-size red onion, finely chopped
½ cup chopped fresh cilantro leaves
3 tablespoons fresh lime juice, or more to taste
1 tablespoon light brown sugar, or more as needed

1. Peel the pineapple, cut it in half lengthwise, and remove the core. Cut each pineapple half lengthwise into quarters. You should have 8 pieces.

2. Set up the grill for direct grilling and preheat to high.

3. When ready to cook, brush and oil the grill grate. Arrange the pineapple pieces, bell peppers, and poblano pepper on the hot grate and grill, turning with tongs, until nicely charred on all sides, 8 to 12 minutes. Transfer the pineapple and bell and poblano peppers to a bowl and let cool.

4. Cut the cooled pineapple into 1-inch chunks. Core and seed the bell peppers and poblano pepper and cut them into them 1-inch dice. Combine the pineapple, bell and poblano peppers, Scotch bonnet, candied ginger, onion, cilantro, lime juice, and brown sugar in a serving bowl and toss gently to mix. Taste for seasoning, adding more lime juice and/or brown sugar as necessary; the pineapple salsa should be highly seasoned. Serve the salsa within 3 hours.

SMOKY APPLE-BANANA SALSA

MAKES ABOUT 3 CUPS; SERVES 4 TO 6

The apple banana (*platano manzano* in Spanish) is one of the tastiest exotic fruits ever to cross the North American table. Short and stubby, it has a tart, "apple-y" banana flavor that makes you want to throw stones at regular bananas. Look for it in Hispanic markets and in some large supermarkets. This is the salsa to serve with grilled duck or chicken; the smoke flavor comes from the chipotle chiles.

1 to 2 chipotle chiles (see Note)
4 apple bananas, peeled and diced (about 2 cups), or 2 large bananas
½ medium-size red bell pepper, cored, seeded, and finely diced
½ poblano pepper or medium-size green bell pepper, cored, seeded, and finely diced
¼ cup finely diced red onion
3 tablespoons chopped fresh mint
3 tablespoons fresh orange juice
2 tablespoons fresh lime juice, or more to taste
1 tablespoon honey, or more to taste

1. If using dried chipotle chiles, soak them in warm water to cover for 30 minutes. Remove the chiles from the water and blot dry with paper towels. Stem, seed, and mince the chiles. If you are using canned chipotles, simply mince them (no seeding necessary).

2. Combine the chipotles, apple bananas, bell pepper, poblano pepper, onion, mint, orange juice, lime juice, and honey in a serving bowl and toss gently to mix. Taste for seasoning, adding more lime juice and/or honey as necessary. This salsa tastes best served within 3 hours of making.

NOTE: Chipotles (smoked jalapeño peppers) come dried and canned (the latter are packed in a spicy sauce called *adobo*). If you are using dried chipotles, you'll need to soak them in warm water for 30 minutes. If you are using canned ones, no soaking is required; simply fish them out of the can and mince them.

MANGO-MINT SALSA

MAKES 3 TO 4 CUPS; SERVES 4 TO 6

When buying mangoes, look for heavy, unblemished fruits. Let them ripen at room temperature until squeezably soft and very fragrant. Many (but not all) varieties turn red when ripe, so you really need to judge ripeness by smell and touch. If you have sensitive skin, wear rubber gloves when handling mangoes: The sap can cause a poison ivy–like reaction. This salsa is delicious made with other fruits, such as peaches, nectarines, or melons, and is a perfect companion to poultry or seafood. Note that the ingredients can be chopped ahead of time, but do the mixing within twenty minutes of serving.

1 pound ripe mangoes
1 medium-size cucumber, peeled, seeded, and cut into ¼-inch dice
½ cup finely chopped scallions, both white and green parts
½ medium-size red bell pepper, cored, seeded, and cut into ¼-inch dice
1 tablespoon minced candied ginger or peeled fresh ginger
1 to 3 jalapeño peppers, seeded and minced (for a hotter salsa, leave the seeds in)
¼ cup chopped fresh mint
3 tablespoons fresh lime juice, or more to taste
2 tablespoons light brown sugar, or more to taste

1. Peel and pit the mangoes. Cut the mango flesh into ¼-inch dice. You should have about 2 cups.

2. Combine the mangoes, cucumber, scallions, bell pepper, ginger, jalapeños, mint, lime juice, and brown sugar in a large serving bowl and toss gently to mix. Taste for seasoning, adding more lime juice and/or brown sugar as necessary; the salsa should be highly seasoned. The salsa tastes best served within 3 hours of making.

MEXICO

"DOG'S SNOUT" SALSA

XNI PEC

ON THE SIDE
MAKES ABOUT 1 CUP; SERVES 4 TO 6

The world's most colorfully named salsa—*xni pec* (pronounced shnee pek)—is also one of the hottest. *Xni* is Mayan for dog, *pec* for nose or snout. Just why it's got this name is a matter of debate. The likely explanation is that the habañero peppers make your nose run, an effect I can readily attest to—and a dog's nose is always wet. Or maybe it has to do with the salsa's pugnacious bite. I've given a range of peppers; in the Yucatán they'd use the full eight (for less heat, seed the peppers). There's more to this fighter than heat alone. The onion, tomato, cilantro, and sour orange juice create a complex play of flavors.

2 to 8 habañero peppers or Scotch bonnet chiles, finely chopped
1 large ripe tomato, cut into ¼-inch dice (with its juices)
½ cup finely chopped white onion
3 tablespoons chopped fresh cilantro
3 tablespoons fresh sour orange juice (see box, page 186), or 2 tablespoons fresh lime juice plus 1 tablespoon fresh orange juice, or more to taste
½ teaspoon salt

Combine the habañero peppers, tomato, onion, cilantro, sour orange juice, and salt in a serving bowl. Toss to mix. Taste for seasoning, adding more sour orange juice as necessary. The salsa tastes best served within 3 hours of making.

INDIA

TWO RAITAS

ON THE SIDE

A cooling condiment made with yogurt, vegetables, or fruits, and aromatic spices, *raita* is the perfect accompaniment to the Indian grilled fare in this book, not to mention an effective soother of any chile-inflamed palate. You'll find two traditional Indian *raitas* here. Both recipes call for the yogurt to be drained to concentrate its richness. If you're in a hurry, you can omit this step, but reduce the amount of yogurt by a half cup. You can make the *raita* with fat-free yogurt, but it won't be quite as rich.

PINEAPPLE RAITA

MAKES ABOUT 3 CUPS; SERVES 4 TO 6

ADVANCE PREPARATION

2 hours for draining the yogurt (optional)

INGREDIENTS

2 cups plain whole-milk yogurt (see Note)
½ teaspoon cumin seeds
1 cup finely diced ripe pineapple
4½ teaspoons fresh mint, or 2 teaspoons dried mint
1 teaspoon Quick Garam Masala (page 496)
Salt and freshly ground black pepper

1. If draining the yogurt, set a yogurt strainer, or regular strainer lined with a double layer of dampened cheesecloth, over a bowl. Add the yogurt and let drain, in the refrigerator, for 2 hours.

2. Meanwhile, toast the cumin seeds in a dry skillet over medium heat until fragrant, about 2 minutes (do not use a nonstick skillet for this).

3. Transfer the drained yogurt to a serving bowl and stir in the toasted cumin seeds, pineapple, mint, and ½ teaspoon of garam masala. Season with salt and pepper to taste. Sprinkle the remaining ½ teaspoon of garam masala on top of the *raita* and serve within 4 hours; the raita may be served at room temperature or cold.

NOTE: If you are not draining the yogurt, use only 1½ cups.

TOMATO-CUCUMBER RAITA

MAKES ABOUT 3 CUPS; SERVES 4 TO 6

ADVANCE PREPARATION

2 hours for draining the yogurt

INGREDIENTS

2 cups plain whole-milk yogurt (see Note)
½ teaspoon cumin seeds
1 small or ½ large cucumber, peeled, seeded (see box, page 454), and finely diced
1 medium-size fresh, ripe tomato, peeled, seeded (see box, page 454), and finely diced
Salt and freshly ground black pepper

1. If draining the yogurt, set a yogurt strainer, or regular strainer lined with a double layer of dampened cheesecloth, over a bowl. Add the yogurt and let drain, in the refrigerator, for 2 hours.

2. Toast the cumin seeds in a dry skillet over medium heat until fragrant, about 2 minutes (do not use a nonstick skillet).

3. Transfer the drained yogurt to a serving bowl and stir in the toasted cumin seeds, cucumber, and tomato. Season with salt and pepper to taste. Serve the *raita* at room temperature within 4 hours of making.

NOTE: If you are not draining the yogurt, use only 1½ cups.

THREE SLAWS

ON THE SIDE

Joined together the Dutch words *cole* (cabbage) and *slaw* (salad) serve as a reminder of the days when Manhattan was a Dutch colony. Amelia Simmons mentions slaw in *American Cookery,* the first American cookbook, which was published in 1796. Here's a sampling of slaws ranging from mild to fiery that would do any barbecue justice.

U.S.A.

YOUR BASIC SLAW

SERVES 6

This is the basic mild and creamy, mayonnaise-based coleslaw that is served at barbecue joints throughout the United States. To make a low-fat version, substitute low- or no-fat sour cream for the mayonnaise.

FOR THE DRESSING

5 tablespoons mayonnaise
3 tablespoons cider vinegar
1 tablespoon Dijon mustard
1 tablespoon fresh lemon juice
2 teaspoons sugar, or more to taste
1 clove garlic (optional), minced
2 teaspoons celery seeds
Salt and freshly ground black pepper

FOR THE SLAW

5 to 6 cups packed shredded green cabbage (about ½ medium-size head cabbage; see Note)
2 medium-size carrots, peeled and shredded or julienned (see Note)
½ medium green bell pepper, stemmed, seeded, and shredded (optional; see Note)
1 medium-size rib celery (optional), finely chopped

1. Make the dressing: Combine the mayonnaise, cider vinegar, mustard, lemon juice, sugar, garlic (if using), and celery seeds in a small nonreactive bowl and whisk to mix. Taste for seasoning, adding salt and black pepper to taste and more sugar as necessary; the dressing should be highly seasoned.

2. Make the slaw: Combine the cabbage, carrots, and bell pepper and celery (if using) in a large bowl. Add the dressing and toss to mix. The slaw tastes best served within 4 hours of making. Season the slaw with more salt and black pepper just before serving.

NOTE: The quickest, easiest way to shred cabbage for coleslaw is to use the slicing disk of a food processor. Shred the carrot and the bell pepper (if using) on the shredding or julienne disk.

JAPAN

SHOGUN SLAW

SERVES 4 TO 6

Ginger, rice vinegar, and sesame oil give this slaw a Japanese accent. Wasabi is often described as Japanese horseradish—the green toothpaste-looking stuff served with sushi. While I've made it optional, it does give the slaw a nice bite. Napa is an elongated Asian cabbage. You could also use green or savoy cabbage. Wasabi, rice vinegar, and black sesame seeds can be found in Japanese markets and in some large supermarkets.

FOR THE DRESSING

- 2 teaspoons wasabi powder (optional)
- 1 clove garlic, minced
- 1 tablespoon minced peeled fresh ginger
- 5 tablespoons rice vinegar, or more to taste
- 2 tablespoons sugar, or more to taste
- ½ teaspoon salt, or more to taste
- 1 tablespoon dark (Asian) sesame oil
- 2 tablespoons black sesame seeds, or 2 tablespoons toasted white sesame seeds (see box, page 113)

FOR THE SLAW

- 3 cups thinly shredded napa cabbage, (about ½ small head cabbage)
- 2 medium-size carrots, peeled and shredded or julienned
- ½ medium-size red bell pepper, cored, seeded, and very thinly sliced
- 4 scallions, trimmed, white part minced, green part thinly sliced lengthwise
- ½ cup snow peas, ends trimmed, strings removed, and pods cut into thin slivers

1. Make the dressing: Mix the wasabi powder (if using) with 2 teaspoons of water in a large bowl and let stand for 5 minutes to form a thick paste. Add the garlic, ginger, rice vinegar, sugar, and salt and whisk until the sugar and salt dissolve. Whisk in the sesame oil and sesame seeds.

2. Make the slaw: Stir the cabbage, carrots, bell pepper, scallions, and snow peas into the dressing and toss to mix. The slaw tastes best served within 4 hours of making. Taste for seasoning just before serving, adding more rice vinegar, sugar, and/or salt as necessary.

HAITI

HAITIAN SLAW

PIKLIZ

SERVES 8 TO 10

About the hottest slaw I've found on the barbecue trail, this owes its firepower to the dame jeanne, a Haitian cousin of the Scotch bonnet chile. As the name suggests, *pikliz* is a sort of pickled cabbage. I call for a range of chiles; the full ten would satisfy even the most pyromaniacal Haitian.

ADVANCE PREPARATION

24 hours for pickling the slaw

FOR THE DRESSING

- 1½ cups distilled white vinegar
- 1½ cups fresh sour orange juice (see box, page 186), or 1 cup fresh lime juice plus ½ cup fresh regular orange juice
- 2 tablespoons salt
- ½ teaspoon freshly ground pepper
- 3 whole cloves

FOR THE SLAW

- 6 cups shredded green or savoy cabbage (about 1 small head)
- 2 medium-size carrots, peeled and shredded
- 2 medium-size ribs celery, finely chopped
- 1 large onion, thinly sliced
- 1 bunch scallions, both white and green parts, trimmed and finely chopped
- 5 cloves garlic, finely chopped
- 2 to 10 Scotch bonnet chiles or habañero peppers, seeded and thinly sliced (for an even hotter slaw, leave the seeds in)

1. Make the dressing: Combine the vinegar, sour orange juice, salt, pepper, and cloves in a 2-quart crock, jar, or large nonreactive bowl. Whisk until the salt dissolves.

2. Make the slaw: Stir the cabbage, carrots, celery, onion, scallions, garlic, and Scotch bonnets into the dressing. Cover the crock with plastic wrap and let the slaw pickle in the refrigerator for at least 24 hours, stirring it several times to ensure even pickling. The slaw can be made up to a week in advance; store it, tightly covered, in the refrigerator.

32 OZ
4 CUPS
2 CUPS

CHAPTER 17

SAUCES

Not so long ago, I served as a judge at the Memphis in May International World Championship Barbecue Cooking Contest. I was dazzled by the virtuosity of the pork shoulders and astonished by the penetrating smoke flavor of the ribs. But what really took my breath away was the sheer diversity of the sauces.

"Woe to the cook whose sauce has no sting."
—GEOFFREY CHAUCER

Sauces have always been a touchstone of a pit master's art. In North America they range from the sweet, tomatoey sauces you find in Kansas City to the vinegar-based sauces of northern North Carolina, and from the mustard-based sauces of southern North Carolina to the fiery salsas of the American Southwest.

Grill jockeys are equally ingenious elsewhere. No South American barbecue would be complete without a garlic-parsley sauce called *chimichurri,* while it's hot peppers that give the North African *harissa* its kick. Spaniards dote on the roasted sweet red peppers and nuts that flavor their *romesco,* and fruit dominates many other of the world's barbecue sauces.

This chockablock chapter includes sauces that are an integral part of other recipes in this book and ones that are ecumenical in spirit—that go well with almost any sort of meat, bird, or seafood. The important thing about any barbecue sauce is for it to complement, not overpower, the meat. In this chapter sweet, sour, salty, bitter, and hot flavors are combined into a balanced, harmonious whole. The goal is a sauce that tastes great on a spoon (or on the tip of your finger) and even better on grilled food.

U.S.A.

BASIC BARBECUE SAUCE

ON THE SIDE
MAKES 2½ TO 3 CUPS

A good barbecue sauce is a study in contrasts: sweet versus sour, fruity versus smoky, spicy versus mellow. Here's a great all-purpose sauce that's loaded with flavor but not too sweet. It goes well with all manner of poultry, pork, or beef. The minced vegetables give you a coarse-textured sauce, which I happen to like. If you prefer a smooth sauce, puree it in a blender.

3 tablespoons vegetable oil
1 medium-size onion, minced
1 clove garlic, minced
¼ green bell pepper, cored, seeded, and minced
½ cup ketchup
½ cup tomato sauce
3 tablespoons cider vinegar, or more to taste
3 tablespoons Worcestershire sauce
2 tablespoons fresh lemon juice
2 tablespoons pineapple juice (optional)
1 teaspoon of your favorite hot sauce, or more to taste
½ teaspoon liquid smoke, or 2 tablespoons meat drippings
2 tablespoons molasses
3 tablespoons dark brown sugar, or more to taste
2 tablespoons prepared mustard of your choice
1 teaspoon dry mustard
½ teaspoon freshly ground black pepper
Salt

1. Heat the oil in a large nonreactive saucepan over medium heat. Add the onion, garlic, and bell pepper and cook until softened but not brown, about 4 minutes.

2. Stir in the ketchup, tomato sauce, cider vinegar, Worcestershire sauce, lemon juice, pineapple juice (if using), hot sauce, liquid smoke, molasses, brown sugar, prepared and dry mustards, black pepper, and 1 cup of water and bring to a boil. Reduce the heat to low and let the sauce simmer, uncovered, until thickened, about 15 minutes, stirring often to prevent scorching. If the sauce becomes too thick, add a little more water.

3. Remove the barbecue sauce from the heat and taste for seasoning, adding salt to taste and more cider vinegar, hot sauce, and/or brown sugar as necessary; the sauce should be highly seasoned.

4. Transfer the barbecue sauce to a serving bowl and serve warm or at room temperature. The sauce will keep, tightly covered in the refrigerator, for several weeks.

U.S.A.

CAROLINA MUSTARD BARBECUE SAUCE

ON THE SIDE
MAKES ABOUT 1½ CUPS

Tomato- or ketchup-based barbecue sauces rule most parts of the country. But in the southern part of North Carolina (and in a few parts of South Carolina and Florida), barbecue simply isn't barbecue unless it's served with a bright yellow sauce made from mustard, honey, and vinegar. If you haven't grown up with such a sauce, the very notion might seem off-putting. But even if you come from tomato sauce country, mustard barbecue sauce quickly becomes addictive.

Tradition calls for using inexpensive ballpark-style mustard and you'll certainly be in good company if you use this kind of mustard. But I like the sharper, more refined flavor of Dijon mustard—particularly an "old-fashioned style" mustard imported from France. Look for the words *à l'ancienne* on the label.

½ cup prepared mustard of your choice
½ cup honey
¼ cup firmly packed light brown sugar
¼ cup distilled white vinegar, or more to taste
Salt and freshly ground black pepper

1. Combine the mustard, honey, brown sugar, and vinegar in a nonreactive saucepan and whisk to mix. Bring to a simmer over low heat and cook gently, uncovered, until richly flavored, about 5 minutes, whisking from time to time. Remove from the heat and taste for seasoning, adding salt and pepper to taste and more vinegar as necessary.

2. Transfer the sauce to a serving bowl and serve warm or at room temperature. The sauce will keep, tightly covered in the refrigerator, for several weeks.

U.S.A.

MARK MILITELLO'S MANGO BARBECUE SAUCE

DIRECT GRILLING
MAKES ABOUT 3 CUPS

Here's a mango-based barbecue sauce that fairly explodes with tropical flavor. Grilled bell peppers and tomatoes pump up the smoke, while Scotch bonnet chiles stoke the fire. (Tender of tongue take comfort: The sauce is piquant but not incendiary.) This sauce was inspired by Florida superchef Mark Militello, who serves it with grilled swordfish. I can't think of a single grilled food that doesn't shine in this sauce's presence, but it goes especially well with seafood and chicken.

SPECIAL EQUIPMENT

1 cup wood chips, soaked for 1 hour in cold water to cover and drained

INGREDIENTS

1 medium-size green bell pepper
1 medium-size red bell pepper
2 large ripe tomatoes
1 large or 2 small ripe mangoes, peeled, seeded, and diced (about 2 cups)
⅔ cup finely chopped red onion
1 tablespoon minced garlic
1 Scotch bonnet chile, seeded and cut in half (for a hotter sauce, leave the seeds in)
⅓ cup cider vinegar
½ cup firmly packed dark brown sugar
2 tablespoons molasses
2 tablespoons Dijon mustard
2 tablespoons Tamarind Water (page 241); frozen tamarind puree, thawed; or fresh lime juice
1 tablespoon soy sauce
1 cinnamon stick (3 inches)
1½ teaspoons fresh thyme, or ¾ teaspoon dried thyme
1½ teaspoons fresh marjoram, or ¾ teaspoon dried marjoram
1 teaspoon ground cumin
Salt and freshly ground black pepper

1. Set up the grill for direct grilling and preheat to high. If using a gas grill, place all of the wood chips in the smoker box.

2. When ready to grill, if using a charcoal grill, toss all of the wood chips on the coals. Brush and oil the grill grate. Place the red and green bell peppers and the tomatoes on the hot grate. Grill the bell peppers and tomatoes, turning with tongs, until charred on all sides, 12 to 20 minutes in all. Transfer the bell peppers and tomatoes to a cutting board to cool.

3. Scrape most of the charred skin off the bell peppers and tomatoes, then cut them in half and core, seed, and

MARK MILITELLO'S MANGO BARBECUE SAUCE

coarsely chop them. Transfer the bell peppers and tomatoes to a large nonreactive saucepan and add the mango, onion, garlic, Scotch bonnet, cider vinegar, brown sugar, molasses, mustard, Tamarind Water, soy sauce, cinnamon stick, thyme, marjoram, cumin, ½ cup of water, and a little salt and black pepper. Let the sauce come to a simmer over low heat and cook gently, uncovered, until richly flavored, about 20 minutes, stirring occasionally. Add water as needed to keep the sauce soupy.

4. Discard the cinnamon stick, transfer the sauce to a food processor or blender, and process to a puree. For extra smoothness, press the sauce through a fine-meshed strainer. Season the sauce with salt and black pepper to taste.

5. Transfer the sauce to a serving bowl and serve warm or at room temperature. The sauce will keep, tightly covered in the refrigerator, for several weeks.

U.S.A.

NORTH CAROLINA VINEGAR SAUCE

ON THE SIDE
MAKES ABOUT 2½ CUPS

North Carolina occupies a unique position in the realm of American barbecue. Unlike the rest of the country, which enjoys tomato-based sauces, the preferred condiment here is a piquant mixture of vinegar and hot pepper flakes, with just a little sugar to take off the sharp edge. The meat it is served with is always pork, and the pork is shredded or finely chopped, not sliced. When you put the pork and vinegar sauce together, you have some of the most delectable barbecue ever to grace a bun. The jalapeño peppers aren't strictly traditional, but I like their added bite.

1½ cups cider vinegar
1 tablespoon sugar, or more to taste
1 tablespoon hot red pepper flakes
1 small onion, thinly sliced
1 jalapeño pepper, seeded and thinly sliced (for a hotter sauce, leave the seeds in)
2 teaspoons salt, or more to taste
½ teaspoon freshly ground black pepper

Combine the cider vinegar, sugar, hot pepper flakes, onion, jalapeño, salt, and black pepper in a medium-size nonreactive bowl and stir until the sugar and salt dissolve. Taste for seasoning, adding more salt and/or sugar as necessary. Use the sauce the day it is made; it does not store well.

CUBA

HONEY-GUAVA BARBECUE SAUCE

ON THE SIDE
MAKES ABOUT 1 CUP

Readers of my previous books will recognize the name Elida Proenza, a good friend and Cuban cook extraordinaire. Elida is forever proving this central gastronomic truth: While anyone can make a great-tasting dish with a lot of ingredients, it takes true talent to make unforgettable food with only two or three. Elida watched with what I imagine was secret amusement as I lined up several dozen bottles of spices and condiments to experiment with barbecue sauces. When I wasn't looking, she blended honey, guava paste, and commercial barbecue sauce to make this exotically fruity sauce, which instantly became a Raichlen family favorite. It is particularly good with chicken and pork.

Guava paste is a thick, fragrant red tropical fruit jelly sold in flat tins at Hispanic markets and most supermarkets. Once opened, it keeps for months wrapped in plastic in the refrigerator. Don't be disconcerted if the paste becomes crystallized or grainy—the sugar will melt back in when you cook the sauce.

¼ cup honey
3 tablespoons guava paste
⅔ cup commercial barbecue sauce (see Note)
Squeeze of fresh lemon juice (optional)

1. Combine the honey, guava paste, and barbecue sauce in a small, heavy saucepan and bring to a boil over medium heat. Reduce the heat to low and let simmer for 5 minutes, whisking to mix. The sauce is ready when all the guava paste is dissolved. If it tastes too sweet, add a squeeze of lemon juice.

2. Transfer the sauce to a serving bowl and serve warm or at room temperature. The sauce will keep, tightly covered in the refrigerator, for several weeks.

NOTE: What's amazing about this recipe is that you can use almost any commercial barbecue sauce to make it. Obvious choices include KC Masterpiece or Bull's-Eye, but you can also use vinegar-based sauces in the style of Arthur Bryant's or even the mustard sauces of South Carolina (for example, a sauce like the one on page 464).

Thinking farther afield, you could substitute peach or apricot preserves for the guava paste—or even a ginger jam from Australia. But, guava has a musky tropical flavor that makes the original version of this recipe hard to beat.

REPUBLIC OF GEORGIA

GEORGIAN PICKLED PLUM SAUCE

TKEMALI

ON THE SIDE
MAKES ABOUT 2 CUPS

A deliciously tart table sauce made with sour plums and cilantro, *tkemali* is the Republic of Georgia's answer to ketchup. Pronounced tek-MA-lee, it accompanies everything from grilled sausages to fish. Since dark red *tkemali* plums are very sour, I suggest using the large underripe red plums found at most American supermarkets. They work well for this recipe. You can also use other tart fruits, like rhubarb (see Note).

1 pound underripe red plums
3 tablespoons fresh lemon juice or red wine vinegar, or more to taste
1 tablespoon extra-virgin olive oil
3 cloves garlic, minced
1½ teaspoons ground coriander
½ teaspoon salt, or more to taste
½ teaspoon hot red pepper flakes, or more to taste
3 tablespoons minced fresh cilantro or dill

1. Fill a large saucepan half full of water and bring to a boil over medium-high heat. Immerse the plums in the water for 1 minute, then drain and rinse under cold running water. Slip off the skins, using a sharp paring knife. Cut each plum around its circumference all the way to the stone, then twist the halves in opposite directions to separate them. Use a spoon to pop out the stone. Cut each plum half in half again.

2. Combine the quartered plums, lemon juice, olive oil, garlic, coriander, salt, hot pepper flakes, and ¾ cup of water in a small nonreactive saucepan and bring to a boil over medium heat. Reduce the heat to low and let simmer, covered, until the plums are very soft, about 5 minutes. Transfer the plum mixture to a food processor or blender and process to a smooth puree. Return the puree to the saucepan and stir in the cilantro. Bring to a boil over medium heat, then reduce the heat to medium-low and let simmer until the sauce is reduced to about 2 cups, about 5 minutes.

3. Remove the sauce from the heat and taste for seasoning, adding more lemon juice, salt, and/or hot pepper flakes as necessary; the sauce should be highly seasoned. Let the sauce cool to room temperature before serving. The sauce can be refrigerated, tightly covered, for at least 2 weeks.

NOTE: You can prepare rhubarb sauce as described in the recipe starting with Step 2, substituting 1 pound of fresh rhubarb, trimmed and diced, for the plums. You may need a tablespoon or so more sugar to balance the rhubarb's acidity.

The Four Styles of an American Barbecue

Everyone agrees that barbecue is a distinctly North American delicacy. But what you get will be very different, depending on where you order it. East of the Mississippi, barbecue means pork, while to the west of the mighty river—especially in Texas—barbecue means beef. Ribs are the stock and trade of Kansas City pit masters, while pork shoulder remains the cut of choice in the Carolinas. To confuse matters further, more and more barbecue joints are serving chicken, a reflection of the general lightening-up of the American diet. As you feast your way along America's barbecue trail, you'll find considerable overlap in meat cuts, sauces, and cooking techniques. Here's a guide to the basic regional styles.

The Carolinas

In the Carolinas barbecue means pork, specifically pork shoulder (also known as Boston butt). Sometimes the meat is rubbed with a mixture of paprika, salt, sugar, and other seasonings. But just as often, pit masters forgo the seasonings. The pork shoulders are smoke cooked over oak or hickory for six to eight hours, or until tender enough to be pulled into shreds with your fingers.

Which is precisely what local pit masters do, for the ultimate Carolina barbecue is "pulled pork," a well-smoked and exceedingly tender pork shoulder, teased by hand into soft meaty shreds. Other pit maestros (particularly at restaurants) prefer to chop the shoulders into tiny pieces with a meat cleaver. The pulling or chopping is important, because it allows the tiny pieces of meat to soak up the sauce like a sponge. Unlike other parts of the country, Carolina-style barbecue is rarely served sliced.

Some cooks use vinegar-based mop sauces to keep meat moist during cooking. Other cooks simply let time and wood smoke do the job, without other culinary artifice. Sometimes, Carolinians go hog wild, barbecuing a whole pig in this fashion. The occasion is called a pig picking, and it becomes a community event.

Another factor that distinguishes Carolina barbecue from that of the rest of the country is the use of sauces. There are three main styles, each different from the sweet, thick, red condiment most Americans think of as classic barbecue sauce. In northeastern North Carolina (the capital of Carolina barbecue), folks favor a thin, clear sauce made of distilled white or cider vinegar flavored with salt, hot red pepper flakes, and a little sugar. In the western part of the state, they often add ketchup or tomato sauce to this mixture. The result is a peppery, tart, red sauce unlike any found elsewhere in the U.S. In southern North Carolina and South Carolina, the preferred condiment is a lurid yellow sauce made with vinegar, a sweetener (sugar, molasses, and honey are all used), and ballpark mustard. This is the sweetest of the Carolina-style barbecue sauces, but even it isn't particularly sweet.

The traditional way to eat Carolina-style barbecue is on a bun with coleslaw and vinegar sauce.

Memphis

Memphis knows its stuff when it comes to barbecue. This Tennessee city on the banks of the Mississippi hosts one of the world's largest barbecue contests, The Memphis in May World Championship Barbecue Cooking Contest, a three-day orgy of beer and barbecue that draws three hundred teams from thirty states and half a dozen countries to compete for tens of thousands of dollars in prize money.

Although you find all sorts of barbecued meats and even seafood in Memphis (locals like to say that the Mississippi Delta begins here), two cuts reign supreme: pork shoulder and ribs. The pork shoulder is slow smoked to fork-tender perfection, then served thinly sliced with barbecue sauce. But the ribs are what set Memphis apart from the rest of American barbecue.

Memphis is the home of the dry rib, a rack of baby back ribs or spareribs thickly crusted with a dry rub, then smoke cooked and sprinkled with more rub before serving. My favorite are the ribs served at Charlie Vergos' Rendezvous, a subterranean restaurant in downtown Memphis. Vergos uses a hybrid method for cooking his ribs: The meat is grilled directly over charcoal, but the grate is positioned high above the coals so the heat is somewhat indirect.

Dry-rub ribs are my favorite. The rub reinforces the flavor and texture of the meat without overpowering it, the way barbecue sauce sometimes does.

Kansas City

Kansas City rivals Memphis as the epicenter of American barbecue. Located on the Missouri River, it boasts more than ninety barbecue joints, ranging from Arthur Bryant–esque "grease houses" to proper restaurants with Tiffany-style lamps. Kansans are ecumenical when it comes to barbecue itself. Like their brethren in Tennessee and the Carolinas, Kansans love pork—especially ribs. Indeed, they've developed a whole vocabulary to describe the fine points of rib cookery.

Rib tips are the crusty trimmings of spareribs—greasy, gristly, and delicious. Long ends are the lean fore sections of a rack of spareribs, and short ends are the shorter, fatter, meatier hind sections. Most succulent of all are baby back ribs, cut closest to the backbone.

But Kansans are also broad-minded enough to share the Texas enthusiasm for beef. Because Kansas City was an important meat-packing center until the 1960s, the stockyards have traditionally supplied pit masters with brisket and less expensive cuts of beef. Like Memphans, many Kansan barbecue buffs rub their meats with a dry rub (a mixture of salt, paprika, and other spices) before cooking, but they don't tend to use mop sauces. Perhaps the most defining characteristic of Kansas City barbecue is the prominent role played by the sauce.

A typical Kansas City barbecue sauce is thick and sweet, a complex blend of ketchup or tomato sauce, brown sugar, corn syrup, molasses, vinegar, onion, garlic, hot red pepper flakes, liquid smoke, and sometimes even apple juice. The most typical Kansas City sauce (certainly the best selling) is KC Masterpiece, a brand created by child psychiatrist turned barbecue mogul Rich Davis. But no survey of Kansas City sauces would be complete without a shot of Arthur Bryant's sauce, a sharp, chalky, no-nonsense (and not the least bit sugary) blend of vinegar and paprika.

Kansas City is home to one delicacy seldom seen elsewhere. Called "burnt edges," they are the crisp, charred ends of smoked briskets. (Beware of burnt edges that are cut from the center of the brisket—they don't have the fat content that makes the real burnt edges so damnably delectable.) The world's best burnt edges come from Arthur Bryant's, the bare-bones grease house immortalized by Calvin Trillin.

Texas

I'll never forget my first taste of Texas barbecue—although it has been more than thirty years now. The place was Bodacious Barbecue in Longview, Texas. And, the meat was beef brisket; it was as smoky as a fireplace as succulent as stew, and tender enough to pull apart with my fingers.

In Texas, beef reigns supreme. (Where else but in Fort Worth would you find a monumental bronze sculpture of a herd of steers?) The preferred cut of meat for barbecue is brisket and the preparation is almost Zen in its simplicity, consisting chiefly of meat, time, and wood smoke. The wood is usually oak. As for the time, a properly prepared brisket spends up to eighteen hours in the pit, resulting in a pinkish-red tinge around the edge of the meat. This is the smoke ring, a naturally occurring band of color found in meats that are lengthily smoked. Most Texan pit masters don't bother to use rubs or mop sauce.

The beef generally comes sliced (not chopped), and it's more at home on a slice of cheap, soft, white bread than a bun. Texan barbecue sauces tend to be based on tomatoes and chile powder and are rather thin, tart, and vinegary. "We don't go in for a lot of sugar," says the pit master of the original Sonny Bryan's in Dallas, who gives his sauce its rich flavor by smoking it in the pit.

Today, there are more than 3,800 barbecue joints in Texas (according to the Texas Restaurant Association), and most of them serve ribs, pork shoulder, sausage, turkey, and other meats. But to taste Texas barbecue at its best, you've got to order brisket.

PHILIPPINES

GINGER-PLUM BARBECUE SAUCE

ON THE SIDE
MAKES ABOUT 1 CUP

Here's a contemporary Asian barbecue sauce, made with tangy sweet plums, that is delicious on duck, pork, and ribs. The recipe was inspired by Romy Dorotan, chef-owner of the restaurant Cendrillon in New York City, and it far surpasses the sugary bottled plum sauces from China. To pit a plum, cut it around its circumference all the way to the stone, then separate the halves by twisting them in opposite directions. Use a spoon to pop out the stone left in one of the halves.

12 ounces ripe plums (4 to 5 plums), pitted
1 tablespoon minced peeled fresh ginger
1 stalk fresh lemongrass, trimmed and finely chopped, or 1 strip lemon zest (2 by ½ inches), removed with a vegetable peeler
1 hot chile, seeded (for a hotter sauce, leave the seeds in)
2 scallions, both white and green parts, trimmed and finely chopped
1 large clove garlic, minced
2 tablespoons soy sauce, or more to taste
2 tablespoons sweet soy sauce (ketjap manis), or 1 tablespoon each regular soy sauce and molasses
2 tablespoons honey, or more to taste
1 tablespoon rice vinegar
2 teaspoons fresh lemon juice, or more to taste

1. Combine plums, ginger, lemongrass, chile, scallions, garlic, soy sauce, sweet soy sauce, honey, rice vinegar, lemon juice, and ½ cup of water in a heavy nonreactive saucepan and bring to a boil over medium heat. Reduce the heat to medium-low and let simmer, uncovered, until the plums are very soft, 5 to 10 minutes. Transfer the plum mixture to a food processor or blender and process to a puree, then return it to the pan. Taste for seasoning, adding more soy sauce, honey, and/or lemon juice as necessary; the sauce should be sweet, sour, and spicy. If the sauce is too thick, thin it with a little more water.

2. Transfer the sauce to a serving bowl and serve warm or at room temperature. The sauce will keep, tightly covered in the refrigerator, for at least 1 week.

BANGLADESH

BENGALI MANGO TAMARIND BARBECUE SAUCE

ON THE SIDE
MAKES ABOUT 1¾ CUPS

This recipe is based on a sauce I never actually tasted prior to making it. But the Bengali cab driver who told me about it described it with such passion I could easily imagine its flavor. The sauce belongs to a family of tamarind chutneys popular throughout the Indian subcontinent. Spoon it over grilled meats, poultry, and seafood.

1½ cups Tamarind Water (page 241) or frozen tamarind puree, thawed
1 cup diced ripe mango
1 medium-size onion, finely chopped
1 piece (3 by 2 inches) green bell pepper, finely chopped
2 serrano or jalapeño peppers, seeded and finely chopped
1 tablespoon minced peeled fresh ginger
3 tablespoons dark brown sugar, or more to taste
¼ teaspoon salt, or more to taste
¼ cup chopped fresh cilantro
1 tablespoon fresh lime juice

1. Place the Tamarind Water, mango, onion, bell pepper, serrano peppers, ginger, brown sugar, and salt in a heavy saucepan. Bring to a boil over medium heat, then reduce the heat to medium-low and let simmer, uncovered, until the mango and onion are very soft, about 20 minutes, stirring often. Stir in the cilantro and lime juice and remove from the heat.

2. Transfer the mango mixture to a food processor or blender and process to a puree. Taste for seasoning, adding more brown sugar and/or salt as necessary; the sauce should be both sweet and sour.

3. Transfer the sauce to small individual serving bowls and serve at room temperature. The sauce can be refrigerated, tightly covered, for several days.

VIETNAM

VIETNAMESE APPLE AND SHRIMP SAUCE

MAM NEM

ON THE SIDE
MAKES ABOUT ¾ CUP

Mam nem is certainly one of the more exotic dipping sauces in the Vietnamese culinary repertoire. Despite the odd-sounding combination of flavors—shrimp and apple—it's extremely tasty and easy to make. I first sampled this sauce in Saigon, where it was made with pureed pineapple. I like the no-fuss sweetness of applesauce. Serve *mam nem* with any sort of grilled fish or pork.

1 tablespoon vegetable oil
1 clove garlic, minced
4 ounces shrimp, peeled and deveined (see box, page 361), then very finely chopped
2 tablespoons Asian fish sauce, or more to taste
1 teaspoon sambal ulek or other hot chile paste or sauce, or more to taste
½ cup unsweetened applesauce

1. Heat the oil in a small, heavy saucepan over medium-high heat. Add the garlic and cook until fragrant but not brown, about 15 seconds. Add the shrimp and cook, stirring, until opaque, 1 to 2 minutes. Stir in the fish sauce, *sambal ulek,* and applesauce and bring to a boil, then remove the sauce from the heat. Taste for seasoning, adding more fish sauce or *sambal ulek* as necessary; the sauce should be highly seasoned.

2. Transfer the *mam nem* sauce to a bowl and let cool to room temperature. The sauce will keep, tightly covered in the refrigerator, for at least 3 days. Let it return to room temperature before serving.

THAILAND

A SIMPLE TAMARIND BARBECUE SAUCE

ON THE SIDE
MAKES ABOUT 1 CUP

Most North American barbecue sauces play the sweetness of sugar or molasses against the sharpness of vinegar and hot sauce. A similar contrast of sweet and sour characterizes the barbecue sauces of Thailand. The following sauce, inspired by one served at the restaurant Bahn Thai in Bangkok, derives its piquant flavor from tamarind. It is particularly good with grilled chicken or fish. I leave the number of chiles you use up to you.

¼ cup Tamarind Water (page 241) or frozen tamarind puree, thawed
¼ cup Asian fish sauce
¼ cup sugar
2 large shallots, finely chopped
1 to 6 Thai chiles or serrano or jalapeño peppers, seeded and thinly sliced (for a hotter sauce, leave the seeds in)

Combine the Tamarind Water, fish sauce, sugar, and 2 tablespoons of water in a small bowl and whisk until the sugar dissolves. Whisk in the shallots and Thai chiles. Serve the sauce at room temperature at once—or at least the same day you make it.

SPAIN

ROMESCO SAUCE

DIRECT GRILLING
MAKES ABOUT 2 CUPS

The most famous sauce in Catalonia, *romesco* is a gutsy puree of tomatoes, garlic, and fresh and dried chiles bound together with two characteristic Catalan thickeners: toasted bread and ground almonds. Traditionally, these ingredients would be roasted in the oven to intensify their flavor before pureeing. That set me thinking about an even better way to heighten the flavor: charring the vegetables and bread on the grill. Catalans would use a dried chile called *anorra.* These are difficult to find in the U.S., but a Mexican ancho or pasilla chile makes a good substitute. (In a worst-case scenario, you could use one to two tablespoons of chile powder.) *Romesco* is traditionally served with grilled seafoods, chicken, and meats. I like to eat it straight off the spoon.

SPECIAL EQUIPMENT

Vegetable grate (optional)

INGREDIENTS

3 dried anorra chiles, or 1 ancho or pasilla chile
1 small red bell pepper
2 large or 3 medium-size ripe tomatoes
¼ cup extra-virgin olive oil, plus more for brushing
5 cloves garlic, peeled
1 small onion, quartered
1 slice country-style white bread
3 tablespoons whole almonds, lightly toasted (see box, page 113)
1 bay leaf
3 tablespoons finely chopped fresh flat-leaf parsley
2 tablespoons red wine vinegar, or more to taste
Salt and freshly ground black pepper

1. Place the *anorra* chiles in a bowl and add warm water to cover. Soak until soft and pliable, about 30 minutes.

2. Drain the chiles, reserving the soaking liquid, and blot the chiles dry with paper towels. If a milder sauce is desired, remove the seeds.

3. Set up the grill for direct grilling and preheat to high.

4. When ready to cook, preheat a vegetable grate (if using) for 5 minutes, then brush and oil it or the grill grate. Brush the bell pepper and tomatoes with olive oil and grill until the skins are nicely charred, 10 to 15 minutes in all. Place the garlic and onion in a small bowl and toss them with 1 tablespoon of the olive oil, then arrange them on the hot grate and cook, turning with a spatula, until nicely browned all over and aromatic, 4 to 8 minutes. Grill the slice of bread until nicely browned, 1 to 2 minutes per side. Grill the soaked and drained *anorra* chiles until crisp and fragrant, about 20 seconds per side. As they are done, transfer the grilled vegetables, bread, and chiles to a platter and let cool.

5. Remove any very charred skin from the bell pepper and tomatoes; core and seed the pepper. Transfer the tomatoes to a food processor or blender and puree to a smooth paste. Add the grilled garlic, onion, bell pepper, bread, and *anorra* chiles, and the almonds, bay leaf, parsley, wine vinegar, and remaining 3 tablespoons of olive oil. Season the sauce with salt and black pepper to taste. Process until smooth, adding enough of the reserved chile soaking liquid to make a pourable sauce. Taste for seasoning, adding more vinegar and/or salt as necessary.

6. Serve the *romesco* sauce at room temperature; it will keep, tightly covered in the refrigerator, for at least 3 days.

NICARAGUA

NICARAGUAN TOMATO SAUCE

SALSA MARINARA

ON THE SIDE
MAKES ABOUT 2 CUPS

Nicaraguans call this tangy tomato sauce *marinara,* but it sure doesn't taste like any pasta sauce I've ever sampled. It is one of the three traditional accompaniments to Nicaraguan grilled meats. The other two are *chimichurri,* a parsley-based sauce (see page 477), and *cebollita*—Pickled Onions (page 445). Serve the *salsa marinara* with Nicaraguan-Style Steak (page 147).

3 tablespoons distilled white vinegar, or more to taste
3 tablespoons ketchup
3 ripe tomatoes, peeled and seeded (see page 454), then finely chopped
2 medium-size onions, thinly sliced
½ medium-size green bell pepper, cored, seeded, and thinly sliced
2 cloves garlic, minced
3 tablespoons finely chopped fresh flat-leaf parsley
1 to 2 jalapeño peppers, seeded and diced
Salt and freshly ground black pepper

Combine the vinegar, ketchup, and ½ cup of water in a small nonreactive saucepan. Bring to a boil over medium heat. Add the tomatoes, onions, bell pepper, garlic, parsley, and jalapeños. Reduce the heat to low and let simmer gently until the sauce is thick and flavorful, 5 to 10 minutes. Remove the sauce from the heat and taste for seasoning, adding salt and black pepper to taste and more vinegar as necessary; the sauce should be highly seasoned. The tomato sauce can be stored, tightly covered in the refrigerator, for at least 3 days.

LEBANON

CHARRED TOMATO SAUCE WITH POMEGRANATE MOLASSES

KHASHKESH

DIRECT GRILLING
MAKES ABOUT 1 CUP

Khashkesh isn't your typical tomato sauce—not by a long shot. Charring the tomatoes lends a distinctive smoke flavor, while the pomegranate molasses adds an unexpected sweetness and tartness. (The pomegranate molasses is available at Middle and Near Eastern markets, but I have also included a recipe for it.)

1 large ripe tomato
1 clove garlic, minced
2 tablespoons Pomegranate Molasses (page 243), or 1 tablespoon balsamic vinegar
¼ teaspoon cayenne pepper, or more to taste
Salt and freshly ground black pepper

1. Set up the grill for direct grilling and preheat to high.

2. When ready to cook, brush and oil the grill grate. ace the tomato on the hot grate and grill, turning with tongs, until charred on all sides, 8 to 12 minutes. Transfer the tomato to a platter to cool.

3. Scrape most of the burnt skin off the tomato, then place it and the garlic, Pomegranate Molasses, and cayenne in a food processor. Season with salt and black pepper to taste and process to a coarse paste. Taste for seasoning, adding more cayenne and/or salt as necessary; the sauce should be highly seasoned. Serve the *khashkesh* sauce, at room temperature, within 4 hours.

JAPAN

CLASSIC TERIYAKI SAUCE

ON THE SIDE
MAKES ABOUT 1½ CUPS

Many Americans think of teriyaki as a marinade, but in traditional Japanese cuisine it's actually a glaze or barbecue sauce brushed on simply grilled meats and seafood. *Teri* is the Japanese word for gloss or luster; *yaki* means grilled. Zen-like in its simplicity, this recipe was inspired by the late Shizuo Tsuji, founder of the Ecole Technique Hôtelière Tsuji in Osaka and author of the seminal book *Japanese Cooking: A Simple Art.*

½ cup dark soy sauce
½ cup sake or dry sherry
½ cup mirin (sweet rice wine) or cream sherry
2 tablespoons sugar

1. Combine the soy sauce, sake, mirin, and sugar in a small, heavy saucepan and bring to a boil over high heat. Reduce the heat to medium and let simmer until the sugar dissolves and the sauce is thick and syrupy, about 5 minutes.

2. Remove the sauce from the heat and let cool before using it as a glaze or as a sauce for serving. The teriyaki sauce will keep, tightly covered in the refrigerator, for at least 2 weeks.

INDONESIA

INDONESIAN KETCHUP

KETJAP MANIS

ON THE SIDE
MAKES ABOUT 3 CUPS

Ask for ketchup in the world's fourth most populous nation, and you're likely to be served *ketjap manis,* a thick, syrupy, sweet, spiced soy sauce. At first glance, nothing could be more different from the blood-red sauce most Americans think of as ketchup. But the two condiments are closely related, kissing cousins as it were, descended from a common historical ancestor.

Here's a homemade *ketjap manis* that makes an intriguing condiment for simple grilled meats and seafood. Mixing equal parts *ketjap manis* and melted butter makes a fabulous basting mixture for grilled fish. For the sake of convenience, I've westernized the recipe slightly, substituting the more readily available ginger and bay leaves for the traditional galangal and salam leaf. If you have the patience to search out these ingredients at an Asian market, your *ketjap* will taste even more authentic.

Throughout the book, I have suggested an even easier substitute for the *ketjap*—equal parts soy sauce and molasses—but if you like Indonesian grilling as much as I do, it's worth buying real *ketjap manis* or making your own.

2 cups soy sauce
1½ cups firmly packed light brown sugar, or more to taste
¾ cup molasses, or more to taste
2 cloves garlic, flattened with the side of a cleaver and peeled
2 slices ginger or fresh galangal (each ¼ inch thick), peeled and flattened with the side of a cleaver
2 whole star anise, or 1 teaspoon anisette liqueur plus ¼ teaspoon liquid smoke
1 bay leaf or salam leaf
1 teaspoon coriander seeds

1. Combine the soy sauce, brown sugar, molasses, garlic, ginger, star anise, bay leaf, and coriander seeds in a medium-size, heavy saucepan. Bring to a boil over medium heat, stirring until the brown sugar dissolves. Reduce the heat to medium-low and let simmer, uncovered, until the *ketjap manis* is richly flavored and slightly syrupy, 8 to 12 minutes, stirring it as it cooks. Taste for seasoning, adding more brown sugar and/or molasses as necessary; the *ketjap manis* should be quite sweet.

2. Strain the *ketjap manis* into a clean jar and let cool; it will keep, tightly covered in the refrigerator, for several months.

CHINA

HOISIN-CHILE SAUCE

ON THE SIDE
MAKES ABOUT 1 CUP

Enjoyed over a huge area, including China and Southeast Asia, this sauce is simplicity itself. It contains only two ingredients: hoisin sauce (a dark sweet sauce made from soybeans) and chile sauce. There are lots of options for the latter: I like a Thai chile sauce, like Sriracha, but almost any good-quality bottled chile sauce will do. You can increase or decrease the proportion of chile sauce according to the intensity of the sauce and your tolerance for heat. Serve this sauce with satés and other Asian-style grilled meats.

⅔ cup hoisin sauce
⅓ cup chile sauce

Combine the hoisin and chile sauce in a bowl and whisk to mix (see Note). Transfer the sauce to tiny bowls to serve.

NOTE: For a more striking presentation, spoon the hoisin sauce into tiny bowls and squirt or spoon a puddle of the chile sauce in the center of each. Mix the sauces in the bowl with the tips of chopsticks as you're eating and use the sauce for dipping.

JAPAN

TWO MISO BARBECUE SAUCES

ON THE SIDE

These creamy, sweet-salty sauces are two of the glories of Japanese grilling. You find them at humble yakitori parlors and at grand restaurants. They owe their rich tangy flavor to miso, a nutritious paste made from cultured (fermented) soy beans and grains. It's impossible to describe the exact flavor of miso, but if you imagine the salty tang of a bouillon cube crossed with the richness of cream cheese, you'll start to get the idea.

Miso is readily available in natural foods stores and Japanese markets, and in the produce section of many supermarkets. Stored in the refrigerator, it keeps almost indefinitely. Here are two miso barbecue sauces used widely in Japanese grilling.

WHITE MISO BARBECUE SAUCE

MAKES ABOUT 1½ CUPS

White miso (actually it's beige in color) is the most readily available miso and is best known as an ingredient in miso soup and miso salad dressing. Called *shiro-miso* in Japanese, it's made with soybeans and rice, which give it a sweet flavor. This recipe breaks with tradition in two ways. First, I've substituted mayonnaise for the customary egg yolks. Sometimes the sauce is served warmed but not cooked, so I prefer not to use raw yolks. Second, I use vegetable stock instead of dashi (a light fish broth usually made with dried bonito flakes and kelp). The purist could certainly use two egg yolks and two tablespoons of dashi instead. White miso sauce is delicious on grilled tofu and vegetables.

1 cup white miso
2 tablespoons sake or dry sherry
2 tablespoons mirin (sweet rice wine), or cream sherry
2 tablespoons sugar
2 tablespoons mayonnaise
2 tablespoons vegetable stock, dashi (see headnote), or water

1. Combine the white miso, sake, mirin, sugar, and mayonnaise in the top of a double boiler and whisk until smooth. Gradually whisk in the vegetable stock. Cook the sauce over simmering water, stirring occasionally, until thick and creamy, about 5 minutes. Remove the pan from over the water and let the sauce cool to room temperature.

2. Transfer the white miso sauce to a serving bowl. It can be refrigerated, covered, for at least 3 days. Let it return to room temperature before serving.

RED MISO BARBECUE SAUCE

MAKES ABOUT 1½ CUPS

Red miso (actually a reddish brown in color) has a deep, rich, salty flavor and isn't quite as sweet as white miso. Known as *aka-miso* in Japanese, it contains barley as well as soybeans and rice. Red miso barbecue sauce is particularly good on grilled vegetables and salmon.

1 cup red miso
2 tablespoons sake or dry sherry
2 tablespoons mirin (sweet rice wine), or cream sherry
2 tablespoons sugar, or more to taste
2 tablespoons mayonnaise
2 tablespoons vegetable stock, dashi (see White Miso headnote), or water

1. Combine the red miso, sake, mirin, sugar, and mayonnaise in the top of a double boiler and whisk until smooth. Gradually whisk in the vegetable stock. Cook the sauce over simmering water, stirring occasionally, until thick and creamy, about 5 minutes. Remove the pan from over the water and let the sauce cool to room temperature. Taste for seasoning, adding more sugar as necessary; be sure to stir any added sugar in thoroughly.

2. Transfer the red miso sauce to a serving bowl. It can be refrigerated, covered, for up to 3 days. Let it return to room temperature before serving.

THAILAND

THAI PEANUT SAUCE

ON THE SIDE
MAKES ABOUT 1 CUP

Peanut sauce is the traditional accompaniment to Southeast Asian satés. There are probably as many individual recipes as there are street vendors. You might find this version—enriched with coconut milk—at a Thai saté stall.

- **2 teaspoons minced peeled fresh ginger**
- **1 to 2 Thai chiles or serrano or jalapeño peppers, seeded and minced (for a hotter sauce, leave the seeds in)**
- **1 clove garlic, minced**
- **2 scallions, both white and green parts, trimmed and minced**
- **⅓ cup chunky peanut butter**
- **⅓ cup coconut milk, canned or homemade (page 522), or more as needed**
- **2 tablespoons Asian fish sauce or soy sauce, or more to taste**
- **1 tablespoon fresh lime juice, or more to taste**
- **2 teaspoons sugar, or more to taste**
- **¼ cup chopped fresh cilantro (optional)**

1. Combine the ginger, Thai chiles, garlic, scallions, peanut butter, coconut milk, fish sauce, lime juice, sugar, and cilantro (if using) in a small, heavy saucepan. Bring to a boil over medium heat, stirring to mix well, then reduce the heat to low and let simmer, uncovered, until richly flavored, 5 to 10 minutes. The peanut sauce should be thick but pourable; thin it with more coconut milk, if needed.

2. Remove the sauce from the heat and taste for seasoning, adding more fish sauce, lime juice, and/or sugar as necessary; the peanut sauce should be highly seasoned. Serve the sauce warm or at room temperature; it will keep, tightly covered in the refrigerator, for at least 3 days.

DUTCH WEST INDIES

DUTCH WEST INDIAN PEANUT SAUCE

PINDASAUS

ON THE SIDE
MAKES ABOUT 2 CUPS

Tamarind lends a fruity tartness to this peanut sauce, a West Indian version of an Indonesian classic. The sauce is designed to be served with Dutch West Indian Chicken Kebabs (page 73), but it's great with any type of saté, as well as grilled chicken or seafood.

- **¼ cup finely chopped onion**
- **1 clove garlic, minced**
- **1 teaspoon sambal ulek or other chile paste or sauce**
- **¾ cup creamy peanut butter**
- **¼ cup Tamarind Water (page 241) or frozen tamarind puree, thawed**
- **2 tablespoons sweet soy sauce (ketjap manis), or 1 tablespoon each regular soy sauce and molasses, or more to taste**
- **2 tablespoons distilled white vinegar, or more to taste**

1. Combine the onion, garlic, and *sambal ulek* in a mortar and pound to a smooth paste with a pestle. If you don't have a mortar and pestle, combine all these ingredients in a food processor or blender and process to a smooth paste. Transfer the mixture to a nonreactive heavy saucepan and stir in the peanut butter, Tamarind Water, sweet soy sauce, vinegar, and ¾ cup of water.

2. Bring the mixture to a boil over medium heat, then reduce the heat to low and let simmer, uncovered, until the sauce is dark and well flavored, about 5 minutes, adding more water as necessary to obtain a thick but pourable sauce. Remove the sauce from the heat and taste for seasoning, adding more sweet soy sauce and/or vinegar as necessary; the sauce should be highly seasoned.

3. Serve the peanut sauce warm or at room temperature; it will keep, tightly covered in the refrigerator, for at least 3 days.

U.S.A.

JAKE'S TURKISH COFFEE BARBECUE SAUCE

ON THE SIDE
MAKES ABOUT 2 CUPS

This isn't like any barbecue sauce Bubba used to make. Not with ingredients like cardamom, coffee, and hoisin sauce. The recipe comes from chef Jake, my stepson, who likes to serve it with grilled grouper and rich meats like pork and lamb.

2 tablespoons extra-virgin olive oil
1 medium-size onion, finely chopped
1 medium-size red bell pepper, cored, seeded, and finely chopped
3 cloves garlic, minced
1 tablespoon minced peeled fresh ginger
1½ cups brewed Turkish coffee or espresso
¼ cup hoisin sauce
2 tablespoons balsamic vinegar
1½ teaspoons unsweetened cocoa powder
2 teaspoons ground cardamom
2 tablespoons honey, or more to taste
Salt and freshly ground black pepper

1. Heat the olive oil in a large nonreactive saucepan over medium heat. Add the onion, bell pepper, garlic, and ginger and cook until softened but not brown, about 5 minutes. Add the coffee, hoisin sauce, balsamic vinegar, cocoa powder, and cardamom. Increase the heat and let come to a boil.

2. Reduce the heat to low and let the sauce simmer gently, uncovered, until thick and richly flavored, about 10 minutes, stirring occasionally. If the sauce seems too thick, add a little water. Puree the sauce in a food processor or blender, adding the honey to give the sauce sheen. Taste for seasoning, adding salt and black pepper to taste and more honey as necessary.

3. Transfer the sauce to a serving bowl and serve warm or at room temperature. The sauce will keep, tightly covered in the refrigerator, for several weeks.

SOUTH AMERICA

BASIC CHIMICHURRI

ON THE SIDE
MAKES ABOUT 2 CUPS

The traditional accompaniment to South American grilled meats, *chimichurri* turns up everywhere, from roadside barbecue stalls to pricey steak palaces, as far north as Nicaragua, as far south as Chile, and in just about every Spanish-speaking country in between. No two *chimichurri* recipes are exactly alike, although the most basic recipe contains just four ingredients: parsley, garlic, olive oil, and salt. This recipe comes from Marono Fraga, owner of the Estancia del Puerto in Montevideo's colorful Mercado del Puerto (port market). Don't be alarmed by the seemingly enormous quantity of garlic. The parsley acts as a breath sweetener.

1 bunch fresh flat-leaf parsley, stemmed
1 medium-size carrot, peeled and cut into 1-inch chunks
1 small head garlic, broken into cloves and peeled (8 to 10 cloves in all)
1 cup extra-virgin olive oil
⅓ cup white wine vinegar or distilled vinegar, or more to taste
1 teaspoon salt, or more to taste
1 teaspoon dried oregano
½ teaspoon hot red pepper flakes, or more to taste
½ teaspoon freshly ground black pepper

1. Combine the parsley, carrot, and garlic in a food processor and pulse to chop as fine as possible.

2. Add the olive oil, wine vinegar, salt, oregano, hot pepper flakes, black pepper, and ¼ cup of water and process to mix. Taste for seasoning, adding more vinegar, salt, or hot pepper flakes as necessary; the *chimichurri* should be highly seasoned. The *chimichurri* will keep for several days in the refrigerator (you may need to reseason it just before serving), but it tastes best served within a few hours of making.

ARGENTINA

RED CHIMICHURRI

ON THE SIDE
MAKES ABOUT 1½ CUPS

Traditional *chimichurri* is a garlicky green sauce made with olive oil and fresh parsley. But many variations exist in Argentina and Uruguay, including red *chimichurri*—a specialty of the venerable Buenos Aires steak house La Cabaña. This *chimichurri* differs from most in two significant ways: It's cooked (most are raw) and it's flavored with anchovies and tuna. The anchovies suggest parentage shared with two other of the world's great steak sauces, A.1. and Worcestershire, while the tuna recalls Italy's *tonnato* sauce, which is so delightful with cold roast veal or grilled beef and seafood. Here's how I imagine La Cabaña prepared the *chimichurri* sauce.

½ cup extra-virgin olive oil
½ medium-size red bell pepper, cored, seeded, and diced
½ medium-size carrot, peeled and diced
2 scallions, both white and green parts, trimmed and diced
¼ medium-size onion, diced
1 medium-size rib celery, diced
1 clove garlic, finely chopped
3 tablespoons drained canned water-pack tuna
1 anchovy fillet, drained and chopped
2 tablespoons chopped fresh flat-leaf parsley
2 teaspoons drained capers
1 cup tomato sauce
½ cup homemade chicken stock, canned low-sodium chicken broth, or water
¼ cup tomato paste
1 tablespoon red wine vinegar, or more to taste
1 teaspoon dried oregano
Salt and lots of freshly ground black pepper

1. Heat the olive oil in a medium-size nonreactive saucepan over medium heat. Add the bell pepper, carrot, scallions, onion, celery, and garlic and cook until softened but not brown, about 5 minutes.

2. Stir in the tuna, anchovy, parsley, capers, tomato sauce, chicken stock, tomato paste, wine vinegar, and oregano. Season with salt and black pepper to taste and cook, uncovered, until thick and fragrant, about 10 minutes.

3. Transfer the sauce to a food processor or blender and process to a puree, then return it to the pan and cook over medium-low heat for 5 minutes. Remove the *chimichurri* from the heat and taste for seasoning, adding more wine vinegar and/or salt as necessary; the sauce should be highly seasoned.

4. Transfer the *chimichurri* to a serving bowl and serve hot or at room temperature. The sauce can be stored, tightly covered in the refrigerator, for at least 3 days.

ARGENTINA

"DRY" CHIMICHURRI

ON THE SIDE
MAKES ABOUT ¾ CUP

This is the simplest of *chimichurris:* olive oil flavored with dried herbs and hot red pepper flakes. I first tasted it at the Estancia Cinacina, a horse ranch in Argentina that also stages barbecues and equestrian events for tourists. Argentinean food markets sell packages of premixed *chimichurri* herbs for people who don't have time to buy and chop fresh herbs. Spoon the *chimichurri* over grilled beef.

¾ cup extra-virgin olive oil
3 tablespoons red wine vinegar
1 tablespoon dried oregano
1 tablespoon dried basil
2 teaspoons sweet paprika
1 teaspoon dried thyme
1 teaspoon hot red pepper flakes
½ teaspoon coarse salt (kosher or sea), or more to taste
½ teaspoon freshly ground black pepper, or more to taste

Place the olive oil, wine vinegar, oregano, basil, paprika, thyme, hot pepper flakes, salt, and black pepper in a mixing bowl and whisk to mix. Taste for seasoning, adding more salt and/or black pepper as necessary. The *chimichurri* will keep, tightly covered in the refrigerator, for at least 3 days.

Chimichurri Variations

There are some cooks who add grated onion to their *chimichurris* (add one small onion to the Basic Chimichurri on page 477), while others add a quarter cup diced red bell pepper or fresh hot chiles.

FROM THE TOP CLOCKWISE:
RED CHIMICHURRI | AT LEFT • BASIC CHIMICHURRI | PAGE 477 • "DRY" CHIMICHURRI | AT LEFT

PORTUGAL

PORTUGUESE HOT SAUCE

PIRI-PIRI

ON THE SIDE
MAKES ABOUT 1½ CUPS

The Portuguese learned to love chiles in their former colony, Brazil. The chile in question here is one of the smallest members of the capsicum family, a bullet-shaped brute one quarter to one half inch in length; its diminutive size belies its ferocious bite. Piri-piri peppers go by the name of *pimenta malagueta* in Brazil and *gindungo* in Angola. Piri-piri sauce has become an indispensable part of barbecue all over the Portuguese-speaking world. If you live near a Portuguese or Brazilian market, you may be able to find fresh or bottled piri-piri or malagueta peppers. Acceptable substitutes include fresh or pickled cayenne peppers; péquin chiles from Mexico; Thai chiles; or in a pinch jalapeños.

The sauce goes especially well with grilled fish or chicken; serve it with any dish you feel could use an Iberian blast of heat.

ADVANCE PREPARATION

At least 3 hours for the sauce to stand

SPECIAL EQUIPMENT

One 1-pint jar, well washed

INGREDIENTS

6 to 12 pimenta malagueta or other hot red chiles
1 teaspoon coarse (kosher or sea) salt, or more to taste
⅓ cup red wine vinegar
¾ cup extra-virgin olive oil

1. Thinly slice the *pimenta malagueta,* then combine them with the salt and wine vinegar in a clean 1-pint jar with a lid. Seal the jar and shake it until the salt dissolves. Add the olive oil and ¼ cup of hot water and shake again. Let the piri-piri sauce sit, in a cool place, for at least 3 hours and up to 2 days.

2. Taste the piri-piri for seasoning, adding more salt if necessary. The sauce can be refrigerated for several weeks. Place a piece of plastic wrap between the mouth of the jar and the lid (to prevent the sauce from corroding the metal lid).

BRAZIL

COUNTRY HOT SAUCE

MOLHO DA COMPANHA

ON THE SIDE
MAKES ABOUT 2 CUPS

This salsalike hot sauce turns up wherever Brazilians grill meats. The chile of choice is a pepper called *pimenta malagueta;* the strength of its fiery bite is inversely proportional to its tiny dimensions. *Pimenta malagueta* come packed in vinegar in bottles at Brazilian markets. Other possibilities for chiles include Thai or bird peppers, serrano or jalapeño peppers, or even hot red pepper flakes. The traditional way to eat grilled meats in Brazil is to spoon this sauce on top, then sprinkle the meat with *farofa* (toasted manioc flour—see page 434 for Rainbow Manioc, a more exotic version).

1 medium-size onion, finely chopped
1 large, ripe tomato, finely chopped
½ green bell pepper, cored, seeded, and finely chopped
1 to 6 pimenta malagueta or other hot red chiles, minced
3 tablespoons extra-virgin olive oil
2 tablespoons fresh lime juice
1 tablespoon red wine vinegar, or more to taste
Salt and freshly ground black pepper

Combine the onion, tomato, bell pepper, *pimenta malagueta,* olive oil, lime juice, wine vinegar, and ¼ cup of water in a small nonreactive bowl and stir to mix. Taste for seasoning, adding salt and black pepper to taste and more wine vinegar if necessary; the sauce should be highly seasoned. Serve the sauce at room temperature—the same day you make it.

NORTH AFRICA

TWO HARISSAS

ON THE SIDE

Harissa is North African hot sauce. The concept is sufficiently broad to include simple fresh tomato purees warmed with onion and hot paprika and complex sauces flavored with preserved lemons and cayenne. Homemade *harissa* is quite different and vastly more tasty than the salty canned *harissas* one finds in specialty food shops and ethnic markets.

A SIMPLE HARISSA

MAKES ABOUT 1½ CUPS

Here's a quick and simple version of *harissa*. Serve it alongside grilled lamb, kebabs, and other North African–style meats.

2 large, ripe tomatoes
1 small onion, or 2 shallots, peeled
3 tablespoons minced fresh flat-leaf parsley
1 tablespoon hot paprika, or 1 teaspoon cayenne pepper (see Note), or more to taste
2 tablespoons extra-virgin olive oil
1 tablespoon fresh lemon juice
Salt and freshly ground black pepper

1. Cut the tomatoes in half and gently wring out the seeds and liquid over the sink. Grate each tomato half on the coarse side of a grater into a bowl by holding the cut side of the tomato half against the grater and grating the flesh just to the skin. Discard the tomato skin.

2. Grate the onion into the bowl. Stir in the parsley, paprika, olive oil, and lemon juice. Season the *harissa* with salt and black pepper to taste; it should be highly seasoned. Serve the *harissa* at room temperature at once—or at least no longer than 4 hours after you have made it.

NOTE: For a milder *harissa,* omit the hot paprika or cayenne pepper.

PRESERVED LEMON HARISSA

MAKES ABOUT 2 CUPS

Here's a more sophisticated *harissa,* one flavored with fresh chiles and preserved lemons. The preserved lemons—one of the most distinctive flavors in Moroccan cuisine—are a sort of pickle made with fresh lemons and salt. You can buy them in North African and Middle Eastern markets and at specialty food shops. A little of this intensely flavored pickle goes a long way.

4 to 10 hot peppers, such as jalapeño or serrano peppers, seeded (for a hotter sauce, leave the seeds in)
3 shallots, thinly sliced
2 cloves garlic, coarsely chopped
1 tablespoon chopped preserved lemon
2 large, ripe tomatoes, peeled and seeded **(see page 454)**
1 tablespoon hot paprika, or 1 teaspoon cayenne pepper
½ teaspoon ground cumin
3 tablespoons vegetable oil
2 tablespoons fresh lemon juice
Salt and freshly ground black pepper

1. Place the peppers, shallots, garlic, preserved lemon, and tomatoes in a mortar and pound them to a puree with a pestle, then work in the paprika, cumin, oil, and lemon juice. If you don't have a mortar and pestle, combine all these ingredients in a food processor or blender and process to a puree. Season the *harissa* with salt and pepper to taste; go easy on the salt—the preserved lemon is already quite salty. The *harissa* should be tart and spicy, but there should be more to it than just heat.

2. Transfer the *harissa* to a bowl and serve it at room temperature at once—or at least no longer than 4 hours after you have made it.

FRENCH WEST INDIES

FRENCH WEST INDIAN "DOG" SAUCE

SAUCE CHIEN

ON THE SIDE
MAKES ABOUT 1 CUP

Literally dog sauce, *sauce chien* is a high-voltage vinaigrette served throughout the French West Indies. How did it get its odd name? One theory holds that the "dog" refers to the fierce bite of the chiles. Another refers to the fact that this is a humble sauce, made without the egg yolks, butter, or cream found in more "noble" French sauces. Whatever its origins, *sauce chien* is an indispensable accompaniment to grilled seafood, chicken, and vegetables.

2 cloves garlic, minced
½ teaspoon salt, or more to taste
½ to 2 Scotch bonnet chiles, seeded and minced (for a hotter sauce, leave the seeds in)
1 shallot, minced
2 tablespoons finely chopped fresh chives or scallion greens
2 tablespoons finely chopped fresh cilantro
2 tablespoons finely chopped fresh flat-leaf parsley
½ teaspoon chopped fresh thyme
3 tablespoons fresh lime juice, or more to taste
Freshly ground black pepper
¼ cup extra-virgin olive oil
¼ cup boiling water, or more as needed

1. Combine the garlic and salt in a mortar and pound to a paste with a pestle. Then work in the Scotch bonnets, shallot, chives, cilantro, parsley, thyme, lime juice, and pepper to taste. Work in the olive oil, then add enough boiling water to obtain a mellow, pourable sauce. Or combine all of the ingredients at once in a food processor or blender and run the machine in short bursts until just coarsely pureed. Taste for seasoning, adding more salt and/or lime juice as necessary; the sauce should be highly seasoned.

2. Serve the sauce at once at room temperature—or at least no longer than 4 hours after you have made it.

TRINIDAD AND TOBAGO

GARLIC SAUCE

ON THE SIDE
MAKES ABOUT 1¼ CUPS

You might think that the staggering amount of garlic in this recipe would render the sauce inedible, but the lime juice and salt have a mellowing effect that makes it mild and palatable. This sauce was originally designed to be served with Grilled Shark and Bake (page 322), although it's hard to imagine a grilled dish that wouldn't benefit from a spoonful of this elixir.

8 cloves garlic, coarsely chopped
½ cup fresh lime juice, or more to taste
½ cup distilled white vinegar
1 tablespoon salt, or more to taste

Combine the garlic, lime juice, vinegar, salt, and ¼ cup of water in a blender and process until creamy and smooth. Taste for seasoning, adding more lime juice and/or salt as necessary; the sauce should be highly seasoned. Serve the garlic sauce at once or refrigerate it, tightly covered, for up to 3 days. Let the sauce return to room temperature before serving.

AFGHANISTAN

CORIANDER SAUCE

ON THE SIDE
MAKES ABOUT 1 CUP

Coriander sauce is a tart, tangy condiment that can be spooned over grilled kebabs, chops, and chicken. (Cilantro is the Mexican—and by extension American—name for the pungent leaves of the coriander plant.) This version is a permanent fixture on the Afghan table. Similar sauces are found as far east as India and as far west as the Republic of Georgia. Walnuts help thicken and bind the sauce.

1 bunch fresh cilantro, stemmed (about 1 cup loosely packed leaves)
3 cloves garlic, coarsely chopped
1 jalapeño pepper or other hot chile, seeded (for a hotter sauce, leave the seeds in)
½ cup walnut pieces
⅓ cup fresh lemon juice or distilled white vinegar, or more to taste
1 teaspoon salt, or more to taste
½ teaspoon freshly ground black pepper
¼ teaspoon ground cumin (optional)

1. Combine the cilantro, garlic, jalapeño, and walnuts in a food processor or blender. Add the lemon juice, salt, black pepper, and cumin (if using) and process to a smooth paste. Add enough water to obtain a pourable sauce (2 to 4 tablespoons).

2. Taste for seasoning, adding more lemon juice and salt as necessary; the sauce should be very highly seasoned. Serve the sauce at once at room temperature—or at least no longer than 4 hours after you have made it.

SPAIN

CATALAN VINAIGRETTE

ON THE SIDE
MAKES ABOUT 1 CUP

This is one of the three sauces that invariably accompany grilled meats and seafood in Barcelona (the others are *romesco*—page 472—and alioli, cousin of the Provençal aioli, a simple garlic-spiked mayonnaise). If you think of vinaigrette as too delicate a sauce to stand up to a steak, try this caper, shallot, and pickle–flavored version. You'll be pleasantly surprised.

2 tablespoons red wine vinegar
½ teaspoon salt, or more to taste
½ teaspoon freshly ground black pepper, or more to taste
½ cup extra-virgin olive oil
1 large shallot, finely chopped
1 small sour pickle, such as cornichon, finely chopped
1 ripe plum tomato, finely chopped
1 tablespoon capers, drained and coarsely chopped, if large

1. Combine the wine vinegar, salt, pepper, and 2 tablespoons of hot water in a small nonreactive bowl and whisk until the salt dissolves. Add the olive oil in a thin, steady stream, whisking constantly to make an emulsified sauce. Whisk in the shallot, pickle, tomato, and capers.

2. Taste for seasoning, adding more salt and/or pepper as necessary. Let the vinaigrette stand for at least 10 minutes and up to 4 hours before serving. If you refrigerate the vinaigrette while it stands, let it return to room temperature before serving, making sure you stir and reseason it.

THAILAND

LEMON-HONEY SAUCE WITH GARLIC

ON THE SIDE
MAKES ABOUT 1½ CUPS

Sweet, sour, slightly hot, and decidedly pungent, this sauce is the quintessence of Thai cooking. To be strictly authentic, you'd use cilantro (aka coriander) root, which tastes like a cross between fresh cilantro and parsnip. If you live near an Indian, Hispanic, or Southeast Asian market, you can probably buy cilantro with the roots still attached. If not, use cilantro leaves—the sauce will be almost as good. Don't be put off by the quantity of garlic and chiles: The lemon juice and honey neutralize these ingredients. This sauce can be served with grilled chicken, beef, or pork, but it's particularly good with seafood.

8 to 10 cloves garlic, minced
3 to 6 Thai chiles or serrano peppers, or other hot chiles, seeded and finely chopped
3 tablespoons minced fresh coriander roots or cilantro leaves
½ cup fresh lemon juice
½ cup Asian fish sauce, or more to taste
3 tablespoons honey, or more to taste

Combine the garlic, Thai chiles, coriander root, lemon juice, fish sauce, and honey in a bowl and whisk to mix. Taste for seasoning, adding more fish sauce or honey as necessary. The sauce can be refrigerated for up to 8 hours.

GREAT BRITAIN

HOT AND SWEET MINT SAUCE

ON THE SIDE
MAKES ABOUT 1 CUP

Mint sauce is such a popular accompaniment to lamb in Britain and other Commonwealth countries that it would seem a grievous omission to leave it out here—even though said sauce is usually served with lamb that has been roasted or boiled, not grilled. To jazz up the traditional recipe, I've added fresh mint and Scotch bonnet chiles.

¾ cup mint jelly
¼ cup distilled white vinegar, or more to taste
1 Scotch bonnet chile or habañero or jalapeño pepper, seeded and minced (for a hotter sauce, leave the seeds in)
3 tablespoons thinly slivered fresh mint leaves, or 2 teaspoons dried mint

Combine the mint jelly, vinegar, and Scotch bonnet in a small nonreactive saucepan and bring to a boil over medium heat. Reduce the heat to medium-low and let simmer gently, uncovered, until thick and richly flavored, about 5 minutes. Stir in the mint leaves and let cook for 1 to 2 minutes longer. Remove the sauce from the heat and, if it tastes too sweet, add a little more vinegar; if it's too thick, add a little water. Serve the mint sauce at once or let it cool and refrigerate it, tightly covered, for up to 3 days.

VIETNAM

BASIC VIETNAMESE DIPPING SAUCE

NUOC CHAM

ON THE SIDE
MAKES ABOUT 1 CUP

Vietnam's national table sauce, *nuoc cham* is a delicate, topaz-colored, slightly sweet, salty, and sour condiment that is obligatory for any Vietnamese grilled fare. Traditionally, finely slivered carrots are added for color and texture. And when I say finely slivered, I mean like dental floss!

1 piece of carrot (2 inches), peeled
2 tablespoons sugar, or more to taste
⅓ cup Asian fish sauce, or more to taste
¼ cup fresh lime juice
2 tablespoons rice vinegar or distilled white vinegar
1 small hot red chile, thinly sliced, or ¼ teaspoon hot red pepper flakes
2 cloves garlic, minced

1. Slice the carrot lengthwise with a vegetable peeler and pile the slices on top of one another, then, using a sharp slender knife, slice the carrot lengthwise into the thinnest imaginable strips.

2. Combine the sugar and ½ cup of warm water in a small bowl and whisk until the sugar dissolves. Stir in the fish sauce, lime juice, rice vinegar, chile, garlic, and carrot strips (see Note). Taste for seasoning, adding more sugar and/or fish sauce as necessary; the *nuoc cham* should strike a delicate balance between salty, tart, and sweet.

3. Serve the *nuoc cham* at room temperature at once—or at least the same day you make it.

NOTE: You can also blend the ingredients for the sauce by shaking them in a sealed jar.

BASIC VIETNAMESE DIPPING SAUCE | AT LEFT

KOREA

ASIAN PEAR DIPPING SAUCE

ON THE SIDE
MAKES ABOUT 2½ CUPS

Readers of this book will know of my unbridled enthusiasm for Korean cooking—a cuisine, I might add, that is grossly underappreciated in the West. This sauce reflects the Korean penchant for combining sweet, salty, and nutty flavors in a single dish. Serve it with any Korean meat dish.

½ cup soy sauce
½ cup sake or dry sherry
¼ cup sugar
1 small Asian pear, peeled, cored, and finely chopped
4 scallions, both white and green parts, trimmed and finely chopped
¼ cup finely chopped onion
2 tablespoons sesame seeds, toasted (see page 113)

Combine the soy sauce, sake, sugar, pear, scallions, onion, and sesame seeds in a medium-size bowl and stir until thoroughly mixed and the sugar dissolves. Divide the sauce among as many small bowls as there are people, so each person has his own for dipping, and serve at once.

VIETNAM

PEANUT CHILE DIPPING SAUCE

ON THE SIDE
MAKES ABOUT 1¼ CUPS

Here's a simple tasty dipping sauce modeled on Vietnamese *nuoc cham.* The peanuts add a characteristic Southeast Asian sweetness.

1 piece of carrot (2 inches), peeled
2 cloves garlic, coarsely chopped
2 tablespoons sugar, or more to taste
¼ cup Asian fish sauce, or more to taste
¼ cup fresh lemon or lime juice, or more to taste
2 tablespoons rice vinegar or distilled white vinegar
1 or 2 jalapeño or serrano peppers, seeded and thinly sliced (for a hotter sauce, leave the seeds in)
3 tablespoons chopped dry-roasted peanuts

1. Slice the carrot lengthwise with a vegetable peeler and pile the slices on top of one another, then, using a sharp slender knife, slice the carrot lengthwise into the thinnest imaginable strips.

2. Combine the garlic and sugar in a mortar and pound to a fine paste with a pestle. Or mash them in the bottom of a bowl with the back of a wooden spoon. Stir in the fish sauce, lemon juice, rice vinegar, carrot strips, jalapeños, peanuts, and enough water to obtain a mild, mellow sauce (5 to 6 tablespoons). Taste for seasoning, adding more sugar, fish sauce, and/or lemon juice to taste; the sauce should be a little sweet, a little salty, and a little sour.

3. Serve the sauce at once at room temperature—or at least no longer than 4 hours after you have made it.

JAVA

A SIMPLE JAVANESE DIPPING SAUCE

ON THE SIDE
SERVES 4

Mention Indonesian saté and most Westerners will think of peanut sauce. Equally beloved in Indonesia is this simple dipping sauce made at the table by the eater, who customizes it by adding the preferred proportions of lime juice, fried shallots, and chiles. Sweet and salty, tart and hot, smooth yet crisp, with bites of fried shallot, the sauce launches a bold assault on the taste buds. And it goes without saying that any food you make and mix at the table is fun food. Serve as a dip with any type of saté or grilled meats.

1 cup peanut oil
1 large shallot, cut into thin wedges
¾ cup sweet soy sauce (ketjap manis), or 6 tablespoons each regular soy sauce and molasses
2 to 4 Thai chiles, serrano peppers, or other hot chiles, seeded and thinly sliced (for a hotter sauce, leave the seeds in)
4 lime wedges, for serving

1. Heat the peanut oil in a small, heavy skillet, over medium-high heat until rippling (350°F). Add the shallot wedges and fry until crisp, about 30 seconds. Using a slotted spoon, transfer the fried shallot wedges to paper towels to drain.

2. Divide the sweet soy sauce among 4 small bowls. To eat sprinkle a bowl of soy sauce with sliced Thai chiles and fried shallots to taste, then add a generous squeeze of lime juice. Use the sauce as a dip; the dipping action will mix the ingredients.

THAILAND

TAMARIND DIPPING SAUCE

ON THE SIDE
MAKES ABOUT 1 CUP

Tamarind is the sweet-sour pulp of a tropical seed pod. Its mouth-puckering tartness makes a bold counterpoint to the grilled fare of Southeast Asia. Serve this lively sauce with satés, but don't stop there. Grilled shrimp, chicken, pork, and even hamburgers shine in its presence.

2 tablespoons peanut oil
2 cloves garlic, minced
2 shallots, or 1 small onion, minced
1 tablespoon minced peeled fresh ginger
1 to 2 hot chiles, seeded and minced (for a hotter sauce, leave the seeds in)
¾ cup Tamarind Water (page 241), or frozen tamarind puree, thawed
¼ cup Asian fish sauce, or more to taste
2 tablespoons sugar, or more to taste
2 tablespoons chopped fresh cilantro (optional)

1. Heat the peanut oil in a wok or large, heavy skillet over high heat. Add the garlic, shallots, ginger, and chiles and cook until fragrant but not brown, about 30 seconds, stirring constantly.

2. Stir in the Tamarind Water, fish sauce, and sugar and bring to a boil over medium heat. Reduce the heat to medium-low and let simmer gently, uncovered, until thickened and the flavors are well blended, about 5 minutes. Remove the dipping sauce from the heat and taste for seasoning, adding more fish sauce and/or sugar as necessary; the sauce should be highly seasoned. Stir in the cilantro (if using) and transfer the dipping sauce to bowls. Let the dipping sauce cool to room temperature, then serve at once.

CLOCKWISE FROM TOP:
ISRAELI RUB | PAGE 492 • MEMPHIS RUB | AT RIGHT • HERBES DE PROVENCE | PAGE 491 • HOT PEPPER SESAME SALT | PAGE 494

CHAPTER 18

RUB IT IN

One of the secrets shared by the world's great grill masters is a savvy use of rubs, marinades, butters, and bastes. Rubs are spice mixes applied to meats to flavor and cure them before grilling. In this chapter you'll find recipes for a wide world of rubs, from Israeli *hawaij* to Indian garam masala, from Puerto Rican *sazón* to Szechuan-seasoned salt.

"He who has spice enough may season his meat as he pleases."
—English Proverb

Marinades are the lifeblood of barbecue, lending distinct ethnic or regional character to commonplace meats, poultry, and fish. Here you'll find recipes for some of the world's best, from the vibrant flavors of Mexican *adobo* to a fiery Berber marinade from the Atlas Mountains.

The butters and bastes in this chapter are designed to combat the one drawback to grilling—its tendency to dry foods out. A diligent program of basting will keep even the leanest meats moist and juicy. As for flavor, well, the Japanese Garlic Butter, Bourbon Butter Basting Sauce, and Vinegar-Based Mop Sauce will keep any meat moist and sizzling with taste.

Use these recipes to customize your grilling and energize even the simplest fare.

U.S.A.

MEMPHIS RUB

MAKES ABOUT ½ CUP

I'm not sure where the American version of a spice rub was born, but if I had to guess a birthplace, I'd name Memphis. Memphans make extensive use of rubs—often to the exclusion of mop sauces or barbecue sauces. This rub is especially delicious used on smoke-roasted ribs and pork shoulders.

¼ cup sweet paprika
1 tablespoon dark brown sugar
1 tablespoon granulated sugar
2 teaspoons salt
2 teaspoons Accent (MSG; optional)
1 teaspoon celery salt
1 teaspoon freshly ground black pepper
1 to 3 teaspoons cayenne pepper
1 teaspoon dry mustard
1 teaspoon garlic powder
1 teaspoon onion powder

Combine the paprika, brown sugar, granulated sugar, salt, Accent (if using), celery salt, black pepper, cayenne, dry mustard, and garlic and onion powders in a jar, twist the lid on airtight, and shake to mix. The rub can be stored away from heat and light for at least 6 months.

NOTE: This makes enough rub for 4 to 6 racks of ribs.

U.S.A.

MIAMI SPICE

MAKES ABOUT 1 CUP

I created this rub to celebrate the launch of my book *Miami Spice*. Use it to give a South Floridian accent to grilled meats and seafood. Scotch bonnet or habañero chile powder are available at specialty food shops and from hot-sauce mail-order companies.

5 tablespoons coarse salt (kosher or sea)
3 tablespoons sweet paprika
3 tablespoons freshly ground black pepper
2 tablespoons ground cumin
2 tablespoons dried oregano
1 tablespoon Scotch bonnet or habañero chile powder

Combine the salt, paprika, pepper, cumin, oregano, and chile powder in a jar, twist the cap on airtight, and shake to mix. The rub can be stored away from heat and light for at least 6 months.

NOTE: This makes enough rub for 6 to 8 pounds of meat, poultry, or seafood.

U.S.A.

CAJUN RUB

MAKES ABOUT 1 CUP

This pungent blend originated as a spice mix for pan blackening (a method popular in Cajun cooking that involves charring highly seasoned foods in a superhot skillet). The rub is delectable when applied to almost any seafood or meat at least thirty minutes before grilling.

¼ cup coarse salt (kosher or sea)
2 tablespoons garlic powder
2 tablespoons onion powder
2 tablespoons dried thyme
2 tablespoons dried oregano
2 tablespoons sweet paprika
1 tablespoon freshly ground black pepper
1 tablespoon freshly ground white pepper
1 to 3 teaspoons cayenne pepper

Combine the salt, garlic and onion powders, thyme, oregano, paprika, black and white peppers, and cayenne in a jar, twist the lid on airtight, and shake to mix. The rub can be stored away from heat and light for at least 6 months.

NOTE: This makes enough rub for 6 to 8 pounds of meat or seafood.

U.S.A.

CREOLE RUB SEASONING

MAKES ABOUT ¾ CUP

Suffused with the warm glow of paprika and cayenne, this seasoning lies at the very soul of Creole cooking. Use it to spice up seafood (especially shrimp and crawfish) as well as chicken.

3 tablespoons sweet paprika
2 tablespoons salt
1 tablespoon garlic powder
1 tablespoon freshly ground black pepper
1 tablespoon onion powder
1 tablespoon cayenne pepper
1 tablespoon dried oregano
1 tablespoon dried thyme

Combine the paprika, salt, garlic powder, black pepper, onion powder, cayenne, oregano, and thyme in a jar, twist the cap on airtight, and shake to mix. The rub can be stored away from heat and light for at least 6 months.

NOTE: This makes enough rub for 4 pounds of seafood or poultry.

FRANCE

NIÇOISE RUB
FOR LAMB AND STEAKS

MAKES ABOUT 1 CUP

The rue Pairolière, located in the Old Quarter of Nice, is a narrow, winding street lined with bakeries, olive shops, and spice vendors. This rub, a specialty of the store called Maison d'Olive, caught my eye—and nose—as a colorful and fragrant embellishment for grilled meats.

½ cup dried parsley
3 tablespoons dried garlic flakes
3 tablespoons cracked coriander seeds, or 2 tablespoons ground coriander
2 tablespoons coarse salt (kosher or sea)
2 tablespoons cracked black peppercorns
2 tablespoons hot red pepper flakes

Combine the dried parsley, garlic flakes, coriander seeds, salt, peppercorns, and red pepper flakes in a jar, twist the lid on airtight, and shake to mix. The rub can be stored away from heat and light for at least 6 months.

NOTE: This makes enough rub for 6 to 8 pounds of meat or seafood.

MOROCCO

MARRAKECH RUB

MAKES ½ CUP

The Herboriste de Paradis is a spice shop in the souk (old market) of Marrakech. This tiny stall, run by Majid Ouadouane, conveys all the mystery and mystique of the spice trade in North Africa. The hundreds of spices and seasonings on sale here blur the traditional distinctions between cooking, cosmetics, and medicine. The spices used range from commonplace coriander and cardamom to antimony for making kohl (eye shadow) and Spanish fly (an alleged aphrodisiac made from dried beetles). Monsieur Ouadouane created this spice blend as a seasoning for grilled lamb. For a quicker version, make a tasty rub using commercially ground spices and omit the toasting.

2½ tablespoons coriander seeds
2 tablespoons cumin seeds
1 tablespoon black peppercorns
½ teaspoon cardamom seeds, or 1 teaspoon cardamom pods
2 tablespoons ground ginger
2 tablespoons coarse salt (kosher or sea; optional)

1. Combine the coriander seeds, cumin seeds, peppercorns, and cardamom seeds in a dry skillet and cook over medium heat until the spices are fragrant and just beginning to brown, about 3 minutes, shaking the pan to ensure even cooking (do not use a nonstick skillet for this). Transfer the toasted spices to a bowl and let cool.

2. Grind the toasted spices to a fine powder in a spice mill or clean coffee grinder, then transfer them to a bowl and mix in the ginger and salt (if using). The rub can be stored in an airtight jar away from heat and light for at least 6 months.

NOTE: This makes enough rub for 4 pounds of lamb.

FRANCE

HERBES DE PROVENCE

MAKES ABOUT 1¼ CUPS

Herbs and spices are the very soul of Provençal cooking. As you drive through this sunny corner of southwestern France, you see purple fields of fresh lavender and shrub-size bushes of rosemary growing everywhere. The fennel is so abundant it grows wild by the side of the road. Sometimes these herbs are used fresh, by themselves, but more often they're dried and mixed to make a perfumed blend called Herbes de Provence.

The formula varies from region to region and cook to cook, but the basic ingredients are rosemary, thyme, marjoram, savory, basil, bay leaf, and for a touch of sweetness, fennel and lavender. Herbes de Provence is sold in most specialty food shops, often in decorative jars at inflated prices. But it's easy to make your own for a lot less money. There's nothing like this fragrant herb blend for enhancing the flavor of grilled lamb, steaks, and even seafood or poultry.

3 tablespoons dried rosemary
3 bay leaves
3 tablespoons dried basil
3 tablespoons dried marjoram
3 tablespoons dried summer savory
3 tablespoons dried oregano
2 tablespoons dried thyme
1 teaspoon fennel seeds
1 teaspoon dried lavender
1 teaspoon freshly ground white pepper
1 teaspoon ground coriander

Crumble the rosemary and bay leaves between your fingers into a small bowl to break them into small pieces. Whisk in the basil, marjoram, savory, oregano, thyme, fennel seeds, lavender, white pepper, and coriander. The Herbes de Provence can be stored in an airtight jar away from heat and light for at least 6 months.

NOTE: This makes enough Herbes de Provence for 8 pounds of meat, poultry, or seafood.

ISRAEL

ISRAELI RUB

HAWAIJ

MAKES ABOUT 1 CUP

Hawaij (pronounced ha-WHY-idge) is the national spice mix of Yemen. Yemenite Jews brought it to Israel, where Israelis of all ethnic backgrounds adopted it with gusto. This recipe comes from my food writer and editor friend Lenore Skenazy, whose husband is a Yemenite Jew. Like Chinese five-spice powder or French Herbes de Provence, *hawaij* is rubbed on meats and seafood prior to grilling. It's also added to soups and stews. There's even a version for sprinkling in coffee. North Americans tend to put salt in their rubs; Israelis do not. I like the way the salt rounds out the flavor.

6 tablespoons black peppercorns
5 tablespoons cumin seeds
1 teaspoon whole cloves
1 teaspoon cardamom seeds, or 1 tablespoon cardamom pods
3 tablespoons ground turmeric
3 tablespoons coarse salt (kosher or sea; optional, see Note)

1. Combine the peppercorns, cumin, cloves, and cardamom in a dry skillet and cook over medium heat until toasted and fragrant, about 3 minutes, shaking the pan to ensure even cooking (do not use a nonstick skillet for this). Transfer the toasted spices to a bowl and let cool.

2. Place the toasted spices, turmeric, and salt (if using) in a spice mill or clean coffee grinder and grind to a fine powder. The rub can be stored in an airtight jar away from heat and light for at least 6 months.

NOTE: This makes enough rub for 6 to 8 pounds of meat, poultry, or seafood.

ISRAEL

QUICK HAWAIJ

MAKES ABOUT ¾ CUP

Here's a *hawaij* that's quick to throw together. It requires no toasting. If you add salt to the *hawaij* that will make it a North American–style rub.

3 tablespoons freshly ground black pepper
3 tablespoons ground cumin
3 tablespoons ground turmeric
3 tablespoons coarse salt (kosher or sea; optional)
1 teaspoon ground cardamom

Combine the pepper, cumin, turmeric, salt (if using), and cardamom in a jar, twist the lid on airtight, and shake to mix. The rub can be stored away from heat and light for at least 6 months.

NOTE: This makes enough rub for 4 to 6 pounds of meat, poultry, or seafood.

FRANCE

PROVENÇAL GRILLING MIXTURE FOR FISH

MAKES ABOUT ½ CUP

The postcard picturesque town of Isle Sur la Sorgue lives up to its nickname "the Venice of Provence." The Sorgue River flows through and around its center, creating broad quays and waterfront terraces. On Sunday (market day), the quays fill with vendors selling Provençal provender and handicrafts. The following recipe was inspired by the spice vendors at the market.

1 tablespoon fennel seeds
¼ cup cracked coriander seeds, or 3 tablespoons ground coriander
2 tablespoons cracked black peppercorns
2 tablespoons hot red pepper flakes
2 tablespoons coarse salt (kosher or sea)
3 bay leaves, crumbled

Combine the fennel and coriander seeds, peppercorns, hot pepper flakes, salt, and bay leaves in a jar, twist the lid on airtight, and shake to mix. The grilling mixture can be stored away from heat and light for at least 6 months.

NOTE: This makes enough grilling mixture for 3 to 4 pounds of seafood.

TUNISIA

NORTH-AFRICAN RUB

TABIL

MAKES ABOUT ½ CUP

Pungent, spicy, and aromatic, *tabil* is a simple spice mix from Tunisia. It adds a complex, earthy flavor to almost any grilled fish, chicken, or meat.

2 tablespoons coriander seeds
2 tablespoons cumin seeds
2 tablespoons caraway seeds
2 tablespoons hot red pepper flakes
2 tablespoons coarse salt (kosher or sea)

1. Combine the coriander, cumin, and caraway seeds in a dry skillet and cook over medium heat until toasted and fragrant, about 3 minutes, shaking the pan to ensure even cooking (do not use a nonstick skillet for this). Transfer the toasted seeds to a bowl and let cool.

2. Place the toasted seed mixture in a spice mill or clean coffee grinder, add the hot pepper flakes and salt, and grind to a fine powder. The rub can be stored in an airtight jar away from heat and light for at least 6 months.

NOTE: This makes enough rub for 3 to 4 pounds of meat, poultry, or seafood.

PUERTO RICO

SPANISH CARIBBEAN SEASONING SALT

SAZON

MAKES ABOUT 1 CUP

A seasoned salt fragrant with cumin, oregano, and garlic, *sazón* is the ubiquitous seasoning of Puerto Rico. Commercial blends are widely available, but most are loaded with MSG. Here's a homemade version chock-full of flavor. It calls for whole spices (peppercorns and cumin seeds) that are freshly toasted before grinding. For a quicker version, skip the roasting and grinding and use preground pepper and cumin—the mixture will still be quite tasty.

2 tablespoons black peppercorns
2 tablespoons cumin seeds
2 tablespoons dried oregano
½ cup coarse salt (kosher or sea)
2 tablespoons garlic powder

1. Combine the peppercorns and cumin seeds in a dry skillet and cook over medium heat until toasted and fragrant, about 3 minutes, shaking the pan to ensure even cooking (do not use a nonstick skillet for this). Transfer the peppercorns and cumin seeds to a bowl and let cool.

2. Place the toasted spices in a spice mill or clean coffee grinder, add the oregano, and grind to a fine powder. Add the salt and garlic powder. The seasoning salt can be stored in an airtight jar away from heat and light for at least 6 months.

NOTE: This makes enough seasoning salt for 6 to 8 pounds of meat, poultry, or seafood.

KOREA

HOT PEPPER SESAME SALT

MAKES ABOUT ⅓ CUP

Sesame is one of the defining flavors of Korean cuisine. In this recipe toasted sesame seeds are combined with salt, pepper, and hot red pepper flakes to make an uncommon seasoning for grilled meats and seafood.

3 tablespoons white sesame seeds
1 tablespoon black sesame seeds (see Notes)
2 tablespoons coarse salt (kosher or sea)
2 teaspoons cracked black peppercorns
1 teaspoon hot red pepper flakes (optional)

1. Place the white sesame seeds in a dry skillet and cook over medium heat until toasted and lightly browned, about 3 minutes, shaking the pan to ensure even cooking (do not use a nonstick skillet for this). Transfer the toasted sesame seeds to a bowl and let cool.

2. Stir the black sesame seeds, salt, pepper, and hot pepper flakes (if using) into the toasted sesame seeds. The sesame salt can be stored in an airtight jar away from heat and light for at least 6 months.

NOTES: If you can't find black sesame seeds, increase the amount of white sesame seeds to 4 tablespoons.

This makes enough Sesame Salt for 3 pounds of meat or seafood.

INDIA

ROASTED SPICE POWDER

GARAM MASALA

MAKES ABOUT ½ CUP

Garam masala is the most ubiquitous of India's spice blends. There are almost as many recipes as there are Indian cooks. You can buy a commercial mix at an Indian market, but most households and restaurants there make their own. The dominant flavors of garam masala are cumin, coriander, black pepper, and green and black cardamom. Black cardamom is a large, almond-shaped black pod with a richly aromatic smoky flavor. I've made it optional, as you have to go to an Indian market or mail-order source to find it. It's well worth tracking down. Garam masala is a key flavoring in Indian tandoori marinades. Make a batch every few months and keep some on hand.

3 tablespoons cumin seeds
3 tablespoons coriander seeds
1 tablespoon black peppercorns
2 teaspoons green cardamom pods
1 teaspoon black cardamom pods (optional)
1 piece (2 inches) cinnamon stick
½ whole nutmeg
2 bay leaves
½ teaspoon mace blades
¼ teaspoon whole cloves
1 teaspoon ground ginger

ROASTED SPICE POWDER | AT LEFT

1. Combine the cumin seeds, coriander seeds, peppercorns, green and black cardamom pods, cinnamon stick, nutmeg, bay leaves, mace, and cloves in a dry skillet (do not use a nonstick skillet for this). Cook the spices over medium heat until lightly toasted and fragrant, about 3 minutes, shaking the pan to ensure even cooking. Transfer the toasted spices to a bowl and let cool.

2. Grind the spice mixture to a fine powder in a mortar with a pestle or in a spice mill or clean coffee grinder. Place the spice mixture in a jar, add the ginger, twist the lid on airtight, and shake to mix. The garam masala can be stored away from heat and light for at least 6 months.

NOTE: This makes enough spice powder for 3 to 4 pounds of meat, poultry, or seafood.

INDIA

QUICK GARAM MASALA

MAKES ABOUT ⅓ CUP

If you are pressed for time and can't toast and grind whole spices, here's a garam masala you can make in just a couple of minutes.

2 tablespoons ground cumin
2 tablespoons ground coriander
2 teaspoons freshly ground black pepper
1 teaspoon ground cardamom
1 teaspoon ground ginger
⅛ teaspoon ground cinnamon
⅛ teaspoon ground cloves
⅛ teaspoon ground nutmeg

Combine the cumin, coriander, pepper, cardamom, ginger, cinnamon, cloves, and nutmeg in a jar, twist the lid on airtight, and shake to mix. The garam masala can be stored away from heat and light for at least 6 months.

NOTE: This makes enough spice powder for 3 pounds of meat, poultry, or seafood.

CHINA

SZECHUAN SEASONED SALT

MAKES ABOUT 1 CUP

Seasoned salt isn't unique to North America. The Chinese version features the tongue-popping aromatics of black and Szechuan peppercorns. Szechuan peppercorns aren't really peppers at all but a reddish-brown, peppercorn-size berry native to China's Szechuan province. The spice has a clean, piney, woodsy flavor that's unique in the world of seasonings. (The name notwithstanding, Szechuan peppercorns aren't especially hot.) They can be found in Asian markets and specialty food shops. Toasting the spices intensifies their flavor and makes this an especially good seasoning for grilled chicken, squab, and shrimp.

½ cup coarse salt (kosher or sea)
⅓ cup Szechuan peppercorns
3 tablespoons black peppercorns

1. Combine the salt and Szechuan and black peppercorns in a dry skillet and cook over medium heat until the peppercorns begin to darken and smoke, 3 to 6 minutes, shaking the pan to ensure even cooking (do not use a nonstick skillet for this). Transfer the peppercorn mixture to a bowl and let cool.

2. Grind the peppercorn mixture to a fine powder in a spice mill or clean coffee grinder. The seasoned salt can be stored in an airtight jar away from heat and light for at least 6 months.

NOTE: This makes enough seasoned salt for 6 to 8 pounds of poultry or seafood.

FRENCH WEST INDIES

COLOMBO POWDER

MAKES ABOUT 1 CUP

Colombo is the French West Indian version of curry powder. What sets it apart is the addition of an unexpected ingredient: toasted rice. The rice acts as both a flavoring and natural thickener. Toasting gives the rice a pleasing nutty flavor and makes it easier to grind.

¼ cup white rice
¼ cup cumin seeds
¼ cup coriander seeds
1 tablespoon mustard seeds, preferably black (see Notes)
1 tablespoon black peppercorns
1 tablespoon fenugreek seeds (optional; see Notes)
1 teaspoon whole cloves
¼ cup ground turmeric

1. Place the rice in a dry skillet and cook over medium heat until lightly browned, 2 to 3 minutes, shaking the pan to ensure even cooking (do not use a nonstick skillet for this). Transfer the rice to a bowl and let cool.

2. Add the cumin seeds, coriander seeds, mustard seeds, peppercorns, fenugreek seeds (if using), and cloves to the skillet and cook over medium heat, shaking the pan, until lightly toasted and fragrant, about 3 minutes. Transfer the spices to a bowl and let cool.

3. Combine the rice and toasted spices in a spice mill or clean coffee grinder and grind to a fine powder, then add the turmeric. The *colombo* powder can be stored in an airtight jar away from heat and light for at least 6 months.

NOTES: Black mustard seeds are hotter than white, but the latter will work in a pinch. The small, rectangular tan fenugreek seeds have a slight but agreeable bitterness. Both black mustard seeds and fenugreek are available at Indian markets, specialty food shops, and natural foods stores.

This makes enough *colombo* powder for 6 to 8 pounds of meat, poultry, or seafood.

GREECE

OREGANO OLIVE OIL RUB

MAKES ABOUT 1 CUP

Here's a simple rub that will give any grilled meat (but especially lamb) or fish a Greek accent. For best results, use Greek oregano—it has a sharper, mintier flavor than Italian or Mexican. Look for it at Greek markets. Olive oil gives the rub a flavorful luster, without making it sticky.

⅓ cup coarse salt (kosher or sea)
⅓ cup cracked black peppercorns
⅓ cup coarsely crumbled oregano, preferably Greek
2 tablespoons dried dill
2 tablespoons extra-virgin olive oil

Combine the salt, peppercorns, oregano, dill, and olive oil in a bowl and stir to mix. The spices should be coated with oil but not stick together. The rub can be stored in an airtight jar away from heat or light for at least 6 months.

NOTE: This makes enough rub for 6 to 8 pounds of lamb or fish.

JAMAICA

JERK MARINADE

MAKES ABOUT 2 CUPS

Jerk is a traditional ethnic food that has entered America's culinary mainstream. In the process, it's lost a lot of its fire, spice, and salt. Here's how they make it in the birthplace of jerk—a town called Boston Beach on the north coast of Jamaica. Count yourself lucky to have a blender. In

CHICKEN WITH JERK MARINADE | PAGE 497

Boston Beach they grind the seasonings in a hand-cranked spice mill. Use the jerk marinade to marinate chicken legs or breasts for three hours, pork for six hours, and fish fillets or shrimp for one hour.

4 to 15 Scotch bonnet chiles, seeded (for a hotter marinade, leave the seeds in)
1 bunch scallions, both white and green parts, trimmed and coarsely chopped
2 shallots, cut in half
1 small onion, quartered
2 cloves garlic, peeled
1 tablespoon grated peeled fresh ginger
2 teaspoons chopped fresh thyme, or 1 teaspoon dried thyme
2 teaspoons ground allspice
3 tablespoons canola oil
3 tablespoons soy sauce
3 tablespoons fresh lime juice, or more to taste
2 tablespoons dark brown sugar
2 tablespoons salt, or more to taste
1 teaspoon freshly ground black pepper

Combine the Scotch bonnets, scallions, shallots, onion, garlic, ginger, thyme, allspice, oil, soy sauce, lime juice, brown sugar, salt, pepper, and 1 cup of water in a food processor or blender. Process until smooth. Taste for seasoning, adding more lime juice and/or salt as necessary. The jerk marinade can be refrigerated, tightly covered, for up to 2 weeks.

NOTE: This makes enough marinade for 4 pounds of meat, chicken, or seafood.

JAPAN

TERIYAKI MARINADE

MAKES ABOUT 1½ CUPS BEFORE BOILING

Here's a sweet-salty marinade modeled on classic Japanese teriyaki sauce. To make a safe glaze for brushing on food while it cooks, I boil the marinade after the food—meat or seafood—has been removed from it.

2 cloves garlic, minced
1 tablespoon minced peeled fresh ginger
2 scallions, both white and green parts, trimmed and thinly sliced
½ cup tamari or soy sauce
½ cup mirin (sweet rice wine) or cream sherry
¼ cup sake or dry sherry
¼ cup firmly packed light brown sugar

Combine the garlic, ginger, scallions, tamari, mirin, sake, and brown sugar in a small bowl and whisk until the sugar dissolves. Marinate meat or seafood in this mixture for 1 hour, then remove the food from the marinade.

If you wish to use the marinade as a glaze, strain it into a saucepan and boil it until thick and syrupy, about 5 minutes. Then, brush it on food during the last 5 minutes of cooking. After boiling, the teriyaki marinade can be refrigerated, tightly covered, for at least 1 week.

NOTE: This makes enough Teriyaki Marinade for 2 pounds of chicken or beef.

MEXICO

SMOKED CHILE MARINADE

ADOBO

MAKES ABOUT 1 CUP

Adobo refers to a large family of marinated meat dishes found throughout the Spanish-speaking world. In central Mexico, the term describes a fiery marinade made with chipotle chiles (smoked jalapeño peppers). Chipotles are sold both dried and canned (in tomato sauce). I prefer the canned ones for this recipe. Look for them in Mexican markets and specialty food shops.

Use *adobo* to marinate seafood for thirty minutes, chicken breasts for one hour, and whole chickens and meat for four to six hours. *Adobo* goes particularly well with pork.

Barbecue Alley: The Mexican Grill

To many North Americans, Mexican cooking means tacos, burritos, and enchiladas. Grill buffs, though, will be pleased to learn that Mexico has a venerable, varied, and lively tradition of live-fire cooking, from the mesquite-grilled steaks of the north to the spicy grilled fish of the Yucatán. There's even a version of pit-cooked barbecue known as *barbacoa,* a term that has different meanings in various parts of the country. In the north, *barbacoa* is made with beef, in the south with pyrotechnically spiced goat, and in Mexico City with lamb wrapped in the leaves of maguey cactus and roasted in a wood-heated brick pit: There is no marinade, no spice rub, nor are there fancy condiments—just lamb cooked to fall-off-the-bone tenderness in a pit.

Mexico offers plenty of interesting barbecue cooked over direct heat, too. Consider the gracious colonial city of Oaxaca in the south-central part of the country. Famous for its *moles* (complex, slow-simmered sauces made from nuts, fruits, and a dazzling array of chiles), Oaxaca is also a hotbed of thrilling grilling. "Barbecue alley," as it is known, in the Mercado 20 de Noviembre (November 20 Market) is a great place to sample the best of Mexican live-fire fare.

To find the "alley," you just follow your nose to a smoky arcade on the east side of the market. Lining the arcade are rows of barbecue stalls—each sending thick billows of smoke toward the skylight. The ordering procedure is a little confusing to newcomers, but it ensures that everything you eat will be hot off the grill. As you enter the arcade, pause at the vegetable stalls on the right or left. (I liked the first stall on the right, where two of the servers, Yolanda and Gloria, delighted in pulling their customers' legs as they take their orders.) Ask for a bunch of scallions and a couple of *chiles de agua.* (The latter are rather innocent-looking peppers that resemble American cubanelles. There all innocence ends.) The vegetables will be handed to you in a paper-lined wicker basket.

Continue down the arcade. To the right and left you'll see a series of meat stalls. There are four or five basic meats to choose from: *carne de res* (beef), *tazajo* (dried beef), *cecino* (cured pork), chorizo (strings of egg-shaped, blood-colored sausages), and ropelike hanks of tripe. The meats are cut into broad, thin strips and are displayed on tables. No, they're not refrigerated, but the high heat of the charcoal acts as a powerful disinfectant.

Pick a stall (I liked no. 189) and point to whatever type of meat you want. The owner will cut off a few pieces of beef, pork, or tripe and weigh them on a scale. Enter a woman who relieves you of your scallions and chiles, nestling them amid the coals of an enormous brazier fashioned from a washtub filled with concrete. She's the *asador* (grill jockey), and as you watch, she'll fire char your vegetables and grill your meats on a wire grate resting directly on the coals. While she does, the tortilla lady arrives and counts out the desired number of tortillas and warms them for you on the grill. Meanwhile, a fifth lady stops to sell you a *nopalito* (cactus paddle) salad, neatly packaged in a tiny plastic bag. Give her a large bill to pay for the salad and she'll place the tray on her head while she makes change.

When the meats and vegetables are cooked, the *asador* returns them to your basket. You go back to the first stall where Yolanda will peel and seed your chiles, scrape the burnt parts off your scallions, and douse both with lime juice and salt. Then Gloria will give you dishes of guacamole and *salsa mexicana,* the colors of which, appropriately, mirror the Mexican flag: green serrano peppers, white onions, and shockingly red tomatoes.

Take your seat at one of the low stone communal tables, and let the feast begin. To eat *carne asado,* place a sliver of meat on a tortilla and top it with charred onions, some chiles, a bit of salsa, and a little guacamole. Roll it up and pop it into your mouth. If you're feeling particularly macho you can eat the chile straight, otherwise wrap it in the tortilla with the other ingredients.

A meal of *carne asado* is fun—you interact with vendors and fellow diners at the communal tables and enjoy a fiery treat you won't soon forget.

6 canned chipotle chiles with 2 tablespoons of their juices
5 cloves garlic, peeled
1 strip orange zest (2 by ½ inches), removed with a vegetable peeler
1 cup fresh sour orange juice (see box, page 186), or ¾ cup fresh orange juice and ¼ cup fresh lime juice
1 tablespoon tomato paste
2 teaspoons dried oregano
1 teaspoon ground cumin
2 tablespoons red wine vinegar
1 teaspoon salt
½ teaspoon freshly ground black pepper

1. Combine the chipotles, garlic, orange zest, sour orange juice, tomato paste, oregano, cumin, wine vinegar, salt, and black pepper in a medium-size nonreactive saucepan. Bring to a boil over high heat and let boil until reduced by half, 5 to 8 minutes.

2. Place the *adobo* in a food processor or blender and process to a smooth paste. The *adobo* can be refrigerated, tightly covered, for at least 3 days.

NOTE: This makes enough marinade for 3 pounds of meat or chicken.

BRAZIL

BRAZILIAN LAMB MARINADE

MAKES ABOUT 2 CUPS

Beef is what generally comes to mind when you think of Brazilian barbecue, but the legendary barbecue restaurant chain Porcão, with branches in Rio, São Paulo, and Miami, also does a lively business in lamb. This is a great marinade for either whole (bone-in) or butterflied legs of lamb. Allow the meat to marinate, covered in the refrigerator, for one day before grilling.

1 medium-size onion, quartered
6 cloves garlic, peeled
1 bunch scallions, both white and green parts, trimmed
½ cup fresh cilantro leaves
2 bay leaves
1 teaspoon salt
1 teaspoon freshly ground black pepper
½ cup dry white wine
½ cup extra-virgin olive oil

Combine the onion, garlic, scallions, cilantro, bay leaves, salt, pepper, white wine, and olive oil in a food processor or blender and process to a coarse paste. The marinade can be refrigerated, tightly covered in a bowl or jar, for at least 2 days.

NOTE: This makes enough marinade for 3 pounds of lamb.

U.S.A.

BASIL MARINADE

MAKES ABOUT 1 CUP

Here's a colorful, fragrant, and intensely flavorful basil marinade that's great for chicken and seafood. Set about a third of the marinade aside to use as a basting sauce. If using the marinade for chicken, allow two hours; marinate seafood for one hour.

⅓ cup extra-virgin olive oil
⅓ cup fresh lemon juice
⅓ cup boiling water
3 cloves garlic, peeled
1 large bunch fresh basil, stemmed
1 teaspoon salt
1 teaspoon freshly ground black pepper

Combine the olive oil, lemon juice, boiling water, garlic, basil, salt, and pepper in a food processor or blender and process to a smooth paste. The marinade can be refrigerated, tightly covered, for at least 3 days.

NOTE: This makes enough marinade for 3 pounds of poultry or fish.

Griller's Guide to the World's Chiles and Peppers

Where there's smoke, there's fire, goes the saying. And where's there's fire, there's heat. Chiles and peppers are absolutely essential to barbecue, whether grilled or on their own; added to myriad marinades, rubs, and spice mixes; or served pickled or straight up as an accompaniment to grilled fare.

If you have sensitive skin, don't handle chiles directly. Instead, wear rubber or plastic gloves. Remember that the hottest parts of a chile are the seeds and veins. If you have a low tolerance for heat, remove them by cutting the chile in half and scraping out the seeds with a small spoon or a blunt knife. When working with chiles, never rub your eyes, nose, or mouth—the oils will cause a burning sensation in these sensitive areas. And always wash your hands (or gloves) thoroughly with soap and water when done.

Here's a field guide to some of the many chiles and peppers you will encounter on the barbecue trail.

AJI AMARILLO: Literally yellow chile, the *aji amarillo* is a fiery, fleshy, yellow-orangish Peruvian chile used as a flavoring for kebabs. *Aji amarillo* comes in three forms: powdered, paste, and pickled. Look for it in Hispanic markets.

BIRD PEPPER: A small (about one inch long), cone-shaped red or reddish-orange chile, the bird pepper is related to the cayenne and found in the Bahamas and elsewhere in the Caribbean. Red serrano or cayenne peppers are substitutes.

BULL'S HORN PEPPERS: Popular all along the barbecue trail, the bull's horn pepper—aka horn pepper or *corno di toro*—has a pleasant flavor similar to that of a bell pepper. Its bite can range from a bit hot to moderately hot. The long, slender shape of the bull's horn pepper makes it a favorite for grilling: Simply thread the peppers crosswise on skewers and char them on all sides.

CAYENNE: A small (two inches long), fiery red chile native to the Gulf of Mexico and Guyana and used mostly in powdered form. Today, cayenne is widely used throughout Africa, India, and Asia. Cayenne is very hot, but its flavor is fairly one-dimensional.

CHIPOTLE: A smoked jalapeño pepper, the chipotle is an essential ingredient in Mexican *adobo* (a smoked chile marinade) and numerous salsas. Chipotles come in two varieties—the small red *morena* and the large tan *grande.* The *grande* has a more complex flavor. Chipotles also come in two forms: dried and canned in a sour orange and tomato sauce. Canned chipotles have a richer flavor. Chipotles are available at Mexican markets and specialty food shops.

DE ARBOL: A long (three to four inches), skinny dried red Mexican chile that is moderately fiery, the de arbol chile is used in the charred tomato salsas that accompany grilled beef in northern Mexico.

GOAT PEPPER: A crinkly, round green chile about one and a half inches long, the goat pepper is similar in flavor and heat to the Scotch bonnet. It's popular in the Bahamas.

GUAJILLO: A long, smooth-skinned, reddish-brown dried chile, the Mexican guajillo is flavorful but relatively mild. It is often ground into chile powder and used to marinate pork in central Mexico.

HABAÑERO: A smooth, acorn-shaped red, green, or yellow pepper, the habañero is similar in flavor and tongue-torturing heat to the Scotch bonnet or the manzano.

JALAPEÑO: A bullet-shaped green or red pepper available just about everywhere. Despite its reputation, the jalapeño is relatively mild as chiles go. The heat of a chile is measured in units that are called scovilles, and jalapeños ring in at about 5,000 scovilles. Compare that to the 200,000 scovilles of the habañero or Scotch bonnet chile. The less familiar guero and Red Fresno peppers can be substituted for the jalapeño.

KOREAN CHILE: A hot dried red chile that's indispensable in Korean cooking. Hungarian hot paprika makes a good substitute.

PIMENTA MALAGUETA: A tiny, ridged red or green chile (usually pickled or dried). The *pimenta malagueta* adds zip to Brazilian table sauces.

POBLANO PEPPER: A large (up to three inches), dark green, tapered fresh chile from Mexico. The poblano pepper is similar in flavor to a green bell pepper, but hotter and more aromatic. Poblanos are great for stuffing and grilling. The dried version is called ancho.

SCOTCH BONNET: To call this Chinese lantern–shaped chile hot would be an understatement: The Scotch bonnet is about fifty times more fiery than a jalapeño. But behind the heat, there's a floral, almost fruity flavor that makes me think of apricots. Mexico's habañero chile, Jamaica's country pepper, Haiti's dame jeanne, and Florida's datil pepper are closely related and make satisfactory substitutes. Scotch bonnets are available at West Indian and Mexican markets, specialty food shops, and at most major supermarkets.

SERRANO PEPPER: A thin, tapered bright green pepper smaller and slightly hotter than a jalapeño. Serranos and jalapeños are interchangeable.

THAI CHILE PEPPER: You need to know about two Thai chile peppers: The *prik kee noo,* a tiny ridged, mercilessly hot chile, the Thai name for which literally means mouse dropping; and the *prik kee far,* a slender, horn-shaped green chile that is very hot, but milder than its little brother. Look for Thai chiles at Asian and Indian markets.

MOROCCO

BERBER MARINADE

MAKES ABOUT 1½ CUPS

The Berbers are a rugged, rug-weaving people who live in Morocco's Atlas Mountains. They season lamb and other meats with this vibrant paste of typical North African seasonings. Fenugreek is a rectangular seed with a pleasantly bitter flavor—look for it in Indian and Middle Eastern grocery stores. I have used this marinade with great success on tuna, pork tenderloin, and sirloin steak. Spread the Berber marinade on the meat, poultry, or seafood and marinate it, covered, for eight hours in the refrigerator. A little of this fiery mixture goes a long way!

- 1 medium-size onion, finely chopped
- 4 cloves garlic, finely chopped
- 2 tablespoons chopped peeled fresh ginger
- 3 tablespoons mild paprika
- 3 tablespoons hot paprika
- 1 tablespoon ground coriander
- 2 teaspoons freshly ground black pepper
- ½ teaspoon ground cardamom
- 1 teaspoon hot red pepper flakes, or more to taste
- ½ teaspoon ground fenugreek (optional)
- ½ teaspoon ground cinnamon
- ¼ teaspoon ground allspice
- ⅛ teaspoon ground cloves
- 4 teaspoons salt, or more to taste
- 1 teaspoon honey or sugar
- ¾ cup extra-virgin olive oil
- ¼ cup fresh lemon juice

Place the onion, garlic, ginger, mild and hot paprikas, coriander, black pepper, cardamom, hot pepper flakes, fenugreek (if using), cinnamon, allspice, cloves, and salt in a food processor and process to a coarse paste. Work in the honey, olive oil, and lemon juice. Alternatively, you can combine all the ingredients at once in a blender and puree to a smooth paste. Taste for seasoning, adding more hot pepper flakes and/or salt as necessary. The Berber Marinade can be refrigerated, covered, for 1 week.

NOTE: This makes enough marinade for 2 to 3 pounds of seafood, poultry, or meat.

PEPPERS & CHILES

The world barbecue trail is booby-trapped (figuratively at least) with chiles and peppers. Grill masters everywhere use them in marinades and salsas, or sliced on top of grilled dishes. And of course, for grilling and serving as a fiery dish on their own. You can't play the game without knowing the players. Here's a scorecard to help you keep some of them straight.

MANZANO PEPPERS

BANANA PEPPERS

GUAJILLO PEPPERS

POBLANO PEPPER

SERRANO PEPPERS

CAYENNE PEPPERS

RED FRESNO PEPPERS

ANCHO CHILE PEPPERS

HABANERO PEPPERS

GUERO PEPPERS

FRANCE

WHITE WINE MARINADE FOR SEAFOOD

MAKES ABOUT ¾ CUP

Here's a simple white wine marinade that's good for any seafood. To give it an Asian accent, substitute sesame oil for the olive oil and sake or mirin for the white wine. Marinate the seafood, covered in the refrigerator, one to two hours.

½ cup dry white wine or white vermouth
¼ cup extra-virgin olive oil
3 tablespoons fresh lemon juice
3 tablespoons chopped fresh flat-leaf parsley
2 sprigs fresh rosemary, or 1 tablespoon dried rosemary
2 bay leaves
½ medium-size onion, thinly sliced
2 cloves garlic, thinly sliced
1 teaspoon salt
½ teaspoon freshly ground black pepper

Combine the white wine, olive oil, lemon juice, parsley, rosemary, bay leaves, onion, garlic, salt, and pepper in a small bowl and whisk to mix. Use this marinade within an hour of preparing.

NOTE: This makes enough marinade for 2 pounds of seafood.

FRANCE

SIX COMPOUND BUTTERS

ON THE SIDE

Back in the B.C.C. (Before Cholesterol Consciousness) era, butter was an indispensable ingredient not only to the chef but also the grill jockey. The French have a venerable tradition of crowning meats with a disk of flavored butter. The butter melts on contact with the hot meat or seafood—anointing, basting, and moisturizing it. This compensates for the tendency of many foods to dry out when cooked on the grill.

Compound butters are easy to make, and a small portion certainly won't kill you. The butter is creamed (beaten until light and fluffy—a stage the French call *en pommade*), then seasoned with intense flavorings. The resulting mixture is rolled in a sheet of plastic wrap or parchment paper to form a thick cylinder. Thus prepared, the compound butter can be stored in the refrigerator or freezer. When you need it, simply cut off a slice and place it atop a piece of grilled meat or seafood.

I keep several compound butters on hand in my freezer, knowing that a moist, memorable, flavorful dish is only a moment away. Here are six traditional compound butters. All keep for one week in the refrigerator or can be frozen for at least 2 months.

MAITRE D'HOTEL BUTTER

SERVES 6 TO 8

Here's an updated version of the most classic of all compound butters—a perfect adornment to a piece of grilled salmon, cod, halibut, or sole.

8 tablespoons (1 stick) salted butter, at room temperature
3 tablespoons chopped fresh flat-leaf parsley
1 clove garlic, minced
½ teaspoon grated lemon zest
2 teaspoons fresh lemon juice
¼ teaspoon freshly ground white pepper

1. Cream the butter in a bowl, mixer, or food processor. Beat in the parsley, garlic, lemon zest, lemon juice, and white pepper.

2. Place the butter at the bottom edge of a piece of parchment paper or plastic wrap and roll it into a compact cylinder. Store the butter in the refrigerator or freezer. Cut off ½-inch slices as needed.

ESCARGOT BUTTER

SERVES 6 TO 8

Garlic-parsley butter is the classic topping for escargots (snails), but it goes with any seafood. I like to spread it on bread and grill the bread to make garlic toast.

8 tablespoons (1 stick) salted butter, at room temperature
3 tablespoons chopped fresh flat-leaf parsley
3 cloves garlic, minced
¼ teaspoon freshly ground black pepper

1. Cream the butter in a bowl, mixer, or food processor. Beat in the parsley, garlic, and pepper.

2. Place the butter at the bottom edge of a piece of parchment paper or plastic wrap and roll it into a compact cylinder. Store the butter in the refrigerator or freezer. Cut off ½-inch slices as needed.

ROQUEFORT BUTTER

SERVES 6 TO 8

The salty tang of Roquefort cheese goes especially well with grilled lamb and beef. You can make Stilton or Gorgonzola butter the same way.

8 tablespoons (1 stick) unsalted butter, at room temperature
2 ounces Roquefort cheese, at room temperature

1. Cream the butter in a bowl, mixer, or food processor. Using the back of a spoon, press the Roquefort through a sieve into the butter and whisk to mix.

2. Place the butter at the bottom edge of a piece of parchment paper or plastic wrap and roll it into a compact cylinder. Store the butter in the refrigerator or freezer. Cut off ½-inch slices as needed.

ANCHOVY BUTTER

SERVES 6 TO 8

Anchovies make great appetizers, as the seventeenth-century English writer Thomas Flatman observed:

To quicken appetite it will behoove ye
To feed courageously on good Anchovie.

Anchovy butter is particularly good on grilled swordfish, tuna, and steak.

6 to 8 canned anchovy fillets, rinsed and drained
8 tablespoons (1 stick) unsalted butter, at room temperature
¼ teaspoon freshly ground black pepper

1. Place the anchovies in a mortar and mash to a paste with a pestle. Or mash them in a small bowl using the back of a wooden spoon. Add the butter and pepper and beat until smooth.

2. Place the butter at the bottom edge of a piece of parchment paper or plastic wrap and roll it into a compact cylinder. Store the butter in the refrigerator or freezer. Cut off ½-inch slices as needed.

CURRY BUTTER

SERVES 6 TO 8

Curry butter is easy to make. It's particularly well suited to seafood. Freeze a batch and you'll always have some on hand so you can throw a quick dinner together.

8 tablespoons (1 stick) salted butter, at room temperature
3 tablespoons minced shallots
1 clove garlic, minced
2 teaspoons curry powder

1. Melt 2 tablespoons of the butter in a small saucepan over medium heat. Add the shallots, garlic, and curry powder and cook, stirring often, until the shallots are soft but not brown, about 3 minutes. Let the curry mixture cool completely.

FROM THE TOP CLOCKWISE:
ROQUEFORT BUTTER • CURRY BUTTER • ANCHOVY BUTTER | AT LEFT

2. Cream the remaining butter in a bowl, mixer, or food processor. Add the curry mixture.

3. Place the butter at the bottom edge of a piece of parchment paper or plastic wrap and roll it into a compact cylinder. Store the butter in the refrigerator or freezer. Cut off ½-inch slices as needed.

MARCHAND DE VIN BUTTER

SERVES 6 TO 8

Reduced red wine and shallots account for the name of this butter, which means wine merchant. The butter is delicious served on steak.

1 cup dry red wine
2 shallots, finely chopped
8 tablespoons (1 stick) salted butter
3 tablespoons finely chopped fresh flat-leaf parsley
¼ teaspoon freshly ground black pepper

1. Combine the wine and shallots in a heavy saucepan and bring to a boil over high heat. Let boil until thick, syrupy, and reduced to 3 to 4 tablespoons, about 7 minutes. Let the wine mixture cool completely.

2. Cream the butter in a bowl, mixer, or food processor. Add the wine mixture, parsley, and pepper.

3. Place the butter at the bottom edge of a piece of parchment paper or plastic wrap and roll it into a compact cylinder. Store the butter in the refrigerator or freezer. Cut off ½-inch slices as needed.

JAPAN

JAPANESE GARLIC BUTTER

MAKES ABOUT ½ CUP

East meets West in this recipe—it's a Japanese butter sauce that can be used as a baste and a serving sauce for grilled vegetables, seafood, and meat.

5 tablespoons unsalted butter
3 tablespoons soy sauce
2 tablespoons fresh lemon juice
1 clove garlic, minced

Melt the butter in a small saucepan over medium heat. Stir in the soy sauce, lemon juice, and garlic and let simmer briskly until the garlic has lost its rawness and the sauce is rich tasting and mellow, about 3 minutes. The butter can be refrigerated, covered, for at least 3 days. Reheat the butter over low heat before using.

U.S.A.

BOURBON BUTTER BASTING SAUCE

MAKES ABOUT 2½ CUPS

Here's a sweet, boozy baste from Tennessee that's great on grilled or barbecued pork. To make a Caribbean version, substitute dark rum for the bourbon and pineapple juice for the apple cider. Use this sauce to baste grilled or smoked pork.

8 tablespoons (1 stick) salted butter
1 cup apple cider
¼ cup firmly packed dark brown sugar
1 tablespoon fresh lemon juice
½ teaspoon salt, or more as needed
½ teaspoon freshly ground black pepper
1 cup bourbon

1. Melt the butter in a medium-size saucepan over medium heat. Add the cider, brown sugar, lemon juice, salt, and pepper. Increase the heat to high and bring to a boil. Let the sauce boil until slightly thickened, about 5 minutes.

2. Remove the pan from the heat and stir in the bourbon. Taste for seasoning, adding more salt as necessary. The basting sauce can be refrigerated, covered, for at least 1 week. Reheat the basting sauce over low heat before using.

INDONESIA

KETJAP BUTTER

MAKES ABOUT ½ CUP

Ketjap manis (spiced, sweet soy sauce) is Indonesia's national table sauce. It is an essential ingredient in marinades and is the traditional accompaniment to Indonesian satés. Cooks at the famous Sunda Kelapa fish house in Jakarta use this *ketjap* butter as a baste for grilled fish and seafood. If *ketjap manis* is unavailable, or you don't have the time to make it, combine equal parts soy sauce and molasses and add a half teaspoon of ground coriander.

4 tablespoons (½ stick) unsalted butter
¼ cup ketjap manis, store-bought or homemade (page 474)

Melt the butter in a small saucepan over medium heat. Stir in the *ketjap manis* and let simmer briskly to blend, about 2 minutes. The butter can be refrigerated, covered, for at least 3 days. Reheat the butter over low heat before using.

U.S.A.

VINEGAR-BASED MOP SAUCE

MAKES MORE THAN 1 QUART

Mop sauces are often an integral part of the long, slow, smoky, indirect grilling method known as barbecue. You find mop sauces in North Carolina, where they're brushed on slow-roasting pork shoulders. You find them in Memphis, where they're used to baste ribs. Mop sauces differ from barbecue sauces in that they're designed to be used for cooking, not serving (they tend to be thinner and much more potent than barbecue sauces). Unlike barbecue sauces, you wouldn't want to eat most mop sauces off a spoon.

The traditional instrument used for basting is a cotton floor mop (a clean, brand-new one, of course)—hence the name mop sauce. Grill shops sell miniature barbecue mops for using on your grill or smoker at home.

1 quart cider vinegar
1 medium-size onion, thinly sliced
3 jalapeño peppers, thinly sliced
4 teaspoons coarse salt (kosher or sea)
2 teaspoons hot red pepper flakes
2 teaspoons freshly ground black pepper

Combine the cider vinegar, onion, jalapeños, salt, hot pepper flakes, black pepper, and 2 cups of water in a large plastic container. Stir until the salt dissolves. The mop sauce can be refrigerated, covered, for at least 3 days.

MEXICO

MEXICAN FISH BASTE

MAKES ABOUT ½ CUP

Tart and salty, this is a baste used by cooks in the Yucatán to heighten the flavor of almost any grilled seafood. Hotheads could add a sliced habañero pepper or two. Sour orange juice (see the box on page 186) is used in the Yucatán; if it's unavailable, you can use lime juice.

½ cup fresh sour orange juice or lime juice
2 teaspoons salt
2 cloves garlic, minced

Combine the sour orange juice, salt, and garlic in a bowl and stir until the salt dissolves. The baste can be refrigerated, covered, for at least 3 days.

FIRE-ROASTED APPLES | AT RIGHT

CHAPTER 19

FIRE AND ICE: DESSERTS

"Some say the world will end in fire, some say in ice," wrote the poet Robert Frost. I hold that a barbecue should end with both.

"The gods give everything to the eater of sugar."
—INDIAN PROVERB

Just because you've finished the main course doesn't mean you should turn off your grill. This truth is not lost on the Bangkok banana vendor, who bastes his fruit with coconut milk and chars it over coconut charcoal. Nor is it lost on the French *pâtissier,* who uses a blowtorch to caramelize the top of his crème brûlée. The high heat of a fire does wonders for caramelizing sugar, helping it acquire an extraordinary depth of flavor. Here you'll find recipes for *crema catalana,* grilled pineapples, grilled bananas, an updated version of s'mores, and other fire-charred desserts.

As for ice, well, many people (myself included) would argue that no barbecue is complete without ice cream. Next to beer, there's nothing like it for refreshing a grill jockey who has been tending a blazing fire. The iced desserts in this chapter range from *kulfi* (Indian ice milk) to *faluda* (a Persian rose water and noodle sherbet) to a freshly made coconut ice cream that comes from Guadeloupe.

U.S.A.

FIRE-ROASTED APPLES

INDIRECT GRILLING
SERVES 8

Once you master the concept of indirect grilling, you can grill pretty much anything you once baked in the oven. Even baked apples. But why would you bother? Well, smoke has a natural tie to sugar, a fact that is apparent in such classic sugar-cured foods as smoked salmon, turkey, and ham. It also seems to bring out the autumnal sweetness of apples, which here are stuffed with a luscious filling of brown sugar and graham cracker crumbs before hitting the grill.

SPECIAL EQUIPMENT

1 cup wood chips, preferably apple or maple, soaked for 1 hour in apple cider or cold water to cover and drained

INGREDIENTS

8 firm, sweet apples, such as Cortlands or Galas
6 tablespoons (¾ stick) unsalted butter, at room temperature
¼ cup firmly packed dark brown sugar
¼ cup dried currants
¼ cup graham cracker crumbs, toasted bread crumbs, or ground almonds
½ teaspoon ground cinnamon
¼ teaspoon freshly grated nutmeg
1 teaspoon vanilla extract
4 marshmallows, cut in half (optional)

1. Lightly grease an aluminum-foil roasting pan. Core the apples, using an apple corer or melon baller, but don't cut all the way through the bottom; the idea is to create a cavity for stuffing.

2. Cream the butter and brown sugar in a medium-size bowl until light and fluffy. Beat in the currants, graham cracker crumbs, cinnamon, nutmeg, and vanilla. Spoon the brown sugar mixture into the apples, dividing it evenly among them. Place a marshmallow half (if using) on top of each apple. Place the apples in the prepared roasting pan.

3. Set up the grill for indirect grilling. No drip pan is necessary for this recipe.

If using a gas grill, place all of the wood chips in the smoker box and preheat the grill to high; when smoke appears, reduce the heat to medium.

If using a charcoal grill, preheat it to medium.

4. When ready to cook, if using a charcoal grill, toss all of the wood chips on the coals. Place the pan of apples in the center of the hot grate, away from the heat, and cover the grill. Cook the apples until soft, 40 minutes to 1 hour. Check the apples after 40 minutes and, if the marshmallows start to brown too much, cover the apples with a piece of aluminum foil. Serve the apples at once.

INDONESIA

BALINESE GRILLED BANANAS IN COCONUT MILK CARAMEL

DIRECT GRILLING
SERVES 6

I like to think of this recipe as a Balinese banana split. Imagine a sugar-crusted, smokily grilled banana served with a silken caramel sauce flavored with coconut milk, lemongrass, and palm sugar (palm sugar is a malty sweetener made from palm sap; it's similar in flavor to light brown sugar). You can serve the grilled bananas in a bowl simply topped with this luscious, offbeat sauce or, if you prefer, with the ice cream I've made optional in this recipe.

The Balinese prepare this dish with finger bananas, sweet fruit about the size of your forefinger. I've called for regular bananas, but if you can find finger bananas or apple bananas (which have a tart, apple-y flavor), by all means use them instead. Choose bananas that are ripe, but not too soft.

FOR THE CARAMEL SAUCE

⅔ cup palm sugar or firmly packed light brown sugar
2 cups coconut milk, canned or homemade (page 522)
1 cinnamon stick (3 inches)
1 stalk lemongrass, trimmed and lightly flattened with the side of a cleaver
2 teaspoons cornstarch

FOR THE BANANAS

6 firm, ripe bananas (each about 6 inches long)
1 cup coconut milk, canned or homemade (page 522)
1 cup granulated sugar
1 quart vanilla ice cream (optional), for serving

1. Make the caramel sauce: Place the palm sugar in a large, deep, heavy saucepan (preferably nonstick) and melt it over medium heat, stirring constantly with a wooden spoon, 2 to 3 minutes. Continue cooking the sugar until it begins to caramelize (turn brown), 3 to 5 minutes longer. You're looking for a rich brown color, but not the dark brown of chocolate. Do not overcook the sugar or it will burn and the sauce will be bitter.

2. Immediately remove the pan from the heat and stir in the 2 cups of coconut milk (be careful, it will sputter and hiss). Return the pan to the heat and bring the coconut milk to a boil, stirring until the sugar dissolves. Stir in the cinnamon stick and lemongrass. Reduce the heat and let the caramel sauce simmer, uncovered, until thick and richly flavored, about 10 minutes, stirring from time to time to prevent scorching.

3. Dissolve the cornstarch in 1 tablespoon of water, then stir it into the caramel sauce. Let simmer for 1 minute; the caramel sauce will thicken even more. Transfer the caramel sauce to a bowl and let cool to room temperature. Using tongs, remove and discard the cinnamon stick and lemongrass. Refrigerate the caramel sauce, covered, until cold.

4. Prepare the bananas: Peel the bananas and cut them into quarters on the diagonal. Place the 1 cup of coconut milk and the granulated sugar in separate shallow bowls at grillside.

5. Set up the grill for direct grilling and preheat to high.

6. When ready to cook, brush and oil the grill grate. Dip the pieces of banana first in the coconut milk, then in the sugar, and place them on the hot grate. Grill the bananas, turning with tongs, until they are nicely browned all over, 6 to 8 minutes in all.

7. To serve, arrange the grilled banana pieces on plates or in bowls. If serving the bananas with ice cream, place scoops of it in bowls and arrange the bananas on top. Spoon the caramel sauce over the bananas and serve at once.

U.S.A.

SPICE-GRILLED PINEAPPLE

DIRECT GRILLING
SERVES 8 TO 10

Americans don't customarily grill fruit, but elsewhere in the world—especially in Southeast Asia—bananas and other fruits are often charred over glowing coals for dessert. Pineapples taste particularly good grilled; the charred flavor meshes nicely with the caramelized sweetness of the fruit. When buying pineapple, go for the gold: Look for fruit with a golden rind. It will be juicier and sweeter than the usual green-rind pineapples.

1 ripe pineapple
¾ cup sugar
1 teaspoon grated lime zest
1 teaspoon ground cinnamon
⅛ teaspoon ground cloves
6 tablespoons (¾ stick) unsalted butter, melted
½ cup dark rum (optional), for flambéing

1. Cut the leafy top off the pineapple, then cut off the rind. Slice the fruit into 8 or 10 even rounds. Using a pineapple corer or paring knife, remove the core from each round.

2. Place the sugar in a shallow bowl and stir in the lime zest, cinnamon, and cloves.

3. Set up the grill for direct grilling and preheat to high.

4. When ready to cook, brush and oil the grill grate. Brush each slice of pineapple on both sides with the melted butter. Dip the pineapple in the sugar mixture, shaking off the excess. Arrange the pineapple slices on the hot grate and grill, turning with tongs, until browned and sizzling, 4 to 6 minutes per side.

5. Transfer the pineapple to plates or platter, arranging the slices in an overlapping fashion. If using the rum, warm it in a small flameproof saucepan on one side of the grill; do not let it boil. Remove the rum from the heat and then, working very carefully, light a long match and use it to ignite the rum. Carefully pour the flaming rum over the pineapple and serve at once.

U.S.A.

FIRE-ROASTED BANANA SPLITS

DIRECT GRILLING
SERVES 4

One of Raichlen's rules of the grill states that if something tastes good raw, baked, fried, or sautéed, it probably tastes even better grilled—for example, that classic

American dessert the banana split. Grilling caramelizes the sugars in the bananas, imparting a smoky, candylike flavor, which is reinforced by a maple syrup basting sauce.

There are two ways to approach this dessert. You can grill and marinate the bananas ahead and serve the banana splits "ice cream parlor style" (cold). This allows you to make the dessert in advance. Or, you can grill the bananas just before serving, in which case you get a hot-cold dessert with a double dose of drama. Either version will give you a banana split that's unlike any you've likely ever tasted.

1 cup maple syrup
½ cup dark rum
¼ cup sugar
½ teaspoon ground cinnamon
¼ teaspoon freshly grated nutmeg
4 bananas (see Notes), peeled
Coconut Ice Cream (page 522), or 1 quart good store-bought coconut ice cream, mounded in 4 shallow dessert bowls
Sweetened Whipped Cream (recipe follows)
¼ cup shredded coconut, toasted (see below)
2 tablespoons chopped macadamia nuts, toasted (see box, page 113)

1. Combine the maple syrup, rum, sugar, cinnamon, and nutmeg in a large bowl and whisk until the sugar dissolves.

2. Set up the grill for direct grilling and preheat to high.

3. When ready to cook, brush and oil the grill grate. Brush the bananas all over with some of the maple syrup mixture. Arrange the bananas on the hot grate and grill, turning with tongs, until nicely browned all over, 6 to 8 minutes in all, basting them with more of the maple syrup mixture (save about half of the maple syrup mixture for serving).

4. Transfer the grilled bananas to a cutting board and slice each in half sharply on the diagonal. Arrange 2 banana halves on top of each bowl of ice cream and spoon the remaining maple syrup mixture over them. Spoon the whipped cream over the bananas and sprinkle the toasted coconut and macadamia nuts on top. Serve the banana splits at once (see Notes).

NOTES: Select bananas that are ripe, or almost ripe, but still a little firm.

To serve the banana splits cold, stir the hot bananas into the remaining maple syrup mixture and let the bananas cool to room temperature. Then, cover the bananas and let marinate in the refrigerator for 3 hours before assembling the banana splits.

Toasting Coconut

To toast coconut, preheat the oven to 400°F. Spread shredded coconut on a rimmed baking sheet and toast it in the oven, stirring once, until lightly browned, four to six minutes.

SWEETENED WHIPPED CREAM

MAKES ABOUT 1½ CUPS

Are you willing to go the extra mile? Made from scratch whipped cream is much superior to the stuff in an aerosol can and it's easy to whip up, too. The trick is to chill the bowl and beaters first—place them in the freezer for thirty minutes. This reduces the risk of the whipped cream separating.

1 cup heavy (whipping) cream
3 tablespoons confectioners' sugar
½ teaspoon vanilla extract

1. Place the cream in a chilled large bowl and beat it with an electric mixer, first on slow speed, then medium speed, then high, until soft peaks form, about 5 minutes.

2. Add the confectioners' sugar and vanilla and continue beating until the cream is thick and stiff, about 2 minutes longer. Do not overbeat the cream or it will separate. The cream is best used within 30 minutes of whipping.

U.S.A.

UPTOWN S'MORES

DIRECT GRILLING
MAKES 8; SERVES 4 TO 8

Anyone who ever attended camp or a Boy or Girl Scout cookout will remember s'mores. To make them you sandwiched freshly roasted marshmallows between graham crackers and chocolate candy bars. The marshmallows melted the chocolate, which got all over your face and fingers. The overall effect was so tasty, you cried out for "s'more" (some more). Here's a s'more for grown-ups, made with chocolate chip cookies and superpremium chocolate.

SPECIAL EQUIPMENT

1 long metal skewer for each person

INGREDIENTS

8 large marshmallows
8 thin squares (each 2 inches) premium dark chocolate
16 chocolate chip cookies, preferably homemade

1. Skewer the marshmallows and set them aside, one per skewer.

2. Set up the grill for direct grilling and preheat to high.

3. When ready to cook, if you are using a charcoal grill carefully remove the grill grate. Roast the marshmallows over the glowing embers or as close to as possible, but not touching, the grate of a gas grill, until darkly browned, 2 to 4 minutes, turning the marshmallows so they roast evenly. Some people (myself included) like to set the marshmallows on fire, then blow them out.

4. Place a piece of chocolate on the bottom (the flat side) of a cookie. Ease a hot marshmallow off the skewer onto the chocolate. Place a second cookie (flat side down) on top of the marshmallow to make a sandwich. Wait a few seconds for the hot marshmallow to melt the chocolate, then eat the s'more like a sandwich. Nostalgia never tasted so good!

U.S.A.

LEMON-GINGER CREME BRULEES

DIRECT FIRE
SERVES 6

This is a book about live-fire cooking, so I thought it only natural to include a few variations on crème brûlée (literally burnt cream). Despite their current trendiness, these burnt sugar desserts have been around a long time. Originally, the sugar was caramelized with a fire-heated poker. Although you could caramelize the sugar by running the brûlées under the broiler, these days there's a better method available—the kitchen blowtorch. This is my favorite way to do this—first, because it's in keeping with the live-fire theme of this book; then, because it gives you a very hot, concentrated, and controlled flame that burns the sugar without warming the custard beneath it. On page 516 you'll find a discussion of kitchen blowtorches.

As for the crème brûlée here, fresh ginger and lemon zest give it a haunting Asian accent that makes for a particularly refreshing summer dessert.

ADVANCE PREPARATION

At least 6 hours for chilling the custard

SPECIAL EQUIPMENT

Kitchen blowtorch (optional); 6 flameproof crème brûlée dishes or ramekins

INGREDIENTS

3 cups heavy (whipping) cream
6 slices (each ¼ inch thick) peeled fresh ginger, flattened with the side of a cleaver
6 strips lemon zest (each 2 by ½ inches), removed with a vegetable peeler
10 large egg yolks
⅓ cup granulated sugar
About ⅓ cup turbinado sugar, such as Sugar in the Raw, or additional granulated sugar

1. Combine the cream, ginger, and lemon zest in a heavy saucepan. Bring just to a boil over medium heat. Remove the cream from the heat and let cool to room temperature.

2. Preheat the oven to 300°F. Bring a large saucepan or kettle of water to a boil.

3. Combine the egg yolks and granulated sugar in a large bowl and whisk just to mix. Whisk the cooled cream into the yolk mixture. Strain this custard mixture into 6 crème brûlée dishes or ramekins. Pour boiling water to a depth of ½ inch into a roasting pan. Place the crème brûlée dishes or ramekins in the roasting pan.

4. Bake the custards until just set, 45 minutes to 1 hour. To test for doneness, gently shake a dish; the top should jiggle just a little. Remove the dishes from the roasting pan and let cool to room temperature. Cover the custards loosely with plastic wrap and refrigerate them for at least 6 hours, or overnight.

5. When ready to serve, sprinkle each of the custards with 2 to 3 teaspoons of the turbinado sugar in a thin layer. Light a kitchen blowtorch following the manufacturer's directions. Or preheat the broiler and set the broiling rack 2 to 4 inches from the source of the heat.

6. Use the kitchen blowtorch to caramelize the tops of the custards, following the instructions below. Or arrange the crème brûlée dishes on the broiling rack and broil the custards until the tops have crusted to a rich, golden brown, about 3 minutes; watch carefully to prevent burning and shift the crème brûlées as needed to ensure even browning. Serve at once.

COOKING WITH A BLOWTORCH

OK, it may not be grilling. But it is live-fire cooking. Many chefs and pit masters use a tool that was once relegated to the workshop to lend a flame-charred taste to their food: a blowtorch. The blowtorch made its appearance in the kitchen in the 1970s when French pastry chefs began using it to brown meringues and caramelize sugar on custard desserts, like crème brûlée.

Using a blowtorch may seem a little daunting at first, but there's nothing like it for creating a high, focused flame and sharp blast of heat. Nowadays there are blowtorches specially created for use in the kitchen. Cookware shops sell them. If you decide to use a blowtorch, keep these watchpoints in mind.

- **Start with the food in a heatproof baking dish or plate. Never torch a pastry that is on a glass plate or platter.**

- **Place the baking dish or plate on top of a surface that is heatproof.**

- **Light the flame and adjust it to obtain a pointed, glowing, red-yellow cone of heat in the center of the lavender-blue flame. This cone is where the heat is concentrated. Hold the flame two to three inches above the surface of the food, moving it back and forth to ensure even browning.**

- **Remember that sugar and meringue will continue to cook for a few seconds after the flame has been removed. Stop torching just before you get the desired degree of doneness.**

LEMON-GINGER CREME BRULEES | PAGE 515

U.S.A.

COCO LOCO BRULEE

DIRECT FIRE
SERVES 6

Here's a twist on classic crème brûlée, not to mention a "wow" dessert of the highest order—talk about drama! The custard is made with coconut milk and coconut cream and is served in a hollowed out coconut shell—an idea I got from chef Douglas Rodriguez of the restaurant Patria in New York City.

Coco Loco Brûlée isn't really grilled, but it does involve the application of live fire in order to caramelize the sugar. I like to do it with a blowtorch, but you can use the broiler. Save the coconut water for making drinks, like Bahamian Sky Juice (see page 55).

ADVANCE PREPARATION

At least 4 hours for chilling the custard

SPECIAL EQUIPMENT

Kitchen blowtorch (optional)

INGREDIENTS

- **3 ripe (hard) coconuts**
- **2 cups heavy (whipping) cream**
- **¾ cup coconut milk, canned or homemade (page 522)**
- **¾ cup canned sweetened coconut cream, such as Coco López**
- **1 vanilla bean, split**
- **2 strips lemon zest (each 2 by ½ inches), removed with a vegetable peeler**
- **About ¾ cup sugar**
- **8 large egg yolks**
- **2½ tablespoons cornstarch**
- **8 cups crushed ice**

1. Cut the coconuts in half. The easiest way to do this is to hold each coconut so that the "eyes" are on top, then to tap the shell repeatedly with the back of a cleaver along an imaginary line going around the middle—its "equator." After 10 to 20 taps, the shell will break neatly in two. Work over a bowl with a strainer to collect the coconut water, if desired, for making drinks. Blot the insides of the coconuts dry with paper towels. Place the coconut shell halves upside down on a baking dish and refrigerate them until you are ready to fill them.

2. Combine the heavy cream, coconut milk, coconut cream, vanilla bean, and lemon zest in a heavy saucepan and gradually bring to a boil over medium heat, 6 to 8 minutes. Remove the pan from the heat and let the cream mixture cool for 3 minutes.

3. Meanwhile, combine ½ cup of the sugar and the egg yolks in a medium-size heatproof bowl and whisk just to mix. Whisk in the cornstarch. Pour the cooled cream mixture into the yolk mixture in a thin stream and whisk to mix. Return this mixture to the saucepan and gradually bring to a gentle simmer over medium heat, whisking steadily. Once the custard thickens, let it simmer gently for 1 to 2 minutes. Do not let it boil rapidly or overcook or the custard will curdle. Remove the pan from the heat and let the custard cool to room temperature. Remove and discard the vanilla bean and lemon zest.

4. Make 6 doughnut-shaped rings of aluminum foil and place the coconut shell halves on top. Spoon the custard mixture into the coconut shells and smooth the tops with the back of a spoon. Refrigerate the custards for at least 4 hours, or even overnight.

5. When ready to serve, sprinkle each custard with 2 to 3 teaspoons of sugar in a thin layer. Light a kitchen blowtorch following the manufacturer's directions. Or preheat the broiler and set the broiling rack so that the coconut shells will be 2 to 3 inches from the source of heat.

6. Arrange the custard-filled coconut shells on top of the aluminum foil rings in a roasting pan. Use the kitchen blowtorch to caramelize the tops of the custards, following the instructions on page 516. Or set the roasting pan on the broiling rack and broil the custards until the tops have crusted to a golden brown, about 3 minutes; watch carefully to prevent burning, shifting the pan as needed to ensure even browning.

7. Divide the crushed ice among 6 shallow bowls. Place a coconut shell half in each bowl and serve.

SPAIN

CATALAN CREAM

CREMA CATALANA

DIRECT FIRE
SERVES 6

Crema catalana is Spain's answer to crème brûlée, and a splendid answer it is. This recipe comes from the Restaurant de les 7 Portes in Barcelona, which opened its doors in 1836.

ADVANCE PREPARATION

6 hours for chilling the custards

SPECIAL EQUIPMENT

Kitchen blowtorch (optional); 6 flameproof ramekins or crème brûlée dishes

INGREDIENTS

- **2 cups milk**
- **1 cup heavy (whipping) cream**
- **6 strips fresh orange zest (each 2 by ½ inches), removed with a vegetable peeler**
- **6 strips fresh lemon zest (each 2 by ½ inches), removed with a vegetable peeler**
- **1 cinnamon stick (3 inches)**
- **About 1 cup sugar**
- **7 large egg yolks**
- **2½ tablespoons unbleached all-purpose flour**

1. Combine the milk, cream, orange and lemon zests, and cinnamon stick in a medium-size heavy saucepan and bring almost to a simmer over low heat. Let the milk mixture cook for about 10 minutes but do not allow it to boil. Let the milk mixture cool to room temperature.

2. Whisk together ¾ cup of the sugar and the egg yolks in a medium-size bowl. Whisk in the flour, then strain the cooked milk mixture into the yolk mixture in a thin stream and whisk to mix. Return this mixture to the saucepan and gradually bring to a gentle simmer over medium heat, whisking steadily. Once the mixture thickens, let it simmer gently for 1 to 2 minutes. Do not let it boil rapidly or overcook or the custard will curdle.

3. Immediately divide the custard among 6 ramekins or crème brûlée dishes. Let the custard cool to room temperature, then cover it loosely with plastic wrap and refrigerate for 6 hours.

4. When ready to serve, sprinkle each of the custards with 2 to 3 teaspoons of sugar in a thin layer. Light a kitchen blowtorch following the manufacturer's directions. Or preheat the broiler and set the broiling rack 2 to 4 inches from the heat source.

5. Use the kitchen blowtorch to caramelize the tops of the custards, following the instructions on page 516. Or arrange the ramekins on the broiling rack and broil until the tops have crusted to a rich, golden brown, about 3 minutes; watch carefully to prevent burning, shifting the ramekins as needed to ensure even browning. Serve at once.

ARGENTINA

CARAMEL CREAM

DULCE DE LECHE

SERVES 4 TO 6

This thick, sweet, saucelike caramel is Argentina's national dessert. It turns up at highfalutin restaurants and homey eateries, spooned over everything from fruit to cake to ice cream. It's also good eaten right off the spoon. *Dulce de leche* (literally milk sweet) isn't particularly difficult to make, but it does require conscientious stirring to keep the caramel from boiling over. Be comforted by the fact that it keeps for months and that a little can go a long way.

- **1 quart whole milk (see Note)**
- **1⅓ cups sugar**
- **1 vanilla bean**
- **½ teaspoon baking soda**

1. Combine the milk, sugar, vanilla bean, and baking soda in a large, heavy saucepan and bring to a boil over high heat, stirring to dissolve the sugar. Reduce the heat to medium and let the milk mixture simmer briskly, stirring often with a wooden spoon, until thick, caramel colored, and reduced by half, 30 to 40 minutes. You'll need to

Barbecue from the Land of Morning Calm: The Korean Grill

When I was a bachelor in Boston, my favorite neighborhood restaurant was a small, unassuming storefront called Korea Garden. At least once a week I would retreat to this oasis of calm and warmth for a sorely needed dose of *mandoo* (garlicky beef ravioli), *kimchi* (fiery pickled napa cabbage), and *bool kogi* (sweet-salty sesame grilled beef).

In culinary matters, Korea tends to be eclipsed by its two giant neighbors, China and Japan. Most Americans have had a lifelong experience with some sort of Chinese cooking, while sushi, teriyaki, and other Japanese dishes are now so popular, they've become part of the North American repertoire. But many Americans would be hard-pressed to name a single dish from Korea.

This is a shame, for Korea offers some of the most refined, sophisticated, and intrinsically healthy food I have eaten on five continents: Dishes designed with a dazzling array of colors, textures, and flavors. Menus remarkable for their sparing use of meats and seafoods and high proportion of grains and vegetables. Korean cooking lacks the oiliness associated with many Chinese dishes, while its flavors are more vibrant than the restrained, disciplined tastes of Japan.

Actually, barbecue was about the last thing on my mind when I visited Korea. The month was February, and the bone-numbing cold had frozen the water in the moats around Seoul's Kyongbukkung Palace. This was the time of year to enjoy hearty soups and stews. Curiously, though, wherever I went, I found barbecue—in showy restaurants, homey neighborhood eateries, and back-alley cookshops. In the process, I discovered that in Korea grilling is done, as often as not, indoors and is popular all year round. Koreans gather around their tabletop charcoal braziers with the same fervor, the same hunger for warmth, that brings skiers to crowd around fireplaces at ski lodges in the Alps.

This truth was brought home to me by a restaurant called Dae Won Gak. Actually, the term *restaurant* is a bit of an understatement. Dae Won Gak is a veritable village of sixty traditional Korean houses on several acres of hillside overlooking Seoul. Some of the structures are large enough to accommodate three hundred people, others cozy and intimate enough to seat only two. Each boasts the gracefully curved eaves, ceramic tile roofs, rope mats, and intricate woodwork of a traditional Korean home.

I took my seat on the floor at a knee-high table with a ceramic brazier in the center. Our waitress filled it with blazing coals, then leaning over with her chopsticks, arranged thin sheets of marinated beef and tiny skewers of garlic cloves on the concave grill over the brazier. Smoke filled our nostrils and the sounds of sizzling meat sang in our ears, as the *bool kogi* was grilled before our eyes.

The traditional way to eat *bool kogi* is wrapped, much like moo shu pork or fajitas (although this is not how it's usually served at Korean restaurants in the U.S.). I placed a snippet of meat and a grilled garlic clove on a romaine lettuce leaf, rolled it up, dipped it in a delicately flavored Asian pear sauce, then popped it into my mouth. The contrast of sweet and salty, of pungent and fruity, of crisp vegetable and chewy but tender meat was as haunting and complex as the twangy *kai ya kum* music that played in the background.

To round out the meal, there was an impressive array of refreshing side dishes: a salad of spicy daikon radish, an onion and lettuce salad, a nutty bean sprout salad, three types of *kimchi,* plates of lettuce leaves, sliced cucumbers, and rice.

Korean Barbecued Ribs

Koreans have raised the beef short rib to the level of art in a dish called *kalbi kui* (literally, grilled ribs). I enjoyed my rib experience in one of Seoul's most famous grill restaurants, Samwon Garden. I didn't enjoy it alone: This behemoth eatery seats seven hundred and serves two thousand people on a busy day. *Samwon* means "three utmosts" in Korean, explained the restaurant's manager, Mr. Park. The three utmosts in question here are cleanliness, kindness, and deliciousness. I might add a fourth utmost, entertainment, as Samwon Garden is a veritable theme park, complete with its own pond, mountain, and waterfalls.

Mr. Park led me down to an immaculate kitchen, where seventy chefs toil round the clock to feed the appreciative multitudes upstairs. One whole room has been consecrated to the preparation of the *kalbi*. The restaurant starts with whole rib sections of beef, which are cut into two-inch cross sections on a band saw, then butterflied into thin strips. According to Mr. Park, *kalbi kui* is a relatively new addition to the Korean repertoire, originating in restaurants, not in the home, in the 1950s. As with *bool kogi, kalbi kui* is cooked on a brazier in the center of the table and it's eaten wrapped in lettuce leaves.

Like most Korean dishes, Korean barbecue is built from a simple palate of flavors: the salty succulence of soy sauce, the sweetness of sugar or honey, the nutty tang of sesame oil and sesame seeds. Accents are provided by the pungency of garlic and scallion, the tingle of ginger, the bite of chile powder and chile paste. What this means in practical terms is that Korean food is much easier to prepare in an American kitchen than, say, Chinese or Japanese. It requires few esoteric ingredients or tricky cooking techniques. Using a relatively limited number of ingredients, Koreans can create an astonishing range of flavors.

adjust the heat, now up, now down, to keep the mixture at a brisk simmer without it boiling over. The traditional test for doneness is to pour a spoonful of caramel cream on a plate. When it gathers in a thick puddle and no longer runs to the edges, the caramel cream is ready. Remove the vanilla bean with tongs and discard it.

2. Transfer the caramel cream to a serving bowl and let it cool to room temperature. You can eat it now or refrigerate it, covered, if you prefer to serve it chilled.

NOTE: You must use whole milk for *dulce de leche*. Skim milk will burn during the reduction process.

INDIA

CARDAMOM PISTACHIO RICE PUDDING

KHEER

SERVES 6

It's hard to imagine a meal of tandoori or kebabs without *kheer,* an exquisitely creamy rice pudding dessert popular in Central Asia and the Indian subcontinent. *Kheer* owes its exotic, perfumed fragrance to cardamom and rose water and its richness to the milk, which is boiled until reduced by almost half to concentrate its flavor.

- 2 quarts whole milk (see Note)
- 12 green cardamom pods, crushed and tied in a piece of cheesecloth
- ¼ cup basmati rice
- ½ cup sugar
- ¼ cup finely chopped unsalted pistachio nuts, plus 2 tablespoons for garnish
- ¼ cup slivered almonds
- ¼ cup golden raisins
- Pinch of salt
- 1 tablespoon rose water

1. Combine the milk, cardamom, and rice in a large, heavy saucepan and bring gradually to a boil over medium high heat. Reduce the heat to medium and let simmer, stirring often with a wooden spoon, until the milk is reduced to 6 cups, about 30 minutes. Remove and discard the cardamom.

2. Stir the sugar, ¼ cup of pistachio nuts, the almonds, raisins, and salt into the reduced milk. Gently let the pudding mixture simmer, stirring often, until the rice is very soft and the pudding has thickened, about 20 minutes longer. You should have about 5½ cups in all. Stir the rose water into the rice pudding and let cook for 1 minute.

3. Remove the pan from the heat and let the pudding cool to room temperature, then spoon it into 6 bowls or wine glasses. The pudding tastes best served at room temperature or just slightly chilled. Just before serving, sprinkle the pudding with the remaining 2 tablespoons of chopped pistachio nuts.

NOTE: You must use whole milk for *kheer*. Skim milk will burn during the reduction process.

GUADELOUPE

COCONUT ICE CREAM

SERVES 4

This lovely ice cream comes from Guadeloupe's Pointe des Châteaux beach, where it's churned by hand by women working under beach umbrellas or from the backs of their station wagons. For the best results, use made-from-scratch coconut milk. In a pinch you can make it with canned coconut milk (try Goya or A Taste of Thai); do not use coconut cream.

SPECIAL EQUIPMENT

Ice cream machine

INGREDIENTS

2 cups coconut milk, homemade (recipe follows) or canned
⅔ cup sugar, or more to taste
1 teaspoon vanilla extract
½ teaspoon almond extract
1 teaspoon grated lemon zest
½ teaspoon ground cinnamon
¼ teaspoon freshly grated nutmeg

1. Combine the coconut milk, sugar, vanilla extract, almond extract, lemon zest, cinnamon, and nutmeg in a medium-size bowl and whisk until the sugar dissolves. Taste for sweetness, adding more sugar if necessary.

2. Transfer the coconut mixture to an ice cream machine and freeze, following the manufacturer's instructions.

COCONUT MILK

MAKES 2 TO 3 CUPS

Coconut milk is a staple on the world's barbecue trail, used in marinades in Malaysia, sauces in Brazil, and in refreshing desserts all across the globe. You can buy reasonably good coconut milk in cans (two widely available brands are A Taste of Thai and Chaokoh), but it's not difficult to make your own. Here's how.

1 ripe (hard) coconut
2 cups boiling water

1. Prepare the coconut, through removing the brown skin, as directed in the box on page 114, setting aside the coconut water. Break the large pieces of coconut into 1 to 2-inch pieces.

2. Place the coconut, reserved coconut water, and boiling water in a blender and blend for 3 minutes. You may need to work in two or three batches to reduce the risk of overflow. Let the coconut mixture stand for 5 minutes, then pour it through a fine-mesh strainer or a strainer lined with several layers of dampened cheesecloth. Twist the cheesecloth tightly to extract as much milk as possible. The coconut milk can be refrigerated, covered, for up to 3 days. It can also be frozen for up to 1 month.

CENTRAL ASIA

CARDAMOM CARAMEL ICE CREAM

KULFI

SERVES 4 TO 6

Grilled fare and ice cream are one of the constants of the world of barbecue. This one, *kulfi,* has a haunting flavor that lies midway between malt and caramel—the result of the long, slow simmering of the milk to reduce it by two thirds. To this add the exotic flavors of cardamom and pistachio nuts and you've got an ice cream quite unlike anything in the North American repertoire.

ADVANCE PREPARATION

2 hours for chilling the kulfi mixture

SPECIAL EQUIPMENT

Ice cream machine

INGREDIENTS

2 quarts whole milk (see Note)
6 green cardamom pods, crushed and tied in a piece of cheesecloth
½ cup sugar, or more to taste
3 tablespoons chopped pistachio nuts
3 tablespoons chopped blanched almonds

1. Combine the milk and cardamom in a large, heavy saucepan and gradually bring to a boil over medium-high heat. Reduce the heat to medium and let the milk simmer briskly, stirring it often with a wooden spoon, until reduced to 3 cups, about 1 hour. Remove and discard the cardamom.

2. Stir in the sugar, pistachio nuts, and almonds and let simmer for 3 minutes. Remove the *kulfi* mixture from the heat and taste for sweetening, adding more sugar if necessary. Let the *kulfi* mixture cool to room temperature, then transfer it to a bowl. Cover and refrigerate until cold, about 2 hours.

3. Transfer the *kulfi* mixture to an ice cream machine and freeze, following the manufacturer's instructions.

NOTE: You must use whole milk for *kulfi*. Skim milk will burn during the reduction process.

IRAN

PERSIAN LEMON AND ROSE WATER "SUNDAE" WITH SOUR CHERRY SYRUP

FALUDA

SERVES 8

One of the most refreshing desserts ever to grace a barbecue is *faluda* (aka *faludeh*). I first sampled it at a Persian restaurant in New York. *Faluda* also turns up in Afghanistan, where it is made with fresh mountain snow. It belongs to a large family of Asian frozen desserts that include Indian *kulfi* and Turkish *sorpa* (sorbet). The Persian version offers the haunting flavors of sour cherry syrup and rose water. But what really sets *faluda* apart is the addition of rice noodles, which creates a wonderfully exotic and unexpected texture.

Rose water and sour cherry syrup are available at Middle and Near Eastern markets. Use a thin rice noodle, like Thai rice sticks or Vietnamese rice vermicelli, for the noodles.

ADVANCE PREPARATION

2 hours for chilling the rose water syrup

INGREDIENTS

⅔ cup fresh lemon juice
⅔ cup rose water
1½ cups sugar
1 skein (1 ounce) rice noodles
8 cups crushed ice
½ cup sour cherry syrup or grenadine

1. Combine the lemon juice, rose water, and sugar in a heavy saucepan and bring to a boil over medium-high heat. Let boil, stirring constantly, until the sugar dissolves and the mixture is syrupy, about 5 minutes. Remove the pan from the heat and let the syrup cool to room temperature, then cover and refrigerate it until cold, about 2 hours.

2. Meanwhile, soak the rice noodles in cold water to cover for 20 minutes.

3. Bring 4 cups of water to a boil in a large saucepan. Drain the noodles in a colander and cook them in the boiling water until soft, 3 to 5 minutes. Drain the noodles in a colander, rinse them under cold running water until cool, and drain again. Using kitchen shears, cut the noodles into 1-inch pieces.

4. Working in batches, combine the crushed ice and chilled rose water syrup in a blender and process to an icy puree. Transfer the rose water mixture to a bowl and stir in the rice noodles. Spoon the rose water and noodle mixture into 8 wine glasses. Drizzle a tablespoon of sour cherry syrup over each *faluda* and serve at once (see Note).

NOTE: You can make the *faluda* ahead and freeze it in paper cups. To serve, let the *faluda* warm for 5 to 10 minutes, then crush it by gently squeezing the side of the cups with your fingers to loosen up the ice crystals. Transfer the *faluda* to wine glasses and drizzle the cherry syrup on top.

SOUTHEAST ASIA

FRUIT COOLER

SERVES 6

A cross between a milk shake and a dessert, this refreshing cooler is sold at street stalls and markets throughout Southeast Asia. Sweetened condensed milk is the dairy product of choice here because it will not spoil in the tropical heat. Feel free to vary the fruits.

3 cups seeded, diced watermelon
3 cups diced fresh strawberries, plus 6 small whole strawberries, for garnish
2 ripe bananas, peeled and diced
⅓ cup fresh lime juice, or more to taste
⅓ cup sugar, or more to taste
⅓ cup sweetened condensed milk
6 cups crushed ice

Working in batches, combine the watermelon, diced strawberries, bananas, lime juice, sugar, condensed milk, and ice in a blender and blend until smooth. Taste for flavoring, adding more lime juice and/or sugar as necessary. Serve the coolers at once in 6 tall glasses garnished with the whole strawberries and straws.

KOREA

KOREAN FRUIT "PUNCH"

SERVES 6

Part beverage and part fruit salad, this cool, syrupy dish is served as a refresher at the end of a Korean meal. I've had it made with everything from dried persimmons to jujubes (a type of date); the ingredients are really limited only by your imagination. I like a mixture of hard fruits, like Asian pears or apples; soft fruit, like bananas or melon; and berries, like strawberries or blueberries.

3 cups mixed diced or sliced fresh fruit
¾ cup sugar
4 slices peeled fresh ginger (each ¼ inch thick), flattened with a cleaver
3 strips lemon zest (each 2 by ½ inches), removed with a vegetable peeler
2 cinnamon sticks (each 3 inches)
2 tablespoons pine nuts, lightly toasted (see box, page 113)

1. Toss the fruit with ¼ cup of the sugar in a serving bowl and let stand for 15 minutes.

2. Meanwhile, combine the remaining ½ cup sugar, the ginger, lemon zest, cinnamon sticks, and 4 cups of water in a saucepan and bring to a boil over high heat. Reduce the heat and let simmer until well flavored and lightly syrupy, about 5 minutes. Remove the pan from the heat and let the syrup cool completely.

3. Strain the syrup over the fruit and stir gently to mix. Sprinkle the pine nuts on top and serve at once. I like to serve the punch in glass bowls or brandy snifters. It's perfectly acceptable to raise the bowl to your lips to sip the syrup.

METRIC CONVERSION CHARTS

Tablespoons and Ounces — Grams

Tablespoons and Ounces (U.S. CUSTOMARY SYSTEM)	Grams (METRIC SYSTEM)
1 pinch = less than ⅛ teaspoon (dry)	0.5 grams
1 dash = 3 drops to ¼ teaspoon (liquid)	1.25 grams
1 teaspoon (liquid)	5.0 grams
3 teaspoons = 1 tablespoon = ½ ounce	14.3 grams
2 tablespoons = 1 ounce	28.35 grams
4 tablespoons = 2 ounces = ¼ cup	56.7 grams
8 tablespoons = 4 ounces = ½ cup (1 stick of butter)	113.4 grams
8 tablespoons (flour) = about 2 ounces	72.0 grams
16 tablespoons = 8 ounces = 1 cup = ½ pound	226.8 grams
32 tablespoons = 16 ounces = 2 cups = 1 pound	453.6 grams or 0.4536 kilogram
64 tablespoons = 32 ounces = 1 quart = 2 pounds	907.0 grams or 0.907 kilogram

1 quart = (roughly 1 liter)

Temperatures: Fahrenheit (F) to Celsius (C)

−10°F = −23.3°C (freezer storage)
0°F = −17.7°C
32°F = 0°C (water freezes)
50°F = 10°C
68°F = 20°C (room temperature)
100°F = 37.7°C
150°F = 65.5°C
205°F = 96.1°C (water simmers)
212°F = 100°C (water boils)
300°F = 148.8°C
325°F = 162.8°C
350°F = 177°C (baking)
375°F = 190.5°C
400°F = 204.4°C (hot oven)
425°F = 218.3°C
450°F = 232°C (very hot oven)
475°F = 246.1°C
500°F = 260°C (broiling)

Conversion Factors

ounces to grams: multiply ounce figure by 28.3 to get number of grams
grams to ounces: multiply gram figure by 0.0353 to get number of ounces
pounds to grams: multiply pound figure by 453.59 to get number of grams
pounds to kilograms: multiply pound figure by 0.45 to get number of kilograms
ounces to milliliters: multiply ounce figure by 30 to get number of milliliters
cups to liters: multiply cup figure by 0.24 to get number of liters
Fahrenheit to Celsius: subtract 32 from the Fahrenheit figure, multiply by 5, then divide by 9 to get Celsius figure
Celsius to Fahrenheit: multiply Celsius figure by 9, divide by 5, then add 32 to get Fahrenheit figure
inches to centimeters: multiply inch figure by 2.54 to get number of centimeters
centimeters to inches: multiply centimeter figure by 0.39 to get number of inches

GLOSSARY OF SPECIAL INGREDIENTS

Grilling is the world's most straightforward cooking technique, but as you grill your way along the barbecue trail, you'll need to know about some special ingredients. Here's what they are.

ALEPPO PEPPER: A round, reddish-brown chile from Syria and eastern Turkey, usually sold powdered or in flakes. Used in a number of preparations—notably in this book in the Onion Relish with Pomegranate Molasses. The Aleppo pepper has a complex flavor that's simultaneously earthy, salty, piquant, fruity, and hot. Look for it in Middle Eastern grocery stores. The closest approximation would be equal parts ancho chile powder and hot red pepper flakes with a sprinkle of salt and lime juice.

ALLSPICE: The perfumed berries of this Caribbean tree are one of the most defining flavors of Jamaican jerk. The best allspice comes from Jamaica: Look for it in West Indian markets and buy the berries whole.

AMBA: A hot, sour pickling paste from India and the Middle and Near East. *Amba* is the Hindu word for mango (think mango pickle here). *Amba* paste, whose main ingredients are vinegar, turmeric, and fenugreek, is the flavoring for the hot pickles that invariably accompany Afghan, Iraqi, and Israeli barbecue.

ANNATTO SEED: A hard, squarish, rust-colored seed with a tangy, earthy, iodine flavor. The spice, also known by its Spanish name *achiote,* is native to the Caribbean and Central America. Annatto is an essential ingredient in *recado* (Yucatecan spice paste) and *tikin xik* (Yucatán-style marinated fish). There are two ways to use this hard seed: Grind it to a powder in a spice mill or soak it in sour orange juice (or water) until soft, then crumble or puree.

BLACK SESAME SEEDS: A jet-black variety of sesame seed known as *gomen* in Japanese. Use toasted white sesame seeds as a substitute.

CANDLENUT: An essential ingredient in Balinese spice pastes, the candlenut tastes like a somewhat bitter cashew. Look for it in Asian markets that carry Indonesian ingredients. There's no taste equivalent in the West, but macadamia nuts and cashews have the right texture and mouth feel.

CARDAMOM: A spice with a sweet, perfumed flavor used throughout North Africa, the Middle East, and India. Actually there are two types: Green cardamom is a greenish-tan, coffee bean–size pod with small, fragrant black seeds inside; black cardamom is the size of a plum pit and has a smoky flavor. Green cardamom is available in the spice rack of almost any supermarket; black cardamom can be found in Indian markets.

CHAAT MASALA: A traditional Indian spice mix sprinkled on salads and cold grilled dishes. *Chaat masala* owes its distinctive sourish, sulphurous flavor to the addition of a sulphur-rich mineral called black salt.

CHICKPEA FLOUR (also known as *besan*): A fine, aromatic flour made from roasted chickpeas. It has a tart, nutty, earthy flavor that's unique in the world of cooking. *Besan* is used extensively in Indian barbecue to thicken and flavor marinades. It is also used in the south of France to make pancakes (*socca,* traditionally baked in a wood-fired oven) and in North Africa to make a sort of french fry.

CHILES: Individual chiles are described on page 504.

CILANTRO (also known as coriander leaf and Chinese parsley): This pungent plant is probably the most widely used herb in the world of barbecue. The leaves turn up in salsas and marinades and are sprinkled whole over grilled fare from Malaysia to Mexico City. Cilantro roots are a key ingredient in Thai and Malaysian spice pastes. The seed of the plant (coriander) is an essential flavoring in North African and Indian barbecue.

Cilantro can also be found at Asian, Indian, and Hispanic markets, gourmet shops, and in most supermarkets. There is no substitute for the fresh herb, and it doesn't dry particularly well. Nonetheless, fresh mint can be used as a substitute in many recipes. Cilantro is one of those flavorings people either love or hate. If the herb tastes like soap to you, you may be mildly allergic to it.

COCONUT MILK: A creamy white liquid extracted from freshly grated coconut. (Contrary to popular belief, it's not the clearish liquid inside a coconut—that's coconut water.) Coconut milk is used widely throughout Southeast Asia and the Caribbean, and in Brazil. On page 522, you'll find instructions on how to make it from scratch. Canned coconut milk will work fine for the recipes in this book and is available at Asian and Hispanic supermarkets. Be sure to buy unsweetened coconut milk, and avoid coconut cream. One good brand is A Taste of Thai.

EPAZOTE: A refreshing, astringent, and strongly aromatic Mexican herb whose peculiar aroma lives up to its English name, pigweed. Sold in Mexican and Hispanic markets.

FENUGREEK: A rectangular tan seed with a pleasantly bitter flavor. Fenugreek is used widely in India (where it's known as *methi*) and in the Middle East (where it's known as *hilbeh*).

FISH SAUCE: (called *nam pla* in Thai and *nuoc mam* in Vietnamese): A salty condiment made from pickled anchovies. Fish sauce is used in Southeast Asia the way soy sauce is used in Japan and China. Its aroma can be off-putting, but its distinctive flavor enriches all that it touches. Look for fish sauce in Asian markets, gourmet shops, and in many large supermarkets. The best quality brands come in glass, not plastic, bottles. Good brands include Flying Lion, Three Crabs, and Squid. A smaller amount of soy sauce can be substituted, but the flavor won't be quite the same.

GALANGAL: A root in the ginger family with a peppery, aromatic flavor (imagine the heat of ginger without the sweetness). It usually comes fresh or frozen in Asian markets. There's also a powdered form from Indonesia that is sometimes sold by the name of *laos*. Fresh ginger mixed with freshly ground black pepper makes an acceptable substitute.

GARAM MASALA: An Indian spice mix with as many as 20 different herbs and spices, including cumin, coriander, green and black cardamom seeds, black pepper, and bay leaves. On page 494 you'll find a recipe for making *garam masala* from scratch. Or use a commercial brand, available at Indian markets and in some gourmet shops.

GINGER: Widely available and best used fresh. Choose "races" (clusters) of ginger that feel heavy in your hand. The thinner the skin, the better. Avoid old, fibrous ginger (break off a small piece to check the state of the fibers). One good way to prepare ginger is to grate it.

GRAPE LEAVES: Sold pickled in jars at Middle Eastern markets and in many supermarkets. It is often used to make the wrapped grilled fish dishes of Turkey and the Republic of Georgia.

GRAPE SYRUP (ALSO KNOWN AS GRAPE MOLASSES): A tart, molasseslike sweetener used in Middle Eastern and Iranian cooking. (Try a little drizzled over grilled kebabs or pork chops.) Grape syrup is sold in Middle and Near Eastern markets.

HUNG YOGURT (also known as yogurt cheese): This is the soul of barbecue marinades from Turkey to Bangladesh. Indians make it by tying and hanging fresh whole-milk yogurt in cheesecloth and allowing the whey to drain off (hence the name "hung yogurt"). In the West, we would use a yogurt strainer or strainer lined with dampened cheesecloth or a coffee filter. Save the whey for one of the yogurt drinks in the Thirst Quenchers chapter.

KACHIRI POWDER: A souring agent made from a small, round dried fruit from Rajasthan, used for marinades in North Indian grilling.

KETJAP MANIS: This thick, sweet soy sauce is Indonesia's national flavoring for satés and table sauces. It is available in Asian markets and in some gourmet shops. You can make the real thing by following the recipe on page 474, but a quick substitute can be made by combining equal parts regular soy sauce and molasses.

LAVASH: These large sheets of paper-thin flat bread are served with grilled fare in Iraq, Iran, and the Caucasus Mountain republics of the former Soviet Union (Azerbaijan, Uzbekistan, Turkmenistan, etc.). Central Asians wrap grilled lamb in lavash the way Mexicans serve beef and pork in tortillas. Look for lavash at Middle Eastern markets and in many supermarkets. Dried lavash needs to be softened in water. Pita bread can be used as a substitute.

LEMONGRASS: The quintessential flavoring of Southeast Asia, where it's used in innumerable marinades and spice pastes. The Balinese grill shrimp mousse on whole lemongrass stalks. Malaysian grill jockeys use the leafy shoots as a basting brush.

Lemongrass looks somewhat like a large scallion, with a bulbous base that tapers to slender, pointed leaves. The top two-thirds of the fibrous stalks are generally trimmed off, as are the outside leaves covering the base and the root. (I like to put them in the cavity of fish or chicken before grilling.) The core that remains has a haunting lemon flavor—without the tartness—that goes exceedingly well with seafood, chicken, and beef.

Fresh lemongrass can be found at Asian markets and in an increasing number of supermarkets. Dried lemongrass can be found at most natural foods stores. There's no real substitute for lemongrass, but fresh lemon zest (the lemon's oil-rich outer rind) works better than nothing. When buying lemongrass, look for stalks that feel firm and heavy. (Press your thumbnail into the base of the stalk: it should feel moist.) To trim lemongrass, cut off the root end and the slender greenish leaves. What remains will be a cream-colored core 4 to 6 inches long and ¼ to ½ inch thick.

MIRIN: Sweet Japanese cooking wine. If unavailable, use cream sherry or sake or white wine sweetened with a little sugar or honey.

MISO: A richly flavored and highly nutritious paste made from cultured soy beans and grains. The Japanese make a barbecue sauce for grilled tofu and eggplant by mixing miso, mirin, sugar, and egg yolks. Miso comes in many colors and flavors, but the white is the most often used for grilling. Look for it at Japanese markets and natural foods stores.

OLIVE OIL: Use the best extra-virgin olive oil you can buy for marinating and basting. (Extra-virgin has the lowest acidity and the most intense flavor.) Every country on the Mediterranean makes olive oil and the flavors vary widely. I like to use Spanish oil for Spanish grilled dishes, Italian oil for Italian dishes, and so on. The best oils for the money come from Turkey, Greece, and Lebanon.

PALM SUGAR: A creamy, light brown sugar made from the sap of the date palm. Used throughout Southeast Asia, it has overtones of toffee and maple syrup. Look for it at Asian markets or use light brown sugar or maple sugar.

PEPPER: One of the indispensable barbecue seasonings. Black is the preferred pepper in North America. Asian and Europeans often use white pepper. Nothing can beat the flavor of freshly ground peppercorns, of course, but I find it inconvenient to reach for a peppercorn grinder when I'm in the middle of cooking (hard to grip with wet hands). My compromise is to pregrind black and white peppercorns in a spice mill every few weeks and store them in jars. That way, you always have a pinch on hand.

POMEGRANATE MOLASSES: A thick, sweet-sour syrup made from boiled-down pomegranate juice. Called *narsharab* in Central Asia, it's commonly drizzled on grilled meats in Turkey, Iran, and the Central Asian Republics of the former Soviet Union. Pomegranate syrup is sold at Middle and Near Eastern markets.

SAFFRON: The fragrant, rust-colored stigmas of a crocus grown in Spain and India. Saffron is a key flavoring in Iranian barbecue, where it's used in both marinades and basting mixtures. Seventy thousand flowers are needed to make a single pound of saffron (each must be processed by hand), which accounts for saffron's high price. Always buy saffron threads, not powder (the latter is easier to adulterate). For best results, buy small quantities in tiny glass tubes. Store tightly sealed and away from light. (I keep mine in the refrigerator.) It will keep for several months. If the saffron lacks an intense aroma when you open the bottle, it's probably past its prime. To grind saffron, place the threads in a small bowl and pulverize with the end of a wooden spoon.

SAKE: Japanese rice wine. An ingredient in teriyaki sauce, as well as the traditional beverage for Japanese barbecue. (If you really want to be traditional, serve the sake in a wooden box with a pinch of salt.)

SALT: The primal seasoning for barbecue; indeed it is the only seasoning for grilled beef in many countries, including Argentina and Brazil. Not all salts are created equal, however. My favorite seasoning is coarse sea salt. (The coarse texture keeps it from dissolving completely, so you get little bursts of salty flavor. Also, the minerals in sea salt add flavor. Besides, I like the way it feels between my fingers.) I also like kosher salt—again for its coarse texture.

SAMBAL ULEK: A fiery red chile paste from Indonesia. Available at Asian markets, gourmet shops, and at an increasing number of supermarkets. Substitute Thai or Vietnamese chile paste or a spoonful of your favorite hot sauce.

SESAME OIL: A dark, nutty oil extracted from roasted sesame seeds, used extensively in Japanese and Korean grilling. One good brand is Kadoya from Japan. Look for it at Asian markets and in natural foods stores. (Steer clear of domestic sesame oils, most of which lack the roasted flavor of the Asian.)

SHRIMP PASTE: A malodorous paste made from fermented shrimp and used in Southeast Asian cooking, especially in Indonesia, where it goes by the name of *trasi,* and in Malaysia, where it goes by the name of *belacan*. A small, pea-size piece goes a long way. It's customary to toast the shrimp paste on the end of a skewer over the fire for a few minutes before using. If your fire isn't in operation when you're preparing to use the shrimp paste, sauté it in a skillet or broil on a piece of aluminum foil under the broiler.

SOUR ORANGE: A citrus fruit that looks like an orange (although much less uniform in appearance), but tastes like a lime. Known as *naranja agria* in Spanish, sour orange is widely used in Caribbean and Central American marinades. If unavailable, substitute 3 parts fresh lime juice to 1 part regular orange juice.

SOY SAUCE: The lifeblood of Chinese and Japanese cuisine. *Shoyu* is Japanese soy sauce made with wheat and soybean starter. Tamari is a naturally brewed Japanese soy sauce made with soybean starter. Its clean, elegant flavor makes it my hands-down favorite. Chinese soy sauce is thicker and sweeter than Japanese. Mushroom soy sauce is a thick, sweet Chinese soy sauce flavored with straw mushrooms.

STAR ANISE: The dried, star-shaped fruit of a small evergreen tree that grows in southwestern China and Vietnam. Its smoky licorice flavor is as unique as its eight-pointed pod. A member of the magnolia family, star anise is one of the ingredients in Chinese five-spice powder. Look for it in Asian and Hispanic markets and gourmet shops.

SUMAC: A sour, purplish powder made from the berries of the Middle Eastern sumac tree. Tart and lemony, sumac is used as a seasoning for grilled meats and seafood throughout the Middle East, the Caucasus Mountain republics, and Central Asia.

TAHINI: Refers both to a chalky paste made from sesame seeds and a sauce made from this paste mixed with lemon juice and water. The latter is a popular accompaniment to Lebanese and Middle Eastern–style grilled seafood. Tahini can be purchased at Middle Eastern markets, natural foods stores, and in the ethnic food section of most supermarkets. Store tahini at room temperature. Stir with a fork until smooth before using.

TAMARIND/TAMARIND WATER: Tamarind is a long brown tropical seed pod whose sweet-sour pulp tastes like pureed prunes mixed with lime juice. Tamarind is a flavoring in Worcestershire sauce and in A-1 steak sauce. It is a staple in the Caribbean, India, and Southeast Asia, and it's finally becoming known in this country. If you live in a city with a large Hispanic or Asian population, you may be able to find fresh tamarind pods. Asian and Indian markets often sell sticky balls of peeled tamarind pulp. Tamarind puree (also known as tamarind water) can be found frozen at Hispanic markets.

TURMERIC: A pungent, orange-fleshed cousin of ginger. Sometimes you can find it fresh or frozen at Asian markets. More often, it's used in powdered form and is available in supermarkets. Fresh turmeric is an essential ingredient in the spice pastes of Indonesia. To approximate its flavor, combine ½ teaspoon ground turmeric with 1 tablespoon fresh ginger.

UMEBOSHI PLUMS/PLUM PASTE: Japanese pickled plums flavored with a basil-like herb called *shiso* (beefsteak leaf). Japanese grill jockeys make a piquant *umeboshi* plum sauce for brushing on grilled rice and other grilled vegetables.

ZA'ATAR: A Middle Eastern spice mix made of sumac, wild marjoram, toasted sesame, and sometimes thyme. (Za'atar is the Arabic name for wild marjoram.) In Israel and Jordan, marjoram predominates, resulting in a green blend. Armenians and Syrians add proportionally more sumac to make a reddish *za'atar*. Elsewhere in the Near East, chickpeas or grains are added to make brownish *za'atar*.

INDEX

(Page references in *italic* refer to illustrations.)

Accompaniments. *See* Bread; Condiments; Pickle(d)(s); Relishes; Rice; Salads; Salsas; Side dishes; Vegetables, grilled
Achars:
mango, 452
mixed vegetable, 448, 449
pineapple, 449
Admov, Housseine, 217
Adobo (garlic-lime marinade), 140
Adobo (smoked chile marinade), 499–501
Afghan cooking, 64
coriander sauce, 482–83
game hens, 288–90
lamb and beef kebabs, spiced *(lula kebab),* 238–39
lamb chops, "onion water" *(o be peyaz),* 209–10
pickles, Central Asian *(torshi),* 440, 441–42
quail, grilled, 299–300
yogurt drink *(doh),* 63
Afghan-style chicken (dish from India), 276
Agoupa (Gosier, Guadeloupe), 316
Ahmad, Mushtaque, 272
Aioli, basil, 393
Aji amarillos, 502
Alder wood, 12
Aleppo pepper, 527
Al Forno (Providence, R.I.), 381
Aluminum foil, making shield for skewers with, *23,* 23–24
Allspice, 527
Amandari (Ubud, Bali), 264, 449
Amanusa (Nusa Dua, Bali), 313
Amba, 527
American Cookery (Simmons), 460
American cooking:
bacon grilled prunes, 88–89
baked beans, quick and smoky, *436,* 437–38
barbecue, four styles of, 468–69
barbecue sauces, 49
basic, 463–64
coffee, Jake's Turkish, 477
mango, Mark Militello's, *465,* 465–66
mustard, Carolina, 464
basil marinade, 501
basmati rice, quick-cook, 424–25
beef
brisket, Texas-style barbecued, 135–36
dinosaur ribs, 169
great American hamburger, 222, 223–25
grilled prime ribs of, with garlic and rosemary, *134,* 137–39
mustard lime steaks, 143–44
beverages
minted limeade, 62
smoky martini, 56–58
bourbon butter basting sauce, 508
bread, grilled
Bruce Frankel's, 130–31
garlic, fingers, 126–27
with garlic cilantro butter, 126
chicken
beer-can, 257–58
wings, Eat It & Beat It, 79–80
desserts
coco loco brûlée, 518
fire-grilled banana split, 513–14
fire-roasted apples, *510,* 511–12
lemon-ginger crème brûlées, 515–16, *517*
spice-grilled pineapple, 513
uptown s'mores, 515
duck with garlic and ginger, 290–92
fish and shellfish
Florida snapper burgers, 350 51
Gulf Coast shrimp, 372
New Orleans-style barbecued shrimp, Emeril Lagasse's, 370–71
oysters with horseradish cream, 375
scallop kebabs with pancetta, lemon, and basil, 373
soft-shell crabs with spicy tartar sauce, 357–58
fruit salsas, 457–58
apple-banana, smoky, 458
mango-mint, 458
pineapple, grilled, *456,* 457–58
goat cheese grilled in grape leaves, 88
grits, grilled, 434
mushroom caps with arugula butter, 414
mushroom-rice burgers with Cheddar cheese, 389–90
pizza, original grilled, 381–84
pork
Memphis-style ribs, 194–96
pulled, North Carolina, 175–77
portobello mushroom sandwiches with basil aioli, 392–93
potatoes à la ketchup, 417
rubs
Cajun, 490
Creole, 490–91
Memphis, 489–90
Miami spice, 490
sides
basic slaw, 460
North Carolina-style coleslaw, 177
two-tone potato salad, 121
soups
grilled corn chowder, 92
tomato, fire-charred, 91–92
turkey
annatto-spiced grilled, 287–88
pastrami, 286

vinegar-based mop sauce, 509
vinegar sauce, North Carolina, 466–67
American Royal Barbecue, 49
Ancho chile peppers, *504*
Anchovy(ies):
butter, 506
marinated grilled peppers with olives and, 415–16
Anderson, Burton, 148
Andouille sausage, *234*
Anguillan cooking:
barbecue sauce, 270–72
chicken, roast, 269–72, *271*
Annato seed, 527
Annatto-spiced grilled turkey, 287–88
Anticuchos, 158–59
de pescado, 344–45
Appetizers, 67–93
bacon grilled prunes, 88–89
beef, 67–73
and basil rolls, 69–73, *70,* 71
and coconut satés, Indonesian (*saté lalat*), 67–68
fiery stick meat (*suyas*), 160–61
flying fox satés (*saté kalong*), 237
jerky, Vietnamese (*thit bo kho*), 68–69
and lamb kebabs, Persian (*kubideh*), 239–40, 242
and lamb kebabs, spiced (*lula kebab*), 238–39
lettuce bundles with, 164–66, *165*
matambre, simple, 152–53
pastrami grilled in grape leaves, 69
roll, stuffed, Montevidean (*matambre*), *156,* 156–57
satés with coriander (*saté age*), 236–37
shish kebabs, Bengali, 159–60
sticks, Saigon market, 167
caponata, grilled vegetable, 99
cheese
goat, grilled in grape leaves, 88
provolone, grilled (*provolone asado*), 86
quesadillas, grilled, 86–87, *87*
chicken, 73–80
breasts, Montevidean (*pamplona de pollo*), 280
kebabs, Dutch West Indian (*boka dushi*), 73
satés, Malaysian, 281–82
satés, schoolyard, 283–84
satés, Sri Lankan, 282–83
satés Jakarta (*saté ayam*), 284–85
satés served in lettuce leaves, 281
silver paper, 74
wings, beer-barbecued, Australian, 75–76
wings, Eat It & Beat It, 79–80
wings, garlic lemongrass, Saigon, 74–75
wings, honey-glazed, Hong Kong, 77–78
wings, spicy chile, 78
wings, star anise, 66, 76–77
wings with Hong Kong spices (Shek O wings), 79
chorizo grilled mushrooms, 411
clams, grilled, with *colombo* butter, 373–74
egg(s)
quail, satés (*saté telor*), 89–90
with Vietnamese seasonings, 90–91
eggplant dips
with tahini, Middle Eastern (*baba ghanoush*), 84–85
Trinidadian (*choka dip*), 82–84
with walnuts, Persian, 84
fish mousse satés, Balinese (*saté lilit*), 349–50
lamb
and beef kebabs, Persian (*kubideh*), 239–40, 242
and beef kebabs, spiced (*lula kebab*), 238–39
in lavash (*lyulya kebab*), 247–48
satés with tamarind sauce (*saté buntel*), 240–42
shallot kebabs with pomegranate molasses (*sogar kebab*), 242–43
mushroom caps with arugula butter, 414
oysters with horseradish cream, 375
pancetta grilled figs, *66,* 89
pork
with Moorish seasonings (*pinchos morunos*), 180–82
rollatini, Brazilian, 179
rolled, Uruguayan (*pamplona de puerco*), 188–89
satés, sweet (*saté babi manis*), 189–91
sardines, Portuguese, 319
satés
beef, with coriander (*saté age*), 236–37
beef and coconut, Indonesian (*saté lalat*), 67–68
chicken, Jakarta (*saté ayam*), 284–85
chicken, Malaysian, 281–82
chicken, schoolyard, 283–84
chicken, served in lettuce leaves, 281
chicken, Sri Lankan, 282–83
fish mousse, Balinese (*saté lilit*), 349–50
flying fox (*saté kalong*), 237
lamb, with tamarind sauce (*saté buntel*), 240–42
pork, sweet (*saté babi manis*), 189–91
prawn, Balinese (*saté udang*), 367–68
quail egg (*saté telor*), 89–90
shiitake and scallion kebabs, 410–11
shrimp (or prawns)
with Bahian peanut sauce, 363–64
dim sum, grilled, 80
Gulf Coast, 372
mousse on sugarcane (*chao tom*), 81
plantation, 369–70
satés, Balinese (*saté udang*), 367–68
snails, grilled (*escargots grillés*), 81–82, 83
soups
fire-charred tomato, 91–92
grilled corn chowder, 92
grilled gazpacho, 93
yogurt-cucumber salad with mint (*cacik*), 85–86
Apple(s):
fire-roasted, 510, 511–12
macadamia sauce, 264
and shrimp sauce, Vietnamese (*mam nem*), 471
spicy fruit in tamarind dressing (*rujak*), 122, 123
Apple-banana salsa, smoky, 458
Apple wood, 12, 13
Argentinean cooking, 7, 154–55
La Cabaña's house salad, 111
caramel cream (*dulce de leche*), 519–21
chimichurri, 154–55
"dry," 478, *479*
red, 478, *479*
eggplant, grilled, 406, *407*
matambres, 152
simple, 152–53

provolone, grilled *(provolone asado),* 86
tomato salsa *(salsa criolla),* 457
veal and chicken kebabs, 170
Armenian cooking:
eggplant, tomato, and pepper salad *(fasouli),* 96
shish kebab, 219–20
Aron, Jean-Paul, 303
Arroyo (Coyoacán, Mexico), 200
Arroz loco, 422, 432–33
Arthur Bryant's (Kansas City), 469
Artichoke(s):
Catalan grilled, 402–3
grilling chart for, 400
salad, 308–11
Arugula:
butter, mushroom caps with, 414
grilled pizza with Italian cheeses and, 384
Asado, 154–55
Ash catchers, 29
Asian pear(s):
dipping sauce, 486
spicy fruit in tamarind dressing *(rujak),* 122, *123*
Asparagus:
grilled vegetables in style of Santa Margherita, *394,* 398–401
grilling chart for, 400
grilling techniques for, 47, 396
Japanese vegetable mixed grill *(robatayaki),* 397–98
Auberge des Glycines (Porquerolles), 307
Australian cooking:
barramundi in Asian-spiced coconut milk, 335–37
chicken wings, beer-barbecued, 75–76
lamb steaks with Szechuan pepper rub, 207
Morton Bay "bugs" with ginger-mint butter, *352,* 353–54
shrimp, honey sesame, "on the barbie," 361–63, *362*
Avocado(s):
guacamole, Oaxacan-style, 455
sauce, 333
sprout, and salsa burgers, 225
Azerbaijani cooking:
lamb in lavash *(lyulya kebab),* 247–48
sturgeon *shashlyk,* 326–27

B

Baba ghanoush, 84–85
Babi guling, 177, 177–78
Baby back ribs, 39
Bacalhao grelhado, 343–44
Bacon:
grilled prunes, 88–89
and smoked-cheese burgers, 225
Bacon (Côte d'Azur), 311
Bademiya (Bombay), 272, 275
Baffle, BBQ, 24
Bahamian cooking:
chicken, grilled, 260
conch, grilled, 375–76
peas and rice, 431–32
sky juice, 55–56
snapper, whole grilled, 304–7
Bahian peanut sauce, 363–64
Baked beans, quick and smoky, *436,* 437–38
"Baked beans," Indian *(dal bukhara),* 435–37
Balinese cooking:
bananas, grilled, in coconut milk caramel, 512–13
chicken with apple-macadamia sauce, 264–65
cucumber salad, 120
long beans with fresh coconut *(urap sayur),* 115
pork, roast *(babi guling), 177,* 177–78
rice, yellow *(nasi kuning),* 430
satés, 451
fish mousse *(saté lilit),* 349–50
prawn *(saté udang),* 367–68
Bamboo skewers, making aluminum foil shield for, *23,* 23–24
Banana(s):
fire-grilled, split, 513–14
fruit cooler, 524
grilled, in coconut milk caramel, Balinese, 512–13
Banana leaf, whole fish grilled in, 305
Sunda Kelapa, 314–16
Banana peppers, *504*
Bandung, 62
Bangladeshi (Bengali) cooking:
mango tamarind barbecue sauce, 470–71
shish kebabs, 159–60
Bani Marine Street beef kebabs, 163
Barbacoa, 199–201
Barbados: Baxter Road grilled chicken, 265
Barbecue(d), 1
American, four styles of, 468–69
brisket, Texas-style, 135–36
chicken
beer-, wings, Australian, 75–76
beer-can, 257–58
Dimples', 255–57
defined, 2
indirect grilling and, 2–3
lamb
Mexican *(barbacoa),* 199–201
Moroccan *(mechouie),* 205–6, 217
origin of term, 184
pork
Christmas Eve "pig" *(lechon asado),* 173–75
pulled, North Carolina, 175–77
Susur Lee's, 187–88
shrimp, Emeril Lagasse's New Orleans-style, 370–71
smoking and, 2, 5
Barbecue sauces, 48, 49
Anguillan, 270–72
applying, 40
Australian, 76
basic (American), 463–64
coffee, Jake's Turkish, 477
ginger-plum, 470
honey-guava, 466–67
Jamaican, 256–57
Kansas City, 469
mango, Mark Militello's, *465,* 465–66
mango tamarind, Bengali, 470–71
miso
red, 475
white, 475
mojo, Cuban, 175
mustard, Carolina, 464
tamarind, simple, 471
Texas-style, 136
Barra Grill (Rio de Janeiro), 152
Barramundi in Asian-spiced coconut milk, 335–37
Barrel smokers, 25
Bashir, Mohammed, 226
Basil:
aioli, 393
beef and, rolls, 69–73, *70,* 71
grilled pizza with tomato, cheese and, 382–84

marinade, 501
sauce, 340
Baskets. *See* Grill baskets
Basmati rice, 424
with cranberries, Persian, 427–28, 429
with golden crust, Persian *(chelow),* 425–27
Indian-style, 423–24
quick-cook, 424–25
saffron rosewater, 424
steamed, Persian-style, 425
Bass. *See* Sea bass
Basting, 27
Basting sauces, 48, 49, 489, 508–9
bourbon butter, 508
ketjap butter, 509
Mexican, for fish, 509
mop, 48
applying, 39–40
vinegar-based, 509
saffron, 211
Bathers Pavillion (Sydney), 335
Batido, 56
Batmanglij, Najmieh, 210, 425, 426–27
Baxter Road grilled chicken, 265
Bayless, Rick, 59
BBQ Baffle, 24
Beans:
baked
Indian "baked beans" *(dal bukhara),* 435–37
quick and smoky, 436, 437–38
black, with bacon, Brazilian *(tutu mineira),* 438
peas and rice, Bahamian, 431–32
Bean sprout(s):
long beans with fresh coconut *(urap sayur),* 115
salad, spicy Japanese, 113
Vietnamese salad plate, *116,* 117
Beard, James, 135
Beef, 33–37, 135–71
and basil rolls, 69–73, *70, 71*
brisket, 36–37
Texas-style barbecued, 135–36
butterflying, 181, *181*
churasco of tenderloin tips *(puntas de churrasco),* 147
dry-aged vs. wet-aged, 34
flank steak
butterflying, 150, *150*
preparing, 103, *103*
grilling chart for, 138
ground. *See also* Beef-kebabs (with ground beef); Beef-satés
hamburger, great American, *222,* 223–25
"slipper" burgers *(chapli kebab),* 226–28
three-meat patties *(ćevapčići),* 228–29
jerky, Vietnamese *(thit bo kho),* 68–69
kebabs (with beef chunks), 157–67
Bani Marine Street, 163
Bengali shish kebabs, 159–60
fiery stick meat *(suyas),* 160–61
lemongrass, with peanuts, 166–67
lettuce bundles with, 164–66, 165
Madeira, with bay leaf *(espetadas),* 163–64
with peanut flour *(kyinkyinga),* 157–58
Persian, quick, 161–62
Peruvian *(anticuchos),* 158–59
Russian *shashlik,* 160
Saigon market sticks, 167
kebabs (with ground beef), 238–40
lamb and, Persian *(kubideh),* 239–40
lamb and, spiced *(lula kebab),* 238–39
oasis *(kofta),* 238
Kobe, 35
larding, 139, *139*
marinating times for, 45
matambres, 152, 153
Montevidean stuffed beef roll, *156,* 156–57
simple (Argentinean), 152–53
Oaxaca-style grilled, 151–52
oxtails, grilled *(kare kare),* 170–71
pastrami grilled in grape leaves, 69
prime ribs of, 37
with garlic and rosemary, *134,* 137–39
rib roast, Brazilian stuffed, 139–40
ribs, 37. *See* also Beef-short ribs
dinosaur, 169
salad, spicy Thai *(yam nua yang), 94,* 102
satés
with coconut, Indonesian *(saté lalat),* 67–68
with coriander *(saté age),* 236–37
flying fox *(saté kalong),* 237
sesame-grilled, Korean *(bool kogi),* 150–51
short ribs, *195*
butterflying, 168
Korean grilled (kalbi kui), 167–69
steaks, 33–36
bone-in vs. boneless, 35
cuts of, 145
factors affecting quality of, 34
Florentine-style *(bistecca alla fiorentina),* 146, 148–49
in garlic-lime marinade *(palomilla),* 140–43
grades of, 33–34
grilling techniques for, 35, 141
from hell, *142,* 143
mustard lime, 143–44
Nicaraguan-style *(churrasco),* 147
Niçoise rub for, 491
rib, with red wine sauce and marrow *(entrecôtes à la bordelaise),* 144–46
seasoning before grilling, 35
testing for doneness, 30
trimming fat from, 158
Beer:
-barbecued wings, Australian, 75–76
-can chicken, 43, 257–58
chicken, Brazilian, 262–63
Belgian endive, in grilled vegetables in style of Santa Margherita, *394,* 398–401
Bengali cooking:
mango tamarind barbecue sauce, 470–71
shish kebabs, 159–60
Ben Thanh market (Saigon), 72, 75–76
Berber marinade, 503
Bergeyre, Jesus Arroyo, 200
Beurre blanc, curry, 359
Beverages, 53–65
leaded, 54–60
coconut shake, Brazilian *(batido),* 56
daiquiri, Brazilian *(caipirinha),* 54
daiquiri, passion fruit, 56, *57*
margarita, Frontera, 59
martini, smoky, 56–58
piña colada, original, 54–55
pisco sour, 58
planter's punch, 55
raki, 60

rum punch, French West Indian ('ti punch), 58
sangria, Madrid-style, 60
Singapore sling, 59
sky juice, Bahamian, 55–56
unleaded, 61–65
ginger pineapple punch *(gingere ananas),* 61
iced coffee, Vietnamese, 63
mango nectar, 61
minted limeade, 62
mint tea, 62–63
peanut punch, 61–62
rosewater cooler *(bandung),* 62
yogurt cooler, Indian *(lassi),* 63–65
yogurt drink, Afghan *(doh),* 65
yogurt drink, Persian *(dugh),* 63
Big Green Egg, 4, 9–10, 17
Bird peppers, 502
Bistecca alla fiorentina, 146, 148–49
Black bass, 305
Black beans with bacon, Brazilian *(tutu mineira),* 438
Black truffles, cooking in coals, 414
Blowtorch, cooking with, 516
Bluefish, 305
For suitable recipes see pages 303–7, 312–13, 314–16, 327–29, 331–33
Boar, wild, 41
Boar Hill (Kingston, Jamaica), 255
Boka dushi, 73
Bool kogi, 150–51
Boon, Ngiam Tong, 59
Bosnian three-meat patties *(ćevapčići),* 228–29
Boston butt, 38–39
Bourbon butter basting sauce, 508
Bratwurst, 42, *234*
Brazilian cooking:
beer chicken, 262–63
black beans with bacon *(tutu mineira),* 438
churrasco, 365
coconut shake *(batido),* 56
daiquiri *(caipirinha),* 54
fish, grilled, with garlic marinade, 322
hot sauce, country *(molho da companha),* 480
lamb marinade, 501
manioc, rainbow *(farofa),* 434–35
pork rollatini, 179
rib roast, stuffed, 139–40
rice, crazy *(arroz loco), 422,* 432–33
samba dogs, *230,* 231
samba sausages *(choriçou),* 235
shrimp with Bahian peanut sauce, 363–64
swordfish kebabs with coconut milk, 346–47
Bread, 125–33
fry, Jamaican (festivals), 132–33
grilled
Bruce Frankel's, 130–31
focaccia, 128–30
garlic, fingers, 126–27
garlic, Tuscan *(bruschetta),* 127
with garlic cilantro butter, 126
papadoms cooked over the coals, 132
pita chips, 125–26
tandoori, Indian, 383
tandoori-baked flat *(naan), 124,* 131
tomato, Catalan *(pa amb tomàquet),* 128, *129*
Breadcrumbs, toasting, 113
Breadfruit, fire-roasted, 403
Brick barbecue pits, 5, 10
Brillat-Savarin, Anthelme, 255
Brines, 47
Brisket, 36–37
Texas-style barbecued, 135–36
British cooking:
hot and sweet mint sauce, 484
Yorkshire pudding on the grill, 439
Bruschetta, 127
Brushes, cleaning grill grates with, 28–29
Bryce Boar Blazers, 257
BTUs, 8–9
Buccaneer chicken *(poulet boucanée),* 265–66
Buffalo, 41
Built-in grills, 5, 10
Bukhara (New Delhi), 364, 383, 435
Bulgarian cooking:
burgers *(kufteh),* 226
tomato salad with feta cheese *(shopska salata),* 119–20
Bull's horn peppers, 502
Burgers:
Bulgarian *(kufteh),* 226
grilling techniques for, 41
hamburger, great American, *222,* 223–25
avocado, sprout, and salsa, 225
bacon and smoked-cheese, 225
cheeseburgers, 224
history of, 225
mushroom-rice, with Cheddar cheese, 389–90
safety concerns and, 224
"slipper" *(chapli kebab),* 226–28
snapper, Florida, 350–51
Butter(s):
arugula, mushroom caps with, 414
bourbon, basting sauce, 508
compound, 48, 505–8
anchovy, 506, *507*
curry, 506–8, *507*
escargot, 506
garlic, Japanese, 508
ketjap, 509
maitre d'hotel, 505
marchand de vin, 508
Roquefort, 506, *507*
shadon beni, 404–5
curry beurre blanc, 359
garlic cilantro, grilled bread with, 126
Butterflying:
flank steak, 150, *150*
pork or beef, 181, *181*
short ribs, 168

C

Cabaña, La (Buenos Aires), 111, 155, 478
Cabbage:
slaws, 460–61
basic, 460
Haitian *(pikliz),* 461
North Carolina-style coleslaw, 177
shogun, 461
wedges, long bean salad plate with, Javanese *(lalapan),* 114, *116*
Cachaça:
Brazilian coconut shake *(batido),* 56
Brazilian daiquiri *(caipirinha),* 54
Cacik, 85–86
Caipirinha, 54
Cajun injectors, 49
Cajun rub, 490
Cakes, cooking on grill, 47
Calçots, 415
Campfire, grilling over, 26–28
Candidos (Pedra de Guaratiba, Brazil), 432
Candlenut, 527

Caper:
red wine, and olive sauce *(raïto),* 328, 329–30
sauce, French West Indian, 318
Cape Town lamb, 202–5, *203*
La Capilla (Oaxaca), 191–92
Caponata, grilled vegetable, 99
Los Caracoles (Barcelona), 128
Caramel:
cardamom ice cream *(kulfi)*, 523
coconut milk, grilled bananas in, Balinese, 512–13
cream *(dulce de leche),* 519–21
Carbon monoxide, 17
Cardamom:
caramel ice cream *(kulfi),* 523
pistachio rice pudding *(kheer),* 521–22
Caribbean cooking:
long beans, grilled, 409
mango nectar, 61
passion fruit daiquiri, 56, *57*
plantains, grilled, 416
planter's punch, 55
seasoning salt, Spanish Caribbean *(sazón),* 493–94
see also specific islands
Carne asado, 500
Carolina-style cooking:
barbecue, 468
mustard barbecue sauce, 464
see also North Carolina-style cooking
Carrot(s):
Central American pickled vegetables *(encurtido),* 443–44
Central Asian pickles *(torshi), 440,* 441–42
mixed vegetable *achar, 448,* 449
and pineapple *escabeche,* 443
Catalan cooking:
artichokes, grilled, 402–3
Catalan cream *(crema catalana),* 519
grilled vegetable salad *(escalivada),* 96–97
romesco sauce, 472
sole with Catalan fruits and nuts, 341
tomato bread *(pa amb tomàquet),* 128, *129*
vinaigrette, 483
Cauliflower:
Central Asian pickles *(torshi), 440,* 441–42
tandoori, 403–4
Cayenne peppers, 502, *504*
Cebollita, 445
Cecina adobada, 183–86
Celery, in Central Asian pickles *(torshi), 440,* 441–42
Cendrillon (New York City), 170, 193
Central American cooking:
pickled vegetables *(encurtido),* 443–44
see also specific countries
Central Asian cooking:
cardamom caramel ice cream *(kulfi),* 523
grilled dilled tomatoes, 421
pickles *(torshi), 440,* 441–42
see also specific countries
Ćevapčići, 228–29, 242
Chaat:
masala, 527
mix, quick, 105
murgh, 104–5
Chao tom, 81
Chapli kebab, 226–28
Charcoal, 11–12
briquettes, 11–12, 19–20
lump, 11, 12, 19
Charcoal grills, 6, 7–8, 10
achieving wood-grilled flavor on, 13
adding fresh charcoal to, *19,* 19–20
adjusting heat in, 17–18, 20
cooking with, 15–20
indirect grilling on, 3, *3*
lighting fire in, 15–17
maintaining and cleaning, 28–29
preheating, 16, 27
shopping checklist for, 8
smoking on, 14, 24
spit roasting on, 22
timetable for, 33
two- and three-zone fires in, 18, *19*
Charcoal Grill Seafood (Penang, Malaysia), 312
"Charmin" test, 32
Chaucer, Geoffrey, 463
Cheddar cheese, mushroom-rice burgers with, 389–90
Cheese, 46
Cheddar, mushroom-rice burgers with, 389–90
goat, grilled in grape leaves, 88
grits, 434
pizza, original grilled, 381–84
with arugula and Italian cheeses, 382
with tomato and basil, 382–84
provolone, grilled *(provolone asado),* 86
quesadillas, grilled, 86–87, *87*
raclette, 384–85
Roquefort butter, 506, *507*
smoked, and bacon burgers, 225
Cheeseburgers, 224
Chef Allen's (North Miami Beach), 350
Chelow, 425–27
Cherry:
cinnamon sauce for duck, 291–92
sour, syrup, Persian lemon and rose water "sundae" with *(faluda),* 523–24
Cherry wood, 12, 13
Chicken, 42–43, 74–80, 255–86
breasts
grilling techniques for, *42,* 42–43, 277
Montevidean *(pamplona de pollo),* 280
Palestinian, 276–77
cutting up, *268–69*
fat, rendering, 285
free-range and organic, 42
grilling chart for, 256
halves and quarters, 260–66
with apple-macadamia sauce, Balinese, 264–65
Bahamian grilled, 260
Baxter Road, 265
beer, Brazilian, 262–63
buccaneer *(poulet boucanée),* 265–66
chile-coriander, Bademiya's, 275
grilling techniques for, 263
with lemon-mustard sauce *(yassa),* 261–62
kebabs
Dutch West Indian *(boka dushi),* 73
four pepper *(kafta),* 252–53
veal and, Argentinean, 170
marinating times for, 45
pieces, 269–76
Afghan-style, 276
roast, Anguillan, 269–72, *271*
with saffron *(joojeh kebab)*, 273–75
silver paper, 74
tandoori *(tandoori murgh)*, 267–69
tikka, sea captain's, 272–73
salads
grilled, with Indian spices *(murgh chaat),* 104–5
with pickles and olives, Persian, 106
satés, 281–85

Jakarta *(saté ayam),* 284–85
Malaysian, 281–82
schoolyard, 283–84
served in lettuce leaves, 281
Sri Lankan, 282–83
seasoning under skin, *261*
spatchcocking, *289*
testing for doneness, 30, 42
whole, 255–60
barbecued, Dimples', 255–57
beer-can, 43, 257–58
grilling techniques for, 259
piri-piri, 254, 258–60
wings
beer-barbecued, Australian, 75–76
Eat It & Beat It, 79–80
garlic lemongrass, Saigon, 74–75
honey-glazed, Hong Kong, 77–78
with Hong Kong spices, grilled (Shek O wings), 79
spicy chile, 78
star anise, *66,* 76–77
yakitori, 285–86
Chickpea flour, 527
Chile(s), 201, 504
coriander chicken, Bademiya's justly famous, 275
frying, 178
grilling techniques for, 396–97
guide to, 502–3, *504*
habanero salsa, grilled, 455
hoisin sauce, 474
jalapeño grits, 434
-marinated pork in style of Oaxaca *(cecina adobada),* 183–86
peanut dipping sauce, 486
safe handling of, 502
and shallot relish, fiery *(sambal chobek),* 444–45
smoked, marinade (adobo), 499–501
Chimichurri, 154–55, 477–79
basic, 477, *479*
"dry," 478, *479*
red, 478, *479*
Chimney starters, 15–16
Chinese cooking:
chicken
silver paper, 74
wings, Hong Kong honey-glazed, 77–78
wings with Hong Kong spices (Shek O wings), 79
duck, Peking, 292–95, *294*
hoisin-chile sauce, 474
pork, barbecued, Susur Lee's, 187–88
shrimp dim sum, grilled, 80
Szechuan seasoned salt, 496
Chipotles, 201, 502
smoked chile marinade *(adobo),* 499–501
Chips, grilled pita, 125–26
Choice beef (grade), 33–34
Choka, 401–2
Choka dip, 82–84
Choriçou, 235
Chorizo(s), *234*
grilled mushrooms, 411
samba sausages *(choriçou),* 235
spicy, 231–32
Chowder, grilled corn, 92
Christmas Eve "pig" *(lechon asado),* 173–75
Chung gao jai, 444
Churrasco, 147, 365
Chutney, pineapple, 454–55
Cilantro, 527
garlic butter, grilled bread with, 126
onion relish, 446, *447*
rinsing and drying, 105
Cinnamon cherry sauce for duck, 291–92
Çirağan Palace (Istanbul), 69, 207–8
Citrus peel, grating, 292
Clams:
grilled, with *colombo* butter, 373–74
grilling chart for, 356
grilling techniques for, 45
Claris (Barcelona), 331
Clod (whole beef shoulder), 37
Çoban *salatasi,* 118–19
Cocktails. *See* Beverages-leaded
Coco loco brûlée, 518
Coconut:
beef and, satés, Indonesian *(saté lalat),* 67–68
coco loco brûlée, 518
cream, in original piña colada, 54–55
fresh, preparing, 114
ice cream, 522–23
fire-grilled banana split, 513–14
long beans with *(urap sayur),* 115
milk, 528
caramel, grilled bananas in, Balinese, 512–13
homemade, 522–23
shake, Brazilian *(batido),* 56
toasting, 514
water, in Bahamian sky juice, 55–56
Coffee:
barbecue sauce, Jake's Turkish, 477
iced, Vietnamese, 63
Cold weather grilling, 18
Coleslaw, North Carolina-style, 177
Colombo:
butter, grilled clams with, 373–74
powder, 497
Conch, Bahamian grilled, 375–76
Condiments, 441–60
chimichurri, 154–55
fish sauce, 100–101
guacamole, Oaxacan-style, 455
pineapple chutney, 454–55
pomegranate molasses *(narshrab),* 243
raitas, 459–60
pineapple, 459
tomato-cucumber, 460
sambals
lemongrass, 452–53
sambal ulek, 73
tomato peanut *(sambal achan),* 453
tamarind water, 241–42
tomato jam, 453
see also Barbecue sauces; Pickle(d)(s); Relishes; Salsas; Sauces
Consommé, *barbacoa,* 199–201
Contests, 49–50
Memphis in May, 10, 49, 173, 257, 463
Coriander:
beef satés with *(saté age),* 236–37
chile chicken, Bademiya's justly famous, 275
sauce, 482–83
Corn:
crazy rice *(arroz loco), 422,* 432–33
grilled, chowder, 92
grilled, with *shadon beni* butter, 404–5
grilling chart for, 400
grilling techniques for, 396
grits, 434
Corncobs, for smoking, 14
Cornmeal, in grilled polenta, 433
Costanera Norte (Argentina), 155
Country hot sauce *(molho da companha),* 480

Covering grill, 23, 27
Crabs, soft-shell, with spicy tartar sauce, 357–58
Cracked wheat and lamb kebabs *(semit kebab),* 250–51
Cranberries, Persian rice with, 427–28, *429*
"Crayfish" with curry beurre blanc, 358–59
Crazy rice *(arroz loco), 422,* 432–33
Crema catalana, 519
Crème brûlées:
  coco loco brûlée, 518
  lemon-ginger, 515–16, *517*
Creole rub seasoning, 490–91
Crêpes, scallion, *294,* 295
Cross-contamination, 36, 49
Crudités plate, Lebanese, 117–18
Cuban cooking:
  Christmas Eve "pig" *(lechon asado),* 173–75
  honey-guava barbecue sauce, 466–67
  mojo, 175
  steaks in garlic-lime marinade *(palomilla),* 140–43
Cucumber(s):
  Georgian pickles, 442–43
  Lebanese crudités plate, 117–18
  mixed vegetable *achar, 448,* 449
  salad, Balinese, 120
  sauce, 316–17
  seeding, 454
  tomato, and onion salad, Shirazi, 118
  tomato *raita,* 460
  Vietnamese salad plate, *116,* 117
  yogurt salad with mint *(cacik),* 85–86
La Cuineta (Barcelona), 341
Cumin, lime, and garlic marinade *(adobo)*, 140
Curaçao: Dutch West Indian chicken kebabs *(boka dushi),* 73
Currants, in rainbow manioc *(farofa),* 434–35
Curry:
  beurre blanc, 359
  butter, 506–8, *507*
  colombo
    butter, grilled clams with, 373–74
    powder, 497
Cutting boards, safety concerns and, 36
Cuttlefish with Macanese "salsa," Fernando's, 379

D

Da Delfina (Artimino, Italy), 295–97
Dademir, Murat, 244
Dae Won Gak (Seoul), 520
Dagwood, Provençal, 392
Dahakte jhinga, 366–67
Daikon salad, spicy, 112–13
Daiquiris:
  Brazilian *(caipirinha)*, 54
  passion fruit, 56, *57*
Dal bukhara, 435–37
D'Ambrosio, Luccia, 179, 180
Danny Edwards (formerly Lil' Jake's Eat It & Beat It; Kansas City), 79–80
Davis, Rich, 469
Dean, Basil, 375
De arbols, 502
Delamotte, Hubert, 354
Delmonico's (New York City), 225
Dengaku, 389
Desserts, 47, 511–25
  apples, fire-roasted, *510,* 511–12
  bananas, grilled, in coconut milk caramel, Balinese, 512–13
  banana split, fire-grilled, 513–14
  caramel cream *(dulce de leche),* 519–21
  cardamom caramel ice cream *(kulfi),* 523
  cardamom pistachio rice pudding *(kheer),* 521–22
  Catalan cream *(crema catalana),* 519
  coco loco brûlée, 518
  coconut ice cream, 522–23
  fruit cooler, 524
  fruit "punch," Korean, 524–25
  lemon and rose water "sundae" with sour cherry syrup, Persian *(faluda),* 523–24
  lemon-ginger crème brûlées, 515–16, *517*
  pineapple, spice-grilled, 513
  s'mores, uptown, 515
  sweetened whipped cream for, 514
Develi (Istanbul), 214, 243–45
Dibi, 209
Dimples' barbecued chicken, 255–57
Dim sum, shrimp, grilled, 80
Dinosaur ribs, 169
Dipping sauces, 484–87
  apple and shrimp, Vietnamese *(mam nem),* 471
  Asian pear, 486
  Javanese, simple, 486–87
  peanut chile, 486
  tamarind, 487
  Vietnamese, basic *(nuoc cham),* 484, *485*
Dips:
  eggplant
    with tahini, Middle Eastern *(baba ghanoush),* 84–85
    Trinidadian *(choka dip),* 82–84
    with walnuts, Persian, 84
  grilled pita chips for, 125–26
  yogurt-cucumber salad with mint *(cacik),* 85–86
Direct grilling, 2, 2
DiversiTech, 17
"Dog" sauce, French West Indian *(sauce chien),* 482
"Dog's snout" salsa *(xni pec),* 459
Doh, 63
Doneness, testing for, 30, 31–32
Don García (Montevideo, Uruguay), 279
Donner kebab, 244–45
Dorotan, Romy, 170, 193
Dressings:
  tamarind, 122
  Thai, 102
Drinks. *See* Beverages
Drip pans, 19, 28, 29
Dry aging, 34
"Dry" *chimichurri,* 478, *479*
Duck, 290–95
  with garlic and ginger, 290–92
  grilling chart for, 256
  Peking, 292–95, *294*
  sauces for
  cinnamon cherry, 291–92
  orange, 292
  testing for doneness, 30
Dugh, 63
Dulce de leche, 519–21
Dumas, Alexandre, 220
Duraflame briquettes, 12
Dutch West Indian cooking:
  chicken kebabs *(boka dushi),* 73
  peanut sauce *(pindasaus),* 476

E

Eat It & Beat It wings, 79–80
Éclade, 374
Edwards, Danny, 79
Egg(s):
grilled, with Vietnamese seasonings, 90–91
quail, satés *(saté telor),* 89–90
Eggplant(s):
dips
with tahini, Middle Eastern *(baba ghanoush),* 84–85
Trinidadian *(choka dip),* 82–84
with walnuts, Persian, 84
fire-charred, "Gentle Al" kebabs with yogurt and, 251–52
grilled, Argentinean, 406, *407*
grilled vegetable caponata, 99
grilled vegetables in style of Santa Margherita, *394,* 398–401
grilling chart for, 400
grilling techniques for, 396
and lamb kebabs *(sezzeli kebab),* 248–50, *249*
with miso "barbecue" sauce, 405–6
Provençal Dagwood, 392
salad of grilled tomato, pepper, and *(fasouli),* 96
salads
Lebanese *(salafat el ahab),* 98
Moroccan *(salade d'aubergines),* 97–98
sauce, 208
Spanish grilled vegetable salad *(escalivada),* 96–97
West Indian grilled vegetables *(choka),* 401–2
Electric smokers, 25
Electric starters, 17
Embers, roasting in, 28
onions and potatoes roasted in coals, 418
Encurtido, 443–44
Eng, Goh Choi, 342
England. *See* British cooking
Entrecôtes à la bordelaise, 144–46
Epazote, 528
Equatorial Guinean fish grill with three sauces, 331–33
Esarn (Thailand), barbecue in, 101
Esarn seasoning, fish with, 317–18
Escabeche, carrot and pineapple, 443
Escalivada, 96–97
Escargot butter, 506
Escargots grillés, 81–82, 83
Espetadas, 163–64
Essaouira (Morocco), seafood mixed grill in style of, 320, *321*
La Estancia (Buenos Aires), 170
Estancia del Puerto (Montevideo, Uruguay), 278, 477
Estancia La Cinacina (Buenos Aires), 152, 154, 478
"Exotic" meats, 41

F

Faluda, 523–24
Farofa, 434–35
Farooq, Muhammad, 201
Fasouli, 96
Fat:
in ground meat, 232
trimming from meat, 158
Fendi (Detroit), 252
Fennel:
grilled, 408
-grilled bass flambéed with Pernod, *302,* 307–8
stalks, drying, 307
Fenugreek, 528
Fernando's (Macao), 296
Feta cheese, tomato salad with *(shopska salata),* 119–20
Fiery chile and shallot relish *(sambal chobek),* 444–45
Fiery stick meat *(suyas),* 160–61
55-gallon steel drum grills, 5
Figs, pancetta grilled, *66,* 89
Filipino cooking:
ginger-plum barbecue sauce, 470
oxtails, grilled *(kare kare),* 170–71
ribs with Filipino seasonings, Romy's, 193–94
Fireplace, grilling in, 26
Fireproof grill pads, 17
Fish, 303–51
baste, Mexican, 509
burgers, Florida, 350–51
fillets, grilled, 306, 334–41
in Asian-spiced coconut milk, 335–37
with Catalan fruits and nuts, 341
techniques for, 44–45, 336
Yucatán-style *(tikin xik),* 334–35
fillets, skinning and boning, *333*
grill baskets and grates for, 44, 45, 305, 350
grilling chart for, 306
grilling techniques for, 44–45
kebabs, 344–49
with coconut milk, 346–47
Pandeli, 347–48
Peruvian, 344–45
Russian, 348–49
souvlaki, 345–46
marinating times for, 45
mousse satés, Balinese *(saté lilit),* 349–50
Provençal grilling mixture for, 493
steaks, grilled, 306, 322–33
with Brazilian garlic marinade, 322
en pipián, 325–26
shashlyk, 326–27
Spanish Guinean, with three sauces, 331–33
techniques for, 44–45, 324
yassa, 327–29
testing for doneness, 32, 305
white wine marinade for, 505
whole, grilled, 303–20
Bahamian-style, 304–7
with cucumber sauce, 316–17
with Esarn seasoning, 317–18
fennel-, flambéed with Pernod, *302,* 307–8
filleting at table, *309*
with French West Indian caper sauce, 318–19
with fresh artichoke salad, 308–11
grilling chart for, 306
Gurney Drive, 312–13
with *sauce vierge,* 311–12
seafood mixed grill in style of Essaouira, 320, *321*
with South African spices (fish *braî*), 303–4
Sunda Kelapa, 314–16
sweet and sour *(pla pow),* 313–14
techniques for, 45, 305
tikin xik style, 335
see also specific fish
Fish sauce, 100–101, 528
Flake test, 32
Flaming prawns *(dahakte jhinga),* 366–67

Flank steak:
- butterflying, 150, *150*
- how to prepare, 103, *103*
- spicy Thai beef salad *(yam nua yang), 94,* 102

Flat iron steaks, 36
Flatman, Thomas, 506
Florentine-style steak *(bistecca alla fiorentina),* 146, 148–49
Florida snapper burgers, 350–51
Flying fox satés *(saté kalong),* 237
Focaccia, grilled, 128–30
Foil-grilled potatoes with Asian seasonings, 417–18
Fontana, Marius, 365
FoodSaver, 49
Ford, Henry, 11
Four pepper chicken kebabs *(kafta),* 252–53
Fraga, Antonio, 278
Fraga, Marono, 278, 477
Frankel, Bruce, 130
Franklin, Benjamin, 441
French cooking, 310
- basil aioli, 393
- compound butters, 505–8
  - anchovy, 506
  - curry, 506–8, *507*
  - escargot, 506
  - maitre d'hotel, 505
  - marchand de vin, 508
  - Roquefort, 506, *507*
- Dagwood, Provençal, 392
- John Dory with *sauce vierge,* 311–12
- lamb
  - with herbes de Provence, *212,* 213
  - kebabs, Latin Quarter, 214
- mussels, grilled *(éclade),* 374
- rib steaks with red wine sauce and marrow *(entrecôtes à la bordelaise),* 144–46
- rubs
  - herbes de Provence, 491–92
  - for lamb and steaks, Niçoise, 491
  - Provençal grilling mixture for fish, 493
- *salade niçoise,* grilled, 107–9, *108–9*
- sauces for duck
  - cinnamon cherry, 291–92
  - orange, 292
- sea bass
- fennel-grilled, flambéed with Pernod *(loup de mer au fenouil flambé), 302,* 307–8
- with fresh artichoke salad *(loup de mer grillé aux artichauts),* 308–11
- shrimp kebabs, Latin Quarter, 359–60
- snails, grilled *(escargots grillés),* 81–82, 83
- tuna with red wine, caper, and olive sauce *(thon grillé au jus de raïto), 328,* 329–30
- white wine marinade for seafood, 505

French West Indian cooking:
- clams, grilled, with *colombo* butter, 373–74
- *colombo* powder, 497
- "dog" sauce *(sauce chien),* 482
- rum punch ('ti punch), 58
- spiny lobster
  - with basil butter, 354–55
  - with Creole sauce, 355–56
- *see also* Guadeloupe cooking

Frontera Grill (Chicago), 59
Fruit(s):
- cooler, 524
- grilled, testing for doneness, 32
- "punch," Korean, 524–25
- salsas
  - apple-banana, smoky, 458
  - mango-mint, 458
  - pineapple, grilled, *456,* 457–58
- spicy, in tamarind dressing *(rujak),* 122, 123
- *see also specific fruits*

Fuels, 11–14

G

Galangal, 189, 528
Gallimore, William, 185
Game, 40–41
Game hens:
- Afghan-style, 288–90
- grilling chart for, 256
- with Moroccan spices, 288
- spatchcocking, *289*

Garam masala, 494–96, *495,* 528
- quick, 496

Garlic:
- basil aioli, 393
- bread, grilled
  - fingers, 126–27
  - Tuscan *(bruschetta),* 127
- butter, Japanese, 508
- *chimichurri,* basic, 477, *479*
- cilantro butter, grilled bread with, 126
- cumin, and lime marinade *(adobo),* 140
- escargot butter, 506
- kebabs, 408
- lemongrass wings, Saigon, 74–75
- lemon-honey sauce with, 483–84
- and lemon roasted potatoes, Greek, 419–20
- sauce, 482

Gas (propane) grills, 4, 7, 8, 10
- BTUs of, 8–9
- cooking with, 20–23
- covering with lid, 23
- direct grilling on, 21
- drip pans of, 19, 28, 29
- indirect grilling on, 21–22
- infrared grills, 10
- leaks and, 20–21, 28
- lighting fire in, 20
- maintaining and cleaning, 28–29
- preheating, 16, 20, 27
- propane tanks for
  - filling, 13
  - measuring amount of propane in, 14
- propane vs. natural gas in, 14
- shopping checklist for, 8
- smoking on, 24
- spit roasting on, 22
- timetable for, 33

Gazpacho, grilled, 93
Gelody, Nancy and Gogetidze, 338
"Gentle Al" kebabs with fire-charred eggplant and yogurt, 251–52
Georgian cooking (Central Asian republic):
- lamb kebabs, Alexandre Dumas', 220–21
- pickled plum sauce *(tkemali),* 467
- pickles, 442–43
- pork and pomegranate sausages *(kupati),* 235–36
- salmon grilled in grape leaves *(kolheeda),* 338–40, *339*
- vegetable kebabs, 395–97

Germon, George, 381, 384
Gill, Manjit, 383
Gin:
- Bahamian sky juice, 55–56
- Singapore sling, 59
- smoky martini, 56–58

Ginger, 528
- lemon crème brûlées, 515–16, *517*

pineapple punch *(gingere ananas),* 61
plum barbecue sauce, 470
Gingere ananas, 61
Glazes, 48
rum, 369–70
Goat cheese:
grilled in grape leaves, 88
Provençal Dagwood, 392
Goat peppers, 502
Goldstein, Darra, 220, 300
Gomes, Fernando, 379
Grape leaves:
goat cheese grilled in, 88
pastrami grilled in, 69
quail grilled in, 301
salmon grilled in *(kolheeda),* 338–40, *339*
Grape syrup, 528
Grapevine trimmings, 12
Great Britain. *See* British cooking
Greek cooking:
different Greek salad *(marlo salata),* 110
lamb
rotisseried leg of, with lemon and butter, 206–7
souvlaki flambéed with Metaxa, 218–19
octopus, grilled *(khtapothi sti skhara),* 376–78, *377*
oregano olive oil rub, 497
ouzo, 60
potatoes, garlic and lemon roasted, 419–20
quail Santorini, 298–99
shrimp kebabs, Latin Quarter, 359–60
swordfish souvlaki, 345–46
Green beans:
grilling chart for, 400
grilling techniques for, 47, 396
see also Long bean(s)
Green onions *romesco (calçots),* 415
Greens:
mesclun mix, 107
salad, rinsing, 106
La Grillade au Feu de Bois (Provence), 310
Grill baskets:
for fish, 44, 45, 305, 350
for vegetables, 405
Grill grates:
adding fresh coals or wood chips and, 19, *20*
best material for, 9
cleaning, 28–29
for fish, 44
grilling without, 21, *21*
oiling, 405
seasoning, 9
for vegetables, 405
Grilling, 1–5
over campfire, 26–28
in cold weather, 18
defined, 1–2
direct, 2, 2
indirect, 2–3, *3,* 6
building charcoal fire for, 15, *15*
indoors, 26
charcoal unsafe for, 17, 18
menu planning and, 33
ten commandments of, 27
testing for doneness and, 30, 31–32
timetable for, 33
tools for, 29–31
Grill marks, making, *38*
Grills, 4–10
backyard pits, 5, 10
BTUs and, 8–9
fireproof pads under, 17
fuels for, 11–14
infrared, 10
Kamado cookers, 4, 9–10
maintaining and cleaning, 28–29
pellet, 10
shopping checklist for, 8
and taste of charcoal- vs. gas-grilled food, 10
Tuscan, 10, 26
types of, 4–5
see also Charcoal grills; Gas (propane) grills
Grits, grilled, 434
Ground meat, 223–53
fat content of, 232
grilling chart for, 228
grinding your own, 232
kebabs with, 236–53. *See also* Kebabs-beef (with ground beef); Kebabs-lamb (with ground lamb)
tips and techniques for, 227
three-meat patties *(ćevapčići),* 228–29
tips and techniques for, 227
see also Burgers; Sausages
Grouper. *For suitable recipes see pages 334–37*
Guacamole, Oaxacan-style, 455
Guadeloupe cooking:
chicken, buccaneer *(poulet boucanée),* 265–66
coconut ice cream, 522–23
"crayfish" with curry beurre blanc, 358–59
snapper
with cucumber sauce, 316–17
with French West Indian caper sauce, 318–19
Guajillos, 201, 502, *504*
Guava:
honey barbecue sauce, 466–67
planter's punch, 55
Guero peppers, *504*
Guichard, Allyne Hazel, 269
Guillet, Joël, 329
Gulf Coast shrimp, 372
Gunung Sari (Jakarta), 451
Gurney Drive (Penang, Malaysia), 312, 342
Guyanese mango fire relish, 446–49

H

Habanero(s), 502, *504*
salsa, grilled, 455
Haitian slaw *(pikliz),* 461
Halibut. *For suitable recipes see pages 311–12, 341, 344–45, 346–47, 350–51*
Hamburgers. *See* Burgers
Hanger steaks, 36
Harissas:
preserved lemon, 481
simple, 481
Hawaij, 492
quick, 492–93
Hawkers' centers, 162
Heat, measuring (Mississippi test), 16, 17
Herbes de Provence, 491–92
Herboriste de Paradis (Marrakech), 491
Hibachis, 4, 23
Hickory nuts and shells, for smoking, 14
Hickory wood, 12, 13
Hock, Lee Chun, 76
Hog, grilling, 40–41
Hoisin-chile sauce, 474
Honey:
-glazed wings, Hong Kong, 77–78
guava barbecue sauce, 466–67
lemon sauce with garlic, 483–84

sesame shrimp "on the barbie," 361–63, *362*
Hong Kong cooking:
chicken wings with Hong Kong spices (Shek O wings), 79
honey-glazed wings, 77–78
L'Hostal (Castellnou, France), 81, 83
Hostellerie des Trois Forces (St. Barthélemy), 354
Hot and sweet mint sauce, 484
Hot dogs, *234*
samba dogs, *230,* 231
Hot pepper sesame salt, 494
Hot sauces:
country *(molho da companha)*, 480
harissas
preserved lemon, 481
simple, 481
Portuguese *(piri-piri),* 480
Hung yogurt, 528
Hyatt Regency (Baku), 247

I

Ice cream:
cardamom caramel *(kulfi),* 523
coconut, 522–23
fire-grilled banana split, 513–14
Iced coffee, Vietnamese, 63
Imam Cagdas (Gaziantep), 242, 244, 250
Inakaya (Tokyo), 412–13
Indian cooking, 383
"baked beans" *(dal bukhara),* 435–37
basmati rice, 423–24
breads
flat, tandoori-baked *(naan), 124,* 131
papadoms cooked over the coals, 132
cardamom pistachio rice pudding *(kheer),* 521–22
cauliflower, tandoori, 403–4
chaat masala, 105
chicken
Afghan-style, 276
chile-coriander, Bademiya's justly famous, 275
grilled, salad with Indian spices *(murgh chaat),* 104–5
tandoori *(tandoori murgh),* 267–69
lamb
leg of "mutton" with saffron and rosewater, 201–2
original Karim's *seekh kebab,* 246–47
peppers, tandoori, 386, *387*
prawns
flaming *(dahakte jhinga),* 366–67
tandoori, 364–66
raitas, 459–60
pineapple, 459
tomato-cucumber, 460
roasted spice powder (garam masala), 494–96, *495*
quick, 496
tandoori
-baked flat breads *(naan), 124,* 131
cauliflower, 403–4
chicken *(tandoori murgh),* 267–69
peppers, 386, *387*
prawns, 364–66
white rabbit, 388
yam and nut kebabs, 390–91
yogurt cooler *(lassi),* 65
Indian Harvest (Bombay), 366
Indirect grilling, 2–3, *3,* 6
building charcoal fire for, 15, *15*
Indonesian cooking:
bananas, grilled, in coconut milk caramel, Balinese, 512–13
dipping sauce, simple Javanese, 486–87
fish Sunda Kelapa, 314–16
ketchup *(ketjap manis),* 474
ketjap butter, 509
long bean salad plate with cabbage wedges, Javanese *(lalapan),* 114, *116*
mixed vegetable *achar, 448,* 449
potatoes, foil-grilled, with Asian seasonings, 417–18
prawns with ketjap butter, 358
sambals
fiery chile and shallot relish *(sambal chobek),* 444–45
lemongrass, 452–53
tomato peanut *(sambal achan),* 453
satés, 450–51
beef, with coriander *(saté age),* 236–37
beef and coconut *(saté lalat),* 67–68
chicken, Jakarta *(saté ayam),* 284–85
fish mousse, Balinese *(saté lilit),* 349–50
flying fox *(saté kalong),* 237
lamb, with tamarind sauce *(saté buntel),* 240–42
pork, sweet *(saté babi manis),* 189–91
prawn, Balinese *(saté udang),* 367–68
quail egg *(saté telor),* 89–90
spicy fruit in tamarind dressing *(rujak),* 122, 123
see also Balinese cooking
Indoor grilling, 26
charcoal unsafe for, 17, 18
Infrared grills, 10
Injector sauce, 48
Instant-read meat thermometers, 29, 32
La Iordachi (Bucharest), 229
Ipoh Famous Roasted Chicken Wings (Penang Island), 76
Iranian (Persian) cooking, 426–27
beef kebabs
lamb and *(kubideh),* 239–40
quick, 161–62
chicken
with saffron *(joojeh kebab),* 273–75
salad with pickles and olives, 106
cucumber, tomato, and onion salad, Shirazi, 118
eggplant dip with walnuts, 84
lamb
and beef kebabs *(kubideh),* 239–40
chops with yogurt and saffron *(shishlik), 210,* 210–11
lemon and rose water "sundae" with sour cherry syrup *(faluda),* 523–24
rice
with cranberries, 427–28, 429
with golden crust *(chelow),* 425–27
steamed, 425
yogurt drink *(dugh),* 63
Iraqi four pepper chicken kebabs *(kafta),* 252–53
Israeli rub *(hawaij),* 492
quick, 492–93
Italian cooking:
caponata, grilled vegetable, 99
fennel, grilled, 408
focaccia, grilled, 128–30
garlic bread, Tuscan grilled *(bruschetta),* 127
grilled vegetables in style of Santa Margherita, *394,* 398–401
pancetta grilled figs, *66,* 89
peppers, marinated grilled, with olives and anchovies, 415–16

pheasant, grilled, Tuscan, 295–98
polenta, grilled, 433
pork loin, rosemary-grilled, 179–80
salmon with basil cream, Pino's, 340
steak, Florentine-style *(bistecca alla fiorentina),* 146, 148–49
Italian sausage, *234*

J

Jack Daniel's World Championship Invitational, 49–50
Jakarta chicken saté *(saté ayam),* 284–85
Jalapeño(s), 502
grits, 434
Jam, tomato, 453
Jamaican cooking:
breadfruit, fire-roasted, 403
chicken, Dimples' barbecued, 255–57
fry bread (festivals), 132–33
jerk, 184–85
marinade, 497–99, *498*
pork tenderloin, 182–83
ribs, rasta, 196–97
Japanese cooking, 412–13
bean sprout salad, spicy, 113
eggplants with miso "barbecue" sauce, 405–6
garlic butter, 508
miso barbecue sauces
red, 475
white, 475
okra, sesame-grilled, 414–15
rice
cakes, grilled, 431
steamed, 430–31
sesame spinach salad, 111–12
shiitake and scallion kebabs, 410–11
slaw, shogun, 461
teriyaki
marinade, 499
sauce, classic, 473
tofu on stilts *(dengaku),* 389
vegetable mixed grill *(robatayaki),* 397–98
yakitori, 285–86
Jasmine rice, 428
yellow, Balinese *(nasi kuning),* 430
Javanese cooking:
dipping sauce, simple, 486–87
long bean salad plate with cabbage wedges *(lalapan),* 114, *116*
Jerk, 184–85
marinade, 497–99, *498*
origin of word, 450
pork tenderloin, 182–83
rasta ribs, 196–97
Jerky, beef, Vietnamese *(thit bo kho),* 68–69
Jicama, in spicy fruit in tamarind dressing *(rujak),* 122, *123*
John Dory with *sauce vierge,* 311–12
Joojeh kebab, 273–75

K

Kachiri powder, 528
Kafta, 252–53
Kalbi kui, 167–69
Kale leaves, grilling techniques for, 397
Kamado cookers, 4, 9–10
Kansas City-style barbecue, 469
Kare kare, 170–71
Karim (New Delhi), 246, 274, 276
Karimuddin, Hazi, 274
Karmel, Elizabeth, 175
KC Masterpiece, 469
Kebabs:
beef (with beef chunks), 157–67
Bani Marine Street, 163
Bengali shish kebabs, 159–60
fiery stick meat *(suyas),* 160–61
lemongrass, with peanuts, 166–67
lettuce bundles with, 164–66, *165*
Madeira, with bay leaf *(espetadas),* 163–64
with peanut flour *(kyinkyinga),* 157–58
Persian, quick, 161–62
Peruvian *(anticuchos),* 158–59
Russian *shashlik,* 160
Saigon market sticks, 167
beef (with ground beef), 238–40
lamb and, Persian *(kubideh),* 239–40
lamb and, spiced *(lula kebab),* 238–39
oasis *(kofta),* 238
chicken
Dutch West Indian *(boka dushi),* 73
four pepper *(kafta),* 252–53
veal and, Argentinean, 170
fish, 344–49
with coconut milk, 346–47
Pandeli, 347–48
Peruvian, 344–45
Russian, 348–49
souvlaki, 345–46
with ground meat, 236–53
tips and techniques for, 227
lamb (with ground lamb), 238–52
beef and, Persian *(kubideh),* 239–40
beef and, spiced *(lula kebab),* 238–39
cracked wheat and *(semit kebab),* 250–51
eggplant and *(sezzeli kebab),* 248–50, *249*
with fire-charred eggplant and yogurt, "Gentle Al," 251–52
in lavash *(lyulya kebab),* 247–48
oasis kebabs *(kofta),* 238
pistachio and, 243–46
seekh kebab, original Karim's, 246–47
shallot, with pomegranate molasses *(sogar kebab),* 242–43
lamb (with lamb chunks), 214–21
Georgian-style, Alexandre Dumas', 220–21
Latin Quarter, 214
Moroccan, 218
oasis *(kofta),* 238
shish kebab, Armenian, 219–20
shish kebabs, real Turkish, 214–15
souvlaki flambéed with Metaxa, 218–19
in Persian cuisine, 426–27
saté origins and, 450
scallop, with pancetta, lemon, and basil, 373
shrimp, Latin Quarter, 359–60
veal and chicken, Argentinean, 170
vegetable, 46–47
garlic, 408
Georgian, 395–97
mushroom and scallion, Korean, 409–10
shiitake and scallion, 410–11
yam and nut, 390–91
Kepidana, lingah, 177
Ketchup, Indonesian *(ketjap manis),* 474
Ketjap butter, 509
Ketjap manis, 474, 528
Kettle grills, 4, 6
smoking on, 14

Khashkesh, 473
Kheer, 521–22
Khtapothi sti skhara, 376–78, *377*
Khyber Pass (New York City), 64, 209
Kielbasa, *234*
Killeen, Johanne, 381, 384
Kingfish. *For suitable recipes see pages 327–29, 331–33*
Kingsford briquettes, 11–12
Kitchen injectors, 49
Kiyi (Istanbul), 245
Knackwurst, *234*
Knockwurst, *234*
Kobe beef, 35
Kofta, 238, 242
Kolheeda, 338–40, *339*
Korea House (Seoul), 410
Korean chiles, 503
Korean cooking, 520–21
  Asian pear dipping sauce, 486
  beef, sesame-grilled *(bool kogi),* 150–51
  daikon salad, spicy, 112–13
  fruit "punch," 524–25
  garlic kebabs, 408
  hot pepper sesame salt, 494
  lettuce and onion salad, 110–11
  mushroom and scallion kebabs, 409–10
  oyster mushrooms, sesame grilled, 410
  short ribs, grilled *(kalbi kui),* 167–69
  sweet potatoes with sesame dipping sauce, 421
  "three hots" salad, 112
Kroc, Ray, 223
Kubideh, 239–40, 242
Kufteh, 226
Kulfi, 523
Kupati, 235–36
Kurobuta pork, 38
Kyinkyinga, 157–58

L

Laab, pork, 102–4
Lagasse, Emeril, 370
Lalapan, 114, *116*
Lamb, 199–221
  Brazilian marinade for, 501
  chops, 209–14
    with herbes de Provence, *212,* 213
    Latin Quarter kebabs, 214
    with onion-mustard sauce *(dibi),* 209
    "onion water" *(o be peyaz),* 209–10
    stall #26, 211–13
    with yogurt and saffron *(shishlik), 210,* 210–11
  grilling chart for, 204
  ground. *See also* Lamb-kebabs (with ground lamb)
    satés with tamarind sauce *(saté buntel),* 240–42
    "slipper" burgers (chapli kebab), 226–28
    three-meat patties *(ćevapčići),* 228–29
  kebabs (with ground lamb), 238–52
    beef and, Persian *(kubideh),* 239–40
    beef and, spiced *(lula kebab),* 238–39
    cracked wheat and *(semit kebab),* 250–51
    eggplant and *(sezzeli kebab),* 248–50, *249*
    with fire-charred eggplant and yogurt, "Gentle Al," 251–52
    in lavash *(lyulya kebab),* 247–48
    oasis kebabs *(kofta),* 238
    pistachio and, 243–46
    seekh kebab, original Karim's, 246–47
    shallot, with pomegranate molasses *(sogar kebab),* 242–43
  kebabs (with lamb chunks), 214–21
    Georgian-style, Alexandre Dumas', 220–21
    Latin Quarter, 214
    Moroccan, 218
    oasis *(kofta),* 238
    shish kebab, Armenian, 219–20
    shish kebabs, real Turkish, 214–15
    souvlaki flambéed with Metaxa, 218–19
  leg of, 199–207
    Cape Town, 202–5, *203*
    Mexican barbecued *(barbacoa),* 199–201
    Moroccan barbecued *(mechouie),* 205–6, 217
    rotisseried, with lemon and butter, 206–7
    with saffron and rosewater, 201–2
  marinating times for, 45
  Niçoise rub for, 491
  and pork sausages, Romanian *(mititei),* 229
  racks of, Çirağan Palace, 207–8
    ribs, *195*
    steaks with Szechuan pepper rub, 207
    testing for doneness, 30
Lam Yam Wing (Macao), 293, 296
Larding beef, 139, *139*
Lassi, 65
Latin Quarter lamb kebabs, 214
Latin Quarter shrimp kebabs, 359–60
Lavash, 528
  lamb in *(lyulya kebab),* 247–48
Lawson, William, 395
Leafy vegetables, grilling techniques for, 397
Lebanese cooking:
  crudités plate, 117–18
  eggplant salad *(salafat el ahab),* 98
  shrimp with *taratoor,* 368–69
  tomato, charred, sauce with pomegranate molasses *(khashkesh),* 473
Lechon asado, 173–75
Ledée, Michel, 355
Lee, Susur, 187
Lemon:
  ginger crème brûlées, 515–16, 517
  honey sauce with garlic, 483–84
  maitre d'hotel butter, 505
  mustard sauce, 261–62
  preserved, *harissa,* 481
  and rose water "sundae" with sour cherry syrup, Persian *(faluda),* 523–24
Lemongrass, 529
  Balinese prawn satés *(saté udang),* 367–68
  beef with peanuts, 166–67
  garlic wings, Saigon, 74–75
  marinade, aromatic, 166
  sambal, 452–53
Leocastre, Angelo and Maria Luisa, 148–49
Lettuce:
  bundles with grilled beef, 164–66, *165*
  La Cabaña's house salad, 111
  Georgian pickles, 442–43
  grilling, 47
  leaves, chicken satés served in, 281
  and onion salad, Korean, 110–11
Lighter fluid, 15, 16–17
Lil' Jake's Eat It & Beat It (Kansas City), 79–80
Lime(s):
  Brazilian daiquiri *(caipirinha),* 54

cumin, and garlic marinade *(adobo),* 140
Frontera margarita, 59
minted limeade, 62
mustard steaks, 143–44
Lobster, 353–57
grilling chart for, 356
grilling techniques for, 46
parboiling, 354
spiny or rock
with basil butter, 354–55
with Creole sauce, 355–56
Morton Bay "bugs" with ginger-mint butter, *352,* 353–54
South African, 356–57
For other suitable recipes see pages 366–67
Long bean(s) (aka yard-long beans):
Caribbean grilled, 409
with fresh coconut *(urap sayur),* 115
salad plate with cabbage wedges, Javanese *(lalapan),* 114, *116*
Lotus (Toronto), 187
Loup de mer:
au fenouil flambé, 307
grillé aux artichauts, 308–11
substitutions for, 308
Lula kebab, 238–39, 242
Lyulya kebab, 247–48

M

Macadamia-apple sauce, 264
Macanese cooking, 296
cuttlefish with Macanese "salsa," Fernando's, 379
Peking duck, 292–95, *294*
Mackerel:
Gurney Drive, 312–13
For other suitable recipes see pages 315–16, 331–33
Madeira-style cooking:
beef and bay leaf kebabs *(espetadas),* 163–64
tuna steaks, 330–31
Madrid-style sangria, 60
Mahimahi. *For suitable recipes see pages 304–7, 311–12, 334–37, 341, 344–45, 349–50*
Maison d'Olive (Nice), 491
Maitre d'hotel butter, 505
Malaysian cooking:
chicken
satés, 281–82
star anise wings, *66,* 76–77
mackerel Gurney Drive, 312–13
mango *achar,* 452
shallot relish, Penang *(chung gao jai),* 444
shrimp with painfully hot salsa, Penganese, 371–72
skate wings with *nonya* sweet-and-sour sauce, 342–43
Mam nem, 471
Mango:
achar, 452
barbecue sauce, Mark Militello's, *465,* 465–66
fire relish, 446–49
mint salsa, 458
nectar, 61
tamarind barbecue sauce, Bengali, 470–71
Manioc:
rainbow *(farofa),* 434–35
toasted, 435
Manzano peppers, *504*
Maple, 12
Marchand de vin butter, 508
Margarita, Frontera, 59
Margherita pizza, grilled, 382–84
Marigot Bay Club (St. Barthélemy), 355
Marinades, 47, 48–49, 489
basil, 501
Berber, 503
Brazilian, for lamb, 501
cumin, lime, and garlic *(adobo),* 140
jerk, 497–99, *498*
lemongrass, aromatic, 166
smoked chile *(adobo),* 499–501
teriyaki, 499
white wine, for seafood, 505
Marinated grilled peppers with olives and anchovies, 415–16
Marinating times, 45, 48
Marlo salata, 110
Marrakech rub, 491
Marrow, rib steaks with red wine sauce and *(entrecôtes à la bordelaise),* 144–46
Martini, smoky, 56–58
Mas de Langoustier (Ile de Porquerolles, France), 329
Matambres, 152, 153
Montevidean stuffed beef roll, 156, 156–57
simple (Argentinean), 152–53
Mayonnaise, in basil aioli, 393
Mechouie, 205–6, 217
Mehta, Manu, 388
Memphis in May World Championship Barbecue Cooking Contest, 10, 49, 173, 257, 463
Memphis-style barbecue, 468–69
ribs, 194–96
rub, 489–90
Menu planning, 32
Mercado 20 de Noviembre (Oaxaca, Mexico), 151, 183, 500
Mercado del Puerto (Montevideo, Uruguay), 278–79
Merguez, *234*
Mesclun mix, 107
Mesón del Champiñón (Madrid), 411
Mesquite, 11, 12
Metaxa, souvlaki flambéed with, 218–19
Mexican cooking, 7, 500
beef
Oaxaca-style grilled, 151–52
steaks from hell, *142,* 143
carrot and pineapple *escabeche,* 443
fish, Yucatán-style grilled *(tikin xik),* 334–35
fish baste, 509
guacamole, Oaxacan-style, 455
lamb, barbecued *(barbacoa),* 199–201
margarita, Frontera, 59
onion-cilantro relish, 446, *447*
pork
chile-marinated, in style of Oaxaca *(cecina adobada),* 183–86
with fiery salsa *(poc chuc),* 186–87
ribs, Oaxacan-style, 191–93
quesadillas, grilled, 86–87, *87*
salsas
"dog's snout" *(xni pec),* 459
habanero, grilled, 455
salsa de chiltomate, 187
salsa mexicana, 192–93
smoked chile marinade *(adobo),* 499–501
swordfish *en pipián,* 325–26
Miami Spice (Hong Kong eatery), 369
Miami spice (rub), 490
Middle Eastern cooking:
chicken, Palestinian, 276–77

eggplant purée with tahini (*baba ghanoush*), 84–85
Israeli rub (*hawaij*), 492
quick, 492–93
oasis kebabs (*kofta*), 238
pita chips, 125–26
Militello, Mark, 465
Miller, Mark, 287
Minot, Darrick, 185
Mint(ed):
limeade, *52*, 62
mango salsa, 458
sauce, hot and sweet, 484
tea, 62–63
yogurt-cucumber salad with (*cacik*), 85–86
Mirin, 529
Miso, 529
"barbecue" sauce, grilled eggplants with, 405–6
barbecue sauces
red, 475
white, 475
Mississippi test, for heat, 16, 17
Mititei, 229, 242
Mitla (Juarez, Mexico), 143
Mitov, Kiril, 119
Mixed vegetable *achar*, *448*, 449
Mojo, Cuban, 175
Molho da companha, 480
Monkfish. *For suitable recipes see pages 326–27, 348–49, 350–51*
Monsoon (Port of Spain, Trinidad), 401
Montevidean cooking:
beef roll, stuffed (*matambre*), *156*, 156–57
chicken breasts (*pamplona de pollo*), 280
Moorish seasonings, pork with (*pinchos morunos*), 180–82
Mop sauces, 48
applying, 39–40
vinegar-based, 509
Moroccan cooking, 216–17
beef kebabs, Bani Marine Street, 163
eggplant salad (*salade d'aubergines*), 97–98
game hens with Moroccan spices, 288
lamb
barbecued (*mechouie*), 205–6, 217
chops stall #26, 211–13
kebabs, 218
marinade, Berber, 503
mint tea, 62–63
rub, Marrakech, 491
seafood mixed grill in style of Essaouira, 320, *321*
shallot relish, 445
tomato jam, 453
tomato sauce, 213
zucchini, grilled, salad, 98–99
Morton Bay "bugs" with ginger-mint butter, *352*, 353–54
Mousse:
fish, satés, Balinese (*saté lilit*), 349–50
shrimp, on sugarcane (*chao tom*), 81
Moutawakel, Muhammad, 211, 216
Mughal Sheraton, Agra, 201
Mung bean sprouts. *See* Bean sprout(s)
Murgh chaat, 104–5
Mushroom(s):
caps with arugula butter, 414
chorizo grilled, 411
Georgian vegetable kebabs, 395–97
grilled vegetables in style of Santa Margherita, *394*, 398–401
grilling chart for, 400
grilling techniques for, 396
Japanese vegetable mixed grill (*robatayaki*), 397–98
oyster, sesame-grilled, 410
portobello sandwiches with basil aioli, 392–93
and rice burgers with Cheddar cheese, 389–90
and scallion kebabs, Korean, 409–10
shiitake and scallion kebabs, 410–11
Mussels:
grilled (*éclade*), 374
grilling techniques for, 45
Mustard:
barbecue sauce, Carolina, 464
lemon sauce, 261–62
lime steaks, 143–44
sauce, 39
Mustard greens, in "three hots" salad, 112

Naan, *124*, 131
Narshrab, 243
Nasik, Ali, 251
Nasi kuning, 430
Natalie's Shark and Bake Shop (Trinidad), 323
Natural gas. *see* Gas grills
New Orleans-style barbecued shrimp, Emeril Lagasse's, 370–71
Nicaraguan cooking:
onions, pickled (*cebollita*), 445
steak (*churrasco*), 147
tomato sauce (*salsa marinara*), 472–73
Niçoise cooking:
rub for lamb and steaks, 491
salade *niçoise*, grilled, 107–9, *108–9*
Nigerian fiery stick meat (*suyas*), 160–61
Nnamah, Dozie, 160
Nonya sweet-and-sour sauce, 342–43
Noor, Mohamed, *64*
North African cooking:
harissas
preserved lemon, 481
simple, 481
rub (*tabil*), 493
see also Moroccan cooking
North Carolina-style cooking:
barbecue, 468
coleslaw, 177
mustard barbecue sauce, 464
pulled pork, 175–77
vinegar sauce, 466–67
Nuoc cham, 484, *485*
Nut(s):
toasting, 113
and yam kebabs, 390–91

Oak, 12, 13
Oasis kebabs (*kofta*), 238
Oaxacan-style cooking, 500
beef, 151–52
guacamole, 455
pork
chile-marinated (*cecina adobada*), 183–86
ribs, 191–93
O be peyaz, 209–10
Octopus:
grilled (*khtapothi sti skhara*), 376–78, *377*
ouzo and, 376
Okra:
grilling techniques for, 396

Japanese vegetable mixed grill *(robatayaki),* 397–98
sesame-grilled, 414–15
Olive(s):
marinated grilled peppers with anchovies and, 415–16
red wine, and caper sauce *(raïto),* 328, 329–30
Olive oil, 529
Oregano rub, 497
Onion(s):
caramelized, potato salad with, 120–21
Central Asian pickles *(torshi), 440,* 441–42
cucumber, and tomato salad, Shirazi, 118
green, *romesco* (calçots), 415
grilled vegetable caponata, 99
grilling chart for, 400
grilling techniques for, 396
and lettuce salad, Korean, 110–11
and potatoes roasted in coals, 418
relishes
cilantro, 446, *447*
pickled *(cebollita),* 445
with pomegranate molasses, 446
roasting in embers, 28
shepherd's salad *(çoban salatasi),* 118–19
Spanish grilled vegetable salad *(escalivada),* 96–97
West Indian grilled vegetables *(choka),* 401–2
"Onion water" lamb chops *(o be peyaz),* 209–10
Orange:
juice, in planter's punch, 55
liqueur, in Frontera margarita, 59
sauce for duck, 292
Oregano:
Greek, 299
olive oil rub, 497
Oriental hotel (Bangkok), 100
Ostrich, 41
Ouadouane, Majid, 491
Ouzo, 60
octopus and, 376
Oxtails, grilled (kare kare), 170–71
Oyster mushrooms, sesame grilled, 410
Oysters:
grilling chart for, 356
grilling techniques for, 45
with horseradish cream, 375

P

Pa amb tomàquet, 128, 129
Pakistani cooking:
burgers, "slipper" *(chapli kebab),* 226–28
chicken tikka, sea captain's, 272–73
El Palenque (Montevideo, Uruguay), 153, 279
Palestinian chicken, 276–77
Palm sugar, 529
Palomilla, 140–43
Pamplona de pollo, 280
Pamplona de puerco, 188–89
Panache (Cambridge, Mass.), 130
Pancetta grilled figs, *66,* 89
Pandeli (Istanbul), 347
Papadoms cooked over the coals, 132
Paraffin fire starters, 15
Parillas, 154, 155
Parsley:
chimichurri, basic, 477, *479*
escargot butter, 506
maitre d'hotel butter, 505
Passion fruit daiquiri, 56, *57*
Pastrami:
grilled in grape leaves, 69
turkey, 286
Patria (New York), 518
Peanut(s):
flour, grilled beef with *(kyinkyinga),* 157–58
lemongrass beef with, 166–67
punch, 61–62
sauce
Bahian, 363–64
chile, for dipping, 486
Dutch West Indian *(pindasaus),* 476
Spanish Guinean, 332
Thai, 476
tomato, 171
tomato *sambal (sambal achan),* 453
Pearl Café (Brighton Beach, Brooklyn), 338
Peas and rice, Bahamian, 431–32
Pecan wood, 12
Peking duck, 292–95, *294*
Pellet grills or smokers, 10
Penang cooking:
mackerel Gurney Drive, 312–13
shallot relish *(chung gao jai),* 444
shrimp with painfully hot salsa, 371–72
skate wings with *nonya* sweet-and-sour sauce, 342–43

Pepper, 529
Pepper(s):
Central American pickled vegetables *(encurtido),* 443–44
crazy rice *(arroz loco),* 422, 432–33
four, chicken kebabs *(kafta),* 252–53
gazpacho, grilled, 93
Georgian vegetable kebabs, 395–97
grilled vegetable caponata, 99
grilled vegetables in style of Santa Margherita, *394,* 398–401
grilling chart for, 400
grilling techniques for, 396–97
guide to, 502–3, *504*
marinated grilled, with olives and anchovies, 415–16
mixed vegetable *achar, 448,* 449
Provençal Dagwood, 392
rainbow manioc *(farofa),* 434–35
safe handling of, 502
salad of grilled eggplant, tomato and *(fasouli),* 96
shepherd's salad *(çoban salatasi),* 118–19
Spanish grilled vegetable salad *(escalivada),* 96–97
tandoori, 386, *387*
West Indian grilled vegetables *(choka),* 401–2
Perez, Ramon "Monchito" Marrero, 54–55
Pernot, fennel-grilled bass flambéed with, *302,* 307–8
Persepolis (New York City), 106
Persian cooking. *See* Iranian cooking
Peruvian cooking:
beef kebabs *(anticuchos),* 158–59
fish kebabs *(anticuchos de pescado),* 344–45
pisco sour, 58
potato mixed grill, 418–19
Peshawar (Jaipur, India), 390
Phamid, Nurul, 284, 450–51
Pheasant:
legs, grilled, 298
Tuscan, 295–98
Philippines. *See* Filipino cooking
Pickle(d)(s), 441–44
carrot and pineapple *escabeche,* 443
Central American *(encurtido),* 443–44
Central Asian *(torshi), 440,* 441–42
Georgian, 442–43
onions *(cebollita),* 445
plum sauce, Georgian *(tkemali),* 467

Picnic shoulder, 38
Pikliz, 461
Pimenta malagueta, 503
Piña colada, original, 54–55
Pinchos morunos, 180–82
Pindasaus, 476
Pine, 13, 14
Pineapple:
  achar, 449
  and carrot *escabeche,* 443
  chutney, 454–55
  ginger punch *(gingere ananas),* 61
  grilled, salsa, *456,* 457–58
  juice
    original piña colada, 54–55
    planter's punch, 55
  spice-grilled, 513
  spicy fruit in tamarind dressing *(rujak),* 122, 123
Pipián, 325–26
Piri-piri (Portuguese hot sauce), 480
Piri-piri chicken (South African dish), *254,* 258–60
Pisco sour, *52,* 58
Pistachio:
  cardamom rice pudding *(kheer),* 521–22
  lamb and, kebabs, 243–46
Pita chips, grilled, 125–26
Pit cooking, 7
Pizza, grilled, 46, 381–84
  with arugula and Italian cheeses, 384
  basic dough for, 382
  with tomato, basil, and cheese, 382–84
Planks, grilling fish on, 44–45
Plantains, grilled, 416
Plantation shrimp, 369–70
Planter's punch, 55
Pla pow, 313–14
Plum:
  ginger barbecue sauce, 470
  sauce, pickled, Georgian *(tkemali),* 467
Poblano peppers, 503, *504*
Poc chuc, 186–87
Pochana, Suay and Pong, 283
Poke test, 31–32
Polenta, grilled, 433
Pomegranate:
  molasses *(narshrab),* 243, 529
    charred tomato sauce with *(khashkesh),* 473
    onion relish with, 446
  pork and, sausages *(kupati),* 235–36
Pompano, 305
  For suitable recipes see pages 312–13, 314–16, 325–26, 335
Pope, Alexander, 173
Porcão (Rio de Janeiro), 139, 179, 346, 501
Porgies. *For suitable recipes see pages 308–11, 312–16*
Pork, 38–41, 173–97
  barbecued, Susur Lee's, 187–88
  butterflying, 181, *181*
  chile-marinated, in style of Oaxaca *(cecina adobada),* 183–86
  chops, sweet and garlicky, *190,* 191
  Christmas Eve "pig" *(lechon asado),* 173–75
  with fiery salsa *(poc chuc),* 186–87
  grilling chart for, 174
  ground
    burgers, Bulgarian *(kufteh),* 226
    chorizos, spicy, 231–32
    and lamb sausages, Romanian *(mititei),* 229
    and pomegranate sausages *(kupati),* 235–36
    three-meat patties *(ćevapčići),* 228–29
  hog, grilling, 40–41
  kurobuta, 38
  loin, rosemary-grilled, 179–80
  marinating times for, 45
  with Moorish seasonings (pinchos morunos), 180–82
  pulled, North Carolina, 175–77
  pulling vs. chopping, 39
  ribs, 39–40, 191–97, *195*
    cuts of, 39
    with Filipino seasonings, Romy's, 193–94
    Memphis-style, 194–96
    Oaxacan-style, 191–93
    rasta, 196–97
    removing skin from, 39
  roast, Balinese *(babi guling), 177,* 177–78
  rollatini, Brazilian, 179
  rolled, Uruguayan *(pamplona de puerco),* 188–89
  satés, sweet *(saté babi manis),* 189–91
  shoulder cuts of, 38–39
  with sweet-tart dressing (pork *laab*), 102–4
  tenderloin, jerk, 182–83
  testing for doneness, 30
  vinegar vs. mustard sauce for, 39
Portela, Emilio Gonzales, 279
Portobello(s):
  grilling chart for, 400
  grilling techniques for, 396
  sandwiches with basil aioli, 392–93
Portuguese cooking:
  beef and bay leaf kebabs, Madeira *(espetadas),* 163–64
  hot sauce *(piri-piri),* 480
  Macanese cooking and, 296
  salt cod *(bacalhao grelhado),* 343–44
  sardines, 319
  tuna steaks, Madeira style, 330–31
Potato(es):
  foil-grilled, 416–18
    with Asian seasonings, 417–18
    à la ketchup, 417
  garlic and lemon roasted, Greek, 419–20
  and onions roasted in coals, 418
  Peruvian mixed grill, 418–19
  roasting in embers, 28
  salads
    with caramelized onions, 120–21
    two-tone, 121
Poulet boucanée, 265–66
Prasertsak, Nilcharoen, 101
Prawns. *See* Shrimp
Preheating grill, 16, 20, 27
Preserved lemon *harissa,* 481
Prime beef (grade), 33
Prime ribs of beef, 37
  with garlic and rosemary, *134,* 137–39
Propane grills. *See* Gas grills
Provençal cooking:
  Dagwood, 392
  grilling mixture for fish, 493
  herbes de Provence, 491–92
  salade niçoise, 107–9, *108–9*
  tuna with red wine, caper, and olive sauce *(thon grillé au jus de raïto), 328, 329–30*
Provolone, grilled *(provolone asado),* 86
Prunes:
  bacon grilled, 88–89
  rainbow manioc *(farofa),* 434–35
Puerto Rican cooking:
  piña colada, original, 54–55
  Spanish Caribbean seasoning salt *(sazón),* 493–94
Pulled pork, North Carolina, 175–77
Pumpkin gratin, West Indian, 420

Pumpkin seed sauce *(pipián),* 325–26
Puntas de churrasco, 147

Quail, 298–301
Afghan, 299–300
grilled in grape leaves, 301
Santorini, 298–99
spiced Uzbek, 300
testing for doneness, 30
Quail egg satés *(saté telor),* 89–90
Quesadillas, grilled, 86–87, *87*
Qureshi, Muhammed Ishtiyaque, 366

Rabelais, François, 53
Raclette, 384–85
Radicchio, grilling techniques for, 397
Radish(es):
daikon salad, spicy, 112–13
Lebanese crudités plate, 117–18
salad plate, Turkish, *116,* 117
Raffles Hotel (Singapore), 59
Rainbow manioc *(farofa),* 434–35
Raisins:
crazy rice *(arroz loco),* 422, 432–33
rainbow manioc *(farofa),* 434–35
Raitas, 459–60
pineapple, 459
tomato-cucumber, 460
Raïto, 328, 329–30
Raki, 60
Ramirez family, 154
Rasta ribs, 196–97
Red *chimichurri,* 478, *479*
Red Fresno peppers, *504*
Red miso barbecue sauce, 475
Red wine:
caper, and olive sauce *(raïto), 328,* 329–30
marchand de vin butter, 508
sangria, Madrid-style, 60
sauce, rib steaks with marrow and *(entrecôtes à la bordelaise),* 144–46
Relishes, 444–52
achars
mango, 452
mixed vegetable, *448,* 449
pineapple, 449
chile and shallot, fiery *(sambal chobek),* 444–45
mango fire, 446–49
onion(s)
cilantro, 446, *447*
pickled *(cebollita),* 445
with pomegranate molasses, 446
shallot
and chile, fiery *(sambal chobek),* 444–45
Moroccan, 445
Penang *(chung gao jai),* 444
Restaurant de les 7 Portes (Barcelona), 519
Rhubarb sauce, pickled, Georgian *(tkemali),* 467
Rib roast, Brazilian stuffed, 139–40
Ribs:
beef, 37
dinosaur, 169
short, *195*
short, butterflying, 168
short, Korean grilled *(kalbi kui),* 167–69
cuts of, *195*
pork, 39–40, 191–97, *195*
cuts of, 39
with Filipino seasonings, Romy's, 193–94
Memphis-style, 194–96
Oaxacan-style, 191–93
rasta, 196–97
removing skin from, 39
Rib steaks with red wine sauce and marrow *(entrecôtes à la bordelaise),* 144–46
Rice, 423–33
basmati, 424
with cranberries, Persian, 427–28, *429*
with golden crust, Persian *(chelow),* 425–27
Indian-style, 423–24
quick-cook, 424–25
saffron rosewater, 424
steamed, Persian-style, 425
cakes, grilled, 431
crazy *(arroz loco), 422,* 432–33
jasmine, 428
and mushroom burgers with Cheddar cheese, 389–90
peas and, Bahamian, 431–32
pudding, cardamom pistachio *(kheer),* 521–22
steamed, Japanese, 430–31
yellow, Balinese *(nasi kuning),* 430
Rice noodles, in Persian lemon and rose water "sundae" with sour cherry syrup *(faluda),* 523–24
Rice powder, 104
Roasted spice powder (garam masala), 494–96, *495*
quick, 496
Robatayaki, 412–13
Japanese vegetable mixed grill, 397–98
Rodriguez, Douglas, 518
Romanian pork and lamb sausages *(mititei),* 229
Romesco sauce, 472
green onions with *(calçots),* 415
Roquefort butter, 506, *507*
Rosario, Aiello, 179, 180
Rosemary-grilled pork loin, 179–80
Rose water:
cooler *(bandung),* 62
and lemon "sundae" with sour cherry syrup, Persian *(faluda),* 523–24
saffron basmati, 424
Rosilowati, Sri, 315
Rotisserie cooking, 22
beef rib roast, Brazilian stuffed, 139–40
chicken, whole, 259
game hens, Afghan-style, 288–90
leg of lamb with lemon and butter, 206–7
pheasant, Tuscan grilled, 295–98
pork
loin, rosemary-grilled, 179–80
roast, Balinese *(babi guling), 177,* 177–78
Rubs, 47, 48, 489–97
Cajun, 490
colombo powder, 497
Creole, 490–91
herbes de Provence, 491–92
Israeli *(hawaij),* 492
quick, 492–93
Marrakech, 491
Memphis, 489–90
Miami spice, 490
Niçoise, for lamb and steaks, 491
North-African *(tabil),* 493
oregano olive oil, 497

Provençal grilling mixture for fish, 493
roasted spice powder (garam masala), 494–96, *495*
quick, 496
seasoned salt
hot pepper sesame, 494
Spanish Caribbean *(sazón),* 493–94
Szechuan, 496
Rujak, 122, *123*
Rum:
coconut shake, Brazilian *(batido),* 56
daiquiris
Brazilian *(caipirinha),* 54
passion fruit, 56, *57*
glaze, 369–70
piña colada, original, 54–55
planter's punch, 55
punch, French West Indian ('ti punch), 58
sky juice, Bahamian, 55–56
Russian cooking:
shashlik, 160
sturgeon kebabs, 348–49

S

Saffron, 529
basting sauce, 211
Persian rice with golden crust *(chelow),* 425–27
rosewater basmati, 424
Saigon, Ben Thanh market in, 72, 75–76
Saigon cooking:
garlic lemongrass wings, 74–75
market beef sticks, 167
Le Saint Bonnet (Yucatán), 334
Sake, 529
Salade d'aubergines, 97–98
Salade niçoise, grilled, 107–9, *108–9*
Salad greens:
mesclun mix, 107
rinsing, 106
Salads, 95–123
beef, spicy Thai *(yam nua yang), 94,* 102
chicken
grilled, with Indian spices *(murgh chaat),* 104–5
with pickles and olives, Persian, 106
pork, grilled, with sweet-tart dressing (pork *laab*), 102–4
salade niçoise, grilled, 107–9, *108–9*
salad plates, 114–18
crudités, Lebanese, 117–18
long bean, with cabbage wedges, Javanese *(lalapan),* 114, *116*
long beans with fresh coconut *(urap sayur),* 115
radish, Turkish, *116,* 117
Vietnamese, *116,* 117
side, 110–23
artichoke, 308–11
bean sprout, spicy Japanese, 113
La Cabaña's house, 111
coleslaw, North Carolina-style, 177
cucumber, Balinese, 120
cucumber, tomato, and onion, Shirazi, 118
daikon, spicy, 112–13
fruit, spicy, in tamarind dressing *(rujak),* 122, 123
Greek, different *(marlo salata),* 110
lettuce and onion, Korean, 110–11
potato, two-tone, 121
potato, with caramelized onions, 120–21
sesame spinach, 111–12
shepherd's *(çoban salatasi),* 118–19
slaw, basic, 460
slaw, Haitian *(pikliz),* 461
slaw, shogun, 461
"three hots," 112
tomato, 320, *321*
tomato, with feta cheese *(shopska salata),* 119–20
tomato and shallot, 119
yogurt-cucumber, with mint *(cacik),* 85–86
vegetable, on grill, 96–99
caponata, 99
eggplant, Lebanese *(salafat el ahab),* 98
eggplant, Moroccan *(salade d'aubergines),* 97–98
eggplant, tomato, and pepper *(fasouli),* 96
Spanish (escalivada), 96–97
zucchini, 98–99
Salafat el ahab, 98
Salmon, 305, 333
with basil cream, Pino's, 340
grilled in grape leaves *(kolheeda),* 338–40, *339*
Kiev, grilled, 337–38
For other suitable recipes see pages 312–13, 322, 325–26, 327–29
Salmonella, 36, 224
Salsa marinara, 472–73
Salsas, 455–59
"dog's snout" *(xni pec),* 459
fruit
apple-banana, smoky, 458
mango-mint, 458
pineapple, grilled, *456,* 457–58
habanero, grilled, 455
salsa de chiltomate, 187
salsa mexicana, 192–93
tomato *(salsa criolla),* 457
Salt, 529
and pepper shrimp, 360–61
seasoned
hot pepper sesame, 494
Spanish Caribbean *(sazón),* 493–94
Szechuan, 496
Salt cod, grilled *(bacalhao grelhado),* 343–44
Samba dogs, *230,* 231
Sambals:
fiery chile and shallot relish *(sambal chobek),* 444–45
lemongrass, 452–53
sambal ulek, 73, 530
tomato peanut *(sambal achan),* 453
Samba sausages *(choriçou),* 235
Sam's Smoker Pro, 24
Samwon Garden (Seoul), 112, 521
Sandwiches:
Dagwood, Provençal, 392
portobello mushroom, with basil aioli, 392–93
see also Burgers
Sangria, Madrid-style, *52,* 60
Santa Margherita (Italy), grilled vegetables in style of, *394,* 398–401
Santorini, Grilled quail, 298–99
Sardines:
Portuguese, 319
seafood mixed grill in style of Essaouira, 320, *321*
Saté Babi Sop Bakut Shop (Jakarta), 189
Satés, 450–51
beef
and coconut, Indonesian *(saté lalat),* 67–68
with coriander *(saté age),* 236–37
flying fox *(saté kalong),* 237

chicken, 281–85
Jakarta *(saté ayam),* 284–85
Malaysian, 281–82
schoolyard, 283–84
served in lettuce leaves, 281
Sri Lankan, 282–83
cooking, 23–24
fish mousse, Balinese *(saté lilit),* 349–50
ground meat, tips and techniques for, 227
lamb, with tamarind sauce *(saté buntel),* 240–42
origin of word, 450
pork, sweet *(saté babi manis),* 189–91
prawn, Balinese *(saté udang),* 367–68
quail egg (saté telor), 89–90
Thai, 101
Sauces, 463–87
apple-macadamia, 264
avocado, 333
basil, 340
basil aioli, 393
basting, 48, 49, 508–9
bourbon butter, 508
ketjap butter, 509
Mexican, for fish, 509
mop, applying, 39–40
saffron, 211
vinegar-based mop, 509
butters, compound, 48, 505–8
anchovy, 506
curry, 506–8, *507*
escargot, 506
garlic, Japanese, 508
ketjap, 509
maitre d'hotel, 505
marchand de vin, 508
Roquefort, 506, *507*
shadon beni, 404–5
caper, French West Indian, 318
caramel, 512
chimichurri, 154–55, 477–79
basic, 477, *479*
"dry," 478, *479*
red, 478, *479*
coriander, 482–83
cucumber, 316–17
curry beurre blanc, 359
dipping, 484–87
apple and shrimp, Vietnamese *(mam nem),* 471
Asian pear, 486
Javanese, simple, 486–87
peanut chile, 486
tamarind, 487
Vietnamese, basic *(nuoc cham),* 484, *485*
"dog," French West Indian *(sauce chien),* 482
for duck
cinnamon cherry, 291–92
orange, 292
eggplant, 208
garlic, 482
guacamole, Oaxacan-style, 455
hoisin-chile, 474
hot, 480–81
country *(molho da companha),* 480
harissa, simple, 481
Portuguese *(piri-piri),* 480
preserved lemon *harissa,* 481
injector, 48
ketchup, Indonesian *(ketjap manis),* 474
lemon-honey, with garlic, 483–84
lemon-mustard, 261–62
mint, hot and sweet, 484
mop, 48
applying, 39–40
vinegar-based, 509
peanut, 332
Bahian, 363–64
Dutch West Indian *(pindasaus),* 476
Thai, 476
tomato, 171
plum, pickled, Georgian *(tkemali),* 467
pumpkin seed *(pipián),* 325–26
red wine, caper, and olive *(raïto), 328,* 329–30
romesco, 472
spinach, 332
sweet and sour, *nonya,* 342–43
tamarind, 241
sweet-sour, 313
taratoor, 368
tartar, spicy, 357–58
teriyaki, classic, 473
tomato
charred, with pomegranate molasses *(khashkesh),* 473
Moroccan, 213
Nicaraguan *(salsa marinara),* 472–73
peanut, 171
romesco, 472
sauce vierge, 311–12
vinaigrette, Catalan, 483
vinegar, North Carolina, 177, 466–67
see also Barbecue sauces
Sauce vierge, 311–12
Sausages, 229–36
chorizo(s), *234*
grilled mushrooms, 411
spicy, 231–32
grilling techniques for, 42
pork and lamb, Romanian *(mititei),* 229
pork and pomegranate *(kupati),* 235–36
samba *(choriçou),* 235
samba dogs, *230,* 231
stuffing, *233*
types of, *234*
Savarino, Pino, 340
Sazón, 493–94
Scallion(s):
brushes, 295
crêpes, *294,* 295
green onions *romesco (calçots),* 415
grilling techniques for, 396
Japanese vegetable mixed grill *(robatayaki),* 397–98
Lebanese crudités plate, 117–18
and mushroom kebabs, Korean, 409–10
and shiitake kebabs, 410–11
Scallop(s):
grilling chart for, 356
kebabs with pancetta, lemon, and basil, 373
For other suitable recipes see pages 345–46
Schoolyard chicken satés, 283–84
Scotch bonnets, 503
Sea bass:
fennel-grilled, flambéed with Pernod *(loup de mer au fenouil flambé), 302,* 307–8
with fresh artichoke salad *(loup de mer grillé aux artichauts),* 308–11
For other suitable recipes see pages 303–7, 311–12, 317–18, 335–37, 346–47, 349–50
Sea bream, in seafood mixed grill in style of Essaouira, 320, *321*

Sea captain's chicken tikka, 272–73
Seafood:
  mixed grill in style of Essaouira, 320, *321*
  white wine marinade for, 505
  see also Fish; Shellfish; *specific seafood*
Seasoning grill grates, 9
Seeds, toasting, 113
Seekh kebab, 242
  original Karim's, 246–47
Semit kebab, 250–51
Senegalese cooking:
  chicken with lemon-mustard sauce *(yassa),* 261–62
  fish *yassa,* 327–29
  ginger pineapple punch *(gingere ananas),* 61
  lamb with onion-mustard sauce *(dibi),* 209
Serrano peppers, 503, 504
Sesame:
  dipping sauce, grilled sweet potatoes with, 421
  -grilled beef, Korean *(bool kogi),* 150–51
  -grilled okra, 414–15
  -grilled oyster mushrooms, 410
  honey shrimp "on the barbie," 361–63, *362*
  hot pepper salt, 494
  seeds, black, 527
  spinach salad, 111–12
Sesame oil, 530
Sezzeli kebab, 248–50, *249*
Shadon beni butter, 404–5
Shallot(s):
  kebabs with pomegranate molasses *(sogar kebab),* 242–43
  marchand de vin butter, 508
  mixed vegetable *achar, 448,* 449
  relishes
    chile and, fiery *(sambal chobek),* 444–45
    Moroccan, 445
    Penang (chung gao jai), 444
  tomato and, salad, 119
Shark, 323
  and bake, grilled, 322–25
Shashlik, Russian (beef), 160
Shashlyk, sturgeon, 326–27
Shek O wings, 79
Shellfish, 353–93
  clams, grilled, with *colombo* butter, 373–74
  conch, Bahamian grilled, 375–76
  "crayfish" with curry beurre blanc, 358–59
  cuttlefish with Macanese "salsa," Fernando's, 379
  grilling chart for, 356
  grilling techniques for, 45–46
  mussels, grilled *(éclade),* 374
  octopus, grilled *(khtapothi sti skhara),* 376–78, *377*
  oysters with horseradish cream, 375
  prawns with ketjap butter, 358
  scallop kebabs with pancetta, lemon, and basil, 373
  seafood mixed grill in style of Essaouira, 320, 321
  snails, grilled *(escargots grillés),* 81–82, 83
  soft-shell crabs with spicy tartar sauce, 357–58
  squid Durban, 378–79
  white wine marinade for, 505
  see also Lobster; Shrimp (or prawns)
Shepherd's salad *(çoban salatasi),* 118–19
Sheraton Rajputana (Jaipur, India), 388, 390
Shiitake(s):
  Japanese vegetable mixed grill *(robatayaki),* 397–98
  and scallion kebabs, 410–11
Shirazi cucumber, tomato, and onion salad, 118
Shish kebabs:
  Armenian, 219–20
  Bengali, 159–60
  souvlaki flambéed with Metaxa, 218–19
  Turkish, real, 214–15
  unskewering, 215, 215
  see also Kebabs
Shishlik, 210, 210–11
Shogun slaw, 461
Shopska salata, 119–20
Short ribs (beef), *195*
  butterflying, 168
  Korean grilled *(kalbi kui),* 167–69
Shrimp (or prawns), 358–72
  and apple sauce, Vietnamese *(mam nem),* 471
  with Bahian peanut sauce, 363–64
  Balinese prawn satés *(saté udang),* 367–68
  butterflying, 363
  "crayfish" with curry beurre blanc, 358–59
  dim sum, grilled, 80
  flaming prawns *(dahakte jhinga),* 366–67
  grilling chart for, 356
  grilling techniques for, 45
  Gulf Coast, 372
  honey sesame, "on the barbie," 361–63, *362*
  kebabs, Latin Quarter, 359–60
  marinating times for, 45
  mousse on sugarcane *(chao tom),* 81
  New Orleans-style barbecued, Emeril Lagasse's, 370–71
  with painfully hot salsa, Penganese, 371–72
  paste, 530
  peeling and deveining, *361*
  plantation, 369–70
  prawns with ketjap butter, 358
  salt and pepper, 360–61
  seafood mixed grill in style of Essaouira, 320, *321*
  tandoori prawns, 364–66
  with taratoor, 368–69
  For other suitable recipes see pages 325–26, 345–46, 353–54, 376–78
Side dishes:
  beans
    baked, quick and smoky, *436,* 437–38
    black, with bacon, Brazilian *(tutu mineira),* 438
    Indian "baked beans" *(dal bukhara),* 435–37
  grits, grilled, 434
  manioc, rainbow *(farofa),* 434–35
  polenta, grilled, 433
  Yorkshire pudding on the grill, 439
  see also Bread; Condiments; Pickle(d)(s); Relishes; Rice; Salads; Salsas; Vegetables, grilled
Silver paper chicken, 74
Simmons, Amelia, 460
Singaporean cooking:
  chicken wings, spicy chile, 78
  at hawkers' centers, 162
  pineapple *achar,* 449
  rosewater cooler *(bandung),* 62

Singapore sling, *52,* 59
Skate wings with *nonya* sweet-and-sour sauce, 342–43
Skenazy, Lenore, 492
Skewers:
making aluminum foil shield for, *23,* 23–24
see also Kebabs; Satés
Sky juice, Bahamian, 55–56
Slaws, 460–61
basic, 460
Haitian *(pikliz),* 461
North Carolina-style coleslaw, 177
shogun, 461
"Slipper" burgers *(chapli kebab),* 226–28
Smoked chile marinade *(adobo),* 499–501
Smoking, 1, 5, 24–25
hot vs. cold, 5
indirect grilling and, 2, 3
Smoky apple-banana salsa, 458
Smoky martini, 56–58
S'mores, uptown, 515
Snails, grilled *(escargots grillés),* 81–82, 83
Snapper, 305
burgers, Florida, 350–51
whole, grilled
Bahamian-style, 304–7
with cucumber sauce, 316–17
with French West Indian caper sauce, 318–19
with South African spices (fish *braî*), 303–4
sweet and sour *(pla pow),* 313–14
For other suitable recipes see pages 307–12, 314–16, 317–18, 325–26, 331–35, 349–50
Sobe, Arsenio Pancho, 331
Soft-shell crabs with spicy tartar sauce, 357–58
Sogar kebab, 242–43
Sole, 305
with Catalan fruits and nuts, 341
Soups:
barbacoa consommé, 199–201
corn chowder, grilled, 92
gazpacho, grilled, 93
tomato, fire-charred, 91–92
Sour orange, 186, 530
South African cooking:
chicken, *piri-piri, 254,* 258–60
lamb, Cape Town, 202–5, *203*
rock lobster, 356–57
snapper, whole, with South African spices (fish *braî*), 303–4
squid Durban, 378–79
South American cooking:
chimichurri, basic, 477, 479
see also specific countries
Southeast Asian cooking:
fruit cooler, 524
see also specific countries
Souvlaki:
flambéed with Metaxa, 218–19
swordfish, 345–46
Soyer, Alexis, 95
Soy sauce, 530
Spanish Caribbean seasoning salt *(sazón),* 493–94
Spanish cooking:
artichokes, Catalan grilled, 402–3
Catalan cream *(crema catalana),* 519
chorizo grilled mushrooms, 411
chorizos, spicy, 231–32
gazpacho, grilled, 93
green onions *romesco (calçots),* 415
grilled vegetable salad *(escalivada),* 96–97
pork with Moorish seasonings *(pinchos morunos),* 180–82
romesco sauce, 472
sangria, Madrid-style, 60
sole with Catalan fruits and nuts, 341
tomato bread, Catalan *(pa amb tomàquet),* 128, *129*
vinaigrette, Catalan, 483
Spanish Guinean fish grill with three sauces, 331–33
Spareribs, 39
Spatchcocking chicken or game hen, *289*
Spiced lamb and beef kebabs *(lula kebab),* 238–39
Spice-grilled pineapple, 513
Spice mixes:
chaat, quick, 105
see also Rubs
Spicy bean sprout salad, Japanese, 113
Spicy beef salad, Thai *(yam nua yang), 94,* 102
Spicy chile wings, 78
Spicy chorizos, 231–32
Spicy daikon salad, 112–13
Spicy fruit in tamarind dressing *(rujak),* 122, *123*
Spinach:
rinsing, 106
salad, sesame, 111–12
sauce, 332
Spit roasting, 22
see also Rotisserie cooking
Spruce, 13, 14
Squab, testing for doneness, 30
Squash, summer:
grilling chart for, 400
grilling techniques for, 397
Provençal Dagwood, 392
see also Zucchini
Squid:
Durban, 378–79
seafood mixed grill in style of Essaouira, 320, 321
For other suitable recipes see pages 376–78, 379
Sri Lankan cooking:
chicken satés, 282–83
pineapple chutney, 454–55
potato salad with caramelized onions, 120–21
tomato and shallot salad, 119
Star anise, 530
wings, *66,* 76–77
Star fruit:
spicy fruit in tamarind dressing *(rujak),* 122, *123*
Vietnamese salad plate, 116, 117
Starters. *See* Appetizers
Steaks, 33–36
bone-in vs. boneless, 35
cuts of, *145*
factors affecting quality of, 34
Florentine-style *(bistecca alla fiorentina),* 146, 148–49
in garlic-lime marinade *(palomilla),* 140–43
grades of, 33–34
grilling techniques for, 35, 141
from hell, *142,* 143
mustard lime, 143–44
Nicaraguan-style *(churrasco),* 147
Niçoise rub for, 491
rib, with red wine sauce and marrow *(entrecôtes à la bordelaise),* 144–46
seasoning before grilling, 35
Stephen, George, 6
Stoner, Winston, 184
Strawberries, in fruit cooler, 524

Striped bass. *For suitable recipes see pages 304–12*
Sturgeon, 348
- kebabs, 348–49
- *shashlyk,* 326–27

Sufferer, Prince Duncan, 185
Sufferer's Jerk Pork Front Line No. 1 (Boston Beach, Jamaica), 184–85
Sugar, turbinado, 54
Sugarcane:
- plantation shrimp, 369–70
- shrimp mousse on *(chao tom),* 81

Sugar snap peas, in Japanese vegetable mixed grill *(robatayaki),* 397–98
Sumac, 248, 530
Sunda Kelapa (Jakarta), 314, 315, 358, 509
Susser, Allen, 350
Suyas, 160–61
Sweet and sour:
- sauces
  - *nonya,* 342–43
  - tamarind, 313
- snapper *(pla pow),* 313–14

Sweet potatoes:
- Peruvian potato mixed grill, 418–19
- roasting in embers, 28
- with sesame dipping sauce, 421
- two-tone potato salad, 121

Switzerland: raclette, 384–85
Swordfish:
- kebabs
  - with coconut milk, 346–47
  - Pandeli, 347–48
  - souvlaki, 345–46
- *en pipián,* 325–26
- *For other suitable recipes see pages 308–11, 312–14, 322, 326–27, 344–46, 348–49*

Syafril, Yuni, 450
Szechuan seasoned salt, 496

T

Tabil, 493
Table grills, 4–5
Tahini, 530
- eggplant purée with, Middle Eastern *(baba ghanoush),* 84–85

Tamarind, 530
- dipping sauce, 487
- dressing, spicy fruit in *(rujak),* 122, *123*
- mango barbecue sauce, Bengali, 470–71
- sauce, 241
  - barbecue, simple, 471
  - sweet-sour, 313
- water, 241–42, 530

Tandoori, 383, 426
- -baked flat breads *(naan), 124,* 131
- cauliflower, 403–4
- chicken *(tandoori murgh),* 267–69
- leg of "mutton" with saffron and rosewater, 201–2
- origin of term, 383
- peppers, 386, *387*
- prawns, 364–66

Taratoor, 368
Tartar sauce, spicy, 357–58
Tea, mint, 62–63
TEC Corporation, 10
Tennyson, Jeffrey, 225
Tequila, in Frontera margarita, 59
Teriyaki:
- marinade, 499
- sauce, classic, 473

Texas-style barbecue, 469
- brisket, 135–36

Thai chile peppers, 503
Thai cooking, 100–101
- beef
  - lemongrass, with peanuts, 166–67
  - salad, spicy *(yam nua yang), 94,* 102
- chicken satés
  - schoolyard, 283–84
  - served in lettuce leaves, 281
- fish
  - with Esarn seasoning, 317–18
  - sweet and sour snapper *(pla pow),* 313–14
- jasmine rice, 428
- pork
  - chops, sweet and garlicky, *190,* 191
  - with sweet-tart dressing (pork *laab*), 102–4
- sauces
  - lemon-honey, with garlic, 483–84
  - peanut, 476
  - tamarind barbecue, simple, 471
  - tamarind dipping, 487

Thanh Nien (Saigon), 72
Thermometers, instant-read meat, 29, 32
Thit bo kho, 68–69
Thon grillé au jus de raïto, 328, 329–30
"Three hots" salad, 112
Three-meat patties *(ćevapčići),* 228–29
Three-zone fire, 18, 19
Thurber, James, 125
Tikin xik, 334–35
'Ti punch, 58
Tkemali, 467
Toasting:
- coconut, 514
- seeds, nuts, and breadcrumbs, 113

Tofu, 46
- on stilts *(dengaku),* 389
- white rabbit, 388

La Tomaquera (Barcelona), 402
Tomato(es):
- bread, Catalan *(pa amb tomàquet),* 128, *129*
- cucumber, and onion salad, Shirazi, 118
- cucumber *raita,* 460
- dilled, grilled, 421
- eggplant, and pepper salad *(fasouli),* 96
- fire-charred, soup, 91–92
- flame-roasted, 87
- gazpacho, grilled, 93
- Georgian pickles, 442–43
- Georgian vegetable kebabs, 395–97
- grilled pizza with basil, cheese and, 382–84
- grilled vegetable caponata, 99
- grilled vegetables in style of Santa Margherita, *394,* 398–401
- grilling chart for, 400
- grilling techniques for, 397
- jam, 453
- peanut *sambal (sambal achan),* 453
- salad, 320, *321*
  - with feta cheese *(shopska salata),* 119–20
- salsas
  - Argentinean *(salsa criolla),* 457
  - "dog's snout" *(xni pec),* 459
  - *salsa de chiltomate,* 187
  - *salsa mexicana,* 192–93
- sauces
  - charred, with pomegranate molasses *(khashkesh),* 473
  - Moroccan, 213
  - Nicaraguan *(salsa marinara),* 472–73
  - peanut, 171
  - *romesco,* 472
  - sauce vierge, 311–12

seeding, 454
and shallot salad, 119
shepherd's salad *(çoban salatasi),* 118–19
West Indian grilled vegetables *(choka),* 401–2
Tongs, 29, *34*
Ton Ton (Tokyo), 113
Torres, Manuela Martinez, 192
Torshi, 440, 441–42
Traeger pellet grill, 10
Travel, locating best barbecue places in, 50–51
Trinidadian cooking:
corn, grilled, with *shadon beni* butter, 404–5
eggplant dip *(choka dip),* 82–84
garlic sauce, 482
grilled vegetables *(choka),* 401–2
peanut punch, 61–62
shark and bake, grilled, 322–25
Trotter, Charlie, 12
Trout, 305
Truffles, black, cooking in coals, 414
Tsuji, Shizuo, 430, 473
Tuğra Restaurant (Istanbul), 69
Tuna:
with red wine, caper, and olive sauce *(thon grillé au jus de raïto), 328,* 329–30
salade niçoise, 107–9, *108–9*
steaks, Madeira style, 330–31
For other suitable recipes see pages 308–11, 313–16, 322, 331–33, 345–47
Tunisian rub *(tabil),* 493
Turbinado sugar, 54
Turkey:
annatto-spiced, 287–88
grilling chart for, 256
marinating times for, 45
pastrami, 286
smoke roasting, 43–44
testing for doneness, 30
Turkish cooking, 244–45
coffee barbecue sauce, Jake's, 477
kebabs
cracked wheat and lamb *(semit kebab),* 250–51
with fire-charred eggplant and yogurt, "Gentle Al," 251–52
lamb and eggplant *(sezzeli kebab),* 248–50, *249*
lamb and pistachio, 243–46
shallot, with pomegranate molasses *(sogar kebab),* 242–43
shish, real, 214–15
swordfish, Pandeli, 347–48
lamb, racks of, Çirağan Palace, 207–8
onion relish with pomegranate molasses, 446
pastrami grilled in grape leaves, 69
radish salad plate, *116,* 117
raki, 60
shepherd's salad *(çoban salatasi),* 118–19
yogurt-cucumber salad with mint *(cacik),* 85–86
Turmeric, 530
Turnip, in Central Asian pickles *(torshi), 440,* 441–42
Tuscan cooking:
garlic bread, grilled *(bruschetta),* 127
pheasant, grilled, 295–98
steak, Florentine-style *(bistecca alla fiorentina),* 146, 148–49
Tuscan grills, 10, 26
Tutu mineira, 438
Two-tone potato salad, 121
Two-zone fire, 18, *19*

Ukrainian grilled salmon Kiev, 337–38
Umeboshi plums/plum paste, 530
Unsal, Ayfer, 446
Uptown s'mores, 515
Urap sayur, 115
Uruguayan cooking, 278–79
chicken breasts, Montevidean *(pamplona de pollo),* 280
matambres, 153
Montevidean stuffed beef roll, *156,* 156–57
pork, rolled *(pamplona de puerco),* 188–89
U.S.A. *See* American cooking
Uzbek cooking:
quail, spiced, 300
quail grilled in grape leaves, 301

Veal:
and chicken kebabs, Argentinean, 170
ground
Bulgarian burgers *(kufteh),* 226
three-meat patties *(ćevapčići),* 228–29
Vegetable baskets, 405
Vegetable grates, 405
Vegetables, grilled, 46–47, 395–421
artichokes, Catalan grilled, 402–3
breadfruit, fire-roasted, 403
cauliflower, tandoori, 403–4
corn with *shadon beni* butter, 404–5
eggplant(s)
Argentinean, 406, *407*
with miso "barbecue" sauce, 405–6
fennel, 408
garlic kebabs, 408
Georgian vegetable kebabs, 395–97
grates and baskets for, 405
green onions *romesco (calçots),* 415
grilling chart for, 400
Japanese vegetable mixed grill *(robatayaki),* 397–98
long beans, 409
mushroom(s)
caps with arugula butter, 414
chorizo grilled, 411
oyster, sesame grilled, 410
and scallion kebabs, Korean, 409–10
okra, sesame-grilled, 414–15
onions and potatoes roasted in coals, 418
peppers, marinated, with olives and anchovies, 415–16
plantains, 416
potato(es)
foil-grilled, with Asian seasonings, 417–18
garlic and lemon roasted, Greek, 419–20
à la ketchup, 417
and onions roasted in coals, 418
Peruvian mixed grill, 418–19
pumpkin gratin, West Indian, 420
scraping blackened skins from, 99
shiitake and scallion kebabs, 410–11
in style of Santa Margherita, *394,* 398–401

sweet potatoes with sesame dipping sauce, 421
techniques for, 396–97
testing for doneness, 32
tomatoes, grilled dilled, 421
West Indian *(choka),* 401–2
Vegetarian food, 46, 381–93
Dagwood, Provençal, 392
eggplants with miso "barbecue" sauce, 405–6
mushroom caps with arugula butter, 414
mushroom-rice burgers with Cheddar cheese, 389–90
pizza, original grilled, 381–84
with arugula and Italian cheeses, 384
with tomato, basil, and cheese, 382–84
portobello mushroom sandwiches with basil aioli, 392–93
raclette, 384–85
tandoori peppers, 386, *387*
tofu on stilts *(dengaku),* 389
white rabbit, 388
yam and nut kebabs, 390–91
Venison, 41
Vermouth, in smoky martini, 56–58
Vietnamese cooking, 72
beef
and basil rolls, 69–73, *70, 71*
jerky *(thit bo kho),* 68–69
lettuce bundles with, 164–66, *165*
sticks, Saigon market, 167
chicken wings, garlic lemongrass, Saigon, 74–75
dipping sauces
apple and shrimp *(mam nem),* 471
basic *(nuoc cham),* 484, *485*
peanut chile, 486
eggs, grilled, with Vietnamese seasonings, 90–91
iced coffee, 63
salad plate, *0* 117
shrimp
mousse on sugarcane *(chao tom),* 81
salt and pepper, 360–61
Vietnam House (Saigon), 70, 72
Villa Roncalli (Umbria), 148–49
Vinaigrettes:
Catalan, 483
French West Indian "dog" sauce *(sauce chien),* 482
Vinegar:
-based mop sauce, 509
sauce, 39
North Carolina, 177, 466–67

W

Walnuts, Persian eggplant dip with, 84
Walnut shells, for smoking, 14
Waris, Nisar, 390
Watercress, in "three hots" salad, 112
Watermelon:
fruit cooler, 524
Georgian pickles, 442–43
Water smokers, 25
Weber Kettle, 6
Wells, Patricia, 83
West African cooking:
beef with peanut flour *(kyinkyinga),* 157–58
see also Senegalese cooking
West Indian cooking:
chicken kebabs, Dutch West Indian *(boka dushi),* 73
pumpkin gratin, 420
shrimp, plantation, 369–70
vegetables, grilled *(choka),* 401–2
Wet aging, 34
Whipped cream, sweetened, 514
White miso barbecue sauce, 475
White rabbit, 388
White wine marinade for seafood, 505
Whiting, in seafood mixed grill in style of Essaouira, 320, *321*
Willingham, John, 10
Wine:
red
caper, and olive sauce *(raïto), 328,* 329–30
marchand de vin butter, 508
sangria, Madrid-style, 60
sauce, rib steaks with marrow and *(entrecôtes à la bordelaise),* 144–46
white, marinade for seafood, 505
Wittgenstein, Ludwig, 199
Wood:
chips vs. chunks, 14
cooking over, 7, 13
"flavors" of, 12, 13–14
smoking with, 13–14, 25
Wooldridge, Jane, 360

X

Xni pec, 459

Y

Yakitori, 285–86, 412, 413
Yam and nut kebabs, 390–91
Yam nua yang, 94, 102
Yank Sing (San Francisco), 74
Yard-long beans. *See* Long bean(s)
Yaseen, Muhammad, 275
Yassa:
chicken, 261–62
fish, 327–29
Yellow rice, Balinese *(nasi kuning),* 430
Yellow squash:
grilling chart for, 400
grilling techniques for, 397
Provençal Dagwood, 392
Yogurt:
beverages
Afghan *(doh),* 63
Indian *(lassi),* 65
Persian *(dugh),* 63
cucumber salad with mint *(cacik),* 85–86
raitas, 459–60
pineapple, 459
tomato-cucumber, 460
Yorkshire pudding on the grill, 439
Yucatán-style grilled fish *(tikin xik),* 334–35

Z

Za'atar, 530
Zucchini:
grilled, salad, Moroccan, 98–99
grilled vegetables in style of Santa Margherita, *394,* 398–401
grilling chart for, 400
grilling techniques for, 397
Provençal Dagwood, 392
Zwoyer, Ellsworth, 11